THE CASTLE DIARIES
1974-76

Barbara Castle and Harold Wilson at the Labour Party Conference, November 1975
(*Evening Standard*)

BARBARA CASTLE

THE CASTLE DIARIES

1974-76

Book Club Associates
London

CONTENTS

Preface	*ix*
Introduction	*1*
1974	*15*
1975	*263*
1976	*619*
Epilogue	*737*
Appendices	*741*
Index	*761*

To Ted
who always stood by me, even when I was wrong

PREFACE

A political diary is the most dangerous art form an author can adopt. It is written under the pressures of the moment, both of time and of experience. It is short-term – no second thoughts. So the person who comes worst out of it is often the author, who dares to reveal all the inadequacies of those immediate judgments that he or she might wish later to modify or polish up. But it is exactly for that reason that a diary is such an important contribution to history, particularly when it is about a period in government. Because government is conducted under pressure. Cabinets have to react to crises that won't wait. Ministers have to go to the House of Commons to make detailed statements on important matters at the drop of a hat, worrying all the way whether their brief is as reliable as they are told it is. A diary records life as it is lived from day to day and in doing so it shows, as no polished treatise can do, how people, including the author, behave in given circumstances.

This diary was typed by me as near the events as possible – sometimes in the early hours of the morning when something dramatic had happened which had to be put down on paper at once; more often at weekends when all the red Cabinet boxes had been gone through and my husband had gone to bed. I have kept a diary on and off all my political life, but when Harold Wilson took me into his Cabinet in October 1974 I felt I was entering a new realm of experience which it would be a crime not to record. So a few months after entering the Cabinet I began to keep a detailed daily diary, which I kept up faithfully. I had no thought of publication then, but the longer I was in government the more convinced I became that governments – all governments – make trouble for themselves by not sharing the processes of decision-making more openly. Sitting round the Cabinet table at No. 10 I often used to think that the people outside would feel far less alienated and hostile if they only knew the sort of problems with which some twenty honest men and women and true were struggling to deal to the best of their ability. The governed might be far more willing to co-operate if only they were taken into the confidence of their governors. I agree with Tony Benn that secrecy is the enemy of democracy. That is why I have decided to publish my diaries, even though they contain many irritable and irrational assessments of the moment, including some of Tony himself.

Diaries can have another value, too. They can provide a crucial check on the official records and *ex post facto* explanations of what is supposed to have happened. Because I do shorthand, and because I laboured hard at some physical cost to keep as full a record as possible, I believe my diaries will help to produce a rounded history of Harold Wilson's period of government. To help this along I have tried to put this part of them, which covers the period 1974–76 when I was Secretary of State for the Social Services, in a framework which will explain why we acted as we did and what inspired the policies about which we were arguing. So I have written the Introduction, the linking passages and the footnotes myself, though I am indebted to Richard Strange and Joanna Roll for their invaluable help with the research. I have also been sustained in these labours by the unflagging competence of my secretary, Janet Anderson. Because I found I had typed about one million words on this two-year period alone, I have had to prune out a number of the details and passages to make the whole thing more readable; but, in doing so, I have not falsified the facts nor left out anything which is essential to the account of what the Government was doing, or of my part in it. The earlier story of my life in government will follow in later volumes.

INTRODUCTION

In January 1974 Britain was in a State of Emergency, the third to be declared by the Conservative Government. After three-and-a-half stormy years Mr Heath, the Prime Minister, had finally trapped himself into a confrontation with the miners. Restrictions had been placed on the use of electricity and shopkeepers were selling their goods by candlelight. Mr Heath had put industry on a three-day week and was obviously preparing to appeal to the country over the heads of the unions. With the Labour Opposition vigorously backing the miners, the stage was set for one of the bitterest clashes of post-war politics.

How had British politics reached this pass? The explanation is essential for an understanding of the period 1974–76 covered by this diary. For Mr Heath's confrontation with the miners was the climax of ten years' struggle by successive governments to deal with Britain's deepening economic problems. Harold Wilson had tried in 1964 and 1966, only to be defeated at Mr Heath's hands in 1970. Now Mr Heath faced the collapse of his policies. And the Labour Party was preparing to have another try, based on a new approach which would embody the lessons of the previous ten years.

They had been years of growing economic crisis. British industry had become uncompetitive and its share of world trade was declining. Investment was low and so was productivity. And so were wages. Each side blamed the other. Industrial weakness had led each government in turn into the same economic trap. Attempts to expand the economy had led to balance of payments crises, inflation and a weakened currency. Attempts to correct these developments by deflation had depressed growth, increased unemployment, reduced the standard of living and led to industrial unrest. Neither Government had broken out of the vicious circle and neither had succeeded in mobilizing the enthusiastic co-operation of the unions and their members on the shop floor.

The failure of these previous policies was the key to Labour's new approach. Some details of them are therefore necessary.

The Wilson Government of October 1964, elected with high hopes of social reform, quickly walked into the economic trap. The starry-eyed new members of that Cabinet, of whom I was one, found they had inherited a record balance of payments deficit as a result of the Conservative Chancellor Maudling's dash for growth over the previous two years. As Labour took office, the pound came under immediate attack.

1

The Bank of England and the City moved in to demand deflationary policies. For four years the Labour Government allowed itself to be driven back step by step into those policies, first as a result of Harold Wilson's determination not to devalue the pound and then, when devaluation became inevitable, because the Treasury insisted that deflation was the only way to make devaluation work. The deflationary policies produced their predictable results. The budget was balanced by severe cuts in public expenditure. Industrial costs were held down by wage controls. By 1970 the record balance of payments deficit had been turned into a record surplus. But it had only been done at great political and economic cost. The growth rate had fallen from 5·5 per cent in 1964 to 2·4 per cent in 1969, and by the end of 1969 unemployment was running at 580,000 or 2·4 per cent compared with 354,000 or 1·5 per cent by the end of 1964. The party's rank and file had been disillusioned and traditional Labour voters alienated.

And so had the unions. The cut-backs of those years had driven a wedge between them and the Labour Government. The unions themselves had been ambivalent about their own role. Though supporting the Labour Party formally, they felt no obligation to share the responsibilities of economic management. During the 1960s, under George Woodcock, the General Secretary of the Trades Union Congress [TUC], they saw themselves primarily as wage negotiators who would strike the hardest bargain they could with any government. Wage restraint was anathema, the Left arguing that it was just a device to make capitalism work. Hugh Scanlon, leader of the powerful engineering union, declared categorically: 'I cannot accept that any wage increase can ever be inflationary.' The unions became increasingly restless as the harassed Labour Government was driven back, first to a voluntary prices and incomes policy and then to a statutory one.

The Government's problems were intensified by a rash of unofficial strikes, often in breach of procedures, for which the unions officially refused to take any responsibility. The industrial disruption this caused was typified by a strike at Girlings car components firm in 1968, when a sudden walk-out of twenty-two machine setters put thousands of car workers out of work. The unpopularity of these strikes among workers themselves was being exploited by Mr Heath. In 1965 Harold Wilson, always tuned in to the public mood, set up a Royal Commission under Lord Justice Donovan to examine the whole field of industrial relations. The result was a report which fended off most of the Conservative attacks on the unions. The main need, it argued, was to reform and strengthen collective bargaining. Strikes were caused by out-of-date procedures which must be reformed by voluntary agreement. Unions should be self-regulating, but their rules should be amended to give greater safeguards for individuals. In general it rejected legal sanctions as inappropriate, but did not rule out in principle the legal enforcement of procedure agreements once they had been reformed or other enforcement powers which might prove necessary in the light of experience.

It fell to me, as Secretary of State for Employment and Productivity, to deal with the report. This I did in a White Paper, *In Place of Strife*, in which I built on the Donovan analysis. If collective bargaining was to be strengthened, I argued, we must begin by strengthening the trade unions. My proposals, therefore, rejected the calls

2

coming from the Conservatives to put legal restraints on the unions and instead substantially extended trade union rights. 'The right of an employee to withdraw his labour,' I wrote, 'is one of the essential freedoms in a democracy.' But I was deeply concerned lest abuse of the strike weapon should damage the trade union movement I sought to help. I was particularly concerned with the spate of unofficial strikes which were disrupting industry. Like Donovan I stressed that conciliation and voluntary reforms must be the key. But in order to give conciliation a chance to work I proposed to give the Secretary of State discretionary power to impose a twenty-eight-day 'conciliation pause' on both workers and management in a strike where procedures had been ignored. Meanwhile management was to be required to preserve the status quo and withdraw the offending action that might have caused the strike. Serious damage was also being done by inter-union disputes over recognition. I therefore proposed to take power to refer such disputes to the Commission on Industrial Relations, which had been set up on Donovan's recommendation and on which the unions were strongly represented, in order that it could try to conciliate and, failing that, recommend a solution. Financial penalties were to be imposed on any employer who failed to recognize the recommended union and on the union which obstructed an employer when he did recognize it. I also originally proposed a discretionary power to order a secret ballot in official strikes which could seriously damage the national economy, but I later abandoned this as counter-productive.

Whether these proposals would have worked is arguable. Harold Wilson backed them enthusiastically but the unions were outraged. They claimed – with some justification as it turned out – that the Conservatives would use my proposals as an alibi for the very different legal constraints they were proposing to place on the unions. Labour MPs mobilized in protest. So did the party's National Executive Committee [NEC], of which I was a member. Some Cabinet Ministers opposed me openly. Others, who had supported me, began to get cold feet. The dispute was finally settled, after protracted talks with the TUC by Harold Wilson and me, by the trade unions undertaking to improve their own procedures for dealing with inter-union disputes and unofficial strikes. The full story of this affair is for another volume, but the row had achieved several things. First, it had compelled the unions to face the need for voluntary reforms. The TUC called on its member unions to overhaul their rules. Vic Feather, now its General Secretary, personally intervened to try to end unofficial strikes. Secondly, it forced them to think more deeply about the need for them to play a positive role in the running of the economy. This was to bear fruit in the Social Contract a few years later. But the row had also revealed the strength of the gut reaction against any tampering with trade union freedoms. It had become obvious that no Labour Government could work unless it carried the trade unions with it and this was to become the dominant aim of Labour policy.

But the bitterness remained. My own standing in the party was damaged, Jack Jones declaring that I had become 'totally politically discredited'. Ironically it was Mr Heath who, on taking office in 1970, did most to heal the breach between the Labour Party and the unions. He had no doubt that Britain's troubles were caused by Labour's welfare policies and what he called the 'monopoly power' of the trade unions. Turning his back on the moderate, middle-of-the-road Conservatism of

Harold Macmillan, Mr Heath deliberately set out to polarize politics. There must, he declared, be a radical new medicine for Britain's ills: more 'incentives', lower taxes, higher profits, less public expenditure. No government interference in industry and no subsidies. People must be made to stand on their own feet. And the unions must be brought to heel. This, and the cold winds of competition that would blow from membership of the European Community, would tone up the whole of British society.

Once in office Mr Heath lost no time in testing his theories. In October 1970, his Chancellor, Mr Anthony Barber, startled the House of Commons with an economic programme designed to secure 'a fundamental reform of the role of government and public authorities'. Harold Wilson's modest interventionist measures were swept away. Labour's Industrial Reconstruction Corporation was wound up. Investment grants gave way to depreciation allowances, which helped the successful firms more. Financial support for industry by government was cut. Ports nationalization was dropped and the capital programmes of the nationalized industries cut back. The Consumer Council was abolished. Even the research councils felt the axe. In return corporation tax was reduced.

Central to the theme was that taxation must be cut to increase incentives. To achieve this the Government adopted every device to reduce public expenditure. Charges were increased over a wide range of public services: prescriptions, school meals, even museum charges. The subsidy for cheap welfare milk was abolished and the supply of free milk to the 7s to 11s stopped. Grants for public transport were cut back. Local authorities were to be compelled by law to increase council rents so as to reduce housing subsidies. Most serious of all, Mr Barber announced that the traditional method of supporting farmers' incomes through deficiency payments financed by the Government would be dropped in favour of import levies paid by the consumer, even though Britain had not yet become a member of the European Community. This meant a tax on imported food and pushed up food prices. Finally, the pledge Mr Heath had given during the election to increase family allowances was abandoned in favour of a much cheaper, means-tested alternative: a new Family Income Supplement for low-wage earners with children. To sugar the pill some modest increases were announced in the spending programmes of the social services. But the net effect enabled the Chancellor to cut the standard rate of income tax by 6d ($2\frac{1}{2}$ new pence), to be followed later by further tax cuts which particularly benefited the well-to-do.

No one could deny that Mr Heath had thoroughly tried out his new ideas. Unfortunately for him, the reaction was not what he had anticipated. When the excitement had died down the average worker was able to calculate what he had gained by the 'incentives' deal and was not impressed. All he noticed was that prices had been deliberately pushed up, though Mr Heath in the election had promised to bring them down. The unions growled angrily. Nor were they mollified by Mr Heath's rejection of a statutory prices and incomes policy as incompatible with his free market philosophy. When, true to his word, Mr Heath abolished Harold Wilson's Prices and Incomes Board, the unions decided to recoup the price increases through wage increases. The inflationary upsurge had begun.

Mr Heath's first answer to inflation was the classic one: to restrict growth. Despite the record balance of payments surplus he had in hand, he refused to expand the economy. Output stagnated. Unemployment rose by over 40 per cent by the end of 1971. The alarm bells began to ring in industry. With demand flat Mr Heath's 'incentives' fell flat too. Firms ran into difficulties. In 1971 Conservative supporters had their first shock when the prestigious Rolls-Royce company faced collapse. Mr Heath rushed to nationalize it by the unprecedented device of a one-clause Bill. But there was worse to come. In 1972 his Minister for Industry, Mr John Davies, a former secretary-general of the Confederation of British Industry [CBI], introduced an Industry Bill giving the Government far-reaching powers to help the 'lame ducks' of industry which earlier Mr Heath had said he would not support, including the right for the Government to acquire shares in these companies in return for financial help.

This first U-turn towards interventionist policies in industry was backed by an equal reversal of economic policy. Rising unemployment became the Government's first concern. In a Maudling-type dash for growth it floated the pound and cut taxes again, but it also increased public expenditure. As a result money supply rose sharply, inflation got worse and the balance of payments ran into another record deficit. International developments became menacing. Import prices rose and oil supplies were under threat as a result of the Middle Eastern war. Faced with these alarming developments Mr Heath took fright. Once again economic policy was put into reverse. By December 1973, credit had been restricted, interest rates increased and public expenditure plans cut back sharply.

During all these chops and changes of policy Mr Heath had never lost sight of his main goal: to curb trade union power. This could be done, he believed, by bringing the unions 'within the framework of the law'. The principles had been worked out by Conservative lawyers twenty years earlier and Mr Heath had fought the election on this central theme. One of the first acts of his Government was to produce a pantechnicon Industrial Relations Bill, designed to regulate by law every aspect of trade union activity. Its basic theme was that strikes could be avoided by setting out 'orderly' procedures for the conduct of industrial relations and giving them the force of law. It also strengthened the right of individuals against their union. So the Bill set out a number of 'unfair industrial practices'. Unions who indulged in them could be brought by their employers, or by individuals, before a new National Industrial Relations Court, presided over by a High Court judge. Although the penalty was the civil one of compensation and orders, defiance could bring the unions under the criminal charge of contempt of court. As a result the closed shop was effectively outlawed. So were sympathetic strikes. So were strikes for union recognition while the procedures laid down were being followed. The statutory right to belong to a union, which I had initiated, was accompanied by a statutory right *not* to belong.

To the unions this approach vitiated their whole history. Unions had come into being as voluntary combinations of workers seeking to control the forces that shaped their working lives. Independence from government was crucial to this struggle. So was solidarity among members. From this struggle grew the concept of 'borrowed strength', with strong unions lending their support to weaker ones through sympathetic action. From it grew also the hatred of the 'free rider', who weakened the

5

collective strength by refusing to join a union, while reaping its benefits. But the most serious part of the Bill from the unions' point of view was the reintroduction of the doctrine of 'agency', and civil liability. This had been propounded in the notorious Taff Vale judgment of 1901 when the House of Lords ruled that railwaymen on strike at Taff Vale were acting as agents of their union, which must be held accountable for the effects of their action. The Lords therefore mulcted the Amalgamated Society of Railway Servants for heavy costs and damages. The judgment roused the whole trade-union world. Unions could see that in future their funds would be at risk in any dispute. The outcry led to the passing of the Trade Disputes Act of 1906 which restored the protection the unions had lost by the judgment – a milestone in trade-union history. Now the Conservative Government was turning back the clock. Unofficial strikes, it said, must be stopped by making a union legally responsible for what its members did. This was to be done by a system of registration, the Bill's centrepiece. Unions could only register if they drew up an approved set of rules, policed by a new Registrar. These must lay down clearly who in the union had the right to call a strike and in what circumstances. The Bill then limited the right to strike to registered unions and their members and officials 'acting within the scope of their authority'. So the unions were in a trap. Failure by registered unions to secure the observance of the new rules could lead to penalties on the union itself. Failure to register could also lead to penalties through the loss of legal immunity. The violence of the union reaction surprised the Conservatives. Once again they had ignored history.

The Bill was bitterly – but vainly – contested by Labour MPs in the House of Commons. Once it became law the unions set out with calculated non-co-operation to make it unworkable. Major unions like the Transport and General Workers' Union [T&GWU] refused to register, thus losing their legal rights. Others, like the National Union of Seamen [NUS], who felt compelled to register in order to survive, were expelled from the TUC, adding to the general bitterness. Union representatives withdrew from conciliation agencies like the Commission for Industrial Relations because these bodies had become part of the new legal machinery. The TUC called on its members to boycott the new court.

Industrial relations quickly moved through tragedy into farce. The T&GWU was the first to be caught by the doctrine of agency. Dockers up and down the country were 'blacking' lorries carrying goods to container depots outside the docks, because they could see their own jobs vanishing. It was the sort of problem which could only be solved by a carefully worked-out compromise. But conciliation had given way to legal rights. Under the new law, the lorry drivers' employers could take the union to court for the dockers' action, and this they did. Sir John Donaldson, President of the National Industrial Relations Court [NIRC], took the court's responsibilities very seriously. The court ordered the blacking to be stopped and, when the dockers persisted with it, it fined the union for contempt.

But the blacking persisted – and so did the applications to the court. Once again the union was threatened with contempt. This time the union decided to defend itself, arguing that its shop stewards were locally elected representatives for whose actions it was not accountable. The argument went all the way up the legal hierarchy. The

Court of Appeal under Lord Denning ruled that the shop stewards were not agents and revoked the fine on the union. The NIRC thereupon decided to proceed against the individual dockers – the very opposite of what the Government had intended – and to the Government's consternation issued orders for the arrest of three London shop stewards defiantly picketing the new container depot at Chobham farm and eager for martyrdom. Disaster – and a nationwide walk-out from the docks – was only averted by the mysterious intervention of the Official Solicitor, a legal official of whom few people had heard until he was wheeled out to save the day. On his representations, the Court of Appeal hurriedly set the arrests aside – a rescue operation which one of the disappointed shop stewards bitterly described as a 'bloody liberty'.

Sir John Donaldson, however, continued to assert the court's authority. When the picketing of the depots continued and another firm complained, he committed five London dockers to Pentonville. This brought 85,000 workers out on strike. There was uproar in the House of Commons. The House of Lords reversed the Court of Appeal's findings at record speed, making the union once again liable. So the Official Solicitor appeared again. Against their will the dockers were released, on the curious argument that, although they refused to apologize for their contempt, they need not remain in prison since action could now be taken against the union. The unrepentant dockers were carried shoulder high by an enthusiastic crowd outside Pentonville.

This farce did more than anything else to discredit the new Act. Serious newspapers began to question it. But the legal juggernaut rolled on. When the Amalgamated Union of Engineering Workers [AUEW] refused to call off a strike to secure recognition at Con Mech Engineering Ltd, the court sequestered £100,000 of the union's assets. It was the Government which had earlier added the richest touch of comedy. Faced with a threatened railway dispute over pay, it applied to the court under the provisions of the Act for a compulsory ballot and cooling-off period on the argument that there was serious doubt whether the union's members supported the dispute. This theory was quickly exploded. In the ballot the railwaymen voted six to one to escalate the dispute into a national strike. Two months later the Government was forced to compromise. The railwaymen got another £2 million. Lord Devlin, a High Court judge, complained that the courts were being brought in to make judgments on matters that were really political. 'The prestige of the judiciary...,' he wrote, 'is not at the disposal of any government.' Even Sir John Donaldson admitted that parts of the Act had been 'thoroughly misconceived'. The assumptions behind the Act had been proved wildly wrong and the Government began to hint that amendments might be necessary.

With his legal curbs on the unions in disarray, Mr Heath turned desperately to other ways of curbing their bargaining power. Inflation was galloping ahead and the employers urgently demanded action to deal with it. His first manoeuvre was to clamp down on wage increases in the public services. He produced the 'N minus One' formula under which each settlement must be 1 per cent lower than the previous one. But by now the unions were up in arms. One after another the dustmen, power workers, postal workers, miners and railwaymen hit back angrily. A series of bitter disputes rocked the economy. From all of them – except the postal workers – the

Government came out worst. In February 1972, after a seven-week strike and a Declaration of Emergency, the miners won a then spectacular wage increase of 25 per cent. By the beginning of 1972 wage settlements were running at twice the level they were at the end of the previous Wilson Government. More working days were being lost through strikes than at any time since the general strike of 1926. The CBI complained that industry was being 'murdered' by wage-cost inflation.

In this situation a chastened Mr Heath made his first overtures of reconciliation with the unions. From July to November 1972, in a series of tripartite talks with the TUC and the CBI, he struggled to win union support for voluntary wage restraint. In doing so he moved dramatically away from his previous attitudes. When the unions pressed the needs of the low paid, he offered an almost egalitarian formula for pay increases, combining a flat rate increase with a percentage one. When they demanded protection against price increases, he accepted the TUC's suggestion of 'threshold agreements' under which every 1 per cent increase in prices above the threshold of 6 per cent would lead automatically to an increase in wages. When they raised the question of pensions, he offered a Christmas bonus. But it was too late. He had driven the unions back into the arms of the Labour Party. At the beginning of the year a Liaison Committee had been set up between the TUC, the National Executive of the Labour Party and the Parliamentary Committee of Labour MPs to heal the breach with the unions. The committee had already spent several months working out agreed social and economic policies. The unions would be content with nothing less from Mr Heath. They demanded the abandonment of import levies on food and of the automatic increases in rents under the Housing Finance Act; a lower rate of VAT; higher pensions and family allowances. Above all they demanded the non-implementation of the Industrial Relations Act. All this was too much for Mr Heath. Matters like these, he told them, must be the responsibility of government.

On 6 November the TUC broke off the talks. Thoroughly alerted now to the need to share in economic decision-making, it complained that Mr Heath had rejected 'a real partnership with both sides of industry in the management of the economy'. That afternoon Mr Heath announced to Parliament a statutory freeze on prices, incomes and dividends. Another reversal of policy was under way. Six months later, under Stage Two of wage restraint, the old apparatus of control was reconstituted. A Price Commission and Pay Board were set up to enforce a new Pay and Price Code. By October 1973, Mr Heath was feeling his way towards refinements of what he clearly saw as a permanent policy. The consultative document on Stage Three, due to run to the autumn of 1974, stressed the need for greater fairness and flexibility. It announced that, within the permitted maximum increase of 7 per cent in a group's pay bills, flat rate increases could be negotiated, if preferred, instead of percentage ones. An additional 'flexibility margin' of 1 per cent was to be provided to deal with special factors and improve efficiency. Threshold agreements could be negotiated outside the pay limits – again on a flat rate basis to help the low paid. These would provide an increase of 40 pence per week for every 1 per cent by which prices rose above the threshold of 6 per cent during the next twelve months. Finally, the document said, the Pay Board was producing a report on pay anomalies which had arisen and had been asked to produce a further report by the end of the year on 'pay relativities' between different workers and different groups. The man who in the election had declared, 'We utterly reject the philosophy of compulsory wage control' was embarked on a fully-fledged statutory prices and incomes policy.

The scene was set for another battle with the miners. In July the National Union of Mineworkers' [NUM] conference had rejected the Government's wages policy. In September the miners had submitted a claim for substantial wage increases designed to recover the ground that had been lost since the settlement of 1972. The miners were in a powerful position, knowing that the Middle East crisis and the huge increase in the price of oil had put a premium on the coal industry. On 12 November they started an overtime ban. By January 1974 this was already having its effect and there was worse to come. On 1 February the NUM balloted its members on a national strike. On a high poll, 81 per cent voted for a strike. This time Mr Heath decided to turn and fight. An election on 'Who Governs Britain?' seemed his only hope.

Throughout all this the Labour Party had been digesting the lessons of Mr Heath's failure and its own previous defeat. Mr Heath's travails had proved two things: that good industrial relations cannot be imposed by law and that an incomes policy cannot work without consent. Harold Wilson's earlier travails – and my own – had driven home the lesson that there could be no future for a Labour Government which set itself at odds with the trade unions. This was not merely because the Labour Party was dependent on union money, but because its rank and file were ready to defend the unions to the death as a vital expression of democracy. The unions' resistance to the Industrial Relations Act was in line with a growing school of thought that democracy is defective unless it also extends into industry and that industrial democracy begins at the shop floor. This had been the theme of the Donovan Report, which complained that the 'formal' system of collective bargaining, with its industry-level agreements, was woefully out of touch with the real – but informal – system in which the effective decisions were hammered out at the workplace. It had also been the theme of speeches by Jack Jones, dreaded leader of the Transport and General Workers' Union, who had been urging the importance of the shop steward as the authentic voice of workers trying to control a major part of their lives: their working environment. A movement had begun on the left of the Labour Party to formalize this belief into a programme for workers' control of industry, in which Tony Benn was an influential voice.

Few Labour leaders were prepared to go as far as this, but all of them realized that the next Labour Government must carry the trade unions with it in its policies. Without this the dream of growth without inflation would be a mirage. Statutory policies to curb trade union bargaining power had failed under successive governments. The only way was to turn that power into something more positive by involving unions in the responsibilities of economic management in return for involving them also in the choice of social policy. It was from this approach that the concept of the Social Contract eventually emerged.

Its evolution was slow. The first meetings of the Liaison Committee were pre-occupied with the unions' basic demand for the immediate, unconditional repeal of the Industrial Relations Act. Gradually the discussion widened. What should take its place? What should be Labour's answer to the problem of strikes? It was Jack Jones, gradually emerging as the most dedicated supporter of a Labour government, who proposed the setting up of a new Advisory Conciliation and Arbitration Service [ACAS] as a means of settling disputes on a voluntary basis. The CBI, with which the TUC had been having talks, welcomed the proposal and readily agreed that such a service must be independent of the Government. In July 1972, the Liaison Committee issued its first joint statement covering these two points.

But the biggest hurdle remained. What were the unions prepared to do to help overcome inflation, which was deteriorating steadily and approaching double figures by April 1973. Incomes policy was anathema. Labour's leaders gave solemn pledges that they would never return to a statutory policy, but this was not enough. So bruised and sensitive were the trade unions that any mention even of a voluntary policy was taboo. When at one of the meetings someone dared to refer to the role of incomes in the management of the economy, Jack Jones jumped in at once: 'It would be disastrous if any word went from this meeting that we had been discussing prices and incomes policy.' The unions insisted that the problem of inflation must be approached from the other end by keeping prices down. Gradually the consensus emerged that the right answer was government action to create a 'climate' to which the unions would respond. This, it was agreed, would involve the reversal of most of the Tories' policies. It would mean price controls, food subsidies, the repeal of the Housing Finance Act, the reversal of Tory tax concessions to the rich, an immediate increase in pensions and other social services, reform of the terms of entry into the EEC, a policy for planned growth, industrial democracy, new public enterprise and greater controls over investment in order to channel public and private funds into manufacturing industry to create new jobs.

By February 1973, these ideas had been embodied in another joint statement, 'Economic Policy and the Cost of Living'. This new approach, said the document, 'will further engender the strong feeling of mutual confidence which alone will make it possible to reach the wide-ranging agreement which is necessary to control inflation and achieve sustained growth in the standard of living'. The politicians were still uneasy, but it was the nearest they could get to voluntary incomes policy.

Meanwhile the Labour Party activists had been rallying their forces. Backed by the left-wing leadership of some of the major unions, the rank and file insisted that never again must a Labour Government be driven to deflationary policies with their accompanying cuts in the social services. At party conference resolutions were carried triumphantly demanding an immediate increase in pensions to £10 single and £16 for a married couple (a campaign led by Jack Jones), improvements in the social services, a major house-building programme, new help for mothers through a child endowment scheme (later known as child benefit), a new deal for the disabled and the ending of social privilege by such means as comprehensive education and the abolition of pay beds in the National Health Service. (The majority of conference wanted to abolish private medicine altogether.) The National Executive Committee of the party, whose membership reflected the party's left-wing bias, responded enthusiastically to this mood and in 1973 embodied these conference decisions in a comprehensive statement of party policy: 'Labour's Programme 1973'. The aim, it declared, must be 'to bring about a fundamental and irreversible shift in the balance of power and wealth in favour of working people and their families'.

Once again the party was in danger of enthusing about ends and neglecting means. Denis Healey, as Shadow Chancellor of the Exchequer, warned that Britain faced the most severe economic crisis since the 1930s. Some of us on the NEC urged that, even with the introduction of a wealth tax which conference was demanding, all the dreams of social expenditure could not be realized at once. As a result of our promptings the NEC published in 1973 a document, 'Paying for Labour's pro-gramme', which we hoped would stimulate 'an informed debate in the party about priorities in spending'. But choice was too painful a process for most conference delegates to face.

The NEC's answer was a new industrial strategy to promote growth and the revival of manufacturing industry. Like Mr Heath, it looked to increased production to solve Britain's problems painlessly. But, unlike Mr Heath, it did not believe that this could be achieved by bribes to private industry. He had tried that and it had not worked. There must, the NEC argued, be more, not less, government intervention, financing and ownership if manufacturing industry was ever to recapture its old supremacy. Rejecting the old approach to public ownership, which tended to saddle the taxpayer with declining industries, it argued that in future the state must invest in profitable industries. So in addition to calling for the nationalization of aircraft and shipbuild-ing, ports and steel because of their importance to the economy, the NEC document demanded that a National Enterprise Board be set up, with government funds, to invest in profitable companies in return for a controlling equity interest. National economic planning must be underpinned by a new system of planning agreements at company level to be concluded by the Government with all major firms as a condition of receiving government aid. These tripartite agreements would give both the Government and the workers in these companies, through their trade unions, a say in deciding the planning objectives of the firm – its export, pricing and investment policies.

It was a new attempt to reconcile public ownership and control with private initiative in a mixed economy. It was also a practical instalment of industrial democracy. Few party members absorbed the details. The more timid Labour politicians had their private reservations. But Harold Wilson embraced the new concept enthusiastically in a speech which brought the 1973 party conference to its feet in the exciting belief that next time things would be different.

But this euphoria concealed dangerous rifts. The swing to the left had not gone unchallenged. A group of Labour MPs had begun to mobilize against what they considered the 'extremism' of the NEC and the party conference. Their ideological leader was Roy Jenkins, who aroused the same devotion among his followers as Hugh Gaitskell had once done. And they had never forgiven the former Bevanite, Harold Wilson, for capturing the succession to their adored leader when Gaitskell died in 1963. But this time, unlike Gaitskell, the 'moderates' had become fanatically devoted to the European cause. Like Mr Heath, they had lost faith in their country's ability to solve her problems outside the wider free trade market of the Community and the assumed economic stimulus it would bring. They denounced the Left's policies as 'little Englandism'. The Left, in turn, denounced this approach as a surrender to free market economics and coalition politics.

It was with this explosive situation that Harold Wilson had to deal. He had personally become a convert to Britain's membership of the Community and as Prime Minister he had persuaded his Cabinet and the party conference to allow him to apply for membership in 1967 on strict terms and conditions, but the application was vetoed by President de Gaulle before negotiations could begin. De Gaulle resigned in 1969 and, on coming into office a year later, Mr Heath had seized his opportunity and re-started talks. These were successfully completed a year later. The Labour Party immediately split. The anti-marketeers denounced the terms, later getting the support of the party conference, a majority of Labour MPs and most of the unions.

The pro-marketeers fought back, making it clear they would put Europe first. Roy Jenkins, in a speech interpreted by the press as an oblique attack on Harold Wilson, called for 'honesty and consistency' in the party's policy. George Thomson, who had been Minister for Europe in the Wilson Government, wrecked the party's line by claiming that the Heath terms were as good as any the Labour Government could have got. (Two years later he gave up British politics to become a European Commissioner.) The bitterness intensified when, in October 1971, sixty-nine Labour MPs, headed by Roy Jenkins, defied the Labour whip and voted for Mr Heath's motion approving entry on his terms, giving him a majority of 112. On Europe the political coalition had become a reality.

As leader Harold Wilson had seen it as his prime function to hold the party together, whatever the cost in ideology. Indeed, his original backers, the Left, complained that he had gone out of his way to conciliate his right-wing critics. Now the party was tearing itself apart again. In February 1971, Jim Callaghan came out against the terms. The party crisis had become a crisis of Harold Wilson's own leadership. He privately told some of us that he was going to come out against the terms, even though he knew it would destroy his credibility. This he did at a special conference of the party in July in such a low-key speech that both Left and Right complained of his lack of leadership. Later he became a convert to Tony Benn's idea of a referendum on Britain's membership as the best way to defuse the situation. This eventually became party policy.

As he had anticipated Harold Wilson was mercilessly pilloried in the pro-Market press. His old ally, the *Daily Mirror*, came out against him, deriding him as a 'tethered sacrificial goat' to party unity. Newspaper after newspaper harped on his 'loss of authority'. On 20 October 1971, *The Times* excelled the chorus by declaring he must never again be Prime Minister. By contrast Roy Jenkins was built up in the press as a 'man of principle'. The more fanatical pro-marketeers began to campaign for a change in leadership. There was increasing talk of the need for a new centre party and in 1972 Dick Taverne, Labour MP for Lincoln, whose local party had passed a vote of no confidence in him because of his vote to support Heath's terms, resigned the Labour Whip to fight as an independent Democratic Labour candidate. He held the seat in a by-election, though he was to lose it at the general election of October 1974.

The strain on Harold Wilson began to tell. He became dispirited and more than once hinted at resignation. But Roy Jenkins had no stomach for political in-fighting. After a series of major political speeches, which the press applauded as an attack on the Left, he resigned the deputy leadership, leaving his supporters dismayed. Denis Healey gladly stepped into his shoes as Shadow Chancellor. Michael Foot, who had run Jenkins close in the elections for deputy, increasingly emerged as a conciliator.

It was therefore a bruised and shaken Harold Wilson who prepared for a general election in January 1974. His party was held together only precariously. Although important steps had been taken towards reconciliation with the TUC, the unions remained suspicious of any hint of a return to the old policies or any curbs on their freedom of action. In readiness for the election, the Labour Party had set up the joint meetings of the NEC and the Parliamentary Committee of the Parliamentary Labour Party which, under its constitution, were responsible for deciding which items from the party programme should be included in the Manifesto. It had drawn up a campaign document, based on the agreement reached with the TUC and resolutions passed by party conference.

Meanwhile the economic crisis was deepening. And the British public groped its way through the mysteries of the three-day week.

1974

Tuesday, 1 January

Another wonderful Christmas over. Ted festooned Hell Corner Farm again with ivy and old man's beard; my food was a success and I even managed to squeeze in the children's play on Christmas Eve. It was a mad, impromptu rush and I would never have coped without Jennie Hall's help in dressing up the children. I was improvising the last act as I went along but the children all rose to the occasion.

On Sunday, the family[1] gone, we gave our adult party. Everyone said it was our best yet. There is no doubt that Ted and I are very good at giving parties. Ted, of course, is the supreme giver of himself and I am happy to dash around feeding everyone. Hell Corner Farm [HCF] looks so lovely on these occasions with the log fire greeting everyone as they walk into the dining room, the flames flickering across the polished tiles. I remember John Freeman saying to me years ago how he envied us – particularly Ted – for our capacity as hosts. Some people, he said rather wistfully, would like to be able to give out as we do, but they just can't.

One unexpectedly nice touch to Christmas: a card from Vic Feather signed 'Affectionately, Vic'. And I had always thought his cards were routine official necessity.

Yesterday we set off for Southampton to spend New Year with Phil and Colin[2] and are just recovering from their New Year's Eve party.

Thursday, 3 January

Terry Pitt[3] has become a menace. With three weeks to do his redraft of the campaign document he has left it to the last minute as usual and has called a meeting of the redrafting committee, of which I have been made a member, today. I am not going to curtail my bit of holiday still further to be there. Terry had to rush his 'redraft' down to Southampton by train yesterday and it turned out to be almost the same wording which we criticized so strongly at the December joint meeting with the Parliamentary Committee. I am waiting for him to phone me for my comments – in vain.

---

[1] My only sister, Marjorie McIntosh, had died in 1961 leaving three children, Sonya, Philippa and Hugh, to whom I became 'proxy Mum'. Childless ourselves, Ted and I made our rambling old cottage in the Chiltern hills the family gathering ground for the three children, their spouses, nine great-nephews and nieces and my mother.

[2] Philippa, my niece, and her husband, Colin Dobson. They have two children, Kathryn and Ben.

[3] Head of the Research Department at Transport House, the Labour Party's HQ.

Friday, 4 January

My hopes of a week's rest after Christmas have been dashed as the Liaison Committee with the TUC has been called unexpectedly for this morning. It is all part of the emergency atmosphere. I make my way to London by train without too much difficulty, though the trains are running spasmodically. The meeting was at Congress House, so Sid Greene [general secretary of the National Union of Railwaymen] was in the chair. The parliamentary side was strongly represented – Harold [Wilson], Denis [Healey], Jim [Callaghan], Wedgie [Benn], Reg Prentice, Mik [Ian Mikardo], Bob Mellish, Douglas Houghton, Ron Hayward and me – but the trade unions were terribly thin on the ground: only George Smith [general secretary of the construction workers' union, UCATT] in addition to Sid and of course Len Murray[1] and his officials. When I arrived Wedgie was reporting on the campaign document as it had emerged from yesterday's redrafting committee, which our visit to Southampton had forced me to miss. He was rubbing in how closely it conformed to the joint statement agreed with the TUC.[2] (One piece of good news: Mike [Foot] has apparently completely rewritten Terry Pitt's mediocre draft.) Jim, who had also arrived late, then chipped in, pointing out that, although the campaign document was now pretty good, it had one serious weakness – its lack of reference to incomes. Without this our posture at the election would not be credible. Could the TUC help us on this? He thought something like the reference in the TUC *Economic Review* for 1972, setting out the terms for voluntary incomes policy, would be a great help. To my surprise Bob backed him strongly: 'I endorse this.' At the recent Parliamentary Labour Party meeting, he said, the theme of our lack of credibility on anti-inflation policy had run through many of the speeches. 'What are we to stand for at the election? A free for all? Could we not agree a form of words with the TUC?'

Harold's turn next. It was true, he said, that this point could be thrown at us during the election; it had already been thrown at him by Robin Day and others on TV yesterday. He thought Basnett's article in the *Observer* last week had struck just the right note. Denis then came in, putting it in the sensible way he always does on these occasions. What was lacking, he said, was a statement of *intention* by the TUC – 'something going beyond what you *think* might happen'. Of course it had to be a realistic statement. We were not asking for any reference to 'norms' or rigid commitment to an incomes policy. But what we needed was an indication that, if the Labour Government fulfilled its side of the compact, the TUC for its part would try to make the economic policy work. 'We shall be suffering a critical handicap in the election if the trade unions can't help us on this,' he urged. Reg Prentice thought it was time for him to make some running for the moderates, too. (He has an image to keep up.) 'I would like us to go a bit further and say we *believe* in an incomes policy, even though we recognize it would have to be voluntary,' he insisted. (Lucky for him Jack Jones wasn't there – I can imagine the explosion at this point!) Still, our side kept up the barrage while the trade union boys sat silent: after all, we outnumbered them by eight to two. It was as though safety in numbers had given MPs the courage to reveal their secret thoughts.

[1] Len Murray had taken over the general secretaryship of the TUC from Vic Feather in October 1973.
[2] 'Economic Policy and the Cost of Living'. See Introduction.

18

Douglas next, with one of the jarring notes he loves to strike. 'What has distressed me over the past years has been to watch the decline and fall of the TUC,' he said. 'It has become a non-body. It is not dealing with any of the major issues on the industrial front: for example, how do you settle pay disputes in the public sector (outside the Civil Service), where market forces no longer operate and in my view will never operate again?' And he went on to deploy his familiar arguments about the problem of dealing with the public sector fairly in a free-for-all situation. I listened to all these speeches rather ironically, remembering the months of discussion in which these people have remained silent on the question of what industrial quid pro quo we should exact for the political commitments we have made to the unions. I thought to myself, 'The imminence of an election concentrates the mind wonderfully. This is the crunch, but we are wasting our time at this meeting because neither of the terrible twins – Jack [Jones] or Hughie [Scanlon] – are here. We ought to call another meeting urgently to go over the same ground with them there.' I was about to say this openly when Wedgie cut in on me. He sits very pontifically these days, looking as though he has access to some secret and superior wisdom. (He also scribbles copious notes and I am convinced he is keeping a detailed diary.) He proceeded solemnly: 'This is an important discussion. The problem is real but what worries me is the increasing implication that the solution is easy. The fact is that there is no answer to the problem except through consent. A form of words won't solve anything. We must not fall into the trap which *The Times* has set for us and seem to accept their argument that wages are the cause of inflation.' He didn't like the idea either, he said, of talking about a voluntary incomes policy. That, too, led us into a trap. Heath had started by talking about a voluntary incomes policy and then said that because it had failed he had been forced to introduce a statutory one. All a Labour Government could do was to create the climate of a just society along the lines we had already agreed and if it did that he believed the response would come.

Mik sat silent through all this at the far end of the table on his own, scribbling some of his innumerable tables of figures. Jim clearly thought it was time to resume his emollient role. 'We don't want a debate between ourselves on this. All we ask is that when our campaign document is published you will study it and see how you can help us on it.' This gave Sid Greene his cue and he seized it readily. He may not have the parliamentarians' fluency, but he is no fool and he was soon getting in some shrewd blows in that drawling way of his. 'Douglas says we are a non-body. I am sorry that we don't impress you, but then you don't impress us.' (A flicker of guilt in the eyes of those of us who had been members of the last Labour Government.) He had a simple formula: 'You won't modify wage claims, but you will modify settlements.' The Labour Government had got an incomes policy anyway: all governments had an incomes policy because they had to control incomes in some way, whether by taxation or social services policy or whatever. 'The question is whether it is an agreed one.' And he concluded, 'There is a great desire in the TUC to get an agreement that will get us a Labour Government.' Final shot: 'We as a TUC have no more control over our unions than you have over your members.' (Wince of amusement from Bob.)

Sid then called on Len Murray, who was at his most impressive. He began fluently: 'I must say after listening to this discussion that if you are relying on some commitment by the TUC to some kind of incomes policy you have got to think again. There ain't going to be any statement like that.' Some of the statements round the table had seemed a bit Bourbon to him – as though some people had learned nothing and forgotten nothing. He then gave us a lecture on the pitfalls of incomes policy. The expectations of working people had changed in the past twenty years and in his view one of the main causes had been incomes policy. Fixing 'norms' merely led everyone to expect certain increases automatically. Why did we want intervention in free collective bargaining? Presumably to try and alter relativities between wage earners and to safeguard the balance of payments. Experience proved that a statutory incomes policy had made no significant difference in relativities and the effect on the balance of payments had been almost nil. This did not mean that the TUC did not recognize the problem or refuse to try to help solve it. 'We have said to this Government time and again that if it would do so and so, the TUC would respond. God help us, we cannot go beyond that.' The greatest disservice the TUC could do a Labour Government was to pretend it could do more than it could: the disillusion from that would be far more damaging than the refusal to make impossible promises in the first place. And Len ended almost appealingly: 'If you want us to go further than what we have said in the joint document we have issued then you had better tell us just what you want.'

His speech relaxed the tension. It was as though, not for the first time, each side had listened to the other's problem and had realized it was well-nigh insoluble. So somehow we had got to get through by the solvent of mutual sympathy. It was noticeable that during his speech Len had never given Wedgie a glance, let alone a reference. Harold took up the challenge: we must study the words in the TUC 1972 *Economic Review*. And Len nodded vigorously when Harold added, 'What we need is more the creation of a mood than a compact.' The give and take grew every minute. Len suggested that the TUC might look at our campaign document and decide what public response they might make to it. Harold replied that the less formality there was about this the better: 'We should not send you anything formally and ask for a compact but anything we get in response from you will be a bonus.' Len asked if the TUC might see the document before publication. Jim pointed out the timetable difficulties. The National Executive Committee were holding their joint meeting with the Parliamentary Committee on 9 January, and, if the document were approved then, we should expect to publish on the 10th. Harold pointed out that we always sent the TUC copies of our policy documents 'as a fraternal courtesy' and it had been known for premature leaks to occur. Sid summed it up by saying, 'We want to be able to say when we see the document that we are in agreement with the policy and will do our best to help implement it.' He added, 'This has been a very valuable discussion.' At that we left it to the manipulators to deal with the mechanics.

We then turned to the current economic situation. Harold treated us to a long résumé of his statement of yesterday on the miners' claim and his TV interviews, which we had already read or seen. He may follow the example of the wise thrush [1]

---

[1] 'That's the wise thrush: he sings each song twice over,
Lest you should think he never could recapture
That first fine careless rapture!'   Browning, *Home Thoughts from Abroad*.

but by God it can make him boring. Only one new point. Harold does not think Heath wants an election, 'though his Pearl Harbor boys do'. The trouble was that Heath had a very low flash-point: if he lost his temper he might go for one. Wedgie agreed with this analysis but said that nonetheless we were in the opening phases of an election campaign. He wanted action (joint meetings with the TUC if possible) to demand the withdrawal of the three-day week and the introduction of an emergency increase in the family allowance while the three-day week lasted. Michael Meacher had told him it would cost £15 million a week. George Smith dismissed these suggestions as 'catchpenny', but he gave even shorter shrift to Reg Prentice who now made a speech of such insensitivity that I am convinced he will never be Secretary of State for Employment in a Labour Government. Reg, remembering how the press have cast him, too, for the role of a 'man of principle' (when *The Times* does that to Labour leaders it is the kiss of death), proceeded to say that he was against joint demonstrations against the three-day week because some restrictions were essential. 'Our duty is to be constructive and show some signs of national unity.' The miners should certainly be paid more, but that did not mean that their action was justified because they were contributing to the fuel crisis and to hardship for other workers. We should say publicly that their action should be called off. 'And what happens when you have made that speech?' snarled Harold. But George Smith outdid him in fury. He had been 'appalled' by Reg's approach and he warned him, moderate as George is, that 'the TUC would never accept that the miners are not entitled to stop doing overtime when for years they have been warning this country about the fuel crisis. We've seen all the documents.' The Labour Party, I thought to myself, may or may not be heading for a 1931 split but I believe that, if a split comes, the right-wing rump will be so small as barely to make a ripple on the political surface. The political 'moderates' haven't got an ally among the trade-union moderates. So for whom do they stand?

I made my way to Marylebone pretty satisfied with the morning's work, except that all our constructive decisions have been taken in the absence of the representatives of the two most powerful unions in the country. Nonetheless, I think Len knew he was speaking for them. Perhaps he can deliver the goods. At the station, when my train eventually crawled in, the ticket inspector (who of course recognized me) was very bitter about ASLEF.[1] I can't blame him: he is losing, he told me, £40 a month. But the most significant fact I discovered was that his take-home *basic* pay is £25 a week. Rates like that, in a still affluent society like ours, are the breeding ground for militancy.

Wednesday, 9 January

Heath has conceded a recall of Parliament to discuss the emergency, so there is talk of a general election on the 'Who Governs Britain?' issue. I have established a 'hot line' to the constituency on the effects of the three-day week and have been tied to my desk for two days, taking the calls. Wedgie's elaborate plans for monitoring the

[1] For several weeks the Amalgamated Society of Locomotive Engineers and Firemen had been operating a ban on Sunday overtime and rest-day working in order to secure better terms for its members under a pay package offered by British Rail and broadly accepted by the other rail unions.

effects of the fuel crisis don't seem to have cut much ice in the constituencies. My 'hot line' idea has had much more effect – he does love to overorganize things. He has made a great splash with his figures on coal stocks to prove the three-day week is not necessary, but the *Sunday Times* has repudiated them. At Information Committee [of the National Executive Committee] yesterday I urged him to get off this tack now and concentrate on possible solutions to the miners' dispute: for example, the coming Relativities Report of the Pay Board on which I have been having secret confabulations with Derek Robinson.[1] But Wedgie would have none of it. We also had a long discussion with representatives of the National Labour Women's Advisory Council on how to attract the women's vote. I have a theory about this. I believe the vote in this country is polarizing, not so much on class lines, as on sex lines. The pursuit of money wage increases is a masculine syndrome; the fight for the social wage is a feminine need. Wage increases, which put up prices, don't necessarily put up the wife's housekeeping money by the same amount. While the chaps talk militancy in the pub the women have to cope with the consequences of that militancy, including the cuts in social services this Government has announced. So our propaganda should concentrate less on wage demands and more on protecting women from cuts in the social wage. Wedgie promised to convey all this to the campaign committee.

Just before Harold got up to speak in this afternoon's debate, David Stoddart [Labour MP for Swindon] said to me, 'If Harold would speak for twenty-five minutes instead of an hour he can't miss. I've sent him this message via Joe Haines.' In the event Harold spoke for forty-five minutes and did well. I managed to intervene in Heath's speech with a question that roused the House: 'If the Pay Board's report on relativities, which I understand is due out shortly, makes out a case for special cases to receive special payment, is the Government prepared to amend the pay code immediately?' Heath stalled, of course, but Elystan Morgan [Labour MP for Cardiganshire] whispered to me, 'That is the key issue. We must pursue it.' Later in Annie's Bar, Charles Taylor [Conservative MP for Eastbourne], of all people, insisted on buying me a drink, saying, 'I have never heard an intervention go to the heart of the matter more than yours did today.' And he went on to say that when I first came into the House he thought I was a bitch. Then as he got to know me he came not only to respect, but to like me. Well, well! I intend to try and speak tomorrow.

Thursday, 10 January

The Speaker called me early – immediately after Enoch Powell – so I threw away my notes and debated ad lib, only returning to my notes to read from the Pay Board's terms of reference to prove that the special increases likely to be proposed under the

[1] In 1973 Mr Heath decided to make his statutory pay policy more flexible. In the White Paper on the second stage of the policy (Cmnd. 5205) he announced that the Pay Board would be asked to report on anomalies that had arisen during the first stage and also to look at the problem of pay relativities and of groups who felt they deserved special treatment in order to improve their relative position in the community. The Anomalies Report was published in September 1973. The Relativities Report, due at the end of the year, had not yet appeared. Derek Robinson, a deputy chairman of the Pay Board, had chaired the enquiry into pay relativities.

Relativities Report were intended to be part of Stage Three. Mike [Foot] and Lena [Jeger] were full of praise. In the corridor I ran into Dick [Crossman], breathless with walking up the entrance stairs. He sank down beside me while I tried to interest him in the Relativities Report. He looked ill; said his tummy was in a bad way. 'They tell me there is nothing they can do: they give me three months or three years.' My poor, darling Dick. I chatted to him as normally as I could, going out of my way to praise his last column in *The Times*, at which he brightened up.

Friday, 11 January

The joint meeting of the National Executive Committee and Parliamentary Committee to finalize the campaign document was again held in the Churchill Hotel, where apparently we have an ally in the manager, who does us well. Michael Hatfield in *The Times* is this morning trying to stir up trouble with a story about how the valiant moderates are going to have a showdown about the need for us to commit ourselves to an incomes policy. It really is pathetic how *The Times* has to invent its heroes and villains. In the event Mike's redraft (which in itself was sensible and constructive) went through practically unchallenged. Frank Allaun [Labour MP for East Salford] was waiting to pounce on the reference to arms reduction and nuclear policy. We had a straight vote on whether we should include the specific figure of a £1,000 million reduction target – and those of us who supported Frank won, to Jim's amiable grumbling. For the rest, we again solved our problem by reverting to former compromise texts as though they were Holy Writ. The longest argument was over the references to public ownership, on which I had scribbled a substantial redraft in order to spell out the reasons why we are going to acquire sections of profitable industries. Mik welcomed my redraft at once, but Frank, backed by Joan Maynard[1] and John Forrester,[2] suspected that I was providing loopholes for *not* taking over profitable industries. After some patient explaining and the incorporation of some words by Mik, with Harold backing me vigorously and saying that we must not go back on the commitments of his conference speech,[3] we reached agreement. Reg Prentice protested that he thought the nationalization list was too long, and Roy Jenkins clearly had some anxieties, but none of the Right put up much of a fight.

Some of our time was spent dealing with Denis's dire warnings about the economic holocaust we should inherit when we took over and how we could incorporate some reference to this in the document. But we *did* agree that the pensions and food subsidies commitments should stand, come what might. I am beginning to suspect that Denis will be an even more stubborn deflationist than Jim. He has, unfortunately, more backbone. I remember those endless struggles with him over the F–111A.[4] He doesn't give up easily.

[1] Miss Joan Maynard, Labour MP for Sheffield, Brightside. Member of the NEC since 1970.

[2] Deputy General Secretary of the Amalgamated Union of Engineering Workers – Technical and Supervisory Section – and a member of the NEC since 1972. He died in 1978.

[3] See Introduction.

[4] During the major review of public expenditure carried out during January 1968 by the Labour Government, of which Denis and I were both members, Denis, then Minister of Defence, fought

One significant little incident at the beginning of the meeting. I sat myself down next to Wedgie, who was positively bubbling with euphoria. He has certainly done a good job over the three-day week and Wedgie only needs a dash of success to become uncontainable. He swamped me with extravagant praise: 'What a *marvellous* speech of yours yesterday, Duckie.' At that moment up came John Forrester with a copy of the *Morning Star* containing the report of a resolution passed by a North-Western group of AUEW lefties pledging full support for Wedgie's efforts in the class war, etc. Immensely gratified, Wedgie assured him, 'Things are really on the move.' Next came Joan Maynard asking him to speak at some left-wing meeting of hers. Wedgie nodded solemnly and took out a crowded diary. He seems to have appointed himself a one-man Popular Front. I am a bit more canny than that myself.

Sunday, 13 January

The papers, starved of any hard news about a 'row' yesterday, are busy trying to create one, some of them making a big point of the fact that the wording of the campaign document did not actually rule out the introduction of a statutory incomes policy. (So much for Michael's tactful redraft.) But then the press must somehow conjure up a victory for the 'moderates'.

Monday, 14 January

Back to work because the recess has been shortened. I still think that Heath may announce an election on 7 February on the 'Who Governs Britain?' issue and I am trying to get my Blackburn boys to get going on the postal votes. My Tory opponent is extremely active and the National Party candidate, Kingsley Read, is digging himself in, helped by the local council's mishandling of the redevelopment issue. I can't get my chaps to learn tactics. My aim is to place the responsibility for refusing to save these housing areas on the Government, but they go at things like a bull in a china shop. My sympathies are all with the old ladies who want to end their days in their own homes and with those people who have spent a lot of money on improvements.

Monday, 21 January

Meeting of the Social Policy Committee of the National Executive Committee at which we made progress with our disablement policy. Dick phoned to ask if I was free to have dinner with him in the Members' dining room. Though inconvenient I said yes at once. He looked haggard and weak. When I said that I was going to buy him some wine he said, 'Not much for me; I'm not allowed alcohol with my tummy.' But then he rallied enough to encourage me to buy an excellent half bottle of dry white wine, of which he drank a glass. He began by ordering some food, but only ate a mouthful. My heart ached for him. We talked relativities, in which I have at last persuaded him to take some interest. He guessed that the source of my information

---

tenaciously to save his order for fifty American F–111A aircraft. Cabinet eventually decided to cancel the order, making a saving estimated at £400 million over 1968–78.

was Derek Robinson, with whom I talk regularly on the phone. Derek is very keen for his report to be used in the miners' dispute and is keeping me genned up about when it will appear. But Dick was *distrait* and seemed to find it too much to concentrate even on light political gossip. 'My tummy is playing me up; no, I've no pain, thank God, but endless discomfort. And then I get so tired. I spend most of the week down in the country. Anne likes that.' I got him talking about his new TV series to try and cheer him up, but, frankly, I don't think he will live to do it. My poor, poor Anne! Their friends feel so helpless.

Wednesday, 23 January

I stood up about twenty times trying to get in on Heath's questions so as to deal with the Relativities Report, but Selwyn [Lloyd] didn't call me. Ran into Willie Whitelaw behind the Speaker's chair and he was fuming about the fact that I hadn't been called. 'Former Employment Secretary and a Privy Councillor and not called! I think it is intolerable.' He even tried to rope in the Tory Chief Whip who was passing by and I had to say mildly that really Selwyn was usually very kind to me. I am puzzled by Willie's friendliness. Is he still grateful to me for bailing him out over my recent intervention[1] or does he need my questions for some ploy of his in the Cabinet?

Went along to the National Executive Committee determined that this time we should issue a statement on the miners. The officers, despite my protests last time, had failed to produce one. Jim[2] said they had considered doing so but had decided that it would serve no useful purpose since everything was being adequately debated in Parliament. Mike again backed me up when I said it was absurd for the NEC not to have a view on issues like the miners' strike: the more publicity we got the better. Jim promised he would take an emergency resolution. Wedgie had already circulated one, just praising the TUC and pledging full support for the miners. I sat scribbling one calling on the Government to enter into immediate negotiations with the National Coal Board [NCB] and the National Union of Mineworkers [NUM] for a settlement of the miners' claim on the basis of the Relativities Report. But when we came to discuss it there was an almost unanimous preference for Tony's version. Even Denis and Fred Mulley said we should just support the TUC's initiative and not spell out anything else. Joan [Maynard] didn't like this because she didn't like the TUC's suggestion that the miners were a special case.[3] 'The Government are not just taking on the miners

---

[1] During his speech in the debate on the three-day week on 10 January, Mr Whitelaw, Secretary of State for Employment, refused several times to give way to Labour MP George Cunningham, and then gave way to me. When Mr Cunningham protested, I defended Mr Whitelaw by pointing out that I was 'one of his predecessors who had to handle prices and incomes policy'. It was clear to me at the time that Mr Whitelaw wanted to give me the chance to press my point about the Relativities Report, which I duly did.

[2] Jim Callaghan was chairman of the Labour Party for the year 1973–74 and therefore presided over the NEC.

[3] On 9 January the TUC Economic Committee had agreed that the miners should be treated as a special case and at a meeting of the National Economic Development Council the same day the TUC had told the Government that, if the miners' claim were to be settled outside the Stage Three limits, other unions would not use this as a bargaining counter in their own negotiations. This offer was repeated subsequently but was rejected by the Conservative Government.

but the workers as a whole,' she insisted. Sid Weighell[1] didn't like the suggestion that the miners were a special case, either. Ominous, that! John Forrester disagreed with the criticisms: 'The TUC has given nothing away. A ritual dance is going on.' Eventually it was agreed to take my two opening paragraphs, referring to the 'Government's summary rejection of every attempt to solve the miners' dispute', and to add Tony's piece, though the wording of both had to be amended to meet the sensitivities expressed. I felt cynical about Denis's attitude. These people who will not even fight for a constructive resolution in the NEC are the first to tell the TUC at the Liaison Committee, privately, that they must make more gestures to make our anti-inflation policy 'credible'. And I'm damn sure that if we were in government Denis would be the first to insist on an incomes policy.

This was all the more inexcusable since earlier Wedgie had had a brush over incomes policy. He at least is consistent. He raised the way in which the press had dealt with this issue in its reports of our special meeting with the Parliamentary Committee, suggesting that we had left a loophole in our document for an incomes policy. 'There seems to have been a lot of briefing on a statutory incomes policy,' he complained. He is carrying his opposition to *any* incomes policy almost to pathological lengths. Jim just said briskly, 'Shall we say "noted" to that? I don't know of any such briefing. Individuals will go on saying what they think.'

Thursday, 24 January

Another determined attempt to get called on the PM's questions in the House. To my astonishment, no luck. Even surrounding backbenchers protested to me about it. So after questions I went to Selwyn and asked him mildly if he could not see me where I sat. 'It looks as if I can't,' said Selwyn, puzzled. So he hadn't noticed me! His failure to call me was also off-putting for BBC 2, which had booked me to record a piece for this Sunday's *Westminster*. However, the recording went ahead and I was able to rub in my points about the Relativities Report.

Tuesday, 29 January

Derek Robinson has changed the whole climate over the Relativities Report[2] by saying over the weekend that it *could* be used quickly to deal with the miners' dispute. And Derek Ezra [chairman of the National Coal Board] is reported in the *Guardian* as having asked the Government to use it. I have spoken to Len Murray as to what would be the TUC attitude to my pressing the Government on this. He said that it would be perfectly okay for me to trail my coat, though the TUC had not discussed the Relativities Report yet and would be chary of getting themselves involved in the proposed machinery. He could not see the TUC being willing to sit down with the CBI: they had had no confidence in them recently. 'We have avoided hooking the long-

---

[1] Assistant General Secretary of the NUR. He succeeded Sid Greene as General Secretary in February 1975.

[2] The report (Cmnd. 5535) had been published on 19 January. It recommended a procedure for considering claims for special treatment under pay policy.

term issue on to the short-term one. All we have said about the report is that manifestly its reference to exceptional cases is relevant to the miners' situation. You might say that obviously there is going to be controversy about the machinery but the PM's reaction to the TUC initiative is very damaging to the longer-term possibility of dealing with these matters by discussion and co-operation.' He was obviously very pleased that I had consulted him and thought that this was the way things should be done.

Armed by this talk I went into the chamber determined to get in on the PM's supplementaries this time. As advised by Selwyn, I had a word with the Speaker's secretary – only to discover to my horror that it wasn't Selwyn in his chair but his deputy. Although I stood up time after time it looked as if I was going to be unlucky and Willie started gesticulating at me frantically. That man's desire for me to get in on relativities can only mean that I am helping him to play some game in Cabinet. He obviously wants desperately to settle with the miners. At last, after some signals of my own to the Speaker's secretary, I was called and made my point[1] to some 'Hear, Hears' from our own side. Afterwards David Ginsburg [Labour MP for Dewsbury] came into my room to tell me that not only had I put a first-class question, but that Willie had told him how pleased he was with it. Well, well!

I was leaving the House later with John Silkin to have dinner with Reggie Paget (who apparently loves cooking for people) when I got an urgent message to go and have a word with Harold. Harold, brandy in hand, was dictating a letter to Heath following up my point and wanted my advice on it. I warned him that we must not commit the TUC on machinery though I was sure we could make capital out of the 'exceptional' cases principle. I left him dictating to Doreen.

Wednesday, 30 January

Harold's letter to Heath has got great prominence, but I am alarmed at the unguarded way he has gone overboard for the whole report, with none of the reservations I had urged on him. He really is the most reckless tactician, always getting himself into corners. As I suspected Heath has seized back the initiative, saying he will apply the report to the miners if the TUC will say openly that they accept both the principles and the machinery: just the trap the TUC wanted to avoid! I went on *Nationwide* to discuss the issue and did rather well, arguing that Heath should go ahead and apply the report himself.

Thursday, 31 January

Off to Blackburn again, where I feel so frustrated by Heath's unctuousness that I give a long press interview saying that I have a peace formula. Two things are essential for a settlement I say: (1) Heath must be able to say it is within Stage Three (which he can

---

[1] I reminded Mr Heath that both Derek Robinson and Sir Derek Ezra were pressing for the report to be used as a basis for a settlement with the miners and I demanded: 'Will the Government face up to their responsibilities, take the initiative and take the necessary steps to secure a settlement on the report – or is the nation to be sacrificed to the Prime Minister's blind bigotry?'

because the Relativities Report was always visualized as part of Stage Three), and (2) the TUC must not be asked to abandon its long-standing opposition to a statutory incomes policy. Heath should therefore immediately refer the miners' case to the Pay Board on his own responsibility. (Who, after all, governs Britain?)

Sunday, 3 February

Talk to Derek on the phone about the report. Even the *Observer* comments that Heath is implicitly asking the TUC to accept his incomes policy.

Monday, 4 February

First meeting of our drugs working party.[1] It is clear that public ownership isn't going to be easy here.

Tuesday, 5 February

Decide I must speak on second reading of the Housing Bill, for Blackburn reasons. But send a note to the Speaker asking if I could possibly speak on the economic debate as well. He says, yes, if I will wait till Thursday – the second day of the debate. 'If there *is* a second day,' I tell his secretary prophetically. The air is full of election speculation again. Clearly a lot of pressure is being put on Heath by his own people, who are furious with him for not going for 7 February. (In that way he would certainly miss some of the bad trade and other figures due to be published during the month.) Make a good speech on housing and am congratulated enthusiastically by Tony Crosland and others. Suddenly, speaking in the House has ceased to trouble me.

Thursday, 7 February

Get into the House early to prepare my notes. In comes Roy Mason. 'There will be no debate today, love. Parliament is to be dissolved tomorrow.' I feel cheated. Everyone in serious huddles. Some Tories are obviously distressed. 'No one wants this election,' one of them told me.

Friday, 8 February

Into Transport House to clear the Manifesto. No panic anywhere. Anyway Heath has enabled us to fight on the new register and we have made a start on postal votes.

Saturday, 9 February

Heath announces he has sent the miners' dispute to the Pay Board himself. Just what I advocated! I feel more cheated than ever that I did not get my speech in. If Harold

---

[1] For some years the Labour Party conference had debated resolutions calling for the nationalization of the pharmaceutical industry. These had been remitted to the National Executive Committee for further study and a working party had been set up.

had only listened to me he could have had the credit for the idea. But Heath's move has taken a lot of the wind out of his own sails. Reds under the bed don't seem so convincing any more.

Sunday, 10 February

Drive to Blackburn with Ted and Alison[1] to start the campaign.

The election campaign was launched in an atmosphere of bitterness when the miners, despite the pleas of their President, Joe Gormley, refused to suspend their national strike. At midnight on 9 February every pit closed down. Labour, first off the mark with its Manifesto based on its campaign document, fought the election on the under-standing it had reached with the unions. Mr Heath fought it on the need for 'strong government'. When Mr Wilson referred to the existence of a 'Social Contract' with the unions, Mr Heath poured scorn on it and demanded to see the piece of paper on which it was written. Mr Wilson replied that he was referring to the joint statement with the TUC *of February 1973: 'Economic Policy and the Cost of Living'.*

Mr Heath's riposte was to try to turn the election into a 'vote against disruption'. While promising amendments to the Industrial Relations Act, he insisted that its essential structure must be maintained. In the Conservative Manifesto, he declared war on 'a small number of militants' who 'manipulate and abuse the monopoly power of their unions' and hinted that social security would no longer be paid to strikers' families. Inflation was the main enemy. He would press ahead with pay and prices policy, 'if necessary stiffening it'. The time had come, he said, to tell the extremists: 'We've had enough.'

Harold Wilson's determination to widen the issues was helped by the official announcement in mid-campaign that the index of retail food prices had risen by 20 per cent in the previous year: the fastest rise at any time since 1947. It was also helped dramatically when Mr Enoch Powell announced that he would not seek re-election as Conservative MP *for Wolverhampton because he would not be a party to an 'essentially fraudulent election', adding later that he had cast his postal vote for Labour because it was the only party offering the people the chance to vote in a referendum on whether they wished to remain in the Common Market. Another blow came three days before the poll with the publication of the trade figures showing a £383 million deficit. The* Times *described this as 'the largest monthly trade deficit that Britain has known'. The following day the final indignity was heaped on Mr Heath when Mr Campbell Adam-son, Director-General of the Confederation of British Industry, called for the repeal of the Industrial Relations Act because it was 'surrounded by hatred'.*

Mr Heath's growing difficulties were increased by his own belated decision to refer the miners' claim to the Pay Board in its new guise as a 'Relativities Board'. The miners'

---

[1] Mrs Alison Morris, then my constituency secretary.

union took full advantage of this to press publicly their arguments to be treated.as a special case. Public opinion was already swinging to their side when, towards the end of the campaign, the Pay Board discovered that the Coal Board's figures had consistently overstated the miners' earnings. This made the disparity between miners' pay and average manufacturing earnings £3 a week greater than had been supposed. The following day a further discrepancy in the Coal Board's figures was discovered which widened the gap by another £2 a week. Harold Wilson maintained this had turned the election into an unnecessary farce.

Nonetheless throughout the campaign the polls consistently gave Mr Heath the lead, though the lead varied from 1·5 per cent to 6 per cent according to the particular poll. A feature of the election was the resurgence of the Liberals. At one point Mr Jeremy Thorpe, their leader, talked of a 'landslide' – even the possibility of a Liberal Government. On polling day morning the Harris and National Opinion Polls were still giving Mr Heath a decisive victory. But as the results began to come in that night the picture changed. With a swing to Labour in the North and Midlands and a big upsurge in the Liberal vote to 19·2 per cent, it was soon clear that Mr Heath's gamble had failed. He had exchanged a working majority of fifteen for stalemate. By Saturday morning, 2 March, Labour had emerged as the largest party with a majority of four over the Conservatives (301 seats to 297), but thirty-four short of an overall majority. Ranged against it were fourteen Liberals and twenty-three 'others', including seven Scottish Nationalists, two Plaid Cymru and twelve Ulster Unionists.

At first a stunned Mr Heath refused to relinquish power. With 38·2 per cent of the voters behind him to Labour's 37·2 per cent, he turned to the Liberals, offering them a coalition with a seat in the Cabinet. Liberal MPs *decisively rejected his overtures. At last on 4 March Mr Heath admitted defeat and Harold Wilson was called on to form a government.*

The biggest surprise in the new Cabinet was the inclusion of Michael Foot. His appointment as Secretary of State for Employment was seen as a brilliant move. With Tony Benn at Industry, Peter Shore at Trade and myself at Social Services, the Left was given its usual niche in a Wilson Cabinet, but once again it was denied the key posts of Treasury, which went to Denis Healey, and Foreign Office, which went to Jim Callaghan. Roy Jenkins was partially back in favour as Home Secretary and Reg Prentice was steered from his shadow post at Employment, where he riled the trade unions, to Education. Newcomers to the Cabinet included Merlyn Rees at the Northern Ireland Office, John Morris as Secretary of State for Wales, Eric Varley at Energy and Shirley Williams in a new department as Secretary of State for Prices and Consumer Protection. Tony Crosland, who had always hankered after the Treasury, became overlord of the new super-department of the Environment which Ted Heath had created. Fred Peart went to Agriculture and Roy Mason to Defence. Willie Ross remained at the Scottish Office and Ted Short became Lord President of the Council and Leader of the House of Commons. New to the Cabinet were also the former Labour Attorney-General, Sir Elwyn Jones, who moved to the Lords as Lord Chancellor, and Lord Shepherd, who became Lord Privy Seal and Leader of the Lords. David Wood of The Times *commented that the Cabinet reflected Harold Wilson's 'loyalty to old colleagues'.*

Sunday, 3 March

Looking back over this curious election I realize what an ambivalent state of mind I have been in. I never expected us to win, but equally I did not think that Heath would get away with his contrived scenario. Quite early on I told Ted that I thought it might be another 1964 – certainly no landslide for the Tories. Even when the polls were consistently against us – and a *Liberal* landslide seemed to be building up – this contrasted with the reception I was getting in my own constituency. Never in all my nine elections can I remember such warmth of personal greeting as I got as I went around Blackburn. One Saturday afternoon in the market when Ted started up with the blower I was positively mobbed for autographs. People would stop me in the street to say, 'Ee, luv, I do hope you get in.' Municipal workers I met cleaning the streets told me: 'If that Heath gets in again, we'll emigrate.' Kathleen, my old friend the chambermaid at the White Bull, said almost with tears in her voice, 'I don't know what we'll do if we haven't got you.' Individuals whom I would have expected to be Tories wished me well. I got a letter from a woman who said she had always been a Conservative but was voting for me. The man at Webster's shop, where I buy my coffee, told me, 'Even Conservatives say you are *the* MP for Blackburn.' One thing I soon realized: my TV appearances help tremendously. People are so delighted to meet one in the flesh afterwards.

Of course there were moments of anxiety. I was worried when the Liberals decided to put up against me, as otherwise I knew most Liberals would have voted for me. Fortunately their candidate, Frank Beetham, turned out not to be very popular, even with his own party. Then there was the National Party, which had polled 4,000 in the municipal elections. With a majority of only 2,800 I hadn't enough margin to cope with that! Kingsley Read, the National Party candidate, had been very skilful in rousing support on local issues like redevelopment, which some of our lads on the council had messed up. But somehow, despite it all, I was quietly confident, not least because of all the intensive work I had done in the constituency in the past two months when I was warning Tom Taylor and Jim Mason[1] that an election was very probable. So I spent over half my time out of the constituency – in the South-West, Yorkshire and all over Lancashire. It was a risk I felt I could afford to take, even if it reduced my majority. They were good meetings, though a mite short of ecstatic, except for Bury and Radcliffe where I was convinced we were going to win. In the event Frank White just missed by 345 votes, in a straight fight, so perhaps Liberal intervention helped us more than the Tories, after all.

Highlights of the campaign: a wonderful reception by the old people in Bradda Close, where I slipped and got myself a great gash in my knee; bitter cold meetings at factory gates; a dash to Manchester twice to be interviewed with Cyril Smith on TV; a long session with the sixth-formers at St Mary's College (afterwards two of them turned up to help us); the canvassing of doubtfuls on the doorstep in rain and wind. This time it was not possible to do my great round of street corner meetings in the evening: I should have lost my voice in no time in that weather. My instinct was to go on the doorstep instead. We tried a couple of school meetings but as only forty people turned up at each I said firmly we should cancel the rest. We can and must beat the

[1] Treasurer and Chairman respectively of the Blackburn Trades Council and Labour Party.

Liberals at their own community politics game. Most people are so politically confused these days that they judge candidates purely in terms of what they can offer them personally. Time and again I got it in various forms of crudity: 'If you help me, I'll help you. That's only right, isn't it?'

Other highlights: Frankie Vaughan's descent on Blackburn as part of a whirlwind tour in support of Labour. He was terrific. I even got him singing 'Moonlight' in the marketplace! A sortie to his show at the night-club near Chorley as his guests. A first-class meeting at the Windsor Hall on the last Sunday night with Jim Callaghan, who was on his way to Nelson and Colne. The arrival of Sonya and Terry with Mark[1] so that Mark could be at my last election, just as Sonya had been at my first. Mark was absolutely thrilled as he toured round with Ted and me in our car on polling day and burst with pride at the count when at last they announced my majority of 6,300.

The turning points of the election were the announcement of last month's price rises; the appalling trade figures; the discovery that the miners had actually been claiming too little; Campbell Adamson's gaffe over the Industrial Relations Act and Enoch Powell's statement that he was voting Labour. Even in 1970 we never had such a series of catastrophes. But the weather was nearly a disaster for us when, at 6pm on polling day, a bitter wind turned into the worst snow-storm I can remember at any election. Even with cars to take people to the poll it wasn't fit to ask a dog to turn out in. Yet my valiant knockers-up ploughed on. At 8pm I told Ted firmly that I was abandoning the futile exercise of trying to get people out by loudspeaker and I too joined in the knocking up. We all got soaked. The irony of this election is that the three-day week, Ted Heath's gimmick, saved us from potential disaster as, with so many people not at work, we had had a record early poll. In some stations the poll was already 60 per cent by 6pm. And the immigrants, bless them, whom we had organized brilliantly, turned up trumps. The existence of a National Party candidate actually helped us. There was a roar of applause at the count when we found Read had lost his deposit.

The result, therefore, is better than any of us had dared to hope, though stalemate means there is bound to be another election soon. I told Tom and Jim as we chewed over the events on Friday morning that I had intended this to be my last election, but Jim said that, with another election coming before long, they just would not release me. So here we go for a bumpy ride. Everyone was astonished when Heath did not resign immediately: he has got a bad press over it. But when I rang Harold this morning he agreed with me that he will be forming an administration before many days have passed. He was chuckling over the situation: some of his old spirit seems to have come back. He is already planning his amendments to the Queen's Speech if Heath manages to cook up a deal with the Liberals. 'Footwork is my strong point,' he murmured modestly. 'That's just what Peter Jenkins wrote yesterday,' I replied. 'We shall go ahead with our full Manifesto,' he continued, 'and dare the Liberals to defeat us. I shall work much more as a committee, keeping myself freer than I did before. And no more lobby briefings: just the *Mirror*, the *Sunday Mirror* and the *People* will have access to me.' 'Oh, Harold,' I murmured, my heart sinking. 'No,' he said firmly.

[1] My niece, Sonya Hinton, her husband, Terry, and their ten-year-old son, Mark. They have three other children, Paul, Rachel and Laura.

'There will be no more of those off-the-record discussions of what the Government is going to do. Instead, Government decisions will be all on the record – preferably announced in the evening in time for the 9pm news.' 'That sounds okay,' I replied, relieved. So long as he doesn't renew that vendetta with the press! Certainly Harold is the only man for this tricky hour. It could be that he has really learned the lessons of last time. As he put it to me: 'After all, we are all experienced Ministers this time,' adding, 'Don't go too far away during the next few days.'

In the evening I rang Derek Robinson to find out what is happening to the miners' report. How had the figures of the miners' real comparison come out? He said that the NCB had always had its own earnings figures and the answer to a Parliamentary Question on 4 February had alerted the Pay Board to the point about holiday pay. When he started questioning Ezra he found he had been including sick pay as well. Figgures[1] had chaired the enquiry, which had been conducted by the full Board. When would it be published? They hadn't made up their minds. After all, a Labour Government might not want the report. How helpful was it, I asked. Pretty good, he replied. He would advise a Labour Secretary of State to take it: 'You could wrap this up.' He would expect the report to be delivered tomorrow to a Tory Secretary of State – if there was one. He thought it was dangerous just to abandon the Pay Board; a number of unions were hoping to 'come through' on relativities. The Board was also due to produce a report on the London weighting in about June. I told him this was just what I feared. I had come to the conclusion that, by making everything explicit, an incomes policy was actually inflationary. Even the *Daily Telegraph* journalists had gone on strike for their instalment of Stage Three. Once have a 'norm', and it becomes a minimum which everyone expects to get regardless of the state of their industry. Yet, if an industry is flourishing, its workers expect to get something on top. Everyone would now be trying to get more under relativities. There would be no end to it. Naturally he didn't agree. I asked him if he would send me a few ideas for strengthening the terms of reference of the Prices Commission, which he agreed to do.

Monday, 4 March

My last day of freedom before I return to the treadmill. I spent it writing letters and walking the dogs in the snow. Tommy [Balogh] phoned to ask me to join Mike and Peter [Shore] for dinner at his house tomorrow. Brian [O'Malley][2] phoned to arrange lunch. Mik phoned to say some of the bods were meeting in his office tomorrow afternoon prior to the NEC meeting on Wednesday morning. At 6pm Radio Black-burn phoned: it looks as if Heath is going to resign. So Harold will be summoned to the Palace at any moment. I wondered how I would get up to town if I were

[1] Sir Frank Figgures, KCB, CMG, Chairman of the Pay Board from 1973.

[2] Brian Kevin O'Malley had been Labour MP for Rotherham since 1963. He had been Deputy Chief Government Whip from 1967 to 1969 when he became Parliamentary Secretary to Dick Crossman at the Department of Health and Social Security. He had already made a name for himself in the House of Commons for his political flair, his debating skill and his mastery of the complexities of Dick's National Superannuation Scheme. While the Labour Party was in Opposition, he and I had worked closely together in the sub-committee of the NEC which was producing an amended Crossman plan. As a result of our ministerial partnership, my respect for him was to deepen into warm friendship.

summoned to No. 10 as Ted has already departed for council[1] work in London. Decided to ring Harold. Got him at the House. He said crisply, 'It looks as though this is it. No, don't come up to town. I am not having anyone come up; I shall just make my announcements later. You'll be Secretary of State and I assume you will want Brian and the rest of John Silkin's team.[2] Yes, Social Services.' 'Brian, yes please. But he must be a full Minister.' 'I'll be announcing the junior appointments later,' was all Harold said. 'Just report to your office in the morning.' And he added with a chuckle, 'You'll be at the Elephant and Castle.' 'God,' I groaned. He was crisp and confident and didn't sound as though he were ready to negotiate anything with anyone. But I shall fight hard to keep my promise to Brian; he is worth ten of the other juniors. It is amusing how one can talk about terms before the event and when it comes to it everything melts away in the excitement and urgency of the moment. But if Harold is more self-assured this time, so am I. A year or two at Social Services and then it will be retirement – or a bigger bid. I am already scratching my head as to whom I can appoint my political 'cabinet'.

Tuesday, 5 March

Still no announcement, so Ted and I drove up to London leisurely. On our way Ted and I kept stopping to listen to the news on our portable radio. At noon there it was: Mrs Castle, Secretary of State for the Social Services. I hardly felt my pulse quicken. How very different from last time! I can't quite analyse my mood. I feel supremely confident that I can do this job and I should have hated to be left out. But there is no stardust left. There is even regret that my private pleasures are to be sacrificed again. Perhaps I shall adjust, but at the moment there is a kind of dread at the resumption of a feverish round of meetings and paperwork. I decide to keep my dental appointment and Ted and I continue to discuss whom I shall have as my political adviser. He comes up with an excellent idea: Jack Straw.[3] I ask him to arrange a meeting.

Back at the House I find Alison in chassis, wondering what is going to happen to her. Sir Philip Rogers, my Permanent Secretary, has been on the phone. I ring and tell him I am going to keep a lunch date (with Brian O'Malley). Arrange for him to bring some people of the department over to the House at 3pm for a short chat before I have to go to the Palace to kiss hands. Then I take Ted and Brian over to St Stephen's for lunch. Brian tells me he is not too keen on coming with me just as Minister of State. That would mean he was no further on than he was three-and-a-half years ago when Harold had already promised that rank to him. It transpired he wanted to be a full Minister of Pensions and I promised I would try and get it for him. He certainly

[1] My husband, Ted, was an Alderman of Islington Council.

[2] Following my defeat in the elections for the Shadow Cabinet for the second time in 1972, and my decision to retire to the backbenches, despite Harold Wilson's willingness to keep me on the front bench, John Silkin, MP for Deptford, had become shadow spokesman for the Social Services in my place.

[3] Jack Straw had hit the headlines in 1969 when he became the first left-wing President of the National Union of Students for fifteen years, defeating a lethargic leadership which had reduced the NUS to little more than a travel agency. Jack set out to turn the NUS into a proper union for students, campaigning on the aim to make the NUS 'respected but not respectable'. But it was as a young councillor in Islington that he had met my husband and impressed him with his grasp of an argument and his enjoyment of debate. Ted also liked him very much as a person – as I was to do. Jack had qualified as a barrister, but his thoughts were on politics. When I retired from Parliament in 1979, he was to follow me as Labour MP for Blackburn.

deserves it. He is the only man who can help me to get a national superannuation scheme painlessly.

Sir Philip (whom I now recall from his Cabinet Office days) could not have been more gentle and accommodating. I think I shall get on with him. Brian tells me that Lance Errington, the second Permanent Secretary whom Philip Rogers brought with him, is very good. It was amusing to see how patently anxious they were not to appear to be swamping me with that 'companionable embrace'![1] A few hurried words with them about urgent matters and then off the Palace to kiss hands – a very muted affair this time: no tea and cucumber sandwiches (and I was dying for a cup). Obviously the Palace is economizing too! I was in the old coat in which I had been campaigning for three weeks; Wedgie and Mike looked as though they had been camping. Sir Martin [Charteris] and the rest were as friendly as ever and we stood in groups chatting for an unconscionable time. At last Harold arrived. Still we waited. I was anxious to get down to work but seized the opportunity to have a word with Harold about Brian's desire to become a full Minister of Pensions. Harold said he saw no objection to that. The Privy Council itself seemed a long and boring affair, though the Queen played her part as pleasantly as she always does. It was comical to see Mike balancing on one knee. Most people walked back normally to their places instead of feeling their way backwards as one is supposed to do. Only Wedgie, Mike, Fred Peart and I affirmed, Roy [Jenkins] clutching his Bible rather self-consciously. There was a moment's fun with the Queen's chaps when they asked those with a Bible if they would mind returning it this time if they had already had one. (More economy!) My chief delight was to see Harold Lever[2] there, leaning heavily on his stick, and I gave him a big hug. He said that he and Diane had been thrilled and relieved to find I was back in the Cabinet – so obviously some people had had doubts.

Our first Cabinet at 5pm. The first shock was the sight of the inside of No. 10. Heath must have spent a bomb on having it done up. Gone was the familiar, functional shabbiness. Instead someone with appalling taste had had it tarted up. New old gold carpeting everywhere; white and silver patterned wallpaper; gold moiré curtains of distressing vulgarity; 'nice' sideboards with bowls of flowers on top. It looked like a boudoir. An attendant came up to me to say solemnly that, if I didn't like the new chairs in the Cabinet room, they had kept my leg covers from the old chair and could bring them back![3] No need: the old brass-studded chairs have given way to expensive new leather-covered ones. An interesting insight into Ted Heath's personality.

[1] While in Opposition I had been asked to address a seminar of senior civil servants at the administrative college, Sunningdale, on the relationship between Ministers and civil servants. I did so with some enthusiasm, telling them that the Civil Service had become a state within a state and stressing the need to strengthen the political power of the Minister against the administrators' 'companionable embrace'. On 10 June 1973, the *Sunday Times* published the speech under the title 'Mandarin Power'.

[2] Harold Lever, who had earlier suffered a slight stroke, had been brought into the Cabinet as Chancellor of the Duchy of Lancaster in the special role of economic and financial adviser to the Prime Minister. As his appointment brought the number of Cabinet Ministers above the number entitled by law to receive a salary, he was unpaid.

[3] In the 1964–70 Labour Government I had repeatedly complained to Harold Wilson that I had laddered my tights on the rough legs of the Cabinet chair I occupied. On one occasion when yet another pair had been spoiled I tossed him a jocular note: 'I shall sue you!' When I arrived at our next Cabinet meeting I found he had had the legs of my chair specially swathed in cretonne.

The next shock was to have Harold say as we assembled round the Cabinet table that he thought we might adopt the custom of calling each other by our first names, adding with a smile to Wedgie, 'So you get your point at last.' How some of us urged this greater informality last time! There was a cheer, only Tony Crosland drawling languidly, 'At least let us call each other by our *sur*names.' No one took any notice of him and Harold was soon calling on 'Michael' to give us his report on the mining dispute. The whole atmosphere seemed transformed by that simple gesture at which the new Secretary of the Cabinet, John Hunt, sat smiling discreetly. He is a far less obtrusive character than his predecessor, Burke Trend – less charisma and therefore I think he will fit better into the new mood. He had already reminded me of the work he did for me on my Railway Steering Group when I was Minister of Transport. Very good work, too. I hope it is not vanity to assume that a lot of this change is due to my 'Mandarin Power' article. (In fact later in the day, when I met some more of my senior officials at the department one of them said to me shyly: 'I was at that famous talk of yours at Sunningdale, so I really got the message.')

Harold's next remark was: 'I should make it clear that it is not compulsory to smoke in Cabinet', puffing clouds into the air from his pipe. More laughter. I notice there is a curious little box in the corner above the picture rail. Perhaps it is an air conditioner. If so, I shall really thank Ted Heath for that.

Mike gave us a rather sombre report on the miners. He said that he thought that what we should do was to authorize the National Coal Board to negotiate. Should we give them any indication of our limit? The Pay Board report[1] wasn't helpful because it proposed to give the faceworkers *more* than the NUM had asked and the surface workers (except for the ex-faceworkers) less. He didn't think the NUM would stand for that: the militants on the Executive Committee mostly represented the surface workers. The miners' full claim, including fringe benefits, was £138 million compared with £113 million for basic increases alone, while the Relativities Report went up to £98 million. He would try to settle at £113 million but might be forced further up. We agreed that the NCB should be told to go ahead and to give Mike and Harold *carte blanche* to settle. I urged that we should make it clear we were rejecting the Pay Board report because I understood (I have had this from Derek) that a large number of unions, far from boycotting the Pay Board, were hoping to get in on the relativities act. There were nods at this, particularly from Denis, who nonetheless maintained that it was essential for us to settle with the miners in the next twenty-four hours. So there was complete harmony in our first Cabinet. We were urged to get on with our bids for the Queen's Speech, which Harold said should contain 'everything we think right for a year ahead'. Thanks to Heath's dallying over giving up office we have lost three days of preparation for the State Opening, which cannot be changed now without the agreement of the House. So it is a mad rush of consultation in our departments to get our bids worked out.

It was a pleasant relaxation to go out to Hampstead to dinner with Tommy at Old

[1] The Pay Board report, 'The Relative Pay of Miners' (Cmnd. 5567), had appeared on 1 March. It recommended exceptional increases for mineworkers consisting of a new allowance for every shift worked underground and a smaller personal allowance for surface workers who had previously served a qualifying period underground.

Bank House; a lovely place, so he can't be as hard up as he likes to make out. Mike was there, modest and diffident. Liz Shore, Peter's wife, went down on her knees and salaamed when she saw me, murmuring: 'My boss, my boss.' I hadn't realized that, as Dr Shore, she is one of my employees! Tommy, said Catherine, had been called to No. 10, and when he came in beaming we realized why: he is to be Minister of State at the Department of Energy in charge of North Sea oil! Harold really does seem to mean business this time. Dick and Anne joined us after dinner. He looks so ill; my heart aches, but one dare not even murmur a word of comfort to Anne, she is so apparently unruffled and bright. Perhaps that is the only way she can keep going and keep Dick going. He is still doing his TV programmes, although he is so weak that the effort is obvious. I told Dick and Liz I didn't want Shirley Summerskill in my team: she just didn't carry enough weight. Who could I have on the health side? David Ennals, they said, so I went and phoned Harold, who told me David was already earmarked. Back I went and we mused again. 'What about David Owen?' said Liz. Back I went to the phone. 'I like that idea,' said Harold approvingly. 'Let me think about it.'

Wednesday, 6 March

Up early to a 9.30am meeting of the NEC, called specially so that we in the Government can reassure them that this time we really mean to keep in touch. Jim, bright and relaxed in the chair, had worked out some ideas for doing this. Harold made a little speech assuring the NEC that 'this time I am going to run this Government very differently'. In the Cabinet he now had 'the most experienced team in living memory', and he added with relish, 'They are going to do the bloody work while I have an easy time.' His job was to be the 'deep lying centre half, not scoring all the goals'. We were going to act as a team. 'My job is to be the custodian of the Manifesto. I have already recruited a political team at No. 10 which will have access to all the documents. I am asking all my colleagues to appoint political advisers to their private office.' Wonders will never cease! I don't think it is euphoria (in fact I feel flat and positively reluctant about my own return to office) but I have a hunch things are going to be very different this time. We *could* turn out to be the most successful Labour Government in history. It is a good move that Harold has not put Roy [Jenkins] back at the Treasury and an inspired move to put Mike at Employment. Harold concluded by saying, 'Our relations with the press will be proper, formal, correct and on the record', and then went on to spell out how he intended to keep any planned leaks for *Labour Weekly* and to build it up. The keeper of the Manifesto! So at last he is blossoming out in the consciousness that his long ordeal in keeping the party together is being vindicated.

Over to the House for a party meeting. The thing that astonished me was the extent and the warmth of the congratulations I received. As our people streamed out of the meeting they queued up to grasp my hand and to tell me how delighted they were I was back in the Cabinet. It was as though they wanted to make good for all the humiliations I had suffered in being thrown off the Shadow Cabinet. Perhaps, like Harold, I shall be vindicated too. Though I do believe that our new concordat with

37

the trade unions is far more hopeful than the arms-length relationship we had last time. Thanks to the shock they have had under Heath they may at last prove that *In Place of Strife* was wrong.

Back at the office a hectic round of meetings to clear the Queen's Speech. And a lot of 'urgent' papers on which the election had held up imperative decisions. I had, for example, to clear overnight the capital programme for the hospitals, reluctant though I was to do so before I had even got a Parliamentary Secretary for Health. Brian, on my instructions, has moved in although his appointment has not yet been announced. We had a two-hour mass meeting with officials to discuss the uprating [of pensions and other benefits].[1] The brief officials had given me said that, with an effort, they could get the increase into payment by 1 September. Brian and I told them that this was politically unacceptable. After a lot of arm-twisting they agreed they might advance the date to 22 July, though they told us there was a lot of discontent among the staff about the pressure of work. They warned that, with such a date, a number of pensioners might get their increases in arrears. *Tant pis*, was all we said, and they went away a bit dazed. All I have to do now is to get it through Cabinet. I already know the Chancellor is talking about an autumn uprating and Jim has said that that is all we promised at the election.

I am losing no time in appointing staff. I rang up Brian Abel-Smith[2] this morning and said simply, 'Will you come to me?' to which he replied equally simply, 'Of course.' What a relief! He is unmatchable. I also saw Jack Straw in the flat: he is Ted's brilliant idea for my political adviser. He was clearly keen to come, though asked for time to talk to the chap he is in chambers with. (I have mentioned him to Harold; no problem there.) But things were very dicey about David Owen. I rang him to ask him if he would come on the health side and he asked if he could come and see me. When he did, he did a Brian O'Malley on me: said that he quite enjoyed being on the back benches; had a lot of things he wanted to do; really didn't think it was worth his while to come merely as a Parliamentary Secretary, which would mean no advance for him on last time. But he added, 'It isn't that I don't want to work with you. In fact I should enjoy that.' Over a drink I listened patiently, merely saying that I really did need someone with his knowledge and ability on the health side. I told him the line I thought we ought to take on health issues and he agreed one hundred per cent. He was obviously wavering and then asked for time to think. He would ring me later that night. When he did it was to say that the last thing he wanted to do was to embarrass

---

[1] In its election Manifesto the Labour Party had committed itself to bring 'immediate help' to pensioners, widows, the sick and unemployed by increasing pensions and other benefits from £7·75 to £10 a week for the single person and from £13·50 to £16 a week for the married couple: the largest increase (28 per cent) since national insurance was introduced. It had also committed itself to increase ('uprate') pensions and benefits annually in proportion to increases in prices or in average national earnings, whichever was the more favourable to the pensioner. These pledges were the outcome of a sustained campaign on behalf of the pensioners by Mr Jack Jones, general secretary of the Transport and General Workers' Union, and formed part of the Social Contract entered into by the Labour Party with the trade unions.

[2] Professor Brian Abel-Smith was and is Professor of Social Administration at the London School of Economics. He had been senior adviser to Dick Crossman as Secretary of State for the Social Services from 1968–70. From the academic and administrative posts he had held and the research work he had done, he had incomparable knowledge and experience over the whole field of health and social security.

me. He was conscious that if he backed out now it might get out and look as though it was something personal. So he would come. But would I do what I could to see that he really got the next vacancy as Minister of State? I said that of course I would: repeated that Harold had assured me the only reason he couldn't make David a Minister of State now was that he was already over the statutory number and couldn't risk legislation to increase it. (In fact I have had a tough time with Harold, who has sent me a message: 'Tell the Secretary of State to stop badgering me over O'Malley.' But he really is in a difficulty over Ministers of State.) To my immense relief David said that on that basis he would come. So that is one hurdle passed.

Thursday, 7 March

Our first real Cabinet. I notice ironically that I have been moved down to the end of the table: no longer the central position I had as First Secretary. Not to worry: I'll be back. I'm no has-been, though I am surprised at my own detached mood. I work as hard as ever but wonder all the time whether the game is worth that mass of paper work. I keep saying to Ted, 'Do you know, I'm *bored*!' What on earth has come over me? I'm ten years older, of course, but my energy is as great as ever: my intellectual grasp seems stronger and I feel completely on top of the job. But I shrink from the idea of meeting the press; have no inclination to try and sparkle; just want to slog on doing a good job. And I deeply resent the work that comes between me and the garden – and the dogs.

A desultory discussion at Cabinet about the negotiations with Europe on the Common Market. Fred is to go over to deal with food prices. Jim wanted the Queen's Speech to say something like this. After referring to the Government's intention to seek a 'fundamental renegotiation' of the terms and to put the results to the British people, we should add: 'So that, if their consent is forthcoming, this country can play a full part in a new and wider Europe.' Fred commented, 'I would like that.' (I hope he is not going to sell us out on behalf of his beloved farmers!) Once again Harold showed how toughly he interprets his role as 'custodian of the Manifesto'. He told Jim, who said he was merely quoting from the party document on the EEC, 'There are two points made in the document. We would have to quote both parts to get a proper balance.' As usual, from my remote position, I could barely hear the chat across the table but eventually they reached some agreement.[1] Next I heard Mike warning us that the miners' settlement didn't mean that we had abandoned Stage Three of Heath's incomes policy. That must stay until he had negotiated the basis of a voluntary agreement with the TUC, otherwise the floodgates would be opened. I told him they already were, as far as the doctors and dentists were concerned. I had already had a letter from the British Medical Association [BMA] asking us to support a new claim (bigger than that under Stage Three, which they had originally been prepared to accept) before the Review Body. 'Tell them they can't have it,' Mike almost snapped. This Government is certainly going to be ideologically interesting!

After Cabinet I had a word with Harold about Brian O'Malley. He told me

---

[1] The Queen's Speech did not include Jim's proposed phrase.

39

categorically that he couldn't – or rather wouldn't – make him a full Minister. Too many other people who also wanted to be full Ministers would be offended if he did. I told him Brian had said it wasn't worth his while to take on the job if he was no further on than he had been before. 'Then there are plenty of people you can have,' Harold snapped, adding: 'He's neurotic.' 'That's very unfair,' I retorted. But I couldn't move him. I went away weary and depressed to tell Brian the news, wrapping it up as effectively as I could. 'Then he's gone back on his word,' said Brian tartly. 'I don't think I like people who go back on their word.' I begged him to think it over and he said he would like the night to think it over.

Friday, 8 March

Brian phoned early, as promised. Reluctantly he agreed. I am delighted. He is very able. So now I have a really effective team. Harold is to make Alf Morris a Parliamentary Secretary for Disablement[1] and has offered me another Parliamentary Secretary to console me for the other rebuffs. So, from his list, I have chosen Bob Brown. But having seen this morning's further list of appointments I am terrified lest David Owen retracts. It really is absurd how many newcomers Harold has made Ministers of State. No wonder he has run out of his number! I am sure Eric Heffer, for one, would have been glad to start as Parliamentary Secretary, though I am very pleased he is in the Government. This whole business has exhausted me: it is just like the exuberance of egos I had to face in our working party on the Industrial Relations Bill. As Ted put it to me: 'It isn't politics that are the worry for you, love; it is people.'

Off to Blackburn to fulfil my promise to come back as quickly as possible.

Monday, 11 March

An early visit from William Armstrong,[2] charm itself. He raised no objections at all to my recruiting Jack Straw – even talking in terms of £8,000 a year. And of course I could have Brian Abel-Smith. I said to him that the whole mood seemed to have changed in the Civil Service: could 'Mandarin Power' have had anything to do with it? 'That and other things,' he replied. He had really come to tell me that Philip Rogers is due to retire this summer but could be persuaded to stay on if I wanted him

[1] Alf Morris, Labour MP for Wythenshawe, had won a national reputation by his work for the disabled and in particular by his success in putting the Chronically Sick and Disabled Persons Act on the statute book as a backbencher in 1970.

[2] Sir William Armstrong had been Permanent Secretary at the Civil Service Department and Head of the Home Civil Service since 1968 and was a former Joint Permanent Secretary to the Treasury. He had signal honours heaped on him by successive governments. On 10 April 1974, it was announced from No. 10 that Sir William would be leaving the public service in July to join the Midland Bank with a view to succeeding to the chairmanship the following year. Not only did Harold Wilson confirm the previous Prime Minister's consent to these arrangements under the two-year rule which prevented senior civil servants from taking without permission certain sensitive outside appointments immediately after leaving the Service, but he allotted Sir William a baronetcy in his New Year's Honours list of 1975. Thus rewarded Lord Armstrong quickly used his freedom to campaign against the Labour Party's proposals to nationalize the banks. In 1978 he was to become a prime mover in setting up a committee of top industrialists to mobilize public opinion against further nationalization generally.

to. I asked for time to think it over: 'Though I get on well with him. I am not out to do a Tommy Padmore.'[1] It was all most amicable. William is – and always has been – almost too accommodating to be true.

At the eve-of-the-Queen's-Speech reception at No. 10 there was the usual euphoria for the first Queen's Speech of a new Government, though I still found the tarted-up rooms an irritant. It was good to see Michael Meacher [MP for Oldham West] there, as modest as ever and a little overwhelmed at being Parliamentary Secretary at the Department of Industry. I told him I would have liked him to come to me but Harold had said he was booked. I am not sure Industry is the right assignment for him, but no doubt it will do him good. Ran into Denis, who was very truculent about my proposed July date for the uprating. 'I shall fight you on this.' 'Cabinet will decide,' I said hotly and went away determined to win. These Chancellors of the Exchequer!

Wednesday, 13 March

Despite the pressure of office meetings on this and that problem which has accumulated during the election period (officials can't wait to unload them), I insisted on going into the House for Wedgie's speech. He was strangely muted, even emollient. I suspect that he too is finding his new feet. In the morning I had had to look in at the regular meeting of chairmen of regional health authorities [RHA] over which Philip presides. I went through my routine about how we had inherited a National Health Service [NHS] reorganization with which we disagreed in many particulars, how irresponsible it would have been for me to reverse it after so much upheaval but how we intended to make what adjustment we could within existing legislation pending reconsideration of the whole thing. Then suddenly the chairman of the chairmen asked me if I would give a guarantee that no boundaries would be changed. I had to think on my feet and fended it off non-committally. David Owen said to me afterwards, 'That was a hot potato and you fielded it brilliantly.' Apparently he wants to be free to make some changes in the boundaries of the London districts.

Thursday, 14 March

Some fun at Cabinet over Harold Lever, whom Harold called 'the Duke'. What else do you call the incumbent of the Duchy of Lancaster? Bob Mellish then reported that the Tories had put down an amendment to the address for next Monday on prices and incomes policy, which led Harold to some musing about tactics. His view was that if we were defeated we should not seek a dissolution but just hang on as if nothing had happened until we were ready to ask for a vote of confidence following the Budget and the negotiations with the EEC. He is even toying with the idea of taking powers to reduce the period of the election campaign, but the rest of us were a bit alarmed at this. It would be too patent that what we were up to was denying the Tories the time we had had in this election to widen the issues on which Ted Heath went to the

---

[1] Sir Thomas Padmore was Permanent Secretary at the Ministry of Transport from 1962–68. When I became the Minister of Transport in December 1965 I tried to get him moved.

country. But it is clear that Harold has got his tail up. Jim then announced that a naval visit to Athens due today had been cancelled and that we were also suspending visits to Portugal, which delighted most of us, though Roy Mason said heavily that cancellation at short notice should be avoided where possible and that he should be brought into the review of our policy. No itch for radical gestures there!

This is only our third Cabinet, but public expenditure is already rearing its ugly head. Denis had put in a memo saying that the economic situation the country faced was possibly the worst we had ever faced in peacetime. Unless something was done inflation this year would be over 15 per cent and the balance of payments deficit would jump to £400 million. There was no scope for increases in living standards this year: the threshold agreement would probably be reached by April, with the agreements being triggered nine times during the year. In order to clear the way for his Budget decisions it would be necessary to decide the total level of public expenditure by the end of the week. There would have to be increases in the prices of nationalized industries; defence should be cut by £250 million and prestige projects reviewed; in his view Concorde should be cancelled. In the meantime, he asked Cabinet to accept that for 1974–75 there should be no increases in public expenditure apart from subsidies – and of course the pensions uprating. Wedgie came in first about his beloved Concorde: 'There is no difference between the Chancellor and me,' he said. He could not have been more disingenuous. All he asked was that we should cash in on the previous Government's refusal to disclose the facts and that he should be allowed to make an early statement revealing those facts. No one could – or did – object to that, though Denis did say wistfully that he would have liked to be able to announce cancellation in his Budget, while Elwyn said that the break clause helped us now and Tony Crosland added that the quicker cancellation came the better as far as he was concerned. I suspect that Wedgie has lived to fight another day.

Reg Prentice was very reluctant to accept the December cuts,[1] even for this year, as their effects were proving even worse than had been visualized and would mean that there would be no new schools except to meet expanding population and a cutback in nursery education. Denis hastened to assure him that, if he had an autumn Budget, he would look at this again. I entered a firm caveat about the proposed increase in electricity prices[2] which Eric, like other Ministers of Power before him, was positively anxious to encourage. If there were a 25 per cent increase as suggested, I said, the position of pensioners would be intolerable and I would want to press for a big increase in supplementary benefit heating additions.

We got our first hint of the diametrically different approach of Harold Lever from that of the Treasury when Denis said that one of the ways out would be to increase export prices. Harold exploded at this: 'I am prepared to support the Chancellor until

[1] On 17 December 1973, the Conservative Chancellor of the Exchequer, Mr Anthony Barber, announced some £1,200 million of cuts in public expenditure for the year 1974–75. Among the major items were cuts of £182 million in education and £111 million in health and social services.

[2] Under Mr Heath's prices and incomes policy the prices of nationalized industries' products had been held down and the industries had run up huge deficits, which had begun to alarm the Conservative Government. In order to correct this, Denis Healey proposed stiff increases in a wide range of their prices. In his Budget statement of 26 March he announced an increase in electricity prices of 30 per cent. One argument was that this was essential to secure fuel economies.

after the Budget; then I shall be forced to express my dissent.' And he added that by the end of the year we might well be becoming uncompetitive again in export markets and we would be mad to rely on pushing export prices up. On defence (how history reverses the roles!) Denis was all for our completing the immediate withdrawal from East of Suez, while Roy Mason was full of the difficulties. Harold hankered after taking powers to abolish the Pay Board in Shirley's Bill,[1] 'though we won't abolish it immediately'. It was disturbing to learn that an expenditure of £500 million on food subsidies would only knock 1 per cent off the rise in the Retail Price Index and so do little to protect Denis from the threshold agreement triggers which he described as the millstone round his neck. It was eventually accepted that there was no escape from Denis's formula for public expenditure in 1974–75, and that we would look at his proposals for later years when his further memo was circulated.

Next into my battle over the date of the uprating. I felt on the top of my form. Mike was very helpful, saying he was briefed by his Department to support me because an early date like July would be important for the Social Contract. Peter Shore backed me too. But the best effort came from Bob Mellish, who said vigorously that this was the sort of point on which we had got to behave politically. There might be – and he hoped there would be – an election at any time. Were we to go into it with the pensioners still not having got their increase? Typically, Shirley, Reg Prentice and Jim suggested that we might go for 1 September as an intermediate date for the uprating, but Harold clearly was on my side. He suggested that the needs of demand management might change: we might even be faced with an increase in unemployment before too long. There were three decisive factors: first, the effect on the TUC and the need to win support for the Social Contract; secondly, the possibility of an early election; thirdly, the fact that we might need an autumn Budget to expand demand. At this Roy came in to say that, as a former Chancellor, he believed he should support the Chancellor, but he wanted to ask him whether he really stood firm on this. Here Fred [Peart] passed me a note: 'Stand firm, you will win.' And sure enough, to my astonishment, Denis's opposition collapsed. He was prepared to 'concede', adding that he rejected 1 September as a 'soggy compromise'. I could have hugged him! I went away to receive the bewildered congratulations of the Department, Brian O'Malley whistling his astonishment at my victory.

Back to the office to work on my speech tomorrow in the Queen's Speech debate. I told Graham[2] I wanted to ad lib but the boys were waiting to snatch every line from me for approval by the Treasury. I finally went home to work on my own notes, promising to let Graham see them in the morning. How one produces anything like oratory in these circumstances I'll never know.

Friday, 15 March

Into the House early to get final clearance from officials. When I walked into my room I found about twenty of them assembled like a lot of grey vultures. It was

---

[1] Shirley Williams presented a Bill on 3 April which authorized food subsidies, introduced additional price control powers and abolished the Pay Board. This became the Prices Act, 1974.

[2] Graham Hart, my private secretary.

enough to daunt anyone. They were carrying a lot of scraps of paper – the last-minute edicts of the Treasury on this and that. No, the Treasury would *not* allow me to announce a couple of minor concessions on prescription charges (which the Treasury had already agreed) because they must be announced as part of the Budget. Harold had apparently backed Denis on this and my attempts to reach him on the phone were met by stonewalling. I was furious but there was nothing I could do. So I went into the House with a lot of turgid banalities to deliver and no kicks. The speech therefore was merely adequate. I vowed I would never allow myself to be trapped in this way again. If Mike can get away with murder, I intend to also.

Monday, 18 March

One of my inspirations – to appoint Jack Ashley as my Parliamentary Private Secretary [PPS][1] – has gone down very well. When I put the idea to Ted, he dismissed it as 'sentimental', but my instinct told me he was wrong. If I am to be head of a 'caring' Ministry, I had better start by showing I care myself. And I have taken the precaution of consulting Philip Rogers and Graham first, explaining that the appointment of a totally deaf man would add to our difficulties. Were they prepared to take on the extra burden involved in communicating with him and including him? Of course, they could not say no. And Jack is thrilled. Harold, too, instinctively warmed to the idea. It is the sort of gesture that appeals to him.

At last I have had to submit to the ordeal by photographer. The press have been clamouring for the 'at work at her desk' sort of picture but I have not been in the mood for it. Having been unable to stall it off any longer, I had my hair done first. But my irritation with all this side persists. Later I got into trouble with the office over my long-delayed first press conference when I discovered it clashed with Mike's speech in the House on the Tory motion on prices and incomes policy. I threw the only tantrum I have done in over six years in government, telling Graham [Hart] and Peter Brown[2] that their job was to save me from my own stupidities, like forgetting there was a historic parliamentary occasion on this day. I was tired of missing every dramatic moment in the House and they must just take into account that, if such an occasion arose, I was in future going to put the House first. Peter was very patient but very serious and I eventually struck a bargain with him: he would delay the conference for three-quarters of an hour if I would undertake to leave the House not one moment later than 4.55pm. So I sat through Mike's speech, feeling like a truant but enjoying every minute of it. It was a *tour de force* and he made Carr look like Johnnie

---

[1] Jack Ashley, Labour MP for Stoke on Trent, South, had gone totally deaf following an operation in December 1967. The courage with which he had carried on his parliamentary work, particularly for the disabled, had won widespread admiration. His affliction had brought home to me how seriously the needs of the deaf had been neglected and I determined to do something about it. Though he was centre-right in many of his political views, we were to work together harmoniously and creatively.

[2] Director of Information in the Department. He had been Chief Information Officer at the Ministry of Housing and Local Government when Dick Crossman was Minister and Dick was so delighted with him that, when in 1968 he became Secretary of State for the Social Services, he insisted on Peter Brown being transferred to him. Subsequently Peter Brown served under Dick's successor, Sir Keith Joseph, and I had inherited him.

Boyd in an off moment. When I crept out to Admiralty House the press was waiting *en masse*, well lubricated by Peter in the meantime. Late as it was, Peter insisted on taking me aside to impress on me: 'I want some of the old Castle charisma this afternoon. Don't forget this is the largest uprating in the history of national insurance. Give it to them.' He was like a film director with a star who needed encouragement. I wonder what dear Dick would make of that? Thus encouraged, I went in with all sails flying and I thought I did rather well. Then into TV and at last back to the House for some tricky office meetings. Into the chamber for the winding up and the delicious moment when the Tories climbed down ignominiously.[1]

Tuesday, 19 March

The main business at Cabinet was Mike's memo on his discussions with the TUC. In fact it soon became obvious that there was no need for a Cabinet at all, particularly as the Tory great attack had collapsed yesterday. (I suspect that Harold had only fixed our meeting as a cover for an emergency discussion if the Tories had defeated us. Their reluctance to do so takes some getting used to.) Mike's memo makes clear that the TUC is very willing to play along with the continuance of incomes control until a voluntary policy can be worked out. Len Murray's statement in the TUC *Economic Review*,[2] as the memo put it, 'constitutes a most helpful advance on what he said about the uniqueness of the miners' case'. Len, at any rate, is clearly determined to make the Social Contract work. Mike suggested we should have an early meeting with the TUC on the whole range of Government policy, without being so inept as to put a 'voluntary incomes policy' crudely in the forefront. (A sideswipe at Reg Prentice?) Separate informal meetings could and should be arranged with the TUC on the establishment of such a policy. He also sought immediate authority to proceed with the drafting of a Bill to repeal the Industrial Relations Act. Cabinet agreed to all these propositions, Harold [Wilson] showing his greater maturity by stressing that we should avoid a panoply of top-level discussions in the glare of press publicity.

Did a whirlwind tour of receptions in order to get the measure of international feeling about the renegotiating of the EEC terms and found the Germans apprehensive and the New Zealanders quietly satisfied with our line. At last on to the 'Husbands and Wives' dinner[3] where Mike, to my sympathy and satisfaction, fell asleep. It is comforting to know that others feel the strain as much as I do.

[1] Although the Opposition front bench had tabled an amendment criticizing the Government's lack of proposals for a statutory prices and incomes policy, it announced at the last minute that it would not divide the House on it.

[2] The review for 1974, published in March, delighted the Government. It not only reiterated the unions' pledge not to quote the miners' settlement in support of their own claims, but called on unions 'to adopt negotiating policies which focus on the need to restrain unit costs'.

[3] The left-wing members of the Cabinet – Michael Foot, Wedgwood Benn, Peter Shore and myself – had decided to try to meet weekly over informal dinner in order to keep in touch. To allay Harold's suspicions of a 'cabal', wives (or husbands) were invited as well. The only non-Cabinet Ministers were Mrs Judith Hart, Minister of Overseas Development, John Silkin, Minister for Planning and Local Government (John Silkin entered the Cabinet in October 1974) and Lord Balogh. The description 'Husbands and Wives' dinner enabled us to book these meetings openly through our Private Offices without alerting the Civil Service network to the fact that regular political discussions were taking place.

Wednesday, 20 March

Met the members of the Supplementary Benefits Commission [SBC] and found them highly intelligent. Harold Collison[1] is a dear and has clearly put an enormous amount of himself into the work. Had an argument with Brian O'M. about the cohabitation rule.[2] More office meetings, including a rather forced initial meeting with Lewin and Stevenson of the BMA. I was at my most charming because, as David Owen says, we shall have to have some showdowns with these lads soon.[3]

Thursday, 21 March

As I thought, Wedgie's retreat on Concorde was only to fight another day. He told Cabinet: 'I am not asking for any decision today.' (He knows he would have lost if he had.) The figures were still not agreed, he said, particularly of the social costs of cancellation. Moreover it would be intolerable to announce it without wide consultation with the unions first. He withdrew his proposal to have the whole matter examined by a Select Committee, but he did press for a small Ministerial Committee to be set up to consider and cost all the alternatives and to study representations from outside interests. We also ought to consult the French Government first before announcing anything. We should go for an announcement, if possible in agreement with the French Government, by early May. Denis didn't like this at all. 'There is no economic case whatsoever for not cancelling,' he declared. We had no right to put our responsibilities into commission in this way. At the very least we ought to agree that cancellation was our ultimate intention. He was strongly supported by Roy [Jenkins]: 'We must not lack will over this.' But Mike backed Wedgie: 'It would be terrible to decide to cancel now and then discuss with the unions afterwards.' We might have to establish a special redundancy scheme at a cost of £20 million. Jim agreed with him. And Elwyn came to Wedgie's rescue: the extent to which we had discussed the position with the French before deciding our course would be important in any legal arguments that might arise. He could not recommend unilateral action, which might be legally dangerous. All that Denis could salvage was permission to say in his Budget speech that we would stop production at sixteen planes and that there would be no further development or production. A small Ministerial Committee is to supervise negotiations and receive representations from unions, etc. We also delayed a decision on the channel tunnel at Tony Crosland's request.

On industrial relations Mike ran into trouble over his proposed transitional

---

[1] Lord Collison, former general secretary of the National Union of Agricultural Workers, had been chairman of the Supplementary Benefits Commission since 1969.

[2] See footnote, page 716.

[3] As soon as I took office Dr Walpole Lewin, chairman of the Council of the BMA, and Dr Derek Stevenson, secretary of the BMA, asked to see me to demand a review of the consultants' contract with the NHS. Officials told me that the BMA had been pressing this for some time and that feeling was running high. I therefore agreed to set up a Joint Working Party under Dr Owen's chairmanship to examine the possibility of a new contract, on the understanding that the working party should also deal with the Government's commitment to phase private beds out of NHS hospitals.

arrangements[1] and particularly over picketing, on which even Jack Straw has briefed me to persuade him to drop them. There was no time to discuss them thoroughly, so Harold proposed that a group of senior Ministers should look into them later that day before getting the proposals urgently to the TUC.

Incidentally, my family planning proposals went through without demur, not even Bob raising a murmur about my wish not to impose prescription charges.[2] And it looks as though Denis is going to let me announce the other prescription charges concessions after all.

One of the issues which was to take up a great deal of my and Alf Morris's time was mobility for the disabled. Knowing as we did that money was limited, it was to test all our ingenuity. The invalid tricycle, which had been issued to some 21,500 disabled drivers, had been a boon, but it had two major defects: it could only help those fit to drive and the disabled driver could not carry a passenger. So he or she travelled alone. The Disabled Drivers' Association had launched a campaign to get the tricycle replaced by a specially adapted car, for which war pensioners and a few others were already eligible. The case was a strong one: a four-wheeled vehicle was obviously safer than a three-wheeled one, it overcame the problem of loneliness and – most compelling – a mass-production small car cost no more, and increasingly less, to produce than a specialized tricycle. The Association had backed its campaign with alarming assertions that the tricycle was unsafe.

It was these arguments that had led Alf Morris to endorse the disabled drivers' campaign. Just before the election Harold Wilson had thrown in his support. So, although there had been no Manifesto commitment, the Government was committed morally. Yet the problem, as often happened, was not as simple as it seemed. The invalid tricycle was originally visualized as a substitute for the walking capacity an individual had lost: an extension, in effect, of the artificial limb. But a car was a development of the quality of life of which a large number of other people dreamed. Above all, it was obvious that once the Government provided a car which could take a passenger, it could not logically refuse that vehicle to the most seriously disabled of all – those unfit to drive. As there were thousands of these 'disabled passengers', who at present received no help with their mobility, the additional cost would be considerable.

My predecessor, Sir Keith Joseph, had bought time by referring the whole issue to Lady Sharp who, as Dame Evelyn, had been Permanent Secretary at the Ministry of Housing when Dick Crossman was Minister, with instructions to take account of

[1] In keeping with the Government's election pledge to repeal the Conservatives' Industrial Relations Act 'as a matter of extreme urgency', Michael Foot had been having discussions with the TUC on the scope of the alternative Bill and on whether it should extend trade union rights on such matters as picketing. His Trade Union and Labour Relations Bill, repealing the Tory Act, was presented on 30 April.

[2] Under the Conservative Government Sir Keith Joseph had announced his intention to introduce, from 1 April 1974, a comprehensive family planning service under the NHS, but he intended to impose a prescription charge on the family planning supplies dispensed. In the Budget debate on 28 March I announced that family planning supplies would be free. I also announced that prescription charges generally would be abolished for children up to sixteen years of age and for women from the age of sixty.

'available resources'. Her report, 'Mobility of Physically Disabled People', had landed on Sir Keith's desk in August 1973. He had not published it. My first aim was to get Cabinet consent to my publishing the report, which I did on 25 March. I also published at the same time the reports of tests on the tricycle which had been carried out at the Department's request by the Motor Industry Research Association [MIRA]. These showed that, although some design modifications were needed, there were no reasons on grounds of safety alone why the tricycle should be withdrawn.

Lady Sharp found that the case for replacing three-wheeled vehicles by four-wheeled ones was unanswerable. But in order to keep down the cost she proposed that eligibility for a car should be limited to those disabled people, whether drivers or not, who in effect needed a vehicle to support themselves or their families. In this way the additional cost would have been kept down to £3 million over and above the £10 million already being spent on the vehicle service, including the private car allowance. Existing holders of a tricycle, who did not qualify for a car under the new criteria, would be able to keep them as long as stocks lasted but no new tricycles would be produced.

Neither Alf Morris nor I found this acceptable. We disliked the proposed needs test and we knew that, despite the campaign against the tricycle, those who possessed one valued it. Our civil servants and special advisers were unanimously opposed to the Government providing cars, not only because of the cost, but because a large administrative machine would be needed to buy and service them. They wanted us to 'get out of cars and into cash' through a mobility allowance available to drivers and non-drivers alike, which beneficiaries could then use in the way that suited them best: for taxis; as payment to a neighbour for the use of his car; to help buy a car themselves. The trouble, as Alf Morris and I well knew, was that we would be unlikely to get a high enough mobility allowance out of the Treasury to enable disabled people to buy a car, yet those who demanded cars expected the Government to provide either the capital or the vehicle. We had to find an answer to all these points.

Sunday, 24 March

Phoned Harold from Hell Corner Farm to see if he was willing for me to make the statement on the Sharp Report tomorrow. No problem there, though he says he wants an early meeting with me and Alf to discuss an idea he has for giving the disabled their cars at half the estimated cost. He is clearly determined, if he can, to fulfil the promise he made to the disabled drivers when in Opposition. He said he intended to get Harold Lever working on his idea: some pact he thinks he can enter into with Morris Motors. 'As you know, I don't intend to have a DEA [Department of Economic Affairs]; Harold is better than any DEA,' he told me. I said it had occurred to me we could link the provision of cars for the disabled with the cancellation of Concorde. Why not open a government factory – or get Morris Motors to open one – in Bristol to absorb the redundant men? In this way we could finance the cars out of the social costs of cancellation. He liked the idea. I next asked him if he would arrange for Cabinet Ministers to meet his 'think tank' so that we could know what it was up to, and he said that arrangements for such a meeting, with graphs, etc., were already in hand. Finally I asked him if it would be all right if I were to invite Bernard

Donoghue's team[1] over to drinks to meet my political adviser and Ministers, and he said, sure, though Bernard hardly had a team as yet. I said I was delighted with the emphasis we were now putting on the political side of government, and he repeated with gratification what he loves to dwell on: how he is going to sit back and do strategic thinking while we do all the work. 'And it's damned hard work,' I replied. 'You know you love it,' he replied unsympathetically. He told me he was working on the problem of mortgages – not easy to solve, but he has some ideas. I don't think this is just Walter Mittery or gimmickry. If he will listen to practical warnings he could prove quite creative. I don't think the conventional administrative approaches are enough today. On disabled people's cars, for instance, I have already warned Brian A-S. that we musn't be too logical. The one thing the disabled crave more than anything else is mobility. A system of mobility allowances, I told him, could just leave the disabled at the mercy of the car market. Government intervention is needed to see they get their cars as cheaply as possible.

Over to our neighbours, the Pawsons, for drinks at lunchtime. Tony Keable-Elliott[2] seized on me and we annoyed everyone by talking interesting shop for ages instead of engaging in small talk like the rest. Tony gave me a lot of ideas I shall follow up and promised he would come and give evidence to our working party on the consultants, 'though I shall get into terrible trouble'.

Monday, 25 March

Diary of a typical day, after a weekend spent with my nose in red boxes. Left Hell Corner Farm at 8.45am for London, reading briefs all the way. Mass meeting with officials at the House at 10.30am to discuss my statement for today on the Sharp Report. Frantic last-minute negotiations with Treasury, who want to take out every word that might seem to commit us to anything (despite the fact that Harold has cleared the statement). Over to No. 10 at 11.30 for Budget Cabinet. This went on till

---

[1] In addition to the 'think tank' which Mr Heath had set up in Cabinet Office in 1970 under Lord Rothschild, Harold Wilson had decided to establish his own personal group of political advisers under Dr Bernard Donoghue. The need for such a policy unit servicing the Prime Minister had been urged by Mrs Marcia Williams, Harold Wilson's political secretary, in the light of her experience of the Labour Governments 1964–70, described in her book *Inside No. 10*. While Mr Heath visualized his Central Policy Review Staff [CPRS] as helping the Government as a whole with iron detachment to improve its collective decisions, she wanted to arm a Labour Prime Minister against the Civil Service by giving him a 'small core of highly qualified, highly expert individuals' to help him initiate policy instead of having it imposed on him by the machine. Dr Donoghue had previously been senior research officer in PEP (Political and Economic Planning) and a lecturer at the London School of Economics. During the two stormy years in which I held office during 1974–76 I never found that either the CPRS or Dr Donoghue's unit had any noticeable effect on the decisions we took. These depended far more on the political muscle and (expertly reinforced) political will of individual Ministers.

[2] Dr Robert Anthony Keable-Elliott FRCGP, Member of the Council of the BMA and chairman of its General Medical Services Committee. One of the ironies of my long struggle with the medical profession was that Tony Keable-Elliott was our neighbour in our remote country retreat. As we both did a lot of gardening we would often discuss our departmental disputes informally over the garden hedge, to the alarm of my civil servants.

after 1pm. Straight back to office for sandwiches and an urgent official meeting on our Uprating Bill. Back to the House at 3pm to be in good time for my statement, which went well, everyone congratulating me on having published the Sharp Report so quickly. (Oddly enough no one congratulated me on publishing the MIRA Report, which had been a much greater struggle to achieve.) Up to my room to do a few constituency letters, then back to the Department for another mass meeting of officials and David Owen. Then a quick change and over to Vincent Square for a few minutes with Dick, who is failing fast. Ted joined me and we dashed to Lancaster House where I had to receive, and dine with, doctors from America and Canada. Left at 9.30pm for the rate support grant vote in the House, only to find it wasn't likely to take place till 11.30pm. Worked on my boxes in my room. Home at midnight. Did some sorting out of my clothes and got to bed at 1am. Another box has arrived, but to hell with it. I have two major speeches, two major statements and Parliamentary Questions to do this week and the burden is oppressive. I do not sleep well.

Budget Cabinet was a very comradely affair. Denis had an engaging frankness which disarmed any criticism. He began by saying that this was an interim Budget in the sense that it was impossible to gauge how things would develop over the next few months, and it had also been impossible to work out complicated administrative changes, like a wealth tax, in two weeks. An autumn Budget would therefore be inevitable. Surprisingly enough, there had been no run on sterling, despite the expenditure implications of the Queen's Speech. In fact the pound had been stronger than under the Tories. Nonetheless we all remembered what had happened in 1964[1] and we had to show we were dealing with the appalling economic situation we had inherited. Although he was going for a broadly neutral Budget, with a demand reduction of only £200–£300 million, it was essential to start cutting back the borrowing requirement substantially in order to strengthen sterling. This meant he couldn't restore any of the public expenditure cuts at this stage, but if unemployment started rising he would look at this again later on. The Tories' threshold agreement had left him with little room for manoeuvre, since he dare not introduce taxes which would push up the Retail Prices Index, though some indirect tax increases were unavoidable. In the meantime he had negotiated an international loan on the best possible borrowing terms (he didn't mention the rate of interest) and without recourse to the International Monetary Fund [IMF], which he wanted to avoid, 'with its strings'. (So much for Barber's claim during the election that a Labour Government would not be able to negotiate as good loan terms as the Tories would!) He then set out the details,[2] to which we all listened without protest, only two specific points

[1] See Introduction.
[2] The Budget reversed nearly all the Heath Government policies. One of his main aims, Denis Healey told the Commons, was to recreate the 'sense of social unity'. His Budget raised the threshold for payment of tax, introduced a new higher rate of tax at a lower starting point and raised the highest rate of all from 75 per cent to 83 per cent. Corporation tax was increased and tax relief withdrawn from mortgages of over £25,000 a year or for second homes. More redistributive measures were promised for the future: a gifts tax in the next Budget and a wealth tax as soon as the administrative details had been worked out, with a Green Paper on this in the summer. But in its effect on demand the Budget was neutral – even slightly deflationary. Though unemployment was running at the seasonally adjusted figure of nearly 575,000 or 2·7 per cent, excluding school leavers – an alarmingly high figure by the standards of 1974 – the Chancellor

being raised. Mike naturally said he would be worried if unemployment rose, and Denis again assured us he would take action if it looked like doing this. Secondly, Tony C., backed by a number of us, said he thought a figure of £20,000 was too low as the ceiling for the first mortgage tax relief: he wanted £30,000. I suggested £25,000. 'I welcome advice on this,' said Denis charmingly: the first time in my memory that Cabinet has ever influenced a Budget in any way.[1]

Twice Denis disarmed us all by replying to some esoteric financial queries from Roy: 'I am ashamed to say I don't know the answer to that.' I think we felt that a Chancellor who doesn't claim to be a know-all is likely to be more successful than one who does. Then Harold Lever, who had been twisting his hands, gave tongue. After a convoluted introduction to the effect that he would always be loyal to the Chancellor both publicly and while he was making up his mind, and that he thought the Chancellor had done a remarkable job in so short a time, etc., he now felt it was his duty to let Cabinet know that he disagreed with the Chancellor's approach. ('That's what you are paid – or rather not paid – for,' Harold W. interjected briskly.) 'I disagree with the Chancellor over his demand management assessment,' said Harold L. rather painfully. 'This ought above all to have been a reflationary Budget.' The essence of our policy was the Social Contract, which, above all, was based on reducing unemployment and going for growth. He thought the Budget would inevitably increase unemployment and we should be in trouble with the trade unions. He then went on to complain that the gifts tax proposals were 'confiscatory'. Much as he was in favour of the redistribution of wealth, we must recognize that an 80 per cent rate would be a 'great shock to the City gents' and might produce repercussions we could not handle. Could we not approach the subject a little more diplomatically?

---

said it was too early to talk of expansion. In February the trade deficit had reached its highest recorded figure, giving a total deficit of £800 million for the first two months. Inflation was rising and the first aim, he argued, must be to reduce the Government's borrowing requirement, which had mounted to over £4,000 million in the previous year. So there could be no hope of immediately restoring the Conservative Government's cuts in public expenditure of December 1973. Indeed, defence spending was to be cut by a further £50 million. The increased spending on pensions – with £200 million more for the house building programme and £500 million for food subsidies – must, he said, be covered by increased tax. So he increased the standard rate of income tax by 3 pence, raised national insurance contributions from 5 per cent to 5½ per cent and put up the duties on drink and tobacco. Nationalized industries, which had been forced to run up massive deficits under the Heath policy, would, he announced, be authorized to increase their prices. The net effect was designed to reduce demand by some £200 million by the end of the year and to cut the Government's borrowing requirement by £700 million. But a substantial deficit remained both on trade and internal borrowing. To finance this the Chancellor announced that the Bank of England through the clearing banks had negotiated a massive ten-year loan of $2½ billion from foreign banks and had arranged an increase in short-term financial help under the 'swap arrangements' with other central banks. 'Borrowing is more sensible in economic terms than trying to cut imports by massive deflation,' Denis Healey told the Commons. 'But no one should imagine it is a soft option.'

[1] Budget secrecy was sacrosanct. This enabled the Chancellor to reach his Budget decisions in the recesses of the Treasury, merely informing his colleagues the day before the Budget. Though departmental Ministers were consulted on individual items of interest to them, only the Prime Minister was given the picture as a whole in time to influence it. In the previous Labour Government Dick Crossman and I led an attack on this convention, arguing that there were many aspects of the Budget which could, and should, be put into commission. Cabinet as a whole, for instance, should decide the target for growth, the mix of direct and indirect taxation and the balance between taxation and public expenditure.

Naturally Mike and the rest of us on the Left had pricked up our ears at the first part. But faced with the promise of an autumn Budget, there was little we could do – save that Mike gave another warning on the unemployment point. Harold [Wilson] then reported on last week's discussion on the Industrial Relations Bill. Mike promised that regulations on picketing would be published before the Bill received the Royal Assent. Also that we would say that appeal against the abuse of the closed shop would be introduced in our second Bill. I then slipped away to prepare for my statement, leaving them all congratulating Fred on his success at Brussels.[1]

Tuesday, 26 March

I am still trying to get a meeting of my political team every Monday morning at 11.30am (Brian O'Malley takes life comfortably and does not get back from Rotherham till then), but so far something has always happened to prevent it. I thought it was symbolic of the new co-operative attitude of civil servants that, without consulting me, Graham had called the meeting for noon today instead. (Only this morning I ran into Fred Peart and his Private Secretary, who said, on being introduced: 'We are all frightened of you.') It was a useful meeting[2] at which I discussed with them whether I should ask Philip Rogers to stay on when he is due to retire this summer. I told them William Armstrong had told me it was up to me. On offer as alternatives were Bill Pile of Education and Ian Bancroft of the Civil Service Department [CSD]. They agreed with my assessment of Rogers: deeply conventional, instinctively out of line with the far-reaching reforms we want to make, but not obstructive. I was delighted to hear Brian A-S. say that he and Tony Lynes[3] were getting excellent co-operation from him and that this time there was no attempt to prevent them from seeing papers, etc. (Another effect of my Sunningdale speech?) He cheered me up as he said, 'All the people lower down the line on the pensions side are thrilled that we are going back to National Superannuation.' We agreed it was better at this stage to leave Rogers in post – he would do what we wanted. But the holding of the meeting meant that I was left with twenty minutes to read through my Parliamentary Questions. I have never gone onto the front bench so unprepared. But I couldn't worry. I still can't analyse my own mood. It is one almost of indifference. Is it a new strength: born of experience? God knows it isn't laziness; I work hard enough. Is it that the whole process of government has ceased to dazzle, so that I get things more into perspective? Or is it carelessness that will bring me a cropper one of these days? Time will show.

[1] At the meeting of the Council of Ministers (Agriculture) in Brussels on 21–23 March, an agreement had been reached on food prices and other arrangements for 1974–75 which protected the British housewife from price increases in the shops.

[2] The meetings became a regular weekly fixture at which we discussed policy with no officials present. In addition to Ministers, those attending included the Parliamentary Private Secretaries, my political adviser and the special advisers. Later I also invited two research assistants at Transport House, who were dealing with social policy and who found it invaluable to be kept in touch with the Government's ideas and problems.

[3] Secretary of the Child Poverty Action Group from 1966–69 and author of the *Penguin Guide to Supplementary Benefit*. As an expert on pensions he was for many years a member of the Social Policy Committee of the Labour Party and I brought him into the department to work with Professor Abel-Smith.

I was afraid I wouldn't be able to keep awake through the Budget speech and at one point I did almost doze off. But then it was so packed with meat I perked up. I thought Denis did very well and the Tories sat silent, clearly not certain whether it was a case for jubilation by them or not. Slipped out towards the end to do urgent constituency letters and get ready for a protracted official meeting which had been called, first to prepare for my uprating statement tomorrow and secondly to deal with a complicated submission on the interim pension arrangements we should introduce next April.[1] My head swam as I tried to read Brian O'Malley's submission. (I don't get much sleep these days.) I had no time to master it before the two Brians and the phalanx of officials moved in, so I did what I had once admired Duncan Sandys for doing when I as a backbencher had gone to make representations to him as a Minister: I just sat and asked questions till I had wormed the facts out of them. Ted came in before we finished to collect me for the 'Husbands and Wives' dinner and sat in a corner of my room listening to the discussion. I think he got an eye-opener about the complexities with which we have to deal. Then over to Lockets, where it was our turn to be hosts, but I was so exhausted I could hardly take in a word anyone was saying. I dimly remember Mike complaining furiously about the fact that Harold had packed the Europe Committee of Cabinet with pro-marketeers and that Jim had produced a terrible statement for him to make at the Council of Ministers. I think he, too, must be feeling the physical strain, because Ted said he had never seen him so vehement. Judith also made some noises about Chile which I didn't take in. I positively flopped into bed.

Wednesday, 27 March

Up at 6am to catch up with my boxes. There is a National Executive Committee meeting this morning and yesterday I was told that Legislation Committee of Cabinet had been called for 10.15am. This would have meant missing NEC altogether,

[1] For some years all parties had been agreed that the Beveridge scheme of national insurance, with its provision for flat-rate pensions in return for flat-rate contributions, was out-of-date as the level of contribution needed to finance a decent pension put too great a burden on the low paid. In 1969 Dick Crossman, as Secretary of State for the Social Services, had produced an earnings-related scheme of national superannuation, but this had not become law when the Conservatives were returned to power in 1970. Sir Keith Joseph, Crossman's successor, abandoned the scheme in favour of a two-tier system consisting of the flat-rate state pension plus an earnings-related pension on top, both to be financed by earnings-related contributions. This became law in 1973. Under it, every employee had to qualify for the second pension, either by belonging to an approved private pension scheme, or by becoming a member of the inferior 'State Reserve Scheme'. In Opposition the Labour Party had bitterly attacked Sir Keith's proposals as a sop to the insurance industry by setting the standards of approved private schemes too low and making the Reserve Scheme less attractive still. Sir Keith had himself described it as being 'of modest dimensions'. One of the most obnoxious features of the Reserve Scheme was that it was to be 'funded', i.e. contributions were to be invested and the level of the reserve pension determined by the yield of those investments, instead of current pensions being financed out of current contributions, plus an Exchequer contribution, as in the basic state scheme ('pay as you go').

In our Manifesto we had pledged ourselves to replace the Conservatives' 'inadequate and unjust' long-term pensions scheme with a comprehensive one of our own and this was to be one of my major tasks. My first problem, however, was that Sir Keith's Reserve Pension Scheme was due to come into operation on 6 April 1975, and I had to decide what to do about the Reserve Pension Board, which had already been set up, and whether to allow the Reserve Scheme to start as planned until we could work out, and introduce, our own 'pay as you go' scheme.

particularly as there is a Parliamentary Labour Party meeting on the Budget at 11am. I was about to send a Minute of protest to Harold – asking that such clashes should be avoided in future – when Graham informed me that the Legislation Committee had been advanced to 9.30am for the purpose of avoiding a clash with the NEC. Fine so far. But the early meeting of Legislation Committee did not solve my problem. First I had to point out, in the committee's discussion on my Uprating Bill (which *must* be published this Friday if we are to get the increases in payment by 22 July), that one vital clause was still being negotiated with Treasury. This is the clause that fixes the date of the next uprating after this. If we are to fulfil our Manifesto promise of annual reviews the date included must be not later than 22 July. The Treasury has suddenly insisted that this limits the Chancellor's power of manoeuvre and that Sir K.'s present wording of 'not later than 30 Nov.'[1] must stand. This would throw doubt on the whole validity of our uprating and I am determined to fight this to the death. John Gilbert[2] made friendly enough noises in the Legislation Committee but had to reserve the Chancellor's position. So when I got to NEC at 10.15 I soon got a message saying that arrangements had been made for me to discuss the matter with the Chief Secretary [Joel Barnett] at 12.30 and that officials would be along to discuss it with me first at noon. This meant I had to miss the party meeting in the House that was to discuss the Budget. I gather that quite a lot of references were made to the uprating and there were some comments on my absence. So much for all our emphasis on 'keeping in touch'.

The meeting with Joel was exhausting. For over an hour he argued with a blind Treasury insistence that the Chancellor must be free to have a later budget next year. This did not mean, we were assured, that the Treasury wanted to go back on our policy of annual reviews, merely that the Chancellor must 'keep his options open'. His options to do what, I asked. To move to a sixteen-month review next year? Not at all, said Joel. First patiently, then passionately, I pointed out that that was just what his suggestion of inserting the November date in the Bill would mean. The Treasury official who was sitting next to Joel interposed that my arguments were 'impressive', but Joel didn't give way. Finally, we broke it off, Joel shaking his head and saying, 'You are a terrible woman.'

I went back to the House limp, to have a coffee and biscuits before my statement. Fortunately the statement was so full of goodies it was easy sailing. So was my press conference. So were the radio and TV interviews. But I got to the Cabinet office late for Harold's meeting with the TUC. When I arrived Sid Greene was drawling out that the General Council had given 'general approval' to the Budget as 'going in the right direction'. There had been 'great approval' of the pension increases, some concern that there was only to be a Green Paper on the wealth tax. There was also some concern about the use of VAT, which the TUC wanted abolished, though they understood the Chancellor's reasons this time. The question of family allowances had also

[1] In his Social Security Act of 1973 Sir Keith Joseph had provided for an annual review of pensions and other benefits in order to keep them in line with price increases over the previous twelve months. Pensions were to be adjusted 'not later than 30th November each year'. Since we had advanced the date of our uprating to 22 July, our next increase would have to be in July 1975, if our own promise of twelve-monthly reviews was to be kept.

[2] Dr John Gilbert, Labour MP for Dudley East, was Financial Secretary to the Treasury.

been raised. Len followed him by taking up the unemployment point: with the Chancellor only going for 2½ per cent growth, instead of the 3½ per cent the TUC wanted, they were afraid it might rise. (Looking over Harold Lever's shoulder at his Treasury brief, which he said I ought not to be looking at as it was private, I saw that it made a point of our 'difference with the TUC' on this, since the Treasury forecast was that unemployment would rise.)

The TUC's main preoccupation was about the repeal of the Industrial Relations Act. Sid had said there was 'some anxiety', but Mike explained that he was pressing ahead with this with the utmost urgency. He clearly charms them with his friendly sincerity and Jack Jones nodded approvingly at everything he said. But Hughie returned to this, not unnaturally in view of the fine he faces over Con Mech.[1] 'Our fear,' he said, 'is that the Act will remain on the statute book until some point arises on which you are defeated in the House.' Mike, trying to control his irritation at their failure to realize that he was as frustrated as they were by the procedural difficulties (how I sympathize!), repeated that he was rushing the legislation through as quickly as possible and hoped to introduce the repeal Bill by 1 May. He was meeting the TUC on Monday to discuss what had to be done to get it through the House, adding: 'We may have to give a concession on picketing.' (They wouldn't have taken that from *me*!) He hoped to have the Act by the end of June but 'we can't give you any guarantee as to what will happen in this Parliament'.

Hughie was also – very interestingly – obsessed with the desire not to be accused of rocking the boat for the Government. He entered into an elaborate explanation of the threatened overtime ban.[2] 'It is the height of stupidity,' he said passionately, 'to face the situation we face in the engineering industry which will virtually put us back on the three-day week. There is no problem in the engineering industry which involves the Government in having to believe that someone is out to break the Counter Inflation Act.' Perhaps the Social Contract is working after all!

After the meeting I grabbed Denis for a quick word about the date of the 1975 uprating. He was very offhand and brusque but I persuaded him to come back to Ted Short's room. 'I can't agree to have my options pre-empted in this way,' he said emphatically and walked out. 'Then it will have to go to Cabinet tomorrow,' I told

---

[1] See Introduction. From September 1973, the Amalgamated Union of Engineering Workers had been in dispute with Con Mech (Engineering) Ltd over union recognition. In October 1973, under the Industrial Relations Act provisions, the union had been fined £75,000 for contempt of court for refusing to call off the strike. Despite the fine the strike had continued until the beginning of March and the firm applied to the NIRC for compensation. Although the Labour Government had announced its intention to repeal the Act, the court on 28 March made an award of £47,000 against the union. With the union refusing to obey the court, Scanlon knew its assets were at continuing risk until the Act was repealed. And so it proved. When the money was not paid, the court sequestered the AUEW's assets. The result was the calling of a national engineering strike. This case – as so many others under the Act – ended on a note of farce when on 8 May the court accepted £65,000 from an anonymous donor to discharge the union's debt. One theory was that a group of employers had put up the money. The Act was eventually repealed in July and the NIRC disappeared.

[2] The ban was in support of the AUEW claim for an increase of £10 on basic rates. Agreement was finally reached in March 1975, on an increase of 31 per cent to be phased in over twelve months. Both sides claimed this was within the Social Contract as minimum basic rates only applied to a small minority of workers.

Ted Short, who agreed to raise it orally, while an anxious official hovered round asking me if I could not agree to the Treasury 'compromise' now proposed. It turned out to be a promise that, if the uprating had to be postponed beyond June next year, the Chancellor would be willing to pay a bonus in lieu. 'Nothing doing,' I said firmly and told Ted Short that any tinkering with the twelve-month date would be politically disastrous. He obviously agreed, adding: 'You had better go and ring up some of your friends.'

Back in the House I tried to do that but couldn't contact Mike or Wedgie. Then I thought of Bob Mellish and eventually tracked him down in the Strangers' bar. I took him into a corner, bought him a drink and told him the whole tale. His response was instantaneous and complete. He would tell Cabinet tomorrow that we had just got to stop bothering about what was right for twelve months ahead and concentrate on getting – and winning – an election as soon as possible. 'I am the only Chief Whip in history who is praying for defeat.' The Tories were working for the exact opposite. That was why on Monday we would have the unprecedented situation of an Opposition not even voting against the Government on the traditional last day of the Budget debate. They would almost certainly not even vote against the repeal of the Industrial Relations Act. They were waiting for an issue – and a moment – that would be embarrassing for the Government. We just could not carry on for long on that basis, so *he* was praying that we would be defeated *now* when it suited *us*. In the meantime we must look at all our decisions in a short-term light and it would be madness to throw any doubt on the value of the uprating. 'If you say that tomorrow,' I replied delighted, 'I'm saved.' But I also took the precaution of having a word with Fred Peart. I passed John Ellis [Labour MP for Brigg and Scunthorpe] at the bar having a drink with John Bourne of the *Financial Times*. 'You're lobbying,' chuckled John Ellis. 'I recognize that look in your eye.' 'Isn't she looking well?' said Bourne. 'Aye,' replied Ellis, 'she's blooming again, now she's back in government.' 'Blooming?' I groaned. 'I'm nearly dead. I've a speech to make in the House tomorrow and I haven't even started on it.' 'Go on with you, you're loving every minute of it,' he retorted.

Back home at 10pm to start going through the pages of a turgid brief for tomorrow's speech in the Budget debate which have been rolling in from the Department. I decided the only thing to do was to speak ad lib as much as possible and damn the consequences. Worked till 1am scribbling out some headings. Then up at 6am to finish it.

Thursday, 28 March

Put on my best dress for the Cabinet official photo and hoped the tiredness wouldn't show too much. As it was cold the chairs had been set out in the upstairs reception room at No. 10, instead of outside. We had all been given a set place and Shirley and I found ourselves on the two outside seats of the semi-circle. 'You wait till the women of the movement learn about this,' Shirley called out to Harold. 'Not to worry, Shirley,' I called back. 'We can do a pincer movement on him. His days are doomed.' Harold just grinned, but I hope he was a bit embarrassed. In Cabinet Bob reported that Anthony Fell [Conservative MP for Yarmouth] had caused panic in his party's ranks by using his private member's time next Friday to put down a motion of no confidence in the Government. Bob was much more relaxed about it than Heath must feel. He said he did not intend to keep any of our people there to deal with that situation. In fact he intended to advise everyone to treat Fell with contempt and either stay away or just not vote.

I hoped that my item would be taken early so that I could get back to my speech, but first we had one of those protracted discussions that arise unexpectedly on an apparently quiet agenda. This time it was naval contracts with Chile.[1] Apparently the Defence and Overseas Policy Committee [OPD] (of which I am not a member this time) had decided that, although we would grant no new export licences for arms, we should honour existing contracts for two frigates, two submarines and the refitting of a Chilean destroyer now in one of our yards. (So that was what Judith was complaining about on Tuesday evening!) I hadn't realized there was a crisis over this. The reason soon emerged: an article in the *Sunday Telegraph* had alerted our people to what might be afoot, so ninety of them had protested to Jim. Yesterday he had merely said that current contracts were under review. So he and Harold had decided it must come to Cabinet. Bob jumped in to warn that there was strong feeling in the Parliamentary Labour Party about this. He begged Cabinet therefore not to go ahead with a decision without consulting the party. Jim should discuss it with the Defence group and then the matter should go to party meeting.

This brought Roy Mason grimly into the argument. He is a competent little right-wing so-and-so and reeled off a list of devastating details: the destroyer was already manned up with a Chilean crew and was ready to go to sea; the frigates and subs were being made in yards in development areas and men working on them would be at risk; we would be liable under Export Credit Guarantees for at least £44 million and so on. I could see that even Mike was shaken. He supported Bob's proposal, while adding that we were bound by the Motion we had moved while in Opposition, to say nothing of the party conference debate. Harold promptly sent for both of them and pronounced that we had already fulfilled 95 per cent of the points in them. Roy Mason said darkly that we would be having a series of similar problems – Greece, Portugal, South Africa, etc. – so we had better deal with them all together and work out a consistent line. Jim protested that he was not going to a party meeting until the Cabinet had decided what line it wanted him to take. In this he was backed by Lever and Healey, the latter raising the awful spectre that the party might actually decide to cancel the contracts and then we stood to lose £70 million.

What amused me was how shocked many of them were at the very idea of party democracy. One of them, predictably, was Fred Peart (I often wonder if the Tribune group realize how right-wing he is). He was all in favour of a decision now, 'otherwise ordinary people will have a veto over Cabinet decisions, which would be absurd'. Elwyn, equally predictably, backed him. (I have long ago abandoned the idea that he is Left; another illusion that dies hard.) Reg Prentice was another one, while Roy Jenkins havered all over the place. There might be occasions when it was right to

[1] See page 63.

consult the party first. Was this one of them? He didn't seem to know, but thought that perhaps Jim should take a 'hard down the line position'. Harold, to his credit, was far more responsive to Bob's reiterated bleat that we really must not repeat the mistakes of the last Government, but take the party with us by consulting them first. He was sure we could trust the party's good sense. This brought renewed protests from Jim and his backers, but Wedgie backed Bob Mellish and so did I, remarking ironically that we in the Labour Party loved to talk about workers' participation but hated practising it. 'The speeches made round this Cabinet table this morning could be echoed in every boardroom in industry,' I said. Finally Jim offered to meet the Defence group, provided he could argue along the lines of the OPD decision without actually committing Cabinet. It would be tricky but he would have a shot.

Next we turned to my item, Ted Short introducing it under Parliamentary affairs. Bob interrupted him to say we were faced with a new tactical situation in the House. The Tory Shadow Cabinet had had a reappraisal of its tactics and was clearly not going to try and defeat us at this time, but to give us enough time to get into difficulties. We must go to the country as early as possible. That meant we must always have immediate political points in mind. Harold followed him to say he agreed with the Chief Whip: he wanted us to 'set out our stall'. He then called on me to put my points 'as briefly as you can, Barbara'. I did so, arguing strongly but reasonably. 'Let me get one thing clear at the outset,' I said. 'I am not asking for more money; I am not trying to jump the gun on anyone. I merely want us to stand by our policy, for which the Chancellor has already budgeted, specifically and publicly.' Smiles all round. I was all set for a protracted debate when Denis astonished everyone by saying sweetly, 'I have decided not to press the point for the reasons given by the Chief Whip.' Relief! I left them discussing Crosland's plea to be allowed to go ahead with Phase Two of the channel tunnel scheme and went back to the House to finish my speech. There I rang Graham at the office. 'You've heard the result in Cabinet.' 'Oh, no, Secretary of State.' It sounded genuine. 'The Chancellor has conceded our point: the Bill will be published tomorrow.' 'Good God! How did you do it?' 'I'll tell you my secret some time,' I replied sweetly. 'I think there wouldn't be any point,' said Graham. 'I suspect it is something chemical.' He then told me he would be over with the last bits of my brief now being cleared with Treasury.

Went into the Chamber with a pile of scribbled notes and found I wasn't nervous at all. I really believe that, before I am through this stint, I shall be speaking in the House with ease and even eloquence.[1] The only bit that dragged was the long piece on family planning on which the Treasury had had to clear every word. I can't wait to hear Mike handle a speech in which expenditure implications are involved! The House was pretty thin, as it was a Thursday and no vote, but our people were delighted with the concessions on prescription charges and heating additions. Then off to more TV on family planning, which is obviously going to be the big news. I was exhausted by this time and was glad to crawl back to the flat with only one more

[1] Referring to the record increase in pensions and benefits, I told the House: 'I refuse to underestimate the size of our achievement in our first three weeks – a shift of £1,250 million of resources to the underprivileged at a stroke.'

speech to prepare (for the British Association of Social Workers [BASW] conference tomorrow). What a week! Again I waded through a turgid brief and decided I must pep it up a bit. But by then I just didn't care what happened and headed for bed.

Friday, 29 March

Rejigged most of the BASW speech – to the consternation of Private Office, who don't like the cavalier way I am dismissing Keith Joseph's studies on 'Preparation for Parenthood' and other academic irrelevancies about the 'cycle of deprivation'. They stood by anxiously, snatching pages off me to type for my hand-out and we nearly missed the plane. But when Janie Thomas greeted me affectionately at Manchester and I saw that audience I just scrapped half the speech, dropping whole pages of it, and ad libbed. I really am not going to read whole speeches from now on. How young Elizabeth,[1] with a lengthy hand-out to check of which I never delivered half, managed with the press I do not know. A swift change into a long dress and over to Wythenshawe for Alf Morris's annual dinner. If I survive, I think I am really going to find my feet in this job. But it is a big 'if', with the papers full of my family planning announcement, gleefully seized on by the *Mirror* as Barbara's 'free love'. My friend, Tom Wood, who took me back to Blackburn, told me the Catholic Bishop of Salford is already on my tail. But I never had a moment's hesitation that the family planning service must be free.

Monday, 1 April

A very useful meeting with my departmental Ministers: at last I have got this on to a Monday morning basis and Private Office is fully reconciled to it. They have also laid on drinks for Bernard Donoghue and his team this evening, as I asked. Graham asked me timidly if I wanted any officials there or not. I said that I would like him and Philip Rogers to be there. Donoghue turns out to be a pleasant – almost ingratiating – chap, but I wonder how much authority he will wield with the PM. It was an encouraging sign that, in addition to a transport economist, he has taken David Piachaud[2] into his team, which means that not only shall we have a voice in the inner advisory circle, but that Bernard wants to give special weight to our field. Whether that is inspired by Harold or not I don't know. Bernard assured Philip that they did not want to cut across anyone but rather to work *with* the Civil Service, and I suspect that Philip was rather relieved to find that this dreaded figure – the No. 10 top political adviser – was not an ogre after all, but 'one of us'. I fear that Bernard may be too much 'one of them' and I wonder why Harold chose him. For some no doubt irrational reason I was a bit depressed by meeting him. What is the word I am groping for: ineffectual? But the truth is that any adviser, however good, is as effectual as his Minister will enable

---

[1] Elizabeth Johnson from my Private Office.

[2] David Piachaud had worked as Professor Abel-Smith's assistant while the latter had been senior adviser to Dick Crossman and had later become a lecturer at the London School of Economics in Professor Abel-Smith's department.

him to be. This team of Harold's could just float on the surface of events unless Harold wills otherwise. In himself Bernard is clearly no tiger.

It was a relief to have an evening at the House to go through my boxes at a reasonable hour. I finished just in time to hear Denis wind up the Budget debate, which he did with great *élan*, even ending up with a bit of political knockabout. I note with approval that he is turning out to be a much more political Chancellor than we have had before – though I doubt whether we could ever rival Tony Barber in that respect.

Tuesday, 2 April

Up early to go to No. 10 for a meeting with the PM on the Sharp Report. In addition to Alf Morris I took Brian A-S. along so that he could develop his thesis about the need to move to cash allowances. Harold asked me to open and I did so by pointing out the financial difficulties of moving from invalid tricycles to cars. Brian had estimated that up to 500,000 people might qualify for cars if we included, as I feel we must include, disabled passengers. On the other hand I said that I did not feel we could move to cash allowances, which would merely favour the middle class. No ordinary poor disabled person would ever be able to afford the capital outlay on a car at any level of cash mobility allowance we could afford. There really must be state intervention to ensure that cars were produced for these people cheaply and in bulk. 'We cannot leave the disabled at the mercy of the car market,' I said. Harold and Alf entirely agreed with this, while Brian sat mum. I suppose that advisers feel themselves to be such non-elected animals that they dare not throw their weight about. Harold had brought in Bernard Donoghue, but he sat mum too. 'You know I made a speech on this,' said Harold and turned to an official to say: 'Ask Albert Murray[1] if he can turn up my speech.' 'I have it here, Prime Minister. We study your lightest word,' I replied sweetly. Harold almost blushed.

After a discussion we agreed that my Department should do a crash job on seeing the motor manufacturers and working out what it would cost to supply a car which they would be willing to take back second-hand at a good offset. This is a favourite idea of Harold's of which I don't see the point myself. But Harold also liked my idea of arranging to manufacture these cars at Bristol and elsewhere as part of the 'social costs' of cancelling Concorde. Harold also insisted that we should start by merely providing cars for the present categories: disabled passengers to come later. But much as I sympathized with Harold's desire to provide cars rather than cash allowances (which obviously pleased Alf), I was wary of a euphoria which could overlook the enormous long-term cost. I am not going to have such a large slice of my budget pre-empted in this way. So I put in a caveat to the effect that some of the 'social costs' money of Concorde would have to come my way to help finance this (to help finance Harold out of his political difficulty, I might have added). Not unnaturally Joel exploded at this and said he wasn't going to have the Concorde savings spent before they had even been incurred. 'I am merely reserving my position,' I replied. Fortu-

---

[1] Albert Murray, former Labour MP for Gravesend, had been brought by Harold Wilson into his personal office to help with constituency and party political correspondence.

nately Joel and I are very fond of each other, following our long battle together in the Select Committee of 1972–73 against the Tory tax credits scheme.

On to a meeting of the Social Services Committee of Cabinet over which Ted Short presides. The first item was a draft statement by Reg on comprehensive education. Jack Straw had done a pertinent comment for me to the effect that Reg's refusal even to hint at legislation wouldn't do. Experience showed that we just wouldn't get a comprehensive system unless we legislated. When I made this point, Ted backed me up strongly and Reg promised to have another look at it, though he said the National Union of Teachers was perfectly satisfied. This is just the sort of job I wanted my political adviser to do: looking at other Ministers' proposals from outside and enabling me to be a more effective general member of Cabinet.

Lunched with Peter Jenkins (of the *Guardian*) at the Ritz (a greatly overrated eating place in my view) and told him why I felt so much happier in this Government. I spelt out how much Harold had changed: as the 'custodian of the Manifesto' he just couldn't twist and turn any more. I got quite carried away about how Harold was playing it straight down the line of agreed party policy. After being crucified for four years for his determination to keep the party together at all costs, he now was determined to justify himself by sticking firmly to the policy we had thrashed out between the Shadow Cabinet and the NEC. That it was a more left-wing policy than we had ever had before would make no difference to him. Whatever the cost we would stick to it – on Europe, too, I warned him – and would just have to face the consequences. But I thought this would be a source of secret strength, like the man of principle who says, 'God helping me I can do no other.' This had been Heath's strength, too, and he had nearly got away with it. Peter and I mourned Dick, still clinging tenuously to life after his collapse last Thursday. I said impishly that after all I should have the laugh of him, for I would be writing the second diary: the diary of the third Labour Government which would make the fears and frustrations *his* diary would reveal seem old-fashioned.

After lunch I went to see Roy Jenkins at the Home Office about an immigration case which I thought I had won with Robert Carr when he was Home Secretary and on which, to my surprise and horror, Roy had turned me down. He greeted me charmingly and we sat alone together by the famous Home Secretary's coal fire. 'Yes, I think it *is* the nicest Minister's room in Whitehall,' he said complacently, adding: 'Much nicer than the Foreign Secretary's.' Roy seems in a rather curious frame of mind. I sense a realization that he will never lead the party and I suspect his regret is not very deep. It has made him more detached. He drawls even more than usual and he is certainly showing no great reforming initiative. It is as though his mind is on other things. He listened carefully while I went through the case; sat up sharp when I said the police had lied. As I talked he thumbed through his papers on the case, looking up once to say with that attractive smile of his', 'My Private Office agree that you do not bother us unless you feel you have a case.' Suddenly he interrupted me to say, 'If you feel so strongly about it I think I should be guided by you. I can't commit myself, obviously, but I will look at it again.' He insisted on seeing me down to the door, where he chatted about Dick. 'You were very close to him, so you will feel it more than the rest of us.' 'I had a love–hate relationship with him,' I replied. 'Well, so did everybody,' he said, 'but yours was more love than hate.' It was all curiously emotionless, though friendly in intention. I suspect that man is still numbed, as Harold was numbed for a long time.

Message that the 'Husbands and Wives' dinner has been cancelled because not enough people could turn up. The beginning of the end?

Wednesday, 3 April

The *Daily Mail* is full of a mysterious story about Tony Field,[1] Marcia and a land deal. Harold seems full of indignant self-righteousness, so I can only hope it is all right.

Almost unnoticed by busy non-Treasury Ministers a deep world recession was developing. The massive increase in the price of oil had not only given inflation a boost everywhere, but had thrown world trade out of gear. In 1974 the oil-producing countries were sucking in extra money from the rest of the world to the tune of $60 billion which their economies were unable to absorb. As their surpluses accumulated unspent, world demand was reduced.

The oil price increase dealt a body blow to Britain's already ailing economy, adding nearly £2,500 million to her oil import bill in 1974. Although in his Budget Denis Healey had rejected 'massive deflation' and rightly chose to finance Britain's deficit by borrowing, there was no organized international attempt to recycle these surpluses and Britain remained highly vulnerable. The Social Contract was the Government's main hope in trying to get inflation down and maintain our competitiveness. In its few weeks of office the Government had taken a number of steps to fulfil its side of the bargain with the trade unions. The TUC was anxious to respond to this new 'climate', but the pent-up resentment against Mr Heath's statutory incomes policy was proving irresistible. One group of workers after another put in for 'catching-up' wage increases, led by the nurses who were demanding a fundamental review of their salaries. Other NHS workers were following suit. The doctors were restive. Michael Foot struggled at the Department of Employment to hold back the tide.

Since an election clearly could not be long delayed, Harold Wilson was preoccupied with issues which could affect the Government's popularity. He was therefore alarmed when the building societies, faced with an actual net loss of funds due to high interest rates elsewhere, threatened to put up the mortgage rate, already running at 11 per cent. This brought Harold Lever into effective play. Another issue on which Harold Wilson had set his mind was devolution. He was firmly convinced that a radical devolution of power to Scotland, and to a lesser degree to Wales, was the only way to head off the Nationalists, who were threatening the Labour Party's survival in some of its traditional Scottish strongholds, and to defuse their growing clamour for separatism. To prepare for this he had to set up a Royal Commission on the Constitution in 1969, first

[1] Brother of Mrs Marcia Williams, Harold Wilson's personal secretary, who later became Lady Falkender.

under Lord Crowther and later under Lord Kilbrandon, to examine the possibilities. The Kilbrandon Report was published in October 1973, setting out seven alternatives. One of Harold's closest advisers on devolution was Lord Crowther-Hunt (formerly Dr Norman Hunt), a member of the Kilbrandon Commission and a keen devolutionist. In October 1974, Harold Wilson was to bring him into the Government as Minister of State at the Department of Education and he was to help Ted Short guide the Cabinet through the constitutional intricacies.

With the Opposition keeping its head down on political issues, sections of the press looked for ways of discrediting the Prime Minister. In March the Daily Mail *seemed to have found an opportunity of damaging him through his associates. On 18 March it carried an exclusive story: 'The Case of Ronald Milhench and his £95,000 land deals', which claimed that Marcia Williams and her brother, Tony Field, who had been Harold Wilson's office manager for two years when he was Leader of the Opposition, were involved in them. The story hung fire until 4 April when the* Mail *revealed that Mr Milhench had earlier shown them a letter to him about the deal at Ince-in-Makerfield which had purported to come from Harold Wilson but which the* Mail *said had been found a forgery. On the same day the* Daily Express *splashed a story about another deal in Warwickshire about which Mr Field had written to the Warwickshire County Council in August 1972 from Wilson's office and on House of Commons notepaper. Harold Wilson promptly issued writs against the two newspapers, but the storm erupted in the House of Commons that afternoon at Prime Minister's Question Time. Tory* MPs *jeered when Harold Wilson retorted in reply to a questioner: 'All my honourable Friends know that if you buy land on which there is a slag-heap 120 feet high which costs £100,000 to remove, that is not land speculation in the sense we condemn it, it is land reclamation.' Tony Field issued a statement claiming that he had bought the land for clearance and had made a total profit from the three sites at Ince-in-Makerfield of £110,000 over seven years. But the press kept up the heat and on 8 April Wilson made a statement to the House in which he said he had known about the land deals, but had not been personally involved in them in any way. He repeated the Government's determination to take development land into public ownership. Later Milhench admitted to the forgery and was jailed on this and other charges for three years. Harold Wilson did not proceed with the writs.*

Relations between the Government and the National Executive remained sensitive. Trouble was liable to flare up at any time. It did so over the question of Chile where, in September 1973, the Socialist President, Señor Allende, had been murdered and his Government overthrown by a military junta. To the Labour Party this was the Spanish Civil War of the 1930s all over again. Party conference promptly passed a resolution demanding that the British Government should withdraw our ambassador from Chile, give all possible assistance to refugees from that country and withhold 'all aid, loans and credit from the military régime'. The Labour Government had gone a long way to meet these demands. It had embargoed all future arms sales to Chile, ended aid and adopted a sympathetic attitude to the refugees, but it had to decide what to do about naval contracts entered into by previous Governments and whether to allow the vessels being built or refitted in British yards to be delivered to the Chilean Government. In this it was embarrassed by the stand it had taken in Opposition. In a debate on 23

November 1973, it had called on the Conservative Government to 'prevent any sale of arms to the junta ... and to withhold future aid and credits from the present Chilean régime'. Mrs Judith Hart had declared from the Opposition front bench: 'We do not believe any of the ships being built should go there, although my understanding is that the trade union movement is taking effective steps here.' In fact, Cabinet was told, there had been little or no trade union action against naval contracts, but only against four Rolls-Royce engines belonging to Hawker Hunter jet fighters of the Chilean air force which were under repair at East Kilbride, where AUEW workers were refusing to handle them. Despite Mrs Hart's speech, Cabinet decided the practical difficulties of cancellation were too great. On 10 April Jim Callaghan told the House the contracts would be fulfilled. The NEC remained unconvinced. At its May meeting, with resolutions of protest pouring in from local parties, it called on the Government to reconsider its decision 'even at this late hour'.

Even more bitter was the argument with the Government over the eleven members of Clay Cross Urban District Council who had refused to operate the Housing Finance Act 1972 obliging local authorities to increase council house rents. In January 1973 they had been surcharged for the lost rent income by the District Auditor. In July they had appealed against the surcharge to the High Court and had not only lost the appeal, but had been disqualified from holding office for five years. The Heath Government then put in a Housing Commissioner. The intransigence of the eleven aroused deep, if illogical, loyalty in the Labour movement. Although some twenty Labour-controlled local authorities had delayed, or refused to carry out the Act and although the rebel eleven had broken the law in other ways such as giving manual workers an 80 per cent pay rise in defiance of Mr Heath's statutory pay limit, the Labour rank and file insisted on singling out the Clay Cross councillors as honoured martyrs. At its 1973 conference the party had passed a resolution demanding that on the return of a Labour Government 'all penalties, financial or otherwise, should be removed retrospectively from the councillors who have courageously refused to implement' the Act. Ted Short, put up to reply for the NEC, had bowed to the storm in an equivocal speech recommending acceptance of the resolution. He admitted that Clay Cross was 'something rather special', pledged that the next Labour Government would remove all disqualifications from the councillors involved, but added unhappily that acceptance of the motion 'must not be taken by anyone to be an encouragement to any Labour councillors anywhere to act unlawfully'. On financial penalties he read out a resolution of the NEC pledging itself to consider ways of assisting councillors in their financial difficulties arising out of their refusal to implement the Housing Finance Acts.

On coming into office the Labour Government faced intense hostility both in the House and the press to any idea of exonerating law-breakers and there were also great anxieties about this in Cabinet. On 18 March Tony Crosland, as Secretary of State for the Environment, had told a deputation from Clay Cross that he would not withdraw the Housing Commissioner unless the Council fulfilled its obligation under the law. In a statement in the Commons on 4 April, Harold Wilson insisted that at no time had any commitment been given to reimburse the surcharged councillors from public funds, but added that the Government was committed to removing the disqualification. This later proved impossible (see pages 418 and 486). The Government's problems were made worse by the fact that David Skinner, one of the rebel eleven, was brother of Dennis Skinner, the redoubtable Labour MP for Bolsover, who was to keep the fight going year after year.

Departmentally one of my main headaches was what to do about Sir Keith Joseph's Reserve Pension Scheme. Should I bring it into operation the following year, or abandon it? Abandonment would mean at least two years' delay before people could start to earn their extra pension and that seemed politically dangerous. Yet the scheme had serious disadvantages. In the first place contributions would be high. Employees would pay 5·25 per cent on their earnings up to a ceiling for the flat-rate pension (which at October 1973 was £7·75p for a single person) and 1·5 per cent on top for members of the Reserve Scheme. In return they would get a meagre second pension which would take forty years to mature; women would get smaller pensions than men and widows only 50 per cent of their husband's entitlement. Most serious of all, since the scheme would be funded and the yield from investments uncertain, there would be no guarantee that the Reserve Pension Scheme would keep in line with prices as the basic pension did.

One option open to me was a compromise. I could let the Reserve Scheme start on time, with all its deficiencies, but alter the way it was financed from 'funding' to 'pay-as-you-go' until we could bring in our own scheme. It was this option which first attracted me.

Thursday, 4 April

I went along with Brian to see Edmund Dell in his role of Paymaster General, determined to get what we called Option B (switching the Reserve Scheme to a pay-as-you-go basis) if at all possible. We met at the Treasury, where Edmund was flanked by Joel and the officials with whom we had had our earlier argument about the uprating date. They obviously now treat me with a healthy respect. For our part we were extremely wary, knowing the Treasury. Edmund started by saying, 'I take it we are all agreed that another half per cent on the contributions would be enough to pay for the new and higher basic state pension.' We thought it was a trap, but after half an hour of argument it became clear that Edmund (who, after all, had served with us on the Standing Committee on Keith's Social Security Bill and had had a research assistant briefing him then) was genuinely concerned that we should have an interim scheme that was politically tolerable. He didn't think we should throw away the chance of getting higher contributions for the new and higher basic pension, but equally didn't think we could justify appropriating the Reserve Scheme fund unless we offered improved Reserve Scheme benefits. 'I am speaking purely for myself – and I don't think officials are agreed on this – but I would have thought we must and could do something to shorten the maturity period out of the extra money we would get from putting contributions up,' he told us. This was an unexpected development which I said we must consider – and anyway I had to go to Cabinet. So we broke up, agreeing to meet again at 8.30pm. I took Brian, who was muttering, 'I don't like it', into the waiting room with my officials, Alec Atkinson and Douglas Overend. 'How much would a half per cent on the contributions raise?' I asked. '£630 million; and with the Reserve fund as well the National Insurance fund would have an enormous surplus,' they replied. 'Exactly,' I retorted triumphantly. 'It is just the old Treasury ploy to make the national insurance scheme carry the burden of demand management.' I sent them off to work out the figures to illustrate this.

When I arrived at Cabinet I found that we were all to parade ourselves in the garden for the benefit of TV. 'The idea is to show that we are a team,' said Harold to me. No one had told me and I hadn't even put my full make-up on! I told Shirley how much I liked her new hair style. 'I had to do something,' she replied. 'I got so many letters telling me how terrible my hair looked. I was letting the party down, they said.' We strolled around in the garden casually forming and reforming groups, the cameramen trying hard to get me and Shirley together with Harold. 'We're not posing,' he snapped. Despite the terrible headlines in the press over the land deal he seemed completely relaxed. At one point I heard him saying confidently to Shirley, 'They don't realize the difference between speculation and reclamation; this was a case of reclaiming land', at which she nodded approvingly. 'Are you going to make a statement?' I asked. 'Yes,' he replied, 'but not in the House. I don't want to give them the chance of asking irrelevant questions.' Despite his self-assurance I felt uneasy. I don't like his response of issuing writs. I would have thought that by far the best thing would have been to set up an enquiry immediately. If he had done that he could have come out of it with credit, as Heath did from the Lambton affair. And I wondered if Goodman[1] had advised him to issue those writs. None of the rest of us get a chance to talk to Harold. I have been trying to phone him myself this morning since the early hours to ask him not to prohibit political advisers from serving on local authorities: another matter which he has dealt with without consulting me, though Jack Straw is one of the few who are involved. But Harold has changed his Lord North Street phone number and a message left with the duty clerk at No. 10 brought no results. Oddly enough I almost mourn the absence of George Wigg! Who on earth is advising Harold? If it is only Ted Short, then all we shall get is even more truculent hostility to the press from that narrow martinet. This is where we shall miss Dick. One of his assets was that he could occasionally bludgeon his way into Harold's confidence.

Photos over, I managed to get a word with Harold at last about Jack Straw, who has got to be renominated for the council elections by noon today. Harold was quite reasonable about it: let the nomination go ahead, he said, though Jack might have to resign later unless Harold found a way out of the difficulty. I pleaded that political advisers ought by definition to remain in active politics. 'Yes,' said Harold, 'but we have got a lot more of them than Heath had and we raised it when one of his advisers became a Tory county councillor.' 'Say frankly that you've changed your mind,' I

---

[1] Arnold Goodman, senior partner in Goodman, Derrick & Co., solicitors, had been a close friend of Harold Wilson's for years and had been given a peerage by him in 1965. Lord Goodman had always been very generous with his legal advice to Labour MPs, including me, and Harold Wilson had used him for a number of assignments, including an exploratory visit with Sir Max Aitken to Ian Smith in August 1968 on the possibilities of a settlement. But Lord Goodman never took the Labour Whip and was ready to use his remarkable abilities under any government for any cause which aroused his interest, notably the arts. He was chairman of the Newspaper Proprietors' Association from 1970–75, in which role he clashed with Michael Foot over the issue of the closed shop for newspaper journalists.

urged, 'and that you would be in favour of a Tory Government having political advisers too.' That was going too far for Harold, who said the answer might be to get the political chaps paid for from outside. 'I'm looking into it.'

At Cabinet no one mentioned the land deal. Perhaps I should have done so, but it is hard to break down Harold's assumption that all this is purely his affair. Again I miss Dick. In the old days he and I would have insisted on raising it. I must build up a new pact with Mike instead, through the 'Husbands and Wives' group.

On Parliamentary business Bob reported that the Opposition are to put down an amendment to my Uprating Bill (on which they have agreed to take all the stages on one day: so my ploy on rushing through the increases has worked) calling for pensions to be reviewed every six months. Bob was all for throwing in the sponge; we would be sure to be defeated on it and he couldn't even be sure of whipping our boys into the lobby against it. Better to accept it than be defeated. I was much more cautious, saying I had so many other things I needed to do in my field which would cost money that it would be better to turn and fight. If defeated I could always use this as an alibi when they pressed me to do more for the disabled, etc. Jim said it wasn't even clear that six-monthly reviews would be administratively practicable. It was agreed that I should put in a paper after consultation with the Chancellor and the Chief Whip.

Our most protracted discussion, typically, was on Clay Cross, on which Harold has to answer Questions this afternoon. Harold was all for making a holding statement. As far as reimbursement of the financial penalties was concerned there had never been any implication that we would use public funds for this purpose. And there were other local councillors involved besides Clay Cross. We didn't know the numbers yet, as the district auditors were still at work, but it might run up to over 200. Jim, agreeing, pointed out that we were committed to remove the disqualifications and should stand by that. He couldn't resist the temptation of pointing out that he had always told the NEC we couldn't possibly reimburse the Clay Cross boys from public funds. (I've got to admit he's right about that.) Someone suggested that the eventual sum involved might be £1½ million, and Shirley pointed out that we couldn't possibly raise that through the party machinery. Someone else pointed out that the only people we had committed ourselves at conference to help were Clay Cross. It was unlikely we should see the total picture till October.

Mike came in rather tentatively. He found it 'very difficult', he said, to agree with what Harold suggested. 'This is the first time I have given my mind to it.' We had agreed at the NEC to ask the Government to 'consider' the conference resolution and he couldn't in all conscience say that he *had* considered it. Couldn't the statement be postponed? Harold said he sympathized with Michael's point, but we would remain under great pressure until something had been said. Clay Cross would dominate every issue and debate until it was cleared out of the way. 'Has an amnesty been considered in this case?' asked Wedgie. 'After all, that is the way the Betteshanger fines[1] were dealt with.' But the overwhelming view of Cabinet was that we had better

[1] On 9 January 1942, 1,600 miners at the Betteshanger colliery in Kent went on strike over pay and conditions. The strike was in breach of the wartime National Arbitration Order; the War Cabinet, against Bevin's advice, agreed to prosecute the miners and 1,000 were charged. Three leaders were imprisoned

say quite firmly that we did not intend to use public funds. Eric Varley clinched it when he declared firmly that there was deep resentment in the East Midlands about Clay Cross; local Labour people felt that many of those involved were Trots. Harold seized on this happily, saying he would add a bit to his statement about the importance of ensuring that whatever action was taken should be fair to the many councillors who had reluctantly implemented the Tory Housing Act.

Next Jim reported on how his statement on the EEC renegotiations had gone at the Council of Ministers.[1] In view of the thunderings in the press about the 'rudeness' of his speech and its disastrous effects, he sounded positively cheerful. He said the public reactions had been 'very strong', the private ones 'much more balanced'. The one point on which they would all part company with us was on the renegotiation of the Treaty of Rome. 'I think our approach is right – to see how far we can get, by changing the policies of the Community, to meet our Manifesto commitment – and I will of course report back to Cabinet.' On political co-operation they had had a long meeting about what should be the nature of our relationship with the US. France had found herself in a minority of one and there was to be another meeting on this early in May. 'What I am particularly pleased about is that this will be ahead of the next negotiating meeting on 7 May,' he said. This meant that we should have established ourselves in a majority position on one issue before he had to table our detailed negotiating positions. Jim's statement was received without a murmur from anyone, especially when Harold said Cabinet ought to meet for a whole day in the Easter recess to discuss our proposals so as to be ready for the next negotiating round.

Tony C. then introduced the memorandum he has circulated about mortgages. I thought it was rather a feeble paper, setting out the difficulties rather wordily and not giving a concrete lead. Tony the indecisive once again! Clearly something must be done to check the outflow of funds from building societies, otherwise the output of private homes will fall to about 100,000 a year. The only way, said Tony, if the mortgage rate was not to go up to 13 per cent, was to give a government subsidy for six months while a high-powered committee was set up to examine radical long-term solutions. Before opening the discussion to general comment Harold chipped in: 'I want to make one thing clear. This is the most important decision we shall take. We must as a firm Cabinet decision get the mortgage rate down: to $9\frac{1}{2}$ per cent if possible. We can't allow this rickety mid-Victorian structure of building societies to bring us electoral defeat.' (Keeping his options open, no doubt!) At this Denis came in very

---

and the others fined, but only nine paid the fine. The strike continued and the colliery owners, now anxious to settle, offered to pay the fines, but were strongly advised not to by the Home Secretary. The three leaders had to be released fom prison to help settle the dispute and the Home Office decided not to enforce payment of the fines.

[1] In its election Manifesto the Government was committed to try to secure 'major changes' in the Common Agricultural Policy [CAP], new and fairer methods of financing the Community budget, acceptance of our opposition to Economic and Monetary Union, the retention by Parliament 'of those powers over the British economy needed to pursue effective regional, industrial and fiscal policies', safeguards for the interests of the Commonwealth and developing countries; no harmonization of VAT which would require Britain to tax necessities. At the Council of Ministers meeting on 1 April, Jim Callaghan set out these terms in a tough speech which brought a particularly hostile reaction from the French Foreign Minister, who said that any terms involving a renegotiation of the Treaty of Rome would be unacceptable.

primly: 'I don't agree that we stand or fall by our success in bringing the rates *down*, though I do agree we must not let them go up. There is no socialist case for an across-the-board subsidy. Our only hope is to get interest rates down generally, and as Cabinet will see later today we have already taken the first step. I am today allowing the banks to release 1 per cent of the special deposits, which should bring rates down by 3 per cent in the next few months.'

During all this Harold Lever was twisting himself up for another of his now famous – and very amusing – counterblasts. (Illness seems to have made a political man of him.) Having expressed his now conventional 'great sympathy' with the Chancellor, he had us chuckling with delight as he vigorously denounced the 'stale pedantries of the Treasury'. (Never has language like this been heard before in Cabinet – and from a Treasury Minister, too!) Warming to his theme, he added, 'This is the stuff of which ruined Labour Governments are made. One gets into the view that one won't be able to make love to one's wife without affecting the borrowing requirement.'

The outcome of his contribution was that he warmly agreed with the PM that we must help the building societies to stop them putting up the rate. What the Treasury didn't grasp was that an increase in the rate would itself be highly inflationary. We should tell the building societies that they must use £500 million of their cash reserves, which they were just sitting on because they got more from investing the reserves than in spending them on building houses. If they would do this we would be breaking our backs to bring down interest rates. He would like permission to meet them and put this to them, telling them we would help them to raise a Eurodollar loan and to arrange a rediscounting facility. It could perfectly well be done if only they wanted it, and he was sure he could twist their arm. If, even so, a subsidy was unavoidable, it must be across-the-board and we could place the odium on them. We all almost cheered this spirited *démarche*. Denis, bowing to the mood, said he would have no objection to Harold having this meeting, providing it was without commitment as to the form the subsidy should take. Harold W. ruled that we should take no decision about a subsidy at all until Harold L. had reported back, at which Tony C. said mildly he would like to be at the meeting, too.

Finally we had a very interesting revelation of Roy Jenkins's mind. He brought up the question of the Speaker's Conference.[1] This, he said, had had unfinished business left over from the last Parliament and he was thinking of reconstituting it. But before he did he wanted to discuss how we should handle the matter of the single transferable vote. If we did not include it in the terms of reference we should look as though we were the only party not interested in electoral reform. As the Liberals were very likely to propose its examination, it would be better for us to take the initiative. He suggested therefore that we should get the Speaker's Conference to examine it in a

---

[1] Since 1916 all-party conferences of MPs under the chairmanship of Mr Speaker had been held periodically to consider questions of electoral reform. Speaker Lloyd's Conference, set up in 1972 to consider various aspects of electoral law, had come to an abrupt end with the dissolution of Parliament in February 1974, and had not finished its work. It was not to resume it and the Speaker's Conference was not brought into play again till July 1977, when Jim Callaghan as Prime Minister was anxious to win the support of the Ulster Unionists by increasing the number of Northern Ireland constituencies. Speaker Thomas's Conference then duly recommended by a large majority that the twelve Northern Ireland seats should be increased to a minimum of sixteen and a maximum of eighteen.

'low pressure way'. Bob Mellish looked alarmed at this, while Mike came in emphatically: 'Once we get into this it will grow and grow and grow,' he protested. 'Why hasten the conference at all? I have always believed the Tories would come down for the alternative vote because it is in their interests.' Nodding approval, Bob added that he was darn sure the Speaker was in no hurry to have the conference reconstituted. Willie Ross, in his lugubrious way, pointed out that all this was linked with the Kilbrandon Report, which had itself recommended a form of proportional representation as the only way of eliminating the perpetual Labour majorities in Scotland and Wales which devolution would produce. If we were not careful we could see the end of any possibility of a Labour Government. Harold reminded us that nothing could stop the Speaker's Conference from producing an interim report – particularly if we put on it some of the Labour maverick types like George Strauss as we had done before. It was obviously best to let this sleeping dog lie as long as possible. So we sent Roy away with a flea in his coalition ear.

I told the office I must get into the House for Harold's Questions as often as possible and made them cancel a couple of office meetings so that I could do so today. The statement about Clay Cross went off better than could have been expected. Even the redoubtable Dennis Skinner didn't make much mileage out of it. But my heart sank as I heard Harold inject into his answer to an earlier supplementary what seemed to me a gratuitous reference to the land deals matter now being blown up into enormous proportions by the press. He trotted out the phrase I heard him use this morning: about there being all the difference between land reclamation and property development. It went down as badly as it deserved to do. I'm afraid he has got himself into a corner here quite unnecessarily.

As part of my intention to establish close and friendly relationships with our staff at the Department one of my first acts had been to invite the staff side of the departmental Whitley Council to my office for informal drinks. But I soon found that they wanted much more than that: Philip Rogers had not exaggerated when he warned me they were seething with discontent (a) about Heath's pay freeze and (b) about the way the Tories had cut down staff. Result: they had taken industrial action – unprecedented in the Civil Service – a couple of years ago. Now they are just not prepared to take my rush uprating on board without some 'tangible' gesture on my part, i.e. a bonus. My department have been warning me off this, but I told them we must wait and see what the mood was. So when I saw the staff side this afternoon I told them I wanted to meet them informally, but I realized there were a number of things they were bursting to raise with me urgently and I certainly wasn't trying to fob them off with a drink. Naylor,[1] the chairman, and the other full-time officials responded very pleasantly and were particularly pleased when I said I intended to send Bob Brown on a tour of the local offices and that I hoped they would invite him to meet their Executives. But they weren't to be headed off their bonus and it was soon clear that the elected members were in a nasty mood. And, of course, being

[1] Mr B. H. J. Naylor of the Society of Civil Servants [SCS] was chairman of the staff side which included representatives of the SCS representing the executive grades and of the Civil and Public Services Association [CPSA] representing the clerical workers. The SCS later became the Society of Civil and Public Services.

good negotiators, they quoted against me the tribute I had paid to our staff in the House with the words: 'On an uprating the Government gets the glory but they get the work.' I talked with them for an hour, giving nothing away on the bonus and chi-iking them on the obvious fact that they couldn't agree among themselves who should get it anyway. 'If you were able to give me good precedents, I'd jump at it,' I told them, 'but I can't be the one to create the precedent.' I left them to Bob Brown, promising to meet them again very soon. I think it was a good start and I flatter myself that I am rather good with trade unions, whatever history may seem to show to the contrary.

At 8.30pm, at the end of an exacting day, we had to go into another long conference with Edmund Dell about our interim proposals for the 1973 Social Security Act scheme. Well briefed with figures by my chaps, I soon punctured Edmund's previous 'offer' to improve Reserve Scheme benefits in exchange for pinching the Reserve Scheme funds *and* putting the basic contributions up. 'How much would your improvements cost?' I asked sweetly. 'I haven't really costed them,' he replied. '£5 million?' Edmund looked uneasily at his official, who replied, equally uneasily, 'I doubt whether it would be as much as that.' '£2 million?' 'That would be nearer it, Secretary of State.' 'So,' I said, rounding on Edmund, 'you want to make us raise another £600 million and give us £2 million back. And you call *that* making the move politically more acceptable!' Edmund had the grace to grin. He really is too honest for the Treasury. The truth was, he confessed, that he didn't think Option B was politically acceptable anyway and would much prefer us just to postpone the whole Reserve Scheme. So the chorus in favour of this grows all the time and I begin to think that my judgment must be wrong. I look at Brian; he nods, and within minutes we had agreed that this was what we would do. But then a thought struck me and I marched after Edmund into his room next door, followed by Brian and a trail of officials. 'But if we do postpone the Reserve Scheme,' I asked, 'what level of contribution would you visualize for the state pension?' '5.85 per cent,' he replied. I exploded. 'But don't you see that would be the worst of all worlds? It is certainly not on politically to put the Reserve Scheme into cold storage, deprive people of two or three years of earnings-related benefits and then put up their contribution rate for the state pension to a higher rate than it would have been under Keith Joseph.' To his eternal credit Edmund not only saw the point immediately, but took it seriously. He started poring over our tables of figures with his officials, and as it was now late, we were all muzzy with fatigue and I still had a lot of work to do, I left him at it, stressing the urgency of the need for me to make an announcement in next week's debate.

Friday, 5 April

Despite my preoccupation with the maddening complexities of the insurance minutiae, I decided I must look in at the Home Affairs Committee of Cabinet to make sure that Roy did not renege on the immigration point. Whether he was still huffed over my criticisms of his proposed line over the Avebury Bill[1] or not, he was

---

[1] In January 1974, the Liberal Peer Lord Avebury had introduced a Bill to declare an amnesty for illegal immigrants from the Commonwealth who had entered this country between March 1968, when immigra-

clearly determined to re-emerge as a liberal radical. In the chair he was at his drawliest, explaining that Avebury had withdrawn his Bill in view of Roy's intention to act administratively, and that he had decided in view of this to go for the more generous date of 1 January 1973 as 'more consistent with the statement of the PM during the election campaign'. (A good job I got Jack Straw to unearth, translate and circulate this statement!)

There then ensued a most extraordinary outburst from David Ennals, speaking to his Foreign Office [FO] brief so passionately that he was clearly in sympathy with it. The FO, he said, could not possibly accept the more generous date as there were so few immigration officials at our High Commissions in India, Bangladesh and Pakistan that applicants with every right to enter were already having to wait eighteen months. The proposed date would lengthen this intolerably and the FO would be compelled to increase staff, which would then fall on the FO vote. I have never heard a clearer exposition of the waiting game that the FO has been playing – just what the immigrants have been complaining of! To my delight Alex Lyon[1] swiped out at him good and hard, saying the Home Office was already in talks with the FO about the need to increase the number of officials for this purpose in the High Commissions. That was surely the answer. I backed him strongly, and Roy gave the *coup de grâce*, saying that he really couldn't have his policy dictated by the fact that the FO had failed to man its posts adequately. Roy's drawl always lengthens when he is angry, which heightens the effect of contempt. Next he disposed equally effectively of Elwyn, who tried to make out that Roy really ought to legislate. How the Lord Chancellor could argue this, said Roy, was beyond his understanding, since the 1971 Act had explicitly placed an administrative freedom of action on the Home Secretary which he merely proposed to announce he did not intend to exercise. Collapse of legal party.

Finally, when Roy declared the committee was agreed to proceed on the lines he proposed, David caused another storm by announcing that in that case he must reserve the Foreign Secretary's right to raise the matter in Cabinet. Roy went so cold with fury he could hardly speak. That was the most gross abuse of the procedures of Cabinet in his experience, he said icily. If one member of Cabinet, who had not even taken the trouble to be present, found himself in a minority of one on a committee and then claimed the right to reopen the matter in Cabinet, he really could not see

tion controls were introduced for them, and six months before January 1973, when the Conservatives' Immigration Act of 1971 came into force. Such an amnesty was necessary because in June 1973 the Law Lords had ruled that the 1971 Act removed from immigrants the right of immunity from prosecution after six months normally enjoyed by anyone committing a summary offence. Many illegal immigrants, who believed that by escaping detection for six months they had become legally settled, suddenly found they were at risk retrospectively and lived in dread of detection and removal. The Lords had refused to give Lord Avebury's Bill a second reading, but during the February election campaign I had persuaded Harold Wilson to issue a statement to the immigrant communities promising a similar amnesty. On 11 April Roy Jenkins told the House of Commons that he did not intend to exercise his powers under the 1971 Act to remove illegal immigrants from the Commonwealth and Pakistan who came to Britain before 1 January 1973 – thus going further than Lord Avebury.

[1] Labour MP for York and Minister of State at the Home Office. When Jim Callaghan succeeded Harold Wilson as Prime Minister in April 1976 he removed Alex Lyon from his job. There were vociferous protests from Labour MPs who believed Alex Lyon had been sacked for being too sympathetic to immigrants.

any point in committees meeting at all. We all backed him up. 'You can tell the Foreign Secretary that this reaction is unanimous,' I said tartly. Poor David looked as if he wished the floor would swallow him and merely said meekly he would report the feeling of the committee to the Foreign Secretary. 'Do that,' said Roy grimly. Altogether a good morning's work, for here is another election pledge we shall have kept and damn the consequences – a healthy attitude for any government.

Down, thankfully, to Hell Corner Farm, where I am determined, despite the red boxes, to do some gardening.

Dick has died and a great abrasive, tonic force has gone out of my political life. I shall miss him terribly.

Saturday, 6 April

Poor Mike is under his first attack from *Tribune* for refusing to budge on the London weighting[1] before the Pay Board reports in June. I wonder what *Tribune* would say if it could see the letter Mike has circulated? 'I remain convinced,' he has written to Cabinet colleagues, 'that any interim concession on London weighting, besides being in itself inflationary, would lead to increasing demands from many other groups pressing for special consideration.' So the Labour Government *has* got an incomes policy after all – and through Mike's agency!

Monday, 8 April

A very useful meeting of my Ministers which I have now turned into a working lunch. I told them that every answer to Parliamentary Questions must be rewritten if necessary in order to make it a vehicle for a positive political point. This is particularly urgent in the family planning field where Cardinal Heenan is in hot pursuit of me, as though I had invented the whole policy instead of merely having decided not to impose prescription charges. Ah well, I'm not throwing in the sponge, but I alerted my troops as to how we could fight back. Next I told them, *à propos* of a list of appointments to the Central Health Services Council which David Owen has worked out for me, that what he had done was to reduce the number of women by one. 'I do not intend that, when I leave this job, it shall be found that the number of women in public posts is actually less than when I came into it,' I told him. Humbled, David said he'd have another look at it.

Bowing to the pressure still growing in the press, Harold has decided to make a statement in the House about the land deals after all. I told the office to clear the decks as I intended to be there for it. The House was of course packed and on the front bench we were almost sitting on each other's knees. Harold was clearly nervous and unwontedly deprecatory. I don't like him when he becomes ingratiating; apart from anything else it is a clear sign that he feels unsure. I found his involved story about 'reclamation' unconvincing – not that he is culpable of anything but

[1] Under previous incomes policies allowances had been payable to certain groups for the additional cost of living and travelling in London. As part of the greater flexibility of his Stage Three policy Mr Heath had asked the Pay Board to review these allowances with a view to increasing them. The Board published its report (Cmnd. 5660) on 1 July – its last report before its dissolution.

impulsiveness. It isn't just a question of his great penchant for loyalty. He could have been loyal to Marcia (and rightly so) without going overboard for Tony Field – a kind enough chap, as I know from those dark days of Ted's illness, but not of the calibre to be worth risking one's whole standing for.

Terry Pitt and his allies at Transport House are throwing their weight about again. First, Liz Arnott has positively railroaded me into calling a meeting of the Social Policy Sub-Committee of the NEC. Secondly, at the meeting the suggestion reappeared in an office memo, in which I see Terry's hand, that future pension policy should be dealt with in the Liaison Committee with the TUC rather than our own committee. (I managed to scotch that one.) Thirdly, there was a long list of proposals for 'future work'. I told them I had already decided to reconstitute the working party on the drugs industry, under David Owen's chairmanship, and to set up a parallel working group in the department, also under David, so that we could get our research done for us. For the rest I think it is absurd to imagine that we shall run out of policy steam if we don't go on cooking up new ideas: there are so many aspects of our existing policies to be worked out, to say nothing of getting them implemented. I also think it is absurd to pretend that, somehow, the NEC groups and committees have a separate (Terry would say superior) existence from the Government's activities. Looking round the room I saw that practically everyone there was already directly involved in Government policy making: David Piachaud, David Owen, Brian O'M., Laurie Pavitt (whom I've invited to our next Sunningdale meeting), Nicholas Bosanquet (who is working with David), the TUC representative, etc. Only John Dunwoody[1] has so far been left out.

The only useful thing to come out of the meeting was the chance to consult them on what our interim action on social security should be. David Piachaud said he thought the best thing would be to postpone the Reserve Scheme; the rest agreed, and that was that. So I have got myself an alibi, but hardly the detailed consideration we have been giving to it in the department.

Later at Home Policy Committee [of the NEC] Terry Pitt's manoeuvrings were still more obvious. We had had a memo circulated on future work: no harm in it (and no very ambitious ideas for the development of policy), but it was the vehicle for a Terry trailer: 'Should NEC members who are Ministers fill the posts of chairmen of sub-committees – especially those which cover the work of their own departments? There are obvious dangers here.' Frank Allaun, of course, was all for ruling out Ministers, which would let him in on the housing side (though Tony C. is not a member of the NEC anyway). Judith then tried a little muddled emollition. Of course one should not say that a Minister should never be a chairman, she said, but he or she should not be chairman of a committee in which he or she has a departmental interest. She would like, for instance, to see Tony Benn chair the working party on Communications and the Media, as he had done before. Tony, who hadn't been listening very carefully up to now, sat up at this and, forgoing shallow populism, launched into some robust common sense. 'But, look, Judith, I am up to my eyes in the detailed job of trying to translate our policy in the industrial field into action. I really could not do justice to my Government job if I were to take on anything else. And I should hate to think that

[1] Former Labour MP and Parliamentary Under Secretary at DHSS under Dick Crossman.

what I am doing at Industry and what the party wants doing are incompatible.' Sitting next to him I egged him on with 'Hear, hears' and then spoke in support passionately. I, too, refused to accept that, once one got into government, there was an inevitable dichotomy. I, too, was up to my eyes carrying out party policy. Was it really impossible for Government and party to work as a team? Terry, a bit flustered, started expostulating. 'This is my last meeting here anyway....' 'Thank God,' I murmured to Tony.

Mik then interposed mildly to say that there had been unfortunate experiences of ministerial involvement with NEC committees in the last Labour Government. He remembered one instance when a junior Minister had come along and solemnly read a departmental brief. Fair enough, Mik, I thought, but then the separatism of the last Labour Government didn't save it from its defects: quite the contrary. And this Labour Government won't succeed, either, if both NEC and Government insist that they must go their separate ways. We need *more* integration, not less, if the thing is to work. And the NEC must not assume that every modification of party policy by a Labour Government is a sign of betrayal rather than closer knowledge of the facts: *vide* Mike and London weighting!

Tuesday, 9 April

Up early for meeting with Edmund Dell. We went along prepared for a protracted struggle to get Treasury to accept a contribution rate for the basic scheme of $5\frac{1}{2}$ per cent instead of the 5·85 per cent on which they had originally been insisting. To our surprise, after a token resistance, Edmund capitulated. I nearly hugged him afterwards, saying what a joy it was to have at the Treasury a Minister who looked at things politically and who knew and cared about social insurance schemes. He beamed happily and I felt a warmth towards him I have never felt before.

Then into Cabinet. On foreign affairs Harold reported on his visit to France for what he called a 'working funeral'.[1] It was noticeable how he curbed his once familiar desire to chat, merely contenting himself with saying he had had an hour with Nixon, who had spoken 'very frankly'. Then to Harold Lever's moment of triumph on the building societies. Tony [Crosland] reported on the famous meeting at which, he said generously, the 'leading role' had been 'brilliantly played by the Chancellor of the Duchy'. The outcome was that the building societies had been offered, and had accepted, a loan of £100 million by the banks for April at $10\frac{1}{2}$ per cent, with another £400 million to follow later at a rate to be agreed. Since the lending rate of the Bank of England was $12\frac{1}{2}$ per cent there would be a small element of subsidy: £$1\frac{3}{4}$ million for an entire year. The condition was that there must be no change in the mortgage rate of 11 per cent. 'I think they will succeed in selling it to their council tomorrow.' In the meantime a high-powered committee must be set up to consider the whole future of the building societies. 'If they turn us down I shall make a statement in the House which will be very damaging to them, threatening to turn them over to Wedgie Benn.' Laughter. (I have often noticed how the official Minutes of Cabinet fail to convey any of the cracks, any of the controversies and damn all of the atmosphere.)

[1] The funeral of President Pompidou.

Denis followed to say that it had been a 'very successful operation in view of the shortage of time'. And he added, 'I pay tribute to Harold Lever as the central negotiating figure in this. He was negotiating with me and Tony apart from the building societies.' Naturally Harold Lever was looking very happy through all this and ventured a quip: 'The reassuring thing is that at the end of the day we are still speaking to each other.' 'What are you saying when you do?' interposed Willie [Ross] with his usual gloomy humour. Congratulations all round. My heart warms to Harold Lever's resurrection after an illness that could have put him out of court for good. And the credit for that resurrection must go equally to Harold W., who thought of an inspired role for Harold L. commensurate with his intellectual fertility and physical limitations.

Next to Wednesday's debate on the National Insurance Bill embodying the pensions increases. Ted Short reported that there seemed no way of preventing an amendment calling for six-monthly upratings being in order under the Money Resolution.[1] We would have to amend it first, which would clearly be impossible. I reported that there were no administrative difficulties in the way of six-monthly upratings either, though the additional cost would be £250 million a year, which I would clearly prefer to spend on something else. Other people (and I can't blame them) were anxious about more money being spent on the OAPs. Personally I agree they have had their share on this round. Denis's attempt to get us to say that, if six-monthly upratings were forced on us in the House, we should announce that we would reverse them after the next election, was repulsed as the piece of Treasury nonsense it was. Finally it was left that, if we were defeated on this, we must accept it without commitment either way as to its continuance. I was left with the unhappy job of working out with the Chief Whip how we should handle the mechanics of a defeat.

Finally on to Chile. Jim's report on his discussions with the party groups was ambivalent, despite his care to appear objective. We were left with no clear indication of the party mood. He admitted that over one hundred Labour MPs had signed the Motion on the Order Paper against the delivery of the vessels, but added that there were only twenty-seven at the meeting, of whom five had spoken out against his proposal for going ahead with current contracts and two had spoken for. He described it as a 'fifty–fifty mood', adding that he had been surprised to discover the extent to which we were embroiled in the sale of arms generally. 'Fifty per cent of the capacity of our naval dockyards is for foreign ships,' he pointed out. (A shrewd diversionary note, this.) Flatly he continued that Chile might cut off our supply of

---

[1] Any Bill involving public expenditure must be headed by a Money Resolution outlining the purposes for which the expenditure may be made and the committee stage of the Bill cannot be taken until the Money Resolution has been agreed to. Proposals for expenditure can only be initiated by the Government, but careless drafting can enable the Opposition to move amendments widening the area of expenditure, as in this case. Governments soon learn to draft Money Resolutions very tightly. A superb example of tight drafting was the Money Resolution to the Pensioners Payments Bill of 1978 which repeated the Christmas bonus for pensioners of the previous year. To avoid embarrassing amendments increasing the size or scope of the bonus the Money Resolution merely provided monies 'under provisions which ... correspond to those made ... by the Pensioners Payments Act, 1977'.

copper if the contracts were broken. This formed 20 per cent of our supply. The ships concerned were not part of a government-to-government contract: they had been ordered direct from the shipbuilders. It might need legislation in the House to cancel delivery. We might have to impound the ships – an action which had never been taken before. It wasn't a question of cancelling export licences, as none were required. For the future, arms licences had been stopped. Taking all this into account, his 'strong recommendation' to Cabinet was that the warships should be allowed to go to Chile.

Listening, I thought it was a masterly demonstration of Jim's technique. Clearly it impressed his listeners. Roy Mason hastened to add that the meeting with the party groups had been 'low-key'. I thought that no one could stand out against this weight of argument and was all the more impressed when Mike spoke up with a kind of defiant desperation. 'Some of us,' he said, 'still hold to the view we expressed last year.' The awkward fact was that the ships were going to continue to go to Chile through a long period. Even more important than our sales to Latin America (which Mason had said would be at risk) was to stick to the view we took in Opposition. That was paramount. Otherwise we lost credibility. When Bob, normally the custodian of backbench views, said sadly, 'I don't honestly see how I could get legislation to cancel the contracts through the House', Mike replied a bit wildly, 'I very much doubt whether the only way is to have legislation.' Only Wedgie backed him up. Even Peter sat silent. I myself wondered whether to suggest that we try to draw a distinction between the ships that were merely being refitted and were already at sea and those that would take some years to complete. That would have met Mike's only real point – and that not really a point of principle.

But while I hesitated Harold ruled that the overwhelming view of Cabinet was that the contracts should be fulfilled, though Wedgie's point about the overhaul of the engines of the Hawker Hunter aircraft sold to Chile now being conducted at East Kilbride should be looked into further. (The main point here is that the unions are restive about these contracts, as they clearly are not about the other ones, despite Judith's speech before the election.) I was sorry afterwards that I had not pursued my idea. I have no doubt that we should not take great economic risks over fulfilling the ships contracts unless the feeling in the party is very strong. Maybe Jim has misled us over this; time will show.

Cabinet ended early to enable those of us who wanted to to go to the service of dedication Harold has arranged in the crypt. The whole idea makes me cringe. Is he really a believer or is he doing a Mary Whitehouse? But when I raised the matter at my ministerial meeting last week Brian O'M. (who is a Roman Catholic) had smiled at me rather shyly and said that he thought no harm could come of it and it might do me good. So I went along with Brian and sang the hymns right lustily as I always do. Actually the sermon, by some bishop I didn't recognize, was a masterpiece and I quite enjoyed myself. It interested me how few people were there. As I was coming out Harold W. asked me if I could spare a moment as he wanted a word with me. We went to his room in the House in great comradeship. He poured me a drink. It was quite like old times. As I sat in that familiar room, with Harold pacing up and down, drink in hand, five years just melted away and we slipped back as naturally as breathing into our old affectionate and slightly conspiratorial relationship. Only this time we were both tougher and more relaxed – subtly more sure of ourselves. Harold no longer glanced at his reflection in the windows as he walked up and down. When Harold told me he was going to the Scillies for ten days at Easter I retorted, 'Thank God you are at last learning some sense. Do take plenty of exercise while you're there and get really fit.' 'I've lost a lot of weight,' he replied, proudly patting his tummy. 'So you have,' I replied and added cunningly to encourage him, 'Ted Heath is getting terribly fat.' 'Isn't he?' said Harold, pleased.

Then he sprang his surprise on me: 'You know how short I am of debating talent in the Lords, and you remember how I always intended to put Ted there, though you had objections to being Lady Castle. Well, you could always insist that you wanted to be known as Barbara Castle, and I hope you wouldn't let that stand in the way because I intend to make some elevations soon and I want to include Ted in them. If Heath can have some resignation creations I can have some non-resignation ones. And we are terribly weak in the Lords and I need Ted there.' I said without a moment's hesitation that I was thrilled for Ted and whatever it cost me I wouldn't stand in the way because it was his turn now. God knows he had sacrificed enough for me. But, jumping up and joining Harold in his perambulation, I grabbed him by the arm and said why didn't he seize this opportunity to strike a blow for women's lib. that would win the hearts of every woman in the land? Why didn't he announce that I would *not* share Ted's title but would be 'gazetted' as Mrs Barbara Castle, or whatever the word was? If necessary, I said, I could go and talk to the Queen and I was sure that I could win her over to my side. 'I don't think it is a question of the Queen,' replied Harold. 'I think that legislation would be necessary and I couldn't get that now. But if we are returned with a proper majority I intend to legislate on Honours anyhow – I want their Lordships to be called Life Peers or something.' 'Yes, Harold,' I cried excitedly, 'what we need is for everyone in the Lords to be Mr or Mrs So-and-so, LP instead of MP.' 'We could do it that way and give those who wanted to the right to retain their title instead,' he agreed.

I felt something remarkably like hope and happiness rising in me. Are we really at last going to do something bold? I asked him if I could speak to Ted? Of course, said Harold, adding: 'but don't you go and persuade him out of it.' Could I ask Jack Straw to make very hush-hush enquiries as to how I could remain Mrs Castle? Of course. We then chatted matily about how well the Government was doing. (The land deals issue still doesn't seem to be bothering him.) I enthused about the quality of Brian O'M. and David Owen, adding that it really was a scandal that David should only be a Parliamentary Secretary while Eric Heffer was brought straight from the back benches as Minister of State. 'I know,' agreed Harold, 'but you realize the reason was political.' I said I had an excellent team; we planned to do so much, if only we got the chance. 'There's life in the old girl yet,' I quipped as I almost skipped from the room. 'There's life in the young girl yet,' Harold called after me.

Saw Jack Straw at the office. He was as pleased for Ted as I was and thought the Islington party would be glad, too. 'Ted has been a very conscientious Alderman,' he said. He hurried straight off to check about legislation. It's very useful having a barrister! Then spent the afternoon on the National Insurance Bill. I dictated a piece for my announcement on the interim arrangements for the Reserve Pension Scheme

I had agreed with Edmund Dell, hoping that Cabinet would ratify it in the morning. Officials came in excitedly to say that the Opposition's first amendment on six-monthly uprating of pensions had been ruled out of order, but that they had put down another one merely providing for 'consideration' of the need for legislation and that was going to be called. Brian and I agreed that this put a different complexion on things. We could hardly go into the election even refusing to consider six-monthly upratings! As someone very recently a backbencher it fascinates me how much consternation an Opposition can cause in a department by its activities.

'Husbands and Wives' dinner in the private room at St Stephens was rather drab. Only seven of us turned up. No explanation of Tommy's whereabouts. I wonder how he is getting on? I tried to interest Mike in the land deals affair and the need for some of us to take Dick's place by advising Harold more on things like this, but he brushed it aside saying it was all a storm in a teacup and none of our business anyway. Judith warned us against Denis's proposed Public Expenditure Scrutiny Committee [PESC] exercise, while John Silkin was still sulking about not being in the Cabinet. I asked him when we should get details of his land policy and he said, almost venomously: 'Not until I am in the Cabinet. If the party wants a land policy – and I'm the only person that has one – then they must first put me in the one place where I shall have the authority to carry it out.' I myself felt muzzy with all the complicated insurance formulae I have been studying. Ted is working very late at Islington Council's Planning Committee tonight, so I shall have to wait till morning to tell him the news I am bursting to share with him.

Wednesday, 10 April

Ted was pretty whacked when I took him his morning tea, which may explain the subdued way he took the news. 'It is ten years too late. I don't know whether I could do it now.' I told him firmly that he had got to snap out of his deeply ingrained instinct for running himself down: he could out-debate those deadbeats in 'another place' any time he tried. But, though he is pleased ('I was only thinking the other day that my real problem is loneliness'), neither he nor I are going really euphoric till it actually happens. It has been snatched away from us so often before.

At Cabinet a long discussion on Mike's Bill to repeal the Industrial Relations Act.[1]

[1] The problem of picketing was to bedevil the Government throughout its period of office. The unions were anxious to adapt the right to picket to the needs of the motorized age by enabling pickets to stop vehicles for the purpose of peacefully persuading the drivers to back their strike and Labour's Manifesto had promised this. On 22 March Michael Foot had told the Commons that a provision to this effect would be included in the Bill to repeal the Industrial Relations Act, but he had reckoned without the police and the Home Secretary, both of whom vigorously resisted any interference with the discretion of the police to prevent obstruction of the highway. Long wrangles took place in Cabinet and the only reference to picketing in Michael's amending Bill, the Trade Union and Labour Relations Bill, was a reaffirmation of the legal right in furtherance of a trade dispute peacefully to picket another person at his place of work 'or any other place where another person happens to be, not being a place where he resides'. The TUC was unhappy at the failure to authorize the stopping of vehicles and kept up the pressure on the Government. In 1975 Michael made another attempt to deal with the problem in the Employment Protection Bill, but Clause 99 of this was considered so inadequate by the TUC that it was defeated in committee with the help of some Labour MPs and the law was still unamended when the Grunswick dispute broke out in 1977. The device adopted by the employer in that dispute, Mr Ward, of bringing non-strikers into the factory in

Mike reported that, although he was personally in favour of including his picketing proposals in the Bill, he recognized that this might not be possible in the present parliamentary situation. Much the biggest difficulty arose over the safeguards for individuals affected by union action. The TUC strongly objected to a generalized provision, which they found insulting and unnecessary; they wanted it restricted to the closed shop situation by a formula dealing with the position 'where a union had behaved unreasonably in refusing or expelling a member and he had as a consequence of the action been dismissed'. Elwyn saw no objection to this. But it was interesting how meekly Mike in his paper had accepted the law officers' dictum that there could be no restrospective quashing of actions which had already started in the National Industrial Relations Court by the time the Second Reading came. Even to take that date had seemed to them to be straining things a bit. It was Bob who started an agitated protest on this. Did this mean that the fines levied on unions in the Con Mech and GAS cases must stand?[1] 'Incomprehensible!' Wedgie backed him: must we really meekly allow individuals and the NIRC to go on operating a repulsive law after we had announced our intention to repeal it in the Queen's Speech?

Harold said he had a lot of sympathy with Wedgie's view. We had said we would repeal in order to take the poison out of industrial relations, but poison was still being injected into them under the Act every day. But as we probed the alternative possibilities it became clear that an earlier date would not really solve the problem. Even if we suspended the provisions of the law from the date of the Queen's Speech rather than Second Reading neither of the two major cases would escape. 'That being so,' said Wedgie, 'it would mean we were watching from a position of powerlessness the imposition of a series of fines.' The only hope was an amnesty – and no one in this situation could say that was an incitement to break the law because the law would have been repealed. 'The constitutional difficulty,' said Harold, 'is that we can't get it through Parliament.' And he added the surprising remark: 'My own view is that if we come back with a substantial majority we should legislate. We might look at the possibility of a backbench amendment which we would accept.' The more we studied it, the more intolerable the situation seemed, particularly when Sam Silkin pointed out that NIRC had announced that the whole of the property of the Amalgamated

---

busloads, and the inability of the pickets to stop the buses to reason with the occupants, caused intense bitterness and led to the mass picketing and violent struggles with the police which ensued. Anodyne as the provision in the 1974 Act appeared at the time, it was later to be quoted by the Opposition as having authorized 'secondary picketing' (i.e. picketing of persons not directly involved in the dispute) by lorry drivers, whose strike caused such havoc during the 'winter of discontent' of 1978–79.

[1] For Con Mech, see footnote to page 55. In its last throes the NIRC had also been pursuing the Transport and General Workers' Union, whose members had been 'blacking' General Aviation Services [GAS], a Canadian owned company brought in to provide ground handling services at Heathrow. After a prolonged industrial dispute the British Airports Authority had withdrawn GAS's concession and the firm claimed compensation against the union of nearly £2 million. The NIRC had found the T&GWU liable and the union had appealed. Before the appeal could be heard, Sir John Donaldson announced that a full hearing of the compensation case would be held in his court on 15 July and refused the union's request for an adjournment. However, on 11 July the union took its request for an adjournment to the Court of Appeal and won. Twenty days later the NIRC was abolished and outstanding cases passed to the High Court. On 1 May 1975, having heard the union's appeal against liability to pay compensation, the Court of Appeal found in favour of the T&GWU with costs.

Engineering Union [AEU] would be sequestered if the union hadn't paid its fine by the end of this month. Heartened – and no doubt surprised – by Cabinet's determination to find a way out if at all possible, Mike seized the opportunity to ask if he could not have continued conversations with the lawyers about the possibility of limiting the dangers of the damages, even if the court cases went on. This was agreed.

Next to my National Insurance Bill. On the amendments, Cabinet promptly endorsed my line. When I said we could not refuse even to 'consider' six-monthly upratings, Denis said, 'Of course. Accept.' But I got into trouble when I proposed my interim solution on the Reserve Pension Scheme, even though Edmund Dell supported me. Crosland complained that he had only had my paper the day before. Ted Short, who wasn't there, has circulated a letter fussing about the political effects. Bob was appalled at the idea of introducing anything that would detract from the impact of this 'magnificent' Uprating Bill. Harold said I could easily get away with another two or three weeks' delay. 'If Geoffrey Howe gets difficult Barbara can deal with him in that charming way of hers and with that throbbing voice we all admire so much.' So that was that! All those late sessions gone for nothing.

Nor did Denis get away with his proposed public expenditure exercise. Though he introduced it ever so innocently, stressing that this was merely a procedural paper, not an economic strategy discussion (that would come later when the exercise had been completed without commitment), we were not fooled. We have all trodden this path before. Harold Lever was soon telling Denis that he himself had gone further than pure procedure in his introductory speech. Harold L., for instance, did not agree with Denis's basic assumption that the balance of payments gap must be closed and there must be a rapid shift to exports. We needed a much clearer definition of public expenditure and an early discussion of basic economic strategy. Peter, too, pointed out that there were alternative ways of dealing with the balance of payments position: (1) further borrowing; (2) direct intervention on trade. There were murmurs of approval when he added, 'We are a party of public expenditure. All the main areas of breakdown in our society are in the public, not the private, field.' Crosland warned that the paper's prognosis showed a 'bad overkill' in the construction industry. Nor did it include any reference to the acquisition of land. (Freudian slip?) Wedgie insisted that we should not agree to anything until the alternative strategies had been put before us.

My departmental brief advised that I should accept the Chancellor's proposals as DHSS did rather well out of them. Even Jack Straw had put in a submissive note. But I punctured Denis with a simple question. Did his proposal to freeze public expenditure at its present level for 1974–75 and increase it by 2 per cent a year afterwards mean that there would be no restoration of last December's cuts for another year and that the 2 per cent 'increase' would include the cuts? If so, how many years would it take for the cuts to be restored? No reply. Joel Barnett, sitting next to me, whispered 'The Chancellor must know he can't get away with this.' I went on to say that it was not enough for us to insist there should be no decisions until after we had seen the results of the 'procedural' exercise. We must insist that discussions on our economic strategy went on *in parallel*. And so it was agreed. It being then late, with two more major items on the agenda, Harold adjourned Cabinet till 6pm.

Despite the casual way I had prepared my Second Reading speech, Ted, listening in the gallery, said it was 'excellent'. And I got away without making my announcement on the interim pensions scheme perfectly easily. Indeed, the House seemed quite impressed when I promised it 'early after Easter'. So much for the anticipatory fears a government has! But it was at the committee stage that I really began to feel a mastery of the House. I managed to accept the six-monthly review amendment while reducing its significance and had the pleasure of hearing Ian Lloyd [Conservative MP for Havant and Waterloo] actually attack Geoffrey Howe for being 'inflationary'. I made an impromptu – and effective – speech criticizing the Tory tax credit scheme and then had the satisfaction, when the vote came, of seeing the Tories defeated by thirty votes. (David Owen whispered to me, 'I'm afraid we've won. It really is time we had some defeats in the House so that we can argue that it is impossible to carry on. We must have an election soon.') But my real moment of triumph came when the Tories suddenly tried to make something of an amendment we had thought was quite innocuous. Brian, who was handling it, was so casual he got into a mess. Then Geoffrey Howe attacked me and gave me a chance to come in – and I really laid about him, angry now. Working by instinct and thinking on my feet, I accused the 'Rt Hon. and so-called "learned gentleman"' of having deliberately misread the clause. No wonder he had been responsible for such a disastrous Industrial Relations Bill! Then, as the ding-dong went on, officials in the box passed me a piece of paper which enabled me to give him the *coup de grâce*. My instinct had been right: he *had* misread the clause. Collapse of 'learned gentleman'. 'Barbara's just given Geoffrey Howe a black eye,' said our lads approvingly. Home at last at 1am, tired but euphoric after a celebratory gin. I have really enjoyed myself.

Despite the debate's excitement I managed to slip into Cabinet for half an hour. On to the proposed price increases in nationalized industries. Harold had asked for a review of their timing and it was soon clear why. They form a melancholy list, stretching from June to October, and, as Harold put it, June was 'socially important'. He managed to get agreement that the proposed increase in railway fares (due in the first half of June) should be deferred for a week and the increase in postal charges (ditto) for two weeks. So it looks like a June election. Jack Straw has done me a note opposing postponement. But, then, he doesn't fly by the seat of Harold's political pants.

Thursday, 11 April

Cleared a pile of boxes; then off to Hell Corner Farm to get ready for the Easter invasion of the family. The Dobsons[1] arrive tomorrow and there is a lot to do. Marcia has done a great apologia over the land deal in the *Mirror*, but I doubt whether it helps.

---

[1] See footnote, page 17.

Sunday, 14 April

One of the loveliest Easter Sundays I can remember. The sun shone. Everything went perfectly. The garden was not only a picture, with its great splashes of daffodils, the cherry blossom unfolding and the flowers on the magnolia tree shining like white lights; it was also a children's paradise. And soon it was full of children, laughing, shrieking, sliding down the slopes, playing hide-and-seek among the trees, searching for the little eggs the Easter bunnies had 'laid'. Sonya and her brood arrived for breakfast, Hugh[1] and his brood at noon. Ted went to fetch Great Gran, whom we ensconced on the terrace wrapped in a rug, holding her latest great-grandchild in her arms. Of course there had to be a run down 'rabbit hill' to collect primroses; another run through the woods where the rapturous children rolled me in the leaves. The lunch which Eileen[2] and I cooked for sixteen of us was a great success. And Great Uncle Ted presided over it all with his usual benignity. I feel so rich on these occasions, my heart stretching to embrace this large, diverse, loving and ever-growing family. This is what I promised you, Marjorie, and this is what I have performed. And I pray that we shall always be able to keep HCF just for this: a place of wonder and delight and peace, not just for the family, but for others who need a refuge and an escape.

Wednesday, 17 April

The clerics are still after me on family planning and I decide the time has come to act. I stir up the office by saying I intend to write a long letter of reply to *The Times* and I dictate a draft over the phone. I gather it is unprecedented for a Secretary of State to reply to letters in the press in this way, so the PM must approve. I must curb my impatience while my draft is rushed out to the Scillies.

Len Murray is doing his stuff on the 'Social Contract'. And Jack Jones is backing him up.[3]

Thursday, 18 April

After a lot of to-ing and fro-ing of messages to the Scillies Harold has ruled that Ministers must not sign letters to the press. But we have got John Cronin [Labour MP for Loughborough] to sign the letter. All this has taken a lot of time.

---

[1] Hugh McIntosh, his wife Miranda and their three children, Christopher, Belinda and Susannah.

[2] Mrs Eileen Wells, our housekeeper, loyal guardian of our cottage and of our two cocker spaniels; famed in the family circle for her superb crême caramel and her home-made bread.

[3] On 15 April the TUC issued a circular to its member unions repeating that the miners' settlement should not be quoted in other pay negotiations and urging negotiators to 'take due account of the needs of the economic and industrial situation and of the policies being pursued by the Government'. In a speech at Rothesay Jack Jones urged unions to be realistic in their wage claims, adding: 'We are not advocating wage control. We are advocating common sense.'

Friday, 19 April

Off to Blackburn for a busy two days. The Easter 'holiday' has vanished without my being able to get much rest.

Sunday, 21 April

Back at Hell Corner Farm the sun shines briefly and I go on strike against the red boxes, doing a hefty half day's digging in the garden. Feel much better for it.

Monday, 22 April

Up to London early for a meeting of the Liaison Committee with the TUC. The two sides faced each other across that rather bleak boardroom at Transport House which makes it so difficult to engender enthusiastic intimacy. The TUC anyway are hardly noted for forthcoming enthusiasm at the best of times, and this time their ranks were rather depleted: no Hughie, George Smith or Sid Greene. Healey, Ted Short and Willie Simpson were missing from our side. Jim, in the chair, exuded his usual urbanity. The purpose was, he said, to decide what the work of the Liaison Committee should be: what should be the discussions here and what was better dealt with by direct contact with Ministers. Personally he thought we should concentrate on the longer-term issues. Len was all for that: we needed to look ahead to the development of future policies and might produce some 'pale green papers' outlining what a future Labour Government might do. But it soon became clear that the TUC was anxious for the Liaison Committee to keep overall control of the processing of current policy. Some issues, Len said, like social insurance, were being processed with different bits of the TUC and the results should be fed back to the Liaison Committee. Wedgie jumped at this. He was already in his department, working on such things as the new Industry Bill, he said, and, although David Lea was associated with this, he would welcome the opportunity of making a progress report to the Liaison Committee. Jack nodded approvingly, but Ron, always election-conscious, said that he hoped we wouldn't get bogged down with too much research, as in June we might be fighting for our political survival.

Jim kept harking back to the longer-term issues: the priorities for a five-year government. 'We must be free to have wide-ranging political discussions, too.' (I suspect he realizes that the TUC have not yet faced the really tough issues that lie ahead.) Alf Allen was as helpful as usual. 'There won't be a long term,' he pointed out, 'unless we are able to sell what the Government has achieved and what *we* have achieved in the Social Compact.'[1] Jack pointed out that there was a lot still to be done on the things we are already committed to do. The TUC side would like to be aware of what was being produced in the fields of social insurance, prices, etc. Jack went on: 'As far as the Social Compact is concerned, one of the most important things from the trade-union point of view is the establishment of the Arbitration Conciliation and

---

[1] At this time there was still some confusion as to whether it was a Social Compact or Social Contract. The latter finally won.

Advisory Service [ACAS]. If we are going to avoid an extension of conflict when Stage Three ends it is essential that ACAS should be in being.'

Harold, saying that of course no one yet knew when the election would be, including himself, nonetheless said it was important that Ministers should rush out White Papers on those issues on which we should not be able to legislate if an early election came. I whispered to Bob, sitting next to me, 'Do you favour June or October?' 'June,' he replied, 'because things will be much worse in October. These folks won't be able to hold their bloody shower.' 'Then there won't be time for White Papers,' I retorted. 'A June election would mean dissolving Parliament at the end of May and *that* would mean Cabinet approving those White Papers next week, or the week after at the latest.' 'That's impossible,' said an alarmed Mike, who had been listening in. I then suggested that the way out was for the Ministers with vital matters under preparation to prepare brief paragraphs covering these points which could be brought before the next meeting of the Liaison Committee so that we could reach agreement on them before the Manifesto was prepared. The rest thought this was a good idea. 'We must have a paragraph on dealing with inflation, too,' said Jim, ever hopeful. 'Inflation will be dealt with direct with the Government,' replied Harold firmly.

At my ministerial working lunch I reported on what had happened and asked them all to get busy preparing paragraphs in their respective fields, particularly Brian on our long-term pension proposals. The passage in the last Manifesto had been too vague. If we played our cards properly we could get the party committed next time to the sort of scheme we wanted. Some of them expressed doubts about a June election, but I pointed out that the Government could have its hand forced by the press building up an expectation that became irresistible. 'It is already starting,' they said.

Amusing meeting with Campbell Adamson and two of his buddies from the CBI. C.A. said they wanted to discuss what was going to happen about the Keith Joseph pension scheme. It was amusing because, in contrast with his two companions, C.A. was at his most truculent. It is clear why, of course: even my officials said that his visit might be to collect my thanks for his having won the election for us![1] Despite C.A.'s truculence the discussion was mild enough, his companions protesting that they recognized there had to be improvements in Sir K.'s terms for recognizing occupational pension schemes. They clearly hope that, apart from these tougher conditions, I am going to keep Sir K.'s scheme.

Tuesday, 23 April

Visit to South Ockendon, where things have clearly greatly improved following the Robert Robertson scandal way back in 1969.[2] Although Dick refused an enquiry then (Brian A-S. tells me Dick felt it would be too disastrous for morale, coming on

[1] See linking passage, page 29.

[2] In March 1972, Miss Barbara Robb, chairman of AEGIS [Aid for the Elderly in Government Institutions], launched a campaign for a statutory enquiry into the death three years earlier of Robert Robertson, a patient at South Ockendon Mental Hospital, which police enquiries had failed to explain satisfactorily. She was also disturbed by more recent incidents. In this she was strongly supported by Professor

top of Ely), he carried through a lot of improvements which have changed conditions there. The Inskip Report is horrifying and fully justifies my pressure in the House about R.R.'s death – a pressure for which all the credit must go to Barbara Robb and Brian A-S. As David Owen has urged on me, we shall obviously have to give mental health much greater priority – even at the expense of other, far more popular, developments.

The evening papers are full of Mike's speech to the AUEW conference. He got a standing ovation before and after it. This is a personal triumph, helped not a little by the announcement that the Government is to cancel the £10 million tax debt incurred by unions which lost the tax relief on their provident funds by not registering.[1] The decision came as a surprise, since it had not been before Cabinet, as some of us were quick to tease him with when he joined us for the 'Husbands and Wives' dinner at Lockets. 'Give me £10 million and I could have the nurses eating out of our hands,' I said mockingly. Nonetheless I think it is a brilliant move. It gets us out of the difficulty of repaying fines, and yet is thoroughly justified in view of Carr's assurances, during the passage of the Industrial Relations Bill, that the Government did not intend even unregistered unions to pay these taxes.

But the evening soon degenerated into acrimony. Mike and Judith were insisting that we must reopen Chile at the NEC tomorrow, for which Alex Kitson[2] had sent in a resolution. Mike was saying we must send a deputation to Jim about it from the NEC. Ted and I retorted that that was a recipe for undermining the Government and bringing us into public ridicule as a divided movement just as we were shaping up for the election. I insisted the Hawker Hunter issue was an entirely different one: 'We shall win in Cabinet on that.' What was more, we deserved to win because the workers involved were ready to risk their jobs. 'I'm not going to be a party to imposing unemployment on workers who have not asked for it, just in order to satisfy our middle-class consciences,' I added tetchily. But though we quarrelled, it didn't go deep. Thank God there is a gathering in which we can fight freely without losing our friendship – just as I used to do with Dick.

Abel-Smith and I took the matter up in the House of Commons. Sir Keith Joseph later agreed to set up a committee of enquiry under Mr J. Hampden Inskip, QC, which reported to Sir Keith in March 1973, and stressed the unsatisfactory conditions under which the staff had been working at the hospital. On taking office I immediately decided to publish the report as Dick Crossman had published in 1969 an equally disturbing report on the ill-treatment of patients at Ely psychiatric hospital (Cmnd. 3975). In the meantime improvements had been made at mental hospitals as a result of the work of the Hospital Advisory Service which Dick Crossman had set up. I published the Inskip Report on 14 May (H. C. 124).

[1] Nothing in the Industrial Relations Act had enraged the trade unions more than the loss of their long-standing right to tax relief on their provident funds if they refused to register on the new terms. The charitable status of these funds for tax purposes had been recognized for over eighty years. In piloting the Bill through the House Robert Carr, then Secretary of State for Employment, had denied that this effect was intended or necessary. Unions, he claimed, who did not wish to register could still get the relief by separating off their provident funds under the Friendly Societies Act and he rejected the legal opinion the TUC had obtained to the effect that in most cases this would raise insuperable difficulties. So it proved and over the previous two years unregistered unions had lost some £10 million in tax relief. Michael Foot therefore proposed that the Government should restore this relief with retrospective effect through a clause in the Finance Bill. This was the first issue on which the Opposition decided to end what Mr Heath himself had described as 'the phoney war'. See page 118.

[2] Executive Officer of the T&GWU and a member of the trade union section of the NEC.

Wednesday, 24 April

I think Ted and I must have had some effect on Mike, because in the event he was very mild over Chile at the NEC. Jim asked permission to leave the chair so that he could speak to it and made a long speech which clearly impressed his trade-union audience. I suspect it impressed the Left, too, because when he had finished there was quite a silence before anyone intervened. The significant thing was that Ron Hayward, who had been reported as attacking the Government on Chile in a public speech, tried to stop the whole discussion taking place. On the International Committee Minutes he chipped in right away: 'Now that a decision has been taken it would be ludicrous for me to take a deputation to a member of our own committee. I hope the NEC will disregard this item in the Minutes.' Jim however insisted on his right to make his position clear: 'You will then have had a deputation to me here.' When he had finished his explanation Judith came in almost hesitantly. She was clearly on the defensive about her reference to trade-union action in her pre-election speech in the House: action which Jim had pointed out hadn't taken place. 'There had at that time been a resolution on Clydeside,' she said. 'The AEU had promised to give support to any grassroots reaction.' But, conscious that there had been no grassroots reaction, she quickly changed the subject from the warships to the Hawker Hunter planes. 'This raises a very important residual point: are we going to supply the spare parts for the planes? This is more important than the frigates and would go a long way to assuage anxieties in the movement.' (Just what I had said last night.) Jim's reply was: 'That is not my direct responsibility.' Mik took up her theme, so Harold intervened to say that the Hawker Hunters were 'being looked at'.

By now Mike had rallied. 'We have to see how we can discharge our obligation to conference,' he said. He didn't accept Jim's arguments. 'Maybe we have to let one frigate go, but not the others. I hope there will be no resolution at this meeting but that our views will be taken into account by the Government and that it will reconsider this.' Not relishing the tables of history being turned on him in this way,[1] Jim said sharply, 'I could not agree that this should be reconsidered. I hope that as Michael's view will undoubtedly go out from this meeting my answer will go out too, because of the effect on other countries if it does not.' Walter Padley crystallized the feelings that were now emerging from the meeting: 'If this is just a question of one frigate it is no great matter, but if this carries the implication that four frigates, Hawker Hunters and the rest are to be serviced and supplied with spare parts and ammunition, the party could not wear that.' Said Wedgie, 'I would like to feel we would let the movement know that all our decisions can always be reviewed.' By now the steam had gone out of the argument as no one was anxious for an open row. I passed Mike a note: 'Is there going to be a vote, because I am already desperately late for a departmental meeting?' 'Of course not,' he replied. So I slipped away well satisfied. I am confident we shall now win on the Hawker Hunter issue, as I said last

---

[1] At the NEC meeting of 26 March 1969, Jim Callaghan had voted for a Motion rejecting the White Paper, *In Place of Strife*, which had just been published by the Government of which he was a member. As a result Harold Wilson, then Prime Minister, dropped him from his inner Cabinet.

night. When I saw my office I told them they must *not* arrange departmental meetings on the mornings of the NEC.

Earlier the NEC had agreed Harold's suggestions for greater liaison with the Government, arrangements which, he pointed out, went much further than any we had had in the last Government.

At Social Services Committee of Cabinet Ted Short agreed my proposals for the interim pension provision without argument: another unnecessary delay! I had then to rush into the Pay Committee of Cabinet, over which Mike presided as though he had been running an incomes policy all his life. The first issue was whether he should use his consent powers[1] in favour of three groups which would have certainly had special treatment by the Relativities Board: teachers, nurses and postmen. Officials had been looking into ways in which some relaxation might be given to them on a selective scale, and the suggestions for the nurses suited me admirably because they fitted in well with the proposals in the Briggs Report.[2] But officials had recommended that the relaxations should not be made because they would do more harm than good. Bob Sheldon, for CSD,[3] was against them, too, and Michael was obviously far from keen, but I weighed in strongly behind all three of them and carried the day, despite some sardonic remarks by Mike about my total disinterestedness. He is taking his role as guardian of the Pay Code so seriously that he is becoming more rigid than Jim Callaghan was in his Chancellor days.

So when we turned to the next item I met a stone wall. This was my plea to be allowed to give my staff a small leave bonus as compensation for the rushed uprating and I warned Mike that an overtime ban had already begun and that we risked having the uprating delayed by several weeks. I might have been talking to myself for all he cared and he outdid Bob Sheldon in warning about the 'repercussions'. Why, he said, the Department of Employment staff who were handling the increases in unemployment benefit might ask for the same treatment! What matter if they do? I replied. If they are going to do as much overtime as our people will do, they should get it, too. Even the Treasury admits the cost is negligible.

By this time half the committee had left. Only Gerald Kaufman[4] spoke up on my behalf and he did so passionately. It would be 'insane' to risk our greatest achievement yet – the uprating – by a piece of nonsensical cheese-paring, he urged. But it was all in vain. In his best headmaster tones Mike told me to go away and try to persuade the staff side that their grievances were met by the proposed improvements in overtime (which haven't even been finalized yet). If that didn't work I could come back to the committee. 'It will be too late,' I said despairingly, wishing it had been

[1] Under Mr Heath's Counter-Inflation Act 1973, the Secretary of State was empowered to give a 'consent' overriding the restrictions of pay policy 'in exceptional circumstances'.

[2] A committee on the structure of nursing education had been set up by Richard Crossman in 1970 under Professor Asa Briggs. Sir Keith Joseph had sat on the report. On 6 May I announced that the Government had accepted the main recommendations. The £18 million Michael Foot was persuaded to allocate to the nurses under his consent powers enabled us to expand the number of nurse tutors and clinical teachers and to strengthen the career structure on the lines Briggs had proposed.

[3] Robert Sheldon, Labour MP for Ashton-under-Lyne, had been appointed Minister of State, Civil Service Department, in March 1974. In October 1974 he became Minister of State at the Treasury.

[4] Under-Secretary of State at the Department of the Environment.

Edmund Dell who had been in the chair. He has shown far more flexible understanding than Mike has done.

At Robin and Brian Thompson's[1] annual cocktail party I ran into Jack Jones and told him about the serious danger to the pension increases from the overtime ban. 'Tell them it's outrageous,' he said, clearly furious that his pet uprating was in jeopardy. 'They must call it off.' (No sympathy here for trade union militancy!) Everyone was very friendly and said I looked well – which is more than I feel after Michael's stupidity. (I was too fair and honest to tell Jack that I could probably have got the ban called off if only Mike had yielded one tiny bit.)

Thursday, 25 April

With Hughie Scanlon calling off the overtime ban in the engineering industry Mike has clearly had a triumph at the AUEW conference, on which he was duly congratulated at Cabinet. I arrived late, having had an early and unhappy meeting with the staff side, trying to persuade them that what I had to offer them in terms of career structure and improved overtime rates warranted them calling off their ban, even though I couldn't give them the cash bonus they had asked for. One of the trade-union team admitted grudgingly that I had put a good case, but the unions have got themselves hooked on this cash bonus and it was clear they would lose face if they just succumbed meekly. If I could have offered them the leave bonus I am sure that it would have done the trick. Just before the meeting my officials handed me a situation report showing that the ban has spread like wildfire through the regions and that in some areas the staff are refusing to work with casual labour or to handle the uprating at all, even in normal hours. The result could be disastrous and I went off angrily to Cabinet to find them holding a strained inquest into Roy Mason's speech on Tuesday apparently threatening to pull the troops out of Northern Ireland. And this despite all the warnings given at the Cabinet just before Easter that we must on no account give the impression to the IRA that they were winning because we were a soft sell! Despite the carefully restrained tones in which Merlyn was speaking when I arrived it was clear he was furious, and matters were not helped when Roy admitted he hadn't cleared this vital bit of his speech with the Ireland office. But that india-rubber little man hardly seemed perturbed. It would take more than that major gaffe to shake his complacency. Harold wound it all up by repeating the familiar refrain that we must all be careful to clear everything with everybody.

Jim, of course, could not let the Chile question pass. Mildly he said that yesterday's proceedings at the NEC had been 'unusual', with some members of the NEC behaving as though they were not members of the Government. Said Harold darkly, 'I cannot accept the doctrine that every dog is allowed one bite, but if they do have one, they will not have another.' (And I had thought we had got away from all that!) Jim went on coolly: 'I don't press that anyone should be thrown out of the Cabinet as I was thrown out of the inner Cabinet five years ago.' Harold replied hastily that, reprehensible as it was for Cabinet Ministers to dodge their collective responsibility, he didn't

---

[1] The Thompsons are solicitors who do a great deal of work for various trade unions. Their party is one of the highlights of the political year.

see any need to tighten up procedure 'at this stage'. When Wedgie said earnestly, 'The question is whether Cabinet is prepared to receive representations for a review of its decisions,' Jim replied that he had expressed his willingness to take the views of the NEC into account 'on matters not yet decided'. And that was that. Jim really is a cool one. He did more than anyone in the whole history of the last Labour Government to rock the doctrine of collective responsibility to its foundations and, far from apologizing for it, he has preened himself on it ever since. Yet when Mike produces a mild and insignificant version of Jim's behaviour, Jim casts himself in the role of the aggrieved party! Nonetheless relations in the Government remain determinedly relaxed. How long it will last remains to be seen.

At last we turned to the main item of business: Mike's Bill to replace the Industrial Relations Act. He apologized for raising the matter yet again, but this time he is in trouble over the clause providing machinery for independent review.[1] His previously modified formula has apparently not done the trick with TUC. In his memo he says that to persist with the clause could cause a 'grave breach' with the unions and he therefore wants to postpone the matter until the second Bill. That was in any case the more logical place for it and he thought the TUC had good grounds for their objections because they say this matter should have been settled at the Liaison Committee. Instead, the TUC view of the matter had been accepted by the Labour Party. (All those cowardly birds coming home to roost!) Harold said that it was more logical to put this in the second Bill, but he didn't want us to get into the position that it wasn't in the second Bill either. Crosland said he was one who normally supported the departmental Minister because we ought to recognize that he or she was better apprised of the position than the rest of us were. (I only wish someone had said that yesterday at Pay Committee. We are all treating Michael as though he was a sacred law unto himself.) However he, Tony, would be worried if there were to be any weakening of the conscience clause. (Mike intervened to assure him that, although the TUC wanted to defer this too, he wasn't proposing this, particularly in view of what had appeared in the press.) Tony drawled on: 'We are putting a great many goodies on the table for the trade unions and it is becoming urgent that we should see what is coming from the other side.' He went on to point out that the 37 per cent vote we had

[1] The unions were still highly sensitive about any legal restraints on their independence and resisted any suggestion of outside interference to protect individual members against unfair treatment by their union. In this they could call in aid the Donovan Report's finding that 'it is unlikely that abuse of power by unions is widespread'. Nonetheless the Report had recommended the setting up of an independent review body (consisting of two trade unionists with a lawyer chairman) to hear complaints by individuals against arbitrary exclusion or expulsion from a union, breaches of the rules and election malpractices. It would have the right to award compensation where, for example, refusal of membership could cost a worker his job. During the discussions in the TUC Liaison Committee before the election the Labour Party representatives had urged that some such safeguards were necessary, particularly as the closed shop was to be relegalized when the Industrial Relations Act was repealed, but the TUC shied away from the idea and the matter was shelved. In the first draft of his repeal Bill, Michael Foot had included provision for such review machinery which, to meet the TUC's objections, he had strictly limited to cases where a worker had been dismissed because of 'unreasonable' expulsion or exclusion from a union, i.e. a closed shop situation. Despite this limitation he had run into intense hostility from the TUC, which argued that, following Donovan, it had been exhorting member unions to overhaul and strengthen their rules on these matters and should be left to deal with them itself.

had at the last election represented the maximum trade union and Labour Party automatic vote. If we were to win the middle of the road or uncommitted vote, we needed to show what the trade unions were doing in return. Reg Prentice (surprise, surprise!) supported him.

Finally I spoke out, sticking my neck out again. I said that it was clear that the reason why the TUC wanted this postponed to the second Bill was that they believed this would mean it wouldn't be in that Bill either. Once the election had taken place and we were back with an adequate majority they would argue that we needn't be looking over our shoulders at the civil liberties lot. But Mike's trouble was that the Opposition would cotton on to this, too. If Cabinet decided, as it seemed to be doing, that it was determined to have this in the second Bill, wouldn't it be wiser for Michael to explain this to the TUC, in which case they might accept the political advantage of doing it now? Roy [Jenkins] also asked Mike the penetrating question: 'If you say that for us to proceed now with this would create a damaging breach with the trade unions, what grounds have you for thinking it would not create a damaging breach to do it in the second Bill?' Once again it was Bob Mellish who pulled us back to earth (reminding us that you can be too clever and too logical). As long as we were committed to wage control by voluntary agreement we had to take the trade unions with us, he declared. 'Michael is working to achieve just that. We must back him all the way down the line.' And I was immensely impressed with Denis, who once again (whatever his faults) managed to bring an earthy hope to the whole concept of the Social Contract. 'I support Michael, with reservations,' he said. 'We fought and won the election on the basis of co-operation rather than confrontation. We are engaged in an experiment. We must trust Michael to get the best he can.' And he went on to declare – fairly enough – that it just wasn't true that the trade unions had given nothing in return: Len Murray, Jack, Hughie had all been delivering far more than we had ever dared to hope they would. So Michael got his own way again (with Harold entering the caveat that the provision *would* be in the second Bill), partly by his own virtues, but not least because we old-timers in Cabinet have learned some lessons the hard way.

Just as Cabinet was breaking up I intervened with my unhappy news about the threat to the uprating from the overtime ban. I poured it out in one minute flat, saying that I believed a small concession must be made if we were to have any hope of saving the day. To his credit Denis nodded understandingly at this. I went on to plead that Michael, Bob Sheldon and I should be instructed to look into it urgently. Harold agreed, but added that I must report back to the next Cabinet. It will be *far* too late by then. It is only at moments like these that I resent Michael's role as the favoured son of Cabinet.

Friday, 26 April

Up early to read my papers for my first Sunningdale.[1] My original idea was that I wanted time with my staff to consider some of the policy issues for the Health Service.

[1] In my previous ministerial posts I had developed the habit of holding departmental weekend conferences at the Civil Service College, Sunningdale, to discuss policy in greater depth than is possible during the working week. Sometimes I invited outsiders to join in the discussions. On this occasion the conference

It was Brian A-S. who suggested we should use the opportunity to examine the effects on our policy generally of Denis's proposed restraints on public expenditure. It proved an excellent idea and I spent two hours trying to master some difficult but essential analyses of the implications for us of a nil increase in expenditure in 1975–76 and a 2 per cent growth annually after that. Graham and Jack Straw picked me up at the flat at 11am and we drove down to Ascot while I still had my head in my documents. I did lift my head once to say with a chuckle that the last time I was at Sunningdale was to make the speech which later became the article 'Mandarin Power'. Graham said he knew all about it because he had gone down to Sunningdale the day afterwards with Sir Keith, who was told all about the stirring speech made the day before by Mrs Castle. 'How did the civil servants receive your speech?' asked Jack. 'With total incomprehension,' I replied. And I added, 'If I were to recap now I would lay much greater responsibility on Ministers.' I went on that the trouble with the last Labour Government was that civil servants had been given a simple remit by the Government, 'Defend the pound', which meant that Ministers like me hardly dared to open their mouths in public. This time the remit was a much more dynamic one: 'Defend the Manifesto'. It made life much simpler.

As I arrived at this neo-Georgian building in its magnificent park, memories came flooding back. This was the place where *In Place of Strife* was born[1] and where I tried to make people face up to the implications of the Government's prices and incomes policy. I was even in my old rooms, way out in one of the many spartan residential annexes. It is only in the main building, where the discussions and meals are held, that the surroundings are lavish – and the meals themselves are far from lavish, though the directorate did us pretty well at dinner on our first night, even throwing in some reasonable wine. Lunch on our arrival was modest. We assembled in a great semicircle in the vast drawing room for our opening session at 2pm. At first I thought that the whole enterprise was going to be a gigantic flop. There was a general and rather discursive discussion during the afternoon. But after dinner (thanks partly to the wine) the whole thing came alight and we found ourselves as Ministers engaged in a liberated argument about social security priorities. It wasn't until later that I realized what an effect this had had on my civil servants. Lawrence Brandes, one of my Under-Secretaries who had been with me at the Department of Employment, said to me in the bar at 11.30pm as we had a belated nightcap, 'It was totally fascinating. We are all saying it is the best show in town.'

Morning came somewhat harshly. Having begged for an early morning cup of tea, I found it cooling on my doorstep when I had given up all hope of it and had emerged to venture into the spartan bathroom for my morning bath. But the discussion begun over dinner continued in a lively way over breakfast and we had a stimulating morning discussing Health Service priorities. I even began to recognize the queue of civil servants who have been trooping into my ministerial room in the past few weeks.

was to be an internal one to enable Ministers and officials to consider what our priorities should be in the field of health and personal social services in the light of the money we were likely to be allocated in 1975–76. The only 'outsider' invited was Mr Laurie Pavitt, MP, chairman of the Health Group of the Parliamentary Labour Party.

[1] See Introduction.

We all emerged as individuals. One of the highlights came when David Owen, who began by saying with that disarming smile of his that he knew the department disagreed with him, said that he thought the restraints of public expenditure meant that we should just have to be more interventionist. Consultants, doctors and the rest would have to realize that, when they were prescribing drugs or demanding hospital beds for their patients, they were making economic decisions. Dr Yellowlees, my Chief Medical Officer, followed on immediately to say, 'It may surprise Parliamentary Secretary when I say that I entirely agree with him.' He was sure this was a time when 'my profession and his' would respond to this kind of argument if only they were brought into the consideration of it. 'Give them the data: put an edited version of our papers to them.'

And so we ended on a happy note, Brian A-S. being the most enthusiastic of all about the value of the exercise. I certainly cleared my own mind and learned a lot of facts. Some concrete decisions were made, not least that we must give the mental health services and health centres priority over a succession of new district general hospitals. And Laurie Pavitt, with his gentle common sense, helped to educate the civil servants in such matters as the philosophy behind our devotion to the abolition of prescription charges. Our two main conclusions, which I summed up at the end, were that the restraints on new capital programmes made it all the more imperative that we should go nap on 'people' – i.e., on those employed in the services: their standards of pay, training and general recognition. Secondly, that we must take everyone – staff, doctors, general public, Parliament – much more into our confidence. One of the things that has come out of this weekend is that I have commissioned a new social survey, based on the papers before us, which will spell out with brutal clarity the size of the need in the field of health and social services and the agony of the choices. And I think I succeeded in making the whole thing *fun* in obedience to my basic belief that the cardinal sin among politicians is pomposity.

Monday, 29 April

It was odd to go back to St James's Square,[1] where our meeting with Mike and Bob Sheldon over the leave bonus for my staff was to be held. The liftman looked at me closely and said, 'It is Mrs Castle, isn't it? You look ten years younger!' Odder still to be in that ministerial room, scene of so many traumatic moments. I told Mike how grateful he ought to be to me for having left him such an aesthetically decorated room. But his mind wasn't on aesthetics and we spent a tense hour hotly arguing about the bonus. Mike still stands out against the thought of giving a consent, saying at one point that I didn't realize how difficult these issues were for him. At this I retorted, 'You are only just starting. This hasn't got anything on the builders' penny!'[2] His people came up with the idea that we should approach the national staff

[1] Headquarters of the Department of Employment where I had served as First Secretary and Secretary of State for Employment and Productivity from 1968–70.

[2] In October 1968, when I was in charge of the Labour Government's pay policy, I had to threaten to standstill the building workers' pay increase unless it was reduced by a penny an hour to bring it within the statutory pay limit. This decision was vigorously attacked at the time by the Tribune group of Labour MPs, including Michael Foot.

side to see if they would be prepared to use part of their flexibility bonus under Stage Three to cover this. 'What?' I scoffed, 'Do you really expect a national body to use its money on behalf of a sectional one?' 'But we've got to *try* it, Barbara,' said Mike desperately. The Civil Service Department man quietly pointed out that once we had offered a bonus in this way we should not be able to withdraw it if the national side disagreed. So it was decided that private approaches should be made by CSD to the secretary of the national side. As we left the liftman still eyed me curiously. 'I can't get over it: you *do* look ten years younger.' 'It is not being here,' I quipped. 'Poor Mr Foot looks ten years older.' At the exit I ran into Frank Lawton, the department's solicitor. The years rolled back as we greeted each other with great affection.

Another worthwhile ministerial working lunch. There is a crisis over the Old Age Pensioners' Federation conference meeting tomorrow. Mrs Green [the General Secretary] tells me the CPSA have written to them saying they are sorry about the overtime ban but they have no choice but to impose it. She says there is bound to be an emergency resolution at the conference; can I send a statement? We spent some time drafting it. I made the office cancel some of my appointments so that I could have my hair done at Xavier, as I discovered that it is tonight I have to preside over the annual dinner for the chairmen of the Boards of Governors of the Teaching Hospitals. Lancaster House did everything as beautifully as usual. The chairmen were an odd lot: Reggie Wilson, Alf Robens, Donald Kaberry, etc. Tories to a man, I suspect, save for Audrey Callaghan and Mary Stewart. I had to make a speech and I sent them away purring while David Owen groaned, 'I couldn't help thinking what a bunch we have got in charge of the NHS!' Jack Ashley was deeply touched that I had included him and even more touched when I told him I was determined to do something effective for the deaf if I survived long enough. I sent him away to discuss with Laurie Pavitt how we could give the needs of the deaf more prominence. I am getting more and more fond of Jack. If we are ever to be a 'caring' department, it is people like him that we should be caring about.

Tuesday, 30 April

I won Jack Ashley's praise again by the firm way I told an office meeting we must do something positive about battered wives. One by one I am trying to take his pet projects on board. But the highlight of the day was the deputation I received from the staff side of the Nurses and Midwives Whitley Council over nurses' salaries. Outside the building a thousand nurses demonstrated, whipped up by the Confederation of Health Service Employees [COHSE] and the National and Local Government Officers' Association [NALGO], and I was told that they had almost stormed the gates. I am glad to read that Mike is reporting to Cabinet in favour of selective increases for the nurses at least. But Griffiths, chairman of the staff side, soon made it clear that Briggs is not the priority. What they are bitter about is that there is now no Relativities Board for them to go to for a fundamental revaluation of their salaries. What they want is the assurance of an independent review. I replied as sympathetically as I could without promising anything. Afterwards David Owen said to me, grinning, 'You really are an old poker-face. You never even gave them a hint that something might be on the way.' 'When you have been through the fire as I have,' I replied, 'you will learn not to count on anything until it has been confirmed by Cabinet.'

The 'Husbands and Wives' dinner at Lockets concentrated mainly on the need for an early election. Mike and Peter are desperate about this. Mike said we didn't need a parliamentary pretext, but what we did need was systematically to build up a realization of the size of the crisis that faced the country. We had failed to engender any atmosphere of crisis at all. I told him that I thought it was impossible for us to go to the country until he had got through his repeal of the Industrial Relations Act and that could not be before the end of July. As for crisis, we had to remember that we had talked crisis in October 1964 and all we got for our pains was a run on the pound. This time we had belied Tory predictions that we shouldn't be able to borrow on favourable terms and the pound had actually strengthened since we came in. They remained unconvinced. However, Peter suggested that a Motion in the Commons supporting the principle of a referendum on the Common Market might provide the pretext, and everyone thought that was a superb idea.

Wednesday, 1 May

At the restive parliamentary party meeting on Chile I asked Harold if he had had my note about how I could arrange to remain Mrs Barbara Castle when Ted goes to 'another place'. He said yes and obviously is not going to raise any objections to what I propose, so I shall get my letter off to Godfrey Agnew[1] right away. But he said the announcement cannot be this week, so our plans for a double celebration on Ted's birthday this weekend have come to naught. I *long* for the uncertainty to come to an end so that I can allow myself to dare to revel in Ted's happiness. A very pleasant lunch with John Cunningham of the *Guardian*, who I find to my surprise is a fan of mine. He told me that the way I handled my first press conference was magnificent. What a relief! I need reassurance as much as anyone. The evening was taken up with a short debate in the House on the Sharp Report: another anodyne subject which this frightened Opposition has chosen for its supply day. I had left the debate entirely to Alf and he did well; his deep sincerity always enables him to get away with anything in the House and we are on good ground here. After all, we lost no time in publishing the Sharp Report.

Thursday, 2 May

When Elizabeth told me there would be half an hour's private discussion at the beginning of Cabinet, I thought it would be about Ted Short.[2] Although I can't get

[1] Sir Godfrey Agnew, Clerk of the Privy Council.

[2] The previous day the *Daily Express* had splashed the story of a payment to Ted Short in 1963 by Mr T. Dan Smith, former dynamic chairman of Newcastle City Housing Committee, who had been sentenced to six years' imprisonment for corruption on 26 April. The press had been alerted by a statement made on TV the same day by Mr Smith, claiming that Mr Short, who was MP for Newcastle Central, had entertained businessmen for him. The *Express* had unearthed letters which had passed between the two men in June 1973, in which Dan Smith offered, and Ted Short accepted, a retainer of £500 'which would be a strictly

Michael interested, I still think a PM ought to take his Cabinet into his confidence when personal issues like this, or the Tony Field business, occur. At present we are expected to be content with what we read in the newspapers. But not a bit of it. When Cabinet met – minus officials – Harold said he thought we ought to have a discussion about our election options. No decision would be made – and indeed he himself hadn't made up his mind. But reading between the lines, I sensed that he was seeking support for his own strong inclination to go for June: just another indication of how lightly Harold sweeps the Short business aside. I was surprised how many there were (Shirley arrived late) who were all for a June election – and strongly too: Eric Varley, Willie Ross, Reg Prentice, Tony Crosland, Roy Mason, as well as Mike and Peter – so the polarization was not on ideological lines. Mike repeated his line that we did not need a 'pretext' for another election if we would begin to tell people that Britain faced a serious crisis, that we needed a strong government to get us through it and that the people must make a choice. He admitted that he would be unhappy not to have got the repeal of the Industrial Relations Act through the House. Nonetheless he believed we could and should take the TUC into our confidence about the difficulties which would increasingly face us if we were to struggle on as a minority government.

Harold then chipped in to say that the TUC would understand if they could see how all the other aspects of our policy that were so important to them depended on our getting a real majority. Ministers should pour out White Papers in the next few weeks. We might even force the Tories to vote on some basic issues of principle, such as North Sea oil and gas (Eric nodded) or land. 'Or', he continued, 'we might bring matters to a head by just putting down a Motion of support for a referendum on the Common Market.' (Has Peter been talking to him?) Roy snapped in at this point: 'I hope you would not try to make this the pretext, Prime Minister. I must tell you you might not find this the clear basis for unity you seem to think.' Harold hastened to reassure him that he certainly would not wish to embarrass anyone.

At this point I could no longer contain myself. 'I have had a very divided mind, Harold,' I said, 'but the more I have listened to you, the more you have confirmed me in favour of September rather than June. We talk about setting out our policies instead of creating a parliamentary pretext which we know the Tories just won't afford us.' Turning to Bob I said, 'If you can get your Budget through without a division, you can get anything.' But if we went to the country on 13 June – the latest date that seemed to be safe in view of the holidays – that meant Parliament had to be dissolved when? '23 May,' Bob interposed. 'Right,' I replied. 'This means that any White Papers that are to be relevant must be approved by Cabinet on Thursday next, 9 May. Will the White Paper on North Sea oil be ready then?' Eric shook his head. 'Land?' I went on. 'Mortgages?' Harold Lever shook his head violently. 'I certainly can't be ready with my White Paper on our long-term pension proposals by then,' I went on. 'What we shall be doing is to deny ourselves the parliamentary platform which will be essential if we are to demonstrate the basic difference between them and us.' I then said how serious I thought it would be for the trade-union movement –

---

confidential matter between us'. Ted Short had issued a statement denying he had ever discussed building contracts with Dan Smith and saying that there had been 'one unsolicited payment of £250' for expenses.

and how demoralizing – if we had not even repealed the Industrial Relations Act before we went to the country. I needed to know what objective factors would be operating against us in September compared with June; what would be the indices of greater unpopularity? Only if Denis could set this out for me would I be willing to go for June.

This brought Denis in, complaining that really no one could answer my question. It was just that things would certainly not be better in September than they were now. Jim came in emphatically: 'I am horrified at the suggestion that this party should be plunged into another election in a matter of weeks.' The organization and money were just not there. And what if the result was a repetition of the stalemate we had now? The Liberals seemed to be holding their own and he was haunted by the fact that we only polled 37 per cent of the votes last time. What if we lost? The trade unions would never forgive us. Fred Peart and Harold Lever had been nodding vigorously through all that Jim and I said.

After an hour of this Harold summed up. The Cabinet was divided, but there was just a slight balance of view in favour of September. There was, however, one point none of us had mentioned and that was if the Tories thought they were safe from an early election, they would be tempted to bring the knives out for Heath, just as they had done for Alec Douglas Home when he, Harold, had said there would not be an election in 1965. What he had to decide was whether that would be to our advantage or not. I still think Harold has made his mind up for June, though he repeated no decision had yet been made.

There was an interesting moment when Ted Short intervened to say he hoped no one would feel inhibited from mentioning his part in the calculations, at which everyone brushed aside the very idea that it had any relevance. Ted then went on to say he was in favour of September anyway, while Elwyn confirmed my growing certainty about his deep conventionality by asking what was wrong with minority government? It seemed to be working very well and he didn't see why we should not go on indefinitely.

At last officials were called back in, and we turned to the item on the proposed register of MPs' financial interests,[1] which took up another hour of our time. It is just

---

[1] For some years there had been growing concern among Labour backbenchers about the activities of public relations firms among MPs on behalf of business concerns and foreign governments. These included offers of lavish hospitality, free holidays abroad and in some cases the payment of retainers to MPs to represent particular interests in the House. The determination to bring these matters into the open had been heightened by the Poulson affair and some Labour MPs had been leading a campaign for a compulsory register of MPs' financial interests. Ted Short had responded to this by drawing up three resolutions for submission to the House. These strengthened and extended the convention whereby an MP was expected to disclose any relevant financial interest he had when intervening in the proceedings of the House, set up a compulsory register of Members' interests and proposed that a Select Committee should consider how the register should be compiled and enforced and what type of pecuniary interest should be disclosed. If directorships of companies were to be registered, for instance, ought not large shareholdings also to be disclosed? Although some members of the Opposition wished to tone down the resolutions, they were carried by the House on 22 May on a free vote and the register was set up in June the following year. By May 1976, 634 Members had registered their interests but Mr Enoch Powell's refusal to do so on principle, and the reluctance of MPs to take enforcement action against him, meant that the register in effect became voluntary.

the sort of thing on which we go round endlessly in circles with a lot of cross-chat at the other end of the table which we at our end couldn't even hear. So, having said 'Hear, hear' loudly to Bob's emphatic opening – 'I hope Cabinet is going to say without a shadow of doubt that it is in favour of a compulsory register' – I gave up the attempt to follow the discussion, particularly Harold's mumblings through his pipe, and read up my papers for the next two items, which were vital to me. Occasionally I gathered that others were raising problems of definition about the 'financial interests' referred to in the proposed resolutions Ted had put before us. Someone raised the question of shareholdings. Shouldn't they include such things as building societies? Everyone was poking fun at Harold Lever, who got his own back by protesting solemnly: 'I resent the suggestion that I should ever be so foolish as to put £100,000 in a building society.' The PM's suggestion that the lobby (whose members, he said, engaged extensively in 'moonlighting') should also be compelled to register was firmly slapped down, though we agreed there would be less objection to supporting a backbench amendment on these lines.

I thought we were just on the point of agreeing that we should announce that the register should be compulsory, when Bob chipped in to say emphatically, 'I should remind Cabinet that we have a Liaison Committee with the backbenchers. It is very new and very sensitive. I beg Cabinet not to reach a decision until we have put all these points to them and a party meeting has been held.' And so the whole thing has gone back into the melting pot until the Liaison Committee has considered it. Personally I thought it was a great pity that Cabinet could not have made its own view in favour of a compulsory register clear without delay. After all, the issue is going to be put to a free vote. By this time it was 1 pm, and Harold adjourned Cabinet till 4.45 pm.

My fears were confirmed when I went in to the House to listen to the anticipated Short-baiting. First, Harold's Questions. His replies were crisp and confident, and I was glad to see he was back on his old form, though he did slip into some of his customary verbosity towards the end. Then on to Business Questions and the matter of the register was quickly raised. Ted's handling was as terse and autocratic as it always is – but then I never thought he was a good choice for Leader of the House. He managed to make it look as though we were evading the issue, and it was the last straw when Willie Hamilton backed Ted Heath in complaining that the Government had had all the consultations necessary and ought to have been ready to put its own proposals to the House. This from a member of the Liaison Committee, which, we had been told, was peeved because it hadn't been given the chance to have its say first! Really, we do have a horde of rogue elephants on our own benches, who manage to ensure that things always appear in an unfavourable light for us.

Back at Cabinet I got my way on the consent for nurses' pay: one breakthrough for my long-term policy! I also backed the consents for teachers and postmen.[1] But, by the time we got to the leave bonus for DHSS staff Harold and Ted had had to go to the party meeting. Bob wasn't there. So it was a tired, tetchy and truncated Cabinet

---

[1] On 6 May Michael Foot told the Commons that he proposed to authorize additional payments above the Stage Three limits to nurses and teachers, but not postmen.

which had to deal with the overtime ban which now disastrously threatens my uprating. Mike is still holding out desperately against having to give a public consent on this. The TUC, he says, is more rigid than the Pay Board in wanting no exceptions at all to the Stage Three policy. The unions are obviously afraid they could not hold their own people if a gesture was made to any one of them. But Mike's department have been trying to think of a way out and have come up with the idea that we should approach the national staff side again, the first soundings having proved disastrous, to see if they would agree for the leave bonus to be met out of the 1 per cent flexibility allowance, only this time against Mike's promise that they would be compensated later when the statutory pay policy no longer operated. Well, that's as good a device as any and I felt I had better accept it as Jim and Denis were making noises of opposition to any leave bonus at all.

Friday, 3 May

In to the office early to talk about the next steps over the leave bonus. Then into an office meeting on Sharp. Dear Alf may be very impressive in his obvious sincerity but when I had waded through his agonizing for fifteen minutes I had to take charge of the policy myself, finally sending Brian A–S., who is superb, away to produce a comprehensive submission along the guidelines I had laid down. These were based on the following principles: (1) all those in the existing categories must retain their right to a vehicle: either car or (if they preferred) tricycle; (2) new categories should be entitled to a mobility allowance, which we should introduce as the first phase in our long-term disability income policy – i.e. as part of the payment for the extra expenses of disablement; (3) we should further explore Brian's idea for a rent-a-car scheme. I think the office were relieved to have some clear guidance at last. Slipped away from the office after lunch to buy Ted's birthday presents. Those two darling dogs were awaiting me longingly at Hell Corner Farm, and as soon as I had swallowed my cup of tea I changed into my old things and braved the north-east wind to take them for a walk. Despite the cold wind everything is unimaginably beautiful. The bluebells are out; the beech is at its most tender green. I picked cowslips and crab apple blossom and filled the house with flowers. My love affair with the countryside will not end until I die.

Saturday, 4 May

My last free weekend before what may be an election and it is too bitterly cold to work in the garden, damn it! The papers suggest that the borough election results give no grounds for an early election. Ted does not agree.

Sunday, 5 May

A quiet birthday party for Ted: just Eileen and me and a meal at home. We have decided to reserve his celebrations till the great announcement is made. Neither of us will have any peace of mind until it is. Jack Straw has done his stuff with the Privy

Council and it looks as though I shall be able to do a Beatrice Webb,[1] thank God.

Monday, 6 May

Another good working lunch with my politician team. I find that these discussions are more and more valuable. The office accepts them quite happily and there is always more to talk about than we have time for.

Tuesday, 7 May

At last I am able to announce our interim pensions proposals and what we are going to do about the Tory Pensions Act.[2] My Parliamentary Questions and statement in the House caused me no difficulty, despite our apprehensions that there would be an uproar over the postponement of the Reserve Pension Scheme. Suddenly I am at ease in Parliament. I don't know why. Perhaps because I am aware that I am on my last lap politically, so I don't worry any more. But Mike's speech on the Second Reading of his Trade Union Bill was a disappointment. Even the parliamentary giant can't score every time.

Wednesday, 8 May

Tough time with BMA deputation over their superannuation scheme. Keable-Elliott was the most impressive of them and I had some sympathy with their case: told Brian to see what he could do about it. It will help us to be tough over pay if we can do something here. In the evening was positively fêted at a reception of the General Nursing Council. *They* at any rate are thrilled over Briggs.

Thursday, 9 May

At Cabinet there were signs that Harold is learning a little sense about the press. There is a press debate on Tuesday and Ted Short urged that Harold must speak. 'I don't want to get into a vendetta position,' said Harold reluctantly. Three cheers! The register of interests matter seems to be sorting itself out all right. The Parliamentary Liaison Committee has agreed there shall be a compulsory register and that a Select Committee should be set up to consider the definition of the interests to be included in it. Ted asked that he should be allowed to proceed along these lines. Jim then

---

[1] In 1929 when Sidney Webb was created a peer by the Labour Government and became Lord Passfield, Beatrice Webb refused to use her title.

[2] On 7 May I told the Commons that the Government had decided to scrap Sir Keith Joseph's Reserve Pension Scheme, due to come into operation the following April (see footnote page 53). Instead the Government would introduce its own, much more generous, earnings-related pensions scheme as soon as possible. Sir Geoffrey Howe, Opposition spokesman for the social services, denounced my decision as 'flat-footed and doctrinaire'. The pensions industry was dismayed. But Labour MPs welcomed the prospect of a better scheme and were particularly delighted by my statement that employees' insurance contributions would not go up again next April, as Sir Keith had planned, but would stay at the 5·5 per cent which had been fixed to cover the July uprating – a point on which I had won my battle with the Treasury.

reported on the Council of Ministers, whose meeting on 6 May had been over-shadowed by Italy's decision to introduce an imports deposit scheme. Clearly the whole EEC is in disarray. Jim described it as an 'extremely grave situation', adding, 'What worries me is the general slide that is going on, for example in Denmark. By the autumn the whole scene in the Community may be transformed.' The Community had decided that inaction was the best thing. 'A new situation is developing in Europe and we must be ready to take advantage of it,' he added. Said Harold complacently, 'We are rapidly reaching the position when we are the senior surviving government in Europe.' Peter took the opportunity to remark, 'One cannot help but be impressed by the total incompetence of the Council of Ministers.' Elwyn added, 'I attended the Council of Europe at Strasbourg. There was deep pessimism by all the Presidents of the Assemblies about the survival of the parliamentary system itself.' After this profound gloom Eric's memo on the Community energy policy seemed irrelevant. Even he was condemnatory: 'It is nothing more in my view than a concerted grab at the UK's oil and gas resources.' Said Peter to him, 'On the whole I approve your line but I think even the proposal to "collaborate" with the EEC in increasing supplies is dangerous.'

Off to Blackburn for two busy days.

Monday, 13 May

Office meeting on Brian A-S.'s examination of the possibilities of negative income tax.[1] He had to admit defeat, though is still hoping to work out a limited scheme for pensioners. But the main event of the day was my mass meeting at the office with the Royal College of Nursing. They mounted a massive array of speakers and arguments in support of their impressive report on the state of nursing. In effect, through Mrs Newstead's speech at the end, they gave me an ultimatum: announce the setting up of an independent enquiry or they would have to tell their members to withdraw their labour and be re-engaged as 'temporaries'. And she added they thought it was only fair to give me three weeks to meet their demand. I replied as best I could, having enormous sympathy with their case, and promised to meet them again in three weeks' time. I then told officials we must get the decision cleared quickly so that I could make an announcement *before* the three weeks were up.

Tuesday, 14 May

Peter Brown has arranged a succession of lunches with some of my critics in the press. 'Who knows, you might convert them.' Today's was with Ronald Butt, my pet hate,

[1] Negative income tax was a more radical form of the Tory tax credit scheme. Although its basic mechanism was broadly the same – the replacement of personal tax allowances by tax-free weekly cash credits – its purpose, unlike the Tory scheme, was to redistribute income in favour of the poor. Despite its attractions, particularly in reducing means testing which was one of the goals of our social policy, we finally decided to apply this approach only to children through our child benefit scheme, plus a premium for single-parent families. For other groups we decided to adopt the more flexible approach of progressively extending cash benefits as of right to neglected groups such as the disabled and of steadily lifting pensioners out of dependence on supplementary benefit through our new pensions scheme.

who turned out to be civil, listened respectfully and I am sure was not influenced at all. A lovely meal in the evening with the General Dental Council. I got on well with the President, Sir Robert Bradlaw, who is a fan of Nye's, and I managed to make a quite amusing little off-the-cuff speech. He followed me with a polished after-dinner one on which he had obviously spent a lot of time. What we Ministers are supposed to turn on at the drop of a hat!

Wednesday, 15 May

Dick's memorial meeting. I was in a panic. I have never found these personal tribute meetings easy and kept remembering how I had boobed at Kingsley's memorial. Besides, when I prepare a speech I have no confidence at all that anyone will be the least interested in what I have to say. I only speak well when I am reacting to an actual audience – or to an attack. Harold was in the chair and read a pleasant speech – too long, of course. Brian A-S. read a polished and very charming one. Then it was my turn. I ad libbed rather desperately from headings, but gained in assurance as I went on. Tony Howard followed with a competent speech without much heart in it. Poor Mike, who was due to wind up, wasn't called till it was already 1pm. He cut his losses and merely said a few words. Afterwards everyone said I was the only one who had conveyed the essence of Dick. I was glad because I loved the old boy and was relieved when Anne wrote and said she was sure Dick would have enjoyed my speech. He would at any rate have appreciated its honesty and would have done the same for me.

Hurried into the House to prepare for my South Ockendon statement and the lobby afterwards. Both went well. At Brian A-S.'s suggestion I've sent a special message (and included a tribute) to Barbara Robb. I never thought when Brian and I had lunch with her two years ago that I would be making the statement on the report for which she was so directly responsible.

Thursday, 16 May

Meeting with Age Concern in the afternoon. I am afraid I get pretty impatient with some of these voluntary organizations who are busy researching the problems we could do with their money to help cure. I cut David Hobman short to go and meet an Association of Metropolitan Authorities [AMA] deputation led by nice Labour chaps who are irritated by the interference of DHSS with the expenditure priorities put forward by local authorities. I told them I agreed that this was no way to treat adult men and women and afterwards instructed my department that I wanted the present nanny-ish procedures changed.

Monday, 20 May

Up early to get to the Liaison Committee with the TUC. Mike gave a warning that we might have a number of defeats in committee on the Bill [the Trade Union and Labour Relations Bill] on the pre-entry closed shop, disclosure of information and independent review machinery. 'In my opinion,' he said, 'we should press on with the

Bill, even with these amendments, making it clear we will raise these matters at Report stage or when we have a majority. It is essential that we should get the main purpose of the Bill.' Harold agreed. 'It is essential we get the Bill and not leave it to the hazards of the election. If we are going to have a June election we must dissolve Parliament this Thursday. But once the June date is passed the Tories may get more aggressive and defeat us on Report. I am thinking out ways we could hold them *in terrorem* and I think I may have got the answer.' (A grin here.)

We then turned to Wedgie's report on the work of his department, which painted his reforming efforts in glowing terms.[1] Wedgie told us he hoped to publish details about the public monies received by the first twenty companies in two weeks' time. He said the planning agreement idea was the first new thought to come out for some time, but he wanted to remove from small companies the feeling that they were going to lose the help they get at present. Cledwyn Hughes, who was there as vice-chairman of the Parliamentary Labour Party [PLP] and who has been coming out increasingly in his true colours since Harold dropped him from the Government, struck a sour note. 'If the Green Paper is published in this form, it is certainly not a vote winner in the next election. What does "full parliamentary process" mean if it doesn't mean a full Bill? My own view is that, if you are going to go round the country explaining the policy as it is set out here, it is not going to win us votes.' Wedgie retorted, 'I personally fought the last election on this. I don't for a moment think we shall have the support of our opponents.' Jim said soothingly we shouldn't give prominence to this until Tony's White Paper was available. Hughie and Jack sat silent. Only Alf Allen came in from the trade union side: 'The intentions are very welcome, though there is some anxiety about the repercussions on employment.' I often wonder what the unions really feel about Tony; I suspect their real hero is Mike.

[1] In his paper Tony Benn had seized the opportunity to jump the gun on industrial policy. Although three weeks earlier he had circulated a Minute to the Prime Minister promising a Green Paper in the summer after consultation with colleagues 'through the normal machinery in the usual way', his paper set out his own proposals in considerable detail. These were much more specific than the Manifesto, which had itself gone much further than any previous one in its attitude to public ownership and intervention in industry. Not only, the Manifesto said, would the Government take over mineral rights and the aircraft and shipbuilding industries, but would acquire profitable sectors and individual firms in those industries where a public holding was essential to enable the Government to pursue its economic aims. Included in the list were sections of pharmaceuticals, road haulage, construction and machine tools. The Government would create a powerful National Enterprise Board [NEB] 'with the structure and functions set out in Labour's Programme, 1973'. There would be a new Industry Act and a system of planning agreements 'which will allow the Government to plan with industry more effectively'. What Tony Benn's paper did was to put his interpretation on this policy before Cabinet had considered it. The firms to be included in the planning agreements' system, it said, 'will initially number about one hundred, controlling about half of manufacturing output'. Government aid would be increasingly channelled through these agreements. The NEB would be initially formed out of existing government holdings in industry 'and will then move to purchase key sector leaders in manufacturing industry'. In addition to the nationalization of the aircraft and shipbuilding industries, which would require specific legislative authority, the Industry Act would empower the Government to extend public ownership by the acquisition of individual companies 'through a full parliamentary process'. All this would be underpinned by a new system of consultation with the trade unions and a bold extension of open government. One example of book-opening he had in mind was to publish details of the 'massive programme of public subsidies' – some £3,000 million over the previous four years – showing the amounts received by leading companies.

Next Shirley explained her prices policy. I then introduced my own progress report, hoping by inference to commit the committee (and Jack Jones) to the principles behind our new pensions scheme. To my surprise the only point Jack made was about the dropping of the Tory State Reserve scheme. Contrary to all the other evidence we have had he was fearful that this would make employers drop progress with occupational schemes. I pointed out that the TUC had officially welcomed my decision. 'It is essential you make statements weekly telling employers they must go ahead,' he replied. David Basnett and George Smith nodded agreement. After the meeting Mik [Ian Mikardo] came up to me full of how impressive the three reports from Wedgie, Shirley and me had been. 'I didn't know myself how much you were doing and I'm damn sure the PLP don't. We ought to tell them. Are you willing to do the same report to a party meeting?' I said of course I was.

Harold passed me a note about Ted: *'Operation Ted*: Announcement likely Thurs for Friday this week.' Cheers!

In the afternoon I helped Harold receive a deputation from the nurses, which covered the same ground as they had done with me. I welcome anything which will persuade Cabinet to give me that independent review of their salaries!

Tuesday, 21 May

COHSE and National Union of Public Employees [NUPE] are a bit offended at my seeing the Royal College [of Nursing], which they feel has stolen the initiative, so I have to agree to see them too – individually. Albert Spanswick warned me that the nurses would insist on an interim payment: something that had *not* been raised with me originally by the staff side. This inter-union rivalry is a curse. I listened courteously. Alan Fisher [general secretary of NUPE] was his usual reasonable self and I could understand that he had to make his mark. But I really do seem to have walked into a pack of trouble. Unions always seem to let their pent-up frustrations explode as soon as there is a Labour Government. Later I received a deputation from Blackburn nurses. There are deputations everywhere, even though I have already promised to consider their case urgently. After all I have now been in office for the grand total of eight weeks!

Wednesday, 22 May

Another deputation from nurses, this time led by Bob Mellish. Two nurses from COHSE were so rude he apologized for them – then they went out and leaked an attack on me to the press. I shall need the patience of a saint to go through these provocations. In the evening snatched a few moments to go to the Africa Day reception at the Commonwealth Institute, where I was almost mobbed by African women fans. Teelock, the Mauritian High Commissioner, asked me when Ted and I were going to come to Mauritius: they had been trying to get us there for so long. 'We could come in August,' I said on an impulse. 'Good,' he replied. 'I will tell my Prime Minister.'

Thursday, 23 May

It is now clear there will be no June election. I passed Harold a note pointing out that Blackburn has its September holiday in the week starting 16 September: I didn't want him calling an election for 26 September! He tossed me a note back saying, 'I killed one PPS by not knowing about Leek.[1] I should not like to kill a former PPS. I have retained your note for my file though I expect my already very exhaustive list will include it.' We then discussed the Christmas bonus, which I wanted to include in my Bill to increase contribution rates. The general feeling was that it was better to introduce it later in a separate Bill instead of crowding all the concessions to pensioners into our first few months. But no one doubted we should have to pay it. To my relief Cabinet then endorsed the decision of Social Services Committee to give the nurses their independent review. I have already sounded out Lord Halsbury,[2] who is tickled pink to do it and told me it ought not to take too long; he could probably let me have the report by the end of July. He has gone away to start work on it. I also won another victory with the Cabinet's agreement to back-date the nurses' increases in due course to this very day. The way is now clear for me to ditch my 'shadow', Geoffrey Howe, in this afternoon's debate.

We then had a quick discussion on the third report of the Top Salaries Review Body.[3] Crosland asked, 'What are we here for? Greater social equality?' To which Harold answered, 'Anything that is going to help Michael must come first', adding, 'There will be no thresholds for anyone.' Later I was delighted when I won my battle on behalf of Jack Straw, whose local government activities had been threatened by Harold's earlier pretty conventional approach. Reg Prentice and Ted Short had both turned up trumps on this and Cabinet agreed that special advisers need not resign from their local authorities. (Graham Hart has been very pro-Jack on this: they have become firm friends.)

But our biggest discussion was on Concorde, on which Elwyn reported the findings of his Committee of Ministers. On balance the committee would prefer the project to be cancelled, provided the agreement of the French Government could be obtained.

---

[1] Harold Davies, Labour MP for Leek, had been Harold Wilson's Parliamentary Private Secretary in the previous Labour Government. In calling the election in June 1970, Harold Wilson had uncharacteristically overlooked the fact that the date clashed with the wakes week in Leek when some 15,000 miners, potters and textile workers took their annual holiday. Harold Davies's vote fell by nearly 9,000 and he lost his seat.

[2] John Anthony Hardinge Giffard, third Earl of Halsbury, industrialist, scientist and Fellow of the Royal Society, had been chairman of the Review Body on Doctors' and Dentists' Pay since 1971. We hoped that the appointment of such a prestigious figure to chair the independent review of nurses' pay would convince the nurses that the Government was taking their grievances seriously.

[3] The Top Salaries Review Body had been set up by Mr Heath in 1971, under the chairmanship of Lord Boyle, to advise the Prime Minister on the remuneration of the chairmen and members of the boards of nationalized industries; the higher judiciary; senior civil servants; senior officers of the armed forces 'and other groups which may be referred to it'. In 1971 it published an interim report, pending the conclusion of its 'substantive review'. This full review was overtaken by the introduction of Mr Heath's pay policy and two further interim reports were issued. The latest of these, which we were discussing, recommended that the groups concerned should receive their Stage Three increases plus threshold payments. In the end the Government accepted the report in full. Meanwhile, the pressure for a 'substantive review' was mounting.

Failing that, we should go ahead with the completion of sixteen aircraft at a cost of £360–£400 million. (The cost of cancellation was estimated at £120 million.) Wedgie's speech was moving and eloquent. We all agreed, he said, Concorde should never have been started, but to go for cancellation now, after having spent £545 million, would mean we should have nothing to show for an expenditure of £800 million. The TUC and the Confederation of Shipbuilding and Engineering Unions [CSEU] were strongly against cancelling. 'For us to go for rupture would be wrong.' We should probe the attitude of the French first, 'but if we fail we should announce the decision to go ahead with the sixteen immediately'. Denis put up a brave fight against impossible odds: 'This is very much the argument used for the past ten years. If we allow the unions not merely to decide our social priorities but what we spend our money on for economic reasons, it will be the death of the whole idea of public participation in industry. Public participation must not be made to seem a device for spending money on white elephants. There are bound to be public expenditure restraints. We should take the decision that we shall seek cancellation. We should tell the French we have decided on this and seek their acquiescence. Maybe they will not sue us, but we should cancel anyway and take the risk. But we need not take this decision till October.'

Roy Mason agreed that on balance the argument was for cancelling, but we should give Wedgie the right to talk to the French and in the end we might have to go for the sixteen planes. Industrial unrest was developing. 'We should be losing the techniques on which we have got the lead in the world.' But Wedgie's most enthusiastic supporters turned out to be Peter and Mike. Said Peter, 'We are faced with unquantifiables and must rely on our own common sense. It is one thing to stop it starting and another to drop it when we have spent so many millions. We should look ridiculous when we have gone so far.' Mike said he believed it was impossible to cancel now. So although Roy Jenkins supported the Chancellor ('Giscard was never in favour of these planes'), we proceeded to endorse Elwyn's recommendations. I had my deep doubts but I sat mum.

When I returned to the office with the good news about the enquiry into nurses' salaries, we hurriedly called the staff side together so that I could inform them before this evening's debate. I unfolded my answer: yes, there would be an enquiry, Halsbury had agreed to chair it and – bull point – the increases would be back-dated to the moment I was speaking to them. They were clearly thrilled. Even Spanswick was impressed and said he would consult his Executive Committee immediately. I then went with relish into the Chamber to listen to Howe's dirge on the state of the NHS. In my reply I played with him, developing an effective attack on the mess the Tories had got the NHS into and leaving my announcement about the enquiry to the very end. There were cheers from our side and a Tory backbencher shouted, 'Why couldn't you say so earlier', obviously furious that I had shot their fox. It was one of the more enjoyable episodes in my difficult life. And, to cap it all, tomorrow is the Whitsun recess! I am determined to have a proper break, so we have hired a boat on the Thames again. The only tragedy is that our friends, the Borhams, can't come.

Monday, 3 June

Back to work refreshed, but to bad news. Despite the speed and completeness with which I have met all that they asked, COHSE are demanding an interim payment and are bringing their members out on strike. And this a union that has never gone on strike before, the union that was expelled from the TUC for registering under the Industrial Relations Act! It makes me sick and I am determined not to give way. The nurses have already had their increases under Stage Three and are getting threshold agreements, which they just ignore. To talk about 'starvation' among their members in view of all this is tommy rot. I am determined that Halsbury's report shall make a big impact and don't intend the effects of it to be frittered away by payments on account.

Thursday, 6 June

In Blackburn I receive a local COHSE deputation only to find that the regional organizer, Eric Cooper, has horned in on it. Eric is extremely truculent, while the Blackburn lassies sit meekly silent. I am patient with them but tough with him. The next few months are going to take all my nerve as the press sensationalizes every incident in every hospital.

Sunday, 9 June

Got up early to do an hour's weeding and taking the dogs for a walk before catching my train to Swansea for the Labour women's conference. I hated leaving HCF, with its garden looking so inviting in the June sunshine, but I got through a lot of work in the train. At the Dragon Hotel I joined Harold and his retinue for a meal in Harold's suite. The PM (late, of course) was in his most relaxed mood – though cross about the Common Market article in the *Sunday Times*.[1] (I wonder who briefed them for it?) I think Harold loves power as much as anything because it enables him to play Father Christmas. He nodded approvingly in the direction of John Morris, saying to me, 'You were the making of that man and he's doing very well.' He then chuckled over the news he had just had that Joan Lestor had run into Frank Judd at Lusaka airport, where they were both on their respective official business: Joan for the Foreign Office and Frank for the Ministry of Overseas Development! Neither are the conventional PM's idea of a junior Minister, but I think it is the joker in Harold which makes him delight in promoting unexpected people – and, as in these cases, he is so often proved right. He was tickled pink when I told him I thought I had solved the dispute over the uprating by telling the unions I was going to go to the House and say I accepted that I

---

[1] A perceptive 'Insight' article in the *Sunday Times* had reported on Harold Wilson's 'calculated, consistent – and so far seemingly successful strategy ... to keep Britain in Europe, though on cheaper terms'. It detailed how the Prime Minister had composed the European Strategy Committee of Cabinet so as to leave the final word with him and Jim Callaghan and described how some 250 civil servants working on the renegotiations were producing a flow of papers to prove that one of the anti-marketeers' key demands – the need to amend the Treaty of Rome – was unnecessary.

had asked too much of my staff and that the uprating date must be delayed. It was the kind of ploy he instantly appreciated and he went into a long companionable reminiscence about how he and I had solved the railway dispute in the last Labour Government. At one point he twinkled at me: 'Don't breathe a word but by next Thursday we shall have completed our first hundred days!' The only sour note was provided by Mary, who slipped sullenly into the room without greeting anyone. She sat silent through our rushed meal, her nose in her plate. I had a sympathetic word with her in their bedroom afterwards. 'Of course I hate it,' she told me. 'But then I always have. But I do my job.' Then she added, almost as an afterthought, 'But I'm glad for Harold. He needed this. He went through such a rotten time.' Nonetheless I feel Harold has an incipient revolt on his hands in that quarter.

Monday, 10 June

Woke at 6am, still ebullient. What has come over me? A kind of liberation. John Morris had greeted me affectionately last night, saying in astonishment, 'You look younger than ever.' 'The vitamin of power,' I replied. Whatever it was it kept me going through an official visit to Reading. I developed some outrageous theories over lunch with the Director of Social Services and his chaps – but then one of them told me he had talked to Dick Crossman ten years ago when everyone was planning programmes for old people's homes. Dick had said provocatively to him, 'I wonder if people will thank us for this in ten years' time?' And they don't. So the outrageousness of today may become the wisdom of tomorrow. One great note of consolation as I was touring an assessment centre for difficult children and adolescents. The absconding rate has risen – despite the very good physical surroundings. I began to despair until I had had a hurried word with the psychiatric consultant they have at last obtained and who had come to do a case conference. 'What should we be doing?' I asked him, almost despairingly. 'What we are doing now – only more,' he replied, adding, 'If it is any consolation to you I have travelled Europe extensively and our social service provision is unparalleled.'

Back at the House I got the good news: CPSA has called off the overtime ban. So my ploy has worked.

Tuesday, 11 June

My statement in the House on the ending of the dispute was a walk-over. Osmond[1] didn't like my insistence on including a reference to the fact that relationships with the staff had been worsened by Tory policy over the past three years. Geoffrey Howe didn't like it either. But, as I said rather wildly, 'History is history and facts are facts.' I don't like Harold's dull reiteration of the virtues of this Government, as though there were no difficulties. But equally I am not going to let this Tory lot get away with the fact that their policy *did* make matters worse. I woke at 6am this morning with a sharp pain in my chest. 'This is it,' I thought and I felt pretty groggy. But I suspect that it is

---

[1] Mr M. W. M. Osmond, my department's solicitor.

merely that I have had a punishing weekend. As John Ellis once put it, I am as tough as an old boot. And anyway I would prefer to go out like a light.

At Lockets the 'Husbands and Wives' dinner was more thoughtful than usual. First Peter reported on Jim's speech in the House on Europe[1] and admitted regretfully that Jim had been extremely skilful, so that it was difficult to fault him. Nonetheless the scenario is being built up, with Harold's help, to enable us to stay in. We agreed to have a row in Cabinet about Jim's lack of consultation. I then had a bit of a row with Wedgie, whom I love but whose unctuousness about 'open government' irritates me, perhaps because I sense the ambition that motivates it. Wedgie had acted smartly in the Home Policy Committee of the NEC yesterday to get approval for the public release by Transport House of his report to the Liaison Committee with the TUC on the work of his department. He must have gone out immediately and released it to the press, because this morning the papers were full of it . . . and this afternoon Heath had been chasing Harold about it at PM's question time. Harold had fielded it loyally but I bet he is mad.[2] Wedgie told us loftily that he believed in taking the people into our confidence, etc., adding that he wasn't trying to get anyone's share of the money that was going because he wasn't allowed to do anything anyway. And tomorrow at the PLP meeting he intended to distribute copies of his industrial policy blueprint to the MPs there. I told him that he might not be trying to pinch my share of the money but he *was* trying to pinch my share of the glory. I, too, could make a great speech at PLP tomorrow about my plans, but I could only do so by embarrassing my colleagues who knew the money was not available for the expansion in public expenditure they would need. And I went into a great passionate diatribe on my old theme: my belief in the doctrine of collective responsibility. I could, for instance, have avoided all my trouble with the nurses if Mike had been able earlier to give me my independent review of nurses' pay. But I recognized that Mike had immense difficulties in moving in orderly fashion from a statutory to a voluntary incomes policy. The socialist virtue lay in knowing when one had to keep one's mouth shut.

Wedgie disarmed me when he suddenly said, completely naturally, 'But you are able to *do* things, Barbara. I am in a department where, at present at any rate, I can do nothing but talk.' I clutched his hand sympathetically. When he is honest like this I

[1] In the House that afternoon Jim Callaghan had reported on his second meeting with the Council of Ministers in Luxembourg on 4 June and had implied a considerable softening of his own attitude towards the renegotiations. In particular he stated: 'We do not propose to renegotiate the Treaties. . . . When I started out on this road I thought that it would be necessary to propose some amendments . . . But why should we go out of our way to make trouble if our objective can be secured without it?' Speaking for the Opposition front bench Mr Geoffrey Rippon welcomed this as 'a considerable advance' (Hansard 11.6.74).

[2] Tony Benn's decision to go public with his plans before he had fought them through Cabinet was to backfire on him. It created a storm in Parliament, industry and the press which his enemies in the Cabinet were to use to clip his wings. Mr Heath had been very effective in the House that day, demanding to know the constitutional position of Benn's document. 'Have the Government now handed over complete control of their policy to Transport House?' Harold Wilson's reaction was to let it be known that he would take charge of the discussions on industrial policy himself and he took over from Ted Short the chairmanship of the Cabinet Committee on Industrial Development, claiming later that he had decided to do this several weeks earlier. But neither industry nor the Tories were appeased. The questions in the House continued and Mr Ralph Bateman, new president of the CBI, announced that industry would campaign relentlessly against any further nationalization or intervention.

will back him to the hilt. And I heartily endorsed his suggestion that we ought to have a special Labour Party Conference on the Market terms before putting them to a referendum.

Wednesday, 12 June

The sharp pains have subsided, leaving me with a general tenderness around the chest and a horrible sense of nausea. Graham and Jack have become quite concerned about me and want me to take a day or two off, but there is too much on in which I am interested. If I could survive the TV programme on political advisers yesterday I could survive ordinary meetings. Graham and Jack have struck up a great friendship. Yesterday, as I got ready for the TV interview, Graham said to me, 'I must admit, Secretary of State, I was against the idea of a political adviser when you mooted it, but now I think it has worked very well.' I don't know whether to be flattered or worried by the fact that No. 10 positively insisted on the programme being done, provided it was done by *my* advisers! Jack and Brian Abel-Smith have a sensible moderation about them that would reassure any viewer. Nonetheless I find the strengthening of my political team – and our weekly lunches – invaluable. I even risked letting the BBC record our lunch discussion yesterday, on the understanding that Jack and Brian would vet the result and report to me. Jack says our discussion on butter tokens[1] has come over very well and the BBC are chuffed to have got what they consider to be a scoop. There was one delicious moment yesterday when, anxious to bring everyone in, I turned to Bob Brown and said, 'What do you think, Bob?' The wretched chap had just taken a mouthful of sandwich and went red in the face trying to swallow it quickly, while the cameras trained themselves on him. I couldn't keep my face straight: in fact, with the cameras behind my back, I laughed outright. Jack tells me the BBC has tactfully edited this bit out.

At PLP meeting this morning Wedgie insisted on doing his bit first and I was glad to let him because I wanted to see what he laid on. As promised (or threatened) last night, he had lots of copies of his statement of departmental work ready for distribution and he spoke just as he had done at the Liaison Committee with the TUC. He had an approving audience – then dashed off to look into the explosion that had just taken place at Bristol. My account of what we were working on went well. The only trouble was that there were only about thirty people there out of some three hundred Labour MPs. As Bob [Mellish] said savagely and audibly, 'This shower only turns up for a row.' Well, according to this morning's papers there will be a Tory row over Wedgie. They obviously see in the publication of his document the electoral opportunity they have been waiting for. This is the point at which we should close ranks against the crude Tory blackmail we shall be subjected to. But I wonder how Harold will react? I

---

[1] Butter tokens enabled one pound of butter per month to be bought at 9 pence per pound (later 12 pence per pound) less than the normal price. The scheme had been introduced by the European Commission in 1973 as an attempt to deal with the 'butter mountain' created by the high prices under the Common Agricultural Policy. Eligibility was restricted to those receiving means-tested benefits such as supplementary benefit and family income supplement, so many pensioners were excluded. Brian O'Malley and I strongly opposed this 'tokenization' of poverty as humiliating and niggardly. Moreover the administrative cost was out of all proportion to the benefits. We persuaded the Government to withdraw the scheme in December 1974.

am under no illusions that the right wing of the party is bitterly against the Wedgies of this world – and indeed against large parts of the Manifesto.

Meeting with the staff side of the Whitley Council section which deals with the Professions Supplementary to Medicine [PSMS][1] to discuss their request that they, too, should have an independent review instead of merely being tagged on to the nurses' increase. Mike, bless him, has turned up trumps and agreed that they can, provided it is done by Halsbury instead of Mike having to announce a succession of special reviews. I got the delegation to agree that the nurses' announcement should be made first. It was a pleasure to deal with such a gentlemanly lot. The NUPE chap told me with relish that the staff side of the Nurses and Midwives Whitley Council had yesterday rejected the demand for an interim increase for nurses. That won't restrain COHSE, which is crudely on the make for increased membership. I am astonished to find that Cronin[2] is one of the parliamentary representatives of COHSE, so he is not coming out against their militancy in the way he would come out against other militancy.

Thursday, 13 June

Still feeling sick, I soldier on. So I have paid the price for last weekend's exacting activity. Heath has really got his teeth into Wedgie, and there are great stories in the press that Harold has decided to take over the chairmanship of the Cabinet committee dealing with economic policy. Only a few of them have the grace to mention that he decided to do this as long ago as last April. Ralph Bateman, new president of the CBI, has seized on the issue to make his mark as a truculent defender of private industry. When we got to Cabinet I wondered what on earth was happening. There was a *distrait* air about the Cabinet room. Harold stood chatting to one or two people; there were no officials to be seen. Finally Harold said he had been waiting for everyone to arrive (Roy Mason and Wedgie were missing and Denis had been replaced by Joel), as he wanted us to have a discussion without officials present, but he suggested we got on to our ordinary business until the others turned up. 'Is he going to announce the election date?' I whispered to Eric. 'Looks like it,' he replied. Officials were called back in and we went through parliamentary business for next week. On Thursday the Opposition have chosen to devote a Supply day to Labour's plans for industry. Ted announced that the speakers would be Wedgie and Eric Heffer and Harold showed his first flicker of reaction to Wedgie's recent *démarche* by saying casually, 'I don't think we should be too certain of the speakers at this moment. If Heath goes in, for instance, I may have to speak myself.'

We next turned to foreign affairs and Jim gave us a circumlocutory tour of all sorts of issues in which we were not particularly interested while we waited to pounce on EEC. Mike jumped in first to say he thought we ought to have a discussion on our

---

[1] The seven professions supplementary to medicine comprise chiropody, dietetics, occupational therapy, orthoptics, physiotherapy, radiography and remedial gymnastics. Speech therapists and helpers are also covered by the NHS Professional and Technical Whitley Council 'A' and they were included in the pay review.

[2] John Cronin, a successful consultant surgeon, was not usually classed as left-wing.

111

strategy for the negotiations. I followed by saying innocently that those of us who were not on the European Committee were left in the dark over developments. We had been grateful for an opportunity to consider in Cabinet Jim's opening statement in Brussels, but his second statement in Luxembourg had been made without any consultation with Cabinet. Harold said hastily that we should postpone the discussion of this till our private session.

So I moved in on the renegotiation of the Chilean debt, on which Judith had primed me again yesterday. I said that on Tuesday the International Committee of the NEC had been told that we were about to let the Chileans off a debt of something like £70 million. If so, it meant that we were putting them in a position to buy the frigates we had said we were forced to sell them because we could not renege on contracts. Without the debt renegotiation the deal would have fallen through anyhow. Everyone smiled at that. Jim said hastily that he didn't accept responsibility, but should point out that in any case all the papers had been before Cabinet. (I don't remember any such papers, but wondered whether this was one of those items I had slipped up over due to pressure of work.) I stood my ground. The International Committee, I said, had approached the Foreign Office and been told it was a matter for the Treasury. The Committee then went to the Treasury and were told it was a matter for the Foreign Office. More laughter, and Harold said that papers should be put before Cabinet by whatever department *was* concerned. (Joel was shrugging his ignorance at me.) 'The agreement is due to be signed in the next day or so,' I warned as my final shot. Not to be outfaced, Jim then said testily that he thought Cabinet ought to know that, as a result of cancelling the sale of the Wasp to South Africa, GEC had lost an order worth seven hundred jobs, adding, 'It wasn't worth it.'[1] Harold picked him up: 'I don't necessarily agree. We have got to balance a lot of things. If we had gone ahead we could, for instance, have lost far more important orders from Nigeria.' Jim just grumbled under his breath.

At last, at 12.15 pm, we got to our private session. Harold walked circumspectly all round his theme, which seemed to be that we were doing very well as a government, that we were not 'co-ordinating' our information about our achievements sufficiently and that it might be a good idea if we had an early meeting between the Cabinet and the NEC to co-ordinate policy. I have no doubt that all this is *à propos* of Wedgie, who wasn't there. I remember now that Wedgie told the PLP meeting yesterday he was going to Blackpool today for the Post Office Engineering Union [POEU] conference. Surely Harold not only knew, but had agreed his absence from Cabinet? But whatever the purpose, it all turned out differently from what no doubt Harold had intended. Crosland complained that no one except Harold could get any press coverage anyway, however many handouts one put out. He grumbled that he had made a detailed speech on the rating problem at the NALGO conference and not a word had been used, even in *The Times*. (How I sympathize!) Then Mike took most of the remaining time with a long speech on our strategy on the EEC and Jim took the rest of it in a tetchy reply, saying (he does go feminine at times) that he refused to be

[1] Harold Wilson had announced in the Commons on 21 May that the export licence for one Westland Wasp helicopter, delivery of which to South Africa was outstanding when Labour took office, had been revoked.

hamstrung over the negotiations and that if he was going to be criticized in this way he would chuck in his hand and someone else would have a go. With a number of us trying to speak, Harold closed the meeting in some disorder, saying we should have to have a full-day meeting of Cabinet before we met the NEC. Everyone said 'Hear, hear' to that. As we were all leaving the room Jim said again to Tony Crosland, 'I shall chuck in my hand.' I turned and said mildly, 'Don't talk like that, Jim,' to which he replied, 'I mean it; I won't have this interference.' I lost my temper. 'We have a right to know.' 'Then you must find someone else,' he snapped. 'Okay,' I retorted. 'I'm ready, for one.' And I swept out.

Jim's petulance is all the more childish when one realizes what a gargantuan effort Len Murray, Jack Jones and others are making to create a reality of the Social Contract. The Economic Committee of the TUC has turned up trumps with a document[1] which, as the NALGO conference makes clear, they will have some difficulty in getting through Congress. They make Jim's tribulations look like small beer. But the real question mark is what everyone – including Mike – will do about Mick McGahey's latest demand on behalf of the miners:[2] pure market economy blackmail. Will Mike find an excuse to resign, or will his honesty and charm succeed in drawing the destructive poison out of the miners' claim? If he solves *this* one, I will acknowledge his superiority for ever.

The political row over Tony Benn's ideas continued unabated during the summer months. Tory spokesmen saw it as their major weapon in the coming election, which they feared they were going to lose. No opportunity was lost of building up Benn as a bogeyman and, for his part, he continued to make challenging speeches about his policies. On 7 June he told a Nottinghamshire miners' gala that his officials were investigating the books of the twenty biggest companies and their 4,000 subsidiaries as part of his determination to reveal the extent of public subsidies to private industry. His Tory 'shadows' took up the trail, flushed out the names of the firms concerned and started a scare that Benn was proposing to bring them all into public ownership. 'Benn widens his Grab Net', screamed the Daily Express *headline on 26 June. 'Ready to pounce on 4,000 little firms.' The* Financial Times, *while reporting Benn's claim that the investigation did not mean that the firms were listed for takeover, added that the Opposition saw the list as 'further evidence that Mr Benn is pushing ahead ominously*

[1] In its document, called 'Collective Bargaining and the Social Contract', the TUC paid tribute to the achievements of the Labour Government and called for an orderly return to voluntary collective bargaining when statutory controls were abolished. In particular it stressed that the twelve-month interval between major settlements should continue to apply. 'Over the coming year,' it added, 'negotiators generally should recognize that the scope for real increases in consumption are limited and a central negotiating objective in this period will be to ensure that real incomes are maintained.'

[2] The Scottish miners, under the militant leadership of their President, Mick McGahey, were supporting the equally militant Yorkshire miners in demanding £20-a-week pay increases. At the NUM conference in July the £20-a-week demand was narrowly defeated, but a Scottish resolution opposing all forms of incomes policy, voluntary or statutory, was carried.

fast with his interventionist plans'. Tony's announcement in July that his department was going to put money into workers' co-operatives seeking to launch a daily news-paper in Glasgow and to reopen production at the former Triumph motorcycle factory at Meriden were greeted in the press as further dangerous pieces of 'Bennery'.

Denis Healey and Harold Wilson, worried about the effects of all this on industrial confidence, rivalled each other in trying to restore the image of the Labour Party's belief in a mixed economy. In May the Chancellor assured the annual dinner of the CBI that the Government had no intention of destroying the private sector or encouraging its decay. At the end of June Harold Wilson told the Socialist International conference at Chequers that 'private industry must have the necessary confidence to maintain and increase investment'. But with labour costs rising, share prices falling and industry complaining that its cash flow had been hit by the Budget and price controls, the CBI reported that business pessimism was growing. On 22 July Denis Healey announced an interim package of measures to check the inflationary tide and the rise in un-employment. The rate of inflation, he said, had risen to 16·5 per cent, but this was not due to excessive wage increases. The TUC guidelines had stressed that wage increases should merely keep pace with price increases. This meant that the Government must do everything in its power to keep prices down, particularly as Mr Heath's threshold arrangement meant that every rise in retail prices above the threshold brought an automatic wage increase. The threshold had already been 'triggered' six times. The rise in nationalized industry prices following the Budget had added 1·5 per cent to the Retail Price Index and he now proposed to wipe out that increase in other ways. He therefore cut VAT from 10 per cent to 8 per cent, released £50 million for food subsidies and introduced £150 million of domestic rate relief. He also increased the needs allowance used for calculating rent and rate rebates and rent allowances. To help company funds he doubled the Regional Employment Premium and raised the ceiling under the price code for annual increases in dividend distribution from Mr Heath's 5 per cent to 12·5 per cent. The effect of this, he said, would be to put back into the economy the £200 million of demand he had taken out in March. But he was still not prepared to risk reflation on any dramatic scale. In fact, he claimed, money supply was now under the strictest control it had known for many years. (A month later economist Peter Jay was to complain in The Times *[23 August] that the Bank of England was superimposing a financial crisis on the economic one by contracting the money supply too quickly and too drastically.)*

In my own field the solution of one problem merely gave way to another one. The settlement of the dispute with my staff over the uprating, by the offer of extra leave rather than a cash bonus and the promise of longer-term improvements in their pay structures and conditions for which the staff had been agitating, meant that the vast majority of pensioners and others got their increases on time. The Halsbury enquiry into nurses' pay, set up on 7 June, had lost no time in starting work. Later it agreed to undertake a similar enquiry into the pay of radiographers and other groups 'sup-plementary to medicine'. It promised that the report on them would follow as quickly as possible after the nurses' one and here again the Treasury had agreed to back-date the increases to 23 May. But this did not satisfy some of the unions – notably COHSE and ASTMS [Association of Scientific, Technical and Management Staff]. They launched a widespread campaign, backed by industrial action in a number of hospitals, to force the Government to pay an interim increase. I was entirely at one with Lord Halsbury in resisting this, agreeing with him that the first ever thorough evaluation of nurses' pay must not be jeopardized. But with protest action spreading and Lord Halsbury's committee refusing to be hustled, the situation became increasingly dangerous.

Disruption in the Health Service was spreading to other fronts. Every section of the service was joining the clamour for higher pay. On 11 June consultants and other hospital doctors in the BMA, meeting in national conference, called for mass resignations from the NHS unless their Review Body came up with a big pay increase and unless the Owen working party, which I had set up, reached speedy agreement on a new contract for senior staff. Urged on by the chairman of their negotiating committee, Mr Anthony Grabham, they called on the BMA to set up its own employment agency to hire their services back to the hospitals if mass resignations became necessary. Meanwhile the undercurrent of discontent among the health service unions over the issue of pay beds erupted at Charing Cross Hospital. This time it was NUPE that took the lead. The new £16 million teaching hospital, completed in 1972, included a private wing on the fifteenth floor – the penthouse suite. Feeling against the privileged services provided in the private wing – built by NHS funds – had been running high among the non-medical staff, from nurses to porters, fed by the discontent over pay, particularly among low-paid workers like kitchen staff and hospital orderlies. The local NUPE branch at the hospital, representing this group and 1,000 strong, was led by Mrs Esther Brookstone, a medical secretary, soon known to the press as the 'battling grannie' for her fight to close the private wing. At the beginning of July the union worked out a compromise with the Area Health Authority [AHA] under which for the time being the private patients would be transferred to general ward beds, releasing private wing beds for NHS patients, with only emergency private cases being admitted from then on. Some consultants objected and the BMA stepped in. Mrs Brookstone gave the AHA till 4 July to carry out the compromise. Otherwise all domestic, laundry, portering and engineering services would be withdrawn from the private wing. The media portrayed her in fighting mood: 'Give in ... or we will starve patients out', the Daily Mail reported her as saying on 2 July. The BMA threatened retaliation. There were questions in the House. The AHA panicked and the problem landed in my lap. Meanwhile sporadic action against pay beds was being taken in other hospitals.

The Charing Cross dispute turned the pay beds issue into one of urgency. With the Government admonishing the unions to leave the phasing out of pay beds to Parliament, it was clear that the necessary legislation ought to be in the next Queen's Speech. Discussions in the department, therefore, were intensified.

Friday, 14 June

A whole-day conference at the department to discuss the proposals the Brians have worked out for our long-term pension proposals. Sick as I still am, I managed to enjoy it – and, I think, master it. There were about thirty of them round my table and I encouraged them all to come in. Gradually they found their tongues and we had a full, vigorous discussion. No one was in favour of going back to the Keith Joseph scheme, though some clearly thought our proposals were too generous to women. It looks as if Brian A-S. is right when he says that the younger members of the department are keen to go for a modified Crossman scheme. Peter Brown, who sat stolidly at the far end of the table, clearly is. He told me recently that he had always been a Conservative, but voted Labour at the last election, not least because he thought the K.J. scheme was criminally inadequate.

Down at last to HCF and a weekend of peace.

Sunday, 16 June

One of those idyllic June weekends when the sun shines and the garden is still fresh with colour. I have crawled around, amazingly weak after my tummy trouble (which still rumbles), but I have enjoyed my inertia. Lunch on the terrace *à la Continentale*. A happy day on Sunday when Ted fetched Mother over for lunch. She sat singing on the terrace and my conscience was at rest about her.

Monday, 17 June

Graham tells me that – as I thought – there has been *no* paper put to Cabinet previously on renegotiation of Chilean debt. Harold has also circulated a Personal Minute, clearly directed at Wedgie, stressing that 'Ministerial speeches must be kept within the ambit of *approved* Government policy and should not anticipate decisions not yet made public'. That would circumscribe me as well as Wedgie!

We are all shaken by the news of a bomb at the House. It went off in a room above a corner of Westminster Hall and fortunately there was only one person hurt. By a fluke my secretary, Alison, had come in early and was just crossing over to Lyons for a coffee at 8.30am when it went off. Naturally it has made everyone feel insecure. If the Price sisters had died I would have no doubt that the women members of the Cabinet would have been at serious risk.[1]

In the afternoon I was called to a meeting of Ministerial Economic Committee to discuss threshold agreements. Denis said inflation was worse than we had thought. It looked as though there would be twelve triggers under the threshold by the end of the year, adding £5 a week to wages. What role did we think these agreements should play in a voluntary policy? Mike was worried by the fact that there were seven to eight million workers not covered by such agreements who therefore would not get their increases automatically. Harold Wilson replied that we should have trouble with the low-paid workers, whatever we did about this. In reply to a question by me he expounded Harold Lever's 'new macro-economics': borrow abroad (we are already

[1] Dolours and Marian Price, who were serving life sentences for their part in the IRA bomb attacks in London, had gone on hunger strike to try to force the Home Secretary, Roy Jenkins, to transfer them from Brixton to a Northern Ireland prison. The IRA had warned that it would exact 'just retribution' if either of the sisters died. On 7 June they had been persuaded to end their strike. Later they were moved to Durham and in March 1975 were transferred to Armagh jail in response to the ceasefire in Ulster.

borrowing £3,000 million).[1] Threshold payments must affect prices, so we should subsidize the cost of living on a massive scale. Roy surprised me by saying there was a sense in which Lever was right, because if you have massive price rises and hold back wage increases you create a slump. We were in a new situation – on the edge of hyperinflation – and therefore needed a new approach. It was clear to me that, however much Denis may have complained about thresholds being a millstone round his neck, we are not going to drop them: we daren't. But what worries me is that those workers who receive them consider them as a kind of bonus and promptly discount them when it comes to wage bargaining. That is what is happening with the nurses and the rest currently demanding interim payments. They just scoff when I remind them they have had their thresholds.

Tuesday, 18 June

Another meeting of the Ministerial Economic Committee, this time to discuss the future of the review bodies.[2] I was astonished to read the Department of Employment paper recommending that the three review bodies should continue their independent activity and should proceed with 'substantive' reviews. (I can see the BMA seizing on *that*!) The paper said it was recognized that the Royal Commission on Incomes 'would infringe on the area of activity of the Top Salaries Review Body [TSRB]', but meanwhile it could continue its work on the basis of comparability. I was equally astonished that Mike was not there. If he had been he would have heard that a number of us were worried. After all Mike's efforts to interfere with the doctors' thresholds under Halsbury it amazes me that he has given up the fight to bring all top salaries into line more quickly. I asked what was meant by 'substantive' reviews and was told it meant thorough reassessment of their salaries in the light of a voluntary policy. I just can't see myself holding the doctors' salaries now. I grumbled: 'This tail is now wagging the dog', but I was overruled.

Graham is being promoted and I have to find a new Private Secretary. Graham is pushing his friend, Norman Warner, whom I interview and rather like. I don't intend to be pushed, even though I think I'll go for Norman, who was a junior in Private Office in Dick Crossman's time and said he found it very exciting. But I tell Graham firmly that I do not intend to let him go till the House rises. I need an experienced chap to help me through the storms ahead.

'Husbands and Wives' dinner at Lockets was a restricted affair: no Wedgie. I am afraid we dealt with him rather critically in his absence; Mike in particular is furious

[1] In fact, I was wrong. The $2½ billion loan announced by the Chancellor on 26 March had not been drawn on by June 1974.

[2] For the Top Salaries Review Body see footnote to page 105. The other two independent review bodies were for the Armed Forces under the chairmanship of Mr H. W. Atcherley and the Doctors and Dentists Review Body under Lord Halsbury, which dealt with the pay of consultants, other hospital doctors, GPs and dentists working for the NHS. In its report of June 1974, the DDRB had recommended that threshold arrangements should be introduced for all doctors and dentists in the NHS. Michael Foot had been resisting this but, as I believed these groups were by no means overpaid, I had been fighting him successfully and the threshold payments were made. 'Substantive' reviews to give these groups the large increases we were resisting for other people were, however, a different matter.

with him for pushing his plan for a special conference of the party on the EEC terms. Mike is obsessed with the need to win the next election and is bitterly opposed to anything that might disrupt the party before then – and is therefore bitter about Wedgie. What interests me is how imperious Mike becomes in these discussions, getting positively irritable. But I don't object: I welcome the fact that Mike has developed such authoritativeness.

Wednesday, 19 June

Snatched an hour off in the evening to go to the wedding of the Teelocks' daughter: a Hindu ceremony at the Commonwealth Institute. Very colourful and posh. The Mauritians were full of our suggested visit there in August, so it looks as though it is on. Got back to the House in time for Denis's winding up on the £10 million clause of the Finance Bill, on which the Tories, goaded by our jeers on their phoney war, have threatened to beat us at last. Denis made one of his most effective knockabout speeches and we were all in a high state of excitement when the vote came. When the tellers announced our defeat there was a roar of delight from our benches. I sat on the front bench clapping my hands exuberantly and crying, 'Election, election!' The Tories looked more frightened at their own recklessness than elated by their success and Carr's tepid intervention brought more jeers from our side. There was no doubt who *felt* they were the top dogs.[1]

Thursday, 20 June

The papers are full of our 'technical' defeat in the House last night. No one seems to think the Tories covered themselves with glory. At Cabinet we discussed Mike's two memoranda on the transition to a voluntary pay policy. He was warm in praise of the TUC draft statement on the principles to be followed in collective bargaining and said he hoped the General Council would approve it in time for it to be issued by 26 June. We agreed with him that it would be better for the TUC to issue it unilaterally, though the Government should make a statement at the same time welcoming it. The difficulty, as always, is going to be how to apply the policy in the public field. Obviously the Government must follow the TUC guidelines as far as its own employees are concerned, but we must be careful not to apply it *more* toughly than it is applied in the private field. Shirley made dire noises about the threat of inflationary pressures if the unions didn't toe the line. I suspect that she and Reg Prentice in particular yearn for statutory controls, but the rest of us have no doubt that our only hope is to try the voluntary way.

Friday, 21 June

Off for an official visit to Kettering hospital *en route* for a weekend of political speaking engagements. It was a hot and exacting tour but I sailed through it, taking all the lobbying by the different groups of staff in my stride. On my arrival, closely

[1] The clause was successfully reinserted in the Finance Act 1975.

trailed by press and TV, I saw a small, rather pathetic little group at the door, standing silently carrying a banner: 'They won't show you the laundry.' I promptly broke ranks and went over to have a little chat with them, saying of course I would call in at the laundry. (Later I did so and found that it was old and inadequate. The chap who had been leading the lobby linked arms with me affectionately.) During my tour a group of nurses were waiting to hand me a letter. It merely said the patients wanted them to get more pay. I held a little meeting, gathering them round me. 'Do you realize that you have already got an increase?' I asked them. They shook their heads, bewildered. 'Well,' I said, 'you have. The Government has already agreed to accept the report of the independent review body and to back-date your increase to 23 May. So you are entitled to it *now*. We are only waiting for Lord Halsbury to put a figure on it.' They dispersed, astonished. Finally, in the radiography department, the chief radiographer said cheekily, 'Will you sign our petition? All the patients have.' I felt like saying that patients will sign absolutely anything. Instead I replied, 'Why not? You are going to get your increase.' Altogether a very successful afternoon. The regional chairman was all over me. 'I cannot tell you how much you have done for morale.'

Monday, 24 June

Liaison Committee with TUC met in sombre mood, only deepened by that sombre panelling at Congress House. H.W. sent apologies. So did Hughie Scanlon, Willie Simpson and George Smith. Also Alex Kitson. But Jack was there, brooding with his usual stern intensity. Our business was to discuss the TUC document 'Collective Bargaining and the Social Contract'. It was already approved by their Economic Committee and due to go to the General Committee this week. As Alf Allen pointed out from the chair, the document was not brought to us for endorsement. At first we hesitated to comment, till Ron Hayward blundered in to say that, with an election imminent, he wished there would be more speeches from the trade union side about their contribution to the Social Contract. They looked hurt: they had obviously expected a warmer welcome than this. David Basnett and others pointed out that helpful speeches never received any publicity, though plenty were being made. Jack retorted huffily that we were bound to have 'exaggerated' wage claims – e.g., the miners' and engineers'. Many speeches, he said, were being made from the trade union side but, by and large, 'the press and TV don't want to know'. He thought the document was a 'pretty good trade union response'. It wasn't just a question of the size of wage claims but, even more important from an inflation point of view, 'how far we can reduce the number of disputes'. And he added earnestly, 'We are genuinely trying to make a contribution to the reduction of tension.' At this things began to warm up. Mike described the document as 'a very fine response; the TUC has been carrying out the Social Contract', unlike the CBI which, having originally been pressing for the removal of statutory controls, was now trying to get the Government to enforce the twelve-month rule by law. Of course he had told them it wasn't on. He did not believe there was any need for a wages explosion to take place.

Denis was equally encouraging. He had just returned from Washington and had

119

found that confidence in the British economy was far greater abroad than it was at home. He thought the OECD forecast of our deficit was excessive, though he had always known it would be about £3,500 million.[1] Despite the steps he had taken that was unavoidable. Our central problem was still inflation: it would be 20 per cent by the end of the year. 'Wages have not played a major part in inflation this year,' he said. There were, however, some signs that commodity prices were falling, so the key to inflation next year would be the attitude we took to wage claims. 'If the unions stick to these guidelines we could begin to reduce the rate of inflation next year.' How far was the TUC envisaging having monitoring machinery? This brought in Alf Allen to explain the objections: 'If you set up machinery for monitoring wage claims you make it look as if wages alone are responsible for inflation.' He was backed by David Basnett (and later by Len Murray), who said that the TUC preferred to do the monitoring *ad hoc*, seeing individual unions: 'That is all that is politically viable.' Sid [Greene] echoed this: 'It is no use asking me to come and talk to the TUC about resolutions on pay that I know will be passed at my conference next week.' All they could do was to try to ensure that settlements would be reasonable. Jack pointed out that the difficulty about trying to revive even the TUC voluntary vetting machinery was that the TUC was then forced to make a judgment about amount. 'Someone comes with an 87 per cent claim which we say is excessive. So, they say, would 50 per cent be more reasonable? And then go out and say we have approved 50 per cent.' I must say I thought the trade unions had the best of this argument.

I asked what the TUC would suggest we did about special cases like the nurses', which couldn't be dealt with under the heading of productivity. Jack brushed this aside: of course there must be some flexibility and the Government would just have to judge each case as it arose, as they did now. I also put in a plea for the trade unions to help us stress the importance of the social wage which was so important for the workers' quality of life. It was working men and women, I pointed out, who suffered from the length of the NHS waiting lists – like those described to me by the Ear, Nose and Throat [ENT] consultant at the weekend during my visit to Kettering Hospital. Because working families could not jump the queue it was their children's hearing that might be permanently impaired. Jack said stiffly that of course they appreciated the importance of the social services (but in fact the reference to them in the document is derisory).

Jim then came in, all ingratiating urbanity. The document, he said, was the complete fulfilment of all we expected from the TUC. 'I regard this as one of the historic documents of the TUC.' He added that he did not think anyone in the year ahead could expect to do more than maintain his standard of living. Public expenditure was therefore a great problem. And he added mournfully, 'Not a very good election background, I'm afraid.' At this Mikardo interjected, to my surprise, 'I'm not so sure.' (The reasonableness of my left-wing colleagues these days is remarkable. Is it that we have learned from experience, or merely that we are all older?) Wedgie further surprised me by suggesting that in future we should widen the wages

---

[1] In its Economic Outlook published in July the OECD forecast that Britain's current account deficit in the balance of payments would be £4,000 million for 1974. In the event the deficit was £3,565 million.

discussion in nationalized industries to include the investment programmes and the prices implications of wages claims. 'The Social Contract should be presented as a way of getting workers to accept a greater commitment to the success of the industries in which they work.' (There's collaboration for you! And there were murmurs of approval even from Jack!) Mik followed him even more moderately. 'If, as I believe, our battle over the next few years is to maintain standards, not improve them, we should say so. I don't believe it would be electorally disadvantageous for us to say this in the election. We must use this document to say that this is the only way we can maintain our standards.'

So on this harmonious note we broke up, considerably cheered with the demonstrations of goodwill between us. Denis, who is really doing very well these days, said realistically that he didn't expect the unions to stick to the guidelines all the time. I urged that we politicians should now go out and proclaim our faith in the Social Contract and so counteract the orchestrated alarmism we would increasingly meet on every side.

Couldn't be in the House to hear Harold make his statement about that nuclear warhead test.[1] Jim this morning denies any knowledge of it. 'It is the PM's sphere and he plays these matters close to his chest.' It is a relief to know that the test is in the past, but appalling that these things can be done without the knowledge of Cabinet. Despite Harold's low-key explanation there will be a row in Cabinet on Thursday. On TV tonight Roy Mason gave one of his disastrous performances; he's another Dick Marsh and his insensitive effort will merely exacerbate the party's mood.

Tuesday, 25 June

The press – and the Tories – are in full cry after Wedgie. I am in no doubt that, however irritated I may be about his political pretentiousness, I must back him publicly. Every one of us is going to be under distorted attack in turn. Divided we fall. I was sorry our weekly dinner was cancelled. There is a lot to discuss.

Wednesday, 26 June

Teddy's day. I had told the office weeks ago that they must keep this afternoon as free as possible so that I could do full honours for him at his induction into the Lords. In the event there was an NEC this morning. Conscious that I had to attend Ted's lunch today, and sit on the steps of the throne while he was introduced (to say nothing of the photos), I got up early to have my hair done and arrived late at the NEC. Bob and others said approvingly, 'You've been to the hairdressers.' To which I replied, 'This is Ted's day and I shan't be able to stay for all these Motions that have been pouring in.' Ted was terribly nervous when I left home and I secretly prayed for him. Ideologically I hate the House of Lords but, as a wife, I know what this means for Ted and I

[1] Harold Wilson told an astonished Commons that a nuclear test had taken place a few weeks earlier. This, he said, had been arranged by the previous Government and was necessary to maintain the effectiveness of Britain's nuclear deterrent. But, he assured the House, it had been conducted fully within the provisions of both the partial test ban and the non-proliferation treaties.

don't intend to let anything spoil it. It is his great chance to take part in Parliament and it is a poor socialism that leaves no room for the illogicalities of love.

At the NEC Wedgie had tabled a Motion calling for a special conference of the party to discuss the renegotiated terms for the EEC and to pronounce on them before the issue was put in a referendum. Denis seized an early opportunity to say he couldn't stay to the end and hoped the NEC would not discuss Wedgie's Motion before there was a chance to consider it at a full Executive. I passed Wedgie a note saying that I, too, would have to be absent when his Motion was discussed and I hoped he would accept Denis's suggestion. (In the event I learned later that he did.)

The routine business seemed to take a lot of time. On the International Committee Mik raised the question of Chile. He explained how the Committee had instructed him to meet both the Treasury and the Foreign Secretary. At the Treasury they were told that Denis was in Washington, but they saw Edmund Dell. 'I must say we were a bit shocked by this meeting,' he went on. 'It could have been any Tory Minister.' He added tactfully that he didn't blame Edmund, who clearly didn't know anything about it and was talking to his official brief. They had still not been able to get a meeting with any FO Minister but on 13 June they had been able to see the PM. When they did so they had been relieved to learn that this matter had already been raised in Cabinet that morning and that a decision had been held up. (Mik has already given me a warm kiss about this: how he learned that I raised it at Cabinet I will never know.) It was clear, he continued, that, contrary to what we had been told, these frigates had *not* been 'bought and paid for'. He concluded by asking, 'Will we ever get to know what has been done?' It was I who suggested that we should write to the PM expressing our anxiety and asking that we be kept informed. This was agreed *nem. con.*

All this took place in the context of a rather roving but restless discussion about the refusal of certain Ministers to keep in contact with the NEC. Some of us were given general clearance – but not Jim. Mik was caustic about the fact that the Foreign Secretary did not attend the International Committee meetings, but sent his political adviser (Tom McNally), who merely stalled. So far the relations with the Government are remaining intact, though fragile. The NEC is still bristling with sensitivity. It being noon I slipped away, faithful to my promise to Ted. Mik told me afterwards that Frank Allaun's emergency resolution regretting the nuclear text explosion, and calling for an end to all such explosions by the Government, was carried without dissent.

Back to the House to powder my nose. Got to Ted's lunch drinks just on time. I was more fussed for Ted by now than he was himself. All I cared about was that my Teddy should do well, and the whole thing came alive for me when we met up with the family in the lobby just before the affair began. I swept the children into my arms and into Moses room where Great Uncle Ted was robing. The badge messengers in the Lords are so charming and friendly that I realized the insidious attraction of the place. (I'll have to keep Ted's feet on the ground with some of my usual acerbity.) Ted was taking it all terribly seriously, but broke off long enough from his staged photo with me to get most of the children into a group with him. Then into the Lords, where Ted carried the whole thing off with dignity and confidence. Finally a super tea with the children (*real* cream cakes in their Lordships' House!) and a lot of fun. One of the highlights was when I took the girls into the Peeresses' loo, where they were enthralled with the pedestal lavatory with its flowered china pan and brass handle. They all pinched pieces of House of Lords writing paper as souvenirs.

Thursday, 27 June

I have agreed to do a programme on the NHS for *This Week* which involves my facing a panel of critics from all sides of the profession, and the department is in a positive tizzy about it. They get me into the office early for a briefing on it before Cabinet. I am determined not to get bogged down in too much detail, but find Jack Straw's material very useful. (He's good, that lad. I like him more and more.) He has unearthed a report by McKinsey on comparative health care in different countries out of which this country comes pretty well: nearly at the bottom of the league on expenditure, but well up the league in effective health care. At Cabinet Harold warned us that we were in for a period of intensive work: Cabinets twice a week, as there were a lot of policy decisions to be taken before the summer recess. We all know what that means: White Papers must be got out before the election. I have been struck how effectively Harold has been delegating work in this Government. It has been a joy to have brief and comparatively infrequent Cabinets which have largely endorsed what has been thrashed out in committees or by letter, with Harold forgoing his passion for making running chat on every subject. I pointed out that we might be defeated on the pensions Motion[1] next week but that I didn't intend to concede the setting up of a Select Committee.

Mike raised the question of nuclear tests, saying he had written to Harold asking for a paper on how, when and why the decision to hold a test had been reached without the knowledge of Cabinet. He wanted a proper discussion of the whole question. Said Harold: 'I only got your message last night when I got back. It has always been the convention of Cabinet that certain things are not discussed in Cabinet: for example, the 1967 nuclear tests. No policy decision has been taken on these tests. That decision has got to be taken by Cabinet when we get the Defence Review, which will be a very fundamental reappraisal. If we had refused to do this test we would have been closing an option. I could not consult Cabinet because a leak of any kind would have very serious effects for reasons I can't give now.' It was the old argument and it didn't convince Mike. He continued to press the matter. 'This is an extremely unsatisfactory position. The question whether a policy decision is involved is for us to decide. Many of us have been put in a terrible position of defending a policy decision in which we had no part.' Bob came to Mike's support. '*I* too had reacted as Chief Whip. This is really an entirely different kind of thing from anything before.' Even Reg Prentice expressed concern, while I pointed out that the French didn't seem to need all this secrecy: they just calmly announced their tests were

[1] The Opposition had tabled a Motion deploring my 'arbitrary decision' not to bring Sir Keith Joseph's Reserve Pension Scheme into operation and calling on me to refer 'any proposals for subsequent improvement of that scheme' to an all-party committee. I moved an amendment endorsing the Government's actions on pensions. The amendment was carried by 282 votes to 280.

taking place. To my surprise Jim then backed us. 'I must say I do see substance in what Michael, Barbara and Reg say. We should examine the extent to which we need to have secrecy.' Faced with this unexpected united front, Harold climbed down. 'I agree that the Ministers concerned should get together to look at the need for secrecy. And there will be no further tests until Cabinet has reviewed defence policy.' Quite a victory!

We next turned to Concorde. Wedgie never gives up and Elwyn reported that Wedgie was now trying to by-pass Cabinet's previous decision, maintaining that a number of events had occurred which put cancellation out of the question. Wedgie wanted permission, if the French showed any sign of resisting cancellation, to go ahead with the sixteen without any further reference to Cabinet. Harold backed Wedgie by saying that he had talked to Chirac [the French Prime Minister] in Brussels yesterday (who incidentally wants to defer progress on the channel tunnel). He had taken the opportunity to ask Chirac non-committally what the French reaction would be to cancellation of Concorde and Chirac had replied tersely, 'Négatif'. It was clear he would resist strongly. Harold therefore suggested that the Ministers concerned should now prepare the brief for his meeting with Giscard on the basis that we were *not* going forward with cancellation, the brief to come back to Cabinet before his meeting with the President. Jim agreed. Denis grumbled. 'We must seek to limit our financial commitment to the utmost possible.' (Chirac has been talking of building two hundred planes!) Roy [Jenkins] thought the decision was 'absolutely disastrous' and I was amused when he added, 'The French get their way to an alarming extent.' Even Shirley said, 'I can't see why we give the French everything they want without asking them for what we want in return.' Denis chipped in sourly: 'What if the French say "négatif" on the CAP?' Wedgie wasn't to be deterred: we should be guided by 'simple common sense', he said, i.e. his constituency considerations, I suppose! Harold said it was sensible to bring all these issues together at the same time and so it was left. Tony [Crosland] then told us that the battle with the building societies over mortgages is still running on. They are threatening to raise the lending rate by a half per cent and the Ministerial Committee had agreed to try to persuade them to run down their reserves instead, against a Government guarantee.

Monday, 1 July

At our Ministerial lunch we discussed the special advisers on Community Health Councils. The office never liked the idea, but David (Owen) and Brian A-S. cooked it up between them and I see no objection to it. David reported however that there was some feeling among our own people that we were not giving enough emphasis to the role of the local authorities and he thought one of the advisers should be from local government. Alf suggested Ken Collis of Manchester, and we agreed he should be approached, but, because Philip Rogers has got touchy about our doing these things behind his back, I said he must be informed first. After all, as overall manager of the department, he has his rights. (This is the only real snag we have run into with officials about our meetings; on the whole they now accept them philosophically.) As for

Graham and Private Office, they collaborate fully and without reservation, even circulating agendas and papers for us. Jack Straw has started producing Minutes of these meetings and it was his idea that copies should be sent to Private Office. This has eased things along. (We even have officials now proposing items for us to discuss!)

In the afternoon Brian O'Malley and I had our hands full in the House. He took the Social Security Amendment Bill through its stages and successfully beat off what could have been an awkward attack. After all, the main point of the Bill is to put up contribution rates and Brian is a tower of strength. He has absolute mastery in this field and is very good at the dispatch box. Moreover I can trust his judgment and know he will foresee all the snags for me. We then moved on to the Motion of Censure against me for not proceeding with the Tory Reserve Pension Scheme. Bob was anxiously anticipating another defeat for us and told me to prepare the appropriate form of words for when it happened. I even had to check up on the constitutional position and was mightily relieved to learn that a Motion of this kind had no statutory force. In the event all went swimmingly. I was in good form and laid about me with a will, hardly using a note. Ted, in the gallery, said it was the best debating speech he had ever heard me make. The only snag was that there were only about ten people in the House. Just my luck! Brian made a first-class winding-up speech. We went home feeling mightily pleased with ourselves. I think it was one of the few debates that really changed people's minds.

Tuesday, 2 July

At Cabinet we agreed Merlyn's White Paper on Northern Ireland without any argument. I was interested when Jim said, 'I haven't read any of my Cabinet papers.' So I'm not the only one who sometimes slips up! Eric then painstakingly outlined his draft statement on North Sea oil.[1] He is a nice chap (Tommy is full of praise for how 'nice' he is); he is also able, not very ideological and will never set the Thames on fire. I was particularly concerned over the renegotiation of existing contracts and Denis outlined a series of fearsome fiscal measures he has in mind, including an Excess Revenue Tax, designed to persuade the companies to negotiate participation agreements. The trouble is to present this in ways that won't violate international law or give Heath a chance to say we are damaging the prospects of getting oil by being 'confiscatory'. Altogether it seemed a pretty good statement to me, and Harold was clearly anxious for us to be seen to be honouring party policy.

We next moved to our long-promised discussion on the progress of Jim's negotiations with the EEC. Jim made a long defensive statement which Mike countered with a critical one. I thought Peter was most impressive when he pointed out we couldn't continue to drift over participation in Community policies pending renegotiation, as on 1 January we were supposed to introduce tariff changes which would concede some of our basic principles. In 1975, too, the whole basis of the budgetary

[1] In our election Manifesto we had said we would ensure 'not only that the North Sea and Celtic Sea oil and gas resources are in full public ownership, but that the operation of getting and distributing them is under full Government control with majority public participation'.

contribution would be changed. He maintained we must make it known now that we would not move along these lines until a satisfactory basis of renegotiation had been agreed. Jim got tetchy about this, and a lot of us were bursting to speak. As it was 1.15pm Harold said we must resume the discussion next time.

The 'Husbands and Wives' dinner at Charing Cross Hotel was a tetchy affair, too – Mike almost snarling at Wedgie from time to time. When Wedgie started saying darkly that Jim and others were heading for a coalition, Mike told him not to be 'hysterical'. The most important thing was the election. 'We must win it with the people we disagree with.' When John Silkin said gloomily, 'By the time the next election comes the whole of the atmosphere is going to be in favour of a coalition', adding that Jim was in favour of one, Mike snapped, 'You have been wrong every time. The idea of Jim going into a coalition is a washout.' To change the subject Peter asked Thomas [Balogh] if he thought we were going to be in an economic crisis before long. Thomas replied, 'No one can answer that. Arab money is accumulating in London at £300 million annually. The situation is now almost inconceivably dangerous. The only person who has been acting in a constructive way is Harold Lever. You will all be terribly lucky if your spending programmes are not cut.' When I chipped in sadly with 'I *am* cut – in the NHS', it was my turn to get the rough side of Mike's tongue. 'Don't listen to her,' he almost shouted. 'Quash her.' I am fascinated by Mike's current mood. He is so passionately dedicated to the success of the Government that it is as if his nerves are on edge about it. (Mind you, he has bullied me affectionately all the time I have known him.)

Wedgie then unveiled his plot to bring the EEC issue before a special party conference and Mike got very ratty with him. 'There is no difficulty about having a breach between the party and the Government. There is no difficulty at all,' he snapped. 'But the whole question is whether you can win the election. If we win the election we are in a very powerful position. I can see that the matter is being rushed and I am not opposed to the suggestion, but we must take into account how we win the election and although we can have great rows on this it is not necessarily the right way to go about it.' Said Wedgie, 'If we win the election by twenty seats that is no better.' Judith: 'If Jim and Fred [Peart] are going ahead as they are doing, that is certainly the recipe for confrontation.' Peter: 'I certainly don't want a row before the election if it can be avoided. What matters is that we enter the negotiations in a more serious way.' I supported them and Mike was almost isolated. He said rather more emolliently, 'It is not easy to see how we can bring this to a head. I agree Jim would like a different outcome from what Peter or I would like. After the election we have a real chance of winning the party on this matter. If a complete anti-Market resolution is carried at conference, it is not an election winner.' Peter for his part insisted that if we went further on the road we were going over the EEC it would be impossible to come back. We broke up late, Mike still muttering about Wedgie.

Wednesday, 3 July

The papers are full of Ma Brookstone's activities against private patients at Charing Cross Hospital. The department is all for keeping out of it and leaving it to the Area

Health Authority, but my bet is that Geoffrey Howe will try to make capital out of it through a Private Notice Question. So I set off for an official visit to Leybourne Grange Mental Hospital, expecting to be called back – and so it proves. I have to cut the tour short and leave behind a tempting buffet lunch, making do with a few sandwiches in the car. A quick confab in the office over the draft officials have prepared, which David [Owen] and I find far too moralistic and admonitory. We tone it down and make it clear that we sympathize with the aims of the agitators, though not their methods. Despite this my reply goes smoothly and I get a cheer from our side as I say emphatically that it is our policy to phase private practice out of NHS hospitals. It is astonishing how a simple statement of principle heartens our own lads, who get disheartened by the cautious conditionals in so many ministerial statements. Then to Xavier for a hair-do and a quick appearance on TV, where I repeat our policy.

Hurriedly I dress in my décolleté for Jim Callaghan's annual diplomatic banquet at the Royal Naval College, Greenwich. I haven't normally much time or inclination for these dress-up do's, but I have always wanted to see the painted ceiling there. I am not disappointed. I like the long low-ceilinged entrance corridor, all white, and the banqueting chamber itself is magnificent. I find myself on the high dais next to the Dutch ambassador, whom I try to pump about his country's attitude to the renegotiation of the Chilean debt – without much success. Jim makes a brief, relaxed and highly competent after-dinner speech to that glittering audience. His poise in these matters is remarkable. (Harold would have written every word of it.) Our programmes warn us that after the meal there will be the Beating of the Retreat, but does *not* warn us that it will be out of doors on a bitterly cold July evening. Judith and I, both bare-shouldered, huddle under my flimsy stole in the evening air, with Ted's arm round us, as the Royal Marines wheel and weave and drum backwards and forwards across the grass between the two wings of that elegant building against a darkly clouded sky. We have probably caught pneumonia but it is worth it. Ted and I are suckers for history. The navy insist on pouring strong drinks down us afterwards and we are late away. It is a poor heart....

Thursday, 4 July

Of course the BMA are after me because I refuse to condemn the NUPE lads and lasses at Charing Cross in the unequivocal terms they demand. And the press join in. That I can take, but there are signs of panic from the AHA. First I have to accommodate Cabinet. Harold returned to his favourite theme that we weren't doing enough to put our policy across and that we must all make more speeches, adding to my surprise, 'Barbara has a very high rating.' This irritated Crosland, who returned to *his* favourite theme: that it was no good any of us putting out press statements because the only one of us who got reported was Harold. It was an 'absolute waste of time'. Wedgie informed us that he took the precaution of tape recording all his public speeches as a protection against the sort of distortion he had had over his speech to the AEU. When Harold assured him that that speech had been 'unexceptionable', Wedgie said with mock meekness, 'Thank you very much. Can I have that in writing?' Jim concluded the discussion on a plaintive note. 'No one ever asks *me* to go on TV.'

We then returned to our great debate on the EEC. (I was interested to see from Cabinet Minutes later that this was considered so sensitive as to be 'recorded separately' and so not circulated.) Denis opened with an attack on Wedgie. 'What is the purpose of this discussion? Here we have Tony Benn last night ostentatiously abstaining on his own front bench against a "take note" vote on the EEC regulations.'[1] Harold added severely, 'For a Cabinet Minister to abstain on a PM's Motion is quite intolerable. But we will deal with this when I receive the Chief Whip's report.' But Wedgie wasn't going to take this lying down. 'Every single member round this table abstained last night,' he snapped, 'because none of them appeared.' He went on to argue that we had got into a muddle over how to handle the Scrutiny Committee debates, but Bob snapped back at him, 'Everyone knew it was a one-line whip. But in the event there was a vote. You were there and you are a Cabinet Minister.' Wedgie was really cornered by now. 'I deeply resent the fact that my colleagues were gallivanting at Greenwich. If votes are to acquire political significance, Cabinet must take a view.' It wasn't a very convincing case and Jim said mournfully, 'I am conscious all the time that Tony Benn isn't co-operating. Although my office asked for a statement of what he was proposing to say on the Regional Fund we did not get one.' Wedgie retorted hotly, 'When Hansard is read Jim will see that I did not put a foot wrong.'

It was interesting that Wedgie got no support from anyone on his behaviour last night. Mike obviously thinks he is obsessed with ambition. The rest of us, who are on his side on policy, are getting a bit sick of his clear determination to strike attitudes publicly whenever he can, regardless of our old friend collective responsibility. Wedgie therefore went on to widen the argument. He claimed that he fully supported what the Manifesto said about renegotiation but he didn't believe that renegotiation would achieve the Manifesto's aims. 'Membership is deeply damaging to Britain's interests. Control of the steel industry has passed from this country: on prices, for example. Shipbuilding capacity and investment could not be engaged in without the consent of the Community. The responsibility of Parliament is undermined.' Harold intervened coldly. 'You reject the Manifesto.'

After the row the contributions of the rest of us seemed mild, though I was interested to hear Reg Prentice express some doubts. 'I fully support Jim,' he said, 'although I was originally opposed to entry. My only doubt arises from a conversation I had in Brussels on an educational visit. The people I talked to there did not take renegotiation seriously.' Peter reiterated brilliantly the points he keeps making about what we will be committed to next year unless renegotiation is concluded first. I said I thought Cabinet should have been consulted about Jim's second speech, which was

---

[1] Pending renegotiations there was an uneasy situation about how to deal with the flood of regulations, directives and other documents coming from the European Commission. The House of Commons had set up an all-party Scrutiny Committee to decide which of them were important enough to merit parliamentary debate and on 3 July two debates had taken place under this procedure on a 'take note' Motion by the Government. Tony Benn was on the front bench waiting to deal with the second debate on regional policy when anti-Market backbenchers staged a revolt on the first Motion to take note of the guidelines on economic policy which the Commission was proposing, demanding their rejection. When they forced a division, Tony Benn openly abstained in sympathy. Bob Mellish, as Chief Whip, was so incensed that he sent backbenchers home, leaving Tony to talk out the debate on regional policy.

undoubtedly different in tone from the first. (Jim muttered angrily at this.) Crosland, typically, played straight down the middle to end up on the Right. 'I find the tone of this discussion very depressing; so would the party. I have been a moderate pro. I have never taken the sovereignty issue as some of my colleagues do. I don't take Michael's view about what feeling in the party and in the country is.' He didn't, of course, want to take any of Peter's initiatives. And so the discussion ended inconclusively, with Jim resentful again about the suggestion that he wasn't toeing the party line. But it at least put some warning shots across his and Harold's bows.

Back to the office to film the programme on special advisers. In the middle of all the fuss Peter and Jack came in to say the press were still chasing the *Private Eye* canards about my having recently been in a private wing in University College Hospital [UCH] under an assumed name. (Rumour has it that the operation was gynaecological!) Peter said he wanted to scotch it once and for all. 'But I have never been in UCH,' I said, bewildered. 'Can I say then,' asked Peter, 'that you have never been a patient in UCH either publicly or privately?' 'Yes,' I replied. 'Ted was in there some time ago for a hernia operation, but he was in a public ward. And of course I visited Beattie Plummer [our friend] in the private wing.' 'That must be the source of it,' said Peter and went off triumphantly.

But in the middle of all the pressures the words 'UCH' rankled in my mind. I have already told Jack in confidence of the time I had sinus trouble as a result of a visit abroad as Minister of Overseas Development. I had gone to have it treated through the NHS, but the office had insisted I had a private room so that I could read Cabinet papers and hold office meetings. I thought it was in the London Clinic. When I got home I told Ted what had happened and he suddenly said, 'Of course your operation in 1965 was in UCH.' Then it all came back to me. While I was worrying over this there came a telephone call. Ted took it. Then he turned round to me: a newspaper was asking for a comment on a story appearing on the front page of tomorrow's *Daily Telegraph* about my treatment in UCH in 1965. He brushed them off. The full horror of my position then swept over me: I had lied in all innocence. I could see what the press would make of this. No one would believe that I had not gone into a private room through choice, but through necessity. They would do a Ted Short on me. I went to bed submerged in wretchedness and doubting whether I would sleep.

Friday, 5 July

Woke with a start at 5am. All my miseries came flooding in and I knew further sleep would be impossible. Got up, made some tea and forced myself to work my way grimly through one of my boxes. When the newspapers arrived I found that the UCH story was on the front pages, together with an interview with the sinus consultant, Kingdom, who had now gone to the reckless length of allowing his name to be used about his treatment of me. Left home at 9am, feeling physically and nervously exhausted before I started. Ted hugged me consolingly as I said, 'This is going to be one of the worst days of my life.' At the office there was an embarrassed reticence about the atmosphere. 'Where's Graham?' I asked. 'Checking about the Private

Notice Questions [PNQ],' replied the girls. Oh, God, I thought, spare me that! I couldn't even begin to turn my mind to the details of today's negotiations before I cleared up my own affair. At last I got Graham, Peter Brown, Jack and Philip Rogers assembled in my room. 'Peter,' I said firmly, 'I owe you an apology.' He looked surprised. 'Last night I unintentionally lied to you and I do not lie to my press officers. I tried to phone you to tell you not to put out my denial but I could not get hold of you.' Peter almost laughed at my agony. 'There's nothing to apologize to me about, Secretary of State. We didn't put out anything that was inaccurate. All the queries were about recent operations. The stories *were* all wrong anyway. Don't think another thing about it. I believe the story is dead anyway. But I want to get a statement out from you today to finish it.'

We then discussed how I could check up on the details of what actually happened. Philip said he would get on to the Ministry of Overseas Development and Jack was despatched to turn up what he could from the cuttings. Graham then came in with the first good news of the day. 'The PNQ is refused,' he said in his genially laconic way. My spirits began, if not to rise, at least to calm and they steadied still more as a result of Peter's unruffled loyalty. 'I do not share your views about private beds, Mrs Castle. But this department is not going to have you hounded. You have done no wrong.' And he made me laugh when he told me that he had to get Dick out of a similar mess when Dick had discovered that Anne [Crossman], unbeknown to him, was a member of BUPA! I began to feel ashamed that I hadn't taken Peter into my confidence. He was obviously in his favourite Svengali element and he kept saying to me, 'You are about to enter into crucial negotiations and you are going to win. We'll settle this other nonsense and I want you to put it out of your mind and do what only you can do.' They were all so charming, gathering round to defend me, that I wondered once again at the unique quality of the British Civil Service: the capacity of its top people to develop a genuine loyalty to a Minister who wasn't here yesterday and will be gone tomorrow.

But the physical damage was done. At an office meeting to discuss our strategy over Charing Cross I had such a headache I could barely concentrate. And this on a day when I needed all my wits about me! The message was that the AHA chairman and Mrs Brookstone's merry men had asked to see me, but that the consultants at Charing Cross were standing aloof. There was also an insulting ultimatum from the BMA in the post threatening industrial action on Monday if I did not intervene, together with a letter to David Owen demanding a meeting to discuss the future of his working party. I said I should reply to the AHA that I would be glad to see them, but only if the consultants came along too. I should then set up immediate, but separate, meetings with the BMA and the national leaders of the unions. Everyone agreed that I was right and that I should ask Len Murray to come along with Alan Fisher and Albert Spanswick. (We decided to include Spanswick because COHSE has been taking action on this issue.)

Various people dashed off to make phone calls. At intervals Jack and Peter came in with drafts of my statement on my treatment at UCH. They said they had tracked down my Private Secretary of the time, John Rednall, who couldn't remember the details of departmental advice to me at the time. 'And, unfortunately, Secretary of

State,' said Philip Rogers, 'your then Permanent Secretary, who would have given the advice, is dead.' But they had established that the department had *not* paid for the private room. Peter and Jack asked me whether I could be sure that I had not received private treatment on any other occasion, as it would be fatal to have other incidents unearthed by the press bit by bit. 'It isn't the press,' I replied grimly. 'The Tories undoubtedly would employ private detectives to do us dirt.' I couldn't remember any, but then my memory could be deceiving me. Jack went off to contact Ted and ask him to get in touch with Colin-Russ, who, even though he had only been our doctor for a few years, would have all my files.

Then back to an office meeting to discuss the state of play on the other negotiations. The report was that the Charing Cross consultants had agreed to come along with the rest. The BMA had also agreed to come. Would I phone Len Murray myself, please? Which I did, only to learn from him that it was impossible for him to get out of engagements that afternoon. 'In any case, Barbara, I doubt if I could be helpful. After all, Congress is in favour of getting rid of private practice.' I explained to him that that was not the point. I was in favour of getting rid of private practice too, but the right way was to negotiate a new contract with the consultants that would recompense them for loss of pay. Surely that was a good trade-union principle? Len saw the point at once and said he would talk to Alan Fisher: the best he could do. I then rang Alan to invite him. He too had an engagement, but he agreed to scrub it and come. Spanswick, I was told by the office, had agreed too. Graham then gently reminded me that John Donne (chairman of SE Thames Regional Health Authority) was coming to see me over a snack lunch. As I had let him down last Tuesday he was sure I would agree that I could not turn him down again. Wearily I agreed. I then asked officials what on earth they thought I could say to the Charing Cross deputation when it came? 'All you can do,' said Philip, 'is to repeat what you have said in your letter to the AHA chairman yesterday.' As the letter had had no impact at all and had merely led to a desperate plea from the chairman to come and drop the problem in my lap, I could not see any formula for success. Yet success was vital if I was to wipe the personal story off the front pages tomorrow.

Jack came in with the report from Colin-Russ, who, it appears, has been immensely co-operative. There was, said Jack, another occasion on which I had had treatment: from a Mr Scott of Guy's who had written about me to Colin-Russ from an address in Guy's, Keats House, which would seem to imply that the treatment had been private. Did I remember it? No, I replied desperately. Jack went off to find out more. Until this was cleared up, my statement had to be held up. Somehow I got through my lunch with John Donne and his administrator, who had come to tell me of the desperate difficulties of their Regional Health Authority. Mercifully David Owen was there, as I myself was so *distrait* I could hardly answer Donne's points intelligently. As I ate a couple of sandwiches I thought, 'Thank God for the obstetricians' banquet tonight. I shall be starving by then.' Little did I know what lay ahead of me!

Before I knew where I was it was 1.30pm and all the Charing Cross contingent had arrived. I tried to rally my thoughts. Jordan-Moss had had the good idea that I should start by asking them whether it was true that they had nearly reached a compromise earlier and if so what was it? (We knew that they had almost agreed to move some of the private wing patients into other parts of the hospital, but then the consultants had gone to the BMA for advice and had been sternly told to sit tight and concede nothing.) As the chairman of the AHA, Mr Meyer, walked in, followed by his troupe, I thought how much nicer they all looked than they had appeared on TV or in the press. (Probably they were thinking the same of me!) Granny Brookstone turned out to be a pleasantly unaggressive person who was clearly bewildered by all the publicity she had attracted and very aggrieved by the nature of some of it. She was accompanied by a thin little girl in a white overall, who turned out to be a medico-physics technician, and a subdued little chap with fuzzy hair: the porters' supervisor. Meyer was deprecatingly grateful for my intervention; his administrator was a friendly, competent chap. Even the two consultants were mild and unassuming: obviously not cut out by nature to conduct a confrontation war.

I began by telling them that, as I had already said in the House, their local dispute was for them to settle. All I could do was to try to clarify the issues for them so as to make a settlement more possible. Was it true that they had at one point almost agreed on a compromise? Meyer said, 'Yes', outlined it and explained that since then the consultants had turned it down. I then pitched rather sternly into the two men about why they had turned it down. By cross-examination I established the fact that their stand was not upon the principle of their clinical responsibility. Were they refusing to move patients because their treatment might suffer? No. (Here Granny B. intervened to say almost pleadingly that she had never asked, and never would ask, that the interests of any patient should suffer.) Their stand was upon the law and order principle, they said. The law allowed private practice and until it was changed it should be enforced. (All good BMA stuff.) When it *was* changed they would abide by it, even if they didn't agree with it. Mixed up with all this was a different argument: that the clinical interests of their private practice patients would suffer if they were no longer to be treated within the context of the NHS – a glorious illogicality which enabled me to pounce. Did they realize that the NHS Act did not *require* me to allow private beds? It merely empowered me to authorize them when – and to the extent that – I as Secretary of State thought it reasonable. That shook them a bit. So, I said, I could have withdrawn authorizations immediately on taking office. If I had done so, would they have accepted it? No, they said, rather cornered now, because they thought private practice within the NHS benefited their private patients. So, I pressed them, 'Your objection is not on law and order grounds at all? You are merely fighting the Government's policy?'

While they digested this I turned to Granny B. Didn't she know that the Government was committed to phasing out private beds? What right had she therefore to disrupt the whole hospital? Disarmingly, and almost apologetically, she replied that she was no politician, but the fact was that her members didn't trust any of us. They were fed up with staff shortages and the fact that people like them had to wait months for beds, while people 'like this pop star', she added contemptuously, throwing a copy of the *Daily Mirror* across the table, could waft themselves up to the private floor, putting demands on the kitchen staff with their extra menus, simply by paying for it. She wanted a full enquiry, not just into pay, but into the whole situation in the NHS. Her silent companions nodded grimly. All they asked was that the privileges of the

132

fifteenth (private) floor should be shared by NHS patients so as to shorten the waiting lists. They had *not* asked for the floor to be closed: merely for some of the beds to be made available to NHS patients. I turned again to the consultants: 'What is your reply?' They shrugged. They didn't have to reply, they said. '*We* are not making any demands. We are merely standing on the *status quo*. Why should we compromise?' 'Even if it means closing the hospital?' I asked. They shrugged again. Again I could see the hand of the BMA. 'Well,' I said, 'it is clear that you are not going to solve this at local level.' The consultants nodded eagerly. I told them I was now due to see the national leaders of both sides. Would they wait? Granny demurred. She was expected back with a report soon, otherwise she would not be able to hold her members. I made encouraging noises and shooed her out, giving instructions that they were all to be made comfortable, given tea and fed. I yearned for the expertise of my old Department of Employment and Productivity, which had been so well equipped for dealing with situations of this kind. As they left, David said to me, 'Those consultants are bastards.' Typically Philip interjected, 'I thought they were all bastards.'

I saw Alan Fisher, Albert Spanswick and his President with only David and Philip present. They were in immensely emollient mood, obviously wishing to be rid of this incubus. Alan tried to say that his members were adamant that private beds must go. I pointed out that they, as good trade unionists, would be the first to object if someone came along arbitrarily to cut their pay before they could even negotiate a new contract. No demur. Finally Alan, backed by the others, said that there might be a way out if the report of the Owen working party on private practice could be speeded up; after all, no one could be sure that there would not be a change of government. I said I would see what I could do about this.

But the BMA, who came next, were a very different kettle of fish. They had rung up to say they were bringing the hospital consultants' breakaway union[1] with them: unity forged in the face of the enemy! In they trooped, about one dozen strong. Lewin was as tight-faced as ever, Stevenson as touchy and truculent. They were flanked by the authoritative – and authoritarian – top brass of the profession, and it was soon clear where the rigidity of the Charing Cross consultants came from. Lewin began by reading me a lecture. They had been shocked by my failure to denounce NUPE's action in unequivocal terms. I retorted by reading out to them just what I had said in the House and in my letter to the AHA. I reminded them of their ultimatum to me: their threat to take industrial action – 'Everyone from top to bottom of the profession is apparently prepared to damage the Health Service to secure his ends: there is no difference between you' – unless I 'intervened' to ensure that the hospital service was kept going without any interference with private practice. I reminded them that we did not live in a dictatorship: I had no power to compel anyone to provide services. The idea obviously appalled them; I could feel the 'Gad, sir, these upstart trade unionists must be whipped' atmosphere. They tried to be lofty about the 'law and order' principle, and once again I had to tell them that the law had given me complete

---

[1] A number of consultants had broken away from the BMA and formed the Hospital Consultants and Specialists Association. It claimed to represent 7,000 consultants out of the 11,000 working in the NHS.

discretion. I could have ruled out private beds from the word go, but I hadn't because I believed that we should negotiate any changes in an orderly way. This led to some nasty exchanges about the role of the working party (David Owen had said to me earlier that they might be coming to announce that they were walking out of it – the last thing I want). One of their chaps, who is a member of it, tried to make out that the outcome had been prejudged. When David and I reminded him that there had never been any secret about the Government's policy, he pretended that the BMA were going into it with an open mind while we were not. Anything further from an open mind than these chaps showed would be impossible! I then told them that I had always held that the Charing Cross situation ought to have been dealt with locally: after all, my responsibility as Secretary of State was to *all* the patients in the hospital, not merely to the private ones. They nodded at this (they had to). But, I said, it had become clear that the Charing Cross consultants were acting under the orders of the BMA. The issue had to be settled nationally and my position was clear: I believed that it was wrong for any changes in the NHS to be made without proper negotiations with the appropriate union. They didn't exactly like the application of this word to them. Lewin put it pompously in a different way: 'We don't think our people at Charing Cross should have the burden placed on them of defending what is a matter of principle.' Mr Astley (the sort of man to be conscious that he held your life in his hands) kept looking up to say, 'I will never agree to any compromise.'

Finally, having established that there was no point of clinical freedom involved at Charing Cross, and having reiterated that I had no power to shoot recalcitrant trade unionists on sight, and also that I had a responsibility to all the patients involved, I told them what Alan Fisher and the others had said about speeding up the working-party report. Lewin pricked up his ears at this. Two hours having now elapsed, and everyone being exhausted (for myself I felt the old strength and stamina flowing back into me), I suggested a break while they considered this. 'And someone must find you a drink,' I said genially. 'You deserve it.'

While I gulped a cup of tea in their absence Peter Brown and Jack came in again to talk about my private treatment. Apparently they had unearthed that Mr Scott was the chap at Guy's to whom I had gone in 1968 about some trouble with my chest. 'God, I remember,' I groaned. 'I got 'flu very badly while down at HCF that January. I developed such an acute pain in my chest that our friends, the local doctors, said I must have an x-ray. So when I got back to the Ministry of Transport the office sent me round to Guy's for one. For God's sake, it was the out-patients' department. I remember going there one afternoon. And they found a shadow on my lung. And the specialist told me to go back for a check-up.' 'But on the second time did you go round to his private room?' they asked. 'I can't remember,' I replied, 'but if I did, he probably asked me to and didn't charge me for it.' After a further rather wild discussion Peter said firmly, 'We must put this statement of yours out now or not at all.' We decided to stick to the wording we had worked out: that I 'normally' had treatment through the NHS. 'I seem to have spent my life queueing in out-patients' departments,' I said desperately.

There then ensued a lengthy lull during which someone, blessedly, produced some sandwiches. It by now being 7pm, I said to Henry Yellowlees, 'We're not going to get to that banquet, Henry.' 'No, Secretary of State,' he replied sadly, 'and it would have been good food.' We chewed our way through some dry bits while the BMA, godlike, took their time. 'I wouldn't blame Granny if she walked out,' I remarked. But it was all so unreal I didn't care.

It was 10pm before the BMA came back. ('Has anyone taken them drinks?' I hissed to Graham. 'Yes,' he replied, 'but we are running out of it.' 'There's some in my room,' hissed back Philip. 'Help yourself when you can get at it.') Lewin was obviously very pleased with himself and lost no time in saying triumphantly that the BMA was only too ready to help speed up the findings of the working party. Provided that I agreed to state more categorically than I had yet done that I deplored the action of the union (with which by now I was feeling increasing sympathy), and that I committed myself to *no* reduction in private beds meanwhile, they were prepared to agree that the working party should report by 31 August. I seized on the first point in white cold temper by now. 'You had better spell out first, Mr Lewin, exactly what you want me to say that I haven't said. What am I – St Joan faced by her Inquisitors? What exactly is it you want me to recant?' They looked nonplussed. But David seized on the last point, appalled. How on earth could his working party produce a report by August? The BMA themselves had originally said the discussions would take eighteen months. By committing myself to 'early next year' in my Commons statement I was already pushing things. August, they surely knew, was impossible. And as he talked it became clear that the BMA's ploy was to kill the work-load studies which we had intended to be an integral part of the discussion on their contract and which Halsbury, as chairman of their review body which would have to price the contract, had welcomed. We would be faced with straight financial blackmail. Lewin looked like the cat that had got at the cream and remarked that *they* were only too willing to speed things up. Obviously he saw himself in the position of being able to say that it was *we* who were holding things up. Gradually David got them to agree to a November date as more reasonable. ('And that will still cost us a lot,' he whispered to me.)

I then turned to their second point, seeing a way of turning the tables on them. I couldn't possibly commit myself not to reduce the number of private beds, I told them, except in the context of a Charing Cross settlement. Didn't they remember that my responsibility was to *all* patients, NHS as well as private ones? Faced with a possibility of all the Charing Cross services being withdrawn, how could I tie my hands? Remember I might be under pressure from the House next week to do something like ordering the withdrawal of half the private beds. Wasn't it possible for there to be a little give on both sides there to make a settlement possible? At this Lewin and his friends looked crestfallen. It was, oddly enough, only the militant hospital consultants who could see the sense of it. They kept nodding sympathetically. Eventually we made another break so that we could both try to work out a form of words that might do the trick.

While we waited I decided to ring up Alan Fisher to see how firm he was prepared to go on his assurances. He was delighted to hear that we had agreed to advance the date of the report to November. Yes, he was prepared to issue a call to all his members that very night to discontinue their action and await the report, but, he added, he couldn't possibly do that unless there had been a settlement at Charing Cross. Couldn't I get the consultants to move at all? I said I'd try. When at last the BMA came back again with their proposed amendments to our draft statement, I was ready for them. Yes, I would reiterate my condemnation of the industrial action; yes, I would be prepared to promise not to introduce any arbitrary reduction in the number of pay beds while awaiting the working-party report. But I could only do that in the context of a Charing Cross settlement. And then I played my trump card: Alan Fisher was willing to call off the action nationally that night if only we could settle Charing Cross. They were clearly shaken. Wasn't any give in their attitude possible, I asked, pressing my advantage. David followed it up. Did we need to talk about reducing the number of private beds there? Couldn't they be merely redistributed? Some of the BMA boys were for going to the stake for no compromise, but again it was the hospital consultants who were nodding at what we said. Finally the BMA agreed to go and talk to the Charing Cross consultants and we settled down for another wait.

I phoned Spanswick. Eventually we tracked him down on a caravan site somewhere on the coast, and over a bad line I heard him say faintly that he was willing to call off the action, too, and to call his executive on Monday to confirm it. Back at last came the BMA, again looking like cats that had got at the cream. They had worked out a formula that did just what David had suggested: did not reduce the number of private beds but *did* redistribute them through the hospital.[1] We said we would try it on the Charing Cross team, though I personally doubted whether Ma Brookstone, who had by now been cooped up for seven hours while we worked out her fate with the BMA, would find it tolerable. We then agreed the final wording of the statement with the BMA, and Lewin, looking mighty satisfied, got up to go. As he started shaking hands all round we said to him, 'Hey, Mrs Brookstone hasn't agreed this yet. There may be a hitch on which we shall need to consult you.' He seemed outraged at the very idea that Ma B. could upset anything *they* had decided, but agreed to stay. So once again the BMA were shepherded into another room while we sent for the Charing Cross contingent.

'You are very near agreement now, Mrs Castle,' said Peter as we waited. 'In my experience,' I replied, 'the biggest snag comes just before the dawn.' It was by now past midnight and Peter was getting edgy lest I miss the press. 'The TV boys have already gone,' he told me, 'but the press are hanging on. As soon as this thing is settled I want you straight down there to see them. Those BMA fellows will be talking

---

[1] The formula they proposed was: 'With regard to the distribution of private beds at Charing Cross Hospital, when private patients are treated for clinical purposes in special units elsewhere in the hospital, the equivalent number of beds in the private floor will be occupied by NHS patients, thus releasing acute beds elsewhere in the hospital.' In the statement we eventually agreed, I also reiterated my call to all concerned to leave the phasing out of pay beds to the Government, accepted the speeding up of the work of the Owen working party with a view to trying to reach agreement by November and undertook not to make any 'arbitrary reduction' in the number of pay beds meanwhile. In return for this the BMA and HCSA agreed to call off their threatened work to rule on the understanding that the other parties would also call off their action against private patients in any NHS hospital involved.

their heads off to the press and it is essential you put the key points of the agreement across.' I told him we hadn't got an agreement yet, and, sure enough, when Ma B. and her two companions came in we soon ran into difficulties. I explained what had been agreed, laying enormous stress on the fact that by her efforts she had got the date of the report advanced by several months. (Lewin himself had suggested to me that I might use this argument with her – the BMA wouldn't mind.) And I made as much as I could of the fact that the private floor would become a mixed ward. But she was no fool and soon realized that they hadn't got the magic formula on which they had pinned their hopes: the release of twenty private beds for the NHS. 'All we have got is one for one,' she complained. 'Yes, Brooky,' explained one of the consultants – now free from the shadow of the BMA to renew his normal friendly relations with Ma B. and her staff – 'but you know that the private floor is always under-occupied. In future these beds will not be kept empty. When we move a private patient to a specialized unit, as we do frequently, we will move an NHS patient immediately into the empty bed.' Could they guarantee a minimum number of NHS patients there? No, they must trust him to play fair. I came in here to say that, by definition, insistence on a minimum number would be inconsistent with the consultants' offer to bring in NHS patients when they moved their private ones on *clinical grounds*. How quickly could they move in NHS patients? Tomorrow, starting with four. Could they make it six? Yes, they could, said the administrative officer.

Eventually, whether she was just tired and fed up with the whole business or naturally moderate, Ma B. said she was inclined to accept if her companions would. They were far more unhappy about it all. Timorously but tenaciously they maintained that in reality they had got nothing and when they reported back the settlement would be rejected. 'You have got the advancement of the date,' I said gently. 'And you have now got a mixed floor instead of a private one.' I could see that this was the bull point with them, so I clinched the business by suggesting we write the words into the statement: 'thus ensuring it becomes a mixed floor'. It did the trick. We started shaking hands all round. Ma B. thanked me profusely, saying she had said some hard things about me and that my statement in the House condemning them had made her very angry. But now she had met me she had formed a very different impression of me. The tense little girl was bitter about her pay and I assured her the medico-physics technicians *were* going to get their increase.

Peter kept tugging at me saying, 'I want you down there with the press before it is too late.' Graham insisted I must report to Alan Fisher and get his commitment to call off his people's action. David reminded me that the BMA were still waiting in another room. I told him to go and report to them that the agreement had been clinched. There was no need for me to consult them again as we had not deviated in any detail from what they had agreed. Long delay while Graham read the whole statement at dictation speed over the phone to Alan. Then a quick word with him while he congratulated me on what I had achieved, Peter almost beside himself with impatience. At last he was able to grab me and rush me downstairs, where a handful of reporters were watching the clock desperately. A hurried interview and three short radio recordings during which I fended off provocative questions and played it absolutely straight with the BMA, throwing away some of the effectiveness of my success in order not to cause them embarrassment. Then upstairs again where I hoped to relax over a celebratory drink, only to find David waiting with a face of doom. 'You ought not to have gone down without seeing the BMA,' he told me. 'You are in deep trouble there.' 'For God's sake, why?' I asked, bewildered. Apparently they had been expecting me to go into them, like a subject to a reigning monarch, to get their final blessing on what had been concluded and were blazing mad to learn I had gone to talk to the press without doing so. David said he had just about quietened them down by a grovelling apology and officials had been 'magnificent'. Apparently Philip Rogers had ticked them off in his mild way while Henry Yellowlees had lost his temper and torn a strip off them. It was now clear that officials were as contemptuous of the BMA's whole behaviour as ever we could be.

In an effort to retrieve the situation I, too, went into them with profuse apologies. Lewin was bridling like a petulant child, Stevenson was spluttering and the rest of the consultants stood around brooding like Henry Moore monoliths. I finally pacified them by sending Stevenson off to talk to the Press Association, who were still standing around, and sent Peter Brown chasing to see if there were any radio people left. I then adjourned to my room with my own team, where we sat over a last drink, not knowing whether to giggle or weep with despair. At 2.30am Lewin and Stevenson finally came in to bid me a stiff goodnight. And off at last went Ted and I to drive to HCF. Having been on the go by now for nearly twenty-two hours I was terrified that I might doze off and so encourage Ted to fall asleep at the wheel, so I forced myself to keep awake by screeching tuneless songs at him until at last we turned into the blessed home lane. The delight of the waiting dogs was, as always, an antidote to the unrealities of the day. To bed at 4am.

Saturday, 6 July

Woke, still exhausted, at 9am. I had barely rallied my senses before a spluttering Stevenson was on the phone. Had I seen the papers? The worst had happened, as he knew it would. The papers had got the BMA attitude all wrong. His telephone had never stopped ringing. He was in terrible trouble with his members and must therefore send me a letter to put it right. He then read out a letter beginning with a vicious attack on me for having kept them 'imprisoned' in a room while I scooped the press. I listened patiently, then, with infinite gentleness, gradually soothed him down. I told him that I would gladly send him a letter in reply confirming his interpretation of the agreement, but would it really have the effect he wanted if it appeared as just part of a row? 'But we understood the statement was to be a joint one,' he almost moaned. 'Oh, no,' I replied. 'You can't have understood that. If you had, why did Mr Lewin come to say goodnight before the discussions were complete?' That floored him and he sobered down. He said he would try his hand at a redraft and phone again – which he did, right in the middle of my breakfast. The redraft was fine – except for a still slightly petulant introduction. 'Why don't you just say that you had hoped to have a better opportunity to talk to the press than was possible owing to the lateness of the hour?' I said soothingly. 'If you will do that I will be glad to send you a reply by hand on Monday confirming your understanding of the agreement unreservedly.' He capitulated, took down my form of words and agreed to do as I said. I returned to my congealing bacon and eggs and breathed again.

Spent the rest of the day dozing on and off in the garden – except, of course, for a run with the dogs, though it was an effort to drive my weary limbs through the woods. In the evening we went over to the Keable-Elliotts for a cocktail party. Neither he nor I mentioned yesterday's event, though Keith Pawson, who was among the guests, did say to me wonderingly, 'How did you do it? I had a bet on with some friends that you would not pull it off.' 'Just a question of stamina,' I replied. Ted and I left early to look in at the *Week in Westminster* on TV, where they were doing our political advisers' programme. It didn't come over too badly.

Sunday, 7 July

Nora Beloff has got a great piece about our Tuesday dinners, half right in detail, wholly wrong in atmosphere. Ted swears it is Wedgie who has leaked. Maybe – but I doubt it. Anyway who cares about what Nora writes?

Monday, 8 July

Graham greeted me cheerfully at the office with the words: 'Seen Nora Beloff? She's incredible.' My ploy about telling him frankly about the dinners at the outset – 'Keep Tuesday evenings free if you can for a "Husbands and Wives" dinner. Some of us are determined to keep *some* social life with our spouses if we can' – evoked an approving response from him. Every week Judith sends me a note heavily marked, 'For the attention of the Secretary of State only', giving details of the rendezvous. I promptly put her note into my box for Graham's attention. It succeeds in defusing the whole thing. The *Daily Telegraph* carries the story that the breakaway consultants, who are meeting in London today, are complaining they have been 'outfoxed' by Mrs Castle. That won't help me over my statement in the House today, for, of course, Geoffrey Howe has put down a Private Notice Question. Derek Stevenson's letter has duly arrived and the office put up a stilted reply to it which I rewrite then and there under my officials' noses. Henry Yellowlees nods approvingly as I scribble out the words: 'I *welcome* the opportunity of confirming what we agreed.' I tell them that, Stevenson having agreed to take all the poison out of his own letter, I must respond generously. My ploy in negotiations is always to respond warmly to a reasonable approach, but to hit back hard against an unreasonable one. I also insist on including in my reply to the PNQ that I am circulating copies of the correspondence in the Official Report Hansard]. This manoeuvre succeeds in foxing Howe who, of course, does not know what the correspondence contains. His supplementaries were, therefore, muted and cautious and the whole exercise went swimmingly. Bob Mellish had approached me anxiously beforehand. 'Is it going to be all right, you darling? I don't want any Standing Order Number Nines.'[1] He was immensely relieved and congratulatory when I got through so easily.

---

[1] Standing Order No. 9 enables an MP to ask leave to move the adjournment of the House in order to debate 'a specific and important matter which should have urgent consideration'. This is raised after Questions and, if leave is granted by Mr Speaker and the House, the debate takes precedence over all public business the following day or, exceptionally, at 7pm the same day.

At Home Policy Committee of the NEC we had a discussion on land policy. As agreed, Silkin came along, bringing with him two other members of the policy group: Robert Neild and Neal Robert. Frank Allaun opened by expressing his doubts about Silkin's interim policy and his rejection of the idea of the land bank. I didn't find John's reply very convincing and it was worrying that the other two didn't agree with him. I have never thought John a particularly tough political figure but I must suspend judgment because he remains supremely confident that he is right.

Tuesday, 9 July

We are now having Cabinets twice a week. This morning's was to allow the long-delayed discussion on the Chilean debt. Edmund had put in a paper designed to establish that the renegotiation of the debt did not amount to a new loan and had nothing to do with the sale of the frigates, since Chile had not defaulted on her cash progress payments. Ownership of the warships had passed to Chile the moment the first cash payments were made. Jim insisted that he had met the points in the Socialist International resolution by the continuing overtures he had made to the Chilean Government about the restoration of human rights. I chipped in firmly to say that we could not deny that by selling the warships we were increasing the amount of Chile's debt. If we didn't reschedule the debt Chile might have to default on her payments and the whole legal position about the sale would be changed. At the very least we should conform to the resolution of our own International Committee and make the rescheduling *conditional* on the release of certain of the political prisoners (e.g. the former Foreign Minister – in whose fate I was sure Jim would take an interest). But the others would have none of it. If we did not reschedule, other countries would, they argued. Chile would get her warships and our creditors would not get repaid. Said Jim, 'The balance of advantage is overwhelmingly on our side.' Mike of course backed me up. Harold however said that at Chequers that weekend the exiled General Secretary of the Chilean Radical Party had been very appreciative of the efforts we had made to restore human rights. Bob let me down by saying the one thing the party would want to know was whether, if we did not reschedule, the Chileans would still keep their warships. When the rest chorused 'Yes' he accepted it. So I lost.

In the afternoon Brian and I trooped over to the Treasury with our officials to discuss, at Denis's request, the family endowment scheme[1] on which I have been working so hard. Denis, after some of his rather mawkish jocularity, which always irritates me, then suddenly proceeded to lecture me. It was all right my coming forward with all these plans, he said, but there was no money for any of them. Gradually I felt cold fury mounting in me. I told him at last that I resented being brought over for a lecture: 'Here's Barbara again with her begging bowl.' I told him that the commitment to a child endowment scheme was in the Manifesto, which *he*

[1] In the Manifesto we had said we would 'help the low paid by introducing a new system of child cash allowances for every child, including the first, payable to the mother'. I was working on this 'child endowment' scheme, which was designed to combine child tax reliefs and family allowances in a new cash payment to the mother and which was later to become known as the child benefit scheme. In the meantime I was pressing the Chancellor to agree to a substantial increase in the family allowance, which had not been increased since 1968 and which stood at £1 for the second and subsequent children in a family.

had helped draw up. All I had been doing was to discharge my ministerial responsibility to try and clothe it in administrative form. If he now wanted to repudiate the commitment he had better tell Cabinet. He climbed down somewhat at that; said it was all very difficult and Cabinet would have to decide its priorities in the light of the public expenditure exercise. After three-quarters of an hour on this I said I had to go and we left it that officials should continue their discussions on the plan without commitment to timing, etc. Baldwin of the Treasury, whom I rather like, looked sympathetic but worried. Brian [O'Malley] and I stalked out, saying audibly, 'Why did we come? It has been a complete waste of time.'

H and W dinner at Charing Cross Hotel. We discussed the Common Market and agreed that Jim, Harold and Fred were pulling their punches over membership. I begged Peter to brief us all on what Fred was up to over beef, but Peter was obviously not keen to take on this chore. I also complained that those of us who were not members of the Ministerial Economic Strategy Committee [MES] did not know what Denis was planning to do in his interim measures. Instead of reducing VAT, why didn't he increase family allowances? Far more selective. And if he wanted to boost the construction industry, what better than to give Housing and Health some of their expenditure cuts back so that I could release some permissions to build hospitals?

Tommy [Balogh] and Catherine [his wife] came in late, Tommy bringing with him copies of a gloomy economic analysis he has drawn up. Always when I read his papers I feel that he is better at analysing doom than explaining what we should do about it. Mike explained to me what is going on in MES: 'Denis and Harold Lever are in favour of borrowing like hell,' he said. And he added, 'I must say I am a Haroldite.' We should borrow what we can, reduce inflation as much as we can. 'The worst part of the programme is to keep public expenditure down. I hope we will reflate a bit.' Peter was far more grim: the world economy was crumbling. 'If you take reflation measures now on the scale that is proposed you will have the most massive effects on the exchange rates.' Wedgie said with relish that we were in a siege economy: Harold Lever, he said, had moved from being a growth man to being a straight gambler. Mike would have none of this extremism. What Peter wanted, he scoffed, was to take the country into great austerity. At this point, it being late and fatigue overtaking me – with a couple of boxes still to do – I left them to it. Ted, who was brought home later by Mike, told me that Mike had complained all the way about Wedgie.

Wednesday, 10 July

Spent the morning chairing my first meeting of the Women's National Commission.[1] Apparently I delighted them all by my robust determination to build up the Commis-

[1] In 1969 Harold Wilson, always anxious to promote the status of women, had responded to United Nations pressure and created a Women's National Commission representing all the leading women's organizations in the country. This replaced the Women's Consultative Council, originally set up by Mr Heath in 1962 to disseminate information about the European Community as part of his drive to get Britain into the EEC. The terms of reference of the Commission were 'to ensure by all possible means that the informed opinion of women is given its due weight in the deliberations of Government on both national and international affairs' and the Government had appointed one of the co-chairmen since its inception. On our return to office Harold had asked me to take this on.

sion and to get the Women's European Committee wound up. Dr Thornton, the Commission's secretary, had such a bad cold she had almost lost her voice. I have never known me catch a cold from someone so quickly that it develops in a few hours, but that is what happened – by the evening I had such a sore throat that I too could hardly speak. Perhaps my fatigue had made me vulnerable. I was in a wretched state when, at 6.15pm, I met Alf Morris, Jack Ashley, Jack Straw and a phalanx of officials in the House to try to settle our policy over the Sharp Report. Alf has been getting nowhere over this and Brian Abel-Smith has taken charge. Brian is pressing us to go for cash payments instead of cars and I can see the sense of it. But the trouble is that, finance being so stringently short, this means that we could not afford to extend to disabled people who can't drive the big cash allowance (£300 million a year) that it would be necessary to give the existing disabled drivers instead of cars. And Alf and I are haunted by the knowledge that very few disabled people would be able to buy their own car on £300 a year anyway. Elizabeth Johnson has been urgently reminding me that we must get a decision soon if we are to clear the policy with Cabinet before the recess, so I said to everyone as we assembled, 'This is jury service. No one leaves this room, eats, drinks or sleeps until we have settled our policy.'

Two-and-a-half hours later I was regretting this. I felt ghastly; my mind was going round and round as dizzily as the argument. Alf had produced a complicated scheme for enabling existing users of invalid tricycles to commute their allowance into a large enough sum in the first year to enable them to buy a car and suggested that this provision be extended to disabled non-drivers who needed a car to get to work or education (Lady Sharp's idea). I don't like these arbitrary categories. But my idea of extending a mobility allowance to every disabled person as the first instalment of our disablement income scheme was slapped down by officials on the grounds of cost. They clung doggedly to their determination to get the department out of the responsibility of providing cars. Finally, almost in despair and my head swimming, I said we would go for Alf's idea. '*Without* offering cars in lieu?' queried Philip. 'Yes,' I replied firmly. Brian O'Malley took me off to eat and bought me a superb bottle of wine, which cheered me up but didn't do anything to get my boxes cleared. When I went up to my room to start on them Jack Ashley came in to tell me both he and Alf felt it was politically impossible for us not to offer cars to existing users of tricycles. Would I allow Alf to reopen the point? I groaned and said 'Yes'. What with votes on the Trade Union Bill and my boxes, it was 2am before I got to bed.

Earlier I had had to give an hour to the RHA chairmen, hearing their views on our proposals for the democratization of the NHS.[1] They are all against our making any

---

[1] The Labour Party had bitterly opposed Sir Keith Joseph's reorganization of the NHS as administratively top-heavy and managerial. Party conference had called for its administration to be democratized and in our Manifesto we had said we would 'transform the Area Health Authorities into democratic bodies'. My difficulty was that the new structure was due to come into operation one month after we took office. Most of the new officials and authority members had already been appointed. It was too late to unscramble Sir Keith's eggs and another immediate reorganization would have been disastrous for morale. David Owen and I had therefore worked out interim proposals to make the new structure more democratic by increasing the number of local authority representatives on the Health Authorities to one-third and by including on them, for the first time in the NHS's history, two elected representatives of the rest of the staff in addition to the doctors and nurses who were already represented. We also proposed

changes at all until the new bodies have settled down. So even this modest instalment of reform is running into difficulties! The only bright note in the day was that Dick Bourton [Deputy Secretary at the DHSS] had managed to get Treasury to cough up £47 million to offset price rises in the NHS and thus avoid the threatened reduction of services. And Treasury have promised to let us have another supplementary estimate later if this sum does not prove enough to do the trick.[1] This meets one of the major worries expressed to me by John Donne last Friday and the RHA chairmen were duly grateful. Dick Bourton used the opportunity to get a dig in at David Owen, whom officials find irritating. Could I please tell Parliamentary Secretary, Bourton asked, to leave these things to him as Parliamentary Secretary had nearly upset the apple-cart by going direct to the Chief Secretary? These things were far better left to officials, as it had been necessary to twist the rules. I listened soothingly. I like David and am glad of his endless policy initiatives, even if some of them are only half thought through and, having started them, he drops them suddenly. I would far rather have someone who thinks for himself and stirs things up, for out of this good always comes.

Thursday, 11 July

At Cabinet Harold Lever reported another victory over the building societies. He had offered them a Government guarantee of their reserves to enable them to maintain the mortgage rate at 11 per cent till the end of the year. They didn't like this at all (they clearly don't like being dependent on the Government for anything), but had agreed to hold the rate for another three months. But most of our time was taken up with an initial private session in which we had a major row. Harold referred to the leak in this morning's *Times* about yesterday's meeting of the Monitoring Committee, set up at Jim's suggestion to enable a joint body of Ministers and the NEC to keep in touch with the negotiations over the Common Market. *The Times* report said that the committee has censured Jim for his 'soft' attitude and Jim was furious. He obviously wanted a go at the anti-marketeers in the Cabinet. Wedgie this time was virtuously in the clear. Although made chairman on the committee originally, he had, at Harold's suggestion, given it up and in fact he wasn't present yesterday. It was on the luckless Peter that Jim turned all his wrath. He hoped, he said, that his colleague had had the decency to denounce the outrageous document that Transport House had circulated.[2] Peter answered him with spirit. When he had been put on the committee, he retorted, it had never occurred to him that he would be the only Minister, but at yesterday's meeting he had found he was. He had been taken by surprise by the document and had certainly not attacked Jim, but his views on what

---

to strengthen the role of the Community Health Councils. Even these modest modifications had caused alarm among the existing membership of the Authorities.

[1] In the event the supplementary estimates for the NHS during the year amounted to over £642 million in England alone.

[2] The purpose of the document was 'to compare, and where necessary contrast, the Foreign Secretary's statement of June 4th with his earlier statements and the Manifesto'. It expressed concern at the Foreign Secretary's 'more conciliatory' attitude. In particular it criticized 'with respect' his statement that everything he had proposed was 'compatible with the principles of the CAP and with the treaties' and his dropping of other Manifesto demands such as the retention by Parliament of powers over the British economy.

we should stand for in the negotiations were well known and he had not hidden them. Shirley pointed out that it was really incredible that Transport House could circulate a document of critical comment without giving the Minister concerned the chance to comment first. We all agreed with that; Harold said he intended to wind the committee up and Jim simmered down. But it is clear we are sitting on a volcano as far as the Common Market is concerned.

The BMA doctors, meeting in Hull, have excelled themselves. The *Daily Telegraph* and others carry the headline: 'Doctors jeer at Castle's cash transfusion.' As Wedgie said to me, 'Could there really be any other group in the country that would jeer at £47 million?'[1] How I am going to cope with that bunch of mavericks, without even any margin of money to jolly things along, I don't know. And David has worried me by suggesting that he is working on the idea of allowing consultants to continue to work full-time in the NHS and do private work *outside* the NHS hospitals. I will never put up with that: it would be a direct incentive to build up a private service outside the NHS. It is clearly essential that I should keep in closer touch with David's negotiations, though he resents any feeling that he hasn't got a completely free hand. It is going to be a tricky situation to handle, particularly as I have to spend so much of my time on these blasted strikes.

This afternoon was an example. First I saw Clive Jenkins,[2] at his request, about the medico-physics technicians, who are threatening to stop the kidney machines by coming out on strike. I have got colleagues to allow their pay revaluation discussions, held up by Ted Heath's pay policy, to be resumed, but the negotiations have got bogged down in the Whitley Council machinery. Clive told me the offer in Whitley had been derisory. He was worried about what might happen. Could I speed things up? I said I'd try and then seized the opportunity to tell him off about the radiographers. He's bringing them out on strike, too, for an interim payment and I told him he knew that that was impossible. Didn't he know also that, by giving them their separate independent pay enquiry, I have given them what they had asked for and that, as their increase was to be back-dated, they had already been granted it? He huffed and puffed a bit and then said he would see what he could do, but didn't I realize how high feelings were running? I said I thought it was because the rank and file had not been encouraged to appreciate just what was being offered them.

Next I had to see Miss Maddocks, staff side secretary with the Whitley Council that deals with the Professions Supplementary to Medicine [PSMS]. She wriggled in her chair uncomfortably as I told her we had to do something abut the nonsense of the radiographers' threatened strike. Her union, NALGO, is not involved in this action for a change and she said that one of the troubles was inter-union rivalry: Society of

[1] On 3 July a meeting of doctors, dentists, nurses and midwives had urged the Prime Minister to set up an independent enquiry into the NHS, claiming that an injection of £500 million was needed to save it from disaster. At the meeting Dr Stevenson maintained that '£40 million is neither here nor there'. Mr Walpole Lewin told the meeting that the BMA had drawn up plans for sanctions in the event of any of the three crises facing the NHS not being solved. These were: the under-financing of the NHS, the future of private practice and new contracts for consultants.

[2] Left-wing General Secretary of the Association of Scientific, Technical and Managerial Staffs [ASTMS] since 1968. After many attempts he was to become a member of the TUC General Council in September 1974.

Radiographers versus ASTMS. Perhaps I could see the staff side? I said (on official advice) that I thought it would raise expectations if I invited them to see me. Could she arrange for them to invite me? She said she'd try and was clearly unhappy about the whole thing, as the press is full of horror stories about the danger to patients.

By now my voice has almost gone. In the meeting we had with Edmund Dell over our long-term pensions proposals I felt so ill I could not concentrate. Fortunately Brian, as usual, was masterly and I left most of it to him. Edmund skirted round every issue wordily and we parted to consider each other's points of view. Late to bed again and wishing I could spend a day in it.

Friday, 12 July

Up early to go to Blackburn, though I wasn't really fit. But with an election in the offing I dare not fall behind with my interviews. Somehow I got through the day and on to the night sleeper where I dosed myself with pills and linctus and slept heavily. But I found the strength to give a press interview condemning the doctors for 'playing politics'.

Saturday, 13 July

At HCF I crawled to bed where I slept most of the day. It was bliss to give in and to be able to read something other than an official document. I found great comfort in *Watership Down*.

Monday, 15 July

One of the things in my box last week was an excellent Minute to Fred, drafted by Brian O'M., attacking the whole idea of beef tokens.[1] I signed it thankfully. I have also caught up in my box with a memo by Denis on Wedgie's industrial policy which is now circulating. Denis begins: 'I am strongly in favour of a substantial extension of public ownership and a more dynamic industrial policy.' He also supports the idea of the NEB and agrees the functions Wedgie outlined for it. But he stresses that 'a further important objective must be to ensure that the manufacturing sector which remains in private hands must be enabled to operate vigorously and competitively'. Therefore we must remove uncertainty as quickly as possible. Nor does he oppose the nationalization of the aircraft industry and shipbuilding. But compensation would have implications for the Government's borrowing requirement and he does not think he should be asked to sign a blank cheque. So programmes should be defined as closely and as soon as possible. On planning agreements he welcomes the

---

[1] Beef tokens were another device for reducing the EEC's food surpluses: this time the 'beef mountain'. As with butter tokens the recipient would present the token in shops and ask for the special reduced price. Understandably many people objected to singling themselves out for hand-outs and had not used their cheap butter entitlement. Despite our criticisms Fred Peart announced EEC approval for a beef token scheme at the end of a marathon negotiating session on 20 September. The tokens were first issued in December 1974, and entitled 8½ million people, mainly pensioners, to claim around 20 pence per week off their meat bill.

intention to introduce these on a limited scale in the first place. He is sure we should not be thinking in terms of the biggest hundred firms, but rather in terms of the sectors most urgently requiring attention – e.g. engineering rather than food or tobacco. We should also go for co-operation rather than sanctions. I must say I find all this common sense.

The BMA have reacted rather interestingly to my Blackburn hand-out about the doctors playing politics (which I gather from Jack Straw alarmed Rogers and Yellowlees!). Lewin and Stevenson are very upset (I would say worried) by my accusation and have asked to see me. Just the reaction I anticipated – and wanted!

We are still agonizing over the Sharp Report. The office is fighting tooth and nail to get the department out of the business of providing cars and I must say that I am rather overwhelmed at the prospect of our having to provide something like 11,000 cars a year – and to service them. This is what would be involved in making cars available for all the existing categories – to say nothing of extending them. B. A-S., too, is all in favour of moving to cash allowances. He takes the line that the provision of a car goes far beyond the 'prosthesis' of substituting an invalid tricycle for a leg and enters the wider realm of social dreams. I entirely agree with him that *all* the disabled should have help with mobility: the chance, for instance, to hire a taxi to get to some social event. The trouble is that, once you get away from the idea of a vehicle, you get away from the qualification of ability to drive – and provision for non-drivers becomes alarmingly expensive. I don't think we can get out of this difficulty without spending some money and I say we must send an SOS Minute to Harold urging him to allow us to provide cars for existing categories, *plus* the beginning of a mobility allowance for other groups as the first instalment of a mobility allowance that would eventually enable us to move completely to cash: cost £25 million. I hope that his recognition of what he himself said to the Disabled Drivers Group before the election will swing him to our side. I think it is time the disabled had a look in.

Tuesday, 16 July

Up early to have my hair done; then into Cabinet. (We never seem to meet before 11am these days.) The main item was Concorde again, and Elwyn introduced the brief for the PM's meeting with Giscard which, he said, had been unanimously agreed by the Ministerial Committee. I had read it with mounting irritation. Conscious as I was of the public expenditure pressures, I was furious at the way we were drifting into a more and more expensive commitment to Wedgie's toy and my fury exploded as I heard Elwyn obviously trimming our resolution not to proceed beyond sixteen planes. He wanted the phrase to run: 'But any agreement to authorize further production or development must clearly define the commitment of the parties.' When he added, 'It will be a real battle to hold them down to sixteen,' I thought the time had come to do something. I said that it was clear to me from the brief that we were retreating before we started. It was obvious that the production of sixteen planes was no use to the French, and if they were convinced that we were firm in our determination *not* to proceed beyond this number, their whole attitude to cancellation might change. The break would then come from their side, which would release us from the legal restraints which were supposed to be governing us. I could see we were drifting inexorably into an open-ended commitment that would knock all our public expenditure plans for six. 'When some of you round this table see what the public expenditure cuts are going to do to the NHS and other social services, you will weep,' I declared passionately. I knew I had impressed Cabinet. Roy Jenkins and Tony C. leaned forward to nod their approval to me. Roy and Reg spoke firmly in support of me and Denis rallied to say he had always warned of the consequences of going ahead. Mike and Peter, Wedgie's firm allies, were silenced and Harold said that all these points must be borne in mind. We were definitely limited in our commitment to sixteen aircraft. I felt I had achieved something.

Next Michael walked his usual tightrope over the Pay Board's report on London Weighting. He said the TUC insisted it must be considered 'not as a straitjacket; simply as a guide to negotiators'. Of course the Government itself ought not to lead the breach of pay policy, but equally there must not be a Government veto on negotiations. That brought Jim and co. into play to express their anxiety. Jim said the unions must realize that the total was fixed; they must therefore negotiate on the 'kitty principle'. Said Mike, 'We would never have settled the miners' strike that way. There had to be a bit more to get a settlement.' Roy J. intervened: 'I thought the miners were a special case?' Bob backed Mike by saying there must be 'free negotiations'; that was the whole basis of our policy. But it was Denis who once again showed what a shrewd realist he is. 'We are embarked,' he said, 'on a new experiment. Sometimes it is cheaper to the economy to settle. There has got to be some latitude.' Harold supported Mike, 'though some in Cabinet have doubts', to which Jim said fervently, 'Hear, hear!' We quickly despatched the remaining business: abandoning Maplin[1] and approving Roy's Sex Discrimination Bill, though Roy did go on an unconscionable time while introducing it. No one had the nerve to rebuke him openly, but there were a lot of *sotto voce* mutterings.

Later I ran into Roy in the corridor. He said to me shyly, 'You once told me that I had forfeited your respect for me. I want you to know I don't feel the same about you. I have a great respect and admiration for you as a Minister and find myself agreeing 70 per cent of the time with your contributions in Cabinet.' I was very touched.

Wednesday, 17 July

Another COHSE deputation on the nurses' campaign for an interim pay increase. These industrial disputes are exhausting all my time. I listened patiently, explained

[1] Work on the new Maplin airport at Foulness near Southend had been suspended after the February election and a committee of civil servants set up to review the need for the £800 million project. They recommended halting work giving three main reasons why it was not as necessary as when the Roskill Commission had reported in 1970:

  1. the expansion of air services had come to a virtual standstill following the fare rises caused by oil price rises;
  2. worldwide inflation was adding to the disinclination of the public to travel;
  3. larger airliners were taking the strain off runways and terminal buildings to an extent unsuspected when Roskill was written.

The British Airports Authority had told the committee that they could cope with existing airports until 1990, which was too far ahead for planning a third airport.

endlessly – and kept thinking to myself how remarkable it is that these 'militant' unions always seem to come out on strike when there's a Labour Government.

Thursday, 18 July

The pace of Cabinet meetings is hotting up. Harold warned that in addition to two Cabinet meetings for the next two weeks, Cabinet might have to meet in the week beginning 5 August. When we all sat up at that, Harold asked, 'How many of you will be away that week?' When a positive chorus broke out, someone said primly, 'You *told* us to get away at the beginning of August, Prime Minister.' I shall be furious if our Mauritius trip gets wrecked. What annoys me is that *this* Cabinet has only been called for 11.30am. I like Harold's new relaxed mood – but not if it doodles us on into August. Before then we have to have Denis's economic statement on 22 July and last night at the H and W dinner I was trying to stir Mike, Peter *et al*. into supporting my attempt to ensure that any reflationary measures he takes shall be directed through the public expenditure field. It remains a continuing contradiction to proper social and economic planning that expenditure decisions are strictly controlled by Treasury, while the rest of us have no control over taxation policy, which is equally vital to demand management. As it is, we have to wait patiently for Denis to disclose what he intends to do; Cabinet control of budgetary policy remains a mirage.

Fred looked hopefully for praise for what he had done to get agreement at Brussels to a scheme for direct premiums for beef producers.[1] The praise was perfunctory because he hasn't managed to prevent the Community from suspending imports of beef. Harold admitted that 'we regretted it', but it did not prejudice our determination to achieve long-term changes in the CAP. I'll believe them when I see them. Finally we turned to a discussion of the proposed increases in Members' allowances. I supported them as a step towards the proper treatment of MPs' secretaries, whose conditions and pay, I pointed out, continue to be scandalous. But when we turned to the suggestion that Peers' allowances should be increased too, I interposed: 'I want to declare an interest; I oppose.' Wedgie, whose wit is a relief from his tendency to excessive seriousness, said he wanted to declare a *non*-interest.[2] He too opposed. We were overruled on the basis of sob stories about some of our Labour stalwarts in the Lords, who came from the North and were out of pocket from the cost of staying in London. I replied that the real answer was to review the whole system so as to

[1] Pending the renegotiations over Britain's membership of the EEC, the Government had suspended the system of 'intervention' buying of beef under the Common Agricultural Policy, on the principle that 'beef was for eating and not for keeping in store'. In July the Community gave reluctant approval to our paying fixed premia per head of cattle to supplement producers' returns from the market, but only on a temporary basis. See also footnote to page 229.

[2] In the early 1960s Anthony Wedgwood Benn had conducted a long campaign to renounce the peerage he had inherited from his father, the first Viscount Stansgate, which had robbed him of his membership of the House of Commons as MP for Bristol South-East. As a result of his brilliant tactics a Joint Parliamentary Commission was set up to consider Lords reform. This led to the passing of the Peerages Act 1973, which authorized the disclaimer for life of certain hereditary peerages. Within minutes of its becoming law, Benn had surrendered his. Some time later he announced that he was dropping the 'Wedgwood' from his name. Unrepentant I continued to call him 'Wedgie' and Dick Crossman once told me: 'You are the only one who is allowed to call him that.'

introduce a differential rate between Peers living in London and those in the provinces. Harold said we would ask the Top Salaries Review Board to do just that – for the next round.

I am desperate about the problem of mobility for the disabled. Another long office meeting, Alf as harassed and unhappy as usual. Eventually I said, 'We can't solve this with less than £30 million. I'm going to send the PM a Minute setting out the problem.' I sat down and drafted it myself.

Monday, 22 July

Up to town early for the Liaison Committee with the TUC. The purpose was to discuss the draft Manifesto circulated by Transport House. Our side was thin on the ground – Michael, me, Wedgie, Mik and Ted Short, with Harold arriving late. On the trade union side Jack Jones was there, as grimly determined as ever. George Smith, Alf Allen, David Basnett and Len Murray were ready for business. Hughie – familiarly now – was absent. The unions were clearly anxious to put their imprimatur on the document. First reactions were on the section dealing with the Social Contract. Jack objected to the reference: 'Unions should not have two bites at the same cherry' (referring to the threshold agreements). Jack described it as 'clearly a Freudian slip' and suggested an alternative: 'so that there should not be two bites . . .' Wedgie seized the opportunity to give us one of his little homilies: 'I understood the Social Contract was an agreement we reached about the whole range of policies, not a mere form of voluntary incomes policy. Could we not spell out what the Social Contract means?' Of course the unions had to endorse this. Said Len, 'This was the point I was going to make.'

Jack pounced too on certain sentences in the EEC section, clearly showing that Harold will have trouble with the T and G if he ever recommends that we stay in. Wedgie, of course, endorsed Jack's line: 'I agree with that wholeheartedly.' Jack, for instance, objected to the omission of any reference to a European defence policy. 'Defence is being skated over, but it is a fundamental part of an economic union. The party is opposed to this.' Next Jack sought to toughen up the section on the referendum, claiming that there must be a firmer commitment to a date for it. 'As the referendum will be an election issue we should say that it *will* take place.' Ted Short backed him: 'I am sure the setting of a fixed period to the negotiations is necessary for our credibility.' Harold's reaction interested me. He intervened to say that he and Jim C. were thinking of a double timetable for this: first, for the conclusion of the negotiations; secondly, for the holding of a referendum. And he added revealingly, 'The pro-marketeers have made a lot of its being a "consultative" referendum. I personally think it must be final and binding.' Jack nodded approvingly through all this. Does it mean, I wondered, that at last Harold is prepared to take on Roy Jenkins?

Jack's next ploy was over pensions. He hoped we would include a Christmas bonus. And, he asked me, what relationship pensions would have to earnings when they became payable in July? Not very hot, I admitted. But I added hastily that we would be dealing with this in our long-term pension proposals. Jack said darkly that we could not be content with pensions at merely 22 per cent of average net earnings and should move towards a higher percentage immediately. Jack also dismissed with contempt the reference to the need for an anti-poverty strategy: 'What does it mean? This becomes a meaningless exercise.' Of course it becomes nothing of the kind and once again I was aware of Jack's inability to see beyond a short-term pensions campaign. Brian and I *must* get our White Paper out quickly!

On nationalization George Smith came in with one of his earthy comments. He wasn't at all happy about the bit on the construction industry. He wanted to avoid the 'airy fairy views of nationalization by some people'. Jack's final shot was over workers' representation on supervisory boards in industry. The representatives must be elected, not appointed – and elected through their unions.

Just before noon Ministers had to leave for the mini-Budget Cabinet. Denis's revelations were as predicted, though he made a good case. I said I was sorry he had chosen to reduce VAT rather than increase family allowances, as the latter would have helped those who were too poor to have much to spend. Nonetheless I appreciated why he was driven to adopt an anti-inflationary strategy. But I flatly denounced his proposal to tackle unemployment by doubling the Regional Employment Premium [REP], which was indiscriminate, rather than through investment in construction in development areas through an expansion of public expenditure on housing and hospitals. Wedgie and Mike supported me on this, Wedgie pointing out that his four alternatives to the REP increase had all been rejected, though they would have been more effective. Mike modified his criticism by saying that it was creditable that Denis had done anything at all and Harold Lever echoed this: 'When I look at what other countries are doing, I have to congratulate the Chancellor on his courage.' Altogether Cabinet was clearly cheered by the attractive package. But I stirred them by my speech, in which I warned them what lay ahead of us on public expenditure: 'When we realize what we are going to have to do with our programmes there will be broken hearts all round this table.' Denis worried me by his response. He said that he was trying to find ways in which to soften the blow and then went out of his way to mention his hope of making another £20 million available for school building and something to help Willie with investment in Scottish industry. Not a word about hospitals. I remembered ruefully how Joel had told Brian and me how feeble Reg P. was as a Minister: he asked for nothing. 'I feel like *pressing* money on him.' So he is to be rewarded while I am passed over as a greedy Minister who has already had too much!

Back to the office for the Ministers' meeting over a sandwich; then into a series of office meetings over the policy documents going to Social Services Committee of Cabinet this week and also – inevitably these days – over the industrial action that is being taken, or threatened, in every section of the NHS. I cleared up some details over our disablement income paper, but it is a bleak outlook over Sharp. I tremble to think what is going to happen to all these policies. It is not my fault that so many of the Manifesto commitments are in my field, and I know that, if I am not careful, there will be nothing left for the health side. That is why I have been busy joining with Treasury in shooting down Harold's series of suggestions for *ad hoc* (and vote-catching) concessions for pensioners, such as free TV licences and making concessionary fares mandatory. We are already landed with the Christmas bonus, thanks to the Tories, who, for all their sneers at Harold's 'gimmickry', have excelled at it themselves.

Next into confabs over the works engineers and radiographers who are threatening to close the NHS down. At the Ministers' lunch the MPs had united against me to say that I must concede an interim rise for nurses and radiographers. I told them stubbornly that the situation was not as simple as that. I agreed with them that it was important to have these disputes settled before the election (and to have a payment in hand for the nurses), but I did not believe that a panic concession on interim payments would necessarily settle the disputes and that our only hope was to get Halsbury to report on the nurses earlier. He has promised to give me a firm date for the nurses' report next week, but I said I would see him before then to discuss the whole problem with him. This we proceeded to arrange.

Then over to the House to struggle with constituency correspondence in the absence of a secretary. This took nearly two hours and it was late before I could get down to tomorrow's papers on our national superannuation scheme. At 8pm Brian O'M. joined me and I went through certain points with him. Tired and hungry, we continued our detailed discussion over a meal. Home at 11.30pm, with two boxes to clear before I could go to bed. No one outside a department has any idea of the pressure.

Harold has replied to my *cri de coeur* over Sharp by saying the matter must go to Social Services Committee. So much for relying on him!

Tuesday, 23 July

To the disapproval of the department I insisted on taking an hour off on my way to the office to try to buy a swimsuit for my holiday. All the ones I have got are ten years old! Of course I have left it too late and there wasn't a swimsuit of my size to be had. When Pearl picked me up she said would I please hurry to the office as they had laid on a meeting with Halsbury. I found him waiting for me and I settled down for a long persuasive talk with him. Having outlined my problem I asked him how he could help: perhaps by producing an *interim* report on the nurses earlier? But he wouldn't budge: an interim report would take as long as a final one. Finally he said reluctantly that he would discuss the position with his committee. On an impulse I asked whether it would help if I were to come and address the committee myself? To my surprise he said it would. So I shall have the fight of my life there!

Took a sandwich to the hairdressers and did some quiet work under the drier. Then to Broadcasting House to record my ministerial broadcast on the uprating of pensions. As always, a good hair-do was like a tonic; careful make-up and I looked positively fresh! Revived, I went on to do battle in the Social Services Committee on the Sharp Report. To my surprise Joel said he didn't want to discuss Sharp at this stage and proceeded to say we couldn't decide anything on anything until the PESC exercise was complete. I began to despair, but Ted Short in the chair was magnificent and in his summing-up ignored the Treasury's caveats, saying we were agreed something must be decided before September and that the committee accepted our proposals in principle. (I thanked him in the House later, and he said in his brisk way,

'Of course we've got to publish these policies. Everything you are putting forward is a vote winner.') We got the national superannuation document through on the same basis and I emerged feeling much less worried than I had been. For the first time in my experience a representative of CPRS[1] was at the Committee to support a paper they had put in arguing that 'Ministers will wish to consider the proposed package against the tight constraints on public expenditure'. No one took any notice of him – whoever he was.

The H and W dinner is off tonight because some of our friends on the NEC are peevish at not being included in these dinners (following Nora Beloff's revelations) and have asked that we NEC members should have a meeting before tomorrow's NEC. Only Wedgie, Michael and I turned up, in addition to Frank [Allaun], Lena [Jeger] and Joan [Lestor]. Mik was in a very sour mood. When I said to Wedgie that I should have to leave the NEC meeting early tomorrow because there was a Cabinet Committee meeting on Kilbrandon, in which I had an interest, Mik said that was just typical of the gulf that was growing up again between the Government and the NEC. 'It is just as wide as it was in the last Labour Government.' Personally I think this is nonsense, but Mik went on to instance Harold's decision to wind up the Monitoring Committee on the EEC negotiations and the failure of the Government to let the International Committee have an answer on the rescheduling of the Chilean debt. Frank and Lena were worried about John Silkin's land policy.[2] Michael and I did what we could to soothe Mik down and we agreed to raise all these points tomorrow.

Wednesday, 24 July

Mik seemed to have sobered down a bit when he raised his various points at the NEC. He was studiously polite and moderate, but this did not prevent a near row between him and Jim, whose behaviour I thought to be unnecessarily offensive. (Perhaps we are all getting tetchy at the end of an exhausting summer term.) When Mik tried to raise the question of what was happening on the Monitoring Committee and moved that the NEC should proceed to replace the four Ministers who, according to the papers, had now been withdrawn by the PM (including the chairman, Wedgie), Jim from the chair just told him brusquely, 'I cannot accept your Motion.' When, keeping his temper, Mik queried this ruling, Jim said, 'It does not possibly arise out of this item,' and even added, 'There isn't going to be anything for this Monitoring Committee to do before the election.' I interposed to ask if Ron Hayward had received any communication about this committee from the PM, and Ron said he had been informed that the four Government members were being withdrawn. I therefore suggested this meant the NEC had a duty to fill their places, but Jim would have none of it. Mik must put down a Motion for next time. 'I am not prepared to accept any Motion on this item, and if Ian doesn't like it he must move me out of the chair.' To my surprise Mik said nothing – but I'm damn sure this isn't the end of it. I had to leave for the MISC [Miscellaneous] meeting of Cabinet on devolution before

---

[1] See footnote, page 48.

[2] One of our key Manifesto commitments was to take land required for development into common ownership and John Silkin was responsible for preparing the legislation.

Wedgie's Motion on a special conference on the EEC was reached, or the one on the Chilean debt, but I learned later that both were carried.

The discussion at MISC showed how deep are the waters into which we have got. Officials clearly don't like the idea of devolution at all and have come out for legislative devolution as being, though dangerous, less so than the sweeping ideas on executive devolution that Norman Hunt had pressed. Willie was as gloomy as usual: we ought not to have gone so far, he said, but, having started the whole enquiry, we had roused expectations we could not resist. 'It will now be impossible to avoid Scheme A [legislative devolution].' But he hinted darkly it might lead to the break-up of the UK. John Morris was far more enthusiastic. Expectations had been built up and we could be in grave difficulties in a few years' time if we did not meet them. A directly elected assembly was essential and had in any case long been part of the Welsh Labour Party policy. It was the haves who were for the *status quo* and the have nots who wanted a greater say. Roy Jenkins clearly disapproved of the whole business: 'I am horrified at the idea of rushing into a decision in the last fevered weeks of July which could affect the shape of Great Britain for a hundred years.' He didn't like the effect of all this on law and order and in any case doubted whether it would influence many votes. Eric and Edmund supported him, but Ted Short said testily that he had spent months on this and time and again had pledged a White Paper before the election. It was impossible for us not to make a statement soon. Eventually Harold ruled that Norman Hunt should submit a modified form of Scheme A for consideration next week. I raised the dangers of introducing a single transferable vote and was assured we would not be recommending this.

The papers are full of Marcia's installation in the Lords yesterday,[1] which I did not get time to go and see. Ted tells me she did it impeccably and with dignity. Whatever else one thinks of her she certainly is a remarkable personality. Personally I always got on well with her, but it is astonishing how many people are outraged at Harold's gesture – including Mik. It is typical of Harold that he should have gone to watch his own handiwork. The cheeky chappie is also a stubborn one. But Ted says their Lordships are disgusted at *The Times* for its profile on Marcia today, revealing that she has two children by Walter Terry. So dog has at last eaten dog! But the hack journalists of the right-wing press must be desperate in their determination to discredit Harold if possible.

Back at the office to spend an hour and a half carefully going through Brian's draft of our White Paper on National Superannuation and amending it in detail. Then a hurried office briefing on PESC, ready for Friday's misery. David [Owen] is desperately worried over the works engineers. He says the management side of Whitley has messed things up and never faced up to the realities. As a result we are faced with widespread industrial action which can cause chaos in hospitals. The press is making the most of it. We draft an urgent letter to Michael asking for more leeway to get a settlement.

I hadn't had time to surface from my papers to see what was going on in the House

---

[1] On 24 May Harold Wilson had announced fifteen new life peerages. Typically, he had responded to the harassment of Marcia Williams over the land deals by including her in the list. She took the title of Lady Falkender and made it clear she would continue to work as his political secretary.

before the division bell rang. In the division lobby Harold came up to me, full of himself: 'My amendment has completely foxed them; there's life in the old dog yet. I know you all think he is finished, but he's up to it still.' I gathered that he had thought up an amendment to Heath's Motion on Denis's economic proposals which would put Heath in the soup. Well, it certainly did the trick.[1] The Tories were in complete disarray and only twenty-five people voted against us. Afterwards I listened with glee to Jeremy Thorpe's impotent protests in the House. It put our people in good heart – particularly because, according to my Ted, Harold had made a good speech. One of our chaps remarked of the Tories, 'That lot is finished.'

Thursday, 25 July

Our joint meeting between Cabinet and NEC on the draft Manifesto took place in the large dining room at No. 10. Looking round the oil paintings on the walls Joan Maynard asked me, 'Is this where you have your Cabinet meetings?' 'God, no!' I replied. 'The Cabinet room is much more austere.' The atmosphere of the meeting seemed relaxed and genial enough and there was considerable agreement during the second reading debate on the draft Manifesto. No one objected when Denis warned there would be little margin for expensive new policies when we got back. True, Reg Prentice, who is growing more overtly right-wing every day, said we should remember that there was a widespread desire for national unity. We should therefore talk more in terms of the national interest. 'Only a minority in this country are socialist.' Roy [Jenkins] also attacked the document as 'too complacent'. Things were going to be very grim. Wedgie made his usually intense speech to the effect that the whole system was breaking down, and John Chalmers[2] said he entirely agreed with him: the system was creaking. And he went on to say that the unions could not hold their members back if they saw a few people doing very well out of it. Michael said we could lose the election if we threw over our plans for public ownership. The country only respected parties who said what they believed, even if it appeared unpopular. I said that I agreed with Denis that the Social Contract was central to our policy. But it would be wrong to present it as merely a contract between the Government and the TUC: it was between the Government and the people. We had got to do a major job of educating the country in what we were trying to do and what the restraints were, and above all to get them involved in the importance to them of the social wage. A lot of people echoed this afterwards. Wedgie returned to his old theme: 'I take the Social Contract to mean a joint programme jointly agreed and jointly implemented,' to which Harold added, 'I agree.'

The real trouble broke out when we came to the Common Market bit. Once again I realized what Harold is up against and what trouble he will be in if he tries to shift the delicate balance in the party in any way. Fred Mulley, in the chair, reported that Jim

---

[1] The Opposition had put down a Motion attacking the Government's handling of the economic situation and Harold had drafted an amendment welcoming the Chancellor's extension of rate relief and other popular concessions in his July package.

[2] Mr John Chalmers, General Secretary of the Boilermakers' Union, was a member of the trade-union section of the NEC.

had sent a message to the effect that he was in favour of a commitment to a timetable for the referendum, but it ought to be a general one of twelve months. Harold seized the opportunity to say we ought to add something to the effect 'and in any case not later than four months after the completion of the negotiations'. We must also eliminate the reference to consultation by means of an election. 'There is a sheer constitutional problem here and I am not certain the Queen would grant the request for a general election.' This roused Roy J. 'I wish to place on record my deep-seated and continuing objection to a referendum and therefore my preference for keeping the options open. We could not keep the use of the referendum to this subject.' Shirley supported him. 'The referendum is a device of right-wing systems. I don't myself share Roy's view that you cannot limit it to one issue, but why change the form of the general election alternative now?' Reg P. said he spoke as 'an agnostic about the Market', adding, 'I have supported the referendum but think now I was wrong to do so. I do not see how, given the sovereignty of Parliament, the referendum can be binding.' Crosland wanted to stick to the wording in the Manifesto.[1] Bob complained: 'Why are we raising all this issue again? I don't find the Market the great burning issue some of you do. Why not leave well alone?' Denis suggested we should fix a time limit (i.e. by the end of 1975) and leave the Government free to have an election or not. Harold climbed down: 'I would prefer to wait till the chairman of the party is here. We are taking no decision today.' And so it was left: the grumbling appendix which, to everyone's relief, has not yet become acute.

Friday, 26 July

The first round of the battle over next year's public expenditure White Paper. Denis introduced his paper to Cabinet in less provocative terms than Jim used to do in the same role. He reassured us by saying there would be no settlement of individual programmes before the recess and that we could not do everything at once by trying to close the *whole* of the balance of payments deficit by 1978–79. Nonetheless we must begin to progress towards it and it was necessary to fix a public expenditure increase limit of $2\frac{3}{4}$ per cent in demand terms. If Cabinet accepted that, it meant that any increases in individual programmes would have to come from other programmes or from the contingency reserve. The claims from health and social security would already absorb the whole of that and we must keep half of it uncommitted. The $1\frac{1}{2}$ per cent increase he proposed for private consumption would just allow wages to keep pace with prices, plus some exceptions identified by the TUC. This would leave £700 million for the annual increase in public expenditure (i.e. $2\frac{3}{4}$ per cent a year).

It was soon clear that Cabinet broadly agreed with him, though Reg piled it on about what this would mean in the educational field and said that, if the figure was agreed, he would be seeking increases at the expense of other people's programmes. I was more challenging. I asked Denis, 'What level of unemployment are you visualizing? According to the Organization for Economic Co-operation and Development

---

[1] The words in the February Manifesto were: 'If renegotiations are successful, it is the policy of the Labour Party that, in view of the unique importance of the decision, the people should have the right to decide the issue through a General Election or a Consultative Referendum.'

[OECD], unemployment is going to rise to 800,000 or one million next year. Is that the sort of scenario a Labour Government can survive? Or are we going to have emergency programmes of less essential items of expenditure brought forward at the last minute to stimulate the employment our cuts in really essential items have reduced? If your cuts reduce growth all your other assumptions are vitiated.' I also pointed out that a lot of my items were transfer payments like pensions which were a form of private consumption, not at its expense. I insisted that it was impossible to agree the figure of 2¾ per cent until we had seen the effects of this on the individual services. What was more, we should never make a success of the Social Contract unless we succeeded in converting trade unionists to the importance to them of the social wage.

Mike echoed me sympathetically. This figure would have grave consequences for our programmes. The whole of the constraints were so great that we must find some other way out (e.g. by stimulating productivity through the extension of industrial democracy). Crosland, on the other hand, accepted the 2¾ per cent while putting in a plug for housing. 'We face the collapse of the housing programme. I hope Denis will have a look at the construction industry.' Wedgie said we must review the whole assumptions behind the Regional Employment Premium. One of our difficulties was that tax reliefs were not decided by us collectively. Harold Lever burst out: 'This is a sterile exercise on assumptions that will not be fulfilled.' I wasn't quite clear what he was driving at, particularly as he went on to say that some of the proposed new expenditures were not sacrosanct (e.g. the land policy). We should also have another look at the school-leaving age of sixteen. And he added darkly, 'Let those who believe in a siege economy say so at the next election.' (I think he was getting at Wedgie.) Harold then summed up in phrases that gave us all something for which we had asked: we must take the 2¾ per cent as a 'guiding principle', but we were only committed to a procedure of examination by officials, not to its detailed outcome.

Monday, 29 July

Bob held a noon drinks party to celebrate his promotion,[1] inviting the lobby and Ministers. Everyone was talking about Roy Jenkins's disastrous speech on Friday.[2] When Ted and I saw him on TV I said, 'That has cost us the election.' Eric Heffer, Mik, Syd Bidwell et Tribune al. haven't made things any better by rushing into public attacks on Roy. One of the pressmen asked me if I was going to join in the fray. I replied no: I thought we should none of us make speeches on anything but our

[1] On 26 July it had been announced that Bob Mellish, as Government Chief Whip, was to become a member of the Cabinet instead of merely attending by invitation. The appointment was to be personal to him. David Owen was made Minister of State at DHSS on the same date.

[2] In a speech at Haverfordwest, Roy Jenkins, while rejecting the 'febrile coalition talk', urged that the Labour Party must win over the 'great body of moderate, rather uncommitted opinion' in Britain and implied that this was being alienated by the left-wing views in the party. For some time a group of middle-of-the-road and right-wing Labour MPs had been meeting to discuss how to counter the growing influence of the left-wing Tribune group of MPs and this move was formalized on 17 December 1974 by the establishment of the 'Manifesto Group' of Labour backbenchers under the chairmanship of a prominent pro-marketeer, Dr Dickson Mabon.

departmental work between now and the election. Ian Aitken of the *Guardian* tried to incite me into an indiscretion, but I merely replied that I liked Roy and thought he was badly advised.

I was *distrait* during our Ministers' lunch, being conscious that I had a major job on my hands that afternoon trying to persuade the nurses and radiographers to accept Halsbury's date.[1] First the nurses. The staff side listened attentively, but only made a non-committal comment. The PSMs were more forthcoming. After considering what I had said they called me back while Miss Maddocks read a statement warmly welcoming the date *by a majority*. The sting was in the tail. The three unions that really matter (the Society of Radiographers, ASTMS and COHSE) had reserved their position. I have told my chaps I must now mount the biggest exercise in individual contact with the unions, leaders and executives that I have ever done.

We started tonight with a series of meetings with the key chaps in my room at the House. Clive [Jenkins] first. 'Will you help me?' I asked, at which he spat out 'No'. He then proceeded to be as insulting as he knew how and told me his union would enter into widespread and destructive industrial action immediately. I was furious enough inside, but my show of temper was deliberate. 'All right then, go ahead,' I told him. 'I can't stop you destroying me and the Government. If that is what you want, it is war.' We screamed at each other like fishwives and officials sat cowed at the most unholy row they had ever heard. I thought Clive would walk out, but he lingered on. As I had guessed, this was the only way to treat him and he was clearly shaken by my determination not to budge. 'I've asked you to meet my members,' he said, 'but you haven't even had the courtesy to reply. You have behaved abominably.' I told him that was a lie and that I was willing to meet his members now – tomorrow if he liked. We finally agreed on Friday. He still hung around muttering and I almost had to throw him out, knowing that his enemy, the Society of Radiographers, were waiting in the wings. In came the Society's Secretary, Denley, and the President. They were polite, but tough. No, they didn't think they could persuade their members to accept Halsbury's date for their interim. Over drinks they softened a bit and said they would see what they could do, but would like me to meet their national council. Finally Albert Spanswick and his President. Albert was positively mellow and I think they will accept the nurses' date. All this took over three hours and I was limp at the end of it. And it is going to go on all week!

Tuesday, 30 July

Up at 6am to struggle through my massive brief on the National Superannuation White Paper which we are bringing before Cabinet today. I had to be in the office

---

[1] Owing to the growing threat to the Health Service from industrial action by nurses and radiographers, I had been to see the Halsbury Committee a few days earlier to plead with them to give me an early date for the publication of their report on nurses' pay. I also suggested that the committee might, on the basis of that report, be able to make proposals for interim payments for radiographers and the rest at the same time. The committee promised to consider my difficulties sympathetically and later agreed that I could announce that they would produce their report on nurses in the week beginning 16 September, on the understanding that there would be no interim increase before then and would produce an interim report on PSMs at the same time.

early for the first of my round of talks with individual union executives: today·with COHSE. Once again I spelt out the case for awaiting the Halsbury report on 16 September. They were immensely friendly and one of them said he was impressed by my obvious sincerity. They grumbled about the Whitley machinery and I promised to consider any proposals for change once the nurses' problem was out of the way. Later I learned that they had agreed to my compromise positively enthusiastically – one success I badly need to brighten a troubled week! But at Cabinet I had another success too. National superannuation went through with only a few manoeuvres, pretty half-hearted ones, by Denis to whittle it down and to my joy he agreed that the White Paper ought to be published before the TUC Congress. The only trouble now is that the HMSO printing dispute shows no sign of ending, so we will probably have to issue it in typed form.

One thing that interested me was the total lack of interest in Cabinet in discussing my scheme. Remembering from Dick's days how complex these matters can seem to outsiders – and how long Dick took to expound his own scheme – I had gone to a lot of trouble to sketch out a summary, but before I had finished delivering it Harold interrupted to say that I really shouldn't assume that my colleagues hadn't read their documents. All I can say is that that is exactly my experience! But Cabinet – and particularly Harold – is in the mood these days to settle everything in committee, so Cabinets get shorter and shorter and the discussions on major policy items more perfunctory. The others were teasing me afterwards about my long oration. Said Bob, 'I said to Tony if she goes on any longer we'll all be old age pensioners.' But I didn't care: I've won and we've got a first-class scheme through with few compromises, despite PESC.

Lunch with Conrad[1] was a matey affair. He called me 'Barbara', sympathized with me in all my difficulties and eventually promised to do what he could to help. His trouble was, he said, that the staff at the Department of Employment was very thin on the ground because of the hiving off. He could ill spare Douglas Smith, for whom I pleaded. I told Conrad that the job I offered could lead quickly to a larger remit: to help sort out the whole Whitley machinery and to evolve a pay policy for the public sector in the light of the new pay policy. He could see the importance of that, particularly as he has no doubt that the voluntary pay policy will break down and that we shall be back to a statutory one before long – under any government. 'Isn't the Civil Service a remarkable thing?' he mused. 'Here am I, well known for my views on the need for a statutory incomes policy – and yet in this job. And Robert Armstrong: he enjoyed working with the previous PM and had built up quite a loyalty to him, yet Harold keeps him on.' I replied that I had always said that I didn't mind what a civil

[1] Conrad Heron, who had been my key man on industrial relations when I was Secretary of State for Employment and Productivity in 1968–70, had become Second Permanent Secretary at the department (renamed the Department of Employment) and now worked with Michael Foot. My aim in taking him out to lunch was to persuade him to persuade Michael to release one of his top conciliators – preferably my former very able Private Secretary, Douglas Smith – to help us at DHSS with the spate of industrial disputes we were experiencing. The difficulty I met was that, since my day there, most of the original functions of the old Ministry of Labour had been hived off to independent bodies. The conciliation work had gone to the new ACAS [the Advisory Conciliation and Arbitration Service]; training to a new Training Services Agency and health and safety to the Health and Safety Executive.

servant's political views were provided he was open about them. It was nonsense to expect any intelligent man to be apolitical. What I liked was to surround myself with civil servants of differing political views and then get them arguing about policy. In that way I was really able to work out the pros and cons.

I asked Conrad how he got on with Michael Foot. 'Oh, what a charming man,' he exclaimed, but I detected something less than idolatry. 'How does he get on with the administrative side?' I asked. 'Ah, well, his only policy is to find out what the unions want,' he replied. One thing nearly drove them to distraction. When Michael had a major speech to make, they put up briefs which they doubted whether he even read. 'We ask: is there anything else you want to discuss with us? He won't put up even an outline of his speech, but will suddenly say he is going out for a walk. He will be gone for about an hour and a half and when he comes back he has obviously worked it all out.' I said I thought that that was the best way to prepare speeches, but Conrad shook his head and said it led to all sorts of slips, 'like his remark about Donaldson,[1] for example'. I insisted that that was a small price to pay. Even the most cautious of us were liable to indiscretions which then dogged us for the rest of our lives. I said that what had astonished me was the way Michael had sturdily shouldered his share of unpopular decisions. 'Ah,' replied Conrad, 'but do you think he will really stay put when the going gets tough?' I said I did. Typically, Conrad repeated that the most short-sighted thing my party had done was to reject *In Place of Strife*. Clearly here is a civil servant who thinks that Armageddon is not far away, yearns for a coalition and thinks the only answer is to contain the unions in a framework of legal restrictions.

After various office meetings, including a discussion with Dick Bourton about how we could get more money under PESC for the NHS, Norman Warner (who has now taken over as my Private Secretary) phoned to say that the Home Secretary was in his room if I would like to see him now. On an impulse I had decided to talk to Roy, whose speech and its repercussions are still headline news. Roy greeted me as warmly as he is capable of and I went straight to the point. 'Roy, I wanted to have a word with you in the greatest friendliness because I am very fond of you. I think that once again you have listened to very bad advice. I have been struck by how harmonious we have been in this Cabinet. You know my views on Europe: I've always been against entry and hope the negotiations will at least get us out of the grandiose implications of the Treaty of Rome. But if the people voted to stay in, I shouldn't leave the Government. I'd stay in and try to make the best of it. Of course the press is waiting to egg you on: you are their mouthpiece for Europe and they are using you. But your friends ought to know better. They are driving you into a course that can only ruin your political career....' At this point, red in the face with sudden emotion, Roy said violently, 'What makes you think I care about my political career? All that matters to me is what is happening in the world, which I think is heading for disaster. I can't stand by and see us pretend everything is all right when I know we are heading for

---

[1] In a Commons debate on 7 May, Michael Foot had said that part of the Conservative approach to industrial relations was to rely upon '... some trigger-happy judicial finger'. Asked if he was referring to Sir John, he said, 'Of course I am referring to Sir John Donaldson'. The Opposition attacked the phrase as 'unparliamentary'.

catastrophe.' More calmly he added, 'It isn't only Europe. It is a question of whether this country is going to cut itself off from the Western Alliance and go isolationist.' I was frankly puzzled. 'I simply don't see where you get that fear from. Are you suggesting we are going Communist?' No, it wasn't as crude as that. At this moment the division bell interrupted us. We stood up and Roy said, smiling affectionately, 'But I repeat what I told you in the corridor the other day. I think you are a very good Minister and 70 per cent of the time I agree with what you say in Cabinet. I appreciate that you have spoken in friendliness.' He squeezed my hand. As we made our way downstairs I persisted: 'But what exactly do you want the Government to do that it isn't doing? What is *your* remedy for our troubles? Personally I think the basic dilemma today is to get people to share responsibility instead of confusing short-term militancy with the need for fundamental change. But that problem remains whether we are inside Europe or outside it.' He had no answer. Awkwardly he said, 'Let us have a talk sometime', and disappeared thankfully.

Hurried meeting with some members of the Tribune group, led by Dennis Skinner, who had asked me to see them to discuss the radiographers' dispute. They were concerned lest I might have to admit defeat and make a panic payment in the middle of the election campaign. I explained to them what had happened and asked them to use their influence with Clive. Jo Richardson, for one, looked anxious to help, but Dennis only said, 'You'll have to give in anyway.' Oh, will I!

No. 10 Committee Room was crowded for Harold's end-of-term speech to the PLP. He read every carefully prepared word of it and I found it pedestrian. But Ted [Castle] said the people sitting round him praised it as extremely skilful. I was sitting on the platform next to Tony C. As Harold went through a long catalogue of our achievements in government it began to be obvious that he was singling out Shirley for special and repeated praise. The rest of us got barely a mention (except Jim) and some Ministers none at all. Tony C. began muttering, 'Shirley 3, Jim 2, Barbara 1, poor Tony nought.' We soon got the giggles over Harold's patent manoeuvres. I whispered to Tony, 'He's making a bid for the pro-marketeers and of course he isn't going to mention Roy.' Tony started to keep a list of mentions, and as we passed housing and land without a single reference to him he scribbled at the bottom of it, 'Unfair to To-to!' I consoled him, 'You are now classed with Michael and Wedgie,' who hadn't been mentioned either, despite the big point Harold made of the repeal of the Industrial Relations Act. Afterwards Ted said to me that from Harold's speech it was clear that our election slogan was going to be 'Shirley for Queen'.

Our last 'Husbands and Wives' dinner before the recess was a bit thin on the ground, as Mike was having a celebratory party for the repeal of the Industrial Relations Act.[1] I asked Wedgie whether the press reports that he had been snubbed over industrial policy were true. He said no. The original draft of the industrial policy White Paper had been pretty unsatisfactory but he thought the latest one was much better. We were on a three-line whip and as John Silkin and I dashed for his car at one division bell (that is the beauty of Lockets: it is on the bell) we were followed out of the restaurant by Roy Jenkins and Reg Prentice, who stood on the steps looking

---

[1] The Trade Union and Labour Relations Act became law on 31 July.

helplessly around them. 'Quick,' we said, 'jump in.' Still they stood bewildered, and we almost had to drag them in. 'I didn't realize you were dining there,' said Roy vaguely. Neither of them had the grace to thank us; perhaps they were embarrassed at being caught in a conspiracy. They had clearly no idea that *our* conspiracy was going on in a private room! As we dashed through the division lobby John said to me, 'That is why I can't bear these right-wingers. They are arrogant, selfish and ...' 'Insensitive,' I added. I am personally convinced that Roy hasn't got it in him to lead the party – only to do a Gaitskell and divide it. And once again I realized that these right-wing and left-wing allegiancies are due as much to the chemical reaction between people as to ideology. To get back into that cosy room at Lockets, with Tommy, Katherine, Wedgie, Caroline, Judith, her Tony [Hart], Rosamund [Silkin] and Ted [Castle] was like getting back into a different world from Roy's.

Wednesday, 31 July

Five hours' sleep, then up to deal with my boxes. Ted tells me Marcia has had a mysterious phone call to contact Clive Jenkins. It turns out to be a message that he wants to see Harold urgently. I gather Clive has been considerably shaken by his row with me. At the office I am told the PM wants me to ring him. It turns out to be about this. I explain the situation and he says, 'Why don't we ask Mik[1] to help? Ask him whether he thinks I should see Clive.' Frantic efforts start to contact Mik. Meanwhile I go through a series of office meetings to give everyone their battle orders (particularly on PESC) before I go away on holiday. Then comes the message: Mik could see me at my room at the House at 1.15pm. Norman puts a sandwich and a carton of milk in my box and off I dash. I explain my *contretemps* with Clive to Mik, who looks worried and says that Clive is under terrible pressure from his rank and file. Mik too hankers after an interim payment for the radiographers, but says there can be no harm in our seeing Clive. I eat my sandwich hurriedly and get over to No. 10 to report to Harold, who gets his office to set up the meeting with Clive.

I would have felt less cheerful if I had known that I was going to spend the next eight hours in No. 10 – just like old times! First a long, wearying meeting of the Ministerial Committee on Industrial Development to finalize the White Paper on industrial policy.[2] I had presumably been invited because of the pharmaceutical

---

[1] Ian Mikardo was a member of the executive of Clive Jenkins's union, ASTMS.

[2] The White Paper which was eventually published, 'The Regeneration of British Industry' (Cmnd. 5710, August 1974), was very different both in tone and content from the Green Paper Tony Benn had proposed three months earlier. Its emphasis was all on the need for government 'partnership' with industry. There would be no statutory requirement on a company to enter a planning agreement. Financial assistance for these agreements would be additional, not conditional. The full range of help under the Industry Act 1972 would 'of course' continue to be available for companies not covered by them. There was no mention of extending planning agreements to one hundred companies: the Government would be 'selective' in its initial approach. The role of the trade unions was played down: the agreements would be bipartite, not tripartite. They would be concluded between the Government and the company, with the unions being brought into close consultation. The extent of public ownership was carefully circumscribed. The Government's proposals for public ownership, said the White Paper, were those listed in the Manifesto. In addition, the NEB would be used to extend public ownership into profitable manufacturing industry, but only by agreement. If in any case it proved necessary to acquire a company compulsorily – for

industry, which David has persuaded me ought to be left out of the list of acquisitions by the NEB, as the acquisition of a single British firm would do nothing to secure the across-the-board control of the drugs industry that we need if we are to get the drugs bill down. As the people at the other end of the table, who have been in the Committee all along, continued their cross-chats in muffled conversational tones, I found myself nodding off and was comforted to see that Ted Short was sound asleep.

Harold began by saying that the draft White Paper was 'too tentative and pussy-footing' on certain issues. There followed a lot of esoteric talk about planning agreements, during which Wedgie said that he had never visualized them being statutory but that he needed some leverage to make the big companies play along with him. He therefore believed that all regional aids should eventually be channelled through them, except the Regional Employment Premium. Otherwise we should find that we could only get firms in by offering expensive additional inducements. I could hardly hear what was going on, but Harold summed up that, although the whole system of regional aid required review, the present system should remain in being for a further year. On the NEB side I suddenly woke up to point out that the key sentence in the document – to the effect that in manufacturing industry the NEB would require to take over certain firms in key industries – was tucked away in the middle of a general paragraph. Was this what remained of previous versions: from twenty-five companies to a specific shopping list? If so we must realize that the Tories would maintain that every company on the country was at risk. Harold snapped that there had never been any idea of saying twenty-five companies. That *hadn't* been passed by conference. Wedgie seized the opportunity to say that the sentence should be lifted out of this paragraph and given greater prominence. I surfaced again to attack a later phrase to the effect that, apart from the action outlined, we would not propose to take over 'any other companies'. 'Other than what?' I asked. 'You already have an open-ended commitment earlier on.' They all agreed the sentence was maladroit. Harold then agreed with Wedgie that we should make it clear in the document that we intended to extend public ownership to profitable industry. At last it was over. To my surprise Wedgie did not mention the pharmaceutical industry. In fact there seemed to me to have been merely minor disagreements.

There was barely time to have a quick briefing meeting in Harold's study for our great confrontation with the BMA and the Royal Colleges over the state of the NHS. I advised him to be sympathetic but to ask them to break down the figure of £500 million they had asked to be pumped into the NHS. If he did so he would find they had just not worked it out. The deputation streamed in, about twenty strong. Harold replied rather sketchily, leaning heavily on his brief to explain why we didn't think a

---

instance, where an important company was in danger of collapse or of passing into unacceptable foreign control – this would normally require a specific Act of Parliament. These proposals represented 'the whole of the Government's policy for public ownership for the next Parliament'. The NEB's main job would be to discharge the functions of the old Industrial Reorganization Corporation in promoting industrial efficiency and profitability. Power to establish these new instruments would be taken in a new Industry Bill. This would widen and make permanent the power in the existing Tory Act to acquire share capital in a company in return for financial assistance, but, as in the Tory Act, it would have to be by agreement and subject to the same parliamentary control. 'We need,' declared the document, 'both efficient publicly-owned industries and a vigorous, alert, responsible and profitable private sector.'

full-scale enquiry into the NHS was necessary. He then asked me if I would like to add anything, and I plunged in. I said they had made an impressive case, but as I listened I couldn't help wondering – and I didn't mean any offence – why the dog had suddenly started barking in the night? (Some of them had the grace to smile at this.) I then read out the comment that Stevenson had made at the time of the Tory December cuts in public expenditure and added, 'If those were the headlines we were getting now we should feel there wasn't any problem.'[1] (My suggestion to Jack that he should turn up these comments has borne fruit.) I thought the reason for the sudden crisis mood had arisen from four things: (1) the chaos caused by the NHS reorganization, to which one of them had referred; (2) the trouble caused by the industrial action stemming from the last three years' pay policy; (3) inflation; (4) the December 1973 cuts. The first three were being remedied, and the important thing was that the Government had guaranteed to inflation-proof the NHS and also would meet any extra expenditure arising from straight pay increases. It was also considering the whole question of public expenditure. I believed therefore that the crisis could, and would, be largely defused. An enquiry wasn't necessary, as my department was already developing sophisticated techniques for keeping in touch with regional and area spending plans and needs, but I would be glad, as soon as we knew the final figures of public expenditure, to hold conferences with the profession and the health authorities to work out with them how the money available could be put to the best use.

Lewin and Stevenson seized on my speech and said it was 'most important'. If what I had said could be spelled out in an agreed communiqué they thought it would go a long way to meet anxieties. Meanwhile they would break down their own estimate of £500 million as Harold had asked. Harold handed me over to them and thankfully disappeared. By now it was 7pm and I could see my pleasant and relaxed dinner with Reggie Paget disappearing down a long corridor of tedious statement-drafting. And so it proved. I was hungry and tired to the point of exhaustion. As Henry Yellowlees, Jack Straw and Peter Brown kept coming in to me with reports of Stevenson's impossible niggling I was near to explosion. At one point Henry came in muttering, 'I'll kill that man Stevenson one day – I swear I will.' Finally I *did* explode and threatened to leave. 'It is intolerable that a busy Cabinet Minister should be kept hanging around while the BMA dictates what the Government is supposed to have said,' I declared. Peter was assigned to the job of calming me down while Norman also kept an eye on me anxiously. Somehow Jack dredged me up a drink – smuggling it into me in his briefcase past the waiting remnants of the delegation. Peter kept reassuring me. 'You have been absolutely wonderful. We have never had anyone at the department who can handle these people as you do – and the unions. Dick [Crossman] was a brilliant man, but you have this special ability.' He admitted the press had never given me a square deal. 'It is true many of them don't like you. They think that in everything you do you have one single thought: how it will serve your

[1] In his crisis public expenditure cuts of 17 December 1973, the Conservative Chancellor, Mr Anthony Barber, had announced that expenditure on the Health Service in 1974–75, instead of increasing as planned, would fall by £111 million, of which £69 million would be in capital spending. Dr Stevenson's public comment had been: 'The Government's need to cut capital expenditure is understood, but the effect on the Health Service will be particularly felt because of the need for more hospitals.'

ends.' I smiled wryly at this. Okay – I *am* single-minded in politics and determined to get my own way, but I should be no good as a Minister otherwise.

At last the agreed statement emerged and I swept into the impatient and disgruntled press conference flanked by Lewin and Stevenson. They played it absolutely fairly and down the line and I think the press were astonished – and disappointed – to find us so harmonious. A groggy interview on TV, some radio recordings and then it was over. So was my dinner. I settled down wearily on the sofa of Joe Haines's room with Lewin and Stevenson for a self-congratulatory drink. We were almost buddies and I couldn't help thinking that my outburst about the doctors playing politics had been as salutary as I intended it to be. Ted had gone down to HCF. I fell into bed at midnight and slept for six hours like a beaten dog. My last act was to send a note to the Treasury on the mobility allowance, arguing that we should allow the disabled to commute the allowance.

Thursday, 1 August

The press is full of Wedgie's announcement about the nationalization of the ship-building industry. He can't complain that he has had none of his own way! But we have also got a good press for our meeting yesterday. Harold ought to give me a vote of thanks, but he won't. Arrived at No. 10 at 9.15am for the meeting with Clive about the radiographers.[1] He was chatting with Harold in his study, which depresses me these days since Heath reclothed it in its expensive trappings. Harold went straight to the point and Clive was in an emollient mood. He explained how ASTMS had always opposed the radiographers' case going to the Halsbury enquiry and wanted a chance to negotiate their pay. If ASTMS and the Society of Radiographers both came to us and asked for the radiographers' reference to be withdrawn from Halsbury, would we agree? Thinking rapidly, I said of course (though I thought my department would have kittens). I had no objection to scrapping Halsbury, Whitley or any other machinery, I said, once it was clear that the unions as a whole wanted something else. Clive said he would have a word this morning with the Society about this. But clearly knowing they wouldn't agree, he kept murmuring about an earlier interim payment anyway. I told him it was impossible. Clive was still murmuring 'interim' when Harold showed us out.

Back for Cabinet at 11.30am. We had a discussion on land policy at which John Silkin maintained that the draft White Paper met all Frank Allaun's points and seemed to answer my questions satisfactorily. No one else questioned him and, as we shall see the final draft later, I let it go, having reminded the PM of his promise that the committee of the NEC which is drafting the Manifesto will be allowed to know the content of the White Papers before they are published. We then had a great to-do about 'social beef' as beef tokens are now called. The Cabinet committee had agreed that we dare not refuse this offer of cheap beef for pensioners, but I lashed out and told them we ought to have more political guts. Were we going to allow the CAP to

---

[1] On 30 July I had persuaded COHSE to await Halsbury's report on 16 September and not to renew the nurses' industrial action, but ASTMS had rejected this and was threatening to step up the radiographers' action, causing severe disruption in hospitals.

drive us to extend means testing? I must have been effective, because Harold insisted we should extend the tokens to *all* pensioners, not just those on supplementary benefit, while Fred [Peart] moaned that the Community would never put up with it.

Once again I bolted a sandwich in my room in the House before departing for Camden Town and my meeting with ASTMS on the radiographers. It had been Clive's idea that I went to his office for the meeting and I had readily agreed, telling my department I would go anywhere to get a settlement. Surprise, surprise: the TV and press had been informed of the meeting (which Clive had originally told me would be kept secret) and were waiting at the door! So was Clive, who greeted me with the utmost friendliness. Over drinks, Clive told me that the Society were not keen on his idea of withdrawing the reference. It was now up to me, he said, to convince his members, who were waiting for me, to await their interim payment. I would see how young they were and in what a militant mood.

He was right. There were about thirty of them and there was no reverence about them. Some of them stood up as I came in, others ostentatiously kept their seats. I was surprised how many young women there were among them and it was they who openly sneered as I spoke. It was quite an ordeal. I spoke off the cuff and without histrionics, starting with: 'Mr Chairman and fellow trade unionists'. (Sneers at that.) As I expounded my case, with Philip next to me and Jack Straw, Peter [Brown], Ian Gillis [Peter's deputy] and Norman [Warner] lining the walls, I had to struggle against more sneers, head-shakings and audible jeers from several of them. But I soldiered on, saying there was no difference between us about ends, but only about means. My difficulty was that I knew they had voted against the Halsbury enquiry, but I met that head-on, saying I had inherited a negotiating machinery which, as trade unionists, they knew that it was not for me to overthrow unilaterally, though I would be willing to discuss any changes in machinery the unions wanted as soon as this dispute was over. On my feet, I suddenly thought up a new idea. Talking about the Government's pledge to get the results of the enquiry into payment as quickly as possible, I said I would undertake to call the Health Authority Treasurers together well before 16 September to satisfy myself that everything possible had been done to speed up the payment machinery. Clive played it completely fair and did not try to influence them.

When I had finished the bitterness broke out as they had their turn and as I listened to their tirade I resigned myself to total failure. But I wasn't going to take it lying down and lashed out when some of them distorted what I had said. I think my passion surprised them. I was interested to see that the young women who had sneered most did not speak. Just as I was despairing a young man stood up and congratulated me rather patronizingly on my 'eloquence'. But how, he said, did I expect them to persuade their members to wait for six weeks for an interim payment of which they did not even know the amount? They had been 'had' before. This struck me as a ray of hope: they would accept the delay if they had some indication of the sum. Clive followed this up (seeing it also as a ray of hope, I think) and asked me whether I could ask Halsbury to say what percentage increase they would get as an interim. I said of course, but I couldn't give any guarantee and warned them that Halsbury was getting fed up at being pushed around. At this point I had to leave and left Jack and Gillis behind to draw up an agreed statement. Clive accompanied me to the door and once again we were photographed shaking hands. I was limp with the effort and dubious of the outcome. In the car Philip was shaking his head about the 'vicious' young women, who clearly frightened him.

The meeting with the Society of Radiographers was in their office and here, too, the TV cameras were waiting outside. This was no modern, with-it Camden Town office but a traditional building in the heart of Harley Street land. The National Council was older, too, and much more polite. No sneering as I spoke and I knew I was on safer ground because the Society had turned down Clive's attempt to withdraw the reference. So I was able to play on this, saying they had got to make up their minds: they couldn't have their Halsbury cake and eat their Castle interim. (They smiled at that.) But when discussion came they, too, spoke of a sense of frustration among their members which they doubted whether they could contain and they, too, stressed how much it would help if Halsbury could indicate the size of the interim. This time I left Peter behind to agree a joint statement and went back to the office to ring the PM. I told Harold what had happened and asked him to invite Halsbury to see him. 'I have twisted his arm as much as I dare and only you can persuade him now to help us out.' He agreed to lay it on. I sent Philip off to try his hand at drafting a statement for Halsbury to issue and to think out a way in which he could indicate the size of the interim.

I still wasn't through: there was the BMA to see again. Henry Yellowlees has begged me to fit them in before my holiday to discuss their pay. With statutory control of incomes dead from midnight on 25 July[1] they are on the warpath for an immediate re-reference of their pay to their Review Body to get another instalment of pay to top them up. Henry assured me they had agreed to a short meeting, really only to be able to tell their members that they had made their mark with me as soon as possible after the end of the statutory policy. But once again he had underestimated them. I had barely five minutes to discuss with Henry and David what I should say before they were streaming through the door, a dozen strong. No sign of yesterday's bonhomie: they were grim and politely threatening, cross-examining me as to whether Halsbury was now free of statutory restrictions and how soon they could go back to him. Grabham was the most outspoken; Tony Keable-Elliott the most reasonable. But there was no doubting Grabham's mood of barely restrained viciousness. They had noted, he said, that militancy paid on every hand and warned me that they, too, had learned the lesson and, unless they got satisfaction soon, they would act on it. As I listened I thought: how can we ever solve the problems of this country when the already well off are ready to fight in the last ditch for their privilege? Yet the pundits in *The Times* and elsewhere are waiting to denounce the Government for not curing inflation by 'standing up' to the trade unions! There was a lovelessness about that bunch that made me sick. Just as they arrived Norman brought me a piece of good news: the Society of Radiographers had agreed to call off its industrial action and wait for Halsbury! As I shook hands with Lewin and Stevenson I said, 'You will be glad to know the Society has called off its action.' 'At what price?' sneered Derek

[1] Section 6 of the Prices Act 1974 gave the Government power to abolish the machinery of a statutory incomes policy. The Order abolishing the Pay Board came into effect on 26 July.

Stevenson. 'No price,' I replied sweetly. 'Just my eloquence.' Not a word of congratulation from either of them.

After nearly an hour of their interrogation I reminded Lewin politely that I had other things to do. Even so he clung on. Eventually it was agreed I should send them a letter setting out the new position under a voluntary policy, though I warned them the Government would want to stick to the twelve-month rule. Then Philip and Peter came in to say they simply couldn't think how we should indicate a figure for the radiographers' interim award. I told them the only way was to indicate the criteria on which Halsbury would recommend their increase and we might get the best idea of this from Halsbury himself. They thought this was a good idea. Home at last to my fourth omelette of the week and to see with relief that my interviews came over rather well on TV.

Friday, 2 August

Up at 6am to pack my things for Mauritius and to rewrite the Health and Social Welfare sections of the Manifesto, which must reach the drafting committee this afternoon. This meant that I was late for Cabinet, in whose business I was too tired to take an interest. Harold reported that it had been decided not to issue a White Paper about devolution, on which a number of people have now got cold feet, but to put a statement later before Cabinet. They turned next to the industrial policy White Paper, which I thought had been more or less agreed – but not a bit of it. Wedgie returned to his theme about planning agreements and regional aid, saying he must have a lever to influence the big companies. He brought a hornet's nest about his ears. One after another his colleagues turned on him, Harold Lever summing it up when he said he could think of nothing more likely to shatter the already fragile business confidence than the suggestion that the aids industry had been promised might be at risk. Mike said nothing. Wedgie fought on alone, saying at one point, 'What is proposed is a major change in the party's policy.' And he accused Harold of going back on his conference speech. I have seldom seen Harold more furiously emphatic. He had never at any time suggested that the payment of regional aids should be made conditional on a planning agreement being reached, he declared, and he sent for his conference speech to prove it. At 11am I left them at it to go to the Treasury for another long inconclusive wrangle with Joel Barnett over disablement policy. At this rate we will never get our disablement policy out before the election.

More work over the now routine sandwich under the hair-dryer; a quick shop for a swimsuit and then back to No. 10 for Harold's meeting with Halsbury, whom we smuggled in through the back door. I warned Harold that Halsbury was touchy, but in the event he could not have been more anxious to please, saying how disturbed he had been over press reports that he had threatened to resign. 'I told the press that my relations with the Secretary of State could not be more cordial,' he assured us. He had been trying to work out a formula to help and thought he might say that the radiographers' interim would be a 'substantial proportion of the nurses' settlement'. I seized on this and then, with typical caution, he backed away from it. I pressed him time and again, pointing out that it had been a triumph to get ASTMS to suspend their action even for a week to see what he produced and I was sure that, if he could say what he had originally suggested, it would do the trick. We left it that he would go back to his office to work something out and I phoned Philip to keep in touch with him and get him to stick to the words he had suggested if at all possible. In the car to HCF at last! Only one box between me and freedom and rest for a whole two weeks. On the way I noted with irony that Terry Lancaster had a piece in the *Mirror* building up Shirley as Harold's darling, the centrepiece of the next election and potentially the next PM. What on earth is Harold up to? I haven't had a word of recognition from him about my efforts in the last three weeks. Yet I have done as much as anyone to save the Government from catastrophe. Philip phoned to say Halsbury refused to stick to his original words.[1] Hell!

Saturday, 3 August

The papers are full of Wedgie's supposed defeat in Cabinet over industrial policy. I wonder what happened after I left – or is it just another press ploy? Jimmie Margach phoned and congratulated me over the way I had 'cooled things' in the past few weeks, which must have been gruelling. When I told him that all I had had for my pains was a great spiel by Tim Raison on the eight o'clock news attacking me as the most disastrous Minister of Health in history, who had gone around 'lighting fires' through the whole Health Service, he was indignant. Ted [Castle] should get on to Bill Hardcastle, he said, and demand I be given the right of reply on *World at One* tomorrow. Ted did this, only to be told by Bill, regretfully, that he had got Harold on *World at One* tomorrow and simply couldn't fit in both of us. Harold ought to deal with it himself. I rang Harold this evening and he said 'That's odd, saying they couldn't have you as well as me: they have been trying to get Bob Mellish tonight to go on the programme.' Another example of the media's prejudice against me? Anyway Harold agreed to deal with it. The happiest moment of the day was this morning when Henry Yellowlees came on the phone to speak to me, swearing to Ted that it was nothing to do with work. 'Forgive me for troubling you,' he said. 'I had written a note to you for the box only to find you weren't having any more and I can't blame you. I didn't want you to go away until I had told you how much I admire how you have behaved in the past few weeks and what you have achieved. The whole department agrees with me. I have never known a Minister maintain themselves as you have done in this difficult time. Have a good holiday.' I was so touched by his warmth I thought I was going to cry.

Off to Mauritius tomorrow! We are staying first with the Governor-General, then with the Prime Minister, and the fleet is in. We shall either be submerged in a boring

[1] Lord Halsbury was only prepared to hint that his report on nurses' pay would be linked with a parallel but interim recommendation for other Health Service workers, including radiographers. This was not enough to prevent industrial action by the radiographers but, while I was away, David Owen had talks with their union, ASTMS. He assured them that high-speed arrangements were being made by the Department to ensure that the radiographers received their interim pay increase recommended by Halsbury, back-dated to 23 May, in their September pay packets. As a result the radiographers called off their industrial action on 17 August.

social round or have the time of our lives.[1] The big thing is that I shall be right away from all this.

Friday, 23 August

Back from Mauritius I find that while I have been away things have gone amiss on a whole list of policy matters which it is essential to get right for publication before the election. The Chancellor has closed the door on my making any announcement about existing pensioners[2] when the White Paper on our new pensions scheme appears, despite the fact that we are still discussing this with the Treasury. Another miserable meeting about Sharp. The Treasury has had kittens about Alf's commutation idea,[3] not so much on the grounds of cost as of its implication that we are still committed to providing cars or their equivalent. Alf is away in Italy, so, if we are to get anything out before the election, I must act. Says Elizabeth primly, 'He knew it was coming up, Secretary of State, so he shouldn't have gone away.' (It is a deep-rooted feeling among civil servants that they have done their duty if they have dumped the problems in Ministers' laps before going away themselves.) I say desperately that I am perfectly prepared to get the Government out of the car-providing business, despite the political difficulties, *provided* I have the political quid pro quo of a mobility allowance for all disabled persons with the same medical entitlement. This would scotch the Tories, who wouldn't dare to attack our failure to give cars to disabled drivers knowing that we had extended the mobility allowance to disabled people who can't drive. The cost of giving *them* cars as well would be prohibitive. I could see that officials were impressed. Even Dick Bourton admitted there would be something very valuable in it for the Treasury. Though the cost would be over £20 million, we should be out of the car business for ever and the long-term implications would be clear and containable. I adjourned the meeting while I myself dictated a letter to the Chancellor.

Next to PESC. Bourton said he thought he might get another £100 million for the NHS, though he had conceded that the Sharp proposals should be taken out of it. I sat up indignantly at that and he looked crestfallen. Just before I went away he had asked me what were my priorities in my PESC list, and I had said, 'The NHS,' adding mischievously that my Cabinet colleagues had a vested electoral interest in the other items, like disablement policy and child endowment. But I can see that officials' hearts are not in my battle to get more money. I suspect that they thoroughly sympathize with the Treasury's traditional retrenchment attitude to public expenditure. And I cannot deny that the economic situation is hardly propitious for expanding it. My difficulty is that I am right in the centre of the 'Social Contract' field. Failure to achieve socially just policies will endanger our whole new approach as a Govern-

---

[1] We had the time of our lives.

[2] Brian O'Malley and I believed that existing pensioners would be resentful if they drew no benefit from the new scheme. We had therefore been working out proposals to give them notional credits under the scheme as though they had been contributing to it over a previous period of, say, ten years, but the Treasury refused to commit any more money.

[3] Alf Morris was working on an idea whereby the disabled could 'commute' their mobility allowance into a lump sum to enable them to buy a car.

ment. As it is, Treasury wants a meagre child endowment figure which will actually make some families worse off. Tony Lynes, who slipped deprecatingly into the meeting (B. A-S. is also on holiday!), pointed out that even my higher figures would mean that the allocation of resources to families would be reduced. (I asked him afterwards to let me have the figures.) Bourton and the rest got impatient at this. Said Bourton, 'The trouble, Secretary of State, is that your bids add up to the total amount available for public expenditure by all departments.' And things are made worse by the fact that even officials (and therefore presumably the Treasury) now feel that another uprating will be essential next March or April because of inflation. I said I would be willing to ditch the Christmas bonus if necessary – an absurd non-selective device which they hate as much as I do – but I could not advocate policies for child endowment which violated my principles. 'What you are saying,' said Bourton, 'is that you do not accept the Chancellor's total for public expenditure.' 'Yes,' I replied. As it is, I am miserably aware that I shall be able to do little for the one-parent families during the coming five years – certainly not Finer's cash payment as of right.[1]

Monday, 26 August

Spent Bank Holiday Monday ploughing through my boxes at HCF. The lassies in the Private Office (in charge while Norman Warner is away) have almost begged me to work down here this week as the department generally is so thinly manned. But I find from papers in my box that the private practice question has reached crisis point. I have been worrying for some time what David was up to on this issue and how the talks in the Joint Working Party were going on – all the more so since we have got ourselves committed to producing its report by November. The papers consist of a long, desperate Minute by Philip Rogers saying he knows officials ought to have let me have their views on pay beds earlier, but they have all been so busy. Now they feel they would be failing in their duty if they did not let me know how opposed they all were to the phasing of private practice out of NHS hospitals. His Minute was accompanied by a succession of submissions about the legal, constitutional and practical objections to phasing out put forward by the department. There was also a copy of a letter to Philip from Sir Douglas Logan [Principal of the University of London] saying that the disappearance of part-time consultants from NHS hospitals would seriously damage medical education. So the forces are mobilizing against us as they did against Nye – only this time the party would not tolerate the sort of concessions that Nye made.[2] Our job is going to be even harder than his.

---

[1] The Finer Committee on One-Parent Families, which had reported in July (Cmnd. 5629), had highlighted the financial difficulties of one-parent families and recommended a new cash benefit for them, the guaranteed maintenance allowance, plus generous child allowances.

[2] Aneurin Bevan, as Minister of Health in the 1945 Labour Government, had a long and bitter struggle with the medical profession over the introduction of the National Health Service in 1948. He was helped by the remarkable alliance he struck up with Lord Moran, President of the Royal College of Physicians, who was anxious to help him to attract top specialists into the new and untried service, which the profession was threatening to boycott. It was as a result of Lord Moran's advice that Nye agreed to allow NHS doctors to earn fees from private patients and NHS specialists to have the use of some private beds in NHS hospitals at the discretion of the Minister. Contrary to what the BMA was to assert in its later battle with me over the

Along with all this came a Minute from David saying rather sourly that he supposed officials had a right to put forward their views, but he was annoyed because this meant that they had not produced the document on the policy of separation of private practice from the NHS for which he had asked. He had himself, however, produced two papers – one of them for the Joint Working Party meeting on 4 September – which he was intending to discuss at an office meeting on Wednesday. Could I let him have my views before then? I read all this very carefully and, although I admired David's initiative of ideas, I grew alarmed as I read some of his proposals.[1] I wrote a long Minute in reply, saying I wanted an office meeting myself on all this next week. I can see that the time has now come for me to get fully involved in David's work on this, though he much prefers to be in full and independent charge. I shall have to handle him tactfully.

Monday, 2 September

Back full-time at the office. Spend most of my time preparing for my crucial meeting with the Chancellor tomorrow about my bids for PESC. Dick Bourton is gloomy about the prospects – even suggests that Denis will insist on my postponing the pension plan, due for publication next week. I gird myself with grimness for the fight.

Tuesday 3 September

In the event the two hours with Denis were a pleasant surprise: no pawky humour from him; no irritating digs. We just sat down, Denis flanked by Joel Barnett and his key officials, Baldwin and Widdup. I was flanked by Brian [O'Malley] and Alf, Errington and the rest. Denis began by saying that my bids took up the whole of the contingency fund for 1975–76 and then drew up an agenda of items for us to deal with. I interrupted to say, 'You have left out the housewives' disablement benefit.' 'Oh, no, that's agreed,' replied Denis, brushing it airily aside. I looked at my officials, who have been bringing me messages, ostensibly from the Chancellor, to the effect that he couldn't accept any commitment to a disabled housewives' benefit and, if I didn't fall immediately into line, he would take the whole thing into Cabinet (where I know only too well I shall have few allies in my efforts to pre-empt some of the PESC discussions). 'But I thought you had reservations, Chancellor,' I said sweetly. (In fact

---

phasing out of these private beds, this concession was not a 'condition' on which the profession agreed to participate in the NHS. On the contrary its violent opposition to Bevan's proposals continued and was only broken down at the eleventh hour by Nye's clear determination to go ahead and by his offer – again on Lord Moran's advice – to embody in amending legislation his frequently repeated pledge that he did not intend to introduce a whole-time salaried service by regulation. The story is told in detail in Michael Foot's biography of Bevan (*Aneurin Bevan 1945–60*, Davis-Poynter, 1973).

[1] In my Minute I told David that two aspects of the paper he had prepared for the Joint Working Party caused me particular anxiety. The first was his proposition that we would allow up to three years for phasing out pay beds in order to provide time for alternative private accommodation outside the service to be built up. Our aim, I said, should be to discourage the building up of the private sector, not encourage it. The second was that we would consider, as one version of the new contract, allowing consultants to opt for a full-time contract, plus the right to practise privately outside the NHS. This was in direct conflict with my policy of encouraging consultants to devote their whole time to the NHS.

I have been compelled by these peremptory messages from Treasury to write them into my document for the Social Services Committee.) Denis looked puzzled. Joel shrugged: 'We reached agreement.' Widdup then protruded his head reluctantly to admit that he had been the author of the diktats. 'You haven't seen this yet, Chancellor,' he said. I felt like exploding at this impudence of Treasury officials, but restrained myself. 'Well, yes,' drawled Denis. 'I'll have a look at this, but I don't see any difficulty.'

Discussions went well for a time: no suggestion of postponing the pensions scheme (we are no nearer solving how to latch in existing pensioners); agreement between Denis and me to sacrifice the Christmas bonus in favour of two pension increases next year, starting in March; a warm welcome by Denis for my new line on invalid vehicles ('I like your new approach'), if only we could find some way of reducing the initial cost. (I felt rather pleased with myself over this – I had had a hunch that I could play on the Treasury's passionate desire to get the Government out of the car business to the extent of extracting a good mobility allowance from them. Alf has accepted this.) But the real crunch came over family allowances and the child endowment scheme. Denis is trying to get the family allowance increase down to derisory levels and to get me to postpone the introduction of child endowment for a year. I told him that both propositions were totally unacceptable and we agreed to leave these issues for the fight in Cabinet. I also warned Denis that I would not be content with the present allocation for the NHS. (I am determined not to let him do a 'divide and cut' exercise between the social security and health sides of the department.) He just noted that. Altogether I went away not too dissatisfied.

Back at the office I told officials to work out a scheme for phasing in the new mobility allowance at smaller cost and hurried to catch my train to King's Lynn for a meeting in NW Norfolk. The meeting was packed and enthusiastic; and confirmed my view that there is a strong current of opinion flowing our way.

Wednesday, 4 September

Up early to get a train back to London, tired but exhilarated. Spoke to the monthly meeting in the department of NHS Regional Treasurers and buttered them up to do their best to get the Halsbury lump-sum payments into nurses' pay packets by the end of the month. Caldwell had produced a scheme for phasing in the mobility allowance which I didn't think was too bad at all, though I insisted on his including a fourth stage in the process, covering everyone up to seventy years of age by 1978–79 at a total cost by then of £20 million. The office is still dazed by the success of my proposals and even Alf is beginning to get enthusiastic.

Thursday, 5 September

Harold has been trying to pep up a draft by officials for the Devolution White Paper, which only too clearly drags its feet. We got Willie's usual belly-ache: he had been travelling down from Scotland, hadn't seen Harold's draft till he arrived, etc., etc. He obviously has a distaste for the whole thing. 'I don't know what the Secretary of State for Scotland will do when this goes through,' he mourned. John Morris welcomed the draft for Wales unreservedly, but others repeated their head-shakings. 'I don't like the situation at all,' said Denis. 'We are moving steadily in a dangerous direction which we have not thought through properly.' Reg agreed: 'I dislike the whole exercise.' Harold was immensely grateful when I piped up to say that if devolution was inevitable we had better relax and at least look as though we enjoyed it. I supported Harold's redraft: the worst of all worlds would be to publish policies grudgingly and reluctantly. John Morris nodded vigorously. Jim then started up a great scare: he had discovered that Transport House was about to publish that very morning a Home Policy statement on devolution, enthusiastically going overboard for it, which hadn't even been to the NEC. 'And it hasn't been shown to either Secretary of State,' added Shirley disapprovingly. Jim rushed out to try and stop it – too late. There were a lot of shocked noises about the cavalier behaviour of Transport House. 'Geoff Bish,[1] again,' said someone angrily. But we had to lump it. Personally I thought the Home Policy statement at least had some vigour and life in it.

Tony C. then introduced the Land White Paper, without any acknowledgments to John Silkin, who was sitting mutely there. I got an assurance that Frank Allaun's points had all been met. We next started what promised to be a major row over the regional policy of the EEC. With time slipping away, I pointed out that I *must* have clearance on my paper on our disablement policy if it was to be published next week, so Harold postponed the regional policy item till next time after Jim and Wedgie had had a go at each other. My paper went through easily, Widdup having been shamed into dropping his attempt to redraft all the life out of it. And Denis did not raise the matter of the commitment to disabled housewives. It makes one feel good to beat those Treasury officials at their own game. Finally we returned to 'social beef'. Fred is still hopeful of persuading Lardinois[2] to accept our more generous version of the scheme, so, as Shirley was still willing to take the cost on her own budget, there was nothing I could do to stop it.

Off to Blackburn for a busy two days, including a very useful visit to the Royal Infirmary and another nurses' dance. No one can say I am neglecting the NHS side of things.

Saturday, 7 September

Back to Hell Corner Farm from the night sleeper to get ready for a weekend visit by Sonya and Terry – very pleasant, despite the rain. But it meant that I could only get down to the Pensions White Paper on Sunday evening[3] and I began to panic at all the reading-up I have got to do for the great launching exercise in the coming week.

Monday, 9 September

Up early to open the Annual World Congress of the Fédération Dentaire Inter-

---

[1] Mr Geoffrey Bish had become Research Secretary of the Labour Party in succession to Mr Terry Pitt. He operated from the Labour Party headquarters at Transport House.
[2] Petrus Lardinois was Commissioner for Agriculture in the European Community from 1973 to 1977.
[3] See Appendix IV.

nationale at the Festival Hall. My speech went down well, particularly my reference to my desire to abolish cost-related dental charges as soon as possible.[1] This was all the more apposite because these charges of 50 per cent are due to go up automatically as a result of our agreement to raise dental fees from 1 October. David Owen and I have decided that, as money is so desperately short for the NHS, we shall have to let it go and merely freeze the maximum cost at £10. Some hunch made me say we had better refer the decision to Harold before announcing it and, lo and behold, he is protesting vigorously. He never misses a political trick! Back at the office we had a meeting to discuss what could be done about Harold's protest, and decided to put a neutral paper to Cabinet suggesting alternative ways of preventing the real totals of charges from going up, while stressing that I had no money to finance the increased subsidy. Spent the rest of the day trying to master the details of the Pensions White Paper, drafting a press statement for the lobby and background notes. I find I have to rewrite most of the department's press statements because my officials have clearly never been trained to present our policies in a way which will make a political impact. (I suspect Keith Joseph positively loathed the limelight.) Peter Brown utters dire warnings from time to time on the political dangers of this proposal or that and he has a good flair for this, but I have never yet met a civil servant who could write vividly.

Tuesday, 10 September

Up early for a hair-do, ready for my terrifyingly imminent exposure to press and TV. I begin to get a bit trembly: how will our pensions policy be received? The more I reread it, the better it strikes me, but one never knows what reaction one will get. This is the great moment for which Brian and I have been working for months – a make-or-break moment – and I almost panic at the thought of the technical minutiae on which I could be tripped up. Then into Cabinet for the deferred discussion on EEC regional policy.[2] Wedgie has put up an alternative draft for the background briefing for officials in the coming meeting at Brussels and at first sight I can see little difference between his and the Foreign Office one prepared by Roy Hattersley. The key seems to be that Roy is arguing for a flexible set of rules (so flexible that I doubt whether the EEC could ever agree to them), whereas Wedgie wants no rules at all – just 'co-operation and consultations' – to achieve the same ends. I can't help feeling that he is taking a rather 'angels dancing on a pinhead' approach and I am interested to see that, when our discussion resumes, Mike concentrates on the risk of seeming to accept the authority of the Commission at this moment in political time. Why not defer the matter? he asked. Denis was impatient with all this: 'I am baffled by the

[1] Under Sir Keith Joseph's system of cost-related dental charges, introduced in 1971, patients were charged an automatic 50 per cent of dental fees, up to a maximum of £10. The system had been attacked by the dental profession.

[2] The party conference had agreed that one of our aims in the renegotiations should be to secure 'the retention by Parliament of those powers over the British economy needed to pursue effective regional, industrial and fiscal policies'. Under the Treaty of Rome, which prohibited any forms of state aid which distorted competition and gave the European Commission the power to enforce this principle, the Commission had been drawing up rules to control the member states' systems of regional aid. Tony Benn argued that this would rob us of our freedom to pursue our own regional policies.

argument. The Minister of State's paper is in line with the policy we agreed.' And he added, 'Governments in practice do just what they like.'

This irritated me into speech. I said I was tired of the argument that it didn't matter what we committed ourselves to in the Community because no one took any notice of the rules anyway – hardly a clarion call of principle. I was against doing anything which strengthened the bureaucratic busybodies in the Commission or that took any step towards an economic and monetary union. The discussion then followed predictable lines, till Harold chipped in to say there must be some rules, but what worried him was the weakness of the Foreign Office paper in not making clear what were our sticking points. 'I am in favour of rules, as this will help us.' Wedgie agreed there must be rules, 'but will their appropriateness be decided by this country?' He then burst into a tirade about how his own freedom of action as a Minister was now circumscribed. 'Everything has to be referred to the Commission. I feel like a man who is bleeding in the bath.' There was some slightly derisory laughter at this, but Bob Mellish could see the advantage of deferring the whole matter; after all there was an election coming on. Jim said that wasn't possible, and Harold summed up that the majority was in favour of the Foreign Office brief but that it should be strengthened to show that we meant what we said.

I slipped away hurriedly to join Ted at St Bride's for John Graham's memorial service.[1] The singing was so beautiful I don't know how Sandy didn't break down and howl. Then a whole bunch of us, led by Bob Edwards [editor of the *Sunday Mirror*] and Sidney Jacobson [editorial director of the *Mirror* newspapers], proceeded to the Press Club for drinks and lunch, which I had to abandon half-way through in order to get back to the lobby conference on the pensions scheme at 3pm. By that time I was feeling pretty tense, but I survived, while Brian was waiting to jump in brilliantly to supplement, with complete mastery, what I said. I had stressed that he had done all the detailed work and I am so grateful that he doesn't in any way resent the fact that it is inevitably called the 'Castle' scheme. Who said that men will never work under women?

Back to the office for a series of meetings with individual leader-writers. Peter has organized these three days like a martinet. 'I arranged for Mr Crossman to do this for his scheme, Mrs Castle, and I want you to agree to do the same.' Of course I acquiesced meekly. And all the time other departmental problems came crowding in on me, notably a continuing argument with Treasury over the wording of our press statement on Sharp, due out on Friday. I had carefully written the statement within the terms of the agreement I had made with Denis, even accepting that the total sum for the mobility allowance could only be £15 million. Every over-expansionary phrase had been toned down, but that did not stop the miserable Widdup from sending ultimata about other passages, because they made me sound like a human being. Even Norman began to be outraged. Charles Regan [Under-Secretary at the department] kept coming in with whole redrafted passages which he said Treasury insisted on. I hit the roof. 'This is what I mean about the arrogance of the Treasury,' I told Norman. 'They will never stick to their own last – which is safeguarding the

[1] John Graham, political correspondent of the *Sunday Mirror* and a long-standing Fleet Street friend of my husband, Ted, had died suddenly of a heart attack. He left a young wife, Sandy, and a small baby.

financial implications – but want to take over mine as well, which is presenting the social aspects in the right way.' He obviously agreed. In the end, by making a few minor concessions, I got most of what I wanted left in, but it was infuriating and wearisome.

At last I managed to get away, very late, to Russell Harty's party. He was terribly anxious to help me in the election and very willing to speak at my main meeting. A lot of the acting world was there. Frankie Howerd was all over me; Jill Bennett intrigued. 'We thought Russell was making it up when he said Barbara Castle was coming,' said one of them. I explained that every minute of my day was earmarked by my officials, adding laughingly, 'They have to know where I am wherever I go so that they can get in touch with me. I could never have an affair.' Later Jill came up to me and said dreamily, 'I have been thinking over your problem. I've solved it. You *could* have an affair. You should say that you have regularly to attend a hypnotist and the whole essence of your treatment is that no one should know.' I told her that, if she thought that would hold off a Private Secretary, she didn't know the nature of the breed! I shouldn't be surprised if someone on TV doesn't now make a play out of it.

Wednesday, 11 September

More individual interviews on pensions. The *Financial Times* seemed friendly; Malcolm Dean of the *Guardian* said openly, 'We like this scheme.' Then into a drinks session with City editors which Peter had specially laid on. To my horror he insisted on my making a little speech, but I needn't have worried. They were exuding friendliness. It was quite clear that most of the journalists there were very impressed and the crowning moment came when the CBI chap came up to me and frankly said that they warmly welcomed our whole approach! Brian and I began to have our tails up. 'I think it is going to be a wow,' I whispered to him. The vast press conference in the afternoon was an ordeal, but there was one thing Brian and I congratulated ourselves on: we took them all completely by surprise. No leaks, despite the continual earlier probing by John Cunningham of the *Guardian*. Then TV. The ITN chap was relaxed and helpful, but Hardiman Scott would not give me an inch to say anything about the merits of the scheme. He kept pushing me into a corner with snide questions like, 'Isn't this all just an electoral bribe?' I am beginning to share Harold's suspicions of the BBC.

Just time after all this to look in at a little drinks party organized by the department's division responsible for pensions policy to celebrate the publication of the White Paper. They are obviously mightily pleased with it. I told them that Brian and I really ought to have given a party for *them* and would do so as soon as the Bill was on the statute book. Cheers at that. Civil servants really are very convivial people and love an excuse for getting together over a modest glass of sherry. On the notice-board in the room they had pinned up a host of ironic suggestions for the title of the White Paper taken from films, such as: '1984', 'Something to Hide', and so on. I told them the one I liked best was 'A Touch of Class', because it reflected the elegantly simple structure they had worked out. 'Which of you thought of that stroke of genius: the twenty best years?' I asked. 'Crocker,' they said. 'He isn't here.' Crocker: that stuttering, rather elderly man who didn't look a bit impressive at first sight! 'Tell him I'll forgive him his evidence to the Tax Credits Select Committee after this,' I retorted amid laughter.

A switch now to Halsbury and how to get the lump sums into payment by the end of this month. The Treasurers say they cannot do it unless they get the figures at once. I say that if necessary I will have to see Halsbury again. Raymond [Gedling, Deputy Secretary at DHSS] is getting almost afraid to ring up Halsbury's secretary, he has been on the phone to her so often! At last a swift change in time for the annual dinner of the British Dental Association. Jack has knocked me out a bit of a speech and I have hardly had time to look at it. But my new gold dress makes me feel better and Dick Bourton, who had insisted on having an urgent word with me about PESC (which comes up tomorrow at Cabinet), dropped his usual Civil Service caution to say, 'May I say, Secretary of State, how charming you look.' I arrive at the dinner feeling drained, but manage to put some fun into the official bits of the brief. I even risk – and get away with – a political joke Bob Mellish regaled me with this afternoon: 'I have been at a little party of journalists and politicians on my way here – and Sir Geoffrey Howe can make what he likes of that,' I said. 'I asked them to give me a joke about dentists,' I continued, 'not too blue: and they couldn't think of one. But one of them told me the latest joke: "Mr Heath has been to see Gerald Ford to ask for a free pardon," adding, "you couldn't tell them that." And,' I concluded, 'with Sir Geoffrey here I clearly couldn't, could I?' They chuckled. I do like to squeeze a bit of humour into every speech, however drained I may feel.

Thursday, 12 September

An excellent press for the pensions scheme, actually helped by the few sour comments of people like Geoffrey Howe. Even the Life Assurance have welcomed it! And Len Murray has said the right things. That is the great bond between Brian and me: we like to be politically clever as well as competent. Harold was delighted; greeted me at Cabinet with the words: 'Wonderful publicity. I am going to send you a note of congratulations, including Brian, of course.' We were almost back on the 'little Minister' terms. Perhaps I am beginning to come out of my eclipse.

At Cabinet Denis had reported on the progress so far with PESC, within his $2\frac{3}{4}$ per cent ceiling. Under the guise of merely discussing procedure for the next stage, he recommended that he should negotiate some smaller items with the Ministers concerned (amounting to a total of £43 million) and that Cabinet should accept his proposals for dealing with the remaining bids for education, health and social security. Dick Bourton has warned me that we have only been allocated a small share of Denis's reflationary construction package of £100 million (£25 million over two years, just about enough to keep the health centre programme going), and that this is going to be our lot for the Health Service. Denis is also trying to cut the family allowance increase next year to 25 or 30 pence and to postpone the introduction of child endowment till 1977. Both of these would be disastrous. I have kept saying I must put in a paper in support of my case. Bourton has kept replying that he was sure this wasn't the moment and, as I only saw Denis's proposals late last night, I have been kept in the dark. (I feel my officials, like Bourton and Rogers, are as much in favour of public expenditure cuts as the Treasury are and so don't really fight for my corner as they should.) I insisted that if Reg Prentice put in a paper I must too, so would they get one ready for that contingency. And sure enough they came to me shamefacedly yesterday to say that Reg P. had 'pulled a fast one' and slipped a paper in. Ours therefore had to be hurriedly circulated late last night. I was redictating whole areas of it to strengthen it while I was having my face made up for TV yesterday. And the department have cobbled together a massive brief – sixty pages of individual submissions from different officials which no one had pulled together and which it was impossible for me to read properly.

Reg made a great spiel about how unfair the Chancellor's proposals were to him, but it was I who, by a divine instinct, put my finger on the weakness of the Chancellor's case. Just as they were going to approve the additional £43 million for 'smaller items' I chipped in. The sums, however small, were additions to what? Presumably to the allocations in the Chancellor's original PESC proposals, which had never been agreed. We had been told that we should be allowed to have a comprehensive look at the distribution of expenditure between programmes generally. Yet here we were being asked to agree the fate of Reg's claims and mine when (a) there was no figure in for defence cuts at all and we were merely being told the review was going on; (b) we had had no discussion on general priorities – whether, for instance, we should continue to spend millions on food subsidies while cutting down the family allowance increases which were so vital for the very poor, and (c) we had been given no indication of the purpose of the 'smaller' increases. What, for instance, did the proposed increase of £2 million or £3 million on 'overseas services' represent? Everyone looked at Jim, who shrugged and said he didn't know. Judith [Hart] said with anguish, 'And I don't accept that the increase for overseas aid is enough.' (I whispered to her, 'Don't worry, I'll fight for you.') There was immediate and total acceptance of what I said. Harold pointed out that even £43 million wasn't chicken-feed. He admitted we *had* been promised a comprehensive discussion and Denis was sent away to produce his own proposals on priorities across the board, including defence. I was really proud of myself.

Back at the office I held a council of war. First I gently pointed out to them that it was cruel to a busy Minister to present her with such an unco-ordinated mass of briefs. 'Don't you ever speak to each other? Can't you set up a committee or something to save me from having to work out a brief from the briefs?' Dick Bourton said, 'I have got to admit, Secretary of State, that we did not serve you very well this time.' He also admitted that there was a good deal of sympathy for us in Treasury about the relative importance of our programmes compared with some others. I sent them away to press our advantage and to make the best use of the breathing space I had won, final decisions having been postponed till after the election.

The question of dental charges came up at the last minute. No one would hear of the dental charges going up in real terms on the eve of an election and I was instructed to freeze them, effectively bringing the relationship of charge to cost to 40 per cent. When I bleated that I just could not afford the £6 million this would cost out of my NHS budget (never miss an opportunity of highlighting one's woes!) Denis said briskly, 'The money has got to come from somewhere.' Finally we cleared the last draft of the Devolution White Paper. Launching is to be next Wednesday. 'And God help all who sail in her,' said Harold.

At the office I rewrote the press statement on our disablement proposals.[1] I had intended to get Alf to deal with mobility at tomorrow's press conference, but he is committed to be in Liverpool, so he will hold a separate press conference there. With disablement out of the way, the only issue remaining before I can relax is Halsbury.

Friday, 13 September

The press conference on the disablement proposals went well. When I asked if there were any questions there was silence. Then one journalist said, 'We are stunned.' So it has worked! I should have thought this issue would have been of wide human interest, calling for TV, but once again the BBC didn't want to know. I think they are getting terrified of the effectiveness of our succession of announcements and are clearly determined to play them down. By contrast ITN agreed to put me on their midday programme live if I could get to the studio on time. With a rush I did, only to hear the interviewer say as he introduced me, 'We have already heard similar proposals by the Conservatives from Sir Geoffrey Howe.' I was staggered: the Tory

---

[1] In 1973 there had been a revolt in the House of Commons against Sir Keith Joseph's failure to improve the social security provision for the chronically sick and disabled. He had been compelled to accept a new clause in his pensions legislation instructing him to review their needs and to report to Parliament by October 1974. This had given Alf Morris and me the chance to press for major reforms and on 13 September, after a long struggle with the Treasury, we were able to announce three important new benefits. (House of Commons paper No. 276.) These comprised a non-contributory invalidity pension to be introduced the following year for people of working age who had never been fit to work, including a 'pocket money' pension for the in-patients of mental hospitals; an invalid care allowance for those forced to stay at home to look after a severely disabled relative, to be introduced in 1976–77; and an invalidity pension for disabled housewives, which it was planned to introduce as soon as the problem of assessing incapacity in these cases had been overcome. We had already announced that invalidity pensioners would be able to qualify for additional earnings-related benefit in our new pensions scheme.

We were able to report at the same time the outcome of the protracted discussions over the mobility allowance. Treasury had at last agreed to pay a mobility allowance of £4 a week covering all the qualifying disabled, whether they could drive or not, to be phased in over three years for some 100,000 disabled, including children, at an initial additional cost of £15 million. In return we had given up the idea that the Government itself might commute the weekly payments into a lump sum, where the disabled desired it, which could be exchanged for a Government-provided car. Instead we undertook to continue to produce the invalid vehicle for those who wanted it, to improve it and to consider what advice and other help we could give to those who preferred to save their allowance to buy a car. The disabled people's organizations warmly welcomed the mobility allowance and said that they would be getting in touch with the motor manufacturers to try to work out a hire purchase scheme.

On 5 September I had also announced that we were going to set up an Institute of Hearing Research to give the problem of deafness the greater study and prominence it needed.

Manifesto is carefully non-committal on its disablement policy.[1] Yet apparently Sir G. has rushed in to announce an identical disablement benefit, saying unctuously that he is glad the two parties agree on this at least. In the car I muse to Peter: 'Someone must have leaked.' But later, in the train to Lancaster, the penny dropped. We must have sent the usual advance copy out of courtesy to Sir G. yesterday! I could have kicked myself.

A succession of hurried office meetings. First with Halsbury himself, who told me with pride that I should receive the nurses' report on Monday after all. I thanked him profusely and got the office drafting a letter to the PM asking for urgent consideration of the report as soon as it was received, so that, hopefully, I could announce the Government's acceptance on the nod.[2]

A good and enthusiastic meeting at Lancaster. True to Eric Cooper's promise, the COHSE people were there in strength, ready to jump up and thank me publicly for all I had done for the nurses.

Saturday, 14 September

A glorious September day at Hell Corner Farm. Days like this make me realize what compensations there would be in losing the election!

Monday, 16 September

Had to get up at 6.30am to get to No. 10 for the joint meeting between Cabinet and NEC on the Manifesto. The draft has been kept under wraps with as much security as if it had been the Crown Jewels, so we had to read it on the spot. No one is going to let it be leaked like the Tory one was in February. Ted Heath is really getting accident-prone, a bad enough sign in government but fatal when you are in Opposition. I have a curiously strong hunch that we are going to win this election – and I am usually a Cassandra. It may be just that I am so conscious of how much we have got through in my department, but I get the feeling that no one could take the other lot seriously. Harold began by saying that, contrary to what had appeared in the *Observer* yester-day (a bit of nasty Nora Beloff, of course) to the effect that he had personally vetted and watered down the draft before going to Paris, 'I never saw a single line till this morning.' That went for me too, so when Jim pleaded that we should do as little redrafting as possible, particularly because the document was a carefully worked-out

[1] Heath's Manifesto in the February election had merely said: 'We shall be carrying out by this autumn our statutory duty to report to Parliament on our proposals for improving the cash provision for the disabled, including the possibility of a disablement income.'

[2] The report recommended an average pay increase for nurses of 30 per cent, backdated to 23 May, together with improvements in overtime and holidays. This was in addition to the threshold payments they had received. As I had requested, Halsbury had worked out the lump sum payments nurses should receive on account and recommended an interim award for the professions supplementary to medicine. The Government accepted the report, which was published on 17 September, and agreed to make extra money available to cover the £170 million cost. The nurses were delighted and Albert Spanswick of COHSE commented: 'We never expected to get increases of this rate.'

compromise between widely differing views, I upped and said that I hoped it would be realized that some of us had not seen the sections on our own departments since we sent our first drafts in at the beginning of August; inevitably they were out of date and some extensive redrafting of my bit would be inevitable. Tony C. snapped at once: 'We really can't have Barbara making any more bids. If she does I am going to put in another big bid for housing.' Undeterred, I started scribbling busily. But, apart from these little personal pettinesses, the atmosphere was one of determined harmony. We even had Mik saying at the outset that the Introduction ought to be strengthened by a warning that 'the timing of all this must depend on economic circumstances, so don't think we are going to have an easy time'. Wonders will never cease! If only the Left had shown a bit more realism when we were in last time. . . . But then it is surely a reflection on the way we handled the party last time that the mood is so different and constructive now – one of the biggest bonuses from the Social Contract.

When we came to my section I was ready with an extensive rewrite. Even Denis nodded approvingly, for, of course, I stuck to what had been cleared with him. There was some teasing as I read on and on, but Bryan Stanley[1] whispered to me, 'Your redrafts are a great improvement. Stick to your guns.' Later, over the lavish buffet lunch Harold provided for us, Bob kept up the teasing: 'You should have heard us at our end of the table,' he cheeked. 'She'll never stop, we said.' Ted Short said quietly, 'She is one of the few Ministers who do their homework.' No one could say that of Fred Peart, who had failed to produce any section on agriculture at all and was sent away to draft something; or of Tony Crosland, whose section on housing was so inadequate that he spent his time profusely thanking Frank Allaun, Joan Maynard and me, consecutively, for the additions we suggested.

At lunch I had a hurried word with Harold about Halsbury. With the report due later today, I want agreement to announce that it will be published tomorrow and also a rapid indication of the line the Government will take on it. Harold washed his hands of the whole business and said that if Mike and Denis would agree a line, so would he. So Mike, Denis and I took our salmon and excellent wine to a little table in the drawing-room to talk it over. Mike was emphatic that we must publish and announce our acceptance of the report as soon as possible. Denis, entirely naturally, said that at least his people must be allowed a look at it, though he didn't see any difficulty. As we grew mellow over stilton and burgundy Denis said, 'You must admit I am the most political Chancellor you have ever had.' 'I do,' I replied, 'and I appreciate it.'

Back in the long dining-room to continue our discussion of the Manifesto, everyone was more talkative, though – a good sign – more jocularly, not more aggressively. As the cross-chatter broke out, Harold said, 'Next time I shall serve lemonade.' Laughter – incredulous. (Not of the next time, but of the lemonade.) But things sobered up as we turned to the section on the rights of the individual and my never very dormant affection for Roy lit up again as I heard him say, 'I am against

---

[1] General Secretary of the Post Office Engineering Union and a member of the trade-union section of the NEC.

entering into a law and order auction.' (Surprised applause from people like Lena Jeger.) The trouble with Roy is that he is so damned civilized. If only he could remain civilized and have an injection of red blood as well. Jim came out in typical colours: 'I agree, but I am rather in favour of dealing with teenage hooliganism', adding that he greatly admired the section on this in the Tory Manifesto and wished we had anything as good on this in ours. Denis: 'Hear, hear!' Bryan Stanley said it was no good talking about the problem without talking about the causes. Everyone then agreed that teenage hooliganism was repulsive, but, while backing the police, we should not go overboard on a wave of reactionary emotion. 'I do not like the phrase "law and order",' Roy insisted amid murmurs of approval from a number of us.

An amusing moment came when someone pointed out that there was no reference in the document to the abolition of the Lords. (It was Walter Padley, I think.) Said Harold, 'Let's have a sentence in about it.'[1]

At last we got Fred's draft on agriculture, which was innocuous enough, but said nothing. I said that I was totally in the dark about our agriculture and could not make out whether we were in this crisis because we had carried out the Common Agricultural Policy or had not. Harold chipped in: 'When we came into office farmers no longer had the guarantees Labour's policy gave them. Labour's Minister of Agriculture insisted on taking the powers necessary to protect them. Everyone at Paris when I was there agreed the CAP is a shambles.' I still didn't think it added up and Peter came in: 'With respect, we have not got the right *yet* to continue our own policy; we have only got short-term guarantees. The Tory Government got rid of the guarantees we insisted on and Fred Peart is mandated to restore them.' Fred said feebly, 'I believe the guarantees should be brought back', and Jim smoothed everything down by telling Fred to go away and do another draft.

This little fracas was merely a lead-in to the only potentially serious row of the day: the Common Market negotiations again. (Wedgie had not raised a murmur about the section on industry, which did not commit us to channel public support for industry through planning agreements.) Bob jumped in at the start to say he understood the words in the draft on renegotiation[2] had been hammered out as a compromise and he hoped we would take them on the nod. But this was expecting too much. First Peter said there was one serious omission compared with our original policy: while the negotiations proceeded we should resist the process of Britain's integration in the Community, the third stage of which was due in January. He moved an amendment on these lines. Roy returned to his old theme: 'We had considerable discussion at our last meeting on the referendum issue. I remain profoundly unhappy about it.' He was against the commitment to twelve months and to the referendum being binding on the Government. 'We can by no means rule out the possibility that the referendum might produce a very low poll indeed.' In that situation it was right that the decision should pass to Parliament. 'I remain convinced that this party will live to regret ever

---

[1] The sentence did not appear.

[2] The words were: 'The Labour Government pledges that within twelve months of the election we will give the British people the final say, which will be binding on the Government – through the ballot box – on whether we accept the terms and stay in or reject the terms and stay out.' The next day *The Times* had a headline: 'Cabinet pro-Europeans bow to referendum.'

having got committed to a referendum.' It was all done very reasonably (nothing like the hysteria of my last talk with him) and for a moment there was silence. Then Reg Prentice chipped in. 'I support Roy. As someone who was originally against entry' (how often we hear that from him these days!), 'I don't like the phrase about the referendum being binding on the Government. The final decision will have to be taken by Parliament.' Mike came in in support of Peter's amendment. Some of them had agreed to compromise in allowing the use of the word 'ballot box', he said. 'It never occurred to me that we were going to abandon the idea of the referendum being binding.'

People came flooding in on different sides of the argument. Alex [Kitson] wanted a shorter period than twelve months; Harold Lever no reference to twelve months at all; Wedgie said we couldn't go back on our solemn pledge; Mike that he wanted the word 'referendum', rather than 'ballot box'. In desperation Bob intervened: 'I move the present words be accepted *in toto*', to which Harold Wilson replied equally desperately that we didn't want a vote. Jim said that, as the one who was conducting the negotiations, he was profoundly unhappy about Peter's amendment. Peter refused to withdraw. Suddenly I hit out: 'Look, I agree with Peter's point and will fight for it in Cabinet. But is the only thing to come out of this meeting really going to be the report of a row over this, drowning all the rest of the news about it? If we have any vote on this it will leak disastrously. Let us leave things as they are.' While Peter still muttered revolt, Harold said smartly, 'I think we can say there is a consensus.' And so, by everyone's silence, there was. We broke up then, congratulating ourselves on the continuing strong undercurrent towards cohesion. Ted Short said complacently to me, 'I have never seen the party more united.' Even Frank Allaun's attempt to get written into the reference to defence cuts the words 'of £1,000 million' foundered after a passionate speech by Roy Mason, saying he was engaged in 'the most searching defence review in our history', which was going to have 'profound effects on every spending department'. We should never, he said, put a figure in the Manifesto because all the correspondents would seize on it and its implications for the constituencies concerned. Mike nodded to me; Frank fell silent. And so it was agreed. No vote. We are no longer tearing ourselves apart publicly to make a Tory holiday. Let them do that to themselves.

Back at the office I called an urgent meeting over Halsbury. Crises abound, of course. Peter said he didn't want to call a press conference tomorrow. It was too risky before everything was cleared with Treasury. I told him the report *must* be published tomorrow or there would be distorted leaks. So we must just go ahead and gamble. Raymond Gedling reported the PSMs had gone away satisfied with their proposed lump sum interim payments (£80 and £60), but there was a terrible snag with the nurses. Thanks to Halsbury's restructuring, which cuts out the juvenile training rates, a few student nurses would only be entitled to a lump sum of £20 if there was not to be a claw-back of overpayment when the increases came into the regular pay packets. The only way out of this would be to make the sums for the nurses £80 and £20. Inconceivable! I put my head in my hands and groaned. These student nurses, of course, are the COHSE lot. Peter insisted that the very mention of £20 would wreck the reception of the whole report.

We went round and round the problem. How many were affected? We didn't exactly know. Perhaps ten thousand. Perhaps less. But there would be a sprinkling in every hospital. News came in that the staff side had asked that some formula should be found for lifting this group, too, to £60. Another of my chaps said the Treasury would never stand for it – to say nothing of the Public Accounts Committee. I said the only way out was to take the payments for this group out of the computer and pay them manually. Could this be done? It was possible, but difficult, and anyway the pay clerks are now threatening to go on strike unless they get a cash bonus for doing the work. Of course this is ridiculous, but their union, NALGO, is sore because ASTMS made such a good running over the radiographers. In the normal way I would sweat this out, but, with the Tories waiting to ridicule the Social Contract in an imminent election, I have not much room for manoeuvre. I send Norman away to try to contact Len Murray to help us over the pay clerks and Gedling away to try to persuade the staff side to agree to leave this small group out of the computer and to meet me to fix their lump sum after we have all had a chance of studying the report.

I then sit down to wait. Message: there have been hitches over duplicating the report and its delivery is delayed. Message: Len Murray doesn't want to see me till he has talked to Audrey Prime.[1] Message: the staff side are bogged down over the problem of the student nurses and want to see me personally. I agree to see them, and at 8pm the staff side troop in, pretty jaded by three-and-a-half hours' non-stop belly-aching. I order Norman to open my drinks cabinet and they perk up noticeably. They are not aggressive: in fact, pleased with what they have heard of the report. But they are desperately anxious how to deal with this small group. So am I. But I explain to them it is going to be difficult enough to get Treasury acceptance of the report without their paying over the odds on it as well. I could not possibly commit the Government to this myself. They see the point of this. Would they like me to delay the payment to everyone, I ask. Vigorous head-shakings at this. Then, I say, the only hope is for them to agree to take this group out of the computer and to meet me on Thursday to discuss, in the light of the report, what extra we might do for them. Reluctantly they agree and go away. The report still not having materialized I go home. It arrives at 10.30pm. Being pretty washed out by this time I say to hell with it and go to bed.

Tuesday, 17 September

Slept till 7am, but I am so sleep-parched that the good night merely makes me realize how much more sleep I need. In for an early office meeting to discuss the press statement. Too early yet to know Treasury reactions to the report. And Gedling has discovered another snag. Halsbury has got some of his figures wrong and has recommended £60 for the PSM helpers, which his full figures do not justify. Crisis while someone goes off to persuade the staff side to accept £40 for the helpers instead. Another long discussion about what we do for the small student nurses group. David has a good idea. Since Halsbury is recommending an 'initial expenses

[1] Miss Audrey Prime of NALGO was the secretary of the staff side of the General Council of the National Whitley Councils for the Health Services.

allowance' for future student nurses to cover the cost of clothing, etc. that they have to buy, why not give this retrospectively to this group and so bring their total up to £40? I seize on it. We decide to try this on Mrs Newstead, secretary of the staff side of the Nurses' Whitley Council, to see if we can announce it this afternoon. Good news begins to roll in: Mike has accepted the report enthusiastically, the Treasury with resignation; the PSMs have accepted the £40 for helpers; Mrs Newstead is frantically ringing around. We go ahead and draft a press statement on the most optimistic assumptions.

The only bad news is from the pay clerks. Audrey Prime has been on the phone in truculent mood. She has obviously had a word with Len Murray and no dice. There will be no pay increases programmed without a cash payment for the clerks and they are obviously furious that we have got the interim lump sums fed into the computers behind their backs. Len Murray has taken to his sick bed and can't be reached. *Tant pis*: we'll face that tomorrow. In the meantime we clear our press statement, £40 and all, Mrs Newstead having got agreement from her side.

So at 4pm I sail into my press conference, still reading the report frantically on the way, and have an easy ride. When I ask for questions after my announcement of the Government's acceptance of the report there is a silence. 'We are stunned,' says one journalist at last. That phrase again! Then into TV after a make-up girl has tried to patch up my haggard face. As I am about to face up to the cameras Peter comes and whispers to me, 'Remember, no smiling. You are still too coy. Norman [Warner] tells me his children mimic you when you smile.' So I speak sternly to the interviewer. When I get home Ted says to me, 'Very good interview, but I wish you had smiled more. After all, it was good news!' Who'd be a politician? Well, I would, for one, after all I have managed to achieve in the past few weeks – just bulldozing things through. The only cloud is the pay clerks. They have got us in a trap: either to submit to blackmail or to hold up the nurses' pay packets. Either way the Social Contract would come out of it pretty tarnished. Peter Brown is full of heavy admonitions about the need to stand firm, but I suspect there is something in the pay clerks' case. There ususally is. I'll just have to give my mind to this tomorrow.

Wednesday, 18 September

I am interested in David Owen's reaction to what I tell him about the Manifesto meeting. When I describe Tony C.'s reaction to my attempt to redraft our section of the Manifesto, David snaps, 'We have had absolutely no electoral bonus at all from the extra money we have allocated to housing. The money has simply been thrown away.' Yet David is naturally aligned with that centrist group.

Sudden call at short notice to a Cabinet meeting. When I arrived, a little late, Harold was announcing the date of the election: 10 October. Officials had been turned out of the room and we had a discursive chat. Harold said Parliament would be recalled on 22 October; the State Opening would be on 29 October. 'I don't want any of you sitting next to a telephone after the poll. If we win I would not expect to make many changes in a winning team. Just catch up with your sleep after the poll and be at your office desk on the Monday morning. If it is stalemate I shall call a Cabinet

at 2.30pm on the Friday afternoon.' He told us he would be making the announcement that afternoon, so that he could make his broadcast tonight. That would mean
Heath would get his right of reply tomorrow. 'I wasn't going to have him broadcasting
at peak viewing time on Friday night.' In the rather rambling political discussion
which followed everyone was calm. I don't think anyone was certain we would win,
but no one seemed to doubt we were right to go to the country – or that, in choosing
the date, Harold had taken every conceivable consideration into account. Jim said we
must not get diverted by the coalition talk. Denis said there must be no exaggerated
gloom: inflation was *not* running at 20 per cent. Wedgie said our thesis should be that
we could make our problems manageable by believing in each other. We dispersed in
some relief that the crunch had come at last.

But back at the office I faced another crunch, for of *course* there is another pay
crisis. The pay clerks are threatening a work-to-rule unless they get an immediate pay
increase – and that means the nurses' increase will not be in next month's pay
package. Bang go all my carefully laid plans! The clerks are already furious with us
because we have staved them off long enough to make sure that the lump sum will
reach the nurses in time. They now want their claim settled immediately or else they
will announce industrial action at their meeting on Monday. In any other context
than today's announcement I would sweat it out, as I did with my own staff over the
pensioners' uprating, but there could not be a more awkward moment than this. I tell
my chaps that I had better see Audrey Prime, to which they agree thankfully.

When she arrives I find that she has been asking to see me: something my officials
had failed to report to me! She is obviously desperately anxious to avoid upsetting the
apple-cart. In her own disarmingly direct way she says frankly that she has never
hidden the fact that she wants the return of a Labour Government again. But it is the
usual story: a group of underpaid workers, whose work load and complexity has
increased as a result of NHS reorganization, suddenly losing patience when they see
other workers like the nurses getting a whacking increase. Audrey defends their case
vigorously – and indeed she would not be earning her pay as their union representative unless she did, for they have a case. And she obviously believes she has met
obstacles that have been created by officials, not Ministers. Gently but firmly I
disabuse her: we are prepared to do a job evaluation exercise on the pay clerks' work
ready for their next pay round, but if we make them an additional payment now on
the grounds that their work load has increased I shall have the CPSA marching
through my door demanding their cash bonus again before they will put the Christmas bonus into operation for pensioners.[1] At one point I say to her, 'We are getting
into the position where the Government cannot announce a pay increase or an
uprating without our own staff demanding a pay increase for handling it. Why don't
we just spell it out and say that staff insist on their commission on every social
improvement? Why don't we fix it at 10 per cent and have done with it?' She can see
the point, bless her, but pleads with me to let her borrow the official responsible for
this side of the department, Jack Woodlock, for an hour. She assures me she can work
out a formula which will not cause repercussions elsewhere. It will merely refer to the

[1] Though Denis Healey and I had been willing to drop the Christmas bonus in order to finance other
improvements, Cabinet had overruled us.

additional *skills* required, not to the additional *work*. And she is prepared to refer to a proper 'reassessment' of the nature of the work, though she jibs at the words 'job evaluation'. I agree to her request. She is so patently anxious to help and I am so determined not to provide grist to Geoffrey Howe's mischief-making mill.

I then turn to the accumulation of work I have to clear before I go electioneering and work steadily. Audrey's hour expands into two, then three. I begin to get impatient. I tell my people I must go home to start writing my election address and pack for three weeks in Blackburn. I am barely home, hungry and tired, when the phone rings. It is Norman. He tells me that Audrey and Jack Woodlock have worked out a formula, but Audrey insists that, for presentational reasons with her own people, she must report it to me personally. I climb back into my coat and return wearily to the office. Audrey is full of apologies but pleased with the formula, which she assures me she will do her best to sell to her members, though it is less than they want. Woodlock clearly thinks it is reasonable. I tell Audrey that I will put it to colleagues, though of course I cannot guarantee that they will accept it. She quite understands that and at last I am released. Woodlock believes the case for more pay for additional skills is made out. (NHS pay clerks have had to take on board all the complications of the pay structures of the workers transferred to the health service from local authorities.) The flaw in the formula, which I can see, is that the pay clerks would get something on account *before* the reassessment of their work skills has taken place: something we have refused to other people. However I agree to sign a minute to Mike recommending the formula and at last get to bed without having started on my election address.

Friday, 20 September

Norman rings to say that the Department of Employment have turned down our formula for the pay clerks. Would I like to ring Michael Foot? I do so, and Mike comes on in his usual diffident but tenacious way. 'Your first reaction was right, Barbara; you would have the CPSA round your ears at once if we agreed to this.' I don't argue, merely say, 'Then you will have to see Audrey, Mike, and I shall have to come up to London from Blackburn on Sunday night to be there.' He is as helpful as he can be, saying he will come back from Ebbw Vale at any time that suits me. My feelings are strangely divided: it will be a near disaster not to get the nurses' pay increase into their packets as planned, but one part of me is weary of this endless yielding to clamant demands. If Mike wants to be tough I am not going to stop him – and there might even conceivably be an election bonus in it.

Off to Oxford to open the campaign. To my surprise, I find myself speaking well.

Sunday, 22 September

Catch a train to Blackburn, leaving Ted to bring up Janet[1] and packing cases by car. I read up my background briefing on the way and do two meetings on my arrival. Am

---

[1] Janet Anderson, my new constituency secretary.

on the top of my form. This pleases me immensely, because I am determined to make this my last election if the results will let me – I want to go out on the peak, not in the trough, of my ability. I hate people who hang on, keeping the young ones out. Catch the night sleeper back for my meeting with Mike.

Monday, 23 September

Into the office first for a meeting with my own chaps. Jack Woodlock is obviously very distressed at the Department of Employment rejection of the formula he worked out with Audrey. *He* clearly thinks the pay clerks have a case. He has been thinking over the situation during the weekend and has come forward with a new version. If Audrey would agree to a job evaluation exercise by our people in the department, it would not be unreasonable to ask them to produce a pilot study of the reassessment of the pay clerks' work in one month's time. This could then be put into the clerks' pay packets. This would mean that Audrey's lads would only have to wait one month for their increase and we could claim rightly that it was based on a revaluation of their work, thus saving the twelve-month rule, repercussions *et al.* I said I would put this to Mike. When we arrived at Department of Employment we found Mike in the middle of anxious consultation over the Ford's deal,[1] Harold having asked him to deal with it at this morning's press conference. He was *distrait* and there was certainly no great fight in him. He asked me to explain what we had in mind and agreed to it almost thankfully. So when Audrey came in it was merely a question of going through the formalities. She huffed and puffed a bit at having been summoned to the pay policy throne; then relaxed into smiles and agreed to go and work out the details with officials. I rushed for my train, feeling that my journey had hardly been necessary, but nonetheless relieved to learn later that Audrey had accepted the new version and got it through Whitley.

A chastened Mr Heath fought the election in conciliatory vein. Gone was the confrontation of February. Nervous Conservatives and Liberals, worried by Labour's lead in the polls, had been toying with the idea of a Government of National Unity. The Conservative Manifesto echoed the theme of 'putting Britain first'. A Conservative Government, it said, would not reintroduce the Industrial Relations Act 'in the interest of national unity'. Other policies would be toned down. A prices and incomes policy was essential, but should if possible be voluntary. Even food subsidies would be retained for the time being. Pensions would be increased at six-monthly intervals. For the rest, public expenditure and money supply would be rigorously controlled. There would be no 'narrow partisan spirit'. After the election a Conservative Government would consult

[1] After a series of unofficial stoppages in Halewood, Dagenham and on Merseyside, the Ford management had decided to scrap their current annual agreement only seven months after it had been signed. This was widely interpreted as a breach of the TUC agreement with the Government to limit pay rises to once a year.

other party leaders about policy and invite people from outside the party's ranks to join in overcoming Britain's difficulties. 'The nation's crisis should transcend party differences.' Mr Heath's new tone disturbed some of his own activists and muted his attack.

The Liberals also took up the theme of national unity. In June the Liberal leader, Mr Thorpe, and his Chief Whip, Mr David Steel, had rashly offered to go into a coalition if no party won a clear majority. This aroused the fury of the rank and file and had to be toned down. Nonetheless Thorpe continued to insist that all parties must try to come together on an agreed policy. He talked confidently of lifting the Liberal vote from the six million of February to eight or ten million.

For its part the Labour Party flatly rejected all coalition talk. The Government continued boldly to elaborate its own policies. In the two months before the election a spate of White and Green Papers had been pouring out of Whitehall: on a wealth tax, capital transfer tax, devolution, equality for women, the regeneration of industry, a National Consumers' Agency, my new pensions scheme. The Social Contract remained the cornerstone of Labour policy. At the Trades Union Congress in September Len Murray had persuaded the AEUW to withdraw its resolution opposing the Social Contract and to present an enthusiastic united front of support for the Government. A few days later Michael Foot issued a consultative document on his proposed Employment Protection Bill which met many of the unions' long-standing demands for an extension of workers' rights. Its provisions included the right to paid maternity leave, better guaranteed week payments, stronger remedies against unfair dismissal, the duty of firms to disclose information to unions for bargaining purposes, the right of unions to refer recognition complaints to ACAS for adjudication and to secure enforceable awards against employers failing to observe the general level of terms and conditions enjoyed by other workers in similar circumstances. It also clearly legalized inducement to breach of commercial contract in a trade dispute. A significant omission was on picketing, where Michael Foot had failed to persuade the Home Secretary to extend the definition of peaceful picketing to enable pickets to stop vehicles. The document merely said the matter was 'under review'. The Labour Manifesto was in the main a recapitulation of the proposals of February with three additional promises: to create elected assemblies for Scotland and Wales, to set up a Co-operative Development Agency and to ensure open government by replacing the Official Secrets Act with a measure to put on public authorities the responsibility for justifying why information should be withheld. In my own field the Manifesto renewed the commitment to a new system of child allowances, or child benefit, a new pensions scheme and the phasing of private beds out of NHS hospitals.

The Conservatives were embarrassed by internal disputes. On 5 September Keith Joseph attacked incomes policy in a speech which reflected the growing support for monetarism among Tory backbenchers. Enoch Powell, who had re-entered the parliamentary lists as Ulster Unionist candidate for Down, South, denounced Mr Heath's frequent changes of line, remarking cruelly: 'I have sometimes permitted myself to wonder whether the strain of office had been too much for him.' Worried by the opinion polls, the Conservatives put up Margaret Thatcher to promise to peg mortgage rates at 9·5 per cent. (They were then 11 per cent.) The Labour Party, too, had its embarrassments. The Common Market issue was still festering. The pro-marketeers in the Cabinet had reluctantly concurred in the pledge to hold a referendum or election within twelve months on the outcome of the renegotiations. Then, early in the campaign, Shirley Williams startled her colleagues by announcing that, if Labour took Britain out of the EEC, she would not be able to stay in the Cabinet or active politics. The following day Roy Jenkins echoed her. Leading anti-marketeer, Peter Shore, was put up to undo the damage. Challenged at a press conference as to what he would do if the British people voted to stay in Europe, he said he would abide by their verdict. On prices Denis Healey laid up trouble for himself in a euphoric speech. Deriding Heath's claim that prices were rising at an annual rate of over 20 per cent, he claimed that over the three months to August the annual rate of inflation had been down to 8·4 per cent. It was an unfortunate use of statistics that was to boomerang.

In the campaign Labour's leaders denounced 'gloom and panic' talk. Britain, said Mr Wilson, faced crisis but not catastrophe. Denis Healey claimed that the balance of payments deficit, apart from oil, had been halved. So had the rate of growth of money supply. Sterling was strong and funds were flowing in. The worrying facts for the Government were growth, which had not fully made up the fall during the three-day week, and unemployment, which in September had risen to the seasonally adjusted figure, excluding school leavers, of nearly 612,000 or 2·7 per cent. Industry remained jittery, complaining of cash shortage. Some big firms, like Ferranti, ran into trouble and had to be helped by the Government. Nonetheless, as the country went to vote, the opinion polls were still giving Labour a comfortable lead. This was confirmed as the earlier results came in, showing Labour gains. They also showed the Liberals slipping everywhere, with their vote dropping to below six million. But when the counting was over Labour's absolute majority was down to three. Its lead of forty-two seats over the Conservatives had been eaten away by the 'third force' parties, the Scottish Nationalists polling particularly heavily and gaining four seats. The 'others', therefore, held the balance: Liberals (13 seats), Scottish Nationalists (11), Welsh Nationalists (3), Northern Ireland MPS (12). Labour's only consolation was that its vote had risen by 2·1 per cent to 39·2 per cent of the total votes, while the Conservative share of the poll at 35·8 per cent was its lowest in recorded electoral history. I myself was back with the highest majority I had ever had: 7,652.

Thus precariously reinforced the new Government faced up to its problems. Problem No. 1 was the renegotiations with the EEC. Expert Wilson watchers had already detected that he was determined to keep Britain in the European Community if at all possible. And although the Labour Party conference continued to be tough over the terms, there were signs of weakening among Labour MPS. In the new session they proceeded to elect an avowed pro-marketeer, Cledwyn Hughes, as chairman of the Parliamentary Labour Party and four pro-marketeers topped the poll in the election for the backbenchers' Liaison Committee with the Government. Harold Wilson's most serious threat came from the dedicated anti-marketeers in the Cabinet, of which I was one.

Meanwhile my own showdown with the medical profession was coming to a head. With statutory incomes controls abolished, both consultants and GPS were getting restive about their pay. Like the nurses before them, they were pressing for an interim *pay increase, for fear that a pay freeze might be slapped on before their annual review of pay could take place in April 1975. They were at the end of the queue for the catching-up pay increases that were taking place and I was determined that they should not lose out as a result of their having to wait twelve months for their turn.*

But the situation was complicated by the consultants' demand for a new type of contract currently being processed in the joint working party under David Owen. Since we had promised the report by November, there was no time to lose. Of the 11,500 or so consultants in the NHS, some 5,000 had full-time contracts which forbade them to do private practice. Of the rest, the majority had opted for 'maximum part-time' contracts under which they were allowed to do private practice but were expected to devote 'substantially' the whole of their time to the NHS. Though they contracted to do the same eleven sessions a week as the whole-timers did, they received only 9/11ths of the salary. In recognition of the fact that the demands of their private patients would be bound to affect their availability for NHS work. This differential in pay for equivalent sessions had rankled for a long time and the BMA was determined to get rid of it. It was therefore demanding a 'closed' contract of ten sessions a week for maximum part-timers and whole-timers alike, with extra work attracting extra pay, the whole-timers allowed to do private practice and an end to the differential. David Owen and I could see merit in a more 'work-load sensitive' contract which would enable us to reward the whole-timers more adequately. Many of them worked long hours of unpaid overtime manning up unattractive areas and unpopular specialities like geriatrics, which offered no rich pickings to part-timers seeking private fees. But there were dangers, too. The BMA's aim was to encourage the spread of private practice and to discourage whole-time work. To combat this aim it was essential to maintain the differential and reform the system of merit awards under which some £10 million a year was secretly allocated by a professional panel in additional payments to the medically distinguished. Under it a top consultant with a large private practice could get as much as an additional £8,000 a year. The whole-timers received only a minor share. We wanted to use the money on a new system of 'career supplements' which would recognize, not merely medical eminence, but dedicated service generally to the NHS. The breakaway consultants of the HCSA wanted to go even further than the BMA, demanding that payment should be by fees for 'items of service'. It was clear that storms lay ahead.

The junior hospital doctors were restive, too – and with stronger cause. The men and women in these training grades had for years been expected to work excessive hours, filling in among other things for the part-time consultants' absence on private work. Their career structure was too narrow at the top. A 'junior' often had to wait till he or she was thirty-six to get a consultant post. Yet the consultant in situ was not anxious to see the consultant grade expanded too much as this increased the competition for private work. There was a great deal of sympathy in the Labour movement for the juniors' grievances. In July the Government had recognized this by agreeing that the extra duty allowances to which they were entitled after 102 hours at work or on call should be paid after eighty hours. But the juniors, too, were set on a new type of contract which would define their working hours more closely and prevent health authorities from exploiting them. They had launched a campaign for a basic working week of forty hours, with all hours above that being counted as overtime. In September the Trades Union Congress had passed a resolution supporting them. Yet, unless carefully handled, their demand could create difficulties for pay policy. The department's officials had been negotiating uneasily and the juniors' discontent had reached boiling point. In the new session the problem was to land on my desk.

Sunday, 13 October

Rang Harold at Chequers. He answered with a croak, a heavy cold having caught up with him after three weeks in top health. I congratulated him on the way he had run the campaign and how relaxed he had seemed. 'I *felt* relaxed,' he replied. 'I've never enjoyed a campaign as much.' He went on to say that he was making practically no changes in Cabinet and only a few among junior Ministers. The trouble was what to do with Bob Mellish: he had shot his mouth off about wanting Housing, and as a result Harold had had Tony C. on the phone at 8.30 this morning, not exactly threatening to resign but getting very near it if *his* team were disturbed. There was also the problem of whom to appoint as Chief Whip in Bob's place. At this point I took a firm grip on my own anxieties and said bravely, 'Although the last thing I want is to lose Brian O'Malley – and God knows how I shall get the Pensions Bill through without him – I think you ought to know that the one job he really wants more than any other is Chief Whip.' 'Yes, of course, there's Brian,' mused Harold. 'If you *do* take him,' I said desperately, 'you'll have to give me someone first-class in his place. Heaven knows how I would manage without him, but he has been so superb that he deserves promotion and my nobility of nature will not let me stand in his way.' 'Your nobility is well known,' quipped Harold.

Phil and Colin brought the children over for the day and we spent it picking apples in the autumn sunshine. I have never known such a crop. The place is submerged in apples and I have filled every window sill. It is bliss to potter in the garden again – and not a red box to darken the horizon. Obviously the Civil Service don't know what to do. It is so different from previous elections, with people streaming up to No. 10 to discuss what appointments they are going to have. All the leaders have gone to ground and a great calm reigns. It all helps to make it look as though it is the most natural thing in the world for us to be in government.

Monday, 14 October

Up to the office for the ministerial lunch I had called. David and Brian said the department didn't seem sure whether they should even continue to give them briefs. I told Norman firmly it was to be business as usual for everyone. We discussed the issues which had arisen in the election. David was full of the complaints he had met about the abuses of social security. I said I was unhappy about the whole running of supplementary benefits. Staff on the social security side were increasingly hostile to what they felt was scrounging. A quite nasty mood was building up and, as a result, even deserving cases were being treated with insensitivity. I shocked Liz by saying that 'open-ended welfarism' was not what I meant by socialism. 'You sound like Keith Joseph,' she said. But David heartily agreed with me. I said I was going to discuss all this with Harold Collison[1] and in particular was determined to make sure that something more effective was done about heating additions. 'I agree we must, but you realize it will cost us a lot of money,' said Brian O'M. gloomily. Brian A-S. said we ought to be launching some long-term studies of social policy: it wasn't too early to start thinking of the next election Manifesto. We all heartily endorsed that and I added that we should also be thinking of the things we could do now that did not cost money. We should be seen to be active on a number of fronts: not just fighting for the next uprating. 'This is where your social plan[1] comes in,' said Jack, and I asked him and Brian to get working on it fast.

Tuesday, 15 October

In early to see Collison before the monthly meeting of the Supplementary Benefits Commission. As if he had been reading my thoughts, he produced a most encouraging answer to my letter about heating additions. The improvements he proposes could be quite dramatic, particularly on central heating, where the commission have forestalled an idea I was going to put to him: namely, that they should ask local authorities to give them an estimate of what the normal heating costs in one of their centrally heated old peoples' flats should be, so that the SBC could make up the difference. I urged him to make a splash about this; why didn't he hold a press conference and get on TV? The more people saw what a kindly chap he was the more it would break down the criticisms – and, not least, the more it would influence the attitudes of his staff. He seemed faintly alarmed at the idea, and then said he had occasionally done joint press conferences with the Secretary of State and preferred it that way – at which I jumped. I also asked him if I and the two Ministers of State could come and have an informal discussion with the Commission.

Into our first Cabinet. No agenda. No officials taking notes, only John Hunt. Harold was very chirpy: said he thought we would like a general chat on the position following the election. Personally he thought the tiny majority was manageable – after all, we had beaten the Tories by forty-two seats. His view was that we should act as though we were facing a full-length Parliament. He wasn't going to make any big changes in his 'winning team'; we should tell junior Ministers to stay at their posts and get on with it. As far as the Queen's Speech was concerned we should 'go absolutely straight ahead with our Manifesto'. He then tried a bit of whip-cracking. Ministers had been free during the election – and indeed for some weeks before – to write articles and generally to trail their own coats. We must now have 'a more cohesive Cabinet, following all the rules'. He didn't even look at Wedgie!

Jim came in first, starting his comments with glowing congratulations to Harold on

---

[1] I wanted to publish a social plan which would comprise a survey of the needs of different groups in society, a description of how far they were being met, what remained to be done and the choices that had to be made.

the way he had conducted the campaign and going on to do his Cassandra act. One of our difficulties was that the middle classes had got into a great state of defeatism. He personally was gloomy about the economy. We must go for the conservation of oil. 'Public expenditure has to be reined back pretty severely if we are to get through.' (Shades of 1966!) The Social Contract had got to be made to work. The Ford's deal was very disturbing. His credentials about the rights of the unions were well enough known for him to be frank: 'There is a real fear of the power of the unions.' And he concluded: 'We are the real national party now.'

Denis refused to be panicked. We could now plan for four years and we were going to get enormous help from oil. Provided we could get through the next year or eighteen months there was no reason why we should not stay in power for a long time. The next year was the tricky year for us. 'The key to everything is the Social Contract.' The scope for public expenditure beyond the figure of $2\frac{3}{4}$ per cent was not there. During the election he had been made aware that there was 'an immense dislike of income tax'. Mike came next. 'I don't agree with the peace and quiet formula at all.' We must have a series of emergency measures – e.g. oil conservation, an attack on unemployment, a move towards the £30 national minimum wage. That was bound to come: it was part of the Social Contract and we must accommodate it by telling people there must be a narrowing of differentials and a holding back of top salaries.

I made a great spiel which seemed to impress. I warned that it was a bit euphoric to assume that we could survive for the length of a whole Parliament. In two years' time we could be forced to the country by a series of by-election defeats and above all by the press predicting that we couldn't carry on. 'The press can force elections.' So I hoped that once again we would not become the architects of Tory victory by our noble sacrifices. 'I am not advocating economic fecklessness,' I said, 'but, shall I say, taking a bit of a risk.' Denis grinned at this. I heartily endorsed what Harold had said about going for the whole Manifesto. I hoped we would not ape Tory language about national unity. The line I had taken during the election was that unity was produced by deeds, not words. We ought to sharpen the distinction between us and the Tories and I hoped therefore that we would publicly reject statutory controls; it was economically necessary, as well as politically, to kill the fears of a freeze. We needed a theme for the Queen's Speech and I thought it should be that we appealed to hope, not fear: to the confidence that we could win through *provided* that certain clearly defined conditions were met. And one of them was that the better off must be ready to see differentials narrowed. And I ended by pleading that we should remember that public expenditure was part of the standard of living of millions. 'If you are talking about a national minimum, they need a minimum, too.'

Tony C. got restive through all this, as he always does when I speak; I think he sees me merely as his rival No. 1 for public expenditure. Reg P. came out in his true colours again, saying we had got to appeal to national unity and give 'priority for measures which are the most relevant'. (We all know what he means by that: no nationalization.) He even went so far as to say that there should be no commitment in the Queen's Speech *not* to introduce statutory controls! Fred [Peart], too, was true to type; he had found that nationalization was not popular and he warned us we could never go back to cheap food. Wedgie was his usual euphoric self; the election campaign had ended cynicism, he said. 'There is no alternative to our policy.' Eric said that a lot of nonsense was talked about energy conservation. The only effective way was a realistic energy pricing policy, and he hoped that this time he wouldn't meet any revolts over night storage heater charges![1] Bob cheered us up by saying that the position in the House was better than it was before and Harold wound up by saying there would be a party meeting next Tuesday, at which the party would be given an opportunity to talk about the priorities for the Queen's Speech. This is an innovation and I suspect it is Wedgie's idea.

Back at the office I called a meeting to discuss the social security headaches that lie ahead: the timing and size of the family allowance increase and, not least, what is going to happen to the child endowment scheme. All these have got to be settled urgently – ahead of PESC – so I have to go to see the Chancellor. Officials were very gloomy, saying that inflation had already boosted the bill for our policies and that the Chancellor was likely to be tough. We discussed what, if anything, I should yield on if I am in a corner. I am not likely to get any mercy from Tony C. or Reg if I appeal over the Chancellor's head to Cabinet – certainly not before the whole PESC is discussed.

Whatever our worries they are nothing to the Tories': they are in real travail over the leadership. Edward du Cann has been trying to jump the gun through the 1922 Committee,[2] but I have bet Ted that Heath will still be leader when the next election comes. He's incredulous and has bet me two to one, but my hunch is strong.

Wednesday, 16 October

Peter Brown came in to see me, congratulated me and pledged renewed loyalty. 'You are a very skilled politician,' he told me, 'and you have done extremely well during the past six months. But now I want you to take things a little more easily.' Just my idea! I am determined to enjoy life to the full – get more fun, more home life and more time to think. A bit more social life too, if I can get it. After all, I haven't many more years left! Yet I never felt more full of energy. Into another tense office meeting, this time over our policy for phasing out pay beds. We are in for a major row here, and the officials have already passed me, with gusto, a letter from the Royal Colleges and the BMA which is practically an ultimatum to us not to touch private practice – or even pay beds. 'This is a declaration of war,' I said sternly, looking round

[1] The increase in electricity prices had fallen particularly savagely on night storage heaters. On 10 May the off-peak rate had gone up by 70 per cent, compared with 30 per cent for the standard rate. This particularly hit old age pensioners, who had been encouraged to install night storage heaters by the prospect of 'half-price' electricity. As a result of the outcry the Government had restored the price differential on 1 August at a cost of £40 million.

[2] Edward du Cann, MP for Taunton and chairman of the 1922 Committee comprising all backbench Conservative MPs, seemed to be trying to force Mr Heath into an early statement of his intentions on the leadership. Du Cann called a full 1922 Committee meeting for 22 October while there was still a strong anti-Heath mood following the second election defeat. This tactical manoeuvre leaked extensively to the press, but was defeated when the 1922 Committee's executive decided to hold the full meeting on 31 October, two days after the Queen's Speech. The full meeting set up an enquiry into procedures for electing a leader and invited Mr Heath to address them on 14 November. Although du Cann was criticized by some MPs for his conspicuous plotting, he was re-elected unopposed as 1922 Committee chairman.

the table. 'No Government could accept instructions to ignore its own Manifesto.' Philip hastily agreed; Henry Yellowlees seemed to agree genuinely. But David says he just doesn't think we can get away with it if, in addition to phasing out pay beds, we try also to prohibit consultants from doing any private practice at all, even outside the Service. I agree, but don't like the alternative forms of contract he is proposing, pointing out that they could result in there being even *fewer* whole-time consultants than there were before. Things haven't been made easier by Halsbury's antics. In an interview in the magazine *Pulse*, he has blabbed in confidence to a journalist (Stevenson, who also writes for the *Mail*) about the doctors' interim pay claim, saying he couldn't see how he could possibly defy the Government's policy on the twelve-month rule. The journalist has leaked! Naturally the doctors are furious, arguing that their case has been prejudged. I'm going to need a lot of time to deal with the mounting troubles in this field.

True to my new determination to have a bit more fun, Ted and I take the night off to go to the theatre. *Saturday, Sunday, Monday* was recommended to us, but we find it a bore. My only theatre trip for two years wasted!

Thursday, 17 October

At Cabinet we had a long report on sugar in the EEC renegotiations, about which I am uneasy, but Jim assured us that the Ministerial Committee on European Questions [EQ] had agreed the line. One thing was clear: the Commission won't have long-term agreements. Since I am not on the committee (and hadn't even received yet the document which has apparently been circulated) there was nothing I could do but rely on Peter. I *did* ask about sugar from Mauritius and was assured we could take all she could offer within the 1·4 million tons from the developing Commonwealth countries to which we were committed – and by which we would stand. So that was that.

The main business was a discussion of a lengthy document on 'Strategy and Priorities' for our work prepared by CPRS, on which the department had briefed me approvingly. Obviously the poor dears in CPRS feel they must justify their existence, but at any rate it had the effect of forcing us to look at things in the round for once. Actually I didn't think the document was too bad, because it did at least have the sense to indicate which decisions were clearly political ones. Harold began by saying that no decisions would be taken on the memorandum, and he suggested that it might be a good idea to have a fuller discussion of it at Chequers before too long, 'though some members of the last Government got a bit fed up with Chequers discussions', he added. A number of us denied this audibly. We welcomed the idea of resuming them. Shirley opened the discussion, saying the document was disappointing. It was 'high on analysis and low on proposals'. She returned to her theme about how we must adopt greater austerity of standards in the buildings, etc. which we provided. Tony C. got in a plug for expansion of the construction industry (which to him means expansion of housing). Denis said the major weakness of the document was that it failed to deal with the international dimension: North Sea oil would dramatically alter our relative position in the world. It would give us a 'very useful start'. Jim was as gloomy as ever: 'We face an economic Dunkirk.' Harold Lever was in maverick mood: 'Are we or are we not going to go for a strategy of growth?' He obviously had little enthusiasm for some of our most crucial political commitments, such as land. 'It is a lunatic absurdity to pour out £100 million a year on the administrative costs in order to satisfy certain soap box commitments.' (There was, noticeably, no angry reaction from Tony C. at this.)

My line was that I welcomed the memo, not because I agreed with all of it, but because it forced us to crystallize our thoughts. We should never manage to relate expectations to resources unless we put the whole problem together and presented people with a choice in the context of concrete illustrations of the size of the need compared with the restrictions that faced us. That was what we in DHSS were trying to do in our social plan. Our prime aim in the coming months should be to take people into our confidence. 'For a party which has staked everything on education and persuasion we do precious little educating.' What worried me about these discussions was that we all made different points but nothing was ever done to pull them together and therefore there was never any follow-up. For the discussion at Chequers we should all put in a paper setting out our comments on the memo and our suggestions for action. To my surprise everyone thought this was an excellent idea.

Mike then made some very telling points which I applauded audibly. We must not lose the impetus of the election. In his view we should draw up a list of measures, including energy rationing, a programme for the construction industry, steps to deal with unemployment, a policy for top salaries which would deliberately aim at narrowing differentials and action on overseas aid. MPs should be encouraged to go and talk to unions, Ministers should accept a cut in salaries and we should at last face the need to televise Parliament. (Fred Peart pulled his usual face at this, but I said 'Hear, hear!' loudly). Wedgie swept all this aside in his best apocalyptic manner. 'This paper is shot through with pessimism. Ideally we should publish this and it would be a revelation that the Establishment has no confidence in the British people at all or their capacity to solve their difficulties. What we are facing is the shrinking of democratic accountability. This paper misses the boat by a hundred miles.' I am afraid I made rude noises at all this, while no one seemed quite clear what he was getting at. I feel these days that Wedgie has got himself launched so strongly on a tide of challenging everything and everyone that all he can do is to shoot the rapids. Harold summed up soothingly. He agreed we should examine the reduction of Ministers' salaries and he hoped that, as I suggested, all Ministers would put in papers for Chequers. They should be 'short and specific'. We should also consider reopening the question of the televising of Parliament. After the meeting Wedgie came up to me in his disarming way. 'What a marvellous speech you made, duckie.' 'I don't know why you say that,' I replied rather coldly, 'as you proceeded to deride all I had said.'

The 'Husbands and Wives' dinner was resumed at Tommy's. I love their quaint little Old Bank House and it was great fun to relax in that familiar, politically bohemian atmosphere. Everyone was full of Norman Buchan's resignation.[1] Dick

---

[1] Norman Buchan, Labour MP for Renfrewshire West and a member of the Tribune group, was Minister of State in the Ministry of Agriculture, Fisheries and Food under Fred Peart. He was strongly opposed to

Clements of *Tribune* (I wonder if his inclusion is to be permanent?) said he had spent the last few days trying to persuade him out of it, but had only succeeded in getting him to put the reasons in a slightly more respectable form. Judith came in late, obviously upset. Half-way through the meal she disappeared and Tony said she wasn't too well as she had just had a great shock. Harold had sent for her and told her she was being positively vetted. When Judith came back she poured out her heart to me. The very idea that anyone could consider her a Communist! It was all no doubt to do with her contacts with Chile. Didn't the fools realize that there were even more non-Communists in gaol there than Communists? Harold had accepted her assurances, but she was clearly shaken to the core.

Down late to HCF to start a long luxurious weekend at home and more apple-picking.

Monday, 21 October

Sir Keith Joseph has made another of his traumatic speeches, this time with very nasty genetic undertones.[1] I have spent the weekend beating off press requests for me to comment on it, but I have refused. I want to think out a considered answer carefully. We spent most of the Ministers' meeting discussing this and they all applauded my discretion. We agreed that I should give my answer when I speak to the Family Service Council in Liverpool on Friday. This doesn't give me much time, but I sent Brian A-S. and Jack away to work on it. I have my hands full with office minutiae, including my crucial meeting with the Chancellor on my public expenditure bids and the developments over Halsbury, in whom the General Medical Services Committee of the BMA has passed a vote of no confidence. God knows when I shall have time to work on the speech, but it must be done this week or I shall miss the boat. Yet on his own admission K.J. has spent weeks on his key speeches.

Douglas Allen pays me a courtesy call as he has now taken over as head of the Civil Service. We have quite a useful chat. He asks first whether I still want Philip Rogers to go in February and I say I think we should get a new chap to take over at the beginning of a new administration. Who can he offer me? To my surprise he suggests Derek Mitchell (I shall have to ask Tommy about him, as I only remember him vaguely from Cabinet Office); also a chap I don't know: Bancroft.[2] I ask him if he has thought of Douglas Smith and his eyebrows shoot up approvingly. No, he hasn't, but it isn't a bad idea. Then he has second thoughts and wonders whether the older

---

the Common Market. In his resignation letter he said he was resigning 'because of increasingly serious disagreements about certain policy matters and about the control and direction of the Department'.

[1] In a speech in Birmingham the previous day, calling for the 're-moralization' of our society, Sir Keith had declared: 'The balance of our population, our human stock, is threatened ... a high and rising proportion of children are being born to mothers least fitted to bring children into the world and bring them up. They are born to mothers who were first pregnant in adolescence in social classes four and five. Many of these girls are unmarried. ... Some are of low intelligence, most of low educational attainment.' I was able to prove that, apart from anything else, his figures were wrong.

[2] Ian Bancroft was Second Permanent Secretary in the Civil Service Department. He moved to the Department of the Environment as Permanent Secretary in 1975 and became head of the Home Civil Service in January 1978.

people in my department might not resent being put under someone so young. I promise to think over the names. Then I ask him: 'I often wonder – not that I want to put ideas into your head – whether civil servants might not suddenly start rebelling like everybody else and challenge some of the conventions which have always dominated their lives. After all, they see governments having to govern on a narrow margin; everything is unstable. Parliaments no longer last their normal term; the civil servants' role has been challenged; outsiders have been brought in. They have to keep switching from one policy to another. Why should they go on being so submissive and loyal? Do you think they might change?' 'Yes,' he said, 'I think they will. The older ones will conform because it has been instilled in them, but the younger ones coming on may well be different. It is not the outsiders as such they object to, but what they do resent is when they are treated less generously than the people brought in from industry or whatever. There was a lot of bitterness when George Brown brought in industrialists at enormously inflated salaries.' I was sorry when Norman came in and broke it up – just as we were getting warmed up!

Home late, too tired to work on my Liverpool speech.

Tuesday, 22 October

At Cabinet we had a preliminary discussion of the Queen's Speech, Harold stressing all the time that we were not reaching any final decisions until after the party meeting had had a chance to express its views. There was some argument about the passage on the Social Contract, Shirley and Jim wanting to stress the issue of inflation more, Mike arguing that the Social Contract was about more than that. Mike was sent off to try and redraft. The section on industry had the reference to the nationalization of aircraft and shipbuilding in brackets and some of them were clearly ready to fight Wedgie on this, when Harold clinched it by saying he agreed with Attlee that one should always do the controversial things in the first session and also with Wedgie that it was essential to end uncertainty. Denis agreed with this, but added that he hoped the timing of the legislation would be considered carefully: 'It is better for private enterprise to cancel planes, not us.' Roy murmured gloomily that he hoped nationalization would not provide the most expensive programme yet for subsidizing uneconomic aircraft.

As a codicil Harold said we should tell our junior Ministers not to make speeches about the Tory leadership crisis. We should leave the Tories to wallow in their own misery.

In the event the long meeting with the Chancellor was more productive than I had dared to hope. He agreed without demur that there must be another uprating of pensions and benefits in April next year and in return I agreed to accept the basis of 'historic' calculation of the relationship to average national earnings, instead of the 'forecasting' method we had sought.[1] The main thing is to have got the timing agreed,

[1] In our uprating legislation, the National Insurance Act 1974, we had bound ourselves by law to increase pensions and other long-term benefits at least yearly in line with the movement of average earnings or prices, whichever was the more favourable to the pensioner. But there were two ways of calculating this movement. Under the 'historic' method, the increase was based on the movement of

particularly in view of Denis's introductory homily to the effect that he now faced bids for public expenditure of up to £1,000 million *more* than the 2¾ per cent increase he was planning would justify. He also agreed to let me double the earnings disregard for supplementary benefit[1] and said he would announce that there would be a second uprating next year.

My real battle came over child allowances [later child benefit]. First he delighted me by saying he was prepared to drop his figure of a 25–35p increase in family allowances next year and go for my figure of 60–50p instead, but only, he added menacingly, if I were prepared to postpone the introduction of child allowances till 1977 and accept his proposal for a lower figure of £1·86p for the first child when the scheme did come in. My jaw dropped. I knew that my priority must be an adequate increase in family allowances next year; also that the department do not think it is physically possible to achieve child allowances by 1976, but to have a lower allowance for the first child as well was intolerable. I told him as much, adding I had expected him to ask *either* for postponement of the scheme *or* for a lower allowance for the first child, but not both. 'Which would you choose if I gave you a choice?' he cracked back. After a moment's hesitation (and to my officials' relief) I replied, 'Postponement.' 'Only because you know you can't bring it in on time anyway,' he twinkled. There then ensued a complicated discussion about when we would have to decide the actual rates of child allowance anyway and we eventually agreed that we would tell Cabinet that we had decided to fix those later. I felt a great sense of relief. Even Treasury officials joined in the exercise sympathetically, Baldwin telling Denis that he was sure they could 'fudge' the public expenditure White Paper so that there was no indication that Denis was hoping to go for the lower rate.

To our surprise Denis then turned to my health budget, a subject which I had been told wouldn't be raised. He said sternly that we couldn't have a penny more for the NHS, at which I said, outraged, that if he intended to leave me out of the construction industry rescue operation I would take it to Cabinet. Philip came in gravely with a warning about the consequences of freezing the health capital programme and Denis suddenly said, 'But you haven't put in a paper saying what you need.' We denied this vigorously and he repented, smiling: 'Put one in now and we'll have a look at it.' We went out congratulating ourselves on what we had achieved.

Back to the office for more key discussions, this time on private practice. Henry Yellowlees has informed me that the BMA has got a little frightened over the Royal Colleges' ultimatum to me over pay beds: he can see that it is an unconstitutional threat to an elected Government. Stevenson is in a positive tizzy about the situation. David gave his usual warnings about the difficulties we were going to have with the

---

earnings and prices over an appropriate past period and was a process of catching up. The 'forecasting' method involved estimating the future movement of prices and earnings up to the date the next increase became payable. At a time of rising prices the forecasting method was obviously more favourable, but with the Chancellor promising another uprating in nine months' time instead of twelve, the time lag was not so serious.

[1] Under the 'earnings disregard', earnings up to a certain level are ignored in calculating entitlement to supplementary benefit. The doubling of the amount which a claimant could earn without his or her benefit being affected was of special benefit to one-parent families and met one of the recommendations of the Finer Report.

consultants. He has obviously already given them an enormous amount of ground on the new contract and I had to fight him all the way on the need to retain the whole-time differential and to redistribute the merit award. 'I have my breaking point, too,' I kept reminding him.

Thursday, 24 October

Up at 5am to struggle on with my speech in answer to Keith Joseph's. If only I had more time to develop it! I was so tired the words would not flow. I was still scribbling when it was time to go and have my hair done and I went on scribbling under the dryer and all the way to Cabinet. Arrived at Cabinet five minutes late to find them discussing the strikes in Scotland, which are playing such havoc with the Social Contract. Of course, the press have been full of the usual illiterate demands for the Government to intervene (and then they complain when Government intervention leads to a settlement which they immediately denounce as inflationary!). Mike was all for standing firm and leaving it to ACAS which, he pointed out, we had, after all, set up for just this purpose. Jack Jones was doing everything he could to get the road-haulage boys into line and Alex Kitson was working nobly. Harold agreed, but said that we should make a statement in Parliament next week if the trouble was not settled till then, while Roy J. said primly that we must go ahead with contingency plans.

The meat of the morning was the row between Mason and Jim over last night's stories that the Foreign Office had told off the Ministry of Defence about the naval visit to South Africa. Jim apologized to Roy about the reports and assured him they had not been inspired by him. Nonetheless, he said, the publicity given to the visit – and the propaganda use which the South African Government had made of it – had been very embarrassing to him diplomatically. We had agreed last March, as part of our arms-length attitude to South Africa, that we would oppose sporting and cultural exchanges and not allow goodwill visits by the navy. Operational requirement visits should only be made sparsely and on a very muted basis. That was obviously not what had happened this time. Personally he doubted whether the Simonstown agreement[1] was worth militarily the trouble it was to us diplomatically: we ought to review the need for it as part of the Defence Review. If the security interest was marginal, we should scrap it. He wanted however to warn us that we intended to veto the Motion coming before the UN to expel South Africa. He thought it essential to preserve the principle of universality in the UN; otherwise there might be moves to expel all sorts of people, including Israel. He thought it was essential to make our attitude to South Africa clear, and he hoped Cabinet would agree he should do so along the lines he had indicated when he made a speech in his constituency the following day. In the

---

[1] The Simonstown Agreement was signed with South Africa in 1955 when the Royal Navy ceased to be the owner and occupier of the Simonstown naval base near Cape Town. Under the agreement the Royal Navy retained the right to use the facilities of the base in peacetime and Britain's allies were given the right to use it in war. In return Britain agreed to conduct joint planning and naval exercises with the South African navy. Following the Cabinet discussion Jim Callaghan announced in Cardiff that the agreement 'should be brought to an end or allowed to wither on the vine'.

discussion no one opposed Jim's intention to veto expulsion; everyone agreed we should review Simonstown urgently and that Jim should make his speech.

We then cleared the Queen's Speech. No changes were necessary as a result of the party meeting, as all the points had already been covered anyway – except the issue of the tied cottage, which nobody mentioned. Ted [Short] made his usual complaint that the programme of Bills was far too heavy and that we couldn't possibly get them all through the House. I had an anxious moment while Jim suggested a list of Bills that could be left out, including my long-term Pensions Bill! However even Ted melted at my look of dismay and said we should just have to soldier on and do the best we could. I tried to get into my section of the Queen's Speech dealing with the NHS a reference to phasing out pay beds, because I want Cabinet committed to that so that I can get extra funds for the new whole-time consultants' contract when the time comes, but Harold said this wasn't appropriate for the Queen's Speech. 'Mention it in the debate,' he said.[1]

Friday, 25 October

When I arrived at Liverpool to visit the mental hostel complex at New Hall, Norman was waiting with the news that there was great press and TV interest in my reply to Keith Joseph, which had been handed out yesterday. I said we must finish the visit early so that I could go through the completed speech, which I had not yet seen, having asked Brian A-S. to polish off certain points. It all became a mad rush, with Norman and me having a long talk on the telephone after lunch while I cleared up some obscurities about the statistics and satisfied myself that my criticisms of Sir K. were watertight. It was a rather snooty cleric who greeted me when we arrived late at the rendezvous with the Family Service Council. He was obviously not too pleased at the incursion of the TV. A hurried bit of back-combing by the make-up girl, which Norman, properly trained now, had ordered for me, and I was on my feet – and potentially on the air. I hated reading the whole thing but went doggedly on. Then into radio recordings and TV. We left to visit a home for battered wives and at last were on the plane home. I bought Norman a drink and as we chatted companionably he admitted to me, 'I am a total convert to special advisers. I don't know what we would do without Brian A-S. and Jack. I sometimes wonder how we managed without them.'

Surprisingly extensive coverage of my speech on TV. I hadn't expected this. Slept a satisfied and relaxed sleep.

Sunday, 27 October

'Insight' in the *Sunday Times* has a long piece explaining the facts as I had revealed them and saying I had wiped the floor with Sir K. So, despite the rush, I have succeeded where K. flopped. Thank God for special advisers!

---

[1] The main measures eventually included in the Queen's Speech were a new Industry Act and Housing Act, Michael Foot's Employment Protection proposals, the establishment of a British National Oil Corporation, my new pensions scheme, the Children's Bill, and Bills to take development land into public ownership and to end sex discrimination.

Monday, 28 October

At the office I had a meeting with Ministers only to discuss the paper I shall put into the Chequers meeting of Cabinet on the CPRS memo on 'Strategy and Priorities'. I spelt out my ideas and Brian A-S. went off to work on them: another example of the value of these special outside chaps. Over our ministerial lunch we had a long discussion on the distribution of the rate support grant. Alf is very worried lest, under the limitation of resources which is going to take place, provision for the disabled is going to get squeezed out. He wants a specific grant, but failing that pleaded that I should fight for the personal social services to be retained as a measurement of need in the distribution of the grant. David briefed me on the details and I agreed to fight for it.

Then Raymond Gedling and Philip asked to see me, full of grim foreboding about Halsbury. Raymond reported that Halsbury had told him in confidence that he wasn't going to be browbeaten into resignation by the threats of the BMA. Instead, to show his independence of mind, he was going to recommend that the twelve-month rule should be breached in their case – and then resign! We couldn't imagine anything more embarrassing for the Government. I said that I thought the PM ought to be brought in.

An awkward session with Dick Bourton, who had come to report what he thought were his great achievements over PESC. He told me proudly that he had got another £30 million for the NHS next year, but it was to be non-recurring. The Treasury refused to allow us any more for subsequent years. Nonetheless this, together with a few other things, meant that, together with my £25 million from the reflationary package, I had in fact got the additional £100 million for which I was pressing. And he sat back well satisfied with himself, awaiting my applause. Part of the deal was, of course, to be that I accepted the offer and would not argue the matter any more in Cabinet. I gulped; then said tactfully that I thought he had done very well, etc. Nonetheless I could not give up my right to demand that Cabinet look at the PESC programmes *as a whole* before reaching a decision. All along I had resisted the attempt to set one side of my department against another, or me against Education, in a series of bilateral deals. How could I accept this offer when I had still no idea what was going to happen to defence, roads or any other programme? (And although Dick Bourton's figuring *sounded* impressive, I was far from clear from his rush report what actually I had gained.) So I still wanted to go ahead and put to Cabinet the paper on social priorities.

Bourton bridled angrily. He was obviously deeply affronted. His reputation as the great fixer on behalf of the department's interests had never been challenged before. (Philip keeps coming to me and saying how marvellous Dick is at getting more than our share out of the Treasury and how wise it is to leave him alone to get on with it, etc.) Dick then warned me darkly that, if I were to question the offer in any way, it would be withdrawn. Maybe, I said, but that was a risk I was prepared to take. I had no idea, for instance, how much Education was going to get. 'A mere £15 million next year and a *cut* of £160 million by 1978–79,' said Dick triumphantly. Maybe, I repeated, desperate by now but still placatory, but I really couldn't commit myself in the short time I had had to study this. And I hurried off to No. 10 for Harold's eve-of-Queen's Speech reception, leaving him in high dudgeon.

At No. 10 I took Brian and David aside to ask for their advice: was I wise to continue to challenge our allocation, knowing how much hatred Tony C. would try to stir up against me? David was in no doubt I should: Tony was a failure anyway. Everyone seemed pretty pleased with the Queen's Speech (junior Ministers have no idea what agonizing struggles lie behind its programme) and I went home more determined than ever not to take my NHS allocation without a fight.

Tuesday, 29 October

At PLP meeting on the Queen's Speech there were no great complaints from the rank and file. I whispered to Harold that I was in trouble over Halsbury and that we were faced with the possibility that he might come out against the twelve-month rule. I then went off to have a hilarious State Opening lunch with Ted and Joan Woodman[1] in the Lords, where we fought for food at the most lordly buffet it has ever been my hard work to queue for. But we laughed a lot and I kept saying to Joan that the oddities around us were supposed to be the highest in the realm. She enjoyed it – and, of course, the spectacle of the opening was as dazzling as ever. I am all in favour of spectacle as long as one does not inhale. I got back to my room to find an urgent message waiting for me: the PM had taken my remarks about Halsbury so seriously that he had called an urgent meeting at No. 10 to discuss the matter that afternoon. Michael, Malcolm Shepherd and Edmund Dell were waiting in Harold's study. I explained our problem and urged Harold to see Halsbury, who thought a lot of him. Everyone agreed with our analysis that Halsbury must be got to resign, but Harold insisted that I should see him first and that *he* should only be brought in as a last resort. So another dirty job lands on my plate.

Wednesday, 30 October

I went into the NEC not expecting any great drama. We discussed how to re-establish liaison between party and Government, and decided to reconstitute the top level Liaison Committee while keeping the Campaign Committee as well. Next we came to the International Committee minutes, on which Mik referred specially to the old EEC Monitoring Committee – which he said was now defunct, following the PM's ban on Ministers attending it. As a result four members had withdrawn, including the chairman. What Mik wanted to know was when and how the committee was going to be reconstituted. At this Wedgie said promptly, 'I have not withdrawn from the chairmanship,' which surprised everyone, in view of Harold's ruling. Wedgie then went on to say that the real trouble had been in the *name* of the committee: 'monitoring' sounded as though the Minister members were supervising their colleagues' work. But if we called it a 'Liaison Committee' there could be no objection from anyone and the committee could be reconstituted as before. In Harold's absence

[1] A family friend.

everyone agreed cheerfully, though I have no doubt Harold will take it as a deliberate snub.

By this time I was getting restive as I had an official visit to pay at 2pm and could see myself missing lunch again, but I felt I must stay for Mik's Motion on South Africa. This was couched in such offensive terms that I did not see how any Minister could vote for it, but I reckoned without the completely slap-happy, let's-have-the-best-of-both-worlds attitude of some of my colleagues. Mik then proceeded to move the resolution: 'That the National Executive Committee deplores the Government's action in holding the recent combined naval exercise with South Africa, which is directly contrary both to party policy and to clear assurances given by the Government itself; and calls upon the Government to ensure that the Ministers concerned do not repeat this gross error.' There was a chorus of approval by Lena and co. I said that, as Jim couldn't be there that day, we should postpone the matter so that he could be asked for an explanation, at which Lena snapped, 'Why should we? He knew this item was coming up and it was up to him to be here.' I protested that Jim had already made a statement making it clear we were reviewing Simonstown in line with party policy, whereupon Joan Lestor moved, and Judith seconded, that we should insert at the beginning that we welcomed this statement, before going on to the rest of the Motion. Even this gesture of solidarity with the Government was too much for Lena: it would only weaken the resolution, she said. So the addition was put to the vote and only scraped through by eleven votes to ten, the Ministers voting for it, Mik against. (Mike, alas, wasn't there.) It was clear to me that most of them were hell-bent on having a row with the Government and nothing would stop them.

I plodded on, pointing out that we could have a Motion which reiterated party policy without attacking the Government and so making it impossible for some of us to vote for it. Could we not delete the words 'the Government's action in holding', which would then leave us free to have time to sort out who was to blame? (I knew, for instance, that Harold and Jim had both been unaware that the visit was to take place, as the Cabinet as a whole had certainly been unaware.) This suggestion was rejected overwhelmingly (though, to do him justice, Wedgie voted for it), and Ron did not help by saying that he was sure the whole international as well as national Labour movement was waiting for us to denounce the visit in no uncertain terms. When the Motion was put to the vote I – and I believe Shirley – abstained, but the rest of the Ministers – Wedgie, Joan and Judith – voted for. As I got up to go I said angrily and audibly, 'I don't like this attempt to get the best of both worlds.' Walter and Wedgie joined me in the lift. Wedgie was seeking to justify himself as ingratiatingly as always. 'What we ought to do,' he said to me pleasantly, 'is to distinguish between past actions of the Government for which we all share responsibility and *future* actions which we must retain the right to try and influence.' 'Exactly,' I replied, 'but that is just what the Motion did not do. I do not believe you had any choice but to abstain, as I did.' 'Well, duckie . . .' he shrugged. Walter, of course, was full of socialist righteousness.

In the afternoon I won a great battle at the Ministerial Committee on the distribution of the rate support grant. John Silkin made a poor case for excluding personal social services from the formula; I made a vigorous case for including them and beat him into the ground. As I left John was talking to his officials. 'I was reminding them,' he said to me ruefully, 'that I had said before the meeting, "If Mrs Castle is there we have lost."'

Thursday, 31 October

Went into Cabinet without having seen my *Times*, so was surprised when Harold beckoned me upstairs to his study before the others came. He was blazing mad at the *Times* front-page story, with its usual line about how he had been 'snubbed' and 'defied' at the NEC yesterday. The story also reported my conciliatory role, so I was Harold's blue-eyed girl that morning. Harold said he wasn't going to tolerate this kind of behaviour; his authority would be completely undermined. I tried to head him off a showdown, but he wouldn't listen and marched into Cabinet room, turning officials out while he let fly at full blast. He was not going to accept such open defiance of collective responsibility, he declared. Some Ministers had better realize that they would have to choose between freedom on the NEC and responsibility to Cabinet. They couldn't have both. He would be in touch with those concerned.

Wedgie sat silent; so did I. Mike tried his usual emollient line. He was in favour of collective responsibility, he said, and agreed it was necessary to sustain it. This had always been Nye's view. But there were problems about the relationship between Cabinet and NEC which couldn't be dealt with properly in the way Harold suggested. His way 'could lead to a furious row'. He hadn't 'any simple solutions to offer' but thought we should have a meeting to discuss it. Harold replied that it was really a matter for the Liaison Committee with the NEC, while Jim gave us a gloomy bit of philosophizing about whether or not Ministers should be members of the NEC. He personally doubted whether it was possible to reconcile the two roles and was ready to come off the NEC himself. He hoped other Ministers would too. There were murmurs of disapproval at this from Mike and Wedgie; and so it was left, uneasily.

It was so late by the time we got on to the Defence Review that the meeting spilled over into the afternoon. Roy Mason made a great show of his proposals, but was rather punctured by Denis, who said that the proposed cuts over ten years were proportionately much smaller than he had made in five years when he was at Defence. Moreover a lot of the cuts had already been agreed in 1968. However, Denis spoiled his impact by wavering: on the one hand he said that Roy's target was too modest and that we should have to reconsider it at a later date; on the other, that it was always better to go for bigger cuts in a shorter time than to have two bites at the cherry, as that was unsettling. Some of us were waiting to back Denis up with all our strength if he asked for more: after all, he should know what is possible. But he ended lamely, 'I recognize that it is difficult to ask the people who have been doing the review to go back and start again.' We agreed that this discussion was only a preliminary run. But we did reach a decision on Simonstown. Roy [Mason] had put up a spirited defence of the agreement, but Harold and Jim were having none of it. The only problem was the legal one: there was no provision in the agreement for unilateral abrogation, so if we went ahead without discussing it first with South Africa we could be in breach of international law. We also wanted if possible to avoid retaliation from South Africa. So it was agreed that we should announce that we were entering into consultations with South Africa 'with a view to terminating the agreement'. Harold was determined to show the NEC that their great attack on the Government was unjustified.

One nasty little moment at the beginning of the afternoon meeting: Mike held up the *Evening Standard*, with headlines about how Harold had ticked off the recalcitrant Ministers that morning. He asked furiously who was responsible for this atrocious leak. Harold replied smoothly that it hadn't come from No. 10. Joe Haines,[1] on his instructions, had merely told the lobby – who were clearly going to follow up *The Times* story – that the matter had been discussed at Cabinet, but nothing else. A likely story. I know my Harold and I bet he was determined to do a tit for tat. It is hard to blame him, though whether he is wise is another matter.

Anyway, Wedgie got his way again on more help for his ailing industries. Treasury had brought to Cabinet a proposal which had been agreed, apparently, in Industrial Policy Committee to let him put £3·9 million into another workers' co-operative; officials are all against this and the Industrial Development Advisory Board has advised against it. But Wedgie had won the committee over by his moving accounts of how he had got the workers to cut their manning numbers down voluntarily and he was furious that the Treasury was still keeping up the fight. Unemployment on Merseyside was 9·5 per cent, he pointed out, and no one had put up any suggestions as to how the workers could be otherwise employed. Denis, Harold Lever and a few others put up a desultory fight. I came down strongly on Wedgie's side. We were not just investing in jobs, I said, but in a new experiment in getting workers to share responsibility. This, I believed, was the only way in which inflation would ever be overcome. Eric, to my surprise, said, 'I'm with Barbara.' So, after five goes in committee and one in Cabinet, the opponents were beaten into the ground and Wedgie won.

Friday, 1 November

Up early to try to knock out some headings for my contribution to the Queen's Speech debate. Jack Straw and Brian A-S. had put up long drafts for me, but I can't use other people's words, so I just took the essence out of them. It went swimmingly. I touched briefly on the NHS and our commitment to phase private beds out of NHS hospitals, adding, 'We shall act on that this session.' The House was empty, of course, and I went down to HCF thinking to myself that the debate wouldn't rate a line in tomorrow's press. To my astonishment my announcement was retailed on the news as a great new event and was accompanied by violent reactions from the BMA and the HCSA. David was interviewed about it on TV and did very well. I went contentedly to bed.

Saturday, 2 November

The papers are still echoing with my 'announcement'. Life really is very odd. I should have thought all I had done was to repeat the obvious.

---

[1] Joe Haines was Political Correspondent on the *Sun* from 1964 to 1968 and had been Harold Wilson's Chief Press Secretary since 1969.

Monday, 4 November

On the eight o'clock news I learned that consultants in the North-East have started to work to rule and were breathing fire and slaughter about me. Ted was obviously worried but I felt strangely relaxed, not to say euphoric: probably something to do with all the heavy gardening I had done. Digging always tones me up and sends me back feeling ready for anything. I told Ted things were turning out just as I wanted. First, a fight on this issue would put me back right where I wanted to be in the NEC stakes. Secondly, whatever the militant unions did now on the pay bed issue it would be the consultants who had started the industrial action. Ted seemed relieved at my cheeriness.

My mood held when I arrived at the office to find an atmosphere charged with menace. Henry Yellowlees wanted to see me urgently, so I said David must be there too. I have never seen Henry so white with anger. He is a very nice chap and not given to doing battle with me, but this time he was really steamed up. He said grimly that he agreed with some of what I was trying to do and had tried to help me to the best of his ability, but by my speech on Friday I had wrecked his credibility with the doctors and he thought he ought to have been consulted. Even David looked shaken. I said to Henry as gently as I could, though firmly, that I was extremely sorry if he had not known what I was going to say, but the fact was that we had all discussed at some length the sentence we should try to get into the Queen's Speech on this. The PM had ruled that the Queen's Speech was not the right place for it but had added that I should deal with it in the debate instead. This I had done, on the basis of a draft speech put up to me which I had assumed had been circulated to all concerned, including him. If it had not been, I apologized, but it was routine for this to be done and I just had not time myself to chase up Private Office. 'Do you realize I only got down to this speech at 5am on Friday morning?' But I would instruct Norman to see that Henry was shown everything I proposed to say on the NHS in future.

Henry calmed down at once and the colour came back into his cheeks. Then Philip came in, even more beside himself than Henry had been. 'I must tell you, Secretary of State, that I believe the health service is in more danger than I have ever known.' I spoke soothingly to him too, but I made it clear by my manner that I was not alarmed. It is so obvious how against this change they all are and I can guess what councils of war they have been holding behind my back. David cheered up and said it was all his fault: he ought to have kept Henry in the picture. I congratulated David on the magnificent performance he had given on TV on Friday night.

We then went into a meeting about the next steps. I told them cheerfully that one could never make any real change in society without a row, but we must look at the things in our favour, as well as the dangers. One of the advantages for us was that it was only when there was a row that the public started to listen and I thought there would be a mass of feeling in the country on our side. The doctors had put themselves in the wrong by their hysterical reaction and even Philip seemed inclined to agree with this. David said dramatically that I had got to make up my mind on the crucial issue: how much time I was prepared to allow for the phasing out. We had fortunately circulated to the BMA his paper on the new forms of contract on Friday, before the storm broke. We spent a good deal of time discussing his second paper on the timing of phasing out. He wants us to allow at least two years, but has also worked out an ingenious plan for moving to 'consolidated' waiting lists by January, under which private patients would have to wait their turn with NHS patients in the medical priority queue. After some chat, with a circle of frightened officials around me, I said we would have to discuss this further at the ministerial lunch. In the meantime press office reported that the BBC were after me both for the nine o'clock news and *Nationwide*, on which they had arranged to interview some of the rebellious consultants. Peter Brown was all for my going on; Philip, typically, for my lying low. The more we discussed it the more convinced I became that I could not let our case go by default. And so it was arranged.

We spent the whole of our ministerial lunch on David's paper. Most of them felt David's plan for phasing out was highly ingenious, but Jack Ashley warned it would infuriate the doctors because what private patients really paid for when they went private was to jump the queue. I was inclined to agree with him, but was certain we couldn't hope to take two years phasing pay beds out unless we were seen to be taking some concrete steps to end queue-jumping by private patients in another way. Finally, after a protracted argument, we agreed we should not commit ourselves to a precise period of time in the document – ('Never give hostages to fortune,' I said) – and David agreed, on my insistence, that we should omit all references to the need to allow consultants time to build up their own private facilities outside the NHS. Fancy our making that our public aim! David keeps saying to me, 'The amusing thing is that the department thinks it is I who am the tough one over all this and that you are so reasonable!' Anyway we decided to insert words like 'over a reasonable period, taking account of all the local circumstances'. 'And what do you say when people ask you what you mean by a reasonable time?' David demanded. 'I should reply that I mean a period to be negotiated with those concerned,' I replied unruffled. Brian A-S. is all for allowing enough time to enable us to take powers to control the private facilities which will grow up outside the NHS, and Theresa [O'Connell] from Transport House warmly agreed with him. There may be something in it.

I then went into a series of office meetings on a number of complicated issues, like briefing for tomorrow's PESC Cabinet, discussions on when to see Halsbury and an examination of the possibilities of introducing family allowance for the first child of one-parent families ahead of our child allowance scheme. I broke off at 4pm to film my bit on pay beds for the 9 o'clock news in Peter's room. Philip, Henry and David had been urging me to be overwhelmingly non-provocative, but when I got upstairs Peter took me aside to lecture me about not giving way. 'You are on to a good point here. There is one word I want you to keep pressing home: queue-jumping. You have a perfect right to do what you are proposing to do.' I felt a split personality by the time I got on the air! Not for the first time I was aware that the department is split into two different worlds: the conventional, change-nothing world of the top Establishment; the challenging, irreverent world of the press office and some of the younger officials. I thanked God for the allies I have got in the ministerial team and for the special advisers. Without them a Minister is almost certainly swamped by the sheer pressure of the top officials surrounding him – or her.

By the time I was on my way to Lime Grove my light-heartedness had come back. I felt almost frivolous. Who are these people to dictate that nothing shall be changed, even by a duly elected Government? To hell with them! I felt on top of the whole situation – and it showed. I knew I had never done a better performance and all the comments I got in the House afterwards confirmed it. I was helped by the fact that the interviewer was tough, knew his stuff and gave the two consultants from the North-East a gruelling time. Seeing these rather tatty creatures twisting and turning and changing their ground reinforced the sense of certainty I had had all day. I may fall flat on my face, but it is better to go down fighting than meekly submit to that autocratic lot.

Tuesday, 5 November

Among all this I had to brief myself for the great PESC discussion in Cabinet. Brian A-S. had drawn up an excellent paper for me to submit on the need to review our priorities in expenditure, which, with a little pepping-up by me, read very well. Denis, in opening the Cabinet discussion, made great play with the fact that the policies he had agreed would mean an increase in public expenditure of £3,000 million over the figure for 1975–76 which the Tories had published last December. He emphasized how much he was doing for me in the social security field and said he would need 'larger and faster cuts in defence' if he was to cover everything. On that basis he asked for general acceptance of the outcome of his bilateral deals with different Ministers. Harold called me next and I had not only to move my paper on priorities, but also, on the Chancellor's insistence, to present the paper embodying what he and I had agreed in the social security field. So naturally that made me look as if I had been very well treated (which was no doubt what he intended). Nonetheless I made an impassioned speech about how we had failed to rejig the Tory priorities (e.g. law and order and roads), while our expenditure on the NHS was going to fall disastrously from 4·2 per cent growth annually under the Tories to 2·8 per cent under us. (I thought this must surely bring Mike up in arms on my behalf.)

Next came Judith, asking for an increase in overseas aid to a figure next year of £30 million. She needn't have worried: every speaker who followed her, Reg P., Shirley, Roy Jenkins *et al.*, insisted that, whatever else suffered, overseas aid must go up to avoid world catastrophe. (What a difference from the miserable battles I had with Dick Crossman, Frank Cousins and the rest of them when I was at the Ministry of Overseas Development![1]) But I got no similar sympathy. Reg P. said he was not prepared to argue for a rejigging of priorities now; Roy J. and Peter were worried about the size of the borrowing requirement; Harold Lever was worried by the 'Chancellor's accounting strategy'; Shirley merely said vaguely that there should be a 'trade-off' between family allowances and food subsidies, but she didn't turn that, whatever it meant, into specific support for me. Even Michael let me down. He muttered something about the 'dangers to the NHS' but wasn't going to challenge Denis's strategy or priorities. All he would stress was the need to get the whole

[1] I was Minister of Overseas Development from October 1964 to December 1965.

situation across: we ought to draw up a Declaration of Chequers – about five thousand words – which should be worked out in advance and which would set out our whole strategy. (Even that was turned down.) Wedgie said he welcomed the emphasis on industry. Harold in summing up said that there was general support for the Chancellor, but Denis should now consider the detailed points and meet the Ministers concerned to see how far he could accommodate them. He should then bring back any unresolved points to Cabinet. I clutched at this life-line and bore it back to the office, where I instructed officials that I was not going to throw in the sponge. I told them to draft a very short list of the items that we should concentrate on trying to get.

In the afternoon I had to face Halsbury. I was dreading it, but it went like a dream. I think in fact he welcomed the whole business coming out into the open and warmed up gratefully when I told him I brought a message of 'affectionate sympathy' from the PM, who wanted him to know he still had confidence in him. Nevertheless, 'I made a mistake and I have got to pay the price,' chipped in Halsbury cheerfully. 'Of course I can see I ought to resign.' 'We *all* drop clangers,' I murmured, 'but . . .' Of course, he saw the point. So we parted, both feeling relieved.

At the H and W dinner at Vitello's I insisted on talking about '*l'affaire* Simonstown', which has now become a *cause célèbre* in the movement. And of course Wedgie is the hero again. Harold has told me smugly that he has received letters from all three Ministers, which are 'entirely satisfactory', adding that Michael [Foot] had been 'most helpful'. But apparently Harold had had to send Joan's back for redrafting before he could accept it. I expect I have once again done myself damage with the Left by my attitude, but I can't help it. I really do find it intolerable for us to be heading down the road of splits again when they are so unnecessary.

Wednesday, 6 November

Up to Coventry to address the Association of Directors of Social Services – a difficult speech to make when expenditure is being reined back. Then a hurried return to the House to move the Second Reading of the Uprating Bill.

Thursday, 7 November

Up early to address the Family Planning Association conference. I tell them I am allotting another £1 million to family planning. Then into Cabinet, where Shirley explained her proposed amendments to the Price Code to give firms some investment relief. The TUC has apparently accepted the changes reluctantly, provided they do not add more than 1 per cent to the Retail Prices Index. So the CBI has won part of its battle to put up prices in order to increase profits. Only Wedgie protested that we hadn't linked investment help to disclosure of information about a company's affairs. 'The exit from the Price Code is through planning agreements,' he argued.

Our main argument arose on sugar. Fred reported on the agreement reached in the Council of Ministers on 21 October, subject to the ratification of the deal by governments. As usual, Fred was full of self-justification about what he had achieved.

It wasn't ideal but it was the only way of getting our supplies next year; it didn't discriminate against cane sugar from the developing countries, etc. He would have liked to have got a separate agreement with Australia, but Australia had made it clear she would not conclude a long-term agreement with us unless the Community endorsed it, so there was nothing he could do. The important point was to get the EEC committed to the import of 1·4 million tons from the developing Commonwealth countries and we ought in any case to examine the whole structure of the British cane sugar industry. Peter, roused at last to the implications of what was happening over sugar, was scathing about the deal. It was, he said, a 'great setback' for us. The increase in the quotas for European beet sugar would effectively exclude Commonwealth sugar from European markets. The Commission's buying on world markets had had a ludicrous effect on prices.

To everyone's surprise Harold then came in with more passion than anyone had heard from him for a long time – whether from conviction or because the memory of the jeers about his criticisms of Rippon's negotiations over sugar still rankled, I wasn't (typically) sure. But he certainly laid about him. Peter, he said, was 'basically right'. The Commission were 'using the present shortage of sugar to achieve long-term ends we have always opposed'. The Commonwealth Sugar Agreement was of great value to us. As for Australia, we had no right to write her off as a source of supply until we had got the renegotiated terms for which we were asking. Of course we could buy from Australia if we wanted to. He would rather Fred had made a breaking-point of this: 'It will be for me,' he added. We must maintain our lifeline to the Commonwealth. 'When it comes to the Commonwealth and sugar you will not find me willing to give in.' We had got to get certainty next week on guaranteed access for sugar from the Commonwealth and for enough raw cane sugar for UK refineries.

Fred intervened mournfully: 'If it does come to the breaking-point where do you get your sugar?' But I backed Harold up vigorously, pointing out that, if the Commonwealth Sugar Agreement was coming to an end, it was no wonder that Commonwealth suppliers were looking around for other markets. And I put in a plea for early sugar rationing, on which Shirley supported me. Of course the Common Marketeers came back at Harold, maintaining that our traditional suppliers were now looking elsewhere, etc. It all typified the insidious vicious circle into which the marketeers have got us: Britain has talked for so long about the need to put Europe before the Commonwealth that the Commonwealth has taken the hint and got out from under first and so the traditional links have been destroyed – perhaps irretrievably. I personally believe we are being inched into the Market by a succession of small *faits accomplis* and that the Commonwealth is dying the death by a thousand scratches. But we may succeed in mutilating the 'European idea' of the fanatics sufficiently to make it tolerable to stay in. And the conclusions we reached on the sugar deal will all help. Harold summed up that we accepted it only on conditions.

In the afternoon I had to receive a deputation from the BMA, led by Dr Astley, steaming with fury at my House of Commons speech. To strengthen their attack they had even brought Dr Brian Lewis, Chairman of the HCSA, and his colleagues with them, dropping their traditional rivalry. I was my usual patient, reasonable self. I stuck by my right to phase out pay beds, but said I was certainly not going to rush into it without consultation, if only they were ready to discuss it. They kept bringing in their demand for a new contract as a test of whether the Government was prepared to safeguard their 'freedom and independence'. I kept telling them that the right place to discuss that was in the Owen working party, where they could discuss private practice too. Would they get back into the working party and try to speed things up? Eventually they simmered down. At the end of all this both Henry and Philip seemed to recover their nerve a bit.

Monday, 11 November
Budget Cabinet.[1] Denis gave a long, slow exposition in his best Ministry of Defence style. There was a shocked silence at first – whistles through the teeth when Denis said the borrowing requirement would have to be doubled, Peter in particular expressing dismay. Shirley and others commented that the Budget would be less severe than people were expecting, Jim describing it as 'agreeable'. Not when people realized how much prices would go up next year, retorted Denis. It struck me that the Treasury are back on their old track of trying to solve inflation by putting prices up. It has never worked and I think the result this time will be disastrous. But Wedgie and Mike were mollified by Denis's attempt to make his aids to industry selective: 'as selective as we can without the instruments to do so, which we shall not get until we have our planning agreements machinery'. And Mike liked Denis's vigorous refusal to precipitate a world depression by being too deflationary. Mike meekly let pass Denis's claim that unemployment should be kept 'under a million'.

[1] The main aim of Healey's autumn Budget was to improve the increasingly desperate financial position of companies. This he did by relaxing the Price Code and deferring corporation tax on profits arising from the abnormal stock appreciation which inflation had caused. For the rest he painted a daunting picture. Oil prices had now increased fivefold in just over a year. The $60 billion surplus in the hands of the oil-producing countries was still depressing world trade. Unemployment and inflation were rising everywhere. With our trade deficit on current account running at about £4,000 million, he had begun to draw on the $2½ billion loan. Resources must be switched into investment and exports. The public sector borrowing requirement, estimated in the spring as amounting to £2,733 million for 1974–75, had doubled as a result of his July measures, wage increases and other cost increases. His proposed reliefs would push it up to the 'disturbingly large' figure of £6,300 million. To attempt to close it in the abnormal world circumstances would mean a fall in output and a massive increase in unemployment. Nonetheless it must not get out of hand. The increase in public expenditure must be held down to an annual average 2¾ per cent over the next four years in demand terms. Wage increases must be confined to what was needed to cover the cost of living, as urged by the TUC. Otherwise the Government would have to take other steps to curtail demand. Energy conservation was vital. To this end fuel prices must continue to go up to their economic level by eliminating subsidies to nationalized industries. He also proposed to increase VAT on petrol from 8 per cent to 25 per cent. The elderly, those on low incomes and families would be cushioned by another increase in pensions and benefits in April and an increase in family allowance. There would also be higher tax allowances for the elderly at a cost of £280 million in addition to another Christmas bonus. Meanwhile the Government was pressing ahead with a capital transfer tax to replace estate duty and with a new tax on the development value of land. The administrative problems of a wealth tax, outlined in the Green Paper, were being referred to a Select Committee. The proposal to lower the starting point for the investment income surcharge from £2,000 to £1,000, which the Commons had rejected in the summer, would be reintroduced, as would the retrospective tax relief on trade union provident funds. As a result of these measures he estimated that retail prices would rise by about 1½ per cent and output grow by 2 per cent a year. This would mean a 'modest' rise in unemployment, though the level would remain well below one million.

I launched into a great speech about how unwise it would be to assume that 'realistic fuel pricing' would solve our expenditure difficulties, as it would be essential to accompany this with rises in the incomes of the hardest hit. I reminded them that Denis had *not* managed to protect *all* families: we were doing nothing for the three million with one child. I wasn't just trying to grab more than my share, I said, because, if I had been consulted on tax changes, I might well have urged him not to give his £280 million higher tax allowances to pensioners who work; there were only 220,000 of them and the money could have gone to meet the cost of doing something for the first child. All this reinforced the case for the Anti-Poverty Strategy Committee which I had urged the PM to set up. (He refused to do so last summer.) We really must have the chance to influence tax policy at the formative stage, I continued. And what about the disabled with invalid vehicles, who were going to be faced with petrol at 75p per gallon? We must discuss all this at Chequers. There were murmurs of agreement. (When I got back to the office I discovered that No. 10 had phoned to ask us to work out something on petrol for the disabled. So I had really shaken them![1])

But our longest row was over Mike's trade union legislation. Elwyn and Sam Silkin pontificated solemnly against Mike's recommendation that we should accept the TUC's offer to set up voluntary machinery to deal with appeals against refusal of admission to, or against expulsion from, a union, in place of the statutory machinery which the Opposition had managed to insert into the repeal Bill.[2] Elwyn read lengthily from the Donovan Report to prove we needed statutory protection for workers whose whole jobs could be at risk from the operation of the closed shop. He argued that the TUC offer had no teeth. Mike argued back that Cabinet had authorized him last spring to tell the TUC that we would be willing to consider any voluntary alternative they might be prepared to set up themselves. Admittedly, the TUC had been very reluctant to consider even that, but, at the eleventh hour, their General Purposes Committee had come forward with this scheme, which he felt met what we had asked for.

The discussion then went on predictable lines: Roy J., Reg Prentice and Roy Mason saying that nothing less than statutory safeguards would do; Shirley expressing serious doubts about the efficacy of the TUC proposals. Mike's most powerful defence came from Bob, who asked us scathingly if we really wanted to repeat *In Place of Strife* and get into a row with the unions at this early stage. Surprisingly, even Fred Peart agreed with him; so did Eric Varley and John Morris. Typically, Harold tried to find a middle way. The trouble with the TUC scheme was that there were no sanctions against unions who defied the review body's ruling, he said. Couldn't we strengthen it, as we had done the Croydon agreement, along the lines of Bridling-

[1] We later decided to pay a £10 a year tax-free petrol allowance to all disabled drivers of invalid tricycles and Ministry-supplied cars.

[2] The Trade Union and Labour Relations Act, repealing the Tory industrial relations legislation, had become law on 31 July. During the passage of the Bill the House of Lords had defied the Government and inserted a clause (Clause 5) giving a statutory right of appeal by aggrieved union members to an industrial tribunal and, where necessary, the High Court. The TUC was pressing the Government to remove this clause in favour of appeals machinery it would set up itself. One of the arguments in Cabinet was whether the Government and/or ACAS should have a say in the appointment of the three-man body the TUC offered to set up.

ton?[1] I pointed out crisply that (1) it would be intolerably unfair to Mike to turn down the TUC proposals now, just because they were voluntary, when we had encouraged the TUC to believe we were ready to accept a voluntary scheme; (2) the TUC's review body would have the same composition as the one Donovan proposed; (3) it would go further than we asked by offering to cover admission as well as expulsion; (4) it proposed reinstatement in the union as the remedy for unfair treatment and this, we all knew, was much more important than compensation. So we might try to strengthen their proposals, but we could not possibly reject them. And so it was agreed that Mike should go back to tell the TUC they must 'require' unions to accept the findings of the review body and that the chairman must be chosen *with the approval* of ACAS. Roy Jenkins, however, asked for his disagreement to be recorded in the Minutes. 'You can send me a Minute and it will be registered,' snapped back Harold. 'We stopped recording disagreements in Cabinet Minutes back in 1964.'

Halsbury has sent Harold his letter of resignation – exactly on the lines I urged on him. But No. 10 have agreed not to announce it until Halsbury has had a chance to tell his committee tomorrow. He has agreed to urge them to stay on, but Raymond Gedling (who is in close touch) thinks the committee has decided to breach the twelve-month rule anyway. They also have the right to go ahead and publish their report without a chairman (or so Gedling says), so our ploy to play for time by getting the new chairman to reopen the whole thing may not work. The BMA has now called outright for Halsbury's resignation (so he would have had to go anyway), but the HCSA is demanding the abolition of the whole review body. Personally I believe that might be a good thing: we will have to argue cash over the new contract if we are to have any chance of getting it accepted. But the department is in a panic over the whole idea. Our troubles in this field are not over!

Tuesday, 12 November

First I was top order for Questions and they went swimmingly. They have no terrors for me anymore. Then the Budget. Even second time round this year Denis had to make a speech of one and three-quarter hours. Harold Lever, sitting next to me, managed to keep me awake most of the time by his chattering. He is in favour of the

---

[1] A reference to the negotiations with the TUC over *In Place of Strife*. At a Special Congress called at Croydon in June 1969 to discuss my proposals the TUC announced that they were proposing to strengthen the Rules of Congress to deal with inter-union disputes and unofficial strikes. While welcoming this as an advance Harold Wilson and I did not feel that the proposed amendments to Rule 11 to deal with 'unauthorized and unconstitutional stoppages of work' went far enough to justify the Government in abandoning its intention to legislate. We urged further amendments to secure compliance by unions with the TUC's instructions, including the use by the General Council of its disciplinary powers under Rule 13 to suspend unions from membership with a view to their possible expulsion by Congress. The long controversy was eventually settled by the TUC accepting our amendments, not as an addition to Rule 11, but in the form of a 'solemn and binding undertaking' that their provisions would have 'the same binding force as the TUC Bridlington principles and regulations'. Under the Bridlington agreement, reached by the TUC in 1939, rules were approved to deal with allegations of 'poaching' and other disputes between unions over membership. Although the Bridlington regulations have not the formality of Rules of Congress, they have been observed and one of Vic Feather's strongest arguments was that they had only been defied in a couple of cases in thirty years.

Budget on the whole, but against Denis's reduction of the surcharge level for unearned income to £1,000. I must say I can't see the demagogic point of it myself. I was called out of the Chamber by Norman before I could hear Heath's speech. Ted [Castle], glued to the gallery, told me it was one of the most effective Heath has made. I am fascinated by the chemistry of politics, which apparently operates in other people as well as myself: the inevitability most times of falling flat when too much is expected of one, and then reviving defiantly just when everyone has written one off. At my office meeting we cleared my letter to the Chancellor: my dogged attempt to get something more for the Health Service out of the PESC round. I told officials it was outrageous that the Chancellor should be able unilaterally to give £280 million away in tax reliefs to the elderly, without even a word to me about the social priorities – and even Dick Bourton agreed.

At the PLP meeting a number of people complained that this was a 'CBI budget', resenting the hand-outs to industry before we had the selective controls ready. I have no doubt that the party just will not tolerate any reversion to traditional solutions for traditional economic crises – and I am not just referring to the Left. The urge for more egalitarian remedies is, I believe, now deeply rooted in our society. That is why I shall get away with the pay beds issue. On the front bench during Parliamentary Questions earlier David had said to me as I was being cross-examined over private practice, with our own side egging me on to abolish it altogether, 'We'd better get the legislation through as quickly as possible and just push it through.' I agree.

Wednesday, 13 November

My main job today was my massive uprating statement in the House,[1] followed by a press conference. I prepared meticulously all morning in the office, as I always do on these occasions, pepping up Peter's press statement, checking on this fact and that, thinking up new pitfalls. To my relief there was to be no TV, so I could concentrate on the substance without worrying whether my hair was okay and went into the House feeling relaxed. Our side roared its approval of my statement and I had the refreshing experience of hearing Frank [Allaun] pay a glowing public tribute to me. I got over tricky points like the non-announcement of the child allowance scheme without disaster.

Thursday, 14 November

I was just leaving for Cabinet when Pam rang from the office. Someone had phoned from the Katherine Knapp home to say Mother had been taken ill; would I phone them. It was the nice deputy matron who answered. Mother had had difficulty with her breathing and they had sent for the doctor. She had given her a pill and she

---

[1] I spelt out in detail the Chancellor's announcement that long-term pensions and benefits would be increased by about 15½ per cent the following April – eight and a half months after the last increase – and that there would be a further increase in December 1975. Short-term benefits would be increased by about 14 per cent. Family allowance would go up by 50 pence at the same time and would be extended to the first child under our new scheme 'in due course'.

seemed better, but I ought to know. Arranging for a message to be got to me as soon as the doctor had been, I went into Cabinet feeling *distrait* and telling the office to cancel my afternoon engagements anyway, so that I could go down. After some mutterings about the Channel Tunnel Bill (which clearly no one but Tony C. wants) we got down to the main business: the concessions Mike had managed to get from Len Murray about the appeals machinery. Mike had just circulated the reply he had received from Len on our two points and he introduced it as something we should accept on its merits, 'though I can't claim it fulfils every point Cabinet was asking for.' As far as consulting the Lord Chancellor on the appointment of the chairman of the appeal body was concerned, Len didn't hold anything against the present Lord Chancellor, but pointed out that it might mean consulting Lord Hailsham one day and they couldn't stomach that. As for trying to inject the Bridlington agreement type of procedure for enforcement purposes Len had said, 'If you press me further there will be no chance of getting it through the General Council.' So Mike added quite frankly that we must take into account the effect on our relationships with the TUC. They might even refuse to take part in any statutory provisions if we insisted on setting them up. 'In my view it would be a particular folly for Cabinet to spurn this response from the TUC.'

Harold, unable to contain himself, chipped in: 'In my view this is better than Croydon', which surprised me, as Len merely proposed to say that there would be a 'clear responsibility' for the union concerned to accept the appeal body's recommendation. Elwyn was pompously uncertain of his ground: the phrase 'clear responsibility' was an improvement, but the duty of the union was still not mandatory. Rule 13 of the TUC rules would not apply. 'We are still in an unhappy situation.' Roy Jenkins was more robust: 'I am more unhappy than I was before, not less.' The change of wording represented no advance. For instance, we had asked that the chairman be appointed 'in agreement with' ACAS. All we were offered was 'after consultation with'. We were, in his view, on a dangerous course and once again he would like his dissent to be recorded. Ted Short said that on balance it was not an unreasonable result. Denis took his usual realistic line. We could not get away from the value of the trade union support for our economic policies. He had been particularly heartened by Len Murray's response to the Budget – it could have been disastrous if he had gone the other way. 'If our relations with the unions break down it will be infinitely more difficult to make any other policy work.' Reg P. of course agreed with Roy J. What was all this about 'negotiating' with the TUC? 'Cabinet does not have to negotiate with anybody.' (There were some jeers of incredulity at that.)

Jim came in as blandly as usual. He hadn't been at the last meeting, so could come to this with a fresh eye, and he must say that he was impressed with what Len was offering. 'This procedure is good.' And he reminded us that the trade unions had a traumatic reaction to the intrusion of the law into their affairs. My contribution was succinct. The points about which we were arguing were presentational ones. The success of the formula entirely depended on the spirit in which the TUC were prepared to operate it and there was only one sanction of any value: their knowledge that, if they failed to deliver as promised, public opinion would force us to introduce a statutory alternative. There was merely one change I should like to make for presentational purposes. Len's letter said that the chairman would be appointed 'after consultation with', etc. This implied a perfunctory nod in the direction of consultation. If the phrase read 'in consultation with' the presentational picture would be complete. Harold welcomed my suggestion and Mike said he would try to get it accepted. So it was agreed that Len should be told to go ahead and try to get the proposition through the General Council on 20 November, the Bill being held up till then.[1]

There was also a slight flare-up on sugar. Jim gave a complacent report on his success in getting the Community to accept 1·4 million tons annually from the Commonwealth countries on a continuing basis. I asked bluntly, 'What about Australia?' Jim, backed by Harold, said that it was doubtful whether Australia would have any sugar for us anyway. She was trying to sell it to Japan, though Harold admitted the Australian trade negotiations with Japan seemed to be breaking down. 'Could Cabinet have a report on the outcome?' I persisted. Harold muttered a reluctant 'yes'. Peter maintained that we needed a long-term contract with Australia if we were to have any hope of diverting her sugar to us, but Jim insisted that he regarded Australian sugar as 'marginal'. In any case there was no point in buying Australian beet sugar at the expense of our own beet producers if the price was too high. 'The important thing is that we have got long-term guarantees for Commonwealth producers,' insisted Harold.

Cabinet over, I hurried to the German Embassy for a private lunch with the Ambassador: the usual preparatory lunch for an official visit to the country concerned.[2] The Ambassador was accompanied merely by his labour attaché (who has worked hard for the reciprocal agreement I shall be going to sign). I was flanked by Norman and by my official who had negotiated the deal. The conversation at lunch ranged over wider fields. I seized the opportunity to warn the Ambassador about the mood of the NEC about the impending speech of his Chancellor to our party conference.[3] I had that morning heard on the radio the report of comments Herr Schmidt had made about what he was going to say to conference: how he was going to warn Britain that we would be cutting our own throats if we decided to leave the EEC. The Ambassador's excellent wine made me fluent, and I told him earnestly that his Chancellor faced a walk-out – or at best a slow handclap – if he tried in any way to lecture us about Britain's attitude to EEC. He had been invited as a *fraternal* delegate, not as a head of a government. The best thing he could do from the point of view of his own objective of keeping us in the Market was to talk to us as a socialist to

[1] Clause 5 was repealed in the Trade Union and Labour Relations (Amendment) Act of March 1976, and the TUC's Independent Review Committee was set up the following month.

[2] I had arranged to visit my opposite number in the Federal Republic, Herr Arendt, Minister of Labour and Social Welfare, in order to sign a reciprocal agreement which would give all UK visitors to West Germany free urgent medical treatment under the German sickness scheme. This was necessary because the German scheme, unlike the NHS, did not cover the self-employed.

[3] The NEC had decided to invite Helmut Schmidt, leader of the German Social Democratic Party and Chancellor of the Federal Republic, to deliver fraternal greetings on behalf of all international delegates to our party conference. Owing to the general election our conference had been postponed from October to November.

fellow-socialists. I waxed quite eloquent, adding, 'Why should I, as an anti-marketeer, give you such excellent pro-Market advice?' We all laughed, but the Ambassador was clearly impressed and told me that everything I had said would be conveyed to Schmidt.

After lunch I headed for Penn, picking up my brother Jimmie on the way. At the home, as we walked towards Mother's room, we heard singing. She was sitting bolt upright in bed, her cheeks pink, looking about sixty years old instead of ninety-one. 'It's my Barbara,' she said as I went in and instantly demanded to know when she was coming home. She didn't want to be in bed; there was nothing wrong with her. Edna was enchanted with her – as they clearly all were. But when I phoned the doctor he said she had had a pulmonary embolism; it might recur at any time and one day it would be too much for her. Little Mother! Reconciled as I am to her approaching death, the sharp prospect of it brings my childhood right back into my consciousness and with it my sense of her as a mother: endearing, much loved and totally exasperating. Time is the oddest thing. There have been many moments in the last few years when it hasn't seemed to exist as a barrier of distance and when the past has been as vivid as the present. Perhaps I too am approaching the threshold. Into nothingness? No, back in a circle to where I began.

Friday, 15 November

Yesterday's rush through driving rainstorms and impossible traffic has left me exhausted. And this too has been an exacting day, including two official meals and two official speeches: the Health Service Treasurers at lunch and the Royal College of General Practitioners in the evening. Neither speech was as spontaneous as I would have wished: that is impossible while one is still feeling the temperature of the water in strange ponds. Tony Keable-Elliott drove me home and we talked about doctors' pay, Halsbury *et al*. The findings, as the Cabinet Minutes would put it, are recorded separately.[1]

Sunday, 17 November

Chequers park looked beautifully peaceful as we arrived for the all-day strategy meeting, but the network of policemen showed that security was there in full force. As we came in by the side gate several policemen came out of the lodge to ask our names and search the boot. Inside the house it was clear that Heath's favourite internal decorator had been at work again (he must have spent a mint of money), but

---

[1] Dr Keable-Elliott warned me that, unless GPs received an interim increase in pay before their annual review the following April in defiance of the twelve-month rule, they would withdraw 100 per cent commitment to the NHS. They believed the Government would be forced to impose a wages freeze before their turn came to have their pay reviewed free from statutory controls. I told him I would fight tooth and nail in Cabinet against any such development. He finally volunteered that, if the Government would announce its intention to implement their Review Body's award in full next April, he personally would do his best to get GPs to withdraw their interim claim. I circulated a Minute on this conversation to David Owen and the officials concerned.

this time she had made an improvement by stripping the dark oak panelling (which I had always found oppressive) in the great hall. I liked the light wood, the careful display of china treasures and the urns of flowers in every corner of hall and landings, but it made everything look so much more *feminine* – another clue to Heath's character? Every room I went into seemed to have been lavishly repapered; *we* would never have dreamed of such extravagance. I was shown into the little bedroom I had stayed in that time in 1969 when Harold had brought me back secretly from Italy and memories came flooding back about that traumatic confrontation with Jack [Jones], Hughie [Scanlon] and Vic [Feather].[1] So near and yet so far – near in time, only five years ago, yet a century away in knowledge and experience gained in the meantime. The Cabinet was very largely the same then as it is now, yet we could not have been more different in approach.

This mood continued as we met in the library. I was proud of the success of my suggestion that we should all put in papers ranging over the whole field of strategy. Most Ministers had done so. They were succinct, concrete, very revealing and undoubtedly helped to concentrate our minds. As the discussion unfolded, revealing problems of almost insurmountable gloom, I had the quiet feeling that so much expertise, sense and conviction of purpose *must* enable us somehow to win through. Though CPRS had drawn up an agenda in four parts, starting with our relationship with the external world, we soon found ourselves in the middle of a second reading debate over the whole field. Ken Berrill, head of CPRS, introduced the discussion succinctly, setting out the problems (the threatening world slump, the petrodollar crisis, etc.) rather than attempting to answer them. Harold Lever then spoke to his own paper. 'We have only a 50 per cent chance of avoiding world catastrophe,' he told us. Getting some international machinery to recycle the petrodollars was the only hope. Everything else, like petrol rationing, was only 'frolics at the margin'. We should broadly back the Americans. Denis admitted that it was very unlikely we could close the whole of the balance of payments gap by 1978–79, even if things went well. But unless we improved our competitiveness our balance of payments position would become disastrous. There was a strong case for an energy conservation programme, if only on psychological grounds.

Roy J. ruminated: 'Your memory is better than mine, Prime Minister, but I believe it is ten years ago to this very day that we sat in this room discussing the Defence Review. The world has changed out of all recognition since then.' He then talked about the changes in the power blocs, adding that those like himself who had expected the coherence of Europe to develop strongly had found the reality 'disappointing'. The Middle East situation was full of menace and he believed a pre-emptive strike by the USA was possible. Eric talked about energy extremely competently, though he insisted that looking for major energy savings was likely to be 'extremely disappointing'. He was 'very opposed' to petrol rationing and maintained that rota cuts, organized systematically, would be the only effective method – and they were out of the question. The only hope was to move to energy self-sufficiency. But the miners' attitude was frightening. He had been speaking only a day or two ago

[1] Part of the story of the negotiations with the TUC over *In Place of Strife*, which is for another volume.

to a miners' meeting attended by what he called the 'Scargill Mafia'. When he told them that the Government could have used more oil at the power stations this summer and so built up coal stocks for the winter against a possible strike, but hadn't, they had merely retorted, 'More fool you', and thanked him for letting them know how strong their position was. He concluded sadly: 'Don't let us frighten the oil companies away.' We needed their investment.

Wedgie then made what I found a very effective speech, pointing out that we had got to look at the problem in domestic as well as international terms. A devolution of power had also been going on at home and all our policy must take account of it. 'We cannot win consent to a technocratic solution. We must redistribute power in this country by peaceful means. Beyond the slump must be the perspective of a better society.' He did not believe the solution lay in bigger and bigger units: he had been immensely struck by the emphasis which Jim laid on devolution in his paper. 'We must show what sort of Government we are.' Were we going to go for impersonal macro-solutions, or were we going to realize that the people were looking to us as their leaders to provide an answer to their difficulties? To them their leaders seemed utterly remote. 'Without consent no solution we work out round this table will have a chance.' Mike said wryly that if, as Harold Lever said, we had only a 50 per cent chance of avoiding catastrophe, we had better work out a contingency plan in case that chance did not come off. Roy M. made a fluent contribution about the added danger of war in the Middle East.

The gathering gloom was compounded by Jim, acting Cassandra as usual. 'When I am shaving in the morning I say to myself that if I were a young man I would emigrate. By the time I am sitting down to breakfast I ask myself, "Where would I go?" ' (Laughter.) Mike had talked about contingency plans for catastrophe, he continued. If we ever got to a siege economy he, Jim, dreaded the effect on our democracy. He didn't think that the US would do a Suez in the Middle East. The more likely prospect was our declining influence. 'One prospect is that we shall lose our seat on the Security Council.' Jim concluded gloomily that in his view we should go on sliding downhill for the next few years. 'Nothing in these papers makes me believe anything to the contrary. I haven't got any solution. As I said, if I were a young man, I should emigrate.'

By this time faces were getting pretty long. I hadn't intended to speak on the external affairs section, but the discussion had widened so much that I came in with the attached remarks.[1] Denis rallied the defeatists with a robust speech: what everyone had said showed how pretentious were some of the demands made by the party for us to interfere here, there and everywhere. 'It is no good ceasing to be the

[1] In my speech I urged that we had to win consent to our policies. This meant putting them in a philosophical context. At home, for instance, we needed an anti-poverty strategy, which must include tax policy. Petrol rationing would be fairer than rationing by price. If the Social Contract was to work it was vital to convince workers that we were not going to return to a statutory policy and we must convince them of the importance of the 'social wage'. Above all, presentation was the key. We must explain the problems and set out the choices. There ought, for instance, to be a popular version of the White Paper on Public Expenditure setting out in simple and graphic terms what our priorities were and why. We should organize a public campaign to explain our policies and demonstrate to the ordinary worker what he gained in financial terms from public expenditure.

world's policeman in order to become the world's parson instead.' But he would have nothing of Jim's gloom. 'If we do join the Third World it will be as a member of OPEC.' He wasn't as pessimistic as Harold L. (who by this time had gone home, pleading that he was suffering from gastric flu). We could not sensibly plan ahead for a doomsday-type catastrophe. He agreed with Wedgie about the dissolution of the power blocs. He rejected the conspiracy theory of foreign affairs. 'International Communism has as much or as little significance as the Commonwealth.' By this time it was nearly 1pm. Harold summed up by saying the discussion had been first-class: 'the best I have ever heard in this type of gathering'. The only concrete conclusion he drew at this stage was that there was a gap in our ministerial provision and that we needed a ministerial committee on overseas economic policy, which he would proceed to set up.

It was a relief to move about and wander into the great hall for a drink. The atmosphere remained unshakenly cordial, with everyone glad of the chance to laugh at anything. When Harold said, 'It will be a do-it-yourself type of lunch,' someone quipped, 'Not the cooking, I hope.' On the contrary, the unobtrusive WRNS and WRAFS had done an excellent job with the buffet meal. During it I found myself next to Tony C., with whom I developed an unexpectedly genial conversation. 'Everyone will be soporific by the time I speak,' he complained. To combat the drowsiness some of us seized the opportunity for a breath of air. I took Mike by the arm and marched him round the park. He was only too glad to share his dilemma over the publication of Dick's diaries. Dick Crossman, he said, had asked him to be his literary executor just at the moment when he knew he was dying. 'So I couldn't refuse.' He also talked to me freely about *'l'affaire* Simonstown'. He thought there had been errors on both sides and had tried to act as a go-between. The three Ministers concerned in the row had got together to draft a letter which Harold had not found satisfactory. Then, before they could meet again, Wedgie had written to Harold again off his own bat, capitulating and leaving the other two high and dry. Joan Lestor was furious with him. 'He's a very odd chap,' said Mike in his typically tolerant way.

During the lunch interval Harold seized the opportunity to talk to me about Jack Ashley. He was tickled pink with his own cunning, taking me aside to say that he had to appoint a Privy Councillor and, having promoted Brian O'Malley to PC as the senior Minister of State, he was left with only Roy Hattersley or Bill Rodgers,[1] and he wasn't going to elevate either of *them*. So he had had a brilliant idea: guess who? As I puzzled he said triumphantly, 'Jack Ashley.' I was dumbfounded with admiration and told him how delighted I was. Denis also took the chance to tell me, in the light of my references to the need for an anti-poverty strategy, 'I was wrong about my tax

[1] Roy Hattersley, MP for Birmingham Sparkbrook, was then Minister of State at the Foreign and Commonwealth Office. W. T. (Bill) Rodgers, MP for Teesside, Stockton, was Minister of State for Defence. Both men were prominent members of the Gaitskellite wing of the party and Bill Rodgers, in particular, had been an effective organizer on behalf of Hugh Gaitskell and later Roy Jenkins and consistently hostile to Harold. Both were appointed to the Cabinet in September 1976 in Jim Callaghan's first major reshuffle.

concession to the elderly in the Budget. I'll admit it to you but I won't do so publicly.' This is what I like about Denis – his sudden bits of fairness and frankness.

Back in the library, the afternoon discussion was opened by Ross, deputy secretary of CPRS. There was, he said, 'no surefire recipe for economic growth'. (He can say that again!) There was a role for general incentives and also one for selective assistance. We needed to find a balance between them and help the regions to help themselves. As I listened to him I thought how good these expert advisers always are at analysing a problem on an either/or basis, when what Ministers are yearning for is a clear indication of what policies will do the trick if only we politicians will have the courage to pursue them. In fact, the experts can't even agree on that. The more I listen to them the more I respect my own amateur profession of politics. Ken Berrill came next with some more question-posing. The Government, he maintained, was more likely to be judged by inflation than by the standard of living. And he believed that was right. Inflation was a straight wage–price–wage problem. 'What policies will impinge at the point of the wage bargain? How do you break into it?' (Wouldn't we like to know!) 'Was index-linking the answer?'

Tony C. followed. Our aim must be to get the perspective right. We didn't know how our relative decline had taken place. 'All we can do is to press every button we've got. We do not know which, if any, of them will have the desired results.' One thing we could do was to use resources less wastefully – for example, in packaging. There had been a lot of waste in high technology. 'I agree there is a lot of waste in housing.' We must have an emergency programme for conserving resources. Curing inflation was more important than faster growth. 'The Social Contract must begin with our own sector as the largest employer of labour.' All we could do was to 'grit our teeth till the oil flows'. (Typical Tony, that!) The only answer was a policy of fair shares and greater equality. There must be a philosophic context to our economic strategy. This roused Mike to come in again. There must be a greater effort to change the atmosphere than Tony suggested, he urged. We must not give up the ghost too soon. It was essential, he urged, to convince people we were not going to go back to a statutory incomes policy. (I said 'Hear, hear' to that.) This winter we might have to take other steps, like temporary subsidies for industries faced with redundancies. We ought to look at top salaries again. There would be a bad psychological effect if the review body[1] recommended a fresh round of pay increases for some of the best paid people in the country. We should set an example by cutting ministerial salaries. We must get ourselves heard. 'That is why I do not believe in the doctrine of business as usual.' We must give the Social Contract time and work out fresh methods of communication.

Bob's contribution was to tell us we were on the edge of '£100 per week coal-miners'. This stirred Roy J. to intervene again with an economic lecture which annoyed Denis. 'We are not giving enough priority to the problem of inflation,' said Roy. 'This could actually destroy society. The borrowing requirement is appallingly large. This requires a higher level of business confidence.' When Denis tried to interrupt, Roy silenced him arrogantly. 'The danger of hyperinflation is the greatest

[1] See footnote, page 105. Following the end of statutory controls, the Top Salaries Review Body had resumed its substantive review and its report was imminent. It was published in December 1974.

that we face. I agree that we need a contingency plan, though not a siege economy. We must face the danger that the Social Contract may fail and include this in our contingency plans.' (The danger of this is, of course, that once Cabinet is willing even to contemplate a return to statutory controls the news seeps out through the very bricks of No. 10 and a run of wage increases starts overnight.) Shirley was equally gloomy. We faced, she said, a rate of inflation of 26–30 per cent next year. 'Can we shore up the Social Contract through a tax on inflationary settlements? Otherwise we may face a terrible choice between the Social Contract and unemployment.' We must eliminate waste and move faster on English devolution. We must follow the devolution of power by the devolution of responsibility.

Elwyn said he was 'disturbed by the mood of despair'. Wedgie then spoke to his paper in which he called for Government subsidies for any firm facing the need for redundancies, a policy which Denis described as one which 'would create paralysis in our economic system, leading to *rigor mortis*'. The trouble with Shirley's idea of a tax sanction against inflationary wage increases, said Denis, was that any sanction implied a norm. We must give the Social Contract until next Easter (unless there was catastrophe first) and then discuss the alternative of unemployment. 'What has worried me in this debate is the degree of deterministic pessimism.' It was after 5pm by now and some of us were itching to get away. (I had to get up very early for my visit to Bonn.) So Harold turned quickly to the third main heading: presentational policy. Once again I spelled out my presentational points and was delighted that Cabinet accepted so many of them. Denis even announced that there would be a popular version of the Public Expenditure White Paper showing where every £1 of tax goes.[1] We broke up, congratulating ourselves on a valuable day. The problem, as always, will be whether we have the time to follow our own lessons through.

Monday, 18 November

At Bonn officialdom was there in force to greet us. Nicholas Henderson, our Ambassador, rode in the car with me to the house of Mr Hibbert, Minister at the Embassy, where I was to stay, and I spent the journey reiterating my story about how disastrous it would be if Helmut Schmidt were to make a propaganda speech about the Common Market when he addressed the Labour Party conference next week. Henderson listened attentively, but these diplomats are clearly out of touch with party feeling on this issue: they just can't see what anyone should worry about if the German Chancellor makes a pro-Market speech to us. Henderson apologized profusely about the fact that he could not put me up himself as he was deeply committed to other engagements outside Bonn during my stay. That did not worry me at all – protocol is an obsession of small minds. And the Minister's house turned out to be lavish enough in all conscience, with a luxurious bedroom for me overlooking the woods to the Rhine and the Peterberg. They told me ten times that that was where Chamberlain had talked to Hitler.

[1] The popular version never appeared.

The Ambassador gave me lunch and talked to me affectionately about Dick Crossman, while I looked out with nostalgia at the Drachenfels, up which Dick and I used to pound during those rather depressing Königswinter meetings. We had a racy discussion during the informal lunch party, attended only by British officials. I held forth on my favourite theme of the excellencies and inadequacies of the British Civil Service: how I welcomed their frankness when they disagreed with me and only asked that their views should be balanced by the attendance round my discussion table of dedicated socialists who were in deep agreement with my policy. Under his relaxed and civilized veneer Henderson was obviously nonplussed and I was grateful when young Norman plucked up courage to say that there was something in my point. I only hope he has not damned his promotion prospects! After lunch, into a formal meeting with Frau Focke, Federal Minister for Youth, Family Affairs and Health. She was a delightful woman, who had insisted on a private word with me before we met the officials. I suspected she, too, wanted to talk about Helmut's visit to Britain and his speech to conference. I repeated my warning that he should make only a throw-away line reference to the Common Market. She said she would pass it on to him, but added almost wistfully, 'You do not surely expect Helmut not to speak also as Chancellor of the Federal Republic?'

Dinner at the Hibberts turned out to be very pleasant and relaxed. They had invited Herr Matthöfer, the Cabinet Minister in charge of science and technology, and two leading trade unionists on the German equivalent of the TUC: Alfons Lappas and Heinz Vetter. I got on famously with all three, not least because they spoke English fluently. After dinner I talked to Lappas about the Community. The Germans' eagerness for Britain to stay in was almost pathetic. Vetter was immensely intelligent and civilized about it all and seized on my remark: 'What you must seek to do in the Community is not more, but less.' He did not disguise the Germans' doubts about the Commission's nanny-ish interference, which I said would only frighten the British away. What surprised and attracted me was their sense of humour and lack of fanaticism. On that basis – with no hectoring and no rigidity of rules – I might almost be tempted to stay in. As I put it teasingly to V., 'The only thing wrong with the Common Market is the Treaty of Rome.' He even took that without flinching.

Up early for the signing ceremony with Herr Arendt. Arendt was waiting for me in his office with all the charm I had been told I could expect from him: 'the most popular member of the Government'. He is a rather impishly avuncular figure, an ex-miner with no heavy pretensions to administrative genius, but he has, I suspect, made a number of breakthroughs in his field of labour and social welfare. It is he, for instance, who has got through the policy of a flexible retirement age and who has launched all the ambitious schemes for rehabilitation of the disabled. I found that the Germans are way ahead of us on a number of things; not least, they have pressed through the introduction of a child allowance scheme in six months – something we have been elaborately preparing for over two years and are still not ready to implement. Arendt didn't like talking about all this too seriously; he was merely there for the ceremonial.

The signing was quite a moving affair. I have never signed an international agreement before – with the TV cameras flashing, the carefully prepared duplicated document, the flanking signatures by ambassadors, the solemn exchange of signed volumes. 'This will go into the treaty archives of the Foreign Office,' said Henderson, picking up our copy. Then Arendt and I shook hands for the photographers and someone brought champagne – at 9.30am! It is all fine, as long as one does not inhale. Arendt then handed me over to his officials for the exchange of ideas about policy. We met again for lunch, and this time he stopped joking and began to talk – as well as one can do through an interpreter. It is clear that the SDP is very worried about the prospects, both economic and political. With a large budget deficit, rising un-employment, a growth rate of 2 per cent and inflation of 7 per cent, they are prepared for an extension of the electoral defeats they are already experiencing. When I asked him why they had run up a deficit he replied simply, 'We have spent too much.' When I asked him why they were losing elections, he quipped, 'The workers expect too much.' But he toasted me warmly after lunch and, surprised to learn of our shortage of sugar at home, promised to send me sugar for Christmas. I replied by saying that what mattered was not only the details of policy but the guiding principles, and that while we were ahead of them on the principles of our NHS, they were ahead of us on the principles of their social policy, not least on the equalization of the conditions of manual and salaried workers, notably the right of all workers to six months' sick leave on full pay. This went down well and Arendt and I rolled down to my waiting car arm in arm.

A quick tour of one of their vast, expensive rehabilitation centres for the disabled and I was on the plane home with an armful of roses, aching feet and a swimming head, having been assured by our Embassy people that the visit had been a huge success. One thing I have established is that it would be administratively possible to push through family allowance for the first child next year if we were prepared to improvise distribution through our local offices, instead of waiting for our centralized system to be ready. It just shows one must check and recheck what officials tell one.[1]

When we arrived in London Edna told me the H and W dinner was on at Vitello's, so I joined the gang there. Only John Silkin was missing; even Tommy turned up for once. We talked mostly about the Common Market and whether we should try and tie Cabinet's hands through a special party conference on the renegotiated terms. Peter, the most fanatical of us over this, was all for it. I argued that we needed the threat of a special conference merely to stop Jim coming along with terms that were conditional on Cabinet recommending them. I wanted a free hand for everyone during the referendum campaign. 'Freedom to choose must feed back from the people into the Cabinet.' Otherwise the party would be fatally split. To my surprise, Caroline, sitting next to me, murmured her total approval all the way through. Mike seemed to agree and Wedgie was confused. He looked a little less wild-eyed than usual. ('He never eats,' Caroline had said to us earlier. 'He never used to sleep either, but he does that a bit more now.') We did not come to any fixed conclusion; we

---

[1] Further study showed that the German system could not be applied in this country, not least because claimants there were paid by bank or post office cheque at two-monthly intervals and not by weekly order books as in the less affluent UK.

seldom do. These are not conspiracy meetings – we are all too individualistic and different. But we enjoy our arguments and they crystallize our minds.

Wednesday, 20 November

Another Cabinet! That will make four this week, including the joint meeting with the NEC which Ron has called for Friday. Everyone is mystified – and a bit mad – about the latter. The press have built it up as a showdown over the role of Ministers on the NEC, which Transport House is now denying vigorously. Bob told us all as we were waiting to go into Cabinet that Ron had told him that the joint meeting was intended to be merely a routine one in preparation for party conference, but agreed it had been handled in a ham-fisted way. Cabinet this morning was for the purpose of allowing us a more relaxed discussion of the Defence Review, in keeping with Harold's promise not to rush us over some of the difficult issues. Harold began by reporting on the initial private soundings he and Roy Mason and Jim had had with the US about our proposals for cuts. The discussions had been very friendly, both in Washington and in Bonn. The Americans had taken our proposals on Simonstown 'very calmly'. They accepted we needed to retrench, but thought our suggestions were 'the limit of what is tolerable'. They were unhappy about the idea of our withdrawing from Cyprus and could see the eastern Mediterranean becoming a Russian lake. They could wear our retreat from the Indian Ocean only if we would agree to extend their facilities at Diego Garcia.[1] Since the talks he had had a communication from President Ford showing that the Americans had had second thoughts and were expressing greater concern generally, but he thought they would wear our cuts if we did not extend them. Mike argued that we could not hand over Diego Garcia in this way without consulting India and was assured that we would not give up our attempt to get arms limitation in the Indian Ocean. Denis rubbed it in yet again that the cuts would be minimal compared with the ruthless reductions he had carried through at Defence.

The main rub came over nuclear policy, on which Harold was clearly expecting trouble. He needn't have worried: Mike's comments were so muted as to be almost token. Harold prepared the way carefully by saying that, though we would keep Polaris and carry out certain improvements at a cost of £24 million, there would be no 'Poseidonization and no MIRV'.[2] The nuclear element represented less than 2 per cent of the defence budget but it gave us a 'unique entrée to US thinking' and it was important for our diplomatic influence for us to remain a nuclear power. Germany, for instance, would not like it if France were the only nuclear power in Europe. And he stressed that the policy was in line with the Manifesto and that the decision on it in

[1] An island in the Chagos Peninsula, a thousand miles south of India, which is administered as a British colony, the British Indian Ocean Territory. Britain and the United States operate air and naval facilities jointly on Diego Garcia. In the Defence Review the Government said it had agreed to American proposals for a 'relatively modest expansion' of the facilities. The Indian Government expressed its 'deep concern' over the expansion plans.

[2] 'Poseidonization' meant the costly conversion of existing Polaris submarines to carry the Poseidon missile developed by the United States. Poseidon carries ten to fourteen MIRV [multiple independently-targetted re-entry vehicles] warheads each of 50 kilotons. In our October election Manifesto we renounced 'any intention of moving towards a new generation of nuclear weapons'.

Defence and Overseas Policy Committee of the Cabinet had been 'unanimous'. Other people took the same line, Jim echoing the importance of a nuclear capability for our world influence ('In other words, we must not go naked into the conference chamber,'[1] Eric whispered impishly to me). Mike came in almost hesitantly. He admitted Harold was trying to keep within the compromise of the Manifesto on this, though we were committed to get rid of the nuclear bases. 'We shall proceed to negotiate this within the overall disarmament talks,' Harold countered promptly. Mike then said that he remained of the view that we should rid ourselves of nuclear weapons, but recognized that he was in a minority and so would not press the matter. Peter and Wedgie said nothing.

I was more emphatic than Mike. It was not only that I was a nuclear disarmer, I said, but I thought the decision was self-contradictory within the context of our own defence strategy. What we were saying was that we needed nuclear weapons in order to exercise influence, yet intended to let them diminish in credibility by refusing to keep them up to date. This exercise in defence futility was not cheap: £24 million a year over ten years meant £240 million, 'and I could use that myself'. ('So could I,' parried Tony C. as usual.) The debate then died away. Harold summed up cheerfully, saying that Cabinet, with a few of us expressing dissent, had endorsed the policy and he added unctuously that he was extremely grateful for the constructive spirit in which those who disagreed with the policy had put their views. He then took himself off, looking pleased with himself, as well he might. The fact is that the spirit of the Campaign for Nuclear Disarmament no longer walks the land.

Spent the afternoon in a *tête-à-tête* meeting with the Supplementary Benefits Commission, accompanied by Brian O'Malley. We had an in-depth discussion with them of a kind I don't think they have ever had before with Ministers. I had been warned by officials that the Commission is touchy about its independence, but we found them only too ready to discuss problems like abuse of social security, Finer and heating additions in order that we could see where they were inhibited by lack of Government action just as much as where they were failing to use their own discretionary powers to the full. The discussion lasted nearly two hours, cleared our minds and highlighted certain courses of action we decided to examine further.

Denis has turned down my last desperate effort to get another £16 million for the NHS, which is needed to restore the Tory cuts last December. He has also rejected my plea for £1 million more for community homes and £7·8 million more for a limited scheme we have worked out to give a family allowance to first children in one-parent families at least. His letter was positively nasty in tone and at the meeting of officials which I had hastily called Dick Bourton sat smugly with an 'I told you so' look on his face. 'I am afraid your letter has made things more difficult, Secretary of State,' he said. 'Treasury officials have noticeably hardened their attitude to us.' I ignored this and said that our only hope now was to concentrate on getting a scratch scheme of family allowance for first children, without which I thought we would be in deep

[1] A reference to one of the most famous sentences in Labour Party history, uttered by Aneurin Bevan, supporter of the Campaign for Nuclear Disarmament, when at the Labour Party Conference in 1957 he opposed a resolution calling on the British Government to ban the bomb. The gripping story of how Bevan shattered his left-wing friends is told by Michael Foot in his biography.

political trouble. David agreed sadly that we must accept Denis's ruling on the NHS (after all, he has given us £35 million) and I asked Brian A-S. and the rest to draft a last-effort paper for PESC Cabinet next week, concentrating purely on our special family allowance scheme. A quick visit to the Disablement Income Group sherry party, where to my surprise and delight Mary Greaves [a former Honorary President of DIG] thanked me for all we were doing for the disabled. 'Such a breakthrough.' I hurried back to the House for the three-line whip on rates. We won the vote easily and it is clear there is no fight in the Tories yet. In the division lobby Joel came up to greet me affectionately. 'You've just sent me a horrid reply,' I pouted, tweaking his ear. 'You should never have sent your letter,' he replied with a poor show of severity. 'All I want is £7·8 million to save this Government from catastrophe,' I pleaded, nestling up to him. 'Just £7·8 million.' 'Just £7·8 million,' he echoed, appealing to those who were around. 'She's a terrible woman. We give her everything. I can promise nothing. I'll see, I'll see.'

Thursday, 21 November

Second Reading of our Uprating Bill[1] today and I haven't even started to prepare my speech. Officials have produced their usual well-meaning and factually thorough draft, but it isn't in language I could use. But first I have to get through Cabinet. Fred has come back from Brussels, flushed with what he considers a satisfactory deal over beef and sugar, but which some of us can see as the thin end of the wedge of capitulation over one of our major negotiating objectives: the transformation of the CAP. The discussion confirmed my worst fears. Fred pleaded that these had been the hardest negotiations he had experienced and we all murmured sympathy. But that was the whole point: he had had to fight like hell even to produce a dangerous compromise. His great triumph, he said, was that he had got the variable premium on beef.[2] There had been great hostility, but they had conceded it in the end 'for a period'. In return he had had to concede some temporary intervention.

[1] The Social Security Benefits Bill embodied the increase in pensions and benefits we had announced. It also provided for two new types of disablement benefit: the non-contributory invalidity pension and the invalid care allowance.

[2] Successive Labour Governments had supported agriculture by giving farmers guaranteed prices and subsidizing them out of taxation through deficiency payments where market prices fell below the guaranteed level. The Heath Government rejected this system in favour of import levies. It was, in any case, incompatible with the Common Market policy, which supported farmers' incomes by artificially forcing up the market price. This was done through fixing 'intervention' prices at which the Community was prepared to buy up and store any produce consumers could not afford to buy. Import levies were also imposed on imports from outside the EEC in order to keep internal market prices up to the required level. Labour's policy for the renegotiations as agreed with the TUC in the joint statement, 'Food Policy and the EEC', issued the previous year, was to return to the deficiency payments system which had been abandoned in 1973. No intervention system had in fact been introduced for beef in Britain by mid-1974 and, with market prices lagging behind rising costs, farmers were suffering. In July the Community had agreed, as a stop-gap measure, that Britain could pay her beef producers a fixed subsidy and was meeting part of the cost from the Agricultural Fund. By November this had proved inadequate for farmers' needs. Fred Peart had therefore secured temporary permission to pay them a premium which varied with the market price – the equivalent of guaranteed prices. But there were three snags. First, he had had to accept a limited amount of support buying, i.e. 'intervention', to take beef off the market for storage to force up the market price.

Peter came in first, being one of the few people who has the knowledge and time to find his way through the agricultural complexities. He began by congratulating Fred on what he had achieved: variable premiums were guaranteed prices in disguise. But the difference was that the benefit was not passed on to the consumer. And he deeply regretted we had accepted any intervention, because this weakened our position for the long-term talks. There had been no acceptance of variable premiums in principle and their cost was to fall on the British taxpayer. Shirley, of course, was more optimistic: 'The crucial thing is that Fred has got this policy on the table.' Jim was positively nasty to Peter: 'He has got it utterly wrong. Fred has got deficiency payments accepted. This is a breakthrough in the ideology of the Commission.' And he added that of course we had to pay for our own variable premiums, 'and so we should'.

This jerked me into speech. I am now convinced that Jim is heading for a patched-up deal to stay in – and is actively pursuing it. I said his speech had alarmed me more than anything else. We had made no inroads at all on the CAP. The Community remained as opposed as ever to deficiency payments. All we had been allowed was 'a little private sin provided we paid for it'. 'Don't you *want* to amend the CAP?' snapped Jim. 'I want to abolish it,' I retorted. Otherwise we should be saddled with all its disadvantages and would have to pay for any improvements we made to it through our own help to farmers. I warned that the real crunch was still to come and we had better not live in a fool's paradise. Denis was his usual realistic self. 'I think we have got to accept the deal. It is not a major victory: it is a skirmish we have won with some losses.' Mike took up my point that the battle had not yet effectively been joined and added that he hoped that the deal would not be presented too glowingly as a victory. Nor should we underestimate the cost: £15 million for two-and-a-half months' respite. Peter added mournfully: 'And in the meantime there is a total ban on imported meat.' We then turned to sugar, with which the beef deal is, of course, intertwined. On this, the more I listened to Fred's explanation the more convinced I became that here too we were heading for modifications of the Community policy which would merely mean that Britain remained enmeshed in it, while having to pay through the nose for any national improvements she wanted to make. But the rest dropped their opposition and the beef/sugar deal was agreed. Afterwards, as I sat next to Peter on the front bench, he said gloomily that he didn't like the way things were shaping at all.

By this time it was 12.30pm and I thought I had better go and do a bit of work on my speech. In my absence Cabinet agreed to Tony C.'s plea that we should not scrap the channel tunnel project right away, despite the unfeasibility of the cost of the rail link, but await the Cairncross Committee's report and allow him to negotiate a year's delay with the French. Mike also reported that the TUC General Council had accepted the proposed appeals machinery, including the substitution of the words I had suggested: 'in consultation with' ACAS. He was trying to find some way of dealing with the problems of the press and the closed shop.

Secondly, Britain herself had to pay the extra cost of the variable premium. Thirdly, our Community partners made it clear that they were not prepared to accept the variable premium system as a permanency and this had to be renegotiated each year.

Mike had a rough ride in the House about the NUJ dispute[1] and for once seemed ill at ease. It was only his patent integrity which saved him. Fred had an even rougher ride over the beef/sugar package. My Second Reading speech went without a hitch. I felt relaxed and I think I sounded it. It was a bore having to rush and change for the Lancaster House dinner for the Standing Committee of doctors of the EEC, but I was hostess. At first, with the debate on our Bill still going on, I was tempted to ask David Owen to deputize for me. Then I thought this was the worst moment to appear to give a slight – however unintentionally – to the BMA. Besides I am uneasy about what David is up to over the consultants' new contract. I think he has some exceptionally good and radical ideas, but he chops and changes them too easily. I certainly intend to keep an eye on things. So I ironed my gold dress in the Lady Members' room and climbed into it hurriedly.

In the event I was extremely glad I had made the effort. Walpole Lewin, this year's President of the Standing Committee, was delighted I had gone and even Derek Stevenson was affable. Henry Yellowlees just said, with those speaking eyes of his, 'Thank you, Secretary of State.' Chatting to Lewin over dinner, I found him much more compatible than I had ever done before. At one point he said to me with conspiratorial mateyness, 'I think we are going to solve our little problem, Secretary of State; we *must* do, because otherwise the consequences for the NHS could be disastrous.' I wondered what David had been up to: near agreement, indeed! After the guests had left, with profuse hand-shaking, David and his wife, Ted and I stood chatting for a few moments. David was chuckling over my Minute about my talk with Keable-Elliott. 'Anyone could see you are a journalist. I loved that bit about the officer class.' I always get on well with David; he has a disarming way of suddenly grinning at himself. Jack says David treats him well too, but not the people lower down the line. But once home my suspicions flared up again. Waiting in my box was a long paper on the consultants' contract with a note from Norman: could I please clear it that night, as it had to be circulated at once in the weekend boxes so that it could be dealt with by the Economic Policy Committee of the Cabinet on Monday. The

---

[1] The dispute was about a pay claim by the National Union of Journalists on behalf of provincial journalists. When this was rejected the union imposed sanctions which included a refusal to handle copy prepared or submitted by anyone other than a member of the union. Jim Prior, Opposition shadow on union affairs, attacked this as 'a threat to the freedom of the press and to editorial rights'. The dispute became entangled with the wider issue of the closed shop in journalism. In the Trade Union and Labour Relations Act the Government had relegalized the closed shop by making it 'fair' for an employer to dismiss a worker who refused to join a prescribed union in a closed shop. It had originally intended that the only exceptions should be where an employee 'genuinely objects on grounds of religious belief to being a member of any trade union whatsoever'. During the debates on the Bill in July, owing to a voting error by Harold Lever, the Opposition had succeeded in inserting an amendment widening the exemptions to include those who objected 'on any reasonable grounds to being a member of a particular trade union'. One of the purposes of the Trade Union and Labour Relations (Amendment) Bill, which had been presented that very day, was to remove this 'Lever amendment' and a deputation of editors had been to see Michael Foot to express their concern at being forced to join the NUJ where it obtained a closed shop. They wanted specific exemption from the Bill or protection from dismissal for editors. Michael Foot told Parliament that their fears were misplaced and their proposed remedies unworkable. He argued that the safeguards should be embodied in the closed shop agreement itself rather than the law. This was a start of heated discussions, particularly with Lord Goodman, then chairman of the Newspaper Proprietors' Association, which were to go on for months.

consultants had threatened that, if they did not get a firm offer next Wednesday, they would take industrial action. I glanced at it hurriedly and saw that it seemed to be weakening considerably the additional inducements we wanted to offer the whole-time consultants in the NHS. I threw it in my box. 'Clear it tonight? Not on your life!' I, too, intend to have it in my 'weekend box' – that euphemism for ten or twelve hours' work. If civil servants can get enough knotty problems into the 'weekend box' they feel they have done their job and can go home with a clear conscience for two days' rest.

Friday, 22 November

It was in resentful mood that I went yet again to No. 10 for the joint meeting of NEC and Cabinet Ron has arranged. The mutterings about this meeting have been growing and a number of people, including Shirley and Renee Short,[1] have refused to alter their engagements and have sent apologies. Ron's letter of invitation has been couched disingenuously: the main purpose of the meeting, it said, was to discuss 'the strengthening of liaison between the NEC and the Cabinet'. Harold began by apologizing that he had to be in the House for Roy Jenkins's statement on the Birmingham bombing and Peter's on the hijacking of a British plane. He would get back if he could. He then disappeared and we saw no more of him. (I suspect he was grateful to terrorists for once.) The first two items were clearly a smokescreen and we went through them perfunctorily. When we got to the liaison item it soon transpired that the meeting was really about Simonstown and all that, after all.

Ron opened with a convoluted statement of wonderful circularity. Finally he came into the open. 'The purpose of this meeting is to clear the air and not have the matter thrashed out in front of the TV cameras at conference.' There was no need for him to explain what he meant about 'the matter' and Mik came in at once, carefully refraining from mentioning Simonstown. He wanted us to revive the tripartite meetings with the TUC, 'the most valuable form of liaison we have', and added ominously that it would have been a good thing if such a meeting had been held at the time of the Budget. Ron promptly told him that a meeting with the TUC was to be held on 9 December. There was a silence. Finally Frank Allaun plunged in at the deep end. There was a problem, he said. What was the use of the party drawing up a policy if the Government could flout it? Members of the NEC had been publicly rebuked for supporting party policy. He wanted to ask for two things: first, that the PM should indicate that in future members of the NEC were not going to be carpeted if they were defending the policy of the party; secondly, that we should reaffirm that elected members of the NEC were responsible 'merely to conference'. This was too much for Reg P. He said he was glad that Frank had raised the issue so clearly, because he thought it was crucial. He had been shocked to see that Frank was billed to speak at a meeting at conference on 'Can We Control a Labour Government?' Such a claim was contrary to all the conventions of the British constitution, which rested on three principles: the responsibility of the Cabinet to Parliament, the responsibility of MPs to

---

[1] Labour MP for Wolverhampton North East and a member of the Women's Section of the NEC.

their electors and the collective responsibility of the members of a government. Some of them were not prepared to see these principles undermined. 'If necessary we will publicly argue our case.' With Shirley and Roy absent and Harold Lever silent no one came to Reg's support. Instead Denis gave us a dose of his vigorous pragmatism. 'It doesn't help to argue this theologically,' he protested. 'The important thing is that we should try to stick together. It won't work if members of the NEC use the NEC as a forum publicly to arraign their colleagues in government. We must all show a little give and take. This means respecting the restraints under which Ministers have to operate. I do hope we are not going to deal with this in a nit-picking legalistic way.' Walter Padley, who had voted for the notorious Simonstown resolution in the NEC, then made what I thought was one of the most effective speeches of the morning. He began by rebuking Reg. 'We make a mistake if we argue this theologically or on the lines of Reg Prentice. Our constitution is very wise. It makes the party conference the policy-making body but it also recognizes the rights of MPs, because the Manifesto on which we are elected has to be agreed by both sides. And it is this which binds the Government.' Joan Lestor took her own typically independent line. She didn't agree with the title of Frank's meeting: 'Can We Control a Labour Government?' and thought he oughtn't to have agreed to speak at it. But we were in a difficulty. How can Ministers carry out their responsibilities to both NEC and Government? 'If the rule is that in a private party discussion our responsibility is always to the Government we are in a confrontation situation.' When she tried to go on to discuss Harold's letter to her about her vote, Jim ruled that he would not allow that to be discussed: the relations between the PM and Ministers were entirely a matter for the PM. So she ended rather feebly: 'Let us put down our ideas on how we overcome this difficulty and discuss them.' Bryan Stanley, a terribly nice chap who is always listened to affectionately, tried another piece of rather confused self-justification: 'I am surprised at the way in which the decision taken by the NEC was taken and was blown up. As to the position of Ministers, those who are elected to the NEC are in a different position from other Cabinet Ministers and have a different role to play. I voted for the resolution because I thought something was being done which was quite contrary to the policy on which we fought the election.' Next came Michael, benign and reasonable as always. 'I hope we are not going to be too mournful and funereal about the situation. This is not about the party constitution. The remarkable thing about our constitution is that it is unworkable – but it works.' He also pooh-poohed the claims about the sanctity of conference decisions. 'I have spent my best twenty years in lively opposition to party decisions.' (Laughter and applause at that.) 'When I thought party decisions were wrong I argued and voted against them in the House of Commons and I think I had a right to do so.' The constitution embodied the concept of two paramount powers which in theory could not be reconciled but in practice were. The fact was that neither paramountcy must be pressed too far. There had been a great improvement in relationships within the party, first because of the unity over the Manifesto and secondly because the Government had carried out its promises. The Government must not press the absolute paramountcy of the doctrine of collective responsibility. In this way we should get through our problems in a practical way. This was particularly important at a time when the Common Market issue did threaten to confront us with great difficulties. 'Neither side must try to drive · the other out, but each must carry the other on the basis of the Manifesto.'

Wedgie made a characteristically amusing and seductive speech. Massive efforts had been made since 1970 to rebuild our relationships in the party, he said. Our difficulties were not insurmountable. Take the Privy Councillor's oath: it enjoined us – Ted Short interjected here to say that it was secret and should not be revealed. Wedgie was ready for him. 'I got it from the library of the House of Commons.' Laughter. It enjoined us, he continued, to defend all 'Her Majesty's principalities and powers', so when Clem Attlee gave away India he was breaking it. More laughter. 'All written constitutions are unworkable,' Wedgie continued. 'The NEC cannot instruct the Government nor can you turn Labour Ministers into civil servants.' More laughter. He then told an elaborate story about how when he held a reception for military attachés recently he found the office had invited the attachés from Chile and Spain without consulting him. 'So if a resolution had been moved here deploring my inviting them I should have voted for it myself.' (Oh, Wedgie, I thought, what a phoney comparison. If you had been there – as Jim wasn't at the discussion on Simonstown – and explained what had happened, no motion of censure would have been moved.) Wedgie concluded: 'We all want the Government to succeed in order to carry out the Manifesto. The dividing line should be: we are all responsible for what has happened in the past but we must all be free to influence what we do tomorrow. The Motion was wrong to deplore the actions of the Government.' (Then why didn't you abstain, as I did, I thought.)

Joan Maynard made a sour little speech, hectoring Ministers with, 'If you ignore party policy you'll lose your jobs.' Mik made a long one in which he tried to justify the terms of his resolution, arguing that it did not accuse the Government of a 'gross error' but merely asked it not to repeat it. (Derisory laughter at that.) But what did emerge interestingly from all this is that the Tribune group is no longer arguing that Ministers should not be members of the NEC. Indeed, Mik went so far as to say, 'An NEC with no Ministers on it is a formula for continuous confrontation', to which even Frank Allaun said 'Hear, hear!' So we progress. I hadn't intended to speak, but I was by now so roused that I could not restrain myself. I said that we were all agreed that no Government could survive unless party and Government were in harmony. But what struck me as ironic was that we were having this discussion at a time when, by common consent, they had never been in greater harmony. So why had we gratuitously given the impression that we were split once again – within a few weeks of the start of another Labour Government – and so caused doubt and anxiety in the rank and file at the very time we needed all our unity to overcome the real enemy? And the irony was, too, that we had done so when we now knew there was no real breach over policy. The fact was that the Government was hurrying to get rid of the hated incubus of the Simonstown agreement. And now we faced a conference in which all our arguments against the Tories and for our own policies would be submerged by this row among ourselves. There was some muttering among Frank, Joan and Lena at this, but I didn't care. I thought the wording of the Motion was intolerably offensive and unfair and that Wedgie, Joan and Judith should not have voted for it. As I pointed out to Joan afterwards, her amendment paying tribute to the Government's decision to review Simonstown was only carried by one vote: no less than ten of our dear comrades had voted against. Jim, who had been muttering angrily earlier, then summed up blandly – perhaps because I had said his angry things for him. He is good at knowing how to get the best of both worlds. We all agreed we did not want to try and draw up any rigid formula, he said, but we would see what we could do to improve liaison. And so we broke up.

To my train to Doncaster for Brian O'Malley's annual dinner at Rotherham. It is hard to have to go these long distances after a heavy week, but I felt I owed it to him and I am very fond of him. In the event I enjoyed myself thoroughly. From the word go I felt among friends. The dinner was excellent, the attendance a record. Brian saw I had plenty of excellent wine and my tiredness seemed to vanish. I hadn't prepared a word of my speech, but when I got to my feet I felt on top of my form. I played with them, made them laugh and made them cheer. They crowded round me to congratulate me. Then, instead of going round solemnly shaking hands with everyone, I swept Brian onto the dance floor and jived round the room joining every group of dancers in turn. I insisted on going into the kitchen and shaking hands with the girls there, wanting to buy them a drink, which the Mayor then insisted on buying them instead. (Anyway, they got it.) Back in the Mayor's parlour the local party chairman said to me, 'You know, if you hadn't been a politician you would have made a great actress.' That is what Peter Brown always says to me. I know what they mean. It isn't that I play a part; it is just that every now and then everything clicks into place and I identify myself emotionally with my audience. I love them, want to hug them, teach them, inspire them and carry them with me along the road of euphoric faith which, after all these years, I still tread.

Saturday, 23 November

Lardinois has made a speech which confirms my worst fears over the future of the CAP, suggesting that our national system of consumer subsidies might be our way of reconciling ourselves with the policy. He even quotes the beef token scheme approvingly! I'll soon put a stop to that and I minute Brian that I must submit a paper to Cabinet denouncing the idea before it takes root in Fred's resumed talks in Brussels.

Monday, 25 November

Reg Prentice, despite the concordat reached on Friday, has been shooting his mouth off about the rights of MPs, the limitations of the rights of party conference and the need for the party to be 'social-democratic rather than Marxist'. That chap has become a menace: he is obviously determined to pinch Roy Jenkins's 'man of principle' halo. As Mike said on Friday, it is always the Right which seeks to tear the party in half. Had to get up to town early for a Cabinet – yet another, but the only one this week because of party conference. In any case we would have needed one to deal with the emergency action we must take following the bombing holocaust in

Birmingham on Thursday, which has shaken the country. This was the first item, and Roy began by saying that he, Harold and Ted Short had had to agree on a statement urgently, promising legislation, and he hoped we would not think they had been trying to pre-empt the rights of Cabinet. (No one could reasonably object in the circumstances and no one did.) There then ensued a long discussion of his proposals, which I listened to with only half an ear as I was scribbling down the points I wanted to make when we reached the final clearance of PESC. I gathered that Sam Silkin was very disturbed by the provision to expel suspected terrorists who did not satisfy the residence rule and Merlyn echoed this. A long debate resulted in which Mike and a number of others pointed out that this would be equivalent to banishing British citizens, while Merlyn stressed that Southern Ireland would be unlikely to accept them and so they would all be dumped on him in the North. Bob also warned that the party would expect a general debate on Northern Ireland soon and that we should face determined attempts to restore the death penalty for terrorists. After nearly two hours of this Harold summed up that we accepted the power to make exclusion orders, but that a promise should be made to review this before the end of the six-month period. Meanwhile Roy should have urgent consultations with the law officers to see if the Bill could be improved by laying down criteria for exclusion. We all agreed we should resist the attempt to restore the death penalty and should offer a separate debate on this if necessary.

When we turned to PESC Denis said he had concluded his bilateral talks with individual Ministers satisfactorily and the strategy was now sewn up, including the cutting of nationalized industry subsidies. Only two issues remained outstanding: defence and my paper.[1] Barbara had come forward with a new proposition at the last minute and, although the amount asked for in 1976–77 was small, he had accepted that the proposal might – 'I only say might' – push up the following year's figure by £100 million. ('No!' I called out.) This could only be met by calling on the contingency reserve and he thought it would be better to wait until next year before deciding anything as we would then know better whether we could accommodate it. ('That will be too late administratively,' I called out again.) Denis ploughed on with some details of the bilateral talks, stressing that Cabinet must face the facts not only that nationalized industry prices would go up, but that his proposals involved an increase of school meal charges of 3 pence each year from April 1975. Reg nodded approvingly at that. All this played into my hands.

Harold then called on me to introduce my paper, 'as briefly as possible, please'. I refused to be flustered and made a telling speech, quoting how our expenditure on family support in real terms was planned to *decrease* steadily up to 1978–79. I said that the matter could not wait, as I was under pressure in the House. . . . At this point Tony C. interjected sneeringly, 'We are all under pressure in the House.' I saw cold red and retorted quietly, 'I should be glad, Tony, if you would contain your hostility till the end of my speech for a change.' Everyone laughed. I then repeated, 'I am under pressure in the House to announce our proposals for the introduction of the

[1] I had put a paper to Cabinet appealing against Denis's refusal to let me introduce a family allowance for the first child in one-parent families, known in the department as 'Special FAM'.

child allowances scheme and I must do so soon.' I pointed out that the decision to raise prices deliberately *before* we had extended family allowances to the first child meant that we were absorbing all the family allowance increase almost as soon as it was granted and making the one-child family catastrophically poorer. I recognized the expenditure restraints: that was why I had been casting round desperately for a way in which we could at modest cost hold our political front and salve our consciences. Harold then went round the table and every Minister in turn explained what sacrifices he had made. (Judith wasn't there because she had won her battle on overseas aid and I am glad.) Tony C. continued his elegant spite. Barbara had talked about pressures in the House, he said, but the greatest pressure was on housing. Anyway he was against having any more *ad hoc* measures to relieve poverty until we had a proper system of social monitoring. Shirley's promised great battle on my behalf dissolved into a few wet words. She was worried about the withdrawal of subsidies until we had made some better provision for the children of poor families, but if it couldn't be done in my way it should be done by taxation (e.g. by treating maintenance allowances as earned rather than unearned income). Perhaps Denis could look at this in his next Budget. Mike tried valiantly to support me but was obviously ignorant of the minutiae. Peter and Wedgie were silent. John Silkin made sympathetic noises off. Denis then came back with a promise that he would see what he could do in his next Budget. I could not contain myself at this, so Harold called me in again. I said, passionately this time, that our whole social policy was based on the fact that relief through the tax system did not reach the poorest who most needed help. I did not object to social monitoring; indeed, I had asked months ago for the setting up of an Anti-Poverty Strategy Committee of Ministers. It had been refused. Since then the Chancellor had found the money to give an additional £280 million tax relief to pensioners and I had not even been informed of his intention. Yet everyone knew that tax reliefs were a loss of revenue that meant a loss of money for public expenditure. Reg had drawn up his programme on purely educational grounds, as he was entitled to do, but he had agreed to help pay for it by putting up the price of school meals. The odium of this did not fall on him: it all landed on my plate to try and meet the social consequences. I think this drew blood, for Denis came in again. He said he accepted that he had been wrong not to consult me and had already apologized to me privately. He now did so again. He welcomed the idea of setting up an Anti-Poverty Strategy Committee in order to avoid future mistakes on these lines, but he assured me that when he referred to being willing to consider dealing with this in his next Budget he meant that he would consider introducing my idea then. 'It takes over a year to prepare these things,' I moaned. It was Harold who came to my rescue. If he had really 'summed up' he would have ruled that Cabinet thought a decision should be delayed. Not a bit of it. He said the view of Cabinet was that we should consider anti-poverty measures as a whole. He would set up the proposed committee immediately. My proposal should be the first item referred to it and the committee should report on it before Christmas. Denis and Joel got very restive at this. Surely Cabinet had agreed they should go ahead with the Public Expenditure report on the agreed lines? 'But you won't publish before Christmas,' said Harold cheerfully. They hummed and hawed a bit and then Denis agreed that, if this item were to be added, they could 'fudge' the White Paper sufficiently. And so I had won, to Tony C.'s obvious chagrin. I went back to the office to gloat over Dick Bourton.

We also had another office meeting on the consultants' contract, this time about our paper for EC(P) [Economic Policy Committee of Cabinet]. David was once again nibbling at the possibility of our surrendering the whole-timers' differential. He said that without a concession on this the talks would break down: he is obviously feeling browbeaten by some of the militants. I said, 'So be it', and reminded him yet again, 'I, too, have my breaking-point.' David vacillates a great deal, sometimes pressing the consultants' case for them and talking gloomily about terrible 'disruption' in the NHS unless we give way, then, later, suddenly and inexplicably perking up and saying he thinks a break is inevitable anyway. The profession have sanctions in the blood and must get them out of their system. I warned him that we were going to have great difficulty with colleagues over the new contract he was so cheerfully advocating and that our only hope of getting it accepted was if it was clearly seen to achieve our social ends and not merely as a straight pay increase. Jack Straw and Peter Brown, who seem to be in ideological cahoots these days, sat nodding at me approvingly from the end of the table. I sent David and the boys away to put a new draft paper up to me.

Tuesday, 26 November

The week's work is disrupted by the delayed party conference. Brief it may be going to be, but it is playing havoc with my departmental work. My first job this morning was the NEC meeting to prepare the agenda, etc. We met in cramped conditions in St Ermin's Hotel and there was not much we could do until the Conference Arrangements Committee had decided which emergency resolutions to take. There was a brief discussion about the speech of Herr Schmidt as fraternal delegate, Mik warning yet again that delegates were likely to walk out unless he refrained from referring to the EEC. Jim played it calmly. 'I hope that won't happen, but if it does conference must do what it thinks best.' I told them of the warnings I had sent: I suspect Jim has, too, though he enjoys playing the calm Olympian. Over our hurried sandwich lunch I talked to the lass who represents the Young Socialists on the NEC. She was full of the fact that the Young Socialists are being taken over by the Trots, whom she hates. Anyway Denis Healey has got his main anxiety over: he *is* to be allowed to speak in the economic debate. And I am to speak on the social services.

Wednesday, 27 November

Up at dawn to have my hair dressed before going to Central Hall. Result: a charming photo of Harold and me on the platform. Edna, my wonderful friendly driver, told me that Pat [John Silkin's driver and her flat-mate] had said Harold and I were obviously playing footsy under the table. It was to be my brightest moment of the conference. I had to sit on the platform wading my way through a succession of boxes sent by a devoted office. Either Wedgie has less work than I have or he has different priorities. As I arrived for every session at the platform entrance, struggling upstairs with two or three of those ton-weights of work, he was out in front, mingling with delegates as they arrived, slapping them on the back, speaking at every fringe meeting there was. His ambition grows by the hour. I believe it is so dominating that it could be his undoing.

Conference opened heavily, with delegates resenting the right that Conference Arrangements Committee had insisted on giving them to approve every iota of the constitutional changes we have got to make this year. There was more than one attempt from the floor to declare this was a stratagem by the NEC to prevent them from discussing politics. So the debate flagged and I panicked at one point lest I might suddenly be called to my feet to discuss social policy. Anyway I wasn't worrying about preparing much: our record is so good in my field, and I know it so well, I surely can't fail this time. In the event the debate on the constitutional points dragged on throughout the whole day.

In the evening, over to County Hall for the GLC reception. Once again I was foiled at the reception in my desire to meet rank-and-file delegates, something I enjoy doing at conferences. County Hall is just a rabbit warren of small rooms and I hardly met anybody, though those I did were as affectionate as they always are. The most interesting part of the evening was running into 'Spud' [Brian Murphy], our old collaborator in election propaganda-making, who had suddenly disconcerted Ted and me by going off to Brussels for an EEC job. He told us he was resigning his Brussels job in January and coming back. He just could not stomach the bureaucracy and the ideological starvation there. He clung to us almost pathetically, pleading to be allowed back into the old irreverent socialist intimacy.

Thursday, 28 November

I was a bit nervous about the NEC election results, though I thought I must surely survive after my record at DHSS. I did, albeit without distinction – slipping a place and coming behind Mik. The old Tribune pull – and indifference to me – is still clearly working. But the big surprise to some (not to me) was that Wedgie went to the top, pushing Mike to second place. As the cheers greeted this, Harold turned and drawled at me, 'He is becoming quite a young hero, and I think it is a pity.' His ambition was in both our minds. Shirley has plummeted from top to bottom of the women's section: the price she is paying for that declaration about the Common Market she made during the election. Okay, so why shouldn't she pay the price of her honest beliefs too?

Highlight of the day was Harold's key-note speech. Personally, I liked it because it was more sober than any conference speech he has made for years. 'I think it is the best I have heard you make,' I told him quietly. 'My best since Scarborough,' he replied confidently.[1] He had been telling me beforehand that he had worked out for himself a new line about planning agreements and the NEB. 'I am going to say this is the most important development since Keynes, as I believe it to be. Treasury was a bit shocked, but I went ahead.' Despite the lack of fireworks in the speech, conference took it well. But then I believe conference is in a sober mood.

[1] The speech on 'Labour and the scientific revolution' which he had made at the 1973 party conference in Scarborough had helped Labour win the election the following year.

'*L'affaire* Simonstown' came up in the afternoon. The great campaign to defend the three defiant Ministers was a bit of a damp squib, largely because Harold had had the genius to propose that one of them, Joan Lestor, should answer the debate.[1] She was pretty nervous about it, being a conscientious lass and not prepared to exploit the opportunity for her personal self-promotion. When she was muttering to me what a difficult speech it was going to be to make, I suggested she tell conference that there could hardly be any serious split between Government and NEC because it was Harold himself who had suggested that she should reply. This she did. She did pretty well, her manner as always being excellent.

Over another sandwich lunch, the NEC had gone through the emergency agenda, available at last. There was an interesting tussle over Resolution No. 1, on the economy, put forward by ASTMS, which attacked Denis's Budget strategy. Mik urged we should accept. Judith (a new woman after Harold's drubbing) suggested remit, which Mike backed strongly. The surprise was Wedgie's line: he backed remit too. So did Alex Kitson and the unions on a vote. So the only post-Simonstown non-penitent is Mik. On the Common Market there was unanimity that we should accept T&GW Resolution No. 14 calling for a referendum, but eventual agreement to remit No. 16 because the renegotiation terms it outlined went further than those conference had previously agreed. Mik complained at this decision, pointing out that No. 16 was the only resolution which committed us to hold a special conference on the terms before the referendum took place, so we should have accepted it. However, Ted Short's line prevailed.

Friday, 29 November

Highlight of the day was Ted Short's boob. He managed to get conference to reject his advice and pass Resolution No. 16 after the most inept speech I have ever heard him make. As he went through a long headmaster's report on the progress of the negotiations so far, I whispered to Harold, 'What right has he to tell conference what "progress" has been made when Cabinet hasn't even discussed the interim results yet and some of us would not agree that "progress" has been made at all?' Harold just shook his head. But if it was Ted's day of disaster, it was Denis's day of triumph. I have never heard him better and he swept Clive Jenkins's carpings at his policies into the dustbin of overwhelming defeat on a show of hands. At the *Daily Mirror* cocktail party afterwards, where I congratulated him, he was beaming with honest delight. 'You know, Barbara, as I do, when you have pulled it off.' Edna Healey was as warm to me as she always is, telling me how much Denis thought of me and how he would come home, even after he and I had had a fight in Cabinet, saying, 'She's a grand lass, that one.'

---

[1] An emergency resolution was moved by the Liverpool Toxteth Constituency Labour Party 'supporting those NEC members who censured the Government over the South Africa manoeuvres' and calling for the party's policy on South Africa to be implemented in full. Joan Lestor accepted it with reservations on behalf of the NEC, welcoming Jim Callaghan's statement on the need to end the Simonstown agreement. The resolution was carried without dissent.

Saturday, 30 November

Helmut Schmidt's day. When he arrived on the platform to sit next to Harold, I thought how handsome and relaxed he looked. His speech was masterly: it was a joy to hear how skilfully he dodged all the pitfalls and how cleverly he played on those emotions in his audience which were most likely to be favourable to him. He followed the blueprint I had given him, via the Ambassador, line by line and embellished it brilliantly, even managing to incorporate the socialist appeal to 'solidarity' into his throw-away sentence about our membership of the Common Market. Above all he had them rolling in the aisles and once again I was surprised to realize what a good sense of humour Germans have. As I listened I felt almost guilty. If I had not sent all those warnings he might have boobed. Instead, I had helped him to strike one of the most effective blows yet for our membership.

My own speech on Friday morning was received politely but tepidly. I am non-plussed by my continuing failure to get over in conference. I had never felt more relaxed and the content was good, even if predictable. Ted said my voice sounded thin – not an accusation that is usually made. Perhaps it is that those blasted fixed mikes are too high for me. Whatever the reason, I left conference feeling depressed. Wedgie, of course, got an ovation for a rousing speech. It is no good my being rousing about anti-poverty strategy when I know what a struggle I have to get every penny out of Cabinet. And I could not be demagogic about pay beds, with the negotiations with the consultants in such a delicate state. On the contrary, I chose my words with great care: I was not going to have Henry Yellowlees complaining that I had rocked the boat. I suppose that in the end I am, and always shall be, more interested in results than in striking popular attitudes.

Sunday, 1 December

Wading wearily through my boxes I found a minute from David covering the first report from our advisers on Community Health Councils. It ran, 'The experiment seems to me to have been a great success.' I minuted him back that it was a good thing that we had stuck to our guns. I remember how it was he who had wanted to chuck in his hand in the face of official pressure against our appointing them. Once again I have been reinforced in my view that the trouble with most right-wingers is that they always capitulate under pressure. My definition of a left-winger is someone who, when a storm brews, battens down the hatches and sails through it. It is part of his professional response. A love of popularity is the beginning of defeat.

I also found in my boxes a long submission from Philip [Rogers] about the need for us to come clean as soon as possible about the implication for the NHS of the reduced capital programme and a draft speech from David for me to make in tomorrow's debate in the House to this effect. Yet we haven't even had an office discussion about our priorities. I had to do some quick thinking about what to do and there is so little time to make up my mind. Finally I decided that, if the truth must out, it was better to deal with it in a fuller speech in a debate than in a bald statement to the House. Worked late redrafting the speech to get it just as I wanted it.

Monday, 2 December

Up early so that I could visit Mother in hospital on my way to the office. She has had to have a clot in her leg removed. She lay crooning in her bed and greeted me. 'It's my Barbara.' Then she sang to me in a high voice all the songs she said Dad had sung to her. When I whispered to her, embarrassed, 'You will wake everyone up,' she retorted, 'They are not asleep and they *like* my singing.' When I went out of her cubicle to talk to the other patients in the ward they assured me it was so. 'Sometimes we join in. She's marvellous.' Sister and the nurse were very touched when I repeated what Mother had said to me: 'They are all so kind to me – just like the sister I never had.' I hope and pray she will die with dignity and not be reduced by a stroke into a vegetable.

At the office I handed Norman my speech as far as I had drafted it and then went into a succession of meetings on subjects which had been piling up while I was at conference. First on the democratization of the NHS, on which David has been conducting a running war with officials. Philip, of course, is pretending that there is no difference of approach except on timing, but it was soon clear that he doesn't want any changes at all. I supported David in his view that we must build up the operational strength and independence of the Area Health Authorities and progressively reduce the RHAS to a strategic planning role in which they will become little more than the regional arm of the DHSS. I agreed with him too that we must get away from the present position in which the money which is available for the NHS is distributed automatically among the regions on the basis of a weighting formula which takes little account of our national redistributive priorities. I liked his idea that we should go for workers' participation on AHAS in a big way, in order to reassure the doctors that they were not merely being placed under local authorities. David is a curious mixture. He has excellent ideas but less good follow-through.

Next into another of our mass meetings with officials to discuss the latest state of play over the consultants' contract. About twenty officials troop in on these occasions and sit round like vultures, waiting to gobble every word. Why they all have to turn up I'll never know, for they seldom contribute anything. We went in detail through the paper I am putting to EC(P)[1] tomorrow and once again I had to spell out what I

---

[1] David Owen and I had come to the conclusion that it would benefit the NHS, as well as being fairer to consultants, to accept the idea of a 'closed' contract. We proposed that this should consist of a basic ten sessions (half days) per week with additional payments for regular extra sessions, for emergency work, for domiciliary and exceptional consultations and for administrative and educational duties outside the normal working hours. Whole-timers, who would still be barred from private practice, would all have a basic ten session commitment plus the right to extra payments if they worked excessive hours, as many of them did. In addition they would be paid a 'complete commitment' allowance, equivalent to the existing 2/11ths differential. Consultants still wishing to practise privately could either retain their existing contracts or move to a new contract consisting of the same ten sessions at the same rate of pay as the whole-timers less the differential, but expressed as '8 plus 2' so that a consultant whose private practice workload was in danger of prejudicing his NHS work could be asked by the health authority to drop one or two sessions with a corresponding reduction in pay. If he did, he would not be eligible for our proposed new system of career supplements to replace the secret 'merit award' system as these awards ran out. These supplements would be of two types: a service supplement administered by the health authorities to reward exceptionally responsible and dedicated service to the NHS and a medical progress supplement

thought we had conceded to the consultants and made it clear to David what were *my* breaking-points: e.g. the need to maintain the differential for the whole-timers and to redistribute the old distinction awards on a basis that would reward service to the NHS. David went through his usual gloomy gamut about how the consultants would break tomorrow, etc. I told him I had always thought they would break, that we would have to carry the argument into the field of public debate and that I thought this would be no bad thing. Peter and Jack Straw sat at the end of the table nodding their approval vigorously.

It was afternoon before we got down to the discussion of my speech for this evening's half-day debate on the NHS initiated by the Tories. It went smoothly until we got to the point where I was supposed to admit frankly that we faced a *reduction* in capital expenditure on the NHS in later years. I protested about being pitchforked into such a traumatic announcement ahead of a general orchestration of announcements by other Ministers and again Peter and Jack were on my side. But the alternative of making a cataclysmic statement to the House one afternoon soon was equally unpalatable. We went round and round the problem for two hours. Finally I suggested an alternative form of wording and told them, 'Geoffrey Howe won't be expecting this and, as I shall be following him, he won't have a chance to comment effectively. Yet we shall have cleared the way for discussion with the health authorities.' And so we broke up. I did some frantic last-minute writing, snatching the last pages from the typists just before reaching the House at 7pm.[1]

In the event, my speech went swimmingly. Ted, in the gallery, admitted it was most impressive and it made Howe's hotch-potch of unrelated comments look cheap. As I said scornfully, Howe had been 'long on gloom and short on remedies'. But of course the House was nearly empty and I had paid a big price in nervous energy. My exhaustion, mercifully, did not show, but how I felt it! The evening was crowned by a pleasant meal with Brian O'Malley. He insisted on buying me a Christmas dinner and a nice bottle of wine and talked with an affection that has been even more deepened by my visit to Rotherham. This stimulating intercourse of minds, warmed

---

awarded on professional advice to those making a major medical contribution to the NHS, including research and teaching. In our paper to EC(P) we justified this restructuring of salaries as a strengthening of the NHS as it would encourage the whole-timers we needed to man up the unpopular specialities and neglected areas. At the same time it would enable us to define more closely the part-timers' contractual obligation to the NHS. Under the present arrangements they had been free to fit in their private work at times that suited their private patients rather than the NHS. Though many of them worked devotedly for their NHS patients, in practice the health authorities had no control over this. But it would clearly be wrong to introduce extra payments for extra work if the basic commitment had not been clearly spelt out. As we put it in our document, the new standard contract of ten basic sessions would normally constitute a 'five-day Monday to Friday working week, from 9am to 5pm, including meal times'. It was this that particularly enraged the consultants' negotiators, who wanted to move away from an open-ended, professional-type contract without accepting the disciplines of an industrial-type closed one. (See Appendix I.)

[1] I pointed out that some £450 million additional money had already been made available to the NHS in the current year to cover rising costs, including pay increases for nurses and others, and I announced that next year the Government had decided to restore some of the December cuts of the previous Government. (£19 million on capital and £10 million on revenue.) But I added: 'I must warn the House that the outlook for the next few years is not encouraging. As things now stand it will not be possible to maintain this increase in expenditure in real terms over the next few years.' (Hansard 2.12.74, col. 1214)

by our deep friendship, is the great consolation for all the stresses, strains and incredible rush of work we go through.

Tuesday, 3 December

Woke after a heavy sleep, still exhausted, to face my meeting of EC(P) on the consultants' contract. David swears that if we don't get clearance for our offer this morning he faces a walk-out of the Joint Working Party this afternoon. Officials had briefed us that we were not going to face serious opposition from my colleagues, but they had clearly not done their job properly because the reality turned out to be very different. Mike was in the chair as the custodian of pay policy and, as one colleague after another denounced the proposals as a violent breach of the Social Contract, he refused to come to my help. Albert Booth, speaking for Mike's department, was the most devastating critic of all. To hear him denounce the continuation of a differential in favour of a whole-timer would have made Nye Bevan turn in his grave. I pointed out he was arguing on the same lines as the most militant consultants were and that I had been fighting for the retention of the differential as vital to our whole policy. All Mike could do was to pronounce gravely that my far-reaching proposals must go to Cabinet.

David was plunged in gloom as Edmund Dell tore us to shreds on behalf of the Treasury. To pay the consultants overtime would lead both to massive pay increases and to repercussions everywhere, he declared. Mike was obviously biased against me and as I pleaded in vain that the new contract would enormously strengthen the NHS (1) by enabling the health authorities to ensure that consultants really did work the hours they were committed to, (2) by meeting genuine grievances of the consultants and (3) by giving long-overdue incentives to the men who worked in under-staffed hospitals and less popular specialities, I thought ironically that Nye never met the obstruction from the Attlee Cabinet that I was meeting from the Department of Employment under Mike. I wonder if Mike one day will write the story of Barbara's battle to bring Nye's reforms up to date with as much approval as he wrote about Nye's compromises!

Back at the office we had a council of war. I refused to be gloomy, pointing out that one seldom got away with a major new idea on the first round. We could yet win in Cabinet. Our trouble was that we were under such pressure from the consultants time-wise that we had not had enough elbow room to win colleagues round gradually. David went into his meeting of the Joint Working Party expecting to be torn apart for not having produced a firm offer, but came out positively cheerful. The negotiators had apparently accepted his explanation that the Government had not yet had enough time to consider their ideas and had agreed to postpone industrial action, though they wanted a decision on 12 December – or else.

Wednesday, 4 December

Spent three hours fulfilling my promise to the departmental staff side which I made during the protracted dispute last year over the uprating: namely that I would arrange regular meetings with the full union executives to discuss progress being made with the long-term problems in which they were interested. It went well and afterwards they all said it was the first such meeting they had ever attended: no Minister had done anything like it for twenty years. I think I am beginning to win their confidence.

Thursday, 5 December

At Cabinet Jim reported that Vorster was beginning to put pressure on Ian Smith to reach a settlement with the Africans in Rhodesia. Clearly events in Portugal had made South Africa realize she must come to terms with black Africa. There was now the possibility of a constitutional conference, though the joker in the pack was still Smith, as we well knew. He thought we should leave the African leaders to make the running and should not intervene ourselves unless asked. Our stock in Africa was now higher than it had been for ten years, not least because we had reversed the Tory position on Namibia. Harold then reported on his talks with Giscard [d'Estaing] and [Helmut] Schmidt. The weekend papers have been full of Schmidt's triumph at the party conference and of his matey talks with Harold at Chequers. No wonder the anti-marketeers are getting worried! I suspect Harold is excited by the whiff of international manoeuvring again. His love of the international stage is enough in itself, in my view, to reattract him to Common Market membership. He'll inhale all right, only this time a little more circumspectly. No one challenged the press communiqué the two had issued and Harold was at pains to stress how much they had talked about the economic situation generally and how he had encouraged Schmidt in his determination to pursue expansionary policies in the German Parliament. There wasn't a murmur from anyone, either, about the statement Harold made in Paris following his visit to Giscard, in which he had said that, for his part, provided we got the terms for which we asked, he would be willing to recommend to the British people that they should accept them. He told us he had assured both men that we were not only concerned with the issue of the Community budget, but that he would stand by all the seven points in the Manifesto, which he had just spelt out again in a speech at Manchester. Giscard had talked in his usual theological terms about the Market, 'but he can keep his theology as long as we get the gravy,' said Harold cheerfully. So Harold and Jim are heading for membership as fast as they can!

Eric Varley had a bad time over his proposals for energy conservation. Personally, I thought they were pathetically wet and urged that we should announce we were studying a two-tier system of petrol rationing. I said it was nonsense not to reduce the speed limit on motorways to save petrol. As for Eric's reliance on raising energy prices to do the trick, we had got to remember that this wouldn't save money if we really took seriously our pledge to protect the poor from the consequences. Mike backed my tough line, but the rest of them were even feebler than Eric was. Tony C. succeeded in reversing the proposal to ban floodlighting: 'For God's sake don't let us plunge the country in gloom.' Nor would they hear of including references to petrol rationing at this stage. Harold summed up that the package was satisfactory as an interim measure, but that we should need another statement in the New Year.

To my surprise Mike got away easily with his report on his discussion with newspaper editors. No one objected to his decision *not* to exempt editors from the closed shop provisions of his Trade Union and Labour Relations (Amendment) Bill, but to leave the matter for discussion between the editors and the union. Nor are we to ask the Royal Commission on the Press for an interim report unless the parties call for it. All this left us with only time for a brief introductory debate on top salaries.[1] Harold said we must examine the report very carefully; personally he had changed his mind and was now in favour of a cut in ministerial salaries. Jim came out strongly in favour of a cut, too. Mike said firmly that we must reject the report: there should be smaller increases, or preferably no increases at all above £10,000. And there it was left until next time.

Friday, 6 December

Helped the Queen open the new hospital in Southampton.

Monday, 9 December

Having come back from Blackburn with a heavy cold, I had to give in and take to my bed for two days. It was bliss to let my responsibilities slide from me and to lie inert in the warmth.

Tuesday, 10 December

Back to work, still groggy, but I can't miss my Parliamentary Questions and Tom Taylor would never forgive me if I wasn't at his celebratory dinner for his CBE. On the way I looked in at Harold Collison's Christmas party. (Christmas is the additional hazard I have to face, with all the parties one must attend on top of arrears of work.) Peter Thomasson and the other union boys were there: very friendly about my conference with the staff side last week. Peter Brown and Ian Gillis were in exuberant form. At my request they had been in touch with David Wood about his snide piece about me in *The Times* yesterday[2] and they were tickled pink by how fulsome he had been about me. He wouldn't have been unfair to me for the world; thought I was a

---

[1] The Top Salaries Review Body under Lord Boyle had at last been able to complete its fundamental review of salaries in the top levels of the Civil Service, nationalized industries, armed forces and judiciary (Cmnd. 5846). It found that pay in these cases had 'fallen seriously behind the minimum required' and recommended substantial increases. The pay of Permanent Secretaries and High Court judges, for instance, should go up from £16,350 to £21,000. Admirals, generals and air chief marshals should jump to the same level from £14,850. The biggest recommended increases were for chairmen and board members in nationalized industries to bring them more in line with salaries in private industry. The chairman of the British Steel Corporation should get £40,000 (from £28,100); the chairmen of British Airways and British Rail £35,000 (from £23,100). Overall this represented an average increase of 28·8 per cent, including threshold payments, but the Review Body argued that this merely worked out at an average annual increase of 11·4 per cent since 1972 when the statutory pay policy came in and was still less than the movement of other salaries during the same period.

[2] He had referred to 'feline gossip' to the effect that I always insisted on the services of the *senior* make-up girl on duty before going on TV.

remarkable woman and admired me more than he could say, etc. Peter said he positively blushed! Well, all I can say is that it would be pleasant if occasionally these private tributes became public ones.

Wednesday, 11 December

Another meeting with the office on the consultants' contract. We discussed what we should do if Cabinet decided tomorrow on a cut-off of all salary increases at £10,000 a year. They thought even the consultants could be got to wear it, provided it applied to absolutely everyone. This is, of course, my line. I have said all along, and still believe, that it is Toryism, not socialism, to hold public sector salaries down while doing nothing at all about the much vaster incomes in private industry. David has sent holding replies to the Joint Working Party negotiators, telling them the Government needed more time to consider the new demands they are now making, but they have made it clear they will expect an answer tomorrow. If I can't get a decision from Cabinet by the time he meets them, then heaven knows what they will do. David reported that they were now asking for extra payment for merely being 'on call', while some of them, like Lewis, were insisting that there should be a joint study of a complete 'items of service' contract and he had promised this. I told him that I should have enough difficulty getting through Cabinet what we had already agreed; to add anything else would just wreck all our hopes. As for a piece-work type contract, the idea was inconceivable and we should do nothing to encourage it. He is, in fact, reconciled to there being a break, whatever we do – and he almost welcomes it. It is clear that nothing less than complete capitulation by the Government on all their points will do the trick.

I managed to get into the House to hear Brian Walden open the debate on capital punishment. His speech was masterly. Sir Keith Joseph then intervened with a contribution of marvellous tortuousness and circumlocution. At one point it looked as if he had convinced himself about the contradictions of his own case; then he swung back to his new tough (and popular with the right wing) anti-abolitionist line. Finally, he almost collapsed into his seat with a plea to the Home Secretary to persuade him if he could that he was wrong. He certainly seems a tortured personality. And, of course, when it came to it, he voted for the death penalty. I believe he is consumed with ambition as well as self-doubt.

At my request Jack Straw has been working out a 'maximum incomes' policy and has been in touch with Derek Robinson and others. He is entirely with me on this and has beavered away, coming out in the end in favour of 100 per cent tax on increases above a certain level of income. He really is an invaluable help to me.

Thursday, 12 December

Woke wearily after five hours' sleep. And this is the day on which I have to do battle over top salaries! This was supposed to be today's priority in Cabinet, but as usual Harold allowed it to be pushed to bottom place while other matters were argued interminably. First, on parliamentary business, we had a long, inconclusive discussion on how to handle 'take note' Motions on EEC directives.[1] It was one of those discursive chat-ins which nearly drive me mad in Cabinet. Since the main protagonists on Europe are all bunched at the other end of the table, keep turning their heads away from our end, interrupt each other and talk in low tones, it is impossible to follow what is going on, while Harold bumbles on inaudibly. In the end I gave up, only to hear Ted Short's clear tones booming out above the chat. 'The trouble is that all this is incompatible with parliamentary sovereignty and there is nothing we can do about it.' What they eventually decided I haven't a clue. I just got tired of saying, 'Please speak up.'

This was only the *hors d'oeuvre* to Harold's report on his EEC summit,[2] for which Mike was waiting avidly, clutching a copy of the communiqué in his hand. It went on for nearly an hour and a half and Harold was at his worst – wordy, defensive and repetitive. On inflation, Schmidt had stressed that unemployment was the worst danger. He was planning massive reflation. Harold also gave us a sketch of himself embattled against Giscard, who had organized the whole thing so abominably that we couldn't even get texts translated properly. At last Harold got to the Common Market renegotiations and I had to strain to catch his rambling résumés. It is a familiar technique: when Harold reduces everything to a boring, and almost bored, low key, I reach for my critical faculties. He had, he said, quoted the Manifesto extensively. There had been proposals on what to do about the Community's institutions, but he had 'washed his hands' of them, because until we decided whether to stay in, we were not involved. In any case, they were 'on ice for twelve months'. On the budget it had been 'very tough indeed'. We faced French intransigence.

Finally, a formula had been agreed about a 'corrective mechanism' for our contribution to the budget based on our line about making it a percentage of GNP. Even Schmidt had been difficult here. The discussion on the Regional Fund had been a 'squalid wrangle'. Eventually they had worked out a three-year temporary plan which gave us 28 per cent in return for a 15 per cent contribution, but he had remained detached about all this because, until we decided to go in, it didn't affect us. 'I was more concerned to get freedom to use our own national aids.' This was one of the aspects of the problem of sovereignty. The second was fiscal policy. The move to greater surrender of sovereignty was much less than he had feared. There was, for example, to be no harmonization of VAT. On industrial matters, he had reminded

[1] See footnote to p. 128.

[2] On 9 and 10 December a meeting of heads of government of the nine members of the Community and their Foreign Ministers had been held in Paris on the initiative of the French President, Giscard d'Estaing. The communiqué which had been published (Cmnd. 5830) was impregnated with determination to move to greater European unity. On economic and monetary union the Heads of Government affirmed 'that in this field their will has not weakened and their objective has not changed'. Mr Tindemans, Prime Minister of Belgium, was invited to submit an urgent report on European union. They called for the renunciation of the veto in the Council of Ministers, for direct elections to the European Assembly as soon as possible and for an extension of the Assembly's 'competence'. They decided to activate the European Regional Development Fund from January 1975, allocating Italy and Britain the largest shares, and held out the prospect of adjustments in Britain's contribution to the Community Budget – one of our renegotiation points. Harold Wilson had signed the communiqué, inserting merely token references to the fact that renegotiations were still going on.

them sharply that there could be no interference with public ownership. But the fact was that economic and monetary union was 'as dead as mutton'. True, they had insisted on putting some words in the communiqué which retained it as their 'ultimate goal', but 'I made it clear it was a goal we do not share'. He had let it go because it was like the form of words always included in disarmament agreements – about complete disarmament being the ultimate goal. But it did not mean any more than that.

But Mike was not to be put off so easily. 'I am,' he said gravely, 'deeply disturbed about some aspects of the communiqué.' There had been serious concessions on the issue of parliamentary sovereignty. First, the veto had been weakened; secondly, we had agreed that direct elections to the European Assembly should be introduced 'as soon as possible'; thirdly, we had accepted that economic and monetary union was the 'ultimate goal'. None of this had ever been discussed in Cabinet. It was no use Harold saying that it wasn't *our* goal: 'the communiqué says the exact opposite'. Some of us had sent Harold a memo saying that Cabinet must face up to these issues. We obviously could not get agreement among ourselves, but we *could* get agreement to differ and we should have an early discussion on how such an agreement to differ could operate. Before anyone else could speak Harold jumped in again with another long justification of what he had done. Some people in the party, he said, had attacked him because he had used the words 'I will recommend'. They seemed to think he was trying to take too much power for himself, but he had used the words exactly because he had had Mike's memo and was not going to commit Cabinet to any line of action. He repeated, *ad nauseam*, that he had not swerved one inch from agreed policy; on every issue Cabinet's position was 'totally reserved'. At this I said quietly, 'If we reserved our position on all these points, ought not the communiqué to have said so?' Even Eric murmured agreement on this. Harold floundered, saying there was a passage indicating that he had made our position clear in the discussions. He searched through the communiqué and at last produced a few wet words which obviously did not meet my point. Wedgie then came in equally simply: 'Is the communiqué the policy of HMG, so that we are all bound by it?' Harold snapped back, 'We have accepted the communiqué and reserved our position.'

Peter was much more dramatic. Having read the communiqué, he said, 'I can only register my own feelings of absolute shock. Our credibility in the country has been greatly undermined. The relaxation of the veto strikes at the heart of parliamentary sovereignty.' Harold got really tetchy at this. 'I resent the suggestions that Jim and I are little innocents abroad.' He had had, he said, more experience of negotiating agreements than anyone else in the room – notably the trade treaties he had negotiated in the old days with the Russians, in which he had had to be very tough in protecting Britain's interests. 'I agree that a lot of the words are objectionable, but we have the last word on every issue. What I did was explicitly in terms of the Manifesto.' It was clearly time for some of the pro-Europeans to come to his defence and they duly did. First Harold Lever and then Shirley said they thought he had done very well and hastened to assure the anti-marketeers that there was a lot in what Harold had told us that they regretted, but they had to accept the compromise position of Cabinet, etc. Harold came in yet again; he talks us down by sheer repetition and it works. By this time it was turned noon and the two crucial items on the agenda had not been touched. I was furious; it looks as though Harold is reverting to his old garrulity: a sure sign he knows he is on a collision course with some of us. (We used to get the same thing over his talks with Ian Smith.) Mike said stubbornly that it was a pity we hadn't had this discussion before the summit talks. An urgent discussion about how we should handle the referendum issue was necessary. Roy tried to demur at this but Harold overruled him. There *were* some aspects of the referendum we should discuss and he would arrange this early in the New Year.

At last we turned to top salaries. Mike has put in a paper saying that the proposed increases (particularly for chairmen of nationalized industries) would wreck the Social Contract and demanding a cut-off for increases at income levels of £10,000 a year. He has also ferociously attacked my proposals for the consultants' contract. He told us that the TUC Economic Council had just come out bravely against the miners' excessive claim, but how could we stand up to the miners' £30 increase claim when we were proposing to give thousands a year more to people already highly paid? He himself had spoken out against the miners' demands, but that meant 'we must take a hard line on all other claims'. The situation in relation to the Social Contract was so crucial that we must take 'extreme measures'. That was why he thought it essential for us to cut our own salaries. I came in next, saying I agreed absolutely that extreme measures were necessary: the trouble was that Mike's measures were not extreme enough. I believed that the threat of runaway inflation was so acute that we needed to snap people out of their 'business as usual' attitudes into a new circuit of thinking, but that could only be done, not by Tory policies of discriminating against the public sector, but by having a maximum incomes policy across the board. What, for instance, was Mike proposing should be paid to Don Ryder when he became head of NEB? There were smiles at this, but then a succession of people proceeded to suggest a repetition of conventional half-way solutions. Reg P. and Merlyn merely wanted to stage the top salary increases and not cut Ministers' salaries, which I had backed Mike in urging. Harold Lever said that 'Michael must not seek an easy way out of his difficulties by general populist claptrap like cutting Ministers' salaries. The public will not be impressed by our cut.' Most people echoed this, Eric saying that a cut would be a 'blatant gimmick'. (I hissed at him, 'A young man like you talking with that kind of timidity! You disappoint me; you are just a reactionary old man.')

Only Shirley backed us up in a superb speech. Barbara was right: we *did* face a crisis situation, we could not tolerate these big increases at the top, but there must be action across the board. But she too proposed what was becoming a clear consensus: that we should not cut Ministers' salaries, merely refer them to the review body while announcing in advance that we intended to freeze our salaries, whatever it proposed, for twelve months. Peter backed her: he wanted more than 'austere staging' of top salaries. We should ignore Boyle and merely work out a proper cost of living increase. The proposed increases for nationalized industries chairmen were ludicrous. But Barbara was right: the policy must go across the board. It would be an 'act of masochism' to cut our own salaries, but we should freeze them for twelve months. Wedgie said any increase in salary above £10,000 a year in private industry should not be tax deductible. Only John Silkin flatly proposed a 10 per cent cut in ministerial salaries. Gradually, a consensus emerged in favour of a 'severe staging' for top salary people, plus an announcement that we were freezing our own salaries for twelve months and some action in private industry. I said that no one could expect dramatic recommendations from a Royal Commission under the chairmanship of Jack Diamond.[1] Laughter. Nonetheless, others pointed out that we could hardly ignore a body we had specifically set up to look at top incomes. Right, I said, then let us announce that we are considering immediate action ourselves to deal with immediate *increases* in top incomes in the private sector, while asking the Royal Commission to speed up a report on what the *level* of top incomes ought to be. Everyone thought this was a good idea. Harold then produced a draft staging document he had hurriedly prepared. He said he must see Boyle quickly if he was to make an announcement, as he must, next week. And so we had to leave him discretion, bearing our points in mind. I asked, 'What does staging mean? That next year's increase is merely postponed till 1976, when these people catch up with time and a half?' John Hunt passed me a note saying that staging meant that the postponed increase was lost for ever. So Harold had his way.

By this time it was 1.30pm, and I was supposed to be lunching with John Cunningham of the *Guardian* in Soho at 1.15pm! Harold turned to my item on the consultants' contract: could it be postponed yet again? In despair – because I certainly didn't want the new contract discussed in that atmosphere – I said I would try to hold the lions at bay for another week, though please could I be top item, really top item, next time? Everyone laughed, Harold said yes, and we broke up.

At a hurriedly convened meeting later that afternoon, I told David Owen and officials just what had happened and said we must put a supplementary paper on the new contract to Cabinet. After all, we don't mind so much having consultants' increases staged if everyone else is being staged. The essential point is to establish the principle of the new contract. But once again I had to warn David that we could make no more concessions to the consultants – some of whom will not be satisfied until they have got complete payment by items of service established, with every difference between the whole-timer and the private practitioner ironed out. David seems to be edging inch by inch towards acceptance of the latter, but I would rather resign than accept it.

Saturday, 14 December

Going through my boxes at HCF, I was appalled to read the Minutes of Thursday's Cabinet. Gone is all the talk of 'staging' in the sense that John Hunt had put it to me; instead, it read that we had agreed that part of the increases had merely been

---

[1] One of the ideas to come out of the discussions in the Liaison Committee with the TUC before the February election was the setting up of a Royal Commission on the distribution of income and wealth. The unions wanted to spotlight the unequal distribution of wealth in Britain and the way in which top incomes managed to avoid the restraints of incomes policy through such means as expense accounts, income from investments, capital gains and top hat pensions schemes. The Royal Commission had been duly set up in August 1974 under the chairmanship of Lord Diamond, former Labour MP for Gloucester and Chief Secretary to the Treasury under Harold Wilson from 1957 to 1970. He had been made a peer in 1970. The Commission's terms of reference were to enquire into 'such matters concerning the distribution of personal incomes, both earned and unearned, and wealth, as may be referred to it by the Government'.

'deferred'. One of the hazards of Cabinet government is that one is at the mercy of the Minutes, which often come out very differently from what one remembered. Yet it is almost impossible to get them altered afterwards, particularly if the PM has a vested interest in the official version.

Monday, 16 December

Harold has circulated his draft of the statement on Top Salaries. Said David when he saw it, 'This is the end of the Social Contract.' I was furious at its tone and contents. It certainly was much more muted than I thought Cabinet had intended and it totally failed to reflect our determination to produce a policy for curbing increases in the private sector, pending the production of the Royal Commission report on the *level* of top salaries. It was mercifully accompanied by a memo from Mike, saying that he was disturbed by the decision to go ahead with the announcement of our policy on top salaries before consulting the TUC and urging that this should be reconsidered. When I went into the House to hear Harold's statement on the summit (a turgid and unimpressive affair) I saw Mike and took him aside. He hadn't seen Harold's statement and I urged him to send in a comment immediately, as I intended to do. The whole situation about incomes policy is getting desperate, as was made vividly clear at a meeting of the Ministerial Committee on Economic Policy. The discussion was so familiar that I might have been taken back eight years or so. Mike made a fair and worried statement about the movement of settlements: they look like working out next year at 30 per cent. There were dire warnings all round the table from Shirley, Edmund Dell and others. Officials had prepared a list of recommendations on how to strengthen the voluntary policy, none of which amounted to a row of beans. Financial sanctions against excessive increases? An anti-inflation tax wasn't on, we were told, because it would involve fixing a 'norm' and that, of course, would seem too much like a statutory policy. 'But we have got a norm, haven't we?' I intervened, losing patience. They looked shocked. 'The TUC guidelines say that there must only be increases to offset rises in the cost of living,' I persisted. 'We can establish historically what the movement in the cost of living has been over any period. If it has been 20 per cent that is our norm. We could tax out anything in excess of that. It is rough and ready, but everyone admits we are on the edge of crisis. The only way to stave it off is to *do* something, however rough and ready, not just sit here belly-aching.' They laughed uneasily. Edmund half agreed. Denis merely said we might have to consider reviewing the whole guidelines, but this was not the place. Mike did not disagree. But later, when I talked to him again about Harold's state-ment, he was as alarmed as I was. I told him I was sending in a Minute of protest, and he agreed to turn up the statement and send in another Minute of protest himself. Worked late at the House and got home exhausted with the prospect of an early rise to go to Nottingham. I have decided I must go and see for myself the site of the ghastly fire at the Fairfield Old People's Home.[1]

---

[1] In the early hours of Sunday 15 December a fire had broken out at the Fairfield Old People's Home in Nottinghamshire, which resulted in eighteen deaths.

Tuesday, 17 December

Not my day. The alarm didn't go off and I had a wretched rush to catch the 8am train, arriving at St Pancras half-dressed to find a photographer lurking in the gloom. Getting up in a rush always jangles my nerves and I nearly hit him. Besides, I had had nothing to wear (all my clothes seem to need a stitch, a press or a clean) and my hair was a mess. I knew that cameras would be there in force, so, in despair, I had slammed on 'Lucy'.[1] After a leisurely breakfast on the train, I began to feel that my exhaustion might be containable. I retired to the loo, finished making up my face and adjusted 'Lucy' carefully. So when we arrived at Nottingham, I was ready for anything that might come – or so I thought. The discussion with the County Council and my experts went well and then we got into cars for the visit to Fairfield. TV and press cameramen and journalists came climbing over the charred ruins in full cry after me as the Chief Fire Officer and others took me round, helping me over twisted girders and ash-strewn mud. 'Lucy' rocked uneasily on my head in the strong wind (ironically, the very wind which had helped to spread the fire), but I managed to cope, looking – and feeling – appropriately subdued. Cameras peeped at me through every aperture as I went through the ruined home, watching my feet in case I tripped. Alas, I did not watch my head and suddenly, to my horror, I felt 'Lucy' snatched from it by a piece of wire trailing from the roof. The officer said, 'Oh!' I snatched 'Lucy' back and somehow pulled her on my head again, askew – and carried on. It was one of those nightmares one dreams about and I froze inside with embarrassment. No doubt some wretched camera had caught the whole thing! But some inner grimness of will always comes to my rescue in these crises and I walked on, looking, questioning, and *willing* my entourage to believe they had imagined it. No one dared to refer to it and so, somehow, I got through the dreadful day and back again. At 6pm I looked in at the news anxiously: no, I hadn't been made a laughing-stock. In fact, I looked very calm and correctly serious as I walked around. What a life!

Mike on the phone, full of anger about top salaries. Harold had replied to his Minute by saying it was too late to postpone a decision as he was seeing the national staff side that afternoon. So Mike had hurried over to see him and had got a promise that the matter could be reopened at Thursday's Cabinet and that no announcement would be made meanwhile. Would I back him up with another Minute? I said of course.

Wednesday, 18 December

At the NEC Mike passed me a rough scribble of a letter to Harold which, he hissed, he hadn't sent yet. It expressed his deep concern that it transpired that Harold was not, after all, willing to reopen the top salaries issue completely on Thursday – just some consideration of the amount of the staging. In the letter Mike said that, if the

[1] My *nom-de-guerre* for a wig I had bought some years earlier and to which I occasionally resorted in desperation when I had to be on show without benefit of a hairdresser.

announcement went ahead, the Social Contract would be in ruins and he would have no alternative but to resign. My eyebrows shot up and he looked unhappy and hesitant: obviously he is deeply uncertain about what to do. I scribbled an alternative sentence for him, 'If this goes ahead I believe it will make my job impossible', which, I pointed out, would hold a threat without committing him. He wavered and put the sheet away, so whether he sent it or not I do not know.

But the rest of the NEC went swimmingly. Frank Allaun had a Motion down condemning the Government's failure to make defence cuts and calling for more. I was amused how, to a man – and a woman – the NEC was obviously determined not to repeat the performance we had had over Simonstown. Frank was shamed into not pressing his Motion.

I had to leave at that point to attend a Privy Council, but I learned later that Joan Maynard's motion on Harold's EEC communiqué had been similarly effectively defused. So Harold's outburst against the Simonstown ministerial rebels seems to have worked – as well as Ron Hayward's efforts in calling the joint meeting with the Cabinet. I was one of those who jeered about it at the time, but this morning's change of mood proves I was wrong.

In the afternoon, I was called into the MES to discuss an official document on the proposals to phase out subsidies on nationalized industry items, notably fuel. Officials admitted that the result (together with other rises in the Retail Prices Index) would be that the April uprating would not be quite sufficient to compensate for the rise in prices, so that pensioners and others would face the later rises with nothing in hand. It is in any case too late now to alter the April figure and they suggested we should deal with the problem through the December uprating. We were all of us agreed that we must start to move towards economic prices for fuel, but the consequences on the Retail Prices Index will be appalling. Shirley predicted that by July it would be up by over 25 per cent on the previous year. The inflation picture is indeed terrible and I get a feeling of being trapped in Cabinet's cotton-wool complacency. They *talk* about the need to do something, but every time anyone suggests a crash programme of action *now* they just drift – and stall on practical suggestions, like a two-tier programme of petrol rationing. There seems to be no realization that only a bold move to remove some of the gross inequalities in our society can save the Social Contract, the economy and the Labour Government. That is why Mike is so right to go on badgering Harold to reopen the top salaries issue. Minutes continue to fly between him and Harold and Norman can't find out just what luck Mike is going to have about it on Thursday. In the meantime, I told MES quietly and gravely that it was not enough just to say we would compensate pensioners through the December uprating. Did they not realize that, by next July, the single pension would be worth 7 per cent less than in July 1974? It was just not on to seek to achieve economic rectitude and fuel conservation at the expense of the poor, whom we had always said it would be our priority to protect. Denis and the rest were clearly disturbed and Harold said I should put in a paper to the next meeting setting out what I proposed should be done. So I told my people to get ahead with preparing it and to work out the implications of the moves I suggested we should take: a higher increase in family allowance in April (which they think is operationally possible), the acceptance of

Special FAM[1] (which Edmund Dell is resisting on behalf of the Treasury) and a substantial increase in heating allowances.

Mike wound up the economic censure motion debate in the House with far less than his usual assurance. True, the Tories were set on roughing him up, but he did not retaliate with his usual sparkle. I think he is a very worried man and I think Cabinet as a whole ought to be far more worried than it is.

Thursday, 19 December

Harold called Cabinet for the unusually early hour of 9.30am and, true to his promise, had put my consultants' new contract item at the head of the agenda. Much good did it do me! In fact, once again, it was only reached well after noon because the first two and a half hours were spent on top salaries. Whether Mike sent that resignation threat or not I do not know, but his pressures (and mine) had had an effect, because Harold began by saying that Mike had made such a strong case for reopening the matter that he, Harold, was going to break all the rules and allow it. Unfortunately for Mike, though, he was really too late. Harold had seen the staff side, given them the broad outline of the proposed staging and so was in an impregnable position to fend off any great change. As Eric whispered to me, 'Mike missed the boat at the last Cabinet; he should have said all this then.' However, Mike put up a determined fight. He began by thanking Harold for allowing him to reopen the matter; he apologized for asking Cabinet to reconsider its decision, but the more he had thought about it the more convinced he was that we must postpone the announcement: at least until the miners' claim was out of the way. Otherwise he would not answer for the consequences. Personally, he opposed the whole report. By supporting it, even with staging, we were giving Government support to a breach of the guidelines by some of the best paid people in the country. 'My top civil servants admit this.' His department was fighting the principle of recoupment for lost pay increases. Every worker in the land could make out a case for catching up on what he had lost: that way lay economic disaster. Harold dealt with him gently. 'All timing is always wrong for these things.' But he knew he had a bull point. He had seen the staff side yesterday afternoon to report on what the Government intended to do. 'All the Civil Service unions from top to bottom attach great importance to this going ahead.' (After all, they did not vote for the Social Contract, I thought.) To go back now on what he had told them would be very difficult.

I objected that we had had no time to discuss Harold's draft statement, which was very different from what any of us had anticipated. We were expected to approve a statement which hadn't even any figures in it, yet the ones Harold had quoted last time were 'not austere staging by any means'. Nor did the statement stress the action we were proposing to take in the private sector. Harold interrupted to say that he was not intending to make the statement that afternoon, so we should not discuss the wording, which he had not worked on himself yet. I persisted, strongly backing Mike on the wider issue. When were we going to have a discussion on our overall economic

[1] See footnote, page 236.

strategy? Cabinet's complacency appalled me. I believed we were drifting to disaster: only a bold break with the present drift would do. Yet when I had raised this at EC(P) I had been told it was a matter for Cabinet. There ought to be a year's standstill on all increases above a certain level of salary. Jim came out remarkably strongly on the same lines. 'I support Mike: there should be a total postponement of this.' He was also in favour of a cut in ministerial salaries. 'If you want to set an example start with yourselves.' Shirley was strong too, saying she agreed with everything I had said. The prospects for inflation were horrifying. 'The only thing to do now is to announce a strict twelve months' delay and cut our own salaries. We can't wait for the Diamond Report before dealing with the private sector too.'

Others were more hesitant. Harold Lever was scathing: 'I am not prepared to descend into an irrelevant and demagogic gesture. We ought to be reviewing the whole of our economic and industrial policy.' At this Harold snapped, 'A wage freeze is totally unacceptable. It would destroy this Government.' Tony C., pragmatic as usual, said that we must go ahead. Roy Jenkins was equivocal. To cut ministerial salaries would be a 'ridiculous gesture'. It would be very bad to go back on what Harold had told the unions. But he was 'torn on timing'. Eric said we should not alter the substance of our decision, but meet Mike on timing. He knew the problem he faced with the miners. Emboldened by all this hesitation, Harold fought back. It would, he said, be 'cowardly to take it out on a handful of civil servants'. The treatment of the public sector was the 'great divide' between us and the Tories. To sacrifice the civil servant because we had problems would be 'like the man who kicked the cat'. These were his employees and he was going to fight for them. But he suggested we should vary our decision as follows: on nationalized industry salaries we should say that we were going to await the Diamond Report before considering their increases; on the Civil Service we should 'honour our agreement' about comparability. Eric reacted angrily on nationalized industry salaries. We were already, he said, having difficulty in recruiting the right people. 'Pay them peanuts and you get bloody monkeys.' But the rest were prepared to settle for Harold's compromise, particularly as the figures Harold had prepared at my request showed that the Civil Service increases net of tax were modest enough. It was also agreed that staging should not affect pension rights. As Brian O'Malley has pointed out to me, we are perpetuating two nations in the pensions field.

When at last we turned to my item the atmosphere could not have been worse for me. Cabinet was irritable and listened impatiently. But I ploughed on, telling them that unless we reached a decision that morning, I would face a walk-out of consultants the following day. And I spelt out the advantages of the new contract to the NHS as well as to some very hard-worked and underpaid men. Edmund Dell once again attacked my proposals viciously, unfairly and unscrupulously. I was, he said, wanting to pay consultants for work that had been unpaid before. The rest of them looked as though they neither understood nor cared. Then Mike came in. There were great dangers in the new contract, he said; the repercussions of paying consultants over-time could be serious. It was hardly the right time to introduce an expensive new pay structure for a highly paid group. My heart sank. I thought I was finished. Then he said reluctantly (obviously ignoring his departmental brief) that if, however, Barbara felt this was the only way she could deal with the difficult situation she faced, perhaps they ought to allow me to go ahead on the understanding that Cabinet was not bound by the findings of the Review Body on the cost and reserved the right to modify them in line with any other decisions we were taking over salaries.

Harold seized on this lead. Cabinet, he thought, was willing to agree with this, but I must clear with colleagues my department's evidence to the Review Body on the new contract and Cabinet would wish to examine this critically. The outcome would depend on the decisions we took on higher salaries generally. Cabinet would have a wider discussion on this, and on the economic situation, in the New Year. Edmund chipped in to say that Treasury could not agree with my offer to find a mere £5 million of the cost of this pay restructuring out of my public expenditure allocation and Harold said that that must be discussed between me and the Treasury. (Heaven help me!) Tony C. then said nastily that there had been no provision made in PESC for the cost of phasing out pay beds (with which Edmund had made great play) and he hoped that no steps would be taken in this direction until the point had been cleared up as to how it was to be paid for. Harold ruled that there should be no progress on this until Cabinet had discussed the timing in the light of developments on the new contract. So my hands are tied on every point! Yet, of course, I will get blamed both for 'intransigence' towards the consultants and for dragging my feet on the fulfilment of our policy on pay beds! But I was relieved to get anything at all and staggered out of No. 10 as limp as a wet rag.

Back at the office I reported the position to another of those mass meetings of officials. David said he did not think it would have been possible to reach agreement in the Joint Working Party anyway. He thought the negotiators would reject the contract, so we should be ready to issue it after the meeting I am to have with them tomorrow and should make arrangements to see that every one of the 11,000 consultants got a copy. There would be disruption for some weeks, but he really didn't think our offer was too bad and he was not too pessimistic about the ultimate outcome. I sent them away to draft the necessary documents. I then looked in at the Transport House Christmas party for an hour and was so tired I actually decided to cut the Fire Brigades Union party – and there is no greater measure of tiredness than that!

Friday, 20 December

It was noon before I got to the office, having in the meantime worked on the draft of our contract proposals and on the press statement, which once again I had to alter substantially. Another office meeting at which I told David it just was not possible for me to keep his promise to the Joint Working Party to set up an enquiry into a 'fee for item of service' contract. In the first place, Cabinet would not wear it; secondly, the whole principle was obnoxious. He and Gedling agreed the concept was a bad one but said they had agreed to an enquiry just to keep Lewis quiet. Personally I believe some of our difficulties arise from the fact that David has not been tough enough with the consultants all along. This may have aroused expectations that he must have known we could not fulfil. I am worried enough about some of the principles of the new contract. I think David should have reported to me on it more regularly and more critically, but they seem to have brainwashed him pretty effectively. However, he is certainly standing loyally by my decisions now and I think he is positively relieved to have the whole matter come to the crunch. He alternates, as always, between gloomy warnings and bursts of optimistic cheerfulness. As we left the meeting after I had gone through the contract paper line by line and made a number of changes, he said, 'Of course this means we shall have to spend some years phasing out pay beds. I always thought it would take longer than you did.'

Just before my meeting with the Joint Working Party [JWP] was due to start, Henry suggested it would be a good idea for me to see the independent members of the working party, who, in general, supported me. In came three of them: Hunter, McColl and Dr Revans.[1] They told me they thought it was a good contract. The chances of the profession as a whole accepting it were 60–40; in the case of the negotiating committee it would be the other way round. As academics, they particularly welcomed my clear rejection of the principle of a 'fee for item of service' contract, which they said would ruin the NHS. David smiled at me and said generously, 'You see, you were right.' By this time I got a message that the meeting was getting restless and that the negotiators were threatening to walk out. Really! Henry, Philip, David and I looked at each other grimly. After all, I was only waiting for the statement on top salaries to be released. Harold was making it in the form of a written answer which wouldn't be available until 3.30pm. We had asked No. 10 to send an advance copy, but it hadn't arrived. We had all agreed that I should be accused of having suppressed essential evidence if I didn't inform the meeting that the statement had been made: they might draw from it conclusions about what was likely to happen to the findings of the Doctors and Dentists Review Body [DDRB] in their own case. But once I told them about the statement they would want to see it. Hence our effort to get a copy before the meeting started. And there was another complication: last night the DDRB deposited on Harold's doorstep their report on the profession's demand for an interim increase. Of course the Government hadn't had time to consider it. But, anxious as we were not to appear to be keeping anything up our sleeves, we had decided after worried consultations that I had better mention it. All this had taken time to sort out, and in any case, I had only kept them waiting ten minutes – time they could well have been glad of to consider the details of the contract we had sent down to them. But the imperious messages kept coming up to me, so, suppressing my anger, I hurried downstairs.

There were some fifty people round the table in the big meeting room. Already, before they knew I was coming to the meeting, they had informed the department that the Joint Working Party was bringing with it Lewin and Stevenson of the BMA (not members of the JWP), the leader of the HCSA and the secretary of the British Dental Association [BDA]. So clearly they were not visualizing an ordinary negotiating meeting of the JWP. In fact it was clear they had come prepared for a showdown. They had already threatened to take industrial action unless the Government

---

[1] Dr Robert Hunter (later Lord Hunter), Vice-Chancellor of Birmingham University; Professor Ian McColl, Consultant Surgeon to Guy's Hospital; Dr John Revans (later Sir John), then Regional Medical Officer, Wessex Regional Health Authority.

announced a 'full statement of its position' on 20 December and they had come along prepared to walk out. We had made a copy of the contract proposals available to them half an hour before the meeting was due to start. I walked in, expecting to be able to explain the proposals quietly to them. Instead I found them lined up for war. When I began by apologizing for keeping them waiting, explaining that the PM was making a statement that afternoon in which they would be interested and I had been waiting for a copy, they bristled with suspicion. What had the statement on top salaries to do with them? Well, I said weakly, we didn't want to withhold any information from them which *they* might consider relevant. When I went on to tell them the review body's report on their interim claim had been received, but that obviously it couldn't be published until the Government had considered it, they bridled still more.

Dr Astley interrupted me rudely: what was the status of this meeting? Was it or was it not a meeting of the JWP? I replied, keeping my temper beautifully, that obviously it wasn't a meeting of the JWP because they themselves had said they wanted to bring other people along. He cross-examined me as though I were a prisoner in the dock. Were they to take it, then, that the JWP was dead? Doggedly I continued that they themselves had wanted to bring the negotiations to a head. I suddenly snapped at them that I had been threatened with industrial action unless the Government announced its decision. Faced with such a threat to the NHS, I had obtained that decision. So the proposals I had brought were on a take-it-or-leave-it basis, they countered. They were, I replied, a statement of the Government's decision, for which they had asked. Were the proposals negotiable? Obviously, I replied, the principles were not negotiable because the Government had carefully considered all the principles involved and reached a view, but the details certainly were. I met a cold wall of hostility. What, asked Grabham, was the borderline between principle and detail? I said it could never be rigidly defined, but obviously there were some of their points which the Government could not accept. I would be misleading them, for example, if I pretended there was any hope of the Government accepting an 'item of service' contract. Lewis exploded at that. Spiritedly I told them that I thought I had done very well in this difficult economic situation to have obtained for them so much of what they had asked for. We all knew that the new contract would be more expensive than the present one. I must tell them that some of my colleagues had been worried by the possible repercussions of paying professional people overtime. But I myself thought the consultants had some genuine grievances. I had been anxious to give them better rewards for the long hours so many of them worked. I had therefore fought for the closed contract and I had won. I had thought they would welcome this.

Despairing by now of any chance to go through the proposals in detail, I asked them to take them away and study them, discuss them with their members and then come back and talk them over with me after Christmas. In the meantime obviously I must release the proposals to the press. It would be fatal if they were to be leaked in garbled form. But I wasn't asking for their answer then. We had, I ploughed on, made arrangements for copies of the contract to be sent to all consultants, so that they could have an informed discussion with them. There was a fussy explosion from Derek Stevenson: really, was I proposing to appeal to their members over their heads?

Outrageous! I said I thought they would have welcomed their members getting the facts on which to base a judgment. And again, I appealed to them to take the whole thing away, discuss it and consider it and meet me again later. After a lot more fuming on their part, Lewin said they wanted to talk privately among themselves.

One of the farces of the evening was that Private Office had arranged to hold its Christmas party and Norman had asked if they could use my spacious ministerial room. Of course, I had said yes, so when I went back there I found it already arrayed with paper chains and drinks. I beat a hasty retreat to Brian O'Malley's room, where David, Henry and the rest of us sat round in the usual state of exasperation and despair we get into when we have been talking with the BMA. Tim Nodder and some others said we ought to give way about the distribution of the contract to individual consultants. David insisted that our only hope was if they had access to the facts. We finally agreed that we should make the machinery of distribution available to the BMA to get the copies out under its own name. It should never be the aim of industrial relations policy to weaken the authority of a union. When the negotiators graciously informed us they were ready for us, we went downstairs again. Astley told us solemnly that the contract as it stood was not acceptable to them. They had hoped that negotiations in the JWP would have continued, but I had stopped all that. (How they can imagine they can get a 'full statement' of the Government's position and then negotiate on it I do not know, but then, unfortunately, they are not professional negotiators.) In view of my 'take it or leave it' attitude, they had no alternative but to reject the proposals. As they were mandated to call industrial action unless the proposals were acceptable to them, call industrial action they would. Once again I asked them to take the proposals away and to meet me after the Christmas holiday. Impossible.

There then ensued a chaotic discussion, different people coming in with different arguments. Grabham, looking rather wild, kept asking me what he considered an essential point: was I prepared, if they accepted the new contract, to agree with them on detailed proposals for pricing it, which we would then put jointly to the Review Body? Of course Cabinet had tied my hands on that. He kept coming back: as far as he was concerned, the decision would depend on my answer to another question. Was I willing to join them in a submission to the Review Body for an immediate increase of 18 per cent? I reminded him that they had already made an interim claim. Hadn't they better wait and read the report which the Government would publish as soon as possible? He dismissed this angrily as equivocation on my part. Stevenson tried to argue that, by saying I would release my proposals to the press that day, I was forcing their hand and closing the door. I said that if I were convinced there would be no leak I would be only too happy to hold up release. But did they really think none of their members would talk to the press, or that it wouldn't get out? Several of them had left already, I pointed out. There were nods at this and, while Stevenson bridled at the very idea, Lewis said suddenly, 'I must say I agree with Mrs Castle over this.' I said, however, that I did not wish to undermine their authority in any way. I was therefore prepared to arrange for them to send the copies out under the BMA's name at government expense. 'Can we also send out our own comments?' demanded Stevenson. 'Yes,' I replied. 'And will you send out your own comments in answer to ours as well?' 'No,' I replied. He seemed incredulous at my generosity. Some of them clearly hesitated at the possibility of an open break. What about pay beds, they asked. I said we agreed it was a separate issue and I hoped discussions would continue on that in whatever forum they thought appropriate.

We then got into arguments about detail. Stevenson tried the line about my threatening the 'independence' of the profession. I insisted that I was only retaining the differential that had existed since 1948 and which formed part of Nye Bevan's compromise. 'But what you really want is a whole-time salaried service,' they challenged. 'I prefer consultants to work whole-time,' I replied. 'But that is only the measure of the compromise I am prepared to make. For my part it is a real compromise. After all, Nye preferred whole-time service too, but he made a compromise and it has been faithfully observed all these years.' I pleaded with them: 'Look at how far we have moved from what you originally feared. There was talk at first that I was going to abolish private practice and impose a whole-time service. The contract shows how different is the reality.' 'Yes,' said Lewis viciously. 'What Mrs Castle is saying now is very different from what she was saying earlier: it is much worse.' Something snapped in me and I said coldly, 'If that is to be your attitude there is nothing for us to do but to submit this matter to public debate.' And so we broke up and I went off to see the press, ending up in the ITN studio at 10pm. I never saw anything of the office Christmas party.

It was past 11pm when Edna and I got down to HCF. Ted had already started decorating the beams and the place was a symphony of ivy, holly and old man's beard. Something of the Christmas spirit began to rise in me as we all sat over a drink and Edna showered us with presents. I then rustled her up some food and unpacked all the provisions we had brought down. It was 1am before I got to bed; 6am when I woke to begin the hectic preparations for the invasion by the family. At least the consultants are not due to strike till 2 January! I am determined to put the family Christmas first meanwhile.

Friday, 27 December

Despite its inauspicious beginning this has been one of the happiest Christmases we have ever had. My food was fine; everyone behaved perfectly and I was happy and at peace to have Jimmie with us, so obviously enjoying himself. The only shadow was Sonya's absence: Terry phoned on Christmas Eve to say she had been rushed to hospital with agonizing pains in her back and had to lie flat. So, although the rest of them came, we were short-handed and how I got through all the work I will never know. Christmas is exacting enough when I am not a Minister and when I can get the domestic help I can't get now. But my aching feet did not spoil the fun. Only I missed my Sonya very much.

Boxes have continued to come down and on Monday David phoned to say the Royal Colleges had written to me asking to see me urgently about the dispute. They want to act as mediators and believe a solution can be found by making concessions on the career structure supplements that are to replace the merit awards. David said that he and Henry advised that we should not rush into compromises at this stage but let things simmer a bit. They believed that the consultants had a strike in their system which had to be allowed to come out before any settlement could even be discussed. He said he would see three of the presidents that afternoon in my place. I told him I did not want to give any impression of snubbing the Royal Colleges and would come up to town on Friday the 27th for a meeting if necessary, although obviously I would prefer to wait until after the holiday. He said that he and Henry strongly advised me to wait till January.

Monday, 30 December

I am surprised how exhausted I am. We gave a little drinks party for local friends yesterday and the spurt of effort needed to clear up and prepare for it took all the small reserves of energy that I have been building up. So I was appalled when Ian Gillis phoned to say that the *Today* programme wanted me to come to London for a programme with Brian Lewis which would discuss his personal attack on me in the *Sunday Express* yesterday. I said I just couldn't face it and anyway it would be better for David to do some of the talking, particularly as the *Daily Telegraph* is running the story that there are splits between us over policy. David was very angry about these stories and told me that the best way for him to deal with them was to appear on TV from time to time and show that we had got an agreed line. But, alas! On this occasion, he was down in Wiltshire, so I told the office that our case would just have to go by the board this time. In the event Brian Lewis's attack on me on the programme was so unbridled and one-sided that it probably did me more good than harm.

1975

Thursday, 2 January

My hopes of two days' rest have been shattered. Ted and I arrived at Southampton on Tuesday afternoon to spend the New Year with Colin and Phil. That meant a late party on New Year's Eve and a fairly festive time the day after and I had been hoping to get away to a hotel for a few days' complete rest. Not a bit of it. Last night the *Today* programme was on to me for a recording for this morning – the consultants' D-day – and Ian Gillis has told me I shall be in great demand all day by the media. So I get up early and hurry to London for a succession of appearances, starting with the *Jimmy Young Show* and ending with Llew Gardner late at night. Cameras followed me everywhere – and here was I in my country trouser suit! However, some of my energy had come back and I survived. When I got into the office Philip Rogers, Gedling and other officials streamed in to see me about the story in this morning's *Daily Express*: to the effect that they had all been threatening to resign in protest at my policies. Gillis told me that the story had appeared without any reference to the department first and Philip and co. were deeply shocked. Philip said he had consulted Henry Yellowlees, No. 10 and Douglas Allen and it had been agreed that they might send a letter of denial to the *Express*. This he had drafted and he wanted to show it to me. I said I thought it was right they should send a letter, but, as the *Express* would certainly not print it, they should send a copy to every other newspaper.[1]

And so the hectic day went on, with me rushing from studio to studio. Altogether it was quite fun and civil servants clearly enjoy the excitement of these dramatic occasions. Elizabeth tends to make a lot of confidences at these times and they are very revealing. For instance, when Ian Gillis said how good Jack had been – coming into the office every day, though he was supposed to be on leave – she confessed, 'When I think how we were opposed to the idea of political advisers I am amazed; we admit now we just don't know how we managed without them. Of course, it depends very much on the person you choose. But there again, when we heard you had chosen Jack Straw we were horrified: the militant ex-President of the NUS! Now we all think he is marvellous.' 'The great thing about Jack,' said Gillis, 'is that he is completely

---

[1] Philip Rogers' letter to Alistair Burnet, then editor of the *Daily Express*, denounced the story as 'nonsense'. Burnet replied curtly that 'I have to assure you that our information is copper-bottomed.' Furious, Philip wrote back repeating his denial and asking for his letter to be published. It was, but with the editor's comment that he stood by the story.

straight. The civil servants trust him.' Again, later, when we were chatting after the Llew Gardner recording, Elizabeth said, 'People do get wrong ideas about politicians. We all thought, for instance, when you were made Secretary of State, that you would be very autocratic and come storming into Private Office blowing us all up. But, you see,' (with a seraphic smile) 'you couldn't be more different.' The Llew Gardner show was quite arduous: it went on for an hour and I felt I was beginning to flag at the end of that busy day. But the sweet make-up girl had done her usual brilliant job on me and had dressed out my hair and my black dress looked good, so all was well. At the end of the recording Llew said to me wryly, 'Game, set and match to Blackburn: three goals to nil.' When I got home I found Ted glued to the set, following every word avidly. He was thrilled with it.

Friday, 3 January

David phoned to say he had seen the show and thought I was very good. He thinks things are going very well. He has done a lot of press briefing: result, an excellent leader in *The Times* and intelligent stuff in the *Guardian*. The *Economist*, he says, is the best of all. Of course, the *Sun* and the *Express* are as filthy as usual, but some of the independent members of the Joint Working Party are beginning to come out of their corner and tell the truth about what really happened. I told David it was important that he should do the next round of TV appearances and he agreed. But he summed up: 'The right course is to go on playing it cool as you have been doing.'

One ironic development recently has been over the self-employed. Weeks ago I told Brian O'Malley that I thought the increase in their national insurance stamp was too steep at one go. He equivocated about it, but the protest has grown and grown. Thanks to Jack's note circulated to all Labour MPs and Brian's brilliant handling in the House we have got away with it, but I am still unhappy. After our last parliamentary debate Brian told my Ted that he realized he had made a mistake and let me down. I don't hold it against him, but I shall be labelled as being ideologically hostile to the self-employed to the end of time. Ah well, that is how political reputations are made. Brian has promised me that he will try to do something to correct the position in our new Pensions Bill.[1]

[1] Brian O'Malley's proposals were actuarially fair. Under Sir Keith Joseph's Act of the previous year the national insurance contributions of the self-employed had been put on a new basis: in part flat-rate and in part related to a band of their profits. This was due to come into operation in April 1975 and the Tory Act had fixed the profit-related contribution at 5 per cent. Since then we had substantially increased pensions and all contributions had to be increased to pay for it. Brian O'Malley, to whom I had delegated these matters, decided to help the self-employed on low earnings by making no further increase in the flat-rate part of their contribution while increasing the profit-related contribution from 5 per cent to 8 per cent and extending the band of profits on which it was payable. The result was that men at the top end of the band found themselves paying a sudden impost of about £3 per week. There was an enormous outcry and the Tories in the House denounced it as 'harsh and vindictive'. While agreeing with Brian that the increase was strictly fair in relation to what employed people were paying, I felt it was too sudden and politically unwise, but he had defended it so brilliantly in the House that it was too late to change it. The row with the self-employed was to go on for months. With the introduction of our new pensions scheme in 1978 the profit-related contribution was brought back to 5 per cent.

Saturday, 4 January

Harold has made one of his great showdown speeches about strikes. If this is to be the way we tackle the economic crisis that faces us, heaven help us. I do wish Harold wouldn't go off half-cock without consulting Cabinet. It is not that the substance of his speech is wrong: merely its tone and timing.

Monday, 6 January

Back to a crowded day of work at the office. David is very proud of the job he has done with the press over the consultants' contract – and rightly. Certainly, it has produced a most helpful leader in the *Observer* – of all places. 'I headed off Nora Beloff anyway,' he chuckled. My long talk on the phone with John Fryer of the *Sunday Times* has also brought results – but not in their editorial comment, which is particularly snide about me. I believe I am in for a sustained 'it is time Barbara retired' campaign in the press. It is not that I am noticeably older than Jim Callaghan or Mike Foot: merely that I am a woman and so more vulnerable to the 'surely she's getting old?' kind of talk.

It was a tribute to the way I have managed to build a team among disparate Ministers that one of the items David raised at the ministerial lunch was the medical directives of the EEC.[1] Laurie Pavitt has sent me a copy of the letter he has written to Jim Callaghan expressing alarm that the directives will undermine the NHS: with their free movement arrangements they will open the door to consultants doing morning sessions in Paris and afternoon sessions on private practice in Britain. I had sent David a Minute about this and he was quite frank about the problem: either we went ahead with the debate in the House on the matter next week and faced a parliamentary row, or we stopped the directives in their tracks and exacerbated our row with the consultants. I said that, if things had been otherwise with the profession at the present time, I would have opposed the directives. As it was, I agreed with David that the best thing was to try to get this item removed from the agenda for the meeting of plenipotentiaries next Wednesday (Belgium is apparently objecting anyway) and from the agenda of the Council of Ministers on the 20th. I sent him off to try and fix this with Roy Hattersley, Jim being abroad. We really are a highly civilized ministerial team.

After lunch we held the first of the top-level discussions for which Philip had asked. He had come in to see me just before Christmas to say that he felt that the people on the health side of the department were less in touch with me than the rest of the department and he would like it very much if each Monday, after our ministerial lunch, I and the two Ministers would hold an informal survey of the whole policy scene with himself, the Chief Medical Officer and Errington. I suspect it is his way of offsetting the dominance of our ministerial lunches. I told him I had no objection at all; indeed, I would welcome every opportunity of getting to know more about the health side.

[1] Ever since 1969 the Commission of the EEC had been trying to get a directive adopted to provide for freedom of establishment for self-employed medical practitioners and dental surgeons throughout the Community. Following Britain's entry, we had become involved in the discussions of the draft directive.

Philip, at my request, had chosen the agenda and the first item was a curious one: our 'relations' with the Treasury. Nervously they explained that what they meant was that Treasury officials had told them there had built up a positive hostility to the department on the part of the Treasury Ministers and this was now affecting our negotiating position. For example, Treasury officials were trying to renege on the commitment to inflation-proof the NHS, 'though I am sure we shall overcome this,' Philip added hastily. We were frankly puzzled; Brian, David and I all said we got on like a house on fire with Denis Healey and Joel Barnett, even if Edmund was a more difficult customer. 'No one can really get to know him,' added Brian. Philip finally confessed, as though it was being dragged out of him under torture, that the trouble had been caused by Special FAM: Treasury felt we were pulling a fast one on them after I had agreed to postpone the introduction of child allowance until 1977. I, conciliatory as always, said that I would bear the point in mind, but Brian got quite truculent, asking, 'What is the moral we should draw from all that? That we should give up fighting for things? After all, a Cabinet can always say no.' Philip beat a deprecatory retreat, but the next item, too, was significant. Errington has sent me a Minute stressing the pressure under which we are putting policy divisions in the department by our constant requests for information on this and that and for the exploration of new ideas. I said I thought that this buzz of creative activity was going to be forced to a standstill anyway by lack of money, while Brian was gentleness itself, because he knows what devoted service he has had from the social security side, above all from the younger ones. These are the great restraints facing reformist Ministers: the Treasury and the sheer over-straining of the administrative machine.

I arrived at Home Policy Committee of the NEC without anticipating anything significant: I had even forgotten we had to elect a new chairman. I had assumed that Jim would continue in the job, but he wasn't there, being on his tour of Africa. The meeting was sparsely attended and when Ron asked for nominations for chairman Frank Allaun promptly nominated Wedgie. John Chalmers seconded. Denis Healey equally promptly said he thought a Minister ought not to be in the chair and he was backed by Shirley. Denis then proposed a succession of people, who refused. And so, by default, Wedgie went unopposed into the chair. I think Frank Allaun would have got the job if he had played his cards less precipitately.

Tuesday, 7 January

Got to the International Committee in good time to make sure Mik got the chairmanship. I need not have worried: he was not opposed. I am amused to read the great press headlines about Wedgie's election yesterday: the *Mail* excelled itself with 'Benn's New Power Grab', while the *Mirror* talked of his 'triumph'. In fact, if the press were a little more literate, and not given to what Nye called 'the politics of demonology', they would realize that there is growing up in the NEC a new coalition between Right and Left behind the doctrine that Ministers should take a back place on the NEC. I think we have managed to defuse the Government–NEC confrontation because Harold is managing to keep a close liaison with the trade unions. Jack Jones's response to Harold's weekend speech on strikes, for instance, has been surprisingly mild.

I hurried from Transport House to St James's Square for a meeting with Mike to discuss what I could say to the GPs when they come to see me tomorrow. There is no doubt we shall be faced with sanctions unless we can satisfy them that, their interim pay claim having been kiboshed by their Review Body, they will be sure to get their full award in April.[1] Of course, Mike hummed and hawed about how we could not give any group of workers an 'absolute guarantee', but he was obviously sympathetic and to my relief volunteered a form of words to the effect that we would not treat them any worse than we had treated the civil servants under the Top Salaries Report. This means that no doctor will have his increase staged, as those on salaries above £13,000 will, because he doesn't get that kind of money. I had myself told Gedling we should press for that formula. But Mike went further and he went up in my estimation enormously when he rejected the suggestion of one of his officials that we must consult Treasury. Apparently, Edmund Dell had written saying that we must agree a form of words and I told Mike that if Treasury officials got in on the act there would be so much nit-picking we should never get anything on which we could avoid a breakdown tomorrow. Mike said in his mild way that he thought we ought to be able to work out something satisfactory among ourselves. His most reassuring words were that he had no doubt that the doctors would have to get their money in April. I as good as intimated to him that I would resign if the doctors were picked on for a unilateral application of an unspoken incomes policy.

Back at the office we spent several hours preparing for the other showdown we face tomorrow: the unexpected ultimatum from the junior hospital doctors.[2] David was very good as we worked out our line. But he and I both became tense as we turned to the consultants' contract. It is clear that David is edging me remorselessly towards a concession on career supplements; he even wanted me to volunteer it. This I refused to do. Eventually we agreed that we would in due course use the Royal Colleges as our mediators. (Henry Yellowlees says that they, while anxious to mediate, are very conscious of the fact that they are the people who are held to have sold out to Nye Bevan all those years ago.) I also said I had never been happy about the offset[3] and

---

[1] Despite Lord Halsbury's resignation as chairman, the DDRB had pressed ahead with its examination of the doctors' and dentists' demand for an 18 per cent interim pay increase. It found (Cmnd. 5849) that the case for special treatment in breach of the twelve-month rule had not been made out, but gave warning of its 'firm intention' to recommend substantial catching-up increases at the annual review in April.

[2] They had told the press that, unless I gave them a written assurance that they could have a forty-hour week from July 1975, they would start an immediate work-to-rule.

[3] In our proposals for the new contract we had pointed out that one of the purposes of the existing system of merit awards had been to bring consultants' earnings in the NHS more into line with those in the private sector. Yet the bulk of the awards had gone to those already supplementing their earnings through private practice. We argued, therefore, that there was no justification for extending our proposed new system of career supplements to consultants with large private earnings. Consultants with private practice would be eligible for the new awards for prestige purposes, but their private earnings would be offset against the value of the supplements and in some cases no money at all would be paid. On 7 January the *Economist* had carried an editorial article endorsing our intention to give greater recognition to whole-timers and expressing surprise at the generosity of the Government in agreeing to a new contract which it described as 'a new deal, which is bound to be costly, for doctors at the top of their profession'.

would have preferred to fight on the basic principle of concentrating the career supplements on the whole-timers. David got tetchy at this and said I should have lost the support of the moderate press if I had (though the piece in the *Economist* does not bear him out). He is convinced I shall have to give way on the offset, and, with Jack Straw and Ian Gillis signalling alarm at his views from the end of the table, I told him that, although it might be possible to make some adjustments here, I was not prepared to surrender the whole aim of getting the merit award money into the hands of those who need it most. But my heart sank when, after the meeting, David said in an unguarded, relaxed moment, 'You will see that the *Guardian* will be saying that this is the way to a compromise.' 'I wonder who will have inspired that?' I replied sweetly. But I am angry at David's determination to railroad me.

Wednesday, 8 January

A most successful day. First the junior hospital doctors turned out to be nice, young, reasonable chaps, though one of them was obviously learning to be tough. They were primarily concerned with the fact that officials had fobbed them off on an exact date for their new contract. They melted when I said there had been a genuine misunderstanding – that I was *not* trying to stall on the date and that we should proceed to discuss the most feasible administrative timetable for introducing it. I had been determined not to let the talks break down and was ready with a formula asking them to come back and see me next week if they had produced unexpected demands which made it necessary. But they didn't. Nonetheless, it became clear as we proceeded that the crucial point was not so much the date as the fact that they wanted to produce a definition of the new contract that would enable them to go to the Review Body for some kind of payment for the hours they work between forty and eighty, instead of giving the second set of forty hours free as they do now. David had wisely warned me beforehand that I could not afford to be put in the position of appearing to argue that they must work eighty hours for their basic pay, for both David and I (and the TUC) think that their present hours are outrageous. But all we conceded was that we knew they would go to the Review Body arguing for a hefty overtime rate, while we would go and argue for a modest one. They merely grinned at this and cheerfully agreed to insert a paragraph into our joint communiqué saying that each side would make its separate approach. But, as always, it took ages to agree on the communiqué.[1] They asked to retire for a moment while we sat and drafted hopefully. As we did I said to Henry, 'Why is it these chaps are so much more rational than consultants?' Henry said he thought the reason was that these boys had been reared in the NHS, while some of the most intransigent consultants went back to pre-NHS days. Whatever the explanation, all went well, and they were warmly forthcoming at the press conference. We were all jubilant at our success and David urged me: 'Whatever else you do

[1] We announced that from July 1975 each junior doctor would be issued with a personal contract stating explicitly the 'units of medical time' for which he had contracted to be on duty. The contract, effective from October, would be based on a standard working week of forty hours with a further commitment to meet the needs of the Health Service at the discretion of the employing authority. The implications for the juniors' pay would be dealt with by the Review Body in April, with each side giving separate evidence as to what the implications should be.

you must get on TV about this, so you are shown to be the Secretary of State who gets agreement, not controversy.' But he and I agreed that officials' naïveté in the negotiating committee had been appalling. It is this second-hand control of negotiations conducted by us Ministers which is so dangerous. I asked Norman, when I had a moment to surface from the rush, what had happened to the processing of my decision to appoint Bill McCarthy as industrial adviser.[1] Norman looked at Raymond, who said that we had all been very busy but he would look into it. My guess is that the department is playing for time in the hope that I will forget it. One thing stuck in my memory from the discussions with the junior hospital doctors and that was when the most vocal of them said that they wanted an 'industrial-type' contract. So do they all in the NHS these days: from nurses to consultants. I don't think they realize it, but the professional middle classes are digging their own graves.

All this meant I was late for the GPs, who eventually came trooping in, looking very serious. Tony Keable-Elliott was their sole spokesman and he made out an impressive, reasonable but firm case. In reply I spelt out, slowly and carefully, the problem that no government could ever give them 'cast iron guarantees' about accepting the report of their Review Body. But I went on to detail the assurances we had worked out with Mike, reading the words he had agreed. They were obviously impressed. They asked to retire, but Henry was sure we had done the trick. And so it proved, though Tony warned me sternly that he could not guarantee what his chaps would do when he reported back tomorrow. We then proceeded to draft another agreed press statement: more time for them to retire, more to-ing and fro-ing by Jack and Ian Gillis. (God knows were Peter is.) My aim now was to get a flicker of warmth into their response, though I appreciated Tony's point that for him to appear to have done a big deal with me would be the kiss of death. They argued that the best way for them to get acceptance of my assurances might be for them to agree to call for post-dated resignations as a counter-assurance for their members if the Government went back on my promises. I said despairingly, 'I do hope we shall stop talking the language of confrontation, or I fear that the NHS may really face collapse.' They all nodded earnestly and my plea did the trick: back they came with the sentence that they felt the talks had been 'worthwhile'. It was enough, and I, feeling pretty limp, had to go into the press conference and onto TV conscious of the fact that the last thing I must do was to appear to have scored a victory. So I played it very muted and Ted, watching at home, was disappointed by my cautious tone. But I remain firmly convinced that the only way to secure the real victories is to forgo one's personal triumph and let it appear that neither side has won.

As we were all waiting in my room for the press statement to be agreed I signed fifty letters to the self-employed over the increase in their insurance contributions. 'This protest will not die down, because it is justified,' I remarked wearily. David grinned: 'When I come to write my diary I shall record that you warned us this would happen.'

---

[1] Dr W. E. J. McCarthy, Fellow of Nuffield College, Oxford, and university lecturer in industrial relations. He eventually joined the department as part-time adviser on 2 April with a special remit to study the workings of the NHS Whitley Council machinery. His report on this, 'Making Whitley Work', was published in 1977. He was made a life peer in 1975.

At 10pm I collected four weary members of my staff into my car, which meant I had to sit on Jack's knee. In this undignified posture we toured London, dropping them off at Victoria and King's Cross and finally arriving at home. I took Jack and Edna upstairs to have a celebratory drink with Ted. I love these dear people, and, despite my tiredness, an unaccustomed euphoria came welling up in me.

Thursday, 9 January

Ted and I were astonished that none of yesterday's achievements got even a mention in the review of the papers on radio, but they did carry my last night's recording on *Today* and I was gratified that at that late hour I had managed to be so articulate. The *Guardian* gave me a good show, but most of the populars hastily downgraded the row that had turned out to be a settlement. I said to Ted without rancour that the selectivity of the press in its treatment of my affairs was eternally revealing. Here were stories carried every day about the uncontrollable progress of inflation, yet the press continued to highlight Shirley as one of our most 'successful' Ministers (*vide* last weekend's *Sunday Times*). Even Ted agreed that, if I had been Secretary of State for Prices, the tone would have been very different. 'The only way I could climb to the top of the league in their eyes,' I told him, 'is if I were to become pro-Market.' For once he did not bridle in defence of his profession.

At Cabinet everyone greeted me warmly: 'You are having a dreadful time.' Harold congratulated me on yesterday's victories. 'I said when I read them that you were pursuing Marlborough's strategy.' (I haven't had time to read up my Marlborough.) He congratulated me in Cabinet too. Wedgie, as always, was warmly adulatory. I am sorry if I think it is a bit calculated, but he certainly does it very well, making one feel successful and wanted just when one needs it most. Perhaps there is a human justification for the formula. I really ought to try it more. I then went on to win my case for Special FAM, perhaps because, resigned to increasing economic difficulties in the country, I was more gentle in arguing it. But I think that the real reason was that Cabinet's conscience has been disturbed. Whatever the reason, Denis was mild in his opposition compared with Edmund Dell. (That chap is capable of more misdirected intellectual horsepower than anyone I know.) Tony C., predictably, said that although he had a lot of sympathy with my argument the greatest problem in relation to poverty was housing, 'and I could do with £9 million to help me deal with it'. Harold was obviously anxious to help, and Shirley played into his hands, saying that she accepted my proposals in principle but thought we should discuss the timing in Ministerial Economic Strategy Committee as part of our package of measures to deal with the effects of the rise in the nationalized industries' prices. Peter supported her and I accepted this qualification willingly. Denis climbed down at once but said he might want to announce the decision himself as part of a Budget statement, because he 'might have to do a very nasty Budget package indeed as far as living standards are concerned'. And so it was agreed: one more victory to make the department wonder how I get away with it. (In fact, I do it by very careful preparation and very well-prepared arguments. That is where people like Brian A-S. and Tony Lynes are so valuable.)

I had given Harold notice that I wanted to raise the EEC medical directives. He got a bit cross because he said I ought to have raised the matter before the recess, but the fact is that I haven't had a moment to gen up on it. I pointed out that Laurie Pavitt had written to Jim saying that freedom of establishment meant that our doctors could whizz over to Brussels in the morning for a bit of lucrative activity on the side, returning home in the afternoon to put in some private practice here. Derek Stevenson has already hailed the directives as a means of escaping from the 'shackles' of the NHS. I said David and I had discussed the matter amicably but that there was bound to be a row in the House. I couldn't leave David to deal with it because he was too pro-directive, but if I dealt with it myself I should be bound to express my alarm and that would still further alienate the BMA. 'I realize,' I said, 'that the free movement of labour is not part of our renegotiation,' at which Peter said angrily, 'Of course it is.' Ted Short said, 'It is all part of the question of sovereignty.' (I suspect that man is getting more anti-Market every day.) Harold said quickly that the whole matter must be discussed at a meeting of European Questions Committee of Cabinet on Monday and that I must put in a paper explaining how all this had come about. The trouble is that I am extremely vulnerable for not having taken this thing on board before.

On the way to St Christopher's Hospice[1] for a long-promised ministerial visit, Henry travelled with me in the car and reported mysterious cloak-and-dagger overtures from Astley and Stevenson of the BMA. They wanted to see him – very hush-hush. Was it all right for him to go? I said, of course. My settlements with the juniors and the GPs have obviously had an effect. The *Evening News* also carried a story that David Owen is to see the BMA secretly with new proposals, and Henry explained elaborately that Astley had been trying to speak to David on the phone. I think David rather fancies the idea, but I have told him sharply that there must be no private enterprise. All *démarches* vis-à-vis the consultants must be discussed and agreed collectively, otherwise we shall find ourselves in a mess.

The people at St Christopher's were overwhelmed that I had come despite all the pressures on me. I told them – and meant it – that it was a refreshment to get out into the field and see them at work. They are the most marvellous bunch of people I have ever met. Dr Saunders particularly impressed me. As I toured the wards I could see for myself what their extraordinarily sensitive approach to terminal illness means to the patients. This is medicine as it ought to be – patient care at its most loving and comprehensive. It took some of the nasty taste of the dispute out of my mouth. It was late when I got on my night sleeper to Blackburn.

Friday, 10 January

Norman phoned to report the outcome of Henry's talk with Astley. Apparently they want to know whether I will agree to modify the existing contract instead of proceeding with the new one and have set out four additions they want to make to it, including payment for extra sessions. Henry, it appears, is inclined to nibble at this, but Philip

[1] An independent hospital specializing in terminal care. Beds were available for NHS patients through contractual arrangements with the regional authority.

has said emphatically that he doesn't see how I could possibly accept. I agree with him. I can see us being inched into a trap, ending up with getting the worst of both worlds. Of course it would suit the consultants to stick to their 'open-ended' contract, with the lack of supervision it entails, if they can get overtime on top of it. Norman says Astley is badgering Henry for my reply. Henry is stalling and saying that he can't get hold of me on a 'secret' line, but he really would like me to give him something to tell them. I told Norman to tell him to go on hedging. I certainly wasn't prepared to comment until we had had a chance to discuss the proposals thoroughly on Monday.

Saturday, 11 January

I am quite enjoying the party's annual local government conference at Manchester. My group's discussion this afternoon on the NHS and the reorganization of local government went very well, though I was irritated to find the press, radio and cameras hanging on my every word. No doubt they are hoping I shall let drop some indiscretion about the dispute with the consultants. But I kept mum. David brought with him the draft of Monday's statement on the dispute which I have volunteered to make to the House in order to forestall Geoffrey Howe (who has written me yet another letter and who is obviously trying to set himself up as a go-between). I tell David I will take the statement to bed with me and we agree to meet at 9.15 in the morning to finalize it.

In the evening Tom Taylor, Jim Mason and their spouses, who had come over from Blackburn, take me off for a meal and we bring Tony Crosland and David Lipsey along with us. I quizz Tony about the use he makes of David (his political adviser) and find that he keeps him mainly on research. David does not brief him on non-departmental matters for Cabinet and Tony obviously thought what Jack does for me was a good idea. Nor does Tony have weekly ministerial lunches: merely a chat with his Ministers once a fortnight. When I asked him if the overlordship system worked, he hesitated. He thought there was enough of a case for it in the field of Environment to warrant keeping the experiment on for a ten-year trial, though he was sure it had been right to break up Trade and Industry. He agreed with me rather wistfully that overlording a team of full Ministers *was* rather difficult: they *did* become rather prima donna-ish. 'If I could have got away with Ministers of State I should much have preferred it,' he told me. I also asked him if being an overlord gave him more time to think out long-term strategy. 'Hopefully it will, though I can't say I was able to do much of that last year; two general elections took up too much time.'

Sunday, 12 January

David Owen and I met early, a little bleary-eyed after a late night of social activities. I had rewritten a large part of the statement and we agreed the final points. In a Minute to me outlining Astley's proposals for amending the existing contract,[1] David had

---

[1] Dr Astley wanted extra payments for family planning sessions, for sickness and exceptional leave, for 'out of hours' work and for being on call to be included in the existing contract without any of the reforms we wanted to see.

commented that this was a very dangerous development, but, typically, this morning he seemed to be wavering. 'I think you will have to concede extra sessions,' he said at one point. I headed him off this sternly by quoting his own Minute at him. It was his turn to take one group session of the conference and he spoke extremely well. He is an able lad with a lot of good radical instincts, but he needs stiffening.

Monday, 13 January

Got up early to see Mother on my way in. She was as defiant as ever, saying she was bored and wanted to come home, though Matron says she is more physically dependent than ever. Then into the BBC to do a piece on International Women's Year for *Woman's Hour*. At the office we had another of our long meetings to discuss the draft statement that David and I had prepared yesterday. These meetings are tremendously exhausting because everyone round the table – Philip, Henry, David, Raymond Gedling, Jack Straw and Peter Brown – queries every word anyone else suggests. We are all very conscious now that one of our biggest mistakes in dealing with the consultants had been to leave the wording of the proposed new standard contract to officials. We should have realized that this was a highly politically sensitive document that ought to have been drafted by politicians. I think the bull point in the overtures we are making to the consultants is the offer to get the new contract priced without the profession first committing itself to it. I believe that fear about money is at the root of the consultants' rejection of our proposals and I have told David time and again that it would be madness to concede on any of the ideological parts of the contract (e.g. career supplements) until we have found out what the chaps' anxieties really are. I believe I have got to stuff their mouths with the nearest thing to gold I can get out of the Treasury.[1]

It was a mad rush to get to the House in time for the statement and I was a bit breathless, but it was a walk-over.[2] Geoffrey Howe made a mess of things, and, while choosing my words carefully so as not to exacerbate the situation, I didn't give an inch. Ted, in the gallery as usual, was delighted. He said my case sounded so reasonable. But there is no doubt that opinion among the consultants is hardening. They are voting against the contract overwhelmingly, even though many of them are drawing the line at sanctions. We had another office discussion as to what Henry might say to Astley and Stevenson. I told him to send them a copy of my statement and to tell them I would be glad to meet them again to deal with any points in it they wanted clarified. We also discussed how we could clear up the widespread misunderstandings that have arisen and decided that the first thing was to see the three presidents of the Royal Colleges tomorrow and see how they could help. We are anxious now to try and save the new contract, because otherwise we could be

[1] I was echoing a phrase used by Nye Bevan about his deal with the consultants when setting up the National Health Service. It is quoted by Professor Abel-Smith in his book *Hospitals*, where he writes: 'The whole Bill was made remarkably generous to the hospital medical staffs. As Bevan remarked to a friend: "I stuffed their mouths with gold."'

[2] I was able to report my settlements with the GPs and the junior doctors. On the consultants' dispute I reiterated that the Government had no wish to impose a new contract on them and was willing to ask the Review Body to cost the new contract before the consultants committed themselves to it.

manoeuvred into concessions on the existing one that would leave us with all the disadvantages and none of the advantages.

Tuesday, 14 January

Ted Short presided over Legislation Committee like a headmaster, giving everyone a bad report because they had not got their legislation ready on time. When it came to me I said innocently that our two Bills (the new Pensions Scheme and Child Benefits) were ready, or almost so, adding that it really was only common sense for us to include Special FAM in the Child Benefits Bill instead of doing it separately. It would certainly save time. Ted, who had been getting ready to tell me I couldn't have the Child Benefits Bill this session, said primly, 'Barbara has got us over a barrel again.' I protested that I couldn't help it if I was a good girl and had done my homework, at which everyone laughed and Bob Mellish said, 'There is only one answer to Barbara: why don't we give her her own parliament?' Ted said he would have to discuss it with me and we would have to get the approval of Cabinet, but I bet I win. I have now got the reputation of being incorrigibly cunning at getting my own way. Wedgie was heavily sarcastic when it came to his turn. The reason why he had made so little progress with his Industry Bill, he said, was that some Ministers kept raising queries and obstructions. Could Ted do something about *that*?

We next had to hurry into a special Cabinet so that we could hear Jim report on Rhodesia. He told us that last August there had been a meeting between Vorster and Kaunda (the first Cabinet had heard of it) which had led to the Lusaka agreement between some of the African leaders and Smith. The agreement was an unwritten one, so inevitably there was now dispute about what it had comprised. But the key thing was that Vorster was extremely anxious to get a Rhodesia settlement and was ready to put pressure on Smith. Now Kaunda, Nyerere and Gowon wanted Britain to call a constitutional conference. Vorster, for his part, wanted Britain to keep out of it as long as possible and Smith to talk to the Africans 'on a realistic basis'. Jim wanted to tell the House that afternoon that he was willing to hold such a conference soon and the date he had in mind was mid-March. He himself would like to hold it in London, but they wanted Livingstone. He was sure we would lose African goodwill unless we agreed to the conference, but thought we should send someone, possibly Tom McNally, to Salisbury first to make sure that Smith would agree.

Acting purely on instinct (because I haven't been following these developments closely) I broke through the approving noises to express my doubts. Smith, I said, would never change and, if he tried to, his hard-liners would ditch him. The only thing that had got him as far as he had gone was Vorster's pressure and I was worried that we were proposing to ignore Vorster's advice that we should keep out of it. It was tempting to see ourselves as holding our last great imperial conference, designed to impose the Pax Britannica on a reluctant Salisbury, but I could see us getting embroiled in a futile exercise, with Smith once again out-manoeuvring us. Vorster was right: a settlement had to be forged in direct talks between Smith and the Africans. If we intervened we should only be caught in the crossfire and could find ourselves becoming the target of both sides (just as we had done in Northern Ireland,

I might have added). Harold didn't like this at all. He reminded me that we had 'juridical responsibility' for Rhodesia. In April he faced another Commonwealth PMs' conference and would be under attack if we had done nothing to respond to the Africans' request. We must restore their confidence in us. But when Roy Mason supported me, with Harold Lever and others nodding approvingly, Jim admitted that there was a great deal in what I had said and agreed to tone his statement down. He accepted my suggestion that he should at least say that there would be no point in holding such a conference unless a considerable measure of agreement had been reached first. Afterwards, Harold Lever said to me that we would be 'on a hiding to nothing' if we called such a conference. The trouble, I replied, was that people like Harold and Jim cannot resist playing on the world stage. Later, when Jim made his statement in the House, Arthur Bottomley made exactly the same point as I had done and said to me in the division lobby, 'I am sure *you* agree with what I said.'

The meeting with the presidents of the three Royal Colleges on the consultants' dispute was a poor do: they were so terrified of being accused by the BMA of selling out the profession, as it was alleged they had done to Nye in 1948. All they did was to say I must emphasize my willingness to negotiate. My statement yesterday had been helpful, but they feared it would not be enough to get the sanctions called off at the CCHMS meeting on Thursday.[1] They would not, however, agree to our issuing a joint statement after the meeting, as a vehicle enabling me to repeat my willingness to talk. And Sir Rodney Smith[2] has gone off unilaterally with a letter to *The Times* which we all think will only make matters worse. Afterwards Norman said to me how shocked he had been at their feebleness; here they were, the leaders of the profession, frightened even to say 'Boo' to the BMA goose. But Henry has had his further meeting with Stevenson and his deputy, Gullick. They were, he said, impressed by my statement yesterday, but wanted a number of points 'clarified'. We decided that I should send a written reply which they can use at their meeting on Thursday and I asked David and Henry to draft something.

I was flagging by now, after a fortnight's non-stop pressure, so I went home to bacon and egg and an early bed.

Wednesday, 15 January

A hurried hair-do and into the car, finishing dressing as I went along to Lancaster House for the inaugural reception of International Women's Year. Rather to my surprise it went like a bomb; Princess Alexandra was utterly charming, with a softness and naturalness her mother never had. She worked very hard at questioning and talking to everybody. Harold came along with Mary [Wilson] and Marcia [Lady Falkender] in tow and stayed to the very end, obviously enjoying himself. Jim was

---

[1] The Central Committee for Hospital Medical Services is a committee of the BMA which looks after the interests of senior medical hospital staff. It consists of eighty-five members elected by all consultants in the NHS on a regional basis and its main job is to determine policy. Proposals discussed in the Joint Negotiating Committee are usually referred to it for approval.

[2] Sir Rodney Smith, a surgeon at St George's Hospital, London, had been President of the Royal College of Surgeons since 1973.

there, and I was particularly touched that Len Murray should accompany Marie Patterson and Ethel Chipchase.[1] The press interest was greater than I'd expected and I did endless radio interviews. By the time it was all over I had no time for lunch. I swallowed three of Edna's digestive biscuits before hurrying to the department for six TV interviews for foreign parts. I could have done without this Women's Year lark at this particular time. The irony of it is that I have always found these women's issues a bore, but, having taken on this job as co-chairman of the Women's National Commission at Harold's request, I intend to make a go of it. Mary Wilson said to me, as we escorted her and Harold from the reception, that she was always telling Harold's office they ought to make more use of her. 'With the Leader of the Opposition a bachelor we have an advantage we ought to exploit, but they won't listen to me.'

David and Henry came over with the draft of their letter to Stevenson. I thought it was very good but changed the emphasis here and there, making it warmer in tone and eliminating anything that sounded a bit truculent.[2] Afterwards, David told me Henry had been tickled pink by my attitude and now had his tail up, having been very depressed yesterday. 'The trouble is,' said David, grinning in his handsome, boyish way, 'that the office don't understand our rows. They don't realize that we can argue like that but that basically we agree.' I replied that if we had had someone like George Godber,[3] who would have argued ferociously with us, we should not have had to conduct so much of the argument between ourselves. He took the point: 'Yes, I shouldn't then have felt I had to put so much of the medical point of view.' He chuckled and said, 'I've been talking to John Morris and we both of us agree that you ...' He let the sentence trail off, as he often does. 'But a year-and-a-half of you is about as much ...' He grinned affectionately. In the division lobby I tackled John Morris: 'So you and David have been swopping notes about how terrible it is to work for me,' I teased. 'Not a bit of it,' he laughed. 'It was marvellous. You taught me everything. One-and-a-half years? I managed two-and-a-half, but I was nearly dead at the end of it. I have never worked so hard in all my life.'

Thursday, 16 January

A short night's sleep and then into Cabinet. We have had a good press for our women's reception yesterday and now Italian TV want a picture of my Ted washing up! They say it will encourage Italian women to strike a blow for equality. The *Evening Standard* said that yesterday I looked as though I had just come from Elizabeth Arden's hands. If only they knew! I haven't had time to sew on a button, or

[1] Respectively Chairman and President of the TUC and Secretary of the Women's Advisory Committee of the TUC.

[2] I stressed yet again that I was anxious not to hold up the consultants' pay review due in April on the basis of their existing contract. If, however, we could agree the general outlines of the new contract over the following few weeks, I would ask the Review Body to put some financial figures on it at the same time so that the consultants could decide whether they wanted to go ahead with it. But I insisted that the differential was not negotiable. I said I could not enter into detailed negotiations while sanctions were continuing, but was willing for there to be an 'initial clarification meeting' within the Joint Negotiating Committee. Stevenson replied at once accepting the offer.

[3] Sir George Godber, a formidable personality, had been Chief Medical Officer at the department from 1960 until he retired in 1973.

get enough sleep, let alone have a face massage. The gossip writer said, 'How does she keep so young?' Answer: because I am fully extended, intellectually and emotionally, all the time; yet, when I get down to HCF to the dogs, the garden, the woods and my home, I can revert to nature in five minutes flat. I love my dual personality life and both sides are equally important to me.

On parliamentary business at Cabinet, Jim grumbled about the backbenchers' attitude to the EEC directives and about the way they kept insisting on querying policy in advance of decisions in the Council of Ministers or of negotiations that are going on. 'They are trying to alter the relationship between Parliament and the executive,' he rumbled. 'They want to give Ministers instructions before they go to Brussels.' But the whole essence of negotiations, he continued, was that Ministers must be given a free hand and then face the music afterwards: *vide* the Agricultural Price Review. Before a row could develop between those of us who feel that mandating the members of the Council of Ministers is not a bad idea and Jim and Fred, who want a free hand at Brussels, Ted Short said hastily that he and Jim would soon be circulating a paper to Cabinet on how we should handle these debates. To do him credit, Ted is not satisfied with the present position, but of course it is endemic in membership of the Community. The EEC only works on the basis of tortuous compromises, under which country X gives up one of its essential positions in order to salvage two others of equal urgency. It is government by the fractionalization of policy: that is why the so-called 'moderates' are so attracted to it. They have a built-in alibi for accepting a third of a loaf. Under such a system it is impossible to mandate anyone, but it is such a break with what we have been accustomed to under our parliamentary tradition of voting on clear-cut blacks and whites that most MPs don't yet realize what is going to hit them. The 'international' government many of them will be voting for will turn out to be merely a Europeanized version of 'national government'.

Before Cabinet Bob said to me, 'Ask Ted Short to read out the letter he has had from John Stonehouse; it is a scream.' But in the event Ted was abrupt about the message he had received and said he was not at liberty to disclose it. The British Consul General was chasing Stonehouse and his lawyer round Australia, but it seemed inevitable that a Select Committee would have to be appointed to get him expelled from Parliament.[1] Wedgie went up in my estimation when he said he hoped we would proceed cautiously. He himself was one of the few people who had been expelled from the House of Commons and he knew how complicated the matter could be. On what grounds were we doing it? Not because of any crime Stonehouse had committed: that had not been proved. His long absence? Other MPs had absented themselves for longer periods (Harold Lever ducked self-consciously at that one!).

---

[1] Some two months earlier John Stonehouse, Labour MP for Walsall North and a former Minister, had disappeared, faking his drowning on Miami beach. He was eventually discovered in Australia, which he had entered on a false passport. He claimed that he was being blackmailed and had suffered a 'brainstorm', but later it emerged that he was in financial difficulties. Pressures had been put on him to resign his seat and in his letter to Ted Short he had agreed to do so. Later he changed his mind and the problem of what to do about the absent MP was to plague the Commons for months. It was finally settled in August 1976, by his trial and imprisonment on eighteen charges involving theft and false pretences. He then resigned his seat and Privy Councillorship.

He thought we should show some compassion for a sick man and that someone should go out to Australia to try to talk to him. We must not be governed by the emotional pressure from some quarters to take revenge on him. When Harold argued that we could get Stonehouse for contempt of the House in passing himself off as dead, Elwyn nervously counselled caution. But Harold insisted that a Select Committee could take into account all Wedgie's points. 'Then we must be careful not to appoint a hanging jury,' I said and Roy backed me on this. Harold summed up that Ted should talk to the Speaker and to the Opposition and keep us in touch as to how we should proceed.

I hadn't expected to get anywhere with my paper reopening the question of whether the 1976 census should contain a question about parents' countries of birth. Home Affairs Committee (which I hadn't been able to attend) had decided overwhelmingly in December to include this question (which Alf Morris had opposed on my behalf) and Harold has circulated a Minute stating that he is normally not going to let committee decisions be reopened in Cabinet unless the Cabinet Minister concerned has reserved his or her position and the chairman has agreed it should go to Cabinet. So the odds were strongly against me, particularly as the Home Office and Employment had argued in committee that the inclusion of this question was essential for their purposes. But I feel as strongly on this issue now as I did in 1970, when we were preparing the 1971 census, and I have the backing of the Registrar General, who has sent me a Minute saying that he will not be held responsible for the damage to the census that will ensue. So I had decided to risk a Cabinet rebuff.

In the event it turned out very differently. After I had put my case strongly and Elwyn (who had been in the chair for the committee in Roy's absence) had slapped me down, a very different picture began to emerge. One after another Cabinet members admitted they hadn't been able to be present at the committee either and one of them – Mike – said that for his part he supported me. Roy stuck to the Home Office line, but unexpected support came from Harold Lever and Eric Varley, who said simply that they would resent such a question being asked of them. In the end I was defeated on the strength of the point that I could see standing out a mile: namely, that the voluntary organizations in the race relations field were now strongly in favour of the question being included. Frankly, I don't believe it. I had asked Norman that this point should be checked up carefully, but of course none of us had had time to do this and the Registrar General's brief on the point was inadequate. Anyway, it was a close thing and if I had had more time to do some checking up myself, I think I should have won. Harold Lever, to whom I had been tossing Polo mints during Cabinet (I keep a pack in my bag and feed my neighbours with them), sent me a consolatory note: 'You've got to lose in Cabinet sometimes. P.S. My vote may not always be bought so cheaply.' 'What has it got to be,' I mouthed at him, 'a two-pound box of chocolates?' Anyway the whole business showed that it is too facile to assume that if a Cabinet committee decides a matter, this necessarily reflects the view of Cabinet. The trouble, as I well know, is that desperately busy Cabinet Ministers tend to skip Cabinet committees if they can and send their juniors. Harold only allowed me to reopen this this time because, as he put it, 'We all know Barbara was tied up with the doctors and could not attend.'

Finally to the channel tunnel. Personally I am relieved that Tony Crosland has decided we can't go ahead. This is not only anti-Common Market prejudice. It is a kind of earthy feeling that an island is an island and should not be violated. Certainly I am convinced that the building of a tunnel would do something profound to the national attitude – and not certainly for the better. There is too much facile access being built into the modern world. Something should remain difficult to achieve. Typically, Tony would have preferred to have kept the scheme ticking over without commitment, but the reaction of the companies has made that impossible. So the crunch has come. Jim's was the only discordant voice. We were, he said, putting ourselves in a very difficult position with the French: 'They will use this kind of thing to damage us.' He was worried about Tony's proposal to handle it 'in this brusque way'. From his diplomatic experience he warned us that we should always 'as far as possible avoid getting into the position of being the *demandeur* with the French: they will screw you to the limit'. I thought this was a very revealing comment from someone who is now working hard to get us into Europe. It was Tony who pointed out that the French had far more to gain from the project than we had: they did not face the need for a highly expensive rail link. Fate had made us the *demandeurs* once again and Cabinet agreed we must be ready to face paying the price of blame. The theory is that the project can be reopened in five to ten years' time, but I don't think Tony is fooled by this.

At the parliamentary party meeting there were renewed rumblings about the handling of EEC directives in the House. Tonight there are some on agriculture and Bob has told Cabinet that he hopes Fred will handle them so tactfully that we can avoid a vote. I wanted to get home to bed, so I paired, though I have considerable sympathy with those on our side who want to tie Fred down in advance on CAP.

Friday, 17 January

An all-day meeting at Chequers of the Ministerial Steering Committee on Devolution. The implementation of the White Paper has raised so many difficulties that Harold has wisely decided we should all get away and concentrate our minds on solving them. The papers we had to read were a foot deep, but they boiled down to the fact that there were about five major issues we had to decide. But first we had a Second Reading debate over the whole field which, despite the fact that Harold said we were all now bound by the White Paper, enabled the doubters over the whole business (Roy J., Reg and Elwyn) to air their views again. The debate crystallized round the question of timing. They none of them liked Ted Short's haste. Tony C. predictably found a diversion from decision-making. We must, he said, put England on the agenda of devolution. He had been very impressed at Manchester to find that the English momentum towards regional government was going much faster than it had been a year ago. 'I found a marked shift of opinion pro-regional.' Unemployment would be the dominant issue in coming months and, if we went for legislative devolution for Scotland, the English regions would wish to follow suit in order to be sure of their share of resources and they too 'will want the whole ministerial paraphernalia'. We could therefore 'slow down a bit'. Certainly there should be no firm announcements in the January debate. Reg pointed out, fairly, that the group which Tony had addressed at the local government conference had consisted exclusively of those interested in regional government, so they could hardly be held to be representative. I said I was glad that Tony had raised the question of English regionalism: until we had decided that matter there could certainly be no progress in deciding the form in which we could democratize the NHS.[1] But I thought feelings were still far more confused than he had made out. I did not mind our taking more time to work out the details, provided this was not used merely as an excuse for not devolving at all. I thought that devolution was only the alternative to, not a step towards, separatism. Those who had voted for the Scottish Nationalists were in favour of devolution, not separatism. (Ted nodded vigorously at that.) The longer we postponed the issue of the White (or Green) Paper the stronger it would have to be when it came. Ken Berrill told me afterwards he agreed with me.

We spent the rest of the morning on the major item: to what kind of executive should power be devolved? The committee which had been studying this under Ted had come out in favour of a Cabinet system in Scotland and a committee system in Wales. Willie said that nothing less would satisfy the Scots, while John Morris said that Wales would not insist on parity with Scotland. I backed this strongly, but the doubters' voices were heard again. Again, Tony C. was all for procrastinating: other options ought to be considered, such as power-sharing, though when Merlyn explained to us just how power-sharing was supposed to work in Northern Ireland it became less convincing as an alternative. Norman Hunt was full of his power-sharing scheme,[2] and Harold ruled that Norman might put in a paper to show how a committee system could be grafted onto a Cabinet system in Scotland. Wedgie gave us another of his apocalyptic summaries: the drive for devolution, he said, was 'part of the collapse of confidence of the English Establishment'. The trade unions knew where the reality lay: they didn't want devolution to destroy a centralized trade union movement. 'Industrial democracy brings power far nearer to where people are than

[1] My aim was to link the Health Service more closely to local government so that elected local representatives, as well as staff in the Health Service could have greater control over it and so that the health and social services could be jointly planned. Unfortunately, Peter Walker, Secretary of State for the Environment in the Heath Government, had produced a reorganization of local government which rejected the Maud Commission's proposal for enlarged authorities at district level to run most services, including the social services. Instead he truncated the district councils, including the old county boroughs, and handed their powers over to the county councils, where the Conservatives were strong. In his parallel reorganization of the NHS, Sir Keith Joseph had followed this pattern by inserting an additional, unnecessary tier of administration at county level, the Area Health Authority, between the functional tier, based on the district hospital, and the regional tier responsible for strategic services, and had given excessive control to the regional authorities. The Labour Party favoured the Maud proposals. It also became increasingly clear to me that the need in the NHS was to merge the AHAs and the districts in one local functional unit, but this only made planning sense if local government was also reorganized along the lines the Labour Party proposed.

[2] In his Memorandum of Dissent to the Kilbrandon Report, Lord Crowther-Hunt had rejected legislative devolution to Scotland and Wales as weakening the strong homogeneity of the UK. Instead he urged the setting up of intermediate level governments in the English regions, as well as Scotland and Wales, with extensive executive powers. The regional governments would be run on the local authority pattern, with a functional committee structure, and not on the Cabinet model. In order to ensure that minorities were represented, election would be by the single transferable vote system of proportional representation and power would be shared by giving the chief minority party the vice-chairmanships of all committees.

any talking shop in Edinburgh for the SNP.' He also warned that we could take no decision on these matters until the central issue of whether we went into Europe had been decided. 'If we are in the Common Market it means the break-up of the UK; if we are not, we can retain centralized government.' I had sympathy with him when he ticked off Roy J. for one of his more pontifical speeches about sovereignty. Roy had been saying that sovereignty came from the sovereign, from whom it had passed to the sovereign's Ministers. Wedgie described this contemptuously as a 'feudal fiction', adding, 'We didn't get our authority as Ministers by kissing hands but by winning votes.' What we were doing was talking about an extension of democratic self-management, he said, adding for good measure that 'the power of the trade unions is as great as that of the old landowners'. At least Roy agreed with him about that! What interested me most in the whole discussion, though, was the extent to which Willie is now committed to making devolution work, on the sensible principle that, having been overruled in the first place, he wasn't going to get left out on a limb by the doubters now.

Monday, 20 January

I had not expected any great public interest in our resumed meetings of the Liaison Committee with the TUC, so when I arrived at Congress House at 10.30am straight from HCF and struggled out of the car in mac and boots, with hair dishevelled by the pouring rain, I was dismayed to be snapped by a battery of waiting cameras. Jack Jones followed me into the building and when I moaned that the cameras had caught me with my tight tweed skirt pulled up above my knees he said almost humanly, 'That should make for good publicity.' I realized after a moment's thought that the news hounds were there expecting a major row – the only reason they ever turn up in strength. Denis's recent speech about the need to tighten the pay guidelines of the Social Contract must have made them lick their chops with expectancy. But the media will never understand this baffling movement of ours and they certainly do not understand the deep-rooted new concordat between the Government and the trade unions. They may envy it, and that is perhaps why they watch hungrily for it to disintegrate.

But when I looked round that panelled room where we meet, in such unrelieved acres of lavish woodwork, and saw Harold chatting to Jack, Denis to Len, and Hughie creeping in almost deprecatingly, I knew there wasn't going to be any row. Only Wedgie and George Smith were missing. Sid Greene was late, so Jack was voted into the chair while the rest of us quipped, 'That'll muzzle you.' Bob Mellish said to me wonderingly, 'Do you realize we haven't met since July? That shows you how time flies.' And as soon as Jack took the chair I realized how important it was for us to meet. Here is the Government, beset by so many economic difficulties it would have sunk us in 1964–70. Here was the trade union movement which had contributed so much to our 1970 defeat. And here was Jack Jones in the chair, who had always been considered by my officials, when I was at Employment and Productivity, as the archetypal trade union villain and who had in fact been arid and negative then. But today Jack sat in the chair as an almost gentle and certainly benign influence. I believe he is the greatest voice in the trade union movement today in favour of what I have always wanted to see: the trade union movement being made socialist. And what is more, he is someone who realizes that politicians have to operate in the real world as much as trade unionists do: in the world of the possible. I wonder if Ted Heath understands how much he has done by his crude clumsiness to create this miracle? I suspect the Tory Party is beginning to realize it.

Len Murray opened by introducing the TUC document outlining what would be the TUC *Economic Review*, 1975. His tone was conciliatory. On the international situation the TUC was 'greatly appreciative' of what the Government had achieved. Domestically the overriding priority was to maintain employment. On the social policy side the TUC put housing first. 'We have chosen to give it particular attention this year.' As far as the Social Contract was concerned, defence of living standards remained 'the root of the guidelines'. As for the Budget, their minds were open. It was all very low-key, with an oblique dig at Denis, who immediately asked if he could come in and then proceeded to give us a twenty-minute speech of political shrewdness plus economic gravity. It was a difficult job, in the face of the suspicions he had aroused among the unions, and as he waded through his notes (he was sitting next to me) I was once again impressed by the way he did not pull his factual punches while remaining in tune with the trade union mood.

He began by saying that this meeting was 'very well timed'. The Government was facing some very difficult problems. But he repeated with impressive emphasis his belief in the Social Contract and when he said it was 'the reason for our success so far' it carried conviction. After all, it was a Chancellor speaking – and no Chancellor in Britain had ever said it before. Then he grew grimmer. The world was now in recession. Employment was the main consideration. There was no chance of pulling out of the recession this year. The threat to jobs came from outside Britain: we had got to get a bigger share of world trade. In March 1974 our trade deficit had amounted to 4 per cent of our GDP. The oil deficit had added another 4 per cent. We had cut the trade deficit by 2 per cent, but this still meant that a 6 per cent deficit had to be covered by borrowing. 'We are spending 6 per cent more than we are earning.' (Echoes of Jim's arguments to Cabinet in 1966! But Denis was arguing in an entirely different political context and speaking a different language: the sort of political language the unions were prepared to listen to.) The borrowing we had made was entirely on commercial terms, Denis maintained, but that meant that inflation could jeopardize it. In the three months to August 1974 inflation had been running at 8 per cent. In the three months from September it had jumped to 19½ per cent. In the same period earnings had risen 28½ per cent. The oil producers were simply not prepared to put their money into a country where its value could be undermined. 'The flurry last December[1] cost us $1,000 million of our reserves.' If inflation undermined commer-

---

[1] In December 1974, there had been a run on sterling following Saudi Arabia's announcement that she no longer wanted to take her oil payments from Aramco in pounds. The 'flurry' was heightened by the publication of the trade figures which showed that the £543 million visible trade deficit in November had been the largest monthly deficit ever recorded. Denis Healey, who had been paying a visit to Saudi Arabia to discuss greater economic co-operation and trade, told the House on 13 December that he had been assured the decision was 'purely to simplify matters' and that the Saudis planned to maintain and increase their investment in Britain.

cial borrowing, Denis continued, one of two things would happen: either we should have to reduce the standard of living by 6 per cent, or we should have to start borrowing from institutions which would impose terms, like a statutory incomes policy, which a Labour Government would find unacceptable. 'There have been no conditions on our borrowing so far.' He didn't want to have to face conditions. Jack had said in a recent speech that unions could bankrupt firms by excessive wage demands. 'You can also bankrupt a nation by excessive wage demands.' The union leaders watched him transfixed as he spoke, Len Murray in particular being barely able to refrain from nodding at this point. 'That is why,' Denis continued bravely, 'I said that it is better to have a lower standard of life for all workers than for some of them to be unemployed.' We simply had to get wage settlements down – above all in the public sector, where they were running much higher than in the private one, where short time and other difficulties were beginning to bite. (My heart sank at this, as I could see Cabinet lining up to resist the Review Body's recommendations on doctors' and consultants' salaries next April. I toyed with the thought: if Cabinet toughens up on wage increases before these people reach their turn, what do I do? Resign my job because I have held out false promises?) Denis concluded on a note of appeal. He was not, he repeated, making recommendations, merely asking them to see his problem, though he would understand it if they said he did not understand theirs. Above all, he concluded, 'we must maintain our unity.' (Vigorous nods from Jack in the chair.)

There was a long silence when he had finished. It was Shirley who broke it first, adding some agonizing details of the rate of inflation to underline what Denis had said. Another silence; then Hughie came in, almost writhing in his seat as he tried to combine honesty with moderation and to curb his usual confident truculence. He welcomed Denis's frankness, he said, 'but it does not soften the blow'. Emboldened, he continued: 'I fundamentally disagree with you.' The disagreement, it transpired, was not with Denis's outline of the difficulties: rather with his proposed cure. 'Slumps are caused by the inability of workers to buy back what they produce.' Hughie groped desperately. 'Somehow we have got to bridge the difference between us. We are in a situation in which industry is definitely not investing or retraining.' And then came the crux: 'We are prepared to uphold the Social Contract' (a great breakthrough, that, for Hughie!) 'as we agreed it.' Denis came in swiftly again. 'I would like to finance an enormous retraining programme and I am determined to revivify manufacturing industry.' The argument was then taken up one by one by the trade unions. Said David Basnett, 'Any chance of renegotiating the Social Contract is just not there. Any attempt to reduce demand by reducing wage demands would increase unemployment.' Len Murray talked his usual practical common sense. 'If we allow ourselves to be pushed into extensive unemployment there will be very bad long-term consequences. The simple solution of retraining is a deceptive one. A fall in demand is as much a disincentive to investment as inflation is. A depression in this country would not help.' Jim was as disarmingly depressed as usual. 'I don't know how we deal with this problem. I am sure we shall get complete unity on that!' What worried him was that Britain's reputation overseas was declining. And he told us how, when he was in Nigeria, he found they were only too anxious to buy Leyland buses. The trouble was that they were told they would have to wait a couple of years for delivery. This brought Mik in: our exports were pretty buoyant, he maintained. What we needed to tackle was the huge increase in imports. What Jim had said about Leylands could be paralleled all over the world. But the problem was much more complex than just a question of prices: the spares problem and so on was still not solved. Mike intervened quietly. One of the policies we had committed ourselves to was to try to reduce the rate of inflation. If the guidelines were followed, the rate of inflation would be reduced, 'but they are not being followed. We should not argue about the guidelines, but merely apply them as they stand.' He went on disarmingly, 'I don't know whether I am supposed to say this' (relaxed laughter at this), 'but I think the Government's mistake' ('You can say that,' quipped Len) 'is that we have not related our policies yet.' (How I agree with him!) Mike ploughed on: 'The Budget is possibly the next occasion when the whole tactics of the Government's position can be made clear. We haven't yet built up the patriotic spirit of the nation.' (There were a surprising number of nods from the trade unionists at that.)

Harold then assured us that the Government was not seeking to change the guidelines and I came in with a brief speech to remind them that the Social Contract was concerned with maintaining living standards – not merely for wage-earners, but for all those whom we were in politics to protect. 'We could have a situation in which we had maintained the living standards of wage-earners and yet had breached the Social Contract because we had reduced the standards of the weakest in our community.' Jack was almost at bursting-point, nodding his agreement vigorously. But by now it had turned 12.30pm, so he had to sum up with great self-restraint. The discussion, he said, had been very valuable and we must continue it. He hoped we would have an economic assessment put before us every month. 'We must disabuse the people of the idea that the Government is trying to force the unions to go further. We must implement the guidelines and above all we must go forward together in understanding and unity.' When we had all said Amen to that we broke up. Cynics might say we had achieved nothing by the morning's talk, but those of us who, like me, have lived through the traumas of the past few years, know differently. Winning consent is a slow process, but I myself am convinced it is the only way. And anyone who heard Hughie this morning would know that we progress. We left Congress House fortified in the belief that, if there is an answer to this country's problems, it lies in this inchoate union between our Government and the unions. I have always believed that our only hope is to make the unions *more*, not less, political. But that means that the Government must be willing to share power. There is certainly no monopoly of democratic expression in the Cabinet room.

At our ministerial lunch we had a long discussion on pay beds. David is all in favour of a two-to-three-year phasing out period, with us legislating next session. I believe we cannot hold the unions as long as that, though my trouble is that I have got no allocation in my PESC programme for the cost of phasing out and I simply cannot find the money from the inadequate amount I have been allowed for the NHS. I suggested that I should hold the fort by announcing a short Bill this session to take the necessary powers, to be followed next session by a more complicated Bill to enable me to regulate the private sector of medicine. Brian A-S. attaches a lot of importance to that – and so does David in theory, though, when cornered, he is liable to say suddenly that regulation will prove extremely difficult. The rest of them were all in favour of my not attempting legislation this session and I accepted their judgment – only to be faced shortly afterwards by a note from Jack to the effect that Bernard Dix of NUPE had been on the phone to him warning that their branches were getting restive, not least as a result of the consultants' action, and were threatening direct moves to force phasing out. The suggestion from Dix was that I ought to see Alan Fisher urgently. 'Of course you will have to see him,' said Philip anxiously.

A long official meeting then ensued on what Henry should say to the consultants at the 'initial exploratory meeting' he is to have with them on Thursday in the Joint Negotiating Committee. He began with a show of life, saying he wanted Ministers to decide if they were really going to entrust this job to him rather than take it on themselves, because if they wanted him to do it they really must allow him to play it his own way, 'though of course within your strictly defined parameters'. Otherwise, he added, he might find that he had let us down. (What he really means, I suspect, is that he fears we might repudiate him.) Of course David and I said we didn't want to go into ministerial discussion but to keep the talks within the more hopeful context of the JNC. But it is clearly going to be a tricky operation, because Henry does not intend to take detailed orders.

Tuesday, 21 January

As someone said afterwards, an historic Cabinet! In it the Labour Government slid easily into a solution of the difficulties which threatened to split it only two or three years ago, while Harold announced a fundamental change in our constitutional convention as casually as if he had been offering us a cup of tea. The occasion was a morning-long discussion on how we should handle a referendum on the EEC. Ted Short had circulated a stack of papers and official reports on the logistic questions which we should have to decide, but we barely referred to them. Instead we spent over two hours on the central political point: how we could deal with the imminent split in the Cabinet – already looming as a result of Peter Shore's latest speech, following Tony Benn's Bristol letter and Roy Hattersley's riposte.[1] Ted began by saying that we ought to aim at a referendum in June, otherwise we should be pushed very near our deadline of October. He hoped the Referendum Bill could be approved by 25 March. Then Harold came in quietly: 'As soon as we have made our decision on the terms I am going to recommend that the minority should be free to campaign in the country on their own point of view.' And he added, 'This is unprecedented.' But in his long-winded way he proceeded to justify it, qualifying his proposal with the implied rebuke: 'But this must apply only after the campaign starts.' And he thought

[1] The battle of words between Ministers over renegotiations had already broken out. In December Tony Benn had published an open letter to his Bristol constituents declaring that 'Britain's continuing membership of the Community would mean the end of Britain as a completely self-governing nation and the end of our democratically-elected Parliament as the supreme law-making body in the United Kingdom'. Roy Hattersley had followed with the counter-claim that the loss of sovereignty was minimal and was outweighed by the benefits of membership. Peter Shore, in turn, had produced a detailed analysis of the economic disbenefits Britain had already experienced.

we should issue some guidelines to prevent the argument from becoming unruly and personalized. There was a long silence when he asked for comments. I think the reason was that people like Mike, Wedgie and me were secretly jubilant, while the pro-marketeers were reluctant to accept openly the course of action they knew was inevitable. Gradually acceptance spread through Cabinet. Roy Mason uttered gloomy warnings: 'The media will personalize our differences, even if we do not.' But when Harold asked him rather sharply what he would propose, he admitted he could not see any other way. Tony C. said grudgingly that the PM's proposal was 'more attractive than either of the alternatives'. Mike thought the proposal was right.

I struck the first note of positive enthusiasm. I was glad, I said, that Harold had come to this conclusion. It was endemic in the decision to have a referendum. The alternative of a general election was never open to us – not merely on the grounds of timing, but because people did not divide on this issue on party lines. And I was not gloomy about the consequences. Tomorrow, I said, the NEC was discussing the same issue and Ron Hayward was suggesting that, even after a special conference on the renegotiated terms had made its views known, every member of the party should be free to campaign on his or her individual views. Our tolerance as a Cabinet would encourage the whole party to be tolerant. The proposal was all the more necessary because I did not believe that either of the extremes Harold had visualized would happen: either that the terms would be so marvellous that we should all agree to accept or so terrible that rejection would be unanimous. I believed that the outcome of the negotiations would be 'a messy muddle in the middle'. They laughed at this and there was more laughter – relaxed, not bitter – as I went on to say that we would all then use the outcome to justify the line we had always taken anyway. 'So all Jim's hard work is irrelevant.' We wouldn't, for example, get the EEC to abandon the CAP. What we would be offered would be a bit of freedom to add a few national aids on top. So we would be back where we started years ago. But there was no reason why we should treat the situation tragically. I was prepared to accept the nation's verdict, whichever way it went. I certainly wasn't going to let such an unimportant thing as the Common Market wreck my political work or my party's socialist unity. (Shirley gave me a wry little smile at that.)

Fred, of course, took up my reference to the CAP with heavy indignation. I had never realized that all he had been doing was to negotiate as he was bound to do. 'I have not changed my basic position.' (Does that mean he is going to vote *against*, after all?) Peter's contribution was as astringent as usual. Harold's proposition, he said, was a generous one: '*very* generous, because the negotiations are not going to succeed. I do not expect to be in the minority.' But the healing thing was that we were all committed to accept the verdict. If, for instance, it went against his own views, he did not know whether or not Harold would still wish him to serve him ('Perhaps it would involve moving you to another post,' chipped in Harold genially): whatever it was, he, Peter, would accept the outcome and do whatever was required of him. Denis was pretty relaxed about the whole idea. The party, too, must be ready to show tolerance and those of us on the NEC must use our influence tomorrow to get the same freedom for individual members of the party. There shouldn't, for example, be a block vote at the special conference. He didn't think it should be held at all. Mike demurred at this. With the Government expressing a view, Parliament expressing a view, and every organization in the country doing the same, it was only right that the party should express a view as well – but that did not mean the imposition of party discipline. Wedgie was even more euphoric than I had been. 'The knowledge that we are free to express our views makes us much more relaxed towards the whole renegotiation.' Roy J. was deeply dubious: 'The idea Harold puts forward is a very difficult one.' Some of them would be in a very uncomfortable position, just as he had been as deputy leader when he had felt he must resign.[1] But even Roy didn't oppose the solution outright. Jim was characteristically Cassandra-like. The referendum would not necessarily be a healing exercise. 'I suspect that brotherly love will wear a little thin.' What he did urge was that the campaigning should not begin until the terms were known. His position, he said, was made impossible when members of the Government started publicly opposing membership in principle and thus breaching the compromise we had reached in the Manifesto. 'The negotiations are being made more difficult because the EEC believe whatever they do to meet us will not make any difference.' That is why he was taking over more of the negotiations himself. 'At least they believe it is not impossible to convince me at the end of the day.' (Some of us winked at that.)

As Harold started to sum up, Ted Short pointed out: 'This means that we are formally committing ourselves to a referendum, not a general election.' Roy J. muttered some subdued token reservations at that, but the rest of us just took it as obvious. Harold then said he would submit a draft of his statement to Thursday's Cabinet. He would say that we would publicize the views taken by the different sides in Cabinet but make it clear we would all abide by the referendum result. Here again there was no reserving of positions by the Europeanists and I suspect that Shirley is now sorry she nailed her colours of resignation to the mast so precipitately during the election. Once again I was struck by our astonishing harmony. It really does look as though Harold's long period of humiliation has not been in vain and that the party's unity is emerging as an exercise in genuine party democracy. There was, for instance, the quite moving moment when Wedgie, in the middle of his speech, turned to Shirley and said, 'When she said what she did during the election I was very angry, but I don't think now that it did the party any harm.' My morning was also made by a friendly note John Silkin tossed to me:

To Barbara in admiration   *21-1-75*

In EEC matters the rôle of B.C.
Is to show that, in Cabinet, there is a key
To the problems, the troubles – above all the riddle
Of Pro and of Anti – and those in the middle.
For Barbara's answer to those who are tense
Or up-tight, is just simply to use commonsense.

                        Love,
                        John

[1] See Introduction.

I have started to complain to Philip about the delay in getting Bill McCarthy into post as my adviser on industrial relations. The department has been stalling on this for three months, but still no appointment, despite three Minutes of reminder I have sent to Norman in recent weeks. Philip agreed with me today that we must get McCarthy installed before we get down seriously to examining the Whitley machinery. I shall be interested to see if they dream up some more delaying tactics just the same.

Wednesday, 22 January

Denis arrived late at the NEC meeting and left early, having obviously timed his brief attendance to be present during the discussion of Ron's memo on the referendum and to beat off what he obviously thought was going to be the imposition of party discipline. He need not have worried: harmony seems to have broken out in the NEC as well as Cabinet, just as I predicted yesterday. Ron spoke well in introducing his memo. 'The party,' he said, 'need *not* destroy itself over this matter. If the NEC puts a statement to the special conference, it should *not* be binding on other members of the party.' The special conference would be 'a sounding board and a safety valve'. The discussion which followed on the logistics of the referendum was friendly and relaxed. Ted Short thought that if we counted the votes centrally, as Ron suggested, there would be an 'almighty row' on the grounds that we were trying to disguise regional differences. Wedgie came down firmly in favour of counting on a constituency basis. This would undoubtedly show that Scotland was solidly against entry, but then 'the effect of membership on the unity of the UK is one of the central issues'. I supported him on the grounds that MPs had a right, and a duty, to know how far they were out of touch, or in line, with their constituents. Walter Padley wanted a county basis, while Shirley urged that a national basis for the vote would be 'a visual demonstration of the unity of the UK'. Alex Kitson and McClusky warned us that, if it were discovered that the English vote had kept Scotland in the Market against her will, the row would go rumbling on till the end of time. They then drew the surprising conclusion that that was the reason why we must have a national vote. Mike drew the opposite conclusion: if Scotland suspected that this was the case, and knew on top of that that we had manoeuvred to keep the truth from coming out, the result would be 'deadly'. Ted said he would report all these views to Cabinet.

Then there was a long argument about the form of the question that should be put, Mik pointing out that every pollster knew there was a built-in bias for the *status quo*. We should *not* therefore ask people to choose whether to stay in or come out. We should merely ask, 'Do you think Britain should be a member of the Common Market?' Shirley said the party had been held together on the basis that we should put the terms to the people when renegotiated and ask them whether they accepted them. That was what the Manifesto said. Mike replied that he thought that might be confusing, but I tossed a possible form of words to him: 'In the light of the terms offered to us, do you think Britain should be a member of the Common Market?', and he nodded that that might be possible. So another crisis in the party has been passed peacefully. I suspect the will to unity in the party, which strengthens every day, is being fed by the growing confusion in the Tory ranks over the leadership. Despite the fact that Margaret Thatcher is now giving Heath a hard run for his money, mine is still on Heath's victory. You can't find two Tories to agree on an alternative to him.

Another meeting with the presidents of the Royal Colleges on the consultants' dispute. This time they had brought their whole conference body, but nothing new emerged and we went over the same old ground, with them emphasizing that I must treat these sensitive individualists, the consultants, gently and me replying that I was only too willing to negotiate. After various other office meetings Henry came to see me in my room in the House (where we are incarcerated by a running whip on the Finance Bill) to rehearse once again what he should say to the BMA negotiators at the 'initial exploratory meeting' tomorrow. He has obviously got himself quite keyed up over this and his personality seems to have toughened up quite considerably, though he still lapses into self-deprecatory diffidence from time to time. He has worked over the earlier compromise plan that he had put to me and has now got it into a much more acceptable form as far as I am concerned. He has met my point that I am not prepared to give payment for extra sessions except in the context of a closed contract (a point which even the Royal Colleges have grasped is a valid one), but he has dressed it up so that it becomes more palpably obvious that the size and form of the differential has not changed. I told him he could certainly have his idea in mind as something we could be working towards, though he was not to volunteer anything concrete to the meeting tomorrow. He went away happy.

It was 2am this morning when I got to bed and 6.30am when I got up, but I still had to stay on in the House, fatigue or no fatigue. At last Jimmy Dunn released me at 11.30pm. The doctrine of our Whips is that Ministers ought to do more late stints at the House than ordinary mortals, not less. If it kills us, worse luck.

Thursday, 23 January

To my great delight we have been soundly beaten on the disabled housewives' benefit in the Committee on the Social Security Benefits Bill.[1] The timing of this benefit does not cause much difficulty. We cannot operationally introduce it before 1977 anyway, but I have always been unhappy about the lower rate for women. I only accepted this in my discussions with Joel last summer as otherwise I should not have got it included at all, but it is immensely embarrassing in International Women's Year! My ploy this morning lay in managing to convey to Cabinet that *I* was not asking for more: merely that we faced inescapable defeat in the House and Bob helped me by predicting this. Finally I was instructed to get Brian to talk to Lewis Carter-Jones to see if he would withdraw his amendment if we said we accepted the principle of an equal rate for men and women, though we could not guarantee to equalize it from the start. If Lewis

[1] Lewis Carter-Jones, Labour MP for Eccles and a great campaigner for the disabled, had successfully moved an amendment on the committee stage of the Social Security Benefits Bill to extend the section on the non-contributory invalidity pension [NCIP] to include the disabled housewife. The effect of this was not to advance the date at which the disabled housewives' benefit would be paid, but to ensure that it was paid at the same rate as the NCIP. This pleased me mightily because Treasury had been planning to pay disabled housewives a lower rate, i.e. the one for 'dependent' women.

refuses I am to talk to Denis again. I think I know what Lewis will say! David was quite shocked when I reported this to him later, together with the fact that I have won on the abolition of the wages stop in Social Services Committee this morning, even Joel agreeing to it.[1] 'There are two things that strike me about this Labour Government compared with the last one,' David remarked. 'The atmosphere is much friendlier and the Treasury much weaker. Too weak,' he added grimly. He is quite masochistic about the suffering he thinks this country must impose on itself. However, I assured him I had backed Denis strongly on the need to resist amendments (promoted by George Cunningham) to reduce and finally abolish the earnings rule. I suggested that, if we were defeated, we should go to the House the next day and make the issue a vote of confidence. Cabinet thought this was a good idea, Harold pointing out that the Tories were hardly in the mood to be accused of extravagant increases in public expenditure.

There was a tense interchange between Jim and me on Cyprus. I have been blaming myself for having been so preoccupied at last week's Cabinet that I did not challenge his proposal to repatriate Turkish refugees from the Akrotiri base. The uproar this has caused among the Greeks proves that my anxieties were justified. When Jim reported on this briefly at Cabinet I asked him tersely, 'Did you expect such a violent reaction?' 'Yes,' he replied brutally. Then he repeated his argument that he had done this on humanitarian grounds. It would have been inexcusable to use these refugees as political pawns in trying to force a settlement. 'Have not the Greek refugees got humanitarian grounds as well?' I retorted. He insisted that our action would influence the Turks to treat the Greek refugees reasonably. I'll believe that when I see it, but no one else backed me up. The trouble is that we are all so busy we just have not time to take up all the points we ought to do.

Another hour passed as we went through Harold's draft statement on the Common Market referendum word by word and line by line. Then there was a great argument as to whether the Government should provide background information on the issues when the time came. Peter insisted that it was impossible to provide information that accurately summed up the cases of the two sides, but I did not agree with him. 'The major source of information must be under our control,' I said. After much to-ing and fro-ing Harold said a group of Ministers must look into the whole thing and report to Cabinet.

Finally we cleared the White Paper on Public Expenditure.[2] Denis has toughened

---

[1] This was a device, introduced in the Supplementary Benefits Act 1966, for reducing the amount of supplementary allowance an unemployed man could claim so as not to bring his income above what he would have earned in his normal full-time job. The number of wage stop cases had fallen to a mere 4,900, but the principle remained an irritant.

[2] In 1969 the Labour Government had inaugurated annual reviews of public expenditure in which a five-year forward programme was rolled forward from year to year. This, crises apart, led to the annual manoeuvring between Ministers in PESC. The White Paper published in January 1974 (Cmnd. 5879) set out the Government's public expenditure plans over the five years to 1978–79 on three different assumptions. The first, or 'central case', was based on a forecast rate of growth of about 3 per cent a year. This, it argued, would require an increase in private investment of 5·4 per cent a year and of 3·6 per cent in investment by nationalized industries. After budgeting for a substantial reduction in the balance of payments deficit, the Government estimated that public and private spending could only increase at an

up the words about the grim options that lie ahead of us, but no one could object to that. Perhaps it will help to show the unions that if they go on pressing unreasonable wage demands they will only suffer a cut in the social wage. But I was dismayed to discover that Denis has dropped the idea of a popular version which he seemed to have agreed to when I raised it at Chequers. Once again all the talk of the need for education and persuasion seems to have come to nothing. Late as it was, with everyone edgy to get away, I insisted on raising it. Denis raised all sorts of difficulties, but to my relief Harold ruled that the Presentation of Government Policies Committee under Bill Price[1] should have another look at it. Harold at any rate can appreciate the importance of what I am talking about.

While Henry was incarcerated with the JNC we had an office meeting on pay beds. Philip, Henry and Brian A-S. have produced a long detailed paper about the measures we might take to control the private health sector and prevent it expanding excessively when the phasing-out takes place. To my surprise David exploded violently. Some of the propositions in it he found quite intolerable, he said. Quantity control, for example, was just not on. Having first welcomed the idea of controls he now seems to have swung to the other extreme. It was ironic to hear Philip explaining to him that we really must regulate standards in private nursing homes, while Raymond Gedling said that when the department started to license nursing homes for abortions we rejected some as unfit, though gastrectomies had been performed there for years! So David quietened down. I said gently that I thought the paper was right to put all the possibilities before us so that we could examine them, even if only to reject some of them. But I thought we ought to have a Sunningdale to do it and invite sympathizers from outside, like Laurie Pavitt and John Dunwoody, and perhaps some discreet people from the unions. This idea alarmed Philip, lest the BMA should hear of it, but I said that we could have parallel discussions with the BMA as soon as I had announced our intention to legislate. We all agreed that we should not broach the pay beds question publicly until the consultants' dispute is out of the way, but that we ought to waste no time in getting a paper to Cabinet, particularly as I persuaded them that we must get a quick one-clause Bill through this session, followed by a control Bill later. I convinced them that this was the only way to prevent the eruption of serious trouble with the unions. The announcement of our intention to legislate, plus some immediate reductions in under-used pay beds and discussions on a common waiting list, would lower the temperature. Philip said he liked the sound of this package and they went away to redraft their paper to Cabinet.

---

annual average rate of 1·8 per cent over the period. Within this it was planning to increase cash benefits and subsidies ('publicly financed consumption') by 4·4 per cent a year and other public expenditure by 1·9 per cent a year, leaving a margin of only 1·1 per cent a year for the growth of privately financed spending. Even so, it hinted, some increase in taxation might be necessary and if the economic outcome was less favourable than hoped, even this margin would not be available. Ominously, the White Paper pointed out that the figures for social security did not include child benefit, which would have to come out of the contingency reserve. There would also be some call on the reserve for the NEB and the proposed nationalization measures as the Government's industrial policies developed. For an analysis of the trend in public expenditure, see Appendix II.

[1] William Price was Labour MP for Rugby and Parliamentary Secretary, Privy Council Office.

At 5.30pm Henry came out of the JNC looking limp and harassed. 'How is it going?' I asked. 'Terrible,' said Henry, mopping his face. He then settled down to spell out in detail the consultants' 'shopping list' and the objections to the new contract he had wrung out of them. Philip and Raymond shook their heads derisively as Henry ploughed on: the consultants wanted the lot.[1] What is more, they were waiting for my reply. Henry said he assumed I would just say 'nothing doing', but David, just before he had to dash off to the House to take a debate, took a different line. He said I should seize the opportunity to get on record the fact that they accepted, however reluctantly, that my two cardinal principles (retention of the whole-timers' differential and rejection of item of service contract) were non-negotiable. Apparently Henry, in opening the meeting, had started toughly by asking them if they did accept this: otherwise there was no point in going any further. (He's developing quite a backbone, that man!) Then, said David, we should go on to say in general terms that, although I could make no detailed comments at this stage, I saw nothing in their proposals to prevent fruitful negotiations from taking place. I liked this approach: it would put paid to the myth of my 'take it or leave it' attitude. But I said we must also reiterate the common objective between them and us of getting a more defined contract, otherwise I could see us being manoeuvred into accepting their new aim, which was to keep the present open-ended, undefined and unpoliceable contract and just add extra payments onto it. After David had gone we sweated for an hour over the wording of my reply. We are now so terrified of putting their hackles up with the wrong phrase. At last we were ready to send Henry back into the lion's den, while I went home to pack for the night sleeper to Blackburn.

Friday, 24 January

An exhausting day after an exhausting night. The sleeper ahead of us got itself derailed and we never moved out of Euston. After various interruptions to my sleep, as the attendant came to report non-progress, I was woken at 6am by the assistant station master with the offer to rush me over to Heathrow for the early flight to Manchester. When I eventually arrived in Blackburn one-and-a-half hours late (and with no breakfast) a posse of reporters was waiting for me. They all thought I had been on the derailed train! Even Tories had been ringing up in anxiety. It was quite a let-down when they all learned the truth. Somehow I got through my crowded day's schedule, ending up with a speech on pensions policy to the North West Pensions and Life Society. Over 150 pensions experts were crowded into a hot room – and I had hardly had a minute to think up a speech. So I improvised on my feet, answered all the

---

[1] The consultants had switched their efforts to improving their existing contract. In this they went well beyond Dr Astley's four points, demanding in addition an emergency recall fee, new capital allowances for cars and phones, amendments to their incremental scale and superannuation improvements. They also wanted the maximum part-timers' commitment to the NHS 'clarified' to mean an obligation to attend for nine sessions of three-and-a-half hours each, including travel time, rather than whole time, i.e. eleven sessions. Above all they insisted that an 'absolutely fundamental' precondition for the lifting of sanctions was the department's willingness to support a substantial pay increase for consultants in their current pay review.

questions with great plausibility and made them laugh. I was rather proud of myself. At least I did better than Sir K., who, the chairman told me, went to a pensions dinner when he was Minister, spoke for ten minutes and in answer to every question said, 'I will see you get a written reply.' I've always suspected that K.J. knew nothing about pensions.

Monday, 27 January

Another office meeting on those dratted consultants. Henry reported that, when he went back to them on Thursday evening, they had mulled over my message, were clearly disappointed with it and had almost pleaded with him to get me to elaborate on it, saying they appreciated I hadn't really had enough time to think over their points. Conciliatory as always, I agreed to elaborate on it and we talked end-lessly round the problem before Henry and co. went away to have a shot at another draft.

My biggest victory of the day was at EQ, where I had to introduce my paper on the EEC medical directives. It was a tricky job, because I knew I was vulnerable through not having cottoned on earlier to the implications of what was going on. I decided the only tactic was to make a clean breast of it. This rather floored Roy Hattersley, who was waiting to slaughter me. He was as sarcastic as he dared and fought like a tiger against my proposal to table a 'qualified Take Note' for the debate in the House. What interested me was the European bias of the committee Harold has set up: Jim in the chair, Shirley, Edmund Dell, Roy Hattersley and Harold Lever on their toes to resist any move to outflank them on their beloved Community. The anti-Europeans were thin on the ground: Peter abroad in Iran, Mike missing and Wedgie busy scribbling next to me, his mind exclusively on his own item of regional policy. I hit back at Hattersley, pointing out that if we put down a pure 'Take Note' resolution, an amendment would be moved in the House; there would be a row and a vote. The qualifications I proposed were very moderate ones, but Nigel Spearing [Labour MP for Newham South] had assured me that they would be enough to prevent an amendment being put down. All it would involve was that in the Council of Ministers Jim would have to ask for the directives to be looked at again. One of the reasons he could give was that they didn't go as far as we had wanted over language tests, which was true. Tougher language tests would also stop British doctors practising over the water as freely as they would like to and so help us to preserve the NHS. This was obviously of no importance to Jim. He clearly had no stomach for any fight in the Council of Ministers. 'I think we should stick to our usual Take Note,' he said casually, and I saw red. 'If we do that,' I flashed, 'I shall go to the dispatch box and say I believe the directives will damage the NHS.' This shook Jim to the core; he hummed and hawed and finally said, 'If Barbara feels like that we had better let her have her Motion.' Roy and Shirley were clearly furious. They hit back again and again, but I stood my ground. Only one person in the whole place spoke up in my support: Bruce Millan [Minister of State at the Scottish Office]. To my surprise he came out on my side vigorously. Finally the harassed Jim turned to me: 'Are you saying that, if we make an attempt to change the directives and fail, Nigel Spearing and co. will then accept them?' 'Yes,' I replied. 'It is a device for enabling a proper debate to take place on the basis of a formula which the critics feel is more neutral than a plain "Take Note" one.' 'But would you yourself accept them then?' Jim persisted. 'Yes,' I replied. That did it, and Jim ruled that we should accept my proposition. Roy Hattersley clearly could not go against his own boss and subsided muttering. He is an able, tough, unscrupulous little tyke and in an argument like that is much more formidable than Jim. Shirley, too, is formidable on the Market. She knows her facts. Later in the lobby Jim came up to see me and said ruefully, 'I've got into an awful row from my friends for giving in to you.' I can just imagine it!

Tuesday, 28 January

The row on the directives erupted again in Cabinet. Bob returned to his favourite theme: debates on directives were rolling out of the Scrutiny Committee and he just couldn't keep the lads late in the House night after night. It was an impossible position, and the only way out was for the Minister concerned in each case to try and reach agreement with the interested backbenchers to avoid a vote. Jim then reported grudgingly that EQ had accepted the Motion on which I had reached agreement with him, adding, 'Barbara's resolution will put me in a position of acute embarrassment because I want to help the party.' But he went on grumbling: 'So many of these documents are not worthy of discussion in the House. The Government may have to take its own decision on what should be discussed.' Shirley complained that there was no give and take: there was no satisfying a certain anti-Market group of MPs. Others tried to make out that it was all a one-man exercise in egotism by Nigel Spearing. But Harold had the sense to see that, if once we tried to overrule the Scrutiny Committee (of which, after all, John Davies, the Europeanist, is chairman), we should reveal that there is no way, under Market procedure, of effectively retaining some parliamentary sovereignty. That is why he has instituted a new procedure designed at last to modify this absurd situation in which we find ourselves. When the Scrutiny Committee decides that a directive should be debated in Parliament, EQ must now first discuss the policy aspects; then Legislation Committee must decide how the debate shall be handled. So Harold ruled that we must try out the new procedure before talking about any change. Wedgie then came in lugubriously. The real problem looming up, he said, was in the field of steel closures, where we had sacrificed our freedom of action to the Community. 'We have lost total control of steel investment.' There would be serious trouble when MPs realized what was happening. To my surprise Harold endorsed him for once. 'This is a very difficult one. I am not happy about this matter. It is at the very heart of renegotiation.' Does this mean that Harold's acceptance of the terms is still an open question?

Bob also reported on the troubles which face us on the Report stage of my Social Security Benefits Bill. I am delighted with the backbench revolt which has forced the Treasury to concede that disabled housewives shall get the full rate of the non-contributory invalidity benefit. But I again backed Denis strongly in his proposal that we should resist George Cunningham's amendment on the rapid phasing out of the earnings rule. My motives were double-edged. Partly I thought it would count unto me for righteousness and do something to counteract my greedy image in Cabinet. But I was also acutely conscious that we were in danger of entering the stage we had got to in 1968–69, when our authority as a government was totally undermined by a succession of successful backbench revolts. It is intolerable that a small number of our own people should be able to hold the Government to ransom for their own pet priorities without having to take account of the whole public expenditure picture as Cabinet has to do. We have really done very well by the pensioners. What I am really desperate about is the NHS. We are having to cancel or postpone new hospital building projects on a frightening scale. If George Cunningham succeeds in mobilizing enough of our softies to win the day – with the help of Tories who would do anything to embarrass us – I can see no hope of my being able to get a bit more easement on the health side. So I urged that we should resist the Cunningham amendment to the bitter end, making it a matter of confidence if necessary. Otherwise I can see ourselves back in the kind of rout we had when we gave way on Lords reform. What amused me was that Mike, whose brilliant backbench filibustering then in company with Enoch Powell forced Dick Crossman to retreat over the Lords, did not utter a word of protest at my line. Circumstances alter cases.

At last we have resumed our weekly dinners. I must say it was pleasant to walk into that private room at Lockets again, even though there weren't many of us who could manage to turn up: just Mike and Jill Foot, Tommy and Katherine Balogh, the Silkins and me. We had a good discussion on the economic situation, which we all recognize is deeply serious. What delighted me was to see no sign that Mike is going to throw in the sponge on what has become an increasingly difficult task for him, thus falsifying Conrad Heron's prognostication that he would quit when the going got tough. Instead Mike told us of a policy he has been working out in his department for dealing with inflation by (a) massively increasing subsidies to hold the cost of living down and (b) a big increase in taxation. I found this an odd doctrine, but Mike says Denis, of whom he thinks quite a lot, had not turned it down out of hand.

I was late getting to the dinner because Henry had asked to see me urgently. The BMA has been in touch with him about my clarification letter, which they want further 'clarified'. After some discussion we decided Henry could give them assurances verbally on certain points but that I should not send them another letter. These clarifications of clarifications are becoming slightly ridiculous! The key question they asked is, as we anticipated, whether sanctions would have to be lifted before negotiations could begin. David suggested a useful formula: namely, that I had gone as far as I could reasonably be expected to go and that it was now for the BMA to take a public attitude. Henry went away well satisfied. His tail is slightly up again because my letter had clearly had an effect on some, at any rate, of the negotiators.

Wednesday, 29 January

Harold is showering us with PM's Personal Minutes. First, he is clearly worried about the coming public debate on the EEC. Not only have we Ministers got to refrain from personalizing the public argument but we must keep our speeches within the framework of the Manifesto and not oppose entry on principle. What is more we must clear the text of any proposed speech with both the PM and the Foreign Secretary. (I suspect Jim has been getting at him.) Secondly, Harold has told us he wants ministerial relations with the NEC to be 'close, intimate and constructive'. It is essential, he urges, that Ministers who are not on the NEC should know what is going on, and when it is intended to publish anything in their field; therefore they should maintain liaison through their political advisers or a junior Minister specially detailed to keep in touch with Transport House. Fair enough!

I met Dr Lowe, chairman of the Association of University Clinical Academic Staff [AUCAS], at his request this morning. The idea is that he wants to be helpful in getting a settlement of the consultants' dispute. I soon realized that the honorary consultants on the academic side are a very different kettle of fish from Brian Lewis and co. It is a satisfactory whole-time contract in which they are interested. He concluded by saying that his Association was having its annual meeting on Saturday and he would be glad to make any statement there that we thought might help. David and I told him I might be ready to issue my clarification letter by then and we would see he got a copy of it.

Great drama in the House over the earnings rule. Brian and I agreed that a Treasury spokesman must wind up the debate, but to our alarm only gentle Bob Sheldon was available. Brian opened well, but that Calvinist, George Cunningham, had dug his heels in and a number of our people were impressionable enough to follow him. It began to be clear that we should lose. I then heard that the Treasury was weakening: that Bob had been put up to promise that some concession on amounts would be made. Blazing mad, I sought out Denis in his room. Didn't he realize there wasn't a penny in my PESC allocation for any more concessions on the earnings rule? Hadn't he himself forced me to drop some urgent items from my list and to hold down the level of things like family allowance increases? Why, then, didn't we turn and fight? Or were we to go through the disintegration of 1968–70 again? Denis was sympathetic but quite relaxed. I have never seen a Chancellor face economic disaster with greater equanimity. 'Are we going to lose anyway?' he asked Bob. 'Yes,' snapped Bob viciously. 'That shower Cunningham....' 'Right,' said Denis. 'Then we'll offer nothing.' Back in the Chamber a small farce ensued while Denis tried to slip a note to Bob Sheldon, now launched on his brief, at the dispatch box. Result, Sheldon mumbled something nobody could understand properly. We were defeated by a good margin, the Tories jubilant. Of course we shan't force a vote of confidence on this, as I would like, because we have not prepared the ground properly. But, despite Denis's fiery words at the dispatch box after our defeat, hinting that he would make the rich pay for this concession, the fact is that some more money has been pre-empted that will have to come from somewhere – and it will come from my allocation and from far more important policies I would prefer to spend money on.

Thursday, 30 January

At Legislation Committee we had another battle over the EEC medical directives. Following my victory at EQ I had thought the marketeers would have let my Motion go through graciously, but not a bit of it. Roy Hattersley returned to the attack, backed by Shirley and Roy J., who pontificated about what a bad precedent we were agreeing to. Only Ted Short's brisk common sense and Bob Mellish's anguished support saved me. As I watched Shirley and Roy J. whispering together I couldn't help thinking that, although the Market no longer splits the party publicly and poisonously, it does so insidiously as much as ever. There is an instinctive camaraderie that characterizes the rival cliques. I couldn't imagine, for instance, having a relaxed social evening with David, as I do so frequently with Brian O'Malley, despite the fact that David and I get on well together.

In the evening I had a group of consultants in for a drink in my room. They were led by Professor Jessof, a whole-time academic, and were all extremely reasonable. The academics are with me to a man in supporting the differential for whole-timers and they are uneasy about the whole idea of a closed contract plus extra sessions because, of course, their salaries, though paid by the University Grants Committee, are linked to those of whole-time consultants, so they would not benefit from the introduction of overtime payments. They nodded uneasily when I warned them that the introduction of costly extra payments might lead the Review Body to fix lower increases in the basic pay. What they want is modest modifications in the existing contract and they were pleased when I told them my priority now was to go for a good pay increase in April.

Friday, 31 January

Another meeting in the office about the consultants. Henry reported that there had been no further noises from their representatives, so we had to drop my idea of releasing my latest letter to them in time for the AUCAS conference tomorrow. Both David and I are getting restive at the delay and David made menacing noises about how we must really explode the notion that the consultants were 'working to contract'. They were doing nothing of the kind: they were breaching it, since even the maximum part-timers were contracted to work 'substantially whole-time' for the NHS. I cheered Henry up again by saying I would not do anything precipitate to wreck his talks.

Later in the House I saw Donnison[1] to discuss at first hand the new role he sees for the SBC. He was reasonableness itself, saying of course he realized I could not give him his head to pontificate about spending priorities. He would be glad to submit his proposed annual report to me for comment, though he did feel a certain amount of independence was essential to strengthen the status of the SBC. I was quite satisfied he is anxious to get some serious discussion going on issues of social policy. (So am I.) I told him I would let him know my decision about the chairmanship of the SBC as soon as possible. When he had gone I told Norman how impressed I had been by his

[1] Professor David Donnison was Director of the Centre for Environmental Studies and Deputy Chairman of the Supplementary Benefits Commission. I was considering him for the chairmanship when Harold Collison retired. Donnison had a lot of ideas for giving the SBC a more positive role in shaping social policy. In particular he wanted it to issue an annual report setting out its views on priorities in the light of its own experience and of studies it would undertake. His proposals alarmed my civil servants, who saw them as an encroachment on Ministers' prerogatives.

reasonableness and Norman agreed. He said he thought his senior colleagues were making unnecessarily heavy weather about the 'machinery of government' points. I like Norman more and more: there is a lot of shrewdness as well as ability in that young head and a refreshing willingness to be frank about his superiors when he thinks they are wrong. I don't think the public realize what this new breed of younger civil servants is really like and how unconventional. I said I would be ready to appoint Donnison on the spot but would wait till I had seen Kay Carmichael,[1] as – other things being equal – I would have liked to appoint a woman as chairman in International Women's Year.

Monday, 3 February

Stevenson's deputy, Gullick, has written to Henry to thank me for my long letter of 28 January.[2] Having considered it carefully they asked whether a second clarification meeting would be possible as the first one had 'run out of time'. Henry has also minuted me saying that he now suspects that the negotiators have been so impressed by the reasonableness of my letter that they are trying to avoid publication of it at all – under plea that it is part of the clarification proceedings which we have agreed shall be confidential. The profession is clearly divided down the middle and my letter would split them further. I said at once that I didn't think I could refuse them a second clarification meeting, though Henry should fire a warning shot to the effect that a document of some kind must be published in due course.

A long ministerial lunch. We now find that there are so many points we all want to discuss that our agenda lengthens every week and we haven't got through it even after one-and-three-quarter hours. There is always a good attendance: Liz Arnott and Theresa O'Connell attending faithfully. Brian has now got young Alf Bates [Labour MP for Bebington and Ellesmere Port] as his PPS, and Alf is obviously fascinated by it all. If only Stafford Cripps and Harold Wilson had had similar meetings when I was their PPS I should have learned a lot more about the complexities of government!

Tuesday, 4 February

That the meeting of the Legislation Committee of Cabinet was up to something special was clear from the crowded room. Even Ted Short had arrived by the time I got there. Conference Room A – scene of so many of my traumatic ministerial

[1] Mrs Catherine Carmichael, Lecturer in Social Work and Social Administration at Glasgow University, had been a member of the Commission since 1968. She was the wife of Neil Carmichael, Labour MP for Kelvingrove and Parliamentary Secretary for the Environment. I appointed her Deputy Chairman of the SBC on 31 July.

[2] In it I welcomed the professions' acceptance of the fact that I was not prepared to budge on the whole-timers' differential and that a system of payment by fees for items of service was ruled out. I also reminded them of my anxiety to reform the system of merit awards. On pay I gave them the same assurance as I had done to GPs, agreed that their incremental scale ought to be improved and said I was ready to consider changes in their superannuation scheme. I hinted that a payment for being 'on call' might be possible, but only within the context of a 'closed' contract.

experiences – is a lofty, beautifully proportioned room overlooking Horse Guards Parade; it is the old Treasury boardroom. The ceiling is attractively moulded, and the whole setting is more appropriate to some leisurely eighteenth-century discussion than to the miserably involved technical details of domestic problems that we conduct there. Behind the chairman's seat is a red velvet throne topped with gilded moulding, last occupied when George III presided over one of the board meetings. It is now roped off to prevent the representatives of the people from sitting on it. It was in this room that I had my struggles with Dick Crossman and Judith Hart over *In Place of Strife*. It was here we used to wrangle over the horrible petty details of prices and incomes policy in 1968 and 1969. If X group of workers got 2d on their hourly rate, wouldn't Y group immediately demand the same, etc., etc? Yet what strikes me now is how much less traumatic our policy problems seem. There is no reason why they should, because, God knows, they are as difficult as ever. Perhaps it is just that I am older and more relaxed. Probably, though, it is due to the fact that when we fell in 1970 the Tories made an even greater mess of things than we did, so we don't feel as desperately on trial as we did in 1964–70.

'All the first eleven are here this morning,' remarked Ted from the chair as Jim Callaghan, Shirley, Peter, Mike, Wedgie, the Lord Chancellor *et al*. squeezed them-selves into the chairs round the big baize-covered table. Everyone grinned, for the subject that had brought us there was not the approval of a motley group of Bills but the crucial issue of the sovereignty of Parliament in the context of the EEC. I was puzzled that the Lord President should suddenly have put before us a memo asking us to decide the vital issue of how, assuming Britain decided to remain in the Common Market, Parliament could control legislation imposed on us by the EEC. (No wonder everyone was there!) But Ted, in opening the discussion, reminded us in that staccato way of his that Legislation Committee last July had asked for some further study to be done on the problem of how 'Community secondary legislation' could be made subject to some formal parliamentary scrutiny. Hence his paper, which con-fronted us with two choices: either to try to get the amendment of Article 189 of the Treaty of Rome (so as to subject decisions of the Council of Ministers to the subsequent approval of the British Parliament), or to strengthen the procedure for discussing matters before they went to the Council: a kind of elaboration of the Scrutiny Committee's work. In presenting the paper, Ted solemnly read out the extract from the Manifesto dealing with the issue of sovereignty. One of the aims of renegotiation, it said, was 'the retention by Parliament of those powers over the British economy needed to pursue effective regional, industrial and fiscal policies'. The committee must decide just exactly what that entailed.

Ted then called on Jim, who, a bit taken aback, said he had really just come to listen; but Jim was soon warming up to his typical pro-Market theme. There was 'no chance whatever', he said, of getting the Community to agree to amend Article 189. The concept of directly applicable Community law was central to the Community system. 'If we intended to challenge Article 189 we shouldn't have made our application in the first place.' The whole purpose of the Community was that 'we should grow together'. The pace at which we did it was a very different matter and here the veto was very important. But, he insisted, 'it would be regarded as an act of bad faith to raise this now'. Mike, sitting next to me, was writhing in his seat. He spoke with his usual mixture of gentleness and firmness. It wasn't fair of Jim to suggest that some of us were only raising this at the last minute, he said. As Ted had pointed out, we had raised it as long ago as last July. It would be intolerable to argue that it was now too late. The right of Parliament to retain control had been at the heart of the party's fight against Heath's European Communities Bill which took us into the Market and everyone round the table had voted for the amendments we had put forward in Opposition to assert that right. But this was really a matter for Cabinet. 'We can't say in this Committee that we decide not to tackle Article 189.' Bob returned to the nitty gritty of the problem of even trying to retain the remnants of parliamentary sovereignty. How was he to keep Ministers in the House late night after night voting on these wretched directives? 'You're never here, Jim,' he challenged; 'you're always in Brussels. It's all right for you.' Jim, who is constitutionally incapable of being stirred by great issues of principle, swept this aside. 'A number of issues,' he retorted, 'are being brought up late at night which would domestically have been within the prerogative of Ministers.' Fred said he knew what Jim meant. Here were attempts being made to tie him down over agricultural negotiations in Brussels which would never have been made over the Agricultural Review at home. It was a lot of baloney. 'We have got to find a way of making sure that we do not put Parliament in a position that it stifles the rights of Ministers.' I sat there musing on how badly I had failed to keep in touch with all this – the perennial problem of the busy Minister. But the more Jim talked the clearer it became that entry into the Market would strengthen the executive against the legislature. That is exactly why it suits Jim's book.

Peter's contribution was surprisingly moderate. Why, he asked, did we need Article 189 at all if the Community had given up supranationalism? He thought the way forward lay through amendments to the European Communities Bill. Wedgie was more eloquent. I always sit spellbound while the words flow out of him. The Industry Bill, he said, was an outstanding example of the problem we faced over the EEC. He had been told that he must send a copy of the Bill to the Commission with a pledge that he would not use its powers in violation of our Treaty obligations. That he would never agree to. We had been told that controlling power would rest with the Council of Ministers, but in the field of trade and industry Articles 92–94 gave supreme powers to the Commission, where the veto did not operate. He then swept us on to a philosophical discourse on the nature of democracy. Law-making, to have any meaning, must contain the power to change the law, but that was exactly what we were asking the British people to surrender. Reg Prentice agreed with him at least on this: it would be wrong for this committee to decide such a basic issue. Cabinet must do that; and we should also look at Wedgie's valid point about the Commission and see whether the veto should not be imported there. If we were to do this, I pointed out, this really meant we should raise Article 189 without delay. To try to get such a major change after the negotiations would really open us to a charge of bad faith. Of course Jim disagreed with me, but Ted Short, summing up, said that we had decided no decision should be reached.

Late that afternoon in the House someone said to me, 'Have you heard the news?

Margaret Thatcher has swept to the top in the leadership poll.'[1] I fear that I felt a sneaking feminist pleasure. Damn it, that lass *deserves* to win. Her cool and competent handling of the cheaper mortgages issue in the last election campaign gave us our only moment of acute anxiety. All right, it was a dishonest nonsense as a policy, but she dealt with it like a professional.

Wednesday, 5 February

The papers are full of Margaret Thatcher. She has lent herself with grace and charm to every piece of photographer's gimmickry, but don't we all when the prize is big enough? What interests me now is how blooming she looks – she has never been prettier. I am interested because I understand this phenomenon. She may have been up late on the Finance Bill Committee; she is beset by enemies and has to watch every gesture and word. But she sails through it all looking her best. I understand why. She is in love: in love with power, success – and with herself. She looks as I looked when Harold made me Minister of Transport. If we have to have Tories, good luck to her! At lunch in the House I found myself at Harold's table. I asked him which of the potential Tory leaders he would fear most. He said at first that he refused to answer that question, then added suddenly, 'Heath.' He may have been serious. On the other hand, he may have felt safe in saying that because Heath had announced his withdrawal from the contest. Does that mean I have lost my £5 bet with my friend, Bob Connor? Not necessarily. If the Tories choose Willie Whitelaw and Heath stays in parliamentary life, I have a hunch the Tories may yet call him back.

A delegation from the TUC about pay beds. Their representations were very low-key, though Alan Fisher warned me we must announce our policy before their union conference in May. I suspect they were not more ferocious because we are busy fixing up a secret dinner with them to discuss how we can best implement our policy. This gives me a great peace of mind, because I am not willing to go along with David's ideas about a protracted phasing out until I have sounded out the unions, whose members are getting restive about our failure to announce progress.

Another insight into Roy Jenkins's character. I had asked him to see me about an immigration case in my constituency. He kept me waiting (which I didn't mind, because I knew he had been at a Cabinet Committee), but when I was summoned into his vast and rather gloomy room at the Home Office he didn't trouble to apologize. In

---

[1] The revolt against Mr Heath's leadership had been growing among Conservative backbenchers. As early as 13 October *The Times* had given it impetus by declaring that 'it is not possible for Mr Heath to remain as leader of the Conservative Party'. After manoeuvres in the backbench 1922 Committee elaborate new election procedures had been devised by a group headed by Lord Home and the demand that Mr Heath should submit himself to them became irresistible. To win on the first ballot a candidate needed to get the votes of at least half the Conservative MPs and have a lead of forty-two votes over the nearest rival. Heath loyalists like William Whitelaw refused to run against him and Heath opponents prevailed on Margaret Thatcher, the rising star, to stand. At the first ballot she and the maverick right-wing Scots MP, Hugh Fraser, were the only challengers, and on 4 February Margaret astonished everyone by polling 130 votes to Heath's 119, with Fraser a bad also-ran with eleven votes. The result was enough to kill Heath's hopes, but not enough for an outright win by Margaret. Under the rules new candidates could join in for the second round and an unseemly scramble was to ensue, with 'Stop Thatcher' candidates putting forward their names.

fact, he was obviously angry that I should have dared to bother him and told me immediately that he wasn't going to argue over the evidence: he supported the immigration officer without question. But, in view of the fact that Roy Martin[1] had written in his letter to me that he was prepared to 'stake his life' on the reliability of the chap concerned, he was prepared to give him a chance to prove himself right. 'But tell him from me that, not his life, but his reputation, is at stake and if I am let down he must never put a case to me again.' It was all done like a judge lecturing a prisoner put on probation, and I was out of the room in five minutes. I found the whole process illuminating. Not for Roy any tortured doubts about the reliability of the immigration officer. And he had begun by telling me severely that none of the rest of his Cabinet colleagues ever troubled him on matters like this. 'I only have to see you because of your pertinacity on behalf of your constituents.' I have no doubt that this quality of mine does not make for my being loved, but I should have no peace with myself if I did not fight for those I believe to be in the right.

The newspapers are all full of the Tory leadership farce. So many brave warriors have now crept out of hiding to rush to climb on the second ballot bandwagon! Margaret looks the epitome of cool courage compared with them. In the House I ran into Stephen McAdden [Conservative MP for Southend East] and whispered to him, 'How did you vote?' 'For Margaret, of course,' he replied loudly. 'I think she might win,' I said. 'I am sure she will,' he replied.

Thursday, 6 February

At an early meeting of MES we discussed a succession of papers on nationalized industry prices. The effect of phasing out subsidies is going to be very nasty indeed, but I was interested to note that Mike didn't really oppose it. He did warn us of the 'colossal consequences of what is proposed' and feared it might lead to the reopening of pay settlements, but once again he is staying – as I did in 1966 – to face the music of what he believes is unavoidable. (I wonder what has happened to that policy he hinted at at Lockets? I really do miss those weekly dinners.) All he suggested was that we must not just let the news loose on the PLP without warning, but should hold a party meeting to discuss it with our people before any announcement was made. I backed him strongly on this. Denis said gruffly that he hoped nobody was going to try and reopen the decisions on which the whole PESC strategy had been built, but we insisted that wasn't the idea at all: merely that we should practise some of that consultation we were fond of talking about. And so it was agreed. Shirley and I urged the not very venturesome Eric to have another look at ways in which fuel increases could be tempered for the consumer of small amounts. He agreed reluctantly. I suspect he listens to his conventionally minded officials too much.

Then we turned to my paper on how to protect pensioners and the rest from the increases. Denis resisted my plea for the second uprating this year to be advanced to October and preferred a summer £10 bonus instead. He even, as my officials feared he might, proposed that the bonus should take the form of fuel coupons! I slaugh-

---

[1] Roy Martin had been my political agent in Blackburn from 1960–68. He had then become an officer of the Race Relations Board in the North-West and later of the Commission for Racial Equality.

tered him. Were we, I asked, going to revert to the 'couponization' of the protection of the poor? Everyone backed me, even Roy, saying that he thought my arguments were 'unanswerable', though he added, with a former Chancellor's traditional loyalty to a sitting Chancellor, that it would help Denis if the second uprating were to be in November instead of in October. Harold said I should look at the coupon idea, but I think I have won. My proposals are not ideal but they are the best that can be done. An increase in the April uprating would be the best answer (including family allowance), but it is too late.

One interesting incident came when someone (I think Shirley) was asking what the relationship of my proposals would be to the counter-inflationary package we had said before Christmas we should be drawing up. 'I am not aware of any sweeping new counter-inflationary package,' said Harold sharply and went on to say he wished Ministers would not talk to the press as though crisis measures were on their way. Denis even said things were a bit better than they had been: the indices were still confused. What *is* going on, I thought. Is there a crisis or isn't there? I'm blowed if I know.

At Cabinet Harold reported on his visit to the US. Despite his new-found caution he could not resist a little touch of the old self-satisfaction at the way he had been received by President Ford. Relations with the US, he said, were 'as good as they have ever been', adding typically, 'The ceremonies of welcome went far beyond anything I have had before.' We then went into a long discussion on how we should conduct the count in the EEC referendum. Ted was recommending a central count, despite the cost and the difficulties. This was the only way to show that it was a national issue. The views of Cabinet divided predictably: The pro-marketeers went for centralism (the two Roys, Shirley, Harold Lever, Roy Hattersley and Reg Prentice, backed by Denis, Fred, Elwyn and, surprisingly, John Morris, who said the Welsh group had been unanimous that this was the only way to prevent separatism); the rest of us supported Mike in wanting a count by counties. Only Wedgie was for a constituency count. But the voices were close: ten to eight.

I am interested to see from the Minutes of Industrial Development Committee, over which Harold presides, that Wedgie has had a shot at getting his policy on redundancies introduced to deal with steel closures. He wants to impose a statutory obligation on BSC not to declare significant redundancies until they have provided suitable alternative employment. Apparently he wants all nationalized industries to diversify rather than declare redundancies. He didn't get away with it and I doubt whether he has really thought it through, but he does stir things up!

I could only manage a hurried talk with Kay Carmichael, but I liked her very much. When she had gone I told Norman that if Donnison had not been on offer I would have been delighted to have had her as chairman of the SBC, but I thought Donnison would have more time for it than she would. I did intend, however, to appoint her as vice-chairman.

At the office I ran into Henry, who was looking jaded. He had been awake since 5am, he confessed, brooding over the consultants' problem. I began to feel quite worried about his health. At another of our now almost daily meetings on the consultants he put forward the idea that, instead of my amending my letter of 28

January, it might be possible for me to reach agreement with the negotiators on a joint statement. This would obviously have much more weight in getting the profession to call off sanctions. Peter looked very disapproving at this. He didn't trust the consultants' representatives further than he could throw them. But Henry insisted that my reasonableness had made a great impression on them and that they were in an entirely different mood. It would be difficult to agree a statement but it would be a 'great prize'. I said I was prepared to have a shot at it, but I repeated I was getting uneasy about the delay. We must aim to get a document to Gullick next Monday with a view to a statement in the House on Wednesday – the only day of the week that is not likely to be swamped by Tory leadership ballot news. Henry looked worried but said he would try.

Friday, 7 February

While I was in the House attending the Abortion Bill debate, Norman phoned to say Henry was having anxieties again about our proposed timetable. Could I possibly fit in another meeting that afternoon? Henry was as apologetic as usual: he knew he was being a great nuisance to me, etc., but he was worried that I was trying to rush things too much. He then went on to explain that the draft joint statement would be in my weekend box. No doubt I would want to discuss it on Monday. Then he had to get it to the consultants' leaders, who might want to suggest some further changes. At that I exploded: 'Oh no, we can't go on allowing them to erode my position bit by bit like this.' It really was all getting a bit undignified. The process would never end. I had a feeling that the issue might erupt publicly at any time. I really wanted to bring matters to the crunch now. David was as impatient as I was, but finally I said that the decision should be postponed till Monday, when I would have had a chance to see how near we were to agreement on a joint document.

In the corridor outside my room I found Peter Brown and Ian Gillis lying in wait. Peter asked me if he might phone me this weekend after I had had a chance to study the document. I said of course, though naturally I was puzzled. There certainly are wheels within wheels in this department!

Sunday, 9 February

True to his promise, Peter phoned. He told me, crisply and firmly, that he thought that to issue a joint statement would in itself be catastrophic. He could just imagine how Stevenson would handle it. The BMA had had the impertinence in their part of the document to reopen the whole question of what they claimed had been agreed in the Owen working party, even though I had made my own position clear. My letter to them of 28 January had been a first-class document. That was why they were so afraid of having it published, as it would show how reasonable I had been. He still thought the right way was for me to send my own letter unilaterally and then publish it. Peter then maintained that there were a number of my officials who were against the whole idea of a joint statement, but might not have the courage to say so round my discussion table. I thanked Peter for his comments, which I found very useful. As I went back to my work I began to appreciate why Dick thought so much of Peter Brown. He is not only politically shrewd, but, if he identifies himself with a Minister, he throws himself wholeheartedly into the job of serving him (or her).

I duly phoned David to get his reactions to the document Henry had sent us. His first comment was that it was 'not too bad', though we should need to toughen up our part of it. The trouble about trying any redrafting was that, according to a Minute from his private secretary, it was 'agreed Gullick-Yellowlees, subject to ministerial approval'. I hit the roof at this. I seized the opportunity (without mentioning my talk with Peter) to say that, if this was so, it made it impossible to issue a joint statement at all, because any amendments by me would now take on a dangerous significance. David rather agreed and said he had never been keen on the idea anyway. We agreed sadly that it was going to be tricky handling the next steps. David believes there will be no withdrawal of sanctions until the consultants have seen the colour of our money in April. He has also changed his tune about the phasing out of pay beds, having been talking to NUPE leaders on a recent visit to the North. 'I am now convinced that three years is too long,' he told me; 'two years is the maximum, if we can get that. But I think this whole thing is blowing up.' I'm glad to hear him face this fact.

Monday, 10 February

Another long office meeting on the consultants' contract. I began by asking Henry what was the exact authorship of his document. Had it been jointly drafted by him and Gullick? He said firmly, 'Not in the sense you warned me about. So no one can say, if you reject this document, that there is any kind of a split between you and me.' I then asked whose idea it had been to have a joint statement and he said emphatically, 'Theirs. It was entirely their idea.' Peter's eyebrows shot up so far at this that I thought they would fly off his face. I plodded on patiently. I said I was concerned at the fact that the format of an agreed statement meant that the BMA set up the scenario and I was put in the position of merely reacting to it. Peter nodded vigorously at this; Philip gave a half-nod, while Raymond tried to hide his agreement by stabbing, head down, at his blotting paper. Henry was not upset. He had, he said, been in two minds whether to recommend this course of action to me at all. I said I felt in my bones we should miss the boat if we didn't get our own statement out quickly. We must act now. David supported me on this and so did Philip, so I sent Henry away to report on these lines to the negotiators and tell them I wanted to make a statement on Wednesday. Henry himself volunteered to tell them he had felt unable to advise me to accept their idea.

Some hours later Henry asked to see me, looking grim. He said Gullick's reaction to my rejection of an agreed statement had been pretty violent. He had threatened to reveal publicly that I had been asked to do this and refused. I snapped back that this revealed the negotiators in their true colours. They were not trying to reach a settlement but to score points. Henry should tell them that I would regard their revelation of the advice my own CMO had given to me as a serious breach of our agreed confidentiality and would openly describe it as an act of bad faith. Philip nodded approvingly at this and even Henry seemed impressed.

Tuesday, 11 February

With an urgent decision to be taken on my letter to the BMA, I had to cut the meeting of the International Committee of the NEC once again. Trying to fit in party appointments, to say nothing of making occasional appearances in the House, becomes increasingly impossible. Departments remain firmly convinced that they have the first – and almost exclusive – call on their Minister's time and with so many crises popping up it is hard to blame them. Henry reported that Grabham had asked to see me urgently that evening with a last plea that I should delay my statement to the House. I replied that of course I shouldn't refuse. I wasn't going to have them say I had been high-handed. I believed I might even convince him that the course of action I proposed was wise. We then discussed my proposed letter; I had practically rewritten the whole draft. As usual, we spent ages on it, with one person after another wanting to query this word and that. Finally we got it done and agreed we should let Grabham have a copy confidentially.

A Tuesday Cabinet, because Harold is off to Moscow on Thursday. Jim reported that Turkey was trying to declare an independent zone in Cyprus – just as I thought! However, he claimed that US and UK intervention had stopped them in their tracks. This was followed by a long discussion on Mike's Bill and the press.[1] Shirley, Reg Prentice *et al*. nagged away about their anxieties. Mike stuck to his guns, saying that by far the most hopeful way of preserving editorial freedom – from proprietors as well as from the NUJ – was to get agreement on the Charter of Press Freedom which the NUJ had offered. The trouble lay with the editors, whose recent statement had been nothing more than a 'polemical attack on the NUJ'. Harold – who dislikes the press – obviously had some sympathy with him, but when Harold said, 'We have an unfree press', Jim promptly slapped him down, saying he should go and see what was happening in Portugal. Eventually Mike was persuaded to say in the House that, if there was abuse of the closed shop, the Government would be willing to take fall-back action. Meanwhile the Royal Commission on the Press would be looking at the whole position. Another long discussion on the EEC referendum. There was a circular argument about what we should do about providing the information which will be necessary for people to reach a decision. Harold summed up that there had been no time to reach conclusions and that Ted should put alternative paragraphs in the draft White Paper he will be circulating.

I had my meeting with Grabham and Gullick in the House. The manner of both was extremely conciliatory. In return I spelt out in the most friendly way why I had not been able to accept a joint statement and why I felt it was urgent to make a statement in the House as quickly as possible, in the interests of consultants themselves. (This obviously impressed Grabham, who all along has stressed the importance of getting an early increase in pay from the Review Body.) I laid this down the line: how I was fearful we should miss the boat on this round of pay increases; how I was willing to meet their point on an incremental scale; how I was anxious to submit joint evidence with them on other things. I also said I did not wish to jump the gun on

[1] See footnote, page 231.

them. I was ready to postpone my statement for a day or two to enable them to draw up their comments in reply and would be glad to place their statement along with mine at the same time in the Commons library. They were clearly considerably shaken. Grabham said I had been 'most persuasive', though of course they could not commit their fellow negotiators. They went away clutching my letter and very glad I had agreed not to make a statement tomorrow.

Elizabeth said to me, 'Have you heard the news? Mrs Thatcher has walked it.'[1] I have had a growing conviction that this would happen: she is so clearly the best man among them and she will, in my view, have an enormous advantage in being a woman too. I can't help feeling a thrill, even though I believe her election will make things much more difficult for us. I have been saying for a long time that this country is ready – even more than ready – for a woman Prime Minister. The 'it's time for a change from the male sex' version of the old election slogan. After all, men have been running the show as long as anyone can remember and they don't seem to have made much of a job of it. The excitement of switching to a woman might stir a lot of people out of their lethargy. I think it will be a good thing for the Labour Party too. There's a male-dominated party for you – not least because the trade unions are male-dominated, even the ones that cater for women. I remember just before the February election last year pleading on the NEC for us not to have a completely producer-oriented policy, because women lose out in the producer-run society. The battle for cash wage increases is a masculine obsession. Women are not sold on it, particularly when it leads to strikes, because the men often don't pass their cash increases on to their wives. What matters to the women is the social wage. Of course, no one listened to me: even to suggest that the battle for cash wage increases might be a mirage is to show disloyalty to trade unionism! I believe Margaret Thatcher's election will force our party to think again: and a jolly good thing too. To me, socialism isn't just militant trade unionism. It is the gentle society, in which every producer remembers he is a consumer too.

The first fall-out from the Thatcher news came quickly: it clearly put Harold on his mettle. At a dinner for the New Zealand PM at New Zealand House Harold not only made an amusing speech. He was more relaxed than I have seen him for a long time, making impromptu jokes, wandering around talking to everybody and conducting the Maori choir in the singing with the relish of a schoolboy on holiday. Nothing like a bit of sex challenge for bringing the best out in a man. Ted and I then went on to Buckingham Palace for a late reception. I couldn't quite make out what it was in aid of but when I saw that all the literati had been invited from the theatre and the media, from Alec Guinness to Robin Day, I suspected it might not be unconnected with the threatened row over the Civil List.[2] (Incidentally, this matter has never been to

[1] To win on the second ballot for the Conservative leadership a candidate only required an overall majority (139 votes). The result announced on 11 February was: Thatcher 146, Whitelaw 79, Howe 19, Prior 19, Peyton 11.

[2] On 12 February the Prime Minister announced an increase of £420,000 in the Civil List payment to the Royal Family, £150,000 of which the Queen had offered to pay. He defended it by saying that about three-quarters of it was to meet wage and salary increases, mainly for manual and clerical staff. The most serious threat of backbench revolt came not from the left-wing Tribune group but from the centre-right Manifesto group, who put down an Early Day Motion that '... Parliament should have full information

Cabinet.) What more apposite than a bit of royal softening up – particularly as the refreshments were modest in the extreme, demonstrating that the royal economy drive is really on: nothing but whisky and some almost undrinkable white wine. Not even a canapé in sight. The Royal Family were waiting in line in force. Prince Charles was as forthcoming as ever, and we joked about how he had lectured me when I was Minister of Transport for introducing the seventy-mile-an-hour speed limit. When with routine courtesy I asked him how he was, he said he was very well, adding for no apparent reason, 'I enjoy my job very much.' Altogether a great night of royal salesmanship. But it was good fun.

Wednesday, 12 February

The first of the series of meetings I have insisted on holding with the chairmen of the Area Health Authorities; all part of the ploy by David and me to start breaking down the hierarchical monstrosity of Keith Joseph's reorganized NHS. We are to have four such meetings: this morning we could only manage to see the area chairmen from three regions. It went extremely well. They were delighted to be taken notice of, and one important fact emerged from the informal discussion, namely that there could be a considerable streamlining of the overmanned administrative structure. So many posts have been created at region, area and district levels that they simply can't fill a number of them – and where they have done so, some of them admitted, the officials just hadn't enough to do. So much for Sir Keith's managerial efficiency! I instructed them not to overstrain themselves to fill posts – I would positively welcome streamlining.

The papers are full of Margaret Thatcher, who is looking as radiant as a bride. Who wouldn't after such a successful courtship? But the only effect on Harold is to make him scintillate too. I slipped into the House to hear him make his announcement on the Civil List. As he passed Jim and me where we sat on the front bench he whispered chirpily, 'I am in for a rollicking.' 'Did you know about this business?' I asked Jim. 'Not a word of it,' he replied. 'Who *does* decide about the Civil List?' I asked, but he only shrugged. But Harold was on the top of his form, congratulating Margaret impishly and obviously ready to take on all comers from either side. No sign of his being constrained, as some feared, by a woman Leader of the Opposition. Margaret, naturally rather tense, made a not very notable intervention, but one which augurs that she will fight every issue with a populist political slant. When I left, Harold was going great guns. Sex moves in a mysterious way its wonders to perform!

Thursday, 13 February

Harold has had his best press for years. So the first fall-out from Margaret is pure gain to us. Nonetheless I remain convinced she will prove formidable and will have us fighting for our political lives. Right: that will be good for us.

---

concerning the effects of the Sovereign's immunity from taxation which she enjoys not only on the Civil List, but on her private wealth'.

Saturday, 15 February

When at last I got down to HCF I found the BMA statement in reply to mine in my box. Norman's comment on it was that it was 'rather disappointing'. I think it is shamefully irresponsible. It is not only that the statement says it thinks it is 'unlikely' that sanctions will be lifted because I haven't gone far enough; its whole tone is calculated to make the retention of sanctions inevitable. Every conciliatory gesture I have made has been played down. When I phoned David about it he retorted, 'They are impossible. They are weak men and frightened of the HCSA.' He was convinced we had got to forget the new contract and concentrate on getting a good pay increase for the consultants on the present one. One thing he told me was new to me: that last year it was the BMA who had refused to press the Review Body for a change in the incremental scale. Now they are making it a test of my good faith! The trouble is that they don't give a damn for the younger consultant and are more concerned with getting a higher ceiling at the top, while we are more concerned with giving a boost to the chap at the bottom: another reason why they are so mad with me! I spent a good deal of time rewriting the draft statement for me to make on Monday.

Mike has made a speech justifying the miners' increase.[1] All I can say is that it has made it even more inescapable that we should do something generous for the consultants. Personally, my sympathy for the miners has completely run out. I can't help remembering the very moving interview which Sid Weighell of the NUR had on *Midweek* on Thursday night. 'What *am* I to say to my railwaymen who move the coal the surfacemen have loaded? Is their job really worth so much less?' One thing is certain: the miners' settlement has given inflation another dangerous upward twist and brought nearer the demand some members of Cabinet will make for restraints on pay increases. All I know is that I am not going to have wage restraint introduced *now* at the expense of my GPs and consultants, who are at the end of the line. Wouldn't it be ironic if I had to resign because Cabinet refused to give them a proper increase?

Monday, 17 February

Henry and Philip liked my redraft very much. David had some different drafting of his own out of which I incorporated some points. Henry didn't agree with me that the BMA statement was as bloody minded as I thought it was. He said that the negotiators had obviously been very divided over it. When he phoned Gullick about it on Friday Gullick had replied that it was 'now being retyped for the umpteenth time'. He thought the fact that there had been no leaks of my letter over the weekend (which David had gloomily forecast) was a sign that they were trying not to close the door. It was just that they were incapable of giving leadership. In the House my statement went extremely well.[2] Even Geoffrey Howe, with Margaret sitting watching him,

---

[1] A settlement had just been reached which raised the basic rates of 246,000 miners by up to 35 per cent, with bonuses in addition for increased output. Michael Foot had defended it as being necessary to carry through 'a much needed . . . reform of the pay structure', which did not conflict with the Social Contract.

[2] I reported some of the discussions which had been taking place in the 'clarification' meetings on the new contract and repeated that certain principles, like the whole-timers' differential, were not negotiable.

didn't try to make any serious political mileage out of it, while our people backed me enthusiastically. I then managed to stay on for a snatched quarter of an hour to listen to Wedgie move the second reading of his Industry Bill.[1] The Tories were giving him a sustained barracking, but he ploughed on, declaring his faith like a young martyr at the stake. (He always gives one the impression of being youthful, despite his grey hairs.) But I do wish he could manage to sound less like a lay preacher helping everyone else to find the right road to God.

Tuesday, 18 February

Eric Heffer had a rough ride winding up on the Industry Bill debate. He didn't make a great speech, but he did have the vital political stamina to plough on regardless to the end. Our majority, in the event, was quite comfortable, some of the Welsh Nationalists having switched. As it has happened, we have coasted through most divisions so far with an easy margin, but all that may change as Maggie leads her troops into a real fight. Life should be fun with an embittered Ted Heath on the back benches, together with the other ex-frontbenchers Maggie sends to join him. Her progress continues to be a triumphal one.

But the dreadful shadow over the day is Patrick Crossman's suicide. I was just getting ready for my monthly meeting with Harold Collison of the SBC when they brought me the news that he had hanged himself. Horrible, horrible, horrible! It is like a Greek tragedy and I cannot get rid of the haunting feeling that this is some grim retribution for the publication of the *Memoirs*, which nobody likes very much and which make Dick's insistence on publishing them seem in bad taste. And the unhappy Anne – coming in to her own kitchen from a shopping expedition with Virginia to find him hanging there! I didn't know what to do to comfort her. Finally I dropped the faithful Tam[2] a note asking for his advice. He sought me out in the division lobby and oddly enough the first thing he said to me was that he couldn't help feeling that the *Memoirs* had had something to do with it. He had consulted Patrick about publishing them and he had been in favour of going ahead because 'it is what Pop wanted'. After

---

I added that we did not wish these discussions to hold up the consultants' pay increase due in April and announced that I was giving evidence to the Review Body in support of that increase and of important improvements in their incremental scale.

[1] The Bill reflected the concessions Tony Benn had been forced to make on the party's industrial strategy. It strengthened the Tory Industry Act by, for example, extending the power to acquire 100 per cent of the shares of a company, but still only by agreement. It set up the National Enterprise Board with funds of up to £1,000 million, but gave it no compulsory powers of acquisition. It provided for voluntary planning agreements between firms and the Government, with no mention of the trade unions, and reassured industry by ensuring that any regional development grants payable under them would not be reduced during the lifetime of the agreement. It gave powers to prevent the control of any major manufacturing company from passing into foreign hands and required the disclosure of information to the Secretary of State, and through him to the trade unions concerned, by important companies, subject to qualifications and safeguards. (Even this provision was later modified when Eric Varley succeeded Tony Benn at Industry.) In his Second Reading speech Benn said hopefully that planning agreements were designed to cover 100 to 150 firms.

[2] Tam Dalyell, Labour MP for West Lothian, who had been one of Dick Crossman's most devoted friends for many years and his PPS in his various Cabinet jobs. As he lodged in Dick's London house, he was in closer touch with him than any of us.

the first instalment had appeared Tam had phoned Patrick again and he had seemed quite content, 'but it may be that when he saw them in black and white it felt different'. Tam added, 'I know you were always against publishing them and it may be that you were right.'[1] At Tam's suggestion I went off to phone Anne, because he said she seemed to find talking a relief. For Anne, she was almost voluble, repeating over and over again, 'What a waste. I just do not know why.' She insisted that Patrick had been happy and doing well at school. No doubt it will remain a mystery. I comforted her as best I could, feeling useless, but she said, 'It does help.'

Wednesday, 19 February

Spent the whole morning at the Women's National Commission. I must be getting feminist in my old age! Then into an office meeting on pay beds. We all agree that I must get a paper to Cabinet quickly, so that we are ready with an announcement, either if we can get into talks with the BMA again, or if the unions break out of the restraints their leaders are desperately trying to keep on them. David is now convinced that we cannot hold the position for three years, but he gets quite tetchy at the idea of our trying to control the *quantity* of beds in the private hospitals that will undoubtedly spring up everywhere. He is far more reactionary about this than my officials are! I say firmly that I see no reason why I should not announce that I intend to keep the number of private beds to the level of the pay beds currently allowed in the NHS. I am convinced that we have got to fight like hell to prevent the building up of a vast empire of private medicine. And with not enough money to keep the NHS expanding and improving as it ought, our whole policy is in danger.

Dinner with the Yugoslav Ambassador. I was interested to see that he and the Turkish Ambassador were convinced Britain would have to stay in the Common Market. Even the Polish Ambassador accepted the idea. I got carried away into a great exposé of the anti-Market case which clearly shook them – and I think impressed them. If there is to be a free-for-all, I intend to have my share of freedom.

Thursday, 20 February

Harold is back from Moscow, immensely proud of his achievements and of the communiqué.[2] And of course he is full of the welcome they received from the Russians. 'They laid themselves out in an unparalleled way by all the standard tests' (e.g. column inches in *Pravda*). On parliamentary business the EEC directives reared their ugly heads again: this time on the Regional Fund.[3] Jim, of course, was all for us

[1] When I had read the diaries through I changed my mind. They seemed to me to have thrown a lot of light on the processes of government and not to have damaged anyone – except, in some people's opinion, Dick himself.

[2] The long communiqué set out an agreed programme of Anglo-Soviet co-operation, particularly in the economic and scientific fields. Both sides agreed 'to aim at achieving a substantial increase in the level of trade'. Britain announced the provision of just under £1,000 million of credits for trade over a five-year period.

[3] The Regional Fund was being set up following the Paris Summit in December and a Community regulation was being prepared which would be 'binding in its entirety and directly applicable in all member states'.

tabling a Motion to 'take note'; Wedgie and Mike would have none of it. Such a Motion would be dishonest because we all knew a three-year commitment was about to be decided on in the Council of Ministers. The House should have the right to take a decision on the merits of the proposals themselves. Jim grew tetchy on this, as he now regularly does if anyone tries to limit his freedom of action in the Council of Ministers – I am now convinced that he is the most ardent pro-marketeer of the lot of us. When Wedgie insisted that the Regional Fund policy would prevent us from operating our own regional policy methods, Jim snarled at him, 'Your department could have discussed this with us, but you have given your officials instructions that they are not to co-operate.' Harold, too, got quite tetchy with Wedgie, saying that this matter was not in the Manifesto as one of the items for renegotiation, that we could not hold up a decision because other countries like Italy needed the money desperately and that quite small administrative changes would meet Wedgie's point. And so it was left. Unfortunately I haven't had time to follow the argument. Nor have I had time to read the brief Jack has prepared, at my request, on Fred's agricultural achievements and the progress we are making on the CAP. I am convinced that Fred's settlement is a patchwork thing and I am desperately anxious to raise it, but I have been up since 6am working against time on a detailed and important speech I have to make to a conference on Finer tomorrow. How does one solve the problem of finding the time to equip oneself to be a fully effective member of Cabinet? I work sixteen to seventeen hours a day non-stop and there is still not enough time.

At last we finalized Ted Short's Referendum White Paper, but not before we had spent one-and-a-half hours arguing about some unresolved details. Jim reported that the TUC had come out in favour of a constituency vote, which makes me *less* in favour of it, rather than more (I don't want any witch-hunting), though I believe the central count we have decided on will be disastrous. There was a great argy-bargy about how much information should be distributed and by whom. There was laughter when I suggested we ought to issue a referendum kit: a plastic hold-all, like one gets at conferences, which could contain the Government's statement on the terms, a pamphlet by the pros and another by the antis. Of course they teased me, but one by one they began to see some sense in it. John Hunt even tossed me an amusing note.[1] I still think it is the best idea.

On parliamentary business Harold surprised us by saying suddenly that he wanted to explain what would be his parliamentary strategy in view of the election of a new Tory leader. As far as Thatcher was concerned: 'I shall answer every question in the

---

[1] John Hunt's note to me in Cabinet:

> *Referendum Kit?*
> Outcome of renegotiation
> Government recommendation
> Case for
> Case against
> Map to polling station
> Polling card
> Opinion poll response cards
> 1 bottle champagne ⎤
>   ⎬ to be taken at choice according to result
> 1 bottle arsenic ⎦

spirit in which it is put. If it is a genuine request for information I shall be informative. I want to concentrate on policy. I don't want to get into the situation I was in with Heath: confrontation.' So obviously he has been giving some anxious thought to it!

As I worked late at the office on my Finer speech, news came through that the CCHMS had refused to withdraw sanctions; but they haven't extended them and they have asked to see the PM. I can't help feeling this is not a bad sign and Henry tells me Grabham tried hard to get them to negotiate with me. So my talk with him seems to have worked. I had to rush into TV interviews and a press conference. We shall have to give careful thought to where we go from here.

At last I have got Bill McCarthy appointed! I wonder if Harold ever wrote that Minute he told me he would to speed things up? He said he would only have to write the Minute for Cabinet Office to get busy, sew everything up with my department and then assure him the Minute was unnecessary.

Friday, 21 February

Up at 6am again in a great rush to finish that complicated Finer speech. I thought it was full of meat, but these pressure groups make hysterical audiences. At last into the car to drive to Sunningdale, where we are to have the first of our consultation meetings on the new strategy we need to cope with the financial straits that now face the NHS. This one was with the regional chairmen as a whole. With one or two exceptions I didn't find them a particularly impressive lot. I get the feeling that these appointed bodies are like a fifth wheel on the coach. They neither speak as elected representatives nor do they have the expertise of their own officials. And their attitude to the Secretary of State and the department is necessarily pretty subservient – they want to keep their jobs! Nonetheless I found the two-day talks valuable, not least because they enabled me to set some time aside to study the details of the grim options that are now open to us. The department's projections of the cost of desirable policy amount to over £300 million of capital expenditure in the NHS alone, whereas our PESC allocation for hospital building by the end of the five-year period will be only £225 million. We had a useful discussion on possible administrative and building economies and I am sure there is some fat we can eliminate. But even having done all that, we face some drastic pruning of essential policies. What worried me was that some of the Tory chairmen seemed positively enthusiastic at the prospect of cutting back spending. I said our dilemma meant that we must make a reality of integration between the health and social services. What would they feel if we took some of the limited growth money of the NHS and used it as 'integration money'[1] – i.e., to spend on community services in conjunction with the local authorities, which would save even more money by not keeping people in hospital who should not be there? They liked the idea and officials promised me they would seriously work on it. Anyway, the chairmen told me afterwards they had enjoyed themselves enormously.

During the weekend David, Philip, Henry, Norman and I discussed the answer the

---

[1] This idea was later adopted in the form of 'joint financing'. Under this, health authorities contribute to the capital and the running cost of local authority services which take people like the elderly and mentally handicapped out of hospital and into the community.

PM should send to the BMA. Philip and Henry said they thought he must turn down the request for a meeting, but David and I agreed we must take a more positive posture and constantly keep putting the ball back in the consultants' court. I liked Norman's idea that the PM might say he would see them if they would withdraw sanctions and I went back to Hell Corner Farm to draft what I think is a rather clever version of it. One of my joys as a Minister is proving that I am a better drafter than my civil servants are.

One amusing moment came when David said to me, 'These people still think they can divide Harold from you, but I keep telling them yours is the strongest political alliance in the whole Government. You stood by Harold when no one else did. You really have a special relationship.' I hope he is right!

With the TUC guidelines being breached on every side, inflation had begun to run away. Over the twelve months to December average earnings had increased by 29·1 per cent and by January retail prices had risen by nearly 20 per cent over the previous year, with more increases in the pipeline. Output was falling and by 10 February unemployment had reached 734,000 or 3·1 per cent, with nearly another quarter of a million people on short time. Though the trade deficit was improving there were signs that this was due not so much to an improvement in Britain's industrial performance as to a big jump in our export prices which would eventually make us uncompetitive. World trade remained depressed, aggravated by competitive deflation among major industrial countries determined to keep out of deficit at all costs. West Germany insisted on remaining in surplus over the whole period. Sterling was under intense pressure and our reserves were shrinking, necessitating further borrowing. The press began to talk of national bankruptcy.

There was growing agreement in the Labour movement that something must be done. The argument was about what was necessary. With the CBI's latest survey reporting a slump in business confidence Harold Wilson had hastened to assure firms that Tony Benn would not be allowed a free hand to intervene in industry. Denis Healey was planning new stimuli for private industry. On 10 February the Financial Times *had noted in its leader: 'It seems reasonable to assume ... that the Chancellor is not planning any further assault for the time being on corporate profitability: he has indeed said it is the aim of the government to maintain private capital investment at as high a level as possible.' For its part the TUC was divided on the need to strengthen the guidelines and was calling for some reflation to save jobs. A new school of British economists, the Cambridge Economic Policy Group, led by Mr Wynne Godley, Director of the University of Cambridge Department of Applied Economics, had produced a challenging new analysis of the conditions for economic recovery, in which import controls played a crucial part. This was to dominate the political argument.*

On the NEC apprehension about the crisis was growing. At the March meeting of the Home Policy Committee Geoff Bish, the party's research secretary, produced, 'with the agreement of the chairman' (Tony Benn), the first of what were to become four-monthly Economic Reviews, setting out 'some of the possible options available to the Government'. The most notable thing about this first Review was the priority it gave to tackling inflation and its bald statement: 'The reality of Britain's position today is that there is very little room for any improvement at all in personal living standards over the next four years.' It also rejected the idea that the Government could simply reflate its way out of unemployment. But it also rejected conventional deflationary policies or the belief that private industry could be bribed to invest in British industry to the extent needed. The answer, it argued, lay in more government intervention in industry through planning agreements, which must be enforced, if necessary, and through the NEB, which should be given greater powers. In the short term, to stop the rot in manufacturing industry, import controls might be inevitable. While seizing on the document's willingness to tighten the guidelines of pay policy, Denis Healey ignored the NEC's plea for a tougher industrial strategy. He was already planning a severe budget and another £1 billion of cuts in public expenditure in 1976–77.

Meanwhile the renegotiations of Britain's terms for membership of the EEC were being hurried on in preparation for a decision at the Dublin summit on 10 March. The anti-Market members of Cabinet found the terms that were emerging totally unacceptable and started to prepare their counter-attack in the referendum campaign which was to infuriate Harold Wilson. The White Paper, 'Referendum on United Kingdom Membership of the European Community' (Cmnd. 5925), which had just been published, said the referendum would be held before the end of June, so there was not much time. In my own department the negotiations with the consultants for ending their 'sanctions' dragged on endlessly. Having rejected the new contract we had offered them as too restrictive of part-timers' activities, they were seeking 'modifications' of their new contract which I could not accept. It was clear that the dispute would only be settled by the Government's willingness to implement in full their Review Body's pay award on their existing contract, due in April: the first review since statutory pay controls had been abolished. Although believing that voluntary restraint on pay increases was essential if the 'social wage', was to be safeguarded, I was determined that consultants, junior doctors and GPs should not be penalized by being the last in the queue in the free-for-all pay round.

Saturday, 1 March

Looking back, I think this has been quite one of the most impossible weeks I have ever had. More than once in the past I have said to myself, 'The pressures this week are intolerable; next week *must* be easier', only to find that the following week has been worse. But this time I really do think I have had to crowd more into seven days (in the form of major policy statements, key speeches and policy crises) than I can ever remember and I have been top for Questions as well. There have been moments when I have felt my head would burst – and moments when my temper definitely has burst. It hasn't so much been the lack of sleep (I can manage pretty easily on five hours a night these days) as the relentless pressure of rushing from one piece of major exposure to the next, without even five minutes to relax and take a breath. It has been the endless worry as to whether I would even have a whole garment and an unladdered pair of tights to wear. Poor old Ted pointed out to me at mid-week that his jacket was torn and that he had a missing button which he couldn't get sewn on. My riposte was to pull out my winter coat, whose lining is falling apart for want of a stitch, and tell him how embarrassed I was when people at functions insisted on helping me into it. Any woman in public life really needs a seamstress and hairdresser to travel with her everywhere if she is to have her mind free for higher things. The Queen does, and, for all her public protestations, I suspect Margaret Thatcher has something much nearer to that than I have.

Monday started early, as I had to be at the Liaison Committee with the TUC at the House of Commons. I arrived a little late to find Wedgie in the chair and a full complement of the trade unions – even Hughie. The subject was ostensibly to discuss the draft of the TUC's *Economic Review*, but we all knew we were bursting to talk about inflation and what on earth the trade unions were going to do to help us about it. The papers are once again full of rumours that certain members of the Cabinet are pressing for a tightening of incomes policy and I have no doubt they would love to do it, if they thought there was a cat in hell's chance of getting away with it. The *Economic Review* was a great, fat document which, among all the massive policy statements in my box this weekend, I just hadn't had time to read, but I skimmed through it as we went along. When I arrived Len Murray was introducing it in those low, slurred tones that nearly drive me mad. The strain of trying to catch what people like him and Harold are saying adds to life's irritations all the time. What the *Review* said, said Len, was that it was wrong to think we could continue to try to solve our problems by wage restraint. Productivity was more important. Also investment. The TUC very much welcomed the Industry Bill, planning agreements and the NEB. Also industrial democracy. 'We are taking this side of it very seriously indeed.' And he added, 'We wish there could be more weekend speeches on the positive things the Government are doing and less bickering about wage restraint.'

Denis echoed this. The Labour Government had reversed the Tory policy on social spending. 'The social wage has gone up by 10 per cent in the past year.' But he went on more gloomily, picking his words carefully: 'But I am concerned as to whether, by and large, the spirit of the guidelines is being observed. I hope the trade union movement will not be looking for ways round them, but for ways to carry them out.' Only 60 per cent of settlements were within the guidelines. The OECD figures for next year showed us as 60 per cent above the average on inflation. Michael was bursting to come in. He certainly doesn't try to hide behind anybody. He said he agreed with Len Murray about the importance of other parts of the policy. His department was already discussing job creation measures and training with the TUC. As for wages, it wasn't for us to discuss detailed cases in this committee. Nor did he think the Department of Employment should pass judgments. He had tried to put the miners' case in a context that was helpful to the trade union movement and the Government. Although in some respects it had gone beyond the guidelines he believed it was a good settlement: good for the country. But, he added, 'if others follow it the guidelines will be bust wide open'. If, moreover, the unions were to take the post-tax situation as the starting-point, there wouldn't be any money for the social wage. Jack Jones spoke with an almost pleading anxiety: 'The fact that we are trying has had an effect. Even the miners' settlement could be much worse. All we can do is to use what influence we can and I hope we shall not fall out on the basis that the unions are backsliding.'

Then came the surprise of the morning as Hughie stirred into speech, writhing in his chair as he always does when he feels strongly about something. 'What we should do is some straight talking within the TUC itself,' he said. 'The position has already been breached. If there is a free-for-all my union wants to be part of the all – and I am talking about the trade union movement.' We all knew, he went on, that his union had abstained on the Social Contract vote at Congress because it wanted to see what the Government would do, but at the meeting of his policy committee last November they had taken a line 'that can only be interpreted as concurrence'. But the guidelines meant 'only one increase a year and that within the cost of living, and if we mean that why don't we say so?' Wonders will never cease! The rest of us could hardly believe our ears, while Alf Allen murmured, 'I concur with that.' (Later someone pointed out to me that Hughie must be sensing the right-wing winds beginning to blow through his union.) Sid Greene rounded it off by pointing out that his union was standing fast by the twelve-month rule for the signalmen. Harold said the Tories were moving into a monetarist policy which would highlight the warning of what was the alternative awaiting us. And so we broke up, still friends, the unions still pleading with us that they were doing their best, and with every one of us aware of the unions' difficulties. Perhaps Hughie's volte-face may signal a tougher line by the TUC in support of the guidelines before too long. But I still think Michael's public reaction to the miners' settlement was too soft and tolerant. I still do not see any alternative to a voluntary policy, but I despair at the Government's failure to orchestrate a firm exposition of what is necessary for the Social Contract to succeed and what steps we will have to take if it doesn't. I am more convinced than ever of the importance of my pamphlet on the social wage.[1]

I slipped off before the end in order to fit in an office meeting on the reply Harold should send to the consultants. I wanted to get it cleared before I saw Ronnie Butt of *The Times* tonight. My vanity was boosted when first Philip, then Henry said they did not want to alter my draft at all, while David added with a grin, 'You will be surprised to know that neither do I.' So it was cleared by No. 10 with barely a change. We next had a long ministerial lunch, with, as usual, so many items of interest that we ran over time. First we had to discuss the social wage document, of which Brian A-S. had done another redraft along the lines we suggested. We agreed it is shaping up nicely now and that we should put it in the hands of a popular journalist to decide how to present it. I am desperately anxious to get it out quickly before Denis's axe falls.

---

[1] Denis Healey having failed to produce a popular version of the Public Expenditure White Paper, I had decided to do one myself. I believed we were failing to get across to working people the cash value to them of the social services and how wrong it was for them to think of the taxes they paid as a pure loss. Brian Abel-Smith had worked out a series of useful illustrations. For example, when a woman had a baby she was entitled to free maternity services worth £300. We estimated that this 'second wage' was worth about £20 a week for every member of the working population.

Next I had to discuss with Jack and Brian A-S. the material I shall require for my speech to the Yorkshire region this weekend. Here again I want to talk about the social wage and I told them the sort of figures I would want. Next we went into the Sextet meeting with top officials[1] where Philip accepted without demur the need for us to bring in a journalist for the social wage job. In a great hurry I just managed to get to my meeting at the House with Ronnie Butt. Peter Brown still seems to think he might do a helpful column for us on the consultants and I have already spent an hour with him on the phone. He still wanted to clear some points, so we went over the ground for yet another hour until I finally had to throw him out, explaining that I had to change and get to a dinner at No. 10 at 7.15pm. I shouldn't be a bit surprised if I had been wasting my time. I did one of my quick-change artist's acts and got to No. 10 *nearly* dressed, pinning on my brooch as I hurried upstairs.

The dinner was one of Harold's quixotic gestures to half-a-dozen voluntary organizations which have banded together to work out an anti-poverty strategy for overseas countries. Harold gave every show of taking their very vague and generalized ideas as if they were major contributions to political thought, offered to set up a 'think tank' at the heart of government, hold recall meetings and heaven knows what. When he, Judith and I had to slip away to the House to vote on the televising of Parliament I pleaded with him to be excused from going back as I had two fat boxes of work waiting for me. We won the radio vote easily,[2] but I was horrified to discover people like Judith and Brian [O'Malley] going to the lobby *against* televising, which was lost by twelve votes. It really seems to me incredibly Canute-like for Parliament to try and hold back the people's right to know. Margaret Thatcher sat on the front bench waving her Order Paper jubilantly when the defeat was announced.

It was late when I got home that night with only half my box work done. Submissions on this and that go on showering onto me and I just cannot get the necessary time to do any work in depth. For instance, I have to make a major statement on mental handicap policy tomorrow at a conference called by the National Society for Mentally Handicapped Children. David, who has been leading an office discussion on this, sent me the draft statement at the weekend: policy okay, but drafting so packed with obscure jargon that I insisted that Jack should simplify it a bit. I couldn't get down to looking at the speech until late in the afternoon. I then tried to master a detailed background brief for the questions it has been agreed I should take at the conference. Really! A detailed Finer statement to produce on Friday; a detailed mental handicap statement to make on Wednesday; a massive detailed brief to master on the Pensions Bill which we were to launch for press conferences on Thursday; a major speech on the social wage to make on Saturday (and a day centre to open on Friday!). No human being could be expected to do all this *in addition* to PQs and all the urgent routine office work. If I survive I deserve to be hailed as a genius.

[1] See pages 124–25. We called the meetings 'Sextet' because three Ministers and three top officials were invited.

[2] Two Motions had been debated. The first, to authorize an experiment in public sound broadcasting of our proceedings, was carried by 354 votes to 182; but the second, to permit the televising of Parliament, was lost by 275 to 263.

Once again it was late when I got to bed and once again my box remained half full of work undone. I decided to slip away early from the NEC on Wednesday morning, at which nothing notable occurred except the fixing of the date of the special party conference on the EEC terms. Even Frank Allaun agreed it should only be a one-day conference. Back at the House I went carefully through the rewrite of our press statement on pensions, which I had asked Peter to do, having dismissed his first one as far too academic. I had made him laugh when I said, 'We all of us think far too much about *The Times* and the *Telegraph*. They aren't read by the people in whom I am interested. What I want to do is to move the *Mirror* and silence the *Sun*.' The rewrite was certainly a great improvement, but I still wanted to clarify and simplify it and worked on it against time till at last I was satisfied and sent it off. I then had to turn to my mental handicap brief, which I tried to master in half an hour over a sandwich and a glass of milk. I arrived at the conference pretty drained and strained, but the policy pronouncements went down well; I didn't make any howlers over the esoteric questions that were fired at me and even gave two radio recordings as though I knew what I was talking about.

The sun was shining and I shocked Elizabeth, who was waiting to rush me back to the office for the next round of crisis confabulations, when I said that I was going to take a quick constitutional round St James's Park. She sat disapprovingly in the car over a newspaper while I walked smartly round the park, loving the crocuses and daffodils so prematurely in full bloom and delighting in those ducks. I keep begging the office to try to fit in this kind of little life-saving interlude, but nothing will cure the civil servant of his instinctive belief that a Minister's every waking minute belongs to the department. Back at the office we discussed a party political broadcast Brian and I are to do on pensions; I signed a pile of letters, dealt with some urgent Minutes and talked to Jack and Brian A-S. about the first outline they have done of my weekend speech. Jack was hurriedly finishing my brief on defence for Cabinet and hasn't had a moment to look at that equally vital item: what should be our reaction to the EEC directives on regional policy. God knows, I thought, when I am going to have time to read my Cabinet papers and I really ought to be turning my mind to the press conference on the Pensions Bill tomorrow.

The result of all this was that I was a bit late for the private discussion dinner arranged for us by the NHS unions. Everyone I had suggested was there: Terry Parry (in the chair), Alan Fisher, Audrey Prime, Geoffrey Drain, Clive Jenkins, Peter Jacques, Renee Short, Laurie Pavitt and my lot. Terry had insisted that on the union side only members of the General Council of the TUC should be there. It was a cosy, amiable meal in Victor's top room at the Gay Hussar, though we had to rush things a bit as we had to get back to vote on the Civil List. But we managed to cover all the ground, in addition to eating a good meal. The whole idea of the operation from my point of view was the education of David Owen, with whom I have been having such difficulty over the pay beds policy. In the event it was intriguing to see how completely he swung behind the unions' view. When I, leaning over backwards to present every side of the case (including his previous view), said that the profession would be expecting at least three years for phasing out, he promptly agreed with the unions that eighteen months would be the absolute maximum. So when we came to the issue of controls over the private sector of medicine I wasn't going to be caught again and said firmly that I thought I would be entirely justified in saying that I intended to limit the increase in the number of private beds outside the NHS to the figure at present obtaining inside the NHS – i.e. four thousand. Clive said he thought that would be acceptable to them, whereupon David said at once that this was undoubtedly the right course! Well, I'm delighted to have him committed. As I told him the other day, he is rather like Dick Crossman in that he likes to put up a line of argument purely for argument's sake, only to abandon it later – and he agreed cheerfully.

I had to get up early to read Jack's brief on the Defence White Paper for Cabinet and also the papers on EEC regional policy. Result: I still hadn't read my detailed notes for the pensions press conferences and I hoped I might do my usual trick and go through them during some boring interlude in Cabinet. I have mastered the art of doing two things at once: working on one subject while listening with one ear to the discussion on another. But not a bit of it! I don't seem to have had any breaks this week. Cabinet agenda was crowded with vital matters from beginning to end.

First Denis reported on the renegotiation of the Chilean debt and recommended no rescheduling this year. At the cost of £1 million we could really bring pressure to bear on the Chilean régime to pay some attention to civil rights, he said. (So the pressure of the NEC has had some effect: another reason why the NEC should maintain a critical role.) Incidentally, Denis told us that inflation in Chile was running at about 60 per cent a year. So much for the critics of Allende's Government! We then launched into a protracted discussion of the regional policy of the EEC and the position over steel. Harold had circulated a memo which said that the Community rules on regional policy met our five specific conditions and that, although constitutionally the Treaty gave the Commission certain formal powers, the 'political reality' was that control was effectively kept by the Council of Ministers.[1] On steel he was more worried, because, although in practice we had found it possible to control steel prices, the ECSC Treaty[2] specifically conflicted with Section 15 of the Iron and Steel Act 1967, which gave us powers to control investment in the private sector; that was why Heath had repealed Section 15. We should therefore clearly have to 'overhaul' the ECSC Treaty, but the rest of the Community would not be willing to consider this

---

[1] The Regulation setting up the European Regional Development Fund (Regulation No. 724/75) was adopted by the Council of Ministers on 18 March. The aim is to correct 'the main regional imbalances within the Community which are likely to prejudice the attainment of economic and monetary union'. Industrial investments can be made out of the fund, provided State aid is already being given. The investments must form part of regional development programmes on which the Commission has been consulted and the Commission 'shall examine them, having regard to the provisions of the Treaty and the decisions adopted by Community institutions'. Article 92 of the Treaty of Rome forbids 'any aid granted by a member State ... which distorts or threatens to distort competition by favouring certain undertakings or the production of certain goods'.

[2] The European Coal and Steel Community was set up by the Treaty of Paris and came into force in 1952 with six founder members, who later became the Six of the European Community. The Treaty of Rome developed from discussion among the ECSC members. Section 15 of Labour's Iron and Steel Act, 1967, gave the Government power to control private investment. Ted Heath repealed it in the European Communities Act, 1972, as incompatible with the Treaty of Paris. It was agreed at the final renegotiation meeting in Dublin that Britain would study how best to reassume these powers, but that this should be done after the referendum. They were not reassumed.

unless and until it was clear that we were staying in. What we should do therefore was to give notice that this would be our objective if we *did* stay in. Wedgie had issued a counterblast to all this in the form of a paper condemning us for not having even tried to retrieve the powers over regional policy which the Treaty of Accession had transferred to the Commission. However liberal might be the current statement of Commission policy, it was clear that it was antipathetic to all forms of aid other than those to investors for their capital expenditure and that, if we let this go with our endorsement in the Council of Ministers, we should be under increasing pressure to abandon other forms, like REP.[1] Moreover, we couldn't pretend even to have tried to fulfil the Manifesto commitment on keeping effective control over regional policies. Besides, the Fund Regulation gave the Commission power to interfere over the whole range of regional policy. This was the 'draconian curtailment of the power of the British Parliament to settle questions vital to British interests' which we had pledged ourselves in the Manifesto to reverse. But Wedgie had also scored a coup in getting hold of – and circulating to Cabinet – the Minutes of a meeting Roy Hattersley had had a few days ago with Wischnewski, his German counterpart. Roy was reported as saying that he had told Ortoli [President of the Commission] that the British Government wasn't going to challenge the document on regional policy, but hoped 'the Commission would exercise caution in the exercise of its functions during the period before the referendum', so as not to lose 'yes' votes! The row which followed Wedgie's revelation was prodigious. Jim first said that we ought not to discuss this in Roy Hattersley's absence, then that he took full responsibility anyway, and finally that he didn't see any harm in it. Peter, Mike and I all joined in the fray, with Harold pouring soothing interpretative oil over everything. We three also argued that the discussion of steel should not have been left so late – and certainly could not be left till after our membership had been confirmed. Finally Harold summed up that Britain should make a holding statement on regional aid at the next Council of Ministers and Cabinet should reach a final decision on it in the general stock-taking at the end of the renegotiations.[2] As for steel, we should have to resume powers to control investment, but here again we should have to decide how best this could be done at the stock-taking. So he has successfully dodged both these issues and will be able to present them as part of his general 'back my successful renegotiation' ploy when he reports back from Dublin.[3] Once again he has done his Houdini act!

All this took nearly two hours, and it was 1pm when at last we turned to defence. I was desperate by now because I should have been having a drink with City editors at

[1] The Regional Employment Premium was introduced in 1967 as a subsidy on labour costs payable to manufacturing employers in development areas if their establishment qualified under the Selective Employment Payments Act 1966.

[2] A few days later Tony Benn wrote to the Prime Minister complaining that, according to the *Economist* of 1 March, the Government was urging the Commission to adopt the same 'lie low until after the referendum' technique towards the powers he proposed to take in his Industry Bill. He also complained that the Foreign Secretary was preventing him seeing the record of the Brussels discussions on regional policy.

[3] Britain's renegotiation of the Common Market terms was completed during a two-day meeting held in Dublin Castle on 10–11 March. Dr Garret Fitzgerald, the Irish Foreign Minister, was the current President of the EEC.

12.30 to launch our Pensions Bill. Frustrated as I was at not being at the christening of my own policy, I was nonetheless determined to fire my ammunition against Roy Mason's phoney figures about his 'cuts'. Harold had clearly been primed by Bernard Donoghue in the same way as I had been primed, because as soon as I started to challenge the assumptions on which Mason had based his figures Harold chipped in to say, 'These figures have already been accepted by Cabinet.' Nonetheless, I said doggedly that the Public Expenditure White Paper had starred these figures as 'provisional', yet the Defence White Paper talked in terms of a firm ten-year plan. Why should defence expenditure be firm for ten years when we weren't given security for our other programmes even for five years? Mike and the rest of our group watched anxiously but silently. They obviously hadn't had time to gen up on this – any more than I had had time to gen up on Wedgie's regional policy. Talk about left-wing conspiracies! We don't have time for them. It was Harold who came to my aid. It was true, he said, that we had used the word 'provisional' in the Public Expenditure White Paper. Why not use it in the Defence White Paper too? Roy Mason fought back like a tiger: it would sow alarm and uncertainty, etc., etc. And that turncoat, Denis, supported him. Harold argued back quietly but unshakeably. Frantic as I was to get to my City editors I could not help but admire his tenacity. Eventually Harold managed to rig the summing up his way, and mine, both approving the White Paper and saying that the point about provisionality should be looked into further. I could have hugged him, for I can see what is coming: further expenditure cuts *now* for the rest of us, while Roy Mason takes five years even to think about his further cuts.

It was 1.30pm before I got to Admiralty House in a fine bad temper at being so late. I pulled myself together and made a belated little speech, paying Brian a big tribute. God knows he deserves it, but God knows he would like to take over the whole conduct of the Bill and is already hinting that there is no need for me to go onto the Standing Committee. But go I shall – and what is more, I shall take my full share of the debates. I am not going to be done out of my part of our joint memorial. Having snatched a shrivelled sandwich I then hurried across the road for the big press conference, of which I took charge. As I said at the beginning, the non-stop pressures of this week have been unprecedented.

Ronnie Butt produced an equivocal piece on the consultants – just as I thought he would. When I think of all the time I spent on him I could kick myself!

I still had my hand-out to do for my weekend speech. I am convinced I must start seriously trying to sell the social wage. Ideally I would have liked to write and hand out a full major speech: my counterblast to Keith Joseph. But it was just impossible. I soldiered on and eventually was quite pleased with it. To bed at 1am.

Friday
Woke at 8am, still in a daze. Finished reading yesterday's newspapers over a cup of tea and packed my bag for the weekend. At 8.30am, on my way to my life-saving bath, I had an idea. Why not ask Jack to call in for the hand-out on his way to the office? 'Get me Jack's number, would you?' I asked Ted. Seconds later I heard Ted speaking on the phone. 'It's Anthea,' he said. 'Jack was going out of the door but she

managed to catch him.' Jack was still breathless when I spoke to him and said he would be round immediately. I gave him the hand-out, finished dressing and finally managed to leave for the office just in time to get ready for the TV recording I had promised to do for *Weekend World*. In the heart of the City Edna exclaimed in annoyance, 'There's a diversion.' I looked up from my papers, cursing, to see policemen at the end of the road leading to Moorgate station. They were waving cars aside. 'Must have been an accident,' I said. 'There are a lot of ambulances down that street.' The diversion made me late and I had another hectic rush through make-up, the recording (on the consultants' dispute) and finally to Southwark to open the Aylesbury Day Centre. By then the news had come through that there had been a crash at Moorgate underground and this helped to temper my hosts' annoyance with me for being late. And fortunately I was once again able to draw on my apparently inexhaustible reserves of energy and make a rousing speech at the opening, with Bob Mellish on the front row nodding delightedly. By the time I got back to the office the full horror of the Moorgate crash had got through to the newspapers. At the office a note from Jack was waiting for me: 'You and Ted may (literally) have saved my life this morning. The train I was about to catch just as you phoned was my regular one, the 8.37 from Drayton Park. It was the one that crashed at Moorgate. So thanks.' My blood ran cold. The thought of Jack being dead or mangled in that wreckage was horrible. And it wouldn't only have been I who would have missed him. The whole of Private Office would have gone into mourning.

More work, more rush. At last I sank into the train to York at 5pm, utterly exhausted. Then a long drive to Scarborough. I did an hour's work on my boxes and at last to bed.

Saturday
Eight hours' sleep! Unprecedented. It was good to be in Scarborough again, even in winter: to hear the seagulls crying and a foghorn mooing mournfully through the mist. My speech to conference came on early. I didn't know how those complicated figures on the social wage would go down with that stolid Yorkshire audience, at least half of whom were trade unionists. I sat down to that steady, warm, sustained applause which showed that my speech had hit home. And when I mingled with some of the delegates afterwards, compliments showered on me. One of the chaps came up to me to ask if he could have a copy of the figures. So my judgment about the message was right. I am convinced that this is the kind of constructive toughness that people are waiting to hear.

Sunday, 2 March
Only the *Sunday Times* has given me any sort of a show – though a good one. For the rest, my speech has been crowded off the papers by a row between Reg Prentice and Mike Foot. Reg has made what seems to me a perfectly valid point about the need for the unions to carry out their side of the Social Contract, but has worded it in his usual crudely provocative way: 'welching' is really an unnecessary word to use about people like Jack Jones, who are doing everything in their power to make the Contract

stick. But I think Mike is quite wrong to have hit back so rudely and publicly, talking about 'economic illiteracy'. Economics anyway is a subject on which I should have thought Mike was slightly vulnerable! I told Ted I didn't approve of what Mike had done. He and Reg would both have been better employed trying to get some of the *facts* across, in words and ways that really get home to chaps like shop stewards. This is what we are trying to do in our social wage document, though God knows whether we shall succeed. But if we don't, neither will the Social Contract. Even the *Sunday Times* today has not given a single one of the figures I used yesterday. How *does* one get a constructive case across?

We broke our weekend's peace to go up to town for dinner with Mike. Since we can no longer afford our weekly Lockets dinner this is the only way our little group can keep in touch. As usual, Jill served up a superb meal and the red wine flowed. To our surprise, when Ted and I arrived (first as usual) Mike was solacing himself with classical music on the hi-fi. I hadn't realized he had that side to him. But the arrival of the Shores, Baloghs and Benns soon put a stop to that. I cross-examined Tommy Balogh about the Petroleum Revenue Tax[1] but he seemed quite happy with it. Peter, who is off to foreign parts again in the morning, wanted above all to talk about the Dublin summit and the EEC. He was all for postponing a decision at Dublin if possible. But after I had listened to the discussion for a couple of hours a clear picture of what we ought to do crystallized in my mind. I said I disagreed with Peter that we must play for time. The first question we had to answer was, under what auspices should we conduct our anti-Market campaign when the time came? I – like the rest of them, no doubt – was being approached by various anti-Market bodies to speak for them. Were we all going to fragment ourselves by appearing on non-party platforms, while the Government conducted a concerted official pro-Market campaign? If, I continued, Mike said we should wait for the terms and then swing the official party machine onto our side, so that we all spoke at meetings arranged by Ron Hayward, he was overlooking two things: (a) Ron would never put Harold willingly at risk, so he was likely to drag his feet, and (b) Jim had manoeuvred Ron into agreeing to call the special conference as late as 17 May and Ron would be unlikely to organize anything until after that date. That would leave us approximately three weeks in which to do our stuff. The moral of this was that, first, we needed a decision on the terms as quickly as possible, so as to leave us time to counter-organize, and, secondly, that we should create our own auspices. These should take the form of a Cabinet-level brains trust of all those members of Cabinet who came out against entry. 'This is the only way to counteract the authority of a Cabinet decision to stay in,' I maintained. We should form a committee as soon as the result of renegotiation was known and offer ourselves as a brains trust to anyone who would like to organize a large meeting for us. If necessary, my secretary would help with the organizing. Peter agreed I might be right, Mike demurred, but Wedgie got quite excited and backed me in his enthusiastic way.

[1] Petroleum Revenue Tax was introduced to ensure that Britain took a sizeable share of the profits made from North Sea oil without deterring the development of marginal fields. It was estimated that it would boost Government revenue from the North Sea by over £500 million in the five years up to 1980.

Monday, 3 March

Back to work, positively refreshed by last night's dinner. We had another crowded agenda for the ministerial lunch. The troops were delighted when I said I intended to have a blitz on NHS spectacles[1] and suggested I should see Marcus Sieff to ask his advice on how I could get a top designer to design new frames which we would then have mass-produced. David said rather wryly that (a) it would cost more money (which I deny) and (b) that top officials were already so overworked that he hesitated to ask them to take on any more. In any case the department was very weak on this side and we really ought to get someone in from outside as a procurement adviser. I thought this an excellent idea and Alf pointed out that he and Jack Ashley had had the same trouble with the department in trying to get a more 'cosmetic' hearing aid under the NHS. The department's instinctive reaction was that private industry should make the beautiful things and the NHS the ugly ones. I said I was determined to change all that. David promised to let me have a paper in three weeks' time. He also had the excellent idea that I should ask Hugh Cudlipp to suggest someone to write up our social wage paper, on which I am keener than ever, following the reception of my speech at Scarborough. At the Sextet meeting which followed I told Philip what I intended to do about the journalist and the procurement adviser. He just swallowed and said nothing.

The consultants have written back to Harold asking him to reconsider his refusal to see them. We decided to postpone consideration of our next step until we have had a chance to study the reply. About eighty Tories have signed an Early Day Motion calling for the appointment of an independent adjudicator to handle my dispute with the consultants. I said I would have no objection at all to the dispute going to ACAS, particularly as this would compel the consultants to spell out just what they thought it was about. This tickled Henry enormously, but Philip was worried at the idea of ACAS handling a dispute in which a Minister was involved and wanted to think about it.

David came to see me about the paper on the 1975 pay recommendations for the non-industrial Civil Service, which was due to come before the Cabinet working group this afternoon.[2] He was deeply anxious about the way the economy is developing: 'I don't think the Government's economic strategy will hold.' The problem of this 26 per cent pay increase was appallingly difficult. He had no doubt we would get industrial action if we tried to tinker with the findings of the Pay Research Unit, yet

[1] I was horrified at the extent to which even working-class families spent large sums on private spectacle frames because the range of NHS spectacle frames, particularly for women, was so limited and unattractive. I believed that attractive mass-produced frames need not be more expensive than unattractive ones and that in any case costs could be reduced by promoting the new frames for export.

[2] The determination of non-industrial civil servants' pay up to the top grades was based on agreement reached following the report of the Priestly Royal Commission on the Civil Service (Cmnd. 9613, 1955). This recommended that pay for this group should reflect 'fair comparison with the current remuneration of outside staffs employed on broadly comparable work, taking account of differences in other conditions of service'. The Pay Research Unit [PRU] was set up to undertake fact-finding on job comparisons and on pay and conditions of service. On 14 April it had recommended an increase of about 30 per cent since the last award in January 1974: an annual increase of about 26 per cent. This applied to roughly 500,000 white-collar and non-industrial civil servants ranging from clerks and cleaners up to the Assistant Secretary grade.

equally there was no doubt about the damage this increase would do. 'The trouble is that we lost out on top salaries.' If we wanted to revise this award we must first back-track on that. This would be extremely difficult, too; perhaps the only thing we could do was to get this award, the power workers' and doctors' pay out of the way and then announce a new tougher policy from July onwards. 'The new formula will have to contain a cut in living standards,' he said. Then he added mournfully, 'But I don't think we have got five months.' It is clear that he is in touch with the middle-of-the-roaders who are getting increasingly perturbed at our economic strategy, because he confessed, 'Some of the people I talk to are lying low on the question of the economy, because they want to get the Common Market issue out of the way first. I think they are wrong, because this situation will face us whether we are in or out.'

Certainly, at the top of the scale the increases recommended are absurd: Assistant Secretaries go up from £8,850 to £11,000, while even Principals go up to £7,550, more than many a consultant gets! When Philip came to discuss the matter with me last Thursday I told him then, 'I expect my salary will fall behind everyone else's for years ahead, but that doesn't bother me: I have a comfortable living and a fascinating job. I don't give a damn about status and differentials.' 'That is a sentiment I honour,' replied Philip. 'But I have to tell you that if the Government does not accept this award it will, I am afraid, just not be able to get its business done.' I shrugged and replied, 'Then let people chase mirages. One day the stick will come down to earth with a thud.'

I went along to the working group meeting on the pay recommendations, quite clear what I must do. Malcolm spelt out the predictable Civil Service view; then Mike came in emphatically. At last Tuesday's MES, he said, the members had agreed to adopt a stronger attitude to pay increases. This was the first test. The increases were not by any stretch of imagination within the TUC guidelines: 'comparability does not figure in those'. Indeed, we were about to try to convince the railwaymen that comparability with the miners was not on. He therefore suggested we should try to get the increases reduced by 5 per cent. He wouldn't propose to overturn the Pay Research Unit, but would approach the TUC and ask for their support with the staff side. Denis said at once that he supported Mike. The MES paper, he said, showed that private sector settlements were tending to fall off, due no doubt, in part, to the rise in unemployment. It was the public sector settlements which were now the problem, because the public sector was insulated against unemployment. It was here we must stand firm. On this award we should if necessary go to arbitration and have the full increase forced upon us. That would be better than conceding it. I came in here – quietly for me – saying what David and I had agreed earlier and pointing out that I would consider the attempt to introduce a unilateral form of incomes policy at the end of a pay increase spree and at the expense of the public sector as 'contemptible'. Moreover I warned them that if I were to be forced now – because the Government was panicking – to go back on a pledge to the doctors which I had made with Mike's full connivance, I should be forced to resign. I repeated that we had one of two choices: either to back-track on our decision on top salaries, which was the cause of all our troubles, or to sweat it out till the end of the first free year's round of increases and then work out a much tougher set of criteria. But what we couldn't do – suddenly, arbitrarily and one-sidedly – was to ditch the machinery we had set up to deal with these cases. Tony C. made the valid point that we must consider this claim in a different, wider committee than this esoteric working group (though he is a natural procrastinator anyway). Denis promised to circulate the MES paper, which most of us hadn't seen. Tony urged again that 'we can't decide in forty-five minutes that fair comparison should go'. Mike, replying to me, claimed that 'the fact that we made a mess over top salaries doesn't mean we should repeat it now', to which I retorted, 'Of course, it does mean just that.' I was interested in Mike's plea: 'This is a decision about the whole pay policy of the Government – if it has a pay policy.' Shades of my own era at the Department of Employment! Finally we agreed that the matter should go to EC(P) [Committee on Economic Policy] for consideration in the wider context of what other demands are coming forward and our likely response to them. I certainly intend to be there and to force Michael to take a more comprehensive and more logically philosophical view. But I continue to admire him for the stamina he is showing in his fight to preserve the Social Contract, with all the unpopular decisions that involves.

When I reported to David he looked gloomy. He was particularly amused at my description of Crosland's line. 'That's the trouble with him,' said David. 'I think he has the best mind in the Government, but he just can't come to decisions. That is why he has never got to the very top.' I suggested to David we should put up a paper to EC(P) and he agreed to go away and have a shot at it.

Treated Ted and Brian O'Malley to a steak in the House. Brian and I talked companionable shop while Ted no doubt puzzled over the deep sense of political mateyness there is between us. We *enjoy* our politics. Afterwards I said to Brian, 'I have an idea. Later this year, when we have got pensions out of the way and I have done as much as I can for the NHS, I've told Harold I wouldn't mind becoming Leader of the House. What about being my Chief Whip?' He was tickled pink at the idea, but thought the party would fall to pieces before then because Bob had shot his bolt and there was no real leadership from the Whips' Office. No, he didn't insist on having a department of his own, but what he really wanted was to be in the Cabinet. I think he and I could do a terrific job together dealing with the party in Parliament in what is bound to be a period of increasing strain.

Tuesday, 4 March

David tells me he is mounting quite an exercise to get the paper on pay policy for which I have asked produced for EC(P). I enjoy working with him, too. He is very different from Brian and me, but he does bubble up with ideas and I find we interact very productively. I am supremely lucky in my team – but then I told Harold the people I wanted. David has sent a Minute challenging (quite rightly) Dick Bourton's conventional Treasury-type reaction to a paper Denis Healey has circulated about the next round of the perennial public expenditure review. Denis just wants to take this year's distribution of the spoils between departments and whittle it down a bit. Dick Bourton obviously believes this is right, but David insists that this is the moment to demand a fundamental re-examination of the Tory priorities we inherited. He and

I agreed that the top brass in our department have a sneaking sympathy with the restrictions the Treasury are trying to put on us (and on public expenditure generally), but I told David to go off and draft a reply to Denis saying we wanted a basic reassessment of priorities. David certainly does work prodigiously. Not all his ideas are sound by any means, but he stirs things up in an entirely healthy way.

At last I have got Private Office to earmark time for me to go in and hear PM's Questions. I want to keep in some kind of touch with the developing drama on the Tory benches. Margaret's election has stirred up her own side wonderfully: all her backbenchers perform like knights jousting at a tourney for a lady's favours, showing off their paces by making an unholy row at every opportunity over everything the Government does. Today they were baiting Harold over Reg Prentice's speech, and once again Harold was getting away with it, not by wit, but by sheer verbosity. Everybody kept glancing at Margaret to see when she would take him on. She sat with bowed head and detached primness while the row went on: hair immaculately groomed, smart dress crowned by a string of pearls. At last she rose to enormous cheers from her own side to deliver an adequate but hardly memorable intervention with studied charm. Roy J., sitting next to me, groaned and I said, 'She's not quite real, is she?' As he agreed, I added, 'If she would only occasionally come in with a smut on her nose, her hair dishevelled, looking as if she had been wrestling with her soul as I do.' He gave me his slow smile. 'I wouldn't say that your hair is ever dishevelled. If that is to be the criterion, then Shirley would win every time.' 'That's why everyone likes her,' I retorted. 'Men never feel at ease with a woman politician who looks as if her hair has just been permed.'

Settled as we are in the House for four nights on a three-liner on the Finance Bill, I have seized the opportunity to ask Hugh Cudlipp over for a drink, to try and enlist his help in getting a popular-impact version of all the work we have been doing on the social wage document. He began by saying that he had guessed why I had asked him over: it was to do, as Dick Crossman had asked him to do all those years ago, a popular version of the 'Better Pensions' plan. When I told him it was something much more difficult than that, and handed him Brian A-S.'s basic document on the social wage, his eyes glazed over and he said he would have to take it away. He told me that he had read the report of my weekend speech and thought it was the best speech made by a Cabinet member for many a long month, though he kept turning to Brian A-S. as if to say, 'Of course, you wrote it.' Hugh then broke off to say he wasn't going to be mobilized in support of the sort of rot Michael had been speaking at the weekend. 'Why on earth did he attack Reg Prentice, who may not be my favourite man – he is so dull – but he was obviously talking nothing but the truth.' Despite my denials, he kept reiterating, 'You know the Government is going to introduce a wage freeze.' I kept heading him back to the matter in hand and he agreed to go away and read all the documents. He left with an elaborate round of hand-kissing, making a particular fuss of Brian. I have a theory that the he-men of politics (Nye, Dick Crossman, Cudlipp, Manny Shinwell) cannot bear to recognize the challenge of independent women, even when they have a sneaking admiration for them. Or because they have. He left Brian highly gratified, Norman amused and me thinking that my plan will work. I don't mind these male histrionics so long as I get things done.

Wednesday, 5 March

I was immensely touched when I got to my room in the House this morning to find a bunch of freesias and tulips on my desk. Who on earth? A card explained the plot. It was Private Office's recognition that today was exactly one year's anniversary of my entry into the job. Ten of them in Private Office and the Letters Section had signed it: 'To the Secretary of State on your first anniversary with us – we've enjoyed the first year enormously and look forward to more. Best wishes from your *very* obedient servants [!]' I sent Janet out to find me an equally impish reply card and she came back with a very suitable one – something to the effect that it wasn't that I had forgotten the anniversary: I was merely in good time for next year! I scribbled on it my thanks for their flowers, card and 'belated obedience', adding 'three surprises at one go'. I get very fond of my civil servants (or at any rate some of them). The outside world has no idea how human they are.

Back to the Treasury boardroom (otherwise known as Conference Room A) for another round of discussion on what we could do about the surrender of sovereignty to the EEC. Once again, Legislation Committee was adorned by all the ministerial top brass, including Jim. Ted Short began by summarizing where we had got: 'We agreed last time that we can't alter Article 189 but must discuss what we can do within the Treaty.' Peter had put in an impressive paper about possible amendments to Britain's own Act of 1972, but we never got to it. Instead we spent an hour on Ronald King Murray's idea that we should make a 'statutory declaration' to the effect that nothing could undermine Parliament's right to undo what its predecessors had done (i.e. that nothing could undermine Parliament's sovereignty). I thought this was a useless and possibly dangerous exercise, because it would lull people into a false sense of security about the control over our own affairs that we shall be giving up, but Peter and Mike thought it would be marginally useful. Sam Silkin denounced the declaration as a 'nullity' in a speech of such portentous length and dullness that I started reading my newspaper. Elwyn, however, backed Sam with such fulsome praise that everyone was taken aback, while I chipped in naughtily, 'Why don't you canonize him?' Once again I had to admire Jim's urbane and disarming honesty. 'We had better really face the issue and not pretend we are not giving up sovereignty,' he said cheerfully. There were only two questions worth asking: (1) is it worth it? and (2) can it be kept within reasonable limits? (We all know that his own answers to both would be yes.) Tommy Balogh was as quietly satirical as usual. The matter, he said, was purely 'empirical'. 'The French have no statutory declaration, but they regularly break Community law,' he said. There were giggles and I slipped away well aware that we shall go over all this ground again in Cabinet.

Lunch with the medical correspondents. Though I had had little time to prepare, I rather enjoyed myself, teasing John Stevenson of the *Mail*, who was sitting opposite (and who is my most persistent persecutor at press conferences). The chairman told me that it was a record attendance, to which I replied sweetly, 'Barbara-baiting is a national sport.' Norman (whom I took for a quick, vigorous walk round St James's Park afterwards) told me that the speech came over well. We ought to use it again, because obviously even these expert correspondents hadn't yet grasped the simple facts I gave them about the financing of the NHS. We were both intrigued by the way Stevenson pursued me through and after the lunch – all the way down the stairs – pleading with me to take some new initiative to resolve the consultants' dispute. We both got the impression that the BMA is getting worried and is desperately anxious to get off the hook.

Further evidence of this lies in the reply the BMA have sent to the PM. Far from spitting in his face, they have urged him to reconsider his refusal to see them until sanctions have been lifted and have now dredged up a rather injudicious answer to a Parliamentary Question Dick Crossman gave some years ago.[1] At a meeting with officials we discussed a draft reply for the PM to send yet again. Henry is nervously feeling the way to a further 'give' on our side, though his initiatives collapse as soon as he sees they aren't popular with the rest of us (including Ian Gillis, who was holding a watching brief for Peter. Where *does* that man get to?). David was all in favour of our sweating it out. Henry looked like a grateful basset hound when I said that in any case the tone (if not the content) of the PM's reply should be conciliatory.

Norman tells me Cudlipp has sent a message: (a) he does think our material can be made into a popular pamphlet and (b) he is finding someone to do it for us. I have laid my plans for Hugh to do the popular version of 'Better Pensions' for us. Life is rather fun. And oddly enough I don't worry about my burdens half as much as I used to do.

Harold has sent round a PM's Minute to Ministers reminding them, first, that they shouldn't make speeches without consulting the relevant colleagues and, secondly, that political speeches should be issued through Transport House and not circulated privately. So that is his official snub to Reg P.!

In the division lobby late at night Wedgie said to me, 'I have done nothing but think about what you said about the referendum last Sunday. You are absolutely right: we must set up an anti-Common Market mini-Cabinet as soon as the terms are known. At the very least we could then issue an authoritative statement. It is essential that our impact should be co-ordinated. But the first question is, who would be the members of it?' We agreed to continue the discussion at the meal we are all to have at Peter Shore's on Sunday night.

Thursday, 6 March

Home at 1am again. Four nights on the Finance Bill this week! The proceedings have been punctuated by a series of Parliamentary storms as Margaret's backbenchers have been demonstrating their new-found political virility. But the papers are full of the row she has created by sacking the Director-General of the Conservative political machine, Michael Woolf, while our people tell me that Margaret's party political broadcast last night was such a sweetly calculated bit of femininity that it was nauseating. Well, it is too soon to say how she will make out, though she is obviously not going to have an indefinitely prolonged honeymoon. At Cabinet we finally

[1] The consultants were still trying to get the maximum part-timer's commitment to the NHS defined as being limited to nine half days a week and had quoted a written reply which Dick Crossman had given to a Parliamentary Question in 1969. Officials assured me that the reply had been misinterpreted.

launched the Defence White Paper on its way. Harold has clearly been hounded by Roy Mason and Denis for the brave fight he put up last week in trying to get the White Paper branded as 'provisional'. He has been forced to circulate a Minute (backed by one from Denis), saying that he now appreciated that the word 'provisional' relating to the defence figure in the Public Expenditure White Paper did not mean provisional in the economic sense, but merely referred to the fact that consultations with our NATO allies had still to take place. As we were waiting to go into Cabinet I tackled Denis. 'Why didn't you back me last week when I tried to get a caveat into the White Paper? Here I am, trying to support you on getting more defence cuts and you let me down.' He replied that Harold had been wrong in the interpretation he had tried to put on things. The fact was, though, that the defence programme was as much subject to review as any other programme and he had reserved his position on that. What a broken reed! When Harold had made his public recantation in Cabinet Denis added his little formula about defence being subject to review; I asked if the formula could be minuted. 'It already is,' snapped Denis, and added with a meaningful look at me, 'I've already made it clear that *all* programmes are subject to review – including yours.' At this I remarked audibly, 'If anybody tries to cut my programme before another cut has been made in defence, I shall resign.' 'You're just a pacifist,' said Fred Peart (who sits opposite me) reprovingly. He is a great armaments man. Pacifist indeed! It is David who, from his experience at Defence,[1] keeps telling me the cuts are phoney and that, if only someone would let him loose on the programme, he could make big reductions.

All this was over by 11.30am, and I was beginning to think thankfully that I could get back to my mound of work. But it was not to be. Harold can never resist filling a Cabinet vacuum with words. He remarked casually, 'Before we break up I should just like to let Cabinet know how I see the way we should proceed after Dublin.' The intention was to bring renegotiations to an end then, though there were still two outstanding issues: New Zealand and steel. If they did end he intended that there should be no lobby briefing. All comment would be on the record and he would make it clear that it would be for Cabinet to recommend the terms or not and he would not say where he stood personally. He proposed that Cabinet should consider the terms on Tuesday 8 March, all the necessary papers having been circulated beforehand. From that date the 'agreement to differ' would start and we faced the prospect of three months' campaigning. He hoped we could agree guidelines for the conduct of the campaign; it might even be desirable to advance the referendum date. This apparently innocent report started a debate which lasted one-and-a-half hours, during which Harold twisted and turned, played down every anxiety, gave way on this minor point and that, while achieving the substance of what he wanted – another triumph for his art of wearing down every obstacle by sheer verbosity.

Peter, the keeper of our EEC conscience as well as of the archives of the detailed issues involved, came in first. Two things, he said, caused him anxiety. The first was the exclusion of major issues from the renegotiation period, e.g. the reform of CAP,

---

[1] He had been Parliamentary Under-Secretary of State for the Royal Navy from 1968 to 1970 and an Opposition spokesman on defence from 1970 until 1972, when he resigned over the party's policy towards the Common Market.

our commitment on the access of cheap food, and steel. The second was over the whole issue of sovereignty, which we had never really discussed. He was concerned, therefore, with the pre-Dublin period. We ought to have a Cabinet meeting to recap where we had got to over the whole field before Harold and Jim went into the final stage. Harold came back at once: Peter had sent him a 'very impressive and useful document', which he had studied carefully. But Peter must remember that we should not be committed on some of the points which might be outstanding when negotiations ended. 'We shall still have power even if we are in the Community.' He and Jim could not go on raising new points like steel and sovereignty. We could fight those battles afterwards. Mike backed Peter. We had never had a recap in Cabinet of the progress made, he said, and ought to have one before final negotiations took place. As for post-Dublin, he thought it would be wrong for Cabinet to reach a decision on the terms before the PLP had had a chance to discuss them. Back popped Harold again (the pro-marketeers know they can safely leave all the running to him at times like these). He thought Michael had a point about consulting the PLP and would like to amend his own suggestion. Let Cabinet meet on the Monday morning, 17 March; then have a PLP meeting on the Monday evening and another Cabinet on Tuesday to reach a decision. This led to a long argument as to when and how one could consult the PLP. Roy Hattersley, in Jim's absence, declared it would be most unfair to the Foreign Secretary to expect him to make a 'neutral' report to the PLP; having spent twelve months in negotiations he couldn't be expected not to defend the outcome. Quite right, said Harold cheerfully: it was obviously his own duty to make the report. And so, after a lot of long-windedness, it was decided, Harold having successfully managed to bury Peter's suggestion for a pre-Dublin Cabinet.

There was a light moment earlier when Harold ruled on whether or not Ministers should take part in *Any Questions*. Apparently Wedgie had raised it with him because an invitation had been extended to him. Harold said on the whole he thought it inadvisable. When Wedgie disagreed with him, Harold repeated his favourite quip. He had, he said, once had an analysis made of the use made by the BBC of Labour MPs and had found that 90 per cent of the invitations were to Mr Benn. Laughter. Unperturbed, Wedgie quipped back: 'If you stop me going on, all that happens is that we get John Mackintosh.'[1]

Another late night at the House on the Finance Bill. David and I had drinks with Lord Platt[2] in my room following his nice letter to the BMA *News* in my defence. He obviously thinks the consultants have got themselves into a mess and wants to help, but feels he would be rejected by the profession as an objective witness since he left the BMA years ago as a result of their row with Nye over the Health Service and what he called the 'abominable' treatment of Nye by Charles Hill. Joe Rogaly, with whom David has obviously done his stuff as effectively as usual, has produced a magnificent article in the *Financial Times* which had clearly impressed Platt. (Ronald Butt's second article in *The Times* is as wobbly as I expected, though I suppose it could have

[1] Labour MP for Berwick and East Lothian, a professor of politics at Edinburgh University, strongly pro-devolution and pro-EEC.

[2] Lord Platt was Professor of Medicine at Manchester University and physician at the Royal Infirmary, Manchester, from 1945 to 1965. He was President of the Royal College of Physicians from 1957 to 1962.

been worse.) Platt went away saying he would talk to some of the Royal College presidents to try and get them to stand up and be counted.

Friday, 7 March

Great panic because I just have nothing to wear for today's opening of the new Queen Mary's hospital at Sidcup. At the last minute I was frantically stitching the bow on my old black dress and decided I should just have to carry off my shabbiness with aplomb. Despite the consultants' threatened boycott of the opening it went off well. I just didn't notice whether the consultants were there or not and addressed myself to the nurses in the audience instead. More work at the office and then off to speak to Woolwich Labour Party. The funny thing is that, despite the short nights and endless strain, people are always telling me how well I look. Frank Allaun last night commented on it, while John Ellis referred to me as 'that pretty girl'. The secret, as I've said before, lies in the fact that the older I grow the more philosophical I become – the more at ease in speaking to and meeting people. All right, I sometimes get so strained that I blow my top, but once the pressure is relaxed I bounce back again.

Saturday, 8 March

I have been catching up with my reading of the flood of background documents that keep circulating among Ministers. Usually I don't get much chance to read overseas telegrams, but my eye was caught by the report of the Council of Ministers' discussion of CAP on Tuesday last. Lardinois's report to the meeting certainly doesn't hold out much prospect of a fundamental renegotiation of the CAP. He emphasized, said the telegram, that 'on balance the CAP had had positive effects and that the present exercise was designed only to improve a policy that was already good'. Fred Peart's intervention at the Council stressed nothing more revolutionary than the need to give 'sufficient weight to the role which direct aids can play in avoiding the conflicts and contradictions to which an excessive reliance on end price support can give rise'. Although he claimed that a common Community organization for the marketing of mutton and lamb was not necessary, he merely added that, if it *were* introduced, the UK would have to safeguard continuing access for New Zealand lamb. Moreover we should want to seek the elimination, 'or at least reduction as far as UK imports are concerned', of the present 20 per cent tariff 'at the earliest opportune time'. To all this Lardinois replied that 'the current national regimes and all the distortions of competition that that involved could not, under the terms of the Treaty, be allowed to continue'. No one could say that our Fred has exactly dug his heels in over a fundamental renegotiation of CAP, and I'm interested to see that he acquiesced happily in the proposal that negotiations should be resumed on 28 April: well after Cabinet has decided whether to recommend that we stay in.

Once again we broke our weekend to come up to London for a Sunday night dinner of our group, this time at Peter's. This is becoming quite a habit, but it wasn't such a wrench to leave HCF in the March sleet. With the EEC issue coming to the crunch, we have at last been driven to recognize the need for something more organized than the dilettantish discussions we have had up to now. The Foots and Harts were there, but no Silkin, no Baloghs, and – at the last minute – a message from Wedgie. He was sorry, but he felt so exhausted he thought he had better go to bed. So even his ever-youthful energy is feeling the strain! Since the papers this morning are full of stories about how Wedgie is using Transport House to foist a new economic policy on the Government through the medium of the Home Policy Committee, I asked Mike what *his* economic strategy was. He said some of them in his department had worked on a scheme for holding the Retail Prices Index down by massive subsidies at key points (e.g., school meals and rents) and then meeting the cost by taxation. But it had turned out that it would cost £500 million in subsidies for each one point of the Retail Prices Index, and the TUC had reeled away from the tax implications: something like £2–£10 a week extra for the better-paid worker. So now he and Shirley were working on a more modest version: what would be necessary to iron out the 'hump' in the Retail Prices Index expected this summer. He thought we had got to toughen up the guidelines and it would help if we could do something about RPI. He wasn't a financial masochist like Peter, he said, but equally he didn't share Harold Lever's view that we could just borrow our way out of our difficulties. I pointed out that I was putting a paper to MES suggesting we delay the phasing out of food and fuel subsidies, because Denis did not want to advance the uprating of pensions to October as I had asked. It would surely be absurd to withdraw these subsidies, which are so vital to pensioners, in order to replace them with new ones, like school meals and rents, which wouldn't help the poorer pensioners at all. I also urged that we should insist on a pre-Budget discussion in Cabinet, so as to prevent Denis pre-empting all our options on public expenditure. Mike nodded at all this, but he always wriggles uncomfortably at the suggestion of any concerted left-wing plan.

Bereft of my ally, Wedgie, I tried to get Mike and Peter interested again in my proposals for organizing our opposition to the Common Market. Fortunately Judith was enthusiastic and said she thought a lot of non-Cabinet Ministers would like to sign a common statement, while Jill Foot got quite excited about the idea. They agreed with me that we must issue the statement promptly and that, between us, we could organize the brains trusts I proposed. Mike and Peter sat shaking their heads, but Judith and I are determined to pursue this at Lockets on Tuesday. These meandering men!

Monday, 10 March

Mike was extraordinarily mild at EC(P) this morning, where we discussed the non-industrial civil servants' pay. No one would have guessed that we had had a flaming row about it last night. (I suspect that Mike's flashpoint has become as low as mine: all these pressures!) As I listen to him I can't help smiling to myself. Here he is now: the most determined advocate of wage restraint and damn the ideological conse-quences. I remember how in the 1966–70 Labour Government he helped to pillory me from the backbenches when I was having to face the realities as he is now. I admire his courage and stamina and would not try to plague him with irresponsible attempts to make things easy for myself in my own departmental field, but I cannot subscribe to panic and inconsistent breaches of our general line. Anyway the only result this morning was that Mike said it was a matter for Cabinet.

What is interesting is the extent to which support is coming from all quarters for the view that we must let the first year's post-statutory controls settlements go through and introduce tougher guidelines after that – i.e. after July. This is, surprisingly, the theme of Geoff Bish's *Economic Review*, which we discussed at Home Policy Committee of the NEC this afternoon. Section 2:7, 'The Next Wage Round', spells out that 'it would not in our view be desirable to produce major new policy initiatives calculated to alter the order of pay increases *within the present round of annual pay negotiations*' (his italics) and then goes on to say that discussions should start now as to how we might get tougher adherence to the guidelines '*during the next pay round*'. This is a perfect paraphrase of my paper to EC(P)! First, Geoff explained that, 'contrary to what the press say', he had himself suggested to the chairman (Wedgie) that Home Policy might care to look at the sort of representations the party would be making to the Chancellor, as they always did, in the pre-Budget period. At this point Shirley surprised everyone by saying that there were 'a lot of excellent things in this paper' and merely warned we should put the import controls section in very green colours; otherwise a lot of dangerous forestalling of import controls would go on. No one objected to that. Secondly, Bryan Stanley chipped in to ask exactly what was meant by Section 2:7: 'The Next Wage Round'. Was there some other document we could expect to see? Yes, if you want to, replied Bish. We had been working on further ideas for the next round of pay talks, like the possibility of strengthening the price code so as to stiffen employers in resisting excessive pay demands. (Nothing very left-wing about this!) At this stage Sid Weighell arrived and the first thing he said he wanted to raise was Section 2:7. Laughter. Well, he said defensively, he wanted to know whether it had been drawn up in conjunction with the Treasury. Geoff shook his head. 'Or with any other Government department?' I asked innocently. 'No,' replied Wedgie emphatically. 'It is merely an office document.' Sid ploughed on. What did Section 2:7 mean? Did it mean that the present round of pay talks should remain as they were? And he added, 'I am not quarrelling about the next round but what is happening now. I don't want anyone breathing down my neck. But I agree something should be done for the future.' And he concluded emphatically, 'I want to honour the Contract but I want everyone else to do so too.' (How I wish Michael had been there!)

We agreed to note Geoff's paper as an official information document and had moved onto the next item when Denis arrived. He interrupted to apologize for being late and said he wanted to make some comments on the *Economic Review*. Wedgie leniently allowed him to do so. 'This is a very useful and worthwhile document,' said Denis firmly. 'I very much deplore the way the media have handled it. There is no question of confrontation over this. In fact I have just had the point about import controls put to me by the Manifesto Group.' (Groans. 'Then the idea must be wrong,' quipped someone.) 'But,' he continued, 'I want to put a point about Section 2:7.' We all exploded into laughter at this, and Denis asked, puzzled, 'Have I boobed?' No, Wedgie assured him, and told him he was only the third person to raise this. It appeared that Denis too was interested to see a further paper about how we could strengthen the guidelines for the next round. So apparently Denis too is looking for changes in the guidelines. The hopeful thing is that two trade unionists there were doing the same thing.

The only other item before I left was Mik's letter (he couldn't be there) suggesting a deputation to the PM about the Industry Bill to make sure it squared with Manifesto policy. Obediently the office had circulated a paper comparing the Bill with what we had demanded in party policy documents – much to the disparagement of the Bill. 'Let's send a deputation to Wedgie,' I suggested cheerfully. (After all, he is the Industry Minister.) Wedgie looked worried: there were a lot of misunderstandings about the Bill, he said. So finally we agreed to write him a letter asking for clarification and assurances.

Earlier there had been panic stations at the department when the Speaker accepted a Private Notice Question from Gerry Vaughan about the consultants' dispute. This, as usual, meant a flurry of drafting, briefing and typing up of the reply. But the whole thing went like a bomb. Once again the Tory backbenchers were showing their new-found militancy, trying to howl at me. But this time our packed benches were ready for them and I got the most rousing cheers of support I have had for many a long time. I stuck firmly and repeatedly to the principle of the differential for whole-timers and our lads loved it. When I got back to my room Norman said, 'I think the Opposition must be sorry they put that PNQ down.'

Tuesday, 11 March

Predictably, the newspapers rushed to portray yesterday's Home Policy Committee as a defeat for the Left. The *Daily Telegraph* excelled itself with a story about a great victory for Shirley Williams, who in fact had hardly spoken at all. In the evening we revived our Lockets dinner, at which Judith and I pressed the points I had been making on Sunday night about the need for us to organize a 'Cabinet Against the Market' group and be ready to present it at a press conference as an authoritative alternative to the inevitable pro-Market line of Cabinet as soon as the decision was known. Once again Peter and Mike seemed a bit diffident, but Judith backed me nobly and we worked out a plan of action to the last detail. Wedgie was given the job of drafting a statement for us to issue and John undertook to check the list of anti-Market junior Ministers and MPs which Jack Straw had hurriedly drawn up for me. We also agreed to meet at our flat for dinner next Sunday and that Jack Jones, Clive and Mik should be invited, so that the whole exercise between Cabinet Ministers, junior Ministers, MPs and unions could be co-ordinated. I went home feeling that something concrete had been decided at last.

At Social Policy Committee of Cabinet earlier I had had a bit of a tussle over my paper extending the role and remit of the SBC under David Donnison. To my surprise, Reg Prentice backed me against the predictable timidity of the Treasury, saying vigorously that he was all in favour of bodies like the SBC acting as pressure groups on the Government – it was good for us. He went up in my estimation. During the debate on the Referendum White Paper in the House I thought Margaret made an effective speech. One of our Whips, sitting next to me, muttered, 'She's just a clever little lawyer.' Well, that is more than you can say about a lot of our Ministers – or the Tory ones.

Wednesday, 12 March

More office meetings on the consultants. Henry has fallen for the idea some of the profession have put forward that an independent 'fact-finder' should be asked to adjudicate on just what the facts are in the dispute. Of course, I would have nothing to do with it, but didn't object to Henry probing as to what Grabham and co. thought the terms of reference should be. That would at least pin them down as to what they thought the dispute was all about. Platt has drafted a superb letter to *The Times* which shows that the talk David and I had with him has borne fruit. Henry frowned his doubts about it, but we slapped him down. He slaps down easy.

Took the night train to Blackpool to open the new maternity unit at the Victoria Hospital.

Friday, 14 March

A most successful day at the Victoria Hospital. I followed my usual practice of stopping to talk freely and friendlily – for instance, to a waiting deputation of anxious mothers, wanting to lobby me about the proposed closure of their hospital. I had some nice photos taken of me talking to them, banners and all. They were overwhelmed that I should stop and listen to them. I also insisted on seeing a couple of junior doctors who had been breathing fire and slaughter about me and demanding to talk to me. I gave them a drink, chatted for half an hour and sent them away in an entirely different mood, with the result that they told the press I was quite different from what they had expected. Finally I held a reception with representatives of every level of staff at the hospital. Norman has at last managed to persuade health authorities that this is what I want and although I gather there were some mutterings on the health authority about it, it went famously. Porters, laundrymen, kitchen staff, nurses, radiographers: they were all given drinks and chatted to me delightedly as I circulated among them. And as the official ceremony went well, with both Sidney Hamburger, the regional chairman, and me making informal and jolly speeches, I went home feeling very satisfied with everything.

Sunday, 16 March

Everybody seemed to decide to turn up at the referendum conspiracy meal at our flat. In the event it meant catering for over twenty people and I had to come up early from HCF to get the food ready. Despite all the preparation I did beforehand, I was inevitably on the go looking after everyone and missed some of the discussion that was going on. Jack Jones was a bit apprehensive of the taramoosalata, though he had two helpings of goulash, but his wife, Evelyn, tucked enthusiastically into everything and appeared in a more human light than I have ever seen her. Clive Jenkins arrived with a couple of bottles of champagne, which was a welcome reinforcement. When I finally joined them after the meal, Mik was in charge and was holding forth about the blitz we must make on the NEC next Wednesday. They were all trying to draft a Motion for the NEC (of which we should have to give a week's notice) and getting nowhere fast. I piped up and said my usual piece: how our most effective counterblast to the Establishment was to come out as *Ministers* and to organize our group under the heading 'Cabinet Against the Market'. Clive was most enthusiastic about this. Wedgie produced the draft statement for the Cabinet Ministers' press conference. Mik said at once that this ought to be the basis of an immediate Early Day Motion[1] and of the Motion for the NEC. And so it was agreed. Jack Jones pledged that the unions would swing into line with us, but he was very anxious for us not to undermine the all-party basis of the anti-Market campaign, as he thought we should need every vote we could get. We broke up late with everything organized. I felt I had done a good evening's work and I knew the concept of 'Cabinet Against the Market' was a winner.

Monday, 17 March

When we assembled at No. 10 for the start of our Common Market marathon I passed Eric Varley a note: 'I'm bored before we start.' We had a pile of papers from Jim in front of us, explaining under the seven headings of the Manifesto targets what he claimed we had achieved in the renegotiations. I groaned at the thought of the tedious charade that lay ahead. We all knew that everybody had made up their minds and that nothing anyone said would change anything. And so it proved. The pro-marketeers kept putting up a powerfully plausible pragmatic case which we had to keep puncturing. For example, on CAP, Jim's line was 'we can live with it because of the prospect of further changes'. Fred claimed his beef régime was a major break-through; I pointed out we had only obtained it for one year, whereat he replied, 'Everything operates only for one year.' On free movement of capital, Denis said that he had not had any difficulty in getting a derogation last March, whereupon I asked under what provision of the Treaty he had managed to do so. He didn't know, so Harold said we must be told in time for tomorrow's meeting. Again, on the budget contribution, Denis claimed that our forecasts of the burden on us had proved wildly over-pessimistic, but couldn't tell us why. Harold, playing it strictly fair, said Denis must circulate an explanatory paper tomorrow. And so it went on, with the pros (including Harold and Jim) putting the best gloss on everything and being challenged line by line by us. On economic and monetary union, for instance, Harold insisted that it was dead, while Mike pointed out that the Paris communiqué had said the exact opposite. Peter made the major running, very impressively, on our side, though Wedgie crossed swords with Jim on regional and industrial policy, ending up by saying, 'Our whole regional policy is designed to distort competition. The Community is nothing but a capitalist club.' It all took a long time and when we adjourned at 1.30pm we still hadn't reached the issue of sovereignty. Harold, stressing that this

[1] Backbench MPs can table a Motion on the Commons' Order Paper on almost any subject they choose. They then collect as many signatures as possible in the hope of forcing the Government to allow an early debate on it. Since this does not often happen, the main value is propagandist.

was merely an exploratory stage and that no firm decisions were being reached till tomorrow, said we must meet in the morning at 9.30am. Groans went up from every side and voices were heard asking whether our misery could not at least be alleviated by coffee. Harold said he would see what could be done.

Later it was the turn of the PLP to be consulted. But first I got the horrible news that the Second Reading of our Pensions Bill has been switched to tomorrow and I have nothing prepared! No time to do anything about it before the PLP meeting, which I felt that, for decency's sake, I must attend. But that, too, turned out to be a ritual. Harold made a low-key introductory speech, running through the Manifesto shopping list like a bored housewife at the grocer's. I suspect that that is his way of playing fair. I had to leave before the end, but I gather Jim had no such scruples and made his own views plain.

Tuesday, 18 March

Up at 6am to sketch out my Second Reading speech on the Pensions Bill. As always, the office is pleading for a text so that they can clear it with Treasury. I send them a few pages and tell them I will have to finish the rest somehow in Cabinet. I arrived a little late at Cabinet to hear Ted Short droning his way through the sovereignty issue. Peter was soon dressing him down, complaining that the treatment of this had been 'the most regrettable feature of the whole negotiations'. To safeguard the rights of the British Parliament would have required an amendment of the Treaty or a Protocol of Derogation in certain areas. That was why it had never been raised: to have done so would have been to raise sharply the whole implications of membership. Obviously a lot of members of Cabinet were uneasy at letting this go so easily, but they found no difficulty in squaring their consciences. Tony C., for instance, began by saying that this was 'much the most disturbing part of the negotiations', but he went on to interpret this as something that once again could be solved pragmatically. He complained that a 'host of minor issues' were coming up from the Commission as a result of the harmonization policy, an example being in the transport field. This, he said, had nothing to do with creating a united Europe: it went back to a 'different and dead concept'. What, he asked, was the possibility of persuading the Council of Ministers to end this 'nonsense' and 'stop passing so much Community law'? There were approving murmurs at this, not least from the pro-marketeers, and I had to remind Tony that this 'host of minor issues' was crucial to the doctrine of the need to get rid of the 'distortions of competition', quoting at him the telegram about Lardinois's comments on the CAP. And I pointed out that this doctrine was embodied in some far from minor issues – e.g. the free movement of labour and capital. And I was able to shoot Denis down over his inexcusably misleading statements yesterday. True to Harold's instructions, Treasury had circulated a paper on this which we were handed as we arrived. Preoccupied though I was with trying to finish my Second Reading speech, I managed to glance at it and found that the 'derogation' of which he had boasted yesterday was a purely temporary one, because we were in balance of payments difficulties. And if we continued to plead such difficulties the Commission could move in on us. But once again no one was listening to anyone else.

Pro-marketeers continued to argue that every country had to give up sovereignty anyway, while Wedgie gave one of his extraordinarily fluent tirades on democracy. His capacity for vivid and telling words is immense. Even Harold nodded as Wedgie declaimed, 'Sovereignty is not omnipotence. It is the right to make your own laws.' But I doubt if Harold was as pleased when Wedgie went on to proclaim the 'historic commitment of the working people of Britain to democratic self-government' and to protest that 'we are conniving at the dismemberment of Parliament'.

At last Harold said the time had come for him to go round the table and get our views, adding – to general approval – that he thought he ought to make his statement to the House the same day. This gave me the opportunity to work away at my pensions speech, as I knew pretty predictably what people would say. I merely kept half an ear open to see how the doubtful ones would vote: Willie Ross, for instance, who was okay anti in his usual lugubrious way; Merlyn, who (as Eric Varley had predicted) came down on Big Jim's side; and Eric himself, who hadn't opened his mouth during the two long discussions. He merely said tersely that he remained opposed to membership, largely on energy grounds (which he didn't specify). When my turn came I said no one would be surprised to know my view was against. My reason was that we were asking the British people to remain in an organization in whose principles we said we did not believe. Harold had said that the theology of the Common Market was dead: long live pragmatic decisions. 'But the pragmatic fact is that, far from rejecting the theology, we have accepted that we cannot challenge it and that the negotiations would have broken down if we had even tried, examples being steel, CAP and the issue of sovereignty. As a party we have always rejected coalitions, but the Common Market is merely an internationalized one.' Elwyn, as I had never doubted he would, swung in behind Harold 100 per cent. Teasingly, Harold left John Morris to the very last, but there was no real suspense. He too, after some ritual expression of anxieties, accepted the new terms. ('He'll never go against Big Jim,' Eric had said to me earlier.) As soon as the result was known I passed Eric a note: 'Some of us are having a press conference this afternoon. Would you like to come along?' He muttered something about considering it. As we broke up I said to him again outside the Cabinet room, 'We're meeting at 5.30pm. Let Peter Shore know if you are interested.' I saw Robert Armstrong [the Prime Minister's Principal Private Secretary] hanging around, but didn't care. We have nothing to hide. Anyway, history has been made this morning. We actually had a break at 11am for coffee to be served!

Spent the rest of the lunch hour finishing my speech for Second Reading over a sandwich. Considering all the difficulties, I was rather proud of it. But in any case, with Harold making his statement today, I knew no one would be interested. Just my luck to have one of the most important items of our social policy taken in the House on trauma day! Just before I went to the House Norman came in looking sheepish. He had had a message from No. 10: would he please tell me that the PM did not wish me to attend the press conference that afternoon. My eyebrows shot up, but 'Thank you' was all I said. Had Eric gone running to teacher? Or was Robert Armstrong eavesdropping? Either way, it was pretty contemptible and I intended to take no notice of the message.

In the House my heart went out to Harold as he ploughed his way through one of the longest and dullest statements he has ever made. Tory sneers and jeers greeted every line. We anti-marketeers on the front bench tried to hide our feelings as the pro-marketeers cheered, but it was hard to do so as Harold claimed that Fred's achievements over CAP had taken us back to Labour's Agriculture Act of 1947. Really! As I anticipated, the House emptied rapidly when the long questioning was over. When I stood up to move the Second Reading of my Bill there was not a single Labour MP on the benches behind me! I got through the speech easily, then slipped upstairs to join the others at the 'Cabinet Against the Market' lobby conference, which Peter conducted with relaxed bonhomie. Then down to the Grand Committee Room to a meeting of anti-Market Labour MPs called by Douglas Jay. There were about eighty of them there and volunteers were quickly at work collecting signatures for the declaration[1] we had tabled as an Early Day Motion. So our plan had slipped smoothly into action, and there were over a hundred signatures on the Order Paper before we went home.

But the work of the department has to go on. The BMA is now pleading for a meeting with me and is clearly distressed by the increased militancy being shown by the HCSA. The BMA now argue that they want to clarify 'misunderstandings' they say exist about the consultants' commitment under the existing contract and of course I said at once that I must see them. This is something very different from negotiations and, if they are getting worried about the way they are losing public support, it is my duty to try and get them off the hook. We had to have an office discussion about all this. David is against my trying to get sanctions lifted before the Review Body reports: he is sure the Government will have to clamp down on the Review Body award and thinks that sanctions will give me the excuse I shall need for not implementing it. Backed by Philip and Henry, I disagreed. I said I would meet the BMA the following day and have an adjourned meeting on Thursday if necessary.

But my stresses and strains are still not over. Tomorrow I am due to address a *Financial Times* high-level conference on pensions policy and I haven't prepared a word yet. Elizabeth suggested I ask Brian O'Malley to take my place, but I wasn't having any. I am already acutely aware of the conspiracy by the Tory front bench to keep me out of the pensions picture. They have been blackmailing Bob to try and get me not to go on the Standing Committee, claiming that the proceedings will be more protracted if I go on. I know Brian would love to handle the whole thing himself, but, as I told my officials, I am always sent in to do the dirty work and intend to get a few of the sweets of policy as well. Of course, I know what the Tories are up to: they want to maintain the 'ogre' image of me which my pensions policy and my conciliatory

[1] The declaration welcomed the referendum. It stated that 'it is the true interest of the British people to regain the essential rights which permanent membership of the Common Market would deny them, namely the right of democratic self-government through their own elected Parliament, the right to determine for themselves how they impose taxes and fix food prices, the right to pursue policies designed to ensure full employment and the right to seek co-operation and trade with other nations in a world-wide framework'. It urged MPs to campaign for the withdrawal of the United Kingdom from the Common Market.

Second Reading speech today disprove. In his winding-up speech Kenneth Clarke even went to the lengths of talking about the 'O'Malley Bill'. That decided me: I'll do the FT conference tomorrow if it kills me and I'll sweat out the committee stage, whatever the cost. I just gave in to my tiredness and went to bed.

Wednesday, 19 March

My speech to the *Financial Times* went like a bomb, despite the fact that I had had to get up at 5am. I even survived some pretty tricky questions and afterwards Alec Atkinson, the Deputy Secretary, said I had covered myself with credit. Frank Byers, who took the chair for me, told me that Geoffrey Howe was 'a hundred per cent' behind our pensions policy and he obviously hadn't much time for Norman Fowler's[1] equivocal line.

But I still had to go through the misery of resumed talks with the BMA. They came in, noticeably subdued: Astley, Grabham, Lewin, Stevenson and Gullick. We went through the first stages of explaining what I thought was the consultants' commitment under their current contract with elaborate patience and mutual courtesies. I couldn't help feeling that if they had only shown half this civility on 20 December we would never have had this dispute. But as soon as we thought we had got one point cleared up and agreed, they were at their old game of changing tack. They nodded approvingly when, for instance, I said that I was not in any way seeking to change the existing agreement – and then tried to manoeuvre me into accepting that the existing agreement meant that a consultant's contractual programme was only for nine sessions a week instead of eleven: something which would, of course, immediately destroy the whole-timer's differential. After over an hour of this I suggested we should adjourn, that I should try to put their contractual commitment into words and that we should meet again the following day. Although they had previously welcomed the idea of an adjourned meeting, Stevenson sat up at this and started protesting with all his old petulant arrogance. Really! Mr Grabham had flown back from Majorca specially for this meeting. Anyway, added Lewin, they had only just started. They wanted to discuss with me the additions to the existing contract I would have to give them if sanctions were to be called off. I groaned and sat back while they reeled off the old shopping list, which I had already told them we could discuss when negotiations were resumed. After another hour of this (while officials for my next meeting stood waiting outside in the corridor) I told them quite sharply that I had another important engagement. Why didn't we meet again when we had all had time to consider how far we had got and what I might be able to do to meet their points? Still they spluttered and finally I asked Henry to take them down to the waiting room to try and get some sense out of them. He kept coming back, head in hands, saying they were 'impossible'. They were now apparently quarrelling among themselves as to exactly when they wanted to meet me again and what they wanted me to do. Finally they were appeased. I was to send them an interim reply to their letter and offer to meet them for exploratory talks. But they had now changed their minds and

---

[1] Conservative MP for Sutton Coldfield and one of the shadow team on the social services.

didn't want this meeting to take place till after Easter! In the meantime I had had another urgent meeting on pay beds, officials telling me that I am compelled by law to increase the charges for them on 1 April. The formula to which I am tied works out at an increase of 60 per cent.[1] I can just imagine how this will be interpreted. Mrs Castle out to kill private practice again! After a long discussion I told them to find a device for reducing the increase to 50 per cent, but nonetheless this will mean trouble.

By now my early start and lack of sleep were beginning to tell. Blissfully I managed to pair at 9pm and had just got home, cooked myself some food and was watching the 10pm news when the phone rang. It was Harold, angrier than I have ever heard him in my whole life. He was almost beside himself. The venom poured out of him. He had generously allowed us to disagree publicly on the Common Market and what had we done? 'Made a fool of me,' he declared. When he had talked about freedom to dissent he hadn't meant that we should rush out and hold a press conference and organize an anti-Government campaign. No one had done more than he had to keep the party together and he had been pilloried and he had had enough of it. I tried to interrupt the spate but he swept on, finally spitting out the words, 'So this is all the loyalty I get. No one would have brought you back into Government but me.' At that something snapped in me and I retorted, 'I have never been so insulted in my life. I thought you had chosen me on merit. I am the best Minister you've got and you can have my resignation in ten minutes flat.' He began to climb down. 'You can have mine. Of course I chose you on merit. But this campaign you are organizing is intolerable. Some of us are having a meeting in my room in the House. You can come if you like.' I groaned. Was I never going to get any let-up? Besides, I felt so angry I didn't care what he did or said. 'Harold,' I moaned, 'it is pouring with rain and here I am, marooned in Islington, without a car.' 'You should be in the House,' he snapped. 'Come if you like; it's up to you.' And he slapped down the phone. 'I'm damned if I'm going,' I thought, but then I knew he had knocked all sleep out of my mind anyway. I didn't give a damn whether he sacked me or not and I was utterly uncontrite about what we had done, but I realized that he was, after all, Prime Minister and I owed him some courtesy. So when Ted came home I got him to run me down to the House.

A gloomy scene met me as I entered Harold's room. Harold was sitting in his chair, obviously in a shattered state. Mike sat at one end of the table opposite him; Jim at the other, head in hands. 'Have a drink,' said Harold morosely and as I helped myself he added, 'I was very insulting to Barbara just now and I apologize. I withdraw what I said.' I went over and kissed him affectionately on the forehead. 'And I'm sorry if I have upset you, but I am afraid I can't withdraw,' I replied. 'Don't I get a kiss?' said Jim gloomily. 'God knows I need it.' So I kissed him too and sat down next to him. 'I can't understand why Barbara is so chirpy,' he almost groaned. 'Because I don't think the situation is tragic,' I replied. 'Harold, you must wear with pride this freedom you have given us.' Harold had obviously calmed down a bit, but he was still in a pretty neurotic state. So for over an hour we had to listen to him. He wasn't going to accept

[1] Under the Health Services and Public Health Act, 1968, the Secretary of State for Wales and I were compelled to fix pay bed charges every year to reflect the average cost of in-patient services at hospitals. We had to take into account rising costs, improvements in the services and a contribution to capital expenditure.

Barbara's resignation or anybody else's, because he did not intend to preside over a rump Government. He must represent the whole movement or nothing at all. But his position was intolerable. Here we had approached Eric Varley within minutes of Cabinet's decision having been taken, inviting him to join a press conference that had been clearly pre-arranged (who the hell did tell tales, I wonder?). The thing which obviously hit Harold was the fact that we had got it all worked out beforehand. If he knew I was responsible for the whole plan, I really would be finished! For the fact is that the speed and cohesion with which we have acted has had a big effect on the press.

As he went bitterly on I gathered that another piece of our plan of action has fallen into place: Mik has sent the Motion for next Wednesday's NEC with all our names on it and has released it to the press.[1] It is this Motion, calling for the party to campaign actively against staying in the Market, that has made Harold declare that, unless it is withdrawn, he will resign. How could he carry on? he demanded of us. What would be his position at the special conference? If the NEC recommended that the party should back withdrawal, would he even be allowed to speak? It was intolerable and if this was the position in which we wanted to put him, he would resign. 'I'll resign with you,' said Jim lugubriously. At this moment Ron Hayward – for whom Harold had also sent – drifted in and proceeded to make delphic, and hardly deferential, utterances. If the NEC instructed him to launch a campaign, campaign he would. 'Out of our deficit?' said Jim. From Ron's manner – at moments almost impertinent – I couldn't make out whose side he was on. I made soothing noises from time to time, but I couldn't help thinking that Harold ought to have foreseen all this. How could the right to dissent have any meaning, I asked him, unless it also included the right to make dissent effective? Weren't the pro-marketeers going to organize? At this Harold said he was as angry at their – particularly Roy's – organizing efforts and said he was going to try to stop them too, which is absurd. Why shouldn't they organize? But Harold went on with his dark hints as to what would happen to the party, and not least to the Left, if he resigned. 'Some people would go straight into a coalition,' he spat out, adding, 'Roy would, like a shot.' I felt pretty unrepentant, but to my surprise Mike suddenly said, 'Of course, we shall have to take account of what you say, Harold. I don't think things are as tragic as you make out, but clearly we must consider what you have said. We cannot go any further tonight.' 'I shall make this the main business at Cabinet tomorrow,' declared Harold, at which I groaned. 'Oh no, Harold. Don't you know we ought to be talking about economic strategy? Don't you realize the Chancellor is demanding savage cuts in public expenditure which could split this party far more than the Common Market could? We are in a 1966 situation again.' 'If we are in a 1966 situation,' said Jim gloomily, 'this party is finished.' And so at 1am we broke up. My patient – and fascinated – Ted was waiting outside Harold's room. Mike grinned and shrugged, saying to him, 'Harold is in a bad way.' Mike, too, had apparently been summoned as I had been, but no one else.

---

[1] It rejected the terms as falling 'very far short' of the party's objectives and its final paragraph recommended to the special conference that the party should campaign for Britain's withdrawal from the Common Market. (For full text, see Appendix III.)

Thursday, 20 March

True to his word, Harold swept all the other items off the Cabinet agenda. As we opened he sent officials out of the room. He was calmer and clearer-eyed, but nonetheless still obsessed with his grievances. He had shifted his line from last night, drawing a distinction between the Motion on the Order Paper and the NEC resolution – though he had a side dig at the fact that 'someone' had approached Eric about the press conference, describing the whole pre-preparation of the anti-Market campaign as 'sly'. But then he went on to attack a 'leading pro-marketeer' (unnamed) who was also to be involved in a campaign. (We all knew he meant Roy.) Some people were preparing a 'pro-Market coalition with the Tories'. (Again we knew he meant Roy.) And then he changed tack, saying dissenting Ministers were perfectly entitled to make their position clear: the statement we had issued was okay. The real trouble was that the Ministers were trying to 'pitch the party line against the majority view of the Cabinet'. This was so different from what Harold had been saying last night that I had to modify what I had planned to say, particularly as Jim had the nerve to say that no one had ever objected to our campaigning. But Mike came in next in his most moderate vein. The NEC, he admitted, did present 'special problems'. We should have to see how they could be overcome. 'If you say to me, Harold, that you feel very strongly about it, of course I take that into account and concede that I may have been wrong about it.' I was positively taken aback by this concession, having been much more unrepentant about things myself last night and being still unrepentant this morning. But as I listen to Mike these days the more conscious I am that, as they grow older, these Foot brothers[1] all merge into one collective Foot type: rational, radical and eminently reasonable. They even speak in the same voice and the same terms; they are natural Liberals. No wonder Paul Foot has rebelled against his elders!

The rest of Cabinet clearly wanted to gag the NEC, Denis suggesting that Ministers who were members of the NEC should steer it away from a collective position and should try to steer the special party conference away from taking a view either. Jim even went so far as to say that Ministers ought not to vote on the NEC resolution. This was too much for me. I pointed out that it was impossible for Cabinet to try to silence the NEC, which considered itself as co-custodian of the Manifesto. After all, the NEC had drawn it up jointly with us and spelt out the conditions we would demand for continuing membership of the EEC. How could we stop it from ruling whether in its view the conditions had been fulfilled? If we even attempted to, we should destroy the unity of the party. And surely it was equally absurd to give Ministers freedom of

---

[1] The four brothers – Dingle, Hugh, John and Michael – were the sons of a former Liberal MP for Bodmin, Isaac Foot, and started life as members of the Liberal Party. Michael, the youngest, broke away first, becoming a socialist while still a student at Oxford. Dingle entered Parliament in 1931 as Liberal MP for Dundee, but joined the Labour Party in 1956, won Ipswich for Labour in 1957 and became Solicitor-General in the 1964–70 Labour Government. Hugh won an international reputation for his progressive views on colonial issues and served as Governor of Cyprus in 1957–60. In 1964 Harold Wilson sent him to the House of Lords as Lord Caradon and made him Minister of State for Foreign and Commonwealth Affairs. In this capacity he became the UK Permanent Representative at the United Nations from 1964 to 1970, the first Minister to do so. John fought a number of Liberal seats without success and was made a Peer on the Liberal nomination in 1967.

action and then say they couldn't exercise that freedom on the NEC? There was a Motion down anyway. Were we going to be told we must vote against it when we agreed with it? Even the guidelines Harold had drawn up recognized that dissenting Ministers would be free to campaign because they talked about 'campaigning Ministers'. And for good measure I asked whether, if Cabinet had decided no, anyone believed Roy Jenkins would have meekly stayed silent? Hadn't the European Movement already organized four hundred meetings? I think my speech had some effect and they started to cool down. Jim suggested that the moral was we ought to shorten the referendum campaign. Once again Mike played an emollient role. We should not try to take any decision here and now, he urged. 'The problem is not insoluble.' It was clear, he continued, that Ron Hayward had some idea as to how things might go at the special party conference. We must have a resolution before that conference and a recommendation from the NEC; nothing could stop that. But that did not preclude speeches from both sides. The Prime Minister and Foreign Secretary could, he was sure, be allowed to state their case. If Cabinet would leave this matter for the moment there could be talks over the next few days over a possible statement by Ron which could supersede the resolution before the NEC. It might be we could all back this, but no decision either way should be taken at the present time. And so it was left and Cabinet adjourned at 1pm, not having dealt with a single item of Government business. During the morning I was dispensing Polo mints on either side of me. Harold Lever, who sits opposite, tossed me a note: 'While we are still speaking – have you a sweetie?' I tossed him one back with a grin.

It was a very disgruntled Mikardo who joined us as the Dissenting Ministers gathered in my room at the House at 7pm. After all, all he had done was what we had all agreed and here he was, being type-cast as the Machiavelli again. And what he had done was based on the Dissenting Ministers' own statement, which happened to include a call to the party to campaign for a 'no' vote. So he began by demanding truculently that he be told 'what has happened since last we met'. Mike replied gently and diffidently. There had, he said, been a 'commotion in Cabinet'. And he spelt out Harold's anxieties, ending with the plea: 'What we could do is to have a statement by Ron re procedure, etc. which at the same time would establish the NEC's rights.' Mik remained grumpy. He had been one of the originators of the proposal of the 'right to differ' in the party, he maintained. It wasn't the Left who had tried to split the party. What was wrong with the Motion? It only 'called on' the party to campaign, it didn't 'instruct'. Peter tried to soothe him down: 'If the party machine is brought into action a situation would be created from which we could not recover.' There would be a great current of feeling and he feared for the party itself. Wedgie was conciliatory too. 'What really happened was that Cabinet misjudged the feeling in the movement. Having said that, the agreement to differ applies here too. We must have NEC guidelines and at conference facilities must be given to Harold and Jim.' Mik looked grim and unconvinced. Mike ploughed on: 'Of course the NEC must not be silent. All I suggest, because I want a solution that does not bring the collapse of the Government, is that you should take the resolution we have signed and lop off what we said about a campaign. All these organizational matters should be dealt with in Ron's statement. If that statement is taken first the resolution can be fought over afterwards.' He ended pleadingly: 'If we knock Harold through the ropes, we also knock the referendum and the Labour Government.' 'Are you saying he will go for a national government?' asked Dick Clements,[1] exchanging some eyebrow-raising with Wedgie, who then muttered, 'There are two ways of destroying the party.' Mik remained stubborn. 'Let's move the resolution first and then have a document from Ron.' No, Mike insisted. We should have Ron's statement first. 'Let's try and get them to the bloody conference, Mik.' 'Let's get our victory before we are generous,' retorted Wedgie. And so it was left, rather uneasily. Mik, still grumpy, gave us details of the five working parties he was setting up among the MPS: one for the preparation of material; one on the House of Commons side of our activity; a public relations committee; a working party on the running of meetings and a fifth on contacts with Transport House. We agreed to meet regularly in my room at the House during the campaign. 'Let's call ourselves the DMs,' grinned Judith. 'My office thinks it is a Cabinet committee.'

Friday, 21 March

A hard working trip to Coventry to open Dick Crossman House, the new hostel for the mentally handicapped, which, at my suggestion, the local authority had decided to name after him in commemoration of all his work in this field. I was immensely heartened by what the local authority is doing in the way of hostels and sheltered employment. Their Director of Social Services, Tom White, is first-class. David and I agree he would be an excellent successor to Joan Cooper[2] if we could get him. Anne Crossman turned up as brave and smiling and self-controlled as ever she was. That woman is a mystery to me. I would have broken down and howled when the moving tributes were paid to Dick. Can she possibly be as serene as she appears?

Monday, 24 March

Our monthly meeting of the TUC Liaison Committee. The only item on the agenda was a discussion on the EEC, which turned out predictably routine. Harold didn't even bother to turn up. Jim gave a report on the progress of the negotiations, playing it pretty low-key. He had, he said, always been an agnostic about the EEC. But he then proceeded to make an apologia for all its defects. The Commission, he said, 'was a dragon whose bark is worse than its bite'. The Treaty was 'very fly-blown'. He thought it would be in Britain's best interests to stay in. 'The co-ordination of regional aids does not harm our areas. The question whether to go in is very different from "shall we come out". Four years ago I was against our going in.' He then entered

---

[1] Editor of *Tribune*, which was to be the voice of the anti-marketeers in the campaign.

[2] Joan Cooper was director of the Social Work Service division of the department. Though she had done an excellent job, her rank of Under Secretary showed that the department did not rate the social services side of our work as highly as the medical, which was headed by the Chief Medical Officer and no less than four Deputy Chief Medical Officers. She was due to retire in 1976 and I was planning to upgrade the director's post to deputy secretary so as to correct the department's bias and attract someone like Tom White, who had first-class experience in the field.

into a diatribe against the efforts being made to swing the party against entry. 'The agreement to differ was not intended to be the freedom to organize a campaign.' (So he has gone back on the progress we made at last Thursday's Cabinet!) 'Above all, if the campaign organized by the party machine is used against the Government, the Government cannot survive. The party machine must remain neutral on the organizational side.' I don't know whether he thought he could get the unions on his side against us, or what, but Jack Jones wasn't letting him get away with it. 'That last aspect is not a matter for this committee,' he said primly. And he added the warning: 'Only a special Congress can change the policy of the TUC.'[1] He went on to assure Jim that the Australian trade unions did not want us to stay in. But we must try to avoid rancour. 'At the end of the road it is much more vital for us to have a Labour Government.' Len Murray trod a careful path: 'We too must set out both sides of the argument and Government should set out all the arguments fully.' David Basnett contented himself with the anodyne statement that 'the purpose of this Liaison Committee is to create unity and it would be our wish that this unity should be preserved'. Nonetheless, he congratulated Jim on what he had achieved in the negotiations, and it was obvious from the way he and Alf Allen whispered together that they were in cahoots. I suspect the Union of Shop, Distributive and Allied Workers [USDAW] is going to switch its line.[2] I suspect too that the unity of the trade-union movement is much less complete than Jack would like. There will be some defectors before the campaign is through. Only Wedgie struck a belligerent note. It would be quite wrong, he said, not to put on record that the Government machine was being used flat out to put the pro-Market case. He himself had been denied the use of the duplicating machine and press office of his department: 'So I have come to Transport House.' At the end of this inconclusive discussion we issued a neutral – not to say neutered – statement to the press.

At the office we returned to the tortuous question of our discussions with the BMA. We went through the officials' draft of our interpretation of the option agreement,[3] and I ruled out the possibility of a joint statement. It would take a month of day and night talks to agree that! Instead we decided to put our view in the form of a letter to

[1] At its last annual Congress in September 1974 the TUC had affirmed its continuing opposition to Britain's membership of the European Common Market.

[2] On 25 April 1975, the day before the special Labour Party Conference on the Common Market, the USDAW delegation did decide to switch and vote in favour of staying in the EEC. Four days later, however, the USDAW annual conference decided to recommend its members to vote 'no' in the referendum.

[3] An agreement reached between the Ministry of Health and the Joint Consultants Committee in 1955 and reaffirmed in 1961. Its purpose was to reassure consultants who wanted to retain the right to do private practice that this would not bar them from whole-time posts in the NHS provided they were willing to give 'substantially the whole of their time' to their NHS work and to give it priority on all occasions. Hospital boards were therefore instructed, when making whole-time consultant appointments, to offer applicants the option of taking a maximum part-time contract instead of a whole-time one, if they so wished. Moreover the applicant need not declare his choice until after the appointment had been made and could move from one type of contract to another, unless there were compelling reasons why the hospital had to have a whole-timer. I was prepared to reaffirm this agreement, but the consultants were pressing me to interpret the commitment to give 'substantially the whole of his time' as meaning nine half-day sessions a week, instead of the whole-timers' eleven sessions, with the obvious inference that any time worked over nine sessions ought to attract extra pay. This I was not prepared to do as it would have destroyed the existing pay differential in favour of the whole-timer.

the BMA. I ruled that we shouldn't offer any answer to the BMA's 'shopping list' of demands at this stage. My heart sinks at the thought of the long, arid arguments that lie ahead. I then had to hurry to No. 10 for Harold's reception for the people who had helped in the Moorgate disaster: ambulancemen, the chaps from Bart's, nurses, St John's Ambulance, the police, etc. This was one of Harold's inspired ideas and, of course, as Secretary of State for the Health Service, I had to be there. I enjoyed talking to the men and women who had done all the work during that horrible time and was interested towards the end of the evening to run into some London Transport rescue squad chaps who were muttering about the fact that no one realized they did jobs like this almost as a routine. The cameras were there in force and at one point one of Harold's entourage came up to me and asked me to get into the act. I demurred, saying that it was the PM's do. 'I am sure the Prime Minister would wish you to be in the photograph, Secretary of State,' she insisted. As I still said no she disappeared and then came back and said, 'The PM wants you to join him.' I knew better and moved to the edge of the radius of TV lights. Harold greeted me grudgingly: no 'come here little Minister'. I knew I was still in disfavour and kept my distance, unconcerned.

Tuesday, 25 March

Harold has gone off to the States, so Ted Short presided over Cabinet, which thereupon proceeded at a cracking pace. Nonetheless, there was such an accumulation of items, thanks to Harold's obsessional monopoly of the last Cabinet, that we had to have a spill-over meeting in the afternoon. In the morning we started with Civil Service pay, on which we came to the reluctant conclusion that there was nothing to do but stand by the principle of comparability, despite Mike's mournful warnings. I again backed Malcolm Shepherd because I am not prepared to have a unilateral incomes policy in the public sector: that is too Heathian for me. We next turned to the draft White Paper on the EEC negotiations, which Peter described as 'riddled with value judgments which make it almost impossible to take it seriously'. So we anti-marketeers let it go through with a shrug of indifference. We then had a long discussion on the draft guidelines which Harold had drawn up for Ministers' conduct during the referendum campaign and, if he had been there, he would have been a bit taken aback at the unity with which we dispatched some of them, agreeing they were far too restrictive and inflexible.[1] Roy, in particular, said he would be bound to appear with members of opposite parties and it was absurd to say we couldn't even appear with Tory backbench MPs. We all backed him up and Ted Short said he was sure the PM 'wouldn't take umbrage' if we altered this. As for the handling of ongoing

[1] Harold's document stressed that Ministers should avoid personalizing the argument. There should be no direct confrontation on a platform or programme. No Minister should appear with an MP of a different political party 'or with the representative of any organization he would not in other circumstances be seen dead with'. Ministers, including non-Cabinet Ministers, should not be free to speak against the Government's recommendation in parliamentary debates and dissenting Ministers should not handle ongoing Community business during the referendum campaign either in Brussels or Parliament. It was Eric Heffer's insistence on speaking in the European debate on 9 April which led to his sacking from the Government.

Community business during the campaign, we again united in rejecting the idea that dissenting Ministers couldn't answer Questions or attend Brussels meetings. 'How are departments to be run?' asked Wedgie, quipping that Harold's proposals would establish 'no go areas' and take dissenting Ministers into 'protective custody'. It was much better, we agreed, to rely on Ministers' good sense. And we didn't like Harold's outrageous suggestion that Permanent Secretaries should take over from dissenting Ministers the responsibility for briefing officials on Community business. Altogether we were far more relaxed about it all than Harold had been.

In the afternoon we at last turned to Denis's public expenditure proposals. His determination to cut £1 billion off the programmes for 1976–77 has come as a traumatic blow so soon after the January White Paper and I am furious at the lack of planning and proper forecasting it reveals. Here we have been struggling in my department to work out forward plans on the basis of the restraints of the Public Expenditure White Paper. We have had the agonizing reappraisal weekend at Sunningdale with the RHA chairmen and encouraged them to face up to the problems caused by the minute size of the increases we could propose. We even got them regarding it all as a challenge and David had worked out a list of agreed schemes on the basis of the White Paper figures. Now it had all gone for nothing: the whole exercise to be done again on an even narrower base. How could we hope to maintain morale on this hand-to-mouth basis? So I was feeling truculent. But Denis was in grim mood. Our credit, he said, was low and falling. Inflation was running at 20 per cent. The borrowing requirement was much too high for comfort and we might get a sudden collapse of confidence. The main source of inflation was wage inflation. He hoped he would be able to work out tougher guidelines with the TUC, 'but we can't take credit for that now'. He didn't want to be 'too nasty' in this year's Budget, because the level of world trade was falling. 'The upturn next year could be very rapid indeed, but we will not have the capacity to take advantage of it.' (How cutting public expenditure is supposed to sustain our capacity I have never been able to understand.) He didn't want to increase indirect taxation too much as that fed directly into the Retail Prices Index, but if he was to put all the burden of combating inflation onto direct taxation, this would mean adding from 5 pence to 12 pence to the standard rate of income tax. 'If we could decide the amount of cuts now we could get away with smaller fiscal burdens than otherwise.' The illustrative package he had put forward, he said, was the least damaging way of imposing the cuts, though we could consider some shifts of expenditure between departments. But the figure he asked for was the minimum necessary.

The discussion then took its predictable course: most of Cabinet resigned to the inevitable and all of us conscious that *something* had to be done to stop the inflationary drift. Tony C. complained again that we didn't know what the overall strategy was. Peter said that the package must contain both public expenditure cuts and tax increases. 'The composition of the package is a matter for Cabinet.' (We all keep saying this, but we are no nearer getting Cabinet control of tax policy.) Peter then proceeded to echo my thoughts: 'If we *just* have a deflationary package, we won't be in a better position at the end of the year to seize our opportunities. There is a missing component in Denis's proposals: an effective element for increasing exports or reducing imports this year.' Wedgie fumed: 'These cuts mean we are abandoning the Social Contract. They constitute a massive deflationary package which will cut productive capacity and investment. As Cabinet knows, I have put forward a paper with proposals of my own, but we are not even allowed to look at the alternative.'[1] I declared this was 1966 all over again. The moral appeared to be: 'A Labour Government can never increase the social wage.' We must have a socio-economic strategy worked out with the trade unions. Why didn't we put the alternatives to them? Once again we had fallen back on cuts: no import controls or social objectives. We faced a negative growth rate in the NHS. I was against the stale old formula of bilateral talks with the Treasury, which merely set one Minister against another and robbed Cabinet of the right to work out an overall redistribution of expenditure. Mike hammered away at his familiar themes: after the election we ought to have had a new course, but we threw away the chance. The turning-point came with our refusal to act on top salaries. Result: 'We are in danger of drifting into a conventional Treasury package with no light at the end of the tunnel.' We should face the trade unions with a direct choice: tougher guidelines or disastrous cuts. By just going ahead like this we were jeopardizing the chance of the 'Social Contract round two'.

But Denis had his allies: positive ones in Roy J. and Reg P., acquiescent ones among the rest. Roy said gravely that this was not 1966: 'the situation is incomparably more serious'. In 1966 there was the alternative of devaluation. There was no alternative now. Wedgie's was not a 'remotely viable alternative'. It would take us into a siege economy. 'It is difficult to discuss the whole strategy because of the ban on any discussion of wages policy.' If Denis could not say something publicly about the borrowing requirement, there might be a collapse of confidence. Reg Prentice was as usual even more forthright about wages policy. He didn't disguise his view that he favours a statutory one. 'A voluntary incomes policy, full employment and high public expenditure are irreconcilable.' We spent too much on social security. 'In concentrating priorities on cash payments we have allowed the structure of society to run down.' (How on earth he expects the poor to live he did not say.) John Silkin said he accepted the amount of the cuts, but wanted a different distribution. Bob let loose a Chief Whip blast: 'Will the House of Commons take it? This means the virtual destruction of the Manifesto and the impossibility of continuing the Social Contract. You are going to see the most major revolt in your history.' Denis gave his usual wordy piece of self-justification at the end. 'The things we counted on haven't

[1] On 11 February Tony Benn had circulated to the Ministerial Committee on Economic Strategy a paper outlining two alternative strategies open to the Government to deal with the growing crisis. Strategy A embodied the conventional economic approach of cutting living standards and increasing unemployment in order to wipe out the balance of payments deficit and reduce inflation. Strategy B put the preservation of jobs and industrial capacity first. It involved large-scale selective assistance to industry through the Industry Act and the NEB, selective import restrictions, rationing and allocation of some imported materials and fuel, work sharing, more egalitarian taxation, control of capital outflows and acceptance of a further downward float in sterling to make us more competitive. The effect, Benn argued, would be to maintain jobs and industrial activity, though there would be a slower improvement in the balance of payments and inflation. He urged his colleagues to adopt Strategy B, but the paper had never been discussed by Cabinet.

happened: the Social Contract and reflation by other countries.' He had been in continuous discussion with the TUC: 'It won't come to them as a surprise.' Our trouble was that we had no industrial strategy and were pouring out money on everything from fruit juice to BB[1] indiscriminately. As a result of the cuts unemployment would only be seventy thousand higher by the beginning of 1977. Of course, he got his way and those wretched bilateral talks with the Treasury are to begin.

After all this my chance of getting Cabinet to agree to advance the pension uprating date from November was minimal. I did my best, stressing that by October we would be spending £500 million less on benefits at an annual rate than what was necessary to restore purchasing power. Some of our lads backed me, but the rest put up no resistance to the Chancellor. It was hopeless. Altogether a dreary afternoon. Why, oh why, won't Harold get off his backside and really go for a public presentation of our problems, appealing publicly to the rank and file of the trade unions? We are drifting to disaster. The trouble is that there are really two Cabinets: those of us who want to develop a *positive* strategy, and the Prentice-ites who won't have a planning package (calling it a 'siege economy') and who seem to be sitting back waiting for events to force us into a statutory incomes policy. The line-up is not, in my view, unconnected with the Common Market argument. Wedgie and Harold Lever are engaged in a war by correspondence over our backbenchers' amendments to the Industry Bill.[2] Even John Horam [Labour MP for Gateshead West] of the Manifesto Group has been backing an amendment giving compulsory powers to the NEB, but Harold Lever is fighting all the amendments tooth and nail. I often wonder why that lad is in the Labour Party. Another battle is going on over industrial democracy. Stan Orme has worked out some exciting proposals for Harland and Wolff, but all Harold Lever can think of is 'restoring confidence'.

Wednesday, 26 March

Of course, the photographers were there in strength when I arrived at Transport House for the NEC. I was a little late and the TV cameras were just leaving. They

[1] Bear Brand (BB) and Kirkby Manufacturing and Engineering Ltd, which manufactured soft drinks and storage radiators, were two firms into which Tony Benn had put government money against the advice of the Industrial Development Advisory Board set up under the Industry Act 1972. Both firms were on Merseyside where unemployment was already 9·5 per cent.

[2] Harold Lever had written to the Prime Minister protesting at the 'far-reaching amendments' to the Industry Bill that were being put down by a group of our supporters at committee stage. These, he said, sought to give the NEB powers of compulsory acquisition; to place a duty on the directors of the company in which the NEB took a stake to have regard to government policy and to the interests of employees of the company and consumers of its products; to allow the NEB to acquire, without the consent of the Secretary of State, a stake of up to 51 per cent or £50 million in a company (instead of 30 per cent or £10 million); to give the Secretary of State a duty (as opposed to a power) to make planning agreements with any company 'whose operations in his opinion affect or are likely to affect national objectives and needs' and to require the company under such an agreement to make wide disclosures of information to the Secretary of State; to give a trade union a right to obtain very detailed information (subject to certain qualifications) from any company with 200 or more employees; to declare the European Communities Act inapplicable to the Bill and to widen the range of companies subject to the powers to prevent them passing into non-resident hands. He demanded, successfully, that Tony Benn must be told not to accept these amendments or modify the policy Cabinet had agreed.

swivelled round and said: 'Here she is.' 'Surely you didn't think I wouldn't turn up?' I replied sweetly. The press were there in force, hoping for a great row over the EEC. One chap even asked me for my comments on it before we started! But once again their hopes were falsified. Yesterday Mike told me he had been in touch with Ron and agreed a statement with him which he had then cleared with Mik. Mike's hard back-room work paid dividends. We found Ron's statement[1] waiting for us on the table, and Ron proceeded to speak to it quite eloquently. His advice was 'the sooner we have the special conference the better', and we were most of us glad that he had managed to get a hall in London for 26 April, though Walter Padley complained on behalf of USDAW that it clashed with their conference. His complaints were swept aside, only Shirley supporting him because she knew USDAW is pro-Market. Ron's second point was that he thought we ought to put to conference an NEC statement rather than a resolution (i.e. implicitly, that it would be better to have his statement – very conciliatory in tone – rather than Mik's resolution). Thirdly, he set out his proposal for giving Harold the opening speech at conference, followed by an anti-Market NEC spokesman, another pro-Market speaker and an anti-marketeer to wind up. As for the use of the party machine, he suggested that any campaign would have to be organized by local parties, though there should be no disciplining of dissidents. He was clearly treading a tightrope, precariously balanced between his instinctive loyalty to Harold as PM and his fierce belief in the rights of the NEC. So he expressed the hope that he would be allowed to circulate to local parties the whole proceedings of conference and added that 'we in Transport House will do our best to service everyone whether they want a pro or anti meeting'. He gabbled on: 'You don't want to impose the views of the majority', at which Mik chipped in, 'No one ever did.' Ron was clearly embarrassed at the conclusions of his own statement, advising conference that Harold's terms 'do not satisfy Britain's requirements', and he said defensively, 'I had to take note of the fact that a majority of the NEC had already declared themselves.' (We had got eighteen signatures to our Motion. And a good job we did, I thought to myself. Otherwise I believe that the anti case would have gone almost by default.) Finally Ron summed up with a passionate plea that we should not tear ourselves apart over this: 'The unity of the party is a damn sight more important to me than the question of the Market.' At this there were the predictable 'Hear, hears'.

Harold had turned up in a much more temperate mood and was choosing his words carefully. 'The speaking arrangements seem okay to me,' he said, 'though I reserve my position at this stage.' I could see us drifting into a situation of total harmony behind Ron's line (with the media claiming a walkover for Harold and capitulation by us), when Wedgie dared to raise his voice. (It was like swearing in church.) He didn't object to Ron's statement but he thought we ought to clarify Ron's references to the party machine. 'Of course, we shouldn't bully minorities or prevent the party's press

---

[1] Ron Hayward had produced a draft statement which he suggested the NEC should put to the special conference in place of Mikardo's Motion. The statement paid tribute to Ministers' efforts in the renegotiations. Though it rejected the new terms and opposed Britain's continuing membership of the EEC, it dropped all reference to a party campaign against membership and called for tolerance of differing views in the 'great debate'.

department from putting out speeches from either side. What we are discussing is whether the majority of the party should have the right to produce its own literature in its own cause.' To this Ron retorted, 'The Government has decided to give money to both sides. I also know that the party is in the red. If you want us to produce literature – which we know that only the antis will order anyway – you will put us even deeper in debt.' Then Mik moved in to stop the rot. First, he protested that the Motion which had been tabled was not *his* Motion: 'I didn't even draft it, I was just the postman.' (I could almost feel Harold pricking up his ears at this: so the dissident Ministers were behind this one too?) What we ought to do, said Mik, was to put the Motion to the NEC and then decide whether to put it or Ron's statement to conference. As for the last paragraph of the resolution about campaigning, which had caused such offence, it had been widely misinterpreted – he believed deliberately. He had personally always supported the freedom to dissent and had never intended the paragraph to mean that we should beat local parties over the head. So he welcomed Ron's paper as spelling out the libertarian attitude and supported it 'one hundred per cent'. The reference to 'freedom to campaign' would be in the context of Ron's paper. This clearly foxed the pro-marketeers. Shirley hedged and Harold trimmed. 'I have never,' he said, 'argued at any time that the NEC should not make a recommendation to conference.' ('That's not true,' I hissed to Mike.) 'My desire,' Harold continued, 'was always that we should have a free debate and a comradely debate. I am deeply concerned about putting the reserves of the party behind a campaign. I am also concerned about the wording, though I certainly believe the NEC has the right to say that certain objectives (for example, on the CAP) have not been met.' Finally, despite his obvious efforts not to relapse into his previous hysteria, it burst out of him: 'I am concerned that certain Ministers on the NEC should put their names to a resolution committing the reserves of the party to fighting the Government line.'

Wedgie then suggested, with every appearance of trying to be helpful, that we should add bits of Ron's statement to the resolution for conference purposes and he was backed by Bryan Stanley, who is clearly going to remain toughly anti. At this point it was clear that the dissidents were making all the running. We had succeeded in getting the whole discussion concentrated, not on whether the NEC was pro or anti the terms, but on what form our opposition should take. Jim could obviously see the trap into which Harold had walked. 'I think I have been treated less than fairly,' he complained. 'I thought when I came here that the first thing that would happen is that I should be asked to give a report on the negotiations.' The resolution was tendentious in parts, he maintained, and, he added viciously, 'It is in the same language as the Motion on the House of Commons Order Paper – a remarkable coincidence.' But even he was forced to claim that he had never doubted the NEC must express a view. It was the reference to campaigning he complained about. At this Mik made a brilliant move. He suggested that we should begin by adopting Ron's paper on procedure which accompanied the draft statement. No one could object to that as it ensured that Harold would speak at conference and adopt it we did – unanimously. After that it was only a matter of time before we won. Shirley in desperation moved the deletion of the last paragraph of our Motion about campaigning. Mik was relaxed: 'I would like it as an addendum but it is not madly necessary.' This time it was Wedgie who stepped in to stop us giving away too much. He said he didn't want to jeopardize our unity, but must support the inclusion of this paragraph. All it meant was that literature must be available from Transport House for local parties to use. Sid Weighell came in snappily. 'My union is split down the middle on this issue. We're going to ask both Tony Benn and Shirley Williams to address us. You know this paragraph is dangerous, Mik, and that is why you won't take it out.' 'I take that as a personal attack,' said Mik coldly. I then suggested we should leave in the paragraph but insert after 'campaign' the words 'on the lines of the General Secretary's statement'. Harold rather liked this and so it was agreed.

But another tussle lay ahead. Harold urged that we should not vote on Mik's Motion. It should merely be accepted as the majority view. (Once again this showed how successful our tactic in tabling the Motion with eighteen signatures had been. It conditioned the pros to surrendering the issue without a fight, as Jim kept tetchily observing.) We antis then in turn expressed our sympathy with Harold's aim. Nonetheless, we could see the danger of not having a clear record of the NEC view minuted. I therefore suggested that we should record that 'the following resolution was passed by a majority'. The Motion, I said, must have the same authority as the Cabinet decision. Harold didn't quite like that, but, after a lot of humming and hawing, my suggestion was approved.

All this over, Jim repeated his mournful complaint. He had come along, he said, expecting to be asked to give a full report of the negotiations before any decision had been taken. Instead the NEC had reached its decisions in ignorance. He really felt that, for the record, he had the right to be heard. So we agreed to humour him and he spoke powerfully for about twenty minutes, while some people chatted and others went to the lavatory or the telephone. I must say I think Jim had a point, but our only hope as antis was to outmanoeuvre him. He and Harold have got the whole government machine with which to bulldoze their views through.

Thursday, 27 March

No Cabinet. Cabinet government barely exists any more and is certainly going to be broadly in abeyance until the referendum is over. We antis noted that the popular version of the Government White Paper is being cooked up somewhere behind the scenes. There is no pretence about getting it approved by Cabinet.

Friday, 28 March, to Monday, 31 March

Easter weekend at HCF. The whole family turned up in strength, so it was sixteen round the table every day, Exhausting but utterly satisfying. I told the office I couldn't possibly start my trip to America until after the Easter weekend, even though it meant curtailing it. I am not going to allow anything to interfere with these great family gatherings. They have absolute priority.

Tuesday, 1 April, to Wednesday, 9 April
Trip to USA.

Having been invited to lecture to the Harvard Medical School on the British Health Service, I had decided to make a quick visit to the United States. I particularly wanted to study their 'certification of need' system of controlling hospital developments, as I thought this might encourage the fainter hearts in Cabinet who were worried about my own proposals for licensing. I found that an increasing number of States, worried about the over-provision of hospital beds, were setting up State health planning agencies to monitor and control new hospital developments – and this in the citadel of freedom in medicine! I also found growing fears that the health care system in the United States was breaking down. Edward Kennedy, with whom I talked, was once again seeking to introduce legislation in Congress for radical reform. At his request, I sent him details of the financing and administration of the NHS. Replying, he wrote: 'I believe that the rapidly rising costs and growing inefficiency of the health care system in the United States is one of the most important, most complex and most difficult problems we face.'

On my return I found that Denis Healey's retrenchment plans were well advanced. On 15 April he introduced a Budget to cut back private consumption and to reduce public expenditure in 1976–77 by £900 million. Wage increases, he argued, had outstripped price increases and inflation threatened to undermine our national credibility. The balance of payments gap must be closed: in 1974 the rise in oil prices had helped to push it up to £3,800 million. Government borrowing must be reduced. If nothing was done the PSBR would rise to over £10 million in the coming year. Resources must be switched to exports and investment. His Budget package, therefore, was double-edged. On the one hand, he announced a number of measures to increase the funds of private industry and to promote the training services provided by government. These would cost money. On the other, he introduced swingeing increases in taxation to reduce demand. Here indirect taxes took the lead, with the top rate of VAT going up to 25 per cent on less essential items, beer taking another 2 pence per pint while the tax on spirits went up by a record 64 pence per standard bottle. Income tax went up, too, by 2 per cent on the standard and higher rates of tax bringing the standard rate up to 35 per cent, only partially offset by a modest increase in personal allowances. These changes, he claimed, would reduce the borrowing requirement by £1,200 million. They would also push up the index of retail prices by 2¾ per cent. Most chilling of all was his admission that unemployment could reach one million by the end of the year. The only consolation for me in the package was his firm commitment to introduce child benefit by April 1977 and his undertaking to extend the family allowance to the first child in one-parent families one year earlier.

On the referendum front my relations with Harold Wilson had become very strained. He would clearly not easily forgive the Dissenting Ministers for having organized their *opposition to his renegotiated terms so promptly and effectively. His anger was deepened by the fact that, not only had he been outnumbered on the NEC, but he clearly faced defeat at the special party conference which had been called for 26 April. But before then he was to suffer further chagrin in the House when on 9 April, in the vote on the terms, he was only to get his massive majority of 226 with the help of Tory votes. Of the 315 available Labour MPs, only 137 supported him and 170 voted against. But the campaign of the 'antis' was hampered by the fact that they had to operate through the National Referendum Campaign, an all-party umbrella organization through which the Government channelled the public funds which the referendum Act, which became law on 8 May, was to make available to each side in the campaign. Moreover the funds – £125,000 each – were derisory when compared with the money raised privately by the pro-Market umbrella organization, 'Britain in Europe' (see page 408).*

Wednesday, 9 April

The night trip back from the States was terrible. We got home about 11am and I got into bed for an hour's sleep. I was back in the office in the afternoon. Denis said he wanted to see me that evening and so officials crowded in to discuss solemnly how I could prepare myself. Denis had refused to say what it was about, but they assumed it must be about the PESC discussion at tomorrow's Cabinet. We had to go through the whole rigmarole about what should be my attitude to Denis's demand for cuts of £1,000 million next year (of which the NHS would have to take £62 million) and how we might stave off the effects on us. We were particularly worried lest this might mean that Denis would not accept the Review Body's report on doctors' pay. There is also the question of dental and opthalmic charges coming up. There will be a shortfall of £16 million in revenue from charges this year as a result of the increased fees to dentists and the Health side told me categorically that the £62 million cut for the NHS would be bad enough without having to find this £16 million on top. So I should warn Cabinet. (Of course, my officials are in favour of charges going up and would probably like more of them.) When I got to No. 11 Denis was at his most affable and relaxed. It transpired he wanted to talk to me privately to explain his Budget strategy, just as Roy Jenkins used to do. I wondered whether he (and Roy) did this to every member of the Cabinet or whether they just tried to win me over because they thought I was a formidable enemy. Denis chatted on about his difficulties. The borrowing requirement was 'terrifying'. He just had to cut back public expenditure. The Social Contract wasn't working. Inflation was getting out of control. Why had the situation changed? His officials had got their forecasts wrong. He was getting away with it in the current year by tax increases, but he was reaching the limit of them, etc. etc. As for an alternative strategy, he did not rule out import restrictions on principle. 'I think I have a less ideological objection to them than Harold has.' But there was always the risk of retaliation and so he was working on a form of countervailing powers which he would use if necessary. I mustn't ask him too much about that. Defence? Yes, he was going to insist on greater cuts. And so on. It is always very difficult to fight back against a tactic like this. What could I say? He sounded so reasonable and so anxious to take everyone's views into account. At last I was able to get to bed.

Thursday, 10 April

Another of those wretched PESC Cabinets. They are getting so drearily familiar! Denis reported he had reached agreement with Ministers on some £870 million towards the saving of the £1,000 million he was demanding, but the bilateral talks had still left him short of what he needed. He was still arguing with Defence, who were only offering a cut of £100 million instead of £200 million, and there were other disputed programmes. Everyone fought his corner. Roy [Mason] fought like a tiger against doing more than £100 million and despite my pressure, (and Denis's frequent protestations to me privately that Defence could and should give up more), no one really hit out at him except me and we only succeeded in forcing him up to £110 million. Tony C. was edged into accepting a bit more of his share. I made a vigorous speech about the consequences to the NHS of the cuts the Chancellor was insisting on from me, but I got no support – not even from Mike, the custodian of Nye's memory. I told them flat that I couldn't take the additional £16 million for dental and ophthalmic fees, but Harold merely said we would discuss increases in charges when the time came. My trouble is that everyone remembers how successfully I fought for the roads programme when I was Minister of Transport and I get teased mercilessly. Bob has a favourite crack: 'What we ought to do is make Barbara Chancellor and then no one would get a penny.' Eventually we managed to get the total cuts up to £900 million and Denis weakly said he would be content – reluctantly – with that. But out of the discussion came a chorus of complaints (led by Tony C. and me) that Ministers were never given the chance of discussing priorities or overall economic strategy. Instead we were faced with *ad hoc* demands from the Chancellor from time to time, pleading sudden crisis or necessity. In particular, I pleaded that we should look ahead to 1979 and decide what objectives we would wish to have achieved by then and which ones we were prepared to sacrifice. How could I get my health authorities to plan the NHS properly when the capital allocations were abruptly changed? Harold expressed sympathy with this and said he would see what he could do. He also agreed the public sector borrowing requirement [PSBR] was becoming a fetish. No other Government had it, but we were stuck with it. And he agreed with Wedgie that we ought not to allow the PESC conventions to force us to lump all forms of public expenditure together as though public investment in industry was a debit, while all forms of private expenditure (even on his favourite example: the Brighton Marina) were pure gain. This too should be looked into.

Still suffering from jet lag, I caught the night sleeper to Blackburn to open a factory.

Friday, 11 April

I was astonished at the size of the anti-Market rally in Manchester. They came pouring into the Free Trade Hall, nearly two thousand strong. Everyone spoke well except me. I felt curiously listless. Perhaps it was jet lag, but I think it was also that I cannot get attuned to the over-simplified extremism of the anti-Market case. Peter was impressive and well received, but Wedgie, with a more fluent flow of rhetoric than I have ever heard from him, was the hero of the hour. There was a more revivalist atmosphere than the movement has known for years.

Monday, 14 April

Up at 6.30am to get to London for pre-Budget Cabinet. It went predictably. Denis spelt out his economic analysis and measures competently, if a trifle wearily. Everyone shook their heads, but no one protested seriously. We all know that, whatever the reasons that got us into the mess we are in, we have little alternative. Mike made a few noises about the unemployment figures. Wedgie backed me when I said that the aspect of the Chancellor's Budget that would be attacked most was its 'ad hocery'. Once again we had been blown off course. What we needed was to fix our goals for 1978–79 on the most pessimistic assumptions and then jib back from that. Only in that way would we be able to work out a strategy of priorities. But no one made any scenes and even Wedgie only hinted in that controlled histrionic way of his that there *was* an alternative, if only we had the courage to follow it. Harold Lever for once said he backed the Chancellor 100 per cent. Once again I felt caught in that sense of inevitability when social democratic dreams come up against the realities of the mixed economy.

But it was all preceded by a very early meeting of EC(P) to discuss my paper on the Doctors' and Dentists' Review Body's report on doctors' and dentists' pay.[1] To my surprise, even the Treasury made no objection to accepting my paper. Once again we were in a 'no alternative' situation. My decision to offer the staging of salaries above £13,000 (contrary to David's and the department's first advice) defused any opposition Mike might have been contemplating. And I further disarmed him by saying that I was willing to enter into any discussions for altering the TUC guidelines, including an adjustment of 'fair comparison', once the first year's round of control-free settlements was over. I even got him to agree to recommend to Harold that, since the recommendation was unanimous, it need not go to Cabinet and that I should be left free to play this Government acceptance of the report at any point in my negotiations with the consultants that I felt was right.

[1] The report, produced under the new chairmanship of Sir Ernest Woodroofe, had been in our hands since 1 April and was later published as Cmnd. 5010 on 18 April 1975. As anticipated, it found that the pay of the professions had fallen 'so substantially behind those of comparable professional men and women, both in the public services and in the private sector, that a measure of structural adjustment is now essential'. It therefore recommended 'catching up' increases averaging 30 per cent, including threshold payments. My paper to EC (P) recommended that the Government should accept the report, subject to the staging over two years of the increases on salary levels above £13,000, as had been done in the case of top salaries. This was agreed and the date of the announcement was left to me.

361

With this under my pinny I went back to the office to discuss tactics in my discussion with the consultants' negotiators, which has been fixed for Wednesday. We went through an elaborate examination of all the alternative 'options' that might face us. I always end these rather exhausting analyses by repeating my favourite hymn: 'One step enough for me.' When we are all round the table – David, Philip, Henry, Raymond, Tim Nodder *et al*. (always with Peter Brown brooding protectively over me) – we build up a remarkable sense of camaraderie. Is this the secret of the British Civil Service: the capacity to identify with the personal fortunes of the current Ministers, without the Civil Service ever losing its sense of separate identity?

Tuesday, 15 April

I have insisted on keeping this morning free to attend the Standing Committee on the Pensions Bill. In the event it worked out rather well, because the committee had just got itself into the middle of the discussion on the Married Women's Option[1] on which the Tories hope to make some political mileage. Brian O'M., brilliant as he is on the details of the Bill, is rather short on enthusiasm for women's rights and hadn't dealt with the debate as convincingly as he usually does. But it also meant my getting up early to read up the previous debates and I found I was nervous as I prepared to go into the fray – so long since I dealt with the details of a committee stage, which a Minister usually leaves to subordinates. But I was heartened by the enthusiasm of – and excellent briefing by – some of our younger civil servants on the pensions side of the department and in the event my intervention was great fun. I was on my feet – frequently interrupted, but received with excitement by our own side – for nearly an hour. After the committee Brian, Alec, Alf and I went to celebrate over lunch and their comments were extremely generous. My insistence on being a member of the committee has paid off. We carried the vote in committee by nine votes to six.

I dreaded the Budget speech in the House because (like many others on the front bench) I always find the compulsion to doze irresistible. My complaints to John Gilbert, by whom I sat, that the speech could have been pruned with advantage by at least 25 per cent were fully justified. Denis seemed a bit tired by the time he limped home. But Margaret Thatcher's riposte was pretty shallow, though I continue to admire her impeccable grooming, even under strain. Query: is such polished coolness an enduring asset or will it be her downfall one day?

Back into consultations over my meeting with the BMA negotiators tomorrow. We examined every possible contingency, but agreed in the end that when it comes to it one can only play such situations by ear. Henry ventured the suggestion that the BMA was now pretty anxious for a settlement before the Review Body report is published. Apparently they don't want to be in the position of still operating sanctions when the

---

[1] Since our new scheme provided equal (or better) treatment for women compared with men, we had decided to phase out the existing right of married women to pay reduced insurance contributions at work in return for reduced benefits and to rely on their husband's insurance for their pension. Under the Bill this option would no longer be available to married women going out to work for the first time. For full details see Appendix IV).

Government has to make up its mind whether to authorize their increase of 30 per cent. They neither want a Government refusal of the money, nor an ultimatum to give up sanctions as a condition of obtaining it.

Wednesday, 16 April

'I'm afraid you face rather a hectic day, Secretary of State,' said Karen [Higgs, of my Private Office] sympathetically. She could say that again! For, first, I faced my two meetings with the section executives of the CPSA [Civil and Public Servants Association] and SCS [Society of Civil Servants] respectively, which last week I had recklessly suggested I should take on.[1] At the briefing meeting before we left I asked Caines [an Assistant Secretary in the Department] what reaction he had had from Thomasson and Christie about my idea: did they think I was sticking my nose into their affairs? On the contrary, he replied, they were delighted. And indeed, when we got to CPSA they had laid down the red carpet for us. Bill Kendall and other national officers were there to greet us, tickled pink that we had come. And even Eric Edwards, the bearded menace from Newcastle, couldn't have been more pleasant, telling the Executive from the chair that I had made history: the first Secretary of State to attend one of their meetings. I talked informally and as persuasively as I knew how for nearly half an hour, saying I had a problem I wanted to put to them, but that I would accept their decision and would not try to impose a programme on them. I then spelt it out. They listened attentively. Only one or two of them spoke (which Eric told me afterwards was in itself significant), but those who did said that, much as they would like to help me, they had not a hope in hell of getting their members to accept any addition to the work-load. So at the end of an hour I thanked them for listening to me and said that we were still friends and that I would never blame them publicly for the fact that I couldn't introduce some of the improved benefits earlier. After that they regaled us with drinks and a superb buffet and we had a whale of a time. ('Rather different from the office sandwich I should have had otherwise,' murmured Errington.) I chatted a long time with Edwards, who is always considered by the department to be tinged with dangerous militancy. But when we discussed the Budget and I asked him what he thought we should do about inflation, he flabbergasted me by replying, 'I think we should have a wages freeze.' Afterwards, in the car on our way to John Adam Street for the meeting with the Society of Civil Servants, I said it was disappointing not to have got anything out of the CSPA but I wasn't sorry I had tried, to which my officials replied in chorus, 'Oh, no! It has done a power of good.' I suspect it was the first time any of them had seen a union meeting in action and they had enjoyed the experience.

With the SCS it was the same routine: great friendliness, great pleasure at seeing me

[1] Denis Healey, having rejected my plea to advance the next uprating to October to help those hardest hit by the withdrawal of food and fuel subsidies, had suddenly offered some small extra allowances for those on supplementary benefit. Unfortunately I knew this extra work would mean more overtime for our staff in the holiday months when it was most resented. I had therefore decided to by-pass the normal channels of consultation and ask the two unions concerned – the CPSA and the SCS – whether I could come and talk to their Executives. Although this did not produce a solution to the problem of staff workload, it produced enormous goodwill. In the CPSA journal shortly afterwards Mr Thomasson was to quote this visit as 'living proof' of 'closer communication and involvement' by the Minister.

– but a firm no. I now have to decide whether it is worth going back to the Chancellor. But in the meantime we had a quick confab on the spot – David, Jack, Norman and I – to clear the drafts of the two letters on the consultants' Option Agreement and the modification of the existing contract that I was to put to the BMA in the afternoon. I dared to hope that the talks with the BMA would not take too long. There was a charming incident when I asked for coffee. The elderly John Adam Street messenger who brought it in to me told me reverentially, 'I have given you Miss Herbison's[1] cup.' He had treasured it all that time!

But my hopes were shattered. We started our talk with the BMA at 4pm at the department. The BMA's 'clarification' group had swollen this time to seven people and it was significant that they started by asking whether a wider group of representatives, which was standing by, could come to the office and wait in another room so that they could consult them if necessary. So they obviously meant business! Though Grabham and Astley were flanked by Lewis, Lewin and Stevenson, mercifully none of these three contributed a word the whole night. It was amusing to sit opposite Brian Lewis, who only a short while ago was castigating me on every TV programme he could reach, and find him transformed. Indeed, they were all transformed. Elaborate courtesy was the order of the day – a painstaking patience and determination to reach agreement if at all possible. If only they had been like this on 20 December! But, as David said at the time, he believed the consultants had a strike in their system and had to work it out. But the trauma was not over yet. Anxious they may have been for an agreement – and time and again Astley and the others were clearly ready to say yes – but with Grabham they had a fanatic in charge and he was determined to try and exact his pound of flesh.

And so began another of those wearying marathons. They said our draft on the Option wouldn't do and put forward some amendments. I said their amendments wouldn't do and we started suggesting modifications. They asked if they could discuss it among themselves and at 5pm we retired, leaving it to them. Tim Nodder came up to say that he had overheard Grabham saying, 'If we reach this about midnight —' and we all groaned. Their old arrogance, their belief that they can command the attendance of the Secretary of State for as long as it suits *them*, may be more muted, but it is still there. Norman started to lay in food. Upstairs we did some more drafting. I said firmly that I wasn't going to spend the night arguing with them. We should use Tim Nodder as a go-between and meantime I intended to get on with some work. They all agreed. Every now and then we reassembled to discuss the latest manifestations from below. It was soon clear what Grabham was up to: he was once again trying to insinuate into the draft a form of words which would imply that the maximum part-timers' commitment is only for nine sessions a week: the perfect jumping-off point for getting rid of the whole-timers' differential through the side door. Neither David nor I would have any truck with it. They twisted and turned endlessly. Finally we sent down a form of words which we insisted was our last

---

[1] Miss Margaret Herbison was a much loved Minister of Pensions and later of Social Security from 1964 to 1967 in Harold Wilson's Government. Her office was at No. 10 John Adam Street, which was still used by DHSS for various purposes in 1975 though the headquarters of the department had been moved to the Elephant and Castle.

concession; and they accepted it.[1] Relief all round. We even started drafting our press notices.

Philip and Henry, who had been beginning to clutch their heads with despair, perked up. We might get to bed at a reasonable hour! But I warned them that in this kind of negotiation the biggest snag always crops up just as one thinks one is home and dry. And so it proved. We still had to agree the letter on future modifications of the contract – and that was to go on for another seven hours. We chewed the chicken legs Norman had rustled up for us, while Philip and Henry shook their heads over the incredible behaviour going on below. But the main burden fell on poor Tim, moving backwards and forwards between the parties during the long night. Every line of our draft was queried; endless petty little redrafts kept coming up to us. By 4am David was beginning to lose his temper, saying we'd better realize we'd never reach agreement and just go home. Henry and Philip expressed sympathy, but I told David that on occasions like these victory always went to the person who had the extra ten minutes of stamina. We would see it through to the bitter end – even though Norman announced tragically that we'd run out of tea. Jack Straw was superb; Norman imperturbable. We then came to the crunch: the passage dealing with the payment for extra sessions. Once again it was clear what Grabham was up to: to get a passage which would link the new extra payments, not to a more precisely defined commitment, but to the existing contract as defined in the Option letter. I exploded. That, David and I agreed, *would* be our breaking-point.[2]

Philip and Henry suggested at this point that perhaps they had better join in the discussions and try to convince the negotiators that it just wasn't on. So down they went. They were gone over an hour while David, Jack and I chatted desultorily. To my surprise I didn't feel a bit tired, only desperately hungry. When Philip and Henry came back it was with a form of words which they in their innocence obviously thought was not too bad, but David and I rejected it instantaneously. Whatever the plausible arguments with which Grabham tried to wrap it up, it would have committed us to basing the entitlement to extra sessions on a contractual commitment as outlined in the Option letter (i.e. the present 'flexible' one, not the new closed contract). 'This is the crunch,' snapped David. 'We had better break. No bad thing if we do.' Philip and Henry looked anxious at this. I stood up. 'I had better go down and tell them this myself,' I said. It was 5.30am. The BMA contingent looked surprised as I walked into the room. I spoke as calmly as I could. We had made a lot of

[1] The letter I agreed to send to Dr Stevenson repeated my acceptance of the Option Agreement but rejected Mr Grabham's interpretation of it (see footnote, page 350). Instead it said: 'The maximum part-time contract has been interpreted in a variety of ways and not always in terms of notional half-days. Where it has been so agreed it has normally been nine, but occasionally ten or eleven. The process of assessment should be conducted flexibly so as to provide both that the consultant will give substantially the same service and time overall as he would have done had he opted for a whole-time appointment, and also to allow him to accommodate his other work.' For full text see *British Medical Journal* 26 April 1975.

[2] In a second letter, which I agreed to send to Dr Astley, I reiterated the improvements in the existing contract I had already told the House of Commons I was willing to make and said I would be ready to discuss other improvements as soon as sanctions were lifted. Their request for payment for extra sessions, however, could only be discussed against a clear definition of the consultants' contractual obligations and an agreed programme of duties. For their part the consultants agreed to discuss the reforms in the merit award system for which we had been pressing. See *British Medical Journal* as above.

drafting compromises during the night, I pointed out. (Nods.) But we were still no nearer a solution, I added. It was getting on for 6am. They would be aware that shortly I would be due at a very important Cabinet. (More nods, apprehensive this time. They obviously thought their Review Body report was coming up.) I really could not be expected to devote any more of my time to this. (Nods again.) It was clear that it was no longer just words that divided us, but a deeper difference of aim on which there could be no agreement. We had better break. Even Grabham looked alarmed. (He had obviously made all the running.) He attempted another round of plausible argument. What difference of aim? He wasn't aware of it. I told him that what they were clearly trying to do in rejecting our last form of words was to say that a modified contract should mean the same flexible commitment as the existing one but with payment for extra sessions. That just wasn't on. I had gone as far as my colleagues would allow me to go. I must tell Cabinet that agreement could not be reached. Panic. They asked for time to talk among themselves again. Back upstairs we went. Within half an hour it was all over. They had capitulated. Lewin asked me anxiously what form of words I needed to help me in Cabinet. I told him they must say categorically that they would recommend withdrawal of sanctions at the meeting of their Central Committee on Friday – and added as an afterthought, 'unanimously'. They fell over themselves to agree. We shook hands all round. I went upstairs chuckling. Little do they know that the DDRB report is not coming up at Cabinet and that Harold has given me full freedom to play the acceptance of the report when and how I think fit. Philip and Henry were full of congratulations. I said it had been teamwork, not mine. 'She's got more stamina than the five of us put together,' said David affectionately.

Jack Straw drove me home, slapping his face from time to time to keep awake. It was 7.30am when I got to bed. Mercifully Cabinet wasn't till 11am, so I set my alarm for 9am.

Thursday, 17 April

I awoke feeling remarkably fresh after one-and-a-half hours' sleep. Mercifully the only business at Cabinet was on the referendum: whether people overseas should be given a vote. Ted Short, who before had argued that it was quite impracticable, is now ready to turn and run in the face of what he presented as an imminent revolt from a number of our own MPs. All the pro-marketeers are in favour of it, Roy J. being positively fanatical, despite the constitutional monstrosity it would represent. ('It is the referendum that is the monstrosity,' Roy remarked coldly.) The day was saved by Jim Callaghan at his most decisive. To have voting without a proper system of registration would be intolerable, he maintained. Tony C. was equally firm. Together they put the case against so well that the rest of us only had to say that we agreed. Harold was toying with the idea of a free vote in the House on this, but Bob said gloomily, 'With Cabinet so clearly taking a view, I must whip.' Mike suggested that we hold a party meeting on Monday to explain our view. Backing him, I said I hoped Jim would speak at it. Ted Short has clearly failed to convince the rebels because he has hardly tried.

But my day wasn't over. We had to have an office meeting to plan our course of action following the meeting of the consultants' Central Committee tomorrow. Peter reported that we had had good press reactions to our agreement. Even Stevenson of the *Mail*, comparing my two latest letters with my previous ones, had asked him, 'What's the difference? I can't see any.' Derek Stevenson, true to his earnest assurances last night, had been pretty moderate on radio. The questions we had to decide were (1) what was likely to happen at the consultants' meeting tomorrow and (2) when we should publish the Review Body report. After going round the problem for some time we decided we couldn't really decide till first thing tomorrow, which means an early meeting, despite the fact I have only had one-and-a-half hours' sleep in the past two days.

We also had to discuss the announcement of the date of the uprating. Matters have been complicated by the fact that, despite their firm noes to me yesterday, both CPSA and SCS have come up with suggestions for enabling me to get some of the extra allowances into payment earlier. So my journey was not in vain! Unfortunately they can't agree what the method should be and their ideas are not very practicable either. But the important thing is that they are *trying*, thus proving to my erstwhile sceptical civil servants that trade unionists can be disinterested human beings if properly appealed to.

Finally, at 4pm, we had a meeting of Dissenting Ministers in my room at the House to discuss the next stages of the campaign. We are trying to hold these meetings every Thursday at 7pm. Wedgie turned up full of a ploy for holding another press conference this Sunday to set out what course of action the Government would take if there were a referendum decision to come out. Mike (who couldn't be present) is apparently in favour. Peter was doubtful, but I said that I thought this was a high-level example of Benn ingenuity. It would 'drive a Wedgie' between the pro-marketeers and those voters who were instinctively in fear of change, the status quo being to remain in membership. While Peter got a bit pedantic about some of the details of Wedgie's draft I said the whole purpose should be to produce a plausible prospectus for 'business as usual' after we came out. It would be just as valid as the rosy pictures from the pro-marketeers about what would happen if we stayed in. It was indeed the kind of 'black propaganda' which would have delighted Dick Crossman's heart. And so it was agreed, though my heart sank at the thought of wrecking yet another weekend. (When on earth will I have a full weekend at HCF again? I am at a loss to understand why, at an age when I ought to be slowing down, I find intellectual and political stimulus more satisfying than ever.) The Dissenting Ministers' secretariat – Jack [Straw], Frances [Morrell] and Tony [Banks][1] – were sent off to amend the draft along the lines we discussed.

At last to bed at 11pm, still full of energy.

Friday, 18 April

Climax day. Will, or will not, the consultants' committee endorse the lifting of sanctions? At our early office meeting we had to try to decide how things would go

[1] Frances Morrell was Tony Wedgwood Benn's political adviser at the Department of Industry, Tony Banks was political adviser to Judith Hart.

and when we should release the Review Body report. David and I were in favour of publishing it today on two alternative formulae: if the decision of the Central Committee wasn't known by 3pm (the latest time for answering the written PQ we had inspired), we could say the Government had accepted the report 'in view of the unanimous recommendation to lift sanctions'. If it *were* known and favourable, we could say 'In view of the decision to remove sanctions—' Once again we went through elaborate discussion of the possible combinations of events and contingencies. At one point someone said suddenly, 'What if the House rises early?' There was consternation until David said with his slow smile, 'That is in my hands. I am dealing with Mrs Jill Knight's Bill this afternoon.'[1] We collapsed in laughter. In fact there was a mood of hilarity in the air. We know we have got a trump card in our hands in the Government's acceptance of the report. Once again I was struck by the remarkable sense of solidarity one's civil servants get with one in a crisis. Certainly, they are all very warm towards me. Yesterday morning, when we reassembled after our long night, Philip said to me, 'If it is not impertinent, Secretary of State, we would like to congratulate you on the way you have handled all this and what you have achieved', while Henry nodded approvingly. Peter said to me, 'You have been very patient through all this and it has paid off.' (Not the image of me outside!) Anyway, it was a great cops and robbers day of an 'if they go here, we go there' kind. We decided to make all the contingency planning we could and decided to meet again at 1.30pm. I asked Henry to ring Derek Stevenson and tell him it was vital that we should have an interim report on what was happening at the consultants' meeting by 1pm. I was just leaving the office for the House when Henry rushed down to catch me in the car. He had spoken to Derek Stevenson, who had expressed surprise that we should have any fear of the outcome of the morning's meeting. Hadn't we heard that a thousand consultants in the south-east had already called off sanctions? Didn't we realize that this particular group contained some of the most active militants who had started it all? Right, I told Henry, get on to Derek again and tell him it is vital that I have the result by 2.45pm. And tell him I mean 2.45pm – 3pm would be too late. He rushed off eagerly. 'This is a happy day, Secretary of State,' he said to me. 'Never say that', I warned. 'That is always the moment when things go wrong.'

When we reassembled back in my room we heard that the consultants had decided to reach a decision before they adjourned for lunch, but were still arguing. Once again we had to adjust our contingency plans. But it seemed clear that a decision was in the bag. At 2.15pm the message came: decision in favour of lifting sanctions carried by thirty votes to two, with six abstentions. A walkover! 'Press conference and TV at 4pm,' said Peter. 'Then make-up girl at 3.15pm,' I replied. We scattered to our jobs: getting the answer to the PQ over to the House, redrafting the press statement, getting ready for all the tricky questions at the press conference. At 3.30pm still no make-up girl. 3.45pm before she arrived. And so, at the end of several weeks now of intense strain – and of this week of forfeited sleep – I ended up as I know all these 'triumphs' end up: in rush, disorder and anti-climax. The girl tried to slap something on my face and bring some order into my disordered hair in fifteen

---

[1] A Private Member's Bill which, as it happened, was not reached.

minutes flat, with agitated emissaries knocking at my door: 'the press have been waiting for twenty minutes' and 'the BBC have missed their early editions'. Something in me snapped and I went into the conference churned up, tense and strained. I was furious. Petty? Yes. But the last straw that breaks the camel's back. Of course, I got through it all, as old pros do, but what should have been my relaxed moment of achievement was ruined. My dear Private Office gathered round me like clucking hens over a chick. 'What a sad end to a good week,' said Norman, sad himself. Evelyn asked me anxiously if I felt all right. 'I just want to get down to the country,' was all I could say. Back in my room I felt utterly drained. I put my head in my hands and said to Norman, hovering protectively over me, 'Go away.' He slipped gently out. Then I howled my heart out – the first time I have cried for years and years. After ten minutes I felt better and wiped my eyes and started to sign the pile of letters waiting for me. One by one they drifted back into my room tentatively. The best thing of all in this incredibly demanding week has been the genuine affection I feel for them and which I think they feel for me.

Looking back over the consultants' dispute, I ask myself what are the lessons? First, I believe, as David said, that they had a dispute in them and that I couldn't have avoided it anyway. Secondly, that if one has a conviction that a certain course is right, the only thing to do is to stick to it, whatever the risks. All through this dispute I have stood firmly by the determination not to give way on the differential for the whole-timers. I think that without me David would have been edged off it. Certainly Henry would – and there is still a tough battle ahead. Grabham won't give up any more easily than I will. Philip and the rest never shared my sense of the importance of this principle: I doubt whether they ever understood why I attached so much to it. But once Philip and co. took on board that this was my sticking-point, they made it their own. Thirdly, the fascination of this whole game lies in recognizing when one is in a weak position and when one is in a winning one. Sometimes I got it wrong. For instance, at the end we were in a much stronger position than any of us realized. I could – I now believe, looking back – have got away with much tougher wording in those final letters than I did, even though we did not give anything fundamental away. Fourthly, these medical specialists are a breed all their own: they really do believe, as one of the presidents of the Royal Colleges put it to me, that they are in a position of 'special authority'. (I would put it that they think they are God.) Finally, that there is never a conclusion to anything. One just gets through one situation in a winning or a defeated position (and, as I said to Norman today, 'Treat those two impostors just the same'),[1] then picks oneself up and gets ready for the next fight that will surely come. I pick myself up now in a situation in which I have broadly won the first round. (Norman came into me today just after I had had my private howl to say, 'You may like to know that No. 10 has just been through to congratulate you on the withdrawal of sanc-

---

[1] From Rudyard Kipling's *If*:

> If you can meet with Triumph and Disaster
> And treat those two impostors just the same ...
> Yours is the Earth and everything that's in it
> And – which is more – you'll be a Man, my son!

tions.') But I am under no illusions about the way in which Grabham is coming out of his corner to try to defeat me in the next round. As David and I have agreed, this is the moment to go into the attack on pay beds. Finally, for all my occasional moans to Ted – 'I'm a failure' – I do believe in my proud boast to Harold the other day: 'I'm the best Minister you've got.' Because I believe that, in politics, guts is all.

Saturday, 19 April

After a good night's sleep I feel fighting fit again. Anyway, HCF always cures any neurosis or strain. And this morning one of the most comical incidents I have ever experienced left me laughing for hours. At 8.30am I went downstairs from our bedroom to the loo, opened the door and saw two bright eyes staring at me from the lavatory pan. It was a sweet little baby rabbit sitting at the bottom of the pan, with its nose and ears just above the water line. I was shaken to the core! I shut the door and went back upstairs to Ted, asking him seriously, 'Do you think I could possibly have DTs? There is a rabbit in the lavatory pan.' He was so scared at the very idea that he had to drink his tea before he went to have a look at it, saying, 'We'll set Printer on it', while I moaned, 'Oh, we couldn't do that. It wouldn't be fair after all it has gone through.' 'We're infested with the things,' said Ted angrily. When he peered into the loo he called out, 'It's drowned anyway'. I peered over his shoulder nervously. Its eyes were shut, its ears were flattened against its head, and it had gone limp. 'Well, it was alive when I looked at it,' I replied. 'If you want to kill it, why don't you get some more water and make sure it really is drowned?' But Ted would hear nothing of it: he *knew* it was dead. So he went and got his gardening gloves and a bucket and scooped out the limp rabbit, walking firmly down our long garden to throw the corpse over the hedge into the field. I was in the study working when I heard a roar of laughter from Eileen, watching through the kitchen window. At the hedge, calling on Printer to stand by, Ted tipped over the bucket. Out scuttled the rabbit, shook itself and was through the hedge before either Ted or Printer realized what was happening. 'It's pure *Watership Down*,' I chuckled. 'Once again, cunning rabbit outwits stupid man and dog.' It made our day. That rabbit *deserved* to escape, for Ted remembered that yesterday Printer had chased a baby rabbit through the garden and they thought it had escaped onto the road. Instead, it must have swerved into the house, through the dining room and into the downstairs loo. It must have been hiding in the corner all the time we were going to the loo last night and then somehow got into the pan. I shall never go to the lavatory again without remembering it sitting there. The dramas of the countryside are endless.

Sunday, 20 April

It was a terrible wrench to leave HCF on the first day of warm spring sunshine we have had this year. The garden had never looked lovelier, with its spread of daffodils and narcissi. All I wanted to do in the world was to get down to some real hard gardening.

Things weren't made any better by the stuffiness of St Ermin's Hotel where we were holding our Dissenting Ministers' press conference, but the conference seemed to go quite well. As always, I marvelled at Wedgie's fluency and I got in a few digs myself. Later we all assembled for food at the Benns'. Their home in Holland Park Avenue is just what one would expect: roomy, comfortable, shabby and littered with political mementoes and some pleasant cultural bric-à-brac. Caroline is clearly no *cordon bleu* and seemed worried lest her cooking was not up to the standard of the rest of us. I suspect she and Wedgie normally get by on mugs of tea and bread and cheese. But it was great fun and they were lavish in everything.

After dinner we discussed (of course!) the strategy of our campaign. Having watched the report of our press conference on TV I said that we were in danger of being given 'equality of trivialities'. We ought to insist on some serious, in-depth programmes on TV. Peter said that all that was being organized by the National Referendum Campaign and that we ought to get ourselves represented on it. I was worried about the superficiality of our campaign so far, but when I said I thought we were going to lose the vote Wedgie, Peter and Michael turned on me. They clearly genuinely believed I was wrong; so I offered to lay some money on it. I also said that I thought Peter Jenkins was right when he wrote in the *Guardian* on Saturday that the referendum would decide the whole political direction of the Labour Party and that Harold, if the Europeanists won, would become the prisoner of the Right. Once again they all turned on me. They just wouldn't have it that Harold would move us all out of positions of influence: Mike insisted that Harold ('though I agree he is naturally to the Right politically') would stick by his regular tactic of conciliating his critics. I don't think I am naturally defeatist or gloomy by nature, but I often marvel at the complacency of my left-wing colleagues. Wedgie was at his most brilliantly ingenious again, telling us how he is intending to answer Questions tomorrow by challenging Margaret Thatcher to say whether the Tories accept the referendum. I almost began to believe in his capacity for party leadership.

Monday, 21 April

I am always taken by surprise at the way the press manage to work themselves into a lather about quite insignificant political occasions. I was therefore astonished to find, when I arrived at Congress House for our routine monthly meeting of the Liaison Committee with the TUC, that the cameras were there in force. They really had persuaded themselves that something portentous was about to happen – all in keeping with today's headlines to the effect that the TUC were going to tell the Government off about the Budget or vice versa. I could have told them better: the TUC are not looking for a showdown with us. They know only too well the alternatives they face. Instead, when they have awkward decisions to take, they prefer to run for cover, and today was no exception. The Government, NEC and the PLP were there in force for this much heralded 'historic' meeting on the Social Contract, but there were, apart from Len Murray and his officials, only *two* members of the General Council of the TUC: Jack Jones (who had to take the chair) and David Basnett. So we were, as it were, talking to the converted for nearly two hours.

When I arrived Denis was going over the old ground about the Budget. He only allowed himself one flicker of warning to the trade unions: 'I've appealed to the unions not to try and make good the increase in the cost of living from the Budget. If they do, the only way I shall be able to deal with the situation is by cutting public expenditure. The level of settlements has been well above the spirit of the guidelines and I hope we can discuss how we can prevent this from happening again.' Len Murray twisted and turned equivocally. He began with a bit of menace. 'History repeats itself, sometimes as tragedy and sometimes as farce, and I can see some strands here of the situation we got ourselves into before.' He then trimmed, welcoming many details of the Budget but rather vaguely casting doubts on its strategy, hinting at the need for import controls. Then he returned to his warnings. Unemployment wouldn't bring down wage demands. As for the coming rise in prices, he couldn't give *any* assurances workers would not try to compensate for them. He then wandered off into the opposite direction. On wage restraint: 'We are less than satisfied with our performance.' But then again we mustn't press them too much. At the coming Congress there was a danger of a coalition against the Social Contract. The sour streak in his speech never turned into virulence. Once again it was Jack Jones who showed himself the most eager to help: the biggest defender of the Social Contract of them all. 'Our difficulty is,' he said apologetically from the chair, 'in explaining to trade unionists the gravity of the situation. More could be done about that.' Once again he insisted that the Social Contract had had an effect, though he made grumbling noises about the way the Price Code had been relaxed and warned: 'There is no prospect at all of strengthening the guidelines.' He then went off at a tangent about pay reviews, saying you couldn't blame railwaymen for wanting compensation for the rise in the cost of living if others got it. And there was no control at all, he continued, over the fees charged by the self-employed. But his main emphasis was a familiar one from him: 'All of us round this table want to sustain the Government.' Harold took up his and Len's points at some length. We hadn't closed our minds to import controls, he said, though in themselves they didn't solve the problem of inflation. The Government remained firmly opposed to statutory controls, but he agreed with Jack that there was growing divergence between the public and private sector settlements that he would like to check. 'How we do it I don't know: the only way in a democracy is by leadership.' He urged them not to pay any attention to rumours in the press about a return to statutory controls. David Basnett harped mainly on unemployment, as he always does. This was the main issue, he said. The second was the effect of the Budget on the lower paid. He recognized the constraints of the Chancellor but agreed with Len's analysis: budgets altered the conditions of the Social Contract. We had got to get away from all this one-sided exhortation about wages. The Social Contract didn't mean exhortation: it meant creating an atmosphere, and we had got to realize that the Budget hadn't helped. Denis jumped in again defensively, declaring none of us believed that unemployment was a cure for inflation. But he came back quite toughly on the general issue. On the Social Contract, the Government had done everything it was committed to do last year on the assumption that wages would rise 2–3 per cent at most above the guidelines. Instead, the increase had been 8–9 per cent. The answer was not to tighten the guidelines, but they *must* be observed, otherwise he would have to cut public expenditure far more drastically.

Wedgie made a stirring speech, giving a potted version of the ten-year industrial strategy he had worked out with his advisers Frances Morrell and Francis Cripps.[1] The aim must be to double investment over the period, using Arab money where necessary, through the medium of the NEB. In the meantime we *must* maintain our manufacturing capacity: 'That is where import controls come in.' Jack, Len and David bucked up visibly, as though someone had thrown them a lifeline when they were about to sink. And they bucked up still more when I gave them my theme of the social wage. Although I backed Wedgie's idea of a more constructive approach, I said it still meant that we had to decide priorities in the distribution of resources. 'It merely means that we should be deciding to set aside for the future more of the seed corn that we have been guzzling.' My problem, I continued, was that I was the biggest spender in the Government ('Hear, hear!' said Denis). But I wasn't salting the proceeds away for a private orgy: I was the largest custodian of the social wage. What we had to do was to persuade the worker on the shop floor that the social wage wasn't an impost: it was an *addition* to his wage and in the form that was most likely to secure real equality. My department was working on a document to explain all this and we would welcome the help of the trade unions in putting this across. Jim, sitting gloomily at the end of the table, said that Wedgie's speech and mine were the only ones to hold out hope. He then went on in Cassandra vein: 'If it is true that workers will demand to recoup increases in the cost of living, it is events that will lash us, not the Government.' I had the pleasure of seeing him slapped down by Jack, who told him grimly that he was making the mistake of 'over-emphasizing the wage factor'. Mike, called on to wind up, said he had nothing spectacular to say. 'I am sorry I have no solution to offer.' But he went on bravely: 'The fact is that we have to deal with the immediate situation. It would be terrible if by September a breach had opened between the trade union movement and the Government.' It was not a question of toughening the guidelines. The trade unions had behaved very well – for example, over low pay. But it was right that we should assess the working of the guidelines in order to learn from the way they had operated. Attacking inflation was a part of the Social Contract too. All this said, we broke up amicably, deciding to study Wedgie's investment plan next time. But the proof that we've done nothing to get at the root of the problem came later in the day, when the papers reported Hughie Scanlon's speech at his union's annual conference, denouncing the Budget as a breach of the Social Contract and warning that his members would insist on catching up with the price increases.

Later in the day I called in at the meeting of the National Referendum Campaign in

---

[1] In it he argued that British manufacturing industry was trapped in a 'spiral of decline' which could only be checked by doubling the annual rate of new investment over the next ten years. The NEB and planning agreements should be the instruments of the new policy. Part of the additional expenditure would have to be financed, through taxation, at the expense of consumption, but half the cost should be met by requiring insurance and pension companies to reinvest a large proportion of their rapidly rising funds in manufacturing industry. In the meantime, as a defensive short-term strategy, the Government should be willing to subsidize unprofitable companies and industries to prevent closures and redundancies.

the House. Neil Marten was in the chair. He's a pleasant chap, but I can't see us ever getting much drive behind our plans under his leadership.

Tuesday, 22 April

A good morning's work getting my Child Benefits Bill through Legislation Committee, and enthusiastic endorsement by Social Services Committee of Cabinet for my paper on pay beds.[1] I can now go ahead making my statement to Parliament whenever I like. Then into a special Cabinet on the Leyland report by Don Ryder.[2] Denis introduced the discussion on behalf of the Ministerial Committee, which has been discussing it. He warned that this massive commitment of investment would determine our industrial policy for the lifetime of this Government. It was a 'tricky gamble' and the return on investment over the next seven years would be poor. Nonetheless, the Ministers had, contrary to reports in the *Financial Times* today, decided to recommend it unanimously. Ryder's report was ruthlessly thorough. What was wrong with Leyland was poor management (Stokes would have to go), grotty machinery and bad industrial relations. What Ryder proposed was the only way of putting it right. The alternative was to accept the unemployment of nearly one million people and the abandonment of a comprehensive motor industry. Harry Urwin[3] had been an invaluable member of the Ryder Committee, accepting that there had been bad overmanning and that industrial relations had been partly responsible for the whole mess. And so, with very little opposition, it was agreed. Even Wedgie warned that we must be cautious and monitor each stage of the development carefully. That would be done by the NEB (i.e. by Ryder himself). Harold Wilson said that we might get some Arab funds involved: not directly through Leyland, but through the NEB. And he added wistfully that Donald Stokes had been a long-standing friend. This would hurt him terribly and he hoped that he might be used in the sort of job he excelled at: as a travelling export promotor for the company. Only Harold Lever really let fly: we were rushing into a 'grandiose folly', he said; it was like a 'bad Pharaoh's dream' in which we weren't even promised seven fat years

[1] David Owen and I had agreed that a statement of our intentions to legislate on pay beds was needed urgently to end uncertainty and I had to obtain Cabinet agreement. I made the statement in the House on 5 May. See footnote, page 384.

[2] In December 1974, British Leyland had run into difficulties and, in giving it short-term financial support, the Government announced that it was commissioning an overall assessment of the company's prospects by a team headed by Sir Don Ryder, who had been appointed by Harold Wilson as the Government's Industrial Adviser. The report argued that British Leyland ought to remain a major vehicle producer as an essential part of Britain's economic base and proposed a number of measures to improve its efficiency. But the main need was for a massive investment programme, amounting to some £2,800 million over the next seven years, most of which, the report admitted, would have to be provided from public funds. An abridged version of the report, 'British Leyland: the next decade', was published on 23 April as a House of Commons paper (H.C. 342 of 1974–75). The following day Harold Wilson told the Commons that the Government accepted the Ryder Report and that, in return for the massive investment of public money, it would acquire a majority shareholding in the reconstructed company which would come under the NEB as soon as the latter had been set up. The NEB's funds would be supplemented, if necessary. The injections of capital would be staged and future instalments would depend on improvements in performance. He expressed the hope that, as a result of those improvements, the workforce could be kept intact.

[3] Deputy General Secretary of the Transport and General Workers Union and a member of the TUC General Council since 1969. He was also a member of the Industrial Development Advisory Board and the National Enterprise Board.

after the seven lean ones. But he didn't cut much ice. My contribution was a swingeing attack on the draft statement on Leyland which Wedgie is to make to the House and which we were told had been drafted by a group of Permanent Secretaries (I might have guessed!). To approving nods I said it didn't begin to reflect the arguments we had heard today: they should take it away and redraft the whole wretched thing. Even Harold was stirred to a wintry smile (he remains very cold towards me). 'Barbara's speech, if a trifle passionate, was nonetheless very useful.'

In the evening I had to be guest of honour at the annual dinner of the ABPI.[1] Since David has just written to them saying we are going to cut their sales promotion allowance to 10 per cent it was hardly an auspicious moment to go. But the President was very charming to me and when my turn came to speak I swept my way through the subterranean mutterings unperturbed. What took me aback was the cordiality with which Derek Stevenson and Walpole Lewin greeted me. All enmities forgotten (for the moment, anyway!). I think they realized I played fair with them, not only by getting them their fat increase, but by not trying to exploit our agreement in any of my public comments.

Wednesday, 23 April

The papers have been full of the row over Geoff Bish's document on the EEC.[2] Jim Callaghan has been reported as threatening to move a hundred amendments to it at this morning's NEC, while the International Committee has reversed the decision of the Home Policy Committee that a copy of the Government White Paper should be distributed to every delegate to the special party conference as well as Geoff Bish's document. So the cameras were out in force when I arrived. And sure enough, we spent the best part of the morning on it. Ron began by warning us that it would cost over £1,000 to distribute copies of the Bish document. Another £600 to distribute the White Paper as well. That morning he had received a hundred amendments from Jim Callaghan. Would the NEC please tell him how they wanted to deal with them? To my surprise, Lena jumped in to move that we should not put round anything at all at conference. No one would have time to read it anyway, she argued. We should circulate a verbatim text of the conference speeches afterwards instead. That annoyed some of the rest of us. However, we all studiously kept the atmosphere as calm as possible. Mik moved that we should distribute Geoff's document and I supported him, pointing out that it would be one-sided if conference was not even allowed to know that the anti-marketeers were able to argue a detailed case. Denis backed Lena: Bryan Stanley backed Mik powerfully. Mik's amendment was carried by fourteen votes to ten, despite Lena's defection. Shirley then moved that we also distribute the White Paper. Again we all argued immensely courteously. Was it really

[1] The Association of British Pharmaceutical Industries [ABPI] represents 155 British manufacturers of prescription medicines. As part of our drive to cut the drugs bill of the NHS David Owen was proposing to cut to 10 per cent of sales the sales promotion costs the companies were allowed to claim under the Voluntary Price Regulation Scheme negotiated between DHSS and the manufacturers.

[2] Geoff Bish had prepared a document for the Home Policy Committee, 'The Renegotiations: An Appraisal of the Terms', which was hardly flattering in its analysis. The committee had recommended that the document should be distributed to the special conference, along with the Government's White Paper.

necessary, I asked, to spend £600 on the White Paper when the Government's case was going to be distributed through every door? Wedgie had an idea. Why not ask the Government if they would give us copies to distribute free? Ted Short said he would have to look into this. Mike appealed to Jim to recognize the right of majority in thé NEC, just as we had recognized the right of majority in Cabinet. For the first time Jim hit back viciously. No, he would not, he said, because the NEC had not handled this matter properly. A document ought to have been drawn up by the appropriate committee, where it could be examined and argued; this one was riddled with major inaccuracies. Once again it was Wedgie who was the conciliator. He was genuinely moved, he said, by the desire not to put Jim into the position of having to criticize a document issued by the NEC. We should therefore issue the document as an information paper and make it clear that it had not been endorsed by the NEC. That struck most people as eminently reasonable, but, with Jim still muttering protest and demanding that we go through it and amend it even if it took all day, Wedgie's proposal was only carried by thirteen to seven. Harold, incidentally, had carefully absented himself.

That over, we turned to the main agenda. But the arguments were not at an end. Introducing the Home Policy Minutes, Wedgie said casually that, among other things, he ought to mention item 71(a), which proposed that another Bish information paper on 'Labour's Industrial Policy and the Industry Bill' should be circulated to the PLP.[1] As most of us hadn't read it anyway this apparently innocuous proposal would have gone through, but Jim was on to it. Surely, he said, it was very odd to have the Research Department publishing documents criticizing Government policy. It ought to have been discussed in the Home Policy Committee and he moved the reference back. 'It was discussed,' said Wedgie innocently. Mik asked what was the use of having a Research Department if it couldn't draw the attention of the NEC to the way in which Government policy was diverging from party policy? And so once again Jim was squashed. The way Wedgie is using Bish to conduct his campaign against his colleagues who are trying to water down his Bill is fascinating – and successful.

A late night on the Referendum Bill. At least we got one consolation: the House voted down a national count by a hundred majority. Peter, Wedgie and I were whipped reluctantly into the lobby to vote against additional money being given to both sides in the campaign and helped to defeat a proposition which would have given us a bit more of a chance to hold our own. What is £125,000 against the millions the European Movement can whip up?

Thursday, 24 April

Harold has effectively de-natured Cabinet. Whether he is just trying to clear the decks for the referendum, or whether it is a deliberate ploy to take any kind of control out of the hands of the anti-marketeers, I don't know. All I know is that Cabinet

---

[1] The paper, which was intended for circulation among Labour MPs, listed the points on which the Government's Industry Bill fell short of Labour Party policy.

agendas have never been thinner and this morning's was a record: not a single item of business, apart from next week's parliamentary business and foreign affairs. So we met at 11am and were out before noon, despite a rather rambling discussion on whether Ted Short should resist a Tory and backbench demand that the decision last night to go for a county count should really mean that the votes were counted in the counties. Stiff-necked to the end, Ted was still personally in favour of counting nationally, even if the result was declared on a county basis, but recognized that he would almost certainly be beaten in the House. At 11.30 the door opened and in processed a row of butlers bearing large trays of coffee (with the usual large mug for Wedgie, on which he always insists). We stared and then broke into a hearty cheer, though Harold Lever whispered across the table to me, 'I am afraid this means we shall be here a long time.' But no. The discussion soon died away and Harold dismissed us like a school going on holiday. He had been chirpy throughout, informing us that he and the Foreign Secretary were going on safari for a fortnight 'in the belief that nothing much will happen while we're away'. (Laughter.) Jim said he hoped no one would think a Commonwealth Conference was a holiday for certain members of the delegation, whatever it might be for others. (More laughter.) And Harold capped everything by saying he was pleased with the way the referendum campaign was going. It had not led to the sort of confrontation he had once feared. It was a strange episode and I left wondering what it was all in aid of. Is Harold genuinely feeling more relaxed about things? Anyway, I was able to get my constitutional in St James's Park: a keep-fit bid I am trying very hard to keep up.

After a lavish and friendly lunch with John Cunningham of the *Guardian* I went back to the House for a rather curious office meeting: what Norman called a purely exploratory meeting about certain aspects of the pay beds issue – so, he said, it wasn't necessary to invite the Minister of State, who had already been through the same exercise. Nonetheless I insisted that David be informed and told that he could come along if he wished to. I am not going to bypass my Ministers of State. (I was very pleased when David said to me off-handedly the other day, 'You certainly do delegate very remarkably.') Anyway, David didn't turn up – only Jack Straw, Lawrence Brandes [Under Secretary at the department], Raymond Gedling and Norman. 'I think it is the smallest meeting with officials I've ever attended,' said Lawrence Brandes. They wanted to spell out to me the difficulties of trying to control the private sector outside the NHS merely by fixing a maximum number of private beds: it would, for instance, be so easy to change the use of the existing ones. They certainly made out a powerful case and I was grateful to them. Once again I was struck by how good most civil servants are, if only you give them the right lead. I said I was convinced by their argument that I must go for general licensing and that I didn't see insuperable political difficulties over this (not least because we should only be imitating the US system of 'certification of need'), but that I thought that within such an all-embracing system it would be counter-productive to say that no NHS facilities should ever be made available to the private sector at any price. This could merely lead to unnecessary duplication of such things as radiotherapy. I thought I could sell that to the unions. Lawrence Brandes said that would greatly ease his administrative difficulties and went off to draft something for our next meeting.

At 7pm we had our weekly meeting of Dissenting Ministers in my room at the House. Wedgie once again was bubbling with ideas for press conferences, questions we should put publicly to the Commission, etc. I groaned at the thought of another ruined Sunday and we agreed to make final decisions about our next press conference at the end of Saturday's special party conference. I said that I thought we should go for more *visual* impact and outlined my idea for taking Joan Lestor, Jo Richardson and myself to Brussels on a much publicized shopping spree that would get the prices issue bang on to TV. Tony Banks and Frances got ecstatic about this and Frances had the bright idea of taking some children along. But Wedgie was more obsessed with political in-fighting and suggested that as soon as it was clear that the special conference was going to say no we should requisition a special meeting of the NEC to plan a party campaign against the Market. Incidentally, he has set alarm bells ringing in the pensions field with his industrial strategy document calling for the earmarking of a certain proportion of pensions funds for industrial investment that the Government considers essential.[1] Brian O'Malley is very worried.

Friday, 25 April

Another meeting with a group of area health authority chairmen. They were delighted to be invited at all, telling me privately that the regional chairmen didn't like this direct approach to them. But David and I are determined to break down the appalling bureaucratic hierarchy in the NHS left us by Sir K. When I asked them how they thought reorganization was working, they came tumbling out with complaints about the duplication of staff at the various levels and about how little freedom of action they were given. Philip and co. joined in the discussion amicably enough, but I suspect they are disguising their irritation at my insistence on talking to AHA chairmen direct. They are instinctive hierarchists.

In the evening I went to speak at the Tribune meeting on the Common Market: the first time I have ever been asked to speak at a Tribune meeting at party conference. It was nice to have the breach healed on an issue which I can endorse wholeheartedly. No one knows how painful it had been to be treated as a political pariah (not of Mike's choosing, I hasten to say). Much of what I did in 1964–70 is now being echoed by Mike, than whom there is no one more scrupulously operating an incomes policy, (and incidentally no one currently more acquiescent about the high unemployment figures). Wedgie spoke first, getting a massive reception for a typically brilliant speech which contained a number of what I can only call distortions about the Community. I was, as usual, inhibited by my agonizing inability to say anything if I am not a hundred per cent sure that it is fair. I got a warm enough reception but slipped away early, doubting myself as usual. It was a balmy night and it was a curiously pleasant experience to be on my own, without the constrictions or comforts of an official car. So I strolled up Whitehall and Shaftesbury Avenue, enjoying the sense of normality as I caught a No. 19 bus.

[1] See footnote, page 373.

Saturday, 26 April

The special party conference on the Market went just as I thought it would. It was better attended than the press had made out it would be. The debate lacked thrills because everyone knew the result was a foregone conclusion, but the vote for the NEC recommendation was only two to one (actually 3,724,000 to 1,986,000).[1] Of course the press had been preparing for this by predicting a sweeping victory for the antis beforehand so that they could report a less than sweeping victory afterwards. Nonetheless, I think the pros have made some headway in the constituencies and of course they have captured (or always had) the GMWU, the UPW and the NUR.

My seniority on the NEC placed me between Harold and Mik on the front row of the platform. Harold was very tetchy before his opening speech: whether it was nerves or his resentment against me I couldn't say. At one point he reached out his glass for water and said nastily, 'And leave the jug here.' I poured him a glass of water and waited till he was on his feet before moving the jug away. (I'm not going to have a large glass edifice between me and the cameras. Two of us can play at that game.) Harold made a down-beat speech, contrary to the exhortations of the pro-Market press. He was obviously unhappy before he began and even more unhappy at the lukewarm reception he received at the end. My heart went out to him because I am very fond of him. Perhaps that is my trouble: I am not ruthless enough. Certainly not as ruthless as John Mackintosh, who made an unscrupulously brilliant speech. 'Since when has that chap been in favour of taking over the commanding heights of the economy?' I asked Mike at lunchtime. To which Jill Foot replied, 'Don't worry, Mike is going to deal with that.' Fred Mulley was a bad chairman and somehow managed to call a number of unattractive antis from the constituencies. (There *are* some unattractive ones.) But whenever I felt like wavering, it only took a few speeches from the pros – including Roy Jenkins's passionate and misleading one – to switch me back again. Jim was as india-rubber as I had warned my Dissenting Minister friends he would be. I got gloomier as the day went on, not about the basic principles, but about our ability to present them. His own speech over, Harold relaxed and more than once voluntarily placed himself in a heads-together-for-the-cameras situation with me. (Of course, the papers won't use such photos *now*. It would spoil their prepared scenario.) At one point I said to Harold, impulsively but genuinely, 'The antis are saying that your speech was very skilful.' He jerked into a gesture of disbelief. 'And so it was,' I continued on my healing mission. 'You lowered the temperature. They are saying Roy made a great mistake in raising it.' Harold came to life. 'I intend to play it low-key throughout. The decision is purely a marginal one. I have always said so. I have never been a fanatic for Europe. I believe the judgment is a finely balanced one.'

---

[1] The major unions voting in favour of Britain's membership of the EEC were the General and Municipal, [GMWU], the railwaymen [NUR], shop and distributive workers, and post office workers [UPW]. Against were the Transport and General, engineers, miners, public employees and firemen. ASTMS representing white-collar workers voted against, but APEX [Association of Professional, Executive, Clerical and Computer Staff], also white-collar, voted for.

Then came Mike's winding up. It was a terrifying responsibility. At one point he repeated a phrase he has used more than once recently. 'I intend to remain at the Department of Employment until the figures of unemployment are going down.' I turned to Harold teasingly. 'Do you hear that? Mike is pre-empting your doorstep, threatening to stay at Department of Employment till unemployment is coming down.' Harold turned to me with a smile: 'I've got news for him. He is going to.' I warmed to him. I felt like telling those right-wing plotters that I had got a message for them: they would never succeed in making a prisoner of Harold. Mike's speech wasn't his best: not enough humour or light and shade. Nonetheless, it had a great peroration which brought a third of that audience to its feet in the first spontaneous standing ovation of the day. Mike is making light of the operation for which he is going into hospital tomorrow. And he is furious that the whole thing has leaked. Asked anxiously by us what it was all about, he replied bashfully, 'It is merely a cyst in a rather awkward place.' But there are always risks in any operation and I shan't rest till he is safely through. But all I said at lunchtime was, 'Be careful they take off the right bit.'

During the conference David chatted to me about office work as though the EEC bored him. He was tickled pink about the ending of the consultants' dispute. 'It is the first time the BMA has ever been defeated by a government.'

Monday, 28 April

The press conference on the Child Benefit Bill[1] went off remarkably smoothly. Peter almost grumbled: 'They let you off far too lightly.' But I am having trouble with David over pay beds. At the office meeting to discuss Lawrence Brandes's general registration plan for the private sector David, who told the trade unions at our private

[1] The Bill provided for a new cash benefit, payable to the mother for every child in the family, to be introduced from April 1977, when family allowance would disappear. The benefit would also progressively replace child tax allowances, thus transferring their benefit from the husband's pay packet to the mother's purse. The great advantage, I pointed out, was that some seven million first or only children would be covered for the first time, that the mother would get an income of her own to feed and clothe the family, and that families too poor to pay tax would receive the benefit of child tax reliefs. But there was no rate of child benefit included in the Bill as I had not yet agreed this with the Chancellor. All the Treasury would allow me to say was that if, as a starting point, we replaced the child tax allowances for children under eleven (then running at £240 a year per child), the rate of child benefit which would involve no extra cost to the Exchequer would be about £1.94 per week and that every 1 pence above that would cost about £6½ million per year. We should therefore, when the time came, have to decide the rate 'in the light of the economic prospect at the time'. The Bill also abolished the wage-stop and provided for the interim payment from April 1976 of family allowance for the first child in one-parent families: what I had been fighting for as 'Special FAM'.

Although the Bill was widely welcomed, there were two time-bombs ticking away under it. The first was the ruling Treasury convention that cash payments like child benefit counted as public expenditure while the loss of revenue from child tax allowances did not. This meant that some of the public expenditure 'cost' of the scheme, which was to come from the contingency reserve, represented the conversion of tax reliefs into child benefit, so it seemed greater than it was. The second was that the switch of child tax reliefs from the pay packet to the mother's purse meant a reduction in take-home pay for the wage-earner, thus rousing the deepest instincts of male chauvinism. Jim Callaghan's Government was to use these two factors in April 1976, after my removal from the Government, to justify an attempt to postpone the introduction of child benefit indefinitely.

discussion dinner with them that he was in favour of quantity controls, has switched his ground again and insisted that he was against the whole idea. I suppressed my irritation and listened patiently. Out it all came gradually. He didn't think the private sector would prove a menace. The one thing to do was to leave the private promoters to burn their fingers, separate them 100 per cent from the facilities of the NHS and let the pressure of high costs do the rest. I told him I thought it was an arguable case, but politically untenable. Henry, of course, backed David, but, to my surprise, Philip said almost reluctantly that he thought I was right and David wrong. David shrugged that he didn't attach much importance to it either way and we then went on to discuss details in preparation for the statement on our pay beds policy which, we all agree, I ought to make as soon as possible, preferably next Monday, to stop the speculative stories that have started to run. David and I then dashed to the House for our meeting with Albert Spanswick, his President, Bickerstaff, and the young research secretary of COHSE. We have decided that, since the other unions would not include them in our last private dinner discussion, I had better keep my copy book clean by having a unilateral private discussion with them. They were friendliness itself: delighted that I was fulfilling my promise to meet them in a 'non-crisis situation' from time to time. I told them in confidence about the statement I was going to make and then put the choice to them: would they prefer me to control the size of the private sector and then agree to sell certain NHS facilities to it as part of my effort to stop the private promoters duplicating NHS facilities (e.g. pathology and radiotherapy), or to adopt an entirely laissez-faire policy, leaving them to sink or swim on their own? They unanimously opted for the former and David acknowledged his defeat with his usual friendly grin at me. I said to him afterwards that I believed our own side would never let me get away with a laissez-faire policy.

Tuesday, 29 April

There is a great furore over the meeting of the NEC which Wedgie and some others have requisitioned for tomorrow following the special conference. Of course, the press is making a meal of it. Fred Mulley is going round cornering every one of us in turn, pleading with us to save the unity of the party. We couldn't throw the resources of the party against the leader and embarrass him, he urged. When I told him I wasn't going to be there anyway, as I had to open a hospital, he expressed regret. What a pity: I would have been a reasonable influence. I told him I would have a word with the others as I am rather surprised and puzzled about what Wedgie is up to. I thought all this had been settled at the last NEC. I told him soothingly not to worry. The only idea was to clear up what exactly the party machine was expected to do. But Fred kept on worrying. 'Why don't we ask Wedgie?' I suggested. 'He is only a few doors away.' In came Wedgie, wearing his earnestly innocent look. 'I am wondering whether to attend myself,' he told us. 'This nonsense has been blown up so much by the newspapers.' He waved Fred's anxieties aside rather vaguely. 'It is only a question of deciding what literature we send out. And perhaps the TUC will organize a meeting, say in Trafalgar Square. Perhaps they will invite a couple of us to speak. But there is nothing more than that. I expect the whole meeting will be over in half an hour.' The division bell rang and he melted away. I told Fred, 'Tell Harold not to worry. We all love him and it will be okay.'

Wednesday, 30 April

Up early for my trip to Surrey to open the Frimley Park hospital, our second 'best buy' hospital.[1] I was interested to see this cost-saving hospital for its own sake – all the more intrigued because the local papers have been full of the story that local Conservatives (and voluntary workers at the hospital) have written to Michael Grylls, the local Tory MP, saying they didn't want me in their area. If there is anything I love it is a situation like that. I know from experience that the normal Britisher loves making hostile noises at a distance and just capitulates the moment one walks up to him (or her). And so it proved – though I must admit that since this great showdown with me was planned there has been the settlement with the BMA, to say nothing of that lavish pay award. Whatever the reason, everything went swimmingly. The Tory Mayor was there, courtesy itself, so was Grylls – all charm and assiduity. Even the voluntary ladies, whom I met after the opening, were very civil.

My great moment came, as usual, with the self-employed. When I was warned that they were mounting a demonstration outside the hospital, and the Police Commissioner at the head of my police guard had assured me the demonstration was some distance away from the hospital entrance and I would not be troubled, I told him that on the contrary I would like to talk to the demonstrators. And so I did, stopping the car so that I could deliberately walk back to them. This almost did the trick in itself; they were overwhelmed by the mere fact that I had not hidden behind my massive guard. And with the press crowding round, I spelt out to them how we were not acting vindictively against the self-employed. The whole exercise was nearly wrecked by one of their voluble sea-lawyers who joined us, waving the Bolton Report[2] under my nose. I thought I was going to be trapped for ages while his tirade was taken down, word by word, by the press. But fortunately he played into my hands. Anxious to prove that they did things better in the EEC, he started: 'The other day I was arranging to send my children over to the continent——' 'But I thought you were ruined,' I replied sweetly, to the grins of the rest of them. 'I don't think you can be quite as badly off as you make out.' And I swept into my car. 'Thank you for speaking to us, anyway,' some of them called after me. 'That went much better than I feared,' said the relieved Commissioner. At the hospital nurses were waving from the windows. Altogether quite a successful day.

---

[1] Frimley and its twin 'best buy' hospital at Bury St Edmunds were experiments in hospital design and planning which had made it possible to cut construction costs by one-third without loss of function. They reflected the growing determination of hospital planners to make the limited resources of the NHS go as far as possible. As I said in opening the hospital: 'By having a nationally organized and financed system of health care we are able to get value for money. We can build economically and we can run our service economically.'

[2] The report of the Committee of Inquiry on Small Firms, chaired by J. E. Bolton (Cmnd. 4811, November 1971), had in fact been set up by Harold Wilson on 23 July 1969. It had called for continued reductions in taxation to restore initiative.

Thursday, 1 May

Another foray into the Standing Committee on the Pensions Bill, this time on a tricky aspect of the occupational pensions side. It meant getting up early to mug up some complex details and although I got a few laughs I didn't sparkle as gaily as I did last time. So I was astonished when Boscawen [Conservative MP for Wells] voted with us and came up afterwards to tell me he thought I had made out my case, and even more astonished when officials said to me approvingly, 'Eleven out of ten, Secretary of State.' I think the reason for this hyperbole is that none of them believed I could master any of this field. I was immensely gratified when, replying to me in the debate, Kenneth Clarke instinctively referred to the legislation as the 'Castle Bill'. So my determination to serve on the Committee and hold my corner on it, whatever the additional strain on time and health, has been justified. God knows, I don't want to claim all the credit for the scheme. It has been a joint effort and it ought to be called the Castle/O'Malley Bill. And so it will be if I have anything to do with the writing of history.

Another Dissenting Ministers' meeting in my room. Wedgie explained that everything had gone in the NEC as he had intended. Ron had explained what the party would do in the way of producing literature, etc. Mik had thanked Ron. And then Ron had launched into what he [Wedgie] could only call an outburst of 'hysteria'. Undeterred, Wedgie went on to produce another statement for DMs to issue, this time written by Frances Morrell. I personally thought it was a rather generalized mishmash of assertions which were exaggerated. But it is so clear to me that there is no co-ordinated or coherent leadership of the anti case – and such a danger of our being annihilated by the Establishment in the referendum (with disastrous consequences for the Labour Party) – that I was prepared to go along with it. Peter, however, entered into a niggling argument about phraseology and we had to leave it to poor Jack, Frances and Tony Banks to sort it out with him. I pleaded for us to get into the National Referendum Campaign organization more effectively. I was appalled by the prospect of Neil Marten, George Gale *et al.* cornering all the anti-Market money and the TV appearances. Peter seemed indifferent. I can't make that man out. With Mike in hospital (and of course the right-wing press trying to make out that he had jumped the queue to get there) Peter is our most experienced and reliable spokesman on EEC matters. But he doesn't seem to be bothering about the practical details of organization at all.

Friday, 2 May

Another impossible day with a speech to make to the assembled hordes of our department's staff at lunchtime and an anti-Market meeting at Oxford in the evening. (To say nothing of Ted's birthday celebrations to prepare – and I am not going to sacrifice his birthday to May Day, Common Market or anything else.) I was pretty flaked out by the time I got on my way to Oxford, but was revived by the sight of a packed meeting, from which we had to turn people away, and by the presence of a band of young pro-Market hecklers from the University. In the event I made one of the great speeches of my life and an honest one which clearly impressed even those who had come to attack. I only wish I had more time to write some of the documents we Dissenting Ministers are putting out. I think the real case against the Common Market – which does not rely on exaggerations – is just not being put across.

Sunday, 4 May

Ted's birthday party! Mercifully the sun shone. The garden looked enchanting. The food, on which Eileen and I had slaved all yesterday, was a triumphant success. Teddy was very happy and everyone enjoyed themselves, most of all Tony Keable-Elliott, who stayed a long time and seemed to revel in the relaxed atmosphere, as he always does with us. I *love* giving parties, even though Eileen and I staggered to bed so tired we could hardly walk.

Monday, 5 May

Still a bit flaked out, but utterly relaxed. I have got the great pay beds debate in the House today. We worked away clearing the statement of policy[1] with every department that tried to put a finger in it – including the PM, who had cabled some amendments from Jamaica. 'He can't have enough to do at that Commonwealth Conference,' grumbled Norman. It was irritating to have to read large chunks of my speech because every word of the text had had to be agreed, but the content was sufficiently meaty for me to get away with it. Obviously the Tories were furious, but the TUC health group whom I met beforehand were delighted and even the BMA was mild in its reaction, thanking me for the courtesy of informing them beforehand and for my promise that the details would be negotiated. David made a first-class winding-up speech in seventeen minutes flat and I thumped him on the back enthusiastically. I continue to believe we are a good corrective for each other. Then I had to turn my attention to occupational pensions, on which I have to make a major speech in Standing Committee tomorrow.

Tuesday, 6 May

Up early to finish wrestling with the technical details of my Standing Committee speech. By now I was pretty drained, but it all went well. I still managed to inject a little teasing into the technicalities. My preoccupation with pay beds yesterday meant I had to miss Home Policy Committee, but I see from today's papers that Wedgie had been forced to retreat on his industrial policy statement as far as pension funds are

---

[1] I announced that we intended to legislate to phase out pay beds as soon as possible. I would therefore be consulting the medical profession about the detailed provisions for phasing out and on the extension of my licensing powers over the private sector. In the meantime I was proposing to reduce the number of authorized pay beds, then 4,500, by about 500 where these were under-used and I urged consultants to introduce common waiting lists for their NHS and private patients. The Government had agreed to make extra money available to compensate health authorities for any loss of revenue from private beds.

concerned. Brian continues to be furious with him for intruding into our field without consulting us. So this is the second setback Wedgie has had in the past few days. The press is now full of the Benn phenomenon, Peter Walker, David Wood *et al.* warning that he has managed to become a major political force. Don't they realize this is all grist to his mill? The danger from his point of view is that, in Adlai Stevenson's phrase, he may inhale.

Standing Committee over, I had to turn my mind to another group of technicalities – this time research into hearing problems for a TV programme with Jack Ashley on the deaf. The pressure continues relentlessly, but it is really my own fault. I will insist on starting new policy initiatives, on checking and challenging every detail of policy action that is put up to me, and on taking on an ever heavier load of speaking engagements of every kind. I am even planning a series of overseas visits to promote our exports in OPEC countries! What interests me is that I feel more than ever the urge to work flat out, even though I have definitely made up my mind to retire at the next election and am reconciled to the fact that, when the referendum is over, Harold may well ditch me. I have a yen to go out at my peak and get a deep joy every time I chalk up another achievement – as on pay beds – before I go.

Wednesday, 7 May

For the second week running there is to be no Cabinet – and no Cabinet committees. Okay, so Harold and Jim are away in Jamaica, but Ted Short is here in full charge and the ordinary business of government ought to be going on. We Cabinet Ministers do not even know the business for next week until we hear it at the PLP meeting and there is no discussion of who should speak on what. And crucial decisions are hanging fire on such issues as what to do about the textile industry, which is collapsing before our eyes. Yet another deputation from the Blackburn weavers has been to see me today. When I last wrote to Harold about it he said the matter was under consideration by a committee under Harold Lever. That was two weeks ago and I do not know whether they have even met. It is all very eerie and it is anybody's guess what Harold (the PM one) is up to. The press is full of rumours about the reshuffle he is contemplating when the referendum is over. Brian O'Malley, with whom I had a meal, is worried. The press stories are that Wedgie is to be moved to my job and that he, Brian, is to be moved to Education. 'I wouldn't work in this department under anyone but you,' he told me. 'And I'm damned if I would work under Reg Prentice. In any case, a sideways move is no use to me.' I told him it was quite on the cards that Harold would ditch me, but we could neither of us believe he would dare to do it too blatantly post-referendum. Brian now says the job he would really like is Northern Ireland – of all things! But he would still enjoy being Chief Whip to my Lord President. We agreed that the press is usually wildly wrong in its sensationalist speculations, but the fact remains that Harold, in this pre-referendum period, is effectively governing without a Cabinet, if governing is the right word.

All this speculation is part of the almost hysterical anti-Wedgie campaign that is building up. The papers are full of his fight with Monty Finniston over steel redundancies,[1] in which Monty is managing to hold his own, egged on by every leader-writer. Wedgie has made the maximum meal of the row, telling the unions that he is going to insist on being boss, and no redundancies. Tonight in the Lords Watkinson has made a swingeing attack on him, more or less threatening a strike of the whole of British industry unless Harold gets rid of him, while Keith Joseph has called him a 'dracula'. But Ted tells me that by far the most telling speech in the Lords debate was one by Robbins, who made Ted's blood run cold with his gloom about the economy. On every hand there is the feeling among our own people that the economy is out of control: a mood which is fed by Harold's absence, making irrelevant speeches about commodity agreements (which are contrary to everything we have done in the EEC), at the Commonwealth Conference. Joel Barnett is in a near-neurotic state, making no attempt to disguise his belief that we are on the edge of disaster. Brian [O'Malley] tells me Joel has been to see Harold, begging to be released from the Treasury. He wants out before the crash comes. The outlook for public expenditure programmes is bleak indeed. I spent the morning soldiering on to complete our draft of the social wage document, but I have a feeling it will never see the light of day. Things have gone too far for that.

Yet the unions go cheerfully on with their demands, as though none of this had anything to do with them. Brian O'M. told me he had just had a meeting with the TUC social insurance committee which had left him in despair. They had unfolded a list of social policy items on which they wanted immediate action, such as increases in unemployment benefit, which would cost millions. I said to him, 'We have heaped goodies on them, but they have delivered absolutely nothing in return.'

As Brian and I were eating Stan Orme joined us and we drifted into one of those philosophical discussions one tends to get into over a carafe of wine at the end of a busy day. Brian and I confronted Stan squarely with the dilemma we were in. He wriggled defensively, but he has learned a thing or two in government and he didn't hit back very hard. Indeed, he went out of his way to pile on kind things about me, saying no one had ever doubted my motives over *In Place of Strife*; that I had had a raw deal in having to operate the prices and incomes policy; and so on. I told him I personally thought there was only one way out. We could have a statutory policy, but that hadn't worked. We could have a voluntary policy, but that wasn't working either. All that was left was a voluntary-statutory-policy, and I reminded him of Hughie's heart-cry at the Liaison Committee meeting a month or so ago: 'We in the trade-union movement must do something about it.' When would the unions face reality and have the guts to stand up and be counted? He had no reply.

The one bright spot in the day was the meeting I had called at the office on export promotion. We know that the OPEC countries have more money than they know what to do with and are itching to spend a lot of it on health care. But they want to buy

---

[1] The British Steel Corporation had announced that it was to make twenty-thousand workers redundant by closing old, high-cost plant in an attempt to reduce its losses, running at £2·5 million per week. Tony Benn was resisting the plans for immediate redundancies, and the sharp correspondence between him and Sir Monty Finniston, Chairman of BSC, was carried on publicly, both sides publishing their letters as soon as they were written. BSC withdrew its plan on 19 May after reaching a compromise agreement with the TUC Steel Committee under which the unions agreed to eliminate unnecessary overtime and to accept voluntary redundancies where there was agreed overmanning.

complete health packages: whole hospitals and equipment plus a training programme for the necessary staff. Were we really taking advantage of this, I asked. David tells me that Sam Davies of our Export and Industries Branch of Supply Division is struggling to cope with inadequate staff and against the deep-rooted conventionality of the department. But David wasn't too pleased when I called for a presentation of the issues involved. He likes to keep all initiatives on the health side under his own control. But I soldiered on and we had a useful one-and-a-half hours' discussion, Sam Davies responding eagerly to my interest. I said we ought to have (a) a central procurement department for all purchases for the NHS, as a base on which to build up our supplying industries; (b) the rationalization of small supplying firms under a planning agreement procedure; (c) arrangements to reimburse the NHS out of the contract price for the training we had to do in our hospitals as part of any health package we negotiated; (d) realistic charging for medical training in universities for these people from rich countries, and (e) an arrangement whereby the department, if necessary through some separate agency like the Crown Agents, entered into a comprehensive contract with the purchasing countries and got our cut from the price as payment for the use of designs of 'best buy' hospitals and the rest which have been worked up in our own architects' department. At present, typically, the private consortia go and get fat orders and profits for themselves on the basis of our designs, for the use of which we don't get a penny piece. No wonder the NHS is starved of cash. Sam Davies even dared to say that he thought we couldn't get the best out of the situation as long as exports were dealt with by the Department of Trade on a geographical desk basis. We needed a subject basis instead, so that we could sell a health package as a whole. Finally I said that David and I ought to go on a series of overseas missions to sell our whole health image. Davies jumped at this and signed me up at once for a visit to Nigeria, which, he says, has the largest social expenditure budget of them all. I told Norman to lay this on for September, adding – to Davies's delight – that I would extend my coming visit to Mexico for International Women's Year to do a bit of health-flag waving at the same time. I am determined to keep this field under my control, despite David's obvious irritation at my intrusion.

Thursday, 8 May

The papers are full of Wedgie again. Apparently he had a row with Shirley [Williams] at Neddy yesterday, accusing her of wanting coalition government.[1] At our usual meeting of DMs tonight he was as usual full of bright ideas, which he launched at us with a high-pitched recklessness. Bob Harrison of the Transport and General Workers' Union cheered us up by turning up to tell us in his boyish New Zealand accent what they are planning in NRC, to which he has been seconded by Jack Jones. He told us *we* cheered *him* up, because NRC was getting on his nerves. With all the campaign money going to a bunch like that I am afraid the swing of opinion against us

[1] At the monthly meeting of the tripartite National Economic Development Council, at which Ministers, employers and unions discussed economic problems, Shirley Williams was reported to have disagreed with a long analysis by Tony Benn of the problems of industry and had called for an 'industrial consensus'. According to the reports Benn had accused her of wanting a coalition.

may turn into a rout. Yet a surprising number of Labour MPs remain instinctively hostile to the EEC. But we are just not being briefed to fight back properly and Peter [Shore] in my view is just not doing his stuff. He is so busy with his own speeches that he is not using his department to get us the material with which to answer the employers' brainwashing in every factory, with employers telling their workers that they will lose their jobs if we come out of Europe. I itch to drop everything else and just take charge, but with so much departmental work on my plate it is impossible. Anyway, we agreed another statement for another press conference (which I can't attend): a much better one this time, based on a succession of questions to the Commission.

Meanwhile the office is beavering away preparing the legislation on pay beds. A surprising number of my officials have no doubt that licensing of the size of the private sector should be introduced to safeguard the NHS.

Friday, 9 May

Another meeting with a bunch of area health authority chairmen. David and I went through the usual routine with them and some of the usual answers emerged: they thought the administrative structure was top-heavy; they were supposed to 'manage' but had none of the freedom of decision of managers as to the disposal of their resources or on hire and fire. As one of the brighter of them put it, 'This isn't management at all, merely administration – a very different thing.' Once again I realized how woefully wrong that arch-exponent of efficiency, Keith Joseph, had got things in the NHS with his McKinsey-type theories.

Down to HCF early, as I am only going to get a few hours at home.

Saturday, 10 May

Off to Edinburgh for a weekend meeting of the Women's National Commission. I only agreed to go because it is International Women's Year and we must show the flag in Scotland. It was almost as dreadful as I had feared. The Lord Provost put on a reception for us and failed to turn up, leaving us to our coffee and Scotch pancakes on our own. I soon gathered that the Scots are the biggest male chauvinists of the lot and that the women there are resentful at not being treated seriously. It amuses me to see myself cast in the feminist role after a lifetime in which I have hated the whole idea, but, faced with the failure of the Secretary of State for Scotland to turn up to our functions as well as the Lord Provost, I find myself getting pretty militant.

Monday, 12 May

At the WNC press conference this morning I tell the media what I think of the Scots male. Then I dash for a plane in time to get to the dinner that Brian A-S. has laid on for us in his charming house in Elizabeth Street. It is for the purpose of putting the NHS unions in the picture about the developments in the pay bed field. Unfortunately only Alan Fisher of NUPE, Audrey Prime of NALGO and Peter Jacques of the TUC could turn up, and David and I had to leave early for a 10pm vote, but it was clear that they were far from unanimous on the matter of the need for controls over the private sector. Peter Jacques, in particular, was all for letting the private sector sink or swim and for denying it any use of NHS facilities. This will strengthen David's hand in opposing controls, which he does on the grounds that they are unworkable. I remain convinced (and to my surprise both Philip Rogers and Raymond Gedling agree with me) that our own people would never let me stand by while the private sector escalated and that, in any case, a free-for-all would do great damage to the NHS. Jack Straw told me afterwards that after we had left he and Brian A-S. had succeeded in shaking Peter's views and had got them all more or less to accept our line.

Tuesday, 13 May

All this meant that I had had no time to prepare my Second Reading speech on the Child Benefit Bill this afternoon, so I was annoyed to find this morning had been pre-empted by a meeting of a Cabinet Committee on Joint Approach to Social Policies. Glancing at my papers, I couldn't even remember what it was all about, so I sent David in my place. He told me afterwards that I clearly should have gone: the PM was in the chair, all the top Ministers were there and they discussed the CPRS paper on a 'joint framework for social policies'. I had forgotten all about it. The pressure of hand-to-mouth work is so great these days that anything more profound one has read some weeks ago gets totally submerged. Since this new committee is part of Tony Crosland's bid for better 'social monitoring' (which is all right in itself, except that it is part of his continuing attacks on my expenditure) I would have liked to be there. There has certainly been no more 'wasteful expenditure' than in the housing field, and I am glad to learn that one of the short-term studies which CPRS proposes is on the social aspects of housing policy – as long as 'social aspects' does not rule out a study of cost-effectiveness. I learn that the CPRS paper is to be published, that the PM is to preside over a ministerial group on strategy, that social monitoring is to be carried out by a 'social group' of senior statisticians in the Central Statistical Office, that the group of Permanent Secretaries is to process all this, and that the first strategic ministerial meeting is to be held at Chequers soon. I certainly must not miss any more of these meetings. Harold must have felt aggrieved that I was not there.

My only consolation was that, having had the morning to prepare my Child Benefit Bill speech, the debate went well. Norman Fowler was moderation itself and Kenneth Clarke's more effective and more critical speech came too late – to an empty House – to have any effect. I was inhibited by the almost certain knowledge that, when the time comes to introduce the benefit, Denis will insist on a derisory rate; but that didn't arise at this point. I got away remarkably easily with my reasons for postponing the scheme till 1977.

Wednesday, 14 May

I continue to wrestle, through all my departmental preoccupations, with the minutiae of the anti-Market argument, on which I am struggling to brief myself. The inadequacy of the anti-Market machine, and of the money that has been made available to us, continues to manifest itself. For the pro-marketeers the highly professional and well-endowed European Movement has swung into action. Janet tells me that Roy Hattersley's secretary has told her that Roy has received a vast tome of speaker's notes from them and detailed briefing on every conceivable aspect. I have to do my own reading as best I can, referring points to Jack for checking from time to time. In the division lobby Judith Hart came up to me looking shocked. She had circulated a memo on 'The Future of the Steel Industry in Britain' for the Industrial Policy Committee of the NEC, and had just received a nasty note from Harold asking her what she thought she was up to. Yet the memo barely mentioned the EEC, merely asking whether Monty Finniston had entered into any agreement with the EEC to cut back production. Harold's reaction is a warning of the grudges he may well be nourishing against some of us.

Thursday, 15 May

Cabinet again at last. Harold was in extraordinarily benign mood, saying he thought the referendum campaign was going as he had hoped it would. Everyone was behaving themselves and had eschewed personalities. But some members of Cabinet had complained to him that the guidelines were inhibiting them from taking part in important meetings and TV programmes, because of the no-confrontation principle, and were asking that in the last week the guidelines might be let up a bit. He thought that was reasonable: 'It will all be forgotten as soon as it is over.' Roy [Jenkins] was the one who pressed this particularly hard. He had not been able to agree to go on a Granada eve-of-poll meeting because Peter and Wedgie had been asked first. This meant that the pro-Market case was to be put by Heath, 'who does not exactly represent my views'. After the pro-marketeers had moaned a bit – Jim complaining he hadn't been asked once to go on TV – I interposed to say that, with every newspaper on their side, I thought they did protest too much. I hadn't been on TV either. Harold looked shocked at this and interposed, 'You ought to ask your male chauvinist colleagues to make room for you.' The trouble was, I replied, that the no-confrontation principle had inhibited me too. It meant that the only person who was always available on the anti side was the Minister who had had the vision to resign, or get himself sacked: Eric Heffer – 'and he doesn't always represent my views either'. Laughter at this. The relaxation was agreed.

The main argument of the morning was about arms: first, arms for Turkey. Harold said that the US Congress had defied Ford by insisting on suspending the sale of arms to Turkey. America was now worried about the exposure of Nato's south-east flank and wanted us and other European countries to make good Turkey's arms deficiency. Overseas Policy and Defence Committee [OPD] had agreed strongly, but he thought it was sufficiently sensitive to bring to Cabinet. Jim argued that France and Germany were going to supply anyway. If we refused, it would merely make the Turks bloody-minded and less likely to make concessions over Cyprus. Only Mike and I really resisted this, Mike pointing out that we had treaty obligations to Cyprus we could not ignore. Couldn't we get common ground with the EEC on the concessions we should exact from Turkey in return? Harold's reply to this one astonished me. 'I am very much against using the EEC as a centralized foreign policy-making body. It would make nonsense of our relations with the Commonwealth Conference and US.' So he really *is* cynical about the pro-European line.

Next we turned to arms for South Africa. To my surprise, Peter Shore had put in a paper pleading that we should now phase out the provision of spares. It seemed so out of character, for Peter has never been an emotional socialist by any means. Roy Mason shot him down pretty successfully, pointing out that some of the equipment he wanted to refuse – such as gas masks – simply could not be used for riot control. Harold added that when the matter was discussed at the Commonwealth Conference we had not been pressed to do any more than we were doing.

A human touch at the beginning. Bob Mellish reported that the pressure of legislation was so great that he was having to keep Members late night after night and some of our older members were feeling the strain. Tony C. suddenly burst out, 'I am surprised how decent men can put their family life at the bottom of the list.' And he went on to demand that we should review the state of our legislative programme so as to allow us all to lead something more like normal lives. Harold promised we would do this after the recess.

The Dissenting Ministers' weekly meeting in my room was its usual shambles, with some having to leave early and others not able to turn up at all. Jack Straw, Frances Morrell and Tony Banks are furious at the way in which they are being played about with. Decisions are reached on press conferences and statements, on which they work all Friday, only to have some Ministers throw them over. But last week's shambles was the worst. We had agreed to issue a series of questions to the Commission. The press conference was summoned and then at the last moment it was cancelled. Result: news bulletins were interrupted all Sunday with a reference to the cancellation. Wedgie was sulking, having made a special effort to return to London, only to be informed that the conference had been called off. I said we ought to issue the questions this weekend. Wedgie shrugged and said they were out of date. I urged that we must undo the impression that the DMs had broken up, and the rest strongly agreed with me. Wedgie grudgingly consented and I was given the job of polishing the questions up. It is all very exhausting and I think it is a miracle we have made the impact we have.

Off to Blackburn by the night train for a weekend's anti-marketeering.

Friday, 16 May

Jack Straw phoned me in Blackburn to say Frances Morrell had been on to him: Wedgie didn't want us to issue the questions as he was now working on an entirely different line. Could we have a DM meeting on Monday to consider it? This was really too much. 'Right,' I told Jack, 'issue the questions in my name as my hand-out for Sunday's meetings.' And I told him for God's sake to try to get some TV for Sunday. I was sick of Wedgie monopolizing everything. 'He is losing us the referendum,' replied Jack gloomily. Did four anti-Market meetings up the Calder Valley – a mad rush but well worth it. We got good attendances and a lot of interest.

Saturday, 17 May

Did a stint in Blackburn market on the referendum with an interested crowd: only hampered by the lack of a loudspeaker that would work. I am convinced that if the antis had had the resources of the European Movement, we could get a clear 'no' majority. As it is, we have got the pros on the run – and on the defensive, as even the newspapers admit. I was just finishing some shopping when I ran into Southern, Chief Superintendent of police. He embraced me with open arms: there was a police search out for me. The PM wanted me to ring him at No. 10. My heart quailed a little: was he going to give me the dressing-down he had given Judith? Not a bit of it. He was affability itself. He had been thinking over what I had said at Cabinet. It was quite right that I hadn't been getting a proper show: the same antis were being put on time after time. He had that morning been speaking to the Chairman of the BBC, asking him to see that the reporting of the antis was spread more evenly, and he would be speaking to Lady Plowden [chairman of the Independent Broadcasting Authority] on Monday in the same vein. I thanked him, pointing out that Wedgie had been on TV again last night. But I couldn't help suspecting that Harold's ploy was more anti-Benn than pro-Barbara.

Sunday, 18 May

An excellent anti-Market meeting at Bradford, though despite all Jack's efforts, there was no TV. Nor was there any at Sheffield either, where I found nearly two thousand people crowded into the hall. If the pros had had a meeting like that, there would have been great coverage. I thought I spoke well, having worked out my facts (not least on sugar) very carefully, but the reception of Wedgie fell only just short of idolatry: a standing ovation before he started and one afterwards. He was on the top of his oratorical form, but as I listen to him, Ella Wheeler Wilcox and all, I can't help thinking it is one thing to enthuse people, another to do it on a criminally over-simplified version of the facts. Anyway, he had scooped us all that morning by holding a press conference. No wonder he wanted the DM statement postponed. I did at least manage a bit of a showing on the news for my questions to the Commission, on which Wedgie congratulated me fulsomely.

Monday, 19 May

Up at 6am to catch the early train in order to attend the TUC/LP Liaison Committee. The theme was to be investment, following Wedgie's speech at our last meeting and the circulation of a paper on investment by what was described as 'the Research Secretaries'. On the way up from Sheffield, over breakfast on the train, Wedgie described it as Geoff Bish's paper and said how good it was. I too thought it was pretty good because of the emphasis it laid on the need to give priority to investment and because it touched on the obvious: 'The need for a dramatic recovery in fixed investment implies that other sectors of demand must be severely restrained.' It even endorsed Denis's last estimate of an increase in public expenditure of no more than

$2\frac{3}{4}$ per cent per year over the next four years. And it worked out a residual increase in private consumption of a total of 5·3 per cent over four years. As I read it on the train I realized once again that Geoff Bish is facing facts pretty honestly and I suddenly saw why I mistrust Wedgie. He is *right* about certain of his themes, such as the need for a crash programme of positive hope through investment and for the involvement of working people in the decisions of industry. But what is so wrong about him is that he never spells out that responsibility involves *choice* and that the choices facing this country are by definition grim for everybody. He really cannot eat his seed corn and sow it. But his whole popularity rests on the belief that he is spreading around: that he – and those he seeks to lead – can do just that.

The Liaison Committee meeting was at the House. The unions were there in greater strength this time, but once again Hughie Scanlon was missing. I suspect he has contracted out of a situation in which he is fighting for his own survival. Harold opened with a few general comments on the investment paper. It had not been discussed by the NEC or the Government, he said. 'If the TUC wanted to go for a plan of this kind we would have to discuss where the resources would come from.' Len came next. The General Council had not discussed this. One of the most urgent needs was not to find more money for investment but to make better use of existing investment. Wedgie (who left early) got in his comment at this point. The key question, he said, was: 'How do you maintain your capacity during a slump? Is it desirable to protect jobs or not? Does the criterion of profitability make sense when the whole country is a lame duck?' And he added that it was an 'absolutely crazy situation we are in'. The only answer was 'democratic planning'. Planning agreements opened up planning at the company level.

There was an uneasy silence among the unions when he had finished. I think they all felt on the defensive, which was no doubt why David Basnett spoke rather truculently. We'd also got to look at the short-term measures, he said. Unemployment was still the issue worrying his members most and we should have a plan for dealing with it (e.g. selective import controls). Denis could contain himself no longer and made the toughest speech I have yet heard from him at these usually mutually conciliatory liaison meetings. Before we launched on extravagant investment plans, he said, we ought to remember that, according to OECD, we had kept up our industrial production in the last three months better than any of our major competitors (i.e. we had the lowest fall). The quickest way of dealing with our problems was by making better use of existing investment. In the period 1964–69 we were increasing our manufacturing investment more than Germany, but they were getting 170 per cent of our output. Our major problem was not the *rate* of investment, but the *return* on it. It was the unions who were holding down the return on investment. The Germans also concentrated their investment where it would do most good (a sideswipe at Wedgie). We must have much stricter criteria and a strategic plan. Even to stick to our present public expenditure plans would mean 10p on income tax. If we were to increase expenditure we must cut down private consumption to below the increase in the cost of living. We must discuss this issue in this forum. Denis ploughed on remorselessly. If we had runaway inflation, the only way to deal with it would be by slashing public expenditure and with it the social wage. 'It would be intolerable for a Labour

Government to be forced by a minority of unions who cannot keep within the guidelines to adopt Tory policies on public expenditure.'

Jack took this better than I would have expected. He agreed with Denis that we could get a great deal more from existing investment. He thought we could get a great deal more production if management hadn't abandoned incentive systems. The biggest mistake had been to go over to time-rate systems which eliminated the incentive element. They had reversed this in the docks with spectacular results. (Bang goes the accepted wisdom of the industrial relations reformers, I thought.) As for his own proposals for the next round of guidelines, he remarked with a wry smile, 'Too much praise here might damn it for good.' But he would argue the case for flat-rate increases with anyone. Otherwise we would be forced to face an increase in tax. There ought to be a more productive use of pension funds. 'The sooner we get round to putting 50 per cent of workers on the management side of pension funds, the better.' Mik made one of his impressively practical speeches. Once again he itemized the failures on the export side. Leyland were in trouble, not because there was not a demand for their products or that they were not competitive in price, but simply that customers could not get spares. (What a simple thing, I thought. How the hell is it that business cannot put it right? And what a pity Mik had never been sent to the Department of Trade.) Planning agreements, continued Mik, were not an ideological thing but 'a way of getting these appalling things put right'. But he then went on in cold fury to denounce the way the Government was throwing away the advantages of its own policy. 'The Industry Bill is being emasculated,' he declared. In Standing Committee some of them had been fighting against its systematic weakening. Planning agreements were being made voluntary. The funds of the National Enterprise Board were ludicrously inadequate. There was even a threat to the provisions for disclosure of information. The Government was being completely cowardly. Our reaction to the suggestion of using pension funds was typical. 'We do more posterior crawling to the City than any other country.' France, for instance, financed the major part of her industrial activity through state funds and institutions. Shirley interjected that we had a short-term problem which planning agreements would not deal with and that was quite simply inflation. And she gave some horrifying figures. I thought it was time I came in. The real issue over pension funds, I said, was that there soon might not be any. Our remarkable concordat with the pensions industry over our Pensions Bill was on the edge of breaking down because of the growing difference between the yield on their investments and the cost of protecting private pensions against inflation. Unless we could find a formula for limiting funds' liabilities in a 'catastrophe' situation there would be massive defunding through a panic decision to contract into the state scheme. Harold nodded sagely at this, while the unions looked worried. We also faced, I continued, an imminent threat to public expenditure which would decimate the social wage which was the key to equality. The main problem that faced us was 'motivation'. How could we make workers realize that they now had more power than ever before, that we had firms practically queueing up to be nationalized, and that it was time to drop the old warring 'them and us' attitude and to realize that it was time to make a go of what was increasingly becoming *their* industry? For, unless attitudes changed, inflation would destroy us all.

'Socialism won't suddenly come overnight,' I said. 'There will never be a situation in which we can say, "This is socialism." It will come gradually; it is coming now and we've got to make a success of it.' It was an eloquent speech and a passionate one. I concluded that I had been working for months on a document on the social wage, designed to get the message across urgently to the shop-floor, 'but I expect it will sit in the Treasury for months'. 'It will do nothing of the kind,' retorted Harold. 'I have just sent you a Minute on it, pointing out that the social wage does cover other departments. It is not Barbara's monopoly.' I shrugged: 'If Reg Prentice wants to limp belatedly into the act, I don't mind. But for heaven's sake let's get the pamphlet out.' Len Murray wound up by saying that he was sorry the discussion, which was supposed to be about investment, had once again got round to incomes policy. Personally, I didn't care if I had trodden on their toes: there is no time to be squeamish in view of what lies ahead. I believe we have been mealy-mouthed too long. Shirley passed me a note: 'You and I disagree on the Common Market but we are the only ones who seem to realize there is a crisis.'

I was supposed to make my statement in the House today about next November's uprating, but Harold has tried to get it postponed till after the Whit recess on the grounds that it might have a bad effect on sterling. Norman asks me whether I wish to fight. I say yes. A statement in the hand – and Brian A-S. has already minuted me about the public expenditure proposals Denis will be bringing before Thursday's Cabinet. We are right in the muck cart again. I shall not be sorry to be inched out of government before the rerun of 1966 takes place.

Tuesday, 20 May

Spent the morning in the final stages of the Standing Committee on the Pensions Bill. Made three speeches and re-established my authority again. I am glad I insisted on taking on the extra chore of the committee. Brian O'Malley has been very good about all this.

At an office meeting this afternoon I was warned that private developers were pressing the department for guidance as to my intention on controls on the private sector of medicine and I said a consultative document should be prepared urgently, pointing out how disastrous a free-for-all in the development of private hospitals would be for everybody.

Wednesday, 21 May

Oddly enough, the most significant incident at the NEC meeting arose on the Staff Committee report – not usually a source of arresting interest. When I arrived the staff were out of the room and the NEC was discussing their claim for a wage increase. God knows, they need one to offset the rise in the cost of living and everyone's sympathies were with them, but Ron was holding forth with more passion and eloquence than I have ever heard from him and the burden of his oratory was that the party was broke. Inflation had reached such levels that we just couldn't carry on. The unions had had to put their hands in their pockets three times in the last eighteen months: two elections and now a referendum campaign. Their kitty was bare. And local parties were struggling with the effects of inflation themselves. 'I say to the Government: unless you come forward with plans for helping political parties with state grants, there will be no Labour Party. This time next year you are flat broke. The Houghton Committee[1] is going to take twelve months to report and we can't wait that long. We know the Conservative Party is in trouble too. Jeremy Thorpe is going round industrialists telling them not to subscribe to the Conservative Party unless they agree to electoral reform.' Result: we had just got to cut out some of our activities. It was no good members asking for this bit of research or that bit of propaganda. The money just wasn't there.

All this was traumatic enough, but the most poignant moment came when Sid Vincent, who is chairman of the Staff Committee and (most pointedly of all) a representative of the NUM on the NEC, said rather haltingly, 'There have got to be wage increases. But even an increase of 20 per cent means an additional bill of £700,000 a year. We must have a paper on the state of the party's finances if inflation carries on.' All this in an unpolished working-class accent. This gave Denis his great opportunity and he took it almost gleefully. It was not only the unions who were hit by inflation, he said, it was the Government. 'The policy we laid down is not being adequately maintained by the unions, who supported it unanimously at Congress last year.' It was all right to say that the Government should bail out the political parties, but the Government was going to need bailing out itself. Once again, Mik came in with an eminently practical approach. 'If this had been a commercial organization we would have been talking about this situation two years ago.' And he went on to give us an analysis of the inadequate, not to say jejune, way in which we controlled the finances of the party. But his follow-up was not the political one we needed. It was merely: 'I see no salvation for this party without state aid.' Bryan Stanley was more direct: 'I hope Sid can put this to his miners.' To which Denis made the addendum: 'Another excessive settlement means unemployment – even in the Labour Party.' The result of all this soul-searching was the decision to get a full statement of our finances next month. But, as Mik pointed out, we shall not be saved by saving candle-ends.

Off to Southampton for a TV programme on the Common Market: me, Clive Jenkins and Richard Body [Conservative MP for Holland with Boston] against Willie Whitelaw, David Steel and Roy Grantham.[2] It got a bit rowdy but I thought we antis won hands down. It occurred to me as I listened that the antis – so clearly outnumbered in the country and with all the Establishment against them – have managed to corner fifty per cent of TV time, as though we were level-pegging: very different from the showing we are given in the press. Which is another reason why I always thank the Lord for TV. And we have managed to put the Establishment on the defensive. No mean achievement.

[1] The report of Lord Houghton's committee on 'Financial Aid to Political Parties' (Cmnd. 6601) was published in August 1976. It recommended the introduction of a system of state financial aid to political parties to be paid at a national and local level providing the party had reached a minimum qualifying level of electoral support. The scheme has not yet been introduced.

[2] General Secretary of APEX, member of the TUC General Council and the Executive of the pro-Market Labour Committee for Europe.

Thursday, 22 May

Harold has reluctantly agreed that I may make my statement on the November increase in pensions today, but has vetted every line of it and of my press statement to render them as low-key as possible.[1] Nonetheless, it was well received and I have got away with murder, knowing as I do what Denis is preparing in the way of public expenditure cuts. The documents which have been circulated for Cabinet visualize a cut of 'at least £2 billion' for 1978–79, compared with the PESC White Paper last year. My department has been studying the implications for our budget, which, if there is to be any expenditure on the NHS at all, will this time have to include cuts in social security plans. Philip Rogers and co., of course, see no alternative to cuts. Errington even hinted hesitantly at our office discussion that we should have to amend the legislation which compels us to increase pensions, etc., in line with average national earnings if that is more favourable to the pensioner than prices. So I went to Cabinet prepared to fight with everything I have got. 'I shall resign first,' I told Errington. My officials watch developments nervously, not knowing how much longer I shall be their boss. But Cabinet began surprisingly harmoniously. Harold was at his most affable, in marked contrast to last night, when he had been almost viciously curt with me. Seeing him stroll through the lobby, I had gone up to him. 'Hugh Cudlipp really has done a first-class job on the social wage document,' I said diplomatically, knowing his affection and respect for Hugh. 'Then it mustn't be all Barbara Castle,' he had snapped back. 'The departments of education and housing contribute something to the social wage too.' 'We can include chapters from them,' I replied. 'Then it will have to be shortened,' he almost spat out, pushing past me. 'Harold really has the knives out for me,' I told my Ted afterwards. 'It may have been the brandy talking,' he replied. And Ted may have been right, because this morning Harold could not have been more genial.

The first item was Harold's own paper on the future procedures for dealing with public expenditure. Here it was, all we had been asking for: a timetable for dealing with public expenditure in the wider context of economic and political strategy, with the whole process starting at an early stage in the annual round. In introducing it he particularly referred to the criticisms Tony C. and I had made in the past and called on us to comment on the way he had tried to meet them. We both of us welcomed his proposals wholeheartedly. I merely asked (a) that the preliminary discussions should include tax policy and (b) that in future procedures the forty-eight-hour rule

[1] I announced that the next uprating would be in November, instead of December as originally planned, but that there would be no Christmas bonus. In keeping with the Government's promise, pensions and other long-term benefits would be increased in line with earnings. Using the 'historical' method of calculation (i.e. the movement of earnings over the preceding eight months up to March 1975), this would give an increase of 15 per cent. Short-term benefits such as sickness and unemployment, which were linked to prices, would go up by 13 per cent. Supplementary benefit would be increased in line with insurance benefits. I was also able to confirm the concessions I had wrung out of the Chancellor: heating additions would be increased and the amount of earnings disregarded in calculating the right to supplementary benefit would be doubled, to the special advantage of the single parent. The new non-contributory invalidity pension would come into operation at the same time. The cost of the total package would be over £1,000 million.

for the distribution of the discussion papers to Cabinet should be replaced by a one-week rule. 'We have today,' I said, 'two major public expenditure papers in front of us dated 19 May. Today is the 22nd. In practice, I got my papers in my box last night, because I had to await the office briefing on them.' Denis fell over himself to accept my first point; Harold agreed that my second one was legitimate. (In fact I discovered later both points were officially recorded in the Minutes.) But Harold was clearly very touched by the enthusiasm with which we had received his paper.

But it was in a different mood that we turned to Denis's paper on the survey of public expenditure after 1976–77. The picture he painted for us could not have been grimmer. It was backed by long official papers setting out the economic assessment for the next few years. What we ought to plan for, said Denis, was the implication for individual programmes of a £3 billion cut in public expenditure by 1978–79 and then study the consequences for our overall political policy. (My officials have welcomed this approach as the only way of getting the right assessment of priorities.) In fact, said Denis, he hoped that only a £2 billion cut would be necessary, but, if we didn't like the effect on certain programmes of such a cut, then we had to have in front of us an indication of what would be the effect of cutting other programmes even more drastically. The assumption of the illustrative figures was that inflation would be as bad in 1978–79 as now. 'If we are able to get the inflation rate down, the prospects for public expenditure will be better, but we have no policy for this at present.' I began to wonder what was the point of the whole exercise. The trouble is that the Treasury is not a *political* policy ministry; it is merely a logistics one. But the two really cannot be separated in this day and age. It is like a general saying: I want a quarter of a million soldiers to be held expendable, but I am not interested in the political purpose of their expendability. That sort of approach went out with World War I. Of course, such a coldly logistical approach has its political implications too. And Denis's political slip started to show. Public expenditure, he complained, had risen over the past twenty years from 42 per cent of GNP to 58 per cent. The biggest increase had been in the last ten years. (Exactly, I thought: that has been the period of the revival of Labour Governments. What the hell are you driving at?) Income tax, went on Denis accusingly, had risen over the last ten years as a percentage of average family's earnings from 5·5 per cent to 18·9 per cent. Most startling of all was the revelation that, even if we confiscated all income over £6,000 per year, we should merely have a £450 million 'once and for all' addition to resources available for public expenditure. All this, I thought, is undoubtedly true. But what are you leading up to: the repudiation of every policy on which the Labour Party has built its strength? It is not as simple as that, or else we had all better become Tories. (And the Tories themselves are bankrupt of policies.) So I was in a highly unreceptive mood when he concluded, 'All this adds up to draconian cuts.'

Equally unreceptive, incidentally, were a number of other members of the Cabinet. Tony C. weighed in first. He said that some of Denis's remarks were disturbingly familiar – notably his protestation that the studies he wanted us to authorize officials to make along the lines he proposed were purely 'procedural' decisions at this stage. 'Procedural decisions eventually become policy decisions,' said Tony firmly, to which I said a loud 'Hear, hear'. We must be given some international comparisons of percentages of public expenditure. And there must be a proper economic assessment before we reached any decisions at all. 'Why are we discussing this? Why has the balance of payments situation worsened since the Budget? The Chancellor's paper hasn't proved the need to create more spare capacity.' This was a crucial decision for the future of the party, he continued. The choice between public expenditure and taxation was a *political* decision. 'This is the first time we have started talking about actual cuts. Before it has only been a reduction in increases. We never did this in 1964–70. The effect on the construction industry is horrifying.' Denis, who has Harold's habit of wanting to chip in to answer every speech, insisted on replying at once. 'I agree the balance of payments deficit will be one billion pounds lower than last year, but export orders are slowing down and the figures will be less good in the second half of the year.' And he added, in what seemed to me to be the biggest ever *non sequitur*, 'We hope to get an upsurge in investment.'

Harold called me next. I agreed first with Tony that Denis's talk of purely 'procedural' decisions at this stage was nonsense. His paper asked us to agree 'guidelines' for officials, and guidelines implied approval in principle. 'When we sing "Guide me O thou great Jehovah" it is because we are ready to approve his guidance,' I quipped. What we needed was the setting out of various options, not guidelines on one option only: 'a draconian cut in public expenditure'. Personally, I rejected Denis's option. 'This is a formula for a self-fulfilling prophesy.' If unemployment went up, so would expenditure on benefit. We should also rob ourselves of any chance of solving our problems by increasing productivity. For what did Denis think these cuts would do for investment? Could he really, incredibly, believe they would encourage it? Besides, his option would mean the permanent abandonment of our own policy and would destroy the party. I had been particularly struck by his implication that public expenditure was wrong in itself. What then were we in business for? His proposals included a cut of £1½ billion in 'other categories' than goods and services, and that meant social security. The only way we could achieve this target was by cutting the statutory link between benefits and average national earnings and that meant changing the law. Did we really think we could get such legislation through our own party in the House? ('No,' Bob almost shouted.) Finally his measures would destroy any hope of getting a voluntary incomes policy. What we needed was to get the unions – right down the line and not just their leaders in the Liaison Committee with the TUC – to discuss and decide with us the national housekeeping. We should put to them a comprehensive package designed to safeguard jobs and the social wage in return for a voluntary wages freeze, or at the very least a voluntary and effective holding of wage increases to increases in the cost of living. I was not against the officials being asked to work out the implications of the suggested cuts, if only so that we could demonstrate to the unions what would be the consequence of their failure to help us. (Joel Barnett nodded agreement at that.) But it must be only one of the exercises in which they should engage. They should also work out other options, showing what we could do in the public expenditure field if wage increases and inflation were held down: a package which might include import controls as a temporary measure. But I could not accept that these proposals of Denis's should be studied on their own.

Wedgie was at his most apocalyptic: 'I do not agree with the diagnosis or the strategy. The problem is very different from the one Denis has outlined. We are on the rim of a deep slump. Investment intentions are falling. His policy must be rejected because it won't work. Public expenditure must be planned in a full employment context. The import content of public expenditure needs examining. My belief is that it is very small. Denis's proposals would put our microeconomic strategy in a strait-jacket. It would mean we couldn't have a strategy for saving jobs. The movement will not accept this. It is a parallel with 1931, when the government of the day refused to accept protection and gave us a depression instead. We need an alternative package: import controls *now*, plus an investment strategy.' As I listened, I thought once again that he was three-quarters right, as usual, but that once again he had left out the vital element: that we face a *choice*. And the unions must be forced to face that choice. Shirley took him up on this. Import controls would not cure inflation, she said. We had three choices: a tougher counter-inflation policy, the destruction of our whole public expenditure policy, or the economic collapse of the country. But she agreed with me that we ought not to go nap on number two before we had put these three choices to the unions. Only Jim and Reg Prentice ran true to form. Jim said gloomily that Cabinet itself should be looking at the other alternatives, such as restraint of wages, while Reg said flatly we needed a statutory back-up for wage restraint and cuts in public expenditure as well. He added unctuously, 'But I would exclude cuts in overseas aid; that is a moral imperative.' And for good measure he went on: 'We have made a fundamental mistake in increasing transfer payments (i.e. pensions and benefits) at the expense of the NHS, education, etc.' (I am now convinced that Reg is shaping up to leave the party – or at least the Government.) Roy Jenkins made a sternly impressive speech. He began by agreeing broadly with Denis's economic analysis, 'but conventional terms are no longer enough'. Inflation was now bankrupting all sorts of institutions – like the railways for example – but it was also bankrupting civilized government. 'How we deal with it is more difficult, but we have got to stop it in its tracks.' It was impossible, for instance, to run a state by cutting the police force by thirteen thousand men, as Denis's proposals would necessitate. He didn't agree with Tony Benn's method or with pushing more and more expenditure on the state. 'The survival of society is threatened.'

Michael was disappointingly weak in his contribution. 'The unemployment road is impossible,' he urged. 'Special methods to keep it down must form part of any package.' But on wages he merely reiterated a vague need to get a 'new round' of the Social Contract, insisting that the reason for the 'failure' of the Contract (the first time he has used that word!) could not be pushed on to the unions. 'Everyone round this table has endorsed breaches in the Contract at some time or another: look at what we did about top salaries. That was a fatal mistake in my view. I have always believed in some kind of package and it must include action on top salaries and import controls.' Denis replied by assuring us, 'Nothing in this exercise prevents us drawing up a package.' Harold summed up a sombre morning by saying we would resume the broad economic discussion after the recess. He insisted that we had taken *no* decision on future guidelines, but the general view seemed to be that officials should start their exploratory work. We could then have a whole day at Chequers in July to examine it. And he accepted my plea that, when we did meet, we should have various costed and worked-out options before us. So far so good. But I still feel we are drifting to catastrophe. I can't feel anyone has got a sufficient sense of urgency. Why, for instance, wait till July before the PM calls the sort of conferences with union representatives for which I have been pleading (and with other sections of society)? 'We ought to have held this morning's discussion in public,' I said to Shirley afterwards.

After all this, the weekly meeting of Dissenting Ministers in my room seemed almost euphoric, despite the usual hectic confusion. John Allen,[1] who has taken to materializing at these meetings (apparently NRC have appointed him their press officer), mooned about ineffectually while Jack and Tony Banks did all the work. Bob Harrison told me he had cleared my Brussels trip to examine the cost of living there, provided I was prepared to make it all-party by going with Mrs Neil Marten. I agreed and got Janet to phone Sonya to see if we could borrow her little Rachel to go with us – Frances's idea. She is most enthusiastic about my trip. And so at last I dashed to Islington for an anti-Market meeting and from Islington to various TV studios. Got down to HCF late and exhausted, determined to get in a few days' gardening to revive myself.

Wednesday, 28 May

Great comings and goings over the Brussels trip. Sonya has done her stuff over Rachel's clothes, dressing her in Marks and Spencer's clothes so that we can compare their prices in Brussels, Jack Straw has got out a food shopping list from the *Daily Mirror* Shopping Clock, Spud Murphy has gone over to Brussels to lay everything on for us. But at the last minute John Allen has tried to mess everything up by getting Enoch Powell to come along to the same press conference at which we are to report our findings. Jack Straw, Bob Harrison and I agree it would be ridiculous for Enoch and me to cancel each other out, but for some unknown reason John Allen refuses to budge and Neil Marten will not assert his authority. So I tell Jack I am going to phone Enoch, who is always very civil with me. He agrees at once that it would be absurd for us to upstage each other. He is free to go to the press conference on the previous day instead and thinks it is much better for him to double with Jack Jones on that day. 'Tell them we both agree that that is best.' I get Jack to convey this message to Allen and go to bed.

Thursday, 29 May

Up to 6.30am to catch the plane to Brussels. Rachel is thrilled to bursting-point and behaves beautifully. Joan Marten turns out to be a very pleasant person; Spud was

[1] Son of former Labour MP for Crewe, Scholefield Allen, he had until recently been a research assistant at Transport House. He had also helped Harold Wilson unofficially.

waiting for us with a car. We work hard at our shopping and do everything as scrupulously fairly as we intended to do. Jack met us at the airport back with the news that Enoch was going to appear with me the next day after all – John Allen had flatly refused to alter anything. 'What the hell does that man think he is up to?' Jack asked. We were both furious – and not a little mystified. Whose side does he think he is on? 'Some one recommended him to us,' says Neil weakly. We get back to the flat where Sonya cooks Jack a meal while he does some converting of our prices and weights into British terms and I wade through a big box. A happy but tired little Rachel goes to bed.

Friday, 30 May

A mad rush to get ready for the press conference. We all meet at the Waldorf, where once again Jack and Neil's two experts do all the work. One of them comes in with the news that the opposition have obviously got wind of our shopping trip and have trumped our ace by sending a housewife to Oslo so as to claim that prices are even higher there, though Norway is not in the Community. Then we get the message: Enoch has cancelled, refusing to wreck my show. At the last minute John Allen puts in an appearance – what to do I'm damned if I know. 'So all you have succeeded in doing is to lose Enoch,' I remark to him coldly. He just shrugs indifferently. The conference goes well: Rachel does her stuff as to the manner born. I beat back a hostile barrage from the journalists. These NRC press conferences are not like press conferences at all, but public meetings with an overtly hostile audience. The spleen of some of the reporters that anyone should dare to oppose their precious Community is almost ungovernable. There is one foreign correspondent with a heavily foreign accent who almost spits at us. However, they tell me I handled him well. But afterwards I say to Jack, 'We have a traitor in our midst and we both know who it is.' 'Of course,' he agrees. Once again I feel frustrated in having to work through an umbrella organization over which we have no real control.

True to form, the press have built up the Oslo lass and sneered at us. They have totally ignored the counter-statement Jack rushed out for me last night saying, 'What have Oslo prices to do with it? No one is asking us to join Norway.' The press have also ignored Neil Marten's report of a poll which NRC commissioned in New Zealand, which shows that 52 per cent of those polled think New Zealand would be better off if we came out. With such a conspiracy of the press against us, how can we win? But I have a feeling we have shaken public confidence in the Establishment case so much that we shall drive large numbers of yesses to abstain. I dash up to town to do a *Nationwide* phone-in at Lime Grove. Hopefully, in the end, it will be TV that counts.

Saturday, 31 May

Reading through my boxes, I find that Denis has sent a terse reply to Wedgie's complaint that he was not consulted about Budget changes which affect his department. 'To be fully effective consultation could mean involving a large number of officials,' Denis wrote, 'perhaps even consulting the industries concerned. I am not prepared to accept the inhibitions and constraints on my Budget responsibilities that this might imply.' That is not the sort of tone in which he writes to me.

Jack [Straw] phones to say he has just seen in the *Guardian*'s referendum diary of yesterday a tendentious and malicious piece purporting to explain why Enoch did not turn up at the press conference.[1] It could only have come from one person and confirms all our suspicions. I tell Jack to tell Bob that the person must not be present at any of our future discussions. I am not going to reveal my plans in front of a spy.

One nice note among the sour. I have been reading the diplomatic report from Ghana by the High Commissioner, Stanley, on Joan Lestor's official visit there. It positively radiates excitement about her 'outstanding success', talking of the great effect she had on the Ghanaians with her 'enthusiasm, interest and easy informality'. I have seldom read in any diplomatic report such praise of any Minister. Yet I've no doubt some of the Jenkinsites sneered when Harold appointed Joan. 'Easy informality' is not their line.

Sunday, 1 June to Friday, 6 June

The climax of one of the oddest fortnights of my life. It must be unprecedented for a government to extend the Whit recess in order to allow all comers, including Dissenting Ministers, to campaign against its policy. I flatly refused to do any anti-Market meetings during the Whit weekend. My sense of values held firm. But after that I was in the campaign up to my eyebrows. The following highlights stick in my memory:

(1) My public meetings in Blackburn. The campaign has been taken over by the Get Britain Out movement, mainly run by idealistic and very charming youngsters with no money and long hair. The meeting was well attended, I spoke on the top of my form and there was a remarkable speaker from Australia saying he had come over at his own expense because he knew that Britain's membership had damaged the economy of his country. He was most impressive, but not a word of it was reported.

(2) Open-air meetings in Blackburn shopping centre. Crowds gathered round and I really gave it to them. But what interested me were the number of women who said, 'How can I choose? I don't know enough about it. If you MPs can't agree how can we make up our minds?' This was linked to the remark of one woman who, having listened to me with her usual respectful appreciation, said to me anxiously afterwards, 'Then why does Harold Wilson take a different view?' I realized then that Harold's identification with the pro-Market cause would be decisive for most Labour voters. People still vote party rather than ideas.

(3) Harold's low-key approach throughout the whole campaign. He's not going to let this issue divide the party.

[1] The report said that John Allen, 'the long-suffering anti-EEC official', had tried to arrange a compromise whereby Enoch appeared at the morning press conference and Rachel and I at a special one in the afternoon, but I would not have it. So Enoch refused to turn up. 'Barbara and her niece steal the show (and disgust the assembled international press) with the Brussels shopping basket and infant underwear.'

(4) The professionalism of the pro-Market campaign. Our campaign has had considerable élan. But (a) the press were against us to a man and only attended our conferences to heckle and smear, and (b) Harold's ploy of putting the (inadequate) Government money into the hands of umbrella organizations delivered us over to a bunch of amateurs.

But the biggest occasion of all was the Oxford Union debate. The President had written to me weeks ago to ask me if I would participate with Peter Shore, ranged against Heath and Thorpe, on the subject, 'This House says Yes to Europe'. He had added that TV had shown great interest. Of course, I jumped at it. It is a habit I have: never turning down a challenge and then wondering afterwards whether I could live up to it. The Union has never been my favourite audience and, as the day drew nearer, all my old phobias about Oxford came flooding back. I was hampered too by my inhibitions about the crudities of our anti-Market case. (And I am *not* referring to Enoch, who, throughout everything, remains intellectually sophisticated.) I happen to believe deeply that membership of the EEC will fatally dilute some of the main motive power of British social democracy and give a great fillip to consensus politics. But my spirit cringes at some of the statistical distortions which bring such tumultuous applause from Labour audiences. Life is more complex than that and there is no doubt that the terms Jim and Harold have got effectively blunt the edge of a simplistic attack. Even my Ted said to me the other day that he couldn't get particularly steamed up about the issue! So I was like a fortress divided against itself and as the day of the debate grew nearer something like panic began to rise in me. Things weren't made any easier as various BBC chaps I kept running into remarked to me: 'See you on Tuesday'. Obviously the debate is going to be one of the TV highlights of the campaign. The BBC have decided to do it live from the main speakers onwards. My busy weekend in Blackburn over, I tried to concentrate my thoughts. As usual, the problem was to select a theme. I had an enormous amount of material and I had Jack rushing about like a scalded cat, checking this fact and that meticulously. I set all Tuesday aside to sketch out my speech (which I was determined not to read) and was still in a state of mental confusion by the time I had to rush to catch the train. Peter Shore was at the station, relaxed and casual, remarking: 'I really ought to jot down a few ideas.' I have never envied him more – never been more conscious of the fatal flaw in my make-up which has always prevented me from realizing my full potential. Oddly enough I believe in myself and in my ideas (I expect my Ted would say I believe in myself arrogantly). But there is a curious hiatus between that belief and its effective expression to a certain kind of audience. Give me a soap box at a street corner, or a hostile crowd of cocky inebriates at an annual dinner, and I can be masterly. But give me time to worry about the intellectual niceties of my case and I can become paralysed. As the train steamed into Oxford station I felt paralysed.

Dinner-jacketed undergraduates met us at the station: all politeness and importance. At the Randolph Hotel the BBC were waiting: would I mind being made-up now, before dinner, as there was so much making-up to do? So I went to the room set aside for me, where a charming make-up girl attended me as efficiently as possible in the short time we had. I had decided to wear the sixty-year-old Edwardian blouse I had discovered among Mother's things. I love it – all mutton-chop sleeves and meticulous beading. 'My suffragette blouse,' I explain defiantly. (If only someone were threatening to forcibly feed me for my views, I should have no fear!) I arrived at the Union just in time for the elaborately organized photograph. It was a sunny evening and the queues for the debate were already long as I arrived on the lawn, head held as high as Anne Boleyn's on her way to the scaffold. (My terror had been made worse when Tony Keable-Elliott had informed me at HCF last week that his son was intending to queue 'for hours' in order not to miss the debate.) Then out of the President's room walked Jeremy, to tumultuous cheers from the queueing undergraduates. He gave them an American footballer's hand-held-high clinch. But the most revealing moment of all came when Heath walked on to the lawn. The catcalls of delight were uncontainable. It was a near pandemonium of enthusiasm and I suddenly realized what we were up against. The only wry satisfaction Peter (who had been greeted coolly) and I had was the realization of what Margaret Thatcher was up against too. Heath was the hero of the hour, as he had never been as PM.

At dinner I sat opposite Jeremy, facing the window. The queuers for the debate gawped in at us as they filed past, scanning the long table which was crowded with celebrities. I felt like a Christian being looked over by the Romans on their way to the arena. Jeremy was obviously in his element, cracking jokes and telling historical anecdotes. At one point we got on to Margaret Thatcher. Jeremy leaned forward and said to me with great deliberation, 'The lady *will not do*.' It certainly seemed to be Heath's night! And so it proved, when at last the protracted meal was over and the BBC had completed its last frantic whirl of making-up. A deadly calm of despair came over me as we filed into the debating chamber. The Union was packed to the ceiling; even the standing room had run out. Peter and I were greeted with catcalls and boos; there was warm applause for Jeremy and a crescendo of adulation for Heath, who took it with a new dignity.

The opening undergraduate speeches were fair enough. Though the girl who supported the Motion read every word, she was treated with gallantry. (That, at least, is something I shall be spared!) Then Peter opened for us. He said nothing particularly new and rather rambled on, completely unworried. I didn't think he did particularly well, but later Ted told me it came over very well on TV. Next Jeremy – and I suddenly realized he was out for a purely debating kill, and he did it brilliantly. His merciless cracks against us had them rolling in the aisles. At one point he turned and tore into us. If we thought membership was so disastrous, what would we do if the vote went against us? Resign – or hang on to office to operate a policy in which we did not believe? Enormous cheers from the audience. 'What answer should I give to that?' I asked Peter nervously. 'Ignore it,' he replied blandly. Then it was my turn. As I rose to my feet every word I had prepared seemed irrelevant. I forgot all about TV, concentrating all my efforts on that overwhelmingly hostile audience, wishing with all my heart that this numbing paralysis would leave me so that my natural debating powers could assert themselves. All I could do, I said to myself, was to get through it somehow and not *look* afraid. So I hit out. I had decided to concentrate on the issue of internationalism: the biggest appeal for the young in the EEC idea. The very title of the debate, 'This House says Yes to Europe', was typical of the sloppy thinking which dominated the pro-Market case, I said. It was necessary to define our terms more closely than that: 'Joad, thou shouldst be living at this hour.' For what did we mean by 'yes'? Yes on any terms? 'Yes,' called out Jeremy, so I turned on him. Exactly. His party had been in favour of entry even on the reactionary inward-looking terms negotiated by Heath. So it ill became him to quote the Lomé convention in aid of the 'internationalism' of the Community. He had voted for entry without *that*! Lomé had only been produced by the people who had rejected the Heath terms. By common consent it had been a triumph for Judith Hart and she remained implacably opposed to our entry. Why? Because even Lomé was not real internationalism: it was neo-colonial paternalism. The whole EEC concept of 'association' for the developing countries visualized lesser mortals rotating in the orbit of a superior power bloc. And what did we mean by Europe? Half its peoples and a third of its territory? The whole essence of the Common Market meant that we had to give priority to the Community over all the other international ties we had built up. And I instanced a whole list of examples: sugar, dairy produce, Malaysian pineapple (jeers at that: 'This audience wouldn't understand or care that this crop is the mainstay of the Malaysian economy,' I spat back). 'Is it internationalism,' I asked, 'to give priority to an Italian over a Malaysian, an Englishman over an Indian or a German over an Australian?' And I got my only cheer of the evening.

But as I began to get into my stride Jeremy was biding his time and he leapt up at this point to interrupt. 'Since the Right Honourable Lady thinks the Community is such a deplorable institution, if the country votes to stay in will she resign from the Government?' There it was: there was no escaping it. The audience went wild with delight. Hoots and catcalls drowned any attempt at reply. I turned and faced them, waiting for the row to die down and then said emphatically and slowly, 'If Britain votes to stay in the Common Market, my country will need me more than ever.' I was rather proud of it – and I meant it anyway. But the audience shrieked with derision, while Jeremy did a little jig in his place, turning his eyes heavenwards and drawing a mock halo round his head. By now my time was nearly up, and I had hardly got through half my material. I galloped to a close and sat down to the thinnest applause of the evening. Peter's congratulations were perfunctory. I knew I had been a flop, but my only feeling was one of relief that I had survived at all.

But the most remarkable phenomenon of the evening was Heath. The audience was all his, and he responded to it with a genuineness which was the most impressive thing I have ever seen from him. He stood there, speaking simply, strongly and without a note. They gave him a standing ovation at the end, and he deserved it for the best example I have ever seen of The Man Who Came Back. Then, mercifully, we were able to escape to the President's room for drinks and the slow stain of the misery of failure began to come through into my soul. Everyone was congratulating Heath and I did too. Everyone said what a first-class, gripping debate it had been. Heath was at his warmest and most natural and thanked me genuinely for the nice things I said to him. Then, about midnight, we heard the result: they had wiped the floor with us. Peter and I drove back to London and I just wanted to die. I don't mind being beaten – except by myself.

Wednesday, 4 June

Last night's debate is the talk of the town. Ted tells me it was superb TV, Heath coming over particularly well. A lot of papers have quoted my reply to Jeremy, which Ted says was 'splendid'. But what *didn't* come over on telly was the attitude of the audience, so no one would have guessed what we were up against.

Friday, 6 June

I didn't bother to go to Blackburn for referendum polling day, though Ted put in some work at Islington. Janet said to me, 'There are lots of letters about the TV debate.' 'Hostile,' I said, resigned. 'No,' she said. 'Only one against. The rest are very congratulatory.' And so, to my utter astonishment, they were – even from people who said they didn't agree with me. Apparently that reply of mine seems to have been a sensation. What interests me is the contempt they express for Jeremy. His Union debating style proved counter-productive with a non-Union audience.

Sunday, 8 June

Congratulatory letters still pouring in: balm to my bruised soul.

On 5 June the referendum campaign had reached its predictable result. For some time it had been clear that the verdict would be Yes, helped by the professionalism of the well-heeled 'Britain in Europe' campaign, dire warnings by British firms about the danger to jobs of a No vote, the prediction by the polls of a Yes victory, but above all by the confusion of Labour supporters when they saw their trusted Prime Minister, Harold Wilson, in conflict with their romantic hero, Tony Benn. The confusion was compounded by the cross-party alignments on the two rival platforms. If it was off-putting to see Roy Jenkins in public pro-Market harmony with Edward Heath and Jeremy Thorpe, it was equally bewildering to see Michael Foot consorting with Enoch Powell and right-wing Tory MPs like Ronald Bell at anti-Market press conferences. The strength of Harold Wilson's appeal was that he kept out of sight, relying on the published popular version of the case for staying in Europe to pull in the loyal Labour vote.

In this unheroic stance Harold Wilson was aided and abetted by the very press which was fond of castigating him for his lack of 'principle'. On the eve of the poll they came out in strength to praise the Government's line. The Daily Mirror *produced one of its famous four-page spreads to whip up pro-Market feeling and reproduced a VE Day cartoon by Philip Zec showing a wounded soldier pleading with the politicians not to throw away the 'peace in Europe' he had helped to win. Commentators everywhere hinted to the fearful that a vote against the Market was a vote for Tony Benn's domestic policies. When the result – a two to one Yes vote on a poll of about 65 per cent – was announced, the* Guardian *reported that the result had been received with satisfaction in financial circles. 'The first beneficiary was the Government', it commented on 7 June, 'which took the opportunity to announce the issue of a further £1,100 million of short-dated government stock to help finance its massive borrowing requirement.'*

The count was held on a county basis, Ted Short having failed to convince the Commons of the virtues of a central count. In the event this strengthened the pro-marketeers' claims because it showed that the vote in all areas approximated very closely to the national result of a 68·3 per cent Yes vote against a 32·8 per cent No. Even Scotland, which many people believed would vote heavily against membership, produced a Yes majority, though a 10 per cent smaller one. There were some slight variations on party lines, strong Conservative counties recording a higher than average Yes vote and turnout and strong Labour ones a lower than average, while some areas seemed to have been influenced by the views of pro- or anti- MPs. But the differences were so minimal as not to counteract the local effect of a national result. Only in London, where the turnout fell as low as 49 per cent in the five most Labour boroughs, was there any hint of the massive indifference to Europe which was to manifest itself four years later in the direct elections to the European Assembly.

The pro-Market press was naturally jubilant. Peter Jenkins in the Guardian *on 7 June described it as a 'Euroslide victory', adding that 'for practical purposes the verdict of the people means that the case is now closed'. David Watt wrote in the* Financial Times *on the same day: 'The Common Market issue is settled.' The* Daily Telegraph *congratulated Harold Wilson on his successful gamble, while the* Daily Mail *declared that 'the effect of this thunderous Yes will echo down the years'. For the most part the anti-marketeers accepted their defeat gracefully, Tony Benn declaring: 'I have just been in receipt of a very big message from the British people. I read it loud and clear. . . . By an overwhelming majority the British people have voted to stay in and I am sure that everyone would want to accept that.' Only Enoch Powell struck a defiant note, declaring that the result was 'provisional' and reminding the country of the words in the Government's own pamphlet: 'Our continued membership will depend on the continuing assent of Parliament.'*

It was not until October 1975 that the accounts of the campaigning organizations were available, whose publication the Government had provided for in the Referendum Act, hopefully as a protection against excessive spending by either side. The White Paper giving the accounts (Cmnd. 6251) showed that this disincentive had not prevented 'Britain in Europe' from spending nearly £1·5 million on the campaign, compared with just over £133,000 by the NRC, including the £125,000 from the Government. The list of contributions to 'Britain in Europe' funds, notably from industry and the stock exchange, filled eight columns of the White Paper, while the NRC could only muster seven private contributions, mainly from individuals, the largest sum being £1,377 from the Transport and General Workers' Union.

Press predictions that Harold Wilson would lose no time after the referendum in reshuffling his Cabinet were quickly vindicated. On Monday 9 June he switched Tony Benn from Industry to Energy, replacing him with Eric Varley. He demoted Reg Prentice from Education to Overseas Development, though forced to keep him in the Cabinet, and replaced him at Education with a right-wing pro-marketeer, Fred Mulley. Judith Hart, losing Overseas Development, decided to leave the Government. Mean-

408

while the economic storm clouds grew ever more menacing. Inflation had reached 25 per cent and Denis Healey was desperately negotiating with the TUC over a tough voluntary incomes policy and was pressing ahead in Cabinet with his plans for further public expenditure cuts in the longer term. Jack Jones was using all his influence to help the Government.

Monday, 9 June

Harold had called a Cabinet for this, the first working day after the referendum result. No agenda. No background papers. The sun was still shining brilliantly when I left HCF and yet I was glad to get back to reality. I remain astonished at the new sense of work vitality which possesses me. I am lured into taking on more and more burdens and instead of wanting to wind myself down from the limelight of responsibility, I am attracted to it like a moth to a flame. Perhaps it is like the drowning man who sees all his life's history concentrated before his eyes. I know I have not much longer to operate in the febrile, exacting and fulfilling world of power and some instinct makes me want to make the most of it.

To our surprise Fred was there, dark blotches under his eyes from the shock of the rail crash in which he was involved. We all commiserated with him. Harold swerved past me without a greeting into the Cabinet room and, when he had called us to order, it was in his best 'I'm going to get tough now', prime ministerial mood. I felt it didn't bode good to any of us Dissenting Ministers, though I doubt whether he will do a clean sweep immediately. That wouldn't be his style: he prefers picking people off one by one. As we waited outside the room I had asked Wedgie, 'Have you heard anything?' He had shrugged in his boyishly disarming way, 'Not a word.' Harold opened by saying rather grimly that he didn't intend to go over past events. With only one or two exceptions Ministers had kept to the guidelines during the recent campaign and he felt that its conduct had been 'reasonably satisfactory'. He then went on to remind us sternly that the agreement to differ ended on 5 June and he now intended to tighten up on some of the rules of procedure, which had become too relaxed even before the referendum campaign. We would have, for instance, to look at relations between Ministers and the NEC and there must be no issuing of speeches without clearance with the relevant Minister. The practice had also grown up of issuing speeches some days before delivery which led to trouble if the speech was later changed. The habit of the press of highlighting any alterations was a warning to us of the sort of morality we could expect from them. (These last two were a dig at Reg P.) Jim then said that he would like to circulate a memo to Cabinet indicating the sort of issues which were likely to be coming up in the EEC and how we should deal with them. He would also like to see EQs continue in being. It is clear that Jim is going to be busy mending his fences with the anti-marketeers from now on. The pro-marketeers as a whole, though not wholly avoiding looking like the cats that had got at the cream, were patently trying to restrain their jubilation. No gloating.

A brief discussion of the Stonehouse debate due on Thursday. Ted Short was on the whole in favour of going ahead with it but I protested that, since Stonehouse had tried to return to this country, however speciously, the public would condemn us for trying him *in absentia*. Shirley and others agreed with me though Eric Varley, who is clearly a secret pragmatist – not to say opportunist – whispered to me, 'If we postpone the by-election, we are less likely to win it.' Bob said robustly that we had been guided by the Select Committee all along and ought to be also on this point and so it was agreed.

At the office I had a lively meeting over my determination to get a better range of NHS spectacle frames. I would love to achieve a breakthrough here before I go. I sent officials away to follow up my ideas and went along to Home Policy Committee of the NEC, where I found the members busy discussing an office document on the nationalization of financial institutions, including the clearing banks. Wedgie was complaining with his familiar air of bewildered innocence that he had had a Question in the House that day suggesting that it was *his* document. It really was an impossible situation, he said, if the Research Department could not circulate a discussion document without him being accused of its authorship. Could we not have a clearer classification of the status of documents? There was a lot of sympathy with this and even Shirley, who attends regularly as a kind of watch-dog for the 'moderates', did not disagree with the document being circulated to the trade unions and others for comment, with a view to our drafting something for the 1976 programme. It was just another example of how the press, in their anxiety to discredit the Government, have made Wedgie, not only a hero of the Left, but a major political force. Every day there are articles about him which, far from doing him harm, turn him into a political giant, particularly as the criticisms are larded with grudging admissions of his abilities.

I have been interested to read in my box a letter from Wedgie to Harold setting out the steps he is proposing to take to establish warm and intimate relations with the Industrial Commissioner of the EEC. He has lost no time in sending Spinelli a personal telegram and even phoning him 'to express my good wishes'. That lad really is brilliant at taking avoiding action! Here am I, ready to accept that I must co-operate now with the Council of Ministers, but still nursing reticences and unhappiness about the Market, while Wedgie has been able to do a complete about-turn emotionally without any sense of inconsistency. I was just brooding on this in my room at the House when Judith came in, somewhat distraught, to borrow a cigarette. She was to be moved, she told me, from Overseas Development. I was taken aback, having been lulled this morning into a false sense of security by Harold's failure to announce any changes in the Government. Judith said Harold had offered her Transport, but she wouldn't take it. Where was everybody, I asked. In Tony's room, she replied. I went along. Tony Benn was sitting at his desk, a figure of tragedy, surrounded by a cortège of political advisers: Michael Meacher, Joe Ashton and other figures I could barely make out, because the curtains were drawn against the brilliant sun. The heat was stifling. 'Have you heard anything?' I asked. 'Yes,' he replied, 'I am to be moved to Energy.' I was staggered, my first feeling being that it was the cleverest move Harold could make. Wedgie said he had talked to Eric

[Varley], who has been offered Industry. Eric had written to Harold saying he would not take the job if Wedgie were to resign, as he seemed to be contemplating. It must be a straight swap or nothing. Wedgie was clearly hesitant. Harold had demanded an instant reply and Wedgie had been 'very rude' to him. He thought he was at least entitled to twenty-four hours to think it over. We all supported him on this. Apparently Michael [Foot] has been in and was ready to act as go-between.

As we sat mulling things over Judith was sent for by Harold again and came back saying she was back at Overseas Development after all. Great rejoicing all round. Had I heard anything? they asked. No, I said. 'Then you are all right. It is clear that you, Peter and Mike are not to be moved.' I consoled Wedgie: 'At least Harold has moved you to another power point in the Manifesto.' 'Yes,' he replied gloomily, 'but I shall have no part in the negotiations with the oil companies. Harold has made it clear that that will remain with Harold Lever's committee.' 'But as Secretary of State they can't keep you out of the picture,' I replied. 'And if things are going the wrong way, you can bring it to Cabinet. It gives you a better resigning position.' I think he had already made up his mind to accept, however reluctantly. After an hour of this I could not stand any more of the airless, sweaty heat, so Ted and I went off to eat with Judith and Tony Hart. We speculated as to why Harold had changed his mind over her job and decided he must have offered it to Reg Prentice as demotion and had been faced by a row. Judith said the rumour was that Roy Jenkins had threatened to resign if Reg Prentice was moved out of the Cabinet. Whatever the reason we rejoiced that she was back at ODM. 'Though Transport would have been a challenge,' said Tony Hart almost wistfully.

Tuesday, 10 June

The newspapers are full of Wedgie's 'triumph' at Questions yesterday, the first time the proceedings of the House have been broadcast live. Some of the most ecstatic comments were from enemy papers. 'Big Benn is the star of the air!' said the *Sun*. 'Commons radio starts with sparkling Benn cut and thrust', said the *Financial Times*. 'Benn a hit in radio Commons', said the *Daily Telegraph*, while even Andrew Alexander talked about his 'dignity and skill'. Which confirms my view that (a) the press are doing more than anyone else to build up Wedgie and (b) that you have got to have certain attributes to be a successful rebel: you must shine on the platform and in the House. Wedgie does both, which is why he can get away with murder.

At Social Services Committee of Cabinet I faced another example of the philistinism of the Treasury. I had hoped to get routine approval for the publication of our White Paper on Mental Illness, on which David has done an excellent job. There has been no inter-departmental disagreement about the policy and we had promised the House publication before the summer recess. But suddenly Treasury started saying the 'timing' was inopportune. Even though the whole purpose of the White Paper was to warn local authorities that the ten-year programme might have to be extended for much longer owing to a shortage of resources, Joel Barnett argued that the setting out of a long-term plan raised expectations of expenditure. I fought hard. Eventually I got off fairly lightly by having to agree that we should discuss the contents of the

White Paper generally with the steering committee of the new joint consultative body the Government has set up with the local authorities and get their reaction.

Alex Kitson came to see me about a health matter and spent the first quarter of an hour talking politics. He was very disturbed about the rumours that Wedgie was to be moved, and about the result of the referendum, but said that Harold could always rely on Jack Jones's 'blind loyalty'. (It fascinates me how completely Jack has forgiven Harold for his part in the *In Place of Strife* saga. The breach between Jack and me has been partially healed during the anti-Market campaign, but I don't think he will ever completely trust me again. Alex remains my devoted slave, hugging me when he arrived. How much loyalties in politics depend on stray incidents! The only thing Alex stubbornly remembers about me is that I was the Minister of Transport who *volunteered* the reduction in lorry drivers' statutory hours.) Alex said that Jack got into trouble with the T and G Executive for his loyalty to Harold. He had had a rough time with them. 'He's the boss,' said Alex, 'so we are loyal to him. "Blind loyalty" if you like.'

Having been up till 1am this morning at the House, I paired so as to be reasonably fresh for the Report stage of our Pensions Bill tomorrow. I got to the flat at 8pm. I had just got out of my clothes into something cool and was planning to eat my bacon and egg while I watched *Edward VII* on TV when the phone rang. No. 10. The PM would like to see me at 9pm. 'We will send a car.' This is it, I thought. We were all being premature when we thought Wedgie was going to be the only one to be dealt with. I dressed again, as relaxed as I always am when disaster strikes. My head went up as I worked out how I would act when Harold told me he wanted me out. He had the right to do it, just as he had a right to move Wedgie. After all, Harold was the referendum victor and there had been little doubt that he would exploit his victory. Not excessively, that is not his way, but to the maximum extent compatible with what the party would tolerate. And as Ted has pointed out to me several times in the last few weeks, Harold has an excuse in my case on the grounds of age. So when the car came I walked down to it with all the poise I could muster, feeling like Anne Boleyn walking to the scaffold in the TV series on Henry VIII: my Dorothy Tutin to Harold's Keith Michell? 'Henry feasted while Anne died', I thought to myself. In the car I chatted nonchalantly to the driver. My thoughts were racing. I have got to go soon. What better way than when my political allies can argue that I have been victimized? But do one's political friends care when it comes to the crunch? I felt very lonely. I doubted they did.

The meeting was to be at the House, though if Harold thought that would disguise the comings and goings he was being very naïve. The private secretary greeted me apologetically: did I suspect sympathy? As I waited in the ante-room I felt – or imagined – that Ken Marks [Labour MP for Gorton and Harold's PPS] and Doreen, one of the secretaries, were embarrassed in their elaborate friendliness. 'Come in, please, Secretary of State,' the message came at last. It was 9.20pm. Harold was pacing up and down in his shirt-sleeves, enjoying himself. 'Sit here,' he said, indicating the chair next to his. He played out the drama, knowing full well what I was thinking. 'Barbara, as I am always loyal and never more loyal to anyone than to you, I wanted to see you to say that I want to take your junior Minister.' I was puzzled while he grinned. 'Alec Jones,' he explained. 'I want him for the Welsh Office.' 'But he's very good,' I protested mildly, 'and we have the Report stage of the Pension Bill tomorrow.' 'But I'm going to give you the one you asked for in the first place: Michael Meacher.' The significance of that remark did not dawn on me then for I was very pleased. 'Oh, he'd be first-class.' 'Right, then,' he said. He was too busy to offer me a drink. 'These reshuffles are hell,' he said, resuming his pacing. 'None of you know what ulcers they give me. All this multilateral moving about. But it's going very well. When it is all over you will say that the old boy has not lost his touch. It is pure poetry.' Then he added defensively, 'What I have done about Wedgie – he's accepted by the way – has nothing to do with the referendum. I planned it as long ago as Easter. And I've dealt with Reg Prentice. I have offered him the one job he cannot refuse: the one he resigned from because he said he believed in it so much.' So Reg has got ODM after all! In the Cabinet I suspect. Otherwise Harold would have faced Roy Jenkins's revolt. I tried to recapture some of our old relationship. 'I must say your move for Wedgie was brilliantly cunning,' I told him. 'I said to myself: "The old basket has outmanoeuvred us again." You have moved him to another power point in the Manifesto.' 'I've moved him to a job where he will be commanding millions of pounds worth of oil as it comes flowing in,' replied Harold. 'I told Wedgie he ought to accept,' I continued. 'You are a good girl,' he replied. 'I could never get you to be a bad girl even in the days when you and I were younger.' (I am always amused by this myth he perpetuates between us. As I remember those days, he never even tried to make a pass at me.) 'But,' I persisted, 'there is one sour note in what you have done. You must not move Judith from ODM. Apart from anything else, she did marvellously. Do you realize how much what she achieved at Lomé helped you in the referendum campaign? If she hadn't, you would have been extremely vulnerable.' He got restive, looking at the clock and moving to the door. 'I have got an announcement to make at 10pm.' I could see the point of that and left, shooting out to the waiting car, thankful to be free at last to cook my bacon and egg, for I was starving.

Back at the flat I had just shed my hot clothes again (we are never equipped for a heat wave in this country) and had started to cook my long-delayed bacon and egg (too late now for *Edward VII* but just time for the 10pm news) when the phone rang again. I cursed. It was Wedgie. 'Barbara, Harold has moved Judith from ODM after all. He has offered her Transport and she has refused. We are all here in my room, except Peter, and we are going to see Harold to tell him we won't take it. Will you come?' 'Oh, God,' I groaned, 'I haven't got a car. And I'm starving. Look, I've just come back from Harold and he is making the announcement at 10pm.' 'Never mind then, duckie. We'll go without you.' 'No,' I shouted, 'but the news is just starting. We must listen to that first. I'll ring you back'. Clutching a charred bit of bacon I hurried to listen to the news. Yes, there it was: Reg P. for ODM. No mention of Judith. I grabbed the phone, only to be told by the House of Commons switchboard that Wedgie had put his absent button on. 'We have been inundated with calls from the press trying to reach him' (for, of course, his new job was announced at the same time). I was distraught. I must get down to the House to support Judith, but taxis are almost unobtainable in Islington. In despair I phoned Ted at the town hall. 'I have to get down to the House. Can you leave your committee and take me?' 'Of course,' said

Ted, identifying himself as always with the dramas in which I am involved. I hurriedly re-dressed, gulping the rest of my charred bacon. Twenty minutes later Ted arrived, announcing, 'I can't take you in my car as I'm out of petrol.' I groaned. Never had a wife a husband who managed to combine complete loyalty with patches of practical unreliability more exasperatingly. The times I have found in a crisis that he had a flat battery, was out of petrol or had forgotten to blow up his tyre. . . . 'I'll get a cab,' he shouted, hurrying downstairs, obviously dreading the worst for me. When I followed him I found him standing in the middle of the road, trying to flag down the most unlikely vehicles. 'It's too late, too late,' I shouted, in despair at the feeling that I had let Judith down. Wasn't she feeling as I had been feeling just an hour or so ago? Then, as always, Ted's luck – the luck of the happy-go-lucky – held. A taxi drew up. On the way down I told Ted the whole story. He was immensely relieved for me. We raced up to Wedgie's room to find the usual crowd of mourners sitting behind drawn curtains in that steamy heat. Judith was holding court. 'Am I too late?' I panted. No, they said. 'Mike and Wedgie are seeing Harold now.' I raced downstairs to Harold's room, sweeping the private secretary aside. 'I'm going in to see the PM,' I announced and walked in. Harold was sitting in his chair, glass in hand, looking tired. Ken Marks was watching, fascinated. 'You were here only a short while ago,' said Harold amiably. The atmosphere was relaxed as Mike and Wedgie greeted me with pleasure. But it was soon clear that, in his inimitably gentle way, Mike was laying it down the line. 'We're not trying to blackmail or threaten you, Harold. You have the right to make what appointments you choose. But then other people have the right to decide their position in the light of those appointments.' Harold gave us the old routine about the agony of these reshuffles. 'None of you know the job it is: the multilateral dispositions that have to be made. None of you know what this does to me.' We said we did. 'But,' said Wedgie, 'you must realize that during these past few weeks the seven of us have worked as a team. We are not going to leave anyone on the battlefield.' Harold tried to make out that the Ministry of Transport was a worthwhile job. 'Look what Barbara made of it.' 'Not outside the Cabinet,' said Mike firmly. Harold was keeping his temper very well. 'I've never discussed Cabinet changes with anyone before,' he said mildly. 'Has no one else threatened to go on strike?' I murmured impishly. He had to admit they had: we knew Roy had laid it down the line on Reg Prentice's behalf. It helped to make our intervention less of an impertinence. 'But I'm already over the number of Cabinet posts,' Harold complained. 'I'd have to legislate.' 'You can do it if you want to,' said Mike tenaciously. 'Unless,' said Harold slyly, lookng at me, 'I were to give Judith Social Services, which she has had before.' 'You can have my job for Judith,' I replied promptly. 'That's no answer,' retorted Wedgie. 'We're not leaving Barbara on the battlefield either.' The circular argument went on, Mike leaving Harold in no doubt that, if Judith were demoted, we would all resign, 'and Peter is with us on this, too'. I spoke eloquently, though I can't for the life of me remember what I said. Wedgie gave one of his amusing little homilies. 'I'm really quite a simple guy, Harold, and I'm certainly not after your job. You once called me an Old Testament prophet and that is just what I am. There are just certain ideas that I think ought to be spelt out and I spell them out.' After nearly an hour of this I suddenly took pity on Harold, having to show infinite patience after a long and exacting day. 'We shan't solve this argument by trying to beat this man into the ground physically,' I told the other two. 'I think we ought to have some mercy on Harold and leave him alone to think over what we have said.' 'There *are* two boxes to do,' said Harold, still mildly. As we got up to leave Mike repeated without menaces that we were not prepared to see one of our team sacrificed. We would like to see Harold again tomorrow if necessary. At the door I said to Harold warmly, 'Thank you for your courtesy', and I meant it. Outside Wedgie and Mike hugged me enthusiastically: 'You were magnificent.' 'Barbara was magnificent,' they told the crowd waiting upstairs. God knows why. 'Not more than these two,' I replied. Judith thanked us effusively. 'We've told him we shall return to the attack tomorrow,' said Mike. 'I think we are going to win', I assured Judith. And so to bed at 1am. 'My early night,' I groaned. But my conscience was at rest.

Wednesday, 11 June

At the office I warned Norman, in strictest privacy, what might happen. 'You may find yourself not only without a Parliamentary Secretary for the Report stage of the Pensions Bill this afternoon, but without a Secretary of State.' 'That would be a great pity,' he replied. But I went ahead, briefing myself on some of the complex amendments I had to move, just in case Harold did give in. Then suddenly Norman came into my room to say that Mrs Judith Hart was making 'a personal statement on Rhodesia' that afternoon. I was flabbergasted. At the House I put my head into Mike's room and asked him if he knew what was happening. He was as bewildered as I was. 'I've been in touch with Harold again and said we would want to see him today to settle this matter,' he replied. 'But I now hear that Judith has been making statements all over the place.' 'She is making one in the House now,' I replied. We hurried down. Judith came into the Chamber rather coyly, notes in hand, and slipped deprecatingly into a seat on the front bench below the gangway. Anyway, one mystery was soon solved. She was making her personal statement *after* Jim's statement on Rhodesia, not on it. As she spoke, announcing her resignation from the Government rather emotionally, I couldn't help wondering what it was all supposed to be in aid of. What was she trying to prove? That she personally had been victimized[1] or that there was a great political point in the return of the Ministry of Overseas Development to Foreign Office tutelage? I certainly deplore that and I am nauseated by the cynical way in which Harold plays ducks and drakes with this whole question of overseas aid. He made a great political point in 1964 about his intention to create a separate Ministry of Overseas Development 'with a seat in the Cabinet'. And he gave me the job. As soon as he had moved me from ODM to Transport he demoted my old Ministry to outside the Cabinet (though it was still a separate Ministry). When we came back to office in 1974 he made ODM a separate Ministry again, giving Judith Cabinet status and charge of her own department. Now, to fit into his reshuffle jigsaw puzzle, he has put Reg P. *in* the Cabinet but as Minister of Overseas Development *under* the FO. It is this kind of behaviour that makes one

[1] In her statement she said: 'Frankly, I can see no reason for the Prime Minister to sack me from my Ministry.' (Hansard 11.6.75, col. 419)

despair of him. He subordinates all considerations, not only of principle but of administrative effectiveness, to his balance of power manoeuvrings. If Judith had stuck to this point, I would have applauded her. As it was I felt slightly embarrassed. Afterwards I learned that it was her political adviser, Tony Banks, who had told her she must make a statement. Mike was furious. 'It's bloody nonsense,' he said to me in the division lobby. 'Here we are, bringing pressure on Harold to put her in the Cabinet at Transport, and we would have won.'

The Report stage on the Pensions Bill went smoothly enough. It began with a discussion on the mobility allowance. Of course, the Tory Opposition attacked the Bill's 'restrictiveness' and wanted more, but when Lewis Carter-Jones and Bruce Douglas-Mann joined in, and it looked like being another defeat for us, I laid about me with a will, saying that of course the Government had to draw the financial parameters. We had been lucky to be able to spend an additional £19 million on this. Enoch sat smiling at my toughness. I thought to myself, 'You've done yourself down again, Barbara. This is no way to win friends and influence people, talking the crude truth like that.' But in the division lobby I was surprised to see all our people there. Lewis came and exculpated himself to me and when later I ran into Douglas-Mann he stopped to load me with extravagant praise about my speech at the Oxford Union debate. 'My wife and I sat glued to the TV, cheering you on. You were magnificent. It was the only time in the whole campaign in which I felt someone was expressing my own doubts.' I remain totally mystified about that debate. I don't *feel* inside me that I made a good speech, but the letters of ecstatic praise come rolling in – forty of them so far.

When I slipped out of the Chamber for some food I joined the table where Mik, Russ Kerr and Jo Richardson were sitting. Mik was at his sourest and I learned afterwards that the Tribune group had just held a meeting at which they denounced Wedgie's move from Industry. 'Five of you could have stopped it in its tracks by just threatening to resign, but none of you were willing to risk your jobs,' he said savagely. 'That's a lie, Mik,' I replied equally savagely. But, looking back, I wondered why none of us had thought of going on strike to stop Wedgie's switch, though we were ready to do so for Judith's. Of course we would have done so if Harold had tried to sack him, but I suspect that we were more than prepared for Wedgie's move. We have all suffered from his habit of writing Labour policy by ministerial edict. The Department of Industry enabled him to be all things to the Labour movement with none of the restraints the rest of us face. 'The prima donnas can look after themselves,' I told Mik. 'And if Harold tries to water down the Industry Bill Wedgie is still in the Cabinet. It is the second eleven you ought to worry about. Harold has been picking them off one by one.' But I couldn't get them interested in Judith. They just shrugged. But it is in fact the second eleven dispositions that worry me most. The penny has now dropped about Michael Meacher. Glad as I am to have him at DHSS, his transfer is just part of Harold's determination to denude the Department of Industry of all its former devotees. And one of the things that shocks me most is the removal of Joan Lestor from the Foreign Office. As that dispatch from Ghana showed, she was obviously a breath of fresh air in that airless institution and I gather that her move was due to personal representations by Jim to Harold. He had found her behaviour 'embarrassing' to him. I shan't forgive Jim for that. She is to go to Education: again, a move no one can really complain about unless they are in the know. But Joan working to Fred Mulley....

Thursday, 12 June

Wore my new striped kaftan dress to Cabinet and the enthusiasm with which it was greeted cheered up my morale. In a private word beforehand Peter told me: 'Of course I would have been with you over Judith. What a mess she has made of things!' Cabinet agenda was so light we did not meet till 11.30am, and even then Harold was late. We began with a lighthearted touch over how we should celebrate the American bicentenary over here. Harold suggested a joint meeting with the United States Congress in Westminster Hall and the presentation of a copy of Magna Carta. Willie grumbled that that had no significance whatsoever for Scotland, but he was swept aside. Someone suggested that we ought to ask for a historic American document in return. 'Why not ask for the Statue of Liberty?' I murmured. Wedgie had us rolling with his proposal that at the joint meeting we ought solemnly to repeal the legislation passed against America 200 years ago, together with the tea tax. But the mood changed when Jim reported on Idi Amin's threat to execute a couple of Britishers in Uganda.[1] Jim said he was taking Kenyatta's advice and he hoped Cabinet would be understanding if we had to make some crawling gestures. Amin was a psychiatric case, not a political one. And he agreed that we really needed a psychiatrist, not a politician, to advise us. Maudling and the Opposition, with whom Jim said he had kept in close touch, were behaving very responsibly. (I doubt if the press will, I thought to myself. They'd risk a man's life for a sensationalist story against the Government.) Harold told us an astonishing story about Amin's pathological state of mind. Amin had written to Harold sympathizing with him over Will Hamling's[2] death. Harold had sent him a very warm reply in return and the chap was absolutely delighted with it. Jim and Harold then launched on a long dissertation on the Middle East, which was as usual mumbled and difficult to follow. The minutes ticked by and then, suddenly, when Harold turned to Denis for comments, Denis burst out with all his suppressed anxieties about the state of sterling. 'This morning we have had the most severe attack on sterling we have ever had. It has cost us 500 million dollars to hold the rate even here. *We have got to stop the slide.* I have been talking to the central bankers in Paris and the real reason for this run is the widespread feeling that we lack the will to deal with inflation. If the railways strike materializes – or, worse still, if we

[1] Denis Hills, a British lecturer in Uganda, had described President Amin as a tyrant in the unpublished manuscript for a book to be called *The White Pumpkin*. For this he was found guilty of treason and Amin threatened to execute him unless the Foreign Secretary flew to Kampala for talks on a series of Ugandan demands. Amin turned down a plea for clemency from the Queen, but later, after mediation by President Mobutu of Zaire, Hills was allowed to return to London from Kampala with Mr Callaghan. Stanley Smolen, the other British subject, was accused of the non-capital offence of hoarding soap and cooking oil, but Amin had threatened to execute him if he was found guilty. The military tribunal trying his case acquitted him on 19 June.
[2] Will Hamling, Labour MP for Greenwich, Woolwich West, and Harold Wilson's Parliamentary Private Secretary, had died on 20 March 1975.

give in to the NUR – the position would be untenable. I am beginning to think that I cannot wait till July.' We just sat silent and worried.

It was late before we got on to the main item: whether we should drop Clause 4 of the Housing Finance Bill by accepting a Tory amendment in the Lords.[1] Tony C. was at his most loftily practical: why risk a humiliating defeat for a clause which in any case had become 'otiose'? After a number of people had supported him I raised my voice, saying that for political reasons it was essential that we should have been seen to have fought to the end to fulfil our pledge to remove the disqualification from the Clay Cross councillors. Wedgie supported me in a speech of his usual analytical fluency. Eventually we won, at least to the extent of Cabinet deciding to resist the Tory amendment and take the situation to the party meeting after that. These pragmatic 'moderates' have no feel for the party's sensitivities at all.

I have decided to outdo Wedgie on the EEC. The Council of Ministers will be discussing social matters next week and so will be attended by social service Ministers. There is nothing of any great importance coming up, so the office had assumed we would be sending the Parliamentary Secretary. Alec Jones's transfer to the Welsh Office gives me an excuse to announce that I shall go myself. I'm sure Hindmarsh [Under Secretary in the DHSS International Relations Division] will be furious at my intervention, which adds to the zest.

Friday, 13 June

NALGO has come out flatly against private medical practice at its annual conference and has called on local branches to oppose all planning applications for private hospitals. If I hadn't made my statement on pay beds last month, we should be in grave trouble now with the unions.

Monday, 16 June

Before I could go to Luxembourg I had to attend another all-day meeting at Chequers, this time of the devolution committee on which Ted Short is trying desperately to force the pace. Harold has got very fond of these Chequers meetings, and it is certainly a pleasanter place to meet than No. 10. The significant thing about this meeting was the attempt of Denis, Roy J. *et al.* to back-track on the whole devolution idea, on the grounds that the Common Market referendum result in Scotland showed that the Scots Nats were a busted flush. Ted was furious because there have been extensive leaks in the Scottish press to the effect that the Government was retreating from its original plans. I backed Ted on the grounds that we could still manage to detach devolution from separatism if we stuck to our guns, but

---

[1] The clause was designed to fulfil our promise to lift the disqualification of the Clay Cross councillors who had refused to implement the Tory Housing Finance Act. The clause was otiose in the sense that the Councillors had already incurred a further five years' disqualification on an entirely separate issue. In the event the Lords deleted the clause. An attempt on 4 August to reinstate it in the Commons was defeated by the defection of a few Labour MPs who refused to condone 'defiant and purposeful violation of the law of Parliament'. (See pages 64 and 486.)

that if we retreated now we should play into the Scots Nats hands – quite apart from the fact that they would cease to support us in Parliament. So once again the doubters were beaten down. The discussion was enlivened by another of Wedgie's scintillating philosophical speeches. The government machine in this country, he said, was 'centralized, bureaucratic, secretive and out of touch'. The English Establishment had lost confidence in itself. 'There is talk of the breakdown in our society, in which I do not believe.' Of course, he continued, there was concern about all the changes that were taking place. 'Metrication has made me an alien in my own country.' (That from the chap who gave us the complications of the Post Code!) In these changes we were dealing with people's 'environment of authority'. We had to remember that democracy grew from below. 'There is something ludicrous in the idea of the Cabinet Office and Dr Gallup giving us a map for the future.' We could not just hand over power at the first sign of trouble. 'People's response must be ready.' So what did all this amount to? Apparently he wanted to 'maintain the impetus and argue for devolution and speak for the people who are alienated'. But again, apparently, we should not impose our solutions from above. 'We are muddling up the role of Moses with drawing up rules for the Knesset.' This meant we must publish our document but 'we will not carry through a change of this size without specific endorsement'. So we might even have to hold a constitutional conference. Once again I was divided in my mind over Wedgie: a maddening mixture of the bogus theoretician and the genuine visionary.

I had to leave early to catch a Defence plane to Luxembourg. On the way John Fraser and I swopped notes on the line we should take tomorrow on the directive on Equality of Rights for Women in Employment – one of those pretentious pieces of EEC 'legislation' which can be as grandiose as you like because everyone ignores them when it suits them. The bit that concerned me was the reference to complete equality of treatment in pension rights, which was a nonsense as it stood and would have cut right across our new Pensions Bill. We arrived at Luxembourg in time for the President's dinner. This year the Irish are heading the Commission and President Ritchie Ryan has been working desperately hard to make an impact with everyone. Luxembourg was as pretty as a picture and looked prosperous. I put on my favourite Mauritian dress and swept into the club where the dinner was to be held, feeling full of mischief. Of course, there was considerable interest in the appearance of this British anti-marketeer and over dinner I got into a lively discussion with the French Minister of Finance, trying to explain to him in my erratic French how counter-productive I thought these ill-thought-out directives were. 'A law is a law and should be drafted with the intention that it shall be enforced,' I said. He was greatly amused. Ortoli, who had shied away from me as if I might bite when we were first introduced, came up to me again more confidently after dinner. (If I could ignore that telegram, why should not he?)[1] 'She is the most Community-minded member of us all,' said the

---

[1] As part of the referendum campaign I had sent a telegram to M. Ortoli, then President of the Commission, on 18 May. In it I asked him the following questions:

1. Will the Commission undertake that the British Government's plan to save British Leyland will not be declared illegal under Article 92 of the Treaty of Rome?

French Minister. All I know is that I have no time for the shambling discussions and hypocritical attitudinizing of which I have had so much at these international conferences. If Britain is in the Common Market, for better or for worse, I want to see that the EEC institutions develop some of the intellectual discipline we have to have in our own Government.

Tuesday, 17 June

True to my intentions, I took the day's discussions *au sérieux*. In fact I made quite a powerful speech, pointing out the implications of the proposed wording about pensions equality. They were clearly staggered when I told them that to equalize the retirement age of men and women at sixty in Britain would cost £1,400 million, 'which my country just has not got at the present time'. But what shook them even more was my revelation that, as the words stood, it would not be possible for any of us to go on insisting that the family allowance must be paid to the mother and not the father. They just hadn't thought the thing out at all. My old friend, Walter Leber, chuckled at my energetic denunciations and backed my amendments. The Commissioner hastened to say he would consider them. The young Irish chairman of the Council egged me on. So, after a wordy debate it was agreed the Commission should take this bit back. I then excused myself gracefully and returned early to London, leaving John Fraser to wrangle for hours over the other points about employment. I was told afterwards that, at a late hour, when the discussion had been going in fruitless circles, the chairman had rapped the table and said reproachfully, 'Gentlemen, what would Barbara Castle say if she were here?'

Worked late on my papers for Friday's crucial Cabinet meeting at Chequers on economic strategy which some of us have been pressing for. The implications for public expenditure are quite terrifying.

Wednesday, 18 June

Quite a show in the press about my EEC debut! And of course my pro-Market ministerial colleagues are teasing me mercilessly. At Legislation Committee (where I had to fight to prevent Ted Short from knocking my Pay Beds Bill out of next year's programme) I whispered to Mike, 'Have *you* got an economic strategy for dealing with the crisis?' 'Some of us ought to meet tonight,' he replied. 'I am trying to fix a dinner somewhere. Can you come?' Of course, I said I could and would, even though it meant missing the Report stage of the Sex Discrimination Bill and getting David to move an amendment in which we were interested. But with the pound still weaken-

---

2. If Britain stays in the Common Market, will you guarantee that we will not be obliged to put further taxes on imported food such as mutton and lamb from New Zealand and Canadian wheat?

3. Do you agree that laws passed by the British Parliament should have priority in the British courts over EEC regulations?

On 29 May his *Chef de Cabinet* replied saying the President felt that 'given the controversial nature of these matters in the current referendum campaign in the United Kingdom, it would not be right for the Commission to make statements on them which would inevitably be quoted by one side or the other in support of their respective positions in the campaign'.

ing, and with the AUEW, despite some rather feeble efforts by Hughie to prevent it, voting at its conference to reject the Social Contract, I had no doubt that economic strategy had overwhelming priority. Before we met at the Gay Hussar I had time to read the document on strengthening the voluntary pay policy which Mike has circulated for Friday's meeting. I also read the TUC's draft statement for Congress on 'The Development of the Social Contract', which has already been through the Economic Committee and is going to the General Council on 25 June.[1] The TUC has certainly gone further than it ever has in spelling out the minutiae of a voluntary incomes policy and has even put its toes in the waters of 'norms', flat rate increases and the Heathian formula of a combination of flat rate and percentage increases. But, as Peter Shore said tonight, can it deliver?

We met in that cosy little upstairs private room of almost Edwardian intimacy where I have attended so many traumatic meetings. I was tense, having spent an hour sketching out some ideas for our line of action for Friday's meeting. Janet had duplicated my notes and I distributed them as people arrived but, with the wives present, the conversation skated over all sorts of scintillating political gossip before we could get down to the hard core of the argument. Mike and Jill were there; also Peter. Caroline arrived, looking as distractingly pretty as always in her fashionably informal clothes and windswept hair-do. She was shrugging her shoulders in distaste about the top brass ceremonial she and Wedgie had just been through as he had been turning on the valve to start the flow of North Sea oil. When Wedgie himself arrived, waving the menu aside with indifference, asking for a coca cola and settling for a bitter lemon ('I can't even get a coca cola at the Dorchester'), we at last got down to the serious discussion. Wedgie sat in brooding silence while the rest of us chattered as the food was served. People glanced at my paper and tossed it aside. Peter, nominated into the chair, spelt out the economic problem, adding that Hughie Scanlon had hardly made our job on Friday easier. Mike agreed, but insisted that there was still no alternative to beavering away at a voluntary policy. The TUC memo was a very good document and he had hopes of persuading the unions to adopt a 15 per cent target of wage increases or a flat £9 across the board. Peter said gloomily, 'If what Michael wants proves possible by September, it will be marvellous. If not——.' Tommy Balogh, appealed to for economic advice, shook his head: 'I believe the answer is not economic but political.' (But he had let show earlier that he still hankers after a statutory incomes policy.) I developed my ideas about getting the message across, right down the line, but no one seemed particularly interested. During all this time Wedgie sat mute until his silence built up into the loudest comment of all. Eventually Peter could no longer resist the 'If only I could tell all——' aura that was exuding from him. 'I think we would all like your views,' he said. Thus encouraged, Wedgie burst out into one of his Old Testament prophet pronouncements. (He is

[1] The first draft of the document embodied six main aims: the need to fix a target for inflation to be achieved by mid-1976; a figure for pay increases, related to this target, in the form of a flat-rate money increase; a cut-off point for pay increases in the case of very high incomes; radical action to limit price increases through the Price Code and subsidies; a major reduction in the level of unemployment in 1976; and the maintenance and development of the Social Contract. At its meeting on 25 June the General Council agreed that these points should be defined more specifically.

hugely pleased with this description of him, as he keeps telling us.) Listening to the discussion, he said, he had been struck by the way the only aspect of the crisis any of us had talked about was wages. 'We are now in the middle of the biggest attack on the unions and the Labour movement in our history.' Every day the press mounted a barrage against the unions; the whole crisis was reduced to their wage demands. There was no talk about the deep crisis in British industry itself, due to the failure to liberate the enthusiasm and self-identification with the future of their country of working men and women. We had talked about the danger of coalition. 'There is already a coalition on the Industry Bill,' he declared. The Government would only be able to get its watering-down of the Bill through the House with the help of the Tories and the CBI. The unions were our last line of defence. 'Now as in 1931 we are selling them out.' Of course, wages played some part in the crisis, but not the whole or even the major part. 'Our first job as a Labour Government is to defend the trade union movement.' Mike could stand no more. 'You are dodging it,' he exploded. 'The best way to defend the trade union movement is for them to have a policy that deals with the country's problems.' ('Sounds just like me on *In Place of Strife*,' I thought to myself.) We just could not run away from the fact, Mike continued, that inflation threatened to undermine everything we were trying to do. The TUC now recognized it in its document. Did he disagree with that document? Wedgie admitted he had not read it yet. I came in equally vigorously to point out that, if inflation was not brought under control, we would face such reductions in the social wage as to knock our whole progress towards social equality for six. 'Of course we must refuse to accept the cuts on Barbara's programmes,' murmured Wedgie, climbing down a bit. And so we left it, nothing concrete having been agreed. But then that is not the purpose of the exercise.

Thursday, 19 June

The fact that we Dissenting Ministers are not an organized cabal was proved at Cabinet. Main item was the renewed discussion on Peter Shore's long-postponed statement on industrial democracy. The committee Harold had set up under the Lord Chancellor to decide what the statement should contain had by a large majority come down against Peter's desire to set up an 'external inquiry' to look into the whole matter. The TUC is opposing this idea, particularly in view of the proposed terms of reference. Mike is backing the TUC, and Peter and his Department had been in a minority of the committee. But, in view of the importance of the matter, Elwyn as chairman had agreed that it could come to Cabinet. Peter opened with a powerful speech. He was sorry to challenge the committee's findings, but what the TUC was seeking was not just workers' participation but 'joint control of the private sector'. That might be the answer, but 'it needs to be thought through'. What this meant was the joint appointment of management and joint control of the financial operations of a company. 'This may be the kind of revolutionary change this country needs, but we have an absolute duty to consider it seriously.' There was one crucial issue that divided us from the TUC: they wanted us to accept in advance that whatever form of industrial democracy was adopted should be based on the trade unions. He thought there were all sorts of people, not in unions, who must not be left out, so the TUC terms were unacceptable.

Mike, as often, began almost hesitantly, but built up to a crescendo of conviction. He reminded us that the Government through its Manifesto was committed to a Bill to implement industrial democracy. The TUC said this was a political matter which could not be settled by an 'independent' committee. Whatever the committee's findings, the Government would have to make up its own mind in the end, so why go through this elaborate, time-wasting device? To my surprise, Tony C. backed Mike, but it was soon clear that the committee (which we learned later had been attended mainly by junior Ministers) did not reflect the views of the majority of Cabinet. A massive counter-attack was soon mounted in favour of an external enquiry, initiated by Roy Mason and followed by every right-winger in turn. Denis even put on the cap of humility. 'We don't understand enough about the workings of industry to make decisions like this, nor do our civil servants.' The alternative of an internal enquiry was therefore no good. We needed a 'broad-based committee to kick the ball around'. But it should have wider terms of reference, covering all aspects of workers' democracy. Jim, who is going through one of his intermittent phases of disillusionment with the unions, agreed with him. We couldn't introduce far-reaching changes without 'winning consent' generally, he said. On that basis, I thought, we should never get any changes at all and I came out strongly on Mike's side. The trouble with this 'external enquiry', I maintained, was that it could actually embarrass us politically. 'You can produce any result you like from any committee of enquiry according to the membership you choose.' I could just see the format: some people from the CBI, some from the TUC and some independent members holding the ring. So the findings of the committee would be in the hands of 'independents', whatever that meant. Of course, the unions were confused and divided on this issue, but there was a strong current of instinct flowing in the direction of greater sharing of responsibility and we should welcome it. And we should lead it, too. We should have an internal examination of all the implications and then produce a Green Paper to act as a catalyst. Because in the end the decision would be ours, however many people had a nibble at it. But nothing would happen unless the Government proposed something. Harold Lever backed Peter and so, to my disappointment, did Eric Varley. He is a very nice lad and, as he sits next to me, I get all his asides. He is a curious mixture, aligning instinctively with what is very roughly called the 'Left' these days, and yet with a deeply ingrained pragmatism which can still lead him astray. He is not theoretical enough to be safe from political oversimplification. On this occasion he once again revealed his antagonism to the unions, telling us that they really didn't want workers' participation at all. He obviously wanted an external enquiry to show up the divisions in the trade union movement. After he had finished his piece he whispered to me, 'The first time I became disillusioned with the trade-union movement was in 1969, when I saw the way they treated you.' Which was gratifying, but not a very objective way of looking at the needs of today. He even said scathingly in his contribution to the public argument, 'I would very much like to see Mick McGahey in charge of one of the pits.' To which I whispered back afterwards, 'But don't you realize that is the whole point of the exercise: the unions have negative power and our job is to *make* them exercise positive power.' Shirley was her usual middle-of-the-road self. She was in favour of an external enquiry, but the terms of reference must be wider; a judge should *not* be chairman and we should commit ourselves to legislation publicly. Then Wedgie came in. We must look at this matter in a wider context, he claimed. We often failed to realize that we still lived in a mediaeval society. He had just come back from turning on the tap of North Sea oil. At the ceremony, whom had he sat next to? Vere Harmsworth and a multinational oil magnate, while the workers who had made it all possible were kept at a respectful distance. We had got to recognize that workers today had a new power. 'I say to Eric, Mick McGahey *does* run the Scottish pits.' Our policy on industrial democracy was intended to be a 'revolutionary change'. We should set our civil servants to work to produce models of workers' participation in different situations and contexts. Obviously there would not be one uniform answer for every case. The Liaison Committee with the TUC should discuss it on Monday before we reached a decision. While he was speaking Eric was writhing with impatience. He pulled towards him a file on which was written 'Meriden'. Pointing it out to me, he said contemptuously, 'It's gone bust', and almost threw it away from him. 'So did the Labour Government of 1929,' I whispered back. 'When you are changing society you don't get it right first time.' And as I probed, still in whispers while Harold looked disapprovingly in our direction from time to time, he admitted it was the US market that had collapsed and that the workers at Meriden had done very well. Meanwhile it had become clear that Peter had won hands down. Harold summed up that we should try to bring the TUC round to our point of view and should give further thought to widening the terms of reference.

Friday, 20 June

Woke at 5.30am in one of the depressed moods I get rather frequently these days. With Ted away at Bristol I could make myself a cup of tea and brood. I am now almost pathologically anxious to finish my job. With the press seeking to edge me out – and with some right-wing backbenchers obviously speculating on when I shall go – the last thing I want to do is to hang on. What pains me is the way the press pick me out for sacrifice while ignoring the longevity of the others in my age group. Why do the press hate me so? I know I do not find fraternizing particularly easy, but then, equally, I am always civil and co-operative. My only problem is to find the right time and reason for going. I do not deserve to be humiliated. And there are one or two initiatives I want to get launched in the department before I go so that my successor can pick them up (if he or she is the right sort of person). I want, for instance, to force the department to reform those wretched NHS spectacle frames and I want to get a great export initiative going in the health field. *Nothing* will be done unless I am there to drive it through. Look at Tony Crosland for instance, still waffling about without a housing policy after fifteen months!

Yesterday we had a long office meeting to discuss what my officials should put forward in the bilateral talks with the Treasury on the 1978–79 expenditure cuts. It was a grim meeting – all the more because it was soon clear even to my officials that it would be politically impossible to cut social security payments by £1½ billion, involving, as it would, altering the law so as to link the annual uprating of pensions, etc. to a lower level in future. This means that Treasury will force us to make even more cuts on the health side. We face an actual *fall* in NHS expenditure. (That might make a good scenario for a dramatic resignation and get me canonized by the rank and file even more than Wedgie, except that the real message we should be getting across to the rank and file is that the cuts are the product of the unions' failure to put a proper value on the social wage – and I am not going to run away from that.) At the end of the meeting I turned to Philip and said, 'All this makes it more imperative than ever that we get our export drive launched. What *is* being done about that?' Philip looked round nervously and said, 'You should get a draft tomorrow of a Minute for you to send to the PM.' But when everyone had gone Jack said to me 'You should realize that *nothing* will be done in the export field unless you push and push.' 'The trouble is that civil servants are no good at this kind of commercial problem,' added Norman apologetically. 'You will have to get someone in from outside,' said Jack. 'And the obvious person is Geoffrey Robinson.'[1] What a good idea! As they left Jack gave me a parting shot: 'And you'll get nothing done on spectacles either unless you insist.'

Incidentally I am amused at the way Michael Meacher is reacting to his new department. Norman has said to me rather anxiously that Parliamentary Secretary was sending back all the letters he was supposed to sign: not so much for redrafting as for reconsideration of policy. But when I had a private word with Michael to welcome him to the department, he was rather self-deprecatory about all this. I told him that I welcomed Parliamentary Secretaries showing the maximum initiative and would look forward to discussing his anxieties at next Monday's ministerial lunch. I outlined what our relationships with the department's officials were: how we had had to beat them about the head of key issues, but after that they had toed the line pretty loyally. 'You obviously have a good relationship with your civil servants', he replied wistfully. I wasn't sure that he approved of our departmental bonhomie.

As Edna raced me to Chequers for our all-day meeting on economic strategy I was amused to read in my *Guardian* that 'at this time most of the Cabinet probably favours a statutory policy', the only real exceptions, it said, being the PM and Mike! (I suspected Harold would be furious at this right-wing build-up and sure enough he was.) There was a mass of documents before us: from Mike, spelling out various ways of toughening the guidelines; from Denis, giving figures of the effect on take-home pay and unemployment of the various alternative policies; from Shirley, suggesting a 'phased norm' for pay increases and demanding that breaches of the norm in the public sector should not be met from increased expenditure. (In the NHS that would mean no inflation-proofing of pay rises beyond the norm and in transport it would mean passing on the excess in fare increases.) There was also a massive document by officials spelling out the advantages and disadvantages of the different courses,

[1] Geoffrey Robinson, a former Labour Party research assistant, held senior posts in British Leyland from 1971 to 1975. He had recently resigned as Chief Executive of Jaguar Cars. In March 1976, he was to stand as Labour candidate in the Coventry North-West by-election and hold the seat with a smaller anti-Government swing than expected.

including a statutory policy. Reg, Roy and others have been demanding that this course of action shall no longer be ruled out of order and I for one welcomed bringing this out into the open, so that they are forced to show their hand. But what interests me is how a norm of some kind is now widely accepted, even by the TUC.

It was a beautiful day and it seemed criminal to proceed to incarcerate ourselves in the long room, with its dark panelled walls and sombre oil paintings. As I looked out on the park with its lush grass, and watched the cows graze under the big bosomy trees, I wondered why it is that crises always occur in that incomparable weather in which the English countryside seems to exude a placid security. Harold called on Mike first to introduce his paper, which he did quietly and without histrionics, but with obvious total commitment to the need to face what had to be done. He began by dismissing a statutory policy, which, he said, 'is only possible with a consent that does not exist'. Last Monday MES had considered the TUC document and had decided to respond to it in discussions with the TUC 'later today'. (Some of us raised our eyebrows at this: so they were losing no time!) What we had to do was to get TUC support for a 'fixed target figure' for pay settlements and he hoped the CBI would be able to give it clearer support. He agreed that the AUEW decision was not exactly helpful, but he did not think it meant that the union would refuse to comply with any vote of Congress. The inflation target must be made public and we should set it out in a White Paper later on. We would have to decide 'how the Government would act to deal with industrial action against the target'. He accepted that a norm of 10 per cent would be better than 15 per cent, but he warned us that it would be difficult enough to get 15 per cent and he didn't think that 10 per cent could be made acceptable. We should insert the actual figure agreed when we reached the end of our discussions in July. We should buttress it with some cost-of-living safeguards and with a policy for higher incomes. It would mean that review bodies, arbitration and so on would have to be suspended and we should have to think carefully about MPs' salaries.

Denis came next, more sombre than I have seen him for a long time, but still sticking firmly to a voluntary policy. The problem, he said, was more urgent than any of us realized. On the balance of payments deficit we had done better than anticipated, but output would still be falling to the end of the year and inflation was 'terrifying'.[1] Borrowing could stop 'overnight'. Anything could trigger off a disastrous run on the pound and force us into £1 billion's worth of public expenditure cuts *this year*. There was not a minute to waste. 'We must have a credible policy by the end of July.' And if we were to get inflation down to single figures, we couldn't go beyond 10 per cent for wages or £5 a week. The problem was how to get compliance. The Government would have to play a central role and prevent public service employees breaching the norm. We should face that problem right away this autumn, when the local authority manuals and NHS ancillaries came up for their pay round. 'So Barbara and Tony [Crosland] will have to be tough.' It also meant the end of review bodies, and we should have to find some way of ensuring that the private sector followed suit.

---

[1] Inflation was running at 26·1 per cent over June 1974.

People had suggested various forms of statutory enforcement. He had gone into the question of a tax sanction and it wouldn't work. Shirley's idea of operating through the Price Code might be a starter. Unfortunately he couldn't risk any demand reflation before April 1976. We should get more exports and that would help. It might be worth seeing whether we could get a guarantee from the CBI about increasing investment. But unless we got a tough and effective voluntary policy he would have no choice but to slash public expenditure. The opening round was completed by Shirley. She was even more alarmist than Denis. 'We can't wait even until July.' A price freeze was impossible. Contrary to most people's beliefs, profits both of wholesalers and retailers had fallen so low that some of them were in danger of going to the wall. A 15 per cent norm was far too high. All in all she was very sceptical whether we could avoid a statutory policy.

When Harold threw the discussion open to general debate Tony C. made one of his drawling contributions in which he always manages to make everyone else sound a fool. The gist of it was that we could only give six months for the voluntary policy to show results. If that failed he would prefer unemployment to a statutory policy. In the meantime we needed a monitoring and relativities body in order to give the voluntary policy more flexibility. Harold Lever interrupted Tony: 'How severe would the unemployment have to be to get results?' To this Tony replied, to Harold Lever's derisive amusement, 'We don't know.' Reg P. was itching to come in – just couldn't wait to tell us, 'I go for a statutory policy *now*.' Roy J. repeated his previous speech about how society was breaking down. We faced an 'excruciating situation'. Unemployment was not an effective way of dealing with wage inflation. And he launched into a great diatribe against public expenditure. (How these people come out in their true colours!) It was 'absurd' that public expenditure should have risen to 58 per cent of GNP. 'We need a critical survey of the return we have had from public expenditure.' We needed a crisis package by July: incomes policy plus cuts in public expenditure. Peter was passionate. There simply was no way, he said, unless we wanted to destroy our movement, of solving our problems except by consent. 'We've *got* to win the argument, starting with the TUC.' It was Harold Lever's turn next. He too spoke vigorously. Workers' net take-home pay had stagnated since 1972, he argued. 'We are suffering from a wage paper-chase that has got to stop.' There had to be a government pledge that 'one way or another we are going to enforce it'. 'What do you mean by that?' cried Mike. 'What I say.' 'But what do you *mean* by enforcement? How are you going to do it?' Harold from the chair tried to silence Mike, but Lever insisted that Mike's question was perfectly fair and he wanted to answer it. 'We could do it if necessary by a sanction against the employers, making it illegal to pay. There need be no reciprocal penalty against the unions.' 'If Harold really doesn't mind interruptions,' I intervened, 'can I say to him, as someone who has had to operate a statutory policy, that I was always told it was impossible to put a penalty on the employer unless one also put a penalty on the union which tried by striking to force him to break the law.' There were murmurs of agreement at this, but Lever said he was unconvinced. Harold said sternly that we really must allow everyone to make their speeches without interruptions. I think he was wrong. We needed the cut and thrust of real argument, not a series of set speeches. Then came Wedgie: the familiar theme. We were in 1931 again, he declared. 'We have got to look at this in a very broad framework indeed.' The answer one gave depended on the problem one was studying. The whole discussion had centred round the discussion of wages. But we were in a slump and the people were not prepared to accept it. The fight for jobs was on in earnest. 'Unemployment is not on as an option.' Nor was a cut in real wages or in benefits. 'The policies suggested round this table are unacceptable.' The course being advocated was a route to coalition. It was also economic nonsense. 'The crisis is taking place against the background of a marked shift of power to the trade unions. We have got to come to terms with 500,000 shop stewards.' Wedgie swept on. 'There must be an attempt to penetrate down to the recesses of the shop floor. I am accused of looking forward to the promised land. This Cabinet is in the desert, looking back to Egypt.' 'If Moses had turned right instead of left he would have struck oil,' quipped back Harold. I must say I thought the honours of wit were even on that one. Wedgie concluded somewhat inconsequentially that he supported Mike.

My turn next. I thought I spoke rather lamely but I ploughed on. I welcomed the fact, I said, that some members of Cabinet had forced the issue of a statutory policy into the open, because this forced us to study it on its merits. And when we did so, as in the official paper, we found that it had as many disadvantages as any of the alternatives. Harold Lever nodded vigorously. But, I continued, the policy had been hovering in the wings for some time as the panacea for all our ills if only we had the ideological courage to seize it. But when officials studied it objectively they found it wasn't a panacea any more than anything else. What emerged was that the only solution to our problems was to win consent. Without that we were in a mess anyway. Harold Lever, I continued, had asked where we would be if we did not get a voluntary policy. I could tell him where we would be: in a coalition. 'A different set of people would be round this table, supported by different votes in the House of Commons.' So the moral for *this* Government was that we had *got* to win consent. In fact we were already beginning to succeed. The TUC document was an astonishing step forward in its acceptance of our analysis. All of us knew there were people in the trade union movement and the PLP who had been arguing for years that wage increases could never cause inflation. Yet here we had the trade union movement admitting officially that that was not true. It was significant that the *Guardian* in a leader only a few days ago was saying that the Government was right to have spent so much time on pursuing a voluntary policy. Now we all knew the problem was to secure compliance, right down the line, as Wedgie had said. It would be wrong for us to leave this to the TUC. 'It is for the Government to win support for the choice the TUC has made: we need an orchestrated Government effort to get this across.' This was the only way to set the crisis in the wider context of our social and socialist economic policies, and so break away from the exclusive concentration on the role of wages to which Wedgie had referred. For months I had been pleading that we should bring home to people the importance of the social wage and how the exclusive concentration on the cash wage was putting it in jeopardy. But we had never begun to get down to this seriously. I stressed the need for a Public Relations Unit to be set up, manned mainly by outside experts in communication. It should be given the job of organizing conferences to be addressed by the PM and other Ministers; preparing graphic material for newspapers to drive home the alternative scenarios that faced us; getting out the social wage document; drafting our White Paper. My speech was received in silence and I thought, 'Well, at least I've tried.'

A few more speeches followed mine. The climax came with Elwyn's. He made the most powerful case against a statutory policy I have ever heard him make. It was a remarkable change from his attitude in 1968 when I was put in charge of the statutory incomes policy Peter Shore had drawn up. I don't remember hearing Elwyn warn Cabinet then of the dangers of legal pay curbs on unions. I thought he would express agreement with what I had said to Lever about the impossibility of having a unilateral legal sanction against employers (it was he who always used to stress this). Certainly he did spell this out and then suddenly, to my astonishment, he turned it into an attack on me: 'I am interested to hear that Barbara is now converted to this view.' I was furious. 'I was too bloody loyal, that was my trouble,' I flashed out. 'Never again!' There was a roar of laughter. 'We all have skeletons in our cupboards,' said Elwyn patronizingly. 'I inherited Peter's policy,' I cried, 'and I had to get it through Standing Committee with half our own side against me.' Peter, to his eternal credit, nodded. 'We'll break for lunch now,' came in Harold. 'Back here at 2.15pm prompt.' I crept out of the room feeling heartbroken. I would never, I felt, live down the myth that I had been the originator of all evil in the 1966–70 Labour Government. The unfairness of it almost crushed me. I went downstairs into the great hall, where they were gathering for drinks, still seething. But the first thing that happened was that Harold came up to me, drink in hand, to say how much he liked my idea of the Public Relations Unit. 'We don't need a large unit, just a few people to run the thing in a way that gets through to people.' 'But they must be outsiders, not civil servants,' I insisted. He agreed. He was all over me. As for Elwyn's intervention: 'We know who was disloyal, don't we? Remember how Jenkins ratted?' Harold was full of ideas for getting over the problem of protecting employers against the pressure of strikes to get them to break the norm. 'We must have a government-financed insurance fund.'

People drifted into the buffet lunch: as always, very nicely done. As I veered into a corner, Mike greeted me with great affection. 'Very good speech,' he said, 'Well done.' He nodded conspiratorially. 'The best speech on the Left,' drawled Tony C. I was staggered. So my rather muted vein had been more effective than a flow of oratory! Jim came up to me. 'I have been thinking about what you said about the problem of the NHS ancillary workers. I think we will just have to get some separate way of dealing with the low-paid through something like the wage councils. I'm afraid I've lost faith in collective bargaining, and, as you know, that is a strange confession to come from me.' Harold Lever came up to congratulate me on my contribution and I hissed at him, 'I'll never forgive Elwyn for that unwarranted attack.' 'Don't worry,' soothed Lever, 'you know we all know you carried the can for the lot. You dealt with Elwyn completely and did you notice that Peter admitted you were right?' 'He's an honourable man,' I replied. As we sat perched on our chairs eating our cold collation off our laps Eric came and sat next to me. He seems to seek me out and poured out his heart defensively to me about Wedgie. 'What is the truth about the Industry Bill?' I asked. 'Is it true that it is being emasculated?' Eric nearly exploded. It was a lot of rot, he insisted. All that was being done about the disclosure of information[1] was to give the Secretary of State the right to decide what information should be passed on to the unions – something Wedgie had never objected to. I couldn't help remarking that I was puzzled at the way disclosure of information had been built up into a *cause célèbre*. It had always been part of *In Place of Strife*.

Back in the long room the discussion came quickly to a close. Finally Harold summed up. This was not a normal Cabinet, he said, and no decisions would be recorded, but the general view seemed to be that we should aim at a wages norm of 10 per cent. And time was running out. There had been an overwhelming rejection of a statutory policy, but the Government would have to be tough with the public sector. There would be no more money for the nationalized industries if they broke the norm. We might consider giving these industries a total wages bill and then letting them get the advantages of any increased productivity they could produce. He also, despite Mike's disagreement, came down in favour of some form of monitoring body. And with that we sent Mike, Denis and Shirley off to negotiate with the TUC. I was thankful that I myself was free to head for home.

As we broke up Malcolm said to me, 'How is Ted's health?' 'Marvellous,' I replied. 'Good,' he said, 'because we are thinking of him as one of the peers' representatives at Strasbourg.' I was thrilled and assured Malcolm with everything I had got that Ted had never been fitter. I went back to HCF, hugging to myself an excited hope that Malcolm had asked me not to divulge at this stage.

Great excitement at HCF. Swallows have started to build in our front porch. I almost began to feel that they must be a sign of good luck! It was fascinating to watch the pair of them come and go, bringing bits of mud and straw to weave their home. At night they perch one on each side of their little edifice to sleep. We peer round the curtain to look at them, afraid to turn on the light.

Monday, 23 June

Yet another chewing over of the TUC document on the development of the Social Contract at the Liaison Committee at Transport House. The cameras and reporters were waiting as I arrived. One journalist asked me the usual idiot questions about what I thought was going to happen, ending with, 'Will the meeting be friendly?' To which I replied, 'Of course.' And friendly it was, but miserably ineffective too. The only trade unionists there, apart from junior officials, were Jack Jones and Len

---

[1] One of the complaints of the Left about the changes being made in the Industry Bill concerned the disclosure of information by companies to unions. Under Tony Benn's original Bill the Secretary of State could require a company making a 'substantial contribution' to a sector of industry to disclose to him information about its commercial activities. He then had a duty to disclose that information to the relevant trade unions, subject to certain safeguards, including the Minister's right to decide that disclosure would be 'undesirable in the national interest'. Following an outcry by the CBI, Eric Varley was in the process of modifying these provisions. Under the Act, which became law in November 1975, the duty of Ministers to pass on the information was changed to a discretionary power to decide what information, if any, should be passed on. When criticized, Eric Varley complained that the amendments written into the Bill merely reflected assurances given by Tony Benn in introducing his Bill that the powers would merely be reserve ones. Nonetheless the legislation's change of emphasis was significant.

Murray. Hughie, we were told, was at his union conference; David Basnett abroad. No explanation from Alf Allen, Sid Greene or anyone else. And no explanation, either, why Denis did not bother to turn up. Harold arrived late to hear Len introducing the TUC document. Len hovered uneasily between endorsing it and putting up a show of belligerency. It was, he said, an officials' document, put forward as a basis of discussion. Meanwhile exploratory talks were going on with the CBI about such problems as control of prices and dividends. There were problems to be faced in the proposals, such as how to deal with the question of comparability, to which a number of unions attached considerable importance. Len rallied into a counterattack on the Government when he stressed the danger of using unemployment as a regulator; we needed an employment target too. Jack Jones – lone, valiant and almost tragic symbol of the defenders of the Social Contract – came in next. 'We are anxious to help you,' he said. But then he too, perhaps conscious of the dangers he himself was running, went into the counterattack. 'Some speeches coming from members of the Government are not helping us to get acceptance of it. It is quite wrong to lay all the blame on wages, as if the unions were the only criminals in the community.' He then went on to pitch into Shirley, saying that the relaxation of the Price Code had been a mistake; she was giving in to the CBI. He gave a warning: 'We can't say to the worker on £30 a week that he can get through next year on 10 per cent.' Workers could see what was going on at Ascot at that very moment. And Jack ended with a plea that reinforced everything I have said. 'If we are going to win over working men and women we have got to explain a little more the nature of our policies. We must talk to workers in the language they understand. Civil servants can't draft speeches.'

The atmosphere was deteriorating into the usual exchange of commiserations and mutual excuses when Harold, in Denis's absence, rallied it a little, though he concluded, 'We are not here to negotiate but to listen.' Bob [Mellish] gave one of his usual rousing speeches about the ordinary lads he represented. 'They are looking for action from us. The militants don't speak for the majority of people.' At which Jack nodded seriously. Jim then came in in his best negative Cassandra vein. 'The document is very encouraging, but inadequate.' He frankly didn't know how Jack was going to deal with his own conference next week. How could he put across the proposition that wages should go up by 10 per cent when prices had risen by 25 per cent? But, as usual, he said he had no answer: he didn't know. The only constructive note he struck was at the end: 'I agree with Barbara. We have got to start selling what the Government has done.' Mike soon cut through some of Jim's mushiness, pointing out that although we should start with an inflation rate of 25 per cent, it would be dropping throughout the year. The TUC document was not a policy for keeps, merely a way of getting round the corner. 'The problem is now to find a figure which will both turn the corner and be acceptable.' There was an urgent need to reaffirm the Social Contract in all its aspects and bring it up to date. Shirley launched into a fluent apologia as to why we couldn't do more about prices and was badly roughed up by both Jack and Len. Wedgie repeated his now routine speech about how this was 1931 all over again. 'Don't let us slip into our opponents' language,' he pleaded. I, too, more or less repeated my Chequers speech. There were nods of agreement when I said I had been trying for months to persuade my colleagues to spell the problem out publicly and both Jack and Len warmly endorsed my proposal that we should issue a statement that morning. But I left Transport House wondering whether our meeting, with its sparse attendance, had not done more harm than good. This impression was confirmed when Roger Carroll of the *Sun* phoned me to ask whether the virtual trade union boycott of the meeting meant that the Liaison Committee had served its purpose and was about to wind up. I said of course it was not.

In the course of the morning, encouraged by what Jack Jones had said, I tossed Harold a note: 'Could you give a personal push to the social wage document? It has been bogged down with Treasury officials for over a month.' He nodded and pocketed it.

At 10pm Jim made a statement to the House on Amin's rejection of the Queen's appeal.[1] It was superbly done, once again showing that our Jim may be a broken reed in an economic crisis but he is God's gift to a parliamentary occasion, particularly one in which we can all combine the emotional luxury of 'Damn it, Sir: we'll stand no more' with high-wire tension over the fate of another human being. The Tories' almost grovelling praise for the way Jim had conducted himself was marvellous to behold, while Margaret sat, hair immaculately coiffed again and pink evening dress low cut, presiding over her party like a female God symbol dressed by *Vogue*. As we all streamed out of the Chamber I said to Harold, '*Why* did Denis not turn up this morning?' To my surprise, instead of brushing me aside, he said out of the corner of his mouth, 'I'll tell you when we get outside.' He took me into his room and poured me a brandy. It then transpired that Denis had tried to get Harold to postpone this morning's meeting on the grounds that he would be embarrassed by having to attend in the middle of his discussions with the TUC. So Harold had suggested that he should attend instead. But what Harold, who was in mellow mood, really wanted to talk about was his favourite theme: how to scotch Roy Jenkins's plot for a coalition. That there is such a plot Harold is convinced and he produced a new piece of evidence. 'We all know he lunched with Heath at Brooks's club, but did you know Heath had been down to East Hendred?' [Jenkins's country cottage in Berkshire]. 'I have that from a source which, by its very nature, makes it reliable, though I can't tell you who it is. Let me say, by way of illustration only, that someone who had to drive him there had reason to complain. . . . Now I know that during the referendum campaign you had to appear with people you otherwise would not have done. But what if you had had them down to your cottage secretly? That would have been a very different kettle of fish.'

Tuesday, 24 June

I was right in my prognostications about the press reaction to yesterday's meeting. They have picked out the most disruptive point they can from Ron's and Len's joint statement afterwards (which wasn't all that apt, anyway): the suggestion that the TUC is insisting on price curbs first, as the *Telegraph* put it. Denis did a party political

[1] See footnote, page 417.

broadcast tonight – not very good. These chaps really must get real journalists to write their scripts.

Wednesday, 25 June

The main item at the NEC was again party finance. Ron had produced the report asked for last time on the state of the party's funds. It contained a detailed list of what Mik would contemptuously call 'candle-ends'. But the day's business started with a sour note from Mik. He raised it on the report of the TUC Liaison Committee, remarking sarcastically that he had read in *The Times* that tributes had been paid to the achievements of the Labour Government in carrying out its share of the Contract. 'What achievements?' he asked. What had happened to our side of the Contract: to the commitment to full employment, to the pledge to produce a 'fundamental and irreversible shift' in wealth and power to working people? What about our commitment to the Industry Bill, which had been 'decimated'? What about the proposed ditching of the Aircraft and Shipbuilding Nationalization Bill? Denis came in savagely. 'Perhaps I can help Mik.' The TUC had accepted that we had repealed the Tory Industrial Relations Act, etc. It also accepted that we could not reflate demand with inflation running at 25 per cent. 'Mik may find it very disagreeable to find himself in a minority, but that is the case.' Mik hit back: 'This NEC has some rights on that Liaison Committee,' he almost snarled. 'In fact, this NEC is the principal custodian of the Manifesto. So don't let us have any snootery about it.' He insisted that we must have a proper discussion of this matter at our next meeting, on the basis of a paper setting out the commitments on both sides of the Social Contract. 'I strongly support that,' Denis snapped back. And so it was agreed.

But when we turned to finance Mik was brilliant. After Ron had warned that we faced an estimated deficit of £700,000 by the end of 1977 he spelt out all his candle-ends, from cutting the expenses allowance of NEC members at party conference (long overdue in my view) to having fewer working parties on policy. It was the latter which aroused the fury of Mik, Frank Allaun, Wedgie and the rest of us. Wedgie was sweepingly eloquent as usual. 'Anyone who believes Government knows anything about the Labour movement is kidding themselves,' he declared. And he told a story about how, at the Department of Industry, he had once told one of his Deputy Secretaries to get in touch with the Confederation of Shipbuilding and Engineering Unions [CSEU], and the civil servant had replied, 'You have the advantage of me, Secretary of State. What is the CSEU?' (Of course the trade unionists on the NEC loved that!) But it was Mik who was particularly telling. The cause of all our troubles, he said, was that we looked at finance in an itsy-bitsy way. He was still waiting for the cash-flow forecasts month by month. 'My guess is that, if you quantify all these things Ron has proposed, you will find they would put back disaster by one month.' Of course, he admitted, we had to find economies, but 'I will resist to the death anything which reduces the policy-making function of this NEC.' And he reminded us that this had been Gaitskell's ploy: he had always wanted to make the Parliamentary Labour Party the policy-making body. One by one the unions came in to back the thesis of the 'Left' that, whatever else we did, we must not cut back on the policy-making function of the NEC. Even Denis, having recovered his temper, said he agreed with almost everything Mik had said, adding, 'I'm glad we've got through the bad-tempered stage.' So it was decided to refer Ron's proposals to the individual committees for examination. The only candle-end we agreed at that stage was to reduce the expenses allowance for members of the NEC at the next party conference.

Slipped away early to have a couple of hours at Wimbledon: the first time I have played hookey for months. After all, it may be the last time I can watch it in style in the royal box at the Centre Court: with strawberries and cream to follow! The sun shone and it was all perfect Wimbledon, but it was rather exasperating to have to watch Rosewall and Feaver when roars of excitement were coming from Court No. 1 where the unseeded Stewart was beating Nastase. But it was all very brief, as I had to get back to office meetings, followed by an eve-of-poll meeting in the by-election at Woolwich West. I told Ron Hayward on Monday that it was absurd to have a school meeting with Mike and me on a hot June evening. All we should do would be to take our activists off the street. We should do a whirlwind tour of street-corner meetings instead, designed to stir the admittedly lethargic Labour voters. Ron said Woolwich wanted it that way, so we'd got to go ahead. Well, I was proved right. Of the hundred-odd people in the hall, ninety were wearing Labour badges and the atmosphere was as flat as a pancake. Will our party never learn? I believe we shall lose the seat because we cannot snap out of our traditional organizational attitudes. Can't we grasp that the difficult job on which a Labour Government is always engaged demands that we pull out every stop of grassroots politics?

I left the meeting early to hurry and change for the midsummer party John Silkin was holding at the Garrick. When I arrived, very late, I found that he had invited an interesting medley of what he called his 'old friends'. I had a long chat with Tom Driberg, who is writing his memoirs and who said with a sly glance at me that he would have to be discreet about his friends. When I replied, with an equally friendly grin, that if he was indiscreet about me I should tell all about *him*, he replied, 'But I am doing that anyway, duckie. The whole idea of the book is that I should come clean.'

The whole day was made particularly happy by the fact that Ted tells me he has been selected for the European Parliament. I am *thrilled* for him. For the past five years I have been putting up a little prayer: 'Lord, I have had a good run for my money. It is Teddy's turn. Please let something go spectacularly right for him.' It looks as though my prayers are being answered. It reminds me of the skipping song we used to sing as children! 'As I go out, you come in.' I wonder what on earth I shall do with myself when I'm retired and Teddy isn't! I wonder if the adjustment will be as easy as I found it when we went into opposition last time?

Throughout June fears about inflation had been causing the pound to slide. On 30 June it took the biggest nosedive yet to a 28·9 per cent depreciation rate since it was floated in 1972. The press highlighted rumours that the Middle East oil interests were about to join the rush to sell sterling. Curiously, it was reported that the Bank of England was 'inactive' in supporting the pound. Wrote John Palmer, then Business Editor of the Guardian: 'Most foreign exchange dealers are startled by the government's willingness to let the pound fall so low.'

Whatever the reason for the run on the pound, it helped Denis Healey clinch a historic deal with the TUC for a voluntary incomes policy. In this he had an unflinching ally in Jack Jones, who secured overwhelming endorsement of the policy from his own union conference. But there were arguments in Cabinet and with the TUC as to what form the new pay limit should take, Denis Healey talking of a 10 per cent increase and Jack Jones urging a flat rate egalitarian one. There were also fierce arguments as to what powers were needed to enforce the policy. Some powers – such as the use of the Price Code – were uncontentious, but Denis Healey hankered after statutory powers to make it illegal for employers to breach the policy. This was resisted by some of us in Cabinet and by the TUC as the thin end of the wedge of a full statutory incomes policy. At a crisis Cabinet on 1 July Denis Healey insisted that he must make an immediate interim statement to stop the rot in confidence. In it he announced a 10 per cent limit in increases in pay and dividends in order to bring inflation down to 10 per cent over the coming year. On powers all we would allow him to say was that if no agreement was reached in carrying out the policy, the Government would legislate to compel employers to toe the line.

Two days later the General Council of the TUC endorsed a pay limit of £6 a week, but only by a majority of nineteen votes to thirteen and in the absence of powerful opponents like Hughie Scanlon. Thus armed Denis Healey returned to the attack, urging that, in order to give credibility to the agreement with the TUC, the promised White Paper on the policy must announce that the Government would legislate at once to secure these reserve powers. But he met with tough resistance, led by Michael Foot, and the White Paper, 'The Attack on Inflation' (Cmnd. 6151), published on 11 July, contained a compromise. Legislation, it said, had been prepared and, if the pay limit was endangered, Parliament would be asked to approve it immediately.

But the battles were not over. Denis Healey struggled to strengthen his package, this time by seeking to announce his proposed cuts of £2 billion in public expenditure in the debate on the White Paper on 22 July. Following strong resistance by some of us he was overruled, though he insisted on warning the House that the existing public expenditure programmes for 1977–78 and 1978–79 were 'quite unrealistic' and would have to be reviewed in order to make way for the expansion of exports and investment he anticipated.

Despite the TUC's acceptance of the policy, the Tribune group of Labour MPs was restive and in the debate of 22 July some thirty-six Labour left-wingers defied the Whips to vote against the White Paper. The Opposition officially abstained, complaining that the Government had failed to cut public expenditure. Challenged during the debate as to what he would do if the Government produced its threatened Bill containing statutory powers against employers, Michael Foot, who was winding up for the Government, admitted frankly: 'If such a Bill were to be introduced, I would hardly be the proper person to do it.'

Thursday, 26 June

A most peculiar Cabinet: no item at all on the agenda apart from parliamentary business and foreign affairs. I have no objection to these short business-like meetings, provided they are supplemented regularly by all-day discussions in depth at Chequers. And it looks as though they may be: Harold has already announced another one for 14 July. The subject is ostensibly to discuss the 'medium-term assessment', but I suspect that is a pseudonym for the economic 'package' Denis is preparing. Jack Jones has managed to get his proposals for a flat-rate increase through the General Council, but it is obvious that there will be resistance from some unions. That doesn't matter so much if the TUC officially gives us the base on which to act. The run on the pound continues unabated. One minute the Bank supports the pound, another it seems to let it rip. I can't make out whether Denis is anxious to stop the rot or is glad of something with which to frighten the unions. I can't make out, either, whether he is in earnest about further immediate expenditure cuts, even if the unions come up with wage restraint. I am willing to join in the chorus of warnings about what will happen to the social wage if the cash wage goes romping ahead: all part of the necessary conditioning of the unions that must go on. But if Denis starts proposing severe cuts for *real*, that will be a very different thing. Some of us won't take it.

Private Office suggested to me that the PM might be intending to raise the guidelines for Ministers. 'Crossman diaries?' I wondered. But nothing happened. Harold postponed Cabinet till noon and then started it ten minutes late. All we did, apart from routine, was to discuss what we should do about the Boyle Report on MPs' salaries:[1] hold it up till we had agreed the economic package; publish it without comment; or publish it, saying that we would accept the increase in expenses (which would at last enable me to pay Janet more than the £2,000 a year which is all I can afford at present), but that the wages element would have to conform with whatever we agreed about wages generally. I urged the latter strongly and eventually, since Mike was worried about the timing of any statement at all, Harold ruled we should return to the matter next week. One thing we all know we shall have to do is to refuse any increases for ourselves as Ministers.

There was also a short discussion on the appointment of our representatives to the European Parliament. It now looks as though the Social Democrats will be the largest party there, but Peter is furious because the parliamentary party has decided that the British Labour Party shall apply for membership of the Social-Democratic group. The trouble is, he says, that the other European socialist parties are federalist. This is

---

[1] The Review Body on Top Salaries under Lord Boyle had produced its report on Parliamentary pay (Report No. 7 Cmnd. 6136). It strongly recommended increasing MPs' salaries from £4,500 to £8,000 as they had last been reviewed in 1971 and were worth less in real terms than they had been in October 1964. The report also recommended (1) increasing the parliamentary salary of Ministers, and other MPs who were paid office-holders, from £3,000 to £5,000; (2) increasing the secretarial allowance from £1,750 to £3,200 a year, and (3) adjusting other expenses such as London weighting and car allowances to bring them into line with appropriate civil service rates. Cabinet decided that MPs' salaries should be increased to £5,750, but that Ministers' parliamentary salary should be frozen.

certainly a problem we shall face very shortly: whether to go for direct elections and all that means. I personally am torn. Does accepting the result of the referendum mean that we merely go through the motions of membership and in fact continue to stymie the development of democratic control of the Community? It is a horrible dilemma, not least because some of the younger anti MPs now see no alternative for us but to go in and run the whole European show ourselves. And there is an equally important tactical point for us to bear in mind: how to help Harold in his now patent desire to break out of the clutches of the pro-marketeers, now the referendum campaign is over, and to resume a central position in the party again. As I put it to him during one of our now frequent conspiratorial chats, 'That is why I went to Luxembourg. I don't think we should let the pro-marketeers corner Europe, because in doing so they corner you.'

Spent the afternoon recording the BBC programme *The Times of their Lives* with Gerald Harrison: a nostalgic journey into the past set to music I had had to choose myself as reminiscent of key points in my life. It was most moving to see how they handled my choice of the *Eroica* because it reminded me of Nye. They wove flashes of his face and hands into the threads of the music, as though he was conducting it, and I nearly blubbed when one flash showed the hand-clasp he gave me when I was elected to the NEC way back in 1951. I am glad to think that this side of my life will remain on the record when I am gone.

I was back at the House, waiting to vote my way through the evening, when Norman rang in some agitation. No. 10 had just come dramatically alive over my social wage document. Harold now wanted it finished by Monday and published in time for a press conference he is giving on social policy on 12 July. Panic stations! Treasury have sent back a turgid redraft and we are all furious – just another example of the way Treasury officials assume they can do every Minister's job better than he can himself. Norman said he was sending over the redraft and our original drafted with journalistic help. Could I let him have my views before I left early in the morning for my official visit to Weston-super-Mare? I hurried downstairs, having barely eaten all day, to have a quick meal in the dining room. I was just finishing when Harold joined our table, affability itself. 'Don't leave, luvvie,' he said as I got up to go and proceeded to tell me how he had acted on my note and how he was planning a great press conference to put our social policy across. ('No more of these off-the-record briefings which the press only use against me.') He wanted me to introduce the social wage document, so it had to be ready by Monday. 'That's why I must go and work on it,' I gasped – and fled. I sat reading through the Treasury redraft almost in despair; then I minuted Norman not to wait for any more clearance by Treasury, but to get on to David Tattersall [a journalist on the *Daily Mirror*] tomorrow, give him both documents, ask him merely to incorporate any new bits by Treasury and get the whole document into a uniform style. All this meant I was late to bed.

Friday, 27 June
Up early to face a gruelling day at Weston-super-Mare, every minute of which had been packed with official visits and talks. I was surprised how perky I felt. My spirits

have risen: I must say it is rather nice to be in favour with the PM again! Even the news that we had lost Woolwich West didn't dampen me; I had expected it. By-election losses and runs on the pound no longer frighten us as they used to in 1966, I think because everyone knows the Tory Party isn't beginning to be a runner as an alternative government. I got through the difficult day (difficult not least because I had to turn down the desperate pleading for a new District General Hospital at Weston) without flagging, helped by my new dress. I was just on my feet dealing with my fifth and last meeting of the day when a message came: could I come to the phone. I sent Jack, who proceeded to pass me a note saying I must leave for London immediately. The trouble, it turned out, was the social wage document. In a long phone call Norman told me that all our plans had come apart. David Tattersall had been willing to do the rewrite, but said he must clear it with his boss: Tony Miles, editorial director of the *Mirror* papers. Tony Miles had turned very nasty indeed after the weeks of delay since we first approached the *Mirror* and had refused to let David do it. Norman had spoken to Miles, but everything the poor lad tried to do only seemed to make things worse. There was nothing, said Norman, but for me to ring Miles. I could get hold of him at his office the next day. I groaned. 'I must say I have a lot of sympathy with him,' said Norman, enlightened as ever.

Saturday, 28 June

Jack Jones has rounded on the 'Left' – obviously a reaction to the Arthur Scargills of this world, who are up to no good at all. It is remarkable how Jack has thrown his hat over the windmill in an overt and unequivocal determination to save the Labour Government. This makes me all the more furious at the botch-up over my social wage document. When I phoned Tony Miles I found him friendly enough, but fuming over the way the Government, having waited for weeks before doing anything about Tattersall's write-up, suddenly wanted a further rewrite in forty-eight hours. 'It just can't be done,' he said. And he was furious at the way the Treasury had messed about with our original version. I soothed him down, pointing out that this was the sort of thing Ministers had to put up with every day of the week. 'I'm not blaming you,' he replied, 'But it's just not good enough. The PM can't have it by Monday, that's all.' Like Norman, I had total sympathy with his complaints, but as I talked to him he climbed down, said Tattersall had gone away for the weekend, that he would try to get in touch with him, and that, if that failed, I could phone Tattersall on Sunday night. It is obvious that I shall have to take charge on my return on Monday, see Tattersall myself and tell him what to ignore in the Treasury redraft. The trouble with Harold's instant action technique is that it makes no allowance for the fact that Ministers may have official visits which they just can't cut. I suspect that Churchill was just as bad. Men call this kind of chaos political virility.

One of the telegrams in my box was from our High Commissioner in Delhi. He takes a gloomy view of the Declaration of Emergency. 'Mrs Gandhi is now on the classic slippery slope towards dictatorship,' he writes.

I am desolate because the swallow in our HCF porch has deserted her eggs. On Friday night, when I arrived home, I found her sitting snugly in her nest, unperturbed by the dogs' high decibels. Yesterday she was nowhere to be seen and had not returned even at night. No sign of her today. I wonder all day what can have happened to her. Our porch is suddenly emptied of life.

Monday, 30 June

Rushed up to the office to deal with the social wage document, only to be told by Norman that David Tattersall is walking the Pennines and won't be back till Wednesday. So that is why I could not get hold of him yesterday! I go through the Treasury draft myself, marking the bits I think we should include with ours, and then hand the whole thing over to Brian Abel-Smith to knock in to the sort of shape David Tattersall can deal with on his return. No. 10's timetable now is that we have till Wednesday to clear our draft.

In the evening I run into Mike at the House. 'How are things?' I ask conventionally. 'Terrible, terrible,' he mutters to my surprise. Drawing me aside he tells me that the pound is 'crumbling', that there is to be a Cabinet early tomorrow, that Denis is talking of statutory controls on employers – though not workers – and that he is just off to see Len Murray with Denis and Shirley, Jack Jones being away at his union conference. So the crunch has come earlier than we thought. 'You'll just have to give us a lead tomorrow in the light of your talks,' was all I could say.

Tuesday, 1 July

Cabinet assembled at 9.30am. To my surprise, there were no cameras waiting outside No. 10. So the press has been taken by surprise as much as we have, despite the fact that the papers are full of the worst-ever run on the pound. It was an apprehensive lot who gathered outside the Cabinet room and John Silkin whispered to me as we went in, 'I have never attended a Cabinet more reluctantly.' I thought to myself, 'Crisis always strikes in the sunshine', and, according to Denis, crisis it certainly was. The pound, he told us, had fallen 1 per cent yesterday and this morning it had reached its lowest devaluation ever: 29·2 per cent. The worst thing was that it was now going down versus the dollar, and we could face a disastrous withdrawal of funds at any time – just what he had kept warning us of. Nigeria, Kuwait and Saudi Arabia had all warned us that, though they were anxious to be friendly, there was a limit to the amount of devaluation they would stand. Nigeria, for instance, had told us she would withdraw her funds if the pound fell below 2·17 dollars and we had now reached that point. We simply had to stop inflation in its tracks. He did not believe that heavy cuts in public expenditure this year would have any effect on inflation whatever. All they would do would be to create more unemployment. We had made enormous progress in our discussions with the TUC: they were now ready to link wage increases to a *forward* target of inflation of 10 per cent by September 1976. This meant there must be a limit on wage increases of 10 per cent or £6 per week, over the coming year. The TUC had not yet agreed that sum and Jack was still talking of £8. The question was: how could we create confidence in compliance with this policy by the unions? Len Murray agreed that it meant there could be no collective bargaining. Yet unless he, Denis, was able to make a statement that afternoon which carried conviction, the run

439

on the pound would continue and the withdrawal of funds would start. He had been considering a series of pay sanctions: cash limits on nationalized industries and local authorities would certainly be part of them. But how were we to control the private sector? We could, as Shirley had suggested, use the Price Code to disallow excessive wage settlements, but this did not have much effect in capital intensive industries. 'I couldn't make this rag-bag look effective from this afternoon.' This is why he had been discussing with the PM, Shirley and Mike the need to impose a legal sanction on employers. They were a law-abiding lot and he was sure they would comply with the law. Nothing less would restore confidence.

Harold came in here. They had discussed all this with Len Murray yesterday, he said. Len was very depressed and didn't think the TUC could approve, but stressed that they wanted the Labour Government to survive. Jack Jones had taken the same view. Harold had made it clear to Len that 'we rule out criminal sanctions against workers in all circumstances'. We must make much more of a show on prices. Perhaps we could relate rent increases to the norm. He had been thinking about the problem till 3am this morning. He thought the answer lay in the 1966 precedent: we should take general powers, but they would not become law except by regulation. The more I listened to Harold the more convinced I became that once again he was fooling himself: first, in imagining that he could take legal powers against employers only, and secondly, that the device of taking reserve powers would help. It would neither create confidence nor allay our own people's fears. On the contrary, I thought it would exacerbate them. To call the 1966 precedent in aid would be merely to make them think we were on the same slippery slope to a statutory policy. But how to answer Denis's case? Once again I realized how much one is at the mercy of Treasury. How could the rest of us possibly check how serious the situation was: what, for instance, was the attitude of the OPEC countries, particularly as Denis had stressed that everything he had said about them was strictly confidential, mustn't be breathed outside? So it was hardly surprising that, when Harold called on Mike, he began hesitantly. 'The more I have thought about it, the more convinced I am that a 10 per cent legal limit constitutes a return to a statutory policy,' said Mike. Jack Jones's reaction had been 'very forcible'. The number of anomalies it would create was enormous and his department was very worried about them. What if the miners went on strike against the 10 per cent limit? We would have to let current arbitrations through, but what about indexation agreements? He didn't believe the TUC would accept a 10 per cent figure. He believed that we could get 12 per cent by negotiation and this would be worth more than anything else. What Denis was proposing would put the whole burden of the crisis on wages and we should be trying to solve it by imposing a wage cut. We really must take more time to try and get an agreed policy. Tony C. began by agreeing with Mike on one thing: 'You cannot produce a workable incomes policy in one night's discussion.' But then, as usual, he went on to prevaricate. 'I don't believe we can get an agreement with the TUC,' he said, his Freudian slip showing. But did we have to make a statement that afternoon? 'The layman can't judge these things.' Harold intervened to say he thought there was a chance of acceptance by the TUC, but Jim was wobbling too. 'I don't know that it is necessary for us to throw it in today in this form,' he said. 'We shouldn't go into details on wages and prices today: merely make a firm statement of our intention and determination to get inflation down and to take all the measures necessary to achieve it. We ought to state our target for wages publicly, which we had never yet done.' 'I've done it three times,' said Denis savagely. 'Well, then, you have cut the ground from under my feet,' said Jim lamely.

Shirley was tougher. We had got to make a statement and should make it clear that if our attempt to get a voluntary policy failed, we would take powers for a compulsory policy. But even Roy Jenkins was less than enthusiastic about Denis's plan. 'There are grave difficulties in patching a policy together in twenty-four hours.' He didn't underestimate the dangers we faced. We were in danger of going into a tail-spin and of hyperinflation. He had himself never believed in floating exchange rates, which led to 'fatal indiscipline'. (Harold Lever nodded enthusiastic agreement.) It was essential to have medium-term control of public expenditure, he concluded. Peter's contribution too was tentative, though he began by defending the floating rate. The great case for it, he said, was that it didn't affect our reserves. (Denis chipped in to say that our monthly reserve figure was down, but, under pressure, he agreed that that figure was not a complete guide. We did 'massage' it a bit.) 'How far is the threat of withdrawals of funds a real one?' Peter persisted. 'There is always an element of bluff.' What had happened to the idea we had once discussed of giving a sterling guarantee to the holders of sterling? We desperately needed more time. 'We must get the maximum consent because we are going to need it,' he concluded. Denis fought back again. Last Thursday and Friday, he insisted, the oil producers had sold £130 million. As for sterling guarantees, they were 'immensely costly'. For our three major suppliers of funds they would cost £500 million. 'But we should look at that again,' chipped in Harold. We waited with interest as Wedgie spoke, but all he said, rather heavily, was that he wanted to ask four questions. (1) What is the size of the wage cut we are proposing? Local authority manual workers, for example, had had a fall of 37 per cent in their living standards between September 1974 and 1976. As for the miners, if we got into a confrontation with them, could we rely on public opinion to support us? (2) What was the estimate of unemployment over the next few months? (3) What was the scale of the public expenditure cuts we were contemplating? (4) What were we going to say to the TUC about import controls and investment? Denis, who can never contain himself, burst out angrily that Wedgie's figures were 'ridiculous'. In 1974 there had been a 9 per cent increase in take-home pay and for the current year there would still be a wage increase of 10 per cent. Wedgie had been talking 'absolute bunk'. To my surprise, Wedgie subsided quietly.

Eric had been whispering to me, 'You ought to tell us about your experience. After all you have lived through all this before.' 'I'm trying to,' I whispered back, 'if Denis will only stop talking.' At last Harold called on me. I spoke confidently. We were all agreed, I said, that our decision that morning was a crucial one. We were deciding whether to put our whole strategy and philosophy into reverse – and we were doing it at the very moment when the TUC was straining every nerve to give us what we wanted and when Jack Jones was on his feet at his conference, putting his reputation with his union on the line to save the Labour Government. Frankly I believed that a holding statement would do more harm than good. I did not believe it would be enough to restore confidence. Once one's enemies thought they had got the Government on the run they did not call off the pressure – they pressed their advantage even more vigorously. Once the gnomes felt they had got the Government in retreat they would not be content until we had gone the whole hog of statutory policy. So, as Roy feared, we should be back next week making a still tougher statement to stop the rot. And did we really think we could rely on the Tories to help us get through the House a policy that put penalties merely on the employers? Margaret Thatcher wasn't going to try to save this Government. I warned my colleagues like Shirley, who had been saying public opinion was on our side, not to be fooled: that had been the situation over *In Place of Strife*. All the polls showed that the people of this country had wanted action to check strikes, including a majority of trade unionists, yet when I introduced just a teeny-weeny element of penal sanction in a massive charter of trade union rights, that hadn't prevented the balloon from going up and it would go up now. I had never visualized that the TUC would be able to enforce compliance with a voluntary policy, but what was imperative was that we should get the 'umbrella of TUC approval', under which we could then do what was necessary to ensure compliance with the policy with which they had agreed. The essential prerequisite was that we should get more time. Denis had dismissed sterling guarantees as ruinously expensive and then put a figure on them of £500 million. Surely that was chicken-feed compared with the disaster that faced us if we abandoned the attempt to get a voluntary policy? There were murmurs of approval from our lads when I had finished, though Harold said primly that *In Place of Strife* wasn't a parallel because we were not now proposing penalties on workers. Roy Mason declared emphatically, 'If you had put *In Place of Strife* to a referendum, ninety per cent of the people of this country would have voted in favour of it.' And he then went on to back Denis 100 per cent, while Fred Peart, Willie Ross and Harold Lever nodded agreement.

Eric meanwhile had been tossing me notes: 'Isn't it ironical that we should be discussing statutory policy when Reg Prentice isn't even here?' 'Can social democracy ever work?' and 'Do you think the Government will still be in office this autumn?' He then made one of his rather tentative contributions. He had doubts about the statement, he said. He thought the unions had let us down badly, but he was doubtful as to whether the employers would be a pushover. So he would rather we held off today and, if necessary, fall back on a wages and prices freeze. Then Elwyn proceeded to warn Cabinet as I had done. 'I am very worried,' he said, 'about the commitment it is proposed to make today to legal sanctions against the employer.' In such a situation a strike to try to force an employer to break the law would be a criminal conspiracy, so we would have to legislate specifically, as we had done in 1966, to exonerate strikers; but we had done it then in the context of providing other penalties against them. Undeterred, Harold summed up that the general view was that we must make a statement today, but it should be in such a form that it would help us to keep the TUC in play. Denis insisted that we must spell out the wages target of 10 per cent 'which we have not done before'. At this Jim exploded. 'But you have just told me the exact opposite.' Denis brushed him aside. If confidence was to be restored we must make it clear that we were determined to secure compliance and must spell out all the sanctions we had in mind. Harold ruled that a small number should draft the statement on behalf of Cabinet: Denis, Shirley, Mike and Peter. And so it was agreed. As Cabinet broke up Mike grasped my hand warmly. 'A marvellous speech: you are the only one who really backed me up.'

I made the office rearrange my engagements so that I could be in the House to hear Denis's statement. I thought it was a pretty ineffectual one, but the Tories roared their ironic delight as the possibility of sanctions against employers was read out. Denis fielded the supplementaries superbly and the protests on our side were fairly muted. But I am not fooled. This is how it all started over *In Place of Strife*. I remember how Charlie Pannell congratulated me after I had explained it to the trade union group, but that didn't mean that he or anyone else stood up in my support once the fury started slowly, but surely, to escalate. Meanwhile I am still doing battle with Ted Short about the inclusion of my Pay Beds Bill in next session's programme. Doesn't the Government realize that this is an essential political sweetener for the unions?

Wednesday, 2 July

One of the busiest days of my ministerial life. With the recess on its way there's everything to do first, so I started with the Cabinet Committee on Miscellaneous Devolution Questions, at which Ted Short got very fierce with those of us who were not ready to devolve everything. He even tried to get my department to devolve drug control. I believe devolution is inescapable, but some things must be retained if there is to be any unity of the UK left at all. Then back to the office to meet the BMA, at their request, to discuss the financing of the NHS. This has been hanging in the air ever since the deputation went to see the PM months ago, a casualty of the consultants' dispute, following which we are now trying to pick up the threads as if nothing had happened. But Lewin and Stevenson had asked to see me first to discuss pay policy. They came in all smiles, as though we were life-long buddies. Denis's statement yesterday didn't seem to have upset them at all, except that they pressed that the control of incomes should be a percentage one and not flat-rate and, of course, it must not interfere with the improvements in the consultants' contract we had agreed to put to the Review Body in April 1976 (a typically smug middle-class reaction that almost made me see virtue in Arthur Scargill). This is something a Labour Government must never forget: that the middle class is all in favour of income control, provided it cures inflation without disturbing their relative advantage.

The meeting on NHS financing was placid enough, but it soon became clear that they are all – from the Royal Colleges to Keable-Elliott – going to use the argument of economic stringency to question the possibility of maintaining the 'comprehensiveness' of the NHS. David's speech about a 'rationed service' has played into their hands.[1] Tony K-E., for instance, argued that the fact that the NHS could not expand as we would like proved the need to allow people to pay that bit over the odds for extras

[1] David Owen had been arguing that, with the increasing sophistication of medical techniques, no health service in the world could provide everything and that there would have to be priorities. The medical profession had picked this up as a call for 'rationing'.

such as complete medical check-ups and do it *within* the NHS. And they all united in declaring that morale in the NHS could not be maintained unless we agreed to an independent enquiry into its financing, obviously hoping that the enquiry would make out a case for additional charging in some form or another. As we listened David tossed me a note: 'Do you *still* want an enquiry?' I smiled ruefully. He is probably right that it would play into their hands.

This over, I hurried to Xavier's for a quick comb-out, while I swallowed a sandwich and tried to assimilate the notes for my speech at the opening of the new day hospital at St Giles for the mentally ill which was to follow. I like these visits very much, but they do add an additional dimension of strain in a hectic week, not least because a woman Minister is gawped at and appearance counts. Kenneth Younger [Chairman of the Area Health Authority] greeted me at St Giles, and I soon found myself fascinated by the detailed, devoted work that goes on in our society on behalf of people who will never produce very much or grace a dining table. Their only claim on us is that they are human beings. I remain firmly convinced that the duty of a valid social democracy is to combine sensitivity for the helpless and hopeless with a toughness about the battle for equality rather than do-goodery. Nye managed to do it.

The visit over, I hurried to the House for my long-overdue appearance before the Select Committee on Violence in Marriage.[1] Seeing that the setting up of the committee had been my idea, which I had had to process through the department against the objections of my officials, my conscience was clear, but I was under no illusion that Willie Hamilton, who has insinuated himself into the chairmanship on Tory votes, would try to make a meal of me. He isn't one for missing a self-promotion opportunity. So in the car I was still frantically reading up the minutiae of the questions they wanted to put to me, as if I were a criminal in the dock. There was a pile of rather inadequately political material from officials which I somehow had to digest and regurgitate into a politically effective answer. That is the whole art of government. How right I was about Willie. Within minutes he was interrupting me rudely and putting me through a cross-examination which implied that I had been caught with my hand *not* in the European till, which was there to be rifled on behalf of the oppressed British poor if only I weren't so obstinately anti-Europe. I knew this was a lie, but my brief was inadequate on facts. I did not feel at all nervous, only coldly angry and hit back as best I could with my material. Winifred Ewing postured like a mini-Hamilton, and I suddenly realized why Ministers who are not as tough as I am dislike Select Committees. Personally I think it is right for Ministers and civil servants to be put through the hoop, however unfairly. It does force them to check up on facts. And it does force Ministers to insist on being surrounded by reliable civil servants. Karen, my lady-in-waiting of the day, who was sitting at the back of the committee, turned out to be one such (as most of my Private Office are). She had obviously gone out to check up on one of the points on which I was being cross-examined and, just before the end, passed a note to me. 'Ah,' I said, 'I have just received some new

[1] As a result of my pressure a Select Committee had been set up in February 1975 to consider 'the extent, nature and causes of the problems of families where there is violence between the partners or where children suffer non-accidental injury'.

information. Would the committee like me to read it out to them?' Intrigued, Willie said yes. 'I haven't even read it myself,' I said sweetly. 'I hope it isn't an official secret.' I then read out the information, which completely shot the hare with which Willie had been running. Thanks to Karen I ended vindicated and I told her afterwards that she was a good girl. Later that evening I ran into Bruce George, a member of the committee, who told me how shockingly he thought Willie had treated me. 'How you kept your temper I don't know. But it turned out all right.' 'Yes,' I thought to myself, 'but you didn't come in once in my support.'

Back in my room, with half an hour to change for an official dinner, I found Norman, Brian A-S. and a couple of our departmental chaps waiting for me with the latest draft of the social wage document. Apparently David Tattersall had come back from his holiday only too keen to help. He had measured every word and line of the text in order to fit it into a popular pamphlet and the result had to be approved by me before I dressed for Jim Callaghan's annual jamboree to celebrate the Queen's birthday. This is the great diplomatic event of the year, at which Cabinet Ministers are expected to help Jim out as co-hosts, and we had all been allowed to pair by the Whips, even though we were in the middle of a three-line whip on the Industry Bill. I flicked through the document, making a number of suggestions and then had less than five minutes to change. But I wanted to go because the dinner was at Hampton Court Palace, which I haven't seen since I was a child and even then I never penetrated inside. Ted – already dressed up in his glory – was marvellously patient as I changed. At last we were on our way, with me busily trying to catch up on the work in my two boxes on the way. It was a gloriously sunny evening and, despite the absurdly intense pressures, I managed to enjoy myself. Hampton Court was everything I had hoped; the meal was good, and I enjoyed quarrelling with my Luxembourg neighbour about the European Community as I looked up at the high ceiling in the dining hall. 'I do hope they play the Post Gallop,' he said as the band rattled on in the Minstrels' Gallery. 'I have never heard anything like it.' And so they did. We then all trooped through the Tudor courtyard to the garden, with its long avenues and beautifully kempt lawns, to hear the marines play The Retreat as they marched and wheeled in perfect formation on a perfect summer evening. I was interested to watch the diverse diplomats – the one in front of me looked like Haile Selassie – studying the whole performance with rapt attention, while Ted and I tapped our feet approvingly to the tunes, unashamedly patriotic. 'This is one of the reasons why I am anti-Market,' I whispered naughtily to my neighbour, as he applauded the Englishness of it all. I love my home and country with a fierce protectiveness. It was nearly 1am before we got back to our flat and as we drove up a young figure emerged from the shadows. It was Paul Chapman [one of the team of special advisers] with yet another urgent document from the devoted Brian Abel-Smith. I thanked him, yawned and went to bed, setting my alarm for 6.30am.

Thursday, 3 July

Routine Cabinet. But there were overtones of Tuesday's crisis Cabinet as we spent nearly two hours discussing MPs' pay. The Boyle Report has put us in a real dilemma:

how could we recommend acceptance of an increase of 25 per cent for MPs at a time when we had just announced a flat-rate increase for the coming year of £6 for everyone else? True, the MPs hadn't had an increase for three-and-a-half years and on the most rigid formula of parity with what other people had had during that period an increase to at least £6,000 was justified, but we all knew the politics of the situation. No one outside Parliament ever accepts that MPs should have an increase at any time. And this is a peculiarly sensitive moment. What angers me is that we have been through this kind of agony ever since I have been in government and I, for one, have been pressing all that time for MPs' pay to be linked automatically to that of some outside group, and to be reviewed annually as other people's pay is. But nothing has been done. What amuses me is how viciously those 'moderate' MPs who have been most vociferous about the need for an incomes policy are now demanding a big increase in their own pay. Harold agreed with Bob Mellish that MPs were 'very angry'. A delegation which he had received last night had clearly torn a strip off him. They were even, we gathered, threatening to refuse to support the Government on crucial votes. Some moderates! We all agreed that some MPs *were* suffering considerable hardship, but I for one thought Boyle had over-egged the pudding with his recommendations. He was a bad choice to do this job: middle class always looks after middle class.

We went round and round the mulberry bush about what modifications we should make to the Boyle Report and how we should present it. Peter had an ingenious formula for totting up how much MPs would be entitled to if they had got all the stages of Heath's pay policy plus the guidelines for last year (which they hadn't). It brought them up to about £6,000 and we agreed we should fix something around that figure. But all the logical totting up in the world won't make any difference to the political spite that will be shown against MPs for getting any increase at all. Michael, who didn't resist the £6,000 figure, pleaded that no announcement should be made till the crucial talks with the TUC and CBI on the pay policy were over. We must tell the TUC what we were proposing in advance. Harold suggested we could keep MPs quiet meantime by promising an early announcement, plus back-dating to 13 June, when the report was signed, and he thought up a typical Harold device: he would get Cledwyn [Hughes, chairman of the PLP] to ask him a supplementary at his Questions today so that he could get this announced without making an embarrassingly formal statement. And we should also seriously explore ways in which MPs' pay could be linked to an outside analogue, even though the Boyle Report has turned down this idea. Jim said that even an increase to £6,000 would make our position impossible, except on one condition: that Ministers took a cut of 10 per cent in their own pay. Denis nodded at this and so did Mike and I. (Fred Peart shook his head vigorously.) Harold said we would consider this too when the final decision was made.

We then went through the proposed legislative programme for next year. Ted Short gave us his best headmaster's head-shaking act. The legislative pressure this year had been 'intolerable', he said. Colleagues really must accept that they could not put in the kind of legislative bids they had done last time. We then all fought passionately for our own bids again. It was a fight with no quarter given by anyone.

When I pointed out that DHSS hadn't got a single piece of legislation accepted for the essential Bills list this year, there were derisory cheers of approval. So I made their blood curdle with warnings of the industrial action health unions would take if I wasn't allowed to legislate for the phasing out of pay beds. (Thank God for the unions!) Harold, at least, cottoned on to this and in summing up included this among the Reserve Bills with the strongest claims for inclusion in the programme. So I went back to the office and told Norman we must have an early meeting to get the policy finalized well before next session. It is the early bird. . . . But once again I pondered on how totally unaware our party rank and file are of the barriers to rapid action in a democracy. It is not just money; it is parliamentary time.

At the office we had a long meeting on David's paper on the reorganization of the NHS. He has argued extremely effectively for the elimination of the regional tier. We must obviously make up our minds in which direction we are going, even if we cannot turn the whole of the present structure on its head overnight. David has got the office to produce some figures of the administrative costs of Keith Joseph's reorganization and these reveal that this 'managerial' approach has merely heavily increased administrative overheads. I am certainly not prepared to cut health expenditure unless we first cut these administrative costs. We talked for a long time round the problems of the new structure. We must resume the discussion soon.

After a long evening's work at the House I had to catch the night sleeper to Preston for a heavy day's work in Blackburn and another sleeper back. Few people know the misery these incessant sleeper trips add to life. How can anyone sleep properly in a noisy little box which starts at tropical heat (or freezing) and ends the night at freezing point (or at tropical heat)? To say nothing of what sounds like milk churns at Crewe.

Saturday, 5 July

This is the weekend of our DHSS Sunningdale conference on how to make better use of women doctors in the NHS. Private Office had put me down to do a token winding-up speech at 4.30pm (and a pretty turgid brief they had put up for me too). But I care very much about this matter. I had carefully vetted the list of women doctors we had invited in order to make sure it included some real rebels and I wanted to listen to them. So I had a bath and breakfast when I got to HCF and turned up unexpectedly at the coffee break in the morning, to everyone's delight. And to mine too, for it enabled me to listen to a first-class symposium by a succession of women doctors themselves, who set out the problems which face them in their medical careers with a wit and aplomb that none of the men could rival. Even Henry, in the chair, was clearly shaken. The conference took a chunk out of my weekend, but, by heavens, it was worth it.

The rumblings about pay policy are still causing some of us anxiety. It is clear that Denis is still hankering after taking his precious statutory reserve powers and this would make Mike's position impossible. If he resigned, I certainly would and I suspect Wedgie (and perhaps even Peter) would, too. I suggested to the others that we all ought to meet on Monday morning, when the TUC line should be clearer.

Monday, 7 July

There really couldn't be a crisis, I thought, as I got up early on a perfect summer morning to finish spraying the roses before I left for town. The caress of the sunshine, the gentle greenness of orchard and woods, belied all the tensions that lay ahead. Somehow I tore myself away from it and hurried to my hot room in the House to await Peter, Mike and Wedgie to discuss what we should do if we were faced with a Chancellor and Cabinet determined to impose statutory controls. To my surprise and delight Eric Varley was there too. Someone must have told him we had arranged to meet and I wondered why he had come to a meeting with us on this issue when he had so carefully detached himself from our group over the referendum campaign. There is something ineffably nice about that lad, even though he is far from being 'Left' in the traditional sense of the word.

Mike began by reporting on the progress of discussions with the TUC. The Economic Committee, he told us, was meeting that morning to discuss the final draft of the TUC document, which was a 'good document'.[1] Of course, they were asking for certain set-offs, such as a tougher line on prices and import controls and wanted an unemployment target as well as a wages one: unemployment to be down to 500,000 by the end of 1976. He didn't pretend that would be realizable, but stressed the TUC wasn't insisting on these as conditions for accepting the figure of £6 for wage increases. If the Government turned all this down it would be very bad. A draconian Bill was being prepared, but the TUC was having further meetings with Ministers that afternoon at which they would spell out their opposition to legal curbs of any kind. There was a 'blurred area' of legislation which might be necessary even if we got agreement with them, such as the notification of wage settlements. The idea was that review bodies should be suspended and the TUC wanted a cut-off with no pay increases at all above £10,000. We five ought to make our views known *before* Cabinet. One thing was clear: we would never get reserve powers through the House of Commons. Jack Jones was very anxious that we should not tear the Government apart. 'If things go wrong I should have to discuss my personal position with Jack Jones.' We all laughed at the idea of Mike piloting a reserve power Bill through the House, though Peter pointed out that if the CBI was prepared to accept unilateral powers against employers, the Tories would let it through. And he added with his charming smile, 'I must be frank with you: this is not to me a matter of principle. But it is a matter of very serious practice.' Mike accepted this. If the TUC was prepared to accept a tough pay policy, we should not complain. 'We must not be more republican than the TUC.' But he reiterated that he was 'absolutely against a statutory policy'. Again he stressed: 'The Tribune-type recrimination against the Government is not being made by the TUC.' 'But what if we face a collapse of sterling?' Peter repeated. 'What has happened about the promised consideration of a guarantee of sterling balances?' I asked. Peter told me it had been considered, but that Denis had firmly turned it down. I said that the threat of statutory powers had obviously concentrated the unions' minds wonderfully. What we needed was enough threat to make the

---

[1] The document, called 'The Development of the Social Contract', accepted a flat rate pay increase limit of £6 a week and declared: 'The TUC will oppose any settlement in excess of this figure.'

voluntary policy work. If it looked as if Cabinet was going to beat us on the issue of including statutory powers in the package, we might propose as a compromise that we insert a paragraph in the White Paper to the effect that we would review the working of the policy with the TUC after, say, a three-month period and decide what further strengthening of the powers was necessary. Peter supported me strongly on this, but Mike looked doubtful. Wedgie and Eric said little. We left it that we would keep in touch and co-ordinate our line. We don't want any unilateral gestures. As Eric had whispered to me at the last Cabinet, 'If Mike can accept it, so can I.'

At Home Policy Committee of the NEC there was a surprising piece of mildness from Mik and Judith. Geoff Bish had circulated another of his Economic Reviews opposing a statutory policy, urging import controls and a few other embarrassing items, though the document was far from being a tearaway piece of left-wing anarchy. Indeed, it even spelt out the sort of public expenditure cuts that might be necessary. Shirley, who was tied up with all the to-ings and fro-ings with the TUC, had sent a message saying that at this delicate time the document should not be discussed, because it was bound to embarrass the TUC as well as the Government. Then Mik upped and said he agreed with her; Judith backed him, and so it was decided that we should merely circulate the document to the rest of the members of the NEC without comment. Wedgie, in the chair, pointed out ironically that, since the document was now headed, as we had previously agreed, by the statement that it was endorsed by no one but the Research Department, it hadn't leaked. I will be interested to see how the press treat this disappointingly (for them) low-key decision today. Could the headlines conceivably be: 'Left Refuses to Attack Government'?

At the office I had my long-planned meeting with Sir John Gray of the Medical Research Council [MRC]. It was originally arranged (at my suggestion) with the idea of my making it clear that I intended to go ahead with the Institute of Hearing Research on the lines Jack Ashley has rightly been fighting for and that, if the MRC stuck to its opposition, DHSS would go ahead unilaterally and finance a chair of hearing research at a university. In the event the MRC has climbed down and agreed to make £500,000 available for a new building to conduct and co-ordinate multi-disciplinary research. It has also accepted our terms of reference for the director, who we are determined shall be someone of international repute. So all I had to do was to mend my fences with Sir John by being immensely civil and respectful. It went very well and David said afterwards, 'It is good for the MRC to know that Ministers are taking an interest in their work.' So once again we politicians have been right and our officials wrong. We have succeeded in imposing some of our research priorities on the MRC without an open breach with it. Of course, officials opposed us all the way. They instinctively shared the MRC hostility to the Rothschild approach.[1] But once again the value of ministerial team-work (and of our weekly ministerial lunches) has been

[1] Lord Rothschild in his report 'A Framework for Government Research and Development' (Cmnd. 4814), published in November 1971, argued that research and development with a practical application as its objective must be done on a customer-contractor basis. 'The customer says what he wants; the contractor does it (if he can); and the customer pays. . . . However distinguished, intelligent and practical scientists may be, they cannot be so well qualified to decide what the needs of the nation are, and their priorities, as those responsible for ensuring that those needs are met.'

proved. Jack Ashley plugged away tenaciously at his views. I backed him a hundred per cent and threw in my whole weight as Secretary of State, while David did his usual intelligent in-fighting with officials on the health side.

After a busy day we started the Report stage of the Child Benefit Bill at 10pm – such is the pressure of parliamentary business up to the recess. It soon became clear that the Tories were determined to keep us late, dividing on all sorts of amendments, even though they were only keeping fifteen of their own people there. It also soon became clear that the Tory party is speaking with two voices. While Margaret is trying to get kudos by demanding tough controls of public expenditure, her lesser cohorts are busy attacking the Government for meanness on a number of specific issues. Kenneth Clarke on the Tory front bench indulged in more political hypocrisy than I have heard for a long time. We eventually got the Bill at 3.30am. Dawn was breaking when I finally got to bed at nearly 5am.

Tuesday, 8 July

As anticipated, the press had done its best with yesterday's non-event at Home Policy. The *Guardian* carries a story by Ian Aitken headed, 'Cabinet fights off Labour hard-liners'. All the glory went again, of course, to Shirley.

To the Lords to see Malcolm Shepherd about the grading of my Social Work Director post. The Civil Service Department have been standing out stubbornly against my request that the post should be upgraded to Deputy Secretary level. Their grounds are that the whole public service is suffering from what they call 'grade creep'. I have a lot of sympathy with this: after all, I know that Keith Joseph's reorganization of the NHS has been a grade creepers' paradise and administrative costs have gone shooting up. But I told Malcolm that, if the policy of integrating the health service with the social services was ever to become a reality, we must give a lead from DHSS by putting the social services on a parity with the health side and with social security. To my relief, he gave me a drink and we relaxed, with his Permanent Secretary, Ian Bancroft, listening sympathetically. I told Malcolm that, if he came to me and said that DHSS was overweighted with medical staff at the top, I wouldn't disagree with him. But in the meantime I could no longer afford to have the social work side eating below the salt. He responded with obvious warmth. From time to time, when I was selling Henry Yellowlees and his boys down the river, I exclaimed to the Private Secretary, who was busy scribbling a note, 'For God's sake don't minute that!' The poor chap would sit up guiltily and put his pencil down. I await the outcome of this *tête-à-tête* with some confidence.

At last I got home to the empty flat. I managed to eat a bit of food, wash a garment or two and flop into bed. It is a good week to be a Euro-widow because I am too tired to notice whether Ted is there or not. I only hope he is having a whale of a time in Strasbourg.

Wednesday, 9 July

After nine hours' sleep I am a different woman, ready for the day of tough policy meetings at the department that lies ahead. The first meeting was on how to control private practice once we have phased pay beds out of the NHS. I have told the department that our only hope of getting the legislation into the next Queen's speech is for us to get the policy cleared up before the recess and a consultative document issued so that Instructions can go to counsel. (It was Wedgie's failure to get policy cleared on time that led to the postponement of the Bill on the nationalization of aircraft and shipbuilding. It just missed the bus and there isn't a minute of parliamentary time left even for Second Reading.) The department has obviously been having agonies of indecision over the private practice policy, not least because officials are divided, Lawrence Brandes wanting to be tough, Gedling dithering and Philip uncertain about everything except the need for some sort of control. So the submission they have made to me consists merely of a list of problems matched by tentative suggestions or just plain question marks.

I opened the meeting by saying firmly (and optimistically) that we would not conclude it until we had reached a decision on every one of the points. It didn't matter whether the decision was perfect. We were merely drawing up a consultative document, not a Bill. Indeed, it was unlikely that even if we sat all day we should produce the perfect answer among ourselves, because, contrary to the belief we tended to nurture, we in the department were not the sole repositories of all wisdom. Philip, entirely agreeing with my line, denied vociferously that the department nursed any such illusion. And so we went through the key points, every one of them bristling with difficulties. To my relief, David no longer spent his time declaring that in his view the policy of control would never work. Instead he put forward a lot of constructive and useful points. When in this mood he is invaluable. He is undoubtedly extremely able. It is his erratic changes of line that disturb everyone and make my job difficult. I have always believed in giving my Ministers of State their head, merely drawing the reins to myself again when vital policy decisions are at stake. And they appreciate it. David said to me with his charming smile the other day, after Harold's mini reshuffle, 'You nearly lost me to the Treasury. Denis wanted me to take the job of Financial Secretary. Don't worry, I refused. I told Denis that a Financial Secretary had no authority. I'd rather stay where I am, where I can get something done.' 'I would have told Harold to ban the move,' I quipped back. It is David's occasional arrogance of manner that gets him in bad with officials. It is a fault he shares with Roy Jenkins. I think Brian and I humanize him.

For nearly two hours we went down the list of queries. As I looked round that table, flanked by anxious and – in some cases – hostile officials, I thought once again how desperately a Minister needs allies if any real policy changes are to be made. The policy we thrashed out began to take workable shape. As usual, I encouraged every agnostic official to voice his views and, as we proceeded, we began to plan fundamental and long overdue reforms in the *quality* controls of private nursing homes and hospitals, as well as quantitative ones. At 12.45 I had to admit that we could not meet my deadline before lunch. Rejecting my usual tray of cheese and lettuce, I disappeared to the House, where I joined Eric Heffer and Caerwyn Roderick for steak and kidney pie in the Members' dining room. They were speculating gloomily about the outcome of the week's manoeuvrings over the pay policy.

Before I could get back to the office I had to attend the special meeting of the NEC requisitioned by Mik and co. to discuss the crisis. Ministers were there in force, except for Harold and, of course, for Jim, who was away in Africa trying to save Hills's life. Mik was soon in full spate with a bitter attack. After the last election, he said, the PM had promised closer contact between the Government and the party. Instead, contact had 'never been worse'. There had been no meeting between the NEC and the Cabinet since the election and the precious Liaison Committee between NEC and Government hadn't met once. Okay, so the Government was constantly talking to the TUC, but what about the party? 'The Government is expressing contempt for the party even worse than in the 1966–70 Government.' It thought that party members were merely 'dogsbodies to go and knock on doors'. Time and again meetings arranged with Ministers were cancelled 'and Peter Shore is the worst'. He ended in a crescendo of viciousness: 'We are heading for direct confrontation between the party and the Government.' Other people were more moderate. Joan Lestor asked how we could hope to sustain the economy by cutting back on services like education or social services which were designed to protect us from unemployment. Sam McClusky of the seamen's union was concerned about what would happen under the new policy to pay claims that were in the pipeline and had been to arbitration. Alex Kitson echoed Jack Jones's line on the need for flat-rate increases instead of percentage ones, more price controls and no statutory powers.

During all this Denis was getting more and more tense. I could see his Irish dander getting up. He spoke eloquently and forcibly, reminding us that the Manifesto was not only against statutory incomes policy; it also said in terms that 'the fight against inflation is the most important job of the next Labour Government'. He laid about him in great style. The Government had kept its side of the Social Contract, he declared, but, thanks to some unions, the TUC pay guidelines had not been observed. We were on a slippery slope. Import controls would not cure inflation. He was so carried away that he got his phrases mixed up, saying that import controls would make things worse by making things 'cheaper'. 'More expensive,' I corrected kindly, at which he snapped, 'Don't talk rot, Barbara.' Everyone laughed, and some, including Ron, called out, 'She is trying to help.' But Denis was so beside himself he wasn't listening. He swept on with his tirade and Shirley turned to clutch my arm: 'Don't mind it, Barbara. Denis has been under terrible strain all the week.' I replied with my usual softness, 'I don't mind, Shirley. In fact, I'm rather amused.' (Later I was rewarded by hearing on the nine o'clock news a report to the effect that Denis, faced with tough opposition by people like me, had slapped me down. When will I learn not to be soft?) On went Denis: 'I sometimes wonder where my colleagues live.' He himself had been talking to miners in his Yorkshire area and they had said to him as he described what he was trying to do, 'It's about bloody time.'

Through all this Mik was doodling furiously. Then Denis left, leaving Mike with the unenviable task of clearing up the wreckage. He spoke with his usual diffidence. 'We can't get through the situation in the next six months without having a policy to get through this side of the problem.' At this point I left. I wasn't going to stay to make a Roman holiday for Frank Allaun, who had insisted that members of the NEC must be free to move and vote on a Motion and was obviously preparing one. I had voted against this suggestion, but it had been carried.

Back at the office we had another long session on private practice, finally conclud-ing the major points for the consultative document. It was David who pointed out that we might have to postpone the final phasing-out date from November 1976 as originally agreed, because otherwise we would be cutting off earnings from pay beds during the very year when we were limiting consultants' earnings under the pay policy. So we might be laying ourselves open to claims for compensation. The path to reform is immensely complicated! Home to read my papers for tomorrow's crucial Cabinet.

Thursday, 10 July

In my box was a note from Norman: would I arrive at Cabinet early, as there would be a redraft of the White Paper on pay policy waiting for us at No. 10 which we were expected to read before Cabinet. So I arrived at 9.45am and was ushered upstairs to the large reception room, where coffee was waiting for us. The second draft was much superior to the first, and, of course, in both drafts there were alternative passages in brackets on reserve powers. But I was still shocked by the total lack of any indication of a socialist strategy. The sections on unemployment and public expenditure were pure Treasury orthodoxy – not even a mention of the NEB! In Cabinet Harold was at his most businesslike. We had got to get the White Paper agreed that morning; we would go through it paragraph by paragraph. But Wedgie intervened to say that some of us had not been in the intensive discussions with the TUC and CBI this week. Could we be told what had happened? Denis, looking rather irritated, skimmed through the events rapidly: there had been agreement with the TUC on the £6; the 'only issue left' was whether the cut-off for increases should be at £10,000 or £7,000. When some of us raised our eyebrows at this he added hastily that the TUC were at first not prepared to discuss any legislation at all, but had later agreed to penal sanctions through the Price Code, legislation to relieve employers of their contractual obligations and the selective application of the rate support grant. The CBI had finally agreed to the use of the Price Code, but were urging that we should have reserve powers against the employer. They didn't like the £6 and preferred a percentage figure. 'We must get on,' intervened Harold.

We went through the other paragraphs, making relatively minor changes, until we came to paragraph 38 on 'action on employment', where I was poised to make a row. But Wedgie got in first. 'I move we delete paragraphs 38 to 45,' he said sternly. 'The strategy in these paragraphs is entirely pre-Keynesian. There isn't even a passing reference to the NEB!' No one supported deletion, not because I (and I've no doubt Mike) didn't agree with him, but because we thought the right way was to amend the paragraphs radically. Even Harold Lever was disturbed by them. There must, he said, be a clear commitment that, if workers would co-operate in the pay policy, 'the Government will get these horrific levels of unemployment down'. Harold Wilson and Denis were soon agreeing to redraft, incorporating references to the NEB. Next we turned to the section on public expenditure. I pounced angrily. The paragraphs, I said, contradicted themselves. First we argued that a pay policy was an alternative to cutting the social wage; next that we had to review public expenditure anyway. I moved the deletion of the sentence which referred to that. Harold said that we should be discussing this question on Monday at a special Cabinet on the medium-term economic assessment, so the sentence was merely a statement of fact. It did not commit Cabinet to any specific decision. I persisted. Wedgie backed me. 'Is this policy an alternative to public expenditure cuts, or is it, as I believe, the first step?' he demanded. 'We've got to do both,' retorted Roy J., giving the game away. Harold insisted the sentence must stay in, but said there could be some redrafting here as well. I nagged on. What target date had Denis in mind when the paragraph talked about the need to 'eliminate' the balance of payments deficit? He hadn't got any specific date in mind, he replied irritably. And so I was overruled, but my suspicions were unallayed. 'Why do you think we're not going to discuss public expenditure until *after* this White Paper?' I whispered to Eric. 'The timing is deliberate.'

By this time it was 12.30 and we broke for coffee, refreshing ourselves for the tussle over reserve powers still to come. I went up to Mike and Peter and said, 'We ought to meet immediately after Cabinet to discuss our line. I'll get my secretary to lay on some sandwiches.' They agreed, but Mike said diffidently, 'I should tell you that I cannot say I will necessarily resign. Jack Jones has been pleading with me to remain in the Government whatever happens.' 'That's why we must talk,' I replied. The tussle began at 12.45 and did not end till 3pm. Denis opened, fighting hard for his reserve powers. The TUC had gone a long way but it was 'absolutely essential that the White Paper carries conviction with our creditors'. We now had a big battery of powers, but the key question was how to secure compliance with the policy. Unfortunately 'the problem of credibility became worse in the past week'. Last year the Trades Union Congress had carried the Social Contract policy by an overwhelming majority, yet it hadn't been observed. What could we expect to happen now, when the General Council yesterday had only carried the policy by nineteen votes to thirteen? We needed reserve powers on employers in the legislation to make the policy work and to give it credibility. In his view it was better to get the parliamentary battle over now. It would be more, not less, difficult later on.

Harold supported him. If the White Paper was not credible we could be bringing Parliament back in August to deal with another run on the pound. He was totally opposed to criminal sanctions against workers, but sanctions against employers were not the same thing. He would like to operate with the agreement of the TUC, but the vote in the General Council had not been 'happy' and had been widely interpreted as meaning that compliance would be unlikely. Elwyn then asked what sanctions there would be on employers? Harold replied, 'Presumably a limited fine and no limit on indictment.' He called on Michael next. As always, Mike started almost hesitatingly. The TUC thought, he said, that they had gone very far. If we were to upset what had been agreed with them, the whole atmosphere might change. It was true there had been no specific discussion with them about reserve powers, but Denis must know that more than once Len had expressed opposition to the idea 'in the strongest possible terms'. ('This is fair,' admitted Denis.) If we went ahead, what would happen, asked Mike, warming up. There would be 'effective action leading to the destruction of the Government'. The parliamentary row would be a threat to sterling the whole time. As for our relations with the trade union movement, the vote in the

General Council yesterday had been 'a disappointment', but he thought the reason for it was that the TUC had gone to extremes in tightening up the policy and some union leaders, like Alf Allen and Alan Fisher, were merely reacting to certain aspects of that tightening. If we took reserve powers there would be an angry debate in the trade union movement and almost certain defeat in Congress. What would that do to sterling? 'We can't run an incomes policy without the support of the trade union movement.'

Shirley followed. Until yesterday she had been uncertain, but the vote in the General Council had decided her that Denis was right. Bob made one of his robust speeches, coming out against the powers, rather to my surprise. 'What would the legislation achieve?' he asked scornfully. Tony C. had the best of both worlds. The issue, he said, was 'trivial' from a counter-inflationary point of view. Nonetheless, the risk of a run on sterling was paramount, so he supported Denis reluctantly. Harold at this stage was signalling for me to come in and I wondered why. Could it be true, as Mike believes, that he is wavering and wanted the case against powers put as early on as possible, so that others would be convinced and so give him an alibi for deserting the Chancellor? My line was to cast doubt on the 'credibility' argument. If it was compliance we were worried about, who was likely to rat on the policy? If it was the unions, we weren't taking powers against them anyway. If it was the employers, why would they be doing it? Employers in this straitened economic situation were hardly likely to be rushing around pressing wage increases on their workpeople. If they ratted it would be because they were under pressure from a strike or threat of a strike. So what would be the scenario in which we would be going to Parliament for authority to activate these reserve powers? A situation in which the policy was being violated as a result of strike action. Was it really credible to try and get Parliament to invoke powers against an employer because he was under a threat? Could we really get the Tories to vote for that? Many of our own people would not vote for penal sanctions against anyone. In the coming debate did we really think this point would not be highlighted? If it was 'confidence' we were after, we really only had two choices: either to go the whole hog, with sanctions against workers, or to build up the effectiveness of the agreement we had got with the unions. And I personally thought it was highly effective. We had a phalanx of legislative measures plus agreement with the unions: it was a formidable package. Someone had said, 'What about Arthur Scargill?' but the fact was that Scargill had been beaten at the miners' conference. Just compare Heath's humiliation at the hands of the miners with what we had got out of them! We must not throw the priceless asset of our agreement away. Mike nodded approvingly at all this. Peter spoke in very similar vein. Roy Jenkins backed Denis, except that – typically – he would have preferred a 10 per cent figure rather than the flat rate. Wedgie read a piece from the Manifesto which he was carrying as he arrived – duly getting himself photographed.

As the contributions rolled on Eric and I began to keep a tally; for reserve powers: Ted Short, Denis, Shirley, Crosland, Prentice, of course (he said he would have been willing to go the whole hog), Roy J., Malcolm Shepherd and Fred Peart. Against them Mike, me, Bob, Eric, Peter, Wedgie, John Silkin. Eric was resigned to our defeat, and then some surprising things started to happen. First, Fred Mulley said he was very unhappy about throwing away our agreement with the TUC. Could we not merely say that we had a Bill ready which we would introduce if the policy looked like breaking down? This would mean that we would not be legislating right away, but would be giving the TUC the chance to deliver the goods. Soon Merlyn was coming down in favour of the same idea, followed by John Morris and finally – biggest surprise of all – by Harold Lever, the author of the whole idea of powers against employers. More surprises. Roy Mason came out vigorously against reserve powers. So did Elwyn and Willie Ross. Eric and I became jubilant. It was clear we had won hands down. But Harold, who, I suspect, had all along been plotting for a compromise, summed up with his usual cunning when he is determined to get his own way. Apart, he said, from the four who wanted a compromise, Cabinet was evenly divided for and against. (The truth was that, leaving out the four, we had won by ten to nine.) He would like to know what the Chancellor felt. Denis promptly squeezed the maximum advantage out of his defeat. Of course, he said, he would have preferred to legislate for reserve powers now. 'Cabinet's attitude imposes a major problem for me personally.' But he would accept Cabinet's decision, provided that we announced that a Bill was already prepared and would be introduced immediately there was a breach of the policy. And if that happened it wouldn't be a question of legislating *reserve* powers; the powers would operate immediately. And, of course, if the package failed to restore confidence in sterling, we would have to use the powers right away. 'We are meeting on Monday,' soothed Harold, 'and can consider the position then in the light of reaction abroad.' For good measure Denis gave us a parting shot with a glare at me. 'Cabinet will appreciate that as the package is weaker than I would like, that will make it all the more necessary for us to be tough over public expenditure.' I was about to protest when Harold hastily wound things up. 'We shall be discussing that too on Monday.' And he designated Denis, Mike and Shirley to form a drafting committee to agree the redrafted bits that afternoon. We broke up, longing for food. 'Can we still have those sandwiches of yours?' asked Eric and I said, 'Of course,' telling Mike, Peter and Wedgie to come along to my room immediately. Merlyn and Fred were looking very pleased with themselves, but assured me there had been no collusion and no one had put them up to it. 'Not even Harold?' I asked sceptically.

Over sandwiches we agreed that we had been manoeuvred into a trap. We couldn't even be sure that Denis would not welcome a run on the pound as a justification for slapping on the reserve powers right away. I asked Mike how he thought the TUC would take the compromise. 'They'll be very relieved,' he replied, grinning with relief himself. He would have been in an impossible position if we had lost.

At last I got back to the office for a meeting on export promotion. The Minute to the Prime Minister about this which Norman had drafted for me has done the trick and brought Philip into action so as not to lose control of the whole thing. He recognizes that I am determined to bring someone in from outside and we had a long discussion about what his remit should be and what kind of person we wanted. I said I wanted a procurement and export executive, headed by an outsider. 'If we can get the man we want, Secretary of State,' said Philip, 'which I doubt.' Finally I asked him to prepare me two alternative scenarios and put up some names. After the meeting Jack and Brian A-S. came dashing back into my room. Could they have an urgent word with me about Monday's Cabinet? They had been studying the Chancellor's paper and the accompanying Treasury paper on the MTA [medium-term assessment] which had arrived while I had been in Cabinet. Did I realize that the Chancellor was going to demand an immediate decision on the £2 billion cuts from 1978–79? He wanted to announce it in the anti-inflation debate next week. I thumped the table furiously. 'So he lied to me this morning. He tried to fool us that no decision was imminent.' I could now see the whole ploy. Denis had kept this back until he had got the White Paper, trying to wangle reserve powers out of us as an *alternative* to public expenditure cuts, knowing all the while that on Monday he was going to demand his full public expenditure cuts as well. At this moment Norman came in to tell me Cabinet had been recalled for 6.30pm, 'but we have been told it will be short'. 'What on earth? – perhaps it is only so that we can approve the redrafts,' I said. 'Give me the papers. I will raise this in Cabinet.' As I read the MTA I made another discovery. The proposed economic strategy is based on our eliminating the balance of payments deficit by 1978. So Denis had lied to me about that too. We had been conned and I was determined to let Denis – and Cabinet – know I knew we had been.

When I arrived at No. 10 the cameras were still hovering. So was the large crowd of gazing holiday-makers. Harold, having got his way, was at his most affable. He and Denis, he said, had seen the TUC and the CBI and given them an indication of the decision of Cabinet. They had both accepted it. But the rest of us were abjured not to breathe a word to anyone. 'It's always No. 10 and Treasury who leak anyway,' I whispered to Eric. Denis then went into a rather emotional spiel about how essential it was to handle the decision properly. 'Foreign opinion will accept our formulation if domestic opinion does.' It was imperative, therefore, that there should be no talk of 'victory' by anyone over anyone else – no gloating that the Chancellor had been defeated. We nodded solemnly, shocked at the very idea of such caddishness. I began to wonder how I could raise my point about public expenditure. In this atmosphere any criticism of Denis would seem an indecency. But I was determined not to let him get away with it and at last I got my point in by asking how we had redrafted the section referring to the policy as being an alternative to public expenditure cuts. 'When I got back to my office this afternoon,' I ploughed on, 'I saw the Chancellor's paper and the one on the MTA. In it Denis is asking us to decide on Monday to accept the £2 billion cuts *as a minimum* so that he can announce it during *next week's* debate. So it would clearly make us look ridiculous if tomorrow we were to publish a White Paper holding out the hope that this pay policy is an alternative.' 'That bit has been rewritten,' replied Denis triumphantly. 'Anyway,' drawled Crosland, 'what is the use of discussing a document that is already in print?' But I could see that some of my colleagues had pricked up their ears apprehensively.

Nonetheless, a sense of hopelessness engulfs me. The only strategy that will be before us on Monday will be one which commits us to unemployment levels continuing at 3 per cent right up to 1978–79, after which, say the Treasury, things should improve economically. But they certainly won't improve politically for us. This is a scenario for another Tory victory just in time for them to reap the harvest of our bitter self-sacrifice. And the price will be the destruction of all our social policies, so that a Labour Government will preside over the biggest cuts in public services since 1931. There *must* be a better way of running a Labour Government. I still back a voluntary wages policy, plus more daring and adventurous appeals to social conscience than we are ever likely to get out of this carefully 'balanced' (i.e. highly conventional) Government. And we are under this difficulty: that none of us are equipped with the sort of economic advice that enables us to stand up to the dubious expertise of the Treasury. All Jack and Brian could do this afternoon, for instance, was to wring their hands at me over the MTA and the consequences Denis wants to ensue. They can spell out brilliantly the disasters that will happen to my department if he gets his way, but it is not their job – and they wouldn't know where to start – to provide an alternative. As Brian put it to me this afternoon, 'I could talk to Worswick of the NIESR [National Institute for Economic and Social Research]; he's a friend of mine. But how could I disclose a Treasury document to him?'

Friday, 11 July

I rearranged my day so that I could be present in the House for Harold's statement on the White Paper.[1] I squeezed in between Harold Lever and Jim Callaghan, whom I congratulated on the Hills affair. 'I thought it might help to distract attention from other things,' purred Jim. 'Ah, but,' I replied, 'our people have been saying why couldn't Jim time it for the morning of the Woolwich by-election?' Harold's statement sounded well, but I nearly went frantic as he fell over himself to conciliate every enemy within sight: from Margaret Thatcher to Ted Heath, who was sitting immobile, staring straight ahead as usual. Harold Lever, trying to contain me, assured me that this was Harold at his most cunning, but to me – blunt and inept Yorkshire as I am – words are words and I just could not stomach my PM saying that he had placed great importance on reaching agreement with the TUC, 'as the Right Honourable Gentleman had tried to do'. Really! Lever kept up a running commentary in my ear and I reciprocated, saying to him at one point, 'Do you know what target date Denis has set himself for eliminating the balance of payments deficit?' Lever didn't, so I told him, '1978.' 'But that's ridiculous,' he replied, adding, 'Let's have lunch together next week. Let me talk to you.' I told him I would welcome it. On one thing we agreed: that Thatcher with her prim and carefully modulated diction flopped. I was reminded of Jeremy Thorpe's words to me at the Oxford Union: 'The lady will not do.' Jeremy didn't 'do' today either. Too fluently slick by half. Incidentally, I noticed how cleverly Harold exploited Cabinet's agreement that we should help Denis as much as possible. He kept referring to 'reserve powers' as though we

---

[1] In introducing the White Paper Harold Wilson described the TUC's agreement to the pay policy as 'unexampled in peace or war by the free democratic trade union movement in this country'. He listed the 'battery of weapons' that would be provided by the legislation to enforce the policy, such as the use of price controls and the rate support grant as sanctions against recalcitrant firms and authorities, and reiterated that legislation had also been prepared, 'for introduction if need be', to make it illegal for the employer to exceed the pay limit. On the prices side the Government was extending strict price controls and intended to ensure that price increases for a range of essential goods did not exceed the 10 per cent. It had also decided to delay the phasing out of food subsidies announced in the Budget and to limit rent increases.

had already taken them. But the Left remained strangely muted. After all, Harold holds the trump card of an agreement with the TUC.

The statement over, I went to the annual conference – the first ever – of the Association of Health Authorities, which I encouraged to become a pressure group for the NHS. During a scrappy buffet lunch they were all over me: I seem fated to live on sandwiches, suppers of bacon and egg or fork lunches largely consisting of rice. But when I made my tough speech about cutting our NHS coat according to our diminished cloth, I suddenly found myself wondering why I was doing the Chancellor's job for him. Certainly my audience was far from enamoured. There must be a more positive message than this.

David Watt in the *Financial Times* has an article, 'Where Common Sense is Not Enough', which reflects most of the things I have been saying in Cabinet. I am sure that, if we in the Labour movement fall too much for the orthodox financial line, we are finished.

Joe Rogaly, incidentally, went to town last Tuesday on the social wage. Norman brought his article in to me, looking rather pale. Obviously the department thinks I have been shooting off my mouth. In fact, as usual, Joe had got all his material before he spoke to me – and I suspect he got it from Treasury.

It was lovely to get home to HCF and find Ted waiting for me, full of interest in his great adventure. He is so sold on parliaments he is obviously ready to be sold on this European one. He told me that by far the most impressive British figure at Strasbourg was Peter Kirk. It is total joy for me to see Ted so fulfilled, even if he is now in favour of directly elected European Parliaments, providing the timing is right. I am ironically amused by all this and remember that, at the height of the anti-Market campaign, when Ted was loyally throwing his whole weight behind the anti-marketeers, he confessed to me privately that he wasn't all that convinced that the issue was life and death. These are the political nuances beneath the monolithic surface of party loyalties.

Saturday, 12 July

The press on Harold's statement isn't too bad, though the 'foreign reaction' isn't as clear-cut as I would like it to be. We could yet be faced with a crisis on Monday – and who can say who will have engineered it? I'm amused to see, incidentally, that Harold has launched the Public Relations Unit I suggested to him. Of course I shan't get any credit for it.

Sunday, 13 July

After a happy day of gardening, work and lunch with our friend, John Fane, at Wormsley House – during which we read the scaffold speech of his regicide forebear, Colonel Scroop and admired Cromwell's boots, I suddenly found that my Ted had been hit again by the press. This time it was the *Observer*, which, in a leader, picked him out for attack, saying he ought not to have been chosen for the European Parliament. Ted pretended not to care, but I know that it has taken the gilt off his bit of long-overdue gingerbread. I was so angry I could have killed the leader-writer. Because, of course, under the guise of dispassionate comment on matters of public interest, whoever it was was merely earning his bread and butter by promoting his newspaper's party line – i.e. to boost the Liberals. To pick Ted out for a sneer, saying he ought to give way to 'more vigorous and better informed Labour men', when what the *Observer* really wanted was that old European hack, Lord Gladwyn, is an old party trick: attack a policy you don't like under the guise of a dispassionate comment on an individual Minister's or representative's ability. I've suffered from it myself.

All this is made worse by the excitement with which Ted has come back from Strasbourg. He is thrilled to have been put on the political committee, is ready to devote himself flat out to the new work and is even planning to take a fortnight's refresher course in French! I suppose the *Observer* would prefer anyone whose name isn't Castle.

Monday, 14 July

Peter [Shore] phoned me yesterday to see if I could come to lunch. He had a few people coming in to discuss what we should do about the MTA and public expenditure. I just couldn't face ruining another Sunday at HCF, even for that, so I arrived at Cabinet at 10am, not having had a chance to co-ordinate strategy with anyone. Another grim morning milling round our economic miseries lay ahead. In my brief Jack and Brian pleaded with me to try and get any announcement of the £2 billion figure of cuts delayed until Cabinet had had a chance to study the detailed consequences. Officials, on the other hand, advised me to accept the Chancellor's recommendations, as they believed there was no alternative. This is exactly why political advisers are so necessary. I have no doubt that most top officials are conventional and conscientious Tories, so *they* are never going to encourage me to challenge the Treasury's fiat.

Harold opened by congratulating himself on this new approach to the public expenditure: 'it has never been done before'. Here were ordinary Cabinet mortals being let into the secret statistics of the MTA before we had to decide such mundane things as cuts. That would come later; we were merely deciding the 'global amount' today. We would have an all-day meeting at Chequers on 25 July to work out the details of the cuts. Then in the autumn we would put the finishing touches to the PESC exercise. Denis then covered familiar ground. There was 'severe imbalance' in the economy, he said. We were spending 5 per cent more abroad than we earned. Internally, public expenditure and loans amounted to 19 pence in the pound more than we were getting in taxes, etc. We had met the gap so far by borrowing and saving, but that couldn't go on. (He wasn't very convincing in explaining why.) We had got to close the balance of payments gap by 1978 – again, not very clear why. And he once again returned to the innuendo that public expenditure had got out of hand, not just relatively, but absolutely. It had grown from 42 per cent of GDP to 58 per cent over the last twenty years, he maintained, and in the last five years particularly had galloped ahead. We couldn't go on diverting manpower from productive industry at this rate. The economic assessment was probably over-optimistic. It was doubtful, for instance, whether we would get an improvement in productivity. 'Every time we come to office we've said we will improve economic performance and every time we've failed.' (Yet all you are advocating is the medicine as before, thinks I.) We couldn't go at the balance of payments more slowly because that would mean increasing borrowing. So, of the prospective yield of growth over the next few years we should have £600 million left to share between private and public spending. And we couldn't take it all in public expenditure. As usual, Harold called Tony C. – the Chancellor-in-waiting – next and, as usual, we got a mixture of brilliant analysis and suspended action. The factual analysis of the MTA document was 'not perfect', Tony pronounced. It had 'not made a sufficient case for a savage change in strategy'. We must wait and see what the policy involved before we accepted the 'absolutely catastrophic nature of the decision'.

More criticisms then came in quick succession. Peter, normally pretty tough about the economy, demanded to know what had changed since the January White Paper on public expenditure. The only change he knew of was the extraordinarily impressive improvement in the balance of payments: so why the flap? He thought it really was time we got back to some 'national strategic planning', as suggested in Neddy. Michael said that, if we announced the £2 billion figure next week, it 'would greatly add to the party's problems'. Shirley was concerned about the way we define public expenditure and about the effect of the cuts on those in poverty. Could we not put more emphasis on productivity? ('That's not for me,' snapped Denis. And when Shirley looked surprised he snarled, 'We've been in office eighteen months and I'm still waiting for some ideas on this to come from the Department of Industry.') Ted Short said he was very worried about unemployment. The 3 per cent estimate was 'wildly optimistic'. He concluded, 'The Treasury should take this paper back.' Even Elwyn thought a crude statement of the £2 billion cut next week would be a 'devastating blow to pay policy'.

Wedgie backed our opposition, while I launched into a speech which had them grinning at its impudence. The sentence that had most struck me in the whole MTA paper, I said, was one appearing in the middle of paragraph 14. It ran to the effect that: 'by 1978, following the elimination of the balance of payments deficit, the strain on resources will be very severe. By 1980 the situation should have eased.' That, I told them, was the scenario with which I had become so familiar during ten years' service in Labour Governments: a Labour Government coming into power, accepting all the adjurations to put the country's house in order, reaching a climax of sacrifice in election year which ensured our defeat and then watching the Tories inherit the harvest we had sown and proceed to squander it in a burst of public popularity. The Treasury, I continued to appreciative laughter, found Labour Governments perfect material on which to impose their rigidly orthodox patterns, which they never managed to impose on any other Governments. The reason was that we were instinctive Puritans. We came in, lavished a bit of money on the poor and then had an immediate guilt complex because we were naturally masochistic moralists who didn't really believe life should be fun. So we were receptive to the argument that our only duty was to be tough. Tory Governments never made this mistake. They knew that government was the art of the possible – which was why they kept us out of power so successfully. We had only scraped back in February 1974 because, fortunately for us, the Tories were led by another moralist who wrecked his party with his fanaticism. (The knowing grins round the table showed that the shafts had gone home.) What we ought to be doing, I continued, was to start the other way round, by asking the question, 'What will improve the standard of life?' Nothing the Treasury proposed ever in any circumstances improved the standard of life. As Denis shook his head vigorously I asked him: 'What course of action in the MTA document will improve the standard of life? A successful pay policy won't: we are now told it makes public expenditure cuts even more necessary. Eliminating the balance of payments deficit won't. That too, Denis has just told us, will make it even more essential for us to dig a "hole" in the economy to make way for the additional exports. No wonder people get cynical and uninterested. Whatever they do, the Treasury says more deflation is necessary. We all know that the only things that will raise the standard of life are increased investment and increased productivity. So why don't we enter into open discussions with the TUC and CBI about the choices we have to make if we are to reach these goals – just as we did over pay policy?' I agreed with Tony C. It was wrong to assume that people would automatically prefer cuts in public expenditure to higher taxes. It depended on which cuts and which taxes. We needed urgently to work out a comprehensive plan with the TUC and CBI.

So far we on the Left had made most of the running in the discussion, but the Chancellor's allies soon hit back. Harold Lever showed once again that, when the crunch comes, he will always tread the path of Treasury orthodoxy. He had, he said, 'no urge to plan the rapid self-sacrificial elimination of the balance of payments deficit by 1978', but we could hardly force the Chancellor to hold back the upsurge in exports that was now taking place. 'We've got to support the Chancellor.' He was soon backed by Roy J., Roy M., Reg P. (who couldn't wait for swingeing cuts to be introduced) and, of course, Fred Peart. Others, like John Morris, Fred Mulley and Merlyn, wobbled. They are making a positive habit of it. Denis replied at length, obviously torn between a determination to be tough and a lack of confidence in his own remedy. Sterling had 'fallen back a little' that afternoon, he told Elwyn. But he added frankly, 'I wouldn't however make too much of that.' All the criticisms made of the MTA strategy really pointed to more stringent cuts, not less. For example, if we didn't get a £500 million increase in investment, GDP would be down and we should need even greater cuts. 'I agree with Tony Benn: we can't go on taking 100,000 people a year out of productive industry.' We couldn't afford to carry a bigger load of interest. 'It is very difficult to know what is *essential* to maintain confidence,' he admitted honestly, but added, 'If I don't say anything next week it might have an effect on confidence.' Of course, the resource effect of different forms of public expenditure was very different, but 'they all have to be financed'. (A lame one, that. For instance, the cost of the child benefit scheme will all be chalked up against public expenditure, even though a large element of it will consist of absorbing Child Tax Allowances, which at present *don't* count as public expenditure. I remain firmly convinced that half the elaborately detailed public expenditure calculations are phoney in economic terms.)

Why had there been such a big change in the outlook since last December?

continued Denis. 'We did not expect so deep a recession.' The Germans and Japan-ese hadn't done nearly enough reflating, but he still thought the world upturn should start next year. As to unemployment, he admitted it would be 'above' 3 per cent till late 1977. He agreed we must move in the direction of a national plan, but the CBI was pressing for cuts in public expenditure. He then went off into a little tirade which was very revealing. A lot of people, he said, believed that too much of the resources of the nation were going on the public services. 'Barbara's social wage document will be very double-edged for us, though I'm in favour of publishing it.' People would be shocked, not pleased, when they saw how much we were spending on the social services. 'Which ones?' I demanded. 'Name them.' 'Oh yes,' he replied. 'Schools for one, and other forms of education.' Suddenly as I listened to him I lost heart totally. Harold Lever tossed me a note adjuring me not to look so miserable. I tossed him one back: 'I see no reason for the existence of a Labour Government. We have adopted the Tory *mores*. The only difference is that we carry out Tory policies more efficiently than they do.' He shook his head, but I felt I had lost all stomach for the fight. As I had said earlier, when Ted Short was moaning that he was worried about our abandoning the Manifesto, it isn't a question of not implementing it; we are committing ourselves to putting it into reverse.

Harold was summing up. He accepted the criticisms of the way we calculate public expenditure (but then, he has been doing it for years and nothing has happened). He returned to his favourite theme about the Brighton Marina: why is private invest-ment of that kind always considered an asset, while public investment in housing is dismissed as a liability? Why indeed? But I've been hearing Harold say this ever since 1968 and the Treasury is still having its own way unchallenged. All this was a cover for Harold's familiar device: trimming his sails while backing Denis. We had, he said, 'no alternative but to support the Chancellor'. In any case 'there *is* some resentment among the public about the level of public expenditure'. But this time there would be no flat cut across the board. Denis chipped in to say that what we were talking about was merely a reduction in the growth of public expenditure, not a cut. This was more than I could bear. I cried out, 'I do not want to be sensationalist, but I *must* challenge what the Chancellor has just said. He is just not telling Cabinet the truth.' To my surprise, Harold let me continue and everyone listened attentively as I read out a passage from my official brief, couched in cautious official language, but which contained figures on the health and personal social services side which showed irrefutably that the Chancellor's proposals would mean that expenditure under this heading would move from plus 4·2 per cent in 1974–75 to minus 1·2 per cent in 1978–79. 'Other departments can show the same,' intervened Tony C., but gently for him. 'I know,' I replied. 'I am not trying to argue a departmental case. I just want Cabinet to realize what it is that we are being asked to agree. For the first time since its inception expenditure on the NHS would show an actual decline. And don't tell me that this time it won't be a flat across-the-board cut. It will be spread over every one of us as it always is.' This stirred up the debate again and roused some of the others to express anxieties.

Finally Harold said that the list of priorities would be discussed at Chequers. In the meantime, he continued, the views in Cabinet as to whether Denis should mention a sum in his speech next week were neck and neck. The balance seemed to be held by those who would be influenced by the way the statement was worded. It was 'absolutely necessary' that something should be said in the debate, but two or three Ministers should have a look at the wording and report to Cabinet later in the week. Denis snapped out, 'I must say to you, Prime Minister, that these matters cannot be decided by a majority in Cabinet.' This was the first challenge to Harold's method of counting heads without calling for a 'vote' that I have ever heard. Harold smoothed him down, unperturbed. I said, equally anxiously, 'Did you say the meeting of Cabinet would be on Friday? I am committed to open part of a new hospital in a Health Service area where morale is already dangerously low.' John Hunt looked amiably worried, as he always does. Denis said savagely that, of course, if we could get an agreed statement there would be no need for Cabinet to meet at all. That merely decided me that I must talk to Michael, one of the drafters, as quickly as possible and, back in the office, I told the ever-eager Norman to lay this on.

Another long meeting at the office on private practice. The whole policy is beginning to take meaningful shape. Then I had to rush to the House for a special meeting of the Home Policy Committee to discuss the industrial policy paper which is to be put to conference.[1] The paper has, of course, been heralded by the press as indicating another bitter clash between Left and Right in the party. True it argues against a statutory pay policy in any form (having been written before the Government agreement with the TUC), and for import controls as an integral part of an expansionist strategy. God knows, I am not against that. It is just that I instinctively mistrust the overkill to which the Left is prone.

Wedgie began by declaring that the document in front of us was 'pushing the frontiers of our policy'. He had always believed that the 'present belonged to the Government but the future to the party', etc., etc. He positively appealed to Ron Hayward to rule how far the committee could go in developing policy – a role Ron didn't relish very much. Judith, whose whole *raison d'être* now consists in her work as chairman of the Industrial Policy Committee, insisted that her document was 'not an alternative strategy to what the Government is doing at the moment. The reality is that the paper goes beyond the present strategy.' And she added, 'I hope Ministers will stay their official hand in considering this paper.' To my surprise, the only Ministers there were Fred Mulley, Shirley and me. I had expected that Denis would be there in all his wrath. For myself, I did not see why I should take the defence of the Government strategy (with which I have not all that sympathy anyway) on to my shoulders. Shirley was typically emollient: there were a number of good things in the paper, she said, but she had certain queries. But Mik was so bitter he roused all my

---

[1] The document set out in indigestible detail the case for doubling manufacturing investment within ten years through the use of planning agreements (to be enforced through new statutory powers) and an expansion of the funds of the NEB, the drive for growth being backed by selective import controls. What worried me were the hesitant references to the possibility of 'requiring' pension and insurance companies to direct a certain proportion of their funds into approved manufacturing investment: one of the 'options' which it said the NEC was studying. This seemed to me to raise the maximum of alarm with the minimum of commitment. But I welcomed the document's realistic statement that 'the need for a dramatic recovery in manufacturing investment means that other demands on the economy must be severely restrained'.

natural combativeness. 'As to how Ministers behave, it is for people themselves to decide, but no doubt party members will note if Ministers decide their jobs are incompatible with membership of the NEC. We can't say that when we are in government the party must give up its policy-making function.'

Ron Hayward, to whom Wedgie kept appealing for papal dispensations, refused to be caught in the policy crossfire. He rode off on a technical tack, saying, 'You will make fools of yourselves because you have got your timetable all wrong. You have got to get it to delegates by September.' Mik tried to argue that the policy statement could be circulated at conference itself and I began to get irritated. I said that the trouble was that the document was too long and wordy: pages spent on spelling out an analysis and the actual policy choices wrapped up in verbiage. We needed a much shorter document so that we could pinpoint the policy options we had to face. Once that was done we could really see what, if anything, divided us. No one, for instance, would persuade me that import controls were the be-all and end-all of left-wing policy. And I added tetchily that I had come to discuss one aspect of the document that particularly interested me: the use of pension funds. I thought that there was substance in a lot of the argument the document used about using such funds for productive investment, but the way it was suggested we present the arguments gave us the worst of all worlds. 'The more radical one wants to be the more important it is to decide policy clearly before saying anything. Never hint; act.' Wedgie then hurried to conciliate me, asking me to spell out the amendments I wanted, while Geoff Bish grumbled, 'By all means let us cut the document. I never wanted a great spiel on economic strategy.' And so I left them and God knows what they did with the document.[1]

This over, I held an office meeting, at Brian O'Malley's request, about the starting date for the pensions policy. He stubbornly wants us to go for 1977, even though the pensions industry is against rushing things. I am all in favour of getting the scheme in the bag but am afraid of raising the matter with Treasury now because of the public expenditure exercise. I ruled that we should leave the matter open till the position is clearer.

Tuesday, 15 July

We had Cabinet today because Jim and Harold are due in Brussels on Thursday for a great Council of Ministers' post-referendum recap. We are in a mess because at the press conference introducing the Anti-Inflation White Paper Harold said that the Reserve Powers Bill would be published before the Commons debate, even though it was not intended to introduce it unless the voluntary system failed. Mike is furious: Cabinet has never agreed this. He has written to Harold demanding that publication should be deferred at least until after the Trades Union Congress: otherwise Len Murray's position will be impossible. Harold trimmed on this this morning, saying that the Bill should not be published during the debate next week, though Ministers should proceed to agree its text on a contingent basis and 'without prejudice'. He

---

[1] It was decided that a much abbreviated version should be put to conference.

knows he has boobed. We then proceeded to another long wrangle over MPs' pay. There have been scenes in the House about this and Harold was anxious to make a statement this afternoon. However, we soon became involved in elaborate statistical calculations. Assuming that one could not give MPs the full Boyle award of £8,000 (which we all agreed), what other formula should one adopt? Cost of living? Heath's pay policy stages? It was all very arbitrary. Eventually it was reduced to a choice between two figures; an increase in pay of £1,500 or £1,250. Typically, the right-wingers were all for giving the MPs the higher figure, but the rest of us plumped for the lower figure and swamped them.

We then turned to the question of a reduction of Ministers' salaries. Mike and I have been pressing for this for a long time and Jim was all in favour of it. Even Harold said he had now become converted to the necessity for it. So, of all people, did Roy Jenkins. But when we came to look at the mechanics we found the snags were insurmountable. It turned out that, under income tax law, if we were to renounce 10 per cent of our salaries we should still have to pay tax on the full amount! The only way out would be to carry an amending Order through the House – and we paled at the thought of what some mavericks might try to do then to our salaries! So in the end we had reluctantly to accept that the most we could do was to forgo the £2,000 increase in our parliamentary salary recommended by Boyle. I don't suppose we shall get any credit for it – and, as Roy Mason lost no time in pointing out, by continuing to freeze our salaries while the cost of living soars, we shall be reducing their value to about £8,000 by the end of this Parliament. Nonetheless, I have no doubt that what we are doing is right. While all the mathematical calculations were going on I passed Harold Lever a note: 'You don't need to be a politician to be a member of this Cabinet – merely a Fellow of the Royal Statistical Society.' Harold Lever scribbled on it: 'Duty compels me to pass on a note Barbara sent me' and tossed it to the PM. Harold read it, poker-faced, then scribbled on the bottom: 'Preferably an ex-President'[1] and tossed it back. It is this lack of stuffiness that endears him to me, despite everything.

We then proceeded in five minutes flat to decide *not* to go ahead with the new parliamentary building in Bridge Street. As I have never liked the design I welcomed this side-effect of the economy drive.

Another long evening of three-line whips in the House. I got Peter, Wedgie and Mike to come along to my room for a drink to discuss the statement on public expenditure Denis is to make next week. I need to know how things are going because I am due to make an official visit to Leigh on Friday and if there has to be a Cabinet I shall have to cancel it. We all agreed to resist with all our strength Denis's desire to mention the £2 billion figure of cuts in his speech and Mike promised to do all he could to get the statement watered down. I was therefore intrigued at David Owen's line when he came into my room later to have a word about public expendi-ture. He is all for getting a circular out to regional health authorities quickly to tell them what their capital allocations are going to be over the next few years – on the most pessimistic basis. I am all in favour of letting RHAs know where they stand as

---

[1] Harold Wilson had been President of the Royal Statistical Society from 1972 to 1973.

quickly as possible. The present hand-to-mouth last-minute basis of allocations is the negation of good planning – and I am the last person to run away from telling them the hard facts, as soon as they *are* hard facts. But I told David I was not willing to issue anything which implied we accepted across-the-board cuts while the battle over public expenditure was going on. He accepted this grudgingly, but surprised me by adding suddenly, 'I ought to let you know that I believe the cuts the Chancellor is asking for are essential. He has been drifting on this too long.' 'I don't necessarily accept that,' I replied, 'but in any case I'm damned if I am going to throw in my hand in the battle of priorities.' He then switched his ground and said he entirely agreed with that.

Wednesday, 16 July

I am very glad that Douglas Allen has proposed Pat Nairne to me as Philip's successor. David Owen first mentioned him to me, having formed a very high opinion of him when Nairne was Denis's Private Secretary at Defence. Denis too raves about him. When I met him I took an instant liking to him and am sure we shall get on. I think too he will be far less the conventional civil servant than Philip, loyal as the latter has been.

Having paired all day I was able to go with Ted to George Weidenfeld's late-night party for Françoise Giroud.[1] I had had my hair done, put on my kaftan dress and felt ready to enjoy myself. I always find George's sophisticated little parties fun. Everybody who is anybody is there, his elegant Chelsea flat is an aesthetic delight, the drinks are good and the conversation spicy. I felt – and looked – young and gay. It did me good.

Thursday, 17 July

Went to the royal garden party with Ted – much against my inclination as I have a lot of work to do, but he took the line that it might be the last time we should take tea in the royal tent. It was a pleasant sunny afternoon and we enjoyed strolling round the garden till the time came for tea. The royal tent was packed with High Commissioners and their magnificently garbed wives of various hues. The general crowd were roped off some distance from the tent like animals in a compound and, the Queen having walked through the people and done her stuff for over an hour, they stood gawping at us favoured few as we drank our tea and iced coffee and ate the Queen's delicious raspberries and cream. I was reminded irresistibly of George Tomlinson's story when, having started life as a half-timer in a cotton mill at the age of twelve, he became Minister of Education in the first Labour Government after the war. The night trains from Manchester back to London were packed and George was one of the lucky ones to be allocated a sleeper. 'Privilege, I suppose,' a sour Tory MP who had been unlucky said to him as they waited on the platform. 'Aye, privilege,' George replied in broad Lancashire. 'I've waited a long time for it and it's very nice now it's

---

[1] Secretary of State for Women's Affairs in the French Government. Weidenfeld and Nicolson had just published her book *I Give You My Word*.

cum.' I am glad to say that Ted and I share all the interests of normal people. No intellectual snobbery about *us*. Ted in particular adores ceremonial and will never willingly turn down a festivity.

Mike has reported victory over Denis's statement on the economy. Denis has climbed down and the fatal figure of £2 billion cuts does not appear. So my trip north tomorrow is on. Meanwhile the commentators are nagging away about the need to cut public expenditure; even Peter Jenkins has a piece on it. As for Joe Rogaly, he is beavering away in the *Financial Times* about the need for cash ceilings in the public sector. I had a chat with him on the phone about it the other day, telling him I thought it was all very sinister. I have only got by in the NHS in the past year because we got Treasury to inflation-proof our health expenditure (i.e., to compensate in full for all normal wage increases and for the excessive rise in the cost of living). Result: we got £600 million of supplementary estimates last year, giving us the highest ever share of the Gross National Product since the NHS started. But of course this didn't build a single new hospital. All it did was to enable us to pay decent wages in the NHS for the first time. I am perfectly willing to accept that the Treasury should not inflation-proof us for any increases above the £6 limit, but to go further than that and to fix rigid cash ceilings, regardless of what is happening to inflation, is merely an economists' technical device for cutting public expenditure – part of the drive to desocialize Britain.

Friday, 18 July

Had to get up at 6am to catch the early plane to Manchester for my official visit to Leigh. As usual (and rightly), the office had worked out a crowded day. I can only get away for these visits with such difficulty that I have to see as much as possible while I can. At the opening of the new ward at Leigh Infirmary I decided to make a largely off-the-cuff speech, and, for all my fights over public expenditure, I showed my usual loyalty to the Government by giving a stirring homily about the need to face economic stringency, to stop moaning about the fact that we hadn't got as much money as we would like and to concentrate instead on getting the best value for it. Once again I found some demonstrators waiting to lobby me as I arrived and I adopted my usual technique of asking that they be invited in to take a glass of sherry with us. It always defuses any damaging press reaction. This time it was an eccentric woman consultant who had got two of her colleagues to protest about politicians running the Health Service. (The other two melted away as soon as I had arrived.)

But the most exciting part of the day for me was at Hope Hospital. I had learned from one of the office papers that had come my way that the department had been sponsoring an experiment there in 'participative management' and I had said I wanted to visit it. So Norman had fitted in a buffet lunch with the workers, management consultants and hospital administrators so that I could discuss what they were doing and how it was going. It turned out to be utterly fascinating. Sid Hamburger [chairman of the Regional Health Authority] had done his stuff well and brought along representatives of all the different groups of staff who had been participating in the experiment: porters, cleaners, laundry workers, and so on. After an excellent lunch and some drinks they soon lost their shyness and when we drew up our chairs for a discussion after lunch, they were raring to go. They were full of excitement about the whole thing. First and foremost, it was great that they were considered important enough to be consulted about their work, but not least because they believed they had been able to suggest ways in which they themselves could be better used and money saved. One simple example: the cleaners pointed out that, when one part of the hospital had been refloored, no one had consulted them. Result: they found their equipment would not deal with the new surfacing. And some bright designer had put a white floor in the casualty ward. Never again! It was the most impressive demonstration of industrial democracy in action I have seen. On the way home Norman, Jack and I got really worked up about it. This, I told them, was what I wanted to see developed throughout the whole NHS. It was the only hope for the salvation of our society. Jack pointed out that the department was about to issue a circular about the experiment which was so down-beat as to be positively discouraging. 'Redraft it,' I told him. And I asked Norman to arrange an office meeting quickly on how we could promote more of the same.

My last visit of the day was to the Hester Adrian Research Institute. I am woefully ignorant about the mental handicap side of my job and wanted to see for myself what Dr Mittler[1] was doing. It was a hurried visit, but that meant they had to cut down the talking and give me the essence of it. As a positivist I find this slow, painstaking work with mentally handicapped children intimidating. My commitment here is intellectual rather than instinctive, but I am ready to instruct myself to give it priority. Altogether a rewarding day.

Monday, 21 July

The press has an odd sense of values. There were no cameras or reporters waiting outside Congress House when I arrived for the Liaison Committee meeting, and yet this was one of the most revealing meetings we have ever had. The press could have learned a lot if they had only probed. They could have learned, for instance, that this time the trade unionists were there in force, even Hughie, whose mute presence was an eloquent testimony to the almost total collaboration we are now getting from the TUC with the pay policy. The agenda of the meeting was to discuss the TUC's document, 'The Development of the Social Contract', and the White Paper on pay policy due to be debated in the House in the afternoon. Jack Jones presided over the meeting like a lynx-eyed guardian of the policy. So we had the ironic situation of people like Mik being in the role of chaps who were defying the trade union movement and getting rebuked by Jack. (My mind went back to the party conference of 1970 when, to Alex Kitson's distress, Jack dismissed me contemptuously in a talk with him with the words, 'She's lost all political credibility.' Alex begged then that I should be forgiven for *In Place of Strife*. Now Jack is denouncing Mik for opposing wage restraint! Such are the strange twists of politics.)

[1] Peter Mittler had been Professor of Special Education at the University of Manchester since 1973. He was a pioneer in this field and I made him chairman of the National Development Group for the Mentally Handicapped which we set up in 1975.

When I arrived Len Murray was speaking. The room was crowded, with only Harold missing from our side. Len was merely asking in moderate tones for some measures to be taken to deal with the increasing unemployment threat. And Denis was replying affably, saying that he had this very much in mind. The unions were also in rather edgy mood over the £6 pay limit. Len said that their aim was to secure its universal application. 'It is not a maximum,' he maintained. At this Denis tried to be stern. The unions were, of course, entitled to press for this, he said, but in the White Paper the £6 was laid down as a limit which in some cases might not be achieved. 'And that is the Government's position.' But Jack came back at him: 'Of course, you are right that, if we say the £6 must be paid in all cases, we're getting near a statutory policy. But will you at least say in the House today that the Government favours the payment of £6?' 'No,' replied Denis. 'This is a situation in which there is a clear distinction between the roles of the Government and the TUC.' Alf Allen came in at this: 'This is important. Some employers are already saying the £6 would finish them. That is not true of all of them. If my people are to be discriminated against before the start of the policy, their opposition will be even greater.' Hughie made his only contribution of the morning. Denis's answer, he said, was 'very disappointing'. He added, 'Where stands the Government as employer on this?' Even David Basnett joined the hunt. 'My executive will support the policy, but it will also support going for £6. I hope you will say this afternoon that you understand our point of view.' Denis dodged all this as best he could.

Wedgie then moved to a no doubt welcome diversion by saying that he wanted to talk about jobs. If the world economy's upturn did not take place, then obviously the outlook for employment would be much more serious. Once again it was Jack who tackled this left-wing deviationism. He said that he already saw signs of confidence among employers. He was sure that, as we were seen to be tackling inflation, investment would revive and this in itself would help jobs. Jim reinforced this by saying that he and Harold had been talking to Giscard and Schmidt and they had promised to consider taking new measures to stimulate investment. The idea had been mooted of a meeting of the European Federation of Trade Unions to discuss the employment outlook with the relevant Ministers, and no doubt Mike and Barbara would be going along. (News to me!) Jack then launched into an earnest appeal for us all to make a great effort to publicize the policy. 'The Social Contract is not dead. We should combine our resources in explaining what the Labour and trade union movement stands for. The attitude of MPs in demanding the right to maintain their percentage increases is not helping. We must put across why we need a Labour Government.' And he added, with an obvious sideswipe at Mik, who was sitting at the end of the room next to me, 'We cannot afford the luxury of boosting our egos.' He grew quite eloquent. 'Can we agree to do this ourselves – quite apart from anything being done by the Government? Very few people know what is in the Employment Protection Act, the Industrial Relations Act and so on.'

Len took up the theme: 'The key is that this is an *agreed* policy.' And he went on to say that he hoped there would be no publication of the Reserve Powers Bill in the immediate future. That would destroy the whole atmosphere we were trying to create. This gave Denis the chance to exonerate himself. 'Frankly, I was staggered when the PM said he was going to publish the Bill,' he told us. 'Of course, that was an unpremeditated answer to a question at a press conference. What I shall have to do this afternoon is to spell out the contents. I shall try to justify not publishing the Bill.' While Len and Jack were nodding approval at this, Mik came in. After all, it is the Tribune group which has been harassing the Government on this as much as the Opposition has. The difficulty, said Mik, was that MPs were being asked to approve the White Paper and the White Paper mentioned the Bill, which wasn't being published. To say that the use of powers against employers was not a statutory policy was absurd. But once again Jack slapped him down. Publication would be disastrous. 'You've got to teach your union [ASTMS] to show a bit of trade union solidarity,' he snapped. (So the row at Congress between Jack and Clive Jenkins is shaping up.) Mike assured Mik that there was no question of anyone being committed to the Bill until it had been presented to Parliament, but I doubt if Mik is listening to Mike these days. The breach between Mike and the Tribune group is now almost as great as the breach was between me and them in the previous Labour Government over *In Place of Strife*.

Shirley ended the proceedings by a great plea on publicity. Could not junior Ministers be mobilized to do three or four meetings each on the policy, backed by trade union representatives? That would give us 1,200 meetings over the next months. ('It's got to be earlier than that,' chipped in Jack.) When I congratulated her on her contribution she said in her nice way, 'It was you who first showed me the importance of this.' 'Why don't you and I take the leaders of Harold's new Public Relations Unit out to lunch to get them to organize this?' I suggested. She thought it was a good idea and would get her office to fix something with mine, but I very much doubt whether I shall hear any more from her about it. Once again I realize that the whole secret of success lies in follow-through. Jack is no doubt going to work very hard at this as far as his writ runs, but there is no co-ordinating machinery. Sometimes I despair, but no one who attends these liaison meetings can be in any doubt how far Jack and Len have gone, or that Hughie and people like Alf Allen, who voted against the policy on technical points, are willing to be silent co-operators in it. Ted Heath would envy us the collaboration we have achieved.

At the office I had to curtail the ministerial lunch so that I could meet the BMA before the opening of the Commons debate on the Anti-Inflation White Paper. They came in all their solemn majesty, with Lewin flanked by Tony Keable-Elliott and a representative of the junior hospital doctors, to tell me how much they disapproved of the flat rate formula and, above all, the cut-off at £10,000, and to ask me a series of detailed questions as to what we intended to do about increments, pension rights, merit awards, etc. under the pay policy. It was a familiar atmosphere: the incredibly complicated fall-out there always is even from an apparently simple pay policy formula. I staved them off, saying all these things were still being examined, but I would convey their views. But the revelation of the deep gulf there is between classes in this country came through clearly, even though this time they behaved with courteous restraint. I pointed out to them, for instance, that a year or two ago no one would have believed that the NUM executive would ever ballot their members recommending that they accept a flat rate £6 increase. And I thought the cut-off had contributed to this miracle. Lewin merely responded to this by remarking stiffly, 'You have confirmed my worst fears, Secretary of State, that we are being sacrificed to placate the miners.' It is at times like this that I know instinctively which side of the class war I am on.

Instead of listening to the debate I sloped off to the flat to cook patés, etc., for Sunday's pensions party,[1] which is now the talk of the department. I adore entertaining, but fitting it in to the pressures of ministerial life does create difficulties. Norman has entered into the spirit of the thing. 'I'll have to produce a fictitious list of engagements for you, Secretary of State.'

Tuesday, 22 July

My back aches and I feel bilious. It must be end-of-term strain. If my great, rich endowment of health and strength ever melts away I shall be in the soup.

Lunch with Harold Lever at Eaton Square. We ate in elegant isolation amid the colour and grandeur of the formal dining room. The pictures, porcelain and silver must be priceless. Even Harold's exquisite ties must cost a bomb. I have never indulged in the politics of envy and there is such a disarming honesty about Harold I always warm to him. We discussed Reg Prentice's troubles at Newham[2] and I told him I thought he, the PM and others who had written in support of him had been wrong to interfere. He agreed in principle, but added, 'If we hadn't, he would have been out; it's as simple as that.' On the contrary, I said, I was sure that the intervention would be counter-productive. Harold then destroyed his own case in support of Reg by telling a jocular story about himself: how he had disagreed with his own local Labour Party about the Common Market and had said he could not conform to their views on this, but had told them they had a perfect right to get another MP if they found his views intolerable. Result: there had never been a move to unseat him. 'Exactly,' I said, 'and that is what you should have said in Reg Prentice's case.'

But when we came to discuss economic strategy I found Harold had lost his old cheeky independence of attitude. He just couldn't keep still, jumping up from the table time and again during the meal to hobble up and down as if to relieve an intolerable tension. He was also firmly committed to the new right-wing line that the level of public expenditure had become excessive and that it should be curbed as a desirable end in itself. I'm afraid I shan't find him much of an ally in Cabinet, but our

---

[1] Brian O'Malley and I had promised the departmental staff who had worked on our new pensions scheme a party to celebrate the passing of the legislation. The Social Security Pensions Act 1975, embodying the scheme, received the Royal Assent on 7 August.

[2] For some time the Newham North East constituency Labour Party had been restive about the political attitude and statements of Reg Prentice as its MP and had called a special meeting for 23 July to discuss a Motion calling on him to retire at the next general election. A letter of support for him had been sent to the constituency party signed by twelve Cabinet Ministers and 160 Labour MPs. The previous day Harold Wilson had thrown his weight into the fray. In a letter to Labour MP Neville Sandelson, a Prentice supporter, he had declared that if the Motion was passed he would feel it his duty as leader and a member of the NEC 'to raise the question of action by small and certainly not necessarily representative groups who have secured a degree of power within a constituency'.

talk did inspire some ideas in me of how to fight the new line. When I got back to the office I scribbled Brian A-S. a Minute asking him to get me a breakdown of the rise in public expenditure in recent years between transfer payments, acquisition of assets and goods and services. I bet I shall find that the increase has gone mainly on transfer payments, which are merely a way of redistributing private income to pensioners and others. I also asked for an analysis of the increase in manpower in the public services.

I got back to the House in time to hear the opening of the second day's anti-inflation debate. Geoffrey Howe was in quite good form, but Denis and Harold behaved like a couple of schoolchildren on the front bench, chattering, shouting comments and generally conducting themselves with levity. Mike, next to me, was writhing with disapproving embarrassment. Margaret sat with her air of knowing primness, immaculately groomed as usual, in a new dress. The general view was that she flopped yesterday. But I had to miss Harold's speech and most of the debate. Later the House was buzzing with excitement about Ted Heath's speech – by common agreement the best he has ever made. Apparently it made Margaret look like a tinny amateur and speculation began to circulate as to whether she could survive. When I went in to hear the winding up, there she was in another new dress. Two in one afternoon was a bit much! But I had to suffer the agony of watching Mike flop – and I knew why. I too have suffered from having to address two entirely different audiences at once, the enemy in front and the ex-friends behind. The Tories, of course, were waiting to pounce and jeer and Mike battled on against their derision and the unbelieving silence behind him, getting wordier and wordier. A flash of the old Mike came when he suddenly admitted that of course sanctions against an employer constituted a statutory policy to which he had always been opposed. And he dealt with dignity with his own position, saying simply that of course he was not the person to deal with a Reserve Powers Bill if it ever had to be introduced. As he finished to pandemonium I congratulated him genuinely on the way he had battled through, but he pushed past me, head down, muttering 'a terrible speech'. One of my frontbench colleagues reported almost with relish that Dennis Skinner had been heard remarking that that was the end of Michael Foot. I only know that he has matured before my eyes during these past months and to me he is worth half a dozen of the negative Left.

Wednesday, 23 July

I had to leave the NEC meeting early to attend a meeting of Misc. 91, the ad hoc group of Ministers who are dealing with pay policy. I had been invited to attend to deal with the treatment of occupational pensions. Brian and I have been fighting to have pension improvements excluded from the pay limit to the extent necessary to enable our new pensions scheme to go ahead. I was furious that once again Harold should have allowed these important committees to clash with the NEC, but then we are working under such intense pressure on every front that I suppose he is at his wits' end to fit everything in.

At the committee we went through some of the detailed points that Mike will have to deal with this afternoon at the Second Reading of the Remuneration, Charges and

Grants Bill. (What a name! Some bright spark must have been determined to·get as unidentifiable a title as possible for the new incomes policy.) I saw Mike beforehand and he assured me he would be reading the statement on pensions in the form he had agreed with Brian O'Malley, which, though it doesn't meet all our points, at least should go far to remove the anxieties aroused in the pensions industry.

I wasn't able to hear Mike's speech in the House as I had committed myself to a rather absurd dinner John Langford-Holt had organized. It was a private gathering of the 'Class of 1945': the MPs of all parties who had been elected in 1945 and who had survived. It seemed mean to refuse to join in, but I was sure it would be a bore and I was feeling rather annoyed with myself as I changed hurriedly. In the event, it was one of the most hilarious gatherings I have ever attended in the House. Everybody but Burnaby Drayson [Conservative MP for Skipton] turned up out of the twenty-two survivors, including Harold [Wilson], Jim [Callaghan], Fred Peart and the Speaker, Selwyn Lloyd. As soon as I arrived we were rushed up to Selwyn's rooms for a photograph and we were all in festive mood. As the only woman there I was fêted, petted and teased. I was sandwiched at dinner between Hugh Fraser and Derek Walker-Smith. Wine flowed and we were all mateyness itself. No one listened to the brief speech Selwyn made and when they forced me to my feet to say a few words I could hardly make myself heard for the ribald din. As we streamed through the division lobby at 10pm, the libels started to circulate. People wanted to know what we had all been up to. 'You should have seen Barbara flirting,' said Fred wickedly, while Harold himself, I was told, had assured everyone that Hugh Fraser had put me over his knee and spanked me. Certainly everyone was high, but not as high as that! I can see I shall never hear the end of that dinner.

Thursday, 24 July

At Cabinet Bob reported gloomily on the parliamentary prospects in the two weeks that still lie ahead before the summer recess. We faced an impossible position, legislation-wise, he said, with the pay policy Bill to get through, the Employment Protection Bill, the Petroleum and Submarine Pipelines Bill and the Community Land Bill – all of them complex and highly controversial. Apart from anything else, there would be a problem in getting the necessary stages through the Lords. As for our own MPs, they faced an all-nighter tonight and three next week – and they were getting very tired. If we were to force through all the remaining stages of Mike's Bill tonight we must be ready to threaten to sit through all Friday as well and if necessary into Saturday. We all groaned and Ted repeated his headmaster's homily about how he had been warning class that it had been taking on too much homework. He hoped we would learn the lesson for next session's legislative programme. After arguing the position all round the mulberry bush we eventually agreed that Ted, Bob and a few others should try to see if they could do a deal with the Opposition on the basis that we would postpone the Community Land Bill to the overspill period. Even Tony C. and John Silkin were forced to accept this reluctantly.

We then had a long rambling discussion on foreign policy on the Parkinson principle that Harold cannot bear to leave an empty space of Cabinet time unfilled. I am sure we ought to have more discussion of foreign policy, but not in this bitty, chattily inaudible way. I must suggest a special Chequers on this. The fact is that it is almost impossible to vet what the Foreign Office is up to. At one point, when we were discussing how to stop the Opposition wrecking our parliamentary timetable, Eric scribbled a jocular note to me: 'The Mrs Gandhi solution is the only way out.'[1] I passed it to Harold impishly and he wrote on it: 'There are one or two potential candidates for the post round this table.' Now who on earth could he have been referring to?

I had a bit of a struggle to get my consultative document on pay beds through Social Services Committee of Cabinet, but I think I've managed it. Most of the points raised were pretty trivial. (Treasury, for instance, which has been very good at making extra money available for my budget to meet the cost of phasing out pay beds, wanted to be sure that the licensing system would be self-financing.) Ted summed up that the committee endorsed the 'main aims' of my document, so that gives me everything I want: total separation of pay beds from the NHS by a date to be included in the legislation; the withdrawal of private out-patient facilities from NHS hospitals; and a licensing system which will ensure that the total of private beds outside the NHS after separation will not exceed the total number of private beds inside and outside the NHS in March 1974. The only retreat I have made is on the final date for separation, largely because David has made some valid points about the difficulties involved in going for November 1976 as I had originally visualized. I agree with him we must have greater flexibility than that in order to meet the problem of consultants who would face a sudden and considerable drop in their income if pay beds disappeared almost overnight, so I am happy to leave the date for further negotiation. I do believe that I am on my way at last!

At the House I settled down to an all-nighter on Mike's Bill: I slogged on through my boxes in my room till fatigue overcame me and I snatched an uneasy hour's doze on my couch. Came dawn and the debate was still going strong. I went downstairs and had a cup of tea. It was obvious that Friday's normal business in the House had gone for a burton, so I went back to my room and did some more work. By 9am the rumour went round that the Whips were allowing people to pair for a short time to enable them to get home for a wash. I grabbed my chance, hurried home, bathed, changed and did some urgent shopping, getting back to the House in time for lunch.

In the dining room I joined an already hilarious group, consisting of Brian O'Malley, Joel Barnett, Bob Sheldon, John Silkin and Alf Bates. Carafes of wine were circulating and our shouts of laughter disturbed the whole dining room. It was one of those bursts of euphoria one gets when one has had no sleep. 'It's a tough life,' said Brian, 'but it's better than a nine till five job any day.' I took him aside to talk some urgent shop. Did he realize that Mike had *not* used in the debate the formula on occupational pensions we had agreed with him? We must ensure that he put this right at the report stage. By 3pm it was all over and we could go home. Thirty hours without going to bed, yet I felt fresh and fit. I got down to HCF and took the dogs a walk. And I had the pensions party to prepare for!

---

[1] On 26 June Mrs Gandhi, Prime Minister of India, had declared a state of emergency.

Sunday, 27 July

The great Pensions Bill party. When Brian and I volunteered this months ago we had no idea how many were involved in the production of the Pensions Bill. Private Office, given the job of preparing the list of invitees, came up with a hundred! So I had given the office the job of dividing the invitees into two groups: one for HCF, the rest for London. (They said there was great rivalry to come to HCF, except among the lawyers, who plumped for London. There must be a moral in this somewhere.) Brian and Kate [O'Malley] arrived last night. Mercifully, this fabulous weather held and this morning we were all busy, putting a bar out in the garden, freezing the drinks as much as possible, while I put the last mad touches to an ambitious cold buffet. Prompt at noon the guests started arriving: I suspect they must have been counting the minutes while they dallied in the lane. It went like a bomb, even the prim Errington waxing poetic about the garden (which Ted had brought to a peak of perfection, despite the drought) and about our kindness in inviting them all. 'What we will never understand, Secretary of State,' said Tom [Crawley of my Private Office], 'is how you can bear to tear yourself away from all this to come to the office.' 'Don't you realize, Tom,' I replied, 'that the whole point of this party is to make Private Office more sympathetic to my needs?' Brian and Kate slaved away carving ham, beef and chicken, while I mobilized Eileen and whomsoever else I could to make salads. They all wandered round the garden, drank a lot of wine, ate a lot of food and thoroughly enjoyed themselves. I told them they were none of them allowed to leave until they had dossed down on rugs on the lawn, slept off the alcohol and had a cup of tea. It was about 6pm when they started to leave. I loved it – and I think they did too.

Monday, 28 July

The press is buzzing with the pensions industry's anxieties. The unfortunate phrasing Mike used in the debate has given the impression that we will not be able to make any progress towards our new scheme under the pay policy. At Frank Byers's[1] reception this evening I did my best to allay these anxieties. He had held it to celebrate the passing of our Pensions Bill; it was an odd feeling to be popular! The pensions industry boys were all over me, particularly when I assured them that I would see that Michael cleared up the confusion during the Report stage of the pay policy Bill. I took the opportunity to find out from them whether they were really opposed to a 1977 starting date. But naturally the thing they wanted most was certainty. Harry Lucas of the General and Municipal Workers was there and I asked him why the unions weren't putting up a fight to get progress towards our new pensions scheme excluded from the pay policy? He admitted the TUC just didn't seem interested and promised to speak to David Basnett on his way home.

Letters have come pouring in from Errington and others about Sunday's party.

---

[1] Lord Byers, Liberal leader in the House of Lords since 1967 and chairman of the Company Pensions Information Centre since 1973.

There is no doubt that they are all very touched by the trouble we took. Jack told me that he had heard one civil servant at the party remark to another, 'Have you ever been invited to a party like this by a Minister before?' To which the reply had been, 'Never. I once had to call at a Minister's house and was given a glass of sherry, but that was all.' What apparently pleased them most was that we included everybody: from the Deputy Secretary to the humblest clerical officer. And, of course, my beloved driver, Edna, was there with her pal, Pat.

Tuesday, 29 July

Today was a day of reckoning for Wedgie over Meriden[1] and he took it with barely a whimper. Eric's paper on the motorcycle industry was the only item at Cabinet and as I got up early to read the documents I expected all hell to be let loose. Not only was Eric recommending that 'no further government funds should be made available to the industry on the basis of present plans', he was rejecting all three of the 'strategy alternatives' worked out by the Boston Consulting Group set up by Wedgie in March to look into the whole situation. And, for good measure, Eric's paper piled on the agony about how we were going to be accused of breach of faith on the basis of a letter sent by Wedgie to the convener of shop stewards at Small Heath on 6 November. This letter, though circumspect on details, contained the deadly phrase, 'the Government is fully committed to securing the future of the motor industry in this country', and Eric had obligingly circulated it to Cabinet along with another literary effort of Wedgie's to Bob Wright of the AUEW. In fact, correspondence has been floating about like confetti as Wedgie has hotly resisted the suggestion he ever went beyond his Cabinet brief. And, to cap it all, Eric inserted a savage little phrase into his paper: 'I shall wish to make it clear in my statement that this is a collective decision in which every member of the Cabinet is involved.' That young man's antipathy to Wedgie should never be underestimated. I began to suspect that he was challenging Wedgie to resign.

In the event, the discussion went remarkably smoothly. Wedgie, with whom I had a word before Cabinet, was mournful rather than militant. All he said was that of course he opposed the decision, but he had to be careful not to appear to be poaching on Eric's territory. Eric made a firm speech, the most telling point of which was that

---

[1] In July 1974 Tony Benn, then Secretary of State for Industry, had announced the Government's decision to help the workers at the Norton Villiers Triumph motorcycle factory at Meriden to form a workers' co-operative. The workers had been resisting the firm's attempt to close the factory down in order to concentrate production at its other two plants. The co-operative started work in March 1975 with the aid of a government grant and loans. At the same time Tony Benn commissioned a study by the Boston Consulting Group of the alternative strategies open to the British motorcycle industry as a whole for recapturing lost markets. The report highlighted the failings of management in the industry and spelt out three alternatives: a high volume strategy which would involve a cash deficit for many years of at least £51 million; a medium volume strategy costing £38 million; and a low volume strategy with a cumulative deficit of only £15 million. With sales of British motorcycles continuing to fall in the face of Japanese competition, Eric Varley had rejected all three alternatives and, having won the backing of Cabinet for his 'no more government money' policy, he told the House of Commons on 31 July that the Government had decided to refuse NVT's request for further funds. Despite this, the workers at Meriden struggled on.

all the members of his reconstituted Industrial Development Advisory Board [IDAB][1] – including George Doughty and Harry Urwin – had reluctantly come to the conclusion that there were no prospects of viability for the industry. The unions involved at Meriden were divided. The Confederation of Shipbuilding and Engineering Unions wanted nationalization, plus the high-volume strategy. Meriden wanted to go on as it was. Norton Villiers Triumph [NVT] wanted nationalization because Poore, its chairman, wanted his money back. 'I don't think an expenditure of £50 million is justified just for supporting 3,500 jobs,' concluded Eric. Michael went through some pretty routine reservations about Eric's proposals. Unemployment would move up from 5·4 per cent to 6·2 per cent in the West Midlands. 'I would still like us to look at the £15 million strategy.' Peter too was rather tentative. Our export of motorcycles had been going up; besides, we had to think of import substitution. Wedgie was emotional about the wonderful efforts made by the lads at Meriden, but not in his usual form.

To my surprise the most forceful speech was made by me. I had got quite stirred up as I waded through the eighteen-page summary of the consultants' report in bed this morning. The picture of British management at work was so appalling that I suddenly realized how it would appear to our activists. Once again our analysis of what was wrong with British industry had been justified; yet we were prepared to risk the hopeful experiment in workers' co-operatives at Meriden. Even Jack Straw, normally balanced in his judgments almost to a fault, had written in his brief to me that he could not imagine a worse time for us to take this step. I began to realize how deeply conventional in his reactions Eric Varley is. Behind that nice, unassuming exterior lies an almost ruthless hardness.

So I found myself carried away into a measured but devastating political analysis. Let us look at this, I said, as our own people would look at it, because Eric was proposing to publish the consultants' report. They would find in it a total justification of our socialist analysis of private industry: a record of incompetence more deadly than I had ever read. And they would compare it with what Eric himself said in his paper: 'The co-operative has shown it can produce machines more efficiently than the factory did before.' And they would also read that 'all the alternatives offer some prospect of profitability once a new generation of models can be produced'. Yet what was our reaction? To turn away from the challenge of a root and branch revolution of

---

[1] The IDAB was the watchdog set up by the Heath Government in 1972 to reassure Tory backbenchers that the new policy of helping the lame ducks of industry through the Industry Act would not be carried too far. The Board had to include people with wide experience of industry, banking, accountancy and finance and its job was to advise the Secretary of State on whether assistance should be given under the Act, the main criterion being an applicant's prospect of viability. The Conservative Government had appointed only one trade unionist, Harry Urwin of the T&GWU. On coming into office Tony Benn had found himself overriding so many of the Board's recommendations that he decided to alter its political balance. He therefore appointed three additional Labour sympathizers: George Doughty, General Secretary, Technical and Supervisory Branch, AUEW; John Hughes, Vice Principal of Ruskin College; and Lord Brown, a former Labour Minister and ex-chairman of Glacier Metal Ltd. But Labour's Industry Act 1975, while strengthening the Government's powers to give financial help, did not alter the IDAB's terms of reference. Indeed, under Eric Varley, the Department of Industry published in January 1976, 'Criteria for Assistance to Industry', which went further than the Conservative Government had gone in spelling out that 'prospect of viability' meant a company's ability to pay its way after selective assistance on a once-for-all basis.

managerial approach and wind up the whole thing on the grounds that this country could not compete – even in the area of motorbike design, where we had an advantage. What was this but a continuation of the 'segment retreat' which the consultants had condemned in the NVT management? When were we going into the industrial attack? For if we always retreated, we would have no industrial base left. I wasn't sentimentalizing, I continued, because I had always been prepared to be tough where it was clear we were in a shrinking market (e.g. textiles), but the world market in motorbikes was still expanding and we were merely accepting the total abandonment of our share of it. The whole country suffered from a 'segment retreat' mentality, and we were throwing away the chance of rallying workers to reject it and face the hard realities. What did we think our people would feel when all we offered them were the negatives of wage restraint?

Harold came in crisply: 'Once again Barbara has given us a passionate speech which is very useful. I liked her points about British management and Eric should incorporate them in his statement.' Nonetheless, he couldn't see any alternative to what Eric proposed. Others were soon agreeing with him and it was all over. Wedgie came up to me afterwards nearly in tears: 'You were wonderful. I couldn't say it as you said it because I was constrained by the feeling I mustn't upstage Eric. But how right you were.' I couldn't help feeling that if only Wedgie would put more practical cutting edge on his visions he wouldn't have lost his job and the Government wouldn't now be so negative.

Earlier, on parliamentary business, someone – I think Peter – warned us about the Ombudsman's report on Court Line.[1] As this would be backed by reports by the Board of Trade inspectors, and as all the reports would be criticizing the Government in general and Wedgie in particular, we had better face the fact that somehow or another we would have to fit in a debate next week. Ted Short nearly had one of his headmasterly fits at this and Harold tried to suggest that a couple of statements by Wedgie and Peter respectively would do, but Wedgie was very opposed to making a statement on an issue for which he was no longer departmentally responsible and on which he would be appearing in his own defence. He is clearly very sensitive about the barrage of criticisms which are now mounting against him. Peter was staunch in

---

[1] Early in 1974 Court Line Ltd, a shipbuilding company also in the package tour business, ran into financial difficulties and appealed to the Government for help to prevent its imminent collapse. In order to save some 9,000 jobs in shipbuilding and prevent widespread cancellations of holiday bookings, the Government decided to acquire Court Line's shipbuilding assets in advance of the nationalization of shipbuilding, which had already been announced. As it had become crucial to restore confidence in the company without delay it was decided that Tony Benn should make an immediate announcement of the Government's intentions. This he did on 26 June and, in answer to questions, used words which were interpreted as meaning that the holiday bookings that summer were safe. Six weeks later, new evidence about the company's financial situation having meanwhile come to light, Court Line went into liquidation and a large number of holidaymakers suffered loss.

In August 1974, Peter Shore had set up a Board of Trade enquiry into the firm's collapse and MPs had also approached the Parliamentary Commission alleging maladministration by the Government. Both reports were now to hand and, though neither report criticized the Government's decisions or questioned Ministers' good faith, both criticized Tony Benn's statement as being too unqualified. Meanwhile the Air Travel Reserve Fund had been set up with government help, out of which the Court Line holidaymakers were being compensated.

Wedgie's defence, pointing out that a debate would enable him to clear himself completely, and Harold came in to say he totally accepted that Wedgie was being unfairly criticized. Nonetheless, Wedgie is going through a bad time. His enemies are itching to claw him down and his confounded capacity for euphoric over-simplification gives them a claw-hole. After a long, circular argument Ted glower-ingly accepted that we should offer a debate next Wednesday. The prospect of release from this intolerable pressure of work and late nights slips further away.

After Cabinet I buttonholed Mike about pensions and the pay policy. He really hadn't got the formula right and the Opposition was ready to go into the attack, scenting that we were trying to postpone the whole scheme by the side door of pay restraint. Could I please have a word with him? Poor lad, he looked harassed. He has been having an appalling pressure of work in the House: what with pay policy *and* the Employment Protection Bill. He has had to be on the front bench night after night and all night, replying to amendments, etc., and it is pretty marvellous how well he has stood up to the strain, considering that he is not strong. But, yes, he would see me in his room at 3pm. So I grabbed Brian O'Malley and officials and together we worked out a form of words on which we would insist. When we went along at 3pm the formidable Derx[1] was there. When I started to outline our problem as reasonably and gently as I could Derx started to argue with us imperiously and Mike said tetchily, 'We really can't allow your problems to wreck the pay policy, Barbara.' At this both Brian and I saw red. 'And we can't allow your pay policy to wreck our pensions scheme,' I snapped back, while Brian launched into an emotional spiel, threatening to resign. 'I'm not going to have years of work thrown away,' he declared. And we were both so angry, we *would* have resigned. Mike, looking more harassed than ever, said he would really have to leave as he had another meeting. Would we try to work something out with Derx? Since Derx was obviously the source of the trouble, we agreed.

Back in my room, Brian spat out, 'That official is bloody insolent and must be shown his place.' Our pensions officials cowered nervously. There then ensued the usual to-ing and fro-ing when a tricky piece of drafting has to be agreed. But in the end we had Derx eating out of our hand. Next stage, of course, was to clear the new form of words with Treasury. That meant dealing with Treasury officials, who always claim the right to speak in the name of the Chancellor, knowing that he will back them anyway. Fortunately, Brian and I know our stuff in this field better than they do and, at the end of an hour or so of this, we emerged triumphantly with a written form of words for Mike which committed him clearly to allowing pension improvements up to the level of our new scheme to go ahead from April 1976. When officials had left, Brian and I jubilated. We had done far better than we had originally hoped.

When I went down to the House for this point in the Report stage the Tories were there in force, obviously anticipating that I would have been defeated and that they could dance a dance of triumph over the indefinite postponement of the pensions scheme. Because of another meeting I arrived late and an ironic cheer went up. 'They've been commenting on your absence,' whispered Mike. I waved to them

[1] D. J. Derx, Deputy Secretary for Incomes Policy, Department of Employment.

airily. And when Mike stood up and eventually read the piece we had agreed with Derx, their faces fell. Kenneth Clarke, their pensions spokesman, slipped out unobtrusively. He knew that our pensions scheme was home and dry.

Thursday, 31 July

Brian is still hankering after a 1977 starting date for the pensions scheme. The trouble about this is that an early date might well jeopardize its success, and, moreover, it would mean a frontal battle with Treasury, who would use this as an example of Barbara trying to get more than her fair share of resources again and would insist on taking the whole question of whether we should even have a 1978 date to PESC. As I talked over the problem with Norman I suddenly saw what I must do: write to Joel[Barnett], saying that he knew we wanted a 1977 date, but, in view of the expenditure restraints, I was ready to drop this – provided he would let me announce a firm 1978 date at my press conference next week to introduce our popular booklet on the scheme. Norman chuckled at this and readily went away to draft it.

A miserable meeting with officials to brief me for the wretched Chequers meeting on Monday about public expenditure.

Saturday, 2 August

The heat wave continues. Why on earth are we going to Corfu for our holiday? The dogs were so limp with it I persuaded Ted to take us to the river so that they and I could swim. Printer, who normally takes to the water like a duck, took fright at something and we had a job to get him in. I think it is his sight which distorts simple things like stalks of grass and floating thistle seeds into terrifying objects. I am now convinced he is going blind and my heart aches for him. But when we threw an enormous bough into the water he suddenly overcame his fears and went in after it time and again, dragging it with enormous effort up the bank. He is a fine, lithe little retriever and I love him dearly.

Sunday, 3 August

Another brilliantly sunny day. What is all that nonsense some scientists are talking about an incipient ice age? I cannot remember more consistently hot weather in all my life. Sonya and Terry brought the children over. They collected Mother on the way and we had one of those perfect summer days. We swam in the Pawsons' pool, ate on the terrace, slept on the grass and picked pounds of redcurrants for the deep freeze. I still hadn't read my tome of briefs for tomorrow's Cabinet by the time we went to bed, so set my alarm for 6am. In any case, there is always an enormous waste of time over these public expenditure exercises. I spend hours mulling up this statistic and that and preparing my case, but in the end Cabinet decides these things on a kind of hunch. A bias builds up for or against this programme and that. If the tide is with one, one wins. Rational argument has little to do with it.

Monday, 4 August

It was still stinking hot as we drove to Chequers. With Eileen away, I had a rush getting breakfast, clearing away, locking everything up and packing the dogs' things. So I felt limp before we started the day and ill-prepared for the discussion. The staff at Chequers oohed and aahed over Printer and Brandy as we drove up to the door. I took them in to see Harold and they sniffed their way cheerily round the furniture in the great hall. It was Harold who, as he fondled Brandy, reminded me we had had both the dogs at the time he came to our silver wedding party at HFC six years ago. I had forgotten that! He never forgets a dog. As we assembled in the library everyone was in shirt-sleeves, but even with every window open we could not keep cool.

Harold opened by telling us he wanted us to work through to a late lunch. The aim of the morning's work was to get 'as near a consensus as possible on priorities': first, our priorities for reductions in expenditure; second, those items we would put first when reflation became possible. Denis then gave us one of his long economic *tours d'horizon*, all about how this year 35·7 per cent of GDP was going on public expenditure in resource terms: 58 per cent if we included transfer payments. But his guns had been spiked a bit by a paper put in by Tony Crosland giving international comparisons of the percentage of GDP spent by different countries on public services – very much the sort of thing I had got Brian A-S. to work out for me. It showed that we were far from being the most lavish in public expenditure; other countries did more than we did in this field. And they too had had increases in non-productive manpower expansion. Ah, but, said Denis, the difference was that countries like West Germany had had unemployed labour to take off the land. We hadn't any fresh source of labour, yet during the 1970s there would be something like 700,000 more people employed in the public services. He assured us he was not trying to cut demand: merely redistribute it between the public and private sectors. Here he digressed into a typical bit of Treasury trickery. We were at present, he said, uprating pensions, etc. by the historical method,[1] which meant that, as inflation was reduced, pensions would actually be ahead of the rise in average national earnings. Was it really right that we should give this preferential treatment to pensioners over wage-earners? I couldn't contain myself at this. 'We've adopted the historical method because you insisted on it,' I chipped in. '*We* wanted the forecasting method, which would have helped pensioners more when inflation was rising.' 'I'm glad Barbara now agrees with me,' he retorted in that unscrupulous way of his. 'She has just made a very important concession which I welcome.' Of course, everyone laughed. The third point, he continued, was how far we stuck to non-selective universal benefits such as housing and rent subsidies. (He didn't dare to mention pensions this time.) Fourthly, how far should we give priority to growth? He agreed with me that nationalized industry programmes should be examined. It really did seem difficult to justify, for instance, the expansion of private telephones planned by the Post Office. This was in line with what Brian A-S. had put up to me and the letter he had drafted for me to send to the Chancellor had obviously had its effect, but I could see Denis trying to wriggle out of the obvious implication: namely, that reductions in nationalized industries' invest-

[1] See footnote, page 397.

ment should count towards his target saving a £2 billion. 'Doesn't this mean we should reduce the demand for public expenditure cuts in other fields?' I asked. But Denis wasn't having any. 'We are not cutting the programmes, merely our commitment. We are leaving it open.' I subsided, grumbling. Finally, said Denis, it was imperative that we produced an overall strategy for industry. Was there a case for more sectoral aid, rather than disbursements purely on a regional basis?

Before throwing open the discussion, Harold issued a warning. We must all limit our speeches to ten minutes and would we please note we were *not* to reopen the general discussion on MTA: merely to indicate what were our priorities for cuts. I was furious at this, since my brief from Brian A-S. challenged the need for £2 billion cuts and called for a mix of increased taxation. I realized that once again we were being manoeuvred into accepting Denis's whole premise, which we were supposed to be there to examine thoroughly. But Tony Crosland, having produced a valuable paper, failed to follow it up, despite his earlier protestations about the whole strategy. All he said was that his paper showed that our non-productive expenditure was *not* going up to the extent suggested, compared with that of other countries. Then he dutifully proceeded to spell out his low- and high-priority areas. He had been ready, he insisted, to reduce housing subsidies more, but Cabinet had decided otherwise as part of the pay policy. Wedgie, to his credit, insisted on discussing wider strategy. What Denis was doing, he said, was to 'blow a hole in the economy': first, by unemployment; next, by pay policy, and now, by huge cuts in public expenditure. What Cabinet hadn't grasped was that there was 'an enormous slump'. The political implications for us of the level of unemployment which we faced were 'hair-raising'.

I had been sitting through all this, struggling with my muzziness. As Harold called on me I ploughed on as best I could. I wanted to deal with a different point. 'I hope this party is not going to fall for the line now being peddled in the *Financial Times* by Joe Rogaly and others that private consumption is automatically preferable to public expenditure and that public expenditure in this country had gone to sinful lengths.' I then tried to summarize the marvellous material Brian A-S. had got for me, but time was against me and I didn't do it well. But I *did* ram home that, if we looked at the breakdown of the rise in public expenditure over the past decade, we found that two-thirds of the increase had been in transfer payments like pensions and these contributed to the 'jingle in the pocket' as much as wage increases. Nor had there been a bonanza in social security increases. They constituted only one-tenth of the increases, the biggest rise being in subsidies. We really would be fooling ourselves if we thought we had given the pensioners a spree. Thanks to the historical method on which the Chancellor had insisted, single pensions had already dropped to the old figure of about 19 per cent of average national earnings. The Chancellor shouldn't imagine it would not be noticed if he changed the rules of the game now because it suited him. I then went on to argue Brian's case for a 'mix' of £1½ billion expenditure cuts plus £1 billion increases in taxation on such things as tobacco, alcohol and other luxuries, including a review of mortgage reliefs, life insurance reliefs and the lowering of the threshold for higher tax rates. 'You're in injury time now,' remarked Harold, looking at his watch. I therefore raced through the list of priorities for cuts Brian had suggested to me, above all, defence. It was ridiculous, I said, that we should be planning extensive cuts without including it. Roy Mason argued, I continued, that his was the only department that had had a thorough review. 'What kind of review has it been?' I asked. 'We have asked the generals and admirals to tell us what they think is their "critical level" of defence spending. If I were to ask the Royal Colleges to do the same for the NHS I can tell you what answer you would get.' They all laughed at that, and Roy [Mason], sitting next to me, nearly had apoplexy. I concluded with a plea that when we next discussed public expenditure we should have before us an assessment of where we wanted to be in 1978–79 in Manifesto terms. 'You took eighteen minutes,' whispered Roy Mason accusingly. Even so I was dissatisfied and felt miserably that I had muffed my chance.

The right wing were soon rallying to the Chancellor's support, led by Fred Peart. Roy Jenkins dismissed Wedgie's analysis contemptuously. 'He is wrong. I ought as Chancellor to have dug a hole faster than I did. The fact was that public expenditure had been out of control.' What had struck him most on coming back into government had been the way in which attitudes to spending had 'completely changed'. (No doubt a dig at Denis as a 'political Chancellor'.) Next Bob Mellish warned us of the trouble we would have with our own party unless we did something about unemployment: he wanted a 'massive programme of retraining'. Michael came back to unemployment. The latest Treasury figures show it reaching a peak of 1,200,000 this winter: 200,000 above the estimate, and, even so, he thought this was optimistic. (Denis nodded at this.) 'These are disastrous figures for us and will wreck the anti-inflation policy,' said Mike. 'It is no good retraining people if they have nowhere to go.' We must therefore, continued Mike, have schemes prepared for this winter, but we also had to work out how much each public expenditure cut would increase unemployment and have an employment table in front of us. (Whoopee. That was one of the points I had wanted to make. It certainly suits our labour-intensive programmes.)

Jim was as bland as usual. The Government had got to emerge at the end of its period with one outstanding success, he said, and he had no doubt that it should be housing. We also needed a strategy for industry. 'We must put it before the social wage.' He then turned on me about defence, putting Roy Mason's case more passionately even than the latter had. 'If we were to make cuts in defence now it would seriously damage our standing abroad.' Harold Lever was as optimistic as ever in his analysis. 'Cuts in public expenditure will not jeopardize employment. On the contrary. I am not in favour of cutting demand, but that is *not* what the Chancellor is proposing.' But he agreed we needed to study how to deal with unemployment without general reflation. Malcolm Shepherd returned to the manpower question. For 1976–79 an increase of 102,585 for the Civil Service Department was proposed. The growth in the Civil Service was ridiculous. 'Departments should not ask for any more civil servants until they have examined what they can do out of their own fat.' He hoped he would be authorized to conduct a thorough review. ('I give you that directive now,' chipped in Harold.) Peter made an excellent speech on the lines of the letter he has sent to the Chancellor. We really must not forget that we were suffering from 'the worst ever demand deflation'. Two of the assumptions on which we were working he found suspect: first, the timing and scope of the pick-up in world trade;

second, that there would be a switch of resources into investment. In 1976–77 there would be no increase at all. Meantime we faced an 'investment hole'. So we must have a mechanism for ensuring that the investment did take place. The increase in British investment overseas had doubled in the past two years: we must have a look at it. We must not commit ourselves in advance to slashing cuts in public expenditure. We could not, for instance, divorce home investment in the nationalized industries from exports. Nor should we forget that, if we *did* get inflation down to 10 per cent in 1976, it would have a big effect on the borrowing requirement. He thought there was room for an increase in taxation. The only spending priority he would insist on was the inner city areas. Ted Short then astonished everyone with an attacking speech. 'I am acutely unhappy about this exercise,' he declared. 'The case for this large cut has not been made out.'

At last, at turned 2pm, Harold summed up: (1) There should be a meeting on unemployment in September. (2) A committee would be set up to consider areas of reflation. (3) Estimates should be produced of the increased unemployment resulting from any cut. ('You can't do that,' jumped in Denis, horrified. 'We can and we shall,' retorted Harold.) (4) There should be a review of staff levels in the Civil Service and of ways of controlling them. The priorities emerging for safeguarding were housing (but not housing subsidies), industrial retraining, and inner cities. The lowest priorities were transport and higher education. There was also a view that there should be more selectivity in social security payments, and JASP[1] should look at this. (I didn't protest. Let them look by all means: they will find the results politically suicidal.) And so we broke up. 'Lunch,' said Harold. 'A drink, I hope,' gasped Denis. We poured downstairs in the greatest amiability. Joel thanked me for what I had said on defence. 'To imagine we can go to the party with these cuts and not include defence is ridiculous,' he told me. He knew ways in which we could save £400 million on it. 'Give me the details and I'll blast away at them,' I said, but he replied that he was intending to use them himself. (I'll believe that when I see it!) I seized the opportunity to tell him of the letter that was on the way to him about the pensions scheme starting date. He was taken aback at my offer to give up the 1977 starting date in favour of a firm commitment to April 1978. 'Your number two won't like that,' he said. 'I know,' I replied. 'He'll be furious with me, but I think the most important thing is for me to announce a firm date on Thursday and I know you won't give me 1977 ahead of PESC.' Joel seemed impressed and said he would consider it. Later, in the House, I told Brian of my ploy and he was tickled pink, entering into the conspiracy with relish.

At the buffet lunch I sat in the same corner as Mike. Denis and Joel joined us and we chi-iked each other over a glass of wine. 'At any rate, you've got to admit I'm the only political Chancellor you've ever had,' said Denis again. 'Oh yes,' I cheeked back, 'but it all depends *what* politics.' My trouser suit – the only garment fit to wear I could find at HCF – caused a lot of favourable comment. One of the civil servants

---

[1] Joint Approach to Social Policy [JASP] stemmed from a report produced by CPRS, 'A Joint Framework for Social Policy', which had been published by HMSO in June 1975. The report advocated regular meetings of Ministers concerned with social policy to co-ordinate their approach.

whispered, 'Every time you come to Chequers, Secretary of State, you wear an even more distracting ensemble. It isn't fair to the secretaries.' Bob said, 'Very sexy.' Fred: 'I always went for her.' Denis said, 'She is just the size of my first girlfriend. I can tuck her under my armpit' – and proceeded to do so. Life is certainly full of surprises! There was I, hair dishevelled, freckled face steaming in the heat, in a cheap mail-order suit, with bare feet and sandals – and in my sixties too! I wouldn't have thought I had a scrap of sex attraction left.

At the House we were due for another late night on a three-line whip, but the heat must have knocked the stuffing out of the Tories because in the event we finished at 11pm. We got through the Lords amendments to the Pensions Bill and Child Benefit Bill easily enough, but then came Clay Cross.[1] As we trooped down for the last crucial vote it was clear we were in for trouble when such impeccably high-minded characters as George Strauss started striking attitudes about the rule of law. And when the result was announced to a crowded House there it was: we were defeated by nine votes. Of course, the Tories cheered and jeered, waving their order papers. I have always thought party conference was intellectually illogical over this. Of course, everyone has the right to defy the law on conscience grounds – otherwise we should have fascism (or communism). But the whole point about conscientious objection is that one must be willing to pay the price of it. On the other hand I can understand the instinctive identification by our party with those idealistic rebels of Clay Cross who are just as high-minded as George Strauss (a great deal more, in fact). So I think we were right to bend the law retrospectively a little in their favour – and certainly right to tell their Lordships to go to hell.

I am becoming increasingly worried about the arbitrary and non-accountable power of the Lords. This has been made worse by Harold's habit of making sentimental appointments of sloppy-minded crossbenchers, who then arrogate to themselves the right to make emotional decisions which cost a lot of money they don't have to raise. Tonight I was sickened by the posturing of the Lords over the 'law and order' issue of Clay Cross. This is power without responsibility: the power to send something back to the Commons in a situation where a Government is walking an economic and political tightrope, so that the Lords have only got to extract one rebel from the Government side to win. And there is always likely to be one emotional renegade in any party. Tonight they found several on Clay Cross and crowed at their own cleverness. Tony C. saved the night by getting up impassively, amid cries of 'resign', to move the next piece of business, as if nothing had happened. I always admire his parliamentary cool and congratulated him on it tonight. It completely defused the Tories. 'You've shot their emotional fox,' I told him. What fascinates me is the way in which a superb parliamentary manner will get anyone, from Left or Right, out of trouble. This applies particularly in this Parliament (on our side) to Wedgie, Jim C., Michael and Tony C. himself. I deeply envy this quality, which I have not got. I have to work hard for my survival.

Harold Lever has sent me a Minute (copied to the PM) saying he is 'greatly

---

[1] The Lords had deleted the Clause in the Housing Finance (Special Provisions) Bill to remove the disqualification of the Clay Cross councillors and we were voting to reinstate it.

troubled' by my proposal to take licensing powers over the private sector of medicine. I have sent him a firm answer back and am praying the PM will ignore him.

Tuesday, 5 August

At Social Services Committee we made further progress with David Owen's pet campaign against smoking. He is very touched that, smoker though I am, I should humour him on this. We agreed he should make his statement this week. I'm certainly leaving it to him, as I am hardly an example of desirable behaviour in this field! Later this evening the *Sun* was on the phone to the flat asking whether it was true I was going to ban sponsorship of sport by cigarette manufacturers. How these things leak! I always tend to blame officials – leaking happens so regularly – but I suppose it could be an interested Minister in each case, doing some log-rolling. Today we were top for Questions and we sailed through. It really is extraordinarily easy to fend off an effective probe by backbenchers when the attacks are disseminated over such a wide range of diverse and detailed subjects. It is when a co-ordinated campaign on one specific and clear-cut issue gets going that Parliament can be effective.

Our Questions over, I sat next to Harold for his. This gave me a full view of Margaret, who slipped into her place as demurely tight-lipped as ever and glossy with her best suburban grooming: fresh flowered summer frock and every wave of her hair in place. How *does* she keep her hair so unchangeably immaculate? It all adds to the feeling of unreality about her political leadership. Somehow that also is too bandbox. She never risks anything: just sits there listening to Harold with a carefully modulated look of disapproval on her face, then produces one regulation intervention per Question time. When she is ready for this great act she starts to lean forward slightly and an atmosphere of 'wait for it' builds up behind her. When finally she rises our chaps cheer ironically. She ignores them and fires her shaft. It never completely misses but is never (or very, very rarely) deadly. The lads behind her cheer lustily. Once again their tame bird has laid her egg.

My main departmental business of the day was the traumatic one: would I or would I not agree to raise dental and ophthalmic charges? The Dental Rates Board has now let us have the details of the new dental fees and David has been bombarding me with the need for me to make up my mind before the recess, so that, if charges are to be increased, the necessary regulations can be laid in time. I have been waiting for him to produce a sweetener on the ophthalmic side in response to my demand that we should produce a more attractive range of NHS specs. Now the submissions are before me, comprising a move from cost-related charges to (increased) flat-rate ones, with some concessions to children on specs (which will be very popular). But the submissions assert that to try and improve the range of spectacle frames would lead to increased costs, which we couldn't afford, and get us into difficulties with the manufacturers. I astonished them all by saying briskly that (1) it was clear that we would have to raise charges, because I wouldn't get any extra money out of the Treasury; (2) all Ministers would be expected to sacrifice at least one sacred cow anyhow (it was always part of the public expenditure cuts ritual), and this would be mine; but (3) the Government would never get away with a succession of dreary negative policies. Our policy must have some charisma. 'It is when you are hard up

487

that you most need that bottle of champagne,' I said. A new breakthrough on spec frames would be our touch of charisma.

Dick Bourton looked shocked at this last point. He had put an offensive Minute on the file to the effect that the public would consider any titivating of frames as 'frivolous' at this time, but David suddenly changed tack and supported me. So we agreed that we should keep this in the statement and I instructed Norman to fix a dinner with Derek Rayner[1] after the holiday at which David and I could seek his advice on how to organize the production of more fashionable frames. Brian A-S. tells me Rayner is brilliant and loves advising government departments on these things. (We also want to use him on the general medical procurement side.) Finally we decided that it would be politically advisable to make the statement before the House rose, otherwise we should be faced with it as first business after the recess. 'Treasury won't like this reference to NHS spectacles in the statement,' warned Dick Bourton, but I sent them off to polish up the statement and to draft a letter to Joel, in which we put the political choice squarely to him (copies to other members of the Cabinet) and made it clear what a sacrifice I was making. No hiding of my light under a PESC bushel for me!

Wading through the telegrams in my box I find a very revealing one from Paris giving a résumé of France's economic situation. I am intrigued to find that Giscard's economic policies have 'been unable to prevent a worse recession than expected', and that actual growth this year will be zero. So Giscard is planning a reflationary programme of 15 billion francs. I have also been reading a series of telegrams about the green pound, sugar, the Lomé convention, etc. all showing that our criticisms and warnings about the Common Market during the referendum campaign were justified. The latest is about a speech by Helmut Schmidt saying that the stronger economies in the EEC would have to go ahead on their own with the European Monetary Union, leaving the weaker brethren like Italy and the UK outside. Just what Giscard said and I warned during the campaign! I only wish I had more time to follow the telegrams. The flood of paper in one's life is so great that one has to let lots of important matters go over one's head, relying on Cabinet colleagues responsible for the matters concerned to keep one alerted to the major issues. In the case of the Common Market, I cannot so rely.

Wednesday, 6 August

The *Daily Express* has got me on the front page as the villain of the anti-smoking campaign. How the press does miscast one! I worked at home all morning waiting for Norman to phone me with Joel's reply to my letter on the pensions starting date. Finally he rings at 12.30pm. The reply from Joel has arrived. It is as cunning as I might have guessed. I can announce 1978 as the firm date *provided* I postpone for one year the very three items Brian O'Malley had been willing to offer in order to get a 1977 date, thus giving a saving of £26 million in that year. I explode. 'So he is trying to pre-empt savings from me before Cabinet decides the cuts!' My naturally militant

[1] Sir Derek Rayner, joint managing director of Marks and Spencer and a member of the Ministry of Defence procurement management executive board.

instinct is to tell them to stuff it and then have the battle out in Cabinet. But a hunch tells me I must control my belligerence and talk it over with Brian.

I race down to the House to have lunch with him. *His* instinct is to go for a firm date at any cost, and as we talk I can see the wisdom of it. We are both anxious about the lack of support we have had from the TUC over the pensions side of the pay policy and we suspect the hand of Jack Jones, who has never, as a ruthless egalitarian, seemed to have much sympathy with occupational pension schemes. Indeed, we recall, it was Harry Urwin, his second-in-command, who, when we were working out our pensions policy in opposition, joined other trade unionists on the NEC in supporting a flat rate pension. So we dare not rely on TUC backing if I take this to Cabinet: the TUC might prefer to give priority to the big increase in unemployment benefit they are beginning to demand. We asked ourselves how the Treasury had hit on the three concessions we were prepared to make. 'Our officials must have told them,' I said indignantly. 'It's not disloyalty,' said Brian. 'It is just how the whole Civil Service works.' Finally Brian suggested a compromise. We would accept postponement of the invalid care allowance and of the abolition of the half test, but not of the improvement in short-term benefits for married women, which, we agreed, was much more sensitive.[1] We summoned officials to my room in the House and I phoned Joel, away home in Surrey. After a bit of our usual sparring I put the proposition to him, developing a ploy that had just occurred to me – namely, that we might even find ourselves before the Equal Opportunities Board if we were to continue to give women unequal benefits for the same contributions when the scheme came in. Finally he said, 'I'll think about it and ring you back in five minutes.' Five minutes! We sat for two hours in that baking room, twiddling our thumbs, getting negative reports from Norman from time to time, and increasingly resenting the Treasury autocracy. Finally we discovered that the necessary Treasury officials had been in the House of Lords all the time and had only just assembled under the chairmanship of the Permanent Secretary to consider our proposal! I decided the moment had come to do a piece of my deliberate temper losing. I phoned up Joel's Private Secretary and tore a strip off him. He cringed. I told him I wanted an answer in ten minutes flat. A quarter of an hour later, when our hopes were at zero, Norman phoned. 'You've won.' We just grinned and I said, 'The press conference is on.' That means another day off my holiday, but it's worth it.

Meanwhile the Court Line battle was being fought in the House. As these great showdowns so often do, it proved a damp squib. I thought the best speech was made by Peter – with his newly acquired impressive air of authority – but, of course, all the attention centred on Wedgie, and once again he got away with it easily. We defeated the Opposition's challenge by a comfortable margin, Mr Heseltine having been effectively reduced to size.

---

[1] The 'half test' was part of the unequal treatment of women under the existing pension arrangements. Under it a woman who had been contributing for a pension while at work could not receive a pension in her own right, unless, after marriage, she had paid contributions or been given credits in half the weeks between marriage and her pension age. This was particularly hard on women who had married, or re-married, late in life. Even more iniquitous was the provision whereby a married woman at work, even if she opted to pay the full national insurance contribution as the men did, only received a reduced rate of benefit if she was sick or unemployed.

Back in my room I continued wading through the last minute pre-holiday boxes that keep pouring in: six already today. They included some very important submissions on the major issues David and I have been raising in the last few weeks. Norman has been doing his stuff remarkably, peppering me with comments and suggestions helping me to see through some of the difficulties. He advised me to accept a Minute from Philip about the export drive, which suggested we put Sam Davies as Under Secretary in charge of a new export division under Collier, while setting up a working group on procurement under David to try and get the regional health authorities buying their requirements centrally. This would give a stronger industrial base to our export drive in such things as medical equipment. I accepted Norman's advice on these things, though insisting that Derek Rayner should be asked to advise David's group. I am continuously impressed by Norman's radical instincts and good judgment.

Thursday, 7 August

Woke at 5.30am again. I can't sleep in this heat. Had my hair done, did some hurried holiday shopping and then swept into the press conference on our pensions booklet. It was crowded and to my relief was in the Fish Room at the Admiralty, where these occasions always seem much more relaxed. 'Please go to town when you speak,' pleaded Peter. 'You've achieved something to be proud of. It *is* a good scheme.' So I held forth euphorically and all went swimmingly. Brian had drafted the press notice so cunningly that the postponement of the two items Joel had forced on us seemed the most natural thing in the world, and no one questioned it. They seemed quite impressed that the increase in the women's short-term benefits is to come into effect immediately. So our great anxieties about the postponements were groundless. And we have got the Government committed to start the pensions scheme in this Parliament, instead of postponing it. Altogether a good session's work, as Peter emphasized to me. As he saw me to the car and wished me a good holiday I said with a wicked grin, 'Poor old Dick Crossman will be turning in his grave with envy.' 'He'll be pleased,' said Peter gravely. 'Don't you believe it,' I retorted. 'That chap had no chivalry.'

Norman clambered desperately into the car with me to clear one last point. The PM had read my statement on charges and wanted it postponed till we came back. We grinned. 'So you've won again,' said Norman. 'I wouldn't be too sure,' I cautioned. 'It may be that he is merely backing the Treasury.' Anyway, I have made my noble gesture and Cabinet will not now be able to blame me for the consequences of the delay.

HCF at last, with only a few hours to go before the holiday. But as Ted and I listened to the news there came the reports of a new disastrous run on sterling. 'I don't believe in this holiday,' I told him. 'You watch: there'll be a crisis Cabinet yet.'

Saturday, 9 August to Saturday, 23 August

A perfect fortnight in Corfu. I slept about nine hours every night and had an afternoon snooze on the beach as well! The consultative document on pay beds was published on 11 August.[1] I preferred to have it come out in my absence than to hold things up.

Wednesday, 27 August

Settling down at HCF – if settling down is the word, for the hot summer days continue distractingly. A box was awaiting my return on Saturday night – even before my fortnight was up! I catch up in a leisurely way with arrears of departmental work or laze in the hammock. It is too hot for gardening. The dogs don't want to stir for a walk until the cool of the evening. I cannot remember a summer like it. On Tuesday we have Mother over for lunch to celebrate her ninety-second birthday. Members of the family make special trips over to see her and she gives us her familiar confused but endearing repertoire: singing 'Old Soldiers Never Die' and reciting the love poem Dad wrote to her seventy-odd years ago. It always moves me very much. On Sunday, as Ted, Eileen and I were dozing in the garden, Sonya and Terry *mit* brood suddenly materialized, asking if they could camp overnight at the bottom of the garden on their way home from their holiday. Altogether a week of rich enjoyment of HCF.

It was good to be home and back at my boxes. Holidays always bore me after a couple of weeks. Among my papers I find a letter from Malcolm Shepherd finally endorsing the appointment of a Chief Social Work Officer of Deputy Secretary rank in succession to Joan Cooper. Victory! It has taken me about six months, but I've won, overcoming all the resistance from the department. Malcolm has been very good, telling me he was totally convinced by my argument that we had to strike a better balance between the medical and the social work side of the department. So the long, slow process of loosening the grip of the medical professionals on the department has begun – just as I managed at Transport to reduce the dominance of the highway engineers. Of course, Henry will be terribly unhappy, but it will be unhappiness rather than anger. No doubt the BMA will be alarmed too, and see this as another sign that I refuse to treat the medical profession as God. These changes are made all the more difficult because one has no spare money with which to sweeten the opponents. I have to challenge some of their deepest assumptions at the very time when I am being forced to cut back on NHS expenditure. I note one easement

[1] The document, 'The Separation of Private Practice from NHS Hospitals', elaborated the statement I had made in the House on 5 May. I repeated our commitment to legislate to withdraw pay beds and the private use of out-patient facilities from NHS hospitals. The date for the completion of this process would be set out in the legislation, 'bearing in mind that the Government first announced their intention in March 1974'. I was willing to consider making certain highly specialized procedures, such as radiotherapy, available to the private sector on a contract basis at full economic cost, provided no fees were paid for such services to individual members of NHS staff. But the main part of the document dealt with licensing. First, I intended to strengthen the Government's powers to regulate the quality of nursing homes and other provision for patients in the private sector. Second, I intended to see that private developments did not jeopardize the needs of NHS patients, by, for example, absorbing 'any undue proportion of scarce skills'. To this end I proposed to set up a licensing system to ensure that, after pay beds had been phased out, the volume of private provision for short-stay patients (i.e. [acute] medical, surgical and maternity cases) would not substantially exceed the number of NHS pay beds and beds in private nursing homes and hospitals at March 1974. For full text see Appendix V.

in the situation: the reaction of the profession to my consultative document, with its control of the private sector, is as muted as I thought it might be. Even the BMA's comments are pretty mild, while the Independent Hospitals Association thinks it is 'fair'. So it is and I believe I can sell it as such, despite Walpole Lewin's ritual moans.

The social wage document is still hanging fire. All attention has been concentrated on the production of Geoffrey Goodman's 'popular' version of the anti-inflation White Paper: not the same thing at all. Robson of the Treasury has written to No. 10 with the final redraft of the social wage document, which has now been tinkered about with by everybody, saying Ministers will wish to consider 'whether there is still advantage in publishing the document'. Really! If Tony Miles only realized what Ministers are up against!

Wednesday, 3 September

The £6 pay policy has been 'overwhelmingly' endorsed by Trades Union Congress. Quite a landmark! Jack Jones has delivered magnificently. The Government must now deliver too. And that should mean no slashing public expenditure cuts.

Friday, 5 September

A visit to Blackburn to catch up with interviews and, at my request, to address a delegate conference of the local party, which is in some political disarray, not least because of Crosland's circular restraining local authority spending. It went according to the usual pattern, with a few vocal ones criticizing the pay policy. Before the meeting Jim Mason pleaded with me to reconsider my decision not to run again next time, but I told him my mind was made up.

Monday, 8 September

I hurried back from an official engagement in Norwich in order not to miss Home Policy Committee of the NEC. This was the last chance to discuss the industrial policy document for conference on which Judith has been beavering away and I knew the atmosphere would be rather strained as Wedgie has done one of his 'Bristol letters', making an overt bid for the headlines on the eve of conference. In six thousand words he has skilfully put himself at the head of all the discontents in the movement – discontents which have been brought to a head by Crosland's circular to local authorities. And, as usual, the media have endorsed his claim to be the keeper of the socialist conscience. Last night he was given a great build-up on TV. This morning the *Guardian* has led with his speech on its front page 'Benn bounces back to fight for jobs' and talks about his emergence from 'relative obscurity' with a 'spirited call' for the fulfilment of the party's Manifesto. Wedgie's speech covers familiar ground: the fact that Britain is now in a 'deep slump' and that only radical policies will cure it. Once again I find a fatal flaw in his analysis: his refusal to tell the movement that, if it wants more investment, it must give up eating the seed corn. But I have no doubt that will make his message even sweeter music to conference delegates.

The room was crowded when I arrived at Home Policy and they were racing through the industrial policy paper. Denis Healey was in a near-savage mood, alternating between saying, 'I disagree with the whole document, but this bit is nonsense', and forcing through some sensible modifications. Wedgie sat in the chair as if butter would not melt in his mouth, being reasonableness itself on every point raised. He really is the most skilled, political practitioner of us all! Today he was at his most emollient, as though the Bristol letter was an invention of Ronald Butt. When, for instance, we came to import controls he leaned over backwards to placate Denis, who said truculently that everyone knew he disagreed with the document, but the only comment he wanted to make was on this passage. If we said we would put import controls on goods 'which directly compete with our own products' we would be putting them on everything. This really was absurd. 'Let's leave out that phrase,' said Wedgie quickly and accepted someone's suggestion that we should insert the words 'for a period' after 'introduce'. Even Mik agreed with that. Again, in the section on the national plan, Denis jeered at the words 'our proposed new plan would rely ... on pressure from trade unionists'. We all knew what that meant, he said: giving in to their pressure to back 'bum firms'. Wedgie said sweetly that perhaps we could put it another way.

There was another tiff over the proposed financing of NEB. 'The Government should take powers to provide capital funds for the NEB of at least £1 billion a year over the next five years,' said the document. Shirley asked in her reasonable way, 'Where is the money coming from?' There was a whole section on financing investment, protested Mik. Denis exploded. 'I totally disagree with this but I won't argue it. To invest £1 billion a year you'll either have to cut public expenditure or increase taxation.' Wedgie said mildly, 'These are the identical words to those in the summary which has been agreed by the NEC.' (It must have been at one of those meetings which I had to leave early.) Denis couldn't contain himself. 'Do let us be honest with ourselves. The fact that the NEC late on in a meeting passed that summary without even discussing it properly doesn't alter economic facts.' And he moved that we add the words: 'Given the public sector borrowing requirement the additional money would either have to be met from cuts in public expenditure or increases in taxation.' Of course, Wedgie wasn't having that, but he soothed Denis down by suggesting we insert a cross-reference to the section in which we dealt with the borrowing requirement. Denis rumbled on, grumbling next at the sweeping references to public ownership. He supposed we would be picking up every lame duck in the place. When Mik said we were certainly not going to invest in white elephants, Denis said sarcastically, 'Good. Cross out white elephants and put Concorde.' Wedgie did not bat an eyelid at this swipe at him, but tried to get his own back later. When once again Denis was muttering about the need to stress that investment must be *productive*, Wedgie suggested sweetly that we insert the words: 'Unlike the most successful economy in Europe, France, we do not intend to build Concorde.' But it misfired as Denis broke into ribald laughter: 'France! Look at the mess she is in now.' And so the war went on.

During all this Mike had sat silent, biding his time, but when we turned to the section on manpower policy he let himself go in true ministerial vein. Not for him any playing to the gallery. He thought the whole of the section must be qualified. 'We musn't raise expectations too much. The total costs of what is proposed here would be considerable.' Were we really committed to a payroll tax before we had considered what it would yield, and so on? The additional levy on employers could push unemployment up. 'The Employment Protection Bill does impose burdens on employers,' he said. We should hesitate before we added to them. Finally he was against the suggested reorganization of the Manpower Services Commission at this crucial time of high unemployment. He hadn't set the thing up, didn't like it much, and would certainly be against putting all his money into its hands, but we couldn't reorganize it again just now. Judith hastened to accept all his qualifications. At this point Denis became reasonable. He was, he said, working on the possibility of a payroll tax, but there were 'enormous difficulties'. So Mike won all his points and it was agreed that the section should be substantially modified. I think the document has a lot of good things in it, but the trouble is that conference won't face up to Shirley's question: 'Where does the money come from?'

We next turned to a remarkable document on 'Jobs and Prices' produced by Geoff Bish. Remarkable because he intended it as an NEC statement to conference, broadly endorsing the pay policy. He succeeded in uniting everyone against him for different reasons. Denis didn't like it because it regurgitated the whole of the industrial policy which we had just been discussing. Mik warned, 'The Government can only get our support if the other things mentioned in the statement are done.' In his view it was too conditional: it didn't lay down what the Government *must* do. Mike said mildly that it was lopsided. 'This document puts almost the whole emphasis on import controls.' We were facing a very critical situation, he continued, and ought to have a meeting with the General Council and discuss what the policies should be before we published anything, just as we had done over pay policy. 'I think that is very wise,' said Denis, and so it was agreed. Ministerial responsibility has certainly transformed Mike. I can't help thinking that he gets more like the rest of the Foot clan every day: constructive, courageous, principled but moderate. Only his political will has a sharper cutting edge than that of the rest of the Foots.

Tuesday, 9 September

The press don't know what to make of the leaks of yesterday's Home Policy. The *Guardian* did its best to find something to sensationalize with the headline, 'Left hurls pay-price gauntlet at Wilson.' But new life has certainly been breathed into the *Guardian* under the new editor. I particularly enjoyed its leader yesterday on the EEC, full of scathing remarks about the CAP and political union. 'Dreams Which the Nine Must Banish,' it called it. Not exactly the sort of thing it was saying during the referendum campaign.

In the morning we had another bit of policy soul-searching in the International Committee: this time over Portugal. While I've been away Judith has apparently been under attack for what she had said following a visit to Portugal paid by her and

Audrey Wise (the choice of companion struck me as significant). So she came along today to justify herself, circulating a long report and a copy of the article she has written for *Tribune*. As she expressed herself to us she couldn't have been more reasonable, but Ron Hayward wasn't having it. When she had finished he burst out vehemently, reminding us that he too had been to Portugal at the NEC's request. 'I must say to you, Judith, there didn't appear to be any encouragement for Mario [Soares] in your article or statement. The Communist Party [CP] *is* trying to get disproportionate power.' And he suggested we invite Mario to address conference. Jim drawled, 'I must say I can't object to anything Judith has said this morning. You may have been misreported, but what caused Harold to repudiate you was that you were reported as saying that the *only* threat to democracy came from the Right.' 'I believe that,' chipped in Judith. Jim pounced. Ah, *that* was where he disagreed with her. The attitude of the CP since the ballot had been profoundly worrying. They were now dismissing the ballot as what they called 'electoralism'. Soares had been man-handled by them at the May Day rally. Unlike Judith, he didn't approve of 'direct democracy'. The Portuguese Socialist Party thought the CP was preparing a communist dictatorship. Mik from the chair said that of course we all supported the SP and Mario. Anyway, we agreed to invite Mario. The problem of picking one's way between the CP trap on the one hand and over-conventionalism in an unconventional situation on the other is very hard. I personally hate the CP and distrust the fellow-travellers, but I watch very carefully that this doesn't manoeuvre me into watering down my socialist goals and getting into the wrong company.

Back we went to Transport House at 2.15pm for the joint meeting of the NEC and the Cabinet, called because of Mik's sneers that the promised 'consultation' of the NEC by the Government had broken down. It was a great yawn. Most of us there meet together several times a week. Of the non-NEC Ministers who turned up – Roy J., Harold Lever, John Silkin, etc. – only Tony Crosland attempted to speak. The theme, of course, was the economic situation and Harold insisted on opening with what he called a 'Parliamentary report', i.e. he raced, head down, through a catalogue of the Government's achievements in a mumble that was almost meaningless. I got on with some office work, Lena beamed vacuously and Wedgie stared quizzically at his finger-tips. 'I am the custodian of the Manifesto,' droned Harold, 'though I gather some claims to that are being made from the extreme Left and Right of the party.' I wondered once again why Harold plays it so uninspiringly. Is it deliberate? I suspect he is as bored with his own speeches as we are, but doesn't care, his sole concern being to get what he wants reported on the record and to defuse any hostile leaks. (I guess that speech had been handed out.)

That over, Frank Allaun led off with the usual hope that we should have a 'frank and free discussion', but he hadn't much new to say. The occasion was notable chiefly for the resumption of the sparring match between Denis and Mik. It was Mik's turn to be as savagely sour as Denis had been yesterday. We all knew the areas where the policies of the party were not being carried out, he said. 'It is not a long list, but there have been a series of departures from policy. There is no point in doing anything more than agree to differ.' As for the international side, 'I cannot recall a single occasion when any representations made to the Government by the NEC have had the slightest effect,' he said bitterly. 'Chilean debt,' called out Denis. 'Hong Kong,' said Jim. Mik said in that savagely slow way of his, 'Since I've been interrupted I shan't proceed. I don't intend to interrupt anyone. I'm just not interested.' And he lapsed into silence. To everyone's surprise, Sid Weighell proved a match for him. He had, he said, agreed to go on an NEC deputation with Mik to the Minister of Defence, but before they had got the Minister's reply Mik had tabled a resolution at the NEC condemning him. 'I made up my mind from that time on not to be used as a decoy for deputations for people merely to push what they have already made up their minds about,' said Sid. Mik stirred himself. 'I went through the Minutes of the International Committee and drew up a list of the cases where party policy has been ignored,' he said sourly. 'It is not the purpose of this meeting to have a confrontation, but I shall publish it when the time comes. The euphoric mood of the Government won't wash.'

With that threat hanging over us we turned to economic affairs. Inevitably the major preoccupation of the unions was unemployment. Chalmers warned it would be the major issue at conference. Bryan Stanley said he greatly welcomed the action taken to tackle inflation, but there was a feeling that the Government was not doing enough to tackle unemployment or investment. The funds available were not enough. Tony C. said the dissatisfaction in the party was due to certain brute economic facts. Our only hope was to concentrate on certain limited priorities. (Housing, of course!) Denis gave us his usual economic analysis. 'What is going to happen to unemployment? I don't know. But I am certain it won't reach two million.' He and Mike were considering some job creation steps this winter, he said. Mik, back in the discussion, said two things were worrying him. First, the failure of regional policy. The gap between the best and worst was not narrowing. Secondly, the redistribution of wealth. 'The gap between the rich and poor is actually widening, as the Child Poverty Action Group [CPAG] has shown.' Denis couldn't contain himself. 'It is atrocious to keep repeating statements that are wrong,' he fumed. He had already disproved the CPAG figures and the Diamond Report now showed that redistribution *was* taking place, he insisted. 'Another paper I'll have to publish, I'm afraid,' sighed Mik with mock regret. (I wish he *would* publish a paper, so that we could examine it.) Once again the dirty job of defending the Government fell to Michael, and he did it bravely. He admitted that 'if we don't get unemployment down this Government will be swept away'. But equally, he pointed out, if we didn't get inflation down that would sweep us away too. And he repeated his plea that we should get into detailed discussion with the TUC on the measures we should take. 'Our £6 policy is going to have a bigger effect on equality than any wages policy we have ever had.' Denis and Roy exchanged patronizing smiles at his vehement loyalty. Wedgie sat silent, no doubt reserving himself for a more worthwhile audience. We broke up thankfully. What Mik thinks the meeting achieved I'm blowed if I know.

Wednesday, 10 September

Another long day's meeting at Chequers: this time on devolution again. There was a mound of bumph to read on which functions should be developed and which not. As

Shirley said to me as we arrived, 'And so boring too.' There was also a paper by CPRS, gloomily questioning whether the whole devolution package was viable. There is no doubt that officials as a whole are deeply alarmed at the whole exercise. Philip Rogers asked to see me last night to urge that we shouldn't rush to publish a Devolution Bill, but allow plenty of time for consultation on the further White Paper we are to produce. He said that officials in the devolution committee doubted very much whether we would be able to get away with devolving a lot of social policy powers and hardly any economic ones. And there is no doubt, either, that the anti-devolution minority in Cabinet is stubbornly determined to fight against it to the end. A mysterious last-minute paper, heavily marked confidential, had been circulated to us, warning that devolution of so many powers to Scotland would make it impossible to retain Scottish and Welsh MPs at Westminster and that the Tories would be almost certain to abolish them if we went ahead. It urged that much reduced legislative powers should be given to both Wales and Scotland instead. Shirley told me she thought it was the best paper of the lot.

So the scene was all set for another row and Ted Short was soon protesting that there was a clear commitment to full legislative devolution for Scotland in the White Paper. He had also distributed another ORC poll, showing that the demand for devolution in Scotland is growing, not diminishing. It soon transpired that – contrary to everyone's belief – John Morris had *not* circulated the last minute paper. On the contrary, he disagreed with it. Mystery! And a rather disturbing one too, because the paper referred to our committee by its official name – DS (75) – so it must have come from someone in the know. Ted's extensive enquiries had failed to reveal the author. A political adviser? Officials don't have to resort to such cloak and dagger methods; all their points can be put through CPRS. So how on earth did the paper get circulated? We never found out. Roy J. then made a bid for us to try and get all-party agreement on the devolution policy before the White Paper was published, but Mike and I said 'no' in a loud voice. I said our interests and the Tories' in this matter were diametrically opposed, while Mike pointed out that it would hardly do our cause any good in Scotland to be advocating a consensus policy. Harold said we should leave the decision about consultations till our October meeting, when we would be able to look at the package as a whole.

By 4pm we had gone through the long, dreary details. 'Aren't we going to discuss the CPRS paper?' asked Denis innocently. Ted nearly exploded. It was asking us to go back on everything we had agreed. Harold backed him up: 'We can't discuss the reversal of the White Paper.' Jim drawled, 'I am beginning to be converted to the least possible devolution.' Denis battled on stubbornly. We should at least have in front of us in October an 'alternative model' produced by CPRS. Ted would have none of this: we had considered all the possible alternative models before picking on this one, he maintained. But with Fred Peart, Roy, Malcolm, Fred Mulley and others making approving noises of support for Denis, Harold was forced to go through the list of items on which CPRS suggested we should ask officials to do further work. We agreed one or two of them. I said that what we needed in October was a document drawing together what we had so far agreed, so that we could see the whole picture. The decision would then be a political one. 'Thank you for your help,' Ted said to me afterwards. He really is deeply committed on this. Philip Rogers admitted to me wickedly that officials talk about him 'Short-circuiting' the timetable.

I think the implications of devolution *are* worrying, but (a) we have no alternative in view of the feeling in Scotland and (b) it is a bit much for Roy Jenkins and co. to express their alarm at the break-up of the unity of the UK when they have done so much to destroy its sense of sovereignty by impaling us on the horns of the EEC. For instance, when we were discussing the devolution of responsibility for the Health Service, someone pointed out that this meant the Scots could wind up the NHS if they wanted to, go over to private insurance and lure our doctors away. Was I prepared to accept that? 'Of course, I hate it,' I replied. 'But if you decide to make a constitutional change like devolution you must accept the implications, just as we decided to make a constitutional change by joining the EEC. I can assure you the BMA is licking its chops at the prospect this offers of lucrative pickings from private medicine in the Community.' That silenced them.

With Eileen on holiday and Ted on his European work in Perpignan, I am having to trail those poor sweet dogs everywhere with me in the car. They behave impeccably, but it is obvious they miss the freedom of their own home. So Edna and I decided to slip over to HCF for the night, where I took them for a run and did some gardening. It made a welcome release for both them and us. The garden is a riot of autumn colour, with dahlias, petunias and gladioli. A great peace always descends on me as I stroll through the orchard and vegetable garden, picking up fallen apples and gathering french beans for the deep freeze. There is no doubt that, like Nye Bevan, I am a peasant at heart and – what is worse – a kulak! There is nothing like the ownership of one's own four acres for making one feel rooted in the earth.

Thursday, 11 September

Back in London in time for the Inter-Parliamentary Union dinner at Lancaster House. I had been in more than half a mind not to go, but I force myself into these sociabilities from time to time, as otherwise one gets completely out of touch. It was a dull do – a lot of empty places and the food not very good – but, as usual, the wine was excellent and it was a recurring pleasure to study the magnificent gilded ceiling and the glorious floral centrepieces on the tables. Harold greeted me affectionately. He was glad to chat as he stood bored at the receiving point. 'Political neophyte as you always were,' he quipped, 'I noticed that you did not fail to observe yesterday that certain people were up to their coalition tricks again.' Of course, he meant Roy. At table I had got myself placed next to the Kuwaiti Minister, so that I could soften him up for the medical export promotion visit I am hoping to make there soon. Once again, of course, I put my foot in it. His wife was sitting opposite us at the table and was explaining to Elwyn that her son was going to America to study computer systems and that she herself was going to attend a course at the Kuwait University. She was a gay, intelligent, bright-eyed, youngish woman, who, I noticed, drank some wine. Her husband stuck to water. As he barely spoke any English and I certainly have no Arabic, conversation was difficult. 'When are you going to give women the vote in your country?' I asked him charmingly. He exploded in positive fury at the thought. 'Parliament? Women? Never!' His wife signalled to me with her kohled eyes. 'Don't worry, it will come.'

Friday, 12 September

Back to HCF to clean the house through for Eileen's return. The liberated dogs raced round the garden in bliss.

Saturday, 13 September

The papers are full of the rowdyism at Reg Prentice's meeting last night. The antics of the Trots play right into his hands.

Sunday, 14 September to Wednesday, 17 September

Off to France for an official visit to my French counterpart, Mme Simone Veil – hopefully to help promote the export of medical equipment to France. Norman isn't coming with me because he is still on leave. I never felt less like a foreign trip as we drove to the airport through driving wind and rain. And I only had summer clothes with me too! In the event it turned out to be one of the most satisfying adventures of my life. Reason: I found all my latent love of speaking French, however ungrammatically, surge up in me. Indeed, I just couldn't talk English even when other people were speaking it to me! So it was fun. I felt young and I looked young. I had no nerves, no shyness, no agonized sense of reserve as I so often do. I went right out to meet everybody in my most relaxed mood and they responded warmly.

It is always a joy to stay at the British Embassy in Paris. The Faubourg St Honoré is in any case my favourite street in Paris and to step into the courtyards of the Embassy is to step out of all the modern noise into the eighteenth-century elegance of de Charost. Napoleon's sister lived here and she filled it with its elaborate furniture. I must say I like splendour – so, incidentally, do Communist governments, who usually preserve theirs carefully for the greater glorification of the people's take-over. My relations with the Tomkinses [the Ambassador and his wife] were soon humanized by the fact that they have two blue roan spaniels. With this common bond – and with the help of their attractive teenage daughter – we spent a relaxed family evening talking dogs and Dutch elm disease. Wedgie, we were told, was due the next day, and I was amused by the flutter of mixed apprehension and curiosity this evoked.

Up early the next day. I was rushed to the big new hospital at Clamart, where Mme Veil was waiting. She was accompanied by the incomparable M. Le Vert, her Directeur du Cabinet, who was to prove such a stimulating companion for the rest of the trip. He is in his late forties, with an intelligently attractive face, a good command of English, a sense of humour and, above all, a racy independence of mind. It was from him, as we travelled later into the provinces, that I learned how the French 'cabinet' system works. Mme Veil's 'cabinet', for instance, consists of about twelve of them chosen by her. They are all, as it happens, civil servants, but she could have brought in someone from outside. They all leave the 'cabinet' with the change of Minister, but the career civil servants among them do not lose their place on the ladder as a result of this diversion in their lives. When I asked Le Vert how a Minister knew which civil servants were likely to suit her purposes best, he replied that, as Mme Veil had been a civil servant herself in the Ministry of Justice, she knew the catchment area well. But I can see how difficult the system could prove for a Minister coming fresh to the administrative scene – perhaps even from outside politics, as Mme Veil did herself. For a French Minister does not have to be an MP and Mme Veil herself is not.

She turned out to be an elegant, rather shy woman in her late forties. I thought the words 'cold charm', which *The Times* has used to describe her, were about right. She is *très sérieuse* and used the occasion of my visit to see some of the hospitals, like Clamart, that she hadn't seen. The Antoine Beclerk was a well-designed modern hospital belonging to the vast 'Assistance Publique' group for the Paris area and seemed well equipped. But it struck me that in France they are still putting nearly all the emphasis on hospitalization. There is no family doctor list system like ours; there are vast out-patients departments and no health centres. I can't imagine how the link with the community services is made, though Mme Veil has responsibility for social welfare as well. Another thing that struck me as we marched miles round the hospital corridors was how clinical and austere it seemed: no colour anywhere, no warmth of atmosphere. The few patients we met in the out-patients seemed sunk in self-obsessed gloom. They don't have the system of wards: two beds to a room at the most. Le Vert told me they had a programme on hand of 'humanizing' their older hospitals. This turned out to mean splitting the accommodation down to single or two-bedded rooms, all coldly white. I thought to myself how much I should prefer to be in one of those modern four-bedded wards of ours, with their gaily coloured curtains, flowers and 'get well' cards everywhere. To say nothing of our cheerful nurses. Apparently one of Mme Veil's most serious problems is the shortage of *infirmières*. French women don't seem to take to nursing like ours do.

Another thing emerged: how incomplete their health care coverage is. The patient, we were told, pays on the spot and then has to recover the agreed percentage refund from social security. What if they couldn't pay the balance? Ah, then, said Mme Veil, they could go to public assistance. And the pro-Europeans have been trying to tell us how superior the social services are in the Community! Incidentally, I was told the consultants work full-time in the hospitals but are allowed to have private patients as well and some private beds are set aside for this.

In between visits I had some long chats with Mme Veil in her car. I congratulated her warmly on her courage over her abortion law reform and she seemed pleased. Le Vert told me she is not a great orator, but she won people over by the sheer logic of her argument. She is also extremely popular with the public, even those who disagree with her, because they feel she is completely honest and straightforward in what she says and does. She is a Jewess and her horrifying experiences in German concentration camps are no doubt responsible for her air of reserve: besides, she is a jurist and therefore no demagogue. But as the day went by she began to melt, and when we concluded the long day with a sumptuous dinner in the private room of a restaurant, she really unbent. She made a friendly little speech of welcome after the meal and I decided to risk all and reply in French. She positively beamed her delight and we parted on terms of mutual warmth.

When I got back to the Embassy Wedgie had arrived and came into my room for a little chat. He seemed untypically subdued, as though he suddenly realized he had been shunted onto a track where he couldn't play the demagogic politics he loves so much. Why was he there? Well, he thought it was time he met his European counterparts, so he was doing a tour of Energy Ministers. I get the impression Wedgie doesn't like administration very much, which means he won't be a very good administrator, but at least he won't get swamped in administration as so many of us do.

Up early to catch the train to Dijon – still in the cold and driving rain. Mme Veil had to stay behind as – amusingly – she had a press conference to launch her own anti-smoking campaign. (How similar are our problems!) That meant that Le Vert, the two women and the three of us from Britain were closeted cosily in our compartment for over two hours. Le Vert was very embarrassed by the quality of train, then came back triumphantly to say he had discovered it was an Italian one. France's honour was saved! At Dijon the sun was shining and there followed a memorable drive through Burgundy to Beaune. It was fascinating to see the famous names of wine coming up along the roadside – Chambertin, Clos de Vougeot. At Beaune, mercifully, we were allowed to indulge in a little 'tourisme'. The Mayor and his entourage were waiting to welcome us at the *hôtel de ville* and to take us round the marvellous Hôtel Dieu, with its incomparable tapestries. And then a great lunch before going to visit the modern hospital built out of the huge funds of the *Hospices*. At lunch the wines were, of course, superb: an excellent Volnay followed by a rare bottle of 1959 Beaune, over which Le Vert and I crooned lovingly. They told us about the great *vente* of wines every year and how the Duke of Kent had been their guest last time, bringing them record sales. And, of course, the *maire* made an eloquent speech after lunch and I had to respond. This time I even ventured some jokes in French. Saluting the 1959 Beaune as *un rêve*, I said how relieved I was to find in these modern times that *l'âge compte*. They had told me, I continued, about the great success of the Duke of Kent's visit: 'Je ne peux pas vous apporter la plus grande vente, mais je vous promets la plus grande consommation.' That went down well, and I was cheered when I quipped back at the *maire*, who had told us that the fortunes of the *Hospices* had been founded on the ransoming of Joan of Arc, 'Il me faut vous avertir que si vous avez les mêmes idées aujourd'hui le gouvernement britannique ne va pas me rançonner, et, quant à moi, je veux y rester.' Altogether quite a triumph and a lot of fun. We poured out of the room together in the greatest amity.

The Beaune visit over, on to Lyons to stay with the *préfet* – a much more conventional type of civil servant than my friend Le Vert. Then in the morning on to the Consul-General's office to hold a press conference. Heaven knows what kind of press reports will come from my unconventional French! And so to the *hôtel de ville* to meet the *maire* of Lyons, a bit of a Chicago-type character who, as we warmed up over a glass of porto (an execrable drink), insisted on showing me round the vast reception rooms, which he had had newly decorated: new silk panels on the walls; the paintings luridly touched up, glittering chandeliers everywhere. While I murmured, 'Je suis éblouie,' the irrepressible Le Vert muttered to me, 'C'est affreux.' And he continued his indiscretions on our visit to the vast Edouard Herriot hospital (three thousand beds), considered a triumph of hospital design when it was put up all those years ago. 'All wrong, much too big,' said Le Vert, and the medical men agreed. It was at the lunch that I had to make my last speech. It was probably horribly pidgin French but they loved it. And when the time came to say goodbye and to make for the airport, our farewells could not have been more affectionate. It was a good 'last time'. I am sad to think I shall never make another ministerial speech in French.

Monday, 22 September

Woke at 5am with agonizing tummy pains, which necessitated several trips up and down the stairs and across the cold tiles to the loo. So I left HCF in no state to face my meeting with Minister Petrovsky of the Soviet Union to launch our joint committee under the Health Co-operation Agreement. Of course, I got through it somehow, helped by the fact that he is an extraordinarily agreeable, fatherly and uninhibited old boy. He is a surgeon, which perhaps explains why he does not seem constrained by the political aloofness of most Soviet visitors. Our Dr Reid told me that, on the trip to Oxford yesterday, he had on an impulse invited Petrovsky to his own home, where they had a most matey and relaxed time.

The opening ceremony over, I hurried to Transport House to attend the Liaison Committee meeting with the TUC. When I arrived they were in the middle of a discussion of the economic situation, which, Mik told me, had centred on the unemployment figures and the possibilities of reflation. *The Times* today has Jack Jones condemning 'Whitehall paralysis', but as far as I could see the discussion was amicable enough, though naturally the union boys (Jack, Hughie, David Basnett, Alf Allen and Len) looked serious. Mike was just describing the package which the Government is considering to create 100,000 jobs. 'You may call them palliatives and so they are,' he said. But they would particularly help school-leavers. Mik was complaining that what Denis had said about import controls was 'far too slow and tentative', adding that an import surcharge of 10 per cent would save £1,000 million of imports. Denis was at his most conciliatory. The Government *were* concerned about unemployment, he said. More training and investment were essential. There must be further discussions between the TUC and Government on the next steps in our economic strategy. 'I want to discuss measures urgently with you.' And so it was left. Anxious as they are, the unions are clearly still ready to extend the utmost tolerance to the Government's difficulties. It is remarkable how the new amity is holding.

We then turned briefly to the NEC document on industrial strategy. While stressing that it was not for them to trespass on NEC territory, the unions were glad of the opportunity to get in a few comments of their own. David Basnett said his own reaction was that the document was all right, but 'rather vague in places'. There were no clear outlines of the new planning mechanisms. (You can say that again!) It also ignored the existing institutions. For instance, there was only a passing reference to NEDO [National Economic Development Office], 'to whose mechanisms the TUC attaches a great deal of importance'. (Wedgie looked down his nose at that.) Hughie said modestly, 'It hardly behoves us to criticize a NEC document, but my concern is: will the Government accept this as a general philosophy? The document itself is a reasonable assessment of the problems and solutions, but will it be acted on?' Wedgie answered him by repeating his old formula. It was for the party to plot the way ahead as a lead to the Government. 'There is a role for the party while we are in Government.' Shirley was her usual down-to-earth self: what we needed was some machinery whereby the TUC and the Government could 'work out the realities'. Wedgie saw this as the trap it was, protesting, 'Is the party never to be able to look beyond what the Chancellor is prepared to do?' But once again the discussion was completely amicable.

I personally think Wedgie's visions would be a good corrective if only they were more rooted in real life. I couldn't resist asking him about the terrific attack on Robert Maxwell (and the *Scottish Daily Express* co-operative) in yesterday's *Sunday Times*, obviously designed to be an attack on Wedgie as well. He replied with his usual boyish innocence. 'I did my best to warn the workers' co-operative. But the Government had wasted £500 million on unemployment benefit while refusing to lift a finger to find the bit of extra money they needed. So you can't blame them for turning to Maxwell. But I saw that they kept the full right to sack him, so what more could I do?'

Cabinet was on unemployment, as promised at the last Chequers meeting. My main aim was to see that DHSS got its fair share of any increased expenditure that was going, whether on work creation or the package to stimulate the construction industry. Tony Crosland overreached himself in his efforts to hog all the money for housing. He had put in a paper attacking the work creation scheme and saying the money ought to be put to housing improvements instead. But his sarcastic ribaldry in introducing it was so selective that it enabled me to shoot him down. What was wrong, I said, in spending £30 million on painting old people's own homes, helping them with their gardens, manning day centres or providing transport for the disabled? In any case it was the most effective way of getting young school-leavers off the dole. That was why, contrary to its normal approach on this sort of thing, the TUC were strongly backing the work creation scheme. But I supported Mike in saying that we had to go further and draw up a package to help the construction industry. But it must be the industry as a whole, not just housing. We had, for instance, in DHSS a backlog of maintenance work in the NHS amounting to £100 million, to say nothing of the long-overdue fire precautions we could not afford to introduce. So Denis gave way and agreed to consider a construction package to follow soon.

An amusing moment came over the proposal to extend the Temporary Employment Subsidy [TES] to the whole country. Roy Hattersley, sitting in for Jim, gave the regulation Foreign Office bleat about how the EEC Commission had to be consulted first, and was waved scornfully aside by Denis and Harold. Even Roy Jenkins, anxious to get the TES for the West Midlands, murmured his disdain. Eric Varley

passed me a note: 'Note for Barbara's diary: Roy Jenkins says: "Ignore the
EEC".'

In the evening, still weak from my tummy, I had to go through an official dinner for
Minister Petrovsky at Lancaster House. He admired the room's ornate beauty. 'This
once was the home of a royal personage,' I said mischievously, 'but now it belongs to
the people.' 'That is familiar with us,' he replied.

Tuesday, 23 September

Weaker still, I got through a day of official pressures, starting with an urgent meeting
with the group of Labour regional health authorities chairmen, at their request.
Apparently all sorts of rumours are circulating about an imminent announcement by
me to the effect that the RHAs are to be wound up and the effect on the morale of their
staff was, they said, disastrous. Such are the penalties of open government and the
risks of reform. I had both to reassure them that no decisions had yet been taken,
even on the lines of what should be our long-term aim, while reserving the right to go
on considering the problems left by reorganization. Anyway, they went away
mollified. I was still half-way through rewriting Brian Abel-Smith's draft for my
speech to tomorrow's Community Care conference. Good as his draft was, I was
determined to sharpen and humanize it. So I stayed on at the office till 10pm to finish
it, fortifying myself with sips of brandy. I was very pleased with it when it was done.

Wednesday, 24 September

Woke in the early hours with my tummy in a dreadful state. I knew I would have to
give in and call our doctor; otherwise I should not be on my feet for party conference.
He diagnosed an infection of the bowel and put me on antibiotics. This meant a great
flurry of cancelling all my engagements and Brian was sent to read my speech for me.
Norman said it was well received, but I was very disappointed not to deliver it myself,
as I think it is one of the best speeches I have done. Worked in bed, feeling very ill.

Thursday, 25 September

I insisted on getting up, for there were a number of things I could not afford to miss
First, Cabinet, at which the main business was my own paper on putting up dental and
optical charges. I had a tightrope to walk here. If I insisted they must *not* go up, Denis
would pounce and say the money must come out of my PESC allocation, and I just
cannot spare that £16 million. We shall build no health centres at all if I lose any more
money! On the other hand, David and I have carefully constructed a package of
charges designed to make some important concessions (and thus reduce the saving). I
had to defend it against a threatened Treasury demand that the savings were not big
enough and that I must give up more. So I delivered my proposals in a flat, quiet tone,
helped by my state of physical weakness. Then, to my astonishment, the storm broke.
Denis welcomed my proposals as 'courageous', but our lads at last came out of their
corner fighting to defend the NHS. Mike said he thought that to increase charges
would be disastrous. (Of course! I suddenly realized the old bogey of 'teeth and

spectacles' had rung a bell!) Wedgie said that, listening to me introducing my paper, he had realized what was meant by the phrase: 'Working without enthusiasm.' Were we really going to tear the movement apart for £16 million? Even Peter said gravely that he thought it would be a 'real mistake', because of the movement's emotive association with the NHS.

Others followed. Only Reg Prentice could not get the cuts in public expenditure increased quickly enough. Then Malcolm Shepherd, to my surprise, said he didn't like the increases either. Could he not come along to my department and look at ways in which we could make administrative economies instead? He was sure he could find ways of saving the necessary £16 million. Unfortunately Harold had had to leave. (I am sure he would have grasped the political sensitivity of this and found a saving formula.) I insisted that any administrative economies possible had already been identified and earmarked to offset the £16½ million cut already made in the health budget. Tony C. objected to the reopening of the PESC decisions in this way. Other people had to deal with sensitive issues, he muttered: none more sensitive than rents, etc. But Mike snapped at him, 'Some of us have to deal with the effects of these decisions on the pay policy. We've helped you over rents.' Harold Lever told me that I could find the money by postponing the phasing out of pay beds – he would! Fortunately Denis nodded when I said that if we did not act, pay beds would be phased out by the unions anyway, but in a disorderly way. Finally Ted ruled that the decisions should be postponed till the Cabinet on 14 October, to enable Malcolm to see what he could do.

Somehow I got through the farewell lunch to Petrovsky and the press conference. Then a rush to the Treasury to discuss the 1977–78 and 1978–79 PESC with Joel Barnett. We went through the 'options' for cuts on the social security side which officials had prepared: Joel wants £500 million from this side alone. I told him I would offer £100 million by reversing the decision to phase out the earnings rule (which has never been my priority), but nothing more. Nonetheless, we went down the list (e.g. abolition of maternity grant, ditto death grant). I just gave Joel a withering look. 'Ah well, I didn't think you'd accept that,' grinned Joel. 'I'm glad she gave *you* that look and not me,' whispered one of his officials. Postponement of the introduction of the child benefit scheme? I countered that by referring to a table in our briefs which showed that our family support provision, despite child benefit, will actually be going down. The suggestion that we should save by postponement was therefore a Treasury fiction. Joel said hastily that he would look into this. His main aim was to get me to agree to switch from the historical method of calculating the pension increases (which, with the fall off in inflation, would now begin to benefit the pensioners) to the forecasting one, which would save the Treasury some £500 million. Brian and I had agreed we would resist this ferociously. Of course, Joel said, 'Then we'll have to get more savings from the health side.' Suddenly I had a good idea. We were talking about the 1976 uprating, yet the proposed public expenditure cuts were related purely to 1977–79. Was there to be a mini-PESC for 1976–77 for Barbara only? I would consider moving to the forecasting method once the 1976 uprating was over and we had given pensioners a fair turn of the wheel in their favour on one round. Peter Baldwin [Deputy Secretary, Treasury] and Joel looked at each other, saying that wouldn't be enough, but we agreed that we should all go away and look at it.

As I dashed for my train to Blackpool for the Labour Party conference, I instructed Norman in the car to use his wits and see that Malcolm's visitation led to some offers of economies in our HQ administration *only*. Norman entered into the idea enthusiastically. I sank into my compartment in the train, feeling like death, and worked quietly all the way to Blackpool, reading up my papers for conference.

Friday, 26 September

Everyone has been predicting terrible rows at this conference. Certainly there have been floods of resolutions denouncing the Government's economic policy and expenditure cuts and demanding massive increases in expenditure on this and that. But there were few signs of dissension at the NEC meeting this morning. The only controversial item on the normal agenda was Alex Kitson's motion on Chile, calling on the Government to impound Chilean assets in this country, such as submarines, for her non-payment of debt. Alex complained that he had been trying to get his resolution discussed for the past three months, and he insisted on going ahead because he couldn't get any satisfactory reply or explanation from the Government. Harold said something involved about how he had written to Jack Jones about this, but Alex said firmly he didn't want Jack brought into it. Finally, as Jim had not yet arrived, we agreed to postpone it till Sunday's meeting, on the promise that we should then have a full explanation of the difficulties from Harold or Jim. On the Finance Committee report, we were faced by a resolution of Shirley's saying that, in view of the party's acute financial difficulties, Ministers should 'consider' meeting the whole of their expenses at conference this year and the trade union boys should ask their unions to meet their expenses. This led to an involved argument, from which it emerged that some union rules would make this difficult. Eventually it was left that Cabinet Ministers only should 'consider' this. I think it is right that those of us who are comfortably off should fork out generously at this time, but I felt aggrieved by two things. (1) Why keep picking on Cabinet Ministers, as though we were Croesuses? It should be done on ability to pay and I bet Mik's income is bigger than mine. (2) I wish it hadn't been sprung on us at the last minute. If I'd known I would have to find £110 or so for conference, I would have told Ted we couldn't afford Corfu as well.

But the main item was to discuss the proposed statement on jobs and prices – and, indeed, whether we should have a statement at all. Mike took the lead on this. He knew, he said, that there were many passages in Geoff Bish's draft which would offend both sides. It committed the party, for instance, to support of the £6 policy, with which it was clear that Mik at any rate would disagree, but equally it embarrassed the Government by stating that 'the most urgent need is for the Government to introduce temporary restrictions on imports'. So why present a statement at all? Mike asked. He didn't think Harold was right in suggesting the Liaison Committee with the TUC had asked for it. 'We could have amendments moved from both sides that could get us into a great tangle.' Harold said he thought a statement was essential, but wanted the drafting done by a small committee. That didn't find any support at all.

Wedgie said he favoured the statement being made unchanged and in its entirety. When Mike said he did not believe that import controls were 'anything like a full answer to the problem of unemployment' Wedgie said smoothly, 'The statement does reflect the views we have discussed with the TUC.' Joan Maynard supported the statement: 'The real cause of inflation is not wages but lack of investment.' (No mention again of not eating the seed corn!) Frank Allaun echoed her dutifully. Mik, surprisingly, backed Mike. But the general view was that the NEC must not be the only people not to have a view on this issue; so that meant going through the document line by line in the afternoon. At the lunch break Mike seized on me almost desperately. 'Come and lunch.' 'Dodging the press?' I asked. 'Not only them,' he replied. I was grateful for his company as we both awaited the arrival of our spouses. 'They're fools to insist on having a statement,' he grumbled over lunch as he ate restlessly. 'We offered them a way out.' He is a very unquiet person these days, but I sense in him an absolute determination to see his job through: an approach I respect and share. His desire to lunch alone with me was significant. This is no situation in which the traditional camaraderie of the large companionable table of the Left could survive.

As we went through the document line by line in the NEC I was surprised by two things: (1) that Mik should let the passage on the £6 limit go through, merely repeating his sour comment that he wasn't going to waste time arguing it; (2) how much Denis was prepared to give to get agreement. He did get some important changes on such things as import controls, entering a caveat, on which the NEC supported him, because he warned of the danger of 'anticipation'. He and I both successfully resisted a snide attempt of Mik's to insert the words, 'and urge the Government not to introduce any further measures increasing the level of unemployment'. Denis protested at the word 'further'. I made quite a little speech, saying that if I thought the aim of this Government was deliberately to increase unemployment I would have resigned from it long ago. But on other points Denis gave away much more that I expected him to, and he was rewarded for his pains by getting the same line-up against him on the final vote as he would have got anyway, Mik, Frank Allaun, Joan Maynard, John Forrester and Nick Bradley (the Young Socialist delegate who sits next to Joan and does everything she tells him to do) voting against the final text as 'inadequate'. In the hotel lobby afterwards I was intrigued to hear Geoff Bish pitching into Denis in passionate complaint that he had given away too much. So much for the politics of demonology that the press is so prone to! If I had been Denis I would have crawled up to my room wanting to die and moaning to Ted, 'I'm a failure.' I suspect Denis has no such self-doubts, which is why he deserves to survive more than I do.

Went to bed still nursing my tum.

Saturday, 27 September

Worked in bed all morning. The red boxes have come rolling up. In one box is a typical letter from Henry Yellowlees. Apparently he was very disturbed by a sentence in my Community Care conference speech in which he thought I had implied that the new Director of Social Work would be on a parallel with him. Typically, he

507

had not stormed into me but moaned to Norman, who had suggested to me that I send him a tactful note, which Norman had drafted. This I did.

Sunday, 28 September

More work in bed in the morning, followed by a stroll in the sun on Blackpool's magnificent sands. I must be getting set in my ways, because I can almost see some virtue in the place. Then into the usual long, gruelling afternoon session of the NEC to discuss the composite resolutions. The resolutions are all demanding massive expenditure increases, and Geoff Bish remarked to me that we really would have to adopt his idea of having a kind of large-scale tote erected at the back of the platform at conference. Every time one of these resolutions was passed we should ring up the cost on the tote, so delegates could see what the total was amounting to. 'And we should also ring up what this expenditure would mean in terms of increased taxes and insurance contributions,' I agreed. Really, the irresponsibility of delegates infuriates me. I agree with Bish: how can they call on the Government to obey conference decisions when they refuse themselves to do any realistic arithmetic? They must learn to choose: either they can continue to pass these resolutions as a relief for their own souls, knowing full well the Government cannot meet them all, or they must impose some revolutionary self-discipline on themselves.

Frank Allaun has been up to me, pleading for my support in getting the NEC to accept the housing resolution, instead of remitting it as the office suggests. 'I know it asks for massive increases in housing, but I will support the same for the NHS when we come to that composite,' he urged. I told him there was one thing I insisted on: all the resolutions calling for money must be treated the same. I wasn't going to have the PESC battle prejudiced by conference. As for the composite on the NHS, it is a shambles – perfectly illustrating the hit-and-miss way conference works. There were nearly twenty resolutions on the agenda, ranging from comprehensive demands from the Socialist Medical Association to resolutions concentrating on one modest specific point, yet when I went to the compositing meeting yesterday afternoon I found that every single point raised in every resolution had been lumped together by the conference arrangements chap into one jumbo composite. Even then people kept adding bits to it, until everybody who had put down a resolution became a party to asking for the earth: massive increases in expenditure, abolition of private practice, total nationalization of the drugs industry, etc., etc. The reference to abolition of private practice was anathema to me, but under the rules I wasn't supposed to interfere. When I did murmur something about the impossibility (and undesirability) of ending all part-time consultant contracts at once, as the resolution demanded, Albert Spanswick nodded approvingly and came out in my support. But we were both swept aside and the composite was adopted *nem. con.* in its entirety. This blather about the sacredness of conference decisions is a nonsense. Here was a composite with parts of which even the NHS unions don't agree (Alan Fisher told me later that his union's policy is separation of private practice, not abolition), but because of the haphazard way our procedure works, both Alan and Albert had to shrug and let it go.

At the NEC we started our consideration of the composites with the housing one. True to his warning, Frank Allaun pressed that we accept it. I intervened to say I thought that we ought to deal with all the resolutions dealing with public expenditure together, so that we could see the implications of what we were asking for. After a bit of an argument it was agreed that we should ask conference to remit the housing composite, which, as Fred Mulley pointed out, meant that, if the delegates wouldn't agree, the NEC would oppose. At this Frank said that he couldn't speak to this effect and someone else had better answer for the NEC. So we chose John Cartwright. I bet Frank leaks his high-mindedness to the press. At the end of the afternoon we had decided to remit almost everything. I don't expect conference will accept this, but the chief thing is that the NEC has shown a sense of responsibility. On anything controversial like this, Mik's little clique (Frank, Joan Maynard, John Forrester, Nick) voted en bloc to demonstrate their socialist purity. It makes me long to see them in government, facing a few facts. The trouble is they wouldn't face them: they would resign from *any* government.

Finally we turned to Alex Kitson's Motion on Chile and the long-awaited arguments by Harold and Jim against impounding Chilean assets. In the event, they did not produce any. It was the most slipshod performance any Minister could give. Jim merely said, 'I would recommend the Government not to do this,' without stating why. It was left to Denis to produce the only real argument: 'The Attorney General tells me we have no right under international law to impound the submarines, which they have paid for, just because they haven't paid other parts of their debt.' Mik shrugged: 'I am unmoved by that argument,' he said, pointing out that all the previous action the Government had taken on Chile had been dragged out of it, the Government protesting at every stage that what was suggested was impossible. When it came to the vote I felt that, whatever the merits of the Government's case, it deserved a snub for having been so cavalier over this, so I voted for the Motion and it was carried by twenty to seven. Harold glowered at me. I noted with surprise that Mike voted with the Government. I thought that was carrying loyalty too far.

In the evening we had our 'Any Questions' eve-of-conference meeting, designed to give delegates the chance of quizzing four Ministers: Mike, Joan, Eric Varley and me. Despite the fact that I had been living for days on antibiotics, the water wagon and boiled fish (or perhaps because of it), I positively scintillated. Nice to end my conference career on a high note – for I have decided not to run again next year for the National Executive.[1]

Monday, 29 September

Highlight of the day was Mike's speech answering the unemployment debate. Since the unions had been streaming to the rostrum to express alarm, he had a horrible job

---

[1] In the event I was persuaded by Ian Mikardo, among others, to stand again. I remained on the NEC until October 1979, when, having left the House of Commons and been elected to the European Parliament, I decided not to run. As a result of a proposal by Tony Benn I became an ex-officio member of the Executive as leader of the British Labour group in the European Parliament.

and triumphed by taking the challenge full on, giving all the emotional voltage he had got. Conference rose to him with a standing ovation, only Mik and co. remaining on their posteriors. Afterwards some people sneered: 'A virtuoso performance, but it had no content.' But I myself, sitting next to him, had been almost reduced to tears by his utter dedication and sincerity. Conference over, I had to go and address one of the many fringe meetings: this one by the Labour Campaign for Mental Health. It seemed so off the main political stream that I cursed myself, not expecting anyone to be there. In the event, about a hundred people turned up and, despite the antibiotics, I found myself on form, laying about myself as once again they asked for the 'massive injection of resources' into their own pet interest. I have been impressed to find – as on Sunday night – how many of our people are involved in constructive do-goodery. Yet these same people will vote to a man for some of the larger lunacies that will be peddled in some of the resolutions this week. This is what political commentators fail to understand: that conference is an essential piece of catharsis for our activists frustrated by the limitations on our actions imposed by reality.

Tuesday, 30 September

I went down to conference quite serenely to hear the NEC election results. Ted has been worrying that I shall be thrown off. Well, it may be so, but I should find it very odd at a time when the papers are full of my row over phasing out private beds. Ted's argument is that the sustained press sneers about my age have reappeared again and will have some effect. Also I am clearly not on Tribune's slate. Ted tells me that at the Tribune brains trust on Sunday morning Judith said she didn't think Ministers should be on the NEC anyway (having ceased to be a Minister herself), while Stan Orme argued that it all depended on the Ministers and then gave a list of the Ministers who *should* be on and omitted me. The only book Mik has been running this year is for bottom place. I put 50 pence on Denis surviving, finding it difficult to believe that the party would be irresponsible enough to inflict this public humiliation on their Chancellor. Ted put 50 pence on my being bottom – for which I was comforted to find the odds were sixteen to one against. But Ted proved to be right. Though my vote went up by 20,000, Wedgie and Mike sailed to the top with over 500,000 each. Mik dropped a few, but still got 6,000 more than I did, while Joan Lestor and Frank picked up thousands more. Even Eric Heffer, coming on to the Executive for the first time, beat me by 5,000 votes, while poor old Denis was nowhere, being only second runner-up even though he got 1,000 more than last time. The big increase in voting all round was symptomatic, I suppose, of the party's mood of protest, though with typical illogic local parties put Jack Ashley, a well known right-winger, in first place as runner-up, giving him 28,000 more votes than Denis! Such are the quirks of democracy.

It was against this erratic background that Harold launched into his major speech. He was obviously proud of it, having shown me some of his best cracks yesterday. But I thought it was one of the worst he has ever made: flat, uninspiring, unfunny, unphilosophical. It only came to life when he ended up with a long and rather obscure diatribe against the machinations of both Left and Right and the odd thing was that conference rose to it, cheering him constantly, the two wings in turn. This movement of ours really is unpredictable. Then on to the debate on economic policy, which gave Denis the chance to make the speech of his life. I couldn't help thinking that there is nothing like defeat for bringing the best out in one. He got a standing ovation and deserved it.

Wednesday, 1 October

Wedgie's turn. The debate was on industrial policy. Judith opened with what I considered a pretty banal speech. Wedgie had decided to play it *sotto voce*. I got the feeling he is trying to shape up more seriously for the leadership. It was, as usual, an impressively fluent speech and brought conference to its feet, only Ted grumbling that he didn't think much of it. In the afternoon it was my turn. As usual I tensed up in quite an absurd way: not so much nervous as unrelaxed. Jack and Ted urged me to make a scintillating speech, but I was conscious of walking a tightrope between the mood of conference, which is calling for the total abolition of private practice, which I opposed, and of the wider audience, including the BMA, which would be waiting to pounce on anything I said about pay beds.[1] In the event, my speech went quite well. I got a lot of applause and it was a pleasant change to have the unions queueing up to congratulate me on what I was doing. But I could still have kicked myself for not being able to make an off-the-cuff speech with the sort of panache I had displayed on Sunday night. No one will ever believe that all my life I have been cursed by this lack of self-confidence, which only disappears in certain circumstances and before certain audiences. Once again, I contrasted myself unfavourably with Shirley, who followed on pensions, making an effortlessly fluent speech on the basis of a few scribbled notes and who was warmly congratulated by Harold.

During the afternoon the rumour ran around that Mik, who was speaking at the Tribune meeting that night, had issued a hand-out savagely attacking Jack Jones and the TUC and claiming that the poor had got poorer under this Government: straight Child Poverty Action Group propaganda of the kind Denis has repudiated. In any case I had decided to go to the Tribune meeting, Mik having told me there was to be a debate between him and Mike. But first to the *Mirror* party, where I congratulated Jack Jones on his speech on pensions. He exuded friendliness. 'What do you think of Mik's attack on you?' I asked. He bridled suspiciously: 'What attack?' 'He's accusing the trade union movement of selling out,' I replied. He shrugged angrily. But I suspect that by alerting him I was responsible for what happened afterwards. Ted and I got to the Spanish Hall at the Winter Gardens at 9pm, in time to hear Neil Kinnock make the funniest collection speech I have ever heard. He's a find, that boy. The hall was packed, the TV lights picking out the baroque moulding at the back of the platform, which gave the whole scene an air of dramatic intensity. The plaster Spanish villages towering on the walls above the speakers' heads added a final touch

---

[1] Despite my caveats about the composite motion the movers insisted on pressing it and conference carried on. *The Times* denounced the decision the next day under the heading: 'Even More Foolish Than Barbara Castle'.

of incongruity. Mik proceeded to read the speech he had handed out, piling selective statistic on selective statistic to give a hostile distortion of the work of the Government. Suddenly out of the crowded aisle where he had been standing leapt Jack Jones, up onto the platform, jabbing an accusing finger at Mik like an Old Testament prophet pronouncing his doom. As Mik had the microphone and Jack had not, all we could hear were a few snatches of what Jack said. 'I detest these attacks on the trade union movement' was all I caught. But he stood there for a full minute, jab following jab with inarticulate shout after inarticulate shout. It was electrifying. The audience split into pro- and anti-Mik arguments and there was pandemonium, which Dick Clements in the chair eventually managed to quell, appealing to Jack as an 'old friend' and saying that Michael would be answering Mik. Jack sat down heavily on the end seat on the platform to which Dick Clements invited him and didn't utter a word after that. Mik finished rather lamely to tumultuous applause from parts of the audience. A few people tried to give him a standing ovation. I wondered how Mike could possibly turn the emotional anti-authority tide. But once again, he dredged up immense energy from somewhere. It must be from his spirit, because it can't be from that emaciated frame of his. He even managed to make the pay policy sound like a socialist crusade, Jack nodding his approval frequently. The audience rose to him. He exuded clearness of conscience – just as I did in the speeches I made to the PLP on *In Place of Strife*. Only a few people remembered, as I did, the contrast between Mike's speech that night and the speeches he had made at Tribune meetings before he became a member of the Government. One of them was a woman sitting in front of me, who hissed, 'He's sold out', and gave the communist salute. To everyone's surprise Dick Clements did not call on Jack to speak. The meeting broke up to the *Red Flag*. That dramatic incident was the talk of the hotel when we got back.

Thursday, 2 October

At the Granada buffet lunch I got into one of my familiar arguments with Joel, asking him if it was true that the Treasury was now asking for expenditure cuts of £5 billion. 'If so, I know one person who will walk out of the Government,' I said. 'Of course,' he replied, 'it would kill the Government.' He tried to pooh-pooh it on the grounds that all the Treasury had done was to point out that, by omitting to mention interest on the national debt in its PESC documents, its proposals would not reduce the borrowing requirement to the extent anticipated. But I know what that means. Denis will come to Cabinet and say that, in view of this, a saving of £3 billion will be the minimum. I simply am not prepared to accept the sort of cuts they are planning for me and feel deeply apprehensive of what faces us when we return. 'I would accept pretty drastic economies,' I told Joel, 'if it was in support of a positive industrial policy. The Government must choose what it is going for: either the soft welfare line or the tough line of industrial reconstruction. What our people won't accept – and I won't accept – is a policy of messing about with everything: a little inadequate bit of investment plus slashing welfare cuts.' He's a nice chap but I don't think he grasps the political realities.

Friday, 3 October

At conference Mik made a bitter little speech on defence, deliberately down-beat. I find it hard to decide what makes him tick these days. Then Auld Lang Syne and home – to enjoy my birthday in private peace. I thanked the Lord it didn't occur in conference this year and so robbed the commentators of their annual jibe at the 'ageing Mrs Castle'. Why did I ever put my birth date in *Who's Who* in a rash moment all those years ago?

Monday, 6 October

Back to a succession of office meetings on this and that which took up every minute of my day. The paper work is flooding in again. We are pressing ahead with the drafting of the pay beds Bill in the hope of getting it into the Queen's Speech.

Tuesday, 7 October

Highlight of the day was the dinner I gave to Derek Rayner of Marks and Spencer. With memories of Aubrey Jones in my mind, I had suggested a private room at the Stafford Hotel for the rendezvous.[1] Present were David and I, James Collier, Brian A-S. and Norman, who was there to record the words of wisdom we hoped to get from Derek on centralizing procurement policy for the NHS as the basis for a great export drive. Rayner stressed that we must take the medical profession along with us in any changes in procurement of equipment, etc., we might want to make. At one stage I summed up his advice: 'Fix your target and then make the consultants think they had suggested it.' 'Exactly,' he chuckled. I had a bright idea. Since the French do a lot of 'cultural' self-promotion, sending their top specialists round the world to talk on this and that, why didn't we do the same? Why didn't we suggest to our top consultants that they should make trips to various key countries overseas to talk about their specialities and we would pay for it? It would not only help exports, but help to defuse the tension in the NHS which the BMA, aided and abetted by Tory spokesmen, are once again working flat out to build up. There is, for instance, a great campaign being launched in the press to suggest that half the top people in the NHS are emigrating. The others thought my idea was good and I told Norman to work on it.

But back at home I suddenly got depressed. With the age thing for everyone to seize on, (which they would never have guessed if I hadn't told them), and with the very people in the movement who ought to be backing me conspiring against the Government in general and me in particular instead, I temporarily but utterly lost heart. 'I want the hell out of it,' I said to Ted as he cuddled me in bed. 'My only problem is: when I go and the reason I give.' And I added viciously, 'Let some

---

[1] When I was Secretary of State for Employment and Productivity in 1968–70 Aubrey Jones, then chairman of the Prices and Incomes Board, used to entertain me in a private room at the Stafford Hotel so that we could discuss our problems unobserved.

of them take this pay beds thing on and let us see what *they* can make of it.' Ted just listened, stroking my head as gently and staunchly as he has done over the years.

With world recovery still fragile and patchy, the economic outlook remained deeply worrying. At home the £6 pay limit was holding remarkably well with the promise of nearly halving the rate of increase in earnings over the coming year and a big reduction in the rate of inflation, even if not quite to the Chancellor's target of 10 per cent. But with world trade flat and workers' living standards being cut, deflation was deepening. Output had fallen and unemployment continued its relentless upward trend. In October the seasonally adjusted figure had risen to over one million or 4·6 per cent and even the CBI *was forecasting that it would reach 1·25–1·5 million by the end of 1976.*

In this situation the NEC *remained restive about the Government's economic and industrial strategy. With other countries balancing their trade by deflating and with the export surplus of* OPEC *countries still running at between $40 billion and $50 billion, it was clear that the world crisis would only be solved by far more imaginative lending and recycling policies than the international institutions showed any sign of developing. This intensified the problems of the weaker economies like Britain and made it extremely unlikely that we could rely on the revival of world demand to stimulate industrial production. In any case our industrial problems were so deep-seated that some fundamental restructuring was necessary.*

The NEC, *therefore, continued to press its alternative strategy on the Chancellor. This laid increasing emphasis on the need for selective import controls to give industry a breathing space to rebuild itself. In October the* NEC's *statement on industrial strategy, 'Labour and Industry', had been put to the party conference. Geoff Bish's first draft had been softened in tone, but the statement nonetheless declared that the Industry Bill then going through Parliament fell 'very considerably short' of the party's original proposals and called for further legislation to provide powers to ensure that companies entered into planning agreements. It also stated that the* NEC *was considering a number of ways in which the banks, pension funds and insurance companies could make a greater contribution to industrial investment. The statement was carried overwhelmingly by conference, not a voice being raised against it. Indeed, it was the moderate trade union leader, David Basnett, who moved a parallel composite resolution calling among other things for the planning agreement system to be supported by 'indirect sanctions' of the kind the* NEC *had been calling for. And it was he, too, who in a forceful speech a few weeks later declared that workers and trade unions ought to have a say in the management of pension funds in order to ensure that they were used more effectively to promote social and industrial needs.*

Undeterred Denis Healey pressed ahead with his more orthodox policies. The battle over public expenditure cuts continued in Cabinet in preparation for the Public Expenditure White Paper of February 1976. On industrial policy the Government hurried to bury the last remnants of Bennery. With conference over, it held a tripartite meeting at Chequers of government, unions and CBI *to work out a consensus industrial policy. The result was a new White Paper, 'An Approach to Industrial Strategy' (Cmnd. 6315), of which the keynote was collaboration with industry. Though making a token obeisance to the new instruments – the* NEB *and planning agreements – to which the party conference had attached so much importance, it laid its main emphasis on a sector analysis. Within this framework, ran the argument, both government and industry would adapt their policies to ensure success. It found a willing collaborator in the* TUC. *Despite the bold words of the* TUC's Economic Reviews, *most union leaders were not prepared to enter into an alliance with the Left against the Government, alienated by the Left's hectoring tone.*

Meanwhile the latent discontent in the Health Service had erupted into open war. This was fed from three sources: the consultants' anger over my consultative document on pay beds; the juniors' discontent over pay; and the general low morale, due partly to worry about lack of funds, but above all to frustration at the top-heavy administrative structure Sir Keith Joseph had introduced. The press wove all three issues together to build up a picture of the imminent 'collapse' of the NHS. *When on 7 October the breakaway consultants in the* HCSA *published figures claiming that 300 consultants were preparing to leave the* NHS *for jobs abroad, the press took up the emigration scare with enthusiasm. 'Patients Put in Peril as Doctors Emigrate', declared the* Daily Mail. *'Scandal of the Sick Health Service', echoed the* Sun. *Even* The Times *expressed concern. In vain I pointed out that most years some 500 doctors emigrated from Britain and 200 returned and that the figures had been at their worst in 1965. There was some increase in intentions to emigrate, but no one could say whether they would materialize – there had been some falling off since the April pay award. Nonetheless the medical profession seized the opportunity to press its grievances. The* BMA *renewed its demand for an enquiry into the state of the* NHS. *Sir Rodney Smith declared that the Service was at the 'point of no return'. Opposition spokesmen blamed it all on me, Norman Fowler, a junior 'shadow', denouncing me as 'the midwife of chaos' to a delighted Tory conference.*

At the same time trouble had broken out again among the juniors. As we had agreed, the new contract I had negotiated with them in January had been priced by their own Review Body. But as I had also warned them, that did not mean that there would necessarily be any extra money available to finance the 'closed contract' for which they had asked. And so it proved. Though the Review Body reluctantly accepted that supplementary payments should start after forty-four hours of work, to replace the extra duty allowances payable after eighty hours, the introduction of pay policy meant that the same amount of money had to be spread over a wider span. As the juniors had had a 30 per cent increase in April, all the Review Body could do was to redistribute the money already available for 'overtime'. They had done so to the best of their ability but, although most juniors were better off as a result, about a third of them suffered the fatal word 'detriment'. In other words, they were actually worse off. Although their own negotiators had grudgingly accepted the report, it was a recipe for conflict. And within days of the report being known, unofficial action on an 'emergencies only' basis had broken out in a number of areas. The BMA *hurried in to blame the Government.*

Meanwhile the pay beds issue was rumbling on. I believed it was essential to legislate quickly to clear the air and persuaded my colleagues to include the following paragraph in the Queen's Speech of 19 November: 'Legislation will be introduced in the course of the session to phase out private practice from National Health Service hospitals. Consultations will continue on My Government's proposals to strengthen and extend existing powers to regulate nursing homes and hospitals outside the National Health Service.'

The BMA's response was to call on all senior hospital doctors, from consultants downwards, to ban all NHS work except emergencies. Similar action by the juniors was made official at the same time. Some people in the Cabinet began to get cold feet. Harold Wilson schemed with his old friend, Arnold Goodman, to force a compromise.

Wednesday, 8 October

Woke to a major blast of hostile publicity on the NHS. On the eight o'clock news the BBC built up a small unofficial strike by some junior hospital doctors into a vaguely generalized indictment of the state of the NHS (the inference being that I was responsible). The *Daily Telegraph* and other newspapers splashed stories about massive emigration of consultants and warnings of the 'collapse' of the NHS. I soon had the *Evening Standard* and *World at One* on the phone: would I give interviews, etc.? I rang Norman and told him to call an office meeting at 10am when we would decide our whole strategy. Peter was there, firm in the view that a blitz was being deliberately organized by the profession to coincide with the health debate on Thursday at the Tory conference. He agreed absolutely that I ought to have a press conference that day. David demurred a bit at this, but said it was 'a matter for your political judgment'. My political judgment backed Peter's, and so it was agreed. A mad rush to check up on a whole catalogue of detail and to get my reply off to the BMA to their memo on my consultative document. I suggested that the ostensible purpose of the press conference should be to announce my reply to the BMA memo.

In the event, the conference went well, helped by the fact that I had suddenly realized we ought to have a press statement. Most of the press get things woefully wrong unless they have something written down on which they can draw heavily. This meant I had to spend my lunch hour scribbling out the statement myself, choosing my words carefully about my willingness to discuss the consultative document with the BMA and my invitation to them for talks. 'It's no good telling the BMA that we have already erected the gallows and that all they can do is to discuss the thickness of the rope,' I quipped. So the drafting was tricky: how to suggest they could discuss anything, while not suggesting I was running away on pay beds? Anyway, it seemed to do the trick, foxing the hostile press. Then into a succession of radio and TV interviews – quite like old times.

Thursday, 9 October

Very good press coverage, which has successfully defused Rodney Smith's sour press conference yesterday. It is now clear that I was right and David wrong and that we have drawn the poison out of the situation before Norman Fowler can get to his feet at the Tory conference. At Cabinet Bob Mellish was ecstatic about my handling of the attacks. 'That "keep cool" line of yours is first-class.' He has the political nous to realize that all this outcry has been organized, but whether Harold will is another matter. He has asked for a full report. Of course, the right-wing press is using the occasion to call for me to be sacked and I know this campaign will be redoubled as the days go by. The *Mirror*, bless 'em, have got a first-class leader in my support. So I must just fight back with everything I've got.

The sole business of Cabinet was to discuss the law of picketing,[1] Mike, as usual, backing the TUC, with Roy Jenkins *et al.* wringing their hands in horror at the thought of a frontal clash with the Lords, to say nothing of rousing the ire of the police. I suggested a compromise: that the TUC should agree to open informal discussions with the police *pari passu* with our tabling the amendment they want to the Employment Protection Bill. 'The police would never stand for that,' snapped Roy. As he was backed massively by Elwyn, Malcolm, Fred Peart and the rest, Mike was sent away to try to get the TUC to change their minds. I doubt they do.

An amusing little interlude on foreign affairs, our Jim taking a good old nationalistic stand on Britain's right to separate representation from the Community at the coming conference of consumers *v.* producers on oil in particular. Harold Lever didn't like this a bit. There was, he urged, a case for accepting a Community mandate. 'I am arguing for an agreed mandate rather than claiming separate representation,' he said. Jim retorted that he, too, wanted an agreed mandate, but he would not give up our claim. Roy Jenkins made some nervous noises, but Harold backed Jim, while I said, 'Hear, hear' loudly. And so it was agreed.

Having snatched a mouthful of food, I hurried to Folkestone to address the Family Practitioners Committee conference. Once again, TV was there in force and I got quite a good coverage. Ernest Colin-Russ [our GP] was in the chair, as overwhelmingly friendly as ever. I got a courteous hearing, with only a bit of heckling from the back, for which Ernest apologized profusely. 'Just a few of our backwoodsmen,' he said. Apparently they had even protested against the TV lights! I only wish there were more Colin-Russes about, but, alas, he isn't typical. Then back to the office to give an interview to Christine Doyle of the *Observer* about the furore over pay beds. She came in oozing frigidity. When I said the policy of separating private practice from NHS hospitals had not been dreamed up by me: it had been put in the election Manifesto before I even knew I would be in the Government, let alone in this job, she replied, 'No one will believe that.' 'Then the historical evidence proves them wrong,' I replied patiently. I gave her over an hour and she began to melt towards the end.

---

[1] Despite earlier failures (see footnote, page 79), the TUC was still trying to persuade the Government to amend the Employment Protection Bill during its passage through the Lords to enable pickets to stop vehicles, but Roy Jenkins refused to budge.

But I suspect she is against me, as so many of them are. It was late before I got home and to bed.

Saturday, 11 October

The papers are full of Margaret Thatcher's triumph at the Tory conference yesterday. I was struck by how blooming she looked after what must have been a week of intense strain: the vitamin of power again. Success in politics does as much for a woman's looks as falling in love. It *is* falling in love – with success and power.

Sunday, 12 October

Christine Doyle has done a rather snide piece suggesting that the row over pay beds is all my fault. She hasn't used a single one of the arguments I gave her. Why bother to try and communicate?

Monday, 13 October

The *Observer* had an interview with Margaret Thatcher yesterday in which she suggested that she managed to cope with all domestic chores herself, as well as do her political work. 'At weekends I cook and do some housework because there is no one else to do it,' she told Kenneth Harris. Sorry, but I don't believe it. Okay, she's not a Minister now, but she *is* Leader of the Opposition, and the amount of reading she must have to do is enormous. Or doesn't she? Because I find that I just can't fit in regular domestic work. Cooking is a special-occasion luxury that I do about six times a year. For the rest, it is done by Eileen, and very well, too. As for housework, it's fun. Nothing more satisfying than a good spring-clean. I'm positively longing to resign so that I can turn out Mother's storage shed. But when I have work to do at the level I have – and presumably Margaret has – it is quite impossible to do one's own chores. Shopping becomes one of the great unattainables.

Take my weekend. Home lateish Saturday evening for a meal Eileen had pre- pared. A good natter to Ted and Eileen, a wee walk with the dogs and then back to the boxes till 11pm. (Barely time to break off and look at 10pm news.) To bed at midnight and up at 8am, this being Sunday. Then out into the garden to help Ted with the rush of autumn work: pulling up the straggling remains of the border plants and replanting the tubs, getting in a few bulbs and picking apples. A short walk with the dogs, lunch, some more work in the garden. Then a cup of tea and down to work: six hours on my boxes non-stop. When, at midnight, I went to bed, there was still a pile of major submissions I hadn't got through.

Up this morning at 7.15am and saw Ted off to his European committee in Brussels. Edna came at 9am and Eileen had our breakfast ready. Leaving all sorts of domestic messages all over the place, I am driven up to town to start a long day of office meetings on all the departmental minutiae. I didn't have time to go to the flat and collect my clothes. Instead, with rumours of an all-night sitting in the air, Edna went up to the flat to collect a rug and a cardigan. As I type this it is 7pm and Walter Harrison has just told me we may be lucky: the Tories may want to throw in the sponge at 2am. What chance have I got for shopping? Fortunately, my inimitable Edna takes a motherly interest in me (to say nothing of her passion for our dogs).

First office meeting this morning was on the junior doctors. The *Daily Telegraph* has been excelling itself again, talking about my 'crude blackmail'. Since I have merely been carrying out the Government's pay policy, which Michael has refused to modify to give the juniors a bit more money, I find this a bit much. Unless I can budge Michael I think we face a long spate of official industrial action, which will, of course, be blamed on me and my 'tactless' way of handling things. I have had about enough and am determined to fight for my own hand. When David suggested that we draft a letter to Mike, setting out the situation objectively and suggesting that as I was carrying out Government policy the Chancellor and Mike ought to make this clear, I said this was not good enough. I said firmly that I would write to Mike, asking that we accept a 'no detriment' clause. 'Then,' I said acidly, 'if he refuses we can leak that Barbara was overruled by Cabinet.' David looked shocked at this, but I know that both Jack and Norman think that the dead-set which the press is now making at me must be taken seriously.

In fact, it is interesting to note that even David now realizes there is a press conspiracy against me which is getting out of hand. I have spent some time this weekend reading the long 'consultative document' on future health and personal social services planning, on which David has spent a lot of time. David has been all for our taking a tough, realistic line about the 'restraints' on expenditure that lie ahead, arguing that people will only respect us if we tell them the truth. The succession of distorted and viciously hostile stories with which the *Daily Telegraph* has been leading all the past week has shaken this simple faith. He even volunteered this morning that he thought our letter to RHAs on the capital allocations for hospital-building in the next few years (drawn up inevitably on the most pessimistic assumptions) ought not to go out in the present hysterical atmosphere. So I chalk up victory number one. David even said to me this morning that he thought we ought to hold up his precious consultative document. I was grateful for David's sudden access of political realism. 'What do you think the Tory press would make of some of your phrases?' I asked him. 'Like "medical benefits might fall"?' He agreed gloomily.

David has obviously been particularly shaken by the *Daily Mail* and *Daily Express* splashes today: 'Axe to fall on hospitals' and 'Hospitals Face Cash Swop Crisis'. Someone has obviously leaked the, as yet unpublished, report of the working party he set up to discuss the reallocation of resources to the needier areas.[1] But, once again, it has been turned into a personal attack on me. 'Social Services Secretary Barbara Castle is about to deal another hammer blow to morale in the NHS', said the

---

[1] This was one of David's most important contributions to the work of the department. The Resources Allocation Working Party [RAWP], manned by civil servants, NHS administrators and medical academics, was set up in May 1975 to secure a fairer distribution of NHS capital and revenue resources among RHAS, AHAS and districts. David had long argued that the NHS had failed to iron out the wide discrepancies in health care between different parts of the country and was determined to get a new system of allocation related to need. RAWP's first interim report, published in August 1975, became the basis of the new policy and caused an outcry from the richer areas.

Express. I think David suddenly felt, as I did, that the British press would again kill the hope of intelligent decisions in our democracy. He insisted we must rush out a press reply at once and only smiled ruefully when I said, 'Henceforth I am going to deal with our NHS problems politically. No more nobility for me. This open government lark is a catastrophe.' Norman nodded approvingly.

We spent most of the ministerial lunch discussing how we could hit back. Jack reported that Ian Wrigglesworth, Roy Jenkins's PPS, is anxious to table an Early Day Motion supporting me. Would we draft one for him? We drafted it and sent Jack Ashley off to collect the maximum number of signatures. In the lobby a lot of our people made friendly noises to me.

Our last office meeting of the day was on (three guesses!) PESC: this time the discovery by Treasury that they will need cuts of £5 billion, not £2 billion or £3 billion, to get any reduction of the borrowing requirement. Philip, Dick Bourton, Errington, Nick Jordan-Moss, David, Brian O'Malley, Michael Meacher and I met in my room as at a wake. The reason for the change in the calculation is that Treasury has overlooked the increase in the interest on the national debt, which arises (1) from the increase in the borrowing requirement and (2) from the fact that our very success in counter-inflation policy puts up the *rate* of interest in real terms. Can you beat it? As I put it, 'Our success in defeating inflation creates the need for more deflation.' Officials just smiled nervously. I held forth passionately. This had been my experience throughout the ages of my ministerial responsibility. Whatever one proposed – or did – was inflationary and had to be curbed. I saw Nick Jordan-Moss [Deputy Secretary at the department] almost grinning his agreement. (As a former Treasury man he ought to know.) 'The only thing to do,' I concluded, 'is to fly by the seat of one's political pants. Send for my abacus.' Brian said that if anyone tried to change the pension calculations from the historical method to the forecasting one, they could count without him. David merely looked gloomy.

I challenged Philip and Dick Bourton to produce the document now being circulated by Treasury outlining their proposals for £1,000 million more cuts. First they maintained they hadn't seen it, second that it wouldn't affect us anyway. 'We understand that nothing more is being asked from this department.' 'Then where is it coming from?' I asked. 'Housing,' they began, but got such a groan from Brian that they stopped short. 'We really don't know, Secretary of State,' they said lamely. I replied that all this was no consolation for me. If nearly £500 million was to be asked from the health and personal social services under the across-the-board 'formula' procedure to help reach £3 billion cuts, I would be told I was damn lucky to get away with this when the total target went up to £5 billion. 'And I just won't accept the formula cuts,' I said firmly.[1] Philip and Dick wriggled and then Philip added, 'I

---

[1] The Chancellor's proposal, first outlined to Cabinet in May, was that savings of £3 billion should be identified for 1978–79, out of which a selection should be made to achieve a saving of £2 billion. Cuts would also have to be made in 1977–78. As a starting point he proposed a formula for across-the-board cuts of 5 per cent and 10 per cent in revenue and 15 per cent and 20 per cent in capital for 1977–78 and 1978–79 respectively. These would apply to goods and services but not to social security. As this would not give him the total he required, further savings of £1½ billion would have to be negotiated with Ministers on a more selective basis.

sympathize, of course, Secretary of State, and of course we must defend our departmental interest. But I must say to you that I have come to the conclusion that we shall
have to accept the formula cuts.' So the whole exercise of trying to get real priorities
in spending cuts will, if officials have their way, become a pantomime. I have never
had any doubts that three-quarters of my officials have been half-hearted in their
defence of our services against cuts. But they had the grace to look ashamed when I
said, 'How could the Treasury lose £3 billion? And how can anyone have any faith in
their accountancy after this?'

As we broke up I told Philip that I wanted to see a copy of the new secret Treasury
document right away. He pretended to agree but added, 'If we can get hold of it.
There is really nothing to get hold of till the Chancellor has formed a view on it.' As
we went through the division lobby that evening David said to me, 'I'm afraid that
public expenditure has got completely out of control.' I don't agree with him. I think
that it is the *reductions* in public expenditure that have got completely out of political
control. The whole stage is being set for the most massive deflation in our history.
Later, when Norman arrived with a couple of boxes, he confirmed my view. Barely
maintaining the pretence of Civil Service objectivity, he told me, 'I must say the
behaviour of some top civil servants over this is incredible.' I am convinced that Dick
Bourton had a copy of the new Treasury document on his lap all the time he was
talking to me. Officials have made up their minds about the cuts and are trying to get
Ministers to carry the can. When I said I must see the document Norman replied, 'I
am doing a note of this meeting which will say you demanded this forthwith.' Later
over food Brian and I agreed we would resign together over this if necessary. 'In the
end things become very simple,' said Brian. 'It is merely a question of whether we
want to do a Philip Snowden.'

Tuesday, 14 October

The most important part of the day was the private dinner at the Gay Hussar with the
health unions to discuss our progress on pay beds and other things. Victor had done
his stuff in that charming upstairs room of his, all draped with Hungarian embroidery
– as cosy as a peasant sitting room. Alan Fisher, Geoffrey Drain and Peter Jacques
were there. Audrey Prime should have come, but it turned out that she had been laid
out with flu. So Jack, Brian O'Malley, David and I outnumbered them. With the
latest IRA outrages filling the press, I said cheerfully at one point, 'This place should
be the next target for a bomb.' The Community Land Bill was going through the
House, so we had been lucky to be allowed to pair at all, and at one point yesterday
Norman had said to me, 'If your Whip won't pair you we will have to switch it to
Lockets.' And lo and behold, Lockets was the target for an IRA bomb last night! Such
is the precariousness of London life these days. This time it was the TUC's turn to
stand the treat and they had ordered an excellent meal.

It was one of those discursive discussions out of which certain hard points of
importance suddenly crystallize. And so we found ourselves getting down first to the
nitty gritty of the 'participative management' exercise in the NHS which excites me so
much. I was delighted to find that Alan and Geoffrey, far from entering stiff union

caveats on this experiment, shared my excitement over its potentialities. They were all for my setting up the press conference on it which officials had tried to stop. On pay beds they once again confirmed their support for my policy of licensing; despite David's secret doubts about my proposals, he had to listen to their enthusiastic adoption of the idea. I seized the opportunity to sound them out about their attitude to the junior doctors' pay. What worried me, I said, was that my officials and the juniors' representatives had got themselves into the situation in which they were going to make one-third of the juniors worse off under the new contract. It was ridiculous not to expect the juniors to fight for the sacred principle of 'no detriment'. On the other hand, we could only ensure no one was worse off under the new contract if we made some extra money available. And this would contravene pay policy. Would the unions stand by us if it came to a strike over this? Alan went into one of his excited spins, saying that of course we must ensure 'no detriment', but Peter Jacques shook his head. He thought the one thing the TUC would demand was that there must be no breach of the pay policy. After all, lots of people had had to postpone restructuring agreements. The juniors ought to postpone their new contract till next April, when more money would be available. I asked him to contact Len Murray and let us know his views.

Wednesday, 15 October

Jack told me Peter Jacques had phoned to say that Len's deputy, whom he had consulted in Len's absence, had said, 'No extra money for the juniors. The TUC would consider this a breach of pay policy.' I told my chaps that it was essential that this should be seen to have been imposed on me by the Department of Employment, so we sent off the letter to Mike, warning him that industrial action was likely on a large scale and asking him to agree to a compromise. The press is continuing its hysterical campaign against me. Never have they carried so many stories about 'crisis' in the NHS and everything is grist to their mill. David is more convinced than ever that we have got to lie low about cuts for a bit.

At MES [Ministerial Economic Strategy Committee] we had a preliminary canter on cash limits for local authority spending. I am increasingly alarmed about Denis's determination to introduce this mechanism. He maintains Cabinet has agreed to it. I certainly don't remember this and made a note to ask Norman to turn it up. My memory is that we merely said we were studying it. Tony C. made his usual attempt to prevaricate, complaining he had only received the paper yesterday, that the whole concept was full of 'grave difficulties' (e.g. if our forecast of the rate of inflation proved wrong it would mean 'capricious cuts' in local authority services) and demanding that it be made part of a general policy on cash limits. I protested that we had never had a Cabinet discussion on the implications of cash limits for social priorities. Denis waved me aside, saying that a cash limit was being worked out for the NHS. (That's the first I've heard of it and, by heavens, I'm going to look into it.) Harold agreed soothingly that Ministers must have more time to study the paper and so, mercifully, the matter was postponed. I bet Tony C. has shot his usual temporizing bolt and will climb down next time.

Hurried over to see Elwyn about family courts.[1] We have the first major debate on Finer in the House next Monday and, through all the pressure of to-ing and fro-ing over the juniors, I am really trying to get to the bottom of what we are doing on Finer and what we ought to be doing. The office has put up the usual impossibly smug draft speech, which just won't do. Elwyn was as charming as usual and convinced me that the elaborate new machinery Finer proposes just is not on. I begged him to get someone to write me a simple human explanation I could use.

Another late night, with a running three-line whip on Mike's Trade Union Bill. It was late before I could get down to drafting bits of my Finer speech. And, of course, there were the usual boxes crammed with the urgent minutiae of my departmental life. Getting time to think through major policies becomes increasingly impossible.

Thursday, 16 October

Mike has sent me one of his charming letters, saying he's awfully sorry but he can't budge over the juniors' pay. In view of the TUC line I must accept that this is right, but I am furious that we (and the juniors' representatives) have allowed ourselves to drift into the position where we are nailing our colours to fighting for the impossible principle of making some people worse off. This is what comes of delegating detailed negotiations to officials – as pressure of work compels one to do. They just are not trained to foresee political storms. I keep telling them they must find a way of providing 'no detriment' within the available money, while not abandoning the introduction of the new contract for the rest. They keep saying it is impossible, but I refuse to believe it is. I got up wearily to read my stuff for Cabinet, to find the main business was a turgid piece from Eric Varley and Denis Healey on 'an approach to industrial strategy' which they are proposing to circulate to Neddy, as the basis of our planning for five to ten years ahead.[2] It is supposed to avoid the snags of the national plan technique by being 'flexible' and moulding itself on what the French, in particular, have done. I thought it was pretty anodyne: all about working out with both sides of industry detailed criteria on a sector basis; so I'm afraid I didn't pay much attention to it. Eric, in introducing it, waxed eloquent about the 'excellent analysis' in the Labour Party industrial strategy document and insisted that he was a 'strong supporter of planning agreements, industrial democracy and intervention in industry'. The trouble was, he said, that the trade union movement had given no thought to this at all but he hoped that this new approach would stir them up. Peter Shore, who has been touring the world these past few months in the most extensive trade visits ever undertaken by a Trade Minister, gave a passionate warning about how British

---

[1] The report of the Finer Committee on One-Parent Families had recommended the establishment of family courts to apply a single, uniform system of family law for all citizens.

[2] The document later emerged as a White Paper with the same title (Cmnd. 6315, November 1975). Though the White Paper described planning agreements and the NEB as 'powerful new instruments' for dealing with our industrial problems, its whole emphasis was on persuasion, not pressure. Management and unions were invited to tripartite discussions with the Government to work out a common industrial strategy, sector by sector. The Government pledged itself to increase the profitability of private industry and to give priority to industrial development 'over consumption or even our social objectives'.

industry just was not conscious of 'competitiveness'. We must start a dialogue with industry and it must relate to exports. He favoured the document as an initial approach, but it was not a 'full industrial strategy'.

I thought I had better seize the opportunity to let Cabinet know the export potential of the NHS and told them what we were doing. It was wrong, I said, to treat our social spending separately from our economic policy. 'We should study how our industrial strategy can feed back into our social services.' And I told them how we in DHSS were working out a central procurement policy for the NHS which could form a strong base for the rationalization of the supplying industries, the medical equipment industry, for example, and therefore enable it to exploit the export markets now available in the OPEC countries. Tony C., who can recognize gamesmanship when he sees it – and no one is better at practising it – chipped in sarcastically to say that he had been interested to hear Barbara's PESC bid. (Our sparring goes on interminably.) After others had made a few generalized noises Ted Short electrified Cabinet by suddenly launching into a scathing attack on Eric's document. It was, he said, a 'terrible paper', full of 'turgid, indigestible officialese'. What it outlined was 'light years away from economic planning'. It visualized that profits would be the only source of finance and talked about 'holding back social consumption'. (In my hurried reading I am afraid I had missed this.) There was no assurance in it, Ted continued, that the fruits of growth would be available for our social policies. It might accept the party document's analysis, but not its conclusions. Economic strategy must be part of our social strategy. Wedgie was quick to follow on, endorsing what Ted had said. An analytical framework was vital, he urged. 'In whose interests do you intervene?' he asked. Mike said he agreed with Ted 'and most of what Wedgie has said'. It would be better to hold up the paper and rewrite it, integrating the conference document's conclusions in it. And once again he maintained that we were 'faced with a political and economic crisis of enormous size'. We had to decide what to do in the next six months, as 'we may not survive'. We had got to take the trade unions with us. 'I doubt if they will respond to this document.'

Harold tried to pacify everyone, as usual. We were all agreed, he said, that our main task was to get more investment. The criticisms of the document had been valid, but could be dealt with. We should include references to procurement policy, the nature of the planning instruments we would use and the relationship of medium-term strategy to our immediate problems. Denis said defensively, 'The French have revolutionized the performance of their industry by this sort of method.' A lot of the criticism was bound up with our present frustration. 'We all know Tony was not satisfied with the Industry Bill he introduced,' he added. 'He wanted planning agreements to be compulsory.' At least we had got a discussion started. 'Another thing we have to decide is whether we want the tripartite approach. I happen to think it is worth getting support from both sides of industry,' he concluded. It was agreed that MES should clear a redraft by Eric Varley and him.

Harold then called on me to report on the position in the NHS. He has been nibbling at the idea of an independent enquiry for some days and had asked me to circulate a paper setting out the pros and cons. I have come increasingly to the conclusion that we shall never get any sense out of the medical profession until we get this obsession of theirs about an enquiry out of the way, though I am fully alive to the danger that the consultants will try to get the pay beds issue referred to it and *that* I am determined to prevent. So I had set out a purely neutral paper, but at an office meeting yesterday my lads and I agreed that the balance of advantage lay in setting up an enquiry. Not the least of our reasons was that the juniors who are now taking industrial action are giving this as one of their aims. Even David, who has been against an enquiry up to now, said he had reluctantly come to accept that it was unavoidable. 'Your political judgment, Barbara, led you always to keep this option open and you have been proved right.'

I told Cabinet that we faced a major industrial dispute with the juniors over pay policy and I wasn't going to oppose Mike on his interpretation of it. An enquiry might help marginally to improve their mood – at the very least it would take away an alibi. But we must stand firm against referring pay beds to it. And one thing I did ask: that it should be made quite clear to the juniors that I was merely operating Government pay policy and I hoped other Ministers would associate themselves with me over this. Of course, Denis was very nervous about the whole idea of an enquiry, seeing it as a potential pressure group for a bigger share of resources for the NHS (which is just what I hope it will become: this is my main reason for wanting it). Tony [Crosland] inevitably opposed the whole idea, while Harold Lever typically wanted to refer the pay beds issue to it – or, at the very least, my proposals for licensing, which clearly terrify him. (He is terrified of every socialist bit of our policy, from getting rid of direct grant schools to the Community Land Bill.) But the PM successfully steered the decision the way he wanted, overcoming all the doubts by saying that a small group of us (including himself, Denis, Mike and me) should meet immediately after lunch to agree the terms of reference, the ones I proposed having been roundly denounced by Denis as holding out the prospect of pressure for more money. The reason for the rush was that I had told Cabinet I was meeting the juniors that afternoon at their request and Harold wanted me to tell them about the enquiry in confidence before he announced it later that day. In this way he hoped my meeting would be easier.

Cabinet over, I grabbed coffee and biscuits before summoning my officials to my room in the House. We agreed that at the coming meeting on the terms of reference I should stick as closely as possible to those I had already worked out: 'To examine the financial and manpower resources of the NHS, their use and management.' But when the small Cabinet group met in Harold's room at 2pm Denis was obdurate. He wasn't going to have anyone looking into the 'resources' of the NHS. That was entirely a matter for the Government. We had a tough battle and eventually I emerged with a form of words which David agreed was not too bad. It means that the enquiry can look at almost anything except pay beds. I had made it clear to Harold I wouldn't stand for that and he agreed to say in his statement that we should proceed to implement our Manifesto commitment on pay beds as soon as parliamentary time was available. (The battle over parliamentary time has still to come.)

Back to my officials to prepare for the juniors' meeting at 4pm. There were three representatives of the junior doctors – Dr Bell, Dr Ford and Dr Mander – but they were firmly led by Grabham, as Chairman of the BMA Central Committee for Hospital Medical Services, the tough egg I have had trouble with before. And, of course, there was the ubiquitous Stevenson. We met in the little ministerial conference room at the House. Grabham was succinct: the BMA, he said, backed the juniors in their claim for extra money to enable us to operate the principle of 'no detriment'. The situation was so serious they thought they should see me and find out what the Government was prepared to do to resolve the dispute. I spoke gravely, firmly. Any extra money would mean a breach of the pay policy. It wasn't Barbara Castle picking on the juniors. Cabinet had felt obliged to reaffirm that view, whatever the consequences. Grabham, who manages to make all his remarks sound politely insolent, said that they were not surprised. It really hadn't required the Secretary of State's 'eloquence'. I kept my temper and turned to the juniors (who had sat in respectful silence while their masters spoke), deliberately bringing them in. Dr Ford, who is clearly desperately anxious for a settlement, merely said that, though he himself could accept my arguments, I had to realize they couldn't carry their grassroots with them. 'We shall be repudiated,' he said. Bell echoed this: 'This will be the end of us.' 'Well, then,' I said, 'if you are going to be finished anyway, why not go down fighting?' Grabham intervened, obviously annoyed at the rapport which was building up between me and the juniors. They would like the opportunity of discussing what I had said among themselves. I agreed at once. He then added, as insolently as ever, that he must ask that no press statement or comment should be made by me pending their decision on what I had said. Again, I agreed, despite Peter Brown's signals of alarm. As we broke up and they prepared to return to BMA House to report back, Dr Bell turned and said to me, 'Here's one who will go down fighting.'

But I wasn't out of the rough. True to Harold's instructions that I could – and should – give the juniors advance notice of the statement he was preparing to make on the independent enquiry that night, I had thrown this into the discussion. In the event, the juniors did not seem interested, but Grabham and Stevenson had pricked up their ears immediately. 'May I ask,' said Grabham, 'whether the enquiry will deal with the issue of pay beds?' I had to think quickly. Realizing that, if I hesitated on this at all, the hounds would move in, I said 'No', firmly. No reaction from Grabham at that stage, but, as we broke up, he and Stevenson asked if they could have a few moments with me privately. Grabham at once proceeded to warn me that, if the Government were to go ahead with setting up the enquiry without agreeing to refer the issue of pay beds to it, there would be 'confrontation'. That was the last thing they wanted. Indeed, they would be prepared to co-operate fully with the Government if I would be prepared to do something which he knew would be difficult for me. He was asking a sacrifice: that I should agree to postpone the phasing out of pay beds for two years while the Royal Commission looked at it. (And until, hopefully from his point of view, there would be a Tory Government, I thought to myself.) I told him he really was asking the impossible, whereupon he demanded to see the PM before any announcement was made, while Derek Stevenson started squeaking his indignation. I said that of course I would convey their request to the PM at once and let them know. At last they agreed to take the juniors away and discuss what I had thought was the key issue of the moment, the juniors' dispute.

Back in my room, I had the job of trying to contact the PM. When Harold came to the phone I was relieved to find he was quite relaxed. I hardly had to do any stiffening.

It would, he said, be quite wrong for him to consult anyone about the setting up of a Royal Commission, which was entirely within the Queen's prerogative. But I kicked myself for having mentioned the Royal Commission to the BMA at all. Next, Norman, David and I worked on the wording of the PM's announcement, which was eventually got out at 6.30pm. Norman waited till it was safely out before phoning Stevenson with the PM's reply. Apparently he took it fairly calmly. The bit about the Queen's prerogative had done the trick. But when Norman went on to ask him where was the statement on the juniors' dispute which we had been promised and were waiting to see, Stevenson coolly informed him that they were just about to issue it! Norman's icy anger was a joy to listen to. He said he found it 'incredible' that, when we were holding up a statement of our own at their request in order to hear their decision, the BMA should proceed to issue its own statement without even informing us. ('Typical,' Peter Brown would say.) Apparently Stevenson blustered a bit and finally read the juniors' statement to Norman over the phone. It ran as follows:

'The leaders of the Hospital Junior Staff have considered the proposal of Mrs Castle on recent unrest over the junior contract. While they do not accept the Government's interpretation of the pay policy as applied to this new contract, they accept that there are overriding national issues at stake. They have decided therefore that the opinion of the juniors should be obtained by ballot. This will be done as quickly as possible. There will be a meeting of the Hospital Junior Staffs Committee to consider the results as soon as they are available.'

Not too bad at all. Ford and Bell are clearly doing their best for us, though we learned that Mander had walked out and resigned. David and I then had to work on my own statement and rush it out. It was late before I could get down to my Finer speech again. After a disjointed hour on it I had to hurry for my night sleeper to Blackburn, where Harold Wilson was due to open our new library. What a day! And an unrestful night.

Friday, 17 October
My spirits zoomed up again after a hair-do and a nice lunch with Tom Taylor. I was all ready for the PM's visit. The only cloud on the horizon was that busloads of textile workers from all over Lancashire were converging on Blackburn to demonstrate against the Government's refusal to impose import controls. There was even talk among officials of taking Harold to the library by car rather than have him run the gauntlet of the demonstrators in the three-minute walk from the town hall, but he wouldn't hear of it. As we emerged from the town hall we saw textile workers lining the route several deep, waving banners and shouting protests. 'Those on the left are the National Front,' I whispered to Harold. 'So ignore them. Go and shake hands with some of the demonstrators over there.' He promptly crossed the street, hand outstretched, and within minutes men and women were leaning over the rails to grasp his hand, shouting, 'Good old Harold.' One woman textile worker called out pleadingly, 'We need you, Harold. We're behind you all the way.' Of course, some booed, but Harold slipped into the magnificent new library, unruffled, to make what even the Tories there said was one of the best and most civilized, opening ceremony

speeches they had ever heard. If only, I thought, Harold would show more of this side of him – his instinctive siding with great social issues, like free access to books. Instead, I couldn't help thinking sadly to myself, as I sat on the platform, that Blackburn County Borough, under Labour leadership, had managed to slip through this exciting development just in time: not only just before Tory reorganization of local government robbed us of Labour control of our town's affairs, but just before a Labour Government moved in, to Tory applause, to check such 'extravagances' as examples of 'public expenditure getting out of control'.

Saturday, 18 October

When I got home this morning after another night sleeper Ted told me the whole incident had come over very well on TV, showing Harold in an excellent light.

Sunday, 19 October

Ted Short has done his stuff wonderfully on my behalf. He was particularly nice to me at Thursday's Cabinet, saying I was having a rotten time over the doctors and a shocking deal from the press, but adding affectionately, 'You are at your best when you are under attack.' Then on Friday his office phoned to say he wanted to make a speech in my support over the weekend and sent round the draft of a searing attack on my critics. Norman said he thought it was a splendid draft and we ought to encourage it. It has come over very well in the press.

There was not much rest this weekend. This morning I had to go up to London to appear on Peter Jay's programme, *Weekend World*, the office having advised that I must not miss this opportunity to counter the hysteria about the NHS which has been built up. So it was about 7pm tonight when, having waded through urgent stuff in two boxes, I at last got down to my Finer speech seriously. I not only wanted to write it all myself, I also wanted for the first time to think through the Finer proposals and assess them on their merits. This meant rereading whole sections of the report. Ted left me to it and went to bed.

Monday, 20 October

It was 2am this morning before I got to bed, taking a plateful of Eileen's crème caramel up with me. But I felt contented because a speech was beginning to take shape of which I could feel reasonably proud. I continued working on it all the way up in the car and again in the office, scattering detailed queries through Private Office like confetti. It is appalling how much checking up of a Ministerial speech there has to be. A casual throw-away line can create a crisis, with all sorts of people writing in to demand an explanation of this and that. After a rather *distrait* ministerial lunch I at last got down to the House with a speech, with Norman, Pat Folger and co. from Private Office pinning pages together in a last-minute flurry as we went in the car. I think Norman, who has a stout heart, rather enjoys this kind of hot-off-the-presses rush, but Pat isn't used to it and looked at one point as if she would faint with anxiety. Civil servants are trained to see that Ministers go into battle without a policy hair out of place. For myself, I prefer to live dangerously, and so, I suspect, does Norman.

One thing I had managed to wangle: the hint of a preferential earnings disregard for one-parent families. I had been engaged in a hurried correspondence with Joel to get him to agree an announcement to this effect. Treasury-like, he had sent me a cautious, but not totally dismissive, form of words which I had decided to embroider up. As I anticipated, that was the part of my speech which went down best. After-wards, in the corridors, he said to me, 'I see you went far beyond what I authorized.' But he grinned. As it will come out of my PESC allocation, I don't see what it has to do with Treasury anyway. What interested me was the muted line of Norman Fowler on the Tory front bench. I think Harold's digs at Margaret's failure to specify her promised public expenditure cuts have had their effect.

Before the debate we had the PM's statement on the Royal Commission on the Health Service. I had spent a lot of time making sure Harold didn't give anything away. In the end, typically, he leaned over backwards to stress the 'importance' of private practice. It is the classic mistake he makes of being unable to distinguish between the need to yield on points of material interest to his critics without throwing the philosophical baby out with the practical bathwater. So we had to have a great piece in the statement about the Royal Commission being able to discuss the 'borderline' between private practice and the NHS (whatever that may mean). How-ever, it might have been much worse and I have drilled into Harold that he mustn't yield an inch on the need to legislate on pay beds concurrently with the setting up of the Royal Commission. The BMA are still fighting back and insisting on their right to see the PM. Of course, I have advised that he should see them: one must never refuse to talk. So this has been fixed for tomorrow. But I am delighted to see that NUPE, without any prompting from me, has written to the PM to stiffen him. They have asked for the right to see him too. And why not? But I doubt Harold will agree.

Tuesday, 21 October

Meeting with the regional health authorities chairmen, who are panicking at all the talk of reorganizing the NHS. Once again they tell me that morale is so low at the prospect of our getting rid of the regional (or some other) tier that the health authorities just can't recruit key staff. It is obvious that I shall have to reassure them, otherwise the work of the NHS threatens to snarl up: the way of the reformer is hard! Apparently my last letter has only partly reassured them: they are still pressing for 'stability'. So I promised I would try to include a form of words in my speech in the NHS debate next Monday that would allay the sense of uncertainty (though I am still determined to keep open my options for evolutionary reform). The debate is the latest expression of the 'crisis in the NHS' hysteria the Tories are building up. They have tabled a Motion to reduce my salary and excelled themselves by asking, not just for the token cut that convention requires, but for a cut of 50 per cent. I am honoured by this precedent! Next I had to make a statement in the House on abortion in the light of the Select Committee's report. David has done a good job in getting action on all the committee's recommendations, thus defusing the demand for even more sweeping reforms. He and I agreed that I as Secretary of State ought to make the statement, which went down very well. But it was a sweat mugging up all the details.

But the highlight of the day was the PM's meeting with the BMA on the Royal Commission. As there was a running three-line whip the meeting had to be in the PM's room in the House, which meant we sat intimately close to our adversaries. Harold had summoned all the Secretaries of State concerned: Scotland, Wales and Northern Ireland as well as me. It proved the best break I've had for a long time. Grabham led the comparatively small but stern-looking contingent from the BMA and proceeded to lecture us severely. He told us the CCHMS had met yesterday. 'Attitudes are hardening.' They deplored the Government's decision to act on part of the remit of the Royal Commission before it had reported. If the Government phased out pay beds it would be breaking the undertaking on the basis of which many medical men had entered the service of the NHS. Successive governments had been paying less and less attention to the views of the medical profession: Sir Keith Joseph on reorganization, for instance. The result was a fall in morale and goodwill. The timetable of the Royal Commission should be adapted to enable it to discuss pay beds; it could always produce an interim report. 'We will resist actively any unfair legislation. The profession is absolutely determined to resist what they see as an attack on their independence.'

After this tirade my ministerial colleagues could hardly contain themselves. John Morris leaned forward and said sweetly, 'I must say I am very puzzled. There are only a handful of pay beds in Wales and I have never heard the profession say they felt they had lost their independence.' Merlyn [Rees] echoed this for Northern Ireland, while Willie [Ross] gave one of his rather opaque pontifications out of which it emerged that the medical profession in Scotland had the highest standards of them all and Scotland had only a couple of hundred pay beds. Grabham looked a bit discomfited, but at that moment the division bell rang. As we went through the lobbies my three colleagues were whistling their astonishment. What an appalling man! They couldn't believe their ears. Now they realized what I was up against. As for Joel, who had also been there, he put his arm round me commiseratingly. 'Having heard that, I must say to you, "All is forgiven." Now I understand.' I suddenly realized, to my relief, that their having been there that day meant that the atmosphere in Cabinet on the pay beds issue would be transformed.

Back in Harold's crowded room, Grabham was sitting in ramrod righteousness; Stevenson was scowling. Harold had been stiffened by their attacks rather than intimidated. He told them dismissively that our policy had been set out in the statement he had made to the House. He was not intending to put the matter of pay beds into the hands of the Royal Commission, or hold up legislation. 'Our freedom to legislate remains absolute. This is our policy and I have not heard anything that will cause us to change it.' I could not have put it better myself. After a rather terse agreement to exchange letters, they left. All I had to do then was to help Joe Haines, who I think is a near disaster, to draft the press statement for the PM. I only hope my colleagues will stand firm when the row breaks – as it will.

During the questioning I extracted one important admission from Grabham. I asked him, 'If, hypothetically, I were to drop the licensing of the private sector, would you drop your objection to our proposals?' 'No,' he replied emphatically.

Wednesday, 22 October

I insisted on going along to Tony Crosland's meeting with the TUC Local Government Committee to discuss the rate support grant settlement. I had had to miss the Consultative Council meeting last week on the same thing and David reported there had been an outcry against the so-called 'standstill' on local authority expenditure next year, which the councils unanimously denounced as meaning savage cuts. They claim that the Treasury figures will leave them £82 million short, even on the 'standstill' formula. I was delighted to learn that the local authorities singled out the social services as the field which would suffer most and which they were determined to protect. Certainly the picture which emerges from the report of the sub-group of the Council dealing with social services is horrifying. The figure the Government is trying to impose would mean, for instance, that residential homes and other residential accommodation would have to be 'mothballed' – some even closed down. It just is not on. I think I am as realistic as anyone about the economic restraints that face us (and certainly don't share Wedgie's belief that there is some sunny, easy alternative), but there are certain things a Labour Government cannot do and should propose revolutionary egalitarianism to avoid – and that is, to reverse engines over social expenditure. Checks on growth in expenditure are one thing, and painful enough, but actual cuts, as far as I am concerned, are out. Anyway, David seems to have put up a good fight for us. But I wanted to gen myself up on what was happening.

Tony C. was surprised (and, I suspect, not too pleased) to see me turn up. The document which had been put before the trade unions was ridiculously general and vague. I was delighted when Alan Fisher led the revolt against the denial of information to them. At one point he remarked, 'No doubt that is why there is such an impressive turn-out of Cabinet Ministers today.' I couldn't resist calling out, 'We're here to watch each other, not you.' Laughter. Eventually Tony was forced to agree that they should be given more details and I went back to the office to ensure that the full manpower implications of the social services cuts should be included in the documentation they received.

Mike has for some time been pressing Harold for an economic strategy meeting of Cabinet before we discuss PESC. Of course, Harold has accepted in principle, but is being very dilatory in fixing it – a familiar trick. Mike readily agreed with me earlier this week that our group ought to meet to plan our line. So we fixed it for tonight. In the event, Peter was abroad and Wedgie tied up somewhere and so only Mike, John Silkin and I were free. I took Brian O'Malley along with me to make up a foursome. We had to dine at Old Russia, within sound of the division bell, as one of those running three-liners is cursing us again. (Lords amendments to the Industry Bill. Their Lordships are keeping us tied to the House day and night with their amendments to this and that and are beginning to get under all our skins.) It was a pleasant enough meal, though not very productive of alternative economic strategies. Tommy Balogh, who has circulated one of his esoteric pieces on economic strategy, couldn't be there either. I don't find his analyses very good guides to political action, I'm afraid. The most interesting part of the discussion was on the Ministry of Defence. We agreed that Roy Mason's determined resistance to any more defence cuts must somehow be overcome. John Silkin,[1] who I am beginning to suspect is one of the failures of this Government, suddenly astonished me by saying that he had a proposal for Mason's successor: himself. I'm afraid I only registered incredulity.

Thursday, 23 October

I went along to Cabinet determined to get pay beds into the Queen's Speech if it killed me. For some inexplicable reason, Ted Short, Elwyn and the other pundits of the Legislation Committee have refused to move my Bill (the only Bill from my department for the forthcoming session) up from the Reserve list. All sorts of non-politically urgent Bills (like race relations, police discipline *et al.*) have been given priority over it. They must have gone mad. Of course, I had put in amendments to Short's draft of the Queen's Speech and I geared myself up for a tough fight. Ted was at his most headmasterly, saying he wouldn't put the PLP through the sort of late night misery of the past session again. There were heaven knew how many days to be devoted to the discussion of devolution and there simply would not be time for a major controversial Bill like mine. I made an impassioned speech about the political urgency of legislating quickly on pay beds, but I was merely met with the prim response that Cabinet would have to suggest what should be dropped to make way for my Bill. Even Bob Mellish was unsympathetic, asking at one point what Bill from my department I would be willing to drop to make way for this. 'This is the only Bill I have got this session,' I retorted. But I only got cheers for that. What saved me was Harold. If Grabham could only have seen how counter-productive his tirades on Tuesday had been! Harold was clearly apprised, as a result of his meeting with the BMA, of the need to get this legislation out of the way quickly. He may even have been influenced by the approach to him from NUPE. He twisted and turned with the tactical skill he always shows when he is determined to get his own way. This certainly was rather an urgent matter, he said. The unions were holding their people back with difficulty. On the other hand, he realized that Legislation Committee had not been able to give this priority over other Bills. However, there might be a way out. Could we find a form of words that would indicate that the Bill would be *introduced* in this session, but not necessarily passed? For example, could we say that legislation would be introduced 'in the course of the session', which wouldn't commit us to exactly when? I saw at once that this was a gimmick that would play into my hands and accepted it with a show of reluctance. There were more rumblings of protest from Ted and others, but finally Harold summed up that this had been accepted. And I knew I had won. Harold at work rigging Cabinet is wonderful to behold. Whether it is welcome depends on which side of the argument one's interests lie. Anyway, this time I blessed him, even though I had to accept a form of words which left the issue of licensing to further consultations.

During the altercation about pay beds Harold Lever put in his oar again. As his

---

[1] He was later to be a dramatic success in the Callaghan Government. As Minister of Agriculture from 1976 to 1979 he waged a tough war in Brussels against the excesses of the Common Agricultural Policy. When I remarked on the change in him he agreed, explaining that it was the first time he had been his own departmental master.

letters to me have shown, he is clearly terrified about the whole idea, but then he is terrified about everything socialist. He spent a long time on the phone to me last weekend, saying he had been speaking to this consultant and that. They all deplored the personal attacks on me, etc., but for God's sake couldn't I yield on the licensing issue or something? When I explained to him that the issue the profession was worried about wasn't licensing at all, but the phasing out of pay beds, he found this incredible. The trouble with Harold Lever is that he plays too much bridge with too many representatives of the Establishment. But at Cabinet I readily settled for a vague phrase in the Queen's Speech about licensing in order to get a firm commitment to legislation on phasing out. I didn't need the reassurance he tossed me in one of his many notes.

The only other argument at Cabinet was about Denis's proposals for alleviating unemployment in the construction industry. Tony C. had, of course, put in a paper trying to grab the whole £30 million for housing. Fortunately, Denis had resisted this, saying that some should go to maintenance work in the NHS (I've plugged the urgency and value of this at every turn) and some for local authorities' services. Of course, Tony fought for it all, but I fought back, painting a gruesome picture about the urgency, for instance, of fire precautions in old people's homes and other urgent maintenance work. In the end Denis and I won. Michael made one of his telling speeches about the need to spend more than £30 million anyway and I said, 'Hear, hear' to that. Denis grumbled a bit at this idea, but I bet he comes round to it. Altogether, not a bad morning's work.

From Cabinet I hurried to one of the intimate little lunches which the Directors of Social Services have taken to giving David and me. I think it was all Tom White's idea as leader of their Association, and he brings three others with him each time. I find it invaluable to talk off the cuff to the chaps who are in the front line. Tom explained how drastic would be the effect of even a 'standstill' in expenditure on social services. He explained that in Coventry there was bound to be an increase in expenditure next year, merely to finance the continuation of present policies. The reason? First, because salaries had increased; secondly, because of the increase in numbers of children in care; and thirdly, because of the cost of bringing new residential accommodation, authorized in earlier years, into operation. I asked him to drop me a note on this for my PESC purposes. As we talked David suddenly said, 'You haven't thanked the Secretary of State yet for getting the Director of Social Work's job upgraded. She had quite a fight, I can tell you.' They were duly grateful and I told Tom White privately that he must see that some first-class people applied.

I had to hurry back to the office for a meeting of the nursing organizations on the consultative document on pay beds. The best of them were the nurse administrators, who said they were in favour of pay beds being phased out, though they wanted it done in an 'orderly way'. Miss Bidulph even admitted they were in favour of licensing: she merely wanted it to be done by the AHAS, rather than by the Secretary of State, saying that Manchester AHA, of which she is a member, had just refused planning permission for a large proposed private development in Manchester. My eyebrows shot up at this, because, as I told her, they really hadn't power under present legislation to refuse planning permission on any but environmental grounds. Afterwards Raymond told me that the refusal was being challenged in the courts as *ultra vires*. That just proves my point!

This is Philip Rogers's last week. I told Norman I wanted to give him farewell drinks and a present. Tonight all we Ministers assembled in my room, together with a few officials and Norman had thoughtfully invited Philip's wife. I handed Philip a very nice briefcase on our behalf, telling him how much we appreciated the way he had loyally backed our policies, even when we knew he thoroughly disagreed with them. 'You have been a fine civil servant,' I told him. I then called on all the Ministers in turn and every one of them spoke warmly and genuinely. Philip was clearly deeply touched, saying, 'I doubt whether, as a good civil servant, I ought to approve of this precedent, but I do.' (Apparently they had never heard of Ministers making a presentation to their Permanent Secretary before.) The other civil servants were tickled pink at our gesture, telling me what a nice chap Philip had been to work for. A very happy and satisfying little interlude.

The IRA bombers have struck again, trying to blow up Hugh Fraser and killing Professor Fairley, the cancer expert, who was passing by. Ted is abroad at his European Parliament again. I've kept the *Evening Standard* cutting to show him, in the hope that at last it will persuade him to lock the boot of the car. With our car having to stand outside in the road at both our homes, we are a sitting target.

Friday, 24 October

David is getting cold feet over pay beds. He came into my room in one of his menacing moods to say he had just sent me a Minute which was for my eyes alone, as he didn't want officials to get any inkling of it. He gave me a great doom-laden warning about the unholy row he thought we were going to face with the medical profession. As I knew, he said, he had never agreed with me over licensing, though he did over phasing out, and he believed my licensing proposals would be the last straw. The only hope was for us to rush a simple short Bill onto the statute book as quickly as possible to do three things: legalize phasing out, fix a date (though he thought we should have to make it 1979), and take a power to control private hospital developments above a certain size. As I replied calmly that of course I would consider this, he began to relax. But the conversation didn't exactly cheer me up: bombers without, tunnellers within and a major censure Motion awaiting me on Monday. It would be lovely to have some allies for a change. But Jack and Norman remain devotees of my policy and my determination not to flinch.

Sunday, 26 October

Before I got down to my NHS speech I typed a reply to David's Minute, determined to get it on the record that I wasn't running amok. I was determined too to emphasize the points on which David had agreed with me, otherwise I could see a great 'split' story leaking into the press. What we must do, I stressed, was to have another private dinner with our TUC friends as quickly as possible and put our problem to them, pointing out that we might lose the legislation altogether for next session if we insisted on the more complicated Bill.

By midnight I was only half-way through preparing my speech, but I felt so wonky I just went to bed. 'To hell with it,' I thought. 'I'll just ad lib.'

Monday, 27 October

In the event I didn't ad lib, but scribbled away at my speech in the car at terrific speed. The words flowed and I got the last bit finished at about 2.45pm. We raced to the House, picking up sheets of typed speech as we fled, only to find two pages missing when we arrived. They were handed to me in manuscript as I was on my feet! I didn't mind. I knew it was a good, meaty speech and I delivered it with great aplomb, despite my cold. I was enormously helped by a crowded House. Even Harold turned up to support me, which he did vocally. Our lads were there in force, cheering me to the echo. I suddenly realized that the press attacks on me had made me a party heroine. They *trust* me again. If David thinks he is going to get me to betray that trust, he is wrong. Norman Fowler's opening attack was feeble: he didn't even mention the juniors! I drove him into a corner, to the delight of our own side. As for the Liberals, I slaughtered them. The contemptible Jeremy had joined the pack at the weekend, howling for my blood. Although the Liberals officially support the phasing out of pay beds, he had found an excuse for voting with the Tories by saying I had 'mismanaged' things. (What things he didn't specify and when Penhaligon came to speak he said he agreed with my line on the juniors!) I had got Jack to turn me up a reference to Lloyd George's battle with the doctors, and, armed with this, I turned on Jeremy: 'Lloyd George would be ashamed of you!' Delirious applause from our side. I got innumerable congratulations afterwards. I was glad that Harold had heard it. I'm not going to have him thinking he is carrying an embarrassing passenger.

The depths to which the press are sinking was again illustrated by today's *Daily Mail*, which carries a front-page story with banner headline: 'New Health Service Row Breaks: Barbara's Top Men Revolt', which claims that my Permanent Secretary and other top officials are threatening to resign over my pay beds policy. Norman told me Philip was furious and, although on leave, rushed out a scathing denial. Of course that won't stop the *Daily Mail*. But I don't care. Our lads in the House are with me to a man, led by – of all people – Ian Wrigglesworth. He may be Roy Jenkins's PPS, but he is with me all the way on this. He has collected 170 signatures to his Early Day Motion backing me and calling for legislation on pay beds to be included in the Queen's Speech. Of course, we can barely get a mention of this in the press, but I hope it will stiffen David's nerve.

It was a sign of my resilience that I forgot all about Norman's rather worried warning to me earlier today. Just when I was in the middle of checking bits of my speech this morning he came into me, looking grave. The police had just been on the phone to say that they had received a card saying that I was on the IRA list of Ministers for extermination. Only a few Ministers, the report ran, had received this. Would I take care? For a moment my heart sank; a few minutes later I had forgotten it. Norman Fowler was a far more important enemy. I went to bed happy because I had demolished him and because, despite the defection of the Liberals, the censure Motion was defeated by a majority of twenty.

Tuesday, 28 October

On the whole a very good press. Even Andrew Alexander had ignored the *Mail*'s policy to the extent of saying I had made an 'impressive' speech. Lots of bibs and bobs all day, including an official deputation from the TUC urging me to phase out pay beds as quickly as possible. The private dinner we have now arranged with them will be far more relevant than these public approaches. But the juniors' dispute continues to be very worrying. The one ray of hope is that the BMA have asked to see me to discuss it. Of course, I have agreed.

Norman is clearly deeply disturbed at the threat to me from the IRA. He came in again this morning to say there has been a further development. Someone claiming to speak for the Ministry of Defence had phoned an official in the department asking for a plan showing the lay-out of the office building. On his checking-up with the Ministry of Defence, they denied any knowledge of such a call. Norman prowled around my room, pointing out that I was a pot shot from the tall buildings opposite. Would I mind keeping the slats of the blinds down? I pointed out mildly that the real security risk was at the entrance to the Ministers' lift, easily accessible from the street, where there hadn't even been a light in the lobby entrance for several days. Norman said he was seeing to that immediately; and so he did. All this adds a new dimension of danger to a life I am already living dangerously. Edna tells me all the government drivers have been issued with torches so that they can look under Ministers' cars for bombs. What a life!

Wednesday, 29 October

When Grabham and the BMA brought the juniors along for the meeting they had requested, it was soon obvious that Lewin and Grabham saw it largely as a formality. They wanted to place on record that they were backing the juniors and maintained, in a vague, grandiose way, that the juniors' claim was perfectly compatible with pay policy. They were in no mood to argue it. I remained painstakingly patient, going through the points again one by one. If the pay policy collapsed, the country's economy would collapse with it and also the NHS. They had said they were going ahead with a ballot which included a question inviting the juniors to support all-out industrial action. Surely we ought to examine whether any other options were open to us? When Grabham tried to sweep this aside, I diplomatically and icily lost my temper. Surely, I said, it was intolerable that with this disaster facing the NHS they were not even prepared to consider whether there was an option open to us which would enable us to go ahead with the new contract within the pay policy, but with no one suffering detriment. Ford and Bell of the juniors were clearly getting restive at Grabham's insolent arrogance and he was shamed into listening. I said I believed there *was* such an option and I asked them to let me spell it out to them. In some confusion they asked for an adjournment. While I went off to another meeting, Jack said he heard them quarrelling among themselves. When we reassembled Lewin said that they had merely come to discuss principles, not to negotiate details: that was a matter for the Joint Negotiating Committee [JNC]. But under continued pressure from me (and, I suspect, the juniors), he and Grabham reluctantly agreed to bring the JNC along the following day. Tim Nodder has produced a new formula as a result of my insistence that there must be *some* way of redistributing the available money without making anyone worse off. It now appears there is, by phasing the new contract in as juniors change jobs. The new money available next April under pay policy would enable us to complete the process without detriment.

Thursday, 30 October

The main agony in Cabinet was over dental and optical charges. My luck was out because two of my strongest allies, Peter and Shirley, were missing. Also the fight seemed to have gone out of Ted Short. I repeated my reluctance to increase charges, but also my insistence that I must have more money if the shortfall was to be made good. Mike was his usual excellent self, repeating that our main problem was how the Government was to survive politically in the next few months and how absurd it was for us to put this political millstone round our necks for the sake of £18 million. But Tony C. wasn't having any: if I got my way everyone would want to reopen PESC. Anyway, teeth and specs were not our social priorities – nor our political ones. Jim backed him, while Wedgie linked this with his general economic line. 'What we are doing is deflating the economy by another £18 million. It is no use saying, as Tony has, that 1951 is a long way away:[1] so is the Battle of the Boyne. We should reconsider our strategy on public spending in the light of unemployment.' Denis, of course, resisted this. Bob said it was 'all a matter of presentation'. (Rubbish. There are some things you can't 'present' to the party.) Fred Mulley moaned that he would have supported me, 'but you all took £30 million off me yesterday'. Harold summed up. 'I very much regret this, but I have no doubt the majority of Cabinet think it must be done.' (I believe he would have supported me robustly if he had been at the previous meeting.) Ted Short just sat silent. So did Eric and John Silkin. So much for one's allies.

Earlier we had had a row over the leakage of Cabinet disagreements over devolution following the last Chequers meeting, which I had to miss. Harold was furious. He said it was obvious there had been deliberate briefing – glaring at Roy. This meant he no longer thought the wording in the Queen's Speech about devolution was satisfactory. If we merely said 'detailed proposals' would be put forward, everyone would

---

[1] In 1951 Aneurin Bevan resigned from Attlee's second Labour Cabinet. Harold Wilson, then President of the Board of Trade, and John Freeman, Parliamentary Under-Secretary at the Ministry of Supply, resigned with him. The ostensible reason was Hugh Gaitskell's insistence as Chancellor of the Exchequer on raising £13 million in his Budget by introducing charges for NHS teeth and spectacles. For Nye this was a threat to the whole principle of a free Health Service but, as Michael Foot's biography of him shows, the reasons went much wider and deeper than that. One of the key elements in Nye's conflict with the Government was its decision, under American pressure, to adopt a massive rearmament programme. Bevan also resented the growing influence of Gaitskell, whom he later described as a 'desiccated calculating machine'. Bevan's resignation launched the bitter Bevan *v.* Gaitskell controversies of the 1950s.

think we were weakening on the policy. We must say, 'Legislation will be introduced.' He agreed that the Bill could not be passed next session, but we must at least publish it. Denis, Roy and Reg mounted an immediate and united resistance, Reg insisting there must be a long public debate before any decisions were taken. Ted Short was furious: 'We've agreed in the White Paper to introduce a Bill. We are committed up to the hilt on it. Unless we introduce legislation this session, I leave the Government.' I soothed things down by suggesting the right formula might be that 'legislative proposals will be introduced'. Harold seized on this, stressing that we all knew it wasn't physically possible to get the legislation through this coming session. And so my formula was agreed, Denis muttering that 'a public display of disagreement would be disastrous'.

At the resumed meeting with the juniors it was as clear as ever that Grabham was trying to prevent an agreement. *He* doesn't want a settlement with the juniors while the pay beds row is still in the air. But it was equally clear that Ford and Bell are angry and impatient with the interference of the BMA and are perfectly aware that they are being used for other people's ends. And so they began by admitting that our new proposals were 'an important advance', adding that they would put them to ballot, but that the proposals would not be enough by themselves to swing support. There were all sorts of safeguards in, and interpretations of, the new contract they would want to work out with us. So we settled down for another long session. Some of the safeguards they wanted, such as an appeals machinery on which they were represented, were perfectly reasonable and presented no difficulty. Others, such as an attempt to interpret their new contract in terms of a 'forty-hour week only' commitment, were far more tricky. All we could agree was to approach this favourably in the longer term. (We would have been in trouble with their Review Body if we had gone further.) It was nearly midnight before the principles were agreed. We gave hurried and cagey press conferences at which Ford and Bell played it extremely fair, but at which we all refused to release details, having agreed to finalize the wording of them next day. All this over, with Stevenson out of the way, David, Jack and I had a relaxed chat with the juniors' representatives which would have astonished the press if they could have listened in at it. These were not the wild, hostile men the newspapers have been trying to make out, full of hatred and resentment of me. These were nice, worried lads who felt their chaps had a grievance, but who hated the industrial action in which they were engaged and wanted a settlement if at all possible. In fact, they even sat plotting with us as to how they could speed up the return of the ballot papers, so that they could be counted and the result announced before the Queen's Speech on 19 November! The last thing they want is to get their dispute mixed up with the consultants' row over pay beds, an issue on which they do not feel strongly. Indeed, one of the healthy things about the juniors' revolt is that they want to break with the system whereby they are exploited as 'juniors' in the hope and expectation that they will be able to exploit others when their turn comes to be consultants. I am more than ever convinced that we must get a better deal for the juniors on the foundation of which we can build a consultants' role which is less high-handed and less exploitatory. The trouble, of course, is that the consultants stand in the way of this just as much as pay policy does.

I had to stay late in London for the *Tonight* programme: the last one in a series on the NHS. I was at my most relaxed and reasonable. People who saw it said afterwards that I made my case sound so eminently fair. One sweet lass in the studio said she had been against me from what she had read in the newspapers, but I had converted her! Got to HCF about 1am.

Monday, 3 November

David Owen is going about glowering these days. I feel he is brewing up some more of his 'I must warn you' private diatribes to me. I find these moods of his very oppressive when, above all else, I am longing for some moral support against the ceaseless attacks made on me in the press. For one thing, I don't think he entirely approves of my oft-stated determination not to accept the formula cuts for the NHS which the Treasury is trying to impose on me in the PESC exercise. He has a masochistic streak in him and likes to go around making *Götterdämmerung* speeches about how tough things are going to be in the next few years and how the NHS cannot escape its share of cuts. I merely shrug and say I have no intention of presiding over the first absolute cut in the NHS and that I'll believe in the need for swingeing cuts when Defence takes its proper share. As he is good on Defence, this usually disarms him. At our first Sextet meeting with Patrick Nairne I reverted to this theme. David did at least back me up in agreeing that we should not issue the NHS capital allocations or the new consultative document on our priorities for health and social services while the PESC discussions are still going on.

Tuesday, 4 November

Ford and Bell have produced a very fair statement of our new formula in the document they are circulating for the juniors' ballot. They remain in constant and intimate touch with Jack. Norman reports that Stevenson has been on the phone about my letter of 8 October, offering consultations on the consultative document on pay beds. The BMA are obviously pinning their hopes on an intervention by Harold, but he is playing it absolutely straight and passing everything to me. The BMA clearly don't know how to deal with my letter and Norman refused to help Stevenson off the hook. David has done another volte-face on pay beds legislation. He has sent me a Minute saying we should not try to introduce any licensing proposals at all – not even the simple control over private developments above a certain size he had himself suggested – but rather rely on voluntary agreement. I haven't bothered to answer it. We are having another of our private dinners with the unions tomorrow night and I can leave them to deal with his points. In the meantime at an office meeting I insisted we go ahead with a three-pronged Bill, including a simple size control.

Wednesday, 5 November

At last I have managed to fit in my visit to Broadmoor. I found it fascinating because the atmosphere was so surprisingly like a hospital – so little like a prison, despite the careful locking of gates at every move. I was completely captivated by McGrath (the senior consulting psychiatrist), impressed by the thoroughness of the assessment centre at which new entrants are received and analysed. I ended by identifying myself completely with the relaxed and unsentimental dedication of the staff. Before I left I had talks with all of them in turn, in groups. What they resent most is the hostility of the media every time a released former inmate repeats his offence. They think no one is backing them and helping their image. Altogether I went away very chastened by the realization that there really is no humane alternative to what they are trying to do. It was odd to talk to some of the inmates, apparently eminently nice and rational men, and to hear McGrath say, 'That chap? He committed a peculiarly nasty offence against a child' or 'He murdered his wife in a rather nasty way.'

Because of the three-line whip on the Lords' amendments to the Petroleum and Submarine Pipelines Bill (damn the Lords!), we had to have our dinner with the unions on the bell. Since Lockets' private room was engaged, we tried Old Russia, which is very pleasant except for the gloomy lighting. In the sepulchral shades of a quiet corner of the room we had one of our relaxed but frank talks. My insistence on these private meetings has paid enormous dividends because we have built up confidence in each other and can genuinely reveal how far each of us can go. There is, moreover, nothing like a good meal for creating camaraderie. Peter Jacques, Audrey Prime, Geoffrey Drain and Alan were all there – and, of course, Brian A-S., David and Jack. Peter began by telling us that he had been putting the Social Insurance Committee of the TUC in the picture on our pay beds problems and they fully realized our difficulties. They would therefore reluctantly accept the shorter Bill, much as they would have preferred the whole consultative document. But they insisted that all pay beds must be phased out within a year and that the licensing should include an overall limit on the size of the private sector as a whole.

I cocked an eye at David at this. He is always extremely charming with them and defers to them – and I think too that he is genuinely impressed by the strength of their feelings. Talking to them is a great corrective to the other Manifesto Group influences to which he is subject. He made good play with the good trade union point that phasing out in certain areas, where alternative private facilities are not available, could mean a sudden and substantial drop in income for some consultants at a time when there was a ceiling on their earnings under the pay policy. Could we avoid an explosion of feeling in a situation like that? As our trade union friends looked impressed I pushed home the point that the right way to deal with it might be by fixing a year as the date specified in the legislation, with provision for me to make exceptions for up to another two years at my discretion. By the end of the evening they had accepted this, with the proviso that, in order to avoid the 'wicked successor syndrome',[1] the power to grant exemption should be only exercisable within six months of the Royal Assent. I rather liked this. On licensing, I pressed away at David's point that a simple control over the larger private developments would be the most appropriate to a quick, short Bill. They agreed – even accepting a figure of

---

[1] My phrase for the fact that a successor Tory Government might seek to reverse our policy and the need to draft our legislation so as to make this as difficult as possible.

seventy-five beds as the starting point for control – though they rumbled away at the need for me to keep an overall total of private beds in mind when operating licensing. David took all this very meekly. One would never have guessed that he keeps bombarding me with near panic-stricken Minutes. The valuable thing about talks like this with good, politically minded trade-union allies is that one can judge so much better where one must strike the balance between their emotional sticking points and their realistic grasp of what we can all deliver politically.

Over drinks before the meal I had casually raised the question of the chairmanship of the Royal Commission on the Health Service. Had they any suggestions? To my surprise, Audrey said enthusiastically, 'Yes, Merrison.' [Dr Alexander Merrison, Vice-Chancellor of Bristol University.] David and I were rather taken aback, but as she had served with him on the Merrison Committee,[1] she was in a better position than any of us to judge his attitude to the NHS and the things in which we believe. She was emphatic that he was a dedicated supporter of the NHS and she was sure he would have no truck with private financing and all that nonsense. David and I agreed afterwards that this made Merrison a very serious contender for the job.

Thursday, 6 November

At Cabinet Mike reported on his protracted attempts to get an agreement with Arnold Goodman on a compromise over the section of the Trade Union Bill dealing with the closed shop and the press. He had decided that compromise was impossible. Any further concession would be bound to involve the enforcement of his proposed voluntary code in the courts, which was our breaking-point. The Manifesto Group would not accept it and it would wreck the hope of a voluntary code. We could of course delete all references to the press, so that the Bill could reach the statute book. This would involve an amending Bill on the press in the next session – and a defeat of the Government at the hands of the Lords. He could not recommend it, he said in his usual reasoned way. The third course was to invoke the provisions of the Parliament Act, which could mean that the Bill would not become law till late in the next session. Clearly he didn't like this, but the TUC agreed it was better than letting the Lords win on a point of principle. The PLP, including the Manifesto Group, were in favour of sending it back to the Lords. Malcolm Shepherd, of course, demurred. 'My concern is to get continuing co-operation for our legislation. I hope we won't use the Parliament Act, but let it go.' Fortunately, Bob was more robust. He said he knew we had no majority, but 'our people in the House would be absolutely furious if the Lords won. I say we should invoke the Parliament Act.' Shirley, of course, trimmed. 'A possible compromise is staring us in the face. Hailsham's amendments are unacceptable, but there are two or three of Goodman's proposals we could accept,' she argued. For instance, his amendment that there should be no limitation of rights under common law was surely acceptable and the provision that breaches of the code could be

---

[1] Dr A. W. Merrison was appointed by Sir Keith Joseph in 1973 to chair the Committee of Inquiry into the Regulation of the Medical Profession, following a dispute between doctors and the General Medical Council over the introduction of an annual registration fee. The Committee reported in April 1975. (Cmnd. 6018.) Dr Merrison was knighted in 1976.

invoked as contrary to public policy by the judges seemed harmless, seeing that we ourselves envisaged that such breaches could be used evidentially. Her siren voice was effectively squashed by none less than the Lord Chancellor. Elwyn rose to some of his old heights in declaring vigorously that to use the reference to 'public policy' would effectively transfer the matter to the courts. Goodman's amendment was itself obscure, but his avowed intention was to make the code legally enforceable. His intervention effectively carried the day, and Harold summed up typically that (a) we should not back down, but (b) another attempt should be made to reach a compromise with Goodman which met some of his points, without in any way opening the scope for intervention by the courts. I can guess what will be the outcome of *that*. I backed Mike.

We had our preliminary economic discussion at Cabinet in preparation for PESC, but it is clear to me that the majority of our colleagues will always toe the Treasury line – including Tony C., for all the oratorical gestures he likes to make. We didn't get far today, either. Michael has been nagging away about the level of unemployment, and, as always, Denis was sympathetic in general terms. The problem was how to finance measures to reduce it without pushing up the borrowing requirement, he said. Cuts in taxation were costly and very slow. The only way was through micro-measures. He was considering some of them, including selective import controls, relaxing hire purchase conditions and identifying bottlenecks. Wedgie then pitched into him with one of his comprehensive denunciations. We were, he said, at 'the turning-point for this Government's strategy'. The present policy was going to fail because it had been sold to the unions as an alternative to unemployment, cuts in public expenditure and so on. 'There is no national consensus for this policy.' We faced a 'grave and accelerating collapse of our industry. It is later than we think.' Senile industry needed a strong wall of protection. Without that we should never recover. There must be a target rate for reducing unemployment, much greater use of micro-methods and a national recovery plan. Michael was, as usual, more temperate. He didn't disagree on the seriousness of the crisis, he said. We faced the prospect of one million unemployed till the end of 1977. The most vulnerable moment would be May–June 1976. 'We have got to have a policy for survival and we must look at our policy of major cuts again.' We needed selective import controls and should bring forward reflation to enable us to survive the next six to eight months, he continued. 'We should study now how this could be done with minimum adverse effect.' Denis chipped in in his irrepressible way. 'Not more than 5 per cent of the borrowing requirement is due to unemployment.' Wedgie's paper on an alternative strategy had some good points. We might have to consider some general controls next year. But Wedgie must face the fact that that would also mean greater cuts in public expenditure to offset the inflationary effect. 'Conventional demand reflation is full of risks.'

Tony C. gave one of his regular digs at public expenditure cuts. 'Cuts put people out of work who can't get jobs,' he pointed out. Harold Lever surprised everyone by urging a 'rolling deal with the trade unions'. He even talked some political sense. 'If,' he said, 'through being over-cautious with the trade union movement over reflation we lose the co-operation of the unions, nothing could be more catastrophic. Reflation ought to be pursued by a series of smaller steps.' I seized on this concept of the rolling deal. At every step we must take the unions into our confidence and win their minds, I urged. We kept on talking about selective import controls, but when were we going to act? Some industries, like textiles, would be dead before we announced anything. Harold Wilson intervened tetchily at this point to say that the matter was being studied urgently and there would be an announcement soon. Undeterred, I ploughed on. I totally supported Peter in his campaign on 'Buy British'. We ought to give it more collective support. Could we not have a 'Buy British' paper for Cabinet to study? I agreed with Michael that we desperately needed another construction package: this was more important, and psychologically right, than relaxing hire purchase controls. There was a lot of job creation work in the field of the Health Service and the social services: the backlog of maintenance, fire precautions, adaptations to disabled people's homes, etc. None of these had revenue consequences. (Tony C., of course, got very restive during this piece of promotion of my departmental interests.) The discussion inevitably reached an inconclusive end, but I can only hope our nagging away on these themes will have some effect in weaning the Chancellor from his pressure for those desperately deflationary public expenditure cuts he is planning.

Friday, 7 November

With President Sadat here on an official visit, it has fallen to me to take Madame Sadat round Charing Cross Hospital. She is an utterly delightful person and I got on with her famously when I paid her a courtesy call at Claridge's yesterday. She is elegant, natural and sweet-natured and chattered away to me about the hospital visiting she does in Egypt to comfort the victims of the October war, who look on her as a mother figure. Our visit to the hospital this morning looked like being threatened by a demonstration by the juniors, but, in view of her presence, they were prevailed on to stand quietly on one side as we passed by, on the understanding that I would speak to them and receive a letter on their grievances, which I did. In the car after this incident Madame Sadat surprised me by launching into a declaration of how much she admired me for standing up to all these attacks and doing what I thought was right. 'How can they strike?' she said in bewilderment. 'How can they damage their country so when you are trying to put it on its feet again?' Such friendly warmth made a nice change!

Monday, 10 November

Into a MISC meeting on the rate support grant. I am immensely relieved that the tough battle to avoid the actual cuts in social services which the Treasury was demanding has been avoided.

Wasily Sakalo, the wild Australian who is stirring it up among junior doctors in the North-West, has excelled himself. The papers are full of his weekend declaration: 'Blame Castle if Patients Die.' I think this beats anything they said about Nye. The juniors are all set to step up their industrial action. The tragedy is that waiting lists grow longer and the level of service in the NHS declines, just as the shortage of money makes it imperative that we use every penny we've got to best effect. One consolation: David is in one of his sunny moods again. Perhaps that dinner with the trade union boys last week had its effect. Anyway, it is a great relief. David's alternations of gloom and charm can be a strain.

At Home Policy Judith has been throwing her weight about as a freebooting left-winger. She has put in a paper full of ideas as to how to tart up the meetings of the TUC Liaison Committee. 'I think the NEC ought to assist the work of the committee by submitting papers, as appropriate,' she urged. Like the papers from her own Industry Committee. Pour soul, she hasn't yet grasped the deeply pragmatic relationship between the trade unions and the Government. The unions have a lot of suggestions and complaints, but they are none of them particularly ideological. Geoff Bish has similar ideas for directing joint NEC-Cabinet discussions. This is all very right and natural, but, try as some of its members may, the NEC cannot conjure up the rift between the party and the Government that existed in 1966–70. This Government is too closely in touch with the unions for that. One document I did wholeheartedly agree with: the one urging the establishment of a joint committee on the EEC between the Home Policy and International Committees. The purpose would be 'the effective development within the EEC framework of our established Manifesto objectives on existing EEC policies'. Since the pro-marketeers won the referendum on a lie – or series of lies – some check-up on what happens afterwards is essential.

Tuesday, 11 November

What you might call an exacting day (and night). It began with Cabinet, at which we had another long discussion about Mike's row with Goodman on the Trade Union and Labour Relations Bill. Elwyn reported that, despite long talks with Goodman, they had not found common ground. An esoteric discussion followed about the content of the proposed press charter and its enforcement which I found almost impossible to follow. What was clear, however, was that Mike was sticking to the principle of voluntarism, while Roy Jenkins and his pedants were ready to get entangled in Goodman's details, which effectively meant surrender. Said Mike, 'Goodman's additions are all attacks on the NUJ and would endanger the chance of having a charter at all. Goodman says he doesn't mind that.' Roy insisted we would be on 'very bad ground' in opposing Goodman's proposals on the contents of the charter, while Malcolm, of course, was only concerned with what he might get Carrington[1] to agree to. It says a lot for the effectiveness of Mike's gentle stubbornness that Harold summed up that Goodman's proposals on the contents of the charter were unacceptable and that we should stick to the amendment of the Manifesto Group. Elwyn, Mike and Malcolm should, he said, make one last attempt to get Goodman to accept this, but none of us thought it would succeed. I take off my hat to Mike.

We then agreed the White Paper on devolution, on which Ted Short has conducted his dogged battle, and turned to Chrysler. Riccardo Chrysler's chairman in Detroit,

[1] Viscount Carrington, Lord Shepherd's opposite number as leader of the Tories in the Lords.

said Eric, had delivered an ultimatum. Either the UK must take over Chrysler by the end of the year, writing off the firm's £75 million loss and finding another £80 million, without a penny contribution by Chrysler, or Chrysler would 'go into liquidation' (in fact, close down) by the end of November. He thought that Chrysler's share of the UK market had probably gone completely and we should concentrate on making British Leyland a success. But 25,000 jobs were at immediate risk. The CPRS report had shown how we were suffering from over-capacity in the motor car industry and he was going over the report with the trade unions that afternoon. There was no clear view coming from local MPs. The press were wrong in saying that Chrysler was asking for money. Chrysler were saying, 'It's your worry; take it over.' He concluded by saying he thought we might try offering Chrysler some money in return for a phased run-down. Harold said that the banks were not willing to put any more money into Chrysler US unless it shed Chrysler UK.

Denis said the central problem was 'how to soften the blow'. Thirty per cent of Chrysler production had been lost through stoppages. This brought Wedgie into play in dramatic mood. This would be the 'biggest industrial collapse in our history' if it went ahead. 'There is a history in this matter,' he declared. In 1964 Chrysler had given a pledge when it acquired a stake in Rootes. In 1966 it wanted to take over the whole of Rootes. 'I got another pledge from Chrysler during that period. Chrysler has been breaking all its pledges.' We should bang a Disclosure Order on them under the party's industrial policy and take control ourselves. Why not send a deputation to Washington to demand that Chrysler fulfil its pledges? In the meantime we should ban the import of Simca cars. ('Unfortunately,' Eric whispered to me, 'those pledges are not legally enforceable.') Wedgie thundered on. 'We are endorsing the lame duck policy of Edward Heath. The truth is that the whole of Britain is a lame duck.' Harold suggested mildly that it was important to distinguish between a lame duck and a dead duck, 'though I agree the legal implications of this should be examined'. Willie then stormed away about the effect of closure on Scotland. Linwood was the only part of the motor industry Scotland had, he declared. 'This will be politically disastrous.' Michael insisted that the whole matter must be examined more fully and carefully before a decision was made. We must set up a committee to consider all possible proposals and put our cards on the table with the trade unions. Jim then gave us a bit of his practical man's stuff. 'What worries me is whether, if we were to take it over as Tony Benn suggests, Cabinet would have the resolution to do what is necessary.' The simple fact was that our productivity here was a fraction of what it was on the Continent. He couldn't see the value of our going to Washington, because the US Government had no responsibility for Chrysler. It was a simple problem of getting our people to work more productively. Harold summed up that the matter would now go to MISC 59, which would supervise continuing negotiations to see if we could save some parts of the Chrysler enterprise. We haven't heard the last of this.

This lengthy discussion made me late for a Fabian lunch and put me in a rush for the rest of the day. At 2.30pm I had to be back for an office discussion on PESC. This is now shaping up to its familiar misery. Only this time it is even worse. Denis has circulated a memo setting out what he claims is the economic case for the biggest cuts he has yet asked for. And we have also had the survey report prepared by officials, ironically known as the 'Red Book', spelling out the effect on departments of a range of cuts. Denis's memo repeats the familiar argument that immediate cuts 'of the kind constantly urged on us by the Opposition' would make matters worse and put up unemployment, but that 'the situation beyond 1976 will be very different'. Why? Because, he argues, by then 'international and domestic demand should have recovered and the forward planning must be based on the assumption that unemployment will be falling very rapidly'. So, if we are to get the 15 per cent increase in manufacturing investment by 1979 visualized in our industrial strategy, plus a modest improvement in living standards, while trying to bring the high level of inflation down, there must be cuts in public expenditure of £3¾ billion in 1978–79. The only alternative, the memo argues, would be an increase in taxation and it goes on at length about what this would mean. Anything less than Denis's full pound of flesh – say the £2 billion of cuts Tony Crosland has been suggesting – would mean an increase in the standard rate of from 5 pence to 9 pence. I can just imagine how these figures will make the Cabinet's blood run cold! My trouble is that I am determined to defend the NHS at all costs, but under the PESC formula that is being considered under the Chancellor's initiative all the normal programmes would have 'formula cuts' allocated to them, i.e. an across-the-board cut of 10 per cent in current and 25 per cent in capital expenditure by 1978–79. This would be disastrous for the NHS. Yet the formula cuts would only produce a saving of £2 billion and Denis wants a lot, lot more. Social security payments, like pensions and benefits, being 'demand led', do not lend themselves to the 'formula cut' technique. Nonetheless Denis has his eye on them. His memo includes an 'illustrative list' of extra cuts necessary to give him the total figure he says he needs beyond 1976 and in it he calls for savings of over £600 million in social security, some £500 million of which he suggests should come from abandoning the 'historical' method of uprating pensions. He justifies this on the grounds that such a method, reflecting past inflation, would be too generous to pensioners 'at a time of *declining* inflation'. If I resist this he will be down on the NHS like a ton of Irish bricks. I realize that.

The only way to save the NHS from this disaster (if Cabinet agrees the Chancellor's cuts, as they will) is for me to accept the £500 million saving on the social security side by switching from the historical to the forecasting method at the next uprating. All this I had to spell out at the office meeting without exactly advocating it, while Brian O'Malley sat tense, suddenly bursting out and saying that as far as he was concerned that was totally unacceptable. 'I'm not prepared to do the pensioners out of another pound a week, to which they are entitled under the method the Treasury has always insisted on. Someone else can do that: I won't.' I listened sympathetically and handled him gently, thinking to myself that we could leave the Jack Joneses of the trade union movement to battle for the pensioners. My problem is that there is no one battling for the NHS. After an hour of this I sent Brian A-S. away to prepare all sorts of defensive briefing for the PESC row. We can make a strong case for the NHS on the basis of demographic factors, the exceptional age of so many NHS buildings, the fact that it has never had its fair share of resources, and so on. But I know perfectly well that all this finessing is wasted when the public expenditure chips are down. It is only political muscle that counts. My one weapon is that I am totally determined not to accept absolute cuts in the NHS – and it is hardly an issue on which the Government could survive my resignation.

A hurried dash to the Consultative Council we have set up with the local authorities to hear Joel Barnett make a brilliant exposition on cash limits. He completely dazzled that suspicious crowd, particularly when he assured them that local authorities would be compensated by an adjustment of the cash limits if the Government's counter-inflation policy did not succeed. This finally disarmed them, with only one mutter from Robert Thomas: 'We do not welcome cash limits with open arms.' I whispered to Joel, 'I'm going to see that I get the same guarantees and assurances for the NHS.' He shook his head at me, grinning, but I am instructing officials not to agree to anything in the cash limits field for my various services until I am satisfied.

Back to the office for a meeting with the TUC on fuel costs. Brian O'Malley has set this up by tipping Peter Jacques off about the fight he, Brian, and I have had to try to get a £10 fuel bonus through Cabinet. We want the backing of the TUC. I am convinced that the bold, brave dash for economic realism by Denis and co. (ably helped by the silence of Shirley, Reg Prentice et al.) on fuel pricing will lead to individual personal disasters in innumerable families. Brian and I have interrogated our officials for hours about the extent to which social security provisions will cover the drastic increase in fuel bills. They always come back with figures to show that the 'fuel component' of the Retail Prices Index adequately reflects the current and prospective increases in fuel bills and that, in fact, the prospective increase in fuel prices in April will only add a few pence to the heating additions for those on supplementary benefit. I just don't believe it, but it is impossible to drive a way through this 'expertise'. Only political action will do it. Of course, at the meeting with the TUC we had to fend them off with pleasant, sympathetic generalities.

All this over, I settled down to an all-nighter on the Community Land Bill. For the first few hours, I was grateful for the opportunity to catch up with my boxes. By 1am I began to feel overwhelmed by a desire to sleep. So I lay down on my couch and fell into an exhausted slumber. I was awakened an hour later by the ringing of my telephone. It was my Whip, Jimmie Dunn. Why had I missed the last division? Horrified, I apologized. I just hadn't heard it in these remote recesses. I promised I wouldn't lie down any more. Nor did I. I got up, had a cup of coffee in the tea-room and returned to work on my boxes. At 3am my work became rather slow. But I soldiered on and managed to see the night through without dozing off any more.

Wednesday, 12 November

By 10am the parliamentary crisis was over and I was able to shake myself free of the House in time to attend a meeting of the Women's National Committee Executive. They were all astonished at my freshness: the sort of pseudo-freshness that comes to one on these occasions. I kept going with a reserve energy through the WNC meeting itself. Another all-nighter faces me on Lords' amendments on this and that.

Fortunately, the Opposition has less stamina than we have. One memory I carry through this Outward Bound course was David saying to me, 'I can appreciate your position with the trade unions over private practice.' That helps.

Thursday, 13 November

Had a word with Ted Short yesterday urging on him how vital it was to legislate on pay beds as quickly as possible. To my surprise, he responded sympathetically. I think the press attacks on me must have aroused his instinctive loyalty and he asked me to put a paper to Social Services Committee.

The opening round of the real PESC agony in Cabinet: the first trial of strength with the Chancellor in his bid for the global sum of £3¾ billion. Denis opened with his now familiar analysis. During 1977-79 output would be 'rising very quickly indeed'. (I have never understood the basis for this claim.) If we didn't get 10 per cent investment a year during that period we should be finished, 'and that is less than in the Labour Party document'. We *must* achieve a balance in our payments by 1978, otherwise the burden of debt interest would wipe out the gains from North Sea oil and gas. It would be a 'recipe for disaster' to accept Tony C.'s proposal for cuts of only £2 billion, with another £500 million of cuts 'kept on the shelf'. At present the public sector was borrowing 20 pence for every pound it spent, and the burden of debt was becoming crippling. We couldn't continue with a borrowing requirement of anything approaching the present £12 billion.[1] Even if public expenditure was cut in the way he proposed, it would still be necessary to increase taxation. Public expenditure over the last three years had risen by more than 18 per cent in real terms, while GDP had probably risen by only 1½ per cent. We still weren't properly controlling public expenditure. The increase in 1975-76 would probably be up by 4 per cent instead of the planned 1½ per cent. It was a formidable case and Tony spent a lot of his speech acknowledging it. His main point was that the Treasury's forecasts of upturn in the economy would probably be falsified, so there would be no pressure on resources by 1978 and the Chancellor would be digging a hole with nothing to fill it. He was prepared to accept the formula cuts of £2 billion as 'politically tolerable', with the commitment to review the position in six months' time. I backed him strongly, but Harold Lever jumped in to back the Chancellor. 'Barbara and Tony would put our full employment strategy in jeopardy.' The PM pointed out that Cabinet had already agreed to reduce public expenditure below this year's level.

Mike intervened as moderately as always: 'If *we* have this kind of argument here we can imagine what sort of argument this will cause in the party. The increase in public expenditure is not the fundamental cause of the crisis. The cause is the world recession, which none of us really understands. Therefore our conclusions should be tentative. If we have a rupture with the TUC we are not going to be able to borrow from anybody. £2 billion would therefore be a better figure.' Jim, of course, backed Denis. 'I go with the Chancellor on his figure, though he knows it will be whittled down.' But he hoped we wouldn't talk of public expenditure being 'out of control'. The trouble was that GDP was too low. 'What the Chancellor has got to show us is that this will help GDP to increase.' (Exactly!) He agreed with Mike that we had to go to

[1] In fact the actual annual figure for 1975-76 was about £10½ billion.

the TUC, but we must decide our own general line first. 'There is a very real danger that, unless we can carry everyone with us, the Government will break up.'

Ted Short then electrified Cabinet with one of his passionate outbursts: 'The kind of cuts proposed in the formula cuts would be disastrous.' He was sure we would be defeated on them. Merlyn too expressed anxiety. 'I am concerned about the philosophy of what we are doing. We don't seem to have priorities within public expenditure: we talk about public expenditure as a whole. I could only come to a decision on the size of the cuts when I am clear about our economic strategy.' Willie gloomed: 'Is it feasible? Even £3¾ billion is not enough for presentation, but far too high for our policies. The figure is probably somewhere between the two.' And he concluded, to Harold Lever's delight, 'There are times when I wish the House of Lords had vented its venom on the Community Land Bill.' (I suspect Tony C. secretly agreed with him.) John Silkin hurried to put in his oar. 'I don't believe you can carry the party on £3¾ billion. I go along with Tony.' Eric predictably agreed with Denis's approach. Bob equivocated: 'If we don't present these proposals properly, there is no chance of getting them through. There's got to be a different form of words.' He then launched into a diatribe about the millions of pounds that could be saved in local government without destroying our housing policies. Take the home loss and disturbance payments. We not only gave people a home for which they had been waiting eagerly, but then paid them to move! 'Let every Ministry ask: where can we save?' His own priority would be to cut roads.

Said Harold, 'My priority would be no cut in the housing programme, but I have doubts about the extent of different cuts. But if we don't cut we shall be in a January 1966 situation.' Roy Mason was another surprise. 'We would do far better to take £2½ billion. The political effects of the Chancellor's statement could be quite appalling.' Reg Prentice, on the other hand, ran true to form. 'We have got to go for the larger figure.' We couldn't hand the strategy decision over to others. 'The worst thing would be for Denis to be forced down by the TUC.' Public expenditure was far too high, he continued. 'Once you get up to the level of over 60 per cent of GDP the argument for public expenditure changes.' But Ted Short was not to be mollified. 'I find some of the Treasury's assumptions incredible,' he said. We must go for a lower figure: 'something just under the figure for the formula cuts' – so he was out-Croslanding Crosland. Wedgie had made his usual speech. Meanwhile Eric and I had been totting up our usual calculation of where the votes had fallen. We made it ten clearly in favour of Tony's figure of £2½ billion; nine for the Chancellor's figure, including Harold himself, and two wobblers: Bob and Jim. We thought the Chancellor had lost, but Harold summed up that there was a 'very slight' majority in favour of the £3¾ billion. Eric kept whispering to me that he thought Denis would have resigned if he had been beaten. What interested me was how close a thing it had been. 'My guess is that in the end the Chancellor will settle for £3 billion,' said Tony C. contentedly to me afterwards. I left Cabinet, feeling like a wet rag, to prepare for my meeting with the BMA on pay beds.

The deputation from the BMA was led by Walpole Lewin and Rodney Smith. The only basis on which they had agreed to come was that there should be 'no preconditions' and, in welcoming them, I repeated this and invited them to give me their uninhibited views on the consultative document. A united hostile chorus then assailed me. Lewin declared that the phasing out of pay beds was not in the interests of the NHS and was a breach of the understanding the profession had had with successive governments. The licensing proposals threatened their independence. In certain areas it would be impossible to put in private specialized equipment. Private practice kept consultants working in ordinary District General Hospitals. 'We still hope you will reappraise your document,' he concluded. Sir Rodney, in that unctuous way of his, said that the Royal Colleges 'should not take part in detailed negotiations'. They were only concerned with standards of patient care, which they believed would suffer if pay beds went. 'I want to listen and take back any changes that may come out of the negotiations.' Bolt, another surgeon, put his case more reasonably than most of them. He was concerned with the nitty gritty of the consultants' interests. If pay beds went, many consultants would not be able to do any private practice at all and would simply emigrate. All this was echoed by Simmons of the HCSA, Allen of the dentists, Gilmore of the juniors and Damerell of the Independent Hospitals Group. It was unanimous and I realized what a united front I was up against.

In reply, I nailed the canard that phasing out was a breach of the understanding on which they had agreed to co-operate with Nye's NHS. I reminded them gently that the profession had continued to oppose Nye long after this concession had been made by him and that they had only been won over to accepting Nye's plans (and then only grudgingly) by his legislative undertaking that doctors would be able to combine private practice with work for the NHS. That I was prepared to reaffirm in my Bill. I also told them that my proposals on licensing had been intended to safeguard the right to private practice by ensuring that private facilities would have an even geographical spread. They were merely put forward as a basis for discussion. If they preferred it, I would be prepared to consider a free-for-all, with total separation of all private facilities from the NHS and no licensing of the private sector. Stevenson bridled at this and said they were not prepared to discuss licensing at all, because they were opposed to the whole principle of phasing out. Was I in effect saying that this was not negotiable? In fact, of course, I was, but I merely said that I could not anticipate the Queen's Speech. I would report to my colleagues what they had said. Could we not meet again when the contents of the Queen's Speech were known? They agreed to that, but obviously had second thoughts afterwards, because Stevenson rushed me a letter saying that their acceptance of another meeting must be dependent on the contents of the Queen's Speech. An epoch of total non-co-operation lies ahead.

The juniors' industrial action, though still unofficial, is becoming more widespread and more dangerous. Ironically, it is led by the lads in the North-West where that wild Australian, Wasily Sakalo, is waving his bush hat about and denouncing me as the villain of the piece. I have had a visit from the panic-stricken Regional Medical Officer of the North-West, who begged to see me to warn me he faced the closure of the NHS in certain areas. The juniors' action, he said, was being fuelled by the consultants, who would 'go to any lengths' in opposing the phasing out of pay beds. Although I discounted some of this, his picture was sufficiently gloomy to be very worrying. Some days ago I had suggested to my officials that I ought to go to Blackburn to see the juniors there, as my constituents. I ought to be able to dispel *some* of the myths that were circulating. Henry looked a bit dubious at first, but the regional chap jumped at it. And so it has been arranged. At my briefing meeting for the trip this afternoon Henry, who has been a bit white about the gills over all this, reported a discussion he had had with Sir John Richardson, of the General Medical Council [GMC]. Henry is firmly of the view that the juniors are in breach of their contract in limiting their work to forty hours and I think he hoped the GMC might be persuaded to impose some discipline. But Sir John had proved as feeble as all the rest of the Establishment. He had told Henry that the GMC would 'have to take action' if any malpractice like refusing patients took place, but wasn't prepared to make a 'general ethical statement', which Sir John said was a matter for the BMA (!). The contrast between the reaction of the medical Establishment to their own recalcitrants and what they all said about the miners grows more marked every day.

Friday, 14 November

My meeting with the Blackburn juniors has escalated into a major meeting with all the leaders in the North-West. So Blackburn Royal Infirmary was seething with excitement when I arrived. First, I went into a cosy confab with the leaders, all of us crowded together in a small room. Dr Torry and the Blackburn lads turned out to be courteous and a little abashed, but Sakalo was there in full voice, interrupting, refusing to listen and only interested in denouncing me. With all the persuasiveness at my command, I explained why the Government could not breach the pay policy: we were not just picking on the juniors. I think I was having some effect on them, so Sakalo jumped up shouting and stalked out. 'I am convinced she would rather see the collapse of the Health Service than pay the juniors their due,' he declaimed to the pressmen waiting outside. But he bobbed up again at the larger meeting we had arranged with all the juniors at the hospital who could get to it. It was a rowdy affair; Sakalo kept up a running hostile commentary. 'When are you going to stop exploiting the juniors?' he shouted, and at last I told him to shut up.

Then into a press conference, where I was asked whether the whole visit had not been, in Sakalo's words, a 'waste of time'. I rejected this and went through the whole argument again gently and patiently. Just as we were getting ready to leave for our plane we heard that Heathrow had been shut down by fog. So we faced another long, weary trek home by train and it was late when I got back to HCF. But I was not dispirited. I remain firmly convinced that the only answer to these situations is to try by every means at one's disposal to get through to the grassroots and I was sure that some of the things I said would stick. Dr Torry's moderate comment to the press afterwards confirmed this view.

The search for a chairman of the Royal Commission on the NHS continues fruitlessly. Harold is playing with the idea of a judge. He would. The BMA is pressing this too. The office has put up some names. David and Jack have been checking them and they are all terrible. It is essential I get this right, for the Royal Commission will be my last legacy to the NHS.

Saturday, 15 November

My 'weekend off', which Norman had carefully arranged for me so that I could enjoy a 'prorogation break', continues to be punctuated by departmental interruptions – and by rain. Impossible to go out and plant any bulbs. And the breakaway Junior Hospital Doctors Association has given a press conference, issuing an ultimatum to me demanding that I see them and negotiate premium overtime rates for everything over forty hours, or else they will move on to a forty-hour week, whatever happened to patients. And they claim that is within the pay policy! (Incidentally, they say the BMA ballot is 'rigged', so they will ignore the results.)

Monday, 17 November

Jack phoned with bad news about the BMA juniors' ballot. Of the 14,000 juniors (out of 20,000) who have answered the questionnaire, 7,000 have voted for industrial action and 5,000 against. Still only a third of all the juniors, but, nonetheless, a majority of those voting on this point. He read over a draft of a statement he had prepared for me and I told him it was too panicky. He said, 'Hell Corner Farm must be doing you good.' I groaned, thinking of the mud and the still unplanted bulbs. Anyway, I stiffened his statement a bit.

At 8pm Edna arrived with a box. The first thing that greeted me was a Minute from Jack, reporting a last-minute panic appeal from David to try and tone down the Queen's Speech on phasing out pay beds. 'He is still concerned,' wrote Jack, 'about the possibility of a major confrontation which may be provoked by the Queen's Speech reference. He agrees that we have to say something, but thinks that it is for consideration whether, for example, the commitment should be made less provocative by saying, "consultations on the consultative document are continuing" (etc. as before) and "in the light of these legislation may be introduced in the session".' Jack added, 'Dr Owen accepts, I think, that you could only do this, if at all, with a certain guarantee from your colleagues that preparation of the legislation continues and that you do not lose your place in the legislative queue.' David must know that it is now far too late to alter the Queen's Speech, even if I wanted to. Indeed, only last Friday David was admitting this to me and saying in my room to my face (and Jack's), 'I am not suggesting that you should do this.' So what is David up to? I have never felt more alone – or more sure that we have no alternative but to press ahead and see this thing through. I can only hope that my allies in the PLP have got more fire in their bellies than this.

Tuesday, 18 November

Up to London again to face the blitz from the juniors. I had told Norman on the phone that I thought I ought to try and see them (through the BMA) today, before the pay beds decision is announced in the Queen's Speech. I want to get the BMA committed on the juniors before the consultants can use pay beds to confuse the issue. But the earliest the BMA are prepared to meet me is Thursday. Well, that lets me off the hook on the question of whether I am treating this as a matter of urgency.

Norman and I also agreed that we had better ask Mike himself to come along. After all, the juniors keep challenging me on our interpretation of the pay policy and he is interpreter-in-chief of that policy.

No time to eat any lunch before I go to the 2.30pm Cabinet. Why we should have one at this odd hour is due to the fact that Harold has been away at Rambouillet, taking part in a summit conference, and has only just got back. He reported with relish on the ensuing Declaration,[1] which he claimed as a success for us because we had encouraged the Americans to be expansionist. But the price has obviously been that we have committed ourselves against 'general' import controls, merely reserving our position on 'selective' ones – under what will clearly be highly restrictive criteria. We also had in front of us Jim's memo on direct elections to the European Assembly, which stressed our commitment to these 'under the Treaty of Rome'. (I only wish I had more time to check up on all these assumptions. Without Jack's help I would be impotent on these non-departmental issues.) All he wanted at this stage was 'some idea' of what Cabinet felt. There was no chance of reaching agreement in the Community on a 'uniform procedure' for the elections, he said, but added 'we have got to have direct elections'. It would have to be left to each country, but he and Harold wanted to 'start talking in some detail' at the Council of Ministers in December. He personally was in favour of an Assembly of 350 members and a common election day. But he thought we should wait until after the December meeting and then issue a Green Paper. The Commission was 'fading into the background'. The coming struggle was between the elected representatives and the Council of Ministers. Typically, he added, 'I don't know the outcome, but this is twenty years ahead.' (We have heard this before.) The next step should be a Green Paper on what was involved. Dear Ted Short, as usual, gave us a combination of his good radical instincts and his practical problems as Leader of the House. Two things worried him. One was the relationship between the European Parliament and Westminster. The other was that this move, plus the devolution proposals and Roy Jenkins's proposed reference of the question of proportional representation to the Speaker's Conference (a later item on the agenda), would build up an 'irresistible pressure' towards changes we did not want. Roy Jenkins said that he 'broadly agreed' with Jim. Peter urged that we didn't have to come forward at this stage with precise proposals. There were 'very serious implications' in direct elections. There should be 'something in the nature of a Speaker's Conference' on the whole question first.

Wedgie was passionate. This was a 'major step towards federalism', he declared. What oath of allegiance would the European parliamentarians give? 'Here is an Establishment that wants elections' – and we should be very careful about *that* combination. We shouldn't proceed on this in this Parliament. I chipped in to say that this was the *basic* dilemma that resulted from membership of the EEC. We were

---

[1] The leaders of Britain, France, Germany, Italy, Japan and the United States had been meeting at Rambouillet to discuss ways of reviving the world economy without rekindling inflation. The meeting ended on Monday 17 November with a public statement promising joint action to lead the world out of recession. The section on import controls said: 'In a period when pressures are developing for a return to protectionism, it is essential for the main trading nations ... to avoid resorting to measures by which they could try to solve their problems at the expense of others.'

tackling the problem the wrong way round. (Jack's brief here.) One should never decide machinery before one had made up one's mind about purpose. What sort of powers would this Parliament have? There should be far more consultation than we had had. Denis argued that direct elections would actually tend to reduce the power of European Parliaments (an argument I totally fail to grasp). The other European-ists who then spoke said they didn't know what we were so frightened of – they would! Harold summed up that we should proceed cautiously. Jim's proposals would form the basis of the line he would take at next month's Council of Ministers, but he wouldn't enter into any commitment and there would be a Green Paper before anything was finally decided – which all sounds very plausible, but is part of the slow but sure manoeuvring in the direction in which Harold and Jim want to go.

After that it was pleasant to have Roy Jenkins slapped down in an attempt to get the question of proportional representation referred to the Speaker's Conference. He gave as his excuse that the Conference ought to be reconvened to discuss certain outstanding items of electoral procedure and that it would be very difficult 'not to refer electoral reform to it at the same time'. What was worrying was that, with Harold's connivance, he had already sounded out the Opposition on this possibility. Ted Short, who ought to know better, supported him. There was, he said, 'great pressure for it', though 'we must watch it very carefully'. But the rest of us turned on them. Denis, with good pragmatic vigour, denounced the idea as 'absolute madness'. Even people like Roy Mason, Fred Peart, Malcolm and Willie Ross were against. Only the hard core of Jenkinsite coalitionists (Harold Lever, Shirley and Reg Prentice) were for. So Harold had to sum up that the idea was turned down. But those rightists will go on beavering away, with Harold and Jim as their instruments, until they have finally destroyed the Labour Party's independence and power to govern single-handedly. Finally there was a tussle between Tony C. and Joel on the level of rate support grant for 1976–77. We leftists backed Tony in insisting on $65\frac{1}{2}$ per cent instead of the $64\frac{1}{2}$ per cent Joel was demanding – and we won.

Hurried back to the office to plot the meeting with the BMA. What is interesting is that the juniors are beginning to lose the sympathy of the press. The decision taken yesterday by the breakaway Junior Hospital Doctors Association to start industrial action in ten days' time, unless I come up with a better overtime offer, has clearly shocked the press into examining the whole position more carefully. The *Evening Standard*'s leader tonight opens with the following significant words: 'The junior hospital doctors are now overstepping the limits of public sympathy' – though, of course, it goes on to say that the phasing out of pay beds would make matters worse. Typically, the *Evening News* manages to blame it all on me: 'There is a growing impression that Mrs Castle's obstinate posture may be based on faulty arithmetic.' Mike's readiness to come openly into the fray will be a great help, bless him.

Another headache is that the decision to raise dental charges has leaked, and I have had an agonized letter from Laurie Pavitt, who is perfectly capable of resigning on this issue. We agree that David should go along to the health group of the PLP on Thursday, when the decision is announced, so as to put it in the best possible light. I say I will try to have a word with Laurie personally.

At last, very late, I got to No. 10 for the eve-of-Queen's Speech reception. Most people there seemed to be fairly pleased with it. David, in sunny mood again, seemed almost to be congratulating me on having succeeded in getting pay beds included. 'It would never have been done without you,' he said approvingly. This is all the more strange, because he continues to bombard me with Minutes seeking to water down the pay beds policy. He has just done this over my paper to the Social Services Committee of Cabinet seeking to get agreement to a short, quick Bill giving legislative authority to phase out pay beds, coupled with a simple size control over private hospitals. It is he who originally suggested this as the best and easiest way to hold the line, pending fuller consultations on licensing. Now he has got cold feet over it. He is also urging that I extend my discretionary power to delay phasing out in certain cases from two years to three, arguing that consultants in certain areas and in certain specialities just won't be able to practise privately outside the NHS. So it is certainly true that, if anything *is* done over phasing out, it will be due to me.

Wednesday, 19 November

The more serious press continues its criticism of the juniors. *The Times* has a useful leader: 'But the Patients have a Case as Well.' The *Financial Times* has an even better one, saying I have no choice but to stand firm on pay policy. This morning I put on my new dress for the State Opening and stood smiling at the Bar of the Lords as the Queen read out the bit about pay beds. Everyone glanced my way.

Thursday, 20 November

Howls from the consultants about the Queen's Speech. But that was only to be expected. Our own people are delighted. 'Government bites bullet on pay beds,' said John Cunningham in the *Guardian*. What mattered to me was that I got my paper on the pay beds Bill through the Social Services Committee of Cabinet: one hurdle crossed, though Ted Short said that, as it involved earlier legislation than visualized in our decisions on the Queen's Speech and contained the power to control private developments above a certain size, he would have to refer it to Cabinet. Despite David's pressures, I have stuck to a final date for phasing out of one year, plus a discretionary power for the Secretary of State to allow an extension of a further two years in exceptional circumstances. No one raised any difficulties about that, so I am pretty pleased with what I have got through as I can return to the attack for a more comprehensive licensing system later in a separate Bill.

But the main business of the day was, of course, with the juniors, in another effort to convince them that their demands were contrary to pay policy. Mike came along to the meeting, looking a bit nervous, but he did his stuff splendidly. Lewin led the juniors into battle, but all he did was to say the BMA were not trying to breach the pay policy and then handed over to Dr Zacharias, the new leader of the militants, a thin, tight-lipped young man, clearly determined to prove he was going to deliver the goods better than his predecessors, Ford and Bell, had done. Zacharias began with an attack on the department, which, he said, had been 'dragging its feet' over the juniors' claim, and he went into a long history of our misdemeanours, designed to show that we had broken faith. He warned that he and the new executive were 'truly representative of grassroots opinion'. All they were seeking was a 'fair interpretation of pay policy'. They accepted the principle of the new contract, but were convinced there was more money available. The pay policy could be interpreted in a way that gave them all they asked. All this in an icy manner bordering on insolence.

I replied gently, but firmly, setting the record straight and insisting that it had been no part of our intention to trap the juniors in the pay policy. I then called on Mike, who began, as usual, rather tentatively. But his very lack of glibness began to have its effect on them in spite of themselves. He stressed that no one else had been allowed to claim that they were a 'special case' and spelt out how strictly the pay policy had been observed. The argument then went round and round. After two hours of this we adjourned to take stock and to have a cup of tea. Over tea in my room I said to Mike, David and my officials that we ought to spike the juniors' guns by offering an independent audit of our figures, to scotch their suggestion that somehow we had cooked up the returns. But when, at the resumed meeting, I offered this, Zacharias rejected it. They were not questioning our figures, he said, but thought they did not represent the 'true position', whatever he meant by that. I also offered to set up a joint examination immediately on the way to reduce the juniors' excessive hours. But Zacharias would have none of this. He said rudely that he saw no point in continuing the discussion and that they had better go. Lewin, knowing I was going to make a statement in the House tomorrow, did not want to be quite so precipitate. He continued his parrot-like assertion that he believed the juniors' claim was not inconsistent with pay policy. It was not that our figures had been 'cooked'. Nonetheless, the figure of £12 million was 'clearly wrong'. I said that in that case the BMA had better submit its evidence of this to us so that we could examine it. Reluctantly he said he would and we broke up. Mike commiserated with me on the kind of people with whom I had to deal. We agreed that no TUC union would behave with such wilful intransigence. You just couldn't negotiate with this lot.

As we left the meeting news was brought to me that the consultants have declared war over pay beds. At a meeting of the CCHMS leaders they had decided to recommend the full meeting on Tuesday to join the juniors in working 'emergencies only' from 1 December, and to start collecting undated resignations from the NHS. When the press asked me for a comment I said like a flash, 'This is a strike against the House of Commons. I find it unique in the history of strikes in Britain that we should be threatened with action about a piece of legislation before Parliament has even seen it.' Personally, I think the consultants have played into our hands.

Harold phoned me to say Arnold Goodman had been onto him. Arnold had, he said, been retained by the Independent Hospitals Group [IHG] to fight the pay beds legislation and was anxious to see if an accommodation of any kind could be reached. Would I be interested in meeting him for a private talk, Harold asked casually? I jumped at it. I have been very anxious to have a talk with the professions about the timing of phasing out and what I have in mind about licensing. I am sure I could allay a lot of their suspicions if only I could get them to discuss anything rationally. But they are impossible. If Arnold was prepared to act as a go-between, he might help me to get them to see sense. (The IHG, for one thing, is far less hung up about licensing and can even see some value in it as helping to secure a better distribution of private facilities.) So I told Harold I would contact Arnold right away and that I assumed the talks would be very hush-hush. Harold confirmed that Arnold wanted to keep them very private too. I then called in Norman, whom I swore to secrecy. I wouldn't tell anyone about this – not even David. One thing intrigued me about Arnold's approach. I am sure it has been inspired by the appalling press the consultants are getting. They may well be anxious to get themselves off the hook.

Friday, 21 November

The Opposition have chosen today for a debate on the Health Service in the Queen's Speech debate, so I had to cancel my visit to Blackburn. They would choose a Friday! I had no difficulty in knocking Norman Fowler round the ring, but the awful thing was that the benches behind us were completely empty. At one stage David and I were totally alone. Jimmie Dunn went off to try and round up some speakers on our side and meanwhile I prevailed on Alan Lee Williams, who had wandered into the chamber, to say a few words. Jimmie said he had found three of our people in the tea-room, but they all refused to come and speak. Later I found out that there was a 'strike' by our people in protest at Harold's decision to send Malcolm Shepherd to represent the Government at Franco's funeral. Really, that man does make some crass mistakes. Of course, this had never come before Cabinet. Norman Atkinson apologized if this 'strike' was an embarrassment to me, but said it was not directed against me, but against the PM. Small comfort! Of course, the Tories made a lot of the emptiness of our benches.

The press is full of the consultants' threat of industrial action. The *FT* reported gravely, 'If both groups of doctors carry out their threats, then day-to-day work in the hospitals could come virtually to a standstill.' The *Daily Telegraph* is continuing its almost daily attacks on me. 'In none of these areas,' said its leader yesterday, 'is there the shambles comparable with the service presided over by the increasingly shrill and vengeful Mrs Castle.' However, there is one bright spot. I had a long talk with Laurie Pavitt yesterday about teeth and spectacles and succeeded in defusing his threatened resignation. I think this is due to the skill with which our package combines increases in certain charges with reductions in others, plus important improvements for children and the blind – for which all the credit must go to David. My contribution has been the announcement that I am going to produce a more attractive range of NHS spectacle frames – about which David is dubious, but our Labour people are delighted.

My debate over, I phoned Arnold. We had an amicable talk and agreed to meet on Monday evening, deciding that his flat would be the safest rendezvous.

Saturday, 22 November

Denis has joined in the fray over the juniors' dispute in a weekend speech. I think Cabinet is now suddenly alive to what I am up against. At Cabinet last week, when I reported on the juniors, I urged every member of the Cabinet to back me up publicly, so that the profession could see that it wasn't my own personal pay policy I was following, but the Government's. Ted Short endorsed this warmly, saying that 'the attacks that are being made on Barbara are quite intolerable'. Denis's speech is the first fruit.

Monday, 24 November

With *The Times* reporting a forceful weekend speech by David Basnett on 'the dire need for an industrial strategy', I expected fireworks at the TUC Liaison Committee meeting this morning. In the event, it was as temperate as usual. The only item was the Queen's Speech and when I arrived I found that neither Harold nor Jim were there. Nor was Hughie. The discussion was desultory. Bob Mellish held forth about his total lack of a majority in the House and the difficulty he was going to have in getting the controversial legislative programme through. 'If we get this Queen's Speech through we will have done brilliantly. If we last a year we will be lucky.' And he went on to say that even some members of the T and G were protesting against the dockworkers' scheme.[1] That was before Jack Jones arrived and as soon as he did he asserted his Cromwellian New Model Army authority. A timidly tentative request by Shirley that the unions should do some propaganda about the dockworkers' scheme, to offset the fears of the food manufacturing industry, met with a stern rebuke that the food manufacturers just didn't know what they were talking about. 'I'm not objecting to the scheme,' said Shirley feebly.

At Tam Dalyell's request from the chair that I should say something about pay beds, I appealed for union pressure on MPs to back our legislation – particularly on the Liberals, who were about to rat, as usual. This provoked an intervention from Danny McGarvey to the effect that my colleagues were leaving me to fight my battles alone. Certainly, he said, the unions should back me, but I ought to get out among the grassroots making my speeches and so should Labour MPs. (As if I hadn't been doing that!) Jack said gravely that the TUC General Council was meeting on Wednesday and would pass a resolution in my support. We ought to pass one today as well, he said.

Jack then went on to ask what the Queen's Speech meant about pensions: when would the next uprating be? I looked at Denis, who said that would depend on the rate of inflation, whereupon Jack warned him that the unions would expect us to do something about pensioners. (I chalked it up in my mind for use in the PESC exercise.) Jack went on to lecture us on the withdrawal of the Christmas bonus. The bonus had been TUC policy and it was regrettable that it had been withdrawn without any consultation with the TUC. They were very concerned about fuel costs and had made

[1] Following the dock strikes of 1971 and 1972 against the increasing transfer of cargo-handling operations to inland container depots (see Introduction), Jack Jones had been pressing for a redefinition of dock work to safeguard dockers' jobs. In March Michael Foot published a consultative document proposing to extend the Dock Labour Scheme to non-scheme ports and to redefine dock work to cover cargo handling within five miles of the ports. This was meeting opposition from other unions, such as the Distributive Workers, who could see themselves losing members to the powerful T&GWU, whose own lorry driver members were also uneasy at the prospect of losing jobs to dockers. The Opposition was whipping up a scare campaign against the proposals, claiming that they would increase handling costs and cause industrial disruption.

representations to me about a possible fuel bonus, which he hoped I had passed on to my colleagues. 'Of course,' I said innocently. Denis merely looked grim. At this stage Judith asked what was being done about unemployment. What were the prospects? Denis said he thought that 'output was bottoming out'. What a glorious phrase! But some increase in unemployment was likely next year, he continued. Indiscriminate reflation was no answer: it took a year for £1,000 million of reflation to produce 30,000 to 50,000 jobs. The short-term measures we had taken were proving very successful (e.g. the number of unemployed school-leavers had been markedly reduced). He realized that we must produce a further package before Christmas and we were also looking at import controls.

Len Murray came in firmly. He hoped the TUC would have a chance to discuss the contents of the package. The situation was obviously deteriorating. Measures were going to be needed to stimulate consumption. 'The main bulwark against inflation is the pay policy,' he said. 'We want it to go on sticking.' David Basnett was equally stern. 'We accept the argument that now is not the time for general reflation, but we shall be coming back to you about another package.' Denis got snappy at this pressure, retorting that our real trouble was that we couldn't get the output we needed. Take Leyland: they could sell the cars all right, but the stocks just weren't there. Jack looked angry. 'You mean the strike?[1] Of course, and we're trying to end it.' But they had brought the strike figures down markedly and there really mustn't be these generalized attacks. Danny McGarvey maintained that there was 'a lot of nonsense talked about overmanning'. As a minor quarrel looked like developing I suggested that each month we should have in front of us a paper on some aspect of industry (e.g. the car industry), so that we could together analyse what was wrong. David, Jack and Len waved this aside: this wasn't the forum for it; they had Neddy and other places to do this and they didn't want to duplicate, etc. So it died away, Wedgie having contributed his usual theme: 'There is the possibility that we may be slipping into a semi-permanent slump.' David Basnett made his parting shot, 'Unemployment is the Achilles heel of the Social Contract', while Len concluded with the plea, 'You've got to help us on this.'

Wedgie is in the news again with a great attack on spending cuts he made to a young workers' conference at the weekend. I am doing my propaganda more subtly. I have told Brian A-S. to draft an attack on the new philosophy which is now spreading, not only in the *Financial Times* but among right-wing members of the Cabinet, to the effect that cuts in public expenditure are positively socially desirable. This is for a speech I am to make to a local government conference on Friday on the social services. Brian A-S. has produced some wonderful stuff, which I polished up and added to at the weekend. Meanwhile the lobby against defence cuts is getting itself mobilized, and, of course, the press is lending a hand. The *Mail* carries front-page banner headlines today: 'Revolt of the Generals.' This campaign, I suspect, is being organized, not merely by Roy Mason, but by No. 10.

[1] There had been a spate of unofficial strikes in Leyland which had resulted over a six-month period in the loss of production of 40,000 cars with a showroom value of £90 million; a further 25,000 were held up in factories by quality faults or missing parts. Leyland's share of the home market fell from 40 per cent in September to an average of 24 per cent in October and November.

This suspicion was confirmed at the 'bilateral' discussion I had this afternoon with Joel on public expenditure. I went along in grim mood. The 'formula cuts' set out by the Treasury would mean an absolute cut in expenditure on the NHS and I told Joel flatly that I would never agree to this. I was prepared to accept a standstill, but, because of demographic changes, this meant I needed an increase of $1\frac{1}{2}$ per cent a year. The poor lad was looking harassed, and no wonder. He just said he would have to report to Cabinet my failure to agree to what had been proposed. Peter Baldwin, coming to his aid in his quietly deadly way as usual, queried whether the demographic argument justified an increase of $1\frac{1}{2}$ per cent for the NHS, but I stood my ground, while David Owen pointed out that the formula cuts for education still allowed present standards in primary and secondary schools to be maintained, while for us they meant that standards would go down. It was agreed that Joel's officials should look into this.

We then turned to social security and the Treasury's proposal that we should switch from the historical to the forecasting method at the next uprating. Brian O'M. predictably resisted this savagely, but I sensed that he was weakening in his resistance, since, bless him, he realizes that otherwise the Health Service will be decimated. So we left it that this change should be considered further in the context of the coming report of the official anti-poverty group now at work. We then went through the list of all the other optional cuts in the social security field and I said no to all of them, including the postponement of child benefit. I got the impression that Joel is not expecting to get away with anything on this side but the change in the uprating method, which will give him £500 million towards his £3¾ billion. I concluded by reading my own list of priorities for savings, which Brian A-S. has worked out for me: defence, roads, environmental research, police and the international space agency. Joel noted them with a grin. Unfortunately, they don't add up to £3¾ billion. Joel hissed to me afterwards, confirming my worst fears, 'You must support us on getting more out of Defence.'

It was against this background that Norman and I raced to Portland Place for our rendezvous with Arnold. We need not have worried: he arrived late. We were greeted at the door by Arnold's housekeeper, Mrs Roberts. She ushered us (it is the only word) into the sort of room I hadn't expected: rather dark and made darker by heavy period furniture and subdued lighting. Superb pictures everywhere, deep armchairs and sofa and a large colour TV. But the whole effect was oppressive. 'I am afraid Lord Goodman has been detained,' said Mrs Roberts, 'but please let me get you some tea.' She did so in a silver teapot and brought in a plate of cucumber sandwiches of such delicate thinness that the Ritz would have been envious.

After we had waited some twenty minutes Arnold breezed in with perfunctory apologies. I had arrived full of affectionate memories of Arnold's kindliness, but his lateness irritated me. However, we chatted amiably. He is a disarming man, always ready to acclaim one's reasonableness and to criticize his own clients' weaknesses. The important thing, he said, was to avoid a collision course and if he could make any modest contribution to this he would be glad. What he needed to do was to get the moderates in the profession to stand up and be counted. 'Mr Grabham must be bypassed.' What his clients wanted, he said, was to get the whole matter of pay beds referred to the Royal Commission. He accepted that that was out, but it might be possible to satisfy them if we could refer the *timing* of phasing out to the Royal Commission, while proceeding to legislate on the general principle. They were also terrified of my licensing proposals, which they considered, no doubt without any serious grounds, to be a threat to the practice of private medicine. He did not share my horror of pay beds, but he was sure I was not proposing to threaten private medicine. However, we had to accept that we were not dealing with people who were entirely rational. If we could refer the whole licensing proposals to the Royal Commission, that would greatly help.

I told him that he must not entertain any false hopes of being able to exclude Mr Grabham, who was the best – and toughest – negotiator of the lot of them. No deal done behind Mr Grabham's back would be worth anything. But I was sure that he, Arnold, could play an invaluable role in helping to clear away some of the more hysterical fears of the professions. As to timing, I had always intended to have a reasonable phasing out period. What I had in mind was to include in the legislation a final date for phasing out, but to give myself, as Secretary of State, power to make exemptions to this date of up to two years or more in order to take account of the difficulties of consultants in the provinces, who supplemented their income in a modest way from a few pay beds and who would never get fat pickings from private practice as consultants in the South-East did. It would be fatal to refer the date to the Royal Commission because this would naturally provoke the unions. 'Don't forget there are two parties to peace in the NHS and one is the unions.' If only he could get the professions to sit down and discuss the problem with the unions, he might find that a solution could be worked out.

Arnold said he found this 'eminently reasonable'. Unfortunately, the people he was working for considered it anathema that in any of their actions they should be responsible to the unions. What about a quadripartite meeting between the professions, the unions, the chairman of the Royal Commission and me to work out a solution? I said that I didn't think that was on (I am not prepared to have the Royal Commission brought into this at any price), but on licensing the situation could be very different. (I know I have no mandate from Cabinet – or the Manifesto – for licensing.) I was sure I could make a concession here. I was not against referring this matter to the RC, but there had to be an interim control, pending the RC's report, in order to prevent private developments from injuring the NHS. I also told him that none of this problem over pay beds need have arisen if only the profession had been willing to take up our idea of common waiting lists. Arnold pricked up his ears at this, said he liked the idea and asked me to send him further details of what we had in mind. This I agreed to do. If only we could get Arnold really committed to common waiting lists we would be half-way home!

The discussion over, Arnold took us on a tour of his pictures, including two portraits of him. The one by Ruskin Spear was a monstrosity (just as Spear's was of me). But I found the one by Graham Sutherland excellent. I told Norman on the way back that things seemed to be going well.

A hurried change for the reception at No. 10 which Harold had agreed to give for International Women's Year. It was packed and everyone was thrilled to be there.

One interesting side of Harold's character: he always likes his invitations to include man and wife, even if it means restricting the guest list.

Tuesday, 25 November

David has sent me another of his admonitory Minutes, this time arising from something I said to officials when we were discussing the formula cuts proposed for the NHS. If these were imposed on me, I said, or any serious cuts at all, I would insist on cutting out one of the management tiers to reduce administrative costs and would like the office to work out what should be done. David has popped in a Minute saying he is 'gravely concerned' to hear I am even contemplating it. I should leave it to him to pursue an 'evolutionary' policy. That lad really is incredible. One minute he is demanding that I have a showdown with everyone to force changes through; the next he is back-tracking hard. But he can spend all his time mastering the Health Service side and does it brilliantly, so I am immensely dependent on him. I decided to ignore the Minute.

The more responsible press continues to be helpful. Today the *Guardian* has a leader saying, 'Undoubtedly this is the most serious crisis the NHS has faced in twenty-seven years', but arguing that it is the consultants, not the Government, who must back down. On Sunday the *Sunday Times* had the best leader yet. It opened with the sentence, 'In its present militant posture the medical profession has lost a lot of respect.' It concluded on pay beds that 'the case for separate systems, private and public, has wide ideological support.... To withdraw labour now, before the Minister's legislative and administrative intentions are tested, and before Parliament has voted, is, again, conduct unbecoming to a responsible profession.' Strong words. Of course, this does not deter a few of the popular papers from continuing their personal vendetta against me. These are the same papers that are dredging up 'abuses' of the social security system to give the impression that thousands of scroungers are getting away with it, which they are not. The real trouble, in the case of large families, is that family allowance is so much lower than the dependents benefits under unemployment benefit and supplementary benefit, that it pays a man with eight or so children to be out of work. The most important reform we could introduce would be a high level of child benefit, but, in this financial climate, I can't see that happening.

An extra Cabinet to discuss the Iceland fishing crisis and Chrysler. Fred reported that Icelandic gunboats have started to harass our trawlers and that the men are threatening to stop fishing unless they get naval protection. Jim said the Icelandic Prime Minister was still offering us a catch of 65,000 tons on a 'take it or leave it' basis. Harold pointed out that the 1974 ruling of the International Court of Justice was on our side.[1] No one raised any objections to the navy going in. As for myself, I

[1] The International Court of Justice in The Hague ruled on 25 July 1974 that Britain was not bound by Iceland's unilateral decision in 1972 to extend its fishing rights from twelve to fifty nautical miles and that Iceland had no right either to prevent British trawlers from fishing or unilaterally to impose restrictions on British trawlers operating in the twelve to fifty mile zone. The court also ruled that Britain and Iceland were obliged to negotiate a settlement of their differences. Iceland refused to recognize the Court's jurisdiction in the case, rejected the verdict and said it planned to extend its limits eventually to 200 miles.

was barely listening. Iceland is peripheral to my own concerns. Nor had I really had time to master the Chrysler crisis, on which we had papers from Eric, Willie and Mike. Eric opened by saying that Chrysler stood by its ultimatum to us: either we took over responsibility for all its future losses in the UK, or they would proceed to wind the company up forthwith. Under pressure, the most they had agreed to do was to put in a fixed amount towards the survival of Chrysler UK, provided its activities were regrouped. But they were not prepared to share in any future losses and there would have to be massive redundancies anyway. The Industrial Development Advisory Board didn't think this option would be viable and the NEB didn't want to have anything to do with the firm. The CPRS report on the motorcar industry, which it had been suggested should be published, made it clear that there was excess capacity in the industry. His firm view was that we had better accept the inevitable, let the company wind itself up, and concentrate on a massive redundancy scheme.

Mike's main concern was to see that the redundancy pay proposed should be big enough, but his own paper indicated that this would have repercussions elsewhere. Willie came out of his corner fighting: the effects in Scotland of a wind-up would be disastrous. The Chrysler offer of a financial contribution should be explored. The discussion which followed was confused. I myself was torn: I had been impressed by the CPRS report, which I had read pretty thoroughly, and so had Jack in his brief to me. This, I thought to myself, was one of those issues on which one had to spend hours before one could judge it properly. Wedgie made one of his contributions about the way in which Britain's manufacturing base was being eroded, but I was far from clear what he was advocating. Harold summed up that we couldn't take decisions until there had been further discussions with Chrysler to find out what their latest offer really meant. Eric muttered to me angrily about this: 'Nothing will come of it.' But we were all thankful to leave it that way. Peter then proposed that, in the event of a complete or substantial closure of Chrysler's activities, we should impose quota restrictions on motorcar imports from all sources, but not commercial vehicles. He had already made informal approaches to the EEC on this, and Gundelach, the Commissioner responsible, had reacted favourably. After a brief discussion Harold ruled that this should be put in cold storage until the Chrysler position had been cleared up. I don't believe this lot will ever impose import restrictions of any importance if they can help it.

Norman has sent Arnold full details of common waiting lists. I await Arnold's conversion.

Wednesday, 26 November

The cameras were there in force outside Transport House for the NEC meeting. Reason? We are to consider Reg Prentice's appeal against his local party's decision not to reselect him as its candidate.[1] The press has been building this up wonderfully.

[1] At its special meeting in July the Newham North East party had carried by twenty-nine votes to nineteen the Motion calling on him to retire at the next election. Reg Prentice had appealed to the NEC, arguing that the complaints against him were due to Trotskyite infiltration of his local party. The enquiry committee set up by the NEC found unanimously that the local party was within its constitutional rights, but

Reg Prentice has circulated a long document, which has been given considerable publicity: any stick will do to beat the Labour Party with. But one begins to suspect that Reg is seriously embarrassing his own friends. The Enquiry Committee, consisting of Tom Bradley,[1] John Chalmers, Alex Kitson and Reg Underhill, reported that it had found no constitutional irregularities in the meeting which had decided to get rid of Reg and therefore dismissed his appeal. But it urged that attempts at reconciliation should be made. Reg Prentice's only response had been to denounce the enquiry publicly and to demand that he be allowed to address the NEC personally. At the Organization Committee a battle royal had taken place, Shirley and Bill John of the NUR trying to get the dismissal of the appeal deleted until the proposed conciliation had taken place (lost by two votes to nine), while Eric Heffer and Nick Bradley wanted no conciliation at all (again, lost two to nine). Mik had proposed successfully that the reconciliation attempt should be made by the General Secretary. When this came up at the NEC Mik said sourly he had changed his mind. He had been all in favour of reconciliation at the Organization Committee, but, in view of Reg's behaviour since, he realized it would be a waste of time. However, his Motion to delete this proposal was lost by four votes to twenty-one. We then turned to Reg's demand to be heard personally. To everyone's surprise it was Fred Mulley who moved that his request be not granted and it was clear that it was carried overwhelmingly. Not even Reg's supporters pretended to fight for him very hard.

While all this was going on Harold suddenly surprised everyone by proceeding to make a long and involved statement which we soon realized he was reading. After he had been going on for some time, Eric Heffer challenged him. What was this all in aid of? (He might have asked what did it mean? It was one of Harold's convoluted 'a plague on both your houses' pieces, including his favourite line, 'I have spent thirteen years so far trying to keep this party together and I do not like what is going on.') Harold then said with injured dignity that he was doing what he always did: reading a prepared text which he had issued to the press. 'I'm sick of having what I say here distorted by leaks.' Eric exploded in righteous indignation. Was it in order? Could we all do the same, etc., etc.? I must say that, while I can sympathize with Harold's desire to be reported accurately, the content and tone of what he was saying was gratuitously provocative. It contained an absurd bit accusing the NEC of ignoring the constitutional role of the PLP, constantly attacking the Government and alienating the moderates. He even threatened there might be a split between the NEC and the PLP, leading to the latter putting up their own candidates against the official Labour ones. While the rest of us sat stunned, Eric grew increasingly vociferous, while Judith said that Harold had widened the discussion so much that other people must be allowed to widen the discussion too. After a bit more of this Bryan Stanley moved next business and the row died down. But Harold has only stirred things up.

Reg Prentice's friends, led by Mrs Shirley Williams, continued to try to find ways to help him. They were later embarrassed when, in 1977, he joined the Conservative Party, crossed the floor of the House and started voting against the Government. Following the Conservative victory in the general election of 1979, he was given a job in Mrs Thatcher's Government.

[1] Labour MP for Leicester East, President of the Transport Salaried Staffs Association and a member of the trade union section of the NEC.

Harold's statement had been linked to Reg Underhill's document on 'Entryist Activities' in the party which has, of course, leaked.[1] Who had inspired Reg Underhill to report on this I could not make out: I suspect it was auto-generated. Of course, it has provided a lot of fuel for the press, stating, as it does, that the Marxist 'Militant' group has full-time organizers and that all but one of the eleven members of the Young Socialists' Executive have 'Militant' tendencies. The Organization Committee had recommended us to let the report 'lie on the table'. Shirley and Russell Tuck (of the NUR) moved the reference back of this. The ensuing debate was in marked contrast to Harold's near-hysteria, Mike arguing moderately and effectively that witch-hunting never solved anything and merely led to the persecution of what even Reg Underhill's report admitted were legitimate pressure groups. Bryan Stanley supported him and the reference back was lost by twelve votes to sixteen, while Harold insisted that the Organization Committee should give consideration to the points he had made. Much good that will do.

Meanwhile Geoff Bish had been up to me to say we ought to pass a Motion of support for me on my disputes with the doctors and he had put a draft in front of me. This not only backed me on pay beds but also on the juniors, putting on record our support for the £6 policy and for the 'Government's position on the junior hospital doctors' pay dispute'. Of course, I could see nothing wrong with this, but I had temporarily forgotten the ASTMS line on pay policy, and of course Mik, Eric and co. objected to this part of it. There was a great hoo-ha, with some people insisting that the £6 limit was the policy of conference, others saying there would be a disastrous leak if we tried to amend the Motion anyway. Tom Bradley, from the chair, cut through all this confusion by saying he was going to put the Motion. This was then carried by sixteen votes to nil, Mik, Eric and a few more sitting on their hands. It is nice to be in line with conference decisions against the 'Left'!

There was only time for a quick lunch before we were all back at No. 10 for the joint meeting of the NEC with the Cabinet on industrial strategy. Eric Varley hit back at his critics passionately and effectively, to my surprise. Eric Heffer jumped in to the other Eric's defence, arguing that 'the battle was lost in the August of the previous year' – i.e. before Eric Varley took over. It was not, he said, 'just a question of the Bill, but of the will'. Had we a list of profitable firms designated by us for take-over? Why had planning agreements not been made compulsory? 'That is not the industrial

---

[1] Entryism, said the report, is the tactic employed by an organization which is ineligible for affiliation to the Labour Party and seeks to overcome this by sending its members into the party as individuals to carry out activities directed by an outside organization. A number of small Trotskyite groups had practised entryism on and off over the years, particularly among the Young Socialists. The most serious challenge now was from the 'Militant' tendency, a Marxist group organized round a paper of that name, which was aiming at a membership of one thousand. Reg Underhill's report extensively quoted a discussion document produced by the group in May 1974, which, he said, 'confirms beyond any doubt whatever that there is a central organization associated with *Militant* with its own membership and full-time organizers'. This made it different from the supporters of *Tribune*, who, as the document itself pointed out, 'have no organized tendency at the present moment'. Underhill made no recommendations for action, but the strong inference of his report was that association with *Militant* by party members should be proscribed. Nonetheless the philosophic and practical objections to proscribing the purchase of a newspaper were obvious.

strategy this party wanted.' Wedgie gave us an apocalyptic speech: the situation was far worse than we realized. We faced 'high and rising unemployment'. And he added, 'No one wants a Barber boom, but even when the upturn comes there is no guarantee that it will absorb the unemployed.' We were undergoing 'a massive monetarist attack on the whole thinking of the Labour Party. If you sack nurses they won't be in manufacturing; they will be on the dole too.' He gave us his familiar theme: 'Viability for a nation is not the same as viability for a company.' But when he had said all this he concluded disarmingly, 'I haven't made any policy proposals, but we must have a shared analysis.' John Forrester was refreshingly frank. 'I don't know any way of avoiding the type of slump that we've got now.'

One interesting little interlude was an attack by Sam McClusky of the National Union of Seamen on the decision to send in the navy to help our trawlermen. Seaman that he was, he didn't like gunboat diplomacy. Iceland had a tremendous economic case anyway, he urged.

During all this I was trying to read up all my notes for my coming appearance on the radio programme, *It's Your Line*. With a vast department like mine, it is an ordeal trying to be omniscient. In the event, it went very well indeed, helped by a consultant who accused me of having been treated in the private wing of a hospital several times – and recently. I got very uptight with him, while Robin Day was magnificent. When I said to this chap that if he continued to make these allegations he could face an action for slander, Robin intervened to say sternly, 'Not slander, Mr Thornton Holmes, but libel. Your allegations are being broadcast.' The wretched doctor stuttered and climbed down. Great fun – but quite a strain at the end of an exacting day. I relaxed thankfully afterwards with my office chaps, Ted and the producer over wine and cold meats in the upper recesses of the BBC. I hadn't had much time to eat!

Boxes waiting for me when I got home, including a Minute from Henry reporting on the meeting of the Central Committee for Hospital Medical Services held today, which confirmed the decision to take industrial action over pay beds from 1 December by thirty-seven votes to three and called on consultants to hand in undated resignations from the NHS. The action is to continue until the Government agrees to hand the pay beds issue over to the Royal Commission. There had also been a meeting of the Conference of Presidents of the Royal Colleges, which decided unanimously that they could not support any action that might harm patients (and about time too). Apparently the Presidents had been to see the BMA, the HCSA and the juniors to put their feelings about the threatened industrial action 'in the strongest possible terms', but they hadn't got anywhere. With typical gloom Henry concluded, 'The outlook is not good.' For myself I don't think things are going too badly at all. David has come up with another Minute worrying lest the unions, quite understandably, should start to take matters into their own hands. He has come out with the incredible idea that I should forestall this by announcing I was going to suspend the right to do private practice in NHS hospitals as long as industrial action continued. I can just imagine what uproar *that* would cause. Anyway, our legal boys have minuted that I almost certainly have no power to do this.

Thursday, 27 November

Arnold has replied to Norman, thanking him for the information on common waiting lists and adding, 'I will not comment on this except to say that it appears to me the information may well be very helpful to me.' Excellent! I have told Norman, however, that I had better see the PM to put him in the picture before my paper on pay beds, supplementing Ted Short's from the Social Services Committee, comes before Cabinet today. Harold agreed to see me in his study in his best conspiratorial mood. In the few moments I had with him before we had to go down to join the rest I told him that I had met Arnold, who was anxious to mediate. With regard to the reference of the pay beds issue to the Royal Commission, for which the profession is hankering, Arnold accepted that this was out, but he had been very pleased when I told him that a reference of the licensing issue might be possible. He could see my point that, when the legislation on phasing out was announced, there could be a rush of private developments to forestall any possible control system and that we needed a minimum holding power, such as a simple size control. He was 'not unhopeful' that we might reach agreement on these lines. The solution, as I saw it, was therefore that we should introduce a size control of limited duration in the legislation, pending the reference of this question to the Royal Commission. In the meantime I should try to negotiate a voluntary agreement on these lines with the Independent Hospitals Group through Arnold. We could then go ahead with my phasing out proposals on the basis agreed with Social Services Committee. Two things, however, were essential. I must have the power to bargain with the profession through Arnold, who must appear to have wrung something from me. This meant that the negotiations must be dealt with on a 'need to know' basis and I could not tell Cabinet what I had in mind. For that I needed his help. Harold responded to all this very happily and, with a friendly 'leave it to me', he hurried me downstairs.

In Cabinet Ted Short introduced his memo on the conclusions of the Social Services Committee very fairly and helpfully, setting out the arguments for early legislation on the basis of my Bill as well as I could have done myself. I backed up his presentation with dire warnings about the risk of industrial action if we did not act legislatively. The consultants were threatening action from next Monday, I said, and there was a real danger of union retaliation if they went ahead. Stevenson and Grabham had both made it clear that, once Parliament legislated, they would accept it, and Norman Fowler was saying that this issue must be a matter for Parliament. So the best way to reduce the temperature was to get the Bill on the statute book. As for the control over the size of developments in the private sector, this was a holding operation pending further consultations over detailed licensing. I had earlier this week been at County Hall, I continued, where the chairman of the Planning Committee had asked me what he could do about the rush of planning applications for private developments which was already coming in to him and I had had to tell him that, under current planning legislation, he had no powers at all to refuse them, except on environmental grounds. But once we announced we were going to legislate on pay beds these applications would come rolling in to beat any possible future ban. It was essential to hold the line, otherwise the NHS might be severely damaged. All I wanted was authorization to go and consult on this particular package.

As I looked down the table at my colleagues I realized that this Cabinet had no fire in its belly for this particular fight. Mike was leaning forward anxiously, obviously ready to be loyal, but – I must face it – he isn't exactly under pressure from Jack Jones to take up the cudgels for this. But Harold Lever is the impassioned voice in Cabinet for the consultants in private practice who share his bridge tables. *He* was ready to fight for *them* to the last ditch. And so he did. He said he held a 'fundamentally different point of view' from me. (Don't I know it! Only last weekend he kept me on the phone for nearly an hour, telling me that my licensing proposals had caused deep alarm among his friends and begging me to drop them. The pressures on me seem to be all one way.) He went on that it would be a 'major policy change' to give me even a holding power. As it was, I was asking for 'total discretion over every bed'. My proposal to phase out four thousand beds in one year would 'bring the Government down'. And for good measure he added, 'A number of our people would not give Barbara the power she asks.' (I wondered whom he thought he was speaking for? Even the Manifesto Group are firm on this.)

Without the PM's backing I would have been lost. Harold tossed me a note: 'If necessary I'll say that I'm setting up a small committee under my chairmanship to supervise the negotiations. I always control membership and I *won't* tell them the committee will consist of two members only.' (How I blessed myself for having taken the precaution of seeing him earlier!) H.W. then proceeded to employ his familiar technique of getting his own way by obfuscating the atmosphere. He said smoothly, 'I think Harold has misunderstood Barbara's position and certainly my position. I am not trying to pre-empt the situation in the private sector at all. On the face of it what Barbara is proposing is very provocative, but no final position will be taken until there have been consultations. What I suggest is that we take no final decision this morning, certainly on timing, but that we should authorize Barbara in contact with me to consult on this; perhaps to set up a small committee under my chairmanship.' Shirley said tentatively, 'Could we try at every stage to build in as much agreement as possible?' Harold Lever came bulldozing back. 'Why should it be necessary to poison the atmosphere by saying we are taking reserve power?' But the other Harold was a match for him. 'For reasons I regret, there are things I can't mention. I do hope Cabinet would leave the negotiations to us.' One can hardly insult a Prime Minister by saying one does not trust him to negotiate, so the rest thankfully sank back into acquiescence. For once, I had reason to be grateful to Elwyn, who observed with judicial authority, 'The purpose of what is proposed is to ensure that the planning procedures do not pre-empt the outcome of the consultations.' Even Harold Lever was forced to observe, 'I would not object to that.' While all this was going on John Silkin tossed me a note: 'The power is not so drastic – I have power to control office building and Eric Varley has power to control industrial buildings over 1,500 square feet.' But when I signalled to him to speak up and say so he merely shrugged.

Finally, we had a discussion on the imposition of import controls on colour TV tubes. Ironically, here it was Eric who was in favour of this, pending a decision on the future of the Thorn plant at Skelmersdale and the restructuring of the TV tube industry in the UK. Peter opposed on the grounds that he had successfully persuaded the Japanese to increase their export prices of tubes voluntarily and that this agreement would undoubtedly break down if import controls were introduced. Other voluntary agreements with the Japs might be at risk. Of course, it is very difficult for another departmental Minister to assess the validity of all this, but, in any case, it was clear that Harold and Denis are very anxious not to do anything very realistic about their 'selective import controls' package for fear of offending the IMF, and so on. Once one has conceded the main outlines of one's strategy – as this Cabinet has by its decision to go into Europe and in other ways – it is much easier for them to win the argument about detail as well. So Eric lost, Harold summing up that the question was linked to the one about import controls on cars: so, if we didn't do the latter, there would be a stronger case for this and we should wait for the package as a whole to be agreed. My guess is that we shan't do either.

One good development amid the darkness: the press is continuing its attacks on the BMA Council's decision last night to endorse industrial action by the consultants. Even *The Times*, in a leader broadly supporting the consultants on pay beds, says, 'It must be asked whether the ends in view justify all this.' The real danger from my point of view is that the pressure to refer the matter to the Royal Commission may become irresistible and it is something I am determined to avoid at all costs, as it would mean a two-year delay and possibly the loss of any phasing out at all as a result. Even the *Guardian* sports the headline: 'Doctors prepare to quit NHS.' Back at the office, I had a chat with Sir Hector Maclennan, chairman of the advisory committee on distinction awards, about merit awards (whose distribution he has certainly tried to improve); I learn that the Royal Colleges have called on the Prime Minister to intervene. This makes me all the more glad that I have got the secret talks with Goodman going: I am not going to have Harold in on this act, despite the fiction about his setting up a 'committee' this morning.

Norman meanwhile has had a telephone conversation with Arnold Goodman, who said he had been trying to get the BMA to postpone its industrial action until 1 January to allow more time for a solution to be found – but without success. Arnold therefore believes that any overtures by the Government before 1 December would be unwise, as they would give the impression that the Government was prepared to concede all the profession wanted. A letter to the profession early next week might be useful, to be followed by a meeting later in the week. If the PM were to be involved in the meeting 'so much the better'. Norman said he had been discouraging about *that*. They agreed to keep in touch.

Friday, 28 November

The juniors' dispute continues to gather pace. Alarmist reports about its escalating effects continue to come into me. We continue unmoved to develop our strategy for dealing with it. Derek Stevenson has duly let me have the BMA's 'evidence' that there is more money available and I sent it at once to the Review Body for comment. Sir Ernest Woodroofe, the new chairman, has replied helpfully, from our point of view, pointing out that the Review Body 'took account of the kind of factors that Dr

Stevenson referred to in his letter and made due allowance for them within the limits of the evidence available to us'. And he has added, 'Incidentally, to the extent that actual hours contracted for prove to exceed those for which we allowed in coming to our recommendations, so will the total amount paid out for hours above forty-four exceed the £12 million paid in extra duty allowance [EDA] in 1975.' Raymond has suggested to Miss Orr [secretary of the Review Body] that it might help if we were to invite the BMA's own statistician, Sir Roy Allen, to have a private discussion with the Review Body as to the basis on which their recommendations were costed and Sir Ernest has agreed to this. I have passed this offer on to Stevenson and he has accepted it. In the meantime Elinor Kapp and her militant men of the JHDA have continued to let off fireworks from the fringe of all this, furious because the BMA won't agree to include them in the negotiations with me. She has written, jumping at my offer of an independent audit, which the BMA refused. The main argument therefore now lies between her and the BMA, and between the BMA and the board, while I continue to sit tight.

The *Daily Telegraph* continues its attacks on me, saying the time has come to 'relieve' me of my ministerial duties, as my 'personality has become an obstacle to a reasonable solution of the pay beds dispute'. The *Mail* has resurrected the old story about my sojourn in a private ward way back in 1965, plus a picture of me with my sinuses strapped up, and Mr Leonard Kingdom has violated his professional obligation to keep his patients' affairs to himself by making a public attack on me about the time he treated me. We discuss in the office whether we should refer this conduct to the General Medical Council, and decide against. One has really no protection against a press and a profession determined to fight dirty. NUPE is making noises about the resumption of industrial action against private patients if consultants refuse to treat NHS ones – and quite right too. Once again, I begin to feel that the only way we shall get phasing out in the end will be by the direct action of the unions.

Among all this I have had to finalize my speech to the conference of local authority associations on the social services and have added whole chunks on my public expenditure philosophy. I am glad to have got on record my repudiation of the 'new wisdom of the Right', to the effect that public expenditure is less desirable than private. I wonder if the press will take up this obvious discrepancy between my line and Roy's – to say nothing of Harold's.

Monday, 1 December

I told the office that the time has come for me to volunteer a statement to the House on the disputes. David, as usual, was for me lying low, but I resisted this. The office draft of the statement was no good and I had to write it myself over the weekend. We had a good tale to tell, including the offer of an independent audit, which the BMA had refused. Even Norman Fowler couldn't make much of it and on pay beds agreed that the consultants should not take industrial action on a matter due to come before Parliament. But, of course, he pressed for the issue to be referred to the Royal Commission and the Liberals are pressing for that too, so I can see us having difficulties in getting the pay beds legislation through. Well, we'll just have to have a bash. Fowler, of course, ended up with a great attack on me as not only leading the

NHS into 'crisis' but into 'catastrophe'. That doesn't worry me, as it is clear that I have our side behind me. Ian Wrigglesworth is backing me up notably.

At the office discussion we agreed we ought to advise the PM to see Sir Rodney Smith, as the Royal Colleges are taking a correct line against industrial action. It might also be a good way of bringing pressure to bear on the BMA through the Colleges: perhaps they have plucked up their courage again! We all agreed it would be disastrous for the PM to see the BMA: a very different kettle of fish from the Colleges, who keep protesting that they are only interested in 'patient care'. Norman and I then decided we had better keep on Arnold's tail to see how he was getting on with his side of the talks. On the phone Arnold told Norman that he was seeing the BMA at 6.30 that evening. It might be his last meeting with them, as he intended to tell them he disapproved of the industrial action they were taking and could no longer accept a retainer from them. However, if he got the chance he was going to try to persuade them to set down their minimum requirements for a settlement, so that he would know whether it was worth while putting this to me. Yes, it might be a good idea if he and I were to meet before he went along to the BMA. So at 5pm Norman and I repaired once again to Portland Place and once again awaited Arnold's dilatory pleasure.

When he arrived he was as amiable and amusing as ever, his thoughts and ideas darting about all over the place. Could we perhaps agree, he suggested, that the profession should accept legislation to separate pay beds from the NHS, on the understanding that the timing of phasing out would be referred to the Royal Commission for urgent report? I rejected this firmly as the delaying device it so clearly was. Could there be, he continued, a discussion with the profession on the timing and extent of phasing out? On the timing, certainly, I replied. I was very willing to discuss with the profession the difficulties that might arise in certain areas, but it must be understood that all pay beds must go after an agreed period. He then flew a new kite: could there not be some kind of review body to pronounce on what rate of phasing out would be reasonable in different areas, in the light of the build-up of private facilities in those areas? He knew what a reasonable person I was, but regrettably the profession did not have the same confidence in me as he had himself, etc., etc. I probed a bit. If, I said, what he had in mind was some kind of committee containing professional representatives to advise me on what was a fair and reasonable timing in particular areas, I would be glad to consider this, but obviously the final responsibility must rest with the Secretary of State, who was answerable to Parliament. Arnold queried this: were there not statutory bodies, like National Insurance tribunals, which acted independently of the Secretary of State? I said that their role was very different. They merely adjudicated on whether the policy defined by Parliament was being correctly applied in individual cases. Arnold let it go at that.

Once again, when I asked him about licensing of the private sector, he saw no great difficulty in a simple interim control over private developments, pending the reference of the issue to the Royal Commission, to which I have agreed. He then told us that Sir Rodney Smith will be going alone to see the PM on Wednesday. He didn't want to take any of the other Royal College presidents because he apparently had some ideas he wanted to put to the PM: Arnold had no idea what they could be. As for the BMA, Arnold accepted that the PM might well be unwilling to meet them while they were taking industrial action. But he was interested in my idea of an advisory committee. He would try it on the professions and report back.

It was late before I was able to contact Arnold again by telephone. He seemed to have his tail up. The 'dreaded Grabham' had not been at the meeting. Instead, he had been represented by his number two: 'a nice little man with glasses' (presumably Mr Bolt). They would be willing to discuss the basis of a settlement which would involve their accepting that there will be legislation, that pay beds will be phased out, that there should be an agreed timetable and that pay beds should remain 'in particular locations' until alternative private facilities were available. They might accept the withdrawal of industrial action as a condition of the settlement. 'Even Dr Simmons nodded at this proposition,' said Arnold with gratification. But it all depended on one qualification: 'the settlement must be consistent with the Government's desire to preserve private medicine'. At the end of the meeting Arnold had told them he did not wish to be retained, as he disapproved of their action. But, I thought to myself, it can't have been much of a rebuke, because he said he went on to tell them he was 'available to act as an intermediary' without a fee. They had been 'a little hang-dog', said Arnold. But he concluded enthusiastically, 'They are not a bad lot. They were more receptive than at any time I have known them.' They had gone away to think about things overnight and he was meeting them at lunch-time tomorrow. 'If tomorrow,' said Arnold, 'they show an inclination to accept this basis, you should consider it. I could contrive that they made this proposal to you, so that you do not have to appear to be offering it.' If I would meet him after lunch tomorrow he was confident we could settle it in forty-eight hours. Of course, I said I would, though there are a lot of fuzzy edges to his proposals which will have to be explored.

Tuesday, 2 December

I have decided we must keep up the initiative with the juniors by offering another meeting as quickly as possible, but they are clearly nervous at this. I have also written to Stevenson, saying I am willing at any time to resume consultations on pay beds. This has clearly nonplussed the BMA and he has sent a stalling reply, saying he must consult his organizations. Meanwhile the juniors keep in unofficial touch with Jack. Zacharias seems as anxious to do this as Ford and Bell were, and their off-the-record talks with him are an invaluable guide to us.

When Norman came to call for me at the House late this afternoon to take me to Arnold's flat, his face was grim. No. 10, he said, had been on to him to say that the PM had agreed to meet the whole BMA tomorrow with Sir Rodney Smith. I was flabbergasted: meet them while industrial action was going on and when it was clear that the feeling in the country against the consultants was growing? It was impossible. I would have to speak to Harold. Norman shook his head. He had been on to Ken Stowe [the Prime Minister's Principal Private Secretary] personally; the PM was in Rome, but No. 10 had been in touch with him on the phone. He had agreed the meeting and the invitations had already gone out. Moreover, the press had been informed. Norman was as shocked as I was: the insult to me was obvious. Here was I, in charge of the negotiations, and Harold had not even consulted me about this key move. 'Arnold is behind this,' I said bitterly. I could see what was happening: Arnold did not think I was sufficiently pliable and was appealing to Harold over my head with the idea that Harold should take charge of the talks. I could just imagine what would happen then.

I went along to keep my rendezvous with Arnold in one of the intensest furies I have ever felt. Whatever happened to me, I wasn't going to be outmanoeuvred in this way. As usual, Arnold was late and the refined Mrs Roberts served us her now regular routine of tea and thin cucumber sandwiches. The gloom of the flat weighed on us oppressively, but couldn't dampen the anger which was smouldering in me. When Arnold at last appeared, as perfunctorily apologetic as ever, it burst into flames. He soon saw something was wrong and cut short the pleasantries. I let fly at him. Did he know the PM had invited the BMA to a meeting tomorrow? 'Of course.' Would he be attending himself? He believed so; it would be up to the Prime Minister. So he knew the invitation was going? 'Yes.' 'Then,' I said angrily, 'you have wrecked the negotiations.' He was taken aback. Surely not. I told him this step had been taken without consulting me. What he had done was to go to the PM over my head without informing me, while we were still in the middle of our discussions. 'I have never been so insulted in my whole life.' I was the custodian of this Manifesto policy and I was answerable to the party for it. I wasn't going to have the talks taken out of my hands in this way. It was clear I had shaken him and he spent the rest of the time assuring me that the last thing he wanted was to offend me and that he certainly didn't want to take the negotiations out of my hands. I said it was extremely bad for the PM's image to be seen receiving the profession's representatives when they were taking industrial action against the Government. He wouldn't accept this, but did accept my suggestion that all that ought to happen tomorrow was for the PM to listen to what the delegation had to say and then hand them over to me. So we left it at that, though I certainly wasn't pacified, particularly as Arnold is harking back to his idea of an independent review body. All this was cooked up at his lunch-time meeting with the consultants today. One thing he said rankled in my memory. When I said that I didn't think Harold realized that the full meeting was being called, adding, 'He wouldn't do this to me', Arnold hesitated and said almost timorously, 'Are you sure?' 'Have you spoken to him?' I asked, suddenly suspicious. 'Yes,' he replied. 'I was in touch with him in Rome by phone.' So Harold could talk to Arnold and not to me!

Back at the House, I was due to get another hour or so in on my speech on Nye, but first Norman and I had a council of war. We both took the gloomiest view of the situation and I got him to tell No. 10 that I wanted to see Harold before the meeting in the morning. No. 10 replied that the PM would not be back till very late tonight or early tomorrow, but they would phone me in the morning to let me know what they had fixed. Next, I decided I had better send Harold a Minute to await him on his return and I had to sit down and draft it so that Norman could take it back and get it typed. In it I stressed the political dangers that we faced if we were to accept Arnold's package, which seemed to visualize that in certain areas pay beds would be continued indefinitely. I urged that at tomorrow's meeting *no* package should be put on the table, but that Harold should tell the profession to get round the table with me in the negotiations I had offered to resume with them. I added this: 'I would urge you should refuse to discuss any proposals for negotiation at all as this would lead to the suggestion that any eventual settlement had only been reached because you had overruled me and this makes my position untenable.' It was a strong Minute and I was rather pleased with it. I concluded by urging that I should have a talk with him before the meeting. Norman promised to get it over to No. 10 that night.

It was 11pm before I was able to get down to my speech on Nye Bevan and I scribbled away into the small hours, drawing extensively on Mike's biography of Nye. The more I write the more I realize how difficult it is to say anything meaningful on the subject I had chosen, 'The NHS Re-visited', at this sensitive time, and hope that I shall be told to cancel the lecture, even at this late hour. At the very least, it is clear that I must circulate a text for the office to comment on and check.

Wednesday, 3 December

As the PM's meeting with the profession was not until 11.30 I had time to work a bit on my still unfinished speech. Norman phoned to say No. 10 had promised to contact me direct as to when I could have my talk with the PM. At 10.30 I had still heard nothing and decided, with mounting anger, to go down there anyway. I arrived at No. 10 at 11.15. An embarrassed Private Secretary said the PM was busy, but he would tell him I was there. (No explanation as to why they had not phoned me.) I began to realize that, if I had not marched in, they would not have phoned at all. As it was, Harold bowed to the inevitable and, with five minutes to spare, I was ushered into the study upstairs.

Harold was pacing up and down, clearly irritable. He started on a long diatribe as to how he had only got back at 3am and how tired he was – what a time he had had in Rome, bailing Jim out of the 'mess' he had got himself into over our seat at the oil talks.[1] 'I have to spend half my time bailing my colleagues out.' Firmly I directed the conversation to my Minute and then he suddenly snapped at me. He wasn't going to be told he couldn't negotiate. 'What am I supposed to be? A cypher?' He had told Cabinet that he and I were going to do the negotiating and he wasn't going to be told now that he had got to leave it all to me. I held my ground, equally angrily. If he took over the talks now my position would be intolerable. Hadn't he seen John Cunningham's piece in the *Guardian* today? ('The PM's ingenuity in conjuring compromise out of deadlock could produce the basis for a settlement....') 'You pay too much attention to the press,' Harold snapped. That from *him*! I was unmoved by his anger. I don't care a damn what he thinks of me. 'You will be playing into the hands of the

---

[1] A world conference on energy was to open in Paris on 16 December attended by eight delegations representing the industrialized countries and nineteen nations representing the oil-producing and developing countries. The conference was to prepare for international co-operation on energy, raw materials, development and related financial questions. The EEC intended to be represented by one spokesman but the British Government had demanded separate representation, arguing that as an oil producer Britain had different interests from other EEC members. Despite a long wrangle at the preparatory EEC conference in Paris, Britain did not get its separate seat, but was permitted to make separate statements in the oil talks provided it did not say anything contrary to the agreed position of the Community. The Prime Minister was later criticized from all sides of the House for having achieved so little after antagonizing other EEC members.

Opposition,' I continued. 'Their whole line has been that you should be brought in because it is my "personality" that is preventing a settlement. They said that about Nye too, when he was fighting to create the NHS. Do you think Clem Attlee would have intervened to take the negotiations out of Nye's hands at a crucial stage?' At this tense moment a Private Secretary put his head round the door nervously. 'Lord Goodman is waiting downstairs,' he said. So that was it: Harold was prepared to see Arnold and not me! My worst fears were confirmed. 'We'd better go,' said Harold and marched downstairs. Arnold was waiting outside the Cabinet room. I stuck firmly to Harold's heels. They had a few moments of embarrassed conversation, with me standing sternly by. Arnold asked if Harold wanted him to attend the meeting. 'I should think so,' said Harold, elaborately casual. He didn't think they should go into details that morning. Of course, if anyone wanted to put forward proposals, we could agree to consider them. But the detailed negotiations would be for me. 'Of course,' said Arnold placatingly. I trailed after Harold into the Cabinet room, more angry than ever, and stood back ostentatiously while the delegation trooped in and he shook hands.

There they were in force: Sir Rodney Smith (no more above the battle than Grabham himself), Simmons of HCSA (with an icy glare on his face), Lewin, Stevenson, Bolt, the dentists' chap, Wardle of the juniors and some secretaries. As I had told Harold, every one of them a surgeon (except the dentist and the junior), and so hardly representative of the medical profession as a whole. With me sitting rigid beside him, Harold started very tentatively, but nonetheless unctuously. Not a word of reprimand about their industrial action! Instead, he pleased them by opening with the remark that 'we are all at one in wanting to see this dispute honourably solved'. Portentous nods. 'I don't want to get into negotiations,' he continued. 'It's not my job.' Stares at that. He then asked Sir Rodney if he would like to speak. Sir R. did so with his usual unctuousness. The Royal Colleges, he said, 'must speak for the interests of patients'. It was the unanimous view of the Royal Colleges that pay beds should not disappear from the NHS, because it would be 'bad for patients'. (You would never have guessed that he is a surgeon with an extensive private practice.) The Colleges would want to put this view to the Royal Commission, he continued. (Not a word about the Colleges deploring industrial action.)

Lewin then took up the tale. The BMA, he said, would wish the dispute solved as soon as possible. 'If this great profession has been brought to this stage there must be something radically wrong,' he prosed. They believed the Government's policy on pay beds would mean loss of individual choice, loss of independence and a loss to the NHS. 'If you refer this matter to the Royal Commission, we will ask doctors to resume normal working.' Far from resenting the BMA laying down its terms for behaving properly, Harold was at his most mollifying. 'We have fully discussed that,' was all he said. 'There is no point in going over the ground again. I want to get to a situation where negotiations can be resumed with some hope.' And he continued, 'I understand Lord Goodman has been applying his mind to this. Healing is his great profession.' But he added hastily, 'We are not negotiating this morning.' Arnold took up his prearranged cue. He must first make clear, he said, that he had 'ceased to be retained' by the Independent Hospitals Group.

He has made a great virtue of this to me, saying that he had done so because he thoroughly disapproved of doctors taking industrial action; but not a word of this escaped him now. He had a proposal to make that might save the positions of both sides. 'If I may say so, Prime Minister, the tone you have set has been impeccable.' He knew we couldn't reach agreement on the principle, but we might reach agreement on the following. (1) If the Government proceeds with the legislation, doctors do not regard this as grounds for continuing industrial action. (2) There must be consultations about timing. 'Doctors find it difficult to understand the imperative haste to phase out on the basis that some other part of the community has to be satisfied.' (3) The Government has declared its intention to maintain private practice. The manifestation of this would be that phasing out of pay beds should be related in some way to the availability of private practice. 'Some method should be devised – some tribunal – to say there are ample facilities.' This body might say that three pay beds here or there might have to stay for some time – 'even for ever'. The criterion would have to be that there was a call for private medicine. The whole matter would be regulated by a governing body. 'It may not be a proposal that has the formal acceptance of doctors, but can a proposal on these lines be put to them?'

Harold, clearly bog-eyed from lack of sleep, began by saying he was not 'commenting' and then proceeded to ramble on in a 'tone' which delighted them, because it clearly implied the package was acceptable. There was a possibility, he mused, of going ahead with the legislation without waiting for the Royal Commission, with the possibility of putting any 'outstanding matters to the Royal Commission' (whatever that might mean). They nodded approvingly. Arnold said hastily, 'If consultation does not produce fruits we would be delighted to put the outstanding points to the Royal Commission. That would be wholly acceptable.' I froze in my seat. Harold must have felt it, for he hurried on, making matters worse with every word. 'Anything the Royal Commission can do,' he said, 'would be on the basis there would be no net loss of beds or facilities; but at the end of the day there would be no less pay beds in the NHS.' They began to look as puzzled as I felt. 'The run-down of pay beds would be *pari passu* with the increase in private practice outside.' I could contain myself no longer. 'Did you say that some pay beds would stay for ever?' I asked Arnold icily. He replied, 'It is a possibility. But there must be a perceptible need for private medicine.' 'The Royal Commission could give advice as well,' Harold ploughed on, getting deeper and deeper into the mire. 'It could work out the criteria.' They could hardly believe their ears. 'Are we agreeing the right of the Royal Commission to look at the whole question?' asked Lewin hopefully. Harold suddenly pulled himself up. 'No,' he repeated, remembering that line at least. 'Consultations should continue and if they reach satisfactory conclusions that is fine. But if anyone felt the Royal Commission might help—— I'm not saying nothing should happen,' he concluded even more incoherently. Arnold was clearly as foxed as anyone else and could see the trap into which Harold was walking and that I would never tolerate this. 'My plan has no relation to the Royal Commission,' he pointed out. Harold rambled on: 'The final safeguard would form part of the legislation.' Lewin seized his opportunity. 'It would mean a big change in the consultative document,' he said. 'The size of the private sector would be related to market need.' Harold seemed to agree with that.

I was in despair as we drifted towards an implied acceptance of the Goodman plan.

Grabham decided it was the moment for him to tie things down. We must, he said, look at any possible solution and they were grateful to Lord Goodman for putting forward his proposals, 'which might lead to a solution'. They would like to explore them. But the likelihood of acceptance would depend very much on the details: for example, the membership of the Independent Practice Commission and its terms of reference. 'This body would have to command our respect. The terms of reference would have to be the maintenance of private practice in this country.' There would have to be private facilities in every district for people who wanted to use private practice. 'These details will be settled in the consultations the Secretary of State will have,' replied Harold blandly – giving the first indication that the negotiations would be conducted by me, not him. As for private practice, 'the duty of this Commission is to make a reality of that'. Grabham, realizing that they would have to negotiate with me, pressed home his point with his usual doggedness. 'Unless there is that expression, "there must be facilities for private practice", we won't accept.' There must be an on-going exercise for the Commission, he demanded. Harold's only reply was to continue his musing. 'It is a thing for us to consider whether this Commission should make annual reports.' He started to wind things up. 'The Secretary of State will want to consider these proposals thoroughly and immediately. I hope Lord Goodman will continue to make himself available.' Simmons then intimated that the HCSA supported the plan, while the dentist did the same for the BDA. Wardle added, 'Juniors are also very concerned about the future of independent practice in this country.' We turned to the question of a press statement. To my relief, Harold agreed that it would not be right to give an outline of the proposals to the press. Arnold suggested that all we need say was that we had had a valuable talk, 'and each side wants time to consider with a view to resumption of negotiations'. Grabham got in a parting shot. He was, he said, 'most anxious' to get the situation 'absolutely clear'. And he went on offensively, 'I personally would have to say that any such discussions with the Secretary of State would not be likely to be helpful, unless it was along the lines of Lord Goodman's proposals. That is, pay beds are to be maintained by one means or another.' 'I note that,' was all Harold said. They filed out, relieved but still puzzled men. As for myself, I was in a turmoil. Harold had set the scene just as Arnold wanted it. On the other hand, he had at least accepted that he must hand the negotiations to me, so I had won that point. (After this morning's performance I began to suspect he knew he was out of his depth and would make a mess of it.) A treacherous road lay ahead of me but I was determined to try and walk it. The alternative was to resign, ostensibly because I wouldn't even try to find a solution. And I knew how little support I would get for that: none from our wretched cowardly Cabinet, a little from the PLP, some from some unions – and a trouncing from the press. I was in a trap and had to spring it as best I could, even if it entailed the loss of a limb or two.

This time Harold invited me upstairs for a drink with him and Arnold, who was very pleased with himself and full of amity towards me, stressing time and again that of course the negotiations must be with me. He also said he would let me have a copy of his formula. I groaned as I saw it was turned 1pm. 'And I've a Nye Bevan memorial speech to finish writing for tonight,' I said. 'I've got to make a memorial speech too,' said Harold cheerfully. 'Perhaps I ought to cancel it,' I continued hopefully. Both Arnold and Harold waved the idea aside. 'So long,' said Harold, 'as you don't refer to this morning's talk.' He thought a review of what Nye had been through wouldn't be at all a bad thing at the present time, while Arnold positively welcomed it. So I went off to the House to grab a sandwich and scribble away at my last sheets. I had to end with my analysis as to why there was talk of 'crisis' in the NHS and I was rather pleased with it. I got it finished in time for an inescapably urgent meeting at the office, while my slaves typed the speech furiously and distributed it around for comment. At last Brian A-S. and I were on our way to Oxford – so late that there wasn't time to eat properly.

The cinema at the Union was crowded for my lecture, a number of doctors from the Radcliffe Infirmary forming a band across the back of the hall. I had to read the speech, for safety's sake, which is always a nuisance, and I was hoarse with fatigue, but they listened carefully and applauded warmly. One of the doctors was the first of my questioners and he began by congratulating me on a 'brilliant résumé' of the NHS's difficulties. It all went swimmingly and I had to tear myself away. Brian Abel-Smith beamed at me: 'That went very well.' 'Did I say anything I shouldn't in reply to questions?' I asked nervously. 'Not a bit of it,' Brian replied. 'You did marvellously.' I lay in the back of the car all the way home, but was too tired to doze.

Thursday, 4 December

The newspapers have done just what I thought they would do with my speech last night. My enemies (the *Mail*, *Telegraph* and *Express*), who were obviously covering it with their own special reporters, have picked isolated bits out of it to headline 'Barbara rocking the boat' sensation stories. 'Castle Rocks Peace Talks', ran the banner front-page headline in the *Mail*, while the *Express* carried a story about 'Dr Harold's Dilemma' (i.e. me) in his noble attempt to get peace in the NHS. Even the BBC picked out one simple sentence about the 'almost reckless disregard of the needs of patients' to spotlight on the eight o'clock news. 'They're after you again,' said Edna, worriedly clutching her *Mail*. What a beginning to the day! My conscience about last night is completely clear and I don't intend to apologize to anyone about it, but this morning's press is hardly likely to help me in my determination not to let Harold do a sell-out. If he decided to bypass me now the right-wing press will say he is justified. I wish now I had followed my hunch and cancelled the lecture. And yet, I don't know: I think it was quite a distinguished speech, considering how hurriedly I had to throw it together, and I am glad to have this testimony to my beliefs placed so firmly on the record before I go – if go I have to.

When I arrived at Cabinet Norman was waiting worriedly in the foyer of No. 10 with a message from Ken Stowe: 'The PM is very disturbed at reports in the *Mail* and *Telegraph* this morning. Were you correctly reported? If so this was at variance with what was agreed between you and Prime Minister.' I told Norman I would draft a reply to the PM in Cabinet, which I would need typed so that I could keep a copy, and he arranged to send someone over for it. So I had a distracted Cabinet, trying to listen to some complicated issues, like Chrysler, while drafting away. I first pricked up my ears when I heard Harold reporting on his Rome talks. No one raised the question of our seat at the oil talks, except that Jim remarked mildly that the press stories to the effect that he was annoyed with Harold were untrue. There was a light moment when Wedgie raised the question of the decision to introduce European passports. He gave us one of his amusingly vivid little speeches, asking why we had to give up our own blue and gold for 'a bit of purple plastic'. Didn't we realize that it was just small symbolic things like this that roused people most? 'You are turning me into an English Nationalist,' he declared. As I said 'Hear, hear' loudly, Harold said defensively, 'No one is more Kiplingesque than me', at which Wedgie quipped, 'If you can walk with the Commission and keep the common touch', and we all roared. Harold capped it by reciting the next few lines, adding, 'You can't teach me anything about Kipling.' He then assured us there was a 'long way to go' on this matter. No design of the new passport had been agreed. 'I had to make a reservation on the subject of the passport.' Jim asserted that 'people are trying to bounce us'. The first thing he knew about the matter was when he read it in his papers for the conference. But when I asked why we needed to give up our own passport anyway, as we would still have to show a passport in Europe, he replied that he and Harold had agreed to a common passport in principle. So we continue on our relentless way to European uniformity.

Cabinet then turned to Chrysler, the massive papers on which I had not had time to study properly. An acrimonious wrangle soon developed. Eric insisted that Scheme B was totally unviable; that we couldn't get any more out of Chrysler's and had better let them go into liquidation. Willie gave us another of his lugubrious forecasts of utter disaster in Scotland if we let Linwood go. Eric was obviously very angry at some of the things Willie said. 'You're now saying I am in the hands of my officials,' he protested. 'For God's sake!' He is obviously deeply riled at the opposition he is getting over this issue and at the attempt he feels is being made to make it look as if he hasn't done his job properly. (I know the feeling!) 'We pressed and pressed for an examination,' retorted Willie. Mike was milder but still critical: 'I do not think it is reprehensible for this Cabinet to take some short-term views as well as long-term ones. I am all in favour of the long-term reorganization of British industry, but I am also in favour of the survival of this Government.' He urged that we take time to try and improve Scheme B's partial salvage operation. But it was Harold Lever who surprised everyone by his rejection of Eric's orthodox 'close things down and toughen them up' line so loved of the Treasury. 'It has not been made clear to me,' said Harold, 'what has been the outstandingly despicable conduct of Chrysler Corporation.' They had behaved commercially as any company should. 'If this were a case simply of putting money in a non-viable industry I would be with Eric all the way, but we are dealing here with an area where with the bathwater we might be throwing out some very useful babies.' For example, there was the Iranian contract, the heavy vehicle capacity, the Avenger engine and spare part business. Was there not some way of saving the viable parts? 'I am not persuaded that the TUC would not help us save something from the wreck.' And to Eric's fury, he added, 'I don't think we are equipped in government to do business negotiations. First-class Ministers and first-class officials and first-class accountants are no substitute for proper business negotiations.' He was sure there was a case for further examination of Scheme B. Eric was writhing in the sort of misery I have been going through: the suggestion that someone else had to be brought in to do his job over his head. But as it was now 1.15pm the PM muttered something about his Parliamentary Questions, instructed Harold Lever to go into the possibilities between now and tomorrow, and adjourned Cabinet.

I hurried over to the House for a bite of food. As I sat in the dining room of the Commons, chatting to Brian O'Malley and others over lunch, Harold joined us. I was completely relaxed. They are not going to get me trembling before the great man, because I no longer think of him that way. Something very near hate is beginning to smoulder in me. I now realize that the contempt I feel for his behaviour is pretty widespread among the PLP. A number of people have stopped me to ask what the hell is going on. Said Dennis Skinner to me, almost in despair, 'We're not selling out on pay beds, are we, Barbara? For God's sake, that is all this Government has got left.' I could only wring my hands in silent agony, muttering something like, 'You know I wouldn't let you down.' At table, before Harold arrived, Joel had been whispering to me to ask how things were going. 'I'm worried,' I whispered back. 'Harold's attitude worries me.' He replied, 'It's terrible.' Joel also revealed that he wasn't going to stay in the House that night and vote on the Civil List.[1] 'I signed the minority report, saying the Queen should not get a penny unless she revealed her sources of private income, or had them taxed. Harold refused even to go and discuss it with her,' he said contemptuously. (I don't remember this being raised in Cabinet.)

When Harold arrived we chatted generally for a bit. 'You must be going to the same funeral as I am,' I remarked, looking at his dark suit. When he found I was going to the memorial service for Professor Fairley he was quite upset that he wasn't going too. 'My officials must have dealt with this. I wasn't told.' He then spent a long time telling us how he had stayed up half the night when Mrs Fairley returned to this country after her husband's death, in order to ensure that she was sheltered from the press at the airport, insisting that the VIP lounge was made available to her. He had had a warm letter of thanks. (He does genuinely delight in these little acts of kindness.) But when I asked casually, 'How did *your* memorial lecture go?' he went sour. 'Very well,' he snapped back. 'But then I didn't answer any questions.' When I replied that I had answered my questions very well, he snapped again, 'I think you have wrecked the talks.' When I replied coolly that I didn't think I had done any such thing he snarled, 'I don't want to discuss it.' As I left Brian O'Malley came with me, saying, as we walked down the corridor, 'The old man was pretty tetchy today', to which I replied that I was desperately worried. I was in a trap. 'They're trying to outmanoeuvre you,' he replied. 'Look,' I said, 'I can't tell you everything just now, but I am in desperate danger. Just do one thing for me. I have no one rooting for me with the press. Just tell any press pals you've got what a big fight I am putting up in Cabinet for the NHS budget. It might help me a bit.' 'That would be nothing but the truth. Of course I will,' he replied warmly.

[1] See footnote to p. 309.

After a dash to Xavier's for a hair comb-out I went to the office for the meeting which Norman had arranged since we agreed I ought now to put people like David Owen, Pat Nairne, Henry Yellowlees and Jack in the picture about exactly what was going on. To my surprise and relief no one complained about my earlier secrecy, and neither David nor Jack seemed to find the proposed package too dreadful. David began to bubble up with ideas. Patrick Nairne assured me that I must go and see Goodman again tonight, however disinclined I might feel. (My own mood had been to tell both him and the PM to go to hell.) Henry sat hunched in dejected silence and when I asked him what he thought he replied, 'I've nothing to say, Secretary of State.' However, under pressure he did report that he had been at a meeting of medicos yesterday and they seemed to know that talks were going on. One of them had said, 'We're to get a tribunal.' I gathered later from David that one of the reasons for Henry's silence was that he was in high dudgeon at having been excluded from the talks with Goodman. To which David had replied that he had been excluded too, but hadn't taken offence. He perfectly understood there were times when discussions had to be limited to a very small circle. However, David did say casually, 'I don't know whether you want me to come with you tonight.' But when I didn't reply he didn't press it. I feel so encumbered with people who are all trying to get into the act and run things for me that I am determined to get the broad principles of a settlement under my control before I allow anyone else to participate in working out the details. Once again I sympathized with Eric!

Brian Abel-Smith then asked for a quick private word with me. His spies, he said, had told him that the Chancellor had just been to a crucial meeting of OPD [Overseas Policy and Defence Committee of Cabinet], where he had been confronted by a massed array of Chiefs of Staff resisting his proposed defence cuts. It had made Denis 'very angry', because from his own knowledge of the Ministry of Defence he knew the cuts were feasible. This demonstration of the Chancellor's mood is all very fine and encouraging, but I can't help being amused, because I remember how when *he* was Minister of Defence he mobilized against Roy the massed ranks of the Chiefs of Staff, threatening resignation if Roy's cuts went through. Times don't change: only people!

It was almost a relief to have to tear myself away from the office to go to St Paul's for the Thanksgiving Service to Professor Fairley. I had been worried this morning because, half dressed, I discovered a note in my box to the effect that Mrs Fairley had particularly asked people to wear bright colours and in no way suggest this was an occasion for mourning. Unfortunately, the only warm coat I possess is black! I arrived one minute late, raced up the front steps, was mercifully recognized by the usher and was directed up the centre aisle to the front row. I tip-toed up that endlessly long aisle while the clergy manoeuvred into place and the organ boomed. As I sank thankfully into my place next to Alf Morris, Angus Ogilvy [husband of Princess Alexandra of Kent] arrived, looking harassed. 'I had a hell of a job getting in,' he whispered to me apologetically. 'Don't worry,' I whispered sweetly, 'I was late too.' He seemed a nice chap, thankful for being treated normally.

After the service a very respectful chap came up to marshal me for the solemn procession of VIPs back down the aisle after the relatives, thanking me profusely for coming. 'I was determined to,' I assured him. It was only from his conversation afterwards that I divined that he was the chairman of one of the area health authorities. (Trust me not to recognize him! And I still don't know which one.) He led me to the family group, waiting to meet all the important people in that vast audience. And then I discovered that the brave, lovely Mrs Fairley, whose statement on her husband's death had so moved me at the time, was herself dressed in dark colours and was in tears. And then the whole service came alive for me. I could only clutch her hand and say how much I had been inspired by what she had said. Then I was taken the round of her teenage children, all in good great human tears. 'What a Dad!' I whispered to the son. 'I know,' was all he could manage to reply. I was so glad I had insisted on going. I know from my own memories of Marjorie's funeral that it *does* help when busy people from high places make the superhuman effort to pay their tribute.

After that the return to Arnold's flat seemed like the descent into the unprincipled and the uninspiring. Once again, Arnold kept us waiting for ten minutes or so. I suspect that gives him a kick: the man who can keep Cabinet Ministers waiting and who knows he has direct access to Prime Ministers. (At least, to *our* Prime Minister.) He started by referring to my Oxford speech, of which I had, for self-protection, sent him a copy. He was typically bland about it. 'I must say I found it remarkably moderate. Not a bit what I would expect from you.' And he assured me affably that there had been no excitement about it among the doctors – 'merely at No. 10'. 'Then you had better tell Harold that,' I said firmly. The smilingly deprecating Mrs Roberts had produced the usual tea tray and thinly exquisite cucumber sandwiches. Arnold offered me something stronger, but I plumped for tea. I have noted that Arnold himself doesn't seem to drink alcohol: it may be weight-watching but it is part of his strength. It is a sign of someone who doesn't need his ego boosting.

I was conscientiously relaxed and reasonable, determined to escape one jaw of the trap: 'She was an impossible woman with whom to negotiate.' But I found Arnold was anxious too. My attack on him on Tuesday had obviously hit home and he spent a lot of time making clear that the last thing he wanted was to bypass me and therefore make my position impossible. So that made progress easier. We went through the formula he had produced for Harold following Wednesday morning's meeting. 'Harold asked me if I could remember what we had offered, so I tried to set something down,' he said casually. The only sticky point was item three; the great concession Harold has allowed Arnold to exact from us, i.e. that the phasing out of pay beds should be subject to the 'solitary safeguard' of the setting up of an 'independent commission'. This, said Arnold's draft, would be composed of three persons appointed by the Government 'after consultations with the professions' (no mention of the trade unions with which this Government is supposed to have a special relationship!). It was this commission (not the Secretary of State) which would certify 'from time to time' that pay beds could be dispensed with in any particular district, because 'sufficient accommodation and facilities for the reasonable operation of private medicine' were available in that particular district. Here was the threat to our whole policy which I had to defuse as much as possible.

I began by saying that I didn't like the word 'commission', for obvious reasons and preferred a board. 'Eminently reasonable,' was Arnold's comment. Secondly, I thought there was a flaw in the logic of the profession's argument: if they said that their aim was to ensure the continuance of private practice *either* in the form of pay beds *or* of private facilities outside the NHS, they ought to be ready to allow us to dispense immediately with all those pay beds in areas where private facilities clearly existed (e.g. inner London). As a show of their good faith, and in order to make the compromise more acceptable to our own side, could we not insert the first list of pay beds to be phased out as a Schedule to the Bill? (This idea has been forming in my mind, as I have thought and thought how we could salvage some of my original policy and avoid the accusations of a 'sell-out'.) Arnold clearly thought this was a very fair suggestion and said that he would put it to the profession's representatives, even suggesting that as many as 2,500 beds might come into this category, though he amended this rather hastily later to 1,000 beds. We could then, I suggested, have three categories of beds for phasing out: (a) the obvious ones, on the basis of the profession's own principles: to be done quickly through the Schedule; (b) those in middle-sized towns, like Chester, where alternative private facilities could be built up reasonably quickly (which could also be in the Schedule, though with a different date), and (c) those in the really difficult sparse areas where it might never be possible to make private facilities commercially viable. Here the terms of reference of the tribunal would have to allow a great deal of latitude and it might be that one or two pay beds would continue for a considerable time; but there must not at any price be the implication that some pay beds would continue in perpetuity. There must be a final date by which they and the board would go. Again, Arnold said he thought all this was 'eminently reasonable' and that he had always visualized a provision that, when pay beds in any area sank to a derisory level, the discretion to phase out could be switched back to me.

Thirdly, I said that where we retained pay beds for phasing out by the tribunal, common waiting lists should operate. Arnold has always liked the idea of common waiting lists and said at once that the profession would accept this for urgent cases. I said this was 'no go', because there were no waiting lists for urgent cases in the NHS. It was the non-urgent cases that caused the queue jumping – i.e., cold surgery, like hernias. He said he would put it to his side, but he saw difficulty. Fourthly, I asked if the profession would accept a ban on private development while the consultations went on about licensing and he said he saw no difficulty in this. I even suggested that the tribunal or board, once it had got into its stride and won everyone's confidence, might develop into the body for licensing private practice. He paled at this and asked me not to raise it at this stage.

Finally, I insisted that I must carry the unions with me at every stage; otherwise we should only exchange one form of industrial action for another. Arnold was shrewd enough to see the force of this and said he was constantly impressing on his chaps that they must take the unions into account: a concept, he implied, that was contrary to their whole instincts. Summing up, Arnold said he was meeting them all at lunch tomorrow; he would put all this to them and if their reaction was reasonable, he suggested that the next stage should be for me to meet them all at his place tomorrow night with a view to clinching things. Once that was done he would tell the PM that they should go into formal negotiations with me on Monday. Speed was essential. In this way my position would be safeguarded: the unwitting offence he had caused me would be expunged (and, by inference, Harold would be kept out of it). I agreed this readily, on one proviso: that I would need to put all this to my union contacts at lunch tomorrow – if I could assemble them in time. And if Arnold ran into any difficulties on any item in the proposals I had made, he could ring me at the Gay Hussar, so that I could put it to the unions over lunch. Arnold thought this was excellent and told Norman they must swap telephone numbers of our respective lunching places. My spirits began to rise.

Norman and I raced to the House to set up the arrangements. We found everyone else at the office had gone home, it was so late, but we soldiered on single-handed. Norman really is superb. This is the sort of service you get from a civil servant when his heart is in your policy. Eventually I got home, made myself an omelette and went to bed.

Friday, 5 December

First, I had to get through Cabinet, with my mind only half on Chrysler again. Yesterday Harold had asked for my comments on the Goodman formula to be put in his weekend box, which I had thought was rather leisurely. Then the message came: would I send them to him by 2pm today? So Norman had the job of drafting something for me hurriedly and sending it to me in Cabinet for me to sign. But just as the Chrysler discussion started a nervous Private Secretary came up to me to whisper that the PM wanted to issue a press statement at once to say that, in view of the progress of discussions, no formal consultations would take place before the weekend. The PM also gathered that the parties might be getting together this evening and, if progress was satisfactory, he would issue a letter to the BMA tonight or tomorrow inviting them to formal talks on Monday. I minuted back that the press statement was okay, noting once again that Arnold was in much closer and more regular touch with Harold than I was – which was a strange way to run a government, to say the least.

I then turned my attention to Chrysler in time to hear Harold Lever admitting that, as a result of his examination of all the material, he had come to the conclusion that Scheme B was not on. 'Eric is 150 per cent right in rejecting this offer.' A once-for-all payment without responsibility for future losses was not on (something Eric has been saying from the start, so he looked smug). But Harold Lever then went on to make a more valid point: namely, that we had got to give much more attention to the presentational aspect. What we had not done was to tell Chrysler what *we* were prepared to offer and put the odium on them of turning down a reasonable offer by us. A lot of members of Cabinet agreed with this tactic. Mike played his usual emollient role, but urged that there must be a positive alternative to Scheme B based on the nationalization of Linwood 'and some other parts'. Peter stressed the importance of keeping the Iranian contract and trying to get British Leyland to pick up some of the bits by offering them extra money. He urged that there *must* be import controls for what was left of the British car industry. Wedgie gave us one of his scintillating analyses of our industrial problems. He rejected Scheme B as 'another example of the long retreat of British industry'. What we were doing was 'to bribe companies to stay as long as they are willing to stay and to bribe workers to take the sack when the companies no longer want to'. We were committed to run down the coal mines, run down the railways and now to run down the motor industry. We had got to stop the rot of decline in British industry. 'My policy is very simple: to defend what we have, even if its equipment is lousy, defend it if necessary behind protective walls and then reconstruct it with the help of workers in the industry and make it viable. The real case for viability comes from the shop floor.' We should 'nationalize the City function'. I thought to myself that this would go down with party audiences to tumultuous applause, but the constant flaw it seems to me is that Wedgie has never faced up to (or asked his followers to face up to) the problem of where the money would come from, and the sacrifices we would have to make, while we were taking over and reconstructing all these unviable companies. Denis muttered that the most difficult part of the package was import controls. Ortoli had been 'very nasty' when sounded out about them. They would only be conceivable if Chrysler closed and if they were limited to one year in the first place.

Eventually we all accepted Lever's presentational point and sent him and Eric off to see Riccardo again and put a firm offer to him of a kind we found acceptable. In the general tetchiness I recognized the sour note of mid-term fatigue that seems to affect every Government these days when they realize the problems they are struggling to master are well-nigh insoluble.

In the meantime I had sent Harold another note: 'PM, I assume that, in view of your conversation with Lord G., you do not now want the comments on his proposals you asked for yesterday.' Harold replied: 'Correct. He didn't make any comments or discuss substance, except to express enthusiasm for (and hopes of getting progress on) a *joint waiting list*. You and he carry on. He and you can keep me informed, though I'm a bit inaccessible.' So he's too busy to horn in, thank God! Which is a blessing because the joint waiting list is a non-starter with the profession in any realistic terms, but is just the sort of thing he would be likely to fasten onto. I think that he is feeling less anxious to get involved in this mess following the horrible pasting he got in the House yesterday over the oil talks. Today he has had the worst press since we came in in February 1974.

I picked up David for our lunch and told him, to his delight, that I'd like him and Patrick to come along to the talks with Arnold this evening. 'I'll cancel my meeting at Chichester tonight,' he said eagerly. The lunch with our union friends was, as usual, in Victor's cosy little private room at the Gay Hussar, of which we are rapidly becoming the most devoted customers. We had managed to rustle up Alan Fisher, Audrey Prime and Peter Jacques and I outlined the rough and ready deal I had struck with Arnold last night. They took it far better than I had dared to hope. Peter Jacques shook his head a bit: 'We've given a lot away already,' he muttered, but Audrey told him categorically: 'We could bring the Government down on this', while Alan admitted that, if we got a Schedule in the Bill getting rid of a considerable number of pay beds at one stroke, his members would feel they were getting somewhere. I got the feeling that they all realized how grimly angry the consultants were, what damage they could do to the NHS and how difficult it was to get our policy through Cabinet. 'You've done marvellously, Barbara,' said Audrey warmly.

But the promised call from Goodman reporting progress with his own side never came through. Jack reported that Norman had not even been able to find out where Arnold was lunching! He had gone to ground, leaving no trace. So we went back to the office more irritated with Lord G. than ever. In the car David remarked what a marvellous article Peter Jenkins had written in the *Guardian* that day, supporting us all the way. 'Yes, but he's managed not to include a single kind word about me,' I grumbled. 'They praise the policy but I don't get a flicker of recognition. Yet if it weren't for me pay beds would never be phased out.' 'That's absolutely right,' Jack and David chorused at once. 'I'll have a word with Peter,' said David. But it won't do me any good. Yet for the policy to succeed at all I *had* to become hated by the medical profession. My only consolation is the flood of letters of support that have been coming in to me, particularly the remarkable letters I have received about my phone-in programme with Robin Day. They are a great reassurance to my anxious soul.

Back at the office I called an urgent meeting on the juniors. They have never been mentioned at the Goodman or No. 10 talks and yet their action is doing far more damage than the consultants' is. The break-away JHDA is trying to horn in on the act by publicly taking up my offer to the BMA of an independent audit of the money we say is available for the juniors, and Dr Kapp, their militant chairman, has had letters in the press attacking me for not responding. We therefore decided to allow the Association to put their 'evidence' on the amount available to officials. This was promptly misrepresented in the press as an agreement to meet the Association myself and equally promptly Derek Stevenson rushed to attack me publicly as 'adding confusion upon confusion'. The BMA is clearly worried at the way the JHDA is taking the initiative and has written to me saying the BMA, too, have got evidence that the latest figures of EDA claims show a big increase and agreeing to my offer of an audit, provided we take the figures up to 5 October. We agreed that we should respond positively to the BMA, while insisting on meeting them to discuss the whole matter next week.

While we were in the middle of this meeting, the phone call came from Arnold at last. Norman reported that Arnold was clearly far from 'clinching things' but nonetheless wanted me to meet them at his place that evening. Arnold suggested that I and my chaps might come along first so that he could put us in the picture over what he saw as the difficulties. Norman had thereupon fixed for us to go along at 6pm. This meant cancelling the phone-in programme I was scheduled to do with Capital Radio. George Gale was extremely abusive to Norman about it, though I had been warning him for some time that I might have to let him down. He obviously didn't believe the cancellation was unavoidable and of course I couldn't tell him why, so we just had to sit mum while a few more insults were hurled around our heads. There has been another nasty story about me by David Loshak in today's *Telegraph*, echoing more demands by the medical profession for my resignation. They are still apparently waiting hopefully for a Wilson initiative to 'break the deadlock'. Even the *Guardian* has a piece expressing surprise that the 'Wilson peace plan' has not yet been delivered to the doctors. If they only knew there will be no Wilson plan! But I've no doubt I shall be castigated for any breakdown.

We had a hurried office confab on the line we should take at tonight's talks. Officials have been beavering away at a rough outline of what beds the Schedule might contain region by region and area by area. I insisted that the Schedule was crucial to the whole exercise: without it the unions would never accept the compromise.

Since Patrick had a funeral to attend and could only join us later, David, Jack, Norman and I made our way to Portland Place alone. The tea tray was waiting and we gathered that the profession's representatives had been herded into the dining room so that Arnold could report to us how things were going. Apart from one or two niggling points (e.g. their fear that the legislation might be amended by backbenchers during the passage of the Bill), the main stumbling block was the Schedule, which the profession said they could not agree to before the passage of the legislation, because this would seem like conniving in the whole policy. When I offered to have completely private discussions with them about the selection of beds for the Schedule, Arnold didn't seem to think this would help. He then trailed a whole series of ideas: obviously his own. Why not get over the difficulty by laying down a finite period of existence for the board? It could be three, eight or ten years, he said airily. (A big difference there, I thought. I could see the profession accepting three years!) And, continued Arnold, when there were only two hundred or so pay beds left, we could consider handing them back to the Secretary of State to deal with at her discretion.

I replied that the important thing was that the phasing out procedure should not become a device for retaining pay beds permanently. Could we not agree that pay beds could be withdrawn in any area when, after a reasonable period, it was clear that the private sector was not going to provide alternative facilities? Wouldn't that be proof that there was no real demand for private medicine? Arnold could, of course, see the logic of this and assured me he had already suggested to the profession that, when pay beds were down to three or four in any area, that ought to be accepted as proof that there was no great demand for private facilities. And he launched into his favourite illustration about 'Cullompton', the little town where there will never be a market for a private clinic or hospital: but he always uses this illustration in two different ways – to suit two different audiences. To me he suggests that the small demand for private medicine in an area like this would justify abolishing pay beds altogether on the *de minimis* principle. To the profession he argues that just because it would never be worth any commercial enterprise's while to provide private facilities in a small place like this, the formula ought to lay down that pay beds would have to be retained in local hospitals as the only way of guaranteeing the right to practise private medicine. He is as slippery as an eel and I knew I should have to be very wary indeed. But he assured me that, although the profession's representatives waiting outside were highly suspicious of me, the dreaded Grabham was not as hostile as he had feared. They might accept that the Government should review the arrangements after a certain period, though he couldn't guess what period they might accept. He even thought the profession might be willing to explore my idea that there should be a standstill on private development. I retorted that my minimum condition was a Schedule and a time limit on the board's existence.

At this point we decided to call the others in. They were there in force: from the BMA, effectively led by Grabham, to Simmons of the HCSA (so the BMA is still looking over its shoulder at the breakaway union!), and the gentle Allen of the dentists. And there among this partisan group was (surprise, surprise!) Sir Rodney Smith of the 'above the battle' Royal Colleges. They trooped into Arnold's sitting room in a kind of defensive tension. Arnold, presiding from a deep armchair, was at his most genial. He didn't think, he said, that we could reach agreement that evening, but we could clarify a number of points. The starting point was that an independent body must be set up to control the phasing out of pay beds, as suggested in the proposals he had put to the PM. (I recognized that I had no choice but to accept this, while Arnold had obviously convinced the other side that they had to accept that legislation would be introduced.)

In the discussion which followed Grabham made all the running: he is by far the ablest (and toughest) negotiator they have got. He was backed all the way by Sir Rodney Smith, fighting hard to retain the surgeons' private practice interests. It was soon clear there were two main points. The first was my idea of a Schedule of beds to be phased out immediately, drawn up by me and included in the Bill. Here again Arnold had obviously convinced them that this was my sticking point, but Grabham was tenacious in his attempt to limit the effect of this, saying that the profession would not be willing to help draw up the Schedule in advance of legislation and trying to get the selection of the beds – and even the number – left open till after the Bill was passed, possibly being referred to the independent board. I wasn't having that and was irritated when David jumped in to suggest that the Schedule might be left out of the original Bill and only included after Second Reading. There might also, he suggested, be some 'flexibility' about the pace of phasing out the beds in the Schedule. Alarmed, I insisted that the legislation must contain a firm date for this.

Arnold tried to divert me by talking about common waiting lists, clearly hoping that if we were to get this it would make the whole phasing out unnecessary. And so it might, but I knew the profession would never agree to something which took away the main reason for going private: i.e. queue jumping. And sure enough Grabham proceeded effectively to demolish the whole idea by saying the profession would agree to it for urgent cases only and then only if there were what he called 'reciprocal arrangements' for private patients. We agreed to leave that issue aside.

The second main point was on specialized facilities. It suddenly became clear that this was Rodney Smith's one real concern and he was strongly backed by that other surgeon, Mr Bolt. The point that emerged was this: the right to do private practice for top surgeons like them depended on their having access to the specialized facilities in NHS hospitals because, with very few exceptions, the private sector could not afford to provide them. As David Owen pointed out, even the Wellington Hospital has no heart or lung facilities. And there were certain other highly specialized fields – such as radiotherapy and neurosurgery – where it would be extremely expensive, and often impossible, for the private sector to duplicate these facilities. Could not, said Mr Bolt almost pleadingly, the surgeon or doctor who did very specialized work continue to have access to the NHS facilities on an occasional basis? Grabham insisted that every doctor or patient ought to have access to NHS facilities as of right and pointed out that the private use of these facilities would be very limited.

I had to think very quickly about this new point. I could see the dangers, but also the advantages. On the one hand, if not properly controlled, this concession could provide a loophole for private practice which could undermine the whole exercise. On the other, the last thing we wanted was to stimulate the private sector to duplicate expensive facilities and to lure our best surgeons and nurses away from the NHS. Besides it wasn't in the field of this kind of urgent surgery that queue jumping was taking place. If we were to charge the full economic cost for the use of these facilities, there would be precious few people who would want to pay the high fees when the same facilities were available equally readily without paying for them. Finally, I could see using this concession as a lever to get my own way on other crucial points such as the Schedule. I therefore said that, if I were to consider it, I should want agreement on the Schedule and on the criteria the independent board was to follow in phasing out the remaining beds. (I had already made up my mind that one of the criteria should embody Arnold's *de minimis* principle.)

By this time it was 11pm and, despite the coffee, sandwiches and drinks Arnold had provided, we were all feeling a bit jaded by the intensity of the discussion and the oppressiveness of that sombre room. Arnold said we should all go away and try to draft a document and he suggested we should meet again on Sunday evening to finalize it. Both Grabham and I put in parting shots. I insisted that a lot was being demanded of me and that in return I would need agreement on dividing pay beds into three categories: those which could go at once; those in areas where a reasonable time was required to enable alternative facilities to be built up; and a third category where the odd pay bed might linger for a longer time, though not indefinitely. For his part Grabham insisted with his usual arrogance that the maintenance of industrial peace in the NHS was a matter for me, not for them. Because they would continue to oppose the legislation, they would not be willing to sign any agreement formally, though, if they were satisfied with its terms, they would call off their industrial action.

On that high-handed note we broke up, but I couldn't help feeling we'd done pretty well. I am beginning to see the shape of an agreement which will safeguard the things which are most important to me and which the unions and our own people will find tolerable. I arranged to meet David and officials at the department on Sunday afternoon so that we could draft a document. At least, I thought as I was driven down to HCF, I shall have a peaceful Saturday.

Saturday, 6 December

It was not to be. I was just going through my boxes when a special messenger arrived, bringing an envelope. It was from David at his most typical. In a covering Minute he said he had cancelled his engagements in Plymouth that night in order to send me a draft statement to put to the consultants which he thought that, even if they rejected it, would strike 'reasonable opinion in the country' as a peace formula. With typical impetuosity he enclosed two spare copies so that I could send one to Arnold Goodman and one to the PM, in the hope that Harold would ring Arnold and tell him he must accept it. (Little does he know my Harold!) David even visualized Arnold being forced into a corner by Harold so that I could 'formally' call in both sides on Monday morning and make a statement to the House on Monday afternoon.

As I read the draft statement my heart sank. True, David was showing his usual inventiveness. His ability to initiate answers to detailed aspects of a problem always impresses me, but his tendency to trim at the first sign of opposition worries me. What he himself called the 'key proposal' of his draft was the suggestion that instead of the Schedule to the Bill being drawn up by me, the independent board should be set up immediately to examine which pay beds could go quickly and publish its first report in time for its findings to be incorporated as a Schedule to the Bill. It was an ingenious idea and David was obviously very proud of it as getting us over the 'vital problem' of the Schedule to the Bill which, he wrote, 'seemed a major stumbling block with the doctors last night'. Recognizing that the list which came out of this process could be 'very small', David suggested that this first round of beds should be phased out within six months 'to protect us against the wrath of the unions'.

What David couldn't see was that this would be a major surrender on my part – and at the very moment when I was confident we were winning on this point. I got on the phone to him immediately to tell him this just wasn't on. I liked certain points in his draft, but on the crucial issue of the Schedule I was not prepared to budge. It was a clear quid pro quo for the other concessions I was being asked to make, particularly in the field of specialized facilities. We ought to be thinking of ways of preventing the abuse of these facilities; there ought to be some reference in our agreement to common waiting lists and, above all, we ought to strengthen the criteria for phasing out pay beds by including a broad declaration in the Bill to the effect that its purpose was to separate private facilities from NHS hospitals. David climbed down at once in his disarming way and said he could see my point. We agreed to amend his draft along these lines when we met the following afternoon.

The press continues its alarmist talk about the effects of the industrial action on the NHS. The *Daily Mail* quotes the personnel officer of the Brent and Harrow AHA as warning that 'accident and emergency services could break down from next Monday'. This is all grist to the consultants' mill, but I remain convinced that they are as ashamed and half-hearted about their industrial action as ever they were and would be glad of a chance to get off the hook, if they could salvage something from the wreck. The main thing is to keep our nerve; to give them what reasonable safeguards we can and to give nothing vital away.

Sunday, 14 December

The end of one of the most intensive weeks of my ministerial life, during which I have battled with Arnold Goodman and the consultants to an uneasy compromise over the pay beds issue, had an all-night session with the junior doctors to reach a settlement of their dispute and fought a great battle in Cabinet over public expenditure. There has been no time to do a daily diary or even to eat or sleep properly. This weekend has been an almost farcical climax during which I have scarcely been off the phone as I have concluded quadripartite negotiations with Arnold, David, Patrick Nairne and Norman to try to tie up a pay beds agreement in time for my statement in the House tomorrow.

The week started last Sunday when David, Patrick, Jack, Norman, Gedling and I assembled at the department at 2.30pm to prepare for our further meeting with Goodman's men. I arrived from HCF bearing a bottle of milk. I wasn't going to be left all day without a cup of tea! The deserted building added to the macabre atmosphere of that Sunday afternoon conspiracy as we gathered round the table in my room. Private Office was empty but for Norman and the typist he had arranged to have standing by to type any document that we produced. I found that the irrepressible David had come in early and redictated his draft statement to take account of the points I had raised with him. His second draft was a great improvement. He had dropped the offending proposal to let the independent board draw up the Schedule and left it to the Government to draw up instead, after consultation with the medical profession. He had included my suggestion about the 'broad declaration', while on common waiting lists he had produced the ingenious idea that the Bill should instruct the independent board to make recommendations within six months of Royal Assent as to the possibility of introducing them. He had strengthened the safeguards against the abuse of the concession on specialized facilities by providing that I, as Secretary of State, would have to be satisfied that there would be 'no detriment' to NHS patients and that these facilities could not be provided in the private sector to a 'satisfactory standard'. So I would retain final control of whether, where and to what extent they were made available to private patients and would ensure that the private patients were charged the full economic cost. He had also had the bright idea of providing that private patients should only be admitted to these facilities on the same basis as NHS patients: a common waiting list! Finally we all agreed he had got the criteria broadly right. Once again I was conscious of how well David and I complement each other: he bubbles with ideas and has a far greater knowledge of the medical scene than I have; I stubbornly defend the main political principles involved and keep a wary eye on every line of the text to make sure they are not being eroded. We make a good pair.

We went through David's draft line by line and word by word for nearly three hours. I insisted on the need to keep referring to private 'facilities' and not just 'beds', as I was determined to end private out-patient facilities as well as pay beds – a point on which I have had some argument with David. Patrick was magnificent, throwing himself wholeheartedly into the job of helping me to carry out my policy. Having redrafted extensively, we left the typist coping with the document on the understanding that Norman would come back for it and went off to Arnold's flat, leaving poor Gedling scribbling away at a Minute for the PM.

At Portland Place we found that Arnold had obviously been having trouble with his principals. He ushered us into the dining room, saying apologetically that his discussions were still going on in the other room. There then ensued one of those

French farce situations with Arnold going backwards and forwards between the two groups. We outlined our proposals to Arnold verbally. He indicated that he personally thought they were reasonable, but every time he reported to the other room he came back with new queries and difficulties. We then gathered that some drafting was going on and that someone had been sent off to get a document typed at BDA House. Eventually Arnold brought copies in to us, rough-typed on sheets of paper torn out of an exercise book. It was headed: 'Memorandum of tentative proposals by Lord Goodman for consideration to both sides on the basis of which the Government will then submit a plan for approval to the doctors.' So the myth that the profession was not 'negotiating' was being carefully preserved!

It was a raggedly-worded document, bearing all the signs of having been put together by a bunch of harassed and disunited men. It incorporated the 'broad declaration' for which we had asked, but apart from that it was terrible. It dodged the issue of the Schedule; provided that the board should continue in operation for an 'initial period' of ten years, with further renewals at five-yearly periods as long as the board considered that necessary; and suggested that all the members of the board should be appointed in consultation with the medical profession and preferably by the Lord Chancellor rather than the Government. Finally, it made no clear provision for pay beds to be phased out where the private sector was making no effort to provide alternative facilities. Despite all the talk on Friday night we were back almost to square one. After we had groaned over it for some time, we suggested to Arnold we should take it away and let him have our comments the following day. It had been a tiring day and we were all thankful to get to bed.

There were, of course, a pile of things for me to do when I got into the office on Monday morning. First and foremost I had to have an office meeting on the juniors at which we agreed the letter I should send to Stevenson. I pointed out that, while we should agree to the independent audit covering the extra duty allowance figures up to the latest available date, it could well be Christmas or later before we had the figures up to 5 October for which they asked. So I stressed in the letter that it would be intolerable if industrial action by the juniors were to continue till the October figures were available. I wanted us to discuss all this at our meeting with them the next day. I made the tone of the letter reasonable but tough.

Next there was Professor Mittler to see. He is thrilled with his new job as head of the National Development Group for the Mentally Handicapped. I also had to clear my PQs for tomorrow and have my last desperate briefing for tomorrow's PESC Cabinet. Brian Abel-Smith had, as usual, produced me some excellent stuff.

At last I was able to turn to the extraordinary document Goodman had handed us the previous night. It was obvious that we ourselves would now have to put in an alternative one and I had spent part of the morning scribbling out the draft for which Arnold had asked. In it I placed the Schedule firmly in the centre of the stage. I also insisted that consultations on the composition of the independent board must not only be with the medical profession, but with 'other NHS staff'. We mulled over my draft for some time and finally produced a document with which we were pretty pleased and which covered all our points on the Schedule, common waiting lists and reserve licensing powers, though we decided not to make any reference at this stage to the number of pay beds to be included in the Schedule or the exact period within which they would have to go.

We rushed the document to the profession's negotiators, arranging to meet them again at Arnold's place at 8.30pm, hopefully to finalize things. I then had to look in at Home Policy Committee before repairing to Portland Place with Patrick Nairne, David, Norman and Jack. When we got there we found the negotiators had not arrived and we gathered from Arnold that they were still arguing heatedly over our document, though he himself had described it to us as a fair offer 'which a reasonable man would have little difficulty in accepting'. By this time we were starving and Arnold took pity on us, calling on the tireless Mrs Roberts to rustle us up some food. She produced some excellent cold meat and salad and a bottle of wine, on which we fell ravenously. 'Poor Arnold will be ruined if these discussions drag on much longer,' I remarked sympathetically. Still no negotiators, though bits of their queries and arguments were relayed to us through Arnold from time to time. Eventually, at 9.45pm, we had to leave for the 10pm vote with Arnold shrugging his apologies. He would try to get some sense out of them and let us have their coherent comments the next day. At the House, the faithful Norman still in attendance, I okayed a Minute to the PM setting out the state of play and adding mischievously: 'I believe Lord Goodman is beginning to realize the difficulties we have in getting the professions to agree among themselves.'

Tuesday morning was, of course, the PESC Cabinet. I got up early to refresh my memory on the key points I had to make in defence of my beloved NHS. I was glad I did, because I needed every one of them. Harold opened by saying that, as a result of the bilateral talks Joel has been having with us all, £2,600 million cuts had already been agreed towards the required £3¾ billion. He praised us all for being so co-operative. However, continued Harold, we were still £1,150 million short of the figure the Chancellor needed and we had to decide how the money should be found in the light of the list of options the Treasury had circulated. (We also had in front of us a possible package prepared by CPRS but no one took any notice of that.) Denis rubbed in the point by giving us another homily about the disastrous consequences of not reaching the full figure, adding with his usual unscrupulousness that this was all the more essential because the figure of £3¾ billion had leaked. (I bet he leaked it.) For full measure he said he had consulted the TUC about what should be the priorities, but they had refused to play. His final *coup de grâce* was that the biggest contributions would have to come from the big spenders: Health and Social Security, Environment and Defence. I was at bay.

Harold then called on me and, though I say it I shouldn't, I made the best speech I have ever made in Cabinet. I had pared down the mass of figures the department had given me to a few key points and they came tumbling out of me. The cuts proposed for the health and personal social services would, I said, mean *absolute* reductions overall and a reduction in expenditure on the NHS for the first time in its history, at a time when demographic and other factors meant we needed 1½ per cent growth on the health side and 2 per cent growth per year in the personal social services just to stand still. I had been prepared to accept a standstill at the already reduced level for 1976–77, but anything else was impossible. On both NHS revenue and capital we needed 1 per cent growth a year just to take account of the fact that people were living longer. Over the next ten years there would be half a million more people over seventy-five years of age and the CPRS document was just plain 'illiterate' in saying this trend would be offset by the fall in the number of children. Older people used the health services more often, stayed in hospital longer and needed more intensive care. The over-sixty-fives cost the hospital and community health services five times as much per head as a child under sixteen; the over-seventy-fives nearly eight times as much. Children occupied 14 per cent of acute beds; the elderly occupied 37 per cent.

The other $\frac{1}{2}$ per cent of annual growth I was asking for was needed just to keep pace with the increased cost of medical technology. Head x-ray and some radiotherapy equipment cost thirteen times more in real terms today than it did twenty years ago. Yet when the present equipment broke down it had to be replaced by the new, more costly one. This wasn't 'improvement', it was necessity, if the NHS was not to deteriorate into a second-class service. Further transfers from capital would merely create a frightening deterioration in our capital stock for the next decade when we already had a far worse legacy of out-of-date hospitals than we had of houses or schools, thanks to long years of neglect of the NHS. The cuts the Treasury were demanding would mean something like a moratorium on new hospital starts and the dropping of twenty-two health centres from this crucial part of our programme. And I whipped out a letter I had received only a day or two earlier from someone working in Maidstone Hospital, which described how the old people had to go out in the rain or up a rickety outside staircase to reach the physiotherapy department of the hospital. (I could see Bob Mellish cringe at that.)

The situation, I continued, was even more serious in the personal social services, which needed a growth of 2 per cent a year to keep pace with the growing number of elderly. The over-seventy-fives were increasing by 2 per cent a year and the number of children in care by $2\frac{1}{2}$ per cent a year. So some growth in expenditure was necessary even if services were just to stand still. And capital cuts in this field merely put a bigger burden on the hospitals. We were in a vicious circle and the Treasury demands would ensure it was a downward one. I sat back breathlessly, knowing I had shaken them. Eric Varley whispered to me: 'That was brilliant.'

But Joel still tried to do his worst. There was, he said ruthlessly, a shortfall of £296 million in the cuts needed from the health and personal social services. He accepted that the personal social services required a growth of 2 per cent. (He had to admit that because the local authorities had recently made it brutally clear to him in the negotiations over the rate support grant.) But, he continued, the same arguments didn't apply to the health side. There a standstill should mean no growth at all and that would give us a saving of £219 million. The Office of Population Census and Surveys [OPCS] forecasts just did not support my demographic argument.

But I had clearly impressed Cabinet and Harold jumped in in his deft way to try to help. Of course he did it circuitously. We all knew, he said, that there were too many chiefs to Indians in the NHS and that in the social services it was even worse. He would take a lot of convincing that there wasn't a lot of fat in these services. Surely we could cut administrative costs without damaging the services? (I groaned inwardly.) Of course, continued Harold, we must take account of any demographic changes. Barbara had made a great point of them. But her figures were challenged by Treasury. So she had better try to clear up this point in bilateral talks. Joel nodded approvingly at this, but before he could draw breath Harold slipped in: 'And she should discuss with the Chief Secretary what would be the least damaging way of saving £100 million.' While Joel gasped I protested vigorously, whereat Harold said disapprovingly that the purpose of the talks would be to set before Cabinet a statement showing the consequences that would flow from a cut of £100 million, so that it could consider this against its priorities generally. Eric gave me a congratulatory nudge and I subsided, realizing that, thanks to Harold, I had already saved £119 million and might yet save the rest.

But I was soon called to do battle again, this time under the heading of social security. Here Joel reported that the main dispute was on the method of uprating. If we switched from the present historical method to the 'forecasting' one (which was only fair when inflation was on the decline), we would save £508 million, but all I was prepared to offer was £200 million. I fought desperately, pointing out that we at DHSS had originally wanted to adopt the forecasting method to protect the pensioners when inflation was rising, but the Treasury would have none of it. To switch methods now, when the factors were moving in the pensioners' favour, would be dishonourable. But I got nowhere, Joel assuaging Cabinet's doubts by assuring them that we were not altering our legislative commitment to the pensioners in any way. In desperation I offered £300 million. Joel was adamant he wanted £508 million. And so Harold ruled that this saving was agreed, with the proviso that we could look at it again when we had the report of Joel's and my bilateral talk on the health and personal social services side. Once again I could see the trap: I could help the pensioners only at the expense of the NHS. I tried one last fling. 'What about the interdepartmental study group on poverty we have set up? We must agree to find some money to deal with its findings.' Joel brushed that imperiously aside. So much for Cabinet's great decision to have an anti-poverty strategy.

I sat back limp. My pals at our end of the table made clucking noises of sympathy. John Silkin, no mean rhymester, tossed me a poem he had been scribbling:

> All things bright and beautiful,
> All projects great and small,
> All things wise and wonderful
> The Chancellor cuts them all.
>
> He cuts the old age pension
> Although he cuts by stealth,
> And when he looks for savings,
> He cuts the National Health.
>
> All things bright and beautiful,
> All houses large and small,
> All things Manifesto,
> The Chancellor cuts them all.

I smiled wanly and then cheered up a bit as I realized that Joel hadn't mentioned one of the items on the Treasury list of options for additional cuts – the postponement of child benefit. At least I've saved that. It will be covered by the contingency fund for which Denis has earmarked £900 million next year. I've also saved the new pensions scheme. Brian O'Malley and I growled so ferociously at the very suggestion that its introduction in 1978 should be postponed that Joel never dared press it.

Next we turned to Environment, on which the discussion was dispatched pretty quickly. Tony C. made a virtue of how co-operative his department had been. It was, he said, responsible for 17 per cent of expenditure but had accepted 38 per cent of the cuts. If other departments had been as helpful (another dig at me), we would have been out of our difficulties. When we turned to Education, Fred Mulley put up a doleful dirge. He had already agreed to cuts of £580 million in the bilateral talks, he said, and now the Treasury wanted another £124 million. Those who offered the most were penalized the most. He went on and on. Poor Fred has such a whining voice and is so humourless that he merely succeeds in sounding comical. John Silkin tossed me another poem:

> He made the mighty Castle;
> He made the lowly Shore;
> But when he made Fred Mulley
> The thing became a bore.

By this time our end of the table was swept by a kind of desperate hilarity. When, during the discussion on further education, Eric whispered to me proudly: 'Did you know that I've been appointed visiting Fellow to Nuffield?' I too was inspired to verse:

> Ruskin gave us Woodcock,
> Dick Marsh, that turncoat gent,
> It even gave us Varley:
> By God, it's time it went!

A kind of PESC madness had descended on us.

But Roy Mason was of a different ilk. When we turned to Defence (Shirley having accepted another £50 million cut in food subsidies by 1978–79), Roy took the floor with a ferocious fluency that one would have thought would have flattened Denis, who was demanding a cut of £350 million on top of the £100 million which was all that Roy had agreed. Roy treated us to a tirade about the break-up of Nato, loss of export orders, etc., etc. Jim, of course, supported him. But a number of us fought back. Tony C. pointed out that defence expenditure was actually increasing. Mike said he didn't dismiss the employment effects as not serious: 'but all these proposals have employment effects'. We would still be spending more of our GNP on defence than the other members of Nato. Denis said the party would never accept cuts in the social services, etc. totalling £3¾ million if defence was only cut by £100 million. Harold then proceeded to get his own way again. It was clear to me he could see the political importance of seeming to be tough over defence expenditure, but equally he wasn't going to have it cut too much. So he suggested that by various devices (such as allowing £100 million for equipment slippage and cuts in HQ staff) Roy could bring his £100 million up to £270 million, i.e., half what the full formula cut would have produced. Roy bridled angrily even at that. He just couldn't do it 'without a major examination of what it would mean'. 'You have three years,' said Harold mildly. No final decision could be taken at that meeting, but Roy should prepare a paper showing the consequences of a £275 million cut. I knew that Roy had got away with it.

At this point Harold said we had gone as far as we could that day and would continue our discussion at the next Cabinet. We streamed out thankfully.

After the morning's trauma my Questions in the House seemed a non-event. But I still had my two other major problems to deal with: the consultants and the juniors. After Questions, Arnold smuggled himself into my room bearing the negotiators' comments on the document I had sent them last night. The comments had been drawn up by his assistant, Montgomerie, who pointed out that a number of them were trivial drafting points. The professions also wanted me to commit myself not to use my discretionary powers to phase out pay beds pending the passage of the legislation. But the other points took us right back to where we started from. The negotiators wanted no reference to common waiting lists or reserve powers for licensing and they wanted a new appendix to deal with the composition of the independent board and its terms of reference. This repeated all the provisions we had already objected to on the life of the board and the criteria for phasing out. I said I would consider all this and let him have my reply.

Back to the office to deal with the BMA and the juniors. I was determined to reach agreement if at all possible, as a settlement with the juniors would strengthen my hand in the pay beds row. That morning *The Times* carried an optimistic leader: 'There is no great distance now between Mrs Castle and the junior hospital doctors ... the parties are separated essentially on a question of fact alone.' The leader-writer little knew the juniors! When I went down to the ministerial conference room to be faced by another of those mass meetings, ten people on the BMA side and sixteen on mine (why so many officials should horn in on these meetings I'll never know), I soon found I was in for a long haul. Despite my being so forthcoming over the independent audit, Zacharias was sitting as tight-lipped as usual. We cleared the details of the audit out of the way without too much difficulty. Faced with my determination to be reasonable, their accusations that we had been out to diddle them began to look pretty thin. (At one point the juniors claimed that a number of area health authorities had never been approached to submit extra duty allowance figures to the department. I got my officials to check up at once with two of the AHAs named and was able to report that both of them had submitted EDA returns for all the periods in question.)

Seizing my advantage I turned the discussion to the need to reduce juniors' excessive hours. The stories of juniors working 120 hours a week or more, which appear regularly in the press, always arouse sympathy in the House of Commons. Every time I tell my officials we've got to do something about it they always reply that the responsibility lies with the consultants, who like to have juniors at their beck and call. And so it proved. Stevenson was lukewarm about my offer of an urgent enquiry as to how we could reduce working hours, saying it was a matter for the consultants through the Joint Negotiating Committee, while Zacharias said darkly that under the proposed new contract there was a positive financial inducement to health authorities to employ staff for long hours.

This brought us to the crux. I was just about to say: 'So we are agreed' . . . when all Zacharias's pent-up fury came pouring out. There could be no agreement, he said, until their grievances about the new contract had been dealt with. He then proceeded to list their demands. The spirit of the new contract which we had agreed last January had been that their basic salary related to a forty-hour week. He accepted that the juniors had an ethical obligation to work above that in 'emergencies and unforeseen circumstances', but health authorities – abetted by the department – had been exploiting this. Some health authorities had been saving money by refusing to fill vacancies in junior staff, or to appoint locums when colleagues went sick, often for months, knowing they could call on other juniors to fill the gap without pay. There was no appeal machinery available to juniors to challenge this. And the department had compounded this exploitation by refusing to give evidence to the DDRB that their basic salary should be related to a forty-hour week, thus leaving them with an open-ended commitment. As I listened to him I recognized the juniors' sense of injustice was very real and I instinctively identified with them over some of their complaints.

But I could see the pitfalls, too. The trouble is that we and the doctors have got ourselves into an almost metaphysical dispute. The juniors clearly want an industrial type contract, with overtime being paid for eventually by premium rates, but they know they can't have it yet under pay policy and they also accept an 'ethical' commitment to fill in without pay in 'emergencies and unforeseen circumstances'. They are furious with their Review Body for continuing to claim that this 'ethical' element makes their contract a professional one and they believe the department has gone back on the January agreement by urging in their evidence to the Review Body that, in recognition of this ethical commitment, supplementary payments should only start to be paid after forty-four hours. In a private telephone call to Jack, one of their negotiators has told him the forty-hour starting point is vital to them and also that they wanted a limit of eighty hours to their working week, any time above that to be paid at locum (i.e. higher) rates. (The way unions and others use Jack as a private channel of communication to me is remarkable and in itself is enough to justify having political advisers.)

Zacharias having set out his demands, we started a long, circuitous argument. I again pointed out that there was no extra money available under the pay policy. They said that what they were interested in was the principle. I insisted that the Government couldn't just override the profession's own independent pay body by accepting the forty-hour week principle off its own bat, particularly as that body had just reported *against* such a proposition. It would be justified in resigning en bloc if we did. The juniors bridled at this suspiciously, but Derek Stevenson could see the point of this and backed me on it reluctantly. He suggested instead that we should agree to make a joint approach to the Review Body saying we recognized the juniors' anxiety to have their salary related to a basic forty-hour week, that the department did not oppose this and that we would like the Review Body to consider the matter from the next round next April, or when pay policy permitted. By now it was late, so I summed up that there should be a joint meeting with officials the next day to agree the details of the audit and that I myself would meet them again on Thursday to continue the discussion on their other points. At this we broke up exhausted and I told Norman that we must get Michael along to Thursday's meeting. I wasn't going to get myself into any situation where I was blamed for breaching pay policy. Any settlement must have his blessing.

But my day wasn't finished: I still had my boxes to do. In them I found a letter from Reg Bird of ASTMS sending me a copy of a resolution on pay beds passed by their AGM three days ago. This declared the union's 'total opposition to any temporizing with the Labour Party's policy' on private practice and its alarm at 'the possibility of compromises'. Good. It would be wrong for all the pressure to come from one side. It also called for immediate negotiations, 'to include the Medical Practitioners' Union section of ASTMS', to achieve a settlement of the juniors' claim 'for fair rates of pay'. This just goes to show the sympathy that can be mobilized for the juniors on our side of the House.

Wednesday brought another succession of battles. It also brought a spate of hostile press comment. George Fitch excelled himself with a foul piece in the *Express* headed: 'As Barbara Castle finally back-tracked on the junior doctors' pay row, The Lady *is* for Burning.' It included such choice comments as: 'The tears and tantrums which got her her way most of the time in the last Labour Government now seem to do no more than demean every issue she touches.' It was not only accompanied by a photograph which made me look twice my age, but it was topped by an equally foul cartoon by Cummings which made me look like a haggard harridan. Not to be outdone, the *Sun* carried a sneering cartoon by Franklin. I tried not to mind and turned to the pay beds issue again.

At an early office meeting on pay beds we went through Montgomerie's comments on our last draft. There were certain minor points of redrafting which we agreed easily and I said I was willing to include a commitment not to use my discretionary power to phase out pay beds pending the legislation. I also agreed to make it clear that two of the four members of the independent board (apart from the chairman) would be members of the medical profession and approved by them. But for the rest I rejected Montgomerie's appendix outright; reiterated my determination to consult with the unions as well as the medical profession; refused to give a guaranteed life to the existence of the board (certainly not ten years!); repeated that pay beds should be dispensed with where all reasonable steps to provide alternative private facilities had not been taken; reiterated the para on common waiting lists and actually strengthened the reference to licensing by providing that, if a voluntary agreement with the private sector could not be reached, 'the Government . . . would take reserve licensing powers in the legislation'. And for the first time I added the suggestion that the reserve powers might be exercised by the independent board.

There remained the vexed question of the Schedule. David, who couldn't be at the morning meeting, had mulled over all this during lunch and produced a form of words which, once again, conceded far more to the professions than I was prepared to do. I could see that the only way out was for us to go boldly for the inclusion in the Bill from the outset of a firm number of beds in the Schedule and had decided to go nap on phasing out 1,000 beds in six months. So we decided to send a 'side letter' to this effect with our main draft.

In the meantime I had also had to turn my mind to the PESC battle and arm myself for the bilateral talk with Joel in the afternoon. This proved to be easier than I had anticipated. When I arrived at the Treasury at 2pm, ready to do battle with Joel over the demographic figures, I was faced with his complete capitulation on this point. His officials, he said, now admitted that my figures were right – and so did OPCS. I was taken aback, musing to myself on the curious way the Civil Service works. My chaps had obviously been on to OPCS, who had confirmed our figures; OPCS had been on to Treasury and the officials had fixed it all up between themselves behind the scenes. So much for ministerial control!

However, Joel's admission did not mean he was giving up the fight to get some more money from me. He insisted that I could still cut the capital programme of the personal social services and reduce the current expenditure on the NHS from $1\frac{1}{2}$ per cent growth annually to 1 per cent on the typically Treasury-specious argument that, as we were going to build fewer hospitals, we should incur less running costs. The illiteracy of Treasury arguments makes me despair. David and I dilated on the unacceptability of Joel's arguments for some time. Eventually we agreed that officials should prepare a short paper for Cabinet on the likely consequences of a further saving of £100 million.

Meanwhile Jack had been having more talks on the side with the juniors and had reported that to them the relating of basic salary to forty hours was 'simply not negotiable'. Dr Wardle claimed that this point was not primarily about money, but about the honouring, as they see it, of the spirit of the January agreement. I grew more and more convinced that we ought to give way on this – and could do so without breaching pay policy – but officials reported to me that the Department of Employment was taking a hard line. Anyway, Michael had agreed to come along to the resumed meeting.

Thursday proved to be the longest and toughest day of the whole week – and that was saying something! It started with the misery and tension of another PESC Cabinet. This, I knew, was my last chance to save the NHS from another large cut. But first we dealt with the other programmes. Fred Mulley, bleating pathetically, had his arm twisted to give up another £50 million, Harold making a positive virtue of this by saying that it was all wrong that the British taxpayer should subsidize well-to-do overseas students, anyway, so savings here would be positively good; and also insisting that savings could quite properly be made on what he called 'evening classes of peripheral importance'. So a Labour Government now considers that evening classes on things like dress-making are an expendable luxury! It is this willingness to reverse all our social thinking that makes me despair of this Government. Public expenditure cuts may, or may not, be unavoidable on economic grounds, but we ought to say publicly that they are regrettable and not try to justify them by Tory arguments. Of course Harold insisted that the Open University must not be touched, because that is his brainchild, but whether this overriding priority can be justified on grounds of social policy, compared with the things we are ready to give up, is another matter.

Next we turned to Environment. Here most of us were ready to take more off roads, only Peter protesting that this programme had already had the biggest cut of all. There was a great wrangle over housing, Treasury suggesting we could save £200 million on local authority mortgages and £100 million on housing expenditure. Harold suggested we should try to get the building societies to take over the lending which the local authorities were doing by offering to guarantee these mortgages: a face-saving non-starter in my opinion. Bob was in favour of saving some money by selling council houses. Others pleaded there should be no cut in house provision. Harold summed up that Environment as a whole should give up another £225 million, leaving it to Ministers to decide how these reductions should be made.

Next we all virtuously agreed to leave overseas aid uncut and Shirley volunteered to take a bigger cut in food subsidies in 1978–79, on the grounds that their main purpose had been to offset the harmonization of UK food prices with those of the Common Market and this would have been achieved by the end of 1977. Mike accepted this reluctantly, on the understanding that there would be no consequential reduction in 1977–78, in view of pay policy.

And so it came to my turn again. Joel opened by admitting that Treasury now accepted my figures of the demographic trends but he still thought I could save another £100 million by restricting growth on the health side to 1 per cent a year instead of the 1½ per cent for which I asked and by accepting the formula cuts on capital in both cases. I fought back desperately. I couldn't accept that we could afford to cut back capital on the social services any more than current expenditure, but if I did concede this, it would save £22 million and that would leave £78 million to come out of the NHS. That would effectively mean a moratorium on new hospital building schemes. It wouldn't be any good any of my colleagues round that table coming to me with pleas for a new hospital in their constituencies. Grimsby's new hospital, for instance, would go for a burton. So would the one at Leeds. (I'd carefully checked up which members of the Cabinet had pet hospital schemes in their constituencies.) I dilated on the backlog we already had in hospital maintenance work and fire precautions. It was a strong case, but I faced a Cabinet of desperate men. They seized my £22 million but wanted more. I volunteered to revoke the next increase in the earnings rule, due in April 1977, saying I was ready to fight *that* one through Parliament as I had never thought it was a priority. That would save another £18 million. Tony C. got nasty, saying everyone else had had to make far worse cuts than I was offering. Wedgie came to my aid with an outburst against the whole exercise. Couldn't we reduce the £3¾ million to what we had got already? Oughtn't the Chancellor to contribute something to closing the gap by selective tax increases or withdrawing tax reliefs to the better off?

Harold came to my help again by going off at a tangent about how much money was being wasted by over-elaborate administration. Did we really have to be so cautious and perfectionist in the running of social security? He was always getting constituency cases where Mrs Bloggs had some small claim or a pensions query and a vast administrative effort was mounted to ascertain whether she was entitled to it. 'That is where the money is going now.' Wouldn't it be better to have rougher justice – or even to have someone getting a few pence more than they were entitled to – than carry these enormous overheads? He was convinced some departments were over-manned. There had been an increase in staff of 22,000 up to October 1975 and a further increase of 23,000 was planned by 1978. Much of this increase was the direct result of new policies and some in the pipeline might have to be reviewed, but he was convinced we could get a saving of 5 per cent in the forecast number of civil servants in 1978–79 by relaxing some of our practices and by increased efficiency. This would save £140 million. Once again I doubted whether Harold's proposition was more than a face-saver, but I jumped at it. So did everyone else, only Denis looked doubtful. The spotlight then switched back to me and Harold said smartly that I had offered £40 million, including the saving on the earnings rule, but Cabinet thought I ought to go up to £60 million, though it was recognized that £18 million of this saving was dependent on our amending the legislation on the earnings rule. I slumped back with relief. What Harold's skilful summing up meant was that I had effectively given up only £42 million, instead of the £100 million Joel was demanding.

But Harold's skill was to be used in ways I didn't approve of, too. He was out to save Defence. Saying airily that Roy Mason hadn't yet had time to prepare his paper showing the consequences of a total cut of £275 million, including the £100 million already agreed, Harold said we should count in an additional saving of £175 million on the understanding that Roy would want to contest it and we should have to consider it further in the light of his paper if this showed the extra saving would damage our ability to fulfil our treaty obligations. I know what that means! Roy has got away with it. Harold then totted up the score so far: savings of £1,033 million or a shortfall of £172 million. However the Chancellor was willing to accept this. ('It'll be nearer £400 million,' I thought to myself, 'when Roy has succeeded in dodging most of his proposed increase.') Denis looked noble at this and we all relaxed till Harold reminded us that the Treasury would have to start another round of bilaterals on the consequential savings which would be needed in 1977–78 and 1979–80. But no one was in the mood to bother about that. Sufficient unto the day....

The Chrysler issue goes rumbling on. Eric and Harold Lever have made some progress in their negotiations with Riccardo, but Eric clearly remains as hostile to the deal as ever. And he is leaking the fact very unwisely to the press. Harold said it was essential to reach decisions quickly. We would then turn to the issue of import controls. I can't see this Cabinet ever agreeing to *them*.

Back at the office I found a Minute from Jack on the pay beds saga, reporting a phone call he had had from Arnold last night on the latest draft I had handed him. Arnold said, 'This is a great advance ... if it is not accepted by them they will be extremely ill-advised.' However I had no time to bother about pay beds as I got ready for the marathon with the juniors that Michael and I faced. But I hadn't anticipated it would be quite such a marathon! We met after lunch; we finished almost at breakfast time.

We opened with both sides deploying familiar arguments, with us maintaining there must be no breach of pay policy and the professions arguing that their demands need mean no such thing. The arrangements for the audit presented no difficulty. I reported that Sir Ernest Woodroofe, redoubtable chairman of the Review Body, had agreed to look at the new contract again in the light of the latest figures the audit revealed of the money available. For their part the juniors agreed to accept the outcome of the audit, whether it produced additional money for distribution or not.

But it was soon clear that the acceptance by us of the principle of the forty-hour week contract was their sticking point. After we had talked round this for some time, and Michael had shaken his head over the implications of this for future pay policy, I suggested we had a break. Michael, our officials and I repaired upstairs to my room for a cup of tea. I told Michael firmly that I could not see how we could justify breaking on this point, when we had already – with his agreement – accepted the principle in January. The real safeguard, from the Government's point of view, was that the whole business had to be priced by the Review Body in the light of pay policy. If the juniors wanted to move from a professional type to an industrial type contract, who were we to stop them, provided no extra money was made available? If the juniors were prepared to wear the implications of this, it was up to them. Mike had clearly been shaken by the juniors' insistence on the principle. David, while not disagreeing with my analysis, pointed out that the 'ethical commitment' to do extra work without pay in 'emergencies and unforeseen circumstances' was vital to the proper running of hospitals: we must insist on that. We sat scribbling away at a form of words. Time passed and the resourceful Norman wheeled in coffee and sandwiches. We gathered that the BMA and the juniors, similarly refreshed, were scribbling away downstairs.

At last our joint meeting was reconvened and a long wrangle ensued about the form of words. We stood firmly by our formula. The juniors kept bringing in additional points. They wanted each junior to have a 'job description' when he took up his contract, so as to prevent his employers from exploiting him by making him do excessive hours, or by making him give indefinite cover for a sick or absent colleague without pay. We for our part insisted that the 'ethical commitment' must not be lost. Drafting became a fine art. I kept adjourning the meeting so that my side could go into another room to argue about individual words, Jack acting as a go-between. By now we were into the early hours of the morning. Mike began to droop – no doubt wondering whether he was dealing in money or metaphysics. Peter Brown hovered, complaining that we were losing the media. 'Media be blowed,' we muttered and drafted on.

Eventually, the bargain was struck word by word and line by line. The reference to the forty-hour week was a semantic masterpiece. We agreed to give joint evidence with them to the Review Body arguing that the basic salary 'should represent' only payment for forty hours, but insisted on defining the basic salary 'as determined by the Review Body from time to time'. The juniors pledged themselves not to use the forty-hour week as an argument to try to get overtime rates for their extra hours and accepted that their supplementary payments (Class A for standby duty and Class B for on call) must be priced 'at rates within the pay policy currently in force'. In return we agreed that, where a junior was expected to provide cover outside his basic contract (our old friends 'occasional emergencies and unforeseen circumstances' always excepted), he should be paid at the standard rate. The fine metaphysical balance had been struck again. Only time would show what its practical effects would be.

These Becher's Brooks crossed we romped home. The final deal was clinched at 3am. Mike sloped off home but, with Peter Brown waiting to pounce, I was not through. He rushed me in to talk to the few remaining flagging journalists. I even had to record an interview for the *Today* programme – never more aptly named. There had to be handshaking and a goodbye drink with the juniors, still a bit suspicious, but on the whole feeling that honour had been satisfied. One of the last points I had to clinch was what they were prepared to do to save the wretched patients from the consequences of their industrial action. The juniors told me (and I realized it was true) that they couldn't get the industrial action called off officially till the full meeting of their members had endorsed the deal. But they did promise to advance the date of the meeting. And Zacharias, mollified a bit now, offered to try to ease the medical situation in any hospital where their action was causing real disruption if I would let him know where dangerous gaps in the service were being caused. I instructed my tired officials to send him that information as quickly as possible and to help him distribute copies of the agreement to his members over the weekend. 'You do realize, don't you,' said Norman as we straggled wearily back to my room, 'that there is a Cabinet meeting on Chrysler this morning?' 'Blow Chrysler,' I said. 'Anyway I shall have to make a statement to the House. Send my apologies to the PM.' I got home with the milk and into bed, setting my alarm for 8am.

Friday morning saw us back at the office early. My statement had to be made at 11am and we barely got it drafted before I was on my way. Of course, with a settlement in the bag which was firmly rooted in pay policy, it was a walk-over. I even got some congratulations in that almost empty House. I was immensely satisfied with the way we had drawn the poison from the juniors' dispute without conceding anything but joint representations to the Review Body over a principle. Nonetheless I realized that the Review Body might not like that principle and that I had to make my peace with it. So I readily agreed with Raymond Gedling that I ought to lose no time in meeting Woodroofe and explaining what I had done and why.

Woodroofe came to my room at the House frosty with disapproval. He told me bluntly that he didn't like the idea of relating the basic salary to a forty-hour week, pointing out that the Review Body had taken account of the extra hours juniors worked in pricing their basic salary and that this might now have to be reduced. I said I had pointed this out to the juniors and that they were prepared to take the risk. He also warned that any reduction in the threshold for the payment of supplements might merely reduce their rate. 'At least he hasn't resigned,' said Raymond with relief behind his departing back.

It was time to turn my attention to pay beds again. Arnold had sent me a letter setting out the profession's comments on our latest draft. His letter opened with the following paragraph: 'May I at the outset say that there can be no doubt at all that this document represents a further substantial advance towards agreement and manifests once again the sincerity of your desire to allay the anxieties of the profession whose interests are, of course, vitally concerned.'

That said, he hoped that I would not be 'unduly impatient that I have not been able to come back with an unqualified acceptance of the document'. There were 'certain further variations' to be recorded 'as necessary on behalf of the profession'. First as to the Schedule: 1,000 beds was the maximum which Mr Damerell – 'our own independent expert' – could assess as available for phasing out over some period of time 'such as eighteen months'. Even that was more than he could safely estimate, but the profession was reluctantly ready to accept it. I promptly said to David I would go nap on 1,000 beds within six months. The remaining changes, wrote Arnold, were not substantial 'although the protracted debate which took place today might have led you to think otherwise'. The doctors wanted a reference to the 'right' to private practice. We agreed we weren't having that. They wanted the criterion for phasing out to be 'the availability of reasonable alternative facilities', instead of our phrase 'the reasonable availability of alternative facilities'. We decided to solve that one by having both 'reasonables' in. They wanted us to specify that the chairman of the independent board should be a legal chap, but I thought that too dangerous. It all depended on what type of fellow we could get. The profession wanted to weaken the safeguards we had built in on the use of specialized facilities for private patients by taking out the proviso that the Secretary of State had to be satisfied before authorizing this use that there would be no detriment to NHS patients. They didn't like the word 'detriment' anyway and thought it ought to be 'injustice'. I said emphatically that I wouldn't take out the proviso, though to soften this blow we decided to suggest the word 'disadvantage' instead of 'detriment'.

On licensing Arnold recognized that this 'is a fundamental matter from your point of view' and had managed to secure their agreement to wording 'which I hope will satisfy you'. This provided first that the Government needed to be satisfied that private developments did not 'significantly' endanger the NHS. Secondly, that the Government would seek 'voluntary assurances to that end'. We decided that the acceptance of the word 'significantly' would do no harm, but that we wanted more than voluntary 'assurances'. We therefore substituted the words 'and will enter into consultation with the medical profession as to how this can be achieved by voluntary means'. The important thing was that the reference to the fact that reserve powers would be taken if necessary remained in.

Last, but by no means least, Arnold turned to the paragraph on common waiting lists. It is significant that our insistence on examining the possibility of common waiting lists terrifies them more than anything. As Arnold put it, this paragraph was 'particularly troublesome'. Some of the doctors felt strongly that it should be taken out, but were prepared to accept it on the basis of amendments suggested by Arnold himself. Yes, there it was: our old friend: 'The professions maintain that if any such scheme is a possibility it can only operate for urgent cases in view of the varied nature of the waiting lists and facilities available at different hospitals.' Well, we decided, they are entitled to their view as long as the Government's contrary view is expressed in the paragraph and that the instruction to the independent board to make recommendations on this matter to the Secretary of State remains. So we accepted this.

It then remained to discuss the heading of the document. We had drafted the following: 'The following statement has been agreed by representatives of the BMA, BDA, HCSA and the Royal Colleges and the Secretary of State for Social Services on the Government's proposals for phasing private practice out of NHS hospitals.' When I gave Arnold the document he once again expressed his appreciation of the changes I had made. He would put them to the professions and he was sure we could now clinch the deal with a view to my making a statement in the House on Monday. I said that it was clearly an essential part of the deal that the industrial action should be called off and that the professions must recommend this to their own people at the same time as they recommended the document. He seemed to feel that that was fair.

Afterwards Patrick said to me: 'You really have done very well, Secretary of State. This really is a remarkable achievement.' I was not so jubilant. I have had to make concessions I would not have made if Harold had not intervened and upset the apple-cart. Nonetheless I believe I have saved the maximum from the situation in which I was placed and safeguarded the major principles of our policy. Given the right kind of board the phasing out cannot be long delayed and at least the existence of the board means that a Tory successor could not reverse the process by an administrative act. David believes we have got an agreement that will now stick, whatever the change of government. I went down thankfully to HCF, relieved to think that the whole messy business was now sewn up.

Disillusionment came rapidly. By Saturday morning Arnold was on the phone full of apologies. First, there were some textual details to wrangle about and I then had to conduct consultations of dizzying circularity: with me ringing Norman, Norman ringing David Owen and Patrick Nairne, David and Patrick ringing me and me ringing Arnold back again. It went on for hours. Every word seemed to terrify Arnold's men. They weighed them up carefully, suspecting traps. As for me, I wasn't prepared to budge on any of my central points. Eventually some minor drafting changes were agreed.

But the main argument raged over the status of the document. Arnold reported that the professions were not prepared to say they had 'agreed' anything. He admitted that this was cowardly, but said that they went further: they were not prepared to admit that they had ever negotiated with me. They actually wanted me to write to them putting these proposals to them as my own! I was furious. I said (after more circular consultations) that I was prepared to leave out the word 'agreed' but I certainly wasn't going to have it appear that I had taken the initiative in work-ing out this compromise. And there must be some commitment on their part to recommend the document and get industrial action stopped, or the deal was off. What about using the words 'joint statement', instead? It certainly wasn't a unilateral one.

Once again Arnold agreed that all this was 'eminently reasonable' and disappeared off the phone to try and sell it to his chaps. And once again he came back to press me to accept some 'modifications'. The professions now wanted a letter, not from me, but from the Prime Minister, following up the meeting they had had with him, with the PM putting the proposals to them as the outcome of the 'clarification' that had taken place. On the basis of this they would be willing to call an early meeting of their constituent bodies to consider them. I said this proposal was even worse: I wasn't going to have the PM humiliated by proposing the compromise, any more than I was prepared to be humiliated myself. These men must really stand up and be counted. They must be ready to commend the proposals for urgent consideration and to recommend the lifting of sanctions at the first meeting of their constituent bodies. We really couldn't have the PM offering concessions to them without even a reference being made to calling off their strike. Once again Arnold heartily agreed and disappeared off the telephone.

By this time we were into Sunday morning and Norman phoned to remind me I must get clearance of the document from the Secretaries of State for Scotland and Wales. Another rush then ensued to track them down. Eventually I got them on the phone and they gave me the clearance readily and thankfully. Back came Arnold, full of apologies for the obstacles being put up by his side and their panicky refusal to give any leadership. But, unfortunately, he said, that was a fact we had to face. What they now proposed, as a device for disguising that they had ever been negotiating with me, was that we should all meet in my office the following day, that he should then produce the proposals out of a hat, we should examine them as though we had never seen them before and simultaneously adopt them on the understanding that the other side adopted them, too. They would then agree to put the proposals to early meetings of their people on the basis that the final decision must rest with them. For its part the Government could make clear that it reserved the right to withdraw the proposals if the full meeting of the professions turned them down or if industrial action was not called off. But they considered a letter from the PM to them to be a crucial element in maintaining the fiction that they hadn't been negotiating. I groaned but promptly started drafting a letter from the PM to them which would preserve the Government's – and the Prime Minister's – dignity. More circular consultations by telephone with David and Patrick to get the wording right. The crucial paragraph, we all agreed, was the following:

I understand from the Secretary of State that clarification has taken place through Lord Goodman and that, as a result, detailed proposals have evolved [!] which you are prepared to commend for approval by an early meeting of the CCHMS and the Council of the BMA. I am writing to inform you that, if the proposals are accepted by the professions as a whole and normal working is resumed, the Government would embody these proposals in its legislation.

Arnold thought this was excellent. By now, over the two days, I must have been on the telephone on and off for at least ten hours. Norman contacted No. 10 to tell them the draft letter was on its way to Chequers by special messenger. I sat down to type out the draft, together with a covering Minute from me to the PM. In it I told him that through the protracted discussions I had had on the letter, 'I have been anxious to preserve your dignity and that of the Government and, I might add, Arnold Goodman is as anxious to ensure this as I am.' And I went on: 'I think that during these difficult talks he has grown increasingly aware of the difficulties of negotiating with the medical profession and increasingly irritated with their lack of courage and leadership.'

The special messenger having arrived and my stuff having been dispatched to the PM, I relaxed. Peace at last! But not for long. Arnold rang again to say the professions had changed their minds about one phrase in the PM's letter. They were not prepared to 'commend' the document 'for approval', merely to place the proposals before the professions' committees and councils. We didn't know whether to groan or laugh. But I was angry at the professions' assumption that they could dictate to a Prime Minister in this way. I said it was up to Harold whether he would swallow it. Privately I had no doubt that he would.

At last I turned to my boxes and a long evening's belated work.

Monday, 15 December

Got to the office exhausted, completely drained by the weekend's activities. We went through the draft I had done of my statement for the House, which everybody liked. But the BMA contingent, who had assembled according to plan in another room, were still making trouble over the PMs letter which Arnold and I had agreed yesterday. They simply were not going to say they were commending the proposals for 'approval'. They were quibbling too over one or two points in the proposals, notably my insertion of the words that consultation over the contents of the Schedule would take place, not merely with them, but also with 'other NHS staff and other interested parties'. Arnold, as usual, was late. When he arrived at nearly noon he was closeted with them for some time, finally coming up to me with a form of words for the PM's letter which said they would put the proposals to their council for 'urgent consideration', plus allowing the PM to add that he understood the proposals would gain acceptance! The arrogance of trying to dictate a PM's letter never occurred to them. 'We simply must not pre-empt the democratic decision of our members in any way,' said Stevenson, whom Arnold had brought up with him. Shades of the anarchic democracy of the BMA, which Mike refers to in his book![1] Eventually we shrugged and agreed.

Out of courtesy I showed Stevenson my statement. He said it was impeccable and thanked me for its fairness. Then we brought the rest of them upstairs into my room for the pantomime of 'discovering' the proposals at Arnold's hands. Those who had turned up trooped in: Grabham, Rodney Smith, Simmons of the HCSA, the dental chap and Bolt. I gave them a drink. We all looked sheepish – and felt it. Grabham had a last fling. He couldn't accept the words about consultation with other NHS staff. 'I can't agree not to consult the unions,' I replied with spirit. 'And we cannot agree to include these words,' he replied with icy obstinacy. It looked like deadlock. Arnold said mildly that I could not be stopped from consulting anyone I liked. I replied that, on that understanding, I did not mind whether the words were in the document or not, 'but I shall certainly consult the unions and I want that minuted'. 'Perfectly reasonable,' said Arnold. And so we skated to safety over thin ice. We all breathed a sigh of relief when they had left. 'I believe I actually saw a faint smile on Grabham's

---

[1] Michael Foot's biography of Aneurin Bevan.

face at one point,' Norman recorded. 'A smile like a silver plate on a coffin,' Gedling quoted.

I was worried as to how our chaps would take my statement in the House. David did some preliminary soundings and reported that people like Ian Wrigglesworth thought it was an acceptable deal. It didn't go too badly, though the only people called from our side were the Bob Cryers and Dennis Skinners, who were mildly critical. 'It's better that way,' said David. 'Too much support from our side would have frightened off the consultants.' My greatest joy was to see Norman Fowler and Gerry Vaughan puzzling over their copy of the statement on their front bench before I spoke – obviously puzzled how to play it. Tired as I was, I put all my remaining force into my delivery. Ted, who had slipped into the gallery with Arnold, told me afterwards it was 'magnificent': no sign of hesitation or fatigue. Thank God for that. All I want now is to get the industrial action called off; the drafting of the Bill, after all, remains in my hands.

It fascinates me to watch how Pat Nairne is settling himself into his new job. In some ways his problem is the same as that of a new Minister: trying to assess the personal quality of the people with whom he has to work, ears open to all comments and even gossip, but knowing that in the end he himself has to select the relevant. I like him enormously. I don't know whether it has anything to do with his long stint at Defence, but he clearly sees his job as to carry out orders: not to query the strategy, but to make sure it works – a welcome change from Philip's and Henry's soul-searchings. On this basis a Minister is in business with his civil servants and can even carry a coward or two. Without this kind of approach from the top brass the doctrine of ministerial responsibility cannot work. To have no power of hire and fire is bad enough (it makes nonsense of the doctrine), but not to be able even to discuss how our manpower is used in terms of the success of strategy is intolerable. Every day at this moment the press is full of stories, innuendoes, and quotes about how 'I' have mishandled the relationships with the juniors. All the juniors' suspicions about the department are personalized by them – and when not by them by the press – in terms of my personal failings of character. It is no use reading me a lesson about how this is the cross that Ministers have to bear. That is nonsense. I have as much belief and pride in my profession as any journalist has in his and I demand the basic equality: equality of respect. So I have a duty to show I deserve it.

Looking back over this whole drama of the juniors one of the things which astonishes me is how any of the negotiators (my officials, the juniors' representatives and the DDRB) could ever have imagined that a deal could be made to stick which actually made one-third of junior doctors worse off. Even in my greenest, crassest days as a young political agitator down from Oxford I could not have negotiated anything as ridiculous as that. And it is now the accepted wisdom of the department that if there had not been this 'detriment' element in the Review Body's supplementary report, the flare-up would never have taken place. The other day, after Raymond Gedling and I had been soothing down Sir Ernest Woodroofe, I drew Raymond aside and asked him how the whole nonsense had ever got accepted in the first place. He said to me (and I have a great respect for him as a shrewd old bird who knows how the whole system works and how to make it work) that once the pay policy was introduced in July it was obvious that any immediate introduction of the new contract (when no extra money could be made available) must mean 'detriment' for some juniors because others of them became better off. That was why, on official advice, I had twice gone back to the Department of Employment in personal letters to Michael, asking that a couple of million pounds extra should be made available as a sweetener. When Michael had refused this (and I do not doubt he was bound to do so) it was up to the Review Body to produce a report making it clear that the new contract could not be introduced on a satisfactory basis under the pay policy and had better be phased in or postponed. Instead, to his – Gedling's – surprise, it had worked out its peculiar scheme and, even more to his surprise, the juniors' representatives had accepted it. What the hell were *we* supposed to do in the face of that?

One bright note: the press comment on my statement yesterday is not too bad, only the *Morning Star* denouncing it as a 'climb-down'. My long telephone conversation with John Cunningham [of the *Guardian*] seems to have borne fruit.

Tuesday, 16 December

I've now had time to look at last Friday's Cabinet Minutes, telling the final rounds of the Chrysler battle. Eric put up a last fight against the outcome of the 'positive offer' Cabinet had decided – over his head – to put to Chrysler. It was clear, even from the anodyne text of the Minutes, that he had been very bitter indeed. The arrangements proposed, he said, under which the Government would put up more money in return for Chrysler getting more deeply committed, were 'thoroughly unsatisfactory'. In effect the Government's commitment would be open-ended; there were no real guarantees of continuity of operation by Chrysler in the UK; we would be attacked by the Select Committee and the Public Accounts Committee and by our own people for putting up money without taking a stake in the industry; we would be surrendering to a multinational company and destroying our own industrial strategy. And so on and so on. The anger obviously came pouring out of him.

Denis was much more relaxed. He accepted a lot of Eric's points, but said the proposals were a great improvement on Scheme B and would save 37,000 jobs. From the recorded discussion it was obvious that this was the governing factor with Cabinet and Ted Short, deputizing for Harold, summed up that 'a large majority of Cabinet' accepted the proposals 'albeit with great reluctance'. However, this acceptance was in principle until a satisfactory agreement with the trade unions concerned had been reached and until Chrysler had accepted profit-sharing arrangements. And so the great Chrysler marathon came to a close, leaving Eric looking a fool because he had publicly threatened to resign and would now have to swallow his words. I know my Eric; he's not the resigning type.

There was another factor obviously weighing with some supporters of the deal – though no one mentioned it. This was the fact that, if Chrysler had closed down, the pressure by Peter Shore and others of us for import controls on motorcars would have been irresistible. Now the majority against this was clear. Peter fought hard for controls, saying it was essential the Government should protect its large investments in the motor industry which, with our trade in cars showing a deficit and with import penetration running at 35 per cent, could easily collapse. Cabinet, he pointed out, had agreed to seek approval for the imposition of temporary restrictions if Chrysler UK closed down, but he had always thought we should do so if there were a substantial contraction by Chrysler and in fact its production would fall by 50 per cent. But his efforts were in vain. The pro-marketeers were too much for him. They tried various arguments to prove that temporary restrictions wouldn't help the industry, but the nub of the matter came to light when Cabinet was told Harold had reached the view, following discussions in the European Council, that there was no prospect whatever of getting the Commission's agreement to import controls. Indeed, the President of the Commission had said that approval would not be granted even in the event of a complete closure by Chrysler UK. So there we are and now we know: however desperate our economic struggles, the Commission will rule that import controls are out.

A long schedule of meetings over, I found it was 7pm and I was already late for the Transport House Christmas party, at which I try very hard to look in each year. 'This year,' I told Norman, 'there are three Christmas parties, which, our travails being temporarily over, it looks as though I should be able to attend. Why not have some belated fun?' He was only too ready to enter into the conspiracy. I arrived at Transport House at 7.15pm. There was a light-hearted crowd there, including a number of journalists, as well as members of the NEC. The journalists, such as Ian Aitken and Matt Coady, had contributed to the political cabaret and were very anxious to watch their own handiwork. 'Come up to the gallery,' said Ron Hayward to me, 'it is the best place to watch the show.' So, with a drink in hand, and a paper plate full of salami snacks in the other, I did so, seating myself happily and affectionately between Coady and Eric Heffer. But, typically, the cabaret was late starting. By 8pm, as the lights dimmed and the curtain went up, I had begun to worry about Edna who, I knew, had a dinner date she hoped to keep. Finally, at 8.30, I got up in despair. 'I must let Edna go,' I whispered to Eric and pushed past him to the stairs, empty glass in one hand, empty paper plate in the other, forgetting that I had my bi-focals still on my nose. As I tried to negotiate the curving fan-shaped steps in the half dark I suddenly felt a violent shock. I was flat on my face, hands down, shin bone in agony, my spectacles spreadeagled in front of me. 'My specs', was all I moaned. Mercifully they were not broken, but everything else in me seemed to be. I noted in a detached way that my fall had made hardly a stir. Eric helped to haul me up, but the only person who really identified with me in that half-dark was Shirley Williams, who was herself on the way out. It was she and some unknown gentleman from Transport House who dragged me to the car. Edna kept saying to me as she hauled me in, 'You should not have worried about me.' I was too racked with pain to care what anyone said. They got me back to the House and somehow up to my room. Shirley took charge of me. She was everything one would expect of her: kind, gentle and competent as she fed me hot drinks and found blankets. 'I'll get the Whips to find a doctor,' she said. 'Who would you prefer?' 'David,' I said, 'or Maurice Miller.'

It seemed ages afterwards, as I lay with my throbbing leg, that there was a stir at the door. 'I couldn't find the others, but here is a doctor,' said a Whip. I then found, to my horror, that the one they had produced was my political 'shadow', that ·smiling sepulchre, Gerry Vaughan [Conservative MP for Reading South and a consultant at Guy's Hospital]. 'I'm sorry it's me, Barbara,' he said. 'I'll go and wash my hands.' I almost clutched Shirley in despair. 'Anyone but him.' But of course, I had to submit. Gerry examined my leg with intense anxiety, finally pronouncing that it was a very bad fall indeed, adding something which I found profoundly contemptible: 'If it were anyone but you, Barbara, I would have sent you for an immediate x-ray.' I knew what he meant: that, with emergency departments shut down by industrial action in a number of hospitals, his wretched profession was waiting to play medical politics with my personal pain. I hissed at him, 'I would not go for an x-ray if I were dying.' Then David, Jack Ashley and a number of them came in, clucking their sympathy. David was very worried that I had to return to an empty flat, Ted being in Brussels, and wondered how I would get upstairs. It ended with him insisting on driving home with me, where he and his driver carried me upstairs. Edna put me to bed.

Wednesday, 17 December

A day of pandemonium, with the press shattering any hope of rest I might have cherished. Our GP, Dr Colin-Russ, was round early and he too said he would like to have my leg x-rayed, as I might well have chipped or cracked the shin-bone. I told him I wouldn't hear of it. Jack came in to help me fend off an *Express* reporter and cameraman who were camped outside the front door, insisting they wanted to take a picture of me in bed. Jack and I worked out a formula for answering press queries about my injuries and why I wasn't having an x-ray. I knew I would be in trouble, whatever I said: if I *did* have an x-ray I should be accused of preferential treatment in an 'emergencies only' situation. If I did not have one, the doctors would complain I was unnecessarily libelling their profession. Indeed, Norman told me that Stevenson had already started murmurings to that effect: 'There is no reason at all why the Secretary of State should not have an x-ray,' Stevenson had told him. As I was trying to rest, the phone never stopped. First, John Stevenson of the *Mail*, as nauseatingly unctuous as ever. 'This isn't a call to get a news story or anything, Barbara, just to let you know how genuinely sorry we all are,' etc. (I later learned he was immediately on to Colin-Russ, pumping him about the x-ray.) Sometime later he phoned again. 'Sorry to disturb you again, Barbara, but one thing frankly puzzles me: just why aren't you having an x-ray?' 'That is a matter between my doctor and me,' I replied and hung up. Next came Norman, gently worried. 'Look, it really is wrong that you should not have an x-ray. I know Colin-Russ would be much happier if you had one and you owe it to yourself. Won't you let me ring round some hospitals in your area to see which are working normally, so that you could attend an out-patients clinic in the normal way?' 'All right,' I said reluctantly, 'but you must not give any indication as to who is making the query or why. If I did go, I should want to go without anyone knowing in advance.' He assured me he would honour this.

When Colin-Russ arrived later he was very amused at the antics of the press, who had been besieging his flat, interrogating his wife and following him when he left. 'They won't get anything out of me.' He told me that Norman had discovered that

Whittington Hospital was operating normally and had an out-patient clinic in the morning. 'If you attend at 11am you won't have too long to wait.' He wanted to ring up the consultant, Peyton, to tell him I was coming, but I forbade him to. 'Just write me a doctor's letter in the usual way. I will slip along without anyone knowing I am coming.' And so it was agreed. I ended an exhausting day with a long session with Janet, who, bless her, jumped into the breach, packed my parcels and finished all my Christmas shopping for me. And I was immensely touched to receive a beautiful bouquet of flowers from David. He is a nice lad.

Thursday, 18 December

I dressed with some difficulty and emerged timorously into the light of day, Edna having assured me that there were no pressmen lurking outside. As she humped me downstairs and packed me into the car we congratulated ourselves on our skill in evading them. (Apparently two turned up at the flat shortly after we had left.) At the hospital we followed Ernest Colin-Russ's instructions and as we turned into the yard outside Casualty Edna said, 'Someone is expecting us.' A uniformed figure waved us on. As the car stopped a man converged on us. 'Welcome, Minister. I am the Area Administrator.' The Nursing Officer emerged and introduced herself next, signalling a porter to bring a chair. Within seconds I was being wheeled smartly up the slope into the hospital. I kept bleating in bewilderment, 'But how did you know I was coming? I didn't want anyone to know.' No reply: they just wheeled me on relentlessly towards their planned destination, a well furnished little consulting room, set apart from the out-patients. A sister and nurse sprang to attention, the door opened and in marched the consultant, Mr Peyton, prim and correct. I felt like a prisoner in a Soviet psychiatric gaol, trapped by their air of medical authority and insistence on what was the 'right' treatment for me. (I'm willing to bet that the consulting room was a private one.) It was all done so swiftly and with such a sense of the proprieties that I felt helpless against it.

What saved me was a sudden onset of delayed shock: I burst into tears and howled my heart out. 'I particularly said I did not want anyone to know I was coming. I want to be treated like anyone else. Look, I've brought my doctor's letter,' I sobbed, pushing it at Mr Peyton. 'I just want to go into the out-patients' department and queue. I don't care how long I wait: one hour, two hours. I've brought my newspapers.' (*The Times* and the *Guardian* were clutched in my bruised hand.) Nurse and sister made soothing noises. 'I'll get you a coffee,' said nurse. 'And some tissues,' I begged, my eyes streaming. Mr Peyton was clearly embarrassed: 'We merely thought, Minister, that a busy person like you would not want to be held up in out-patients, though I can assure you you won't have to wait very long anyway, as clinic is nearly over. We were not trying to give you special treatment, merely to be helpful.' If he had been more human-looking I would have clutched his arm. 'I know you meant it for the best,' I said, 'but none of you have any idea how I am persecuted by the press. They have been trying to break into my flat to photograph me in bed; they never stop ringing up, so I can't get any rest; they watch the flat door day and night and follow my doctor over on his visits to me.' 'I can assure you that the press will not learn of this visit,' Mr Peyton replied rather stiffly. 'Mr Peyton,' I pleaded, 'you don't know the press. They would bribe every patient in the building to find if I had been here.' Mr Peyton succumbed. 'I think you had better register Mrs Castle at the out-patients in the normal way,' he told sister.

So sister, a very charming woman with a detached kind of gaiety, whirled me along the corridors to registry, everyone gawping as we swept by. By this time I was near to giggles: I expect this is the first time any of them have seen a Secretary of State in floods of tears. They all carried it off with great aplomb from then on. Sister dutifully deposited me in the corridor outside Mr Peyton's room. Slamming on my brakes, she said, 'I don't think you will have to wait very long.' Nor did I. The room was much barer than the earlier one, but perfectly adequate. Mr Peyton examined my leg gravely: it certainly did look a mess. He said, 'I think it is unlikely that you have broken anything, but I want to have an x-ray to make sure,' adding, with a rather wintry smile, 'I would do the same for anyone else.' So x-rayed I was and all was well, though as he bandaged my leg (very competently), Peyton told me there was always a danger of ulceration in a case like this and I must take that very seriously, resting the leg as much as possible. I thanked him – and sister – warmly and was on my way. Back in the flat without mishap, I fell into an exhausted sleep.

Later Norman phoned to suggest that we ought to forestall press enquiries by putting out a statement about my x-ray. One paper was already asking, 'Did she have to wait or did she walk straight in?' (So all my instincts were right.) Norman more or less confessed that he was responsible for tipping them off that I was coming and when I rebuked him he said, 'Well, people want to be helpful. As the Area Administrator put it to me, "She'll never believe this, but we really are quite fond of her." ' He also said John Stevenson had been trying to get in touch with me. 'Tell him from me,' I said, 'that after his poisonous piece today I intend never to speak to him on a personal basis again.' 'Delighted,' drawled Norman. 'The piece really is abominable.' For, of course, John Stevenson had managed to imply that I was tight when I fell. So it gave me great satisfaction to read in my *Standard* that Harold has taken a writ out against the *Mail* for a piece suggesting that he is 'tired' (i.e. brandy-soaked) and wants to quit. It might frighten them off some of their poison-pen work about other people.

I have had to leave David to handle the further 'clarification' meeting for which the juniors have asked. It is clear from what Jack tells me that at the meeting with their members on Tuesday Wardle and Zacharias played it pretty straight and genuinely tried to sell the agreement. He thought the decision to ask for further clarification was as much as anything else presentational. No doubt, too, it reflects the years of mistrust and a genuine desire for reassurance on certain points. The consultants' reaction to the pay beds settlement is far more contemptible. Norman phoned to report that their Central Committee decided today to continue its industrial action while it takes a leisurely month to ballot its rank and file on the Goodman proposals. Apparently Arnold is pretty furious, because his little group have so obviously abdicated all leadership, while Grabham positively led a revolt against the proposals he himself had agreed. What is more, they have treated Arnold more cavalierly than usual, failing to tell him what line they were taking or what was going on. Personally, I think this is all to the good: the more badly the professions behave, the more they let me off the hook – and the more they alienate that powerful objective witness, Arnold Goodman, the man they themselves retained. I decided to sleep on it. My plans to go down to HCF tomorrow remain unchanged. Apart from anything else, that fall has shaken me up more than I would have believed and my leg hurts like hell.

Friday, 19 December

Our statement on my x-ray has managed to stall off most of the papers, but the *Express* carries the headline, 'Emergency my foot!' and the *Telegraph* has sunk to its usual depths, saying that, even though I went as an out-patient under the NHS, 'she was seen by a consultant surgeon, a privilege for which many NHS patients have to wait months'. Ernest Colin-Russ was so furious at this blatant lie that he swore he'd cancel his order for the paper. I never thought to suggest he should write a letter, as my GP, to repudiate it.

I found the last remnants of my Christmas shopping a great strain and it was late afternoon before Edna and I got down to HCF. Arnold was on the phone to me, full of the poltroonery of his clients. He said he found their intention to carry on their industrial action totally unforgivable. As chairman of the Newspaper Proprietors' Association, he had offered them facilities for printing their ballot papers more quickly, but, when I snorted at this, he hastily agreed it really didn't go to the heart of their iniquity. So he was proposing to write a letter to *The Times*, saying how inexcusable it was to continue industrial action in this situation, particularly as it had been highly unconstitutional in the first place. Might he respectfully suggest that I should hold up any press comment I was considering making until he had drafted his letter and read it over to me? Of course, I agreed. No thunderings by me will have half the impact of a caustic letter by the 'independent' Arnold. He told me he had offered to go and speak to today's meeting of the consultants and describe the proposals, but they had not even done him the courtesy of informing him whether his offer was accepted. He was left to gather that it wasn't. It may prove, after all, not to have been a bad thing for this peculiar chap – half high principle and half unashamed pragmatism – to have been brought into personal dealings with this autocratic profession and to experience at first hand the kind of behaviour that has been driving Ministers of Health to despair for years. As he put it to me once during our long negotiations, 'I said to them that, when it comes to compromise in the most honourable sense of the word, she is a professional and you are a bunch of amateurs.' If he really produces this letter to *The Times* I shall begin to have some faith in him.[1]

As we talked I mentioned Harold's libel writ against the *Mail*. 'Will he win?' Arnold was unhesitant. Of course. Harold could not lose. Although, as chairman of the Newspaper Proprietors' Association, Arnold couldn't act for him, he had advised Harold that he had a watertight case. The *Mail*, for all its bravado, would be bound to climb down. Said Arnold, 'I have been a friend – I might say a close friend – of Harold's for many years now.' (My ears pricked up at this.) 'I have talked with him late into the night, during which he has sipped his brandy and water. At no time in our

---

[1] His letter, condemning industrial action by the consultants, duly appeared in *The Times* on 22 December.

late night talks was his judgment ever impaired. You just can't get away with suggesting that Harold Wilson, Winston Churchill or anyone else was incapable of governing the country because they sipped brandy.' I found his ringing faith very touching, but what struck me once again was the danger I had been in when Harold first tried to cook up the deal with Arnold on pay beds behind my back. It says a great deal for Arnold's judgment that he realized my anger that night was for real, and that, if I had been double-crossed, I could have destroyed his 'close friend' by resigning.

I limped around on my gammy leg, putting the Christmas goodies away and getting ready for my great Christmas *cordon bleu* exercise.

Saturday, 20 December

Tony Keable-Elliott came in, all warm and friendly, to commiserate about my leg, offer any help he could and, above all, to cope with the cholera injection that my wretched Private Office had belatedly realized I will need for my Middle East trip[1] in a few days' time. This is going to be some Christmas! While Ted and Eileen went shopping I limped round the kitchen, getting my delicacies ready. I also managed to make up the beds, write a charade for the children and generally mount this major military exercise of Christmas. Of course, my leg ached and I could not put it up as much as I should have done.

Sunday, 21 December

Went to the Pawsons' lunch-time drinks party. Two small gins and I nearly passed out. It must be that cholera injection! Spent the afternoon with my leg in the air, trying to stop it throbbing.

Monday, 22 December

Ted has come back from Brussels well below par. He has obviously caught some kind of flu bug. He is not ill enough to give in, so droops round the house, trying to put up his traditional decorations, complaining they are no good and refusing to go to bed. I manage to pack him off there each night at 6pm, but he leaves a trail of half-finished decorations behind him which he refuses to allow me to complete. I begin not to believe in this Christmas.

Norman has been on the phone about one item in my box: the appointment of the new Chief Social Work Officer. Pat Nairne has sent me a Minute about the findings of the Selection Board, consisting of the First Commissioner, Otton[2] and himself. I didn't know anything about the chap they have chosen, but what annoyed me was a footnote by Gerald [Johnson]: 'I am afraid that, under the misapprehension that you had already cleared this Minute, an approach was made to the PM and he has approved. However, the invitation to Mr Utting has not yet gone.' I have never heard of Mr Utting, nor have I interviewed him. Why the hell, therefore, should either the

---

[1] I had arranged to visit Saudi Arabia, Kuwait and Iran to do what I could to promote the export of medical equipment, drugs and NHS know-how generally.

[2] G. J. Otton, Deputy Secretary, Administration and Social Security Operations Group, DHSS.

PM or I be asked to 'approve'? I had quite a session on the phone with Norman about this. I had no objections, I said, to a system which said Ministers could not and should not interfere with such appointments. I could see arguments for that (though I thought they were exaggerated), but what I strongly objected to was the fiction that I had the right to approve or not approve the appointment of Mr Utting. The Civil Service really could not have it both ways: on the one hand, to keep these appointments within their closed vestry control and, on the other, claim that Ministers were responsible for all the actions of all the members of their departments. Could I please be told (a) whether I had any right to reject or select and (b), if not, how it could be made clear the choice was nothing to do with me? Norman was typically sympathetic, but he inevitably came back with the routine answer: these were matters for Selection Boards and not for Ministers, so the Minute should not have been put to me for approval. Which really does not answer my second point.

Wednesday, 24 December

Ted carried on nobly till the end of the evening's proceedings and then gave in and went to bed, not to emerge for two days.

Friday, 26 December

I carried on till the end of Boxing Day and then more or less collapsed with flu, not to emerge for a week. Not one of my happiest Christmases. All that food for Sunday's party wasted! Fortunately, the children had a whale of a time, despite the maladies of the adults. But an accumulation of overwork, that horrible fall, the cholera injection and virulent flu proved too much for me. I was so weak, I even had to cancel our visit to Phil and Colin for New Year's Eve! 'You'll never get to Kuwait unless you go back to bed,' Tony Keable-Elliott had warned me. I sent Ted off to Southampton on his own while the devoted Eileen nursed me splendidly.

One bright note in the darkness: the juniors on Tuesday accepted the results of the 'clarification' talks and are going back to work. Wasily Sakalo has sent me an unctuous series of letters, Christmas cards and calendars, declaring that there had never been anything 'personal' in our dispute. (I am getting a bit bored with these retrospective confessions of amity; they remind me of the succession of acts of contrition over nurses' pay I had from the unions at the last election.) One genuine comfort is the flood of Christmas cards I have had from total stangers this year, saying they believe I have been appallingly denigrated and unfairly abused and wanting me to know how much they admire me. That sort of thing counts, because, unlike Sakalo, these senders do not release them to the press for self-glorification. Another comfort is a glorious letter to *The Times* from George Godber,[1] following up Arnold's. I wish now I hadn't hung fire on the department's proposals to put Godber in the Lords. A few voices like his in that ghastly place and it might begin to mean something.

[1] The letter criticized industrial action by doctors. Its most telling sentence was: 'If the present course is continued I believe that many who, like myself, have been members of the BMA since qualifying will be forced to decide whether we can remain members of a body which is prepared to pursue its objects by methods harmful to patients.' (*The Times*, 31 December 1975.)

Finally there has been a belated letter from Harold. I know we have all been preoccupied, and no one more than he, but I did feel I deserved a mention in Cabinet, or a message of congratulations, for having settled the juniors and brought off this deal with the consultants. But not a word from No. 10. As far as the consultants were concerned, I was quite reconciled to the fact that Harold was probably nursing a grievance over the brutal way I had pushed him out of the picture – something in which I have been strongly backed by his pal, Arnold. But I did feel the triumph with the juniors deserved a nod. Now, unexpectedly, I have received a letter of 'appreciation' from Harold for the 'hard work and long hours' I have put in over the consultants' 'package'. I found it a bit stilted, but Ted thought it warm. 'You know who has inspired that, don't you? Arnold,' he said.

1976

Friday, 2 January

Box-loads of work have arrived for me to do before I go away. Norman reports that Goodman has been on to him about the covering document on pay beds the BMA are to send out with the ballot form. Arnold says it amounts to encouraging rejection and regards this as 'complete treachery'. However, since he is no longer sufficiently trusted by the BMA to be fully consulted about this, there is little he can do about it, he says. He is pinning his hopes on BUPA, who have decided to write to all doctors encouraging them to accept the proposals and have asked him to draft a letter for them. I told Norman that any split in the profession could only help us. I hoped Arnold would not give the impression that pay beds would continue indefinitely and I did *not* consider it wise to suggest that the unions supported the proposals. Considering the way the consultants were behaving, I wouldn't be surprised if they were to reverse that support anyway. I gather from my talks with Arnold that he wouldn't be surprised (or shocked) if they were to proceed to phase out pay beds by industrial action.

Monday, 5 January

Into the office for a mad last-minute rush of meetings, including one on the instructions to parliamentary draftsmen on the contents of the pay beds Bill. I had done a detailed Minute in reply to David's, and on the whole we did not disagree, though I stressed that the criteria for phasing out to be followed by the independent board were crucial and must be spelt out more clearly than in the Goodman proposals. A highlight was the meeting with Merrison, to invite him to chair the Royal Commission on the NHS. When at last I manoeuvred my way round to this point he said bluntly that he had rather guessed I was going to offer it to him. No false modesty about that man! He asked some searching questions, saying that he needed to be reassured that the Commission would be completely free and independent. Take the terms of reference, for instance: Mrs Thatcher had pointed out to the PM in the House that they did not preclude the discussion of pay beds. They were indeed very wide. For himself, as a product of a left-wing family, he was instinctively against pay beds (so Audrey Prime was right about that!), but he thought there was a case to be examined and he could not see that the Royal Commission under its terms of reference could be excluded from examining it. Some people would say that the issue was intrinsic to the future of the NHS. My heart sank and I decided to be as blunt back – so blunt as to be almost discouraging. I began to wonder whether David had not been right after all in resisting the setting up of the Royal Commission. (The decision to do so has not, in the event, had any influence on the junior doctors' dispute at all.) I told him that the Royal Commission would be free to discuss anything it liked relating to the NHS, but the Government too had its right to freedom and independence and the Government had decided that this was an issue of principle that ought to be decided by Parliament. He kept on quibbling about this, but I stood my ground, stressing that the Government intended to go ahead with its legislation in parallel with the Royal Commission's work. I was quite relieved when he indicated that the Commission might involve him in too much work and I sent him away to think about it. The worrying thing is that Derek Stevenson has indicated to Patrick Nairne that the BMA would welcome Merrison; but Audrey Prime insists he is first-class from our point of view.

Hurried to change for the reception Mike has organized to celebrate the full implementation of equal pay. Generous soul that he is, he has insisted that I must be the guest of honour as the author of the Equal Pay Act and I got a lot of greetings at the reception to that effect. Quite a pleasant occasion at the Banqueting Hall.

My export promotion tour of the Middle East started in Saudi Arabia. Our Embassy people there advised me to wear a long dress all the time and cover my arms in order not to offend the Saudis' susceptibilities. Apparently the Duchess of Kent on a visit there had insisted on wearing normal clothes and had got away with it, but her security guards had had an anxious time. Apparently, too, I was the first woman Minister ever to visit Saudi Arabia, so I thought I had better not expect them to make too many adjustments at the same time. I found in my wardrobe a long cotton summer evening dress with high neck and long sleeves which did perfectly, though after I had lived in it for two-and-a-half days I began to look rather creased.

To my surprise my opposite number as Minister of Health, Dr Al Jazairy, treated me perfectly naturally. This young and highly intelligent surgeon knew his country and his job and was soon grilling me about some of the more ambitious plans for health care development put forward by British consultants and British firms. He knew, as they did not seem to have grasped, that health care planning for five million people scattered over 920,000 square miles of mainly desert, served only by primitive roads, required improvization of the simplest kind. I noted in my diary: 'As I listened I was struck by ideas that were to recur throughout my whole trip. First, these oil countries have become deeply suspicious of the foreign firms, consultants and experts who, they think, have flooded their areas with impractical schemes to get their oil money. Secondly, their increasing anxiety about the finite nature of their newly acquired wealth has made them very cost-conscious. Thirdly, these men at the top are of high calibre whom we patronize at our peril: moreover, they are very well-informed about what is going on in the world and are not to be hoodwinked easily. Fourthly, whatever else the UN has or has not done, it has universalized the best thinking in every social field, including health: these Ministers of Health have learned a lot of things from WHO [World Health Organization]. Fifthly, one must not be misled by the calibre of these top men: there is nothing beneath them but a mass of poverty and illiteracy. Finally I realized how insular we are. We think there are great pickings to be garnered in these developing countries just by passing on our Western concepts. We have no exploratory humility.'

One highlight was my visit to King Khalid and Crown Prince Fayd. I asked Al Jazairy how I would know that the royal audience was at an end. *'They will serve first a cup of coffee, then of tea, then of coffee again,'* he told me. *'That is to symbolize the old custom of the desert. When the third cup has been served, you can rise to go.'* Promptly on the hour we were summoned into the King's audience chamber. The King himself, speaking no English, talked banalities to me through an interpreter. On the other side of the room was a real personality: Prince Fayd, swarthy, vigorous, self-assured and sophisticated. *'Welcome to my country,'* he said with outstretched hand. (I noted the *'my'* with interest.) Greetings over, Fayd retired to the other side of the room where he engaged in earnest conversation with a fellow Arab during the whole interview. He reminded me of a kind of Arab George Brown. Al Jazairy's advice to me proved wrong. They didn't bring coffee first, but tea. Then came the bitter coffee. Then nothing. Where were the three cups: the three days of the desert? Eventually in despair I signalled to the ambassador. Was I expected to get up and go? Yes, came the message and, by a kind of telepathic communication, we all rose in unison. Crown Prince Fayd broke off his conversation to rush across the room to say once again *'Welcome to my country'*.

At the end of my talks I offered to send out a group of my officials to study Saudi problems and advise on hospital design, costs of construction, health clinics and other medical services. The Minister accepted gratefully. *'One great thing in my favour,'* I wrote in my diary, *'was the respect in which they all hold the* NHS.'

On to Kuwait across desert wastes where the gas flares from the oil fields stood out in the darkening night. My Westernized reception at the airport made me feel an anachronism in my long, crumpled dress. Greeted by TV lights, cameras and flowers, the women all in short dresses, I was in a different world. I was soon engulfed in the warm welcome of Dr Awadhi, as enthusiastically pro-British as most of the Kuwaitis are. And I was sustained throughout my visit by the export-promotion enthusiasm of Britain's remarkable ambassador, Mr Archie Lamb. But here again I found that oil-rich Kuwait, in which every other person seemed to be a millionaire, suspected Western businessmen of trying to rob this tiny state of its sudden wealth. Dr Awadhi soon made it clear that, although his Government was prepared to spend millions on a national health service, it was not going to throw its money away. Cabinet, he assured me, had insisted on competitive tendering for all hospitals. He was ready with a long shopping list of requests for Britain's technical help: the specialists, nurses and other experts he wanted me to send out to them to train their personnel. In reply I gave him a long list of what Britain had already done in this field and was prepared to do, adding that in return I would expect British firms to get their fair share of that 'competitive tendering'. Enjoying each other's frankness, we parted in the greatest amity.

One of the things which worried the Kuwaitis, with their great faith in the NHS, was how their people could get medical treatment in Britain when pay beds were phased out. I told them that, when the legislation was passed, it should be possible to enter into *an agreement with Kuwait under which some 200 patients a year might be placed in* NHS *beds for specialist treatment (at full economic cost) and with no queue jumping.*

In Iran another contrast awaited me. In this huge country, the size of Western Europe, most of the population of thirty-two million live in the few towns. Teheran, I noted, was one of the dirtiest and most disappointing capital cities I had ever seen. 'Iran has a Parliament,' I wrote, 'but it is clear the Shah is boss. His picture and Farah's are everywhere.' One of my main reasons for going was to clear up problems that had arisen over a British tender for a big hospital and I soon found I was up against the familiar oil states phenomenon: a deep suspicion of foreign firms. The Minister of Social Affairs, Dr Shaikh, another surgeon, was an aggressive ball of energy who knew his facts and clearly was not going to be a pushover for anyone. So there ensued some days of hard bargaining, with Dr Shaikh insisting that the British tender was preposterously high. Our wrangle was only resolved during my visit to the Prime Minister, Mr Hoveyda. I had been warned he was a tough customer, with a remarkable survival record of ten years, but we found ourselves in unexpected harmony as a result of his obvious fascination with the NHS. *He congratulated me on my fight with the British doctors, declaring that doctors had become 'the bandits of society'. I seized my advantage, pointing out that the British firms whose tender had been so much criticized had built an exactly similar hospital for the* NHS. *This gave him an idea. Why didn't Shaikh send someone to look at it? If the hospital was okay and the firm's price was fair, they would build one in Iran and, if all went well, would standardize on it. Dr Shaikh and I responded enthusiastically and so it was arranged.*

Throughout my visit I was struck by how far Westernization had advanced: at any rate in Iran's top society. The position of women was significant. Dr Shaikh's Vice-Minister was a woman and Mrs Afkami, the delightful Minister for Women's Affairs, had just been appointed the first woman Cabinet Minister in Iranian history. But the people I met were clearly not typical and the Embassy warned me there were undercurrents of unrest. 'For all its talk of development plans for the social services,' I wrote in my diary, 'this country endures enormous contrasts of wealth and poverty: it salves its conscience with charitable works under the patronage of the Shah's family.'

I returned home feeling I had made an important breakthrough. Dr Shaikh kept his word and sent two of his top officials to study our NHS *hospitals. They declared themselves very impressed but Dr Shaikh continued his running war about the British firm's price. The dispute had not been settled when the Iranian revolution broke out. Mr Hoveyda was one of the first to be executed.*

Friday, 16 January

On the plane I got the first indication that I was back to the home stint. This was a big story in the *Daily Telegraph* with a banner headline: 'Castle Plans Pay Beds for Foreigners.' It was the sole product of the long press conference I gave yesterday, where the *Express* and the *Telegraph* were lurking purely to stir this issue up. Not a word about all we had done for the export drive. Indeed, the suggestion was that the main reason I had gone to the Middle East was to arrange private treatment for foreigners. (The only place at which it had been mentioned to me was Kuwait.) I suddenly realized why the trip had done me so much good: it was because I had been engaged in constructive discussions all the time, with a lot of tough argument, but no carping criticism. Now I am back to the steady drip of denigration, day by day. Well, to hell with them. I intend to enjoy life.

I told Norman in strict confidence on the plane that I intend to retire this autumn, as soon as the pay beds legislation is through. 'I want to go out of government at my peak,' I said. He said he thought I was wise. 'We are in for a nasty few months,' I told him. 'I don't suppose it will be easy to get the Bill through and no doubt my departure will be a messy business.' But I am undismayed: full of the knowledge that I have done a good job in the Middle East.

I did not allow anything to spoil my homecoming. I distributed the presents I had brought back, like an oil sheikh distributing largesse. Everyone said how blooming I looked. As for the photos Shaikh had given me of his reception for me at the mountain club, Ted said he had never seen better ones of me. 'It is a fraud to pretend the woman in those pictures is about to become an old age pensioner,' he declared. The glow continued unabated, even while I waded through three red boxes. Among the papers was the Radcliffe Report by the group of Privy Councillors Harold had set up to consider the rules for ministerial memoirs. 'The attached was discussed at Cabinet today,' minuted Gerald. 'I think you have an interest!' I have indeed – and read it at once. I have never read anything more pompously written, but it did at least say that confidentiality between colleagues was a matter of honour and not for the courts, and recommend that the period of confidentiality be reduced to fifteen years. I see from Thursday's Cabinet Minutes that, though Harold wanted to publish and accept the report at once, some members of Cabinet wanted to go further towards open government. So Harold had to allow Cabinet more time to make up its mind.

I also see that Roy Mason has, as I anticipated, got away with it on public expenditure. He has only to find defence cuts of £193 million, compared with the £400 million Denis originally asked of him. So Denis's total saving is down.

Jack has sent me a copy of the *British Medical Journal*, reporting the special meeting of Council in December on the Goodman proposals. Of course, Lewin and Grabham gave distorted reports, implying that the initiative in pressing the Goodman proposals on them had come from the PM, who had urged that they should be agreed. But, they said, they had resisted this. What cowards they are! And how essential it is that I should have kept a detailed record of what actually took place.

Monday, 19 January

The *Daily Telegraph* is keeping up its line on what I am supposed to have done about pay beds in the Middle East, whipping up the maximum distrust of me again. All this has done is to harden my resolve not to yield another inch on the pay beds issue. It won't necessarily be a bad thing if the Goodman proposals are turned down.

Spent the day working myself in at the office pretty peacefully. I doubt if it will be as relaxed as this much longer! Norman tells me he keeps being peppered with messages from No. 10 to the effect that Ministers must not retain expensive gifts they acquire on their foreign travels: anything worth more than £30 must become the property of the department. 'I'm afraid we'll have to hang the Persian picture Shaikh gave you in the office,' he said, 'for a time, at any rate!'

Tuesday, 20 January

Office meeting on the Royal Commission. Merrison has accepted the chairmanship, with no serious further demur about the right to deal with the pay beds issue. Indeed, he has been exchanging confidential letters with Patrick Nairne, in which, while reiterating again the need for the Royal Commission to be, and be seen to be, completely independent, he has said he wouldn't like the issue of pay beds to be referred to them for an interim report. While I was going through every line of Merrison's conditions carefully, David sat looking down his nose in one of his frosty moods and suddenly burst out that he didn't see what I was being so suspicious about. That lad spoils a great deal of natural charm with these sudden flashes of insolent arrogance – just like Roy Jenkins. It seems to be a failing of the Manifesto Group. It is very irritating when what I really need is support against the relentless pressures of the Establishment. I am far more in danger – just as any Labour Minister is – of relaxing my guard too much than of being too bloody-minded. These civil servants are so damned reasonable – and politics isn't. I insisted, despite David's attitude, on redrafting the press announcement of Merrison's appointment and including in it a repeat, not only of the PM's statement on the terms of reference, but of his specific exclusion of the pay beds issue.

I am also wondering uneasily how the junior doctors' issue is going to turn out. Gedling has reported to me on the progress of the joint oral evidence we are giving with them to the Doctors and Dentists Review Body. While I have been away Jack, David *et al*. have done an excellent job in handling the juniors, but it is clear there is a danger of a breach developing once again between the juniors' leaders and the rank and file. The former realize that the amount of 'extra' money the audit has revealed is too small to meet the extravagant illusions that have been fostered – but the rank and file do not. I doubt we shall get through all this without another explosion, Jack being particularly worried about the insistence of the new leaders that 'no detriment' is no longer an issue. He thinks it is.

Wednesday, 21 January

To my fury, tomorrow's Cabinet has been switched to this morning, which means I shall have to miss the first of the series of informal meetings with chairmen of local authority social service committees that I have arranged with such difficulty. Just my luck, to launch an important new initiative and then not be able to be there! It is all the more irritating because the only item for Cabinet, apart from parliamentary business, is the Radcliffe Report. Mike has sent an apologetic Minute to the PM, saying he is sorry to stand between the Cabinet and complete harmony on this, but he thinks it ought to be further discussed. Wedgie, too, has minuted the PM along the same lines, saying he hopes the PM will be able to give an open verdict on the report when presenting it.

Harold opened the discussion with a long dissertation on the report. He confessed that he had given oral evidence to the committee, so it wasn't surprising that he thought the report was 'very good'. He thought it was right that, up to fifteen years, the onus of proof should be on the memorialist; over fifteen years the onus of proof should be the other way (presumably on the Cabinet Office and the PM). The real problem, Harold continued, was that of the memorialist who dies before publication: one could not appeal to his better feelings then. So he had one piece of advice to give to colleagues: not to die, or else to make 'adequate testamentary disposition' of their memoirs if they did. He concluded that the Government must 'take a view' on the report.

Mike began, more diffidently than ever. He didn't, he said, agree with Dick Crossman in many respects. He didn't take a 'lax view of the way in which these matters should be conducted'. (He sounds more like Hugh Foot every day.) 'I strongly believe in the confidentiality approach.' But (and here he didn't sound like brother Hugh) he didn't think Radcliffe's proposals were the right way. They had skated over the way in which Churchill had behaved. He who had 'pilloried Auchinleck'. Nor was he sure that they had got the enforcement side of it right. 'The legal advice to us on the Crossman case was that the Official Secrets Act could be invoked.' That really ought to be cleared up. In fact, leakages from Cabinet ('And they have been getting more frequent recently,' Harold chipped in) were much more damaging. 'Obviously some members of Cabinet have talked,' said Mike. He therefore could not wholeheartedly accept the report and thought it ought to be publicly discussed first. (He didn't mention the Boy Scout pledge we are all supposed to sign now.)

Elwyn next, who characteristically supported the acceptance of the report. Then came Roy J. in one of his civilized, but rather inconclusive, contributions. He said it was a 'good report on an unimportant subject'. Perhaps the period of silence was too long. But on the whole he didn't object to the report. In the end it came down to a matter of the individual judgment of Ministers as to how it was right to behave. I followed him up, saying he was right to say this was an 'unimportant subject'. We in Cabinet tended to over-exaggerate the effect even of such leaks of confidentiality as Dick's memoirs. All right, when Dick's book was serialized it was very irritating to see banner headline quotes in the *Sunday Times* to the effect that 'Barbara was impossible': a judgment which everyone round that table knew could not be correct. (Grins.) But it was a 'one-day wonder'. And my turn would come to get my own back on Dick. (Reg P. nodded at this.) I therefore agreed with Mike that we should publish the Radcliffe Report for public discussion before we stated our own views. I thought we would be surprised to find how far ahead of us were not merely the newspapers, but politicians generally and even civil servants. (I was strengthened in saying this by the brief Jack had put up to me, calling not only for a shorter ban than fifteen years, but for greater accountability by civil servants, who today wield such power. To this Norman had appended a Minute: 'As one of those thought to be in need of care and protection, can I say how much I agree with Jack Straw. Fifteen years is far too long. An equally important issue is whether any civil servant criticized in a Minister's memoirs should have the right to answer back. If this could be agreed I would be inclined to reduce the fifteen years.')

Of course, all this was far too advanced for our Harold. Even Wedgie's highly amusing speech failed to penetrate Harold's cocoon of conventionality. 'What we think about each other is hardly news,' chuckled Wedgie and he proceeded to give a hilarious account of an interview Anthony Part had given on TV about what it had been like to work with Wedgie as a Minister and how he had set about resisting his wilder views. Wedgie had us rolling with laughter. But Harold remained unimpressed. He agreed with me that press leaks were the biggest example of the breaches of confidentiality we were supposed to deplore. Nonetheless, he had little difficulty in getting acceptance of the report through that supine Cabinet. So I face having to sign a bit of paper saying I won't do anything in breach of the report, while my colleagues – including Harold – will go on merrily briefing the press. As I told them, 'I am constitutionally incapable of leaking to the press.' And I don't intend to sign anything which prevents me putting distorted records straight.

My Nye Bevan memorial lecture has been duly turned into a Fabian pamphlet, embargoed till Monday. I was immensely pleased when Laurie Pavitt stopped me in the division lobby to tell me it was the best résumé of Nye's fight with the doctors he had ever read. And he heartily agreed with my general line. So I'm glad I went ahead with it after all – though the publication on Monday may well raise another storm about my 'rocking the boat'. But the consultants' ballot will be over by then. It is good to have this political testimony on the record because I am under attack from the Nick Bradleys of the NEC (and from Stark Murray in *Tribune*) for having 'sold out' on pay beds. Heaven save one from one's comrades!

I am also in the middle of a major row on abortion. The Labour women MPs have secured a discussion in party meeting tomorrow on whether the Select Committee should be re-established.[1] They have been begging me to say, in replying to the discussion, that I am against it being set up again. David has told them he is sure I will and he and I have been working on a draft speech giving the reasons why I think the Select Committee has finished its useful work. I have made up my mind that the time has come for me to stand up and be counted on this and I have arranged for my speech to be released to the press in full. Somehow all this has leaked and in the lobbies this evening I have been besieged by irate Catholics. Jimmy White threatened to resign from the party if there was any tinkering with the free vote. Bob Mellish took me aside to talk to me like a Dutch uncle, though a friendly one. 'I know that with all your savvy you'll realize this issue is dynamite.' I kept my nerve, refusing to answer those who came up to me asking what I was going to say tomorrow. 'You'd better come and listen, hadn't you?'

Finally Harold waylaid me and took me to his room. His eyes were baggy and I noted that he was in one of his 'I'll get the hell out of it' moods. (I personally think he

[1] For some time there had been determined attempts in certain quarters of the House to limit, or even reverse, the provisions of the 1967 Abortion Act which legalized abortion in certain circumstances. One of these efforts, a Private Member's Bill introduced in November 1964, by James White, Labour MP for the highly Catholic constituency of Glasgow (Pollok), had aroused intense controversy and led to the setting up of a Select Committee to examine it. By the time the previous session had ended the Committee had only been able to make some relatively uncontroversial recommendations for strengthening the safeguards against abuse, on which David Owen and I were already acting, but the anti-abortionists were demanding that the Committee be reconstituted in order to consider more fundamental changes. It was this that David and I were resisting because we believed that the Act was basically sound, but the Government had agreed to put the matter to the House.

is getting ready to chuck things up.) Pouring me a brandy he said he had given up brandy himself in order to lose weight, arguing that for some unknown reason he had actually lost weight since switching to beer. 'I drink five pints a day,' he boasted, but proceeded to pour himself some Madeira. The pleasantries over, we proceeded to have a major row. He told me categorically that he wasn't going to have me splitting the party. 'I'm sick of pulling this party back from the brink. If this goes on I shall throw in my hand – and then see how some of you will get along.' 'Like who?' I replied, at which he gave me a hostile look, as if to say, 'You'd go, for one.' Does he realize how little his threats worry me? Harold then laid down the law: I could say how I was going to vote personally, but I must not give any reasons. If I did I must give both sides of the issue, or another Minister would have to put the reasons the other way. I quite liked this latter idea, but he did not. 'Perhaps someone else had better speak tomorrow: John Silkin, for instance,' Harold went on. I told him John was as much against re-establishing the Select Committee as I was. 'And imagine what will be said if I do not speak now,' I continued. He went on menacing me about how neutral I must be in my arguments, ending nastily, 'Think about it.' I did, going to bed wondering how I could salvage something from this wreck. Clearly the speech David and I have drafted will not do.

Thursday, 22 January

Got up early to rewrite my abortion speech. I was rather pleased with it, having, I thought, rather skilfully implied the case for not reappointing the Select Committee without defying Harold's fiat or putting backs up. And, of course, I stated that I would be voting against. Jack and David thought it was excellent, though David looked grim at Harold's ruling. 'It is going to make our position very difficult in the debate,' he said.

The meeting of the PLP was exceptionally well attended, for a Thursday night. All the abortion antagonists were there. As Shirley slipped into a seat next to me on the platform she whispered, 'I've come to the conclusion that your job is even worse than mine.' In the debate Kevin McNamara demanded that I should not disclose my own views, as this would inevitably carry the weight of a Secretary of State. Brian Walden, on the other hand, made a passionately eloquent speech, demanding that the party should have the courage of its convictions and I of mine. I sat there calmly, convinced that the speech I had prepared would strike exactly the right note between the two. And so it proved. It was temperate, cunning and firm and it did the trick. 'Ten out of ten,' said Bob Mellish loudly afterwards. Even Jimmy Dunn thanked me, while Shirley said, 'No one could object to *that*.' And yet it had left the party in no doubt where I stood. 'That is my conviction, Brian,' I had said and he came and congratulated me on it. So did innumerable others, including the women who were delighted that I had not been frightened off the one thing they wanted: a statement of how I intended to vote myself. 'Never in my life have I been accorded such unanimity,' I said to Norman, back in my room. 'I wouldn't have believed it would be possible on that subject,' he replied.

Earlier I had had a deputation from the NEC on pay beds, led by Tom Bradley. He explained that, in view of my unavoidable absence from last month's NEC, due to my fall, it had been decided not to take Nick Bradley's resolution condemning me until a deputation had heard my views. I have been worrying what to say to the deputation because, of course, they will have to report back and that will be reported to the press. So I cannot disclose my whole strategy. However, I managed to make some bull points, David backed me up and Tom and Lena nodded approvingly. Even Renee Short was not too hostile. I doubt whether I have shaken Nick Bradley from his belief that it is only 'a few men at the top of the profession' who are fighting my policy, and Geoff Bish looked unconvinced, but Tom promised me he would consult me about what he would say in his report to next week's NEC. So it wasn't too bad at all. The right kind of resolution could actually help me, but what the 'Left' want is an attack on me personally.

Sunday, 25 January

My constituency conscience is at rest after a two-day visit to Blackburn. Ted is at home for the weekend, his hospital tests having so far proved negative.[1] But he has to go back for more tonight. Going through my boxes I find the *British Medical Journal*, with its report of the BMA Council meeting on 7 January. Once again, I note how Lewin and co. are wriggling over their responsibility for the Goodman proposals. Lewin was reported as repeating that the PM had asked Goodman to prepare the proposals. 'The meetings which were held over the next few days with Lord Goodman were simply to enable the profession's representatives to act as technical advisers,' he declared. Really!

Monday, 26 January

The cameras were outside Transport House as I arrived for the anticipated row over unemployment at the TUC Liaison Committee. Harold and Jim were missing, no doubt because of the Iceland crisis, but the trade unions were there in force – even Hughie Scanlon. The original purpose of the meeting was to discuss the Devolution White Paper, but Tom Bradley, in the chair, suggested we took unemployment first. Jack Jones said grimly he would walk out unless we did. Len led off for the TUC, saying there was 'great concern' for the effect that unemployment could have on relations between the TUC and the government. 'There is scope for selective action.' He then set out a list of proposals for job creation; job protection ('Thorn Industries for example. We are appalled that the Government is prepared to stand by and let Skelmersdale go down'); help for people on low living standards like pensioners ('though we understand it must be within available resources'); investment promotion; training; export promotion and import saving, and selective import controls. All this, he said, was 'quite consistent with the need to keep down inflation'. He

---

[1] My husband had been losing weight and appetite and his consultant had sent him to the London Hospital for blood tests.

ended passionately. 'We shall be looking for action and *must* be looking for action. Let there be no doubt about this.'

Jack Jones came in to support that. 'The NEB should give backing to firms facing redundancies,' he urged. The allocation of £1,000 million to the NEB over the next five years was not sufficient. The amount should be brought forward now. Selective import controls was not just a question of colour TV tubes: 'We've done damn all about Japan.' Why not lift HP restrictions on British goods and not on foreign ones? (He must realize, surely, that membership of the EEC prevents that!) We should have three-quarters of a million people in training. Local authorities should be encouraged to look at community work schemes. Even refuse collectors were being laid off. Then take pensions: 'There is a need to encourage spending by those who will spend it on essentials.' There should be a pension increase of £6 a week over the next six months. The unions would like to feel the party was united. 'There must be a statement at the end of this meeting.'

David Basnett followed. 'We see a problem that we must solve together, unlike what the media are trying to whip up. But we must preserve our credibility. We must also stop the collapse of British industry.' That meant more money for the NEB. School-leavers should know that they would have a job or training to go to. 'Let us have a little imagination and say these things,' he concluded. Hughie Scanlon was almost desperate. 'Whatever we do, we have missed the bus and it is going to be calamitous. Do you ever listen to us? We've put the points to you about Japan time and again. Please tell us the truth. Are you afraid of GATT, EEC or what? I'm not yet convinced that a degree of reflation is not necessary, but, leaving that aside, there are all those other steps the Government could take.' Hughie went on to castigate poor Shirley's Prices Ministry. 'What has been happening on prices makes nonsense of what we have been saying. When is publicity going to be given to how many applications for price increases have been made and how many refused?' Alf Allen was sombre: 'The issue of credibility is crucial. I hope we are not all going to lose our nerve and indulge in virtuoso solos. Any criticism of each other in public does irreparable harm to what we are trying to do.' I found it all desperately moving, like a Greek drama. We all feel caught in a web and are fighting to keep our human identity. Denis welcomed the 'tone' of the discussion and promised to consult the TUC about the rate of reflation and to consider the particular suggestions. Mike hinted that the Government was considering the sort of ideas Len had spelt out, though obviously it would be wrong for him to commit himself before Cabinet had approved them. In the end the trade union boys were somewhat mollified – and obviously deeply anxious to preserve our unity and the Government.

A long meeting back at the office on Instructions to Parliamentary Counsel for the Private Practice Bill. I began by saying that that title (which the office had cooked up) would not do. This wasn't a Bill to safeguard private practice, but to phase out pay beds. So we agreed on the title of the 'NHS (Miscellaneous Provisions) Bill'.[1] (We are hoping to include in it mandatory vocational training for GPs, anyway.) We then went

[1] We later changed it again to the Health Services Bill, which became the Health Services Act in November 1976.

through it line by line, with me examining every dot and comma to ensure that we were not entering any trap. I noted with relief that most of the text covered the phasing out of private out-patient facilities from NHS hospitals as well. This is crucial, because, if consultants were able to continue these private out-patient consultations, even after pay beds had been phased out, they could use them to jump their private patients to the top of the queue for NHS beds.

Tuesday, 27 January

Our Parliamentary Questions went smoothly, not to say boringly. The Opposition is so muted these days it is hardly fun. Patrick Jenkin, making his first appearance on the front bench against me, didn't take me on. It was left to Gerry Vaughan to make some snide remarks about my Middle Eastern trip. I was sorry that my PQ on this was not reached. I sat in a glow of secret virtue over what I had done and a sense of satisfaction that Margaret Thatcher has ditched that posturing emptiness, Norman Fowler, and moved him to Transport. After his fiasco in trying to bring me down, it is hardly surprising, but I take it unto myself as a compliment. It is I, not he, who has drawn blood.

In the House, Norman dug up Tom Bradley to talk to me about tomorrow's meeting of the NEC. Tom told me in the most friendly way that he wanted to help. He was going to make a report on our recent meeting in general terms and try to get the NEC to refer Nick Bradley's resolution condemning me on pay beds to the Home Policy Committee for consideration, so as to give me a breathing space. I only know that I am not prepared to be made a Roman sacrifice for the muddled emotionalism of the so-called Left. I told Tom that a resolution in the right form could actually be a help to me. Unfortunately, one cannot, in a democracy, dictate the terms of one's support. I am out at the moment to secure my deserts, which means I am not prepared to be pilloried for Harold's failings or for the necessities of practical politics.

Wednesday, 28 January

Obviously Tom had been talking to Ron Hayward, because, when I arrived at the NEC, I found Ron was most anxious to help too. When I had a word with both of them before the meeting Ron told me he had that morning received a letter from NUPE denouncing my compromise. 'We've got to stop that coming before today's meeting,' he said firmly. Tom told the NEC that the report of their deputation's discussion with me was so detailed it ought to go to Home Policy first. Nick Bradley dismissed this as unconvincing and said he intended to press his resolution. 'I have here the copy of a letter from NUPE which was intended to be dealt with at the same time as this item.' (So NUPE must have slipped him a copy.) Then Ron Hayward weighed in. There was, he said, a ballot of the consultants going on and it was a good principle, which we always observed, not to do anything which interfered with a union ballot. This did the trick, Eric Heffer observing that, as a former Minister, he could appreciate the importance of this point. 'If Nick insists on pressing his Motion I shall certainly support it, but if he can be present at the Home Policy Committee and speak to his resolution there, I suggest to him he should withdraw it now.' Eventually Nick did so, with the greatest reluctance. What always interests me is the readiness of the 'Left' to condemn their colleagues before they are heard.

Another example of this comradely tendency of the NEC came on a Motion by Mik on the Honours List: 'That this NEC notes that a life peerage has been bestowed, presumably on the recommendation of the PM, on the head of the company which is the largest contributor to the funds of the Conservative Party and its allies, and expresses the hope that the object of the exercise was not to encourage increased donations to those funds from other companies.' It transpired Mik was referring to the chairman of Guest, Keen and Nettlefolds. I asked at once how we could be sure that it had been done on the recommendation of the PM, but Mik brushed me aside, saying it must have been approved by the PM as an industrial award. Wedgie then said he was intending to put a document on the reform of the Honours system before the next meeting of Home Policy. 'As I wrote it ten years ago, it is quite ready,' he quipped. Bryan Stanley and I welcomed this, but, as Wedgie failed to put this piece of information in the proper form of an amendment to Mik's resolution, Tom, from the chair, said sadly that he had no alternative but to put Mik's Motion to the vote. At once all the sheep-like hands shot up in support of it. Only Mike and I voted against. I did so on the grounds that there was no firm evidence on which to condemn the PM. Our dear comrades of the NEC condemn easy, as I well know. Wedgie, canny as usual, abstained.

On one thing I did support Mik: the reference back of the item in the Organization Committee Minutes about the re-selection of sitting MPs. Mik's motion at the committee giving a Constituency Labour Party the right, at the discretion of its General Management Committee, to hold a selection conference during the life of each Parliament, even where it had a sitting Labour MP, had clearly been fiercely debated in the committee. Curiously, all five trade union members present at the committee had opposed it strongly: all the MPs had supported it. The vote had been five to five with John Chalmers voting twice, to give his casting vote against as chairman. So Mik was clearly within his rights in reopening it. And he did so on the grounds that this was the only way to take the heat out of situations in which CLPs *did* wish to get rid of their MP. I agreed with him. Bryan Stanley, to my surprise, opposed the reference back vehemently. Mik's proposition, he said, would be a 'recipe for disaster', adding, 'I oppose it with all my strength.' His reason was that 'we've got to give MPs a reasonable sense of security'. (I couldn't help thinking that the very nature of our job denies us that.) The local party, he went on, would be 'in constant turmoil'. Where was the right of appeal? I found it all very odd. There must be some innerness of the trade union movement involved here: perhaps a fear that all trade union offices would be in danger of becoming elective if we set this example. Anyway, Mik only carried his reference back by twelve votes to ten.

I also supported Wedgie on his proposition that chairmen of committees of the NEC should have the right, at their discretion, to hold press conferences after their committee meetings, together with the General Secretary. This strikes me as entirely the right way to defuse press sensations. Jim, of course, opposed. It would be terrible to have 'blow by blow' accounts of what went on, he maintained. I said the 'blow by blow' accounts appeared in the press anyway as soon as anyone thought we had something to hide. The press were only interested in forbidden fruit. Anyway, despite Jim's opposition, we carried it. It occurred to me afterwards that the first occasion on which the experiment will be tried will be next Home Policy, when pay beds will be discussed. Well, I don't mind the party expressing a strong view on this matter as soon as the BMA ballot is out of the way. It will be good for the medical profession to realize that theirs is not the only lobby. It might educate Arnold Goodman.

On the International Committee Minutes Judith Hart raised the question of the World Bank loan to Chile, with the inference that once again the Government was going to sell the party out. Jim, asked about this, just said he didn't know anything about it, which, in my view, justifies a lot of Mik's complaints about him. If he had read his Minutes he ought to have realized that this would be a highly sensitive issue and informed himself. I passed Judith a note saying I would raise it in tomorrow's Cabinet.

One little flicker of genuine comradeship. When we came to the item of Mik's report on the annual conference of the Irish Labour Party, Fred Mulley went out of his way to praise it as a 'literary gem', adding: 'It is one of the few reports coming before this NEC that I actually enjoyed reading.' He was right. Mik writes racily and perceptively. But it will be nice when both sides of the ideological argument always go out of their way to praise where they can praise genuinely.

Incidentally, as I thought, the press have picked up my Fabian pamphlet on the NHS: I even heard long quotes (and alarmist ones) on the BBC news on Monday morning. Good. Perhaps now some of the 'Left' will realize that I am hardly in the mood for selling out.

Back at the office I called in David and Jack to tell them what had happened at the NEC on pay beds. I asked Jack to check up with the health unions to see if I could get any support against a NUPE attack. And I turned the tables on David by saying to him: 'I warn you that, if the BMA ballot is unfavourable, it will be impossible for us to go ahead with the Goodman proposals. The party and the unions will demand that we go ahead with our legislation as originally planned.' And I added, 'If Harold and Cabinet try to force me to overrule the party on this, I shall resign. I do not intend to end my ministerial days with another *In Place of Strife*.' I think David saw the force of this. When I said, 'We shouldn't be in this mess if Harold had not cooked up that meeting with Goodman and the profession behind my back', he nodded vigorous agreement. 'That Rome business was outrageous,' he said.

Thursday, 29 January

I am interested to see from *The Times* that Harold has rushed in furiously on the Honours point. As I suspected, Ray Brookes's Honour was in the Opposition leader's gift. No wonder Harold is mad, and, if I were Wedgie, I'd feel rather small. But Harold does not come out so well from the *New Law Journal*'s comments on the

Radcliffe Report – and quite right too.[1] Cabinet this morning was called for the unearthly late hour of 11.30am, which, in my view, is to devalue it. I am all in favour of shorter, crisper Cabinet meetings, but this is to truncate its whole status. One of the reasons for putting back the time may be the fact that Harold, having told me last week that there would be a discussion on Europe, including direct elections, has at the last minute withdrawn this item. Poor Jack, who has been working overtime on it, has been thrown out of gear. He failed, as a result of concentrating on this item, to prepare a brief on the question of whether we should take up our option for British Nuclear Fuels to get another 1,100 tons of uranium from Namibia in 1977–82. This was raised by Wedgie, who had put in a paper saying that we should even cancel the existing contract,[2] but in his argument in Cabinet he simply said that the situation had changed since 1974. The argument went on predictable lines, because OPD had endorsed taking up the option by an overwhelming majority. Harold had the sense, however, to realize that it must come to Cabinet.

One interesting moment came when Harold asked Jim to put the OPD case. Jim bridled and refused. He didn't see why he should put the pro-option case 'for the benefit of the memorialists'. Why didn't Harold put it himself? Harold, taken aback, said all right, but he hadn't really prepared it – and then made rather a thin case. Peter and Mike backed Wedgie in saying the option should not be taken up at the present time, when the whole southern Africa position was in the melting pot and Namibia might soon be independent of South Africa. Eric backed the pros on the grounds that there were no reliable alternative sources of supplies. (Anyone who thinks that lad is anything but a confirmed right-winger is badly misled by his personal charm.) Harold had undermined this line of argument by admitting that the extra supplies were 'marginal'. He then cut short the discussion, as we had already run out of our truncated time, by asking if anyone else agreed with Wedgie. I said yes, and so did John Silkin, Shirley and Reg P. ('Fancy Shirley doing this,' a shocked Fred Peart whispered to Harold Lever.) And so we were outnumbered. Afterwards Harold Lever came up to me and asked me in his innocent way what was the moral difference between the original contract and the option for more. 'Just a simple question of expediency, my dear Harold,' I said to him sweetly. 'It is always good policy to be on the winning side. And the Africans are winning.' That silenced him.

Harold's reason for withdrawing direct elections from the agenda was explained by

---

[1] In an editorial on 29 January the *New Law Journal* criticized the Radcliffe Committee for giving too little weight to the public interest in the disclosure of government proceedings and in particular its recommendation for a fifteen-year delay in publication unless the Cabinet Secretary and Prime Minister concurred. The editorial went on: 'What Cabinet Secretaries and Ministers are capable of taking exception to has recently been revealed by the Crossman *Diaries* affair: but on what grounds they took exception, claiming that publication would be damaging to the public good, is not known even now – even, that is, after the question has meanwhile had a thorough going-over in the courts.'

[2] The existing contract was originally negotiated in 1968 between Riofinex and the UK Atomic Energy Authority. In December 1974, it was assigned to the publicly-owned British Nuclear Fuels Ltd and provided for the delivery of 7,500 short tons of uranium oxide over the period 1977–82. On 9 December 1974 Joan Lestor, as Under Secretary of State at the Foreign and Commonwealth Office, announced the Government's decision not to cancel the contract. This decision was based on the Law Officers' opinions and was re-affirmed by Tony Benn in a written answer on 12 April 1976.

Jim, who said we needed consultations with everybody before producing our own White Paper. Some of us, led by Mike, tried to argue that we should have had a Cabinet discussion before going into consultations at all, but we came up against Jim's and Harold's inexorable ruling that we were committed to direct elections anyway by the Treaty of Rome. We pointed out that this had hardly been highlighted during the referendum campaign: it hadn't even been mentioned in the Government's Red White and Blue document. But foresight won't avail us now. I remember making a major speech in Blackburn during the campaign, pointing out this issue, but of course the press never reported it, despite my very factual hand-out. The responsibility of the press for closed government should never be underestimated. They say they want to know everything, but don't report what they don't want the country to know. Jim got out of the present row by reading the letter he had sent to Ron Hayward, to the chairman of the PLP, *et al.*, asking for their views on how this inescapable commitment could best be carried out. The British people were blinkered in the referendum campaign and now we are trapped.

When I raised Chile, as I had promised Judith I would do, Denis said in surprised innocence that of course we were going to abstain in the World Bank discussions on this contested loan. When I told Mik afterwards that everything was going to be all right, he agreed with me that the Government was mad in not making its good decisions better known.

I had arranged to do a two-day tour of our offices at Newcastle, which I have had to postpone so often, and to go north this afternoon, but once again I have been foiled by a three-line Whip, this time on the unemployment debate. This means, if I am to get to Newcastle at all, that I must catch a very late night sleeper tonight. The unemployment debate ended in its usual débâcle for the Tories, who, I am convinced, are terrified at the thought of power, for all Margaret's irrelevant posturings over the Russian menace. (She can't be a more ardent devotee of that than Roy Mason.) My heart went out to Mike, who had to wind up. He began, as he always does, by quietening the House by his very manner. But, of course, the Tories tried to hot it up and he had the horrible job of having to speak to two audiences: the one in front and the one behind. What I admired was not his oratory (this was no occasion for that), but his guts. Despite the silence behind him and the catcalls in front, he battled on and was obviously not nonplussed by the impossibilities of the situation. That is the test of a real politician. I love him dearly.

Friday, 30 January

A dreadful journey in a freezing sleeper. The winter has taken an icy turn. Even young Gerald said to me that he had slept 'dreadfully'. There was a howling nor' easter waiting for us at Newcastle, but a warm breakfast in the hotel suite soon revived my spirits, which weren't even dampened when the Controller, Whitaker, told me that the CPSA had called on its members at our Newcastle office to demonstrate in their thousands against the proposed manpower cuts when I did my tour. Apparently this had been sparked off partly by an article in *Labour Weekly*, saying that the cuts must inevitably concentrate on places like Newcastle. My trouble was that I had a great deal of sympathy with the CPSA over this. Reading my briefs for the visit last night, I was shocked to discover how officials have interpreted the implications of the manpower cuts in their 'confidential' preliminary talks with the staff sides. They take them to imply an actual reduction in the manpower figures for 1978–79 *below* those operating last year. This isn't at all what I – and I am sure other members of Cabinet – had in mind when agreeing to Harold's rather hazy proposals for £140 million cuts on administrative costs. It seemed at the time a face-saving formula for reducing the size of cuts in our individual programmes, so we jumped at them. Now it is clear from letters flying around from Malcolm Shepherd that he is taking this very seriously; it won't be just a question of reducing growth in Civil Service numbers; and, once again, the cuts will have to be concentrated on the main spending departments. Malcolm says they will amount to at least 8 per cent and that they can only be met by postponing certain policy developments, such as child benefit. I certainly do not intend to accept the postponement of any of my new policies: the new pensions scheme, child benefit, etc. This would be merely to impose on me by a side wind the sort of PESC cuts I have successfully resisted – at a time, too, when Roy Mason has been allowed to include manpower cuts in his castrated contribution to PESC.

So I felt inhibited in dealing with the demonstration which faced me. I told Whitaker that I wanted above all not to seem to be running away from the demo. I wanted the car to stop short of it, so that I could be seen to be walking voluntarily towards the crowd, not bulldozing my way through it. And so it was arranged. A mass of people was awaiting me as the car drew up. I got out and walked towards my excited staff, with hand outstretched. The women at the front seized my hand eagerly; the rest crowded round in good-humoured curiosity. Only a few shouted hostilities. Some lads at the back tried to get some boos going, but even these were as much in fun as anything else. Somehow I pressed my way through the dense crowd. Inside the corridors the jam was even worse, and the security chap got worried, not from fear of violence, but that he or I might fall and be trampled on. But I came through unruffled and all was well. We estimated there were about a thousand people there: a figure which was inflated to eight thousand on the twelve o'clock news.

Later I met the staff representatives, who were a bit apologetic about the demo, though determined to discuss manpower cuts. I told them it *was* true that the Government was considering manpower economies as part of its overall public expenditure cuts, but that it was *not* true that any detailed decisions had yet been made. As we broke up the meeting the one woman among them insisted on saying a word: 'I wanted you to know that we think the way you behaved with the crowd was magnificent.' Then on to sherry and a buffet lunch (in which I had insisted the staff side should be included), a press conference and TV. Finally another tour, where a small demo was waiting for me outside the family allowance section: a very muted and amiable one. Altogether a very stimulating and successful day. Even a freezing journey home (the heating on the train having failed again) could not knock the glow out of me. Ted said when I got home that the incident had come over well on TV. 'You were smiling so much.'

One thing I learned from this informative visit was that it would have been quite impossible to have introduced child benefit before April 1977, whatever Brandon Rhys Williams might say. I found too that it was a happy office, despite the strong undercurrent of International Socialist militancy that such a large establishment is almost bound to have. There is only one way to beat *that*, and that is to have personal contact with the grassroots, and I think my visit achieved that. People told me that my off-the-cuff speech over the tannoy to all the staff came over well.

Saturday, 31 January

It is amusing to see that the *Guardian* didn't even mention yesterday's 'mobbing': I think they have dismissed it as a non-event. It is also amusing to see that the North-West Economic Planning Council is threatening to create a break-away power block 'from the Mersey to the Humber' if devolution gives too many powers and privileges to Scotland and Wales. It is a pity that the English regions didn't get off their backsides earlier.

Monday, 2 February

My life is temporarily becalmed. Not only are there two days running with only one-line whips, but the office pressure has died down. Of course, the *Sunday Telegraph* is continuing the *Daily Telegraph*'s regular harassing and yesterday carried the headline: 'British doctors will be exported to Persian Gulf: Mrs Castle's deal.' But that does not worry me. I merely enjoyed my lull before the storm. Hopefully, pressures will be less intense during my final months in this job. As I said to Gerald, a Minister really ought to have three years in a department. The third year, by definition, is more relaxed and one can read oneself into much greater depth on one's subject instead of carrying on a hand-to-mouth guerilla warfare with one's colleagues, with the medical profession, etc.

Jack has sent me a memo on NUPE's new line on pay beds, vigorously attacking my compromise. Well, it won't do any harm for the profession to be made aware of NUPE's militancy. The juniors, led once again by the North-West, are beginning to stir things up about pay beds. Sakalo, foiled of his great triumph over the juniors' contract, is turning his attention to this issue to disguise his failure, and David tells me he himself had a rough time with juniors from the South-West last week.

Tuesday, 3 February

Lunch with Fred Catherwood[1] to try and get his Overseas Trade Board to give money to the British Health Exports Council [BHEC] and to win his general support for what we are trying to do. Sir Fred is a bit of a dull stick, but he got positively excited about

---

[1] Sir Frederick Catherwood, former Director General of the National Economic Development Committee, had been chairman of the Overseas Trade Board since 1975. In 1979 he was elected to the European Parliament as Conservative Euro-MP for Cambridgeshire.

my export drive and what I had achieved in the Middle East and he left completely committed to our support. Norman said to me in the car afterwards, 'You have converted me to this policy of yours about private lunches: they really do do the trick.' Well, that's how private business works and I do not see why we in the public service should be less enterprising. A leisurely lunch over good food gives everybody time to lower their guard.

I popped into the House to see the tail-end of the 'retirement of a Speaker, election of a new one' ceremony. The House was packed: it really does love the oozy unctuousness of consensus politics. Every modest little joke raised an enthusiastic laugh. Half an hour of it was enough for me.

Back at the office I found everyone in a tizzy. Wedgie had phoned about a Minute he is proposing to send to the PM. Stung by attacks from Labour MPs that he and his department are doing nothing to protect the aged from the intense cold, he is threatening to write to Harold, saying roughly, 'We must tell people we don't want anyone to die of cold, so those at risk should Switch On, not Switch Off, and then tell someone that they are doing so.' Such rashness filled my officials with horror. My only objection was the incompleteness of his policy: if people *did* switch on, who did he suggest should pay their bills? My officials wanted me to demand that we sent a joint Minute, but, having talked to Wedgie on the phone, I decided it was better for him to go ahead on his own. He is too much of an individualist to collaborate with – as I found during the referendum campaign. I merely instructed my chaps to prepare a Minute for me to send to the PM on the urgent need to agree a fuel bonus.

I am glad to see in the *Mail* that Andrew Alexander has 'sent up' yesterday's saccharine ceremony in the House.

Wednesday, 4 February

Wedgie's Minute has turned out to be much more anodyne than he had threatened. I think his officials must have got at him. I decided to circulate mine at once and when I showed it to Wedgie in the House he was as flattering as usual and said he would back it at Thursday's Cabinet. Later a message came from Harold, saying that it would not be taken till next week and asking Wedgie for concrete proposals. In the meantime I have this morning done a *You and Yours* programme on BBC radio, in which the heating problem naturally figured. I seemed to cope well enough, despite the fact that the papers are full of allegations of deaths from hypothermia. My medical advice is that the number of these deaths runs at about twenty-five a year. Hugh Faulkner (of Help the Aged) is talking dramatically of 'hundreds' of pensioners dying of cold each week. I can only hope these exaggerations will help me to get my fuel bonus through. I think it is intolerable that we should have forced these fuel price increases through so brutally: the price of electricity has doubled in the past two years.

I am angry with Harold for another typical piece of cowardice. My officials, working with their usual scrupulous correctitude, have been busy trying to see that we achieve our target of getting the Second Reading of the pay beds Bill before Easter. Bob Mellish has warned us all that any Bills coming up later than that won't have a cat in hell's chance of reaching the statute book. So, in addition to beavering away at Instructions to Parliamentary Counsel, officials have been planning to get ahead with provisional consultations with health authorities on the contents of the Schedule, and have prepared a document warning the authorities they will have to go into a quick huddle with the medical profession on this as soon as the results of the BMA ballot are known. No. 10 has now vetoed this, saying we must await the outcome of the ballot. This is to play straight into the hands of the BMA, which hasn't exactly been hustling. Indeed, Arnold has complained to me more than once about their leisureliness. So I wrote to Harold pointing this out – and the fact that it is in the interests of the BMA to delay things until it is too late to legislate. (They have now announced that they have messed up the ballot. Some consultants never got their papers, so a supplementary ballot has got to be held!) Harold has replied through Ken Stowe to the effect that he still does not want me to proceed. If he sells me out over this I shall resign and denounce him publicly. My request to have a word with him has been turned down on the grounds that he has two speeches to prepare.

Harold has also got cold feet over the political advisers. He has ruled that Denis Healey's chap, Adrian Mann, may not attend the Finance and Economic Committee of the NEC and has done it in such a way that the position of other advisers on other NEC committees is uncertain. Jack and Brian A-S. are utterly dismayed. They cannot, apparently, continue to service the Social Policy Sub-Committee. The sheer short-sightedness of Harold's attitude alarms me as much as his trimming over the role of the very political advisers he agreed to create. I rang Denis to get his support in resisting this, but all he said was that he had told Harold he wasn't prepared to have his chap treated any differently from other special advisers, adding, 'I don't feel quite the same way as you do over this.' I finally decided in despair that I must take this up with Harold myself, which I did in another Minute. Fortunately, he replied that Jack and co. could continue to serve, pending a discussion of the whole matter in Cabinet. I cannot believe that Harold's trimming to hostile prejudice does him any good with anyone.

Yet, combined with this deep instinct for conventionality, Harold has a wild streak of recklessness running through him. He has got all steamed up about the Jeremy affair,[1] telling some of us at lunch in the House that he believed that it was all a plot to discredit Jeremy, set up by agents of the South African Government because the Liberal Party had opposed South African policies. He hinted darkly that he knew all about that sort of thing and had his spies working on it, because he had been the victim of it: the theft of his own confidential papers. Well, he may well be right, but I

---

[1] On 29 January Mr Norman Scott had been charged in a Barnstaple court with dishonestly obtaining £14.60 in supplementary benefits, and alleged that he was being hounded because of a sexual relationship he had had with Jeremy Thorpe. Jeremy had immediately denied the allegations, but the press had been full of revelations about the payment of money to Scott by Peter Bessell, former Liberal MP, and others. Thorpe's position as Liberal Leader had already been weakened by the publication on 29 January of a critical Department of Trade report on the collapse of a fringe bank, London and County Securities, of which he had been a non-executive director. On 5 February he survived a grilling by his fellow Liberal MPs, but Scott's allegations continued to multiply and in May Thorpe resigned as party leader, claiming that a 'sustained witch hunt' by the press had made his and the party's position impossible. In December 1978 he was committed for trial at the Old Bailey with others for conspiracy and incitement to murder Scott. After a sensational trial he was acquitted the following year.

wish he would deal with it coolly, discreetly and silently, as a calculated expression of political principle, instead of in this erratic and dramatic Goldfinger way.

Thursday, 5 February

Cabinet has finally cleared the White Paper on Public Expenditure [Cmnd. 6393]. I was rather pleased with the draft, because it demonstrated vividly how much more successful I have been than some of my colleagues in defending my programmes. In fact, the section on social security listed all my department's policy initiatives on the disabled, child benefit, the new pensions scheme and so on as established fact, actually giving the dates for their implementation. Poor Fred Mulley, goaded by the summary at the end of his section (which showed a list of nothing but reductions), protested against the draft. 'You are just handing our critics their speeches in the House, ready written,' he moaned. Denis, relieved no doubt at having got a total of £3 billion reductions on expenditure in 1978–79 out of us, was in a generous mood. 'I will accept Cabinet's view on this.' So, with Bob backing Fred, it was agreed that the summaries at the end of each section, pointing out the changes from the previous PESC White Paper, should be deleted. Fortunately, I discovered before it was too late that this would eliminate all the list of Treasury's commitments to me. So the decision was amended to say that, although the separate heading on changes in expenditure should be omitted, Ministers should have the discretion to incorporate what parts of the substance they wanted in the main draft. I made a mental note that I would include most of the bits of mine. I intend to tie Treasury down in print.

Denis prefaced all this by saying that we should be attacked for not doing enough to reduce public expenditure. There would be big increases this year (5 per cent instead of the estimated $2\frac{1}{2}$ per cent), and next year as well, when there would be an increase of $1\frac{1}{2}$ per cent instead of an anticipated fall. The reason for the 1978–79 cut-backs in programmes was the big increase in expenditure on industry, so we should have to emphasize how much we had tightened control through such things as cash limits. History had shown that control by Cabinet was very weak – particularly under the Tories. He also emphasized that there would be no cuts on present jobs in the public service as a whole – which is rather contrary to what CSD and departmental officials are putting out.

We then turned to the problem of students. I am all in favour of ending the farce by which they flood our local offices with claims for social security during the short vacations, when they have no hope of finding a job and are merely looking for a supplement to their inadequate maintenance grants. So I backed the idea of concentrating those vacation grants into the short vacations, leaving them to sign on for jobs, if they want to, during the long summer vacation. But Joel, typically, on behalf of the Treasury, pushed his luck by trying to get us to accept the principle of legislating students out of the right to any unemployment benefit at all and even, however real their need, to supplementary benefits. That Treasury should even try on such an idea is ludicrous. Fred bleated his protest and I backed him vigorously. We successfully slapped Joel down. Shirley said afterwards how much she had agreed with my speech.

Finally, at a late hour, to the development tax on land.[1] John Silkin spoiled a good case by speaking for over twenty minutes (I would never have been allowed to get away with that!). Edmund Dell argued in his usual intellectually able way in favour of a 66¾ per cent top rate of tax instead of 80 per cent, but the most of us were against him, only Jim, Roy J., Fred Peart and Harold Lever voting for the Treasury. When Harold ruled that the Treasury had lost, there was a howl from the right wing, but Harold stood firm. But he did make a gesture on 'roll-over reliefs' (a piece of terminology that caused a lot of mirth) by saying that if the Treasury and Environment Ministers could come to a different agreement, that would be okay by him.

One little flick of parliamentary business. Bob said we might be in trouble next Tuesday over the Dock Labour Bill:[2] with luck we might have a majority of three. So every Minister must cancel his engagements and be there. Tony C. murmured that the trade unions in his constituency were very steamed up about the Bill. Had Mike got agreement on it among the unions? 'Complete agreement,' said Michael firmly.

At lunch in the House Harold came over to me to say he wanted a private word with me. He has got a new idea for his plot to expose the anti-Jeremy machinations, on which he said Albert Murray was already working and 'in which the Lady Falkender is naturally taking a great interest'. He believes that the Tories, or someone even more sinister, put Scott up to announcing his alleged association with Jeremy. 'The Tories had this information as long ago as 1972. Why didn't they use it then? My theory is that they thought it would rebound on Heath. But now they see their opportunity to destroy the Liberal Party. They wouldn't be beyond paying Scott to make his allegations now. And what better way of getting maximum publicity than to do it in a court case? So I want you to make some discreet enquiries about the prosecution your department brought against Scott for fraud. How did it originate? How was he discovered? Did he even volunteer the information on which he was prosecuted?' I said I would put Jack on to it as, apart from anything else, he was a barrister. Harold thought this was a good idea and wanted the information by Monday. So, back at the office, I passed the message on to Jack and Norman in confidence. Norman spoke to the Permanent Secretary and Jack went off to do some ferreting.

Officials have now produced the analysis of the implications for the department's

[1] The Development Land Tax Bill fulfilled our 1974 Manifesto pledge that we would 'heavily tax speculation in property'. The profit on realized development value of land was to be taxed at 80 per cent; the first £10,000 was to be exempt and, until March 1979, a lower rate of 66¾ per cent was to be levied on the next £150,000 to encourage owners of relatively small parcels of land to sell or develop. 'Roll-over reliefs' referred to the possibility of staggering sales over the period to 1979 in order to qualify for the lower rate of tax in each of the three years.

[2] In the event the Dock Work Regulation Bill survived its Second Reading by eight votes but later the Lords emasculated it by reducing the five-mile cargo handling zone to half a mile and by excluding the small ports altogether, thus increasing Labour MPs' mounting fury with the Upper House. On 10 November 1976, the Government tabled Commons Motions to reverse these amendments, but by then the Government's overall majority was down to one. Many Labour MPs were unhappy about the Bill and two of them, Brian Walden and John Mackintosh, refused to vote with the Government. The Government was defeated in its attempt to restore the five-mile zone and only succeeded in reversing three other Lords amendments with the help of the Deputy Speaker, who cast his vote for the Government as was customary following a tied vote. The Bill in its emasculated form received the Royal Assent on 22 November 1976.

work and policies of the three options to which CSD has said we must work in fulfilment of Cabinet's remit on manpower cuts in the Civil Service. These options are cuts of 5, 10 and 15 per cent and are designed to enable Cabinet to choose the right mix to secure an eventual cut of 8 per cent in manpower overall. Norman, at my request, has turned up the Cabinet Minutes and added his own covering note, 'They completely vindicate the line you have taken' – i.e., my contention that Cabinet had never visualized cuts on the scale now proposed or realized that they would involve cuts in the levels of Civil Service manpower obtaining *now*. And, indeed, Harold's summing up makes it quite clear that we were conned. After a discussion highlighting the prospective growth in Civil Service numbers up to 1978, Harold summed up that there was 'general agreement that there was scope for a major exercise to bring about a reduction in the *forecast* [my italics] level of Civil Service numbers'. And he concluded: 'The aims should be to achieve a reduction of 5 per cent in the forecast number of civil servants in 1978–79, a reduction which would secure savings of some £140 million.' Since that decision, of course, Roy Mason has got away with his reduced contribution to PESC and been allowed to include his manpower savings in it, thus pushing up the percentage manpower cuts for the rest of us to eight. This was slipped in while I was away in the Middle East. ('You don't think they didn't *know* you would be away?' David Owen remarked to me mockingly.) It is this which has led CSD to talk about a cut on present levels and so caused a furore with the staff I don't think Cabinet ever contemplated.

At the office meeting to discuss all this we had before us three lists of possibilities. List A would achieve staff reductions of 2 per cent by 'better housekeeping', and neither David nor Brian saw any problem in reaching that figure. Indeed, there would merely be an increase in efficiency. List B would produce a further 3 per cent cut in staff by more fundamental changes, but, here again, they both thought a lot of suggestions could be accepted without catastrophe. It was when we turned to List C, giving an additional 10 per cent cut, that we ran into the real difficulties. The social security list, for instance, would involve big reductions in supplementary benefit visiting: a sensitive area at a time when we are all anxious to identify the elderly people living alone who might be at risk. Worse still, it would involve the postponement of the invalid care allowance, the non-contributory invalidity benefit for disabled housewives, extensions of mobility allowance to other categories, the child benefit scheme and the new pensions scheme. I told Patrick firmly that he could forget all those. 'I am afraid I should not be carrying out my remit properly if I did,' he murmured. 'It is my writ that runs over you, not CSD's,' I retorted. 'I have given you a different remit.' He smiled, but squirmed anxiously. I then told them triumphantly that we had that morning agreed the Public Expenditure White Paper and that that spelled out in terms our commitment to go ahead with all these policies and actually spelt out the dates. 'So, of course, we are bound by that,' I added sweetly. They all laughed. When Patrick pointed out that commitments in Public Expenditure White Papers had been overthrown before, I replied that in that case the figure of £140 million manpower cuts set out in the White Paper could also be overthrown. I had just got through a PESC exercise, I went on, in which I had salvaged the starting date for all these policies and I wasn't going to have a mini-PESC imposed on me through a side door. 'The figure of £140 million has no overriding validity,' I declared. So I sent Patrick away, muttering, to work out a List C which did not include the postponement of these policies. 'I don't think I can do it, Secretary of State,' he kept saying in that nice way of his. 'The results would really be seen to be absurd.' 'Okay, then,' I retorted (Brian backing me strongly, bless him): 'put up absurdities. Say we would have to close half the Newcastle office down or halve unemployment benefit. This is no more absurd than postponing policies which this very morning Cabinet has confirmed.' He grinned, but I expect he will come back at me.

One thing has emerged clearly from all this: that if we were to adopt one option suggested by Malcolm Shepherd (i.e. to postpone child benefit), we would have to do so till 1980 – long after the lifetime of this Government. Otherwise we should merely push the peak of recruitment of new staff to the key year of 1978–79, because the numbers of staff are swelled *ad interim* until we get the saving from the absorption of family allowance into child benefit. So 'postponement', I shall be able to argue, would mean abandonment, and surely even this Cabinet is not asking for that?

On David's side of the department things are rather different. He positively welcomes the pressure on manpower, even in List C, because it enables him to revive his pet aim of reducing the department's 'monitoring function' over RHAS and AHAS: in other words to devolve these functions on to the regions, while making the regions an arm of the department. This resurrects the problem of whether we should have to turn regional officials into civil servants, a problem we never resolved in the discussion we had some months ago. So the whole idea has lain doggo. With Patrick (more adventurous than Philip) now in charge, we may be able to work out something. David sent me a very sweeping Minute on this yesterday, but, typically, when I raised it at the meeting he was much more tentative. Instead of entering into a great row with officials, as I had expected, he climbed down and said that he had agreed with them that 'precipitate action' could not be taken and that we should merely go on examining it. So that means we shall not get much from him out of List C.

I am constantly impressed by David's lively mind and imaginative initiatives. The trouble is that he chops and changes so. I believe he could produce great creative changes if only he was less didactic to begin with and climbed down less dramatically. Nonetheless, it is to him I owe the changes to make the NHS more democratic and the opening up of the whole question of changes in the structure of the NHS. He also has to his credit the policy for redistributing the resources of the NHS more fairly and the insistence on selecting better priorities, such as mental health. And he is the sole author of the Children's Act. As I brooded on this I realized how we had parcelled out the initiatives. Mine have been the prominence we now give to battered wives (the Select Committee would never have been set up without my insistence), the idea of joint financing of schemes by local authorities and the NHS, the emphasis on exports, the victories in PESC, the action on pay beds, the resistance to the worst features of the consultants' proposed new contract, the defusing of the juniors' dispute by accepting their need to move to a forty-hour week and a number of smaller ones. Among these I include the regular ministerial lunches, the new rapport with Transport House in our field, the push I have given to participation in management, and, not least, the improved relations with the staff. This has been helped enormously by my insistence that, when I pay official visits, members of the staff from top to bottom shall share in the junketing. David's initiatives have made the whole health side of the department hum with new thinking and he has toned up the whole administration there. I could not have done this job so fully without him, any more than I could have done it without Brian on the pensions side.

Friday, 6 February

Meeting with the staff side of the departmental Whitley Council about those cuts. It was nice to hear Naylor, Leslie Christie and Peter Thomasson say how much staff relations had improved since I took over, even if they did go on to express the fear that the manpower cuts would take us right back to the days of confrontation in 1972. I assured them, 'As long as I am Secretary of State there will be no going back to that', that everything was fluid and nothing firmly decided, and that I would take them into detailed consultation before any decisions were made as to how the cuts would apply in DHSS. I doubt that satisfied; they are against any cuts at all. After a long day in the office I had a mad rush to Sunningdale for the weekend's discussions with the organizations for the disabled. I suggested this to Alf Morris months ago, when he was fretting about his inability to get all the money he wanted. Now the time has come I am cursing at having to take such a big chunk out of a busy weekend. But I was cheered up by the obvious pleasure of so many of them at the whole idea and I managed to get home to HCF for the night.

Saturday, 7 February

Back to Sunningdale for the afternoon plenary session. Most people there felt the enterprise had been well worth while and, even in my snatches of conversation with them over lunch, I picked up a lot of points. I was impressed by the way they had all applied themselves, not to setting up demands for more money, but to making the best use of what resources we have. There is no doubt that these Sunningdale conferences are a first-class idea. My only regret is that pressure of work prevents me from participating in these in-depth discussions as much as I would like. I was glad to see that Alf had invited members of the all-party group on the disabled. Sir George Sinclair [Conservative MP for Dorking] turned up and said the whole thing was a good idea. Alf seems to have run it well.

At HCF two crammed boxes awaited me. I fear I am going to have trouble with David again over pay beds – but that's for Monday. There is a nice telegram in my box from Kuwait: from Marshall, the Commercial Counsellor, to Laurie Walker, saying that they have had a visit from Gavin Ellis, marketing director of Cementation, who was 'unreserved in his praise of Mrs Castle, whose recent meeting in London with contractors he had attended, for the work she is doing to assist British exporters'. Well, that makes a welcome change from Patrick Jenkin and the *Telegraph*, who are jointly pursuing me over the export deals I am trying to pull off. I would love British firms to pull off big contracts in Iran, thank me publicly and show up the critics.

The personal venom in the right-wing press against me and Ted shows no bounds. Poor old Ted has just had a taste of it. When he went into the London Hospital three weeks ago for the tests his excellent consultant, Brigden, has been planning for some time – they are worried about his traces of diabetes and his loss of weight – he found, to his poor dear innocent delight, that, unbeknown to him, Brigden had put him in a side room of the ward. Then, a few days later, the secretariat of the hospital rang Ted up to say the press were trying to see him and Ted told them to tell the press to get stuffed. Suddenly a charming young lass from the *Mail* walked into Ted's room brandishing a notebook and he saw her to the door. The poor innocent still didn't know what was going to hit him, but there it all was the next day in the *Mail* – 'The privacy of a single room for battling Barbara's Ted' – plus a picture of the two of us at his inauguration into the Lords, ermine and all. Ted was furious – he even toyed with the idea of taking it up with the Press Council – but I headed him off. I told him that you just have to accept that you can't win with the press and the next instalment of this thrilling drama proved it. When Ted returned to the hospital to continue his tests he was told that his single room had been needed for a man in a violent state (which the man certainly was), so he had been put in the general ward. Ted went into the ward perfectly happily, because he is a naturally gregarious chap anyway. However, the press hadn't finished with him. The next day the *Telegraph* and *Mail* carried stories to the effect that Lord Castle had been moved as a result of their revelations. This time Ted only shrugged. He is learning to take it. But the drama wasn't over. I was thankful Ted was in Brussels, his tests having proved negative, when the *Mail* delivered its final (?) shaft. There was a prominent piece in Nigel Dempster's diary on Monday to the effect that the whole ward had been thankful when Lord Castle left, because he had thrown his weight about and had obviously resented not being treated as a VIP. This brought savage rage rising into my gorge. I repeated something I often say bitterly to Ted, 'The press does not report news; it invents it.' Ted used to have great rows with me about this attitude and – to do him credit – he probably still would.

Monday, 9 February

Office meeting on the juniors to tidy up some last points on their new contract. Also a discussion on exports policy, with which Collier, catching my enthusiasm, is faithfully pressing ahead. His procurement policy working group is just about ready to submit its report to me on how we can rationalize the procurement of supplies in the NHS. In the evening I had the ordeal of fighting Nick Bradley's Motion on pay beds in the Home Policy Committee of the NEC. I'd prepared a great speech, expecting to be ganged up against by Nick, Joan Maynard, Frank Allaun, Eric, Mik, Judith and co. In the event, Judith was anxious to be helpful and readily agreed to move the amendment which I had privately suggested to her.[1] And I had the ironic satisfaction of hearing Bryan Stanley complain that even the amendment went too far! So, in the

---

[1] The amendment reaffirmed the party's Manifesto commitment to remove private practice from the National Health Service and called on the Government to carry this out 'immediately and in full'.

end, a most anodyne expression of support for the Manifesto policy on phasing out went through without any difficulty. I was rather pleased with the eloquent speech I had made, but afterwards Joan Lestor and Fred Mulley said to me outside the meeting, 'You nearly talked yourself out. We don't know what you were worried about.' I decided the moral of this little affair was that most people in the party realize full well how difficult the medical profession is to handle and that I shall do damn well to get away with any phasing out policy at all.

Tuesday, 10 February

I had insisted on accepting the *Financial Times* invitation to address their conference on pensions, even though it meant mugging up a lot of up-to-date technical details. In doing so I discovered that we are about to make a number of regulations on such important matters as equal access for women to firms' pensions schemes, so I told the office to hold them up till I could announce them in my speech. So it became quite a major one, Brian O'Malley co-operating willingly in my hogging the announcements in this way. There is a very real comradeship and loyalty between us. His trouble now is that he hasn't got enough to do and is bored. He would love a change of job.

Meeting on the Elizabeth Garrett Anderson hospital. I accepted the case for closing it, though we know there will be a row, and told the AHA to transfer it as an identifiable woman-only unit into a local DGH. We have had a bigger lobby on this than on any other closure proposal, but if we are ever to carry out our strategy for the NHS we shall just have to stand firm on the need to close uneconomic hospitals.

Despite Cabinet's panic about the Dock Work Regulation Bill, we sailed through with a majority of eight.

Wednesday, 11 February

Long office meeting on the pay beds Bill, now renamed on my insistence the NHS (Miscellaneous Provisions) Bill. One of the problems over the Schedule is that if we attempt to give too much detail we shall run into hybridity.[1] So we must give merely an aggregate figure for the pay beds to be abolished in each area, making it clear that the figure has been based on a formula. I insisted that the Bill must allow the withdrawal of *all* pay beds in a hospital where this met the formula and suited our book. David was very restive about this. However, I stood firm. On licensing, I said we should try and get the profession to take the initiative in indicating the lines a voluntary system might take and that, for a start, officials should approach the IHG. I also told the office to prepare a Minute to the PM, asking for permission to go ahead with consultations, now that the outcome of the ballot is imminent. The biggest worry

---

[1] A Public Bill may be declared hybrid, or semi-private, if it affects in part only a small, identifiable group of persons. In addition to the stages of a Public Bill, hybrid Bills are subject to lengthy Select Committee examination.

is the provision in Goodman allowing part-time consultants to continue to use specialized facilities in the NHS. We have strengthened the safeguards against abuse of this as much as possible, but I suggested an additional one: an obligation on the Secretary of State to make an annual report to Parliament on the use of these powers. I think it will provide a useful check.

In the morning I had had an amusing time addressing the annual conference of Local Optical Committee representatives. Once again, it meant reading up all sorts of technical details ready for the question time I had agreed to take, but I volunteered to go because officials are so full of dire anxieties about my proposals to improve NHS spectacle frames. They have hinted at incipient revolt among opticians and had studded my brief with cautions about the need to play this down, say as little as possible, etc. This is, of course, because they don't want to try to do anything seriously on this anyway. But my tactic is always to face up to trouble as the only way to get something done. In the event, the occasion turned out to be surprisingly amicable. First, they were delighted I had volunteered to come; secondly, they were naturally courteous; thirdly, I teased them and made them laugh; fourthly, I presented my proposals as the reasonable development of the NHS, which they are. It went swimmingly and my relieved officials could not believe their ears. 'This will prove very helpful in our discussions,' said the one of them who had been foremost in advising me to play my proposals down.

One unexpected snag nearly floored me: most of my notes for questions were, as usual, prepared for me in dim and almost illegible type, which I can't read without my glasses. Yet the frames of my glasses were obviously private ones and, although I have never hidden the fact that I do wear private frames, and indeed make a point of the fact that the unattractiveness of NHS frames forces most women to do so, I knew the press photographers would be there and that the only thing the press would report of my speech would be my private frames: plus a large photo. So I decided to manage without my glasses somehow, which I did by dodging the illegible statistics and quipping my way through the answers, to the audience's delight. But it was a near thing.

Thursday, 12 February

I hurried into Cabinet early to give Harold the résumé Jack has done of the Scott file. Harold's face dropped a bit when I told him it seemed to show Jeremy's relationship with Scott had been longer and more domesticated than he had so far admitted. My aim is to warn Harold against going overboard for Jeremy too recklessly. He has already made a rather hysterical attack on the press for 'hounding' Jeremy and has exposed himself to an attack in a *Mirror* leader today. He really is an incredible mixture of caution and recklessness. Anyway, Harold thanked me for the work Jack had done, so perhaps it will do the political advisers a bit of good.

At Cabinet we also had a couple of timid papers by Malcolm Shepherd on the political rights of civil servants and the application of the closed shop in the Civil Service. He was suggesting we refer both of them to an independent enquiry headed by a judge and manned by political figures from both parties, 'preferably retired'! We all agreed that the first might be so referred,[1] though there was a spirited exchange between Jim and Ted Short – the former urging us to 'stand up to the staff' who are pressing for greater freedom of action, while Ted told him in vigorous terms that his ideas were 'as dead as the dodo' and that we really ought to modernize our ideas about the political activities of civil servants. 'It would do them good to go canvassing: it might brighten their ideas up a bit.' Our Ted goes overboard every now and then in a most un-headmasterish way about things in which he believes. I think he is far better value than most of our own people realize. But we all also – almost to a man – backed Mike when he said that the question of the closed shop was purely for us as employers. We shouldn't farm this issue out, but set up a small committee of Ministers to discuss its application among our own employees. (That lad really does talk a lot of sense on industrial relations. Jim, by comparison, is a timid old Tory, notwithstanding his great gesture of 'solidarity' with the unions over *In Place of Strife*.)

The two questions in which I was particularly interested were Denis's anti-unemployment package and the White Paper on direct elections to the European Parliament. On the first, I was very angry because there was no paper in front of us. Indeed, I have found it very difficult to find out what is going on, because no letters or Minutes have been circulated. Instead, we had an oral report by Denis on what he is proposing to announce this afternoon. Since his package will contain a not inconsiderable commitment of public expenditure (£220 million gross: £137 million in 1976–77), including £50 million on the construction industry, it is extremely relevant to the expansionist activities of our different departments. I cornered Mike in the House a few days ago and gathered, from his rather evasive response, that all the money was going to go on housing improvements – I suspected with his approval. And so it proved.

Denis began by telling us that the package had been approved in detail by the MES committee of Cabinet and he kept a wary eye on me while he spelt it out: all £220 million of it. As soon as he had finished I leapt in with my complaint: why had we not had a paper? Why should all this be drawn up by an 'inner Cabinet deciding a mini-PESC'? I had a lot of old people at risk in old people's homes with inadequate fire precautions, and a terrifying backlog of hospital maintenance work; why could this not have been included in the construction package? Housing old people was 'housing' as much as anything else. Mike came in at once to say, 'I must say Barbara has a case.' But his remedy was to increase the amount Denis was making available. Denis, of course, was not willing to do this. Harold made soothing noises to the effect

[1] Harold Wilson announced on 19 May that he was setting up a committee to 'review the rules governing the active participation by civil servants in national and local political activities'. The chairman was Sir Arthur Armitage, Vice-Chancellor of Manchester University and Professor of Common Law. Judith Hart was one of the original members but when, to everyone's surprise, she accepted a post in Callaghan's Government in March 1977, Jim Callaghan asked me to take her place as I was then out of the Government. On the committee I worked closely with Stanley Mayne, former General Secretary of the Institute of Professional Civil Servants, and together we succeeded in edging the committee towards a greater liberalization of the political activities of civil servants than it would otherwise have proposed. The committee's report was published in January 1978 (Cmnd. 7057), but by the time of the general election in May 1979, Jim Callaghan had not accepted or acted on it.

that the Chancellor had said he might need another package. The claims of the rest of us might be considered then. I persisted. 'I hope it will be minuted that there has been an additional allocation of £50 million to housing under PESC, and that, when the Chancellor has another round, it will be the turn of the rest of us.' 'I have no doubt that those who are responsible for drawing up the Minutes have already noted your points,' Harold drawled.

But my major concern was over the White Paper on direct elections, which we turned to at the derisory hour of 12.15pm. Once again, this was typical of how to lead a Cabinet by the nose. Jim introduced the draft White Paper complacently. 'The Prime Minister and I have both given undertakings to the Community to support direct elections,' he said. We should therefore publish the White Paper, have a debate in the PLP, then a debate in the House, and it would then go to the European Council. Roy J. and Ted Short said they had nothing to add to what Jim had said. I'm not surprised!

Peter opened for the Dissenting Ministers by demanding that the paper should be labelled Green. Among other defects, 'the question of the relation of the European Parliament to the British Parliament is not looked at at all'. I then became airborne. The implications of the White Paper, I said, would have far-reaching consequences, yet it was suggested that the matter should be 'finalized' at the European Council in April. It was outrageous to rush this vital discussion through so quickly. We had never discussed this matter fully in Cabinet and now we were proposing to have an amorphous debate in the PLP, followed by an equally amorphous debate in the House and then off Jim and Harold would go to 'finalize' it. Jim kept interrupting me to say that all the White Paper was doing was to quote the Assembly's suggestions, not to recommend them. I retorted by quoting paragraphs which showed that was not true. And I ended by pointing out that Article 138 of the Treaty of Rome expressed the intention to move to direct elections by a 'uniform procedure'. Now the European Council said it was too soon for that. Okay, then if it was too soon for uniformity, there was no commitment to rush the decision on direct elections either. Harold tried to dismiss my fears by insisting that there was 'not a cat in hell's chance of getting this settled in April'. This was a White Paper 'with very green edges'. Denis backed him heartily. We were committed to the publication of a White Paper, he said. Jim assured me that I had misunderstood his interruptions. In fact, he agreed with a lot of what I had said. 'I don't give a damn whether the paper is Green or White,' he said, but we must give the PM 'a sensible bargaining position'.

All this only justified everything I had said, as Mike hastened to point out. In his view it ought to be a Grey paper (i.e. one which made it clear no one was committed to it at all). 'A bargaining position in April commits us all.' The best proposal was to refer the matter to a Speaker's Conference and not take any decisions till then. Wedgie capped it all with one of his witty cracks. He thought we needed a new type of classification: this should be a Blue Paper, like a firework. 'One lights it, stands back and waits for it to explode.' We all laughed, but there were some sly grimaces at the aptness of the description. Haven't we drifted into this constitutional dilemma as a result of Harold's and Jim's ad hoc-ery: pretending the problems wouldn't be there until they were on top of us? And Wedgie went on devastatingly to describe how relentlessly we were confusing the channels of democratic decision-making. The British people had been trained to look to their Parliament as the repository of democratic power. Now we were busy fragmenting this: there was to be a Scottish Assembly, a British Parliament and then a European one as well. Where would power really lie? What would be the authority of a British Labour Government if, mid-term, Margaret Thatcher were to sweep the polls in a European election? I thought his case was unanswerable and Harold bowed to it to the extent of hastily agreeing that the paper should be labelled Green and that it should make clear that no final decisions would be reached in April. So our row did some good.

But all this time I had been getting restive. It was by now 1.15pm and I had been supposed to be at a lunch at the *Mirror* at 1pm. I was furious when Harold said we must now turn to the text of the White Paper, on which I had a lot of points I wanted to make. It really was intolerable for Harold to put this vital item last on the agenda, so that there was not proper time to consider it. People were already beginning to drift out and I had to go. The *Mirror* lunch was very important to me and I was already going to be half an hour late for it. Harold's behaviour was typical of the tactics of the pro-Europeans: refusing to take the future of the British House of Commons seriously. There is a story in today's *Times* to the effect that John Roper [Labour and Co-op MP for Farnworth] has written to Jim, on behalf of the Labour Committee for Europe, sending him a long memorandum on how direct elections should be organized. It even hints at the necessity for us to accept PR! That would put paid to any hope of a Labour majority: either here or in Europe. But I have always believed that the aim of the Jenkinsites is coalition government.

The *Mirror* lunch was a little private one with Tony Miles, editorial director, Mike Molloy, the new editor, and Terry Lancaster. I took Jack Straw along with me. It arose from a leader on the junior doctors the *Mirror* did some days ago which was so unexpectedly unfair and untrue it took my breath away. True to my new determination not to take these misrepresentations lying down, I got on to Tony Miles, who promptly invited me to have lunch with the three of them. It was a very pleasant affair. Tony admitted that the leader had been a bit much; we explained the facts. Great camaraderie. Just as we were finishing Jack was called to the phone. It was the result of the BMA ballot on the Goodman proposals. Fifty-three per cent poll. Good: it shows that pay beds is not the burning issue the BMA makes it out to be. Only two thousand odd (15 per cent of all consultants) were for handing in undated resignations. Again, good. But alas, a two to one majority (of those voting) for accepting the Goodman proposals. My face dropped. 'Bad,' I said to Jack. This means I am saddled with the Goodman proposals and my hopes of modifying them are gone. Yet I am saddled with them in a situation in which it is clear that we need never have accepted this fudged and dangerous compromise, if only Harold hadn't panicked and played into Goodman's hands. I face a terribly difficult bit of tightrope walking now.

My realization of this was strengthened when, back at the office, I met a deputation from NUPE to discuss the pay beds issue, at their request. The union's Executive had come out firmly against the compromise. Alan Fisher was obviously a bit embarrassed and put their case against the Goodman proposals moderately. I put a good face on it, while David made a telling plea for us to go for a solution that would 'stick' and that a successor government would not feel able to undo. I could see that Alan and the union president were impressed with this, but David was followed by an Executive member who clearly was *not*. A quiet, elderly man, he dismissed what we had said with contempt. 'We have a great admiration and respect for you, Mrs Castle. Nonetheless, we will not accept what you propose.' Bernard Dix[1] went even further, hinting that if the legislation did not fix a terminal date for phasing out pay beds, not only would the union mobilize the whole Labour movement against us, but take industrial action. Well, I'm not sorry to see that the trade unions have some life in them. This strengthens my hand in that craven Cabinet. But it is going to make great difficulties for me politically. I longed to go out with a pay beds triumph to my credit as the last achievement of my career. Now the last image of me will be smeared.

One thing I am determined: I am not going to let the BMA delay the legislation as it clearly intends to try to do. News has come in that the consultants' Central Committee has had a hurried meeting on the ballot result and passed two resolutions: one saying they will continue their out-and-out opposition to the legislation (fine: that helps me); two, that they will seek further 'exploration' of the Goodman proposals. If anyone thinks I am getting into a huddle with Goodman again, they are wrong. Typically, I heard David and Patrick agreeing that the result was 'good'. Patrick even told me it was a great success for me and the Government. We just don't begin to see eye to eye on this! It made me all the more determined to rush a Minute to Harold, setting out the position to date and saying we must go ahead with the legislation immediately. I must say that David was all in favour of our going ahead and publishing our Bill without further consultations with the BMA, except on the two points on which we are committed to consult by the Goodman proposals: the contents of the Schedule and the prospects of a voluntary agreement on licensing. We don't expect to reach agreement on the latter by any stretch of the imagination, and agreed that we should include the reserve powers in the Bill. After all, they are *reserve* powers. Moreover, to give the independent board licensing powers could make that body more acceptable to our people. If Harold has any guts at all he will give me my head from now on.

Saw Geoffrey Smith of *The Times*, at Peter Brown's suggestion, to discuss public expenditure: all part of the big public relations exercise we have decided to launch to put across our part of the Public Expenditure White Paper due to be published next week in as favourable a light as possible. Geoffrey Smith only wanted to talk about the way in which these PESC exercises are run, but it was interesting to hear him say that I had obviously done well out of this round: my colleagues complained that I had 'got away with murder'. Well, that is all balm to my soul, but I hastened to stress to him that 'success' in this PESC round was relative. I don't want there to be a backlash when everyone finds that I have had to cut the capital spending on hospitals, even though I have secured an increase in health and personal social services overall.

At last, home to pack for Blackburn, while Edna cooked us our bacon and egg. On to that hated night sleeper.

---

[1] Alan Fisher's Assistant General Secretary for Research in NUPE.

Friday, 13 February

Peter Jenkins has got a piece in the *Guardian* urging Roy Jenkins to put his head above his parapet and go for a meaningful job like Northern Ireland. It is obvious that Roy's friends are shaping up for the succession to Harold and haven't given up the intention of pressing Roy for the leadership.

Saturday, 14 February

I see from my Cabinet Minutes that the points I made on Denis's construction package *have* been duly recorded, as Harold said they no doubt would be. But I note that he has carefully avoided committing himself or Cabinet to my points in his recorded summing-up.

Monday, 16 February

Peter Brown has laid on the most intensive pre-briefing of journalists on the PESC White Paper I have ever undertaken. It arises from a decision we DHSS Ministers reached last week that we would make a great 'interpretative' effort on the White Paper in order to boost morale in the NHS and prevent the press talking about 'crisis cuts'. Peter has thrown himself into it with gusto and I found myself in the deep end today with the *Guardian* first (Malcolm Dean and John Cunningham), next Joe Rogaly, and finally dinner with Tony Shrimsley of the *Mail*! Peter assured me that if I made it clear my comments were unattributable, and that any use of the material I gave them was embargoed till Thursday, they would play the game. So I found myself in the unusual situation of 'leaking' like mad in the knowledge nothing would be used. All the journalists were immensely grateful for this chance to digest one aspect of what is going to be a very detailed White Paper well in advance of the publication rush and I developed quite an effective line of patter, spelling out how much better the NHS had done than we dared to hope. And I could not resist pointing out that my cut was the smallest of all (essential to the NHS morale-boosting process). God knows what will come out of it, but they seemed impressed. Tony Shrimsley, over an excellent meal at Overtons, got so carried away he asked me if he might do an advance story about how Barbara Castle had saved the National Health Service in the PESC battle, swearing that he wouldn't put in any figures or details. I'm afraid I fell. It would be such a remarkable change to have the *Mail* reporting anything to my credit that I don't suppose the story will be used.

Tuesday, 17 February

At the monthly meeting of the RHA chairmen it was decided I must give them an advance glimpse of the White Paper on the health side, again strictly in confidence. Once again, the words flowed: no absolute cut; overall growth rate for health of $1\frac{1}{2}$ per cent per annum; expansion of health centre programme; yearly growth of family practitioner services of $3\frac{1}{2}$ per cent; no need to cut back services; capital programme levelling out at £250 million a year; joint financing to the tune of £20 million by 1978–79; enough elbow room to move towards the better system of regional allocation under the Resources Allocation Working Party criteria, based on deprivation; the greater flexibility in switching between revenue and capital which Dick Bourton has won from the Treasury (I paid him a public tribute on this); last, but not least, greater flexibility in carrying over spending from one year to the next (1 per cent instead of the ¼ per cent we had won for them this year). Tough, but not catastrophic. They listened like prisoners let out on parole: it was so much better than the dire warnings David had been giving them with such relish. Donne, as chairman of the chairmen, congratulated me warmly – and congratulated Dick Bourton, which he certainly deserved. We swept out of the room in an atmosphere of near euphoria. Even Henry had his tail up. 'Things are going very well, Secretary of State,' he said to me in the lift afterwards.

Then on to more briefings of the press. As I said to Ted when I got home, (he was home from Brussels for once), 'No doubt the stories will be that B.C. has gone round boasting of her achievements.' All this briefing, in fact, is alien to my nature, but I was determined this time to get a bit of credit where credit was due.

In my box I found a joint memo from Eric Varley, Peter Shore and Fred Mulley for the MES meeting on 'Planning Agreements: the Next Steps'. What interested me, in view of some stories in the *Financial Times* that the whole planning agreement business has been watered down, was their unanimity in moderation. They reported that consultation with the TUC had been 'helpful'. The TUC did not want the trade unions to be formally parties to the agreements and accepted that the arrangements for disclosure should be 'flexible'. The CBI, said the trio, had 'softened' their attitude. And they concluded, 'It does look possible to secure sufficient co-operation from a number of companies to make a start provided we adopt a flexible, evolutionary approach in which the scope of a planning agreement, and the extent of related consultation, develops over a period of time as all concerned gain experience of operating the system.' Well, well. Nothing could be more pragmatic than that, my dear Peter.

Harold has replied to my long Minute on the meaning of the consultants' ballot by saying I must bring the matter before Cabinet and not enter into any consultations meanwhile. I exploded to Patrick that if this was not put on Cabinet agenda this week, we should lose the legislation. 'And then,' I warned him, 'I will resign, the unions will go on strike and the PLP will go through the roof.' He said anxiously that he would get on to Ken Stowe in the Cabinet office. Whether that did the trick, or whether Harold would have done it anyway, the item is coming up this Thursday. If Cabinet delays the legislation, I shall walk out without a moment's regret.

Wednesday, 18 February

To my horror, I found that Shrimsley had got his story into the *Mail*: 'Barbara's Threats Halt Health Service Cuts.' How my colleagues will hate my guts! To make matters worse, Geoffrey Smith has produced his piece in *The Times*, including a reference to the fact that I had got away with 'assault and battery'. I steeled my courage for tomorrow's attacks in Cabinet. Anyway, my colleagues do this kind of thing to me every day of the week and I have at least offset the headlines which would otherwise inevitably have flowed in, like the one in last night's *Evening News*: 'London Faces Savage Cuts in Health Service.' (In quotation marks: but the origin of the quote was not identified.) At the Consultative Council with the local authorities Joel and Tony gave a preview of what the PESC White Paper will reveal (again in confidence). With me there watching him, Tony couldn't spread himself when Bob Thomas[1] and other Labour municipal leaders complained about the cut-back on public transport spending and asked how much switching there could be. Thank God, I've secured a 2 per cent revenue growth for the personal social services. They are far more important than bus fares. But on the whole the reaction to the grim picture painted by Joel was muted.

Peter Jenkins has gone up in my estimation by writing a piece in the *Guardian* attacking, by inference, the Roy Jenkins line that public expenditure is becoming a threat to democracy. Some sense at last!

Thursday, 19 February

I don't know why I've worried about my 'briefing' of the press. The papers yesterday were full of a real leak on the Civil Service manpower cuts, particularly as they affect Mike and me. I think this *must* have been a civil servant: there is no political axe-grinding involved here. Cabinet was reduced by flu: Jim and Roy J. being smitten, while Wedgie was in the US talking energy policy. That meant I had one less ally, but two less enemies, for my two major items: pay beds and fuel bonus. Harold has obviously felt compelled to bring my Minute on pay beds to Cabinet and looking back at the 27 November Cabinet Minutes, I can see why. He only got away with his ploy then by promising we would report the outcome of our 'consultations' to Cabinet. But I was far from sure to what extent he was now ready to back me up. I introduced my paper with a carefully prepared résumé of the state of play, stressing the fact that the BMA ballot had been a 'flop' and that only 2,048 consultants out of 13,000 had voted to hand in undated resignations – only slightly more than the 1,834 who had voted *in favour* of the separation of pay beds. So the anger against our proposals was not as profound as some had made out. Nonetheless, we were stuck with the Goodman proposals, since a two-to-one majority of those voting was in favour of them. But the proposals were a total package and we had to go ahead explicitly on that package, though personally I would much have preferred not to have compromised at all. But if we were now to delay legislation, while the profession 'explored' matters still further, we should be giving them an effective veto over our policy and would face an unholy row from the NEC, the PLP and the health unions, who were already unhappy about the compromise.

Harold cut me off at this point. It is no part of his tactical instinct to win a political argument. He chipped in impatiently to say the question before us was the extent to which I should be allowed to proceed with the publication of my Bill, since consultations on the two points I had mentioned in my paper had not been completed. And,

---

[1] Sir Robert Thomas, Leader of the Greater Manchester Metropolitan County Council and chairman of the Association of Metropolitan Authorities from 1973 to 1977.

typically, he managed to sound as though he was against the whole idea. A long wrangle then ensued. Ted Short said primly that Cabinet had never agreed that the Bill should be passed this session, only introduced, though he admitted that Social Services Committee of Cabinet agreed with me that for political reasons we should now lift it into the essential list. Harold Lever, of course, fought me with all his strength. It would be absurd to ruin the effect of the Goodman proposals, he urged, by proceeding to publish the Bill before I had held more talks on the Schedule (he seems very well informed about all this), or by including any reserve powers of control in the legislation. Mike did his valiant best to help me and the PM seized the opportunity to sum up far more favourably than I had dared to hope. First, he said that Cabinet 'agreed' I should introduce my Bill with a view to Second Reading before Easter (though I cannot say I noticed it!). Secondly, he suggested that I shouldn't include powers on licensing in the Bill at the outset, but publish a White Paper setting out my proposals, on which consultations with the profession could continue. In the light of those consultations a reserve power could be added at the Report stage of the Bill, if Cabinet agreed, and the long title should be framed to allow this. Finally, he ruled that I could send out my consultation letter on the Schedule to AHAs without further delay. As I hesitated, Mike nodded at me to accept this formula, so accept I did, though it has only postponed the day of battle over licensing.

My second battle – over fuel bonus[1] this time – also ended in a draw. I always knew it was a forlorn hope to get £110 million out of the Chancellor, but Brian O'Malley and I had agreed that we must try. In calling on me to introduce my paper, Harold made some snide remark about my never giving up in my quest for more money, but that only made me put my case more strongly and effectively. 'I would,' I said coldly, 'be failing in my duty as Secretary of State for the poor if I didn't bring this matter to the attention of Cabinet.' When deciding to phase out the fuel and other subsidies, I continued, Cabinet had agreed that we would take steps to protect the weakest in our community against the effects. 'I am afraid it is true that we are not protecting the poor from the effect of the fuel increases.' And I reeled off some of the figures in my paper. To my surprise, Shirley came in warmly in my support. 'I am glad Barbara brought this forward. At some stage Cabinet ought to consider this problem: the machinery for discussing it is very inadequate.' In Wedgie's absence John Smith[2] gave moral support from the Department of Energy, saying that 'very severe increases in electricity prices' were on the way. Mike backed Shirley.

Faced by this united front, Harold and Denis started to change their tone. Denis said he obviously couldn't resist the proposal to look at it afresh, but he wanted to make it clear that 'I am not going to allow Cabinet to go outside the contingency reserve'. Tony C. muttered that the worst public sector price increase was in bus fares and no one was suggesting anything should be done about that. Harold summed up that Cabinet rejected the bonus, but felt there should be a wider study covering the ways of mitigating the effect on the poor of public sector prices

[1] Brian O'Malley and I wanted a special payment for pensioners and poor families to offset the steep rise in the cost of fuel.

[2] Labour MP for Lanarkshire North and Parliamentary Under Secretary at the Department of Energy.

generally. MES should look at it. Not bad at all, I thought. It was worth running the gauntlet of Cabinet ridicule!

On foreign affairs, I asked Jim what was happening in Rhodesia. Harold said that this was causing considerable concern. Ian Smith was being completely intransigent and he and Jim were now considering sending a senior emissary to Salisbury to urge him to be more responsive to Nkomo. It might be that Smith would now wish us to become involved in the negotiations. I sat up in indignation at that: just what I suspected! Before we knew where we were Smith would be asking us to guarantee any settlement. Denis took alarm at this prospect, saying there must be 'no intervention'. Harold soothed us all down, saying the talk of military intervention in the press was absurd. Cabinet would be kept informed of developments.

Monday, 23 February

This is the day when, all the press tells us, we shall have a major row at the TUC Liaison Committee over the Healey cuts. 'Jones signals Pay Policy Dangers' runs the *Guardian* headline and, of course, Joan Lestor's resignation from the Government[1] on the public expenditure cuts has been given great prominence over the weekend. So the press was massed expectantly outside Congress House, hopeful of blood. In fact, as I had anticipated, the union attack was far more muted than the ragings of the Tribune group might have led one to expect. There is no doubt that they are worried men – and angry at not having been consulted beforehand about the cuts (why didn't Denis listen to Mike and me when we urged they should be?). But they have no patience with irresponsible talk about bringing the Government down.

Denis opened with a rather heavy-going analysis which lasted twenty minutes. It covered the usual ground about the need to avoid further tax increases, etc. 'There is no way of avoiding this by soaking the rich: if we were to confiscate everyone's income over £6,000 a year it would only raise £450 million, and that once and for all.' He rubbed it in about the burden of debt interest; the extent to which public expenditure growth had outstripped output. 'Next year we will be spending £1,200 million more in real terms than we spent this. So the real cut in public expenditure is *nil*.' He then touched on the heart of everyone's anxieties. 'How can I be sure that economic expansion will fill the gap left by the cuts? Of course, I can't be sure, but I am sure of one thing: if you don't cut, you are *guaranteeing* you won't get exports and investment, because you won't have made room for them.' If, in the context of world recovery, we got back to normal growth, then the need for the cuts would be inescapable. (It was the Achilles heel of his argument, and he hurried on to more pleasant things.) 'We are not touching pensions,' he continued, 'nor social benefits.' The housing programme, social security and overseas aid hadn't been cut at all. Education: three-quarters of the cuts were a reflection of the falling birth-rate. Roads: we had hit them particularly heavily. The net effect on employment in the public services was 'no significant change'. In the Civil Service there would be a cut of

---

[1] Joan Lestor had resigned the previous Saturday from her post as Under-Secretary of State for Education. In her letter of resignation she particularly criticized the cuts in education.

15,000, or 2 per cent in manpower (where the hell does he get that figure from?), and, with annual wastage running at 40,000 a year, that should create no problems.

He then grew more heated and launched into a self-defensive peroration which didn't go down very well. 'No Government in history has ever taken the Labour movement as much into its confidence as this one,' he declaimed. And he went on, to Jack's obvious annoyance, 'You can't have special treatment without accepting responsibility. As long as people are in the Government they have a responsibility to the nation as a whole.' We had a majority of one. If we failed we would get the most right-wing Tory Government for years. Some of our critics in the party were trying to make out that we were adopting Tory policies. 'If they think the real struggle is between the Labour Government and the Labour Party they are out of their tiny Chinese minds' (an obvious reference to Judith's weekend speech).[1] And he ended in a furious climax: 'Some of the things being said by some of our people are sabotage of all we hold most dear.'

Len Murray followed him calmly. He wasn't going to be diverted by any perorations. 'We have all said this last part time and again. Of course, we must accept responsibility. We are prepared to accept responsibility' (deliberately said, this) 'for those things on which we have reached agreement.' Unfortunately, the White Paper set out 'dogmatic assertions on a take-it-or-leave-it basis. This appears to pre-empt some of the decisions that have to be taken in the Budget.' Denis, no doubt conscious that he had gone too far, jumped in again in his irrepressible way. He could give Len the reassurance for which he asked. 'The White Paper is not the final word.' Len continued, unmoved, 'I hope we can begin the reassessment of this White Paper, starting *now*. We don't want people turned out of jobs without any idea how they are going to be absorbed by industry. We must have clear intentions and a clear mechanism for getting these people into employment.' He had just come from the West Midlands, where there was a 'primeval reaction' to the White Paper, with our people saying, 'Here they go: stealing the Tories' clothes again, just as they did over *In Place of Strife*.' Len agreed that 'if we will a different end, we have to will a different means and discussion on this should be open between us'.

Next it was Jack's turn. He too had been looking stern. Certain things they found quite unacceptable, such as the cut in the food subsidies. The housewife wouldn't benefit from any reduction in taxation: she would merely see prices going up in the shops. 'We hope you will reconsider that.' Jack continued implacably, 'If you imply this is a change of strategy or philosophy on the lines of Margaret Thatcher, we are finished.' ('I agree,' chipped in the unsilenceable Denis.) 'Unfortunately,' Jack continued relentlessly, 'we did not have a chance to discuss with you what you were proposing. We *must* do some reshaping.' And he concluded, 'There are some things this party must defend, or we go down eventually.'

David Basnett then took up the refrain. 'We want unemployment down to 600,000 in 1978, not 1979.' The White Paper would have a 1 per cent deflationary effect and the increase in nationalized industry prices would 'hit hardest the people we rep-

---

[1] Judith Hart had attacked the cuts in welfare, education and housing as 'the greatest kick in the teeth for the welfare state since the war'.

resent'. The unions were coming up to the conference season and the White Paper provided ammunition for anti-Social Contract speeches. 'We don't want that: we want to stay together. So do let us talk about it.' Ian Mikardo came next. The education cuts were a change in our policy of securing an 'irreversible shift in wealth and power'. The industrial strategy was 'not what we fought the election on'. We didn't need any 'curtain lectures' from Denis about taking our share of responsibility. 'I cannot think of any case,' he continued, getting sourer, 'where any representations made by the party on industrial policy have had the slightest effect.' He had been talking to a TV commentator the other day, who told him people in the City were very pleased with the Labour Government because it had managed to sell to the unions a policy the Tories never could.

This remark brought the trade union boys out of their corner fighting. (Mik gets carried away by his own sourness, just as Denis does by his natural bully-boy streak.) Alf Allen interposed angrily from the chair, 'They did not sell us the part of the Social Contract we still have, nor did they ever try.' David Basnett chipped in, 'Mik's allegation is completely wrong.' Judith, sensing the gulf opening between Mik and her and the unions, tried to restore the atmosphere by pained reasonableness. She appreciated that there were three good elements in the White Paper: the protection of housing, social security and overseas aid. 'But I cannot accept the defence figures or the industrial strategy. We have never had any move from the Government in the direction of our industrial strategy. Just where are we going?' Michael then hummed and hawed his way into the argument. 'Of course, everyone in the Labour movement feels very strongly that there are cuts,' he said gently. 'I certainly don't accept, and I don't think Denis does, that there is some magical percentage of public expenditure we must not exceed.' ('Hear, hear,' said Denis.) There had been the biggest increases in public expenditure ever under this Government. Mike continued, 'I hope we shall have a complete discussion with the TUC on the whole position that faces this Government. And I hope we shan't use the word "betrayal". The worst possible betrayal any of us could be guilty of would be to allow the Tories to run this country. We must keep the Liaison Committee in active being. I don't believe this White Paper is putting Tory policies into operation.' Shirley, too, made a placatory contribution. She agreed that we must watch the underlying assumptions of the White Paper and, if they were being falsified, we must make the necessary adjustments (e.g., if world recovery did not take place, or if the fall in food prices we were anticipating didn't happen. If they *did* the White Paper would have been proved right).

Perhaps the most dramatic speech of all came from Hughie Scanlon: once the arch-opponent of any incomes policy, now almost abject in his support of the Government. Johnnie Boyd's victory[1] must have concentrated his mind wonderfully. 'I cannot convince myself,' he said, 'that there are going to be great alterations in this

---

[1] In the elections for the general secretaryship of the AUEW held the previous year John Boyd, a moderate, had convincingly beaten the 'Broad Left' candidate, Bob Wright, by 164,276 votes to 96,216. A few months later Terence Duffy and Gavin Laird, two moderate candidates who supported the Government's £6 pay limit, had beaten Bob Wright and Jimmie Reid in elections for the Executive of the union. This right-wing trend was to continue when in 1978 Hughie Scanlon retired from the presidency and was succeeded by Terence Duffy in a decisive victory over Bob Wright.

White Paper. Yes, it is true that the trade union movement has taken policies from this Government we would never have taken from a Tory Government. I am deeply apprehensive, not only about the cuts, but the level of unemployment. The level of wages has fallen well below purchasing power, plus a demonstrable inability to control prices. There is no need to apologize for accepting that, because one was convinced the overall economic strategy was correct: for example, the need for industrial expansion. If that overall strategy is correct, I believe there will have to be cuts in the Civil Service, etc., but we have done this in the hope we will have some results. It is no good Denis saying he can't *guarantee* the strategy will work, merely that if we don't do this it will fail. That makes me worry.' He ended almost pleadingly. 'If the Budget doesn't ensure that industry does get the investment, you are going to make our position almost impossible.'

Denis wound up with another long spiel in which he busily mended some broken fences. He didn't, he said, intend the cuts to have any deflationary effect at all: tax reliefs, for example, could take up any slack. There were two points he wanted to make. 'There has been no change whatsoever in the philosophy of the Labour Party or the Labour Government. It is absolute nonsense to say that a 60 per cent level of public expenditure is too high.' (One in the eye for Roy Jenkins.) Secondly, we should never forget the magnitude of the task we faced when we took over. He concluded cheerfully that he had been 'extremely heartened' by the 'tone' of the discussion. And, indeed, when I left the building with him to face the cameras, he was in ebullient mood, turning to the journalists with enthusiasm when they asked him to comment. 'Yes, an excellent meeting; very good spirit.' I suppose one has to be made of india rubber to survive in his job at all.

At the office, I realized that the sore throat and raw chest with which I had awoken this morning indicated incipient 'flu – again! David and the CMO persuaded me to go home and stop infecting everybody. I lay in bed reading a piece of nonsense by David Wood in *The Times* on 'Mr Tomney's test case in Hammersmith'.[1] Not a word about the fact that Tomney is already sixty-seven. I can imagine what short shrift of sympathy *I* would have had if I had complained at not being allowed to fight another election at seventy!

Wednesday, 25 February

Still feeling groggy, but decide I must get up because there is a three-line whip and a tricky meeting of the NEC. As usual, the agenda was full of a series of critical Motions,

---

[1] Frank Tomney had been Labour MP for Hammersmith North since 1950. He had been brought into the constituency by Transport House to fight the sitting independent left-wing Member, D. N. Pritt, KC, and had been at odds with some members of his constituency for his uncompromising right-wing views ever since. A special meeting of the General Management Committee had been called for 26 February to discuss a Motion calling on him to retire at the next election and David Wood had leapt to his defence, denouncing the GMC meeting as a 'drum-head court martial' and claiming that 'if Mr Tomney goes down the spreading attacks on right-wing and moderate Labour MPs will be intensified'. The GMC duly carried the Motion, the NEC found there had been no irregularities and Tomney did not contest the 1979 election.

starting with one by Joan Maynard calling for a special conference on unemployment. Even Harold had turned up for that. (Jim is still off with 'flu.) Joan's Motion
was adeptly phrased, calling for a special conference 'on the question of unemployment and the economic situation generally, with a view to drawing up socialist
proposals for dealing with the situation'. This vague wording enabled its supporters
to put whatever interpretation on it they wanted to – which Mik and Wedgie
proceeded to do, after Joan had made it clear that *she* visualized the conference
covering the whole spectrum of economic policy, including pay policy. 'The
Government's policy is now running absolutely contrary to the party's policy. We
must show the movement there are alternatives we must put to the Government,' she
said.

Mike came in immediately and boldly to oppose the Motion. A conference would
do no good, he said. We must discuss unemployment targets with the TUC and at the
NEC's joint meeting with the Cabinet. Bryan Stanley backed him equally categorically: 'Joan says she wants the conference to discuss pay policy and its relation to
unemployment, because it has held down purchasing power below prices. When we
in the trade unions accepted the policy, we understood fully that that was the
situation. Are we now to reopen that policy just as it is beginning to show results? It is
far too early to get a discussion at conference on public expenditure cuts, on which it
is our intention to have discussions with the Government.'

This brought Mik into the debate at his silkiest and most plausible. He was sorry
Michael, of all people, was opposing the Motion, because he had always been a
'doughty exponent of the need to allow the rank and file to express their views'. He
then went on in his best 'reasonable man' tone to admit that 'we haven't got anything
like the alienation of the party from the Government we had in the last Government
yet', but warned, 'it is beginning to grow and I look on the special conference
as a way of putting a brake on the growth of that alienation'. Shirley argued that
there was no grassroots demand for a special conference and anyway 'it isn't the
rank and file who come to conference'. Bob Mellish was scornful about the idea.
'The last two or three years have been the most exciting in the history of the Labour
movement. We have built a real link with the trade unions. What would a conference *do*?'

Joan Lestor made an effective speech. The case, she said, was not clear-cut, but she
had come down in favour of the conference because 'the party feels no one is
listening'. As *I* listened to *her* I began to wonder if she wasn't right and whether the
conference could not be turned into a great consultation exercise. It is true that we at
the top and in the know forget how little of what we know percolates down the line.
(My Blackburn party, for instance, has passed a unanimous resolution denouncing
the cuts – without even mentioning my success in protecting the NHS. Can I blame
them? What have I done to put my own members in the picture?) Ted Short,
however, was robustly against. 'Mik and co. have not a monopoly of concern about
unemployment. We have plenty in the North-East, but my party supports the
Government's strategy absolutely. A conference like this would do immense damage
to the party. I do wish that just once in the history of this party we could count on the
support of the whole of this movement.' Ron then dealt crisply with the modalities:

even a one-day conference in London would cost nearly £10,000. The timing was difficult. 'I have not exactly been inundated with requests for a special conference.' That settled it as far as I was concerned. My hand shot up against and the Motion was lost by sixteen votes to eleven. Afterwards I learned that only John Forrester and one other among the trade unionists had voted for it. Significantly, Alex Kitson of the T&GWU voted against. It is clear that we now have a situation in the party in which the Government has succeeded in detaching the trade union movement from the left-wing critics and Jack Jones is increasingly losing patience with them.

The Reg Prentice issue came up again. Mik asked why we had not had a report from Ron on the progress of his 'conciliation' mission between Reg and his local party. Ron then burst out into a thinly disguised diatribe against Reg. 'Mik says he wishes we'd never suggested this mission. Let me tell the NEC no one wishes that more than I do. I went to the GMC [General Management Committee] meeting, as I was asked to do by the NEC, and I must tell the committee this: a nicer bunch of people I would never hope to meet in the party. I have been invited to the Annual General Meeting tonight and Reg Prentice is going as well. If you tell me not to go, I shall be delighted. I remain convinced of one thing: this matter need never have arisen, with a little give and take. The bone of contention between Reg Prentice and me is that I regard the Newham party business as family business and he regards it as public business.' This reference to Reg's recent public outbursts kept his pals on the NEC mum, while Mik expressed himself satisfied, as well he might.

Lunch at No. 10, where Harold was entertaining the Prime Minister of Luxembourg, Gaston Thorn. These occasions are always fun, because Harold invites a very catholic collection of guests and today was no exception. I was glad to meet Henry Moore [the sculptor], a small, pleasant, unassuming man with whom I swopped Yorkshire anecdotes. To balance him was Don Revie from the football world, the writer Margaret Drabble, Nancy Banks-Smith of the *Guardian* and Alan Howard, currently playing the lead in *Henry V*. And, of course, politicians and trade unionists. Jeremy Thorpe insisted on kissing me on the cheek. I found Jeremy's gesture rather distasteful in view of the barrage of personal attacks he has kept up against me, from the Oxford Union debate onwards. Perhaps he feels in need of friends, or perhaps he really did think I looked nice, because he said to me over lunch, 'I can't get over it. You look ten years younger than at any time I have seen you in the last ten years.'

The horseshoe table in the panelled dining room was ablaze with daffodils. It was a good meal and the wine was excellent. Afterwards Harold made a little speech and read every word of it, hunched over his pieces of paper as if he had never made a speech in his life before. I am at a loss to understand why he doesn't ad lib more, because his impromptu asides are usually very witty. At the very least, I can't understand why he reads his speeches in such a flat way, as though it was all a bore. He kills even the most dramatic occasion – in the House as well – in this way. Ted's contemptuous comment on his style afterwards was 'careless'.

I felt I had to look in at the party meeting on public expenditure. It was packed, but once again the atmosphere was far less intense than one might have anticipated. And the speeches were evenly balanced for and against the Government. I felt so rotten with my 'flu that I left before Denis spoke, but Ted told me he laid about him in great style.

Thursday, 26 February

A late Cabinet at which the only business was parliamentary and foreign affairs. The purpose was clearly to square us on what Harold and Jim have been up to in Rhodesia. I was furious to read yesterday that they had dispatched Greenhill[1] to Salisbury to 'explore' Ian Smith's mind. Will they never learn? For us to get into a private huddle with Smith is ridiculous. Jim is still in bed with 'flu, so David Ennals, his number two, took up the tale, gabbling through his report as if he didn't want us to take it in. Smith, he said, had sent two indirect messages to us (one through Banda, of all people) indicating that he would like us to become involved in the negotiations with Nkomo. Jim had been very doubtful about Smith's intentions, so had sent him a telegram to clarify how seriously he was prepared to negotiate. Smith's reply had been 'characteristically ambiguous'. Nonetheless, Jim had decided there was enough to justify our exploring Smith's mind 'without commitment'. So Greenhill had gone out to talk to Smith – but not to negotiate. If Greenhill's appreciation was that there was an opportunity to secure a settlement, we should have to decide our next step. Jim might want to send him, Ennals, out to consult with Kaunda and Nyerere. If, as seemed more likely, Greenhill's report was 'discouraging', we should have to consider if there were any other ways in which we could 'influence the negotiations'.

'Any questions?' asked Harold casually. No one else spoke, but I could not contain myself. The decision to send Greenhill, I declared, was in conflict with the line we had agreed at last week's Cabinet when we had said we should not offer to intervene. What was there in this intervention for us? If Smith really were ready to make an acceptable offer, he would make it to Nkomo. Our overture would merely enable him to confuse the situation, as he always did. Smith hadn't changed. On TV only last night I had heard him telling his Parliament that he would never agree to majority rule. Yet, by sending this emissary, we were tacitly accepting responsibility for a solution and when things went wrong, as they would, we would be expected to be involved. I believed Smith will never negotiate a settlement and that bloodshed will be inevitable. I can then just imagine how Harold will rush in to condemn it and to moan about the 'splits' among the Africans!

As I spoke, Harold kept interrupting me and he cut me short with all sorts of assurances that he would clear up what he called my 'confusion' and quieten my 'anxieties'. Barbara had got it wrong, he said. We were not 'getting into negotiations'. We were trying to find out whether there was any movement in Smith's position. 'Personally, I believe he will produce a formula that is no good.' If Smith *did* produce any concessions, he said, he would be overthrown by his own right wing anyway: the 'laager mentality' boys. Nor was there any possibility of our getting involved in military activity on behalf of the white minority. 'I don't accept they are our kith and

---

[1] Lord Greenhill, former head of the Diplomatic Service and now a company director, had gone to Rhodesia, accompanied by Mr Callaghan's political adviser, Tom McNally, to 'explore' the situation.

kin. Most of the post-war immigration into Rhodesia has been from South Africa.'
He then went off at a tangent, saying he had sent an emissary to Vorster to see if his
attitude was still as 'robust' towards Smith as it had been, but it had been found his
attitude had 'hardened'. He insisted that Greenhill had taken 'no proposals' and
Ennals chipped in to say Kaunda and Nyerere knew in advance that Greenhill was
going and there had been 'no criticism' from them.

The more Harold talked the more my worst fears were confirmed. Mercifully Mike
came to my support. 'I do share some of Barbara's anxieties. Smith is trying to get us
more involved because he is more frightened.' Wedgie went further. 'What I am
afraid of is a diplomatic initiative ending in a diplomatic triumph. Smith may well say,
"Yes, if you will give me backing." Before we know where we are Rhodesian soldiers
will be soldiers of the Queen again.' Denis had yet another theory. 'The risk lies in
our being drawn in on the *right* side.' But there was no echo in his speech of his robust
demand last week for 'no intervention'. He merely said tamely that he thought we
were right to make this last overture, but we must resist being drawn in at all costs.
Shirley echoed this. 'We had to be seen doing something of this kind. We are
implicated by history.' Harold wound things up with repeated protestations that we
were not going into tripartite negotiations with Smith and Nkomo. Military intervention was out of the question. 'We couldn't mount it anyway, thanks to the defence
cuts,' was Roy Mason's parting shot.

The pay beds question is now coming to the crunch. Yesterday the BMA Council
met to consider the two resolutions passed by the consultants' Central Committee.
Apparently they took all day over it and ended by agreeing a resolution which was
remarkably evasive. After reiterating the council's 'total opposition' to my consultative document and the legislation, it went on, 'The Council has however agreed to
take part in exploratory discussions with the Government in the light of the PM's
stated guarantee to the House of Commons on October 20th, 1975: "I have made it
clear in my statement that the Government are committed to the continuation of
private practice. We expect to see it continue and we shall guarantee it in our
legislation." To this end the Council has agreed to suspend sanctions and to recommend normal working of consultants.'

Once again, I am left fuming at the consequences of Harold's unnecessary and
embarrassing embroidery of my undertaking to repeat Nye's guarantee in our new
legislation,[1] and the way he has hoisted me with his wretched 'compromise'. Suspend
sanctions, indeed! Even David keeps agreeing that they were never operative anyway. So Harold has paid a totally excessive price to buy off a profession whose
opposition has proved a busted flush. (Jack has sent me a Minute saying that,
according to Laurie Pavitt, the junior doctors' great lobby against our legislation last
Tuesday was 'the biggest non-lobby fiasco of the year', with only forty juniors turning
up.) But I was determined on one thing: I am not going to let these boys delay things
any more. Fortunately, the pressures on us have been relieved somewhat by a letter
from Bob Mellish about our timetable for the Bill, in which he says that, provided
the Bill is introduced before Easter, we can have the Second Reading after Easter

[1] See footnote to p. 170.

and still get it through. That gives me a bit more time for the remaining 'consultations', on which the cowards in Cabinet lay so much emphasis.

At the office meeting I called to discuss our next steps Henry Yellowlees reported that he had had a phone call from Stevenson in which Stevenson had almost pleaded that I should issue an invitation to them to come and talk. The reason, Henry insisted, was that Stevenson was worried about the wording of the BMA Council resolution, which elaborately avoided any direct reference to Goodman. Stevenson wanted me to make it clear to them all that 'Goodman' was still on and that we were going ahead. I said that we had got to get our letter on the contents of the Schedule out to the AHAS immediately; otherwise I should not be able to show I had left enough time for the promised consultation and that would give Harold Lever another opening in Cabinet. If Stevenson and Lewin would come and see me that very day, I would agree, but I wouldn't tolerate any further delay. Henry went off, with his usual hang-dog air, to phone Stevenson and came back to say that Stevenson was sorry, but Lewin, who had been in London for three days, had left for Cambridge and that he couldn't get him back before Monday or even Tuesday of next week. I said that wasn't good enough. Why didn't they bring Lewin back this evening and I would give them both a nice meal at the Gay Hussar? My officials all laughed and Henry looked rather shocked. But I insisted that this was only a civilized thing to do and a nice meal would make us all relax anyway. Back went Henry and came back yet again with the news that Stevenson appreciated my problem, but that unfortunately it was impossible for Lewin to come back again today. Would I see him and Dr Gullick? I agreed at once, with the proviso that we must get a letter round to them from me by hand, setting out the purpose of the meeting. No illusions about having 'exploratory' talks about the Goodman proposals! Norman went off to draft this: I can rely on him to get it right.

We then turned to the other area of Cabinet sensitivity: reserve control powers. Tim Nodder had put up a first shot at the White Paper for which the PM had called. But, as so often happens with legislation, the Parliamentary draftsmen reported another snag: we could not (they said) just tack reserve powers on at committee stage unless there were a far more direct reference to them in the Bill than we proposed. We spent some time discussing how this could be done within the PM's remit and decided that it was impossible. I would have to take a regulatory power unto myself in the Bill at the outset. That means I shall have to minute Harold – and heaven knows what will happen then.

Stevenson and Gullick, when they arrived at my room at the House, could not have been more conciliatory. I spelt out to them that, as the ballot had shown a majority in favour of the Goodman proposals and sanctions had been lifted, the Government would stand by its side of the agreement and was proceeding to draft the Bill strictly on the basis of those proposals, with a view to introducing the Bill before Easter. (They did not bat an eyelid at this.) Two remaining matters had to be the subject of consultation: the contents of the Schedule and control powers. I then spelt out the way we proposed to proceed with the drawing up of the Schedule. No problem there. Next I turned to licensing, read out the relevant section of the Goodman proposals to them and proceeded to extract the last ounce of advantage from it. (I think the wording of this bit is one of our greater successes.)[1] I reported that all sorts of queries were coming into us from private developers, asking if it would be okay for them to go ahead. Of course, we had had to keep to a completely neutral line (Gullick nodded at this), saying we could neither refuse the applications nor give them any assurances. The effect of this was to 'blight' all private developments. We needed to know what the profession hoped to deliver in its 'voluntary' agreement with us to check undesirable developments. (They looked anxious at this.) If we arrived at no satisfactory 'voluntary' arrangements, the Government was free under the proposals to introduce 'reserve' powers. What would they feel about the independent board exercising them? The sooner we got this point cleared up the sooner the universal blight would be lifted. They seemed most impressed. Gullick, in particular, seemed attracted to the idea of using the independent board. They raised no objection to the consultation letter going out to the AHAS tomorrow. All Stevenson asked was that I should explain this to Mr Lewin and to perhaps one or two more, as he was sure they would like to hear these explanations from me personally. Would I meet Lewin on Thursday of next week? I said firmly that I really couldn't hold up my preparations for yet another week. I wanted to be helpful, but the meeting must be on Monday at the latest. David frowned at what he considered my high-handedness, but Stevenson took it meekly enough. I am determined not to allow the BMA to indulge in any more delaying tactics.

Friday, 27 February

Spent a pleasant and instructive day in Nottinghamshire, visiting the mental hospital and day centre for the physically handicapped at Balderton. I was particularly interested in the medium security unit at Eastdale Villa. These units are an essential link in the chain of resettlement in the community.

Norman phoned to say there had been no difficulty in fixing Monday's meeting. Lewin was bringing the whole range of representatives with him – including Grabham!

Monday, 1 March

The day began with an office discussion on David's proposals for the pharmaceutical industry. I am worried at their modesty, but Brian A-S. assured me passionately that this was the most we could get. David genuinely does want the National Enterprise Board to create a research-based publicly-owned firm and planning agreements. I agreed to David's proposals for tightening up on advertising and promotion expenses, but I insisted that we must have a further meeting on pricing policy. I won't accept without further examination David's premise that we have got to allow firms to increase their drug prices to the NHS as an incentive to foreign firms to invest more here. I think firms could earn good profits from larger export sales at NHS prices, on the lines I discussed in Iran.

[1] See Appendix VI.

Loshak in the *Telegraph* is stirring it up again over pay beds, saying doctors have had an urgent meeting with Goodman, having 'suddenly' learned that legislation is 'imminent'. And, indeed, when I faced Lewin and representatives from every group except the Royal Colleges across my table today at the Elephant and Castle, it was soon clear that their mood was very different from that of Stevenson and Gullick on Thursday. Lewin was set on drawing the battle lines again. Fortunately, Patrick, who has good judgment on these matters, had advised me beforehand not to allow myself to be diverted from the purpose of the meeting, which was to cover the same ground as I had done on Thursday, and to take the initiative. So, in my opening remarks I plunged straight in, telling them exactly what I had said to Stevenson and taking it for granted that we must now go ahead on Goodman, no more and no less. I concluded by saying we must get clear what was the status of the meeting: whether it was private or public and whether we were going to issue a joint statement at the end of it.

Lewin bridled immediately and said they must be free to make a public protest at the unrealistically short time I was allowing for consultations and on their desire for further 'explorations' of Goodman. I came back at once, politely but firmly. It was quite untrue that we were foreshortening consultations. They had taken ten weeks to consider the Goodman proposals. I wasn't complaining at that, but it was part of Goodman that the Government should now proceed to legislate as announced in the Queen's Speech and that meant that the Bill must be introduced before Easter. Even so, we were able to allow them six weeks to give their first comments on the Schedule. And, of course, consultations would go on through all stages of the Bill and after-wards. That shook them a bit and Keable-Elliott, who is the most sensible of them all, was obviously gratified at my decision actually to include a statutory right for GPs to do private practice in health centres, instead of merely setting this out in the Model Rules. (I have been told that GPs' suspicions about my intentions are leading some of them to turn down plans for health centres.) Grabham, of course, insisted on having a brush with me over the timetable. He even said that the sending out of the AHA letter was 'bad faith, an erosion of the compromise'. But I soon disposed of *that*, pointing out that it was really absurd of him to demand that I should consult on how I should consult. I don't think the others had much sympathy with him.

They then turned to another issue about which they are clearly furious. They are trying to assert that the one thousand beds to be set out in the Schedule included Northern Ireland. Thoroughly briefed on this, I confronted them with a pile of evidence to the contrary, concluding with the statement I had made to Parliament on 12 December, which Dr Stevenson had read beforehand and approved. This specifically mentioned Scotland and Wales, but not Northern Ireland. 'And that,' I said sweetly, 'is conclusive.' Wouldn't I agree to let them consult Goodman on the interpretation of his proposals, asked Grabham. I emphatically rejected this. After about an hour and a half they simmered down, Lewin even agreeing that we didn't want to rush into an open war in the press. In the end the press statement they agreed could not have been better from our point of view.

The next step was to see Arnold Goodman to find out how he saw things develop-ing. He came to my room at the House – late, of course. I didn't think he was looking too well after his spell in hospital and, indeed, it soon became clear that he wanted to disembroil himself from the whole business. He even told me he wouldn't speak in the Lords on the pay beds Bill. However, he toyed with some ideas for licensing. He personally didn't think private practice would be much threat. Nonetheless, he accepted that under his proposals there had to be an attempt to get a voluntary agreement, with reserve powers if necessary. What about a control through man-power numbers, rather than buildings? I said I didn't think that would work and told him how interested Gullick had semed to be about the possibility of bringing in the independent board. He agreed to talk to the profession again. Yes, he would let me know the outcome privately before anything was put to me officially.

At one point he hinted that the real cause of the trouble was that the profession were worried about the board's membership. Would it not be possible to announce the chairman's name in advance of the Bill? I certainly wasn't going to have *that* and managed to head him off it by pointing out that no one in whom the profession would have confidence was likely to accept an appointment before the battle to destroy the Bill itself had taken place. Fortunately, he saw the sense of that. He also tried to get me to show them the Bill before it was published, but I refused emphatically. On Northern Ireland, he agreed that he couldn't remember it being mentioned at all. So far so good.

The day concluded with a most pleasant dinner at Brian Abel-Smith's house in Elizabeth Street. It arose from the TUC's request for a private discussion with us on our long-term priorities for social security. Terry Parry had brought Audrey Prime, Harry Urwin and Peter Jacques along and we were not at all clear what was behind their move. I took the initiative by stressing the need for us not to sacrifice child benefit to our other priorities, pointing out that, apart from anything else, this was the best way to help the low paid and get rid of the scandal under which a family man could get a bigger income when unemployed than when he was at work.[1] Harry Urwin got really interested and impressed, so their pressure was somewhat muted when they turned to pensions. It suddenly became clear that the whole purpose of the evening was to get us committed to – and fighting for – an increase of £3.50 for a married pensioner couple this July, thus bringing the pension increase this year up to £6 a week, the same as the flat-rate pay increase, Jack Jones's face-saver. We couldn't give them much encouragement, because Brian O'Malley and I know Denis will never agree to that. Nonetheless, we all enjoyed the evening, Terry remarking wistfully, 'We ought to have one of these every month.' But what they will say when they find Denis has forced us to abandon the historical method of uprating I tremble to think.

[1] In February 1976, an unemployed man was entitled to draw £3.50 per week for his first child and £2 for each subsequent child. When at work he received nothing for the first child and a family allowance of £1.50 per week for his second and subsequent children. This discrepancy was an important factor in reducing the incentive to work, particularly in the case of a man on a low wage with a large family, who could find himself better off when unemployed. Harry Urwin and Terry Parry quickly grasped the importance of this point and became enthusiastic supporters of the need to introduce a substantial child benefit for every child. It was their influence in the TUC which helped Labour MPs like myself to secure a reversal of Jim Callaghan's attempt, after I had left the Government, to postpone the introduction of child benefit indefinitely. By 1979 child benefit had been increased to £4 per week per child and in its election Manifesto that year the Labour Party pledged to increase it still further with a view to bringing it eventually into line with family support for the unemployed, which had also increased.

Tuesday, 2 March

The papers carry stories of a coming battle over pay beds. The profession's realization that legislation is definitely coming must be getting through. There is also a most remarkable attack on Margaret Thatcher by Joe Rogaly for her weekend speech wooing the trade unions. *The Times* attacks her in a leader too. Much more worrying, from my point of view, is the gloating now going on in the press on the extent to which the NEB has been emasculated. It is this which will fuel the fury of the Left over the Government's economic policy. Gedling has reported to me on the discussion he and Nodder had with Damerell of the Independent Hospitals Group yesterday. Damerell was apparently in a much more truculent mood than he was formerly, saying our proposals for the Schedule were a 'clear breach' of the Goodman proposals. And he obviously isn't going to be very helpful in drawing up ideas for voluntary, or any other, controls. Well, we must just plug away.

Wednesday, 3 March

George Brown has resigned from the Labour Party. Last night on TV he was clearly incapable. Today the *Guardian* and *Mail* honourably carry pictures of him, prostrate in the gutter after his broadcast. If it had been anyone on the Left they would certainly have printed the pictures, and the sight of George Brown whole-seas-over did something to offset the myth hastily being manufactured that he alone is a man of principle and that his resignation is proof of the further collapse of the Labour Party into the hands of the 'Marxists'. *The Times* excelled itself in the worst leader I have ever read, which included the incredible phrase, 'George Brown drunk is a better man than the Prime Minister sober.' I should think even Harold's enemies would be ashamed of it. When I remember what Harold put up with from George all those years.... At the Association of Municipal Corporations party I chatted to Geoffrey Drain of NALGO about pay beds, among other things. I thanked him for the helpful line his Executive had taken and he replied, 'I think you have done pretty well. No other Minister has even tried.'

Harold, however, has obviously got cold feet over my suggestion that I should put a reserve licensing power in the Bill. No. 10 has replied to my Minute asking me to put a paper to Cabinet.

Thursday, 4 March

I went along with some scepticism to the meeting of MSP [Miscellaneous Social Policy], Harold's committee on long-term social policies. The Think Tank was due to give a presentation of its 'synoptic' view of social policy as the first stage of its 'fundamental' review, of which I have always been highly dubious. For the occasion a projector and screen had been set up in the Cabinet room. All the spending Ministers turned up, together with Joel, who was clearly as dubious as I was. Harold was in the chair. In the event, it turned out to be quite illuminating. Ken Berrill introduced a succession of his younger experts, who proceeded to show slides which effectively illustrated some of the things I have been arguing in PESC, e.g. the relative advantage education had enjoyed over the years in public expenditure, despite the move of demographic factors in favour of the health and personal social services. Tony C. drawled his complaint that this exposition ought to have been given *before*, not *after* PESC Cabinet, adding later, 'Barbara would not have got away with blue murder as she did.' I retorted, 'On the contrary, it proved all my arguments.' What particularly interested me were the international comparisons on which Tony C. has been insisting. They showed our expenditure on the social services to be below the European average and scotched another of Tony's insinuations to the contrary. When it came to questions I couldn't resist a dig at Roy J. 'Would it be possible to give these international comparisons for public expenditure as a whole?' I asked sweetly. 'There have been some rather sweeping statements recently to the effect that our level of public expenditure is so high that democracy is threatened and it would be interesting to know if democracy is collapsing all over Europe.' The solemn CPRS boys earnestly assured me that the information was available. Roy smiled rather sourly, while Michael and Joel chuckled openly. 'That was very funny,' said Tony C. afterwards. 'Of course, the figures will show that other people's public expenditure is as high as ours.'[1]

Then into Cabinet. There was a fat draft of Roy Mason's Defence Review, which I hadn't even looked at, and, with poor Jack Straw still missing, mourning his dead baby, I had no briefing at all. 'Have you read it?' I asked Wedgie. 'Of course not,' he replied. 'I have enough of my own paper to struggle through.' So Roy's draft went through on the nod – and heaven knows what hostages he has given to our fortunes. This, as Norman agreed, was just another example of how indispensable political advisers are. Jack would have read it all and alerted me to any dangers.

The main business which interested me in Cabinet was Rhodesia. With Jim absent in Iran David Ennals gave the report on Greenhill's mission. Greenhill had reported that Ian Smith's attitude had 'not shifted far enough to justify our intervention in negotiations'. Nkomo was anxious for us to take the chair at his talks with Smith, but the trouble was that it would commit us to Nkomo against the rest. (I was glad that he could at least see the danger of that.) Jim, said David, 'has not reached his

---

[1] In March CPRS circulated its 'Review of the Social Services' to Cabinet. Far from showing inordinate profligacy by Britain, it revealed that, compared with other countries, our spending on the social services had been on the modest side. Though social spending in Britain had grown rapidly since 1952, by 1972, the latest date for which figures were available, we were still spending a smaller proportion of our Gross Domestic Product on social programmes, excluding housing, than Germany, Italy, the Netherlands and Denmark and were spending less per head than most EEC countries. Taking social security and welfare benefits on their own, Britain was almost at the bottom of the table of spending. This, said the report, was due to our relatively low level of family benefits, invalidity benefits and war pensions. The steps Britain was taking to overcome these deficiencies could substantially affect future comparisons, though, the report pointed out, similar developments would be taking place in other countries. For some incomprehensible reason the CPRS review was labelled 'Confidential' and not published by the Government. My request that it should include comparisons for public expenditure as a whole had not been met, but other statistics published later showed that, here again, Britain was not out of line. On the contrary, in 1976 general government spending in Britain as a percentage of Gross National Product was lower in Britain than in Sweden, Norway, Denmark and Germany. (National Accounts of OECD countries, 1976, Vol. 11.)

conclusions'. Anything we did would have to get the acquiescence of the four presidents[1] and Jim was considering various 'options' that were open to him. That morning a message had come from Smith saying he wanted to send two emissaries over here tomorrow. Jim hadn't yet made up his mind what to do about this. Harold then took up the tale. 'We have made it clear that we have no responsibility.' There was a deep split in the Tory Party, though Tugendhat[2] was taking a statesmanlike line. There would be a lot of flak from the Tory Right, but we just had to 'sit it out'. When, however, I pressed that Jim should not decide on any of his 'options' before he had first consulted Cabinet, Harold became his most devious. First, he evaded answering; then, under my pressure, said elliptically that Jim would consult him and he would see that there was 'no serious involvement' – whatever that may mean. I shall continue to watch all this like a hawk, but Harold will be as slippery as ever.

In the evening I went back to No. 10 for my private meeting with Harold.[3] Tony C. had had an audience too, and, as he came down from the upstairs study, he quipped at me that he had told Harold I was no doubt going to ask him for more money. 'I told him I didn't believe him,' said Harold amicably as he poured me a drink. He was relaxed and talkative, full of his ploy on privacy and the press, which he told me with great satisfaction he was going to develop in a speech that weekend, and I sank back in the sofa cushions to wait my time. 'Well?' he said at last. 'I'm going to ask you a very peculiar question,' I replied. 'When are you going to have your next Cabinet reshuffle?' He jumped up and started pacing up and down. 'I'm in no hurry,' he said; paused and added, 'I don't intend to be in this job much longer.' 'That's funny,' I replied. 'I came to tell you I want to get out too.' He raised his eyebrows in surprise, then settled down in his chair and swore me to secrecy.

'I want to talk to you as an old friend who has always been loyal to me,' he said. 'You are the only person I know who never leaks. I am getting tired of this job. I've spent thirteen years trying to keep this party together and it's been a pretty thankless task. Do you know I've only been to the theatre about twenty times in all those years? Because I have had to keep on top of everything that is happening. Every weekend I have about ten one-hundred-page documents to read – and I read them all. It's the only way. I have to think of everything. Do you know what I did during our arguments over Chrysler? At one point in Cabinet I thought Eric was going to resign, so I wrote him a note, but, so that no one should know I had done so, I rang for a secretary, told him to take it outside, wait for ten minutes and then bring it in to Eric as though it were a message from his office. You have to think of all these things, but it is very tiring. When I became PM this time I told the Queen the date on which I would retire from this job. She's got the record of it, so no one will be able to say afterwards

---

[1] The four 'frontline' presidents most involved in the Rhodesian situation were Julius Nyerere of Tanzania, Kenneth Kaunda of Zambia, Samora Machel of Mozambique and Seretse Khama of Botswana.

[2] Christopher Tugendhat, MP for the City of London and Westminster, South, was Conservative front-bench spokesman for Foreign and Commonwealth Affairs. In 1977 he became a member of the European Commission with special responsibility for the budget and financial control.

[3] Having made up my mind to resign in the autumn when my pay beds legislation was through, I decided to see Harold and tell him in confidence so that, if he were preparing a Cabinet reshuffle, I could time my own resignation to precede it.

that I was pushed out.' 'You work too hard,' I agreed, thinking how yellow and lined he looked. 'I hope you are taking Paddy [his dog] for those walks now.' (It is my panacea for everything.)

He obviously longed to talk. 'Tell me,' he said, 'who do you think will succeed me when I go?' When I said Denis Healey he shook his head. 'The Left hate him.' 'But they would never have Jim, and Roy ditched himself years ago,' I replied. 'There are three groups in the Left,' he continued. 'There is what is now called the "soft" Left, to which you and I and Michael always belonged. There is a middle group and then there are the really vicious group.' He thought they'd go for Wedgie first and let someone other than Denis in. 'But it has got to be someone who is willing to work at it, not going out to dinner all the time, like Roy. Eric is too young, though he's very good and his turn may come. I'll tell you who I think has developed remarkably: Peter Shore. He's really become very impressive.' (I agreed with that, remembering the air of authority he developed during the referendum campaign. But whether he has an emollient enough temperament to lead our stormy party, I very much doubt.)

'What are you going to do when you give this up?' I asked. 'Go into academic life?' 'Heavens, no. I shall just retire to the backbenches and enjoy myself. I've told my local party I will fight another election and have one more Parliament. Then I'll retire.' I could see time slipping away and managed to inject my own problem into the conversation. 'Harold, I want to get the pay beds Bill through Parliament, then give up my job.' 'Why?' he asked, puzzled. 'Because I've had a good run for my money and it's time I made room for one of the younger ones. There are a lot of able young MPs pressing up from below. For your own sake, Harold, you ought to make room for them.' He shook his head. 'It's very difficult.' 'I shall give up my seat: I'm not running again,' I continued. That really surprised him. 'So there'll be two Castles in the Lords,' he grinned. I ignored that. 'But,' I persisted, 'I want to go with dignity. I don't want the press to be able to say that I've been pushed out.' 'This conversation is proof that you haven't been. We'll minute it if you like,' he replied. 'Heavens, no,' I cried. 'It would be round Whitehall in a flash. These civil servants leak like mad.' 'Not the No. 10 ones,' he said rather grandly. 'I want to go by the end of the summer recess,' I continued. 'That is why it is so essential that the pay beds Bill isn't dropped.' 'It won't be,' he assured me. 'What I think we should drop is Weights and Measures: horribly boring anyway.'

He thought a moment, then said, 'Your timetable ought to fit into mine all right.' 'What *is* the date you told the Queen?' I asked. He shook his head. 'I told it her on Privy Council terms.' 'Well, I'm a Privy Councillor,' I replied. He still shook his head, adding, 'I may be forced to stay another six months or so: Rhodesia, for instance, or Northern Ireland.' I began to suspect that his date wasn't as firm as he had implied. At that moment a secretary put his head round the door. 'Lord Goodman is waiting.' I nearly laughed outright. What are those two up to *now*? We parted amicably and I was glad I had spoken to him. After all these years I would hate to resign on him and I know he will play it so as to help me to achieve my ends, complete the jobs I've got on hand and retire with my tail up.

In the hall I spoke to Arnold, who told me he had had a meeting with the medicos and got them thinking out a scheme for controlling the private sector. He promised he would let me have details. I doubt whether it will amount to very much, with the professions sounding off already about the phasing out of the thousand beds.

Friday, 5 March

All day meeting at the House of the Social Policy Committee of the NEC to complete our chapter for the 1976 programme. Brian O'Malley grumbled to me that he didn't know why we needed to spend so much time on it, but I replied that he and I wanted to leave a good memorial to ourselves in the party's policy. Over lunch I told him I had spoken to Harold and that it was clear there wasn't going to be an Easter reshuffle. Of course, I said nothing more than that. 'Is he really going to keep Merlyn on at Northern Ireland?' he asked incredulously. 'It looks like it,' I replied. I am fascinated by Brian's hankering after the Northern Ireland job and suspect he has calculated that it is his best way of getting into the Cabinet. He had told me frankly he couldn't do my job. 'I don't know anything about the health side.' And it is clear that David couldn't take over the department either, because he knows nothing about social security. These two are the specialists – and very able too – but I have had to be the presiding political protagonist, straddling both sides.

Saturday, 6 March

I kept my promise to attend Alec Jones's local party's annual dinner at Rhondda. As we drove past the heads of the valleys and as I talked to the Mayor, a mineworker, I felt I was taking part in the *How Green was my Valley* TV serial. This feeling was deepened as I went to change at Alec's house, one of a terraced row of stone cottages shooting up the mountainside. The women in the street stood at their doors, all dressed up ready for the dinner, to wave to me as we arrived. And the same atmosphere of warm exuberance greeted me at the community centre, where the dinner went with a whoosh. The room was packed. Fortunately, I was on form and I danced like a twenty-year-old afterwards. As I rose to go to catch my night sleeper, the singer on the platform got them all to their feet in a magnificent rendering of 'There'll be a welcome in the valleys', which nearly brought tears to my eyes. I really felt part of Wales.

In the car back to Cardiff Alec's wife, Mildred, provided a hilarious climax to the evening by telling me about the sheep. Sheep, it appears, dominate their municipal politics. 'The only intelligent sheep in existence are in the Rhondda,' said Mildred. They have discovered the riches of the street and its dustbins and by hook – and not by crook – they find their way into it from the mountainside. So the night is made hideous by the clatter of dustbin lids as the sheep nose out the titbits. Cars are damaged as sheep jump onto them, while Alec had a whole row of pansies he had just planted in his front garden whipped out by the sheep in five minutes flat while he was making a cup of tea! 'When you go canvassing in the local elections,' said Mildred, 'all people want to know about is what you are going to do about the sheep.' The local council had exhausted its resources in trying to keep them out. There had been a special issue of sheep-proof dustbins, but the sheep soon learned to kick them over and knock off the specially fastened lids. The council had put up high wire fences, built cattle grids, the lot. But somehow the sheep got to the other side of them. 'They bring their lambs with them,' said Mildred, 'and once a sheep has had a taste of the street there is no keeping him out again.' 'Yes,' said Denis, the mayor's driver, 'they're so cunning, they know when the dust-carts have been round the street and don't bother to come that day.' I went to bed chuckling and happy about my day.

Sunday, 7 March

Home for Sunday breakfast: tired but still happy. I even did some digging in the bitter wind. Alan Watkins, in the *Observer*, has a piece about Harold's imminent retirement: 'Harold: This Year, Next Year, Sometime——' I hope Harold doesn't think I have been talking to him! Alan advances one interesting theory: that Harold is planning to leave in 1977, after he has helped to celebrate the Queen's Jubilee year. Well, now I come to think of it, I can't see him missing that. If so, I have plenty of time to work out my own ploy.

Monday, 8 March

Ted had to get up at 6.30am to catch his plane to Brussels, so it hasn't been a particularly restful weekend. Nonetheless, I feel relaxed – almost euphoric, now I have settled things with Harold. At the office I told Norman what had transpired and agreed to see Patrick at his request that afternoon. 'Is he going to suggest the right person to succeed you?' I asked Norman, who has been warning me that Establishment Division is preparing to move him. Norman assured me that the chap to be offered to me was the 'best buy'. (I suspect Graham will have had a hand in choosing him, so that will be okay by me. After all, he chose Norman for me.) When Patrick started to outline why it was necessary to start thinking about a successor for Norman, whose stint in Private Office has run its normal course, I chipped in, swore him to secrecy, and told him what I had told the PM. He was his usual charming self about it, thanked me for taking him into my confidence, said how much they would all miss me. 'You get younger all the time. I have never worked for a Minister who had so much vitality,' he said and promised to gear Norman's departure to suit my convenience. Private Office have overwhelmed me by depositing a sheaf of spring flowers on my desk, accompanied by an anniversary card. I had forgotten that this was two years to the day since I came to DHSS. 'We couldn't let your second birthday go uncelebrated,' they said. So I invited them in to a drink, bless them. After all they have suffered!

At Home Policy there was a great load of documents to wade through. First, there was a pile on economic strategy, in which Geoff Bish and Judith had conspired to bombard the joint meeting of Cabinet and NEC, and later the TUC Liaison Committee, with a counter-analysis to the Government's. Their line was that the medium-term assessment shows a gloomier outlook than the Government admits, including unemployment still running at 1¼ million at the end of 1977. All this activity is very right and proper. I happen to know that the Treasury deliberately put a misleading figure for unemployment into the Public Expenditure White Paper.

It is perfectly true that Harold Lever, Denis and Eric have succeeded in emasculating the party's industrial policy. The report presented to us of the NEC's delegation to Denis, Eric *et al.* on this last month was proof, if that were still needed. Denis was recorded as saying that 'the NEC approach did not have any chance of gaining support from employers', while Eric apparently said that there was no chance of getting one hundred planning agreements this year, nor of making them compulsory, as this would require a new Act. So this great plank of our policy, which Harold [Wilson] lauded at the 1974 conference as the greatest thing since Keynes, looks like being a damp squib. But having had to face backwoodsmen like the consultants myself, I can just imagine what obstruction and downright sabotage we should face from industrialists if we tried to impose the party's policy on them. The trouble is that we just have not got up a sufficient head of revolutionary steam in the country to win in a showdown. But the Varleys and Healeys don't even try to win consent for more radical policies. As for Harold Lever, he is capitalism's Trojan horse in a Labour Cabinet.

Next, we turned to Geoff's paper on the 'Machinery of Government', which was leaked in the weekend papers as terribly left, but turned out to be a rehash of some old and pretty moderate ideas. And then there was Wedgie's paper on Honours, which he proudly told us he had written in 1964. I could see its authorship being reported to the press after the meeting, so I reminded him, and the committee, that Wedgie and I had both made representations to Harold on this theme during the 1966 Government. (I had got the office to turn this up, and No. 10 has come up with a copy of the letter I sent to Harold in August 1966: a very spirited one, taking very much the line for which Wedgie was claiming credit now.)[1] Wedgie looked surprised and said, 'I must look that up.' We then agreed we would refer the papers on both these subjects to a working group to draft something for inclusion in the 1976 programme. Both Wedgie and I said we were too busy to go on it. (Incidentally, come to think of it, I never got a reply to my letter from Harold.)

When I got home to my boxes I discovered a Minute from Harold to Wedgie in haughty tone, expressing outrage at the NEC decision to allow him to hold press conferences after meetings of Home Policy. 'I cannot agree that you, or any other Minister who is a member of a party committee or sub-committee, should make statements or become identified with statements made on behalf of the committee, in a non-ministerial capacity .... Ministers cannot speak publicly in a non-ministerial capacity. In all cases they speak as Ministers and the principle of collective responsibility applies.' Really! Does Harold have to come barging in in this posturing way? Will he never learn? What he should have done was to take Wedgie aside – and some others of us – and find out what it was all about. If he tries to make an issue of this, he'll only lose.

---

[1] Tony Benn's main proposals were that a way should be found of putting people in the House of Lords without ennoblement, that those whose public service it was desired to recognize should receive a parliamentary medal and that awards for gallantry should be democratized. I had particularly pleaded that the social stratification of awards should be ended.

Tuesday, 9 March

Work at the department is so slack I even had time to attend the meeting of the International Committee of the NEC. When I arrived I found to my surprise that Jim was there. It has been Mik's continuing complaint that Jim, though Foreign Secretary, never comes to the committee and ignores its representations; indeed at first it looked as though the proceedings were going to consist of a feline sparring match between Mik and Jim. The subject was the meetings of the Socialist International: Mik said silkily that he objected to Harold telling the leaders of the socialist parties to ignore the NEC's representatives on the SI as they were 'irresponsible'. Jim replied equally smoothly that we must speak frankly to each other and the fact was that he received constant complaints from our socialist comrades in the SI about the attitude of our representatives. Mik and Ron then joined to do a hatchet job on Jim, setting out at great length and impressively that their disagreements with the other members of the SI had not been about policy, but about the incompetent organization of this body. Ron, in particular, got eloquent about this, telling in detail about how he had struggled to put the finances of the organization into some kind of order. Jim, who had been doodling sceptically on his pad, suddenly looked up and said that if they would let him have their concrete proposals for reforming the SI he would be willing to have a word with some of the SI leaders about it all. Mik and Ron exploded in unison about this. 'But you've got the report. It was written by Tom McNally[1] two years ago. Tom – your own man in your own office – can tell you all about it.' Collapse of slim Jim. I couldn't help wondering how a Labour Foreign Secretary could get as badly out of touch with his own party as that.

Jim then tried to repair his fences by talking freely (with many asides about how he hoped all this would be kept confidential) about Rhodesia. He said that he personally didn't trust Smith, but he was inundated with requests for Britain to intervene, notably from the four African presidents. He hoped we were all agreed that it was important to avoid bloodshed if at all possible. So his line was to say to Smith that he would never negotiate with him, but if Smith would let him have in writing (even if it were kept private) what he was willing to offer, Jim would take it from there. This taking of the committee into his confidence had a magical effect: there were adulatory nods all round the table. It was left to me to say, 'And if Smith were to respond what would you do then?' 'Don't press me for details, Barbara,' pleaded Jim. Really, considering how easy it is to get away with the minimum of deference to the party, I am astonished that Jim doesn't do more of it. The trouble with Foreign Secretaries is that they are only second to Chancellors of the Exchequer in their God-complexes.

I was just finishing my lunch in the House when Harold joined the communal table in the Members' dining room. He was soon involved in a long dissertation on his resignation from the 1950 Labour Government,[2] over which he and George Strauss swapped memories – or, rather, Harold swept on, with George trying vainly to get a word in here and there. Through Harold's out-of-the-corner-of-his-mouth asides I

---

[1] Callaghan's political adviser, who had been head of the Labour Party's International Department.
[2] See footnote, page 537.

gathered that he had been far more concerned with the rearmament side of the issue than Nye had been. George managed to slip in a comment on how he, as Minister of Supply, had warned Cabinet that the proposed rearmament programme just was not achievable. 'You were the only one to support me, Harold.' 'Yet Gaitskell insisted on basing his Budget on the assumption that the programme would be fully achieved,' Harold said. 'Gaitskell's behaviour really was extraordinary. It was out of this that the £13 million for teeth and spectacles arose. But Nye didn't latch on to the rearmament issue until later.' And he added darkly, 'One day the story will be told. Do you realize, George, that we are just getting to the point when the thirty-year rule[1] will not apply to that period?' 'I thought it was now fifteen years,' I chipped in. But Harold shook his head. 'That will only apply to the future.' That was a new one on me, but, as we have not yet – mercifully – been asked to sign the undertaking visualized in the Radcliffe Report, I didn't press the point.

By this time most of the people round the table had slipped away. Harold was by now so carried away by his compulsive need for conversation that he launched on a not very clear but very protracted revelation about what he was going to say at his Question time that afternoon. He had, he said, turning to me, established that BOSS [the South African Bureau of State Security] had been involved in the Thorpe affair. 'It's been a great detective exercise, I can tell you. Detective Inspector Falkender has been up to her eyes in it. I've got conclusive evidence that South African money has been involved. After all, she's been through the same thing. So have I. No Minister or political party is safe unless we expose this. Of course, I can't reveal my sources but, then, neither could Macmillan when he invited me to come and talk to him. If the Right Hon. Lady, the Leader of the Opposition, likes to challenge me to reveal them, I'll invite her to come and talk to me.' Those of us who were left were by this time completely mystified, but Harold was like a Boy Scout playing cops and robbers. He was chuckling at the way he had arranged to make his great announcement that afternoon through the medium of a Question that was only remotely to do with it. 'I have got one of my most vociferous critics to ask a supplementary. I'm rather good at drafting questions.' 'Not Willie Hamilton,' I pleaded, appalled. 'No,' he replied: 'Jim Wellbeloved.' I was astonished at his recklessness. If he *was* fixing Question time in this way, one would have thought he would have kept mum about it. But not our Harold. 'What number Question is it?' I asked. 'Number 4.' 'But how can you be sure it will be reached?' 'It will be,' he replied knowingly. 'Of course,' he added, 'I shall have to say the South African Government isn't involved, because we need their help over Rhodesia.' I almost despaired of him. I can see him getting involved again in a complicated manoeuvre which will merely make him look devious rather than a Sir Galahad. He has been obsessed with this defence of Jeremy for weeks and I have no doubt he is right that the South African security forces are active in this country and are capable of anything. But I couldn't see quite why they should pick on the Liberals, a spent force, rather than us. 'They have already picked on me,' Harold explained.

[1] Under the Public Records Act 1958, classified state documents held in the Public Record Office were not available for public inspection for fifty years. On Harold Wilson's initiative this had been reduced to thirty years in 1967.

'But they believe it was the Liberal intervention that let us into office and the first thing we did was to stop arms for South Africa.' 'Are you saying that there was nothing in the Jeremy–Scott affair and they have been inventing it, or that there *was* something and they are exploiting it?' I asked. 'I dare say there may have been something at some time,' said Harold indifferently, 'but they are out to destroy the Liberal leader and they would destroy any successor to him. There is big money involved in this.' I decided I had better rearrange my afternoon engagements so that I could be present at the unveiling of this mystery.

When I slipped into the chamber for Harold's Questions Jeremy rushed in just ahead of me. He clearly knew what was coming. It was fascinating to watch the plot unfold. Question Number 4, asked by a Tory, seemed a most unlikely vehicle: something about Harold's next visit to the UN, which enabled the Tories to keep up their barrage about Russian intervention in Angola. Then George Thomas dutifully called Jim Wellbeloved, who, without looking at a note, carefully rolled out his prepared supplementary: 'Has my Right Honourable Friend received any evidence about the involvement of South African agents in the framing of leading Liberal Party members?' Harold took up his cue in an opaque reply which began crisply: 'I have no doubt at all that there is strong South African participation in recent activities relating to the Right Honourable Gentleman the Leader of the Liberal Party.' He then tailed off into an apologia for the South African Government: he had 'no evidence at all' that it had any connection 'with these unsavoury activities'. I thought he had succeeded in destroying the whole impact. Most people in the House looked puzzled. Jeremy sat with his ear glued to the amplifier. Chattering among the Liberal ranks. Jeremy was nodding to John Pardoe and Pardoe got up. But George Thomas was playing his part to perfection. He called Tory after Tory, who kept up the anti-Russian refrain. I thought George had lost his cue, but, in contrast to the speed with which he had raced through earlier questions, he was timing this perfectly. After the Tories had had their run he called Pardoe, who rose to ask, in view of the 'extremely serious and important statement' the Prime Minister had made, what action he proposed to take. Harold came back ponderously, egging the pudding of his exoneration of the South African Government. 'I said there is no evidence of South African Government participation in this matter.' He then went off at a tangent. Jim Callaghan was sitting next to me. 'Did you know about this?' I asked. He shook his head. 'What is it all about?' I went on. 'I haven't a clue,' he replied. Question Number 4, having taken as much time as the first three put together, had exhausted the PM's Question time.

I waited for the nine o'clock news, fascinated. Harold's instinct hadn't deserted him. The news led on this incident and included an interview with Pardoe, who exactly echoed Harold's line about the reasons why South African 'business interests' should be interested in destroying the Liberal Party. I don't suppose Harold will worry if the 'police enquiries' don't lead anywhere. But the significant thing was the way Margaret Thatcher had been caught unawares. She was not prepared for anything like this, with one of her carefully worked out and stylized interventions and she wasn't politician enough to react instinctively. If she could only have improvised, she could have driven Harold into a corner. He really is an incredibly rash and romantic man. Why go overboard for Jeremy, for heaven's sake? For the political moral Harold was hinting at was so set about with equivocations that it could not really get home.

The publication of the White Paper on Public Expenditure on 19 February (Cmnd. 6393), providing for cuts of £3 billion in 1978–79, had widened the rift between the left wing and the Government. Despairing of the direction which the Government was taking, thirty Tribune MPs abstained in the vote on the White Paper on 10 March, thus ensuring the Government's defeat. Two days later left-wing union leaders, Jack Jones and Hugh Scanlon, combined with moderate David Basnett to issue a call for unity behind the Government and an end to the 'splits and divisions which have recently emerged'.

Nonetheless doubts were deepening as to whether the growth visualized in the 'central case' of economic projections in the White Paper could be achieved. This central projection was based on a growth in GDP of just under 3·5 per cent per annum between 1974 and 1979, and the White Paper proposed a flattening out of public expenditure after 1976–77 to make way for it. The cutback was to be underpinned by the widespread introduction of cash limits and by pressure on the local authorities through the Consultative Council and the rate support grant to achieve a similar standstill in their current expenditure. But after two years of a slump in growth and investment, this central case called for a far higher rate of recovery than from past performance seemed possible. True, there were some encouraging signs. In March unemployment fell slightly for the first time in two years, though still over one million. The pay policy was holding – so was industrial peace, the number of working days lost through strikes in 1975 having been the lowest for seven years. Export volume was up. But there were as yet no signs of world recovery on the scale required. Nor was it likely that Britain, with her chronic tendency to import, would be in a position to take advantage of it. At the end of March Mr Wynne Godley and his Cambridge colleagues reiterated their warning that unemployment would rise to between one-and-a-half million and two million by the end of the decade unless imports were controlled. The NEC continued to urge a modified version of the Cambridge policy on the Government.

The pleas fell on deaf ears. At the end of 1975 Denis Healey had negotiated with the IMF a drawing of £1,000 million special drawing rights under the oil facility and a further stand-by credit of £700 million. In his letter of application he had not only reiterated his intention to continue with his present policies, but undertook not to impose new restrictions on payments or trade without prior consultation with the Fund. On the industrial front the Government was spending more on industrial promotion and its job protection schemes, but it remained adamant about the need to pursue consensus policies. In February Denis Healey flatly told a deputation from the NEC that he was not going to shift from the tripartite approach to industrial strategy.

Meanwhile he was preparing a budget designed to persuade unions and workers to accept another round of wage restraint. The present pay limit, he argued, should cut the inflation rate by well over half by the end of the year, but, if we were to keep in line with our competitors, inflation must be halved yet again by the end of 1977. That meant that the pay limit in the coming year must be halved as well. To secure this he proposed to bribe the unions with tax concessions, offering to increase income tax reliefs by about £1,300 million in two stages: the first £370 million increase being unconditional, the second £1,000 million being dependent on the unions agreeing to a pay limit of around 3 per cent. The majority of workers, he told the House of Commons on 6 April, would be better off with a lower pay limit and the extra tax reliefs than with a higher limit and lower reliefs, adding that the package would slightly boost demand and would increase confidence. He looked forward optimistically to the recovery gathering speed over the next twelve months, with growth reaching 4 per cent per year, investment reviving, unemployment beginning to fall and inflation down to less than 10 per cent.

In my department we were enjoying a temporary lull. Morale in the Health Service had been improved by our success in coming out of the public expenditure exercise relatively well. At the end of March David Owen and I published a consultative document setting out our priorities for the health and personal social services in the new situation, one of the first attempts at planning in this field. My pay beds legislation inched its way slowly but surely through Cabinet. On 16 March Harold Wilson astonished all of us by announcing his decision to resign the premiership and my own fortunes took a dramatic turn.

Wednesday, 10 March

The press and the BBC are extracting the last ounce of excitement out of Harold's statement – but it isn't helping Jeremy. Cyril Smith is busy rocking Jeremy's boat from his hospital bed and the *Mail* carries a centre spread on Cyril and his Ma which reduces the whole business to a roaring farce. The *Mirror* has taken up Harold's cue on its front page (all prearranged by Harold, I suspect), but even the *Mirror* hasn't been able to resist a centre spread on 'Thorpe's Follies'. So Harold has thrown away his great revelation in the wrong cause.

As I went down to the House in the evening the air was electric with the message: 'We are going to be defeated tonight.' Despite all Bob's ingenuity in trying to head off a Tribunite revolt on the White Paper on Public Expenditure, (a) by drafting the Government Motion in the most emollient form possible[1] and (b) by provoking the Opposition to put down the sort of amendment on which we could all unite,[2] it had become apparent that massive abstentions by our 'Left' were planned. By 10pm Bob was pale with fatigue and almost heartbroken. 'Some of these rozzers aren't the old Tribune group at all,' he told me. 'They're just thugs.' As I worked in my room,

[1] The Government Motion read: 'That this House, in rejecting the demand for massive and immediate cuts in public expenditure which would increase both unemployment and the cost of living, recognizes the need to ensure that manufacturing industry can take full advantage of the upturn in world trade by levelling off total public expenditure from April 1977 while keeping under continuous review the priority between programmes.'

[2] The Tory amendment deleted all after 'That this House' and substituted: 'declines to approve a White Paper which will lead only to lower living standards, fewer jobs and higher taxes.'

waiting for the vote, Eric Varley put his friendly head round the door. 'How are things?' 'Gloomy,' I said, 'and I'm not referring to the vote: I'm referring to these Cabinet papers. Have you read Denis's assessment of the economic outlook?' 'Not yet,' he replied. I read a bit of it out to him: 'The most obvious change since the last medium-term appraisal is that the world recession has been deeper and more prolonged and the upturn so far more sluggish than we had reckoned on.' And I read on: 'If our anxiety should prove well-founded, we should have to pursue our national objectives on employment and the balance of payments in an international environment more difficult than at any time since World War II. The economists suggest that in this case it would be dangerous to base resource planning on the firm assumption that we can devise a combination of policies which will enable us, by 1979, to achieve the state of affairs represented by the central case in the White Paper projections.' And of course Denis added the warning: 'It reinforces previous warnings about the need to avoid over-optimism in planning public expenditure.' As for the CPRS paper which accompanied Denis's, I had never read so many negatives: 'we do not know how fast the world will recover from the slump' and 'we do not know how fast our exporting and import-saving industries could expand, given strong demand for their products'. Eric shuffled round my room uneasily and I said to him, 'I hope tomorrow you will give Cabinet your assessment of what we ought to do. I almost don't care what that assessment is so long as it is clear and firm.' He shook his head and disappeared.

The vote on the Tory amendment presented no problems: a majority of thirty. In the division lobby on the Government Motion rumour was running wild. 'We're defeated. It looks as though thirty have abstained.' When the tellers came to the table before a crowded House a great cheer went up from the Tories as the Opposition Whips took their place on the right-hand side. We had been defeated by thirty-seven votes. Of course, Margaret was on her feet in a flash: tense and rather attractive in a vivid green. Poor Ted Short, ramrod and colourless at the best of times, was no match for her. And suddenly the rumble went round the House: where was Harold? Ted promised a statement somewhen. The Tories fed their anger on this evasiveness. George Thomas was disastrously weak in the chair and even the most faithful of us began to mutter at Harold's absence. Half an hour of farce ensued, during which I once again regretted that the sobering effect of TV was missing. Eventually Ted Short was forced to offer a statement tomorrow. Somehow, eventually, the hubbub died down and the House adjourned, the rest of the night's business having been sacrificed. As we streamed out I asked Bob why Harold hadn't been there. 'You know him as well as I do, duckie. He just said he would keep out of this.' A great mistake in my view. 'I wonder if there will be any sterling left tomorrow,' a Tory MP said to me.

Thursday, 11 March

'I don't think there will be any normal business discussed at tomorrow's Cabinet,' Roy Jenkins said to me last night. (He had also said, commenting on the parliamentary uproar, 'As you know, I don't think we can continue much longer with

681

the system of "first past the post".')[1] In the event, the atmosphere in Cabinet was remarkably calm. Harold looked refreshed and disposed of the 'confidence' matter quite briskly for him. One would never have thought he had been 'humiliated'. Having thought things over during the night, he had concluded that the best thing was for us to take the vote right away today on the Motion for the Adjournment, which he would then make a question of confidence. Some of us were a bit taken aback by this: it looked rather weak and might be misinterpreted. Surely we needed a substantive Motion reaffirming the Government's policy? We were then informed that it was too late for that: the Motion should have been tabled last night. (This reinforced my astonishment at Harold's behaviour last night. He had received full warning that we were going to be beaten and ought to have had his strategy thought out, if necessary calling a quick Cabinet after the vote.)

A long discussion ensued as to which was the lesser evil: to act today without a substantive Motion, or to postpone a vote till Friday or Monday, with all the risks to sterling. I had been fulminating last night that we ought to resign: I could see us drifting into the position in the 1960s, when we just couldn't get our policies through the House, but Roy pointed out that an election wouldn't solve anything. Even if we won, the unresolved clash would still remain. All I did was to ask Bob if the abstainees had realized we would be defeated, to which he replied, 'No doubt at all. They are counting on a vote of confidence to bail them out.' Mike said he thought it wasn't a bad idea to have the debate on the adjournment anyway. There was the precedent of 1940 and Churchill had done the same once. We shouldn't be surprised that the Public Expenditure White Paper had caused so much stir. We had argued about it for months in Cabinet, but we had told the party to take it or leave it. Jim snapped, 'That is dodging the problem. These people should be made to face up to the consequences of their actions. If they can't support the policy, let us get out.' He was all for a tough substantive Motion and a vote tomorrow. Roy supported him. Bob said he thought he could mobilize his troops, even on a Friday, as they would know it would be life or death for them. Once again, Mike mildly counselled tolerance: there should be no question of trying to make people eat humble pie. 'There is no need to get into a panic,' he said. Bob rounded on him. 'I have some genuine outright thugs in that Tribune group,' he declared. Some of them had been telling him they wouldn't vote on anything until Des Warren was released.[2] It wasn't the old Tribune group as Michael had known it, at all, he insisted. Denis said that if we tabled a Motion today

[1] A colloquial expression for the British electoral system under which there is one MP per constituency and victory goes to the candidate with the largest number of votes, even if she or he has polled a minority of the votes cast. Roy Jenkins, as a pro-European, was committed to bringing Britain into line with one of the systems of proportional representation on the continent. The Treaty of Rome visualized that the direct elections to the European Assembly would eventually take place on the basis of a uniform electoral system and, as Britain was in a minority with her own 'first past the post' method, this could only be achieved if Britain switched to a method of PR. In any case, Roy Jenkins was temperamentally more suited to the refinements of PR which, while more delicately reflecting the nuances of the electorate's preferences, tended to reduce the vigour of political argument and to lead to middle-of-the-road coalition governments.

[2] Dennis (Des) Warren and Eric Tomlinson were found guilty at Shrewsbury Crown Court of conspiring to intimidate building workers and causing an affray while leading a 'flying picket' during a building strike. They were sentenced on 19 December 1973 to three years' and two years' imprisonment respectively. The

for debate on Monday he thought he could hold sterling. Then Ted Short settled the whole thing by pointing out that we certainly wouldn't be able to discuss any Government business until the confidence vote had been won. We all therefore accepted the inevitable and agreed to take the matter today, Denis and Harold saying with relish that they would rub in the fact in their speeches that they would be taking the vote tonight as an endorsement of the Government's economic policies. 'You'll have a rough time winding up, Denis,' someone said. 'I shall enjoy that,' he replied with his best bully-boy laugh.

Harold then tried to skip the foreign affairs item, but I asked for a report on Rhodesia. Jim reported that two white businessmen had been over from Rhodesia to see him, probably as emissaries of Smith. They wanted three wise men, drawn from the Lords and representing all parties, to go over from here to draw up a new constitution. 'As you can imagine,' said Jim, 'I sent them away with a flea in their ear.' The trouble was, he continued, that there were 'public and private layers' of view among the participants. For the time being he, Jim, was 'holding it at arm's length', but he was preparing 'our own complete package settlement', including help in resettling Europeans over here, against the day Smith declared that he would accept majority rule. Nobody else in Cabinet seemed interested, so I couldn't pursue it, but I remain convinced that Harold and Jim will get us fatally involved if we don't watch them. What Jim had said, for instance, hardly tallied with the contents of a telegram of 25 February from Dar es Salaam, in which Strong[1] reported that Nyerere had summoned him to express his anxiety lest we should misunderstand the whole situation and get involved in a deal between Smith, Nkomo and Muzorewa which was unacceptable to the guerillas. 'He was very concerned that Britain should find herself on the wrong side facing the guerillas,' ran the telegram, adding, 'It had to be realized that the freedom fighters were a third force whose acceptance of the terms of any agreement was fundamental.' For that reason Nyerere believed it was 'too late for a negotiated constitutional settlement'. I hope to God that Jim's deep conventionality does not prevent him from taking this message on board.

At last we turned to Denis's interim economic assessment, the first stage in our preparation for next year's Public Expenditure White Paper, which Denis hopes to get out by November this year and which everyone agrees we must start to discuss in good time. Denis began by saying he wanted to put us in the picture over sterling. Since floating began the Government had not intervened to influence the rate when it was subject to 'market forces arising from genuine economic conditions', only when extraneous forces were at work. Since last November the success of the pay limit had kept sterling at about 30 per cent devaluation until last week, when there had been a succession of events which had caused the run (e.g. the publication of a series of economic reports), but the bank had *not* intervened to bring the rate down and it wasn't true that Nigeria was selling sterling; so, though the pound had depreciated by 4 per cent since last Thursday, the Treasury had allowed for a fall of this size and

---

Court of Appeal dismissed their appeals in October 1974 and the Home Secretary, Roy Jenkins, told a joint Labour Party–TUC delegation in December that there were no grounds for him to recommend early release.

[1] John Clifford Strong was counsellor and Head of Chancery in Dar es Salaam from 1973–78.

there was nothing to worry about. 'The market has misunderstood the situation,' he said.

Thus encouraged, we turned to Denis's own economic assessment paper. We shouldn't, he said, 'muck about with this year's public expenditure'. We weren't proposing to take any decisions that day anyway. Once again he played the situation down. 'It is probable that we won't achieve the central case as quickly as we thought last year,' he remarked off-handedly. But the unemployment indicators were 'astonishingly encouraging'; so were the trade indicators. He saw no reason for any great readjustments of our plans. Michael came in at once to make it clear that 'an unemployment target above the one million mark is not accepted'. We were to discuss the target with the TUC. Shirley queried the chances of achieving the growth rate predicted, but Denis was studiedly optimistic again. 'Next year we can do better than the 3½ per cent indicated,' he assured us. 'It is a different question whether we should then run into capacity restraints, bringing a lower growth.' I suspect Denis has now developed the deliberate tactic of being buoyant about our prospects, so as to silence us until near catastrophe is upon us and it is too late for us to avoid the retrenchments he was planning anyway. So I challenged him to answer the main fact that emerged; namely, that our central case was going to be falsified. What if the upturn of world trade, on which our whole policy depended, did not take place? Instinctively he turned on the optimism again. 'All the forecasts are becoming more optimistic,' he declared. But then he suddenly flashed out at me. 'What if the upturn does not take place? I can't make Niagara flow uphill. I am waiting anxiously for someone to tell me how it can be done.' Peter dodged this. The analysis in the paper, he said, was inadequate. 'The other factors in the situation have to be made to fit the unemployment target and they obviously don't. There is no forecast, for example, of what will happen to imports when growth starts.' But he added disappointingly, 'I am not wishing to open a major debate now.'

Wedgie, however, with his usual verve, took Denis on frontally. 'The TUC is asking us for a strategy of protection,' he pointed out. The Chancellor's alternative was devaluation, but that meant another wage cut and could affect our sterling balances. 'This argument does merit serious discussion.' Denis's defences began to come down. 'I would welcome a discussion,' he said. 'I have never been theologically opposed to import controls: all I am afraid of is devastating retaliation.' That, of course, was dishonest of him: he knows that our membership of EEC has made a 'strategy of protection' well-nigh impossible. So I wasn't surprised when Harold Lever said, 'I prefer currency depreciation to import controls,' adding, 'I'm sorry to have to tell my colleagues this, but the fact is that we are dependent on world trade.' Jim rounded the discussion off with one of his typical bits of gloom. 'The projection of the past into the future would not lead to the figures in this paper,' he said. 'The central case is unlikely to be achieved. We must all of us reckon over the next few years that real growth in public expenditure is likely to be very small indeed. I agree we do need a proper examination of the case for import controls. We shall be lost as a country if the TUC disagree with this Government. Let us have an agreed assessment of this.' While everyone nodded solemnly at this I interjected passionately, 'And let us work out an agreed assessment with the NEC too. There will be a series of papers from the NEC before the coming joint meeting with the Cabinet: let us treat them seriously. Don't let us just wave them aside as the outpourings of Judith Hart and Geoff Bish. Let us recognize with due humility that there is no indication whatsoever that our own policy is going to succeed.' To my surprise, there were no protests at this. On the contrary, everyone, including Denis himself, nodded approvingly.

Finally to Fred Peart's disastrous deal over EEC agricultural policy.[1] Since I asked No. 10 if it could be put on the agenda Fred has rushed in a defensive paper, and I have got Jack, back at last, to do me a full brief. Jack's analysis of the deal is devastating, and I have been reading it all up to go into the attack. Mercifully, Shirley did it for me. I have never heard her tear a strip off a colleague as she did off Fred – though in her usual gentle way. Even Jim, while claiming that Fred had been in a 'difficult position', admitted that things had gone wrong. He listed the lessons to be learned: the structure of the Common Agriculture Policy Committee was bad (over-weighted with agricultural interests); Schmidt was opposed to the CAP, but, because of his coalition, was represented on the committee by a Free Democrat Minister who needed the farmers' votes; long before the next price review we should tell the Council of Ministers that we wanted a review of the whole policy. 'Next time we must be ready to block an agreement,' he concluded.

All this was not enough for Shirley. There had been a meeting of EQ, she reminded Jim, which had laid down 'precise negotiating objectives'. On 5 March Fred had phoned Edmund Dell from Brussels and had also spoken to her the same evening. Both had told him the matter should come back to Cabinet. She had told him he ought to break. She was sure he hadn't heard what she had said(!), but the fact remained that we had passed up an opportunity to do much better. Lardinois was fighting for his price targets, but we had let him be overruled. Britain had proved to be the only country not ready to press its case. Food prices would be up 4 per cent this year. She asked that at the April Council of Ministers it should be made clear that there would be no further price increases for milk until there had been structural changes to deal with the surpluses and, secondly, that we should lay it down that in future, where precise negotiating targets had been laid down by EQ, the Minister must return for further instructions if he couldn't achieve them. Preferably he should have a Treasury or Prices Minister with him.

After this uncharacteristic outburst by Shirley all that was left for me to do was to say that I doubted whether the CAP could be reformed at all. In fact, far from getting it reformed, we were slipping back. In my view the surrender at Brussels would make it

---

[1] Three days earlier there had been uproar in the House when Fred Peart had reported on the Community's agricultural support and prices for 1976–77 which he had agreed in Brussels. It was clear that, although he had succeeded in retaining the beef premium scheme on a precarious basis for another year, in return he had accepted a wide range of price increases, notably for milk, which were higher than the Agricultural Commissioner, Monsieur Lardinois, had proposed. Even the Conservatives objected that he had secured no structural reform in the Common Agricultural Policy to deal with the food surpluses which would now inevitably increase. The Council of Agricultural Ministers' decisions to try to contain the milk mountain by compelling farmers to incorporate skimmed milk powder in animal feed was attacked as adding to producers' costs and so pushing up food prices still more. Peart's failure to carry out the party's policy was so obvious that I had asked for a discussion in Cabinet.

impossible for us to phase out food subsidies. John Silkin passed me a defeatist little note: 'Yes, my love. But what is the point of arguing it out now? It's already been done!' Peter said it was no use crying over spilt milk: even if it *was* dried. The fact was that we had got to make up our minds. By committing ourselves to growing more of our own food we had made these price increases inevitable.

Harold, unfortunately, missed all this: he had slipped out to prepare his speech for this afternoon. But it was clear that the pro-marketeers were deeply embarrassed and that was reason enough for having a row. But in any case, now we are in, the least we can do is to try to modify the major monstrosities of the EEC. Every day it becomes clearer that the warnings we antis gave during the referendum were 100 per cent justified. It is also clear that Britain's built-in commitment to raise food prices over the next few years under the terms negotiated can wreck our counter-inflation policy.

Half way through Cabinet we were all taken aback and delighted when in trooped a file of waiters and waitresses carrying trays of coffee. Spontaneously we all burst out, singing, 'Happy birthday to you': the only celebration Harold is likely to get today. The papers are full of his sixtieth birthday. Marjorie Proops has drooled over him in the *Mirror*, while Jo Grimond has written a surprisingly friendly piece in the *Mail*, telling us we should be grateful 'for the skills, application and integrity and good temper with which Wilson Governments have discharged our affairs'. (Someone pointed out to me that, typically, the *Mail* had left the words 'the application and the integrity' out of the headline quote.) The BOSS story is also still running strong, Patrick Keatley in the *Guardian* vindicating Harold's argument.

Of course, there were office meetings conflicting with the start of the great debate on the vote of confidence so Harold was nearing the end of his speech when at last I got into the crowded chamber. 'How's he doing?' I whispered to Shirley. 'Very well,' she replied. 'He's been laying into the abstainers and they have just been sitting mum. I don't think they are too happy.' Certainly Harold seemed to be in confident form and sat down to great cheers, though, having told us this morning he was only going to make a 'very short' speech, he had gone on for nearly three-quarters of an hour. Margaret was shorter and, I thought, effective, because she just harped on one simple theme: that Harold could no longer command his own side's loyalty. She sat down to ecstatic cheers from her own side. Later I slipped into the chamber to hear one of the abstainers: Tom Litterick. He certainly wasn't in apologizing mood and made a particularly nasty personal attack on Mike. The mood in the party is growing ugly on both sides. Certainly the abstainers have succeeded in taking the gilt off the ginger-bread of the Coventry victory.[1] We now no longer look like a winning Government. Is that what they want? For their revolt won't change the Government's policy. That is far more likely to be done by people like Mike, Peter, Wedgie and me wearing away at Denis's strategy with the help of the TUC.

This assessment of the situation was confirmed when I talked to David Basnett at the reception for the new American Ambassador. David dismissed the abstentions as

---

[1] Although the Labour vote fell by 4 per cent, and the Conservative vote went up by nearly 6 per cent, Geoffrey Robinson held the seat for Labour.

'stupid' and said that the TUC would be discussing sensible modifications of policy with the Chancellor. The next meeting of the Liaison Committee would be the key one. Mrs Ambassador Armstrong turned out to be a well-groomed woman in an elegant gown, who was obviously anxious to make friends with everyone. Norman, who accompanied me in Ted's absence, suggested I might try to have a word with her about the reciprocal health agreement with the USA on which Elliot Richardson, her predecessor, is faithfully following up the overtures I made to him. And some of the Embassy officials I spoke to seemed really keen. So, as I was leaving, I asked Mrs Armstrong if I could come and have a word with her soon about a matter I had discussed with Mr Richardson. She responded warmly. 'Shall I call you or will you call me?' she asked. As I said to Norman, I would like to pull off this agreement before I go.

Back into the chamber in time for Denis's winding-up. He was almost bellowing and, as I sat crammed among his pals like Edmund Dell, both they and I became increasingly embarrassed. It was an appalling speech: arrogant, offensive and near-hysterical. 'He must have gone off his rocker,' I muttered. 'If he hasn't lost us this vote, he ought to have done.' But of course he hadn't, and the emptiness of the abstainers' gesture was shown when they meekly filed into the Government lobby after a speech which deserved to provoke a revolt. So this was Harold and Denis making up for the fact that we couldn't have a substantive Motion! However angry I may have been about the abstainers' folly, I would never accept Denis's right to insult them in that frenetic way – or in any way at all. Well, he's now lost one vote for the leadership. The final irony was that we won the division by a majority of seventeen. Enoch Powell, the master maverick, persuaded most of his fellow Unionists to sit on their hands.

Friday, 12 March

In Blackburn I sounded out as many of my party's members as I could about their reaction to our defeat. Our local party chairman said he thought the abstainers were right and when I said the union leaders didn't think much of them he said, 'We now call Jack Jones a fascist.' I blew him out of the water for that – and he had the grace to look ashamed. Much more significant was Jim Mason's reaction. He represents the responsible Left and he was furious about the public expenditure cuts. He and I had one of our friendly up-and-downers over lunch, in which I said to him I would have respected the Blackburn GMC if they had passed a resolution saying they would only tolerate the cuts if they were to make way for more investment in support of an expansionist industrial policy. But pure romanticism about have-your-public-expenditure-cake and eat-your-industrial-expansion was childish in this country's desperate economic situation. I think he took that point.

Monday, 15 March

Great activity on the pay beds front. Norman reports that Goodman would like to see me today; Patrick has been having off-the-record talks with Stevenson. Patrick tells me that Stevenson talked frankly to him, admitting that the profession would never volunteer any proposals for a voluntary system of licensing, but would acquiesce in any reasonable proposals put forward by us, even though screaming aloud about them publicly. It appears that the fight has gone out of the consultants and the only question mark now is about the attitude of the juniors and Keable-Elliott. Apparently also the BMA is pretty well in the know about the divisions in the Cabinet over licensing.

I arranged to see Arnold in my room at 3.45pm. He arrived at 4.15pm, saying something about having been detained by Harold. What about I can only guess. Arnold was in amusing and expansive mood, rambling on about how sure he was that the medicos would negotiate a settlement on licensing – though he admitted later that he had only discussed this with Robb of BUPA and Gullick, who are hardly representative. He made great comical play about the profession's disarray. 'They asked me what the prospects were for defeating the Bill, and I said "Nil",' he told me. Nor could they count on the Government falling. 'Mrs Thatcher is unable to achieve a change of Government as things stand at present.' He said he had impressed on them that it was their obligation to come to me with a plan and if they didn't reach an agreement with me, I would take powers in the Bill. He then went off at a tangent about the ridiculous paper Sir Rodney Smith was now circulating, saying that what the profession was worried about was the threat to private practice. Arnold seemed to think it was a criminal waste of money for the profession to produce great costly advertisements to that effect, particularly after Sir Rodney had agreed to his [Goodman's] proposals, 'which ensure that no pay bed will go till there is another private bed in its place'. (I let that pass.) Nor, said Arnold, had he ever been impressed by the 'geographical full-time' argument. But the problem was that 50 per cent of the profession was 'motivated by politics'.

After he had wandered round the scene like this for some time I proceeded to tie him down. Did he accept that paragraph 3(f) of the Goodman proposals meant that, if a voluntary agreement was not reached, the Government had the right to legislate unilaterally on controls? 'Of course,' he replied. Secondly, did he realize that our information was that the profession would never volunteer any proposals of its own? His answer to that was that he would have to talk to them and make them take a line. Perhaps I could just put in the Bill some general vague right to make regulations on this in order to give more time for discussions? I said that would be fine by me, but that the profession would have to suggest it: if it came from me it would be regarded as sinister. He saw this at once, saying, 'They must start by putting proposals to you, otherwise you are walking into a trap.' Finally, I stressed the urgency of the timetable: could he let me have a report on his talks by Thursday? He said he would try. I left him with the idea that the best way out would be to put something firm in the Bill along the lines of giving the independent board licensing powers for all developments over a certain size. I even suggested to him that he should tell them to demand in return that I should abandon the overall size control for the private sector outlined in my original consultative document. 'If I got something firm in return I might consider this.' (I knew I couldn't get the consultative document proposal through Cabinet anyway.) He went off, quite taken with this idea.

The real trouble is that the profession and I will never agree over the size of private hospital developments which would escape control. They are talking of exempting all hospitals with less than two hundred beds and I won't go further than seventy-five beds at any cost. I only know that if I get any control mechanism at all into the legislation it will be a miracle, given the opposition I've got in Cabinet. I then sat down to an office meeting, at which we agreed it was premature for me to put any paper to Cabinet and that it would be better for me to send an explanatory letter to Harold at this stage.

Tuesday, 16 March

I arrived at Cabinet, all unsuspecting that Harold's time-bomb was about to go off. As we settled down in our seats Harold said calmly that he had just come from the Palace and had a statement to make to us. He then read a lengthy statement announcing his 'irrevocable' decision to give up office. As he went through it, personal copies were circulated to each one of us, which he had signed individually. He certainly has developed a flair for drama. The statement was very movingly worded – and included typical Harold statistical touches about how he had presided over 472 Cabinets and answered more than 12,000 Parliamentary Questions. It included some propaganda for the achievements of Labour Governments and he informed us that he was releasing the statement (indeed, had already released it) to the press. It also very skilfully set out the identikit for his successor: he must be loyal to the counter-inflationary policy and to Nato, be ready to work himself to death ('these are not the easy, spacious, socially-orientated days of some of my predecessors') and make a point of getting out into the country and meeting the people. 'Above all remember the Party is the Party in the country – not the Palace of Westminster, not Smith Square.'

We listened in stunned silence. Eric passed me a note: 'Were you aware he was going to do this?' I hesitated, then scribbled back: 'I can't answer that question.' Harold then embroidered his statement with a few casual and almost inaudible explanations. He had made up his mind to do this when he won the election two years ago, he told us. There was never a 'right time' to carry out such an intention, but he thought he had chosen the best possible. He had considered resigning before the last party conference, or at Christmas, but decided the pay policy was in too delicate a balance. However, it was right to go before we became embroiled in the next pay policy round. He had thought of his sixtieth birthday as an excellent moment, but unfortunately there turned out to be two by-elections on that day. He had thought of waiting till the summer, but decided that would be awkward for his successor, who ought to have a chance to play himself in before the House rose for the recess and before the next party conference. So there it was.

The silence which followed this was, I thought, the most moving tribute we could have paid to him. There was no rush of ready falsities. Ted Short blurted out something almost incoherent about what an appalling shock and blow this was. Another silence, then Jim hesitatingly took up the theme. He didn't, he said, want to 'pre-empt' what anybody else might want to say. There would be other occasions to pay proper tributes. But he couldn't let this pass without expressing his thanks to Harold for all the generosities he had always showed to him. He remembered, for instance, how, when Harold had won the leadership thirteen years ago, he had at once turned to him and said: 'Of course you'll carry on, Jim, as shadow Foreign Secretary.' Jim concluded haltingly, 'Thank you, Harold, for all you have done for us.' More silence. I felt near to tears, I don't quite know why. Tears of farewell to the friendly familiar? Eric passed me another note: 'It's a very emotional moment.' To which I replied: 'What's your reaction?' Eric: 'I think he's wrong.' Me: 'I think it will prove how difficult it is to replace him.' Harold then asked us to excuse him, as he had various people to talk to, including the chairman of the PLP with whom he had to discuss the quick holding of an election for his successor. He told Ted Short to take the chair and disappeared just as, once again, the waiters filed in with those welcome cups of coffee.

When he had gone we fumbled for the right procedure. I think it was Shirley who said we should minute a tribute to Harold right away and I said we ought to issue something to the press. Anyway, we both found ourselves sent away to draft something, which we did, short and sweet but making it quite clear that the Cabinet had been taken by surprise. After some amending by Jim and Roy it was agreed and issued, John Hunt adding the discreet prefix that the statement had been agreed 'in the Prime Minister's temporary absence'. These civil servants think of everything.

While Shirley and I were drafting upstairs I asked her what she thought. 'Very sad,' she said and I think she meant it, though I don't think she was heart-broken. Impulsively I said, 'There is only one compromise candidate: Michael.' She didn't protest, but she didn't exactly endorse it either.

When we returned to Cabinet from our drafting session we found them in the middle of discussing the newspaper industry. I barely listened, though Jack had briefed me to amend Peter's statement on the Royal Commission's interim report to make it quite clear we were not committing ourselves to any form of government help. Other people, I found, had taken this up anyway. By this time Ted in his turn had disappeared and Jim was in the chair. It began to feel like Alice in Wonderland, and some irreverent questions about Harold's whole manoeuvre began to creep into my mind. Okay, so a man has the right to decide he will give up office, and whatever date he chooses will have its snags, but for Harold to do this so gratuitously and so apparently senselessly, in the middle of a perfectly reasonably successful term of office, almost looks like frivolity. Has one the *right* to throw one's party into turmoil for no apparent cause, to face them with a *fait accompli* because one knows they would plead with one to stay if they knew in time? What exactly *was* Harold up to? More than had met the eye, I had no doubt. And he certainly hadn't bothered a whit about the effect of the timing of his retirement on my own. That cosy conversation had not amounted to a row of beans. Through all this musing I heard Jim sum up that Peter's statement on the press must be considerably modified.

It was Eric's turn next to give us a catastrophic run-down on the shipbuilding industry. He did it almost with relish. I get the feeling he enjoys telling people how appalling things are: some politicians seem to get a sense of power from it, even while they protest they are powerless to prevent catastrophe. It was, he said, a 'gloomy picture'. A Bill to nationalize shipbuilding was before the House. The industry wasn't fighting it particularly hard, perhaps because it knew there would soon be no industry left to nationalize. 'There is no point in nationalizing unless we are prepared to help the industry,' he said. First and foremost, we ought to put pressure on the shipowners to buy British ships. If voluntary methods failed we should have to consider legislation. Otherwise, we should be left with no shipbuilding industry at all – entirely at the mercy of the Japanese.

Peter agreed, but warned that our ability to force shipowners to buy our own ships was 'very limited'. We must examine all possible alternatives, including the role of the Ministry of Defence – which gave Roy Mason the chance to jump in and say that MOD was by far the industry's biggest customer and that he could bring forward MOD orders worth £160 million over the next six years, if only extra resources could be found for him. He would! Denis agreed Eric's general line, but pointed out that very difficult decisions would be necessary. There was enough shipping capacity in the world to meet current needs, even if there was not another ship built for the next five years. If MOD orders were brought forward, savings would be necessary from other departments. Harold Lever was against giving *carte blanche* to any measures. 'I would like to record my implacable opposition to ruining a profitable industry like shipowning to save an industry which is doomed,' he quipped. Wedgie, of course, rejected this. He supported Eric absolutely. 'We pull out of every industry where we run into difficulties. The time has come when we had better look at our real assets: the generations of skill that exist among our workpeople.' Shirley wanted us to concert action through the EEC and reach an agreement to share the market and keep out the Japanese. I pleaded that the facts facing the industry (including our low productivity) should be discussed not just with the union leaders, but with workers at every level of the industry. 'Let us have a teach-in with the rank and file,' I pleaded. Summing up, Jim said we all agreed that 'this industry must be kept alive'.

As Cabinet broke up I grabbed Michael. 'You've got to stand for the leadership,' I said. Peter endorsed this warmly. 'Perhaps. We must discuss it,' said Mike and I realized he had made up his mind to fight. In his new tough mood I wouldn't be surprised if he fought hard.

I rang up Norman and found him in a tizzy about the news. (Of course, it was all round Whitehall before we'd left Cabinet.) When I said I wanted to go into the House for the PM's Questions he replied, 'Of course. Don't you want to cancel all your office meetings this afternoon?' I told him not a bit of it: it was business as usual. Everybody I met in the House over lunch seemed shell-shocked. As I walked into the crowded chamber behind Jim the Opposition put up a great ironical cheer (for Jim, not me). The front bench was squashed almost unbearably. As we sat chattering like sparrows I said to Jim, 'Did you know?' He tried to pretend he didn't, failed, and, when I challenged him, just smiled deprecatingly. (So there may be something in the rumour already circulating that Harold has set the whole thing up for Jim.) Bob Mellish has told me he didn't know and that Ted Short had been told ten minutes before Cabinet. As for Denis, 'Harold told him in the lavatory.' We consulted anxiously on the front bench as to whether we should stand up for Harold when he came in for his

Questions. Jim thought we should; then decided we had better wait and see what the backbenches did. In the event, the backbenches cheered heartily enough, but had no truck with standing ovations. Some people waved Order Papers. The gallery was crammed. Harold was obviously enjoying himself. He was on form. He just played with Margaret Thatcher, who sat, as she usually does before a parliamentary effort, head down and lips pursed, as if summoning up some superior wisdom of which we ordinary mortals do not know. Her intervention, when it came, was not in my view exactly masterly. 'She can't rise to an occasion,' an impatient backbencher behind me said. Jeremy spoiled a good intervention by long-windedness. Not for the first time it was left to Ted Heath to dominate the House from the Opposition side. His tribute to Harold was unrestrainedly generous and Harold replied in like form. 'The House of Commons at its best,' I could imagine those people saying who love the glutinous.

George Thomas achieved his best moment yet in the chair when Harold said that he had informed Mr Speaker of his intentions only last week. 'That's correct,' George boomed. The tension dissolved in laughter. 'It *is* the end of an era,' Harold Lever whispered to me. The nagging query grew in my mind: 'What is the old maestro up to?'

The orgy over, I went into two key office meetings in the House: the first about child benefit and the second on our proposed new procurement policy for the NHS. I've no doubt my officials are wondering where I stand now, with Harold gone. For myself, I have no doubt that I stand as Secretary of State until I know to the contrary, so I am going to tuck as many policy decisions under my belt as I can before it is too late.

Brian O'Malley came into my room for a drink, obviously worrying where *he* stands now. I told him we'd got to root for Mike and he agreed. Mike called in too, to tell me he would stand. I asked him if Wedgie was standing and he havered a bit. Obviously, he said, it would be better if Wedgie didn't stand, but he wanted to talk to him and tell him he didn't want to get in his way. 'I'll talk to Wedgie myself,' I replied and went at once to Wedgie's room. I found him closeted with Joe Ashton and Joe's wife. 'I thought you'd been sacked,' I said jocularly to Joe.[1] 'Technically, I have been,' he replied, but it was clear he was still spiritually and practically Wedgie's PPS, only just this side of idolatry. I felt a bit constrained, but said bravely to Wedgie, 'The future is with you, but not this moment. This election is a forceps delivery.' Looking a bit haggard, he seemed to agree. Joe was passionate: this election was not about personalities, but about policies. Dennis Skinner was right, he insisted: every candidate for the leadership should be made to set out the policies for which he stood. The important thing, I suggested, was to stop Jim. 'Don't worry,' said Joe grimly. 'The "Stop Jim" movement is already under way: from the Right as well as from the Left.' Both he and Wedgie agreed that they would rather have Denis than Jim, just as Mike had done earlier. My Ted came in hotfoot from Brussels, for once cursing the European Parliament that had kept him away from a great occasion in the Parliament

[1] Joe Ashton, Labour MP for Bassetlaw and Parliamentary Private Secretary to Tony Benn, had abstained in the vote on the public expenditure cuts the previous week and Harold Wilson had demanded that he be sacked.

he really loved. Wedgie, the teetotaller, gave us drinks from his cabinet. At last I was able to get home to bed.

Wednesday, 17 March

Jack Jones, David Basnett and Hughie Scanlon have ironically issued in this morning's papers an astonishing joint appeal for united support for Harold by the movement. Too late! But it shows how impatient they are with the so-called 'Left'.

Woke with eyes streaming and feeling wretched. I suppose I have never given myself a chance to get rid of my last bout of 'flu. Undeterred, I went to the Devolution Committee of Cabinet to protest at the White Paper on English regionalism that Ted Short and his minions have prepared. I laid about me with great effect and successfully led a substantial revolt, pointing out that one could not have a White Paper of any meaning at all on English regionalism which ruled out any further reorganization of local government, such as Tony C. is trying to do. Roy Jenkins and Shirley backed me enthusiastically. Nonetheless, Ted summed up from the chair that the matter would now have to go to the PM's committee on devolution 'with our comments'. (The power of the chairmen of these committees is formidable. They are the arm of Prime Ministerial government.) Somehow I got through a lunch with the General Medical Council, controlling the streaming of my eyes. I got through the 7pm vote, and then even Jimmy Dunn agreed I ought to be in bed.

Thursday, 18 March

Woke in a sad state. I just couldn't see to read. I hoped that a day in bed would do the trick. With streaming eyes I got through my boxes as best I could. Several items interested me – one of them being a note from John Hunt about the valedictory 'photographic record of Cabinet' Harold wants us to have and the draft Minute on this which the Prime Minister had done himself upon it: 'the first time he has undertaken such a task (despite some stories to the contrary) since he served in the Cabinet Secretariat during the War', wrote Hunt. Our Harold's attention to the detail of his own record of history remains legendary. Another thing which interested me was a note Harold had circulated on Soviet–Cuban involvement in Rhodesia. In it officials opined that, if driven to it, the Africans would seek Cuban and Soviet assistance and that the latter would respond.

I have also amused myself reading all the press comments on Harold's dramatic move. It must give him great satisfaction to read the belated tributes to him while he is still alive. Even Bernard Levin writes a friendly piece on him today ('Making my peace, finally, with Mr Wilson'), while the *Sun*, of all papers, carried a leader yesterday headed: 'Thank you from all of us.' So much for the venom that has been poured on Harold all these years. We shall have the doctors canonizing me yet! (In fact, George Godber has written a very balanced article in the *British Medical Journal*, in which he says they ought to be grateful to me for getting more resources for the NHS.)

The press is laying heavy odds on Jim winning the leadership. He is the favourite with them, though some papers plump for Roy. Denis has not put his name forward yet and there is talk that he may stay out of the contest. This thought worried me no end. To be left with Jim would be too terrible! So on an impulse I got the office to get Denis to ring me, which he did as soon as he emerged from Cabinet. I told him frankly I was rooting for Mike, but that I thought he, Denis, ought to stand as he would certainly be my – and a lot of other people's – second choice. He was equally frank back. He had given a lot of thought to it, but the advice from his friends was that he shouldn't. And the statistics were against him. He calculated that on the first ballot Jim would get a hundred votes, Mike ninety and Roy about seventy, which would leave about forty votes to divide between Wedgie, Tony and him. So he would be eliminated humiliatingly. I replied that it was true he ran the risk of humiliation on the first ballot, but if he could only survive into the second his chances would improve enormously. He must realize that there were a lot of people – more than he probably guessed – who, next to wanting to see their own man in, were leading a 'Stop Jim' campaign. They wanted somebody else than Jim to vote for in the last resort. He agreed, adding, 'I think I am the only person who could defeat Jim: Mike couldn't.' I also told him that a very telling campaigning line would be to say that what the party needed above all things was to keep the Foot/Healey axis round which the Government revolved. It was a winning combination. He liked that. Finally I told him that Alf Bates[1] had been doing a head-count for Brian O'Malley. Would he like Brian to have a word with him at the division that night? Denis thanked me and said he would.

Next I rang Michael to make sure that he agreed it would be helpful to him if Denis ran. He said, 'Of course.' Finally I rang Brian to put him in the picture. 'Denis won't run,' he told me firmly. 'Both Joel and Denis's own PPS, Mark Hughes, have been urging him not to.' I said that it was worth a try anyway and he agreed to see Denis as I had arranged. Later, on the nine o'clock news, I heard that Denis had decided to run after all and let out a hoarse 'Whoopee!' Who knows, I may have secured Mike's victory by that timely phone call.

Saturday, 20 March

The press seems to think that Healey's intervention changes the odds on Jim markedly. Hurray! As my eyes were still streaming I called in the doctor, who put me on antibiotics. I wrapped up warmly and Edna drove me to HCF and bed.

Cabinet Minutes for last Thursday include Jim's report on Rhodesia. Jim said he had had a pressing message from Kaunda to the effect that Zambia now had to fall back on the second method of achieving majority rule (i.e. armed intervention). But if there was still time to reach a peaceful solution it was for us to work for it. Jim added that he was awaiting a reply from Kaunda and Nyerere to his proposal that at the right moment the four presidents and HMG might jointly put forward comprehensive proposals for a settlement. Personally, I doubt the presidents would agree to that.

---

[1] Alf Bates, Labour MP for Bebington and Ellesmere Port, was Brian O'Malley's Parliamentary Private Secretary from 1974 to 1976; he became an assistant Government Whip in 1976.

Sunday, 21 March

With my sinusitis somewhat abated, I did a spell in the garden, took the dogs for a walk and then got down to work. Raymond Gedling has put up a draft of the paper on pay beds I am to put to Cabinet next week and has reported on the consultations officials had with the professions last Thursday. Deadlock has been reached with Grabham and co., but the men from the Independent Hospitals Group seem ready to vest control powers in the independent board, though they want 'smaller' hospital developments exempted from control – i.e. those involving fewer than 200–250 beds. 'Smaller', indeed! There would be only a handful left. The worrying thing was, Raymond said, the growing resistance by the GPs to any form of control – even though I have met the GPs on all their points about health centres, etc. On the phone Raymond told me that he feared we were in for a 'major row' if we went ahead with any form of licensing. David has sent me one of his typical Minutes, first stressing the alarmist aspects of the situation and then going on to propose an ingenious but, in my view, non-viable plan. He suggests we should refer the whole question of licensing not to the Royal Commission, but to the independent board, with a remit to report within a year as to what should be done. The interim period would be covered by a voluntary agreement with the IHG. So once again the pressures are building up on me to give way. As if I didn't have enough trouble with Cabinet!

I brooded on all this for a while, imagining everything David would press on me at tomorrow's meeting to discuss the draft paper, then went and phoned Jack to find out what he really thought. He was, heartening. He might be wrong, he said, but he thought that, if we did press ahead with licensing, it would be very difficult for the consultants to get the GPs and juniors out on strike. 'My feeling is that there isn't a head of steam about this,' he said. One junior, for instance, had told him, 'We've had our orgasm over our pay.' Moreover, if I didn't get some kind of licensing into the Bill this year, it 'wouldn't happen at all'. Just imagine what another Minister would do in a year's time – perhaps under J.C.'s premiership! Incidentally Dr Beddard had told him it was clear from the discussions with the profession that they knew exactly the arguments that were going on in Cabinet.

Next I decided to ring Arnold. We began chattily. 'When did Harold tell you he was going to resign?' I asked boldly. 'Well before Christmas,' he replied, 'but he never indicated a precise date, except to say he didn't want to stay after Easter.' We discussed the mystery and Arnold agreed he couldn't understand why Harold should do it, 'except that he was absolutely tired and fed up'. Arnold also believed that Mary [Wilson] had had a great deal to do with it. I mused on what Harold would do now. 'He isn't exactly God's backbencher.' Arnold agreed with this, but said that he thought Harold hadn't taken this fact on board. 'I have not cross-examined him on this – he is not an easy man to cross-examine – but I think he has romanticized a situation that is not real.' I next teased him about the prospect of Michael Foot as PM. He said it didn't alarm him. 'I've always got on well with Michael until recently,' and he hoped to do so still, 'if he acknowledges his error.' He added impulsively, 'I have always loved Michael.'

I then turned to licensing, telling him that tomorrow I had to finalize a paper for

Cabinet and we were getting nowhere in our discussions with the professions. He rejected this as too gloomy, said that, although he was no longer 'the blue-eyed boy of the situation', he was in close touch with Robb and Gullick and believed from what they told him that an agreement with the IHG was possible. And if we got that, the consultants would have to fall into line. I stressed the urgency of the situation and he pledged himself to get in touch with Robb tomorrow and try to get the IHG to put firm proposals to me. From what he said it would appear that I could accept their ideas, except that they want to exempt from controls all developments of under 250 beds, which even Arnold said was 'too high'. I told him that my limit was seventy-five beds. He did not quail, but promised to chase Robb tomorrow urgently. Thus fortified, I went and typed a reply to David which I hope will stiffen his nerve before we meet tomorrow afternoon.

Monday, 22 March

Because our meeting of the Liaison Committee was at the House of Commons there were no cameras waiting, though David Basnett had described this meeting to me as 'crucial'. We had before us, not only the TUC *Economic Review* for 1976, but the NEC document on economic policy options prepared by Geoff Bish. With everyone predicting that we would have a major showdown with the TUC on unemployment, public expenditure cuts *et al.*, it was once again fascinating to note how low-key were Len Murray's opening remarks. In fact, it seemed at first as if he wasn't going to bother to cover the now familiar ground. 'We have discussed all this before,' he said. But he gathered emphasis as he went along. 'We are not looking for massive reflation through a consumer boom,' he insisted. 'But we are more doubtful than some about the expected upturn in world trade.' They therefore thought there was the need for a 'modest stimulus' through the Budget: '£2,000 million or so.' What the TUC was seeking was an improvement in pensions: with 'tax moves' to pay for this; an increase in child allowances; selective cuts in VAT; and 'direct action' on the balance of payments. (Presumably he meant import controls.) 'The case for this would be understood by other countries if properly presented.' Two things were of central importance: first, a return to 'high levels of employment'; secondly, prices. The TUC believed there was a strong case for a return to subsidies.

Harold decided he had better come in at this point. Unfortunately, he said sarcastically, his papers for this meeting had not been put into his weekend box, 'so for greater accuracy I have obtained a copy of this morning's *Guardian*'. He then proceeded to tantalize us (because we knew the latest unemployment figures were due out that morning) and tell us that there were signs of a very big change in the employment situation. Everyone looked duly impressed, but Jack pressed on with the argument, saying he wanted to underline everything Len had said. There might be signs of a pick-up in some industries, but the progress was 'patchy'. The case for selective import controls was very strong for some sectors of industry. 'Somewhere we should be clearly seen to be making an attack on prices.' We had lost a great deal of ground on pensions. People were conscious that we had increased them, but argued that pensioners had lost the Christmas bonus. He hoped there would be a

Budget announcement that would help. (I thought to myself, 'I knew I could leave the battle on pensions to Jack.')

Mik then came in on the NEC document. Obviously the Left on the NEC thought this was the moment when they could detach the unions from their loyalty to government policy. There was, he said, a 'large area of common ground with the TUC'. The trouble with selective import controls was that no one had spelt out what was meant by 'selective'. Somebody should start having a look at this question of import controls sector by sector. But David Basnett wasn't going to be lured into a united front with the rebels. He interrupted Mik quite nastily: 'This is precisely what we have said in our *Economic Review*. The NEC does *not* say the same as the TUC. It is long on analysis and short on proposals. The NEC policy is centred on a 15 per cent surcharge on all manufactured goods. We reject this.' Having disposed of Mik, he turned to Denis, insisting that there must be a target for reducing unemployment. He had more resolutions down for his union conference on this than on any other issue. But he concluded, 'We do not want import controls for their own sake. They must be integrated with our industrial strategy.' Shirley then launched into a defence of our prices policy – rather effectively, I thought. The prices situation, she said, was 'not bad'. The turnaround in the last three months had been 'quite dramatic', she said. But there were three jokers in the pack. First, there was the CAP, where we had got to insist on better control and we needed to look again at food subsidies. Secondly, nationalized industry prices. Here she reminded them that both the party conference and the TUC had endorsed the policy of making nationalized industries financially viable as the only way of restoring their self-respect. Thirdly, there was the need to deal with the balance of payments. 'Whatever road we go down, it is going to have a regressive effect on prices,' she warned. And she made her usual appeal in the direction of Alf Allen. 'Food manufacturers say that 21,000 jobs have been lost by price controls.' 'I would like to see the food manufacturers' figures broken down, because I think they are lying,' Jack said coldly. He added that Shirley had said the TUC had supported the policy of making nationalized industries economically viable through price increases, but what they were worried about was the size of the increase: couldn't it be spread over? David backed him: 'What matters is the rate of progress towards viability.'

At last Denis, who had been bursting to come in after every speech and had been held in check by Bob in the chair, was allowed to answer all this. Once again he painted a rosy view. 'I think the forecasts at the moment are much too pessimistic. The rate of increase of unemployment is falling much faster than we anticipated. Indicators, like the number of vacancies, are also much more favourable. The volume of exports is going up.' If we were to improve our industrial performance it was crucial that we should maintain the alliance between the Government and the TUC. 'But in the end I have to make up my own mind as to what is right for the nation's interests. I cannot put that in commission anywhere.' The question was how could we get an increase in the rate of growth. First, we must tackle bottlenecks. 'I am ready to spend more on training any time anyone comes to me with realistic proposals.' Secondly, there was the balance of payments. 'As long as we float our currency we shall be able to maintain our competitiveness, but at the cost of inflation.' Thirdly, there were import controls. 'I am not against them in principle.' There would be no retaliation if they were put on in a period of growth. 'Now there would be.' He concluded, 'I would welcome the chance of discussing all this after the Budget, but let us look at this, commodity by commodity, realistically.'

The trade unionists listened respectfully: I think they can take Denis's tough line as long as he shows sensitivity to their difficulties in delivering from their own people what they personally may have accepted as inevitable. Jack was soon demonstrating this. The major problem, as he saw it, was unemployment and that depended on investment. 'But investment is much more influenced by the rate of inflation than by import controls, particularly if you are only going to keep them on for two years,' he said. The best way to maximize exports was to lower internal costs. The £6 pay limit was beginning to bring prices down. The TUC target of 10 per cent inflation next year meant a similar pay increase next year. I thought as I listened to him how the role of the trade union movement has been transformed. By now it was noon and Harold was gathering his things to go. 'Before the PM leaves,' said Jack, 'I would like to place on record the very great debt the whole movement owes him. We appreciate his contribution to the unification of the party. He has shown the importance of having toleration in leadership.' Harold was obviously pleased. So the meeting broke up in amity. Once again, we had defused a potentially explosive situation just by facing the facts together and thrashing out difficulties.

At the office I had a meeting on private practice. We discussed the latest print of the Health Services Bill (as the pay beds Bill is now called), with which I was far from satisfied, and went through my draft paper for Cabinet. David accepted my weekend Minute very meekly.

I then went to the House to await the arrival of Lord Goodman in my room. He was late as usual, which gave me the chance to slip into a campaign meeting in Mike's room just down the corridor. I was very pleased to see lively youngsters like Neil Kinnock [Labour MP for Bedwellty] (and of course Brian O'M.) taking such an active part. John Silkin, as Mike's campaign manager, had his tail up, but then I don't trust his euphoria. When Arnold eventually arrived he said he had had a hopeful talk with Mr Robb of the Independent Hospitals Group, who seemed willing to reach a voluntary agreement along the lines I have always been prepared to visualize, i.e. licensing to operate above a certain size of development and to be run by the independent board. The figure at which licensing should start to operate, continued Arnold, would be 250 beds. Of course I told him that was impossible and he agreed it was 'ridiculous'. I stressed that the figure of seventy-five beds was not negotiable. I had already given away too much. But if we could agree the figure, I would be prepared to give up overall control of the size of the private sector. (I don't know whether Arnold realizes I would never have got that through Cabinet, but he agreed solemnly that I was making a big gesture.) Arnold said he was due to see the whole bunch of representatives the next day. If they were not prepared to endorse this compromise, he would be prepared to float it publicly himself. I decided this was worth recording in my paper to Cabinet, which we hastily amended after Arnold had left.

Tonight was the great farewell dinner Harold had promised us. I found time to make up my face and put on my long black velvet dress. Marcia was there, as elegantly groomed as always. She was in a huddle with Eric Varley and we teased them: 'What is going on between you two?' Harold wandered around with a rather detached air. I suspect that levitation has begun. After we had chatted for about twenty minutes or so over champagne the news went round that we were waiting for Shirley – late as usual. She blew in at last, in the same rather crumpled white frock that she had been wearing all day, her hair uncombed. An ironical cheer went up. Harold then asked us all to come into the main reception room, where TV and other cameras had been set up. I realized for the first time that this was the time we were to have an official valedictory Cabinet photo taken with him. Shirley and I both protested when we found that, once again, we had each been posted on the far outside of the front row: typical of the way the party treated women, we said. With a lot of laughter and quipping we all at last settled ourselves down and smiled.

When we moved into the dining room I found to my annoyance that Harold had played safe with the seating arrangements and exactly reproduced the order of sitting in Cabinet, which meant I was between Malcolm and Eric and opposite Willie Ross and John Silkin. I have nothing but regard for any of them, but it would have been more interesting to have had a change. 'This is just like a Cabinet meeting with food,' I said disgustedly. Harold's promised menu turned out to be lavish, but not particularly imaginative. 'Watch Bob's face when he finds it is duck,' said Eric to me wickedly. 'He told me it is the one thing he can't stand.' Eric even passed him a note to this effect, but Bob was too impressed by the occasion even to smile at it. The one innovation was that Marcia and Douglas Allen were at our end of the table, so I enjoyed talking to them. The wines, as usual with government catering, were superb. But as the evening went on I felt there was something artificial about it. It did not come alight. This was a real event, Harold's abrupt and unnecessary departure, and I felt that this ought to be expressed spontaneously in some way. Coffee was served and Ted Short, on Harold's left, stood up to make a speech. It was of almost painful banality. Harold followed him. He talked in that curiously toneless and emotionless way he has almost made a virtue of, so that his natural wit and liveliness were tossed away. 'Ted said I didn't bear grudges,' he began, promisingly. 'If I had, I would have had the smallest Cabinet in history.' He then went on to tell us that 'even on placement tonight I have been vigilant to the end'. That was why he had reproduced a replica of the Cabinet seating, so that no one could read anything into anything. He went on: 'The time to go is while they are saying why do you go, not why do you stay.' What was he most proud of? The Open University. As for his obituary, he was 'amazed to be canonized so quickly'.

After Harold had finished there was a flat pause. I felt desperately that we should all have been asked to say something, however impromptu, going round the table. Wedgie jumped in with some of his witticisms. He told us a funny story about how he had been asked in 1965 to contribute to a TV programme on Harold's obituary. And he repeated the crack: 'If Harold falls under a bus, find out who is driving the bus.' For a moment I thought he had brought the evening to life. Roy followed him with a few polished sentences of tribute. I hoped others would follow, but the life soon fizzled out of the occasion. We broke up raggedly and I went home feeling dispirited.

Tuesday, 23 March

The whole day was supposed to be set aside for a joint meeting of the NEC and Cabinet. In the event, the meeting thankfully took up Tom Bradley's suggestion that we should try to finish by 1pm. One of the reasons, I am convinced, was that yesterday's meeting of the Liaison Committee with the TUC had taken the wind out of the sails of the 'Left'. Certainly we went over the familiar ground with wearisome repetitiveness, Mik trying to assert, without carrying much conviction, that it wasn't true that the NEC document differed markedly from that of the TUC. I worked through my boxes during all this; in particular, I had to clear the answers to my PQS, as I was top for Questions that afternoon.

My attention only perked up when we moved from general economic to industrial policy. (Peter, incidentally, made a brave and brilliant speech about import controls, pointing out that this was not a simple panacea.) Tony C. made one of his effective analyses about the philosophy of public expenditure, though he concluded that 'Denis was absolutely right to impose constraints.' Bryan Stanley contributed his usual common sense: 'I agree we have reached the limit of taxation, so I can accept the argument in the White Paper on Public Expenditure. But what I am not clear about is how the investment in the private sector is going to be obtained. The will to invest is not there.' Roy Jenkins claimed there was no change in our basic position on public expenditure. 'It is a question of balance' (the evasion of the year!). But the argument got nearer the bone when we got on to industrial policy. John Chalmers wanted to know if Eric Varley saw any real success in the sectoral discussions under Neddy. Eric made an evasive reply, claiming that he had 'inherited' the industrial policy. It would require legislation to change it. But the NEB was doing very well. 'The trade union members of the NEB are pretty satisfied.' The amount of money for the NEB was being kept under review. He didn't think we should get a hundred planning agreements this year; we should be lucky if we got twenty. Eric Heffer, who I suspect is of the 'soft' Left, immediately exonerated him. 'I agree that the idea of a hundred planning agreements in the first year was never on. It would have meant the creation of a new unit in the department. The battle for compulsory planning agreements was lost in 1974.' It was Judith Hart who cut through this old boy net complacency. Would Eric Varley wish to see new legislation to overcome the deficiencies to which he had referred, she asked. Eric hedged carefully: 'We have got to examine whether we need legislation, but this is a matter of collective responsibility.' I tossed a note to Mike, who was sitting opposite to me: 'My recollection is that E.V. was never in favour of compulsory PAS.' Mike wrote back: 'Yes, but Eric Heffer is right – the whole change took place before the 1974 election.' That doesn't quite meet my point. Eric, as Minister for Energy, would have been in the appropriate Cabinet committee, as I was not and I am damn sure he would be against compulsory PAS. He is deeply right-wing.

As all this was going on I sent Harold a note: 'Remember our conversation in your study? I think it would be a good thing if you were to dictate that Minute after all!'[1] Harold wrote back: 'I'm pretty sure I had it minuted at the time – as I knew what was going to happen. If not, I'll get it retrospectively recorded.' Over lunch after the meeting I thanked Harold for last night's dinner. He said complacently that he thought it had gone very well. 'Ted made a very good speech.' And he proceeded to explain to me what a problem he had had about the seating arrangements. 'If I had altered the seating at all, someone would have read something into it. So I decided the best thing was to stick to the Cabinet seating.' I suggested mildly that he might have drawn the seating out of a hat: heaven knows who would then have been sitting next to whom. He responded to the idea immediately: 'I never thought of it.' He chuckled at the thought of Wedgie Benn finding himself next to Roy J. 'Or the other Roy, come to that.'

As we DHSS Ministers assembled on the front bench for Questions Brian O'Malley said to me, 'I don't feel like Questions today. Come to think of it, I don't feel like work at all.' That was so unlike him I was rather surprised. He answered Question No. 4 with his usual fluency. I was just in the middle of answering Question No. 5 when I heard him say rather thickly, 'Take Question No. 6', which he was due to answer. I thought it was some kind of silly joke and waved him aside impatiently as I tried to catch the supplementary question that was being addressed at me. The next thing I knew was a flurry on the bench, Brian hurrying out and David saying to me, 'Brian's not well. I'll take Question No. 6.' Questions over, I hurried to Brian's room, to find him white and drawn. He had been vomiting and was complaining about his head. As they wheeled him off to the ambulance he muttered to me, 'Anyway, I've voted.' (It would be for Mike, of course.) Next he said, 'Don't tell my wife.' Of course, we took no notice of that and someone went off to telephone Kathleen. We all hung around anxiously, trying to find out what was wrong. Later Maurice Miller told me it was a 'subarachnoid' haemorrhage – not a cerebral one – and everything should be all right. But we were all deeply disturbed. I told Janet to send lots of flowers and find out when I could visit him.

Later that evening I went to the Thompsons' annual party. Though Ted was in Brussels, I didn't want to miss it. One meets more union chaps there than anywhere else. Hughie was there, full of bonhomie. He is so moderate these days he is unrecognizable. I asked him if he had known about Harold's intention to resign. He said it had come as a complete surprise – and he thought it was a surprise for Jack Jones too. When Jack had asked him to sign the joint statement of support for the Government earlier this week, he had readily agreed. Then, when he read Harold's announcement, he wondered if he had been had. But he had satisfied himself that Jack had acted in complete innocence.

Wednesday, 24 March

A great battle in Social Services Committee of Cabinet over child benefit for non-resident children.[1] I beat Treasury (in the arid person of Mr Edmund Dell) into

[1] See page 672.

[2] With the introduction of child benefit, child tax allowances were to disappear. Since these had been

the ground on every point. Incidentally, Alex Lyon backed me up to the hilt, but said a transitional period of two or three years would be useless unless Cabinet insisted on the Home Office speeding up the period of waiting for entry visa interviews. I said this should be reported to Cabinet. I then found it was too late to go to NEC if I was to do any preparing for my press conference on the Consultative Document on Priorities in the Health Service, on which David and I have worked so hard and which we are launching this afternoon. As this might indeed be my swan song I decided to give it priority and was rather pleased with the way the conference went. David has really done a superb job on this and we have produced the best bit of planning the NHS has ever had.

Next I had to prepare for my meeting at the Treasury with Denis on the next uprating of pensions and benefits. As I walked into the room I said to Denis and Joel: 'There's no fight in me today. I'm too sick at heart about Brian. You will be able to walk all over me.' Brian has had a brain operation and has not yet come round. The unhappy Kate is by his bedside. We are all suspended in misery and uncertainty. I thought of how Brian and I would have come into that meeting with Denis together, ready to do battle for the earlier uprating on which we have set our hearts. We would have passed the ball backwards and forwards to each other in a piece of high-speed play as we always did. Worrying about him, the heart has gone out of me. Joel shared my wretchedness. He is as fond of Brian as I am. In the event, Denis took the wind out of my sails by saying he knew he had to do something to meet the TUC policy on pensions: so what he proposed was to pay the TUC's suggested rate of £13.50 for a married couple in November instead of the £13 that would be due under a straight interpretation of the forecasting method. I pointed out that the TUC had been asking for this rate to be paid in *July* not November and that payment in November would mean he would only be giving back £45 million of the £500 million he had saved by switching from the historical method and urged him at the very least to advance the uprating by three weeks. An October uprating would make all the psychological difference. He said he would look into it.

Still no news from the ever-effervescent Lord G. so I spoke to him on the phone. He told me he had met the Independent Hospitals Group, the BMA *et al.* yesterday. Incidentally, Gerry Vaughan was there! There had been a 'slightly acrimonious discussion'. The consultants and juniors were very 'bolshie' and wouldn't accept anything he proposed. He had to accept, said Arnold, that they were 'highly political'. The scheme I had suggested was acceptable to IHG apart from the question of numbers of beds. They had decided to adjourn the meeting. Robb was coming in at noon tomorrow to tell him what the figure of beds should be. (That is a bore, said I to myself, because I shan't know the figure in time to report to Cabinet. But I simply can't afford to postpone the item yet again.) If the IHG came forward with a 'reasonable' figure, said Arnold, there might be a settlement. 'I am not unhopeful and

---

available for non-resident children, while cash allowances like family allowance never had been, parents with children living abroad faced a serious reduction in take-home pay through the loss of tax reliefs without anything to replace them. This would particularly hit immigrants whose children had not joined them in this country, but whom they were supporting, and I was urging delay in abolishing child tax allowances for them.

I am prepared to foster-father the plan up to the question of the figure, where I reserve my judgment.' All this came after a quite amicable meeting I had with the BMA this afternoon on the next phase of incomes policy. Of course they want a percentage scheme and no ceiling at all on pay increases. I assured them the policy was still in a formative stage and that their ideas would be fed into the pool.

Thursday, 25 March

I have had my best press yet on the consultative document. There are flattering leaders in *The Times* and *Guardian*. So if I go out, it will be on a less controversial note. They won't be able to say that all I've been interested in is pay beds. At Cabinet I was all keyed up for my paper on pay beds in which I reported my discussions with Goodman so far, asked for permission to embody control powers in the Bill from the outset along the lines I had spelt out to the IHG and plumped for seventy-five beds firmly as the starting point of licensing. But first we had to go through a number of other items. On Rhodesia Jim reported that the reactions to his statement in the House had been generally favourable. South Africa had told him the economic stranglehold on Rhodesia would soon become apparent and that Jim's policy statement had been 'exactly right'. Nyerere was delighted with it. The US was backing us. Only Smith and Nkomo had rejected it. He proposed to send David Ennals to see Nyerere. There would be no more overtures to Smith. More worrying was the situation in Nigeria where the Head of State had sent Harold a letter about Gowon,[1] cleverly worded but amounting in effect to a demand for his extradition. That, of course, wasn't on, but it did look as though Gowon had been indiscreet in meeting people who might have been involved in the plotting and we might have to restrict his activities.

We then had a perfunctory discussion on the guidelines for the next public expenditure survey. All that interested me was that Denis suggested we should maintain the general priorities between programmes we had already agreed, which suits me, but when Fred bleated again about how education had been milked, I was able to puncture him by asking for Denis's tables of relative growth of programmes to be given us in cost terms instead of just volume ones. This would show that education had, in fact, got an increase, not a reduction, and that the growth in social security programmes was much less than had been claimed. Denis agreed.

At last we came to my pay beds paper. I introduced it by supplementing it with a report on my phone conversation with Arnold yesterday. Harold seized on this to railroad my proposals through. Once again he faced a determined opposition from Harold Lever, backed this time by Shirley. Harold Lever was all for consultations continuing, however much more time they took. (Of course he would be only too

---

[1] General Gowon, who became head of the Federal Military Government of Nigeria in 1966, was overthrown in July 1975 in a bloodless coup, after which General Murtala Muhamed became head of state. Seven months later, General Muhamed was assassinated during an attempted coup. The Nigerian Government claimed that Gowon, who had come to Britain and enrolled as a student at Warwick University, knew and approved of the coup and asked Britain to return him; Gowon emphatically denied any involvement and the Government took the view that extradition was a matter solely for the courts.

pleased if we lost the Bill through the delay.) The PM swept that aside by saying that of course talks could go on, but, if there was a change in the situation, the Bill could be altered during its passage in the House. Shirley then said we would be 'attacked' for the licensing proposals. The form of control by the independent board was okay, but she was worried about the figure of seventy-five beds. If we discouraged the building of private hospitals, we should lose a lot of foreign exchange from rich overseas patients. Denis backed her pontifically. Harold Lever came nagging back. We really should get this matter into perspective. What did a few private hospitals matter compared with the breakdown of morale in the NHS? We must realize that the view of the profession was that we were trying to undermine private practice. Despite all this the PM nobly discharged his last obligation to me and got all my proposals through. On the figure of beds, however, I suppose it was inevitable he should show his 'neutrality' by yielding a bit. Unfortunately I played into his hands by saying I would be prepared, if it would get agreement, to agree to one hundred beds in London and fifty in the provinces. Harold seized on this to say: 'I suggest one hundred in London and seventy-five in the provinces.' The rest looked at me as if to say, 'That's reasonable: accept it, Barbara.' 'But Arnold may actually get agreement on a lower figure than that for all I know,' I moaned. 'Then let's say seventy-five and one hundred unless a lower figure is agreed,' said Denis cheerfully. I jumped at that, repeating after him: 'All right then, unless a *lower* figure is agreed.' And so it was clinched. The most important thing from my point of view is that, whatever Arnold comes up with now, I can't be forced higher. Not too bad at all.

In the evening I had the first of my 'export' parties: an informal gathering over drinks for medical equipment manufacturers to tell them what I had been up to in the Middle East. As usual the office had been a bit diffident about my intention to make this a relaxed social occasion. They can't get used to my passion for doing business over food and drink. Anyway, Norman had entered into the spirit of the thing as usual and the caterers had turned my room into an attractive buffet. All the invitees streamed in dead on time and I was astonished to find some of them had come from as far afield as Glasgow and Devon. An invitation to meet the Secretary of State seems to have more pulling power than I had imagined. We all got on famously. They were extrovert types with whom I found it easy to get on to familiar terms. They were all so keen to chat to me individually that I couldn't get away from them, but eventually I managed to break away, called them to order, perched on the edge of the table and talked to them rousingly about the export possibilities in the Middle East. I told them why I had gone and what I was trying to do to help them export and ended up with some frank comments about where they were going wrong: notably their failure to organize proper servicing. Their response was remarkable. They frankly admitted I was right; exchanged ideas audibly among themselves about what they could do to remedy this; agreed there ought to be collective action among the smaller firms and promised me, hand on heart, to organize all this through the BHEC. When at last they left, lining up to offer their profuse thanks, James Collier looked dazed at the success of it all. I went home contentedly aware that I'm rather good at this sort of thing.

I had been surprised that David Owen was missing from the party. The explanation came when he turned up at the end, admitting that he had been at a meeting of

Jenkinsites, discussing with their leader what he should do as a result of the vote he has got in the first ballot for the leadership: only fifty-six votes to Jim's eighty-four while Michael tops the poll with ninety. David was clearly pretty worked up: 'We decided he should withdraw,' he told me pugnaciously. I was staggered and told him so. This further display of political daintiness proves conclusively what I have always known: that Jenkins will never lead the Labour Party. I bet Denis stays in the ring, despite his derisory thirty votes. But then, he's a pugilist, not a patrician. Wedgie's withdrawal in Mike's favour was a foregone conclusion. His thirty-seven votes will now almost certainly switch to Mike. I was not surprised by Crosland's dismissal with a mere seventeen votes. Despite the endless build-up he gets in the press, he isn't a serious contender at all.

Friday, 26 March

This was to have been our all-day meeting at Chequers to discuss EEC policy. In view of Harold's imminent departure, it got itself downgraded rapidly. First it was transferred to No. 10; then Harold opened by saying he gathered a number of people wanted to get away. Could we finish at 1pm? In fact, if it weren't for the fact that we had been promised the right to brief the PM and Foreign Secretary on the question of direct elections before they go to the European Council of Heads of Government, I think Harold would have cancelled it altogether. As it was he said that Cabinet would no doubt like the opportunity to comment on the line the Government should take in next week's debate. It was soon clear that Cabinet would like to comment. I myself had got up early to wade through a mass of documents, including a 'draft Convention' on direct elections which the President of the Commission has circulated as the basis of decision-making next month and on which Jack had done me a first-class, thorough briefing, raising all sorts of alarm calls on various points. Above all, he pressed me to insist on the Select Committee being set up for which over 100 Labour MPs are now calling in an Early Day Motion. So I was ready to do battle all on my own, if necessary, but I soon found that the majority of Cabinet was ready to do battle too. Faced with the implications of that draft Convention, everyone had clearly had second thoughts and we ended the morning's discussion by reversing nearly everything we had been saying as a government previously.

When Jim began, he clearly didn't know what was going to hit him. Next week, he said, at the European Council he and Harold would be faced with a number of points. On powers, there was *no* prospect of the European Parliament getting extra powers: the French were adamant on this. But with the added legitimacy of direct elections, the Parliament would certainly press for them. Giscard's whole aim in setting up the European Council had been to offset the role of the European Parliament. In his (Jim's) view the practical difficulties of organizing direct elections made it impossible to achieve the date of May 1978, though he knew the problem the present situation created for the Whips. Roy Jenkins was all against our making a snap decision on the Select Committee. 'We should wait and see how the debate goes.' Bob, on the other hand, thought the case for a Select Committee was powerful. 'It is the question of powers that worries our people.' And he dilated on his own difficulties in having to allow thirty-seven of our Members to keep popping over to Brussels. It would be quite impossible if he had to increase that number to sixty-seven, as the proposals in front of us suggested, so the idea of a 'dual mandate' was unworkable.

Peter then made a major statement. The central point was the relationship between the European Parliament and the British one. This linked up with the question of size, whether there should be a common date, the dual mandate issue – even the name itself: Assembly or Parliament. 'It is frivolous that we should decide these matters after a two-day debate on a procedural Motion. The great argument developing in the party now is: what kind of EEC is it to be?' Separate representation would create immense difficulties. 'Our view of Europe – the confederal one – is very different from that of the socialist parties in Europe. It should be an essential condition that anyone elected to the EP must be a member of the British Parliament.' Denmark, Luxembourg and Ireland had very similar views to us and the French were ambivalent. We had a duty to delay this matter for a further period of time.

Shirley's response to this was predictable. 'The House of Commons is not going to regain its sovereignty over these matters. The choice before us is that either we go on and create some form of parliamentary accountability or have no accountability at all.' (At this point the procession of butlers appeared again bearing coffee in elegant china cups, plus Wedgie's mug. Harold is floating out of office on a sea of sociability.)

Wedgie took up the argument. 'We must discuss the sort of Europe we want to see,' he told us. 'There is no demand for direct elections. That demand comes from those already in power in Europe to legitimize that power. The federal dream is beginning to fade, except among the British Establishment. The British people did not vote for federalism. The role of Ministers vis-à-vis officials is the central issue. The objective should be to strengthen the role of Ministers. I would make the Council of Ministers the focal point, not the Parliament.' I then backed Peter one hundred per cent. We should make no commitment on such issues as a common date for the elections, or the ruling out of the dual mandate, until the Select Committee had been set up. There wasn't a detail in Jim's paper that could be separated from the issue of powers, the demand for which would grow the moment the Assembly got its democratic legitimacy. Denis, too, expressed some robust doubts. Wedgie, he said, had raised the central issue, because there had been far too little discussion of direct elections. Pressure for them had been building up from the Whips. He believed we should have the same date for the European elections as for the national ones: staggered representation would be perfectly feasible. He had therefore come to the conclusion (1) that the movement towards direct elections would be slow; (2) we shouldn't let France, who also had doubts about this, hide behind us and put the blame on us; (3) we should give Jim the 'maximum freedom of manoeuvre'. (I didn't like the sound of this. I knew how he would use this to commit us.)

Harold summed up reassuringly. It was agreed, he said, that in the Commons we should give the Select Committee a fair wind but see that it was chaired by a Minister. We would not impose the 1978 date but would discuss the difficulties, while not ostensibly dragging our feet. We would make it clear that the Government will make no firm commitments at this stage and Cabinet itself would reach no final decision until after the Select Committee had reported. Jim then thanked us all fulsomely. 'I won't commit us,' he promised, 'but I hope you will allow me to let the French take the heat.' And so we had to leave it, hoping for the best.

Monday, 29 March

The Cambridge Economic Policy Group has come out with dire forecasts about our prospects for 1980 if we continue to manage our economic affairs as we do now. Their remedy: a protectionist policy. Denis, of course, rejects their forecasting as unreliable. I am not expert enough to judge. In this leadership election atmosphere we are all poised on the edge of uncertainty. Jack and Brian Abel-Smith, for instance, tell me that they have been served with the sack. The PM has circulated a Minute saying that their appointments 'cease automatically with the end of the Administration in which they were appointed'. So at the moment of the PM's resignation (i.e., the end of the leadership election) they will go. Hopefully they will be immediately reappointed, but that will depend on my being confirmed in office. Jack has told me that, if I go, he would like to stay on as political adviser to someone else, provided another Minister he is in sympathy with offers him a job. Apparently the attractions of the Bar are no substitute for politics! Norman is organizing office meetings on this and that because I want to get my potential successor committed on as many things as possible. (We are hurrying out the circular on joint financing this week.)

An essential part of all this is to get Lord Goodman sewn up before it is too late. On Friday we at last received a letter from him setting out in rather obscure terms his draft of a possible agreement with the Independent Hospitals Group over licensing and I arranged to see him this evening. This morning we had an office meeting to discuss our line. The outline of the Goodman structure for licensing is pretty well along the lines I had in mind, i.e. handing it over to the independent board suitably augmented. The outstanding snag is over the number of beds at which licensing would start. Goodman says the IHG is still standing by 250, which he knows is unacceptable to me, and adds in his letter that he himself has an idea of the figure he would suggest but 'I am hesitant to put it on paper lest it gives you apoplexy'. My guess is that he has a figure of 150 in mind: double what I have told him is my maximum.

In our office discussion we agreed to try to detach the question of the figure from the structure, get an agreement on the latter and agree to differ on the former. I also said that I didn't want any agreement which emerges to be labelled a 'Goodman' one: after all, it is I who have had to fight single-handed to get any licensing provisions included at all (they were never in the Manifesto or the Queen's Speech). So I want to be able to claim this unto myself for righteousness in the eyes of our own side. I suggested we tell Arnold that the IHG must write me a letter putting these proposals to me and I asked officials to draft a form of words which would broadly cover the points Arnold has sketched out, but more lucidly and leaving out the figure of beds. Our problem is that, if we are to keep to our publication timetable, the print of the Bill must be settled by Wednesday of this week. If necessary we shall just have to undertake to introduce Government amendments at the committee stage.

In the afternoon I had a traumatic meeting with Joel over the rate of child benefit.

Brian Abel-Smith and officials have produced an excellent briefing showing that the rate of benefit at which no one will be worse off, including one-parent families and larger families, is about £2.60 a week. Anything below that would require the payment of a special premium to these groups at enormous administrative complication and cost. The figure which would take us back to 1971 levels of family support would be £2.85. I told officials my fall-back figure would probably have to be £2.70 a week, at which Tony Lynes glowered. When we arrived at the Treasury Joel embraced me with his usual affection, asking anxiously after Brian O'Malley. I told him he was expected to make a full recovery, but it would be slow: he had still not come round from the six-hour brain operation at the weekend. Joel then asked me to suggest my figure for child benefit. Quietly I spelt out my analysis of the minimum need for family support, particularly in view of the continuing price increases under CAP and the fact that we should have added 50 pence per week per child to the cost of school meals by November 1977. I would not, I said, be unrealistic and expect us to get back to the level of family support obtaining in 1955 (about £10 a week for a family of three children and on standard rate of income tax) but it did seem to me reasonable that, in launching this major aspect of our social policy, we should get back to 1971, i.e., a rate worth £7 for three children. They watched me avidly as I said slowly: 'And that gives us a rate of £2.85 a week.' Joel exploded with laughter at his officials' dismay. 'I told you,' he spluttered, clutching Pliatzky's[1] arm, 'you don't know her as well as I do. And what would this sumptuous figure cost?' 'We don't know,' said Pliatzky, tearing his hair, 'the Secretary of State has gone right through the top of our table.' 'It would cost £217 million,' I said sweetly, 'only slightly above the £200 million which is the top end of the amount earmarked in the Contingency Fund for this purpose.' 'Nothing is "earmarked",' said Joel desperately. 'Don't you realize that the claims on the Contingency Fund already exceed it several times?' He then tried to assert some kind of control over the situation by spelling out the figure *he* had in mind: £2.40 plus a premium of 22 pence a week for one-parent and large families to ensure they did not actually lose. It was my turn to give an incredulous laugh. The Treasury wasn't actually suggesting, was it, I asked, that we should spend Civil Service manpower, which we had been asked to cut, on paying out little extra driblets of money to a few families because we were in the process of making them poorer?

Joel then went into one of the now fashionable diatribes against universal benefits. Here were we with our backs to the wall and I was proposing an across-the-board increase in family support which would give help to families who did not need it. He waxed eloquent about the wickedness of universal benefits and the need for greater selectivity. It is at moments like this that I despair of this Government, dominated as it is by people who don't believe in the policy on which they fought the election. Denis can say till he is blue in the face that the public expenditure cuts don't reflect any abandonment of Labour's philosophy, but here was his right-hand man talking exactly like Roy Jenkins – or, worse still, like Margaret Thatcher. 'I really don't know why you don't join the Tory Party,' I told Joel coldly. 'Because the policy of *our* party

---

[1] Leo Pliatzky was Permanent Secretary for Public Expenditure in the Treasury.

is to extend the payment of benefits as of right on the basis of functional need and then to take back from those who don't need them the value of those benefits in taxation.' Joel merely said testily that I was talking sentimental nonsense. It is this kind of attitude that makes me fight for my own departmental corner absolutely ruthlessly. Not only am I and others on the left in Cabinet excluded from the centres of real power (Harold has consistently given them to right-wingers and at present there isn't even an inner Cabinet: just Harold and Jim in a huddle) but I am expected to accept meekly the reinterpretations of party doctrine which the Treasury (ably aided by right-wingers like Roy Jenkins, Fred Peart, Fred Mulley and Jim) just imposes on us. Not on me, they're not going to, as long as my talons remain long and sharp.

The atmosphere was beginning to get quite nasty, but once again I was saved by the Treasury overreaching itself. Miss Jennifer Forsyth[1] started asserting that there would be no administrative difficulties at all about operating a selective premium. I thereupon brought in Tony Crocker, who stammered painfully as usual, but nonetheless wiped the floor with her. Lance Errington, of all people, clinched it by pointing out that every one-parent or large family would have to have *two* books in order to get another miserly 22 pence per week. Collapse of Treasury party. 'The line at which we break even,' I pointed out, 'is £2.60 per week.' Joel pounced: 'Does that mean that you'll accept £2.60?' 'Not at all,' I replied smoothly, 'my minimum is £2.70.' Joel said that was impossible and the matter would have to go to Cabinet unless I would come further down than that. I refused, saying I would be delighted for this to go to Cabinet: a rate of £2.70 would still enable us to continue child tax allowances for non-resident children and yet keep within our maximum of £200 million. So we broke up, Joel and I embracing affectionately again to the bewilderment of his officials. (Mine are used to my histrionics by now and they know they pay dividends.) But in the corridors of the Treasury afterwards my officials clucked like anxious hens: they hadn't expected the Treasury to be quite as tough as that. I told them that the only thing for us to do was to keep our nerve.

We gathered in my room at the House at about 6pm to approve the draft officials had been drawing up to present to Arnold as the basis of the letter the Independent Hospitals Group was to send to me. I was perfectly happy with most of it until I came to the paras dealing with the issue of exemption certificates from licensing. We had earlier agreed that it would be of immense value for the independent board to know of all proposed private developments, whether above the licensing figure or below. So we had, I thought, decided that *all* applications should go to the board, either for an exemption certificate or for an authorization. Tim Nodder's draft unfortunately said that it would be for the developer to decide whether to apply for a certificate. I let out a howl; Patrick agreed this was wrong; we cast about us as to how we could get this retyped before we met Arnold at his flat, notionally at 7pm. There was no time to get back to the office to do it. Everyone hastily redrafted these paras and my inimitable Jack said he would willingly retype them, if he could find a typewriter. A

---

[1] Miss Jennifer Forsyth was the Under-Secretary in the Treasury who headed the division scrutinizing social service expenditure.

mad search for a typewriter followed. Finally I broke into Roy Jenkins's room, which was empty, and found his secretary's typewriter. Armed with Jack's rather shaky retype, we eventually were on our way to Portland Place.

Arnold was full of apologies for having dragged me there, so I didn't have to apologize for being late (which I wouldn't have done anyway, because he has kept me waiting so often). As soon as a butler let us into the flat we knew we were intruding on an 'occasion'. Arnold explained that he was holding a farewell dinner to the Newspaper Proprietors' Association, from whose chairmanship he was retiring. (Some evil voices are to be heard saying he was pushed.) The butler showed us into his Lordship's study, where we were offered a drink. I said tea, please, which must have upset Mrs Roberts, busy preparing the meal in the kitchen. Arnold said tea, too, so tea it was, while the rest had something stronger. Arnold was, not surprisingly, a bit *distrait*. I went through the routine I had agreed at my meeting with officials. We could broadly agree with the points in the draft he had sent us, I said – though they might be better stated. But what was the figure of pay beds which he had said would give me 'apoplexy'? As we had guessed he said '150'. I shook my head and said we had really better agree to disagree on the figure. After all, the profession could always continue its battle to get it amended in the House. He thought that there was probably sense in that and said that he would submit my draft to the IHG. He also accepted my idea that IHG should write a letter to me direct – and not through him. If he was disappointed he didn't show it, for he couldn't dispute my point that the profession had promptly dissociated themselves from the last lot of Goodman proposals and pretended that they had fallen from heaven in some mysterious way. 'Don't I know it,' Arnold agreed. 'And I have told them what I thought of their behaviour.' So the whole discussion went very well, Arnold even accepting the urgency of the timetable and the fact that any agreement would have to be concluded in the next few days, if it was to be incorporated in the print of the Bill. We then released him for his dinner and sped home ourselves thankfully, his promise to let us have an answer the next day ringing in our ears.

While we were talking in Arnold's study, I kept glancing over my shoulder at the Graham Sutherland life-size portrait of him which was propped against the wall behind me. 'I keep thinking there are two of you in the room,' I said. 'That must be very unnerving,' Arnold replied. 'It is,' said I. But we both agreed it was a superb portrait: 'The best he's ever done,' said Arnold complacently.

Tuesday, 30 March

Of course there is no news from Arnold. In the meantime we went ahead with an office meeting on finalizing the text of the Bill. I said we would go ahead and put Cabinet's figures in the Bill, whatever the figure Arnold came up with (as it certainly wouldn't be lower). But when I asked Norman to turn up the Cabinet Minutes of last Thursday, I was furious. Despite all Norman's efforts the PM was reported as summing up that the figures would be one hundred and seventy-five 'unless the outcome of Lord Goodman's latest consultations *suggested otherwise*'. 'That's not what we agreed at all,' I exploded. 'I distinctly remember repeating that we had decided firmly on the figures *unless Goodman's figure was lower* and everyone agreed. I'm sick of fighting and winning major battles in Cabinet only to have all my work undermined by inaccurate Minute-taking.' They tried to soothe me down, saying they didn't think the wording would make much difference, but it was the principle of the thing that angered me.

However, I was pleased by my success in strengthening the clause in the Bill which contains the 'broad declaration' in Goodman that private beds and facilities shall be phased out of the NHS. The draftsmen, even in the second print, had produced a wishy-washy phrase to the effect that the provisions of this part of the Bill 'shall have a view to' separating private facilities and 'to that end securing the progressive *reduction* of the extent to which accommodation and services are available' for private practice in the NHS, etc. I could not imagine anything more likely to rouse the suspicions of our side that the Goodman proposals were a device for keeping pay beds indefinitely. Anyway I've now got it changed to 'shall have effect for the purpose of securing the separation of facilities' and 'to that end securing the progressive *withdrawal* of accommodation and services'. That is a fair interpretation of Goodman, to which I am sticking rigidly.

Two bits of good news in the papers: (1) Hughie Scanlon has ordered the Leyland strikers back to work; and (2) Don Lander has made an optimistic speech saying that Chryslers are recovering better than he had dared to hope. It would be wonderful if we could prove that government by consent can really transform society!

The declaration of the result of the second ballot for the party leadership was a bit of an anti-climax. The excitement went out of the contest when Mike dropped to second place, with 133 votes to Jim's 141, with Denis collecting a mere 38. At our campaign meeting in Mike's room afterwards John Silkin was as blandly optimistic as ever, but I think the rest of us knew it was all over bar the shouting. Mike would need to get 24 of the Healey votes to win. I said I would make myself responsible for trying to get two of those votes: Joel Barnett's and David Owen's. Mike remained clearly determined to fight to the end. I have been very interested to note how firmly and unequivocally he is going for the leadership. There is a hidden toughness in Mike and it is showing now.

Wednesday, 31 March

I've been amused to see that Roy Jenkins can get annoyed about Cabinet Minutes too. His private secretary has circulated a letter challenging the Minute on jubilee medals. I must deploy this device myself sometime. If we all kept up a barrage of complaints we might get some results. The trouble is that it is almost impossible to beat the condominium of PM and Cabinet secretary unless the rest of Cabinet forms a united front.

Another long office meeting on private practice. First, the BMA have written to Gedling trying to suggest that I have refused to allow them to discuss any parts of the Bill at all, except the Schedule and licensing, and I know this will be used against me by Gerry Vaughan and co. as proof of my 'arrogance'. (In fact it was David who advised that I should refuse to consult them over the details of the Bill as, if I did, we should be enmeshed in wrangles for months, and he was quite right.) I said that I ought to sign the reply to the BMA and give them an indication of the scope of the Bill, without going into details. This was agreed and we eventually finalized a draft between us which Norman said ought to stand us in very good stead in the battles ahead. We rushed it round to the BMA by hand so that they could have it for their council meeting.

A phone call has come from Arnold: the talks with IHG are going well, but he must have more time. He thought he could get them to write to me next Monday. The trouble about this, of course, is that the Bill must go to the printers today if it is to appear before Legislation Committee of Cabinet next Tuesday. Gedling then reported that the Legislation Committee meeting had been postponed because of the change of 'administration' due to take place on Tuesday. Apparently all government goes into limbo until Harold's successor has announced his dispositions! This worried me, because I am anxious to get the print of the Bill circulated before Jim takes over, in case he sacks me. It will be invaluable for me to have that on the record, because I shall keep up the battle on pay beds from the backbenches. I therefore said we should go ahead and circulate the Bill on Friday: together with my Minute to the PM, reporting on the outcome of my talks with Arnold. I decided I wouldn't send it till the last minute as I don't want to give Harold Lever and co. the chance to try and reopen the Cabinet decisions.

At lunch I got a welcome opportunity to talk to Joel about the leadership. He told me flatly: 'I'm going to vote for Jim', but I worked on him very skilfully, I thought, and it may have had some effect. Back at the office I had, in Brian O'Malley's absence, to receive a deputation from the pensions industry boys about the next stage of incomes policy. In fact I was rather glad of the opportunity to meet them face to face and I found them much easier to deal with than the Grabhams of this world. They were gentle, courteous and easy to handle. In the end, having started by demanding the complete removal of any restrictions on pension increases in the next round of pay policy, I got them agreeing to send us proposals for a limited relaxation – and I did it by hinting that if it all got too difficult the Government might abandon the attempt to get any incomes policy at all. That shook them!

Later I managed to get a word with David about the party leadership, or rather several words, when I saw him privately. 'Have you voted yet?' I asked him. He laughed and said: 'I rather thought you wanted to talk to me about that.' We then talked for three-quarters of an hour very matily. I developed a new tack: Mike had no chance of winning now, but if the final ballot revealed that practically all the Healey votes had switched to Jim, I believed the Healey/Foot axis on which the Government was founded might well collapse. There would be an immense sourness among the Left, many of whom would have been willing to vote for Healey to stop Jim, but who would discover that, when the chips were down, all the Healeyites wanted to do was to stop the Left. He said he hadn't finally made up his mind and would consider what I had said. We then had a discursive chat about what would happen if Jim won. 'Don't worry,' David said. 'They'll keep you on. They'd be mad not to. No one else could get the pay beds thing through. And we *will* get it through: I think we are out of the wood now.' 'I'd like to see the Bill through and then go,' I told him. He was sure that I would be able to do that. As for himself, he wanted a move. Where to? Either Chief Secretary at the Treasury ('we really have to be tougher over public expenditure') or Minister of Defence ('I'd get some real cuts'.) And we must safeguard Brian's position, he added affectionately. I couldn't help thinking what a camaraderie we have forged. I told David we couldn't spare him yet. We still had policy initiatives to finish on the health side. 'Looking back, you know,' I said, 'we really have some remarkable achievements to our credit in the past two years. We've transformed this department – and I couldn't have begun to do it without Brian and you. We've been a magnificent trinity.' He agreed, saying he had enjoyed every minute of it. 'You really are remarkable in the way you delegate,' he told me. 'And you have had the sense to concentrate on general policy and not just departmental policies as so many Ministers do.' Altogether it was a very pleasant talk which warmed my heart.

Finally I phoned Denis: a last way-out throw to help Mike. I repeated the line of argument I had used to David, hoping that Denis would see its significance for the next leadership election. He was friendly enough and I told him I wasn't expecting him to make any statement publicly. 'I just leave you to settle this between your conscience and yourself.' But I suspect these 'radicals' are all cowards at heart.

Thursday, 1 April

No Cabinet! Whether it is that Harold's sense of emancipation has gone to his head, or what, I don't know. Instead we had a meeting of Devolution Committee with Ted Short in the chair and a mass of documents in front of us about 'override' powers which should be retained by Westminster. Everyone agreed that we had got to limit the override powers on general policy grounds: it is a wonder that we ever thought we could get away with *that*. Ted Short recommended a compromise: no legislative override at all and override of executive actions to be limited to those concerning non-developed powers. Jack had briefed me that this concession didn't go far enough, but Willie said he was perfectly happy with it. Elwyn, as cautious as all Lord Chancellors become, wanted a limited policy override in the legislative field as well.

What interested me most was Roy Jenkins's outburst: 'I am absolutely convinced now that we must go ahead with our devolution policy. There can be no going back whatsoever.' But we ought to have as much judicial review as we could. We should write certain principles into the Act itself which would then be interpreted by the courts. We needed a major paper dealing with judicial review over the whole field. (This new declaration of faith by Roy confirmed something David had said to me last night. When I said that I gathered Roy would only take the Foreign Secretary's job, David interjected that wasn't true. What he would like to see Roy doing was to take responsibility for bringing devolution into effect.) The more I think about it the less I like the idea of Roy taking over responsibility for devolution. We should end up with PR, a written constitution and a Bill of Rights, for which people like Shirley are pressing hard. Willie Ross brought us all back to earth with a bit of common sense: 'If things go wrong it would immediately lead to separation.' And he reminded us that what had caused all the outcry was our proposal to take general policy 'override', even in the devolved field. So Ted's compromise went through, subject to Roy's request for a paper on judicial review.

Another office meeting on private practice. We approved the Minute to go to the PM tomorrow. We also discussed Arnold's suggestion that it would help very much towards an agreement, not only if we would say the chairman of the independent board would be legally qualified, but actually gave his name. I have had Jack ferreting away to clear certain names with Bill Wedderburn[1] and others and was all for submitting them to the PM so that, once again, it would be on the record what I had proposed and what Harold's successor had run away from (if he did). However, Patrick raised some very powerful objections to our including this in the Minute, e.g. we were committed to consulting on the appointment, not only the professions, but the trade unions. I then came clean and said my problem was that, at my coming press conference on the Bill, I was not prepared to say we had agreed that the chairman should be legally qualified unless and until I knew that the sort of names I had in mind were likely to be accepted by the PM. Patrick, who is a completely honourable man, who considers his overriding duty is to his own Secretary of State and who never tries to twist things to meet his own personal views, immediately saw the strength of this. We thereupon decided to send a separate letter to the PM on this point, setting out the three top names on Jack's list. Hopefully, even the new PM will be able to give me a reply on this point before the Bill is introduced.

With the prospect that I may be out of a job by Monday I decided I would take Friday off. (In any case I want to catch up with my diary.) As I worked late at the office clearing things up, Raymond came in to report the result of his meeting that afternoon with the Joint Consultative Committee on the Schedule to the Bill. It was obvious, he said, that they were completely divided, some of them trying to make an issue of how little time I had allowed for consultation, others admitting they would never have agreed anyway on what the Schedule should contain. In the end they were ready to leave the real negotiating to the IHG, who were at the meeting. The professions just wiped their hands of the whole thing. But what Raymond has divined from his chats with IHG is that they are going to suggest a compromise on the number of beds to be subject to licensing. This fits in with a telephone conversation we have had from Arnold's secretary. 'So, if I may say so, Secretary of State,' said Raymond, 'it would be advisable to get your Minute off to the PM without delay, before the IHG letter arrives.' He's a good chap, is Raymond and has entered marvellously into the spirit of my tussle with the consultants.

Friday, 2 April

I woke this morning with a streaming head cold. It is obvious that my sinusitis is not cleared and that, as soon as I stop taking the antibiotics, I am back in trouble. Two things in my boxes amuse me very much. First is a letter from Joel Barnett to David Owen about David's proposals for giving the drug company Merck, Sharp and

---

[1] K. W. Wedderburn, barrister and Cassel Professor of Commercial Law at the London School of Economics. He became a Labour Peer in 1977.

Dohme International their head over price increases for pharmaceutical products sold to the NHS in order to encourage them to pursue inward investment in this country. David has been putting great pressure on me about this but, in all our discussions on pharmaceutical industry policy, I have refused to endorse his attitude to pricing, saying I wanted a special office meeting to consider the manifold aspects of this. (I remain convinced that, by helping the drug companies to expand the volume of their exports – as we certainly can – we can ask them in return to keep their prices down: not put them up.) And back from Joel has come a reply after my own heart, saying that the proposition that MSD International should be allowed to increase their profitability was not as simple as it looked and wanting to know a great deal more about what the company proposed. Bully for Joel!

The second is a letter from Crossland of Smith's Industries Ltd, the medical equipment people, thanking me for the party I gave them and for my 'most constructive and instructive talk' and promising they will get cracking on remedying the defects on servicing I had pointed out. This confirms my unshakeable belief that I have been a good Minister. The number of initiatives that David, Brian and I have to our credit in this department is legion. My great contribution has been to see where the gaps in policy are and to insist on taking the obvious steps to remedy them. I am sure the department thought I was mad to hold that drinks party for the medical equipment people. They were wrong and I was right.

Sunday, 4 April

The Sunday papers are full of the inevitability of Jim's victory and how he is spending the weekend preparing a major reshuffle of the Cabinet. So tomorrow evening I may be out of a job. I am quite indifferent. The advantages of being asked to carry on for a while would be that the press would be made to look silly again and it would be quite clear that I hadn't just been Harold's old retainer. Also I would have the fun of fighting my Bill through the House. The disadvantages would be that I would face a hectic week in the House: a late debate on Tuesday on occupational pensions; a statement on the pensions uprating on Wednesday following the Chancellor's Budget statement and a major speech in the Budget debate (since I gather that the Opposition is likely to choose this as one of their subjects during the week). Lance Errington and co. are fighting magnificently on my behalf to get the Chancellor to spell out in his Budget statement the fact that we have switched from the historical to the forecasting method instead of leaving the dirty work to me. I can leave it to them to do the in-fighting.

I have at least got the Chancellor to agree that I shall announce the details of the improvements we have obtained from him in short-term benefits. I feel a deep obligation to my poor Brian in all this. He is still unconscious after his operation. David tells me that this is not unusual after major brain surgery, but none of us will be at peace until he comes round and we know that the prognosis is okay. Until that happens he is obviously critically ill. I am still not allowed to see him. I talk on the phone to Kate from time to time but she won't leave his bedside and come and have a meal with me, though I am sure it would do her good to pour out her heart to someone at greater length than she can do on the phone. Joel and I do a piece of joint mourning every time we meet. I miss Brian so: keep looking towards the corner table in the Members' dining room where he and I used to have so many good plotting meals – either alone or with Joel and Bob. 'I've never known a more popular person in this House,' Joel keeps saying to me, shaking his head. I only know that I have fought Brian over a number of issues. He is instinctively a bit of a male chauvinist pig; he opposed the Supplementary Benefit Commission under David Donnison being given a new role and was against reforms of the cohabitation rule,[1] etc., etc. But I love him dearly and have a natural chemical affinity with him over so many aspects of social and economic policy. He has been the real architect of the new pensions scheme. All I have done is to inject certain refinements into it and have defended and fought it through Cabinet. I cannot bear the thought that, in my retirement, I shall not be able to watch his progress and do anything I can to promote it.

This morbid train of thought has been fed by my streaming cold. I felt so ill I just had to go to bed, where I slept hour upon hour. Ted got quite worried at my low state and I made up my mind to grab some more antibiotics the moment I got back to London. I can't get through this heavy week until at least my streaming eyes clear up. Things aren't made any better by the fact that Denis has turned me down over my plea that he should advance the next uprating date. Moreover he is wriggling about our demand that in his Budget speech he ought to make it clear that we are switching methods of calculating the pension – and why. He clearly intends to leave that to me. Trust a man to pass the buck to a woman!

Monday, 5 April

With my sinusitis slightly more under control I was able to face the Budget Cabinet, despite the crowds and cameras outside No. 10. It was embarrassing to know how to greet Jim C., who we all know will soon be PM. How to avoid being ingratiating without actually seeming rude? Well, Mike managed it successfully when we came to comment on Denis's Budget proposals, which Denis took nearly fifty minutes to spell out to us. He told us he had to have a neutral Budget which put all the emphasis on the need to improve industrial performance. So that meant balancing tax concessions with tax increases. He had a dig at Harold (Wilson) when he said that he was going to exclude pipe tobacco from the tobacco price increases: 'Retired people smoke pipes and may find themselves in reduced circumstances. So, as a farewell present to you, Harold, I am not increasing pipe tobacco.' We all laughed and Harold chuckled through a wreath of pipe smoke: 'You're not going to say *that* in your speech.' 'I certainly am,' retorted Denis.

Denis said his target was 5 per cent to 7 per cent inflation by the end of 1977, but

[1] The rule whereby an unmarried couple who cohabited could be treated as man and wife for supplementary benefit purposes, thus depriving the woman of entitlement to benefit in her own right. I had been urging that the rule should be relaxed.

that meant that wage increases must not exceed 3 per cent. So he had worked out a scheme for conditional reductions in direct taxation which would depend on this figure being achieved. Harold praised the Budget as 'ingenious and well-directed'. I, too, thought it was pretty ingenious. It was Mike who sounded a cautious note. It was very unlikely, he said, that we should get wage increases limited to 3 per cent, which meant a mere £2 a week. Above all it was essential to get a figure the TUC would recommend and we shouldn't jeopardize getting agreement, even if the figure eventually was a bit above that. Jim was stern. We must 'fight like hell' for the 3 per cent. It was essential that we got it at all costs, otherwise we should be in the economic soup. Mike wasn't having this. Unawed by Jim's imminent new status, he came back doggedly: 'I don't think that is the way to do it. What we have got to fight like hell for is agreement with the trade unions and what they are prepared to recommend.' Jim immediately became a bit more emollient: 'I am not trying to teach Michael how to put it to the TUC,' he said. But he insisted that if we failed to get 3 per cent we should be in grave trouble.

In this, Jim was backed by Roy, Shirley, Harold Lever and co., Roy adding that he was worried about the Chancellor's reference to the depreciation of sterling having made us more competitive. 'I do hope we are not going down any further,' he said. Denis retorted that unless we maintained our competitiveness in this way, the only alternative was import controls. I sensed that the lining up on each side of the argument was already taking place. There is no doubt that a victory by Jim will strengthen and embolden the Right in the Cabinet and I foresee trouble ahead as soon as the courtesies of the contest are over. My heart is low in my boots, partly because I don't like the feel of a government led by J.C. and fear the worst for the party. But my greatest sadness is over Brian O'Malley, about whom the news is now pretty disastrous. John Silkin passed me a note saying that his condition was deteriorating rapidly. This whole sudden tragedy is too horrible to believe. I was near to tears.

Back at the office we went through the routine of work, though everyone is obviously wondering whether we will all be there tomorrow, while Brian's condition cast a deep gloom. David was obviously as deeply moved as I was. Somehow I managed to polish up my putative statement on the benefits uprating and my notes for tomorrow night's speech on occupational pensions. By 4pm sharp we Labour MPs were all crowded into No. 14 committee room for the leadership election result, with the press massed outside. There it was at last: the predicted victory for Jim, only sadly Mike had done slightly less well than we had hoped: 139 votes to Jim's 176. There then followed an orgy of speeches. Jim's was quite fluent (though he had prepared it, he admitted, over the weekend and he read it out). Significantly Jim remarked: 'I shall be making changes and asking some of my colleagues who are doing a compe-tent job to make way for younger ones.' 'He can't mean you, Barbara,' audibly remarked Dennis Skinner, who has become quite a fan of mine. Harold's speech was almost a casual throw away. Then came Mike's turn. He stood up without a note, soon had everyone laughing and yet injected a note of political seriousness without a cliché or a touch of pretentiousness. I thought as I listened what a joy it was to have a touch of quality brought back into our political dialogue. Mike is the only one to give it to us since Nye died. I believe this country is hungry for a bit of political spontaneity. Anyway Mike got even warmer applause than Jim. Harold got the biggest reception of all, with a standing ovation. I think everyone in the room realized that in his own funny way he had been a big man.

As we broke up to leave the room, Mike whispered to me: 'I want a word with you.' When I went to his room I found about a dozen of us there. Mike was quietly and authoritatively in command. He told us he had been to see Jim that morning and said to him that he thought he, Jim, would win. But he wanted to warn him that he should be very careful in the changes he made. ('Mike won't let Jim be nasty to you,' whispered Jill [Foot], who was sitting on the sofa next to me.) I felt warmed and comforted by the comradeship of that room after the cold winds of exclusion that had been blowing around me. Suddenly I realized I desperately wanted to stay in the Government: that my elaborate assumption of indifference was merely my rationalization of what I felt inside me was necessity – like steeling myself to face the hostility of the doctors. As we broke up to go Mike said to me: 'I must make a phone call. Then I want to talk to you. I'll come to your room.' I sat waiting with a new hope that I might be safe.

Mike came in with a slightly harassed air. He had talked to Jim about me that morning, saying I mustn't be moved, and Jim had said he had been told I wanted to go anyway. Was that true? So Harold had betrayed my confidence! I explained to Mike what I had said to Harold about a month ago, but stressed that I had always made it clear that I wanted to stay until I had got my Bill through and that I wanted to go with dignity, not just be sloughed off in a mass reshuffle. 'They owe me that.' Mike said he was having another talk with Jim tomorrow and would rub this in. I wasn't to worry: Jim hadn't indicated that he was going to drop me. 'Did you try to stop Jenkins becoming Foreign Secretary?' I asked. 'Yes,' said Mike, 'I told Jim it wouldn't be received at all well.' I settled down to a night's work on my boxes, took my penicillin and went to bed, gloomy at heart about the political future that faces the party now.

Tuesday, 6 April

I had a long exhausted sleep and woke up feeling rather ill. Obviously penicillin doesn't suit me after all. I dare not take any more. As I was finishing my bath the phone bell rang. It was the Press Association. Was I aware that Mr O' Malley had died at 6am that morning? 'Oh, no. . . .' Would I care to dictate a tribute to him? 'Oh, yes . . .' The words poured out of me: his brilliance, the memorial to him in the new pensions scheme and, not least, his personality. 'He was one of the nicest people I have ever met.' I had to go to an early meeting of Legislation Committee to get my pay beds Bill cleared but I was haunted by the need to see Kate [O'Malley]. I rang Norman and asked him to try to find out where she was.

At Legislation Committee there were a few snags on the text of the Bill itself, but there came a nasty moment when Bob tried to create difficulties. 'The Secretary of

State had to report to Cabinet on the result of her latest talks with the profession on licensing,' he insisted. I blessed Ted Short for one of his bursts of no-nonsense radicalism. 'Barbara circulated a letter at the weekend and any member of Cabinet had the right to comment if they wished to,' he said. 'No one did.' Bob subsided, obviously having failed to read his documents. So everything went through. I then passed Ted a note saying that I hoped he would excuse me if I did not stay for the Devolution Committee meeting as I wanted to try and contact Brian's widow. Ted interrupted the proceedings at once to say that he was sure they would all excuse me and ask me to pass their condolences to Mrs O'Malley. There were murmurs of approval and I slipped out thankfully.

My faithful Edna was waiting and rushed me to the House. Norman, bless him, had tracked down Kate at the hospital, where I gathered she would be glad to see me, and said he was coming over to accompany me. That lad has a genius for knowing the moment to bring me the sustenance of his company. We sped to the Nervous Diseases Hospital in Bloomsbury – no time to warn anybody, thank God, that the Secretary of State was on her way. I am not normally morbid about hospitals, but as we walked through the corridors and up the lift to Brian's floor I said to myself: 'There is a smell of death in the air.' My own head was muzzy; there seemed to be intolerable pressures on my brain. Why shouldn't my membrane split suddenly, too, or anyone else's for that matter? I was haunted by man's physical frailty – the thin line that stands between him and death, the line that should have held for Brian and which proved too thin. 'I'll wait outside till you need me,' murmured Norman as we knocked on Kate's door. She stood there, thin and distraught after nine days of hell, then fell on to my shoulder and sobbed bitterly. The young Elizabeth stood there, prettier than I remembered her, so like Brian it was almost unbearable.

Eventually we got down to discussing the funeral. Kate said it would be next Tuesday in Rotherham. 'May I come?' I asked hesitantly. Her face lit up. 'Oh, would you?' It was clear that the one thing she wanted for Brian was full parliamentary honours, because she knew that Parliament had been his life. Elizabeth comforted her with that uncanny maturity which had struck me when last year I attended Brian's party's annual dinner and visited their home. 'You must make your mother eat,' I admonished her. 'Brian loved good food. He has stood me more good dinners than I can count. He would want you to eat something good now. What about smoked salmon?' Elizabeth wriggled with delight at the very thought. 'The hospital food hasn't been very nice,' she said.

So when at last we left the hospital, I told Norman we must find some smoked salmon at any cost. He rang up Pat [Folger] on the car telephone to ask her if she knew anywhere we could get it in Bloomsbury. She was a broken reed. 'Things aren't what they were in the Civil Service,' said Norman, putting down the phone. 'Civil servants don't lunch off smoked salmon any more.' 'Right,' I said, 'then it's Fortnum and Mason's.' At the delicatessen counter I filled a basket of goodies. Edna said she would be only too delighted to take them to the hospital. It was for all three of us as though a member of our own family had died.

After such an emotional morning the Budget speech, over two hours long, seemed an anti-climax. I certainly wasn't going to sit through all of it and went up to my room to work through the first hour. Wedgie also absented himself, saying audibly that the first hour of any Chancellor's economic analysis ought to be written into the record as they do in America. I slipped back on to the front bench in time to hear Denis deal with social security. All my officials' valiant efforts to make him stand up and be counted on the change from the historical to the forecasting method for the pensions uprating have failed. He skimmed over it and so got a cheer from our side for the amount of the increase, whose relevance they did not understand. Once again I thought how ironical it was that Brian, who reluctantly accepted the change under my pressure in order to save the budget of the NHS, should be safely out of the way before the political bill – which I shall have to pay tomorrow, Jim willing – has to be paid. I remain convinced that my ploy was right: I shall sit back and watch Jack Jones and co. fight for even more for the pensioners. There is no similar lobby, alas, for the NHS. I also remain convinced that Denis's offer of tax cuts *v.* pay restraint will prove popular, though many of my Cabinet colleagues are nervous about it. I also happen to think it makes sense, though I wouldn't have put it so much in the form of an ultimatum as he seemed to do.

Earlier I had seen David Donnison about his desire to publish his current tables about the real value of the supplementary benefit increases. As it happens, the present figures are favourable to us, but I still think we should publish them, even when the indicators are less our way. Unless we tell people the truth I don't think there is a hope of survival for democracy.

Ran into Dennis Skinner who said to me: 'If they sack you, it won't be because of your age, but because of your pay beds policy.' Nice to have the backing of the Left again.

I dodged the PLP meeting on the Budget in order to prepare for the debate on the occupational pensions schemes regulations for which the Opposition have asked. I wanted to take this anyway, once Brian fell ill, in order to dispel any suggestion that I can't handle the technical intricacies of the pensions scheme. But as things have turned out I was very glad to have the opportunity of dealing with this tonight, so as to pay my first parliamentary tribute to Brian. The pensions officials from the department turned up for a briefing meeting and, emotionally drained as I was, I had to force myself to master all the esoteric details of the regulations. Eventually I was satisfied and Gerald [Johnson] and I sat down to wait for 10pm. I say 'sat', but all I wanted to do was to wander restlessly about the room, trying to come to terms with the horror of Brian's death. 'What I need,' I said to Gerald, who watched sympathetically, 'is a good howl, but I haven't got a shoulder to howl on when I get home.' Ted *would* be in Brussels this week of all weeks.

I got through the debate pretty well, all things considered, though my voice nearly broke when I paid my tribute to Brian. The Tories were obviously as shocked as we were and their tributes came pouring out of them. I took the wind out of Kenneth Clarke's sails when I told him I had met the pensions industry last week to discuss pay policy – the very thing he was obviously intending to lecture me for not doing. By 11pm it was all over. My officials were very pleased with me and it gave me a bit of inner warmth with which to return to our empty flat and my sad thoughts. For myself,

I felt I had proved myself to be a real old trouper: the show had gone on under impossible circumstances.

Wednesday, 7 April

Up early for a hair-do. I have to make my uprating statement today and hold a press conference and I don't intend to *look* ill at this particular moment, however ill I feel. My stomach has gone back on me and I am fighting a wretched sense of nausea. I cannot shake off my feeling of shellshock: in the literal sense the end of an era, with Harold suddenly pulling the rug from under everyone's feet; the election of an alien right-winger as leader of a party that I was beginning to think might go somewhere exciting; then Brian's death. At the office David was as downcast as I was. He said he wanted to come to Brian's funeral but, as parliamentary business stood next week, he would be tied to the House by a debate on the Children's and Young Persons Act. Would I write to the Chief Whip and try and get it postponed? Of course I agreed. He was also gloomy about the outcome of the leadership election, though he kept repeating 'They won't move you', whether to reassure himself or me I was not clear.

I held an office meeting on the child benefit rate: officials reported that the Treasury might try to lure us to accept the low rate of £2.50 with the bait of a 50 pence premium for one-parent and larger families. After discussion I agreed with Brian Abel-Smith, despite Tony Lynes's pleas for a special rate for large families, that we should resist this and go for the highest possible rate for everyone as the base on which we could build other things eventually. Brian's steady, informed and perceptive help is a tower of strength. I then struggled through my nausea to master the intricacies of the detail of the uprating, conscious that I faced a difficult time in the House over the switch to the forecasting method, on which there has already been considerable comment in the press.

As I stood up to make my statement I noticed that Jim had slipped into his place next to me and wondered vaguely why. But I wasn't concerned about him, but once again about Brian, to whom I was determined to pay an official tribute in a full House. The words I had drafted were received with great murmurs of approval. I then read the rest of the statement in a firm voice. Patrick Jenkin moved in at once to attack Denis for not having had the courage yesterday to accept responsibility for the change to forecasting: I handled him easily. It was more difficult dealing with our own side, but when I answered one question from George Cunningham rather well, Jim murmured, 'a very good answer'. Afterwards, he said to me: 'Well done, Barbara. There are an enormous number of figures to remember, aren't there?' If, I thought to myself, he came along to see whether I can still perform effectively in the House, I have nothing to fear.

My press conference also went swimmingly. I took the issue of the change of method head-on in my opening remarks and didn't get a murmur from anyone. In the TV interviews afterwards I got the inevitable question: did I think I would survive? 'I never answer hypothetical questions,' I replied loftily, which tickled Peter pink. 'I've never heard a less hypothetical question in my whole life,' he said. 'Anyway, it nonplussed them,' I replied, unabashed. The result of this successful warding off was, of course, that not a word of my interviews was used.

The Tories are genuinely shocked at Brian's death. Paul Dean came up to me to plead that there should be a memorial service – so many of them wanted to come.

Back to the office to discuss private practice. I am amused at the reply we have had from Dr Gullick to my letter setting out pretty detailed replies to the points the BMA have raised about the contents of the Bill. My letter has clearly half appeased and half foxed them, but Gullick has risen, as I thought he would, to my carefully injected phrases about the 'detailed negotiations' we had had over the Goodman proposals, and has insisted that there had been no 'negotiations'. However, he concluded with 'best wishes', so perhaps we progress. More important was a letter from Grey-Turner [deputy Secretary of the BMA] about the Schedule to the Bill, first complaining once again that Northern Ireland beds were not included in the figure of 1,000 beds in the Schedule and secondly asking me to reconsider the position. That, of course, I am not prepared to do. But Tim Nodder reported on the outcome of the consultations through AHAs on the contents of the Schedule and also the comments of the IHG. His suggestion was that the two were so much on the same lines I might wish tactically to adopt the IHG comments holus-bolus and thus give myself the virtue of having been eminently reasonable towards their suggestions. I could see what the dear lad had in mind, but that shrewd old operator Raymond Gedling had his doubts and so did I. I said that we should take the AHA suggestions on their merits, which would give us part of the IHG pattern of distribution of phasing out, but would not merely underwrite it. Raymond nodded approvingly.

We also had some anxious words on the way the new overtime payments for juniors are working out. There is no doubt that the new system is costing AHAS hundreds of thousands of uncovenanted pounds. The reason is that the ratio of A units (those for stand-by duty in hospitals) to B units (those for on call at home) has turned out to be nearer to 95:5 than the 50:50 that the Review Body estimated. Raymond was at pains to point out to me that the estimate was *not* the department's. It was just that the DDRB had got it wrong. Not that any of us expect the press will make this clear. Raymond wanted to know whether he should raise this with the DDRB. David and I agreed that this would be suicidal: Wasily Sakalo *et al.* would be on the warpath immediately, saying we were wrecking the agreement that had been reached. In any case we believe there is a good deal of public sympathy for the juniors, which we share. So we told Raymond to lie low. The real answer, I said, was first, to get AHAS to accept their management responsibilities by explaining to consultants (who are suspected of being in cahoots with the juniors in inflating some of the returns) that the agreement was not expected to cost extra money and that none would be made available. So that money which went on these overtime payments would not be available for other things, such as more equipment of the kind the consultants want. Secondly, we must improve the career structure in the NHS. We must, I said, work for the introduction of a new grade between the juniors and the consultants, a sort of sub-consultants' grade which would not have overtime payments attached to it. And we must above all things fight any attempt to reopen the consultants' contract argument, which the BMA is now trying to do, no doubt with the aim of introducing overtime payments for consultants as well.

Norman and I have taken another precautionary step. In case the worst happens I want, if I can, to sew up the chairmanship of the independent board which will phase out pay beds. So I've sent Jim Callaghan a letter suggesting three names of legal luminaries Jack has drawn up for me and who, he assures me, could be relied on to interpret the legislation progressively. We don't want any High Court judge!

Thursday, 8 April

I woke slightly refreshed. The nausea had abated a bit and with my greater clarity of mind I began to wonder just what Jim was up to. The Cabinet agenda this morning consists merely of parliamentary business and foreign affairs so Cabinet isn't till 11am. That should at least give me a bit of time to fill some gaps in my diary. (Must continue to do some contingency planning!) Jim having shown no signs of a reshuffle, I said to myself that I am going to participate in a Callaghan Cabinet meeting after all and shall be able to compare his and Harold's style. But the papers still continue to refer to coming changes: the eight o'clock news and *Today* talk of Jim wanting his changes completed by Friday, when he is due in Cardiff. So where do we all stand?

I suddenly decide to ring Mike and I catch him just as he is going out. 'What the hell does Jim think he is playing at?' I ask. 'Some of us have policy matters to settle urgently and don't know where we are. I, for instance, have to introduce the pay beds Bill on Monday. Or have I?' Mike was as earnestly reasonable as always. He thought it was only right that Jim should have time to consult people and he himself was going to see him again at 10am that morning. He would tell him again that it was wrong to say I wanted to retire now and that I ought to be given time to complete my pay beds legislation. I told Mike I didn't want him to just fight *my* battles. What mattered was the political balance in Cabinet. 'Look,' said Mike, 'Cabinet shouldn't last very long. Let's meet in your room in the House afterwards.' So I bathed, climbed into a dressing gown and sat down in our cramped little dining room, swamped with papers, to type my diary.

Nine-thirty am Pat phoned from the office to say Cabinet was cancelled. Good, I thought at first, more time to do diary. Then I realized the significance of that remark and typed all the more frantically. Ten am Pat phoned again. The PM wanted to see me at 10.30am. 'But Edna hasn't arrived yet,' I wailed. 'Tell him I'll be late.' There ensued one of my frantic attempts to get myself dressed and made up to the degree necessary to face what I knew would be a battery of cameras. But I was still calm. I did not believe Jim would sack me. I didn't deserve that.

Edna and I tore out of the flat with me having to put my lipstick on in the car. (It reminded me of the real wartime blitz when I always used to put on lipstick every time the sirens went.) Yes, there were the cameras outside No. 10 in a solid phalanx and a small crowd of onlookers. I was thankful I had had my hair done yesterday and waved jauntily as I got out of the car. The press, hemmed in behind crash barriers, called out: 'Look this way, Mrs Castle.' I sailed into No. 10. Inside I got a curious message from the policemen. 'The duty secretary has told us to tell him when Mrs Castle has arrived and not to let her past here till he knows.' I paused a moment, puzzled, then walked defiantly through to the outer lobby of the Cabinet room, with them bleating ineffectually behind me. The appropriate private secretary rushed out and said: 'Please come upstairs, Mrs Castle.' (Not Secretary of State, I noted.) Out of the corner of my eye I saw Shirley perched on the window-sill near the lobby telephone from which I have so often phoned my office. She just looked at me blankly. I was hurried upstairs to the lobby outside the PM's study. One thing struck me as curious: the display cabinets which surround the walls and which are normally filled with the treasures of a Prime Minister's period of office were all empty. It looked as though the bailiffs had moved in. When I got upstairs I was, to my surprise, guided into one of the drawing rooms: the very one in which I had worked out the minutiae of the *In Place of Strife* argument – and many other industrial battles of the 1966–70 Wilson era. Nigel Wicks [assistant Private Secretary at No. 10] appeared, solicitous. 'I'm afraid we are running late, Secretary of State. Would you like some coffee?' I said indeed I would. He disappeared to get some. As I sat in the drawing room I noticed that it was rather bare of ornaments, too. I feared the worst and said to myself wryly as I sat on the lavishly covered sofa and looked round at the damask-covered chairs and at the other elaborations of décor for which Ted Heath was responsible: 'They are burying me with satin.' But I still didn't believe that a Prime Minister could cut across a legislative programme in mid-session so crudely, so indifferently. If government is not about policies, what is it about?

A quarter of an hour later Nigel Wicks arrived to fetch me. 'Haven't you had your coffee yet?' he asked me anxiously. 'Don't worry,' I said lightly, 'I'll get it afterwards.' I swept into Jim's study, my head in the air. As I went I said to Wicks: 'What has happened to everything in the display cabinets?' 'Oh,' he replied, 'they were Harold's and he has taken them with him.' 'I bet they cost more than £30 each,' I said sweetly and he grinned. He knew the Prime Ministerial Minute I was referring to! Jim was sitting tense in the study, which struck me as being pretty bare of bric-à-brac, too. He waved me to a seat and said quickly: 'I don't want to soft soap you, Barbara. I must reduce the average age of Cabinet and I want to ask you for your portfolio.' I felt detached. 'Did someone tell you that I wanted to retire at Easter?' I asked. He shrugged. 'It was Harold,' I went on. He replied: 'Whoever it was, this isn't the reason.' I paused and then said: 'I never intended to hang on indefinitely. But I did see Harold about a month ago to tell him I wanted to see my pay beds Bill through Parliament. Then I would wish to retire – with dignity. You do realize that I am due to introduce that Bill on Monday?' He shrugged again and looked miserable. I continued: 'It is, of course, your right to ask for my portfolio. In fact, as I understand it, you have got it already. I received, as we all did, a letter from Harold saying that our portfolios were at the disposal of the incoming Prime Minister and that we should carry on meanwhile. So there is nothing I can do.' 'Do you want to go into the Lords?' said Jim. 'Good God, no,' I replied. 'Thank heavens,' said Jim (it would have meant a by-election), 'though I can't refuse it to you any time you ask for it.'

Another pause and I added: 'Who else is going?' 'Ted Short, Willie Ross and Bob Mellish,' said Jim. 'Not Fred?' I said ironically. 'Not yet,' said Jim. 'There will be other changes later.' 'May I ask who is to succeed me?' 'I can't say that,' said Jim wretchedly, 'because there are two people in it and I don't know yet which it will turn out to be.' Another pause, then Jim burst out: 'Harold said to me that the worst thing about this job would be the Parliamentary Questions. It isn't that: it is this.' 'Harold thought that, too,' I replied sweetly, 'that's why he didn't do it.' Another pause and Jim said with a semblance of briskness: 'So you will let me have a letter saying that you are putting your job at my disposal in order to make way for someone younger.' 'Oh, no,' I replied even more briskly. 'So you are going back on what you have just said,' replied Jim with a show of nastiness. 'Not at all,' I replied. 'What I have said is that I have no choice. But I am not doing this voluntarily. I want to stay to finish my legislation. And that is what I shall say in my letter to you. And I shall hold a press conference to spell this out. I shall go on to the Standing Committee on the Bill and shall defend it line by line.' 'Heaven help your successor,' he replied mournfully. 'Don't worry, Jim,' I said cheerfully, 'I shan't attack you personally, I shall just tell the truth. When will it be known?' 'The announcement will be made at 5pm and I must ask you not to tell anyone else meanwhile.' I told him that was nonsense: I was due back at my office to clear a paper on the rate of child benefit for Tuesday's Cabinet. He himself had commissioned it and it had to be cleared before noon. If I stopped that now, the cat would be out of the bag. After hesitating he said I had better go ahead with the paper and I could tell my Private Secretary, if he was reliable.

I got up to go and Jim held out his hand: 'Wish me well, Barbara.' I shook his hand and said: 'Good luck.' He said almost desperately: 'You should know that Mike has fought for you very hard. I had to tell him this was one thing I could not give him. Perhaps this is the first mistake I have made but, as Harold said to me, I must make my own mistakes.' I said nothing and Jim said to me impulsively: 'Will you let me do this?' and kissed me on the cheek. I said 'Cheerio' and walked out of the room. Outside the waiter was waiting with my tray of coffee. 'How kind of you,' I said, drank it and walked outside to the waiting cameras. 'Have you anything to say to us, Barbara?' asked one journalist pleadingly over the crash barrier. I waved airily and walked to my car. The crowd put up a cheer as I left and I waved to them. I couldn't even tell Edna, who was as anxious as I was to learn my, and therefore her, fate. I asked her to drive me to the House.[1]

In my room I rang Mike. He was just hurrying into the Standing Committee on the Dock Work Regulation Bill and I could forgive him for being *distrait*. He merely made clucking noises when I told him what had happened and we arranged to meet in my room at 3.30pm that afternoon. I couldn't help thinking of that night when Mike, Wedgie and I and all of us had moved in on Harold to tell him that if he sacked Judith he sacked us all. I suppose solidarity gets watered down a bit when one of the victims is sixty-five. Yet the thought stubbornly persists in me that this argument wears a bit thin when the new PM himself is sixty-four – and Mike is nearly sixty-three.

I then faced a dilemma: how to prepare my day's activities when I was not allowed to share my news? I was determined to have a farewell party at the office. I also had a

---

[1] Some months later I was chatting in the Commons to Merlyn Rees, one of Jim Callaghan's strongest backers, and he recalled how much Jim had hated dismissing me. 'He told me it spoilt his day,' he remarked apologetically. 'It spoilt my session,' I retorted.

letter to prepare to send to Jim. I scribbled a draft and hurried to the office to find a strained atmosphere of uncertainty and Jack and Brian Abel-Smith waiting nervously outside my room. I discovered that my devoted Norman, on whom I was relying to see me through this mess, had taken the day off to help his wife move house! Jack assured me that Norman had asked I should phone him if necessary, which I did. When I told him: 'I'm leaving,' Norman's voice almost broke. 'I really am terribly, terribly sorry.' He would hurry back to the office immediately and meet me at my room at the House. I gave Jack and Brian my draft reply to brood over and arranged to meet them all later, telling them that what really worried me was what would happen to them. Their treatment is even more brutal than mine. I then went into the Members' dining room for lunch (not that I felt like any) and sat deliberately at my usual place at the collective table. I found Mervyn, Joel, Jimmie Dunn, Bob and others discussing Brian O'Malley's funeral. They wanted to attend it and I had to sit coolly play-acting while Joel pleaded with me to try and postpone our joint paper on child benefit which is due to come before Cabinet on Tuesday. I solemnly said I would try to see if it could be done. Joel clearly had no idea that he and I would not ever again be presenting joint papers to Cabinet.

I found a saddened Norman waiting for me when I got up to my room. Yet it isn't my room any more: within a few hours' time it will be my successor's. I shall be as homeless and powerless as the next. What interests me is the stubbornness of my sense of power and authority. When we lost the last election I never had this rooted belief that I was part of government. I lapsed into obscurity, almost with a sense of thankfulness. Now I find it inconceivable that I shall not be at Tuesday's Cabinet; not fighting for a proper rate of child benefit; not introducing the pay beds Bill on Monday; not coping with the new problem of the juniors; not conducting our discussions on the consultative document on health priorities; not fighting for the proper treatment of pensions in the next round of pay policy. Authority is ingrained in me in a new way and I just don't believe anyone can discharge it better in DHSS. An unaccustomed self-assurance. And a deep sense of nostalgia. As I paced round the room I said to Norman wryly: 'I always knew I should not live to see the redecoration of this room complete.' (I had been planning it for some time.) I looked out of the window at the still half-finished landscaping of New Palace Yard. 'This view will be worth having soon.' Norman said stoutly: 'Think of all you have achieved. You have crammed five years' work into two.' But I wasn't comforted. My own governmental death stirred up again my deep sense of tragedy over Brian: how ironical that it should be I who had lost my job and he who had died before he could inherit it! Yet I wondered very much whether Jim would have had the generosity and political flair to put Brian in the Cabinet. (Jim had refused to pay the tribute to Brian in the House: something I would have done if I had been PM.) I thanked Norman for all he had done for me and said I'd told Patrick Nairne he was outstandingly the best Private Secretary I had ever had.

Jack and Brian arrived with some emollient additions to my letter to the PM. Norman hurried off to get it typed and to arrange a farewell drinks party at the office for 5pm. I sat down in some confusion, wondering where I should put all my papers: I haven't even a desk allocated to me as a backbencher and I am under instructions from Jim not to breathe a word to anyone before 5pm. Just before that hour I broke the news to Edna and Janet. They had sensed something and were deep in gloom. Jack phoned to say that Mike was to become Leader of the House. He would like to work for him. Could I put in a word for him? I said of course. He also said my successor was to be David Ennals. I was shocked. None of us trust him since his Common Market switch. But I scribbled a note of congratulations to him in order to put in a word for my special advisers, suggesting he might consider keeping them on. Jack's desire not to go back to the Bar is interesting: it shows that, like me, he is a politician to his finger tips. He is a great lad. He has been invaluable.

Mike came into my room, sorry but not desolate. He said he had tried very hard to get Jim to change his mind about me, but without success. There was nothing more he could have done, short of threatening to resign. 'Perhaps I should have done that.' I didn't reproach him, but I had a profound sense that the Left has been weakened in this new Cabinet. We wouldn't have let Harold get away with this! Clearly Mike had been preoccupied with three things: first to get the leadership of the House himself; secondly, to stop Jenkins getting the Foreign Secretaryship; thirdly, to get Albert Booth as his own successor at Employment. He obviously thought that a score of three out of four was satisfactory. Perhaps he felt that the falling off in his vote in the last ballot had weakened his position. And he said worriedly that Tony Benn was furious with him, because he thought, if Mike was going to move, *he* should have been given Employment (which he obviously thinks is a much better political base than Energy). I told Mike about Jack's wish to become his political adviser. Had he got one? He said no, looking apprehensive at the whole idea. I told him Jack had specialized on the devolution issue for me and knew all the details. Moreover as a barrister he would be of particular use on constitutional and legal matters. Mike pricked up his ears on this: I can't see him enjoying the details of the devolution side of his remit! He said he would think about it and hurried off like the White Rabbit, nervously looking at his watch.

Ted phoned from Brussels to commiserate with me about Brian's death. I broke my own shock news to him. He burst out with violent expletives about 'that ... Jim Callaghan'. He told me not to worry about transport at the weekend. We'd cope somehow. He wished more than ever that he was at home with me. So did I.

Although a number of civil servants were at Sunningdale for a conference, they all hurried back for my farewell party: except Henry, from whom not a peep. First into my room was David Owen, who was visibly moved. He kissed me affectionately and sadly on the cheek. I have never felt closer to him. Michael Meacher was outraged. My officials filed in to tell me how much they would miss me, even Charles Regan assuring me it had been 'very stimulating'. As for my dear old Tony Crocker he said: 'I can tell you now what I have always said about you: "She's not only a very good Minister, she's a honey."' (I wish civil servants could talk to the press!) Patrick Nairne was, I think, genuinely sad. I took him aside to thank him for the unswerving loyalty he had always shown to me, at which he protested that it was he who should thank me. 'You are so young,' he said. David Donnison was there, too, to my surprise and pleasure and warmed me with his thanks and praise. Brian Abel-Smith said it had been such 'fun' – I gathered he had himself already written to David offering his services. Jack was utterly dejected. I had insisted on the entire Private Office being invited, as well as Stan, the messenger, and Edna. The youngsters from the outer office were inconsolable. They produced a bunch of flowers ('all we could get in the time') and a good luck card and said that life would never be the same again: 'even tho' there will be less work to do'. I began to feel near to tears.

David then interrupted the proceedings to give us the latest list of appointments which he had had monitored on his office radio. Stan Orme to be the new Minister of State at DHSS; Peter to Environment, etc. And he then went straight on to make a little speech about what a remarkable Minister I had been; what I had achieved; how good I was to work with; how well I had delegated, etc., concluding with his conviction that, on the pay beds issue, we had produced a solution that would stick. I was so moved by his warmth I thought I was going to blub.

Swallowing hard I made my valedictory speech, warning David that he had dangerously softened my stiff upper lip. I then thanked each group in turn: my remarkable Ministerial team, my political advisers ('I think you know you could not manage without them now'), Patrick Nairne, my officials, my Private Office. 'What I shall miss most is the comradeship – and I am not talking in some sinister Marxist sense.' It was the comradeship of battle in which we all pulled and plotted together for victory. I told them I had never accepted the conventional criticisms of civil servants. It was their duty to tell the Minister frankly the dangers and snags they saw in her policy: 'It is far better that they should be voiced and faced in this room than for the Minister to encounter them for the first time at the dispatch box or in the press.' We needed strong civil servants and a strong Minister to digest their advice and make what use of it she thought fit. The words poured out of me though I hadn't prepared anything. Patrick then insisted on saying a few words. 'The sight of you sitting at the top of that table and pulling out your pen to draft something before our eyes is an object lesson none of us will forget.' At last we broke up. David was in a savagely depressed mood. 'I don't want to stay here. I want to get out. This has been a marvellous two years. I don't suppose I shall ever again be so happy in a ministerial job.'

Earlier Norman had said to me unhappily: 'I do hope you will forgive me if I slip away from the party: David Ennals wants to see me.' I said of course. His new master must come first. But I realized later amid the confusion that Norman had come back again. He was quietly organizing the collection of all my personal papers and anything else he could do to help. He whipped my Persian picture off the wall, saying firmly: 'You're taking *that*.' 'Well,' I replied, 'if the PM can take his treasures, so can I.' I recorded an interview for the *Today* programme, turned down requests for TV (I must have been looking pretty tear-stained by now), and got Norman to cancel my dinner with Geoffrey Smith of *The Times*. All I wanted to do was to go to cover till I had collected myself but, alas, I was due to catch the night sleeper to Blackburn. Suddenly I realized that technically I had no transport any more. Edna ceased to be mine from that moment on. But Norman wasn't having any of that nonsense. He said he would square it with the government garage that she was to take me to the train (just as, on Tuesday, he had fought and won a battle with them to get Brian's driver to drive Mrs O'Malley and Elizabeth back to Rotherham). I shook hands with Gerald and Pat. Then Norman escorted me to the car for the last time. As he helped me in he leant forward impulsively and kissed me on the cheek. At that I really did nearly howl! A downcast Edna drove me to the flat and cooked us bacon and egg while I tried to collect my wits and my things.

The phone went endlessly: the press wanting interviews; family and friends who had just heard the news. One call particularly interested me: from Janet and David Hill, who said they were just having a 'wake' with a number of their political friends. My sacking and the new appointments had shocked them all: I must go on to the backbenches and fight this reactionary new Prime Minister. It then transpired that Roy Hattersley, to whom David Hill remains curiously loyal, was furious at having been passed over in favour of David Ennals. I guess Jim will make as many enemies among those he doesn't promote as among those he sacks! All of this took so much time, and I was so *distrait*, that I nearly missed my train. Then I read for a long time before I tried to sleep.

Friday, 9 April

It was a hectic day I faced in Blackburn and it would have been a strain at the best of times. As it was, I knew it would require all my famous reserves of energy to get through the pressures and press queries. One lass from the *Evening Standard* even booked herself into the sleeper next to mine in the hope of getting an interview. I gave it her in the morning in the car from the station, out of compassion and because she was very sweet. My reward was that she left all the morning papers with me; no great comfort for me in any of them and a typically nasty piece in the *Daily Mail*.

Breakfast over, my first concern was to go and have a comb-out. (The Castle motto throughout the ages: 'When the sirens sound, make sure you look your best.') I could then face with aplomb the cameras that materialized from nowhere. Finally I had to succumb to insistent requests and agree to interrupt my lunch with the North-West Tourist Board to give interviews on Granada and BBC. (Mercifully I managed not to look as exhausted as I felt.) Once again I realized that perhaps my greatest asset in life has been my stamina: I ought to have been dead! It was curiously natural and comforting to slip back into ordinary constituency work: to talk to the shop stewards of the British Aircraft Corporation at Samlesbury and have them say worriedly that they didn't like my being sacked but hoped I would be active on the backbenches; to go and see old people about their electricity bills and to promise to take up their problem with the chairman of the SBC(!); to have my local party at our evening meeting express their anger at my treatment and their delight that I had said I wanted to remain a commoner.

The most unnerving moment of the whole day came when I returned to the party offices after lunch for constituency interviews and found waiting for me in the hall Mrs Green, general secretary of the National Federation of Old Age Pensioners' Associations, and her deputy, holding a magnificent bouquet. They thrust it into my hands saying that it was an expression of gratitude for all I had done for the pensioners – and they are a couple of Tories too! That really undid me: the ice melted and the tears came. To hell with Jim Callaghan's ingratitude. 'That is quite the nicest thing that has happened to me,' I told them through my tears. 'We hoped you'd feel that,' they beamed and hurried away.

Saturday, 10 April

It was a brilliantly sunny morning and Tom Wood came to drive me to Lancaster. I have been wanting for a long time to go and see Mother's friend, poor old Clarice Hiley, who, at eighty-two, has been knocked down by a car and has been in hospital for months. When I finally decided I would stay in Blackburn overnight and go this morning, Pat had said: 'We shall have to inform them you are coming, Secretary of State.' In the event, no need! So I arrived unannounced but the news went round the hospital like wildfire and soon the secretary of the hospital was hurrying in to pay his respects; the men in the next ward were clamouring to see me and sister was offering me some lunch. I knew I still felt their Secretary of State – and that they felt it too. I spent a happy hour with Clarice and then went in to say hello to the men's ward. They were tickled pink. One of them said, 'Very glad indeed to meet you, Mrs Castle, though mind you, I've felt like giving you one sometimes.' 'Not now,' I replied, giving him one of my best smiles and holding out my hand. 'Not now I've met you,' he replied, grasping it. Human relations are a funny thing. I've always thought that three-quarters of aggression is theoretical: it is anger against the *idea* one has of a person, not the person himself.

Sunday, 11 April

Back to the consolations of HCF and Ted's company. The *Sunday Mirror* has been nice to me this morning: it makes a change. I remain strangely stirred to my very depths by a sense of finality and nostalgia. And I am deeply hurt by Jim's cavalier discarding of me like so much old junk. I know – and have always known – that I am one of the best Ministers in this Government: and certainly the toughest fighter for our party's policies. And I am at the peak of my powers. To turn me out for *Ennals* – really! I wouldn't have minded if my going had led to some real rejuvenation of the Government – if, for instance, Jim had brought Judith Hart back. (Incidentally it shows how superficial is our party's devotion to the cause of promoting women that Jim could so complacently reduce the number of women in his Cabinet.) If Shirley had gone to my job, I could have understood it, too – though on second thoughts I realize she couldn't have taken it, because she disagrees with my policy on pay beds. One of Norman's last little pieces of mischief just before I left had been to suggest to me that I ask Harold Lever and Shirley Williams to be among the sponsors of my pay beds Bill. I duly did so. They both refused, Harold in a letter of nauseating hypocrisy. Ted is still rumbling with anger over Jim's action. It is a great comfort to have him back and we talk long and tenderly. He tells me that Bob Mitchell was boasting at Strasbourg when the news of the changes came through that 'we' (i.e. the Right) had told Jim Callaghan that they would not tolerate any attempt to get rid of Reg Prentice. So the Right was strong enough to save that anti-party man while the Left was not strong enough to save me. It is this wider significance of my going that is so disturbing.

Phone call from Eric Heffer to say how outraged he was at my sacking. We had had our disagreements, but no one doubted I had more socialism in my little finger than the rest of the Cabinet put together. 'Thank God you are still on the NEC.' I hadn't intended to run again but this made me wonder whether I should. Another heart-warming surprise was a note from Tony Keable-Elliott, which he pushed through the door. It said that, despite our disagreements over pay beds, he wanted to thank me for all I had done for the primary care teams and the NHS. I hadn't expected that!

In the evening Jack phoned to tell me that DHSS was 'like a morgue' and he doubted that he could stay, though David Ennals had asked them all to stay on. David had come in on Friday for a general talk and Lord Goodman had been in to see him. It was fascinating to see the difference in Arnold's manner towards David. 'None of the amusing *bonhomie* he showed with you,' said Jack. 'He blatantly tried to bully him, actually making out that it had been agreed that no pay beds were to be phased out unless and until an equivalent amount of private beds had been provided in their place. I just couldn't keep quiet and told him he was talking nonsense. It was a good job I was there.'

One of my major problems now is transport. With Ted so much in Europe he isn't available to do his old job of chauffeuring me. I can use public transport, up to a point, but I can't carry around with me the masses of food and other things we ferry down to the cottage every weekend. We shall have to make some uncomfortable adjustments, starting with tomorrow morning when Ted is off to Brussels again. We shall have to get up at an early hour so that he can drop me at High Wycombe station on his way to his plane.

Monday, 12 April

Climb into the train at High Wycombe. I wish I weren't so recognizable. One can never be a purely private person again: everyone nudges his neighbour and points me out. It is like asking Harold Wilson to travel incognito. Catch a bus to the flat, clutching my piles of parcels. Change into a pretty dress, because this is my day to say goodbye to the Queen. The office rings: David Ennals would like to talk to me. David comes on thanking me effusively for my note of congratulations and saying of course he would be delighted to keep on my advisers. He knew and respected Brian Abel-Smith from the old days. As for Jack Straw, he had checked up with people at the office and they all spoke highly of him. (If he checked up with Norman he would get a panegyric – those two are close buddies.) Yes, he was going ahead with the press conference introducing the Bill that afternoon. But he first had to see the BMA: they had asked for it and he couldn't refuse. I wished him well and thanked him for letting me continue to use his ministerial room until he needed it. Hugh Macpherson phones breathing anger at my dismissal and saying he was going to write an angry piece in *Tribune* about it. That will be nice!

Caught the underground to the House and then realized I was not coming in by ministerial car and I hadn't got my security pass with me. The policeman in New Palace Yard just smiled at me and waved me on. It was as natural as breathing to go up to my old room. There I found Janet waiting for me and a magnificent bowl of roses on my desk: it was from her and Vince. Once again I felt my eyes dampening, particularly when I read the note which accompanied it: 'To those of us who grew up with the names of Nye Bevan and Barbara Castle it is the end of an era – and we are sorry!' I rebuked her: 'You'll make me cry.' 'Then read those,' she replied, pushing a pile of letters under my nose. As I read them I was engulfed in a warm tide of affection, regret, anger and gratitude. They were letters from unknown old age pensioners, from Tory chairmen of AHAS, from party workers, from nurses, from trade unions, from MPs (including some Tory ones like Teddy Taylor) all saying that they were sorry and/or it was a scandal I was going; all thanking me for what I had done. Among the ones which pleased me most were those from Peter Jacques and Liz Arnott; the most surprising included letters from Merrison, Philip Allen of the Occupational Pensions Board and Derek Stevenson, who actually thanked me for 'the time and trouble you always took over your negotiations and discussion with the BMA'. The two most perfunctory were from Elwyn and Wedgie Benn. I could read their minds: 'Hard cheese, but she can't really complain.' Oddly enough there was only one abusive letter in the whole pile: from a consultant in Sutton Coldfield who wrote: 'I thank God you have been sacked.' I think, however, that the most moving letter of them all was from young Michael Meacher. He is no time-server. He is extremely able and a genuine radical. It was a matter of pride to me that he should write about my 'patent burning sense of socialist purpose and drive', and my 'capacity to inspire'. The ice began to melt around my heart, but my anger against Jim Callaghan's petty 'reconstruction' of his Government grew. Every newspaper has commented on the swing to the Right in the new Cabinet.

It was the last day of the Budget debate and I saw Mike's name go up on the indicator. I went down to hear him and had to stop myself at the door of the Chamber from walking onto the front bench. I crept instead onto the third bench above the gangway and sank thankfully next to nice Tam Dalyell, feeling the eyes of the whole House and the press gallery were on me in my reduction to the ranks. I listened to Mike rather distractedly. No doubt it was my fault that I found his rhetoric a little unreal. Then it was time to go and see the Queen. Once again I wondered how I was supposed to get there. Janet asked me if she should order a taxi, but I didn't like the idea of its clock ticking up endlessly in the courtyard of Buckingham Palace. I felt there ought to be a way of going with slightly more dignity. So I rang up Ted Short who was due to go at the same time and asked if I could cadge a lift, expecting he would have his own car. I went down to Speaker's Court to wait for him. The drivers were there, coping in their usual friendly way with ex-Ministers. Winnie, Mike's driver, took pity on me and insisted on my sheltering in Mike's car from the cold wind. 'You know you could have had a ministerial car to go to the Palace,' she said to me. 'It is absurd the way no one explains this to you.' And sure enough Ted Short arrived in a ministerial car. Anyway it was nice to have his company. He had been at his office clearing out his things. He didn't attempt to hide his bitterness. 'You and I backed a loser, Barbara, and we are paying for it.' 'So you didn't vote for Jim?' 'I voted for Denis, then switched to Mike. This fellow we've got is no good.' 'Are you going into the Lords?' 'Not yet, anyway.' He brooded a bit, then said: 'The irony is that I feel at the top of my powers. I don't feel tired or stale. I expect you are the same. You ought to have been allowed to finish your pay beds legislation. I would have liked to finish my work on devolution. I have spent months on it.' More brooding, then: 'You and I, Barbara, are going to have difficulty in filling our time.' It was the only thing on which I disagreed with him.

At the palace the staff greeted us courteously. 'The audience is upstairs.' We traversed the long carpeted corridors and climbed the stairs to a small boudoir. Martin Charteris, the Queen's secretary, greeted the former Lord President affectionately. 'How are you, Ted.' 'Fine, Martin.' 'I'm afraid we're running late,' said Charteris. 'It's been a busy day. We had a Privy Council this morning at Windsor.' (I knew that – I had been supposed to attend it.) 'Then there were the new Ministers to receive. Now this. These farewell occasions are always very sad.' 'Was Michael Foot there this morning?' I asked. 'Because he was on his feet in the House at 3.30pm.' 'We had to give him a hurried lunch,' said Charteris. 'He only had one course.'

We looked out on the garden, which Charteris remarked was looking very beautiful. 'Not as beautiful as ours at Hell Corner Farm,' I replied truthfully. 'You drew me a picture of your cottage once in Cabinet,' said Ted with his rather wintry but honest smile. 'Those were the days when you were Chief Whip,' I replied, 'and we sat together at the bottom of the Cabinet table.' I noticed idly that the polyanthus in the floral decoration on the table were wilting. The tiny room was crowded with bric-à-brac. Still we waited. Willie Ross joined us. I was interested by the order of precedence: first the Lord President, then me, then the Secretary of State for Scotland. What *would* the Nationalists say? We were joined by Charteris's deputy, Philip Moore, recently recruited from the Civil Service. He asked about Patrick Nairne: 'We always used to say he was the best of the whole bunch of us.' I agreed he was an excellent civil servant indeed. Norman Crowther-Hunt drifted in last, red-faced and cherubic. He explained that this was the right time for him to go because his period of leave from his academic job was nearly up, but he had enjoyed every minute in government. (I am always intrigued by the fascination which public life has for academics.) Willie chatted knowledgeably to Charteris about Scottish nationalism. No doubt the Queen's secretary must keep in touch. I couldn't help thinking that we 'golden oldies', as Ted put it, weren't feeling like has-beens at all. In fact we were feeling rather superior and arrogant.

At last the message came: the Queen was ready. Charteris jumped to attention and Ted was out through the door in one minute flat, calling over his shoulder to me: 'I'll wait for you.' As we sat there someone asked where Bob Mellish was. 'He asked to be excused because he wasn't feeling well,' said Charteris. This amused me because earlier I had heard Bob declaring over lunch in the House that he was blowed if he was going to say goodbye to the Queen: 'During the whole time we have been in government she has never once asked my wife and me to any function, so she can keep her thanks.' Ted came out and I was whisked in to the Queen. She was sitting on an elegant sofa in a larger room. I noted with approval how nice she looked: hair well groomed, a charming simple woollen dress, blue which she seems to prefer, with a bow at the neck. I noted for future non-action how well a circle of real pearls looks on a round neckline. She chatted easily and informally, talking about how difficult my job had been, remembering her visit to the new Southampton hospital and what we had talked about, quoting Dick Crossman (not for the first time). I admired her as a fellow professional. After ten minutes she said: 'I want to thank you, Mrs Castle, for all you have done.' I bowed and thanked her for receiving me. I was out and collecting Ted Short. We were escorted courteously to our car. Back to the House.

Tuesday, 13 April

Tuesday, the thirteenth: an appropriate date for Brian's funeral. Jack, all consideration, had insisted on collecting me and being responsible for my rail ticket. I wondered distractedly what to wear. The sun shone and the flat was warm. It was to be a formal funeral at Rotherham's Roman Catholic church. So I supposed I must wear black – and a hat. I have no Private Secretary to advise me now. Jack had borrowed Anthea's best black hat for me but it was straw. I teetered between my dress with Anthea's hat or my black coat with fur collar and no hat. I ended in my confused state by emerging with neither hat nor coat. Outside the wind was icy. Jack wanted me to go back for my coat but I was afraid of missing the train. I soldiered on. We strap-hung on the Victoria line to King's Cross with me worrying about my clothes and then deciding that the best tribute I could pay to Brian was to be wrongly dressed: the accolade of sincerity.

In the train I was soon engulfed in the warmth of comradeship. Our compartment began to fill up with an impressive parliamentary array. We crowded into the dining car for breakfast. There was Walter Harrison and Stan Orme, me and Jack and Brian Abel-Smith, Alf Bates and Michael Meacher. At the last minute David Owen arrived. 'I thought you had a debate on the Children and Young Persons Act,' I said to him (my efforts with the Chief Whip to get it postponed at David's request having failed). 'I told them to stuff it,' he replied valiantly. 'I have got Alex Lyon to deal with it. One has to get one's priorities right.' I have never like David more. Then I noticed Margaret Jackson,[1] as inadequately and thinly clothed as I was. I thought to myself that Brian could not have had a more eloquent testimony. I discovered that we were all to walk behind the coffin to the church. 'You'll all be back shortly for my funeral,' I warned them. 'But, when I die of pneumonia, I shall instruct Ted that the ceremony will be at Hell Corner Farm and you will have the biggest booze-up you have ever had.' There was an extraordinary feeling of closeness among us in that dining car. Jack told me that the BMA's meeting with David yesterday had been a scream. The BMA boys had been at their worst, Grabham telling David that he was behaving abominably. So the target has changed with dramatic speed! Jack also told me my officials were still subdued. Tim Nodder, particularly. He had told Jack how illuminating the past two years had been to him. For the first time in his life he had learned the value of words. 'We were rather good at drafting,' I replied complacently.

At Doncaster station a fleet of ministerial and mayoral cars were waiting to take us

---

[1] Labour MP for Lincoln and Under-Secretary of State for Education.

to Rotherham. There were refreshments waiting for us in the mayor's parlour. I was astonished how many of Brian's colleagues came crowding in: Joe Harper,[1] Merlyn Rees, John Silkin, Alf Morris, Alice Bacon,[2] Dennis Skinner, Guy Barnett,[3] Joel Barnett. It was a long way for them all to come. From the office had come Alice Perkins, Brian's devoted Private Secretary, and the gentle Alec Atkinson, who Brian always said was the best civil servant on the pensions side. They grieved openly. Alec took me aside to say what a 'remarkable' farewell speech I had made to them. That pleased me a lot. Then came the order to fall into line behind the coffin. Despite the cold wind the streets were lined with onlookers. We shivered under the grey skies.

At the church Merlyn was shocked when the usher directed me into the second row, Cabinet Ministers and the mayoral party sitting in state in front. I didn't give a damn, thankful to rest my head against the wall, drained of all vitality. The rather homely service left me unmoved. I watched Kate as she stood there dry-eyed and dignified, doing what she thought Brian would want her to do. As we left the pews Merlyn, typically nice, insisted on standing back and making me walk out first with John Silkin. It was as though they were burying me with honours, too! As we stood outside in the biting wind, waiting for our cars to come, a woman in the crowd recognized me: 'It's Barbara.' Within minutes I was surrounded by a crowd of women wanting to shake my hand. My colleagues looked on in amusement as I was lost in a sea of excited women. 'That's star quality,' said David. 'Her successor won't have it.'

Back in the town hall there were coffee and buns for the horde of mourners. 'I thought you had child benefit at Cabinet this morning?' I said to Joel. 'I got them to postpone it,' he said. 'I was determined to come here.' We chi-iked about the rate of benefit that should be fixed. 'I'm ready to settle at the figure I know you would have accepted,' said Joel. 'What's that?' I replied. '£2·65?' 'You know you would have settled below that,' he said. 'I know nothing of the kind,' I retorted. It was quite like old times. Suddenly Joel burst out: 'It is absurd that he should have sacked you.' 'It's not absurd, it's bloody wicked,' snarled Dennis Skinner. 'God knows what's going to happen under this man,' gloomed Joel. 'I told you not to vote for him,' I quipped. 'I myself would have voted for Denis if Mike had been knocked out.' 'I know, I know,' he murmured uneasily.

John Silkin, who had come in his ministerial car, insisted on my driving back with him. He said he wanted to talk to me. It turned out that he wanted to theorize about the reasons for Harold's resignation. He didn't think we had got to the bottom of it yet and was sure Harold was planning to come back in some way. But not, he thought, a coalition. It was all very inconclusive. What he was obviously more preoccupied with was his own fate. He was sure he would be sacked on the next round. Mike had tried to get him the job of Environment, but Jim had said he 'hadn't a very high opinion of my capacities'. John was all very relaxed about it, as he is about every-thing. He is the kindest chap, but has not yet proved himself a political heavyweight. I snuggled down between him and Guy Barnett in the back seat and fell sound asleep.

[1] Labour MP for Pontefract.
[2] Former Labour MP for Leeds, now Baroness Bacon.
[3] Labour MP for Greenwich and Under-Secretary of State at the Department of the Environment.

Epilogue

The pay beds Bill duly received its Second Reading on 27 April, David Ennals being anxious to show that he was not reversing my policy. After an argument with the Chief Whip I managed to get myself on to the Standing Committee on the Bill, ready to pounce if the Government looked like giving way to the medical profession on any important point. The Bill became law, substantially unchanged, in November 1976. Some 1,000 pay beds were abolished at once and the Health Services Board was set up to deal with the rest. Thanks to the vigilance of its two trade union members, Bernard Dix of NUPE and Ray Buckton of ASLEF, and to the fairness of its independent chairman, Lord Wigoder, it proceeded to apply the Act scrupulously. I was particularly glad of the provision under which the Board had to produce a report on common waiting lists within six months. This it did in May 1977 (Cmnd. 6828), recommending that private and NHS patients should be placed on the same waiting list and should move up it on the basis of the same criteria. Consultations over the report dragged on endlessly and no action had been taken by the time the Government fell two years later. Moreover the Board ran into difficulties over the criteria for phasing out pay beds, partly because of the failure of the medical profession and the DHSS to provide the information it required. It was clear that the Act needed strengthening, but my attempt as a member of the NEC to get a passage promising this into the Manifesto for the 1979 general election failed.

There were even greater setbacks over child benefit. Although when I left the Government Cabinet had been about to agree the rate at which it would be introduced in 1977, silence fell until 25 May when David Ennals announced that the scheme had been postponed indefinitely. Instead, family allowance of £1 a week would be introduced for the first child. The excuse given was that the trade unions had shied away from the cut in their members' take-home pay which the loss of child tax allowances would mean, even though the family as a whole would benefit. Labour back-benchers, particularly the women MPs, were furious and I persuaded the TUC Liaison Committee to set up a working party to argue things out. The trade union members of the working party – Alf Allen of USDAW and Terry Parry of the Firebrigades Union – proved devoted allies of child benefit and, faced with their determination, the Government was forced to accept a compromise under which the scheme was phased in over three years. By the time the general election came child benefit had been fully introduced at a rate of £4 a week with the promise of more to come and the Government was glad to claim it as the cornerstone of its policy for the family.

The summer of 1976 saw the political turning point for the Government. With the pay policy holding well and the emphasis of public spending being switched to industrial investment, confidence in Britain's economy began to revive, money started to flow in and the pound strengthened. This sharply raised the question of the deep-seated uncompetitiveness of British industry. Until this could be corrected there were two choices: either to rebuild our manufacturing base by a positive investment strategy behind protective walls, or to rely on the devaluation of sterling to enable us to undercut our competitors. Treasury advisers preferred the latter, import controls in any case being ruled out by the commitments the Government had made to the IMF and the EEC. In March 1976, almost unnoticed, the Bank of England began to sell sterling because it was becoming too strong. The new-found confidence was undermined, the pound fell sharply and the decline continued throughout the year.

This made way for the familiar deflationary scenario. In July the trade unions and the Labour Party were torn apart by Denis Healey's well publicized demand to Cabinet for another emergency package consisting of £1,000 million more cuts in public expenditure and a £1,000 million increase in employers' national insurance contributions. Inflation was down to 13·8 per cent. In June the TUC had endorsed the latest round of pay policy. Moreover in mid-July unemployment had reached the post-war record of 1·3 million, which did not indicate an over-stretched economy. The trade unions and the left wing in the Cabinet protested at further deflation, but were overborne by the run on sterling and the argument that tough measures were necessary to restore 'confidence'. Reluctantly they acquiesced.

Inevitably, the package did not do the trick. By October Denis Healey was raising minimum lending rate to 15 per cent. Inevitably, too, this raised the borrowing requirement, already swollen by the high cost of unemployment benefit and the loss of revenue from a depressed economy. The vicious spiral of decline gained momentum and in December Denis Healey accepted a further package of expenditure cuts as the price of an IMF loan of some £3 billion, maintaining once again that cuts would make way for growth. All the time the Bank of England remained vigilant to ensure that the revival of sterling did not go too far.

The Government struggled on through mounting difficulties, kept alive by a pact with the Liberals and the cynical tolerance of the Ulster Unionists. The deeper it got into the mire, the more stubbornly it refused to consider the alternative strategy pressed on it by the NEC or even the modest demands of the TUC. The only planning agreement entered into with any company was with Chrysler, a client company, and the NEB was concentrating most of its resources on keeping British Leyland alive. The Government tried to staunch the growing wounds of unemployment with the job creation and preservation schemes, which by mid-1978 provided 275,000 jobs at a heavy cost in subsidies. It was able to claim some successes. It had made considerable progress towards its target of bringing inflation down to single figures by 1979 and the balance of payments deficit had been substantially reduced, but only at the cost of stagnant output, high unemployment and falling living standards. Investment remained low and no one had much confidence in the long promised world recovery. By September 1978, the patience of the trade union movement reached breaking point. The TUC's plea for more reflation had fallen on deaf ears, in spite of the fact that the public sector's finances turned out to be in much better shape than had been forecast. In the two financial years 1976–77 and 1977–78, the Treasury over-estimated the PSBR by as much as £3,000 million. The new system of cash limits was chopping some 3½ per cent off the planned level of public spending, over and above the specific packages of cuts which had been announced in 1976. Moreover, a change in the presentation of the public expenditure figures in 1977 showed that because of the Treasury's strange accounting conventions[1] the true level of public expenditure had for many years been much less than that stated. Without the agreement of the TUC, the Government had been operating a third round of incomes policy and seeking to enforce a 10 per cent pay limit by administrative means, with some success. When, however, in the summer of 1978 it declared that pay increases must be halved in the coming year to 5 per cent, well below the rise in prices, the trade union movement openly rebelled. At their Congress that year the unions voted almost to a man for a return to free collective bargaining and, at the Labour Party conference despite Michael Foot's pleas, an even tougher resolution, rejecting 'totally any wage restraint by whatever method' was carried by four million votes to nearly two million, some unions being alarmed by its uncompromising tone and by its demand that the NEC should organize a campaign against wage restraint. Jim Callaghan shrugged his acceptance of defeat, but showed no signs of being willing to switch his policy.

In the dark months of late 1978 the unions' exasperation spilled over into wide-spread strikes in the 'winter of discontent'. The Government, snarled up in its devolution policies, had lost Labour support in the House on vital votes. It had also lost its strongest electoral argument: its understanding with the trade unions. In May 1979, the Government fell and Margaret Thatcher was returned, committed to uncompromising monetarist policies.

[1] This included the double counting of certain debt interest, and the charging of all capital investment by the nationalized industries as public expenditure, even though much of it was financed by their own retained profits.

Appendices

I

A NEW CONSULTANT CONTRACT – STATEMENT BY HEALTH
DEPARTMENTS, December 1974

This paper summarizes the principles of a consultant contract that the Health
Departments would be prepared to agree with the professions.
2. These principles are put forward following discussions in the Consultants' Joint
Working Party which started work in May 1974. The Working Party membership
included representatives of the medical and dental professions appointed by the
British Medical Association, the Hospital Consultants and Specialists Association,
and the British Dental Association; members of the Department of Health and
Social Security, the Scottish Home and Health Department and the Welsh Office;
and six independent members.
3. The Department's agreement to the principles set out in this paper is on the basis
that the new contract is taken as a whole.

Objectives of Government Proposals
4. The Government recognizes the dissatisfaction of some consultants with a contract which has stood substantially unaltered since 1948. Their proposals aim to meet
the main grievances, and so make NHS work more attractive. In particular:
  a. the consultants' obligations to the NHS would become closely defined;
  b. the contract would be workload sensitive – those in difficult areas working long
     hours and coping perhaps with staff shortage would be better rewarded;
  c. the distinction awards system would be replaced by career structure supple-
     ments which would reward hard work for the NHS and real contribution to
     medical progress.

Forms of Contract
5. The main principles of the new contract would be as follows:
  a. existing consultants would be entitled to retain their present contracts (see
     paragraphs 25 and 26 below);
  b. there would be a new standard five working-day contract with two options, one
     of which would carry the right to private practice (see paragraphs 10 to 13
     below);

741

    c. there would be a limited session contract for those consultants who because of infirmity or personal obligations (e.g. family commitments) can only work a limited number of hours each week (see paragraph 27 below).

6. The new contract would include as at present some elements paid by items, including emergency calls to the hospital at night or weekends when not on sessional work (which is a new provision), and domiciliary and exceptional consultations as now defined. The details are in paragraphs 17 and 18 below.

7. The new contract would be 'closed' – i.e. unlike the present one it would define the contractual obligations of a consultant in such a way that remuneration would be more closely linked than at present to the individual's workload, and, where appropriate, adjusted in the light of significant alterations in his regular commitment. But it would be inconsistent with professional status for the contract to be drawn in industrial terms; and 'clock watching' and 'overtime' payments are not, therefore, a feature of it.

8. The contract would be for a fixed number of basic sessions. A consultant would be committed to NHS work throughout the period of time of each basic session for which he is contracted. Private practice would be permitted to any consultant who opted to engage in it (the arrangements are described below in paragraphs 12 and 13). Additional sessions, over and above the basic, would be worked at the Health Authority's request and provided the consultant agreed.

9. The basic session would be of four hours. The content of a basic session is described in the Annex. The new standard contract would be for ten basic sessions, normally constituting a five-day Monday to Friday working week, from 9am to 5pm including meal times. During these hours the consultant would be expected by his employing authority to be present at his normal place of NHS work except when obliged to travel between one place of NHS work and another, and would not be free to undertake any private practice (as defined in the existing terms and conditions of service), except where a private patient already under his care required emergency treatment.

Options

10. There would be a Standard Five Day Contract with two options:

    Option A – contracts would be an eight plus two sessions basis as described in paragraph 12, and would carry entitlement to do private practice (as at present defined);

    Option B – contracts would be for ten sessions and would not permit the holder to do private practice.

Obligations within the ten fixed sessions would be identical under either option. Outside those sessions, the obligations of a consultant who had chosen Option A would be divided between his private practice and the NHS, whereas the obligations of a consultant who had chosen Option B would arise solely from NHS patients.

11. These two alternative new contracts are very similar to the existing contracts held by the majority of consultants – the whole-time and maximum part-time contracts – which have existed in their present form since 1955. The remuneration

differential between them has been generally accepted as being 2/11 of the whole-timer's salary. The acceptance and exercise of the obligations to devote oneself entirely to the NHS is of real value to the NHS, and a consultant under Option B (without private practice) would therefore continue to benefit from the present 2/11 differential.

12. A consultant with an Option A contract may wish to spend more time on private practice than would be consistent with a ten-session obligation to the NHS. Under this contract a consultant could, after three years (or earlier if so agreed between himself and the authority), and subject to six months notice, drop one or two sessions.

13. A consultant should not attempt to carry so large an outside commitment as to prejudice his NHS work, but if his NHS employing authority had reasonable grounds for believing this to be the case in an individual instance – on review after three years, or subsequently – it would be entitled to call on him to drop one or two sessions. There would be a right of appeal to a local appeal body. A consultant who had accepted a Standard Five Day Contract on an eight plus two basis, and dropped to nine or eight sessions, would be paid pro rata and retain all the other parts of the Standard Five Day Contract, except the career supplements referred to below.

Additional Sessions
14. Where the Health Authority required more work of the kind referred to in the Annex to be undertaken than could be performed within the basic sessions for which consultants had contracted it could agree with a consultant that he should work extra sessions. This may arise in three ways:
   a. Long-term heavy workload – the job might require a commitment of more than ten sessions; in that case it would be a condition of the consultant's appointment that he would undertake the extra session(s) required so long as necessary;
   b. developments in the service – the workload of a post might increase after the consultant had been appointed, e.g. because of changes in the population served, or the introduction of new services. The consultant could be offered, but would have the right to refuse, the resulting extra sessions;
   c. temporary staff shortages – as at present, staffing levels should suffice to cover normal annual leave, training courses, or sickness absences of colleagues. However, when a colleague was absent through sickness, etc. or a vacancy was unfilled for a considerable period, it would be open to the authority to offer consultants extra session(s) instead of appointing a locum. The consultant would have the right to refuse the session(s) offered.

15. These additional sessions would be available only to consultants who had contracts for at least ten sessions and preference would be given to those who had taken Option B. Additional sessions would either be held for a specified period, or be terminable either by the consultant or his authority with reasonable notice. Whatever the number of sessions contracted for, they would be paid for pro rata to the basic ten sessions.

Increments

16. Basic salary should reflect the fact that from first appointment all consultants carry full professional responsibility, as well as the value of seniority and experience. This would be recognized in a salary scale on which new increments would be paid as follows:

> First increment – 2 years after appointment (about age 40)
> Second increment – 6 years after appointment (about age 44)
> Third increment – 11 years after appointment (about age 49)
> Fourth increment – 17 years after appointment (about age 55)

Work not Covered in Basic Sessions

17. *Emergency work* – the Standard Five Day Contract would include provision for emergency work at night and weekends to be separately paid for. Payment would be related to the length of time spent at the hospital as a result of the call.

18. *Domiciliary and exceptional consultations* – there would be the same provision for these consultations as in the existing contract.

19. *Administrative, teaching and research* – work of this kind which was accepted as part of a consultant's duties but not done in sessional time for which he was being otherwise paid would be separately recognized in the Standard Five Day Contract. It would include work done as a member of the District Management Team, some teaching of other doctors and dentists, and approved research, over and above the sessional work for which he is already paid. Since the burden of such work is difficult to evaluate in terms of time and the range may vary a good deal from place to place, an allowance would be paid by the employing authority. It would be for the authority to assess the allowance within a defined range. Guidance would be given on the type of work attracting an allowance.

Item of Service

20. Work referred to in paragraphs 17 and 18 above would be the only item of service elements recognized in the Standard Five Day Contract and there would be no specific payment for on call or stand-by liability.

Career Structure Supplements

21. One of the purposes of the Distinction Awards scheme is to create earnings differentials and enhanced earnings of the kind that are found in the private sector. A large proportion of awards have gone to consultants who have private practice and therefore the opportunity to adjust their earnings to their professional status (e.g. 50 per cent of consultant surgeons and physicians have awards, and 88 per cent of surgeons and 68 per cent of physicians do private practice). Furthermore:

> a. in spite of considerable efforts to achieve a more balanced distribution, some specialties and localities are still favoured; while others, notably those to which recruitment is in any case difficult, appear to do relatively badly;
>
> b. the criteria for giving awards – both generally and in individual cases – are not specific enough to create the incentive effects and the encouragement of a

healthy distribution of consultants that so large a discretionary expenditure ought to achieve.

While all existing award holders, whether whole or part-time, would retain their present awards if they remained on their old contracts, the scheme would not be continued and no further awards would be made.

22. In place of distinction awards for those taking the new contracts there would be two types of career structure payments:

    a. *Service supplements* whose specialty and regional distribution would be centrally supervised by the Health Departments and which would be paid at the discretion of the NHS authority for a particularly useful contribution to the running of the service nationally or locally. The criteria would need detailed consideration; but their general aim would be to reward exceptionally responsible and dedicated service to the National Health Service. The responsibilities involved in founding, or rebuilding, a department, or of maintaining a service under exceptionally difficult circumstances (e.g. chronic shortage of staff or under-equipment), willingness to apply for and perseverance in unattractive posts and the less popular specialties, would be recognized in these supplements;

    b. *Medical progress supplements* awarded on professional advice would be aimed at rewarding innovations of particular value to the NHS, covering major original research and academic contribution.

23. Both kinds of supplement would be available in one or two values. The selection of recipients of service supplements would be by the Regional Health Authority (with appropriate arrangements in Scotland and Wales) after considering professional advice. The selection of recipients of medical progress supplements would be by a predominantly professional body. The names of recipients would not be confidential.

24. The Departments consider that there is no justification for paying either kind of supplement to consultants with large private earnings. Consultants taking Option A of the Standard Five Day Contract would be eligible for career structure supplements, but to draw any such supplements would have to provide formal evidence about their earnings from private practice. In the absence of such evidence the supplements would be awarded but no money would be paid. Where appropriate, supplements would be awarded less the amount of net private practice earnings: if those earnings exceeded the value of the supplement, the consultant would receive nothing, though his selection would be notified.

Existing Contracts

25. Existing consultants (i.e. those who hold substantive posts on the operative date) would have the right to retain their existing contracts on the old basis, including any distinction award in payment, and their existing right, if any, to do private practice. These would continue to be open contracts under which the consultant's work was not limited to his sessional commitment. Consultants would not have the right to take only part of the new closed contract: the choice would be between taking the whole of the new contract and retaining existing rights and obligations. Remuneration,

including that part attributable to any existing distinction award, would be subject to such increases as the Review Body might recommend.

26. The Departments recognize that some consultants may find it difficult to weigh the advantages of opting for the new contract against retaining their existing one. This might be particularly difficult where a consultant held a distinction award and had to balance possible earnings (including the possible award of a career structure supplement) under the new contract against his present position. Transitional arrangements, including the position of distinction award holders, would need to be further considered.

Limited Session Contract

27. There are some consultants who because of ill health or family commitments, for example, would be unable to take a Standard Five Day Contract. The precise extent of an individual's sessional and other obligations would be discussed between the consultant and the Health Authority concerned. Such consultants would not be permitted to undertake private practice.

Superannuation

28. Superannuation arrangements would have to be considered in consultation with the profession's representatives.

Pricing

29. If the professions decide to accept the principles of the new contract set out in this paper, it would be referred to the Review Body for pricing.

University Clinical Teachers

30. These proposals from the Government are related to the needs of the NHS and those who serve in it. The Universities are responsible for the remuneration of their own clinical academic staffs, and if these new NHS contracts are accepted the implications for these staffs will be the subject of further consultations with the Health Departments, the University Grants Committee and the other appropriate bodies.

Summary

The contracts proposed are:
Existing whole-time contract
Existing 'maximum part-time' contract
Existing part-time contracts for
9 sessions or less

For existing holders (see paragraph 25).

Standard Five Day Contract:
Option A – allowing private practice
Option B – not allowing private practice

For newly appointed consultants; as an option for holders of existing whole-time, maximum part-time or 9-session contracts; and for others, by arrangement.

Limited Session Contract:
For those consultants whose personal circumstances preclude their working a normal working
week.

Summary of New Standard Five Day Contract
Monday to Friday 9am to 5pm week of ten four-hour sessions for NHS work only.
Additional Sessions
Payment for emergency work, domiciliary and exceptional consultations.
Recognition of extra administrative and teaching work.
Recognition of the value to the NHS of consultants who have no private practice.
Increments after 2, 6, 11 and 17 years in the grade to recognize seniority and
experience.
Service supplements and medical progress supplements, adjusted for private practice
earnings.

CONTENTS OF SESSIONS
The basic sessions would cover the consultant's:
   a. out-patient work, ward rounds, operating sessions, laboratory work, diagnos-
       tic and therapeutic procedures;
   b. clinical teaching of his own juniors associated with his own clinical work;
   c. administrative work immediately associated with a. and b., e.g. necessary
       liaison with GPs, other hospital departments and members of other health
       professions, and participation in the administration of the consultant's own
       Division/Department;
   d. travelling time between NHS hospitals resulting from work from a. to c. above;
       and
   e. any arrangements that may be agreed for the professional appraisal of his own
       and other's clinical work.
The commitment would be assessed in advance on the basis of the time that would be
taken on the programme by the average practitioner in the specialty concerned (as at
present), account being taken of the main relevant features of the individual's
professional environment (e.g. facilities and staff).

Travel time between home and NHS hospitals or private consulting room and NHS
hospital would not be included in the basic session or covered in the new contract.

Family planning work should be regarded as part of the session, as it is frequently
impracticable to distinguish this from other clinical work.

747

II

PUBLIC EXPENDITURE TABLES

1. The Trend of Out-turn of Total Public Expenditure since 1968–69

| | (a) In volume terms[1] | | (b) In cost terms[2] | |
	Per cent change from previous year	Index figure (1968–69=100)	Per cent change from previous year	Index figure (1968–69=100)
1969–70	−0·4%	99·6	−0·7%	99·3
1970–71	+2·0%	101·6	+2·9%	102·3
1971–72	+1·9%	103·5	+1·7%	104·0
1972–73	+4·3%	108·0	+5·6%	109·7
1973–74	+3·8%	112·1	+8·0%	118·5
1974–75	+8·8%	122·0	+12·4%	133·3
1975–76	+0·4%	122·4	+0·5%	134·0
1976–77	−2·5%	119·4	−2·4%	130·8
1977–78	−6·0%	112·2	−5·4%	123·8
1978–79	+5·6%	118·5	+5·7%	130·8

N.B. Due to certain changes in the definition of public expenditure within the past ten years, the runs of index figures are not perfect. But the year-to-year changes give an accurate indication of the change each year on the definition in use some years later.

2. Public Spending as % of GNP, 1959 to 1978

Year	Public Expenditure as percentage of GNP[3]	
Calendar Years:	1959	33·0%	
	1960	32·8%	
	1961	33·4%	Tories
	1962	33·7%	
	1963	33·6%	
	1964	33·7%	
	1965	34·7%	
	1966	35·3%	
	1967	38·6%	Labour
	1968	39·3%	
	1969	37·5%	
	1970	37·3%	
	1971	37·3%	
	1972	38·3%	Tories
	1973	38·5%	
Financial Years:	1973–74	39·8%	
	1974–75	45·2%	
	1975–76	46·0%	
	1976–77	43·8%	Labour
	1977–78	40·3%	
	1978–79	41·5%	

Sources: Written Answers, 2 August 1978, Hansard cols. 407–8; Written Answers, 24 July 1979, Hansard cols. 175–6.

[1] Excludes relative price effect.
[2] Includes relative price effect.
[3] Gross national product at market prices.

3. *Trend of Public Spending under Labour and the Tories*
(Average Annual Percentage Changes)

	(a) In volume terms		(b) In cost terms	
	Tories 1970–71 to 1973–74	Labour 1973–74 to 1978–79	Tories 1970–71 to 1973–74	Labour 1973–74 to 1978–79
Defence	−0·8%	−0·7%	+0·7%	+0·5%
Housing	+5·6%	+1·1%	+15·2%	−1·9%
Roads and transport	+3·1%	−2·3%	+4·1%	−1·7%
Education and science, libraries and arts	+6·2%	−0·1%	+3·9%	+0·3%
Health and personal social services	+5·2%	+2·1%	+5·3%	+3·7%
Total public expenditure	+4·4%	+1·0%	+5·4%	+2·0%
Total excluding distorting items[1]	+4·3%	+1·5%	+5·4%	+2·4%

[1] Excludes investment grants (phased out in favour of higher tax allowances in the early 1970s) and the refinancing of fixed rate export credits and of home shipbuilding lending. The latter have been substantial items which have fluctuated violently in recent years, sometimes being negative.

N.B. Relative price effect is the process whereby the cost of providing public services becomes gradually more expensive in comparison with the cost of producing manufactured goods, over and above general inflation, because increases in productivity tend to be concentrated in the production industries. The RPE is not a steady and even figure from year to year as it is affected by trends in public sector pay compared with private industry.

III

MOTION SUBMITTED BY THE UNDERSIGNED MEMBERS OF THE
NATIONAL EXECUTIVE COMMITTEE

Wednesday, 26 March 1975

'This National Executive Committee welcomed the referendum on the Common
Market and reaffirms the undertaking in the Election Manifesto that the Government will accept it as binding;

appreciates that the Government has obtained some promises of alleviation of some
of the most unfavourable terms accepted by the last Conservative Government, but
recognizes that these fall very far short of the renegotiation objectives which have
been Party policy for more than ten years and were embodied in our last two Election
Manifestos;

believes that it is in the true interest of our people to regain the essential rights which
permanent membership of the Common Market would deny us: the right of democratic self-government through our own elected Parliament; the right to determine
for ourselves how we impose taxes and fix food prices; the right to pursue policies
designed to ensure full employment; and the right to seek co-operation and trade
with other nations in a world-wide framework; and therefore

recommends to the Special Conference of the Party that the Party should campaign
for the withdrawal of the United Kingdom from the Common Market and should
invite our fellow-citizens to join us in this campaign.'

Frank Allaun	Len Forden	Joan Lestor
Tony Benn	John Forrester	Sam McCluskie
Nick Bradley	Judith Hart	Joan Maynard
Barbara Castle	Bert Hickling	Ian Mikardo
John Chalmers	Lena Jeger	Renee Short
Michael Foot	Alex Kitson	Bryan Stanley

IV

THE NEW PENSIONS SCHEME

The purpose of the scheme, which came into operation in April 1978, is to provide an earnings-related pension for some twelve million people not covered by good occupational schemes. For low earners the new pension will represent half pay or more on retirement.

Its main features are:

1. The pension is in two parts: the basic component equivalent to £1 for every £1 of earnings up to the level of the flat-rate state pension currently in payment and an additional component at the rate of 25p for each £1 of additional weekly earnings up to the scheme's ceiling of seven times the flat-rate pension.

2. Apart from those working wives and widows who have retained a personal right to pay a reduced contribution, all full-time employees must contribute to the basic pension. For the additional pension, members of approved occupational schemes can be contracted out of the state scheme under strict conditions.

3. Though employees must contribute substantially throughout their working lives, the additional state pension will mature over twenty years from 1978 so that older employees are able to earn a full pension by the time they retire.

4. After the twenty-year maturity period, the additional pension will be calculated on the basis of an employee's twenty best earning years so as to help those, particularly manual workers, who pass their earnings peak some years before they retire.

5. To help those, mainly women, who have a break in employment to bring up a family or look after a sick or elderly person who needs attendance, all pension rights earned will be safeguarded during these periods of home responsibility.

6. The build-up to the new pension is continuous so workers retiring after only one year of the new scheme obtain some benefit.

7. The £1 for £1 element of the scheme particularly helps the lower paid. It means that the lower a worker's wage, the higher the percentage of his earnings on which he will retire.

8. A central feature of the scheme is to protect the pension against inflation. The Labour Government committed itself by law to uprate the basic pension annually in line with prices or earnings, whichever was the more favourable to the pensioner. Under the new scheme the additional pension is also protected against price increases but, equally important, the earnings on which it is calculated are revalued annually in line with the general rise in earnings so that, when it comes to be paid, the pension is not out of line with the earnings it is designed to replace.

9. Women get a new deal. They receive the same pension as men for the same earnings, even though they retire five years earlier. They have been given the same right as their male colleagues to join their firm's private pension scheme. Widows over fifty and widowed mothers inherit their husband's full pension entitlement.

10. In return for women's new rights, the married women's and widows' option to pay reduced contributions is being phased out. In future any woman not already opted out of full contributions or who, having once opted out, spends two or more

years outside the labour force, will have to pay the same contributions as men with the same earnings.

11. A widow who has earned additional pension in her own right will be able to draw it on top of any earned for her by her husband's contributions, up to the maximum payable for a single person. For the first time a widower will enjoy the same right. If he is ill when his wife dies, he will be able to base his invalidity pension on her earnings if they have been better than his own.

12. The flat-rate invalidity pension is replaced by an earnings-related benefit, determined in the same way as the new retirement pension.

13. An employer may contract the members of his occupational scheme out of the additional part of the state pension provided his own scheme gives them at least as good benefits. The state will carry the cost of protecting the guaranteed minimum pension against inflation, of providing invalidity pensions and of making up the widow's pension to 100 per cent of her husband's entitlement.

14. Contributions are earnings-related and, at the time the scheme came into operation, they totalled $16\frac{1}{2}$ per cent, of which the employer paid 10 per cent. These contributions must be paid by everyone up to the basic pension level. Above that level contracted out employees and their employers have had their contributions reduced by $4\frac{1}{2}$ per cent and $2\frac{1}{2}$ per cent respectively.

V

THE SEPARATION OF PRIVATE PRACTICE FROM NHS HOSPITALS
A CONSULTATIVE DOCUMENT

Preamble

1. The Government's policy is for the separation of private practice from National Health Service hospitals. During the debate on the Queen's Speech on 15 March 1974 it was announced that a Joint Working Party had been established with representatives of the consultants to consider (among other things) arrangements for private practice. Further references to the Government's commitment to this policy were made during that Session. In September 1974 a detailed explanation of the Government's views was put to the Joint Working Party with the Consultants in a paper.

The Government's commitment to this policy was reiterated in the October 1974 election. On 1 November 1974 during the debate on the Queen's Speech it was announced that the Government had decided to act upon the commitment during the current session (Official Report col. 545).

2. On 5 May 1975 the Secretary of State for Social Services announced (Official Report vol. 891, cols. 1092–1103) that the Government had decided to introduce legislation as soon as parliamentary time was available to phase out private pay beds from National Health Service hospitals (col. 1096), and to consider the extension of existing powers to enable the Government to regulate more closely the operation, extent and development of the private sector (cols. 1099–1110). The Secretary of State went on to say that within the broad framework of the policy she had announced she was anxious to consult fully with the medical profession and the staff of the National Health Service, and those representing the private medical sector.

3. This memorandum, which is published as a basis for discussion, gives further details of the Government's proposals relating to the phasing out of private practice from NHS hospitals, and to the future operations and developments within the private sector.

The Secretaries of State for Scotland and Wales are associated generally with the proposals in this Consultative Document. References to 'The Secretary of State' and 'The Department' should be construed accordingly, having regard to the present constitutional position. The licensing arrangements would of course need to be reviewed in the light of the Government's proposals for devolution to Scotland and Wales and their detailed practical application would in any case probably differ in some respects from those in England having regard to relevant differences in circumstances.

Phasing out of Private Practice from NHS Hospitals

4. The Government propose that their policy should be put into effect by means of legislation to repeal the present sections of the Health Services and Public Health Act 1968 authorizing the provision of facilities for private practice. The legislation will

also set out the date on which the separation is to be complete, bearing in mind that the Government first announced their intention in March 1974. The Government wish to strike a fair balance between giving a reasonable period of notice and ending the present uncertainty so as to allow Health Authorities to plan future developments taking into account the additional resource of existing pay beds.

Out-Patient Services

5. Legislation will also provide for out-patient facilities in NHS hospitals to be withdrawn. But the private sector at present relies on the availability in National Health Service hospitals of certain highly specialized procedures, such as radiotherapy, and the Secretary of State is willing to examine the possibility of arrangements which, for shorter or longer periods, could make such services available for private hospitals or clinics on a contract basis. Any such arrangements would require payment to the National Health Service of the full economic cost, and would exclude the payment of fees for such services to individual members of NHS staff.

Future Developments of Private Sector

6. The present statutory provisions for the regulation of private nursing homes (including private hospitals and clinics) in England and Wales have been drawn from a variety of sources stretching back over forty years and more. These sources include the 1936 Public Health Act, which in turn consolidated and amended earlier legislation, some of it going back to the nineteenth century; the 1959 Mental Health Act which provided that mental nursing homes should be subject to the same provisions as to registration and supervision as were ordinary nursing homes in the 1936 Act, but with the important addition that under the 1959 Act the Minister of Health (now the Secretary of State) was given power to make regulations in relation to mental nursing homes, although no such power existed in relation to ordinary nursing homes under the 1936 Act; the 1963 Nursing Homes Act which provided that the Minister of Health could make regulations as to the conduct of ordinary nursing homes; and the 1973 National Health Service Reorganisation Act which transferred the functions of local authorities in relation to the supervision of all nursing homes to the Secretary of State. This diversity of sources has had the inevitable consequence that the present scheme of regulation is both over-complicated and in some respects inadequate, and the recent consolidation in the 1975 Nursing Homes Act has done nothing to alter the nature of the present unsatisfactory schemes of regulation. Indeed in their fifth Report (9 April 1975) the Joint Committees of the House of Commons and the House of Lords on Consolidation Bills drew attention to anomalies in several clauses of the 1975 Bill but pointed out that in such a pure consolidation Bill there was no alternative but to leave these unaltered.

6A. In Scotland the provisions are embodied in the Nursing Homes Registration (Scotland) Act 1938 and the Mental Health (Scotland) Act 1960, both as amended by the NHS (Scotland) Act 1972. The main differences are that mental nursing homes (called private hospitals) are registered with the Secretary of State not the health board: and the Secretary of State's power to make regulations is restricted to matters of record keeping.

7. The deficiencies of the present provisions are likely to become even more marked as highly complicated treatments which are at present generally carried out only in NHS hospitals are carried out in the private sector as well. The Government therefore intends to use the legislative opportunity to revise existing legislation to strengthen the regulation of the quality of provision for patients in the private sector. They also intend to establish a licensing system to control the total volume of private provision for medical care. The aim will be to ensure that the total provision for private medical care after pay beds are phased out, shall not materially exceed, either regionally or for Great Britain as a whole, that which obtained within and outside the NHS in March 1974. Powers will also be taken to regulate the advertising of private medical, surgical or maternity facilities to the general public.

A Licensing System
8. The proposals for attaining these objectives envisage new legislation to replace and supplement the present nursing homes legislation. The new proposals to be included in the Bill would modify the present system of registration by Health Authorities acting under powers delegated to them by the Secretary of State (health boards in Scotland) by requiring all private establishments to hold a licence to be granted by the Secretary of State, though it is intended that Area Health Authorities (health boards in Scotland) will play a major part in the process of licensing. The granting of a licence would depend initially on meeting certain specified conditions set out in detail below, and hospitals or homes would be required to accept inspection and to make statutory returns of facilities and of work carried out. The granting of a licence would be subject to national, regional and local considerations and applications for instance would need to be consistent with Health Authorities' plans for future developments and with local authorities' structure plans. Details are given in subsequent sections.

The Aim of the Licensing System
9. The aim of the proposed system of licensing would be twofold. First it would seek to ensure that patient care in the private sector complies with minimum criteria and that all work is carried out by properly qualified staff in an acceptable environment with appropriate operational policies. It is not however proposed to lay down in detail in the legislation such matters as space standards or staffing ratios. Area Health Authorities (health boards in Scotland), subject to direction or guidance from the Secretary of State, and with appropriate professional advice, would play a leading part in this aspect of the system of control by exercising discretion as they do now in connection with registration, though in future this would involve a wider range of considerations.
10. The second objective of licensing is to ensure that development of the private sector does not operate to the detriment of the patients in the NHS. It would not be allowed to make it more difficult to provide a comprehensive national health service by absorbing, either nationally or more locally, any undue proportion of scarce skills achieved by training at public expense. National, regional and more local factors will therefore all influence a decision on an application for a licence and the Secretary of

State is examining the possibility of establishing local enquiries along the lines of local planning enquiries to hear all the relevant evidence, including possible detriment locally to NHS patients. Given the need to exercise control over the size of the private sector nationally it will also be appropriate in considering any application for development in a particular area to consider whether this would unreasonably pre-empt prospective private practice provision elsewhere.

The Size of the Private Sector
11. In Great Britain at March 1974 there were some 25,000 beds in total in private nursing homes and hospitals and of these some 4,000 were estimated as suitable and available for short-stay (acute) medical and surgical work and for maternity cases. The rest were used for the elderly and other groups of patients requiring long-term care and many of the places in these homes were used on a contractual basis for NHS patients. In addition to the 4,000 short-stay beds in the private sector the NHS in Great Britain had some 4,900 pay beds available for private patients and used mainly for acute patients. Statistics show that pay beds for the NHS had an average occupancy of only just over 50 per cent (there has since been some reduction in the authorized number) and there is some evidence of under-use in the private sector also. The Government proposes to ensure that the volume of provision for short-stay patients in the private sector in Great Britain as a whole does not substantially exceed the level of NHS pay beds and beds in private nursing homes and hospitals at March 1974. The legislation will enable the overall level of provision for private short-stay patients in each region and in a particular area at March 1974 and the use made of those facilities to be taken into account in the process of judging whether the granting of a licence would be likely to achieve this aim.

The Method of Licensing
12. It is proposed that applications for licences should in the first instance be submitted to the AHA who will be responsible for immediately informing the Department. If the application concerns the establishment of a hospital or nursing home entirely devoted to work outside the acute sector of medicine and surgery and outside the maternity service, the Health Authority or board will, save in exceptional circumstances, process the application in a similar manner to the existing procedure for registration. Where the effect of any proposal would involve the provision of new or expanded facilities in the acute sector, the Secretary of State would first have to decide whether, having regard to any overriding statutory duties it was an application which could be allowed to proceed. Where it was, a public enquiry, held by an Inspector (Reporter in Scotland) appointed by the Secretary of State, would normally be automatic. The application would be advertised in newspapers circulating within 100 miles of the proposed site. It would be open to all interested parties to give evidence to the enquiry. The Inspector would prepare a report for the Secretary of State which would be confidential in the first instance but would be published when the Secretary of State's decision was announced. Where the Secretary of State decided that the application should not be allowed to proceed, it would be open to the County or London borough council within whose area the proposed development

was situated and to the district councils, community health councils (local health councils in Scotland) and Area Medical Committees in that same region or area to request a public enquiry which would then have to be held. It is intended to make the new licensing system self-financing by charging an annual licence fee.

Licences for Existing Establishments
13. Subject to satisfactory reports following inspection as to quality of provision licences will be automatically granted to nursing homes and private hospitals which are registered on the 1st day of September 1975, provided that they do not subsequently change the type of work done in the home or hospital or extend their facilities. Provided that there has been no such change of use or extension between the date of publication of the consultative paper and the commencement date of legislation, existing nursing homes and private hospitals can therefore be assured that they will not be caught up in licensing controls related to the size of the private sector. No such guarantee can be given to establishments which are registered after 1 September 1975 or which are in the planning stage when the Bill becomes law. The procedure for dealing with such applications will be the same as that for later new developments, and the granting of a licence will depend on satisfying the kind of criteria set out in this document. The Secretary of State is prepared however to arrange for applicants to discuss the matter with Departmental officials during the interim period while a Bill is in preparation and passing through its stages in Parliament. On the basis of such discussions the Secretary of State will be prepared to indicate whether the size or nature of the proposed establishments is likely to conflict with the principles on which future applications are likely to be judged, even though such advice cannot be binding either on Parliament or another Secretary of State. It is however one of the purposes of this document to ensure that developers are given appropriate advance notice of the kind of conditions which will govern both the granting and, later on, the holding of a licence.

Offences
14. The present legislation on registration of nursing homes contains a list of possible offences which can lead to proceedings and penalties. It is proposed to re-enact similar provisions, making it an offence to run a nursing home or hospital without a licence or to fail to observe such conditions or limitations as may be incorporated in the licence.

Variation, Revocation and Renewal of Licences
15. Under present legislation, the Secretary of State may at any time and without appeal vary or revoke an approval issued under the 1967 Abortion Act, and has wide powers to withdraw at any time the registration of a nursing home under the nursing homes legislation, subject only to a right of appeal to the magistrates court (in practice very rarely used); although in every case the Secretary of State is of course required to observe the rules of natural justice.

These present powers are, therefore, extremely wide and may potentially be the subject of arbitrary application. In the new situation it is considered that such wide powers might produce an unfair level of uncertainty; and it is therefore intended to

757

follow a scheme similar to that laid down in the 1968 Medicine Act (Section 28) in respect of the licensing of medicinal products by which the power to revoke or vary a licence for a nursing home could only be exercised by the Secretary of State on certain specified grounds. These grounds might include the furnishing of false or incomplete information about an application; the material contravention of the provisions of a licence; the failure by a licence holder to facilitate an inspection of the premises or to furnish information as required under legislation; or that a material change of circumstances had occurred in relation to any of the matters to which a licence related. Provision would be made for a licence-holder to have the right to make representations where any variation or revocation of his licence was being considered; and for the licence holder to have a right of appeal to the High Court against revocation in certain circumstances. Licences would be issued for a period of five years; but an applicant would be entitled to have his licence renewed for a similar period save in exceptional circumstances (for example, similar grounds as those for variation or revocation, or where there had been a significant change in the ownership or control of the establishment).

Availability of NHS *Services to Patients Outside the* NHS
(I) OVERSEAS PATIENTS
16. Because of the high international standing of British medicine, overseas patients come here or are sent by their Governments for specialized treatments which are not readily available in their own country. It is proposed to allow Health Authorities to provide and charge for specialized services for such patients provided that they can satisfy the Secretary of State that there will be no detriment to NHS patients. Details of such arrangements will be regularly notified to the Department. Charges including an element for a professional fee would be made to these patients (or, in the case of patients sponsored by overseas Governments, to their Governments) and there would be no subsidy by the NHS. No professional fees would be received by NHS staff for their personal benefit, but an element of the total charge would be retained by the Health Authority, or in the case of an academic unit, the University Department to be used for research or development work. Such an arrangement would be similar to the practice which already exists in respect of academic units by which fees for private treatment are received by the practitioner but are passed on to the unit's research funds.

(II) BLOOD TRANSFUSION SERVICE AND OTHER DONOR SERVICES
17. The Blood Transfusion Service where blood is provided free of charge will continue. In so far as private hospitals undertake work involving the use of any other donor material there would similarly be no charge for the material, though as in the Blood Transfusion case there would be administrative and scientific services which would be charged for at economic cost.

Consultation
18. The proposals in this paper contain the main substance of the draft legislation which the Government has in preparation and intends to put before Parliament. In the process of preparation the Secretary of State will welcome comments from all

those concerned, whether professional or lay, whether inside the health service or outside it. Appropriate discussions will be arranged with Departmental officials to enable the Secretary of State to take into account all comments and proposals before submitting a Bill to Parliament.

Department of Health and Social Security
Scottish Home and Health Department
Welsh Office
August 1975

VI

THE 'GOODMAN PROPOSALS'

PROPOSALS CONSIDERED AT A MEETING ON 15 DECEMBER
1975 BETWEEN THE SECRETARY OF STATE FOR SOCIAL
SERVICES AND REPRESENTATIVES OF THE MEDICAL AND
DENTAL PROFESSIONS

1. The Government's policy, as the Queen's Speech made clear, is that legislation will be introduced in the course of this session to phase private practice out of NHS hospitals, and this remains the policy of the Government. As the Secretary of State indicated in her letter of 8 October to Dr Stevenson the legislation would reenact the existing guarantee on the right of consultants to combine NHS and private practice. In announcing the setting up of the Royal Commission on 20 October the Prime Minister also made clear that the Government are 'committed to the maintenance of private medical practice in this country' and 'intend to guarantee this in the legislation'. The problem is to relate the phasing out of pay beds to the preservation of the right to practise medicine privately.

2. The legislation would contain first a broad declaration that private beds and facilities should be separated from the NHS; secondly, an expression of the Government's commitment to the maintenance of private medical and dental practice in this country through the renewal of the provision in the 1949 Act which maintains the right to private practice by entitling doctors and dentists to work both privately and in NHS establishments; and thirdly the establishment of an independent Board to relate these two commitments.

3. Despite its continuing opposition, the medical and dental professions acknowledge that the phasing out of pay beds in NHS hospitals may, through legislation, become the will of Parliament. In that event the phasing out should be subject to the safeguards outlined below:

    a) The criterion for phasing out shall be the reasonable availability of reasonable alternative facilities (including accommodation, services and equipment) within a reasonable geographical distance and to which reasonable access is available to those patients and practitioners desiring to avail themselves of it.

    b) Subject to Parliament's decision, it is accepted that there are some pay beds and facilities which could be phased out from the NHS without undue delay, there being already reasonable alternative beds and facilities; and that the Government will publish in a Schedule to the Bill the location of 1,000 pay beds to be released to general NHS service within six months after the Bill has received Royal Assent. In determining this Schedule the Government will wish to consult fully with the medical and dental professions and with those responsible for providing private medical and dental facilities outside the National Health Service. The Government will also wish to consult at the level of the individual hospital. The criteria for use in these consultations and in determining the content of the Schedule shall be the extent to which the pay

760

beds are being used and the reasonable availability of alternative beds and facilities for the practice of private medicine.

The legislation will supersede the existing powers of the Secretary of State to authorize pay beds and it is not her intention pending the passage of the legislation to vary the existing numbers.

c) It is also accepted that the phasing out of the remaining private facilities should be subject to the creation of an independent Board appointed by the Government. The Board will have an independent Chairman (the appointment of whom will be the subject of consultation with all interested parties) and four other members appointed by the Government. Two would be members of the medical profession and it would be the Government's intention to ensure that these members were acceptable to the profession. The remaining two would be appointed after consultation with other NHS staff and other interested parties.

d) In determining the phasing out of pay beds and facilities from the NHS the Board shall be guided by the following criteria:

    i. that for the retention of beds or facilities for private practice in NHS hospitals there should be reasonable demand for private medicine in the areas of the country served by those particular hospitals;

    ii. that for the abolition of beds or facilities for private practice in NHS hospitals there should be available sufficient accommodation or facilities for the reasonable operation of private medicine in the areas of the country served by those particular hospitals;

    iii. that in those areas of the country presently served for private practice by a particular NHS hospital, all reasonable steps had been or were being taken to provide private beds or facilities outside NHS hospitals and that this would be kept under continuous review;

    iv. that where all reasonable steps to provide in the area of the country concerned alternative private beds and facilities outside an NHS hospital that could be taken were not being taken this would, after due warning, be itself grounds for recommending the withdrawal of facilities for private practice in that particular NHS hospital.

e) The Board shall not necessarily retain existing private facilities for the purpose of specialized operations, treatments and investigations where the NHS is prepared to make such accommodation and equipment reasonably available on an occasional basis for individual requirements in specified circumstances and at an appropriate charge. The Bill would propose to allow health authorities to provide and charge for such specialized services for patients provided that they can satisfy the Secretary of State that there will be no disadvantage to NHS patients, and that such patients – whatever their country of origin – are admitted on the same basis of medical priority as an NHS patient. The Secretary of State will also have to be satisfied that these specialized services cannot reasonably be provided in the private sector to a satisfactory standard in this country. Details of such arrangements will be regularly notified to the Department. Charges will be made to these patients, (or in the case of patients sponsored by overseas Government, to their Governments) and there would be no subsidy by the NHS. No professional fees will be received by whole-time NHS staff, for their personal benefit, but an appropriate element of the total charge will be retained by the health authority, or in the case of an academic unit, the University Department, to be used for medical and dental research or development work. Such an arrangement would be similar to the practice which already exists in respect of academic units by which fees for private treatment are received by the practitioner but are passed on to the unit's research funds. Staff on a part-time contract would be entitled to receive fees from these patients (or sponsors of such patients) and the amount would be determined in the usual way by agreement between the parties concerned.

f) As stated in the Queen's Speech the regulation of the private sector following the separation of pay beds will be subject to further consultation with the professions. In the meantime the Government needs to be satisfied that developments in the private sector do not significantly endanger the service the NHS gives to its patients and will enter into consultation with the medical and dental professions as to how this can be achieved by voluntary means. The consultations would cover the point as to whether any reserve powers that it proved necessary to take in the legislation, might be exercised by the independent Board.

g) The Government believes it is for urgent consideration that a common waiting list should be achieved between NHS and private patients in NHS hospitals. The professions maintain that if any such scheme is a possibility it can only operate for urgent cases, in view of the varied nature of the waiting lists and facilities available at different hospitals. The Government maintains that it is possible to devise common waiting list arrangements by which all NHS and private patients are admitted on grounds of medical priority alone. These are matters for detailed discussion. The Bill will instruct the Board within six months of Royal Assent to make recommendations to the Secretary of State (taking into account the representations of the professions and all other relevant considerations) on the best possible procedures to be undertaken in NHS hospitals covering those beds and facilities that are still to be phased out.

Index

Abel-Smith, Prof. Brian
(Barbara's Special Adviser):
appointed, 38 and n; and the
disabled, 49, 60, 99, 142; and
civil servants' co-operation,
52; and mental hospital, 86
and n; at Sunningdale, 92, 93;
and negative income tax, 101;
at Dick Crossman's memorial,
102; value of, 110, 272; and
new pension scheme, 116;
and Community Health
Councils, 124; and private
sector of medicine, 209, 420;
and social wage document,
439; and public expenditure
cuts, 457, 559; and
Community Care conference,
504; and procurement policy,
513; and NHS lecture, 578;
Barbara at house of, 388,
668; and dismissal notice,
707, 726; and child benefit,
721; and Barbara's dismissal,
726, 727–8; retained by
David Ennals, 731; at Brian
O'Malley's funeral, 734
abortion, 529, 628 and n, 629
ABPI, see Association of British
Pharmaceutical Industries
ACAS, see Advisory Conciliation
and Arbitration Service
Adamson, Campbell
(Director-General, CBI), 29,
32, 85
Advisory Conciliation and
Arbitration Service (ACAS),
10, 84, 158n, 189, 215, 217,
327
AEGIS, see Aid for the Elderly in
Government Institutions

Afkami, Mrs (Iranian Minister),
624
Age Concern, 102
Agnew, Sir Godfrey (Clerk to
Privy Council), 95
AHA, see Area Health
Authorities
Aid for the Elderly in
Government Institutions
(AEGIS), 85n
Air Travel Reserve Fund, 479n
aircraft industry, 103n, 145, 451
Aitken, Ian (Guardian), 450,
611
Aitken, Sir Max, 66n
Al Jazairy, Dr (Saudi Minister),
622–3
Alexander, Andrew (Daily
Mail), 411, 536, 639
Alexandra, Princess, 277
Allaun, Frank (MP (Lab) and
NEC member): and campaign
document, 23; on Ministers
chairing NEC committees, 74;
on nuclear test, 122; on land
policy, 140, 152, 164; at joint
NEC/Cabinet, 181, 183, 232;
and tribute to Barbara, 216,
335; on defence, 254; at 1975
Annual Conference, 507,
508–9
Allen, Alf (Lord) (General
Secretary, USDAW): at Liaison
Committee, 84, 103, 119–20,
149, 319, 350, 737; at TUC
General Council, 455; on
incomes policy (1975), 470,
471
Allen, Douglas (Head of Civil
Service), 198–9, 467, 699
Allen, John (NRC Press Officer),

401 and n, 402, 403n
Allen, Mr (BDA), 550
Allen, Philip (Lord)
(Occupational Pensions
Board), 732
Allen, Sir Roy (BMA), 570
Allende, President (Chile), 63
allowances for MPs, 148
Amalgamated Engineering
Union (AEU), 80, 87
Amalgamated Society of
Locomotive Engineers and
Firemen (ASLEF), 21 and n, 737
Amalgamated Union of
Engineering Workers
(AUEW), assets sequestered, 7,
55n, 80; and Chile, 64; April
1974 Conference, 86, 89; and
Social Contract, 189, 421,
426; and EEC, 379n; elections
in, 659n
Amin, President Idi (Uganda),
417, 432
Anderson, Janet (Constituency
Secretary), x, 187 and n, 421,
436, 613, 732
Annual Conference of Labour
Party: (1973), 239n; (1974),
238–41; (April 1975,
special), 379–80;
(September/October 1975),
506–13; (1978), 739
Anti-Poverty Strategy
Committee of Ministers, 214,
237
APEX, see Association of
Professional, Executive,
Clerical and Computer Staff
Approach to Industrial Strategy,
An (White Paper), 515, 523
and n

Area Health Authorities (AHAS), 115, 130, 132–3, 242, 282n, 310, 378, 388, 533, 722

Arendt, Herr (German Minister), 218n, 225–6

Armitage, Sir Arthur (University Vice-Chancellor), 649n

Armstrong, Mrs (US Ambassador), 687

Armstrong, Robert (PPS to Prime Minister), 158, 342

Armstrong, Sir William (Lord) (Head of Home Civil Service), 40 and n

Arnott, Liz (Labour Party HQ), 74, 192, 300, 732

Ashley, Jack, MP (PPS to Barbara), 44 and n, 94, 142, 209, 222, 385, 449–50

Ashton, Joe, MP (Lab), 410, 692 and n

ASLEF, see Amalgamated Society of Locomotive Engineers and Firemen

Association of British Pharmaceutical Industries (ABPI), 375 and n

Association of Health Authorities, 459

Association of Professional, Executive, Clerical and Computer Staff (APEX), 379n, 396n

Association of Scientific, Technical and Management Staff (ASTMS), 114, 157, 164–6, 379n, 565, 599

Association of University Clinical Academic Staff (AUCAS), 298, 299

Astley, Dr (BMA), 134, 212, 259, 260, 273–4, 364, 365n

ASTMS, see Association of Scientific, Technical and Management Staff

Atcherley, H. W. (Chairman, Review Body), 117n

Atkinson, Alec (Deputy Secretary, DHSS), 65, 735

Atkinson, Norman, MP (Lab), 557

Attack on Inflation, The (White Paper), 435

AUCAS, see Association of University Clinical Academic Staff

Australia, 212, 218

Avebury, Lord, 71n, 72n

Awadhi, Dr (Kuwaiti Minister), 623

Bacon, Alice (Lady), 735 and n

balance of payments, 1–2, 4, 426, 461, 462, 697, 738

Balderton (Notts), visit to, 666

Baldwin, Peter (Deputy Secretary, Treasury), 171, 505, 560

Balogh, Catherine (Lady), 141

Balogh, Tommy (Lord), 36–7, 45n, 126, 141, 197, 331, 422, 531

Bancroft, Sir Ian (Permanent Secretary), 198 and n, 450

Banks, Tony (Political Adviser), 367 and n, 378, 383, 391, 416

Banks-Smith, Nancy (Guardian), 662

Barber, Anthony (Lord), 4, 42n, 60, 163n

Barnett, Guy, MP (Lab), 735 and n

Barnett, Joel, MP (Chief Secretary, Treasury): and pensions uprating, 54; and Concorde, 60–1; and public expenditure, 81, 171, 386, 481, 485, 488–9, 505, 560, 594–6, 600, 641; and one-parent families, 529; and cash limits for LAs, 547, 554; and Civil List, 580; and child benefit, 707–9, 726, 735; and leadership election, 711, 712; and drugs industry, 714–15; at Brian O'Malley's funeral, 735

Basnett, David (General Secretary, GMWU); at Liaison Committee, 104, 119–20, 149, 285, 350, 372, 393; on incomes policy (1975), 470, 559; on industrial strategy, 502–3, 514, 558; on unemployment, 631, 658–9, 697; and unity behind Government, 679, 686, 693

BASW, see British Association of Social Workers

Bateman, Sir Ralph (CBI President), 109n, 111

Bates, Alf, MP (Lab), 300, 694 and n, 734

BB, see Bear Brand

BDA, see British Dental Association

Bear Brand (BB), 354 and n

Beaune, visit to, 501

Beddard, Dr, 695

beef tokens, 145 and n, 164, 173

Beetham, Frank (Liberal candidate), 31

Bell, Dr (JHD), 525–7, 538, 555

Bell, Ronald, MP (Cons), 407

Beloff, Nora (Observer), 139, 152, 180

Benn, Caroline, 161, 226, 371, 421

Benn, Tony (Wedgie), MP (Industry Secretary, then Energy Secretary): and secrecy, ix; and workers' control, 9; and EEC, 12, 110, 126, 128 and n, 174, 183, 226, 287 and n, 288–90, 302, 314, 323 and n, 332, 340, 342; and EEC referendum, 355–7, 361, 371, 376, 381, 383, 391–2, 407–8; and EEC direct elections, 553, 650–1, 706; and election campaign (January 1974), 18–21; and miners' dispute, 22, 24, 25; and incomes policy, 26, 120–1, 427–8, 441, 447–9, 453–5; appointed Industry Secretary, 30, 35; and Concorde, 42, 46, 106, 124; at informal dinners, 45n; and Clay Cross, 67, 418; and chairing NEC committees, 74–5; and Chile, 77, 87; and union fines, 80; and industrial policy, 84, 162, 167, 168, 197, 312, 323n, 338, 376, 378, 384–5, 393, 430n, 464, 492–3, 503, 584–5; and report on Department, 103 and n, 109 and n, 110, 113–14, 121; estimate of, 109–10, 121, 128, 197, 239, 272, 279, 312, 371, 419, 501; press campaign against, 121, 385–6, 387, 410; and coalition fears, 126; and tape recording of speeches, 127;

and renunciation of peerage, 148n; and shipbuilding, 164, 451, 691; and S. Africa, 205; and workers' co-operatives, 207, 503; and economic strategy, 221–4, 353 and n, 373, 400, 422, 449, 483, 537, 542, 548, 563, 566, 684; and NEC/Government relations, 234; at Labour Party Annual Conferences, 238–9, 507, 511; elected to NEC, 239, 510; NEC Committee Chairman, 268; and John Stonehouse, 279–80; and devolution, 282–3, 419; and steel, 296, 305; and *Any Questions*, 334; appointed Energy Secretary, 408, 410–11; and Cabinet changes, 414–15; and industrial democracy, 424; and Meriden, 477 and n, 478–9; and Court Line, 479 and n, 480, 489; and Bristol letter, 492–3; in France, 499, 501; and Chrysler, 545; and speech on spending cuts, 559; and passports, 579; and Radcliffe Report, 627–8; and Honours system, 633, 675 and n; and Namibia, 635 and n; and heating for aged, 639; and Rhodesia, 664; and leadership election, 692, 705; at Harold Wilson's farewell dinner, 699; and Barbara's dismissal, 732

Bennett, Jill (actress), 176
Berrill, Ken (Head of CPRS), 220, 223, 282, 669
Bessell, Peter (former Liberal MP), 640n
Betteshanger Colliery, 67n
Betts, Mrs Annie (Barbara's mother), 116, 216–17, 219, 242, 275, 491
Betts, Jimmie (Barbara's brother), 219, 261
Bevan, Aneurin (former Health Minister), 170n, 228n, 244, 275n, 537n; memorial lecture, 574, 578, 628
Bickerstaff, Mr (COHSE), 381
Bidulph, Miss (nurse administrator), 533

Bird, Reg (ASTMS), 599
Birmingham bombing, 232, 236
Bish, Geoffrey (Secretary, Labour Party Research Department), 173 and n, 316, 337, 375 and n, 393, 449, 494, 507–8, 544, 565, 674
Blackburn (Barbara's constituency), 24, 27, 32–3, 107, 173, 187, 246, 403, 492, 551, 687, 729–30
Blackburn Borough Council, 24, 528
Blackburn Royal Infirmary, 551
Blackpool, 506, 508
BMA, *see* British Medical Association
Body, Richard, MP (Cons), 396
Bolt, Mr (Royal College of Surgeons), 550, 572, 575, 588–9, 608
Bonn, visit to, 224–6
Booth, Albert, MP (Minister for Employment), 244, 727
Bosanquet, Nicholas (assistant to David Owen), 74
Boscawen, Robert, MP (Cons), 383
BOSS, *see* South African Bureau of State Security
Boston Consulting Group, 477 and n
Bottomley, Arthur, MP (Lab), 277
Bourne, John (*Financial Times*), 56
Bourton, Dick (Deputy Secretary, DHSS), 143, 159, 169–70, 177, 178, 203, 228, 329, 488, 520–1, 654
Boyd, Sir John (General Secretary, AUEW), 659 and n
Boyle, Lord, 105n, 246n, 251, 446
Bradford, visit to, 392
Bradlaw, Sir Robert (President, General Dental Council), 102
Bradley, Nick (NEC member), 507, 564, 630, 632–3, 646
Bradley, Tom (MP (Lab) and NEC member), 564, 565, 629–30, 632
Brandes, Lawrence (Under-Secretary, DHSS), 92, 377, 451

Brigden, Mr (consultant), 646
Briggs, Prof. Asa (and Report), 88 and n, 94, 100
Brighton Marina, 360, 463
British·Aircraft Corporation shop stewards, 729
British Airports Authority, 80n, 147n
British Association of Social Workers (BASW), 59
British Dental Association (BDA), 177, 258
British Leyland, 374 and n, 545, 559 and n, 711, 738
British Medical Association (BMA): and salary claim, 39, 115, 166–7; and consultants' contract, 49n, 191, 212, 273, 332, 343, 350–1, 723; and superannuation, 100; and Charing Cross dispute, 115, 127, 130, 133–8; and NHS financing, 144, 162–4, 443; and 'playing politics', 146; and pay beds, 195, 549–50, 571, 575, 588, 608, 621, 640, 651, 652, 655, 702, 711–12; and DHSS staffing, 491; and private practice policy, 491n; and enquiry into NHS, 515, 529, 530; and junior hospital doctors, 554, 586, 603; and industrial action, 569, 664; and meeting with Harold Wilson, 571; and incomes policy, 703; and Health Services Bill, 711–12; and meeting with David Ennals, 731, 734; *see also* consultants, junior hospital doctors, Lewin, Dr Walpole, pay beds, Stevenson, Dr Derek
British Medical Journal, 625, 630, 693
British Nuclear Fuels Ltd, 635 and n
British Steel Corporation (BSC), 386n
Broadmoor, visit to, 539–40
Brookes, Ray (Guest, Keen and Nettlefolds), 633, 634
Brookstone, Esther (NUPE), 115, 126, 132, 136–7
Brown, Bob, MP (Lab), 40, 70–1, 110

Brown, George (Lord) (former
Labour Minister), 669
Brown, Lord, 478n
Brown, Peter (Information
Director, DHSS): and press
conferences, 44, 45, 136-7;
and previous posts, 44n;
arranges press lunches, 101;
and pension proposals, 116;
and political views, 116; and
Barbara's private treatment,
130, 135; and attitude of
press, 163; and drafting of
press statements, 174;
arranges meetings with leader
writers, 175; and Halsbury
Report, 183, 185;
congratulates Barbara, 195;
and consultants' contracts,
209, 306-7; and David Wood
(The Times), 246-7; estimate
of, 307; and pre-briefing of
journalists, 653
Brussels, visit to, 401-2
BSC, see British Steel
Corporation
Buchan, Norman, MP (Lab), 197
and n
Buckton, Ray (ASLEF), 737
Budgets: (March 1974), 50-2;
(July 1974), 114, 148, 150;
(November 1974), 213 and n,
214, 215-16, 240; (April
1975), 358, 359-62;
(April 1976), 716, 720,
732
building societies, 62, 68, 75-6,
143
Burnet, Alistair (Daily Express),
265n
Butt, Ronald (The Times),
101-2, 319-20, 324, 334
butter tokens, 110 and n
Byers, Frank (Lord), 476

Cabinet Committees, see
Devolution; Economic Policy;
European Questions; Home
Affairs; Industrial
Development; Legislation;
Miscellaneous; Miscellaneous
Devolution Questions;
Overseas Policy and Defence;
Pay; Public Expenditure
Scrutiny; Social
Services

Caines, Mr (Assistant Secretary,
DHSS), 363
Calder Valley, meetings at,
391
Caldwell, Mr (DHSS), 172
Callaghan, Audrey, 94
Callaghan, Jim, MP (Foreign
Secretary, then Prime
Minister): and EEC, 12, 39, 68
and n, 100-1, 107n, 109 and
n, 112-13, 125-6, 129, 141,
143-4, 183, 230, 245, 279,
289, 295-6, 301-2, 314, 331,
349-50, 376; and anti-EEC
campaign, 345-6, 356-7; and
EEC agricultural policy, 685;
and incomes policy, 19-20,
120, 440-1; and miners'
dispute, 25; appointed
Foreign Secretary, 30; speaks
for Barbara in election, 32; as
Party Chairman, 37, 57-8,
152; and Chile, 64, 76-7, 87,
89, 112; and long-term issues,
84-5; and In Place of Strife,
87n; and collective
responsibility, 90; and nuclear
test, 124; at Greenwich
banquet, 127; and devolution,
173; and hooliganism, 182;
and trade unions, 194, 217;
and S. Africa, 201; and
gloomy outlook, 221; and
defence, 227, 484; and top
salaries, 206; and Rhodesia,
276-7, 663, 676, 683, 703;
and Cyprus, 292; and child
benefit, 380n, 668n; and Joan
Lestor, 416-17; and Uganda,
417 and n, 432, 452, 458; and
industrial democracy, 423; at
Class of 1945 party, 474; and
Chrysler, 545; and EEC direct
elections, 553, 650, 705-7;
and energy conference, 574,
579; and Namibia, 635; and
Armitage Committee, 649
and n; and Socialist
International, 676; and
confidence vote, 682; and
economic outlook, 684, and
Harold Wilson's resignation,
689-90, 691; and leadership
election, 692, 693, 705, 711,
717; appointed Prime
Minister, 72n; and April 1976

Budget, 717; dismisses
Barbara from Government,
723-5 and n, 732
Cambridge Economic Policy
Group, 316, 707
Campaign for Nuclear
Disarmament, 228 and n
CAP, see Common Agricultural
Policy
capital punishment, 247
Caradon, Lord (Hugh Foot),
347n
Carmichael, Catherine (Deputy
Chairman, SBC), 300 and n,
305
Carr, Robert, MP (Cons),
86n
Carrington, Lord, 544n
Carroll, Roger (Sun), 432
Carter-Jones, Lewis, MP (Lab),
291 and n, 416
Cartwright, John, MP (NEC
member), 509
Castle, Barbara, MP (Social
Services Secretary): on diary
writing, ix; first Cabinet
appointment of, ix; as
Employment and Productivity
Secretary, 2-3, 93n; with
family, 17, 82-3, 99, 192,
261-2, 357, 481-2, 518,
616-18, 730; at Liaison
Committee, 18-21, 373,
394-5, 430-2; and debate on
emergency, 22-3; and
Relativities Report, 22, 23,
24-5, 26-7; and miners'
dispute, 25; and housing
debate, 28; appointed Social
Services Secretary, 30, 34
35; and February 1974
General Election, 31-2; and
incomes policy, 33, 428-9,
441-2, 447-9, 453-9; and
reflections on post, 34, 37,
39, 52, 100; and comments
on Civil Service, 35n, 36, 169,
174, 209, 225, 328-9, 331,
362, 368-9; and Cabinet
room, 35 and n; and laddered
tights, 35n; affirms oath of
office, 35; and recruitment of
colleagues and staff, 34,
38-9, 44, 158; on being
photographed, 44, 56, 66,
283; and informal dinners,

45n; against Budget secrecy, 51n; and immigration cases, 61, 303; and relations with unions, 70–1, 386; and relations with NEC, 74–5, 234; and Cabinet Minutes, 75, 251–2, 710–11; and religious services, 77; and husband's peerage, 78–9, 121–3; and public expenditure, 81, 155–6, 194, 210–11, 243, 360, 399–400, 461–2, 483–4, 492, 520–1, 542–3, 546–7, 593–6, 601–2; and National Insurance Bill, 81–2; and Chile, 86, 112, 127, 140; and bonus for staff, 88–9, 91, 93–4, 98–9; and election options, 96–7; at memorials, 102, 175; and enquiry into nurses' salaries, 105, 106–7, 151, 157n; health of, 108, 110, 111, 115, 141–2, 145, 246, 335, 504, 509, 617, 660, 693; and nuclear policy, 123–4, 228; and censure votes, 125, 535; and private treatment at hospital, 129–31, 134, 570; and Concorde, 146–7; and negotiations with NHS unions, 144–5, 147–8, 150–1, 157, 158, 165–6, 183–7, 363; and personal approach to Roy Jenkins, 159–60; and political allegiances, 161, 412; and industrial policy, 162, 465; and media prejudice towards, 168; and devolution, 173, 497; and Treasury, 175–6, 268; and election Manifesto, 180–3; and reply to Keith Joseph, 201, 202; and personal social services, 205–6; and EEC, 212, 245, 279, 288, 295–6, 313, 404; and October 1974 General Election, 190; and November 1974 Budget, 214; and TU legislation, 217; at Chequers meeting, 219–24; in Germany, 224–6; at 1974 Annual Conference, 238–41; and NEC elections, 239, 510; and top salaries, 250–1,

255–6; and 'Lucy', 253; and Christmas parties, 246, 257, 260, 261; and press campaign against, 267, 513, 517, 570, 586, 599; and Rhodesia, 276–7, 663, 683; and 1976 census, 280; and train derailment, 294; and earnings rule, 297, 298, 505; and strain of office, 317–18, 320, 385; and anti-EEC campaign, 326, 332, 336, 338, 339–40, 345–8, 361, 367, 378, 383, 391–2, 396; and reflections on future, 329, 385, 424, 513–14; in United States, 358; and adventure with rabbit, 370; and trip to Brussels, 401–3; at Oxford Union debate, 404–6; and Cabinet changes, 412–15; in Luxembourg, 419–20; and industrial democracy, 423–4; and social wage document, 437–9; and scenario for Tory victory, 457–8, 461–2; at Royal Garden Party, 467–8; at *Class of 1945* party, 474; at Pensions Bill party, 476–7; and Meriden, 478–9; decides to retire from Parliament, 492, 509n, 672; and Communist Party, 495; in France, 499–502; and Health Co-operation Agreement with the Soviet Union, 502, 505; at 1975 Annual Conference, 506–13; proposes to retire from NEC, 509 and n; elected to European Parliament, 509n; press conspiracy against, 519, 522; on IRA death list, 535–6; and EEC direct elections, 553–4, 636, 650–1; and accident to, 611–15; in the Middle East, 622–4, 704; decides to retire from office at appropriate time, 624, 671 and n, 672, 674, 690, 701, 718; and Radcliffe Report, 627, 677; and Namibia, 635; and rights of civil servants, 649n; and Denis Healey's unemployment 'package', 649–50; and press 'leaks',

653; and economic outlook, 684–5; and EEC agricultural policy, 685–6; and Harold Wilson's resignation, 671–2, 690; and prospects of losing office involuntarily, 714, 715, 718, 721–2; and Brian O'Malley's illness and death, 715–16, 717, 718–19, 720, 721; dismissed from Government, 723–5; farewell party for, 726, 727–8; tributes to, 727–8, 730, 731, 732; at Brian O'Malley's funeral, 734–5;

Comments by, on, Tony Benn, 24, 109–10, 121, 128, 197, 239, 272, 279, 312, 371, 419, 501; Dick Crossman, 23, 61, 66; Lord Elwyn-Jones, 57; Roy Hattersley, 296; Roy Jenkins, 147, 159–60, 303–4; Harold Lever, 35, 76, 354, 472, 525, 533; Brian O'Malley, 78, 243–4, 718; David Owen, 171, 644–5; Fred Peart, 57; Reg Prentice, 21, 235, 338; John Silkin, 532 and n; Margaret Thatcher, 309, 310, 330, 362, 405, 518; Eric Varley, 125, 424, 448, 635; Harold Wilson, 21, 316, 323, 358–9, 379, 397, 432, 437, 527–8, 557;

Visits by, to, Balderton, 666; Blackpool, 506–13; Bradford, 392; Broadmoor, 539–40; Brussels, 401–2; Coventry, 211; Folkestone, 517; France, 499–502; Germany, 224–6; Greenwich, 127; Kettering, 118–19; King's Lynn, 172; Lancaster, 180, 730; Leigh, 468–9; Liverpool, 202; Luxembourg, 419–20; Middle East, 622–4; Newcastle-on-Tyne, 636–8; Norwich, 492; Nottingham, 253; Reading, 108; Rhondda, 673–4; Rotherham, 235; Scarborough, 325; Sheffield, 392; Southampton, 17, 246, 265, 396; Swansea, 107; United States, 358; Weston-super-Mare, 437–8; Woolwich, 434;

Visits by, to – *contd.*
Wythenshawe, 59; *see also*
Blackburn; British Medical
Association; child benefit;
consultants; Halsbury, Lord;
Hell Corner Farm; junior
hospital doctors; National
Health Service; pay beds;
pensions; private practice
policy
Castle, Ted (Lord) (Barbara's
husband): with family, 17,
82-3, 99, 261, 265, 318, 370,
518, 616-17; at February
1974 election, 31-2; on
Islington Council, 34n, 78;
and Peerage, 78-9, 99-100,
121-3; and Chile, 86;
birthday celebrations, 99,
383-4; and Wilson's speech
to PLP, 160; and *World at
One*, 168; at memorial
service, 175; and TV
interview, 185; and Barbara's
speeches, 243, 265, 271, 275,
609; and EEC, 404, 459; and
loyalty of, 414, 513-14; as
member of European
Assembly, 430, 434, 450,
459-60, 498, 518, 674, 692,
731; at Royal Garden Party,
467-8; and HCF garden, 476;
and NEC elections, 510; and
press venom against, 646; and
Barbara's dismissal, 727, 730
Catherwood, Sir Frederick
(Chairman, Overseas Trade
Board), 638 and n, 639
CBI, *see* Confederation of British
Industry
CCHMS, *see* Central Committee
for Hospital Medical Services
Cementation Ltd, 645
Census, 1976, 280
Central Committee for Hospital
Medical Services (CCHMS),
277 and n, 315, 530, 556,
566, 614
Central Health Services
Council, 73
Central Policy Review Staff
(CPRS), 49n, 152, 196, 220,
389, 489n, 497, 545, 563,
670n, 681
Chalmers, John (General
Secretary, Boilermakers, and

NEC member), 154, 496, 564,
633, 700
Channel Tunnel, 46, 58, 124,
217, 230, 281
Chapman, Paul (Special
Adviser), 445
Charing Cross Hospital, 115,
126, 127, 130-8, 543
Charles, Prince of Wales, 310
Charteris, Martin (Queen's
Secretary), 35, 733
Chequers meetings, 219-24,
281-3, 418-19, 425-30,
482-6, 496-8
child benefit (family/child
endowment): Manifesto
commitment to, 140 and n,
177, 189; attempts to
postpone, 172, 177, 200, 638,
644, 668 and n; sent to
Cabinet committee, 237;
included in Budget, 358; for
non-residents, 701; rate of,
707-9, 721, 735; phased in
by 1979, 737
Child Benefit Bill, 276, 374,
380 and n, 389, 450, 486
Child Poverty Action Group
(CPAG), 52n, 496, 511
child tax allowances, 701n
Chile, 53, 57, 63-4, 76-7,
86-7, 112, 122, 140, 322,
506, 634, 636
Chipchase, Ethel (TUC), 278 and
n
Chirac, Jacques (French
Premier), 124
Christie, Leslie (Whitley staff
side), 645
Chrysler, 544-5, 563, 579,
584-5, 602, 610-11, 711
Civil and Public Services
Association (CPSA), 70n, 94,
108, 187, 363 and n, 367, 636
Civil List, 309 and n, 310, 321,
580
Civil Service: comments on,
35n, 209, 225, 331;
discontent in, 70, 88-9, 91;
Pay Research Unit, 327-9,
351; projected growth of,
484; manpower cuts, 637,
643-5; political rights,
649-50 and n
Clarke, Kenneth, MP (Cons),
383, 389, 450, 481, 720

Class of 1945, 474
Clay Cross Councillors, 64,
67-8, 70, 418 and n, 486
and n
Clements, Dick (*Tribune*), 198,
349 and n, 512
closed shop, 52, 66n, 90n, 231n,
246, 308, 541, 648-9
Coady, Matthew (journalist),
611
COHSE, *see* Confederation of
Health Service Employees
Colin-Russ, Ernest (Barbara's
GP), 131, 517, 612-13, 615
Collier, James (DHSS), 490, 513,
646, 704
Collis, Ken (DHSS adviser),
124
Collison, Harold (Lord)
(Chairman, SBC), 46 and n,
193, 246, 299n
Commission on Industrial
Relations, 3, 6
Common Agricultural Policy
(CAP), 68n, 148n, 182, 230,
235, 281, 288, 335, 340, 685
and n
Common Market, *see* European
Economic Community
Commonwealth Sugar
Agreement, 212
Communist Party (CP), 495
Community Care conference,
504, 507
Community Health Councils,
124, 241
Community Land Bill, 474, 521,
547
comprehensive education, 61
Con Mech (Engineering) Ltd, 7,
55n, 80n
Concorde Aircraft, 42, 46, 48,
60, 105-6, 124, 146-7, 493
Confederation of British
Industry (CBI), 85, 119, 316,
426, 453
Confederation of Health Service
Employees (COHSE), 94, 104,
107, 111, 114, 147, 157, 158,
164n
Confederation of Shipbuilding
and Engineering Unions
(CSEU), 106, 433, 478
construction industry, 150, 503,
533
consultants: negotiations over

new contract for, 191, 247, 256–61, 275, 287, 294 and n, 295, 297, 300, 344; work to rule by, 208–9; sanctions by, 260, 275, 294n, 317, 344, 366, 367–8; and ACAS, 327; option agreement, 350 and n, 364, 365n; lessons from dispute with, 369–70; terms of contract with, 741–7 (Appendix I)

Cooper, Eric (COHSE), 107, 180

Cooper, Joan (Under Secretary, DHSS), 349 and n, 491

Corfu holiday, 490

Counter-Inflation Act, 1973, 88n

Court Line Ltd, 479 and n, 489

Coventry North-West by-election, 425n, 686 and n

Coventry, visit to, 211

CP, see Communist Party

CPAG, see Child Poverty Action Group

CPRS, see Central Policy Review Staff

CPSA, see Civil and Public Services Association

Crawley, Tom (Private Office), 476

Cripps, Francis (Political Adviser), 373

Crocker, Tony (Under Secretary, DHSS), 176, 709, 727

Cronin, John, MP (Lab), 83, 111 and n

Crosland, Tony, MP (Environment Secretary): appointed Environment Secretary, 30; in Cabinet, 36, 81, 194; and channel tunnel, 46, 58, 281; and mortgages, 51, 68, 75, 124; and Clay Cross, 64, 418; and unions' treatment of members, 90–1; and press coverage, 112, 127; and Harold Wilson's PLP speech, 160; and housing, 181, 272; and economic strategy, 222–3; and energy conservation, 245; as overlord, 274; and devolution, 281–2; and incomes policy, 329, 427, 440, 455; and EEC, 341; and

legislative programme, 391; and public expenditure, 398–9, 461, 463, 482–3, 503, 537, 542, 596, 670, 700; and industrial democracy, 423; and local authority expenditure, 492, 522, 531, 554; and docks, 642; and leadership election, 705

Crossman, Anne, 25, 37, 102, 130, 312–13, 349

Crossman, Dick, MP (Lab): illness of, 23, 24–5, 50; and TV series, 25, 37; and Peter Brown, 44n, 163; and superannuation scheme, 53n; Barbara's relations with, 61–2, 86, 225; death of, 73; and report on hospital, 86n; and old people's homes, 108; and consultants, 332 and n; Diaries, 222, 627, 635n

Crossman, Patrick, 312–13

Crowther-Hunt, Lord (Norman Hunt), 63, 153, 282 and n, 733

CSEU, see Confederation of Shipbuilding and Engineering Unions

Cudlipp, Hugh (Daily Mirror), 327, 330, 397

Cunningham, George, MP (Lab), 25n, 292, 296–7, 298, 721

Cunningham, John (Guardian), 95, 251, 377, 555, 574, 610, 653

Cyprus, 227, 292, 390

Daily Express, 63, 95n, 113, 265 and n, 266, 488, 519, 578

Daily Mail: and alleged land deals, 62, 63; Harold Wilson's writs against, 63, 614, 615; and Tony Benn, 268; and EEC referendum, 408; and NHS, 515, 519, 535, 590; and defence cuts, 559; attacks Barbara, 570, 578, 729; attacks Ted Castle, 646; reporter dines with Barbara, 653; and George Brown, 669; and Cyril Smith, 680; and Harold Wilson's retirement, 686

Daily Mirror, 12, 83, 168, 240, 268, 407, 517, 651, 680, 686

Daily Telegraph: journalists on strike, 33; attacks Barbara, 129, 519, 557, 578, 615, 624, 625; and consultants, 139; and alleged split between Barbara and David Owen, 262; and Shirley Williams, 338; and EEC referendum, 408; and Tony Benn, 411; and NHS, 516; attacks Ted Castle, 646

Dalyell, Tam, MP (Lab), 312–13, 558, 732

Damerell, Mr (Independent Hospitals Group), 550, 605, 669

Davies, Harold (Lord), 105n

Davies, John, MP (Cons), 5, 296

Davies, Sam (DHSS), 387, 490

Day, Robin (BBC), 309, 566

DDRB, see Doctors' and Dentists' Review Body

Dean, Malcolm (Guardian), 653

Dean, Paul, MP (Cons), 722

defence expenditure, 324, 333, 513, 559, 581, 596–7, 602, 670

Dell, Edmund, MP (Paymaster General): and Reserve Pension scheme, 65, 71, 75, 81; and Chile, 122, 140; and long-term pension proposals, 145; and consultants, 244, 256–7, 272; and land tax, 642; at confidence debate, 687; and child benefit, 701

Denley, Mr (Secretary, Society of Radiographers), 157

Denmark, 101

Denning, Lord, 6

dental charges, 174 and n, 179, 487, 504, 537, 554, 557

Derx, D. J. (Deputy Secretary, Employment), 480

development land tax, 642 and n

Devlin, Lord, 6

devolution, 62–3, 153, 172–3, 179, 281–3, 418–19, 443, 496–8, 537–8, 544, 638, 693, 713

Devolution Committee of Cabinet, 281, 693, 713

DHSS is Department of Health and Social Security (not indexed)

Diamond, Jack (Lord) and Report, 251 and n, 496

Dick Crossman House, Coventry, 349

Diego Garcia, 227 and n

DIG, see Disablement Income Group

Disabled Drivers Association, 47

disabled housewives' benefit, 291n, 296

disabled persons, policy for, 24, 47–9, 60, 99, 167, 173, 179 and n, 180, 229n, 645; see also Sharp Report

Disablement Income Group (DIG), 229

Dix, Bernard (NUPE), 287, 652, 737

Dobson, Philippa and Colin, Kathryn and Ben (Barbara's niece, her husband and children), 17 and n, 82, 192, 265

Dock Labour Scheme, 558n

Dock Work Regulation Bill (dockworkers' scheme), 558, 642 and n, 647, 725

dockers, 6–7, 558n

Doctors' and Dentists' Review Body (DDRB), 117n, 258, 269n, 361 and n, 609, 626, 722

doctors, emigration of, 515, 516

Donaldson, Sir John (President, NIRC), 6–7, 80n, 159 and n

Donne, John (RHA), 131, 143, 654

Donnison, Prof. David (Chairman, SBC), 299 and n, 338, 716, 720, 727

Donoghue, Dr Bernard (Political Adviser), 48 and n, 49n, 59–60

Donovan, Lord Justice (and Report), 2–3, 90n

Doughty, George (AUEW–TASS), 478 and n

Douglas-Mann, Bruce, MP (Lab), 416

Doyle, Christine (Observer), 517, 518

Drabble, Margaret (authoress), 662

Drain, Geoffrey (General Secretary, NALGO), 321, 521, 540, 669

Drayson, Burnaby, MP (Cons), 474

Driberg, Tom (former Labour MP), 434

drugs industry, 28 and n, 74, 162, 666, 714–15

Dublin, EEC summit at, 323n, 326

Du Cann, Edward, MP (Cons), 195 and n

Duffy, Terence (President, AUEW), 659n

Dunn, Jimmie, MP (Lab) (Whip), 547, 557, 629, 693, 726

Dunwoody, John, former MP (Lab), 74 and n, 293

earnings rule, 292, 297, 298, 505, 602

EC(P), see Economic Policy Committee of Cabinet

Economic Policy Committee of Cabinet (EC(P)), 238, 242, 252, 329, 336, 361 and n

Economic Policy, Ministerial Committee on (MES), 116, 117, 141, 254, 304, 522, 649, 657

Economist, The, 266, 270

ECSC, see European Coal and Steel Community

Edna (Barbara's driver), 261, 272, 425, 477, 518–19, 613, 615, 652, 719, 723, 728–9

Edwards, Bob (Sunday Mirror), 175

Edwards, Eric (CPSA), 363

EEC, see European Economic Community

electoral reform, 69–70, 554, 682n

electricity prices, 42 and n, 195n

Elizabeth Garrett Anderson Hospital, 647

Ellis, John, MP (Lab), 56, 109, 335

Elwyn-Jones, Lord (Lord Chancellor): appointed Lord

Chancellor, 30; and Concorde, 46, 124, 146; and Chile, 57; and Council of Europe, 101; and TU legislation, 217, 542, 544; as Cabinet Committee chairman, 280, 423; and John Stonehouse, 280; and census, 280; and incomes policy, 429, 442, 454, 456; and public expenditure, 461, 462; and Finer Report, 523; and Barbara's dismissal, 732

emigration of doctors, 515, 516

Employment Protection Bill, 189, 474, 494, 517 and n

Energy Conference, 1975, 574n; see also Rome talks (energy)

Ennals, David, MP (Minister of State, Foreign Office), 37, 72–3, 663, 670, 703; (Social Services Secretary), 727, 730, 731, 737

entryism, 565 and n

EQ, see European Questions, Cabinet Committee on

Equal Pay Act, 1975, 622

Errington, Lance (Permanent Secretary, DHSS), 35, 171, 476, 709, 715

European Assembly (Parliament): direct elections to, 249, 553–4, 635–6, 650–1, 705–7; Ted Castle selected for, 430, 434; appointment of representatives to, 436–7; Ted Castle at, 450, 459–60, 498, 518, 674, 692, 731

European Coal and Steel Community (ECSC), 322 and n

European Economic Community (EEC): devotion to, by moderates, 11; Britain's entry to, 12; renegotiation of entry terms to, 39, 45, 68 and n, 107 and n, 125–6, 143–4, 149, 174–5, 190, 220–30, 248–50, 314, 323n, 333–4, 340–3; referendum on membership of, 95, 96, 149, 182–3, 226, 287–9, 290, 292, 305, 314, 317, 351–2, 355–7, 359, 366,

375–6, 383, 390, 407–8;
motion on referendum at NEC,
750 (Appendix III); Council
of Ministers meetings, 101,
211, 335, 418–21; and beef,
148 and n, 229 and n, 685n;
Monitoring Committee on,
wound up, 152, 204; and
draft election manifesto,
154–5; and sugar, 196,
211–12, 218, 230; German
view of, 225; at Labour Party
Annual Conference (1974),
240; and medical directories,
267, 273, 279, 295–6, 298–9;
and legislative control over,
301–2, 331; and regional
policy, 322–3; special Labour
Party Conference on,
379–80; and TES, 503–4; and
passports, 579; and
agricultural policy, 685 and n,
686
European Questions, Cabinet
Committee on (EQ), 53, 112,
196, 273, 295, 296, 409, 685
and n
European Questions, Cabinet
Committee on (EQ), 295, 296,
409, 685 and n
European Regional
Development Fund, 128, 248
and n, 313 and n, 322 and n
Evening News, 554
Evening Standard, 278, 516,
554, 729
Ewing, Winifred, MP (Scot Nat),
444
Ezra, Sir Derek (Chairman,
NCB), 26, 27n, 33

Fairfield Old People's Home,
252–3
Fairley, Mrs, 581–2
Fairley, Professor, 534, 580,
581
Falkender, Lady (Mrs Marcia
Williams), 49n, 62, 63, 82,
153 and n, 277–8, 642, 677,
699
family allowances, 140n, 172,
177, 200; special (FAM),
236n, 237, 268, 272, 276,
358, 380n
family courts, 523 and n
family endowment, see child

benefit (family/child
endowment)
family planning, 47 and n, 58–9
73, 83, 211
Family Practitioners' Committee
conference, 517
Fane, John (family friend), 459
Faulkner, Hugh (Help the
Aged), 639
FBU, see Fire Brigades' Union
Feather, Victor (former General
Secretary, TUC), 3, 17, 215n
Fell, Anthony, MP (Cons), 57
Ferranti Ltd, 190
F-111A Aircraft, 23 and n
Field, Tony (Lady Falkender's
brother), 62 and n, 63, 74
Figgures, Sir Frank (Chairman,
Pay Board), 33 and n
Financial Times, 113, 334, 343,
408, 411, 459, 468, 555, 557,
559, 647
Finer Committee and Report,
170 and n, 228, 523 and n,
528
Finniston, Sir Monty
(Chairman, BSC), 385–6, 390
Fire Brigades' Union (FBU),
257, 379n
Fisher, Alan (General
Secretary, NUPE): and nurses,
104; and Charing Cross
dispute, 131, 133, 135, 137;
and pay beds, 321, 388, 521,
540, 585, 651; and private
practice policy, 508; and
incomes policy, 455; and local
government expenditure,
531
Fitch, George (Daily Express),
599
Fitzgerald, Dr Garrett (Irish
Foreign Minister), 323n
Focke, Frau (German Minister),
225
Folger, Patricia (Private Office,
DHSS), 528, 719
Folkestone, visit to, 517
Foot, Dingle, MP (Lab), 347n
Foot, Hugh (Lord Caradon),
347n
Foot, Isaac, 347n
Foot, Jill, 326, 336, 379, 718
Foot, John (Lord), 347n
Foot, Michael, MP (Employment
Secretary): elected PLP

Deputy Leader, 13; rewrites
campaign document, 18;
appointed Employment
Secretary, 30, 35; and miners,
36, 311 and n, 318–19; and
prices and incomes policy
(Social Contract), 44, 62, 88,
119, 194, 244, 250, 286; and
repeal of Industrial Relations
Act, 45, 79–81, 86, 90–1; at
informal dinners, 45n, 79;
and EEC, 53, 111, 112, 126,
183, 249, 288, 290, 380; and
Clay Cross, 67; Tribune
attacks, 73; and Chile, 77,
86, 87; and 'consent' powers,
88, 93–4, 99; and concern
over next election, 95, 96,
118, 126; and Trade Union
Bills, 100, 214–15, 217, 230,
246, 541, 544; and Concorde,
110; and nuclear test, 123;
and public expenditure, 156,
468, 484, 548; and view of
staff on, 159; and Halsbury
Report, 181; and NHS pay
clerks, 187, 188; and
Employment Protection Bill,
189; at Chequers meeting,
221–2; and NUJ dispute, 231
and n; and NEC elections, 239,
510; and NEC/Government
relations, 233–4; and top
salaries, 250, 252, 253–4,
255–6; and censure motions,
255; and GPS, 269; and
inflation, 297, 373; and Reg
Prentice, 325–6; and pay
increases, 328–9; and
anti-EEC campaign, 345–8,
407; operation on, 380; and
Cabinet changes, 414–15;
and economic strategy, 422,
506–7, 531; and industrial
democracy, 423; and incomes
policy (1975), 425–7,
429–30, 435, 440, 447–9,
452–5, 473, 496; and MPS
salaries, 446; and manpower
policy, 494; and job creation, 502,
503; and health charges,
504–5, 537; at 1975 Annual
Conference, 506–7, 509–10;
and industrial strategy, 524,
542, 563; and JHDs, 555–6,

Foot, Michael, MP – *contd.*
602–4; and Chrysler, 579,
584; and Radcliffe Report,
627; and Namibia, 635; and
unemployment debate, 636;
and pay beds, 656; and
Rhodesia, 664; and
confidence vote, 682; and
economic outlook, 684; and
leadership election, 691, 692,
695, 705, 711, 717–18; and
April 1976 Budget, 717, 732;
and Barbara's dismissal, 718,
723, 725, 727; appointed
Leader of House, 727
Foot, Paul, 347
Ford, Dr (JHD), 525–7, 538,
555
Ford Motors, 188 and n, 194
Ford, President (USA), 305, 390
Forrester, John (NEC member),
23–4 and n, 26, 507, 566,
662
Forsyth, Jennifer (Under
Secretary, Treasury), 709 and
n
Fowler, Norman, MP (Cons),
344, 389, 515, 517, 535, 557,
570, 609, 632
France, 68 and n, 75, 124, 248,
390, 493, 499–502, 553n
Franco, General (Spanish
Leader), 557
Fraser, Hugh, MP (Cons), 303n,
474, 534
Fraser, John, MP (Employment
Under Secretary), 419, 420
Freeman, John (former Labour
MP), 17, 537n
Frimley Park Hospital, 382
and n
Fryer, John (*Sunday Times*),
267
fuel bonus, 547, 558–9, 639,
656 and n

Gaitskell, Hugh (former Labour
Party Leader), 11, 222n,
537n, 677
Gale, George, 383, 586
Gandhi, Indira (Premier of
India), 438, 475n
Gardner, Llew, 265, 266
GAS, *see* General Aviation
Services
Gedling, Raymond (Deputy

Secretary, DHSS): and
Halsbury Report, 177, 183,
184, 203, 215; and
consultants, 257; and alleged
resignation threat, 265; and
private practice policy, 451;
and AHAS, 534; and junior
hospital doctors, 570,
609–10, 626, 722; and pay
beds, 669, 695, 711, 714, 722
General and Municipal
Workers' Union (GMWU), 379
and n
General Aviation Services
(GAS), 80n
General Dental Council, 102
General Election (February
1974), 29–32
General Election (October
1974), 185, 188–90
General Election (May 1979),
739
General Medical Council (GMC),
551, 570
General Nursing Council, 100
general practitioners (GPs), 269,
271
George, Bruce, MP (Lab), 445
Germany, West, 218 and n,
224–6, 390, 553n
Ghana, 403
Gilbert, Dr John, MP (Financial
Secretary, Treasury), 54 and
n, 362
Gillis, Ian (Deputy Information
Director, DHSS), 165–6, 246,
262, 265, 306
Gilmore, Mr (JHD), 550
Ginsburg, David, MP (Lab), 27
Giroud, Françoise (French
Minister), 467 and n
Giscard D'Estaing, President
(France), 124, 245, 248 and
n, 488
Gladwyn, Lord, 460
Glasgow newspaper, *see Scottish
Daily Express*
GMC, *see* General Medical
Council
GMWU, *see* General and
Municipal Workers' Union
Godber, Sir George (BMA), 278
and n, 617, 693
Godley, Wynne (economist),
316, 679
Goodman, Arnold (Lord)

(solicitor and Chairman,
NPA): and Harold Wilson's
writs, 66, 615–16; and
Rhodesia, 66n; and the arts,
66n, 561, 710; and NPA, 66n,
231n, 615, 710; and NUJ
closed shop, 66n, 231n, 541,
544; and pay beds, 556–7,
560–1, 567, 569, 571–3,
575–8, 582–4, 586–93, 597,
602, 604–9, 614–15, 618,
621, 640; and consultations
after BMA ballot, 667–8,
672–3, 688, 696, 698, 702,
707, 710–12, 731; and Harold
Wilson's resignation, 695; and
the Goodman proposals,
Appendix VI, 760
Gormley, Joe (President, NUM), 29
Gowon, President (Nigeria),
703 and n
GPs, *see* general practitioners
Grabham, Anthony (Chairman,
CCHMS): and consultants'
contract, 115, 166, 259,
308–9, 364–6, 370; and
junior hospital doctors,
525–6, 538; and Royal
Commission, 526, 530; and
pay beds, 561, 577, 587–9,
608–9, 614, 625; and
consultations after BMA ballot,
667, 695, 734
Graham, John (*Sunday Mirror*),
175 and n
Graham, Sandy, 175 and n
Grantham, Roy (General
Secretary, APEX), 396 and n
Gray, Sir John (MRC), 449
Greaves, Mary (DIG), 229
Greece, 57
Green, Mrs (OAP Federation),
94, 729
Greene, Sid (General Secretary,
NUR), 18, 54, 120, 319
Greenhill, Lord, 663 and n,
664, 671
Greenwich, visit to, 127
Grey-Turner, Dr Elston
(Deputy Secretary, BMA), 722
Griffiths, Mr (Whitley Council
chairman), 94
Grunwick dispute, 79n
Grylls, Michael, MP (Cons), 382
Guardian: and miners, 26; and
consultants' contract, 266,

270; and EEC referendum, 371, 403, 407; and run on sterling, 435; and NEC Home Policy Committee meeting, 450; and Tony Benn, 492; and pay beds, 555, 562, 569, 586; and Barbara's visit to Newcastle, 638; pre-briefing of journalists on, 653; and George Brown, 669; and BOSS, 686; and consultative document on private practice, 703

Guinness, Alec (actor), 309

Gullick, Dr (BMA), 277, 300, 307, 308, 665–6, 688, 696 722

Gundelach, Commissioner (EEC), 563

Haines, Joe (PMS Chief Press Secretary), 207 and n

Hall, Jennie, 17

Halsbury, Lord (Chairman, DDRB): appointed chairman of review on nurses' pay, 105 and n, 106; and extension of review, 114–15; and DDRB, 117n; pressed for report, 151, 157n, 177; and radiographers, 167, 168 and n; and doctors' claim, 196, 203, 204; resignation of, 211, 215

Halsbury Report, 180 and n, 181, 183–5

Hamburger, Sidney (Chairman, RHA), 339, 468

Hamilton, Willie, MP (Lab), 98, 444–5

Hamling, Will, MP (Lab), 417 and n

Hampton Court Palace, 445

Hardcastle, Bill (BBC), 168

Harland and Wolff, 354

Harmsworth, Vere, 424

Harper, Joe, MP (Lab), 735 and n

Harris, Kenneth (Observer), 518

Harrison, Bob (TGWU), 387, 401

Harrison, Gerald (BBC), 437

Harrison, Walter, MP (Lab), 734

Hart, Graham (Private Secretary, DHSS), 43 and n, 44, 52, 58, 92, 105, 110, 117, 125, 130, 137, 674

Hart, Judith, MP (Overseas

Development Minister, 1974–75): and informal dinners, 45n, 139; and Chile, 53, 64, 86, 87, 198, 634; and chairing of NEC committees, 74; and public expenditure, 79, 658n, 659; and EEC, 126, 336; and security vetting, 198; and S. Africa, 205; and televising of Parliament, 320; and reprimand by Harold Wilson, 390; resigns from Government, 408, 410–11, 415; and Economic Reviews, 449; and industrial policy, 464, 492, 494, 544, 659, 700; and Portugal, 494–5; at 1975 Annual Conference, 510, 511; and Harold Wilson's speech at NEC, 564; and pay beds, 646; and Armitage Committee, 649n; and economic strategy, 674

Hart, Tony, 161, 411

Harty, Russell, 176

Hatfield, Michael (The Times), 23

Hattersley, Roy, MP (Minister of State, Foreign Office), 174, 222 and n, 287 and n, 295–6, 298, 323, 503, 729

Hawker Hunter Aircraft, 76, 86, 87

Hayward, Ron (General Secretary, Labour Party): at Liaison Committee, 18, 84, 119; and Chile, 87; and Monitoring Committee (EEC), 152; and joint NEC/Cabinet meetings, 227, 232; and EEC, 288, 290, 346, 348, 355 and n, 356, 375, 383; and party finances, 395–6, 433–4; and industrial policy, 464–5; and Portugal, 495; at Xmas party, 611; and pay bed policy, 632; and unemployment conference, 661–2; and Reg Prentice, 662; and Socialist International, 676

HCF, see Hell Corner Farm

HCSA, see Hospital Consultants and Specialists Association

Healey, Denis, MP (Chancellor of the Exchequer): as Shadow Chancellor, 11, 13; at Liaison Committee, 18, 119–21,

284–5, 318, 372, 393–4; and campaign document, 23; and miners' dispute, 25; appointed Chancellor, 30; and uprating pensions, 41, 43, 55, 58, 363n, 716; and public expenditure, 42–3, 81, 155, 171–2, 178, 194, 200, 236–8, 319n, 352–4, 398–400, 435, 460–4, 468, 482–6, 546, 548, 593, 641, 738; and March 1974 Budget, 50–1, 60, 62; and mortgages, 69, 76; and industrial relations, 91; and Concorde, 106, 124; and mixed economy, 114, 115; and July 1974 Budget, 114, 148, 150, 154; and family endowment, 140–1; and industrial policy, 145–6, 493–4, 675, 679; and EEC, 174–5, 288, 340–1, 347; at joint NEC/Cabinet, 181–2, 233, 496; and inflation, 190, 297; and North Sea Oil, 196; and November 1974 Budget, 213, 240; at Chequers meeting, 220–4; and Special FAM, 272; and earnings rule, 298; and incomes policy, 337–8, 396, 425–6, 430, 432, 435, 439–43, 452, 453–8, 470, 679–80; and April 1975 Budget, 358, 359–62, 372; on industrial democracy, 423; and devolution, 497; and unemployment, 502, 503, 542, 559; and health charges, 504–5; defeated in NEC elections, 510, 511; and NHS enquiry, 525; and Chrysler, 545, 610; and defence cuts, 581; and political advisers, 640; and unemployment 'package', 649, 657–8, 660; and EEC direct elections, 650, 706; and Rhodesia, 664; and economic outlook, 681, 683–5, 697–8; and confidence vote, 682–3, 687; and shipbuilding industry, 691; and Wilson's resignation, 691; and leadership election, 692, 694, 705, 711, 713; and April 1976 Budget, 716, 720

Healey, Edna, 240

Health Co-operation
Agreement, 502
Health Exports Council, 638
Health Service Treasurers, 217
Health Services and Public
Health Act, 1968, 345n
Health Services Bill/Act, 1976,
631n, 698; *see also* pay beds,
Bill on
Health Services Board, 723, 737
Heath, Edward, MP (Prime
Minister, then Leader of
Opposition): and
confrontation with miners, 1;
exploits unpopularity of
strikes, 2; as Prime Minister
(1970-74), 3-9, 12, 21; and
emergency debate, 21-2; and
Relativities Report, 27-8;
General Election defeats,
29-30, 32, 33, 188-9; and
Cabinet Room, 35, 164; on
Benn's report on Department,
109n, 111; and attacks on
leadership, 195 and n, 291,
303n; and November 1974
Budget, 216; and Chequers
redecoration, 219-20; at
Oxford Union debate, 405-7;
and Roy Jenkins, 432; and
incomes policy (1975), 473;
and Wilson's resignation, 692
heating allowances, 363n, 397n
Heenan, Cardinal, 73
Heffer, Eric, MP (Minister of
State for Industry, 1974-75),
40, 78, 312, 351n, 451, 510,
564, 565, 611, 632-3, 700, 731
Hell Corner Farm (HCF), 17, 73,
82-4, 99, 116, 173, 180, 357,
370, 430, 438, 476, 490-1,
498, 615, 730
Help the Aged, 639
Henderson, Nicholas (British
Ambassador), 224-5
Herbison, Margaret (former
Labour Minister), 364 and n
Heron, Conrad (Permanent
Secretary, Employment
Department), 158-9, 297
Heseltine, Michael, MP (Cons),
489
Hester Adrian Research
Institute, 469
Hibbert, Mr (Embassy
Minister), 224-5

Higgs, Karen (Private Office,
DHSS), 363, 444-5
Hiley, Clarice (Barbara's
mother's friend), 730
Hill, David and Janet, 729
Hills, Denis (lecturer in
Uganda), 417n, 452, 458
Hindmarsh, Mr (Under
Secretary, DHSS), 418
Hinton, Mark (son of Barbara's
niece), 32 and n
Hinton, Rachel (daughter of
Barbara's niece), 32n, 401-2,
403n
Hinton, Sonya (Barbara's
niece), 17n, 32 and n, 83,
173, 261, 401, 402, 481, 491;
and children, Paul and Laura,
32n
Hinton, Terry (husband of
Barbara's niece), 32 and n,
173, 261, 481, 491
Hobman, David (Age Concern),
102
Holmes, Thornton (consultant),
566
Home Affairs Committee of
Cabinet, 71, 280
Honours List/system, 633, 634,
675
Hope Hospital, Leigh, 468
Horam, John, MP (Lab), 354
Hospital Consultants and
Specialists Association
(HCSA), 133n, 136n, 212,
258, 343, 515, 550
hospitals, 38, 94, 150, 382 and
n, 500, 502, 519
Houghton, Douglas (Lord),
18-19, 396 and n
House of Lords, 122-3, 182,
214n, 486, 531
Housing Finance Act (1972), 8,
10, 64
Housing Finance Bill, 418
Hoveyda, Mr (Iranian Premier),
624
Howard, Alan (actor), 662
Howe, Sir Geoffrey, MP (Cons),
82, 100n, 106, 108, 139, 177,
180, 243, 274, 275, 309n,
311, 473
Howerd, Frankie (comedian),
176
Hughes, Cledwyn, MP (Lab),
103, 190, 446

Hughes, John (Ruskin College),
478n
Hunt, John (Cabinet Secretary),
36, 193, 251, 314, 690,
693
Hunt, Norman, *see*
Crowther-Hunt, Lord
Hunter, Dr Robert (Lord)
(University Vice-Chancellor),
258 and n
'Husbands and Wives' dinners,
45 and n, 53, 62, 67, 79, 86,
95, 109, 117, 126, 139, 141,
160, 197

Iceland, 562 and n, 563, 566,
630
ID, *see* Industrial Development
Committee of Cabinet
IDAB, *see* Industrial
Development Advisory Board
IHG, *see* Independent Hospitals
Group
IMF, *see* International Monetary
Fund
immigration, 61, 71-3, 702n
import controls, 316, 337, 493,
502, 527, 553 and n, 568-9,
610-11, 697
In Place of Strife, 2, 38, 87n, 92,
159, 214, 215n, 220n, 386, 442
income tax: cuts, 4, 50n, 680;
increases, 50n, 51n, 358, 398
incomes policy, 425-30, 447-9,
453-8, 492, 514, 679-80,
703, 712, 738, 739
Independent Hospitals Group
(IHG), 550, 556, 567, 575,
695, 696, 702, 709
industrial democracy, 354,
422-4
Industrial Development
Advisory Board (IDAB), 207,
478 and n, 563
Industrial Development
Committee of Cabinet (ID),
109n, 161, 305
Industrial Relations Bill/Act, 5,
8, 9, 29, 45, 46n, 55, 79, 86n
Industry Bill/Act, 1975, 312,
323n, 354 and n, 376 and n,
429-30 and n, 531
inflation, 3-4, 7, 10, 51n, 114,
116-17, 254, 284-5, 311,
316, 352, 426 and n, 439,
514, 738

Inskip, J. Hampden (and Report), 86 and n
Institute of Hearing Research, 449
International Court of Justice, 562 and n
International Monetary Fund (IMF), 50, 679, 738
International Women's Year, 275, 277–8, 387, 561
invalid care allowances, 229n, 489
invalidity pension, 229n, 291n, 296, 397n
Iran, 616n, 623–4, 645, 670
Irish Labour Party, 634
Irish Republican Army (IRA), 116n, 521, 534, 535–6
Iron and Steel Act, 1967, 322 and n
Italy, 101, 553n

Jackson, Margaret, MP (Lab), 734
Jacobson, Sidney (*Daily Mirror*), 175
Jacques, Peter (TUC), 321, 388–9, 521, 522, 540, 547, 585, 668, 732
Japan, 553n, 569, 631, 691
JASP, *see* Joint Approach to Social Policy Cabinet Committee
Jay, Douglas, MP (Lab), 343
Jay Peter (economist), 114, 528
Jeger, Lena (MP (Lab) and NEC member), 152, 182, 375, 630
Jenkin, Patrick, MP (Cons), 632, 645, 721
Jenkins, Clive (General Secretary, ASTMS), 144 and n, 157, 161, 164–6, 240, 321, 339, 396
Jenkins, Peter (*Guardian*), 61, 371, 408, 468, 586, 653
Jenkins, Roy, MP (Home Secretary): supports EEC, 11, 12, 155, 190, 289, 379, 407; resigns as Deputy Leader, 12–13, 289; and campaign document, 23; appointed Home Secretary, 30, 35; in Cabinet, 57–8, 96, 280, 353, 400, 462; attitude of, 61, 147; and electoral reform, 69–70, 554, 681, 682n; and

immigration, 71–3, 303–4; and Concorde, 106, 147; and devolution, 153, 283, 497–8, 693, 713; and speech at Haverfordwest, 156n, 159–60; at joint NEC/Cabinet, 181–3, 700; and TU legislation, 215, 217, 544; at Chequers meetings, 220–4, 484; and top salaries, 256; and incomes policy (1975), 427, 441, 454–5; and alleged coalition plot, 432; and TES, 503–4; and Radcliffe Report, 627; press on change of post for, 653; and Shrewsbury pickets, 683n; at Wilson's farewell dinner, 699; and leadership election, 705; and EEC direct elections, 705; and Cabinet Minutes, 711; and April 1976 Budget, 717
Jessof, Prof. (consultant), 299
JHD, *see* junior hospital doctors
JHDA, *see* Junior Hospital Doctors Association
job creation schemes, 502, 503, 630, 738
John, Bill (NEC member), 564
Johnson, Elizabeth (Private Office, DHSS), 59, 95, 142, 169, 193, 265
Johnson, Gerald (Private Office, DHSS), 616, 720
Joint Approach to Social Policy Cabinet Committee (JASP), 389, 485 and n
Jones, Alec, MP (Parliamentary Under Secretary, DHSS), 413, 418, 673
Jones, Aubrey (former Chairman, Prices and Incomes Board), 513 and n
Jones, Evelyn (Mrs Jack), 339
Jones, Jack (General Secretary, TGWU): critical of Barbara, 3; and shop stewards, 9; and ACAS, 9, 84–5; and incomes policy, 10, 83 and n, 435, 440, 448, 469–71, 492; and pensions, 38n, 89, 104, 149–50, 489, 511, 558, 631; and Social Contract, 83, 113, 119, 149, 201; at Liaison Committee, 283–4, 394, 430–2, 502, 558–9; and EEC,

339–40, 350; at *Tribune* meeting, 512; and unemployment, 631; and public expenditure, 658; and unity behind Government, 679, 693; and forthcoming budget, 696–7
Jones, Mildred (Mrs Alec), 673–4
Jordan-Moss, Nick (Deputy Secretary, DHSS), 131, 520
Joseph, Sir Keith, MP (Cons) 44n, 47 and n, 53n, 142n, 179n, 189, 198 and n, 202, 247, 295
Judd, Frank, MP (Lab), 107
junior hospital doctors (JHD): negotiations on new contract for, 191–2, 269 and n, 270 and n; problems of, explained, 515; TU views on, 522; Cabinet discussion on, 525; discussions on avoiding detriment to, 526–7, 536–7, 538–9; industrial action by, 543, 550–1, 554, 569; ballot of, 552; post-ballot discussions on claim by, 555–6, 572, 586, 597–9, 600, 602–4, 609–10, 614, 617; and new overtime payments, 722
Junior Hospital Doctors' Association (JHDA), 554, 570, 586

Kaberry, Donald (Chairman of Hospital Governors), 94
Kapp, Dr Elinor (JHDA), 570, 586
Kaufman, Gerald, MP (Under Secretary, Environment), 88
Kaunda, President Kenneth (Zambia), 276, 663, 664, 671n, 694
Keable-Elliott, Dr Robert Anthony (Tony) (BMA): as neighbour of Barbara's, 49 and n, 139, 384, 405, 616; and superannuation scheme, 100; and salary claim, 166; and GPs claim, 219 and n, 271; and financing of NHS, 443–4; and incomes policy, 471; and pay beds, 667; and Barbara's dismissal, 731
Keatley, Patrick (*Guardian*), 686
Kendall, Bill (CPSA), 363

Kennedy, Edward (us Senator), 358

Kent, Duke of, 501

Kenyatta, President Jomo (Kenya), 417

Kettering hospital, 118–19, 120

Khama, President Seretse (Botswana), 671n

Kilbrandon, Lord, 63, 282n

Kingdom, Leonard (consultant), 570

King's Lynn, visit to, 172

Kinnock, Neil, MP (Lab), 511, 698

Kirk, Peter, MP (Cons), 459

Kirkby Manufacturing and Engineering Ltd, 354n

Kitson, Alex (NEC member), 86, 183, 201, 290, 412, 469, 506, 564, 662

Knight, Jill, MP (Cons), 368

Kuwait, 439, 498–9, 616n, 623, 645

Labour Campaign for Mental Health, 510

Labour Weekly, 37, 636

Laird, Gavin (AUEW), 659n

Lamb, Archie (British Ambassador), 623

Lancaster hospital, 730

Lancaster House, 94, 231, 498, 504

Lancaster, Terry (*Daily Mirror*), 168, 651

Lancaster, visit to, 180

land deal allegations, 62, 63 66–7, 70, 73–4, 79, 82

land policy, 140, 164; *see also* Community Land Bill

Lander, Don (Chrysler), 711

Langford-Holt, John, MP (Cons), 474

Lappas, Alfons (German TUC), 225

Lardinois, Petrus (EEC Commissioner), 173 and n, 235, 335

Lawton, Frank (Solicitor, Employment Department), 94

Le Vert, M. (Directeur du Cabinet), 499–502

Lea, David (TUC), 84

Leber, Walter, 420

Legislation Committee of

Cabinet, 53–4, 276, 296, 298, 331, 421, 712, 719

Leigh, visit to, 468–9

Lestor, Joan MP (Lab), 107, 152, 205, 233, 240, 378, 403, 416, 452, 635n, 657 and n, 661

Lever, Diane, 35

Lever, Harold, MP (Chancellor of the Duchy of Lancaster): appointed Chancellor, 35 and n; as 'the Duke', 41; opposes Denis Healey, 42–3, 51–2, 81; and disabled drivers, 48; and unemployment, 55; and mortgages, 69, 75–6, 143; and public expenditure, 156, 462, 472; and industrial policy, 167, 354 and n, 675; in Cabinet, 197, 250, 277, 280, 348, 424, 505, 542; at Chequers meeting, 220; voting error by, 231n; and EEC, 249; and top salaries, 256; and British Leyland, 374; and textiles, 385; and incomes policy, 427–9, 442, 453, 456; Barbara's lunch at Eaton Square with, 472; and pay beds, 525, 527–8, 568, 656, 703–4, 730; Barbara's comments on, 525, 533; and Chrysler, 579–80, 584, 602; and Namibia, 635; and economic outlook, 684; and shipbuilding industry, 691; and Wilson's resignation, 692

Levin, Bernard (*The Times*), 693

Lewin, Dr Walpole (Chairman, BMA Council): initial meeting with, 46 and n; and consultants' contract, 258, 260, 344; and Charing Cross dispute, 133, 134–5, 137, 138; and NHS financing, 144n, 163–4; and salary claim, 166–7; at dinners with Barbara, 231, 375; and incomes policy, 471–2; and pay beds, 549–50, 575–6, 625, 630, 667; and junior hospital doctors, 555–6

Lewis, Dr Brian (Chairman, HCSA), 212, 247, 257, 259–60, 262, 364

Leybourne Grange Mental Hospital, 127

Liaison Committee (TUC), 8, 9–10, 18–21, 84–5, 102–4, 119, 149, 283–6, 318–19, 349–50, 371–3, 393–5, 430–2, 469–71, 502–3, 558–9, 630–1, 657–60, 696–8

Liberal Party, 30, 189, 570, 738

Lincoln by-election, 12

Lipsey, David (Political Adviser), 274

Litterick, Tom MP (Lab), 686

Liverpool Toxteth Constituency Labour Party, 240n

Liverpool, visit to, 202

Lloyd, Ian, MP (Cons), 82

Lloyd, Selwyn (Speaker), 25, 26, 474

local authority expenditure, 522, 531, 679

local government conference, Labour Party (Manchester), 274, 281

local government reorganization, 282 and n, 528

Local Optical Committee conference, 648

Lockets, 53, 86, 95, 160–1, 297, 326, 338, 521

Logan, Sir Douglas (Principal, London University), 170

London weighting, 73 and n, 147

Loshak, David (*Daily Telegraph*), 586, 667

Lowe, Dr (Chairman, AUCAS), 298

Lucas, Harry (GMWU), 476

Luxembourg, 419–20, 662

Lynes, Tony (Barbara's Special Adviser, DHSS), 52, 170, 272, 708, 721

Lyon, Alex, MP (Home Office Minister), 72 and n, 702, 734

Lyons, visit to, 501–2

Mabon, Dr Dickson, MP (Lab), 156n

McAdden, Sir Stephen, MP (Cons), 304

McCarthy, Dr W. E. J. (Lord) (Adviser, DHSS), 271 and n, 290, 315

Maclennan, Sir Hector (Advisory Committee Chairman), 569

McCluskie, Sam (NEC member), 290, 452, 566

McColl, Prof. Ian (Consultant Surgeon), 258 and n

McGahey, Mick (NUM), 113 and n, 424

McGarvey, Danny (Boilermakers), 558, 559

McGrath, Dr (Broadmoor), 540

Machel, President Samora (Mozambique), 671n

McIntosh, Hugh (Barbara's nephew), 17n, 83; his wife, Miranda, and children, Christopher, Belinda and Susannah, 83n

McIntosh, Marjorie (Barbara's sister), 17n, 83, 582

McKinsey Report, 123, 388

Mackintosh, John, MP (Lab), 334 and n, 379, 642n

McNally, Tom (Political Adviser), 122, 276, 663n, 676 and n

McNamara, Kevin, MP (Lab), 629

Macpherson, Hugh (Tribune), 731

Maddocks, Miss (NALGO), 144–5, 157

Maidstone Hospital, 594

'Mandarin Power', 35n, 40, 92

Mander, Dr (JHD), 525, 527

Manifesto for February 1974 Election, 28, 155n

Manifesto for October 1974 Election, 154–5, 167, 181–3, 189

Manifesto for 1979 Election, 737

Manifesto Group, 156n, 309n, 540, 541, 626

Manpower Services Commission, 494

Mann, Adrian (Political Adviser), 640

Maplin airport, 147 and n

Margach, Jimmie, 168

Marks, Ken, MP (Wilson's PPS), 412, 414

married women's benefits, 489 and n, 490

Marten, Joan, 401

Marten, Neil, MP (Cons), 373, 383, 401, 402

Martin, Roy (Race Relations Board), 304 and n

Mason, Jim (Chairman, Blackburn Labour Party), 31, 274, 492, 687

Mason, Roy, MP (Defence Secretary): appointed Defence Secretary, 30; in Cabinet, 42, 43, 277, 360, 391, 423, 462; and Chile, 57, 77; and Northern Ireland, 89; and TV performance, 121; and defence review, 183, 227, 324, 484, 531, 596–7, 602, 664, 670; at Chequers meeting, 221; and EEC, 288; and incomes policy, 442, 456

Matthöfer, Herr (German Minister), 225

Maudling, Reginald, MP (Cons), 1, 417

Mauritius, 104, 118, 168

Maxwell, Robert (former Labour MP), 503

Maynard, Joan (NEC member), 23–4, 25, 154, 181, 234, 254, 507, 509, 661

Mayne, Stanley (IPCS), 649n

Meacher, Michael, MP (Under Secretary, DHSS), 21, 410, 413, 416, 425, 727, 732, 734

medical equipment manufacturers, 704, 715

Medical Research Council (MRC), 449

medium-term assessment (MTA), 457–8, 460–2

Mellish, Bob, MP (Chief Whip): at Liaison Committee, 18–19, 431; in Cabinet, 41, 43, 123, 353, 391, 541; and pensions uprating, 56, 58, 67, 81; and electoral reform, 70; and union fines, 80; and PLP, 110; congratulates Barbara, 139; official appointment to Cabinet, 156n; and EEC, 175, 296, 302; and MPs salaries, 446; and incomes policy, 455; and legislative pressure, 474, 642; and public expenditure, 549; and abortion, 628, 629; and TU links, 661; and

Tribunite revolt, 680, 682; and Harold Wilson's resignation, 691; at Harold Wilson's farewell dinner, 699; and EEC direct elections, 705–6; and Brian O'Malley's funeral, 726; dismissed by Jim Callaghan, 724, 733

mental health, 85–6, 320–1, 349, 469 and n; White Paper, 411–12

Merck, Sharp and Dohme International, 714–15

Meriden motorcycle factory, 114, 424, 477 and n, 478–9

Merrison, Sir Alexander (Royal Commission Chairman), 541, 621–2, 626, 732

MES, see Economic Policy, Ministerial Committee on

Meyer, Mr (AHA Chairman), 132

Middle East, visit to, 622–4, 625, 704

Mikardo, Ian (MP (Lab) and NEC member): at Liaison Committee, 18–19, 104, 120–1, 394, 469, 471, 502; and Ministers on NEC committees, 75, 204, 465; concern at Government/NEC relations, 152, 232, 452, 661; and ASTMS, 161; at joint NEC/Cabinet, 181, 232, 234, 495–6; and S. Africa, 205; and NEC elections, 239, 510; as NEC International Committee Chairman, 268; and EEC referendum, 290, 339–40, 348–9, 356–7, 375; and party finances, 396, 433–4; and Cabinet changes, 416; and Economic Reviews, 449; and industrial policy, 493–4, 659, 697; at 1975 Annual Conference, 507, 509, 511–12, 513; and Reg Prentice, 564, 662; and Honours List, 633; and re-selection of MPs, 633; and Socialist International, 676

Miles, Tony (Daily Mirror), 438, 492, 651

Milhench, Ronald, 63

militant tendency, 565 and n

Millan, Bruce, MP (Scottish
Secretary of State), 295
miners, 7, 9, 25, 67n, 113, 220,
250, 311 and n
Ministerial Committees, see
Anti-Poverty Strategy;
Devolution; Economic;
Economic Policy;
Miscellaneous Social Policy;
Overseas Economic Policy
ministerial salaries, 436n, 446,
466
MISC, see Miscellaneous
Committee of Cabinet
Miscellaneous Committee of
Cabinet (MISC), 152-3,
543
Miscellaneous Devolution
Questions, Cabinet
Committee on, 443
Miscellaneous Social Policy
Committee (MSP), 669
Mitchell, Bob, MP (Lab),
730
Mitchell, Derek (Cabinet
Office), 198
Mittler, Prof. Peter (Chairman,
Group for Mentally
Handicapped), 469 and n,
592
Mobutu, President (Zaire),
417n
Molloy, Mike (Daily Mirror),
651
Money Resolutions, 76n
Montgomerie, Mr (Lord
Goodman's assistant), 597,
599
Moore, Henry (sculptor), 662
Moore, Philip (Queen's Deputy
Secretary), 733
Moorgate underground crash,
325, 351
Moran, Lord, 170n
Morgan, Elystan, MP (Lab), 22
Morning Star, 24, 610
Morrell, Frances (Political
Adviser), 367 and n, 373,
378, 383, 391
Morris, Alf, MP (Under
Secretary, DHSS), 40 and n,
47-8, 59, 60, 95, 142, 169
and n, 581, 645, 735
Morris, Alison (Secretary,
Blackburn Labour Party), 29,
34, 116

Secretary, 30, 107, 108; and
devolution, 153, 172, 282;
appreciates working with
Barbara, 278; and EEC, 342;
and incomes policy, 456; and
public expenditure, 462; and
pay beds, 530
mortgages, 51, 62, 68, 75-6,
124
MPs, re-selection of, 633
MPs salaries, 436 and n, 445-6,
466
MRC, see Medical Research
Council
MSP, see Miscellaneous Social
Policy Committee
MTA, see medium-term
assessment
Muhamed, President Murtala
(Nigeria), 703n
Mulley, Fred, MP (Transport
Minister, then Education
Secretary): and miners, 25; as
Chairman of Party
Conference, 379; and EEC
referendum, 381-2;
appointed Education
Secretary, 408; and incomes
policy, 455; and public
expenditure, 462; and
devolution, 497; and Reg
Prentice, 564; and education
cuts, 596, 600, 641, 703; and
Ian Mikardo's report on Irish
Labour Party, 634
Murphy, Brian ('Spud'), 239, 401
Murray, Albert, MP (Lab), 60
and n, 642
Murray, Len (General
Secretary, TUC): at Liaison
Committee, 18-20, 284-6,
318, 350, 372, 430-2; and
Relativities Report, 26; and
Social Contract, 45, 83, 113,
189; and March 1974 Budget,
55; and Halsbury Report,
184, 185; at International
Women's Year reception,
278; and incomes policy
(1975), 430-2, 440, 470,
559; and unemployment,
630-1; and public
expenditure, 658; and April
1967 Budget, 696
Murray, Ronald King, MP (Lab),
331

Murray, Dr Stark (Tribune),
628
Muzorewa, Bishop (Rhodesian
African leader), 683

Nairne, Patrick (Permanent
Secretary, DHSS): appointed,
467; and NHS expenditure,
539; and pay beds, 581, 609,
709, 714; and Chief Social
Work Officer, 616; and Civil
Service cuts, 643; and
Norman Warner's transfer,
674; and Barbara's dismissal,
726, 727; tribute to, 726,
733
NALGO, see National Association
of Local Government Officers
Namibia, 635
National Association of Local
Government Officers
(NALGO), 94, 113, 184, 418
National Coal Board (NCB), 30,
33
National Development Group
for the Mentally
Handicapped, 469n, 592
National Economic
Development Council (NEDC
or Neddy), 25n, 387 and n,
503
National Enterprise Board
(NEB), 11, 103n, 145, 161n,
250, 374 and n, 394, 453,
493, 631, 700
National Executive Committee
(NEC) of the Labour Party:
and In Place of Strife, 3;
policy statements (1973),
10-11; and campaign
document, 23; and miners'
dispute, 25-6; and relations
with Government, 63-4,
74-5, 89-90, 122, 152, 205,
206, 232-5, 254, 268, 298,
409, 452, 514, 564; and
Chile, 87, 122, 322, 634; and
land policy, 140; and joint
meetings with Cabinet,
154-5, 180-3, 204, 232-5,
495-6, 565-6, 700; elections
to, 239, 510; and EEC
referendum, 290, 355-7,
375-6, 750 (Appendix III);
and Economic Reviews,
316-17, 337, 449; and party

finance, 395–6, 433–4; and Social Contract, 433, 452; and industrial policy, 464 and n, 492–4, 502–3, 679, 738; and Reg Prentice, 563–4, 662; and entryism, 565; and pay beds, 629–30, 634, 646–7; and Honours List, 633; and re-selection of MPs, 633; and press conferences, 633–4, 675; and unemployment, 661–2

National Health Service (NHS): reorganization of, 41, 142 and n, 143, 163, 242, 282n, 378, 447, 529; and public expenditure restraints, 92–3, 243, 359, 397, 425, 546–7, 593–4, 601–2; disruption in, 115, 150, 163, 515; TV programme on, 123; state of, 162–4; budget for, 200, 203, 210, 228–9, 241; at local government conference, 274; Sunningdale consultation on, 315; and spectacle frames, 327, 410, 425, 487–8; and export promotion, 386–7, 425, 456, 490, 499, 524, 616n, 622–4; financing of, 443, 459, 468, 503, 504–5, 720; woman doctors in, 447; charges, increases in, 487, 490, 504; resolution on, at Annual Conference, 508; procurement policy for, 513, 646, 692; 'collapse' of, 515–16, 529; enquiry on, 524–5, see also Royal Commission on the Health Service; regard for, abroad, 623–4; Fabian pamphlet on, 628, 634; and boost for morale, 653; and consultative document on, 680, 702, 703; see also British Medical Association, consultants, junior hospital doctors, pay beds, private practice policy

National Industrial Relations Court (NIRC), 5, 55n, 80 and n

National Institute for Economic and Social Research (NIESR), 458

National Insurance Bill/Act, 1974, 76, 78, 81–2, 199n

national insurance contributions, 266

National Referendum Campaign (NRC), 359, 371, 373, 383, 387, 402, 408

National Society for Mentally Handicapped Children, 320–1

National Superannuation Scheme, see under pensions: new (earnings-related) scheme

National Union of Journalists (NUJ), 231 and n, 308, 544

National Union of Mineworkers (NUM), 36, 113n, 379n, 471

National Union of Public Employees (NUPE), 104, 111, 115, 379n, 529, 532, 570, 632, 638, 651–2

National Union of Railwaymen (NUR), 379 and n, 418

National Union of Seamen (NUS), 6

National Union of Students (NUS), 34n, 265

National Union of Teachers (NUT), 61

nationalized industries, price increases in, 42 and n, 82

Naylor, B. H. J. (SCS), 70, 645

NCB, see National Coal Board

NEB, see National Enterprise Board

NEC, see National Executive Committee of the Labour Party

NEDC, see National Economic Development Council

negative income tax, 101 and n

Neild, Prof. Robert (NEC Study Group), 140

New Law Journal, 634, 635n

New Zealand, 333, 335, 402

Newcastle, visit to, 636–8

Newham North East Labour Party, 472n, 563n

Newspaper Proprietors' Association (NPA), 66n, 710

Newstead, Mrs (Royal College of Nursing), 101, 185

NHS, see National Health Service

NIESR, see National Institute for Economic and Social Research

Nigeria, 285, 387, 439, 683

NIRC, see National Industrial Relations Court

Nixon, President (USA), 75

Nkomo, Joshua (Rhodesian African leader), 657, 663, 664, 670, 683, 703

Nodder, Tim (DHSS), 260, 362, 364, 537, 665, 669, 722, 734

North Sea Oil, 37, 96, 125 and n, 326n, 421, 424

Northern Ireland, 69n, 125, 236

Norwich, visit to, 492

Nottingham, visit to, 253

NPA, see Newspaper Proprietors' Association

NRC, see National Referendum Campaign

nuclear policy, 121 and n, 122, 123–4, 227–8

NUJ, see National Union of Journalists

NUM, see National Union of Mineworkers

NUPE, see National Union of Public Employees

NUR, see National Union of Railwaymen

nurses, 62, 88 and n, 94, 98 and n, 104, 147, 157

NUS, see National Union of Seamen or National Union of Students

NUT, see National Union of Teachers

Nyerere, President Julius (Tanzania), 276, 663, 664, 671n, 683, 694, 703

Observer, The, 180, 267, 459–60, 518, 674

O'Connell, Theresa (Labour Party HQ), 209, 300

OECD, see Organization for Economic Co-operation and Development

Office of Population Census and Surveys (OPCS), 594, 600

Ogilvy, Angus, 581

oil prices, 62

Old Age Pensioners' Federation, 94, 729

O'Malley, Brian, MP (Minister of State, DHSS): 33 and n, 38;

O'Malley, Brian, MP – *contd.*
appointed Minister of State,
39–40; and SBC, 46; and
political team meetings, 52;
and reserve pension scheme,
65; at NEC sub-committee
meeting, 74; at service of
dedication, 77; value of, 78,
243-4; and pension proposals,
85; and butter tokens, 110n;
and parliamentary debate,
125; and beef tokens, 145;
and possible future posts,
192, 385, 647, 673;
appointed Privy Councillor,
222; and annual dinner at
Rotherham, 235; and
self-employed, 266 and n; and
TV in Parliament, 320; and
Pensions Bill, 362, 472n, 475,
476; at economic strategy
meeting, 531; and fuel costs,
547; and pensions uprating,
560; and NHS budget, 580;
and leadership election, 692,
694; illness of, 701, 702, 708,
715–16, 717; death of,
718–19, 720, 721; funeral of,
726, 734–5
O'Malley, Elizabeth, 719, 728
O'Malley, Kate, 476, 701, 702,
715, 718–19, 728, 735
one-parent families,170 and n,529
OPCS, *see* Office of Population
Census and Surveys
OPD, *see* Overseas Policy and
Defence Committee of
Cabinet
Open University, 600, 699
Organization for Economic
Co-operation and
Development (OECD), 120
and n, 155–6
Orme, Stan, MP (N.I. Minister of
State), 354, 386, 510, 728, 734
Orr, Miss (Doctors' Review
Body secretary), 570
Ortoli, M. (President, EEC
Commission), 419 and n
Oslo, 402
Osmond, M. W. M. (Solicitor,
DHSS), 108 and n
Otton, G. J. (Deputy Secretary,
DHSS), 616 and n
Overend, Douglas (Deputy
Secretary, DHSS), 65

Overseas Economic Policy,
Ministerial Committee on,
222
Overseas Policy and Defence
Committee of Cabinet (OPD),
57, 58, 581, 635
Overseas Trade Board, 638
and n
Owen, David, MP
(Parliamentary Secretary,
then Minister of State, DHSS):
appointed Parliamentary
Secretary, 37, 38–9, 40, 49n;
and RHAS, 41, 131; and
Central Health Services
Council, 73; and drug
industry, 74, 375; Barbara's
estimate of, 78, 143; and
mental health priority, 86; at
Sunningdale Conference, 93;
and hospital chairmen, 94;
and Community Health
Councils, 124, 241; and pay
beds, 130–8, 293, 321, 384,
475, 522, 534, 540, 552, 555,
566, 581, 588–91, 599, 651,
711; and NHS reorganization,
142n, 447, 562; and
consultants, 144; and works
engineers, 153; appointed
Minister of State, 156n; and
proposals for Joint Working
Party, 170–1, 191, 244; and
Halsbury Report, 184; and
Manifesto meeting, 185; and
contracts for consultants, 196,
200, 208–9, 231, 242–3, 247,
251, 257–8, 261–2, 274–5,
278, 294, 299, 306–7, 364–6;
and EEC medical directives,
273; and defence, 333 and n;
and financing NHS, 443 and n,
560; and private practice
policy, 451, 453; on public
expenditure, 466–7, 531; and
smoking campaign, 487; and
procurement policy, 513; and
resources reallocation, 519
and n; in oppressive mood,
539; and JHDS, 614; and
Royal Commission, 626, 695;
and abortion, 628n; and Civil
Service cuts, 643–5; and
consultative document on
priorities, 680, 702; and
leadership election, 704–5,

711, 712; and possible future
posts, 713; and Barbara's
dismissal, 727–8; at Brian
O'Malley's funeral, 734–5
Oxford, speeches at, 187,
383–4, 404–6

Padley, Walter (MP (Lab) and
NEC member), 87, 233, 290,
355
Padmore, Sir Thomas (former
Permanent Secretary,
Transport), 41 and n
Paget, Reginald, MP (Lab), 27
Palmer, John (*Guardian*), 435
Pardoe, John, MP (Lib), 678
Paris, visit to, 499–501
Parliamentary Labour Party
(PLP), 95, 110, 160, 216, 341,
629
Parry, Terry (FBU), 321, 668
and n
Part, Anthony (Dept of
Industry), 628
Patterson, Marie (TUC), 278 and
n
Pavitt, Laurie, MP
(Assistant-Whip), 74, 92n,
93, 94, 267, 321, 554, 557,
628
Pawson, Keith (family friend),
49, 139, 481, 616
pay beds: Government
commitment to phase out,
49n, 127, 189, 207–9, 216,
384 and n, 491n; dispute
over, at Charing Cross
hospital, 115, 130–8; and
Joint Working Party, 170,
171n; BMA letter on 195;
discussions with unions on,
287, 293, 303, 321, 381,
388–9, 447; and Cabinet
papers on, 293, 313, 475,
703; increased charges for,
345 and n; licensing of, 377,
491n, 522, 534; consultative
document on, 490–1 and n,
515, 549–50, 702–3, 753–59
(Appendix V); Bill on
(*ultimately* Health Services
Bill), 513, 567, 621, 631 and
n, 639–40, 647–8, 655–6,
665, 698, 714, 722, 737;
referred to in Queen's
Speech, 516, 552, 555, 558;

and Royal Commission, 526, 561, 567, 575–7; protracted discussions with BMA and Lord Goodman on, 556–7, 560–1, 569, 571–3, 575–8, 582–93, 597, 602, 604–9, 614–15, 618; BMA ballot on, 655; further consultations after ballot on, 664–9, 687–9, 696, 698, 707, 709–12; independent board (Health Services Board) to phase out, 723, 737

Pay Board, 8, 22 and n, 28, 30, 33, 36, 43n, 166n

pay clerks (NHS), 185, 186–7, 188

Pay Committee of Cabinet, 88, 90

pay policy, voluntary, 118; *see also* incomes policy

Peart, Fred, MP (Agriculture Secretary); appointed Agriculture Secretary, 30, 35; in Cabinet, 57, 194, 211–12, 446, 462, 635; and EEC, 126, 141, 145 and n, 148 and n, 165, 229–30, 288, 314, 335; at joint NEC/Cabinet, 181–2; and rail crash, 409; and incomes policy, 442; at *Class of 1945* party, 474; and devolution, 497; and EEC agricultural policy, 685 and n

Penhaligon, David, MP (Lib), 535

pensions: July 1974 uprating of, 38 and n, 43, 45, 51n, 54, 89, 100n; increases in, 38n, 58n; new (earnings-related) scheme (National Superannuation) for, 53n, 100n, 104, 149–50, 151, 152, 153, 157–8, 176–7, 395, 480–1, 751–2 (Appendix IV); discussions on date for next uprating of, 54 and n, 55–6, 58; six-monthly upratings of, 76, 79, 81; discussed at Liaison Committee, 104, 394–5, 558, 631; occupational, 104, 383, 473, 475, 480, 488–9, 717, 720; and Christmas bonus, 105, 149, 151, 186n, 397n, 558; White Paper on new scheme

for, 150, 153, 157–8, 176; April 1975 uprating of, 199 and n, 216 and n, 229, 254, 305; method of calculating uprating of, 199n, 595, 721; November (originally December) 1975 uprating of, 216n, 254, 304–5, 354, 397 and n; speeches on policy for, 294–5, 343–4, 647; discussed with TU representatives, 668; 1976 uprating of, 702, 717, 721; *see also* Reserve Pension Scheme and Social Security Pensions Bill/Act, 1975

Pensioners Payment Act, 1977/Bill, 1978, 76n

Perkins, Alice (DHSS private secretary), 735

PESC, *see* Public Expenditure Scrutiny Committee of Cabinet

petrol, 245

Petroleum and Submarine Pipelines Bill, 474, 540

Petroleum Revenue Tax, 326 and n

Petrovsky, Minister (Soviet Union), 502, 504, 505

Peyton, Mr (consultant), 613–14

pharmaceutical industry, *see* drugs industry

Piachaud, David (Political Adviser to PM), 59 and n, 74

picketing, 52, 79n, 80, 517 and n

Pitt, Terry (Secretary, Labour Party Research Department), 17, 74–5, 173n

planning agreements, 11, 103n, 145, 161n, 162, 167, 312n, 394, 464n, 654, 675, 738

Platt, Lord, 334–5

Pliatzky, Leo (Permanent Secretary, Treasury), 708 and n

PLP, *see* Parliamentary Labour Party

POEU, *see* Post Office Engineering Union

Polaris submarines, 227

political advisers, 37, 66–7, 110, 139, 265, 640

Pompidou, President (France), 75n

Portugal, 42, 57, 494–5

Post Office Engineering Union (POEU), 112

postmen, 7, 88, 98 and n

pound sterling, *see* sterling (pound), run on

Powell, Enoch, MP (U.U.), 29, 32, 97n, 189, 401, 402, 403 and n, 407, 408, 687

Prentice, Reg, MP (Education Secretary, then Overseas Development Secretary): at Liaison Committee, 18, 21; and campaign document, 23; appointed Education Secretary, 30; and comprehensive education, 61; and industrial relations, 91, 118; and nuclear test, 123; and EEC, 128, 155, 183; and Manifesto draft, 154, 183; and public expenditure, 155, 353, 400, 462, 505, 549; in Cabinet, 194, 217, 338, 635; at joint NEC/Cabinet, 232–3, 235; and Social Contract, 325, 330; appointed Overseas Development Secretary, 408, 413; and incomes policy, 427, 455; and constituency problems, 472 and n, 499, 563 and n, 564 and n, 662; remains in Callaghan Government, 730

prescription charges, 44, 47, 58

Price Code, 431, 435, 440, 453

Price sisters (IRA), 116 and n

Price, William, MP (Lab), 293 and n

Prices Act, 1974, 43n, 116n

prices and incomes policy, 2, 4, 8, 18–20, 41, 44; *see also* incomes policy

Prices Commission, 8, 33

Prime, Audrey (NALGO), 184 and n, 185, 186–7, 188, 321, 388, 540, 541, 585, 668

Prior, Jim, MP (Cons), 231n

Private Eye, 129

private practice policy, 171n, 420, 451, 453, 464, 491n, 492, 516, 753–59 (Appendix V); *see also* pay beds

Privy Council, 35, 254

Professions Supplementary to
Medicine (PSMS), 111 and n,
144, 157, 183
Proops, Marjorie (*Daily
Mirror*), 686
PSMS, *see* Professions
Supplementary to Medicine
public expenditure: cuts in,
under 1964–70 Labour
Government, 2; cuts in, under
1970–74 Tory Government,
4, 163 and n; White Papers
on, 155–6, 292–3 and n, 352,
457, 641, 652, 675, 679;
analysis of trend in, 293n,
748–9 (Appendix II); new
approach for dealing with,
397–8, 460; survey of, after
1976–77, 398–401; and
medium-term assessment,
457–8, 460–4; and priorities
for cuts in, 482–5; and
further cuts in, 520–1, 542–3,
548–9, 738–9; international
comparisons of, 670 and n
Public Expenditure Scrutiny
Committee of Cabinet (PESC),
79, 153, 169, 177, 203,
210–11, 236, 360, 505, 520,
548, 593, 600
public ownership, 23, 103n,
161n
Public Records Office, 677
Pulse, 196

Queen (Elizabeth II), 35, 246,
309n, 467, 671, 733–4
Queen Mary's Hospital, Sidcup,
335
Queen's Speech (March 1974),
36, 38, 39 and n, 41;
(November 1974), 193, 202,
204; (November 1975), 555,
558

Radcliffe Report, 625–8, 635
and n, 677
Rambouillet Conference, 553
and n
radiographers, 144, 151, 157,
160, 164
Raison, Timothy, MP (Cons),
168
RAWP, *see* Resources Allocation
Working Party
Rayner, Sir Derek (Ministry of

Defence procurement board),
488 and n, 490, 513
Read, Kingsley (National Party
candidate), 24, 31, 32
Reading, visit to, 108
Rednall, John (former Private
Secretary), 130
Rees, Merlyn, MP (Northern
Ireland Office): appointed to
N.I. Office, 30; in Cabinet,
89, 342; and terrorists, 236;
and incomes policy, 456; and
public expenditure, 462; and
pay beds, 530; and Barbara's
dismissal, 725n; and Brian
O'Malley's funeral, 726,
735
Regan, Charles (Under
Secretary, DHSS), 175, 727
*Regeneration of British Industry,
The*, 161n
Regional Employment Premium
(REP), 114, 150, 156, 323 and
n
Regional Fund, *see* European
Regional Development Fund
Regional Health Authorities
(RHA), 41, 142–3, 242, 315,
352, 466, 504, 529, 653
register of MPs financial
interests, 97 and n, 98, 100
Reid, Dr (DHSS), 502
Reid, Jimmie (AUEW), 659n
Relativities Report, 22 and n,
23, 24–5, 26–7, 28
Remuneration, Charges and
Grants Bill, 474
REP, *see* Regional Employment
Premium
research and development,
449n
Reserve Pension Scheme, 65–6,
71, 74, 78, 81, 100 and n,
104, 123n
Reserve Powers Bill, 465, 470,
473
Resources Allocation Working
Party (RAWP), 519n, 654
Retail Prices Index (RPI), 50,
254, 336, 547
Revans, Dr (Sir) John (Regional
Medical Officer), 258 and n
Revie, Don (football manager),
662
RHA, *see* Regional Health
Authorities

Rhodesia, 245, 276–7, 657,
663, 670–1, 676, 683, 693,
694, 703
Rhondda, visit to, 673–4
Rhys Williams, Sir Brandon, MP
(Cons), 638
Riccardo, Mr (Chrysler
chairman), 544, 585, 602
Richardson, Elliott (US
Ambassador), 687
Richardson, Jo, MP (Lab), 160,
378, 416
Richardson, Sir John (GMC),
551
Rippon, Geoffrey, MP (Cons),
109n
Ritz Hotel, 61
Robb, Barbara (AEGIS), 85n,
86, 102
Robb, Mr (IHG), 688, 696, 698,
702
Robbins, Lord, 386
Robens, Alfred (Lord)
(Chairman of Hospital
Governors), 94
Roberts, Mrs (Lord Goodman's
housekeeper), 560, 582, 593,
710
Robert, Neal (NEC Study
Group), 140
Robinson, Derek (Deputy
Chairman, Pay Board), 22
and n, 25, 26, 27n, 28, 33,
247
Robinson, Geoffrey, MP (Lab),
425 and n, 686n
Roderick, Caerwyn, MP (Lab),
451
Rodgers, Bill, MP (Lab), 222
and n
Rogaly, Joe (*Financial Times*),
334, 459, 468, 483, 653,
669
Rogers, Sir Philip (Permanent
Secretary, DHSS): as
Permanent Secretary, 34–5,
55; possible retirement of,
mooted, 40, 52, 198; and
political advisers, 59; and
staff discontent, 70; and need
to be kept informed, 124; and
Barbara's private treatment,
130–1; and BMA, 138; and
radiographers, 165–6; and
Lord Halsbury, 168, 203; and
pay beds, 170, 293; and

public expenditure cuts, 178, 203, 241, 520–1; and consultants, 208; and alleged resignation threat, 265 and n; and Treasury, 267–8; and export drive, 425; and private practice policy, 451; and devolution, 497, 498; retirement of, 534

Roll, Joanna, x

Rolls-Royce, 5

Rome talks (energy), 572, 574, 579

Roper, John, MP (Lab), 651

Ross, Mr (CPRS), 223

Ross, Willie, MP (Scottish Secretary): and electoral reform, 70; gloomy humour of, 76; and devolution, 153, 172, 282–3, 713; and EEC, 342; and incomes policy, 442, 456; and pay beds, 530; and Chrysler, 545, 579; at Wilson's farewell dinner, 699; dismissed by Callaghan, 724, 733

Rotherham, visits to, 235, 734–5

Rothschild, Lord, 48n, 449 and n

Royal College of General Practitioners, 219

Royal College of Nursing, 101

Royal College of Surgeons, 277n

Royal Colleges presidents, 275, 277, 291, 369, 550, 566, 571

Royal Commission on the Civil Service, 327n

Royal Commission on the Constitution, 62

Royal Commission on the Distribution of Income and Wealth, 117, 251 and n

Royal Commission on the Health Service, 526–7, 529, 530, 541, 551, 561, 567, 575–7, 621–2

Royal Commission on the Press, 246

Royal Naval College, Greenwich, 127, 128

Royal Statistical Society, 466 and n

RPI, see Retail Prices Index

Ryan, President Ritchie (Eire), 419

Ryder, Sir Don (Government Industrial Adviser), 250, 374 and n

Sadat, President and Madame (Egypt), 543

St Christopher's Hospice, 273 and n

St Giles Hospital, 444

Sakalo, Wasily (JHD), 543, 550–1, 617, 638, 722

Saudi Arabia, 284n, 439, 616n, 622–3

SBC, see Supplementary Benefits Commission

Scanlon, Hugh (President, AUEW): and wage restraint, 2, 435; and Industrial Relations Act, 55; absence from Liaison Committee, 149, 393; at Liaison Committee, 285, 319, 469, 503, 631; and Social Contract, 421; and unemployment, 631, 659–60; retirement of, 659n; and unity behind Government, 679, 693; and Harold Wilson's resignation, 701; and British Leyland strikers, 711

Scarborough, visit to, 325

Scargill, Arthur (NUM), 443, 455

Schmidt, Helmut (German Chancellor), 218 and n, 224, 241, 245, 248, 488, 685

Scott, Hardiman (BBC), 176

Scott, Norman, 640n, 642, 648

Scottish Daily Express (Glasgow newspaper), 114, 503

SCS, see Society of Civil Servants

self-employed, 266 and n, 271, 382

Sex Discrimination Bill, 147, 420

Shaikh, Dr (Iranian Minister), 624, 625

Sharp, Lady (Dame Evelyn) (former Permanent Secretary, Housing), 47–8

Sharp Report, 47–8, 95, 99, 142, 146, 151, 169, 175; see also disabled persons, policy for

Sheffield, visit to, 392

Sheldon, Robert, MP (Minister of State, Treasury), 88 and n, 93, 298

Shepherd, Malcolm (Lord) (Lord Privy Seal): appointed Lord Privy Seal, 30; and Lord Castle, 430; and grading of DHSS post, 450, 491; and growth of Civil Service, 484, 637; and devolution, 497; and health service charges, 505; and TU legislation, 541; at Franco's funeral, 557; and political rights in Civil Service, 648; at Harold Wilson's farewell dinner, 699

shipbuilding industry, 103n, 145, 164, 451, 690–1

Shore, Dr Elizabeth, 37

Shore, Peter, MP (Trade Secretary): appointed Trade Secretary, 30; at informal dinners, 45n; and public expenditure, 81, 461, 484–5; and an early election, 95; and EEC, 101, 109, 125–6, 128, 143–4, 182–3, 190, 212, 226, 230, 249, 287 and n, 302, 331, 333–4, 341, 383; and Concorde, 106; and S. Africa, 391, 635; at Oxford Union debate, 404–5; and industrial democracy, 422–4; and incomes policy, 427, 447–9; and MPs salaries, 446; and industrial strategy, 523–4; and EEC direct elections, 553, 650, 706; and Chrysler, 563, 584, 610–11; and import controls, 569, 700; and economic outlook, 684; and EEC agricultural policy, 686; and shipbuilding, 691; appointed Environment Secretary, 728

Short, Renee, MP (Lab), 232, 321, 630

Short, Ted, MP (Lord President of the Council): appointed Lord President, 30; and pensions, 56, 76, 81; and Clay Cross, 64; and Barbara's comments on, 66; allegations about, in press, 95 and n, 98; and election options, 97; and register of interests, 97n;

Short, Ted, MP – *contd.*
replaced as Committee
Chairman, 109n; and Sharp
Report, 151–2; at joint
NEC/Cabinet, 181, 183; at
1974 Annual Conference,
240; and EEC, 248, 273, 287,
289, 290, 351, 377; at
Legislation Committee, 276,
301, 331, 421; and
devolution, 282, 418, 443,
497, 538, 693, 713; and
legislative pressure, 446, 474,
532; and industrial strategy,
524; supports Barbara, 528;
and pay beds, 528, 548, 567;
and public expenditure, 549,
681; and EEC direct elections,
553; and civil servants' rights,
649; and unemployment, 661;
and defeat on White Paper
debate, 681; and Harold
Wilson's resignation, 689,
691; at Harold Wilson's
farewell dinner, 699;
dismissed by Jim Callaghan,
724, 732–3; and leadership
election, 732–3
Shrimsley, Tony (*Daily Mail*),
653, 654
sickness benefits, 397n
Sieff, Marcus, 327
Silkin, John, MP (Minister for
Planning and Local
Government): and dinner
with Reggie Paget, 27; as
shadow Social Services
spokesman, 34n; and informal
dinners, 45n, 79, 126, 160–1;
appointed to Cabinet, 45n;
and land policy, 79, 140, 164;
and talk of coalition, 126; and
personal social services, 205;
and ministerial salaries, 250;
and poems to Barbara, 289,
595–6; and midsummer
party, 434; and incomes
policy, 439, 455; Barbara's
comments on, 532 and n; and
public expenditure, 549; and
leadership election, 698, 711;
at Harold Wilson's farewell
dinner, 699; and Brian
O'Malley's illness, 717; at
Brian's funeral, 735
Silkin, Rosamund, 161

Silkin, Sam, MP
(Attorney-General), 80, 236,
331
Simmons, Dr (HCSA), 572, 575,
577, 588, 608
Simonstown Agreement, 201n,
202, 222, 227, 234–5, 240
and n
Sinclair, Sir George, MP (Cons),
645
Skinner, David, 65
Skinner, Dennis, MP (Lab), 65,
160, 473, 580, 717, 720,
735
Smith, Cyril, MP (Lib), 31,
680
Smith, Douglas (Private
Secretary, Employment), 158
and n, 198
Smith, Geoffrey (*The Times*),
652, 654, 728
Smith, George (General
Secretary, UCATT), 18, 21,
104, 149–50
Smith, Ian (Rhodesian
Premier), 66n, 245, 276,
657, 663–4, 670–1, 683,
703
Smith, John, MP (Parliamentary
Under Secretary, Energy),
656
Smith, Sir Rodney (President,
Royal College of Surgeons),
277 and n, 515, 517, 549–50,
571, 575, 588, 608, 688
Smith, T. Dan, 95n
Smith's Industries Ltd, 715
smoking, campaign against, 487,
488, 501
Smolen, Stanley (British subject
in Uganda), 417n
Soares, Mario (Portuguese
Socialist Leader), 495
Social Contract, 3, 9, 29, 45, 62,
83, 84, 113, 119, 154, 189,
199, 284–6, 319, 371
social plan, 193 and n
Social Security Act, 1973, 54n,
65, 71
Social Security Amendment
Bill, 125
Social Security Benefits Bill,
229n, 291 and n, 296
Social Security Pensions
Bill/Act, 1975, 362, 383, 394,
395, 416, 472n, 486; party to

celebrate passing of, 472n,
476
Social Services Committee of
Cabinet, 105, 151, 292, 374,
411, 475, 487, 567, 701–2
social wage document, 319 and
n, 324–5, 330, 373, 397, 432,
437–9, 463, 492
Socialist International, 114,
140, 676
Society of Civil Servants (SCS)
(*later* Society of Civil and
Public Services), 70n, 363–4,
367
Society of Radiographers, 157,
164, 166
South Africa, 57, 112 and n,
201, 205, 240n, 391, 640,
677–8, 703
South African Bureau of State
Security (BOSS), 677, 686
South Ockendon Mental
Hospital, 85 and n, 102
Southampton, visits to 17, 246,
265, 396
Soviet Union, 313 and n, 502
Spanswick, Albert (General
Secretary, COHSE), 104, 106,
130, 131, 133, 136, 157,
180n, 381, 508
Speaker's Conference, 69 and n,
553, 554
Spearing, Nigel, MP (Lab), 295, 296
Special FAM, *see under* family
allowances
spectacle frames, 327, 410, 425,
487–8, 648
Stanley, Bryan (General
Secretary, POEU and NEC
member), 181 and n, 182,
233, 337, 375, 496, 564, 633,
646, 700
Steel, David, MP (Lib), 189, 396
steel industry, 296, 305, 322–3,
385–6, 390
sterling (pound), run on, 417,
426, 434–5, 436, 439, 490,
683, 738
Stevenson, Dr Derek
(Secretary, BMA): initial
meeting with, 46 and n; and
consultants' contract, 258,
260–1, 277, 344, 365n, 367;
and Charing Cross dispute,
133, 138, 139; and NHS
financing, 144n, 163–4; and

salary claim, 166–7; at dinners with Barbara, 231, 275; and EEC medical directories, 273; and JHDS, 526–7, 569, 597–8; and pay beds, 530, 550, 575, 608; and Barbara's accident, 612; and consultations after BMA ballot, 665–6, 687–8; letter of thanks from, 732

Stevenson, John (*Daily Mail*), 331–2, 367, 612, 614

Stewart, Mary (Chairman of Hospital Governors), 94

Stoddart, David, MP (Lab), 22

Stokes, Donald (Chairman, British Leyland), 374

Stonehouse, John, MP (Lab), 279 and n, 280, 410

Stowe, Ken (PM's Principal Private Secretary), 572, 578, 640, 654

Strange, Richard, x

Strauss, George, MP (Lab), 70, 486, 676–7

Straw, Jack (Political Adviser): appointed Barbara's political adviser, 34 and n, 38, 40; background of, 34n; becomes Barbara's successor as MP, 34n; as London councillor, 66, 105; and Barbara's position as wife of peer, 78, 99; and public expenditure, 81; and Sunningdale Conference, 92; and relations with civil servants, 99, 110, 265; and TV interview, 110; and minutes of political team meetings, 125; and Barbara's private treatment, 130, 134; and Sharp Report, 142; and NHS finances, 163; and radiographers, 165–6; and speech for BDA, 177; and consultants, 247; and Moorgate crash, 324–5; and anti-EEC campaign, 367, 383, 391; and private sector of medicine, 420; and export promotion, 425; and Hope Hospital, 469; and pay beds, 581, 695, 709, 731; and JHDS, 626; and Radcliffe Report, 627; and EEC direct elections, 635, 705; and family

bereavement, 670; and EEC agricultural policy, 685; and dismissal notice, 707, 726; and Barbara's dismissal, 726–7, 728; retained by David Ennals, 731; at Brian O'Malley's funeral, 734

strikes, 2–3, 7, 9–10, 30, 201, 267, 679

student grants, 641

subsidies to private industry, 103n, 113

Summerskill, Shirley, MP (Lab), 37

Sun, The, 266, 411, 432, 515, 599, 693

Sunday Express, 262

Sunday Telegraph, 638

Sunday Times, 22, 107, 202, 267, 325, 503, 562

Sunningdale Conferences, 91–3, 315, 447, 645

Sunningdale Speech on Civil Service, 35n, 52

supplementary benefits, 397n

Supplementary Benefits Commission (SBC), 46, 193, 228, 299 and n, 338, 716

Swansea, visit to, 107

Taff Vale Judgment (1901), 6

Tattersall, David (*Daily Mirror*), 437–9, 445

Taverne, Dick, MP (Ind), 12

Taylor, Charles, MP (Cons), 22

Taylor, Teddy, MP (Cons), 732

Taylor, Tom (Treasurer, Blackburn Labour Party), 31, 246, 274, 527

teachers, 88, 98 and n

Teheran, visit to, 623

televising of Parliament, 197, 320 and n

Temporary Employment Subsidy (TES), 503

Terry, Walter, 153

TES, *see* Temporary Employment Subsidy

textile workers, 527

TGWU, *see* Transport and General Workers' Union

Thatcher, Margaret, MP (Leader of the Opposition): and mortgage rates, 189; and leadership battle, 291, 303 and n, 304, 309, 310; and TV

in Parliament, 320; at PM's questions, 330, 678; and Tory Party machine, 332; parliamentary speeches of, 338, 362, 458, 681, 686, 692; and appearance of, 362, 432, 473, 487, 681; at Tory Party Conference, 518; and domestic chores, 518; and pay beds, 621; attacked by press, 669; wins General Election, 739

Think Tank, *see* Central Policy Review Staff

Thomas, George, MP (Speaker), 678, 681, 692

Thomas, Janie (BASW), 59

Thomas, Sir Robert (Chairman, AMA), 655 and n

Thomasson, Peter (CPSA), 246, 363, 645

Thompson, Brian and Robert (Solicitors), 89, 701

Thomson, George (EEC Commissioner), 12

Thorn, Gaston (Premier of Luxembourg), 662

Thornton, Dr (Secretary, Women's National Commission), 142

Thorpe, Jeremy, MP (Liberal Party Leader): and February 1974 General Election, 30; and parliamentary speeches, 154, 458, 692; and coalition offer, 189; and EEC referendum, 405–6, 407; and pay beds, 535; and events leading to his resignation as Party Leader and trial, 640 and n, 648, 677–9, 680; at lunch with Luxembourg Premier, 662

threshold agreements, 8, 107, 114, 116

Times of their Lives, The, 437

Times, The: and Harold Wilson, 12, 206; and Dick Crossman's column in, 23; and incomes policy, 23; and Jim Callaghan, 143; and Lady Falkender, 153; and Barbara, 246, 511n; and consultants, 266; and Jack Jones, 502; and pay beds, 511, 569; and JHDS, 555, 597; and Honours List,

Times, The – contd.
634; and Margaret Thatcher,
669; and consultative
document on NHS, 703
Tomkins, Ambassador (France),
499
Tomlinson, Eric (Shrewsbury
picket), 682n
Tomlinson, George (former
Education Minister), 467–8
Tomney, Frank, MP (Lab), 660
and n
Top Salaries Review Body
(TSRB), 105 and n, 117 and n,
149, 246 and n, 250–2, 436n
Torry, Dr (Blackburn Royal
Infirmary), 551
Trade Disputes Act (1906), 6
Trade Union and Labour
Relations Bill/Act, 1974, 46n,
79n, 100, 102–3, 160n, 214n,
231n
Trade Union and Labour
Relations (Amendment)
Bill/Act, 1976, 218n, 231n,
246, 541
Trades Union Congress (TUC):
and *In Place of Strife*, 3,
215n; talks with Heath, 8;
Economic Review, 1974, 45
and n; on March 1974
Budget, 54–5; and Social
Contract, 62, 113, 120, 421
and n; and picketing, 79n, 80,
517 and n; and unfair
treatment of members, 90 and
n, 91, 214–15, 217–18; more
rigid than Pay Board, 99;
against cancelling Concorde,
106; and miners, 250;
Economic Review, 1975, 284;
and guidelines, 316; and
industrial democracy, 423; on
incomes policy, 421 and n,
426, 435, 448 and n, 453–5,
492, 738, 739; and industrial
strategy, 515, 738
Transport and General
Workers' Union (TGWU), 6,
80n, 379n, 408, 558 and n
Teelock, Sir Lekratz (Mauritian
High Commissioner), 104, 118
Tribune, 73, 495, 565n, 628, 731
Tribune Group, 57, 156n, 160,
378, 435, 471, 511–12, 657,
679

Trotskyists, 238, 499, 565n
TSRB, *see* Top Salaries Review
Body
TUC, *see* Trades Union Congress
Tuck, Russell (Senior Assistant
General Secretary, NUR, and
NEC member), 565
Tugendhat, Christopher, MP
(Cons), 671 and n
Turkey, 390–1

UCATT, *see* Union of
Construction, Allied Trades
and Technicians
UCH, *see* University College
Hospital
Uganda, 417 and n
Underhill, Reg (National Agent,
Labour Party), 564, 565
unemployment: under Tory
Government, 2, 5; and March
1974 Budget, 50 and n; and
trade union concern, 55, 496,
502, 630; OECD forecast on,
155–6; rising figures of, 316,
514, 738; Denis Healey's
forecasts on, 354, 358, 559;
and 3 per cent estimate of,
457, 461; Cabinet on, 503;
debated at 1975 Annual
Conference, 509–10; in
construction industry, 533;
declining figures of, 679
unemployment benefits, 397n,
738
Union of Construction, Allied
Trades and Technicians
(UCATT), 18
Union of Post Office Workers
(UPW), 379 and n
Union of Shop, Distributive and
Allied Workers (USDAW), 350
and n, 379, 558n
United States (USA), 227, 305,
351, 358, 553n, 703
University of Cambridge
Department of Applied
Economics, 316
University College Hospital
(UCH), 129, 130–1
Uprating Bill, 54, 81, 229
UPW, *see* Union of Post Office
Workers
Urwin, Harry (Deputy General
Secretary, TGWU), 374 and n,
478 and n, 489, 668 and n

USA, *see* United States
USDAW, *see* Union of Shop,
Distributive and Allied
Workers
Utting, Mr (Chief Social Work
Officer, DHSS), 616–17

Value Added Tax (VAT), 114,
141, 150, 248, 358
Varley, Eric, MP (Energy
Secretary, then Industry
Secretary): appointed Energy
Secretary, 30; and Clay Cross,
68; and North Sea Oil, 125;
and energy prices, 195; at
Chequers meeting, 220–1; and
energy conservation, 245; and
top salaries, 250, 256; and
EEC, 342, 346, 503; appointed
Industry Secretary, 408, 411;
and Barbara's estimate of,
424, 635; and industrial
democracy, 424; and Industry
Bill and strategy, 429–30 and
n, 523 and n, 565, 675, 700;
and incomes policy, 441–2,
448–9, 455–6; and Meriden,
477–8 and n; at 1975 Annual
Conference, 509; and
Chrysler, 545, 579–80,
584–5, 602, 610; and import
controls, 568; and Namibia,
635; and Harold Wilson's
resignation, 689, 690; and
shipbuilding industry, 690–1;
at Harold Wilson's farewell
dinner, 699
Vaughan, Frankie (singer), 32
Vaughan, Dr Gerard, MP
(Cons), 338, 609, 612, 532,
702
Veil, Mme Simone (French
Minister), 499–501
Vetter, Heinz (German TUC),
225
Victoria Hospital, 339
Vincent, Sid (NUM), 396
Violence in Marriage, Select
Committee on, 444 and n,
445
Vorster, John (S. African
Premier), 245, 276, 664

wages stop, 292 and n, 380n
Walden, Brian, MP (Lab), 247,
629, 642n

Walker, Peter, MP (Cons), 385
Walker-Smith, Derek, MP
 (Cons), 474
Wardle, Dr (JHD), 577, 600, 614
Warner, Norman (Private
 Secretary, DHSS):
 appointment of, 117, 159;
 and radiographers, 165; and
 Treasury, 175–6; and Royal
 College presidents, 277;
 Barbara's estimate of, 300;
 and export drive, 425, 490,
 704; and social wage, 437,
 438; and procurement policy,
 513; and public expenditure
 cuts, 521; and JHDS, 527; and
 Finer Report, 528; and pay
 beds, 572, 578, 584, 730; and
 Barbara's accident, 612, 614;
 advised of Barbara's
 projected retirement, 624–5;
 and Radcliffe Report, 627;
 and transfer from post, 674;
 and USA health agreement,
 687; and Brian O'Malley's
 death, 718–19; and Barbara's
 dismissal, 726, 728–9
Warren, Dennis (Shrewsbury
 picket), 682 and n
Watkins, Alan (Observer), 674
Watkinson, Lord, 386
Watt, David (Financial Times),
 459
wealth tax, 54
Webb, Beatrice and Sidney
 (Lord Passfield), 100n
Weidenfeld, Sir (later Lord)
 George, 467
Weighell, Sid (General
 Secretary, NUR), 26, 311, 337,
 496
Wellbeloved, Jim, MP (Lab),
 677, 678
Wells, Eileen (Barbara's
 housekeeper), 83 and n, 99, 370,
 384, 476, 498, 518, 616–17
Weston-super-Mare, visit to,
 437–8
White, Frank, MP (Lab), 31
White, Jimmie, MP (Lab), 628
 and n
White, Tom (Social Services
 Director), 349 and n, 533
Whitelaw, William, MP (Cons),
 25 and n, 27, 303 and n,
 309n, 396

Whitley Council, 144, 153,
 184n, 271n, 290;
 departmental staff side of, 70,
 111, 645; Nurses and
 Midwives, 94, 111, 185;
 Professions Supplementary to
 Medicine, 144
Whitaker, Mr (DHSS
 Controller), 636–7
Whittington Hospital, 613
Wicks, Nigel (Assistant Private
 Secretary to PM), 724
Widdup, Mr (Treasury), 171,
 172, 173, 175
Wigoder, Lord (Chairman,
 Health Services Board),
 737
Williams, Alan Lee, MP (Lab),
 557
Williams, Marcia, see Falkender,
 Lady
Williams, Shirley, MP (Prices
 and Consumer Protection
 Secretary): appointed Prices
 Secretary, 30; and Prices Act,
 43n, 104; and hair style, 66;
 and inflation, 118, 224, 394;
 and Concorde, 124; and EEC,
 144, 154, 173, 190, 249, 289,
 290, 295–6, 375; praised by
 Wilson, 160, 168; in Cabinet,
 196, 211, 424, 635, 641; and
 NEC elections, 239; and top
 salaries, 250; and Special
 FAM, 272; and pay policy,
 337, 338, 425, 427, 430, 431,
 441, 455, 471; and 'industrial
 consensus', 387; and public
 expenditure, 461, 493, 596,
 601; and devolution, 497,
 693; at 1975 Annual
 Conference, 506, 511; and TU
 legislation, 541–2; and Dock
 Labour Scheme, 558; and
 Reg Prentice, 564 and n; and
 entryism, 565; and Barbara's
 accident, 611–12; compares
 jobs with Barbara, 629; and
 fuel costs, 656; and Rhodesia,
 664; and economic outlook,
 684, 697; and EEC agricultural
 policy, 685; and Harold
 Wilson's resignation, 690; and
 shipbuilding industry, 691; at
 Harold Wilson's farewell
 dinner, 699; and pay beds,

704, 730; and EEC direct
 elections, 706
Wilson, Harold, MP (Prime
 Minister): appoints Barbara
 to Cabinet, ix; as Prime
 Minister (1964–70), 1–3; and
 planning agreements, 11; and
 EEC, 12, 107, 141, 149, 175,
 212, 245, 248–50, 273, 287,
 289, 296, 297–8, 317, 323,
 333–4, 340–3, 403; under
 strain, 12–13; at Liaison
 Committee, 18–21, 431; and
 debate on emergency, 22; and
 campaign document, 23; and
 letter to Ted Heath, 27; and
 General Election (February
 1974), 29–30; appointed
 Prime Minister, 30, 33; and
 the press, 32–3, 100, 308,
 574, 614; in Cabinet, 36,
 247–8, 376–7; and political
 advisers, 37, 640; and
 Government appointments,
 37, 39, 40; and pensions
 uprating, 58, 107–8; and the
 disabled, 60; and mortgages,
 62, 69; and devolution, 62,
 153, 172–3, 537–8; and land
 deal allegations, 63, 66, 67,
 70, 73–4; and Clay Cross, 67;
 and service of dedication, 77;
 and Lord Castle, 78; and
 union fines, 80; and election
 options, 96–7; and love of
 power, 107; and Tony Benn's
 report on his Department,
 109 and n; takes over
 Committee chairmanship,
 109n; and mixed economy,
 114; and nuclear test, 121
 and n, 123–4; and publicity,
 127; and Denis Healey's
 economic proposals, 154; and
 Government achievements,
 160; and industrial policy,
 162, 167, 316, 524, 675; on
 World at One, 168; and
 dental charges, 174, 480, 537;
 at joint NEC/Cabinet, 180–3,
 495; and General Election
 (October 1974), 185; and
 collective responsibility,
 206–7, 675; and TU
 legislation, 217; at Chequers
 meeting, 222–4; and nuclear

Wilson, Harold, MP – contd.
policy, 227–8; at 1974
Annual Conference, 238–41;
and top salaries, 252, 255–6;
and strikes, 267; and
Rhodesia, 277, 663–4, 671;
at International Women's
Year reception, 277–8; and
Margaret Thatcher, 309, 310,
314, 692; and Russians, 313;
Barbara's estimate of, 316,
323, 379, 397, 432, 437,
527–8, 557; and defence,
324; and anti-EEC campaign,
345–8, 355–7, 358–9; and
British Leyland, 374; at
special (April 1975)
conference, 379–80; at
Commonwealth Conference,
377, 385, 391; and EEC
referendum, 407; and Cabinet
changes, 408, 412–15; and
industrial democracy, 424;
and incomes policy, 427,
429–30, 440, 453–9, 465;
and Roy Jenkins, 432; and
MPs salaries, 446, 465; and
public expenditure, 460–4,
485, 549, 594–5, 600–2, 681;
as statistician, 466 and n; at
Class of 1945 party, 474; and
Meriden, 479; at 1975
Annual Conference, 510; at
Blackburn, 527–8; and pay
beds, 530, 532, 556–7, 567,
568, 572–8, 580, 584–7, 618,
639–40, 655–6, 703–4; and
Chrysler, 545, 563, 579; and
entryism, 564; and Rome
talks, 574, 579; and writ
against Daily Mail, 614–16;

and Radcliffe Report, 626–8,
634; and abortion, 629; and
Honours List, 634; and
Thorpe case, 640, 642, 648,
677–9; and Armitage
Committee, 649n; and EEC
direct elections, 650–1, 706;
confides resignation intentions
to Barbara, 671–2; discusses
his 1950 resignation, 676; and
sixtieth birthday, 686; and
confidence vote, 686; resigns
as Premier, 689–90, 692,
735; farewell dinner, 698–9,
701
Wilson, Mary, 108, 277–8, 695
Wilson, Reginald (Chairman of
Hospital Governors), 94
Wimbledon, 434
Wise, Audrey, MP (Lab), 495
Women's Advisory Council,
National Labour, 22
Women's Conference, Labour
(June 1974), 107
Women's National Commission,
141 and n, 278, 313, 388, 547
Wood, David (The Times), 30,
246–7, 385, 660 and n
Wood, Tom, 59, 730
Woodcock, George (former
General Secretary, TUC), 2
Woodlock, Jack (Assistant
Secretary, DHSS), 186, 187,
188
Woodman, Joan, 204
Woodroofe, Sir Ernest (Review
Body Chairman), 361n,
569–70, 602–4, 609
Woolf, Michael
(Director-General,
Conservative Party), 332

Woolwich West by-election,
434, 438, 458
works engineers (NHS), 151,
153
World Bank, 634, 636
Worswick, Mr (NIESR), 458
Wrigglesworth, Ian, MP (Lab),
520, 535, 571, 609
Wright, Bob (AUEW), 477, 659n
Wythenshawe, visit to, 59

Xavier (hairdresser), 94, 127,
444, 581

Yellowlees, Dr Henry (Chief
Medical Officer, DHSS): and
restraints on public
expenditure, 93; and Charing
Cross dispute, 135 and n,
138, 139; and BMA secretary,
163; and consultants' pay,
166; praises Barbara, 168;
and pay beds, 196, 200, 208,
551, 566, 581, 665; upset
with Barbara, 208; at
Lancaster House dinner, 231;
and consultants' contract,
273–4, 277, 291, 294, 297,
300, 305–7, 362; and DHSS
staffing, 491, 507; absent
from Barbara's farewell party,
727
Young Socialists, 238, 507, 565
Younger, Kenneth (Chairman,
AHA), 444

Zacharias, Dr (JHD), 555–6,
572, 597–8, 604, 614
Zec, Philip (Daily Mirror), 407